MW01258109

wwnorton.com/nawr

The StudySpace site that accompanies *The Norton Anthology of World Religions* is FREE, but you will need the code below to register for a password that will allow you to access the copyrighted materials on the site.

WRLD–RLGN

THE NORTON ANTHOLOGY OF

WORLD
RELIGIONS

CHRISTIANITY

THE NORTON ANTHOLOGY OF

WORLD
RELIGIONS

CHRISTIANITY

Lawrence S. Cunningham
JOHN A. BRIAN PROFESSOR OF THEOLOGY, EMERITUS
UNIVERSITY OF NOTRE DAME

JACK MILES, *General Editor*
DISTINGUISHED PROFESSOR OF ENGLISH
AND RELIGIOUS STUDIES
UNIVERSITY OF CALIFORNIA, IRVINE

W · W · NORTON & COMPANY
NEW YORK · LONDON

W. W. Norton & Company has been independent since its founding in 1923, when William Warder Norton and Mary D. Herter Norton first published lectures delivered at the People's Institute, the adult education division of New York City's Cooper Union. The firm soon expanded its program beyond the Institute, publishing books by celebrated academics from America and abroad. By midcentury, the two major pillars of Norton's publishing program—trade books and college texts—were firmly established. In the 1950s, the Norton family transferred control of the company to its employees, and today—with a staff of four hundred and a comparable number of trade, college, and professional titles published each year—W. W. Norton & Company stands as the largest and oldest publishing house owned wholly by its employees.

Manufacturing by RRDonnelley Crawfordsville
Composition by Westchester Book
Book design by Jo Anne Metsch
Production Managers: Sean Mintus

LIBRARY OF CONGRESS CATALOGING-IN-PUBLICATION DATA

The Norton anthology of world religions / Jack Miles, General Editor, Distinguished Professor of English and Religious Studies, University of California, Irvine; Wendy Doniger, Hinduism; Donald S. Lopez, Jr., Buddhism; James Robson, Daoism. — First Edition.
     volumes cm
   Includes bibliographical references and index.
   ISBN 978-0-393-91899-1 (hardcover)
   1. Religions. 2. Religions—History—Sources.   I. Miles, Jack, 1942– editor.
II. Doniger, Wendy, editor.   III. Lopez, Donald S., 1952– editor.   IV. Robson, James, 1965 December 1– editor.
   BL74.N67 2014
   208—dc23
                                                                        2014030756

Christianity (ISBN 978-0-393-91899-1): Jack Miles, General Editor; Lawrence S. Cunningham, Editor

W. W. Norton & Company, Inc.
500 Fifth Avenue
New York NY 10110
wwnorton.com

W. W. Norton & Company Ltd.
Castle House, 75/76 Wells Street, London W1T 3QT

1 2 3 4 5 6 7 8 9 0

Contents

LIST OF MAPS AND ILLUSTRATIONS   xxi

PREFACE   xxiii

ACKNOWLEDGMENTS   xxxv

GENERAL INTRODUCTION
How the West Learned to Compare Religions   3
JACK MILES

CHRISTIANITY   43
Introduction: The Words and the Word Made Flesh   45
LAWRENCE S. CUNNINGHAM

The Apostolic Era, 4 B.C.E.–100 C.E.   75

CHRONOLOGY   81

THE OLD TESTAMENT   83

GENESIS   83
Genesis 1–3. ["'I was afraid because I was naked'"]   84
Genesis 12:1–3. ["'All the families of the earth shall
  bless themselves by you'"]   88
Genesis 15:1–6. ["And because he put his trust in the Lord,
  He reckoned it to his merit"]   88

Genesis 22:1–19. ["'Because you have done this and have not withheld your son, your favored one'"]   88

EXODUS   89
Exodus 19–20:23. ["You shall have no other gods besides Me"]   90

DEUTERONOMY   93
Deuteronomy 6:1–15. ["You shall love the Lord your God with all your heart"]   93

SAMUEL   94
1 Samuel 2:1–10. ["And Hannah prayed"]   95
2 Samuel 7:8–17. ["I will be a father to him, and he shall be a son to me"]   96

PSALMS, PROVERBS   96
Psalm 22. ["My God, my God, why have you forsaken me?"]   97
Psalm 23. ["The Lord is my shepherd"]   99
Psalm 110. ["The Lord says to my lord, 'Sit at my right hand'"]   99
Proverbs 8:22–31. ["I was by his side, a master craftsman"]   100

ISAIAH   101
Isaiah 9:1–6. ["And he is named Wonderful Counselor, Mighty God, Everlasting Father, Prince of Peace"]   102
Isaiah 11:1–9. ["The wolf shall dwell with the lamb"]   102
Isaiah 40:1–8. ["Prepare ye the way of the Lord"]   103
Isaiah 52:13–53. ["A sheep silent before shearers, he did not open his mouth"]   103
Isaiah 56:1–8. ["My house shall be called a house of prayer for all peoples"]   105

JEREMIAH   106
Jeremiah 31:31–34. ["I will make a new convenant . . . and inscribe it upon their hearts"]   106

EZEKIEL, DANIEL   107
Ezekiel 37:1–14. ["Son of man, can these bones live?"]   108
Daniel 7:1–14. ["Behold, one like the Son of man came with the clouds of heaven"]   108

THE NEW TESTAMENT   110

JOHN   110
John 1:1–18. ["In the beginning was the Word"]   111

LUKE   111
    Luke 1–2:14. ["'You will find a child wrapped in bands
      of cloth and lying in a manger'"]   112

MATTHEW   116
    Matthew 5–7. ["'When someone strikes you on your right
      cheek, turn the other one to him as well'"]   117
    Matthew 19:16–26. ["'Go, sell what you have and give to
      (the) poor'"]   123
    Matthew 25:31–46. ["'I was . . . in prison and you
      visited me"]   123

LUKE   124
    Luke 10:21–37. ["'A Samaritan . . . went to him and
      bandaged his wounds'"]   125
    Luke 15:1–32. ["'This brother of yours was dead and has
      come to life; he was lost and has been found"]   125

MARK   127
    Mark 1:1–13. ["'The voice of one crying out in
      the wilderness'"]   128
    Mark 5:35–43. ["'The child is not dead but sleeping'"]   129
    Mark 6:45–52. ["He came towards them walking
      on the sea"]   129
    Mark 8:27–9:8. ["'One for you, one for Moses, and one
      for Elijah'"]   130
    Mark 14–16:8. ["'My God, my God, why have you
      forsaken me?'"]   131

JOHN, ACTS   136
    John 20. ["Except I . . . thrust my hand into his side,
      I will not believe"]   137
    Acts 2:1–8, 12–46. ["Divided tongues, as of fire, appeared
      among them"]   138

LETTERS OF PAUL   140
    2 Corinthians 10–11. ["Are they Israelites? So am I"]   140
    Romans 7–9. ["Wretched man that I am! Who will
      rescue me . . . ?"]   144
    Galatians 3:6–9, 23–29. ["There is no longer Jew or
      Greek, there is no longer slave or free, there is no longer
      male and female; for all of you are one in Christ Jesus"]   144
    Philippians 1:27–2:11. ["He made himself nothing"]   151
    1 Corinthians 15:12–19, 35–44, 51–58. ["The trumpet
      shall sound, and the dead shall be raised incorruptible"]   151

HEBREWS, JAMES   154
    The Letter to the Hebrews 11–12:2. ["Witnesses in a
      great cloud all around us"]   156
    James 2:14–24. ["'Faith apart from works is barren'"]   158

REVELATION   159
   Revelation 20–21:8. ["Then I saw a new heaven and
     a new earth"]   160

The Patristic Era, 100–600 C.E.   163

CHRONOLOGY   165

EARLY CHRISTIAN WORSHIP   167

SAINT JUSTIN MARTYR (ca. 100–165)   167
   From The Apology   168

ANONYMOUS (early second century)   171
   The Didache   171

EGERIA (late fourth century)   177
   From the Travels of Egeria   178

SAINT JOHN CHRYSOSTOM (ca. 347–407)   180
   From The Eucharistic Prayer in the Byzantine Liturgy   181

THE ROMAN PERSECUTIONS   186

TACITUS (ca. 56–ca. 120)   186
   From the Annals   187

PLINY THE YOUNGER (ca. 61–ca. 113) and
THE EMPEROR TRAJAN (53–117)   188
   Letters   188

ANONYMOUS (early second century)   190
   From The Martyrdom of Polycarp   191

ORIGEN (185–ca. 254)   193
   From An Exhortation to Martyrdom   194

ANONYMOUS EDITOR (early third century)   197
   From The Passion of Perpetua and Felicity   197

OTHER CHRISTIAN GOSPELS   200

ANONYMOUS (mid-to-late second century?)   200
   From the Gospel of Thomas   201

ANONYMOUS (mid-to-late second century?)   203
   From the Protoevangelium of James   205

ARTICULATIONS OF CHRISTIAN BELIEF 207

IRENAEUS OF LYONS (130?–202) 208
  From Against the Heresies 208

TERTULLIAN (ca. 160–225) 210
  De Spectaculis 211
    [On Roman Circus, Theater, and Gladiatorial Games] 211

THE FIRST ECUMENICAL COUNCIL (325) 213
  The Nicene Creed 214

THE SECOND ECUMENICAL COUNCIL (381) 214
  The Creed of Nicaea-Constantinople 215

THE THIRD ECUMENICAL COUNCIL (431) 215
  The Formula of Union at Ephesus 216

THE FOURTH ECUMENICAL COUNCIL (451) 217
  On the Person and Natures of Christ 217

SAINT JOHN OF DAMASCUS (ca. 675–749) 218
  Three Treatises on Images 219
    From the Third Treatise 219

PSEUDO-DIONYSIUS THE AREOPAGITE (fl. ca. 500) 220
  On Mystical Theology 221
    From Chapter One 221
    Chapter Four 222
    From Chapter Five 222

BIOGRAPHICAL AND AUTOBIOGRAPHICAL TEXTS 223

SAINT JEROME (ca. 347–420) 223
  From Letters 224

SAINT AUGUSTINE OF HIPPO (354–430) 226
  Confessions 227
    From Book Eight 227
    From Book Ten 230
  The City of God 230
    From Book XIV 232

SULPICIUS SEVERUS (ca. 360–ca. 420) 236
  Life of Saint Martin 237
    Chapter II 237
    From Chapter III 238
    Chapter X 239

SAINT PATRICK (late fifth century) 240
  From Confession 241

ANONYMOUS (eighth century)   243
    Saint Patrick's Breastplate   243

            EARLY CHRISTIAN HYMNODY   246

PRUDENTIUS (348–411?)   246
    From Ode in Honor of the Blessed Martyr Lawrence   247

SAINT EPHREM THE SYRIAN (306?–373)   249
    Hymns on the Nativity   250
        Hymn 7   250

SAINT ROMANOS THE MELODIST (early sixth century)   251
    The Standing Hymn   252

ANONYMOUS (eighth century?)   258
    From The Dream of the Rood   259

            THE ASCETIC TRADITION   261

SAINT ATHANASIUS OF ALEXANDRIA (ca. 296–373)   262
    From Life of Anthony   262

SAINT GREGORY OF NYSSA (ca. 335–ca. 395)   264
    Life of Macrina   265
        [Saint Macrina's Last Words]   265

ANONYMOUS (fourth and fifth centuries)   268
    From Sayings of the Desert Fathers   268

SAINT BENEDICT OF NURSIA (480?–543)   270
    From Rule of Saint Benedict   271

            The Middle Ages, 600–1300   277

CHRONOLOGY   281

            MISSIONARY EXPANSION   282

SAINT BEDE THE VENERABLE (673?–735)   282
    Ecclesiastical History of the English People   283
        From Book Two   283

RUDOLF OF FULDA (800?–ca. 862–65)   287
    The Life of Abbess Leoba   287
        [*From* Prologue]   287

ANONYMOUS (early twelfth century)   289
   From the Russian Primary Chronicle   289

MEDIEVAL MONASTICISM   294

SAINT ANSELM OF CANTERBURY (1033–1109)   294
   Meditations   295
      Meditation on Human Redemption   295

SAINT HILDEGARD OF BINGEN (1098–1179)   300
   Scivias   300
      Vision Twelve: The New Heaven and the New Earth   300

SAINT BERNARD OF CLAIRVAUX (1090–1153)   306
   Sermons on the Song of Songs   306
      Sermon 3: The Kiss of the Lord's Feet, Hands and
         Mouth   306

THE MENDICANT TRADITION   310

SAINT FRANCIS OF ASSISI (1181 or 1182–1226)   311
   The Testament   312
   The Canticle of Brother Sun   314
   Little Flowers   315
      [Saint Francis Preaches to the Birds]   316

SAINT THOMAS AQUINAS (1225–1274)   317
   From On the Lord's Prayer   318
   Summa contra Gentiles   322
      [On Knowing the Creator through His Creatures]   323

MEDIEVAL LATIN HYMNODY   328

ANONYMOUS (ca. ninth century)   329
   Ave Maris Stella   329

ANONYMOUS (late eleventh century?)   330
   Salve Regina   330

WIPO (died 1050)   331
   Victimae Paschali Laudes   331

SAINT THOMAS AQUINAS (1225–1274)   332
   Pange, Lingua, Gloriosi   332

ANONYMOUS (thirteenth century)   333
   Dies Irae   333

The Late Middle Ages and the Renaissance, 1300–1517   337

CHRONOLOGY   341

VISIONS OF HELL AND HEAVEN, CREATION AND CREATOR   342

DANTE ALIGHIERI (1265–1321)   342
  The Divine Comedy   342
    Inferno   344
      From Canto I   344
      From Canto III   346
    Paradiso   348
      Canto XXXIII   348

MEISTER ECKHART (ca. 1260–1327)   352
  [Sermon 15: On Poverty of Spirit]   353

ANONYMOUS (late fifteenth century)   356
  From The Summoning of Everyman   356

SAINT CATHERINE OF SIENA (1347–1380)   360
  The Dialogue   360
    Prologue   360
    The Bridge   361

JULIAN OF NORWICH (1342–ca. 1416)   365
  From Showings   366

THOMAS À KEMPIS (ca. 1380–1471)   371
  The Imitation of Christ   372
    From Book One   372

OUTSPOKEN WOMEN AND THE FIRST STIRRINGS OF REFORM   375

WILLIAM LANGLAND (ca. 1330–1387)   375
  Piers Plowman   376
    Passus VII   376
      [On Sloth and a Slothful Monk]   376

MARGERY KEMPE (ca. 1373–1438)   379
  The Book of Margery Kempe   379
    [Examination before the Archbishop of York]   379

GEOFFREY CHAUCER (ca. 1343–1400)   383
    The Canterbury Tales   384
        From The Wife of Bath's Prologue   384

Reformations and the Wars of Religion, 1517–1700

                                                        389

CHRONOLOGY   393

PILLARS OF THE PROTESTANT REFORMATION IN
GERMANY, FRANCE, AND ENGLAND   398

MARTIN LUTHER (1483–1546)   399
    From The Freedom of a Christian   401
    Large Catechism   406
        The Sixth Commandment   406
    Small Catechism for Ordinary Pastors and Preachers   408
        [Preface]   408
    A Mighty Fortress Is Our God   411

JOHN CALVIN (1504–1565)   412
    The Institutes of the Christian Religion   414
        [On Predestination]   414

THOMAS CRANMER (1489–1556)   416
    The Book of Common Prayer   417
        From The Order for the Administration of the Lord's
        Supper or Holy Communion   417

DUELING MARTYROLOGIES:
CHRISTIAN CONTRA CHRISTIAN   422

ELIZABETH, A DUTCH ANABAPTIST (sixteenth century)   423
    The Mirror of Martyrs   423
        Letter   423

HENRY MORE (1586–1661]   426
    The Elizabethan Jesuits   426
        [The Trial and Execution of Robert Southwell]   426

SPANISH MYSTICS OF THE CATHOLIC
REFORMATION   429

SAINT IGNATIUS OF LOYOLA (1491–1556)   430
    The Spiritual Exercises   431
        [*From* A Meditation on the Two Standards]   431

SAINT TERESA OF ÁVILA (1515–1582)   434
    The Book of Her Life   435
        Chapter I   435

CHRISTIANITY REACHES THE NEW WORLD
AND CHINA   437

BARTOLOMÉ DE LAS CASAS (1484–1556)   438
    Rules for Confessors   438
        Prologue   438

SOR JUANA INÉS DE LA CRUZ (1651–1695)   441
    From Reply to Sister Philothea   443

NICHOLAS TRIGAULT (1577–1628)   446
    [A Seventeenth-Century Jesuit Missionary in China]   447

BAROQUE DEVOTION IN A CENTURY OF
CONVERSION AND COUNTERCONVERSION   450

ROBERT SOUTHWELL (1561–1595)   450
    The Burning Babe   450

JOHN DONNE (1572–1631)   451
    Death, Be Not Proud   451

GEORGE HERBERT (1593–1633)   452
    The Holdfast   452

RICHARD CRASHAW (ca. 1613–1649)   452
    From To the Noblest and Best of Ladies, the Countess
        of Denbigh   452

EPICS OF SALVATION   454

JOHN MILTON (1608–1674)   454
    Paradise Lost   455
        From Book I   455
        From Book XII   455

JOHN BUNYAN (1628–1688)   458
    The Pilgrim's Progress   458
        From The Second Part   458

PROTESTANT CATHOLICS, CATHOLIC PROTESTANTS, AND BEYOND | 461

BLAISE PASCAL (1623–1662) | 462
From Pensées | 463

ROGER WILLIAMS (1603–1683) | 465
From The Bloody Tenet of Persecution, for Cause
of Conscience, in a Conference between Truth
and Peace | 466

Encounters with Modernity, 1700–1914 | 469

CHRONOLOGY | 473

THE BIBLE WITHIN THE LIMITS OF REASON ALONE | 475

HERMANN SAMUEL REIMARUS (1694–1768) | 476
Apology for Rational Worshippers of God | 477
[Contradictions in the Gospels' Resurrection Accounts] | 477

JEAN-JACQUES ROUSSEAU (1712–1778) | 478
Emile, or On Education | 479
From Profession of Faith of the Savoyard Vicar | 479

FRIEDRICH SCHLEIERMACHER (1768–1834) | 481
On Religion: Speeches to Its Cultured Despisers | 482
From On the Religions [*from* Fifth Speech] | 482

ADOLF VON HARNACK (1851–1930) | 484
From What Is Christianity? | 485

ALFRED FIRMIN LOISY (1857–1940) | 488
The Firmin Lectures | 488
From The Individualist Theory of Religion | 488

ROMANTICISM, NATURE, AND THE CHRISTIANITY OF THE HEART | 493

NICOLAS VON ZINZENDORF (1700–1760) | 494
From The Brotherly Agreement at Herrnhut | 495

JONATHAN EDWARDS (1703–1758) | 498
From Personal Narrative | 499

JOHN WESLEY (1703–1791)   501
    From Journal   502

CHARLES WESLEY (1707–1788)   504
    Love Divine, All Loves Excelling   504

JOSEPH SMITH (1805–1844)   505
    Pearl of Great Price   506
        From The History of Joseph Smith, the Prophet   506

CHARLOTTE ELLIOT (1789–1871)   510
    Just as I Am   510

JARENA LEE (1783–ca. 1849)   511
    The Life and Religious Experience of Jarena Lee   512
        My Call to Preach the Gospel   512

THOMAS WENTWORTH HIGGINSON (1823–1911)   515
    From Negro Spirituals   515

JULIA WARD HOWE (1819–1910)   519
    The Battle Hymn of the Republic   520

ANONYMOUS (mid-nineteenth century)   520
    The Way of a Pilgrim   521
    From Chapter 1   521

      SCANDAL AND PARADOX, FEAR AND FAITH   525

JOHN HENRY NEWMAN (1801–1890)   526
    Apologia pro Vita Sua   526
    From Chapter V   526

SØREN KIERKEGAARD (1813–1855)   531
    Fear and Trembling   532
    From Preface   532
    Tuning Up   533
    From Eulogy on Abraham   536

G. K. CHESTERTON (1874–1936)   540
    Orthodoxy   541
    From Paradoxes of Christianity   541

      THE SEA OF FAITH: EBB OR FLOOD?   545

THOMAS HENRY HUXLEY (1825–1895)   546
    From Agnosticism and Christianity   547

MATTHEW ARNOLD (1822–1888) 551
    Dover Beach 551

EMILY DICKINSON (1830–1886) 552
    [He Fumbles at Your Soul] 553
    [Some Keep the Sabbath Going to Church—] 553

GERARD MANLEY HOPKINS (1844–1889) 554
    The Windhover 555

DAVID LIVINGSTONE (1813–1873) 555
    From Missionary Travels and Researches in South Africa 556
    [Livingstone Makes His First Convert] 556

ALBERT SCHWEITZER (1875–1965) 559
    From Christianity and the Religions of the World 560

The Twentieth Century, 1914–2001

The Twentieth Century, 1914–2001 563

CHRONOLOGY 567

JANE ADDAMS (1860–1935) 569
    From A New Impulse to an Old Gospel 570

WILFRED OWEN (1893–1918) 572
    The Parable of the Old Man and the Young 573

T. S. ELIOT (1888–1965) 574
    Journey of the Magi 575

BERTRAND RUSSELL (1872–1970) 576
    From Why I Am Not a Christian 577

KARL BARTH (1886–1968) 579
    Our Anxiety and God 580

REINHOLD NIEBUHR (1892–1971) 583
    Why the Christian Church Is Not Pacifist 583
    The Truth and Heresy of Pacifism 585
    The Contribution of a True Pacifism 586

DIETRICH BONHOEFFER (1906–1945) 587
    From The Cost of Discipleship 589

W. H. AUDEN (1907–1973) 593
    Friday's Child (In Memory of Dietrich Bonhoeffer,
        Martyred at Flossenburg, April 9th, 1945) 593

WILLIAM TEMPLE (1881–1944)   595
    From German Atrocities: Aid for Refugees
    [Resolution on Behalf of the Jews of Europe]   596

SIMONE WEIL (1909–1943)   598
    From Reflections on the Right Use of School Studies
    with a View to the Love of God   599

MOTHER MARIA SKOBTSOVA (1891–1945)   602
    From The Second Gospel Commandment   603

DOROTHY DAY (1897–1980)   607
    From The Duty of Delight   608

PAUL TILLICH (1886–1965)   610
    Dynamics of Faith   611
        From What Faith Is   611

PIERRE TEILHARD DE CHARDIN (1881–1955)   614
    From The Mass on the World   615

THOMAS MERTON (1915–1968)   618
    From No Man Is an Island   618

C. S. LEWIS (1898–1963)   621
    The Four Loves   621
        From Charity   621

MARTIN LUTHER KING, JR. (1929–1968)   624
    I Have a Dream   625

THE SECOND VATICAN COUNCIL (1965)   628
    Nostra Aetate   629

GUSTAVO GUTIÉRREZ (born 1928)   632
    From The Task and Content of Liberation Theology   633

DESMOND TUTU (born 1931)   638
    From The Rainbow People of God   639

RIGOBERTA MENCHÚ (born 1959)   643
    I, Rigoberta Menchú   644
        The Bible and Self-Defence: The Examples of Judith,
        Moses, and David   644

CZESLAW MILOSZ (1911–2004)   647
    Campo dei Fiori   648
    You Who Wronged   650
    Readings   650

The New Millennium, 2001–the Present

The New Millennium, 2001–the Present ... 653

CHRONOLOGY ... 655

YEONG MEE LEE (born 1966) ... 658
From A Political Reception of the Bible: Korean Minjung
    Theological Interpretation of the Bible ... 659

CHRISTIAN DE CHERGÉ (1937–1996) ... 666
    Spiritual Testament ... 667

LIU ZHENYING (BROTHER YUN; born 1958) ... 669
    The Heavenly Man ... 670
        From Back to Jerusalem ... 670

POPE JOHN PAUL II (1920–2005) AND ECUMENICAL
PATRIARCH BARTHOLOMEW I (born 1940) ... 673
    Common Declaration on Environmental Ethics ... 674

CHRISTIAN WIMAN (born 1966) ... 677
    From My Bright Abyss ... 678

Glossary ... A3

Selected Bibliography ... A19

Permissions Acknowledgments ... A26

Index ... A33

Maps and Illustrations

MAPS

The World of the Apostles, 4 B.C.E.–100 C.E.   82
Religion in Europe, ca. 1590   396
World Christian Population, 2010   656

CHRISTIANITY

Christ as a young shepherd with a lamb draped around his
    shoulders (fourth century)   46
Christ Pantocrator (sixth–seventh century)   52
University of Bologna lecture in progress   57
Calvinist church interior, Utrecht, Netherlands (1645),
    by Pieter Sanraeden   63
Søren Kierkegaard   65
Pope Francis   70
Saint Paul Preaching in Athens (1515–16), by Raphael   75
Ossuary of Joseph son of Caiphas (first century)   131
Alexamonos graffito (early third century)   152
The Virgin Mary as the Mother of God, Hagia Sophia, Istanbul   163
Joachim and Anna fresco, by Giotto   204
Funerary tablet from the Catacomb of St. Sebastian, Rome
    (ca. 200 C.E.)   231
Mosaic of the martyrdom of Saint Lawrence (fifth century)   247
Hildegard of Bingen   277
Non Angli sed Angeli (1793), by William Blake   284
Saint Thomas Aquinas, by Fra Bartolomeo   318
Dante Alighieri, sculpture by Emilio Demi   337
Catherine of Siena, by Ambrogio Bergognone   361
The Wife of Bath, from the Ellesmere Chaucer   383
Detail from The Holy Communion of the Protestants and Ride
    to Hell of the Catholics, by Lucas Cranach the Younger 389
Martin Luther (ca. 1526), by Lucas Cranach   400
Engraving of John Calvin (1597), by Janus-Jacobus Boissard   413
Saint Teresa in Ecstasy (1647–52), by Gian Lorenzo Bernini   434
Sor Juana Inés de la Cruz (1750), by Miguel Cabrera   442
Engraving from the 1778 edition of Rousseau's Emile,
    by Jean-Baptiste Simonet   469
Adolf von Harnack   485
Portrait of John Wesley (1766), by Nathaniel Hone   501

Jarena Lee as painted in 1844   512
Dresden, Germany, after firebombing   563
Dietrich Bonhoeffer at the Tegel Military Prison   588
Martin Luther King, Jr., at the March on Washington   626
Desmond Tutu receives the Nobel Peace Prize   640
Czeslaw Milosz   648
Yoido "Full Gospel" church in Seoul, Republic of Korea   653
Brother Yun   669

Preface

Welcome to *The Norton Anthology of World Religions*. The work offered to you here is large and complex, but it responds to a simple desire—namely, the desire that six major, living, international world religions should be allowed to speak to you in their own words rather than only through the words of others about them. Virtually all of the religious texts assembled here are primary texts. Practitioners of Hinduism, Buddhism, Daoism, Judaism, Christianity, and Islam have written and preserved these texts over the centuries for their own use and their own purposes. What is it like to read them, gathered as they are here like works of religious art in a secular museum?

For practitioners of any of these six religions, who number in the hundreds of millions, this anthology is likely to provide some of the surprise and fascination of a very large family album: some of one's religious ancestors trigger an immediate flash of recognition, while others look very distant and perhaps even comical. For an army of outsiders—those whose religion is not anthologized here, those who practice no religion, those who are "spiritual but not religious," and those who count themselves critics or antagonists of religion—the experience will be rewarding in different ways. No propaganda intrudes here on behalf either of any given religion or of religion in general. The goal at every point is not conversion, but exploration. The only assumptions made are that the most populous and influential of the world's religions are here to stay, that they reward study best when speaking to you in their own words, and that their contemporary words make best sense when heard against the panoramic background of the words they have remembered and preserved from their storied pasts.

Many of the texts gathered here have been translated from foreign languages, for the religions of the world have spoken many different languages over the course of their long histories. A few of the works—the Bhagavad Gita, the *Daode jing*, the Bible, the Qur'an—are readily available. Many more are available only in the libraries of a few major research universities or, though physically available, have not been intellectually available without detailed guidance that was impossible for the lay reader to come by. Bibliographic information is always provided for previously published translations, and a number of translations have been made especially for this anthology. A central concern throughout has been that the anthologized texts should be not just translated but also framed by enough editorial explanation to make them audible and intelligible across the barriers of time and space even if you are coming to them for the first time. When those explanations require the use of words in a foreign language with a non-Roman writing system, standard academic modes of transliteration have sometimes been simplified to enhance user-friendliness.

Globalization, including international migration in all its forms, has brought about a large-scale and largely involuntary mingling of once-separate religious communities, and this historic change has created an urgent occasion for a deeply grounded effort at interreligious understanding. Yes, most of the world's Hindus still live in India, yet the Hindu Diaspora is enormous and influential. Yes, many Jews have migrated to Israel, but half of the world's Jews still live in deeply rooted Diaspora communities around the world. Conventionally, Islam is thought of as a Middle Eastern religion, yet the largest Muslim populations are in South and Southeast Asia, while the Muslim minority in Europe is growing rapidly. By the same token, Christianity is not thought of as an African religion, yet the Christian population of sub-Saharan Africa is growing even more rapidly than the Muslim population of Europe. In a bygone era, the six religions treated here might have been divided geographically into an "Eastern" and a "Western" trio, but we do not so divide them, for in our era they are all everywhere, and none is a majority. Religiously, we live and in all likelihood will continue to live in a world of large and mingling minorities.

This involuntary mingling has created a state of affairs that can be violently disruptive. Terrorism in the name of religion, more often within national borders than across them, has turned many minds against religion in all forms. And yet, paradoxically, religious violence during the twenty-first century has persuaded many that, contrary to innumerable past predictions, religion is by no means fading from modern life. And though the threat of religious violence is a dark challenge of one sort, the bright new opportunities for cross-cultural and interreligious learning present an unprecedented challenge of a different and, in the end, a more consequential sort. On the one hand, whatever some of us might have wished, religious violence has made religion a subject that cannot be avoided. On the other, for those who engage the subject in depth, the study of religion across cultural and political borders builds a uniquely deep and subtle form of cosmopolitan sophistication.

In all its formal features—the format of its tables of contents; its use of maps and illustrations; its handling of headnotes, footnotes, glossaries, and bibliographies; its forty-eight pages of color illustration in six inserts—*The Norton Anthology of World Religions* announces its membership in the venerable family of Norton anthologies. As was true of *The Norton Anthology of English Literature* upon its first publication more than half a century ago, this anthology is both larger and more rigorously realized than any prior anthology published in English for use by the general reader or the college undergraduate. It opens with a generous introduction addressing a set of basic questions not linked to any single tradition but affecting all of them. Each of the six religious traditions is then presented chronologically from its origins to the present (the Buddhism volume also uses a geographical organizing principle). Each presentation begins with a substantial overview of the tradition being anthologized. Each is also punctuated by period introductions tracing the history of the tradition in question. And yet this work is not a history merely enlivened by the inclusion of original texts. No, history here is simply the stage. The texts themselves are the performance, displaying as only they can the perennial and subversive power of religious literature. The difference might be compared to the difference between English history with a bit of Shakespeare and Shakespeare with a bit of English history. The histories come and go, but Shakespeare is irreplaceable. Shakespeare is, to use a term that originated in the church, *canonical*.

Derived from the Greek word for a ruler or measuring rod, *canon* came to mean a rule or criterion of any kind. By extension, the same word came to mean the church rule or "canon" law governing the contents of the Bible: which books were to be included and which excluded. And by yet a further extension, canon came to refer to the understood list of acknowledged masterpieces in English or some other literature. So, the Bible has a canon. English literature has a canon (however endlessly contested). But what works of religious literature constitute the world religious canon?

Aye, dear reader, there was the rub as plans were laid for this anthology. In 2006, when the editorial team began work in earnest, no canons existed for the literatures of the world's major religions. There were limited canons within that vast expanse of written material, the Bible itself being the paradigmatic example. But the literature of Christianity is larger than the Bible, and the situation grows only more complicated as one ranges farther afield into traditions whose concentric canons are more implicit than explicit. Even though more than one canon of the Bible exists, Bible scholars can easily handle that limited variety and still quite literally *know what they are talking about*: they can deal with a clearly delimited body of material within which evidence-based historical interpretation can go forward. But what canon of religious texts exists to help define the entire field of religious studies for religion scholars? The field has never had an agreed-upon answer to that question, and some of the most sweeping theoretical statements about religion turn out, as a result, to rest on an astonishingly small and vague empirical base.

Granted that no master canon in the original religious sense of that term can ever be devised for the religions of the world, the lack of a limited but large and serious study collection of texts is one major indication that the study of religion remains at an early stage of its development as a discipline. For the religions of Asia, especially, it has been as if the Elizabethan theater were being studied without ready access by students to the plays of Shakespeare or with, at most, access to *Hamlet* alone. This lack has been particularly glaring in the United States for reasons that deserve a brief review. Until the early 1960s, the study of religion was largely confined to private colleges and universities, where, thanks to the country's Protestant intellectual heritage, it consisted overwhelmingly of biblical studies and Christian theology. Often, the department of religion was a department of philosophy and religion. Often, too, there was a close relationship between such departments and the college chaplaincy. In public colleges and universities, meanwhile, the situation was quite different. There, the traditional constitutional separation of church and state was understood to preclude the formal study of religion, perhaps especially of the very religions that the student body and the faculty might turn out to be practicing.

But then several events, occurring at nearly the same moment in both the public and the private spheres, created a new climate for the study of religion, and "religious studies" emerged as a new academic discipline distinct from philosophy or theology, on the one hand, and even more distinct from the chaplaincy, on the other. We are still reckoning with the consequences of this shift.

In 1963, Associate Justice Arthur Goldberg wrote for the Supreme Court of the United States in a concurring opinion in *Abington v. Schempp* (374 U.S. 203, 306): "It seems clear to me . . . that the Court would recognize the propriety of . . . the teaching *about* religion, as distinguished from the teaching *of* religion, in the public schools," language that seemed to clear a path for the study of religion in tax-supported schools. Significantly, Goldberg was a Jew; just three years earlier, Americans had elected John F. Kennedy as their first Roman Catholic president. American religious pluralism was becoming increasingly inescapable at the highest levels in American public life; and as it came to be understood that university-level religious studies was to be the study of various religions at once, including but by no means confined to the religions of the United States, the Founding Fathers' fear of an imposed, national religion began to recede from the national consciousness. American pluralism was now as powerful a factor in American religious life as the Constitution itself.

This anthology is published on the fiftieth anniversary of an event little noticed in the cultural ferment of the 1960s but of great importance for the study of religion—namely, the 1964 reincorporation of the National Association of Biblical Instructors (NABI), the principal association of college professors teaching these subjects, as the American Academy of Religion (AAR), whose current mission statement focuses pointedly on "the understanding of religious traditions, issues, questions, and values"—all in the plural. The formal incorporation of the AAR was intended first as a quiet but magnanimous gesture of invitation by a Protestant academic establishment toward the scholars of America's Catholic and Jewish communities, but this was just the beginning. Others would soon be drawn into a conversation whose animating academic conviction is well captured in a dictum of the great nineteenth-century scholar Max Müller: "He who knows one religion knows none."

Catholics and Jews had had their own seminaries and their own institutions of higher learning, but scholarship produced in them tended to remain in them—partly, to be sure, because of Protestant indifference but also because of defensive or reactively triumphalist habits of mind among the residually embattled minorities themselves. But this was already changing. Optimism and openness in the Roman Catholic community had been much assisted in the earlier 1960s by the Second Vatican Council, whose byword was the Italian *aggiornamento*—roughly, "updating"—as employed by the benignly bold Pope John XXIII. American Jews, meanwhile, profoundly traumatized as they had been during and after World War II by the Shoah, or Holocaust, Nazi Germany's attempted genocide, breathed a collective (if premature) sigh of relief in 1967 after Israel's stunning victory over its Arab opponents in the Six-Day War. During the same period, the Reverend Dr. Martin Luther King, Jr., had spearheaded a revolution in American race relations, as segregation ended and the social integration began that would lead to the election of a black president, Barack Obama, in 2008. In short, the mood in the early 1960s was in every way one of barred doors swung open, locked windows flung up, and common cause undertaken in moral enterprises like the interfaith campaign to end the war in Vietnam.

One influential scholar saw the shift occurring in the study of religion as cause for academic jubilation. Writing in 1971 in the *Journal of the American Academy of Religion* (which had been, until 1966, *The Journal of Bible and Religion*), Wilfred Cantwell Smith clearly welcomed the change that was taking place:

> Perhaps what is happening can be summed up most pithily by saying that the transition has been from the teaching of religion to the study of religion. Where men used to instruct, they now inquire. They once attempted to impart what they themselves knew, and what they hoped (of late, with decreasing expectation) to make interesting; now, on the contrary, they inquire, into something that both for them and for their students is incontrovertibly interesting, but is something that they do not quite understand.

And yet there was a shadow across this scene. The newborn American Academy of Religion had bitten off rather more than it could chew. The spread of religious studies to the state university campuses that were proliferating in the late 1960s and the 1970s was vigorously pluralist. Jewish studies experienced an enormous growth spurt, and so did Hindu studies, Buddhist studies, Islamic studies, and so forth. Smith, a scholar of comparative religion who had made his first mark as a specialist in Islam, could only welcome this in principle. But others, writing later, would be troubled by growth that seemed to have spun out of control.

Recall that in 1971, *globalization* was not the byword that it has since become. The Hindu Diaspora in the United States was still tiny. Christian Pentecostalism, though well established, had not yet achieved critical mass in Africa. Europe's Muslim minority, if already substantial, was relatively dormant. Mainland China's population was still in Maoist lockdown. And in the United States, Americans had not yet begun to grasp the coming effects of the passage of the Immigration and Nationality Act of 1965, which removed quotas that had been in place since the 1920s; the resulting explosive growth in Hispanic and Asian immigration would by 1990 make non-Hispanic Caucasians a minority in Los Angeles, America's second-largest city. Americans still saw themselves as a colonized people who had achieved independence, rather than as a colonizing people. The rhetoric of European postcolonialism had not yet been applied to the United States, a superpower whose world hegemony was quasi-imperial in its reach and neocolonialist in its effects. Worldwide, the transformative interrogation of religious traditions by women and about women had barely begun.

While all of these changes, as they have brought about the multiplication and intensification of religious encounters, have made the study of world religions more important than ever, they have not made it easier. They have not, in particular, lent it any internal intellectual coherence. They have not created for it a new study canon to replace the narrowly Protestant study canon, as the founding of the AAR seemed in principle to require. The creation of religious studies as a field had been an academic gamble on a barely perceived religious future. Had the bet paid off? An eminent senior scholar, Jonathan Z. Smith, wrote in 1995 of the change that had taken place: "The field made a decision to give up a (limited) coherence for a (limitless) incoherence."

That limitless incoherence was the context in which we took up the challenge to produce *The Norton Anthology of World Religions*. How ever were we to begin?

There came first the recognition that we would be creating for the field of religious studies a first draft of the very canon that it lacked—a canon covering nearly four thousand years of history in a score of different languages, aspiring not to be authoritative regarding belief or practice but to be plausibly foundational for the study of the subject.

There came second the recognition that though canons, once achieved, are anonymous, they do not begin anonymously. They begin with somebody who declares this in and that out and defends his or her choice. This realization shifted the decision to be made from *What?* to *Who?*

There came third the question of whether the answer to the question *Who?* would come in the singular or in the plural and if in the plural, how multitudinously plural. For each of the traditions to be anthologized, would a large board of specialist advisers be assembled to determine what would be included? Would the selections be formally approved by some kind of plebiscite, as in the verse-by-verse ratification by translators of the language included in the King James Version of the Bible? Would the work of annotating the resulting selections be divided among committees and subcommittees and so forth? Would some governing board formulate a set of topics that each editor or team of editors would be required to address so as to confer a sturdy structure upon the whole? Would there be, for example, a different board of consultants for each period in the long history of Judaism or each language across the geographic breadth of Buddhism?

Our decision was to reject that kind of elaboration and gamble instead on six brilliant and creative individuals, each with a distinct literary style and a record of bold publication, and then to impose no common matrix of obligatory topics or categories on them, nor even a common set of chronological divisions. (Does China have its own Middle Ages? When does modernity begin in Turkey?) It was understood, however, playing to an institutional strength at W. W. Norton & Company, that the prose of these editors, formidable though they were, would be edited very heavily for explanatory clarity even as we second-guessed very lightly indeed their actual anthological choices. To what end this blend of laxity and severity? Our aim has been simply to enhance the intelligent delight of students in religious literature both as literature and as religion. "Intelligent" delight does not mean the delight of intelligent people. The reference is rather to the delight that a strange and baffling ancient text can provide when a great scholar, speaking in his or her own voice, renders it intelligible for you and you recognize, behind it, a human intelligence finally not all that unlike your own.

If that has been our aim for students, our aim for professors has been rather different. Professors of religious studies often find themselves called upon to teach insanely far beyond their area of trained academic competence. For them, we hope to have provided both an invaluable reference tool and a rich reservoir of curricular possibilities. For their graduate students, we hope to have provided breadth to complement the depth of doctoral study at its best. A student studying in depth and probably in the original language some particular religious text can discover here what *else* was being written in the same tradition at the same time. What preceded that text in the life of the religious tradition? What followed it? Who celebrated it? Who attacked it? The fine art of page flipping, crucial to the unique operating system of an ink-on-paper anthology, enables just this kind of exploratory learning. Over time, by repeated forays backward and forward in the evolution of a religious tradition, a serious student can come to know its literature like the interior of a large residence. But this is just the beginning. Comparable forays into the development of other traditions can by degrees situate the target religious tradition in the global religious context. Finally, to further aid all users, the companion website to *The Norton Anthology of World Religions* will provide, over time, both supplementary substantive content—other religious traditions, to begin with—not included in the print anthology and an array of aids for the use of teachers and students.

Beyond these conventional services, however, lies something riskier. We acknowledge that we have provided the professoriate a target to shoot at: "How could you *possibly* omit X?" some will exclaim. And others: "Why on *earth* did you ever bother with Y?" We welcome all such objections. They betray nothing more than the real, existential condition of a field still in many ways struggling to be born. Disciplines do not spring into existence overnight. They are negotiated into existence over time through trial and error. The more vigorously our colleagues find fault with this first draft of a canon for their field, the more productive will be the ensuing negotiation.

Intuition based on deep scholarship and teaching experience has surely played a role in the choices made by the six associate editors responsible, respectively, for anthologizing the six religious literatures covered: Wendy Doniger (Hinduism), Donald S. Lopez, Jr. (Buddhism), James Robson (Daoism), David Biale (Judaism), Lawrence S. Cunningham (Christianity), and Jane Dammen McAuliffe (Islam). They have all sought to include those incipiently canonical texts that few of their colleagues would dare exclude. More intuitively, they have sought to include neglected works of beauty and power whose very appearance here might help them become canonical. The editors have even included occasional attacks on the religious traditions anthologized—for example, excerpts from Kancha Ilaiah, "Why I Am Not a Hindu," in the Hinduism anthology and from Bertrand Russell, "Why I Am Not a Christian," in the Christianity anthology. As these two contrarian entries nicely demonstrate, the canon of texts regarded as permanent and irreplaceable in a religious tradition does not coincide exactly with the canon of texts arguably crucial for the study of the tradition. Coping with all these complications, the editors have coped in every case as well with the painful space limitations that we have had to impose on them even after allowing the anthology to grow to nearly twice its originally envisioned size.

One large question remains to be addressed in this brief preface: *By what criteria did you choose to anthologize these and only these six religions?* This question has a theoretical as well as a practical dimension. How, to begin with, do we distinguish that which is religious from that which is not? Is atheism a religion, or at least a "religious option"? Whatever atheism is, it is certainly no modern novelty. *The Cambridge Companion to Atheism* (2007) begins with a substantial chapter, "Atheism in Antiquity," by the distinguished Dutch classicist Jan Bremmer. Whether atheism in a given ancient or modern form should be considered a strictly religious option may depend on how a given atheist "plays" it. The novelist Alain de Botton, nothing if not playful, dreams or artfully feigns dreaming of a floridly religious enactment of atheism in his *Religion for Atheists: A Non-believer's Guide to the Uses of Religion* (2012). Meanwhile, a 2010 survey by the Pew Forum suggests that the religiously unaffiliated might actually be both more interested in and better informed about religion than the affiliated. But back to the question at hand: If we cannot clearly distinguish religion from irreligion or the "strictly" from the "casually" religious, how can we be sure that we are choosing six versions of the same thing? Arcane and obscure as this question may sound, it did bear rather directly on one of our six key choices, as will be explained below.

In the end, in making our choices, we fell back to an infra-theoretical, practical, or "working" criterion for inclusion: we required that the religions anthologized should be the six most important *major, living, international* religions, a rubric in which each of the three italicized words counted.

Because we anthologize only *living* religions, we do not anthologize the religions of ancient Mesopotamia, Greece, and Rome, despite the fact that these religious traditions loom large in the history of the study of religion in the West, thanks to the dominance of the Bible and of the Greco-Roman classics in Western higher education.

Because we anthologize only *international* religions, we do not anthologize folkloric or indigenous religions, which are typically and symbiotically confined to a single locale, despite the fascination that these religions have had for the sociological or anthropological study of religion, from Johann Gottfried Herder and Émile Durkheim in the late eighteenth and nineteenth century to Clifford Geertz in the twentieth.

Geography, except as the difference between national and international, is not the principle of organization in this anthology. One consequence, however, of our anthologizing only literary religions and then applying a mostly demographic criterion in choosing among them has been the omission of indigenous African religion. While it is true that Yoruba religion is now international and that some texts for it are now available, no such text has become canonical even for practitioners themselves. Rather than saying anything about the limitations of African or other indigenous religious traditions, notably the rich array of Amerindian religions, our decision says something about the inherent limitations of any text-based approach to the study of religion. Texts can indeed teach much, but they cannot teach everything about everybody.

As for the key criterion *major*, we apply it demographically with one glaring exception. Religious demography tends to overstate or understate the size of a religion depending on whether and how that religion counts heads. Roman Catholicism, which counts every baptized baby as a member, probably ends up with somewhat overstated numbers. Daoism, by contrast, probably ends up with its adherents undercounted because formal affiliation is not a recognized criterion for basic participation in it.

Yet even after these difficulties have been acknowledged, there can be no quarrel that Christianity and Islam are demographically major as well as living and international. The same goes at almost equal strength for Hinduism and Buddhism. The obvious exception is Judaism, whose numbers worldwide, though far from trivial, are small even when the question "Who is a Jew?" is given its most broadly inclusive answer. Too small to be reckoned major by a head count, Judaism is too important on other counts to be reckoned less than major. It is the exception that breaks the rule. Its categories, its legends, and many of its practices have been decisive not only for Christianity and Islam but also, arguably, for Western secularism.

As many readers will have noticed by now, this grid of six does not stray very far from the textbook areas of religious studies, as is only right and proper in a reference work, yet this claim of relative "normality" calls for qualification in two final regards if only to provide the occasion for a pair of disclaimers.

First, this anthology does not deal with several religious traditions that, though fully literary and indeed of great intrinsic interest, do not meet its stated criteria. Three that might be named among these are Sikhism, Jainism, and Shinto, but several other traditions commonly enough included in textbooks might easily be added to the list. No judgment of intrinsic worth or importance should be inferred from their exclusion, just as none should be inferred from the omission of indigenous African or Amerindian religion. A less ample presentation of a larger number of religious traditions would always have been possible. Our choice, and all such choices come at a cost, has been to produce ampler presentations of plausibly canonical texts for those most populous religions traditions that the world citizen is likeliest to encounter in the new religious environment that we all inhabit.

To name a second perhaps surprising choice, our grid of six, though generally familiar, has "Daoism" where most textbooks have "Chinese religion." The usual textbook grid resorts to geography or ethnicity as a naming criterion in and only in the Chinese case. Why so? Though, as noted, the designations "Eastern" and "Western" do still have some textbook currency, no one speaks of Christianity as "European religion" or of Islam as "Afro-Asiatic religion." Why proceed otherwise in the Chinese case alone?

Our decision, breaking with this practice, has been, in the first place, to anthologize Chinese Buddhism within the Buddhism anthology, allowing that sub-anthology to become, by the inclusion of its Chinese material, the longest of the six. Our decision, in the second place, has been not to anthologize Chinese Confucianism at all. We have a secondary and a primary reason for this second decision.

The secondary reason not to anthologize Confucianism is that the People's Republic of China does not regard it as a religion at all. The government recognizes only five religions: Buddhism, Daoism, and Islam plus (as separate religions) Catholicism and Protestantism. Confucianism it simply defines as altogether out of the category *religion*.

Properly so? Is Confucianism a religion, or not? This question is notoriously one that "the West has never been able to answer and China never able to ask," and we do not presume to give a definitive answer here. It is true, on the one hand, that at many points during its long history, Confucianism has seemed to be neither a religion nor quite a philosophy either but rather a code of wisdom and conduct for the Chinese gentleman scholar—or, perhaps better, the aspiring Chinese statesman. Yet at other points in Confucian history, it must be noted, Confucius has been accorded the honor of a virtual god. We choose to leave that question in abeyance.

Our primary reason, in any case, to set Confucianism aside and dedicate our limited space to Daoism is that while the Confucian canon has been widely translated and, as ancient religious texts go, is relatively accessible, the Daoist canon has only recently been rescued from near death and has never before been presented for the use of nonspecialists in an overview of any historical completeness.

While two pre-Daoist classics—the gnomic *Daode jing* of Laozi and the tart wisdom of Zhuangzi—have been endlessly translated and are in no danger of disappearance, their relationship to the Daoist canon as a whole is, to borrow from an observation quoted in James Robson's introduction to the Daoism anthology, like the real but distant relationship of Plato and Aristotle to the Christian canon. What would we know of Christianity if Paul, Augustine, Dante, Luther, Milton, and so on down the hallowed list had all been lost and only Plato and Aristotle survived?

Such a fate did indeed very nearly befall Daoism. In the nineteenth century, leading up to the establishment of the first Republic of China in 1912, Qing dynasty authorities systematically confiscated Daoist temples and turned them into schools and factories. Having begun as an underground movement in the second century, Daoism—long out of official favor—was largely forced underground only again and more deeply so after the establishment of the Republic, which condemned it as superstition.

For the Daoist canon, the cost of this persecution was nearly outright extinction. By the early twentieth century, few copies of Daoism's canon of eleven hundred religious texts survived in all of China. But then, remarkably, circumstances eased enough to permit the reprint in 1926 of a rare surviving copy of the full 1445 Ming dynasty canon. This had been the last great effort at canon formation in Daoist history before Daoism's long decline commenced. As this reprint reached the West, scholarship on the history of Daoism and the interpretation of its texts slowly began. Nonetheless, particularly after the establishment of the Communist People's Republic of China in 1949, with its aggressive early persecution of all religions, many in the West believed that the actual practice of Daoism had finally died out in its birthplace.

They were mistaken. Over the past few decades, reliable reports have made it clear that Daoism is still alive and indeed is growing steadily stronger, having survived as if by taking Mao Zedong's advice to his guerrillas that they "move among the people as a fish swims in the sea." Just as the fish in the sea are not easily counted, so the Daoists of China escape the usual forms of Western quantification and Communist surveillance alike. But the Daoist fish are numerous, even if they have reason to swim deep.

Meanwhile, the work of translating and contextualizing the recovered texts has attracted a growing corps of Western scholars—initially in France and more recently in other Western countries, including the United States. As their work has gone forward, the world has begun to hear of Daoist messiahs and utopian dreams of peace; Daoist confession rituals and community liturgies; Daoist alchemy and proto-scientific experimentation; Daoist medicine, bodily cultivation (as distinct from asceticism), and sexual practices; Daoist prayer, including Daoist letter-writing to the gods; and Daoist pageantry, costume, magic, and music. In short, a lost religious world—the central, popular, indigenous, full-throated religious world of China—has been brought back to textual life. Our decision was to bring our readers a major sampling from this remarkable recovery.

The major religions of the world are probably better grasped, many scholars now insist, as a set of alternative customs and practices in loose organization—worship liturgies, pilgrimages, dietary restrictions, birth and burial practices, art, music, drama, dance, and so forth—than as a set of contending ideologies. Millions of men and women, even when they practice religions that we rightly regard as literary, are themselves illiterate. Yet when writing remade the world, it did remake religion as well. The major religious traditions of the world would not be major today had they not become literary traditions as well.

Because it is *written*, religious literature can be and has been shared, preserved through wars and persecutions, transmitted over time and space, and, most important of all, *taught* with ease and delight. When all else perishes, the written word often survives. The work before you is a self-contained, portable library of religious literature. You may read it on a plane, in the park, or in a waiting room and trust that every foreign or otherwise strange term will be explained on or near the page where it occurs. No foreign alphabets are used. Transliterations have been simplified to serve pedagogical utility rather than philological perfection. Diacritical marks have been kept to the absolute minimum. Though, as noted, a few of the large theoretical considerations that religion raises as a subject for human inquiry will be addressed in the general introduction, the emphasis in this work is overwhelmingly pragmatic rather than theoretical. For in this domain, more perhaps than in any other, outsiders have historically been as important as insiders, and beginners as welcome as veterans. So, to conclude where we began, whether you are an outsider or an insider, a beginner or a veteran, we welcome you to the pages of *The Norton Anthology of World Religions*.

JACK MILES
IRVINE, CALIFORNIA

Acknowledgments

*T*he *Norton Anthology of World Religions* would not have been possible without the help of many generous and able friends. We are grateful for the help of those named below as well as of others too numerous to list.

From W. W. Norton & Company, we wish to thank Roby Harrington, head of the college division, who conceived this volume; Pete Simon, its first editor, who contributed its title; Carly Fraser Doria, who has managed the assembly of illustrations and ancillary materials with intelligence and taste; developmental editors Alice Falk, Carol Flechner, and Kurt Wildermuth, who have tamed its prose to the demanding Norton standard; Adrian Kitzinger, who created the beautiful maps; Megan Jackson and Nancy Rodwan, permissions experts; art directors Debra Morton Hoyt and Ingsu Liu, designer Chin-Yee Lai, and artist Rosamond Purcell; production managers Sean Mintus and Julia Druskin; managing editor Marian Johnson, whose project-editorial wisdom is quietly evident on every page; and, most of all, Julia Reidhead, editorial director, whose taste and managerial finesse have preserved and advanced this work sagaciously for fully seven years.

Wendy Doniger wishes to thank Velcheru Narayana Rao for finding "Sita Lost in Thought" for her, and for finding and translating "Kausalya in Fury"; Vasudha Naranayan and Richard Fox for the Southeast Asian materials; Eleanor Zelliot, Gail Omvedt, and Dilip Chitre for the Dalit materials; her student assistants, Jeremy Morse and Charles Preston, for assembling all the texts; and Anne Mocko for help with the pronouncing glossaries.

James Robson wishes to thank Stephen R. Bokenkamp, for helping to get this project started; Alice Falk, for helping to get it completed; and Billy Brewster, for help with the pronouncing glossaries.

David Biale wishes to thank Ariel Evan Mayse and Sarah Shectman for research assistance beyond the call of duty.

Lawrence S. Cunningham wishes to thank his beloved wife, Cecilia, and their two daughters, Sarah and Julia.

Jane Dammen McAuliffe wishes to thank her splendid research associates, Carolyn Baugh, Sayeed Rahman, Robert Tappan, and Clare Wilde, and to recognize with appreciation both Georgetown University and Bryn Mawr College for their support of this work.

For generous financial support of this project, Jack Miles wishes to thank the John T. and Catherine D. MacArthur Foundation, the Getty Research Institute, and the University of California, Irvine. He thanks, in addition, for early editorial consultation, his publishing colleague John Loudon; for generous technical assistance, Steve Franklin and Stan Woo-Sam of UCI's information technology office; for invaluable assistance with the initial enormous delivery of texts, his former student Matthew Shedd; for helpful counsel on Asian Christianity, his colleague Tae Sung; for brilliant assistance in editorial rescue and rewrite, his irreverent friend and colleague Peter Heinegg; and for her sustaining and indomitable spirit, his irreplaceable Catherine Montgomery Crary.

This work is dedicated—in gratitude for all that they have preserved for our instruction—to the scribes of the world's great religions.

THE NORTON ANTHOLOGY OF

WORLD
RELIGIONS

CHRISTIANITY

The relation of the various peoples of the earth to the supreme interests of life, to God, virtue, and immortality, may be investigated up to a certain point, but can never be compared to one another with absolute strictness and certainty. The more plainly in these matters our evidence seems to speak, the more carefully must we refrain from unqualified assumptions and rash generalizations.

—JACOB BURCKHARDT,
The Civilization of
the Renaissance in Italy (1860)

GENERAL INTRODUCTION

How the West Learned to Compare Religions

BY JACK MILES

How to Read This Book: A Poetic Prelude

*T*he *Norton Anthology of World Religions* is designed to be read in either of two ways. You may read it from start to finish, or you may pick and choose from the table of contents as in a museum you might choose to view one gallery rather than another or one painting rather than another.

Imagine yourself at the entrance to a large museum containing a great many strange works of religious art. If you enter, what will you do? Will you devote equal time or equal intensity of attention to every work in the huge museum? Or will you skip some works, linger over others, and shape as you go a kind of museum within the museum? In the latter case, what will be your criteria? Those, too, you may well shape as you go. You may not entirely know even your own mind as you begin. You may not know exactly what you're after. You may be detached, and yet—disinterested? No, you are not exactly disinterested. You're looking around, waiting for something to reach you, some click, some insemination, a start. Entering is sometimes enough. You do not need a briefing by the curator to begin your visit.

So it is with this anthology. Take the works assembled here as lightly as you wish. You will still be taking them properly: you will be taking them for what they are. A new path begins to open into the consideration of religion when it is regarded as unserious, un-adult—but only in the way that art, poetry, and fiction in all its forms (including the theatrical and the cinematic) are so regarded. They all deal with made-up stuff. And yet will we ever be so adult as to outgrow them?

The Western cast of mind has undeniably had an intrusive and distorting effect in many parts of the world as Western culture has become a world culture, and yet that cast of mind has also had a liberating and fertilizing effect. It has opened a space in which the once incomparable has become comparable. Looking at the religions of others even from the outside but with a measure of openness, empathy, and good will can enable those of any religious tradition or none to see themselves from the outside as well, and that capacity is the very foundation of human sympathy and cultural wisdom.

In church one morning in the eighteenth century, the poet Robert Burns spotted a louse on a proper lady's bonnet and started thinking: If only she could see herself as he saw her! He went home and wrote his wonderfully earthy and witty "To a Louse, On Seeing One on a Lady's Bonnet, at Church 1786." The fun of the poem is that it is addressed to the louse in a mock "How dare you!" tone almost all the way to the end. At that point, however, it becomes suddenly reflective, even wistful, and Burns concludes, in his Scots English:

> O wad some Pow'r the giftie gie us
> To see oursels as ithers see us!
> It wad frae monie a blunder free us,
>   An' foolish notion:
> What airs in dress an' gait wad lea'e us,
>   An' ev'n Devotion!

Burns dreams, or half-prays, that some power would "the giftie gie us" (give us the gift) to see "oursels" (ourselves) as others see us—to see, as it were, the lice on our bonnets. Our fine and flouncing airs then "wad lea'e us" (would leave us). But it might not be simply vanity that would depart. The last words in the poem are "an' ev'n Devotion!" (and even devotion). Even our religious devotions might be affected if we could see ourselves at that moment just as others see us. So many of the cruelest mistakes in religion are made not out of malice but out of simple ignorance, blunders we would willingly avoid could we but see ourselves as others see us. Looking at other traditions, you need to see the bonnet and not just the louse. Looking at your own, however you define it, you need to see the louse as well as the bonnet.

Can Religion Be Defined?

What is religion? The word exists in the English language, and people have some commonsense notion of what it refers to. Most understand it as one kind of human activity standing alongside other kinds, such as business, politics, warfare, art, law, sport, or science. Religion is available in a variety of forms, but what is it, really? What makes it itself?

Simple but searching questions like these may seem to be the starting point for the study of religion. Within the study of religion, they are more precisely the starting point for the *theory* of religion. And readers will not be surprised to learn that academic theoreticians of religion have not been content with the commonsense understanding of the subject.

The theoretical difficulties that attend any basic element of human thought or experience are undeniable. What is mathematics? What is art? What is law? What is music? Books have been written debating number theory, aesthetic theory, legal theory, and music theory. It should come as no surprise then that the theory of religion is no less actively debated than are those other theories. Some definitions of religion are so loose as to allow almost anything to qualify as a religion. Others are so strict as to exclude almost everything ordinarily taken to be a religion (prompting one recent contributor to the *Journal of the American Academy of Religion* to give his article the wry or rueful title "Religions: Are There Any?").[1]

The inconvenient truth is that no definition of religion now enjoys general acceptance. In *The Bonobo and the Atheist* (2013), the primatologist Frans de Waal writes:

> To delineate religion to everyone's satisfaction is hopeless. I was once part of a forum at the American Academy of Religion, when

someone proposed we start off with a definition of religion. However much sense this made, the idea was promptly shot down by another participant, who reminded everyone that last time they tried to define religion half the audience had angrily stomped out of the room. And this in an academy named after the topic![2]

A survey of competing theories, if we were to attempt one here, could quickly jump to twenty-three entries if we simply combined the contents of two recent handbooks—the eight in Daniel L. Pals's *Eight Theories of Religion* (2006) and the fifteen in Michael Stausberg's *Contemporary Theories of Religion: A Critical Companion* (2009).[3]

Though no one writing on religion can entirely escape theoretical commitments, *The Norton Anthology of World Religions* is foremost an anthology of primary texts. By the term *primary* we understand texts produced by the practitioners of each of the anthologized religions for their fellow practitioners. Such an anthology does not collect theories of religion, for the simple reason that such theories are secondary texts. They belong not to the creation and practice of religion but, retrospectively, to its study and analysis. Accordingly, they have rarely been of much interest to religious practitioners themselves.

Religious practitioners are far from unique in this regard. "Philosophy of science is about as useful to scientists as ornithology is to birds," Richard Feynman (1918–1988), a Caltech physicist, famously quipped.[4] The philosophy (or theory) of religion is of as little use to, say, the Buddhist as philosophy of science is to the scientist. Just as the scientist is interested in her experiment rather than in the philosophy of science and the painter in his painting rather than in the philosophy of art, so the Buddhist is interested in the Buddha rather than in the philosophy of religion. The term *religion* itself, as an academic term comprising—as indeed it does in this work—many different religious traditions, may not be of much practical utility to the practitioner of any one of the traditions.

And yet we who have assembled this work may not excuse ourselves altogether from addressing the question "What is religion?" simply on the grounds that our pages are filled with primary texts, for introducing, framing, and contextualizing these texts are the words of our six anthologizing editors as well as the general editor. The seven of us speak in these pages not as practitioners of the religions anthologized here but as scholars writing *about* those religions. Scholarship at its most empirical cannot escape theory, because, to quote a dictum from the philosophy of science, all data are theory-laden. A theory of some sort will be found operative even when no explicit theoretical commitment has been made.

If, then, some tacit theory or theories of religion must necessarily have informed the choices made by our associate editors, given the general editor's decision to impose no single theory, has any silent theoretical convergence occurred? Now that the results are in and the editors' choices have actually been made, do they reflect a working answer to the question "What is religion?"

As general editor, I believe that they do, though it would take some rather elaborate spelling out to explain just *how* they do. Something more modest but more readily discernible must suffice for this introduction—namely, the claim that the choices made by the respective associate editors reflect a common method or, more modestly still, a common approach to the task of presenting a major religious literature with some coherence. In brief, the six associate editors have approached the six religions whose texts they anthologize as six kinds of practice rather than as six kinds of belief. In common usage, religious and unreligious people are divided into "believers" and "unbelievers." The editors have departed from this common usage, proceeding instead on the silent and admittedly modest premise that religion is as religion *does*. Even when speaking of belief, as they do only occasionally, they generally treat it as embedded in practice and inseparable from practice. Monotheism in the abstract is a belief. "Hear, O Israel, the Lord is our God, the Lord alone" as sung by a cantor in a synagogue is a practice.

When religion is approached as practice, what follows? Clearly, Daoist practice, Muslim practice, Christian practice, and so on are not identical, but the substantial differences *within* each of them can loom as large as the differences from one to another among them. *The goal of this anthology is to present through texts how this variety has developed and how the past continues to shape the present.* Thus, the body of material put on exhibit here serves less to answer the question "What is religion?" in any theoretically elaborate or definitive way than to question the answers others have given to that question—answers such as those offered by, for example, the twenty-three theories alluded to above. Whatever fascinating questions a given theory of religion may have posed and answered to its own satisfaction, it must also, we submit, be able to account for the complexity of the data that these primary texts exhibit. Rather than serving to illustrate some fully developed new theory of religion, in other words, the texts gathered here constitute the empirical evidence that any such theory must cope with. In the meantime, the working focus is squarely on practice.

Each of the religions anthologized here has contained multiple versions of itself both over time and at any given time, and the anthology does not attempt to drive past the multiplicity to the singular essence of the thing. Practitioners, of course, have not always been so neutral. Many have been or still are prepared to deny the legitimacy of others as Hindu, Muslim, Christian, Jewish, and so on. But for the purposes of this anthology, those denials themselves simply become a part of the broader story.

Syncretism, moreover—namely, the introduction of a feature from one religion into the life of another—is in itself an argument that the borrower and the lender are, or can be, related even when they are not, and never will be, identical. Multiple religious belonging—double or triple affiliation—sometimes takes syncretism a step further. And while borrowings across major borders are an additive process, adjustments within borders can often be a subtractive process, as seen in many statements that take the form "I am a Buddhist, but . . . ," "I am a Catholic, but . . . ," "I am a Muslim, but . . . ," and so forth. In such statements, the speaker takes the broad term as a starting point and then qualifies it until it fits properly.

Yet we do not claim anything more than practical utility for this default approach to the subject, knowing as we do that a great many scholars of religion decline to define the essence of religion itself but do not find themselves inhibited by that abstention from saying a great deal of interest about one religious tradition or another. Rather than name at the outset the one feature that establishes the category *religion* before discussing the particular religion that interests them, they make the usually silent assumption that the full range of beliefs and practices that have been conventionally thought of as religious is vast and that each religion must be allowed to do as it does, assembling its subsets from the vast, never-to-be-fully-enumerated roster of world religious practices. Having made that assumption, the scholars take a deep breath and go on to talk about what they want to talk about.

Twenty-first-century religion scholars are prepared to acknowledge coherence when they find it but determined never to impose it. They are aware that the entries made under the heading *religion* may not all be versions of just the same thing, but they are equally aware that the overlaps, the innumerable ad hoc points of contact, are also there and also real—and so they find the continued use of the collective term *religion* justified for the enriching and enlightening comparisons that it facilitates. All knowledge begins with comparison.

In telling the life stories of six major, living, international religions through their respective primary texts, the editors of *The Norton Anthology of World Religions* have neither suppressed variability over time in service to any supposedly timeless essence of the thing nor, even when using the word *classical*, dignified any one age as truly golden. Each of the stories ends with modernity, but modernity in each case is neither the climax nor the denouement of the story. It is not the last chapter, only the latest.

How Christian Europe Learned to Compare Religions

Most people, we said earlier, understand religion as "one kind of human activity standing alongside other kinds, such as business, politics, warfare, art, law, sport, or science." Another way to say this is that they understand religion to be one domain among many, each separate from the others. Broadly compatible with this popular understanding is a widely influential definition of religion formulated by the anthropologist Clifford Geertz (1926–2006).

In "Religion as a Cultural System," first published in 1966, Geertz defined religion as

> (1) a system of symbols which acts to (2) establish powerful, pervasive, and long-lasting moods and motivations in men by (3) formulating conceptions of a general order of existence and (4) clothing these conceptions with such an aura of factuality that (5) the moods and motivations seem uniquely realistic.[5]

Geertz does not claim that all cultures are equally religious. In fact, toward the end of his essay he observes that "the degree of religious articulateness is not a constant even as between societies of similar complexity."[6] However, he does tacitly assume that religion is if not universal then at least extremely widespread and that it is a domain separate from others, such as—to name two that he explores—science and ideology.[7]

But just how widespread is religion, and is it truly a domain separable from the rest of culture? Can religion really be distinguished from ideology? In Geertz's terms, wouldn't Marxism qualify as a religion? In recent decades, some have argued that even a thoroughly secular anthropologist like Geertz, in whose definition of religion neither God nor Christ is mentioned, can be seen as carrying forward an ideological understanding of religion that originated in the Christian West and has lived on in Western academic life as a set of inadequately examined assumptions. That religion is a domain separate from either ethnicity or culture is one of two key, historically Christian assumptions. That religion is a universal phenomenon—in some form, a part of every human society and even every human mind—is the other key assumption.

Perhaps the most widely cited historical critique of these assumptions is Tomoko Masuzawa's revealing *The Invention of World Religions, Or, How European Universalism Was Preserved in the Language of Pluralism* (2005). Masuzawa's book is not about the invention of the world's religions themselves but about the invention of *world religions* as a phrase used in the West to talk about them, postulating their parallel existence as separable and separate realities, available as an indefinitely expandable group for academic discussion.[8]

When and how, she asks, did this omnibus-phrase *world religions* come into the general usage that it now enjoys? She concludes her influential investigation with the candid confession that the invention and, especially, the very widespread adoption of the phrase remain something of a puzzle—but her analysis traces the usage back only to the nineteenth century. Our claim below is that though the phrase *world religions* may be recent, its roots run much deeper than the nineteenth century, as deep in fact as early Christianity's peculiar and unprecedented self-definition.

To say this is not to undercut the strength of the criticism. Christian explorers, traders, missionaries, and colonists encountering non-Western societies, especially after the discovery of the Americas and the colonial expansion of the West into Asia, have often isolated and labeled as "religions" behaviors that they took to be the local equivalents of what they knew in the West as Christianity. This process of isolating and labeling was a mistake when and if the societies themselves did not understand the behaviors in question as constituting either a separate domain or merely one instance of a more general phenomenon called religion. Moreover, when those purporting to understand non-Western societies in these historically Christian terms were invaders and imperialists, a perhaps unavoidable theoretical mistake could have grievous practical consequences. And when, in turn, ostensibly neutral, secular theories of religion—not imposed by conquerors or missionaries but merely proffered by Western academics—are alleged to make the same historically Christian assumptions, the entire project of comparative religious study may be faulted as Christian imperialism.

Because the viability and indeed the enormous value of such study are premises of this anthology, the challenge calls for a significant response, one that necessarily includes substantial attention to just how Christianity influenced the study of what the West has defined as world religions. The intention in what follows, however, is by no means to make a case for Christianity as inherently central or supreme among the world's religions. We intend rather, and only, to trace how, in point of fact, Christianity began as central to the Western *study* of religions and then, by degrees, yielded its position as more polycentric forms of study emerged.

Let us begin by stipulating that Christians did indeed acquire very early and thereafter never entirely lost the habit of thinking of their religion as a separate domain. Once this is conceded, it should come as no great surprise that as a corollary of this habit, they should have adopted early and never entirely lost the habit of thinking of other religions, rightly or wrongly, as similarly separate domains. This would be simply one more instance of the human habit of beginning with the known and with the self and working outward to the unknown and to the others.

But we must stipulate further that Christians made a second assumption—namely, that theirs should become humankind's first-ever programmatically "world" religion. The idea of universally valid religious truth was not new in itself. Ancient Israel had long since been told that its vocation was to be the light of the world. In the book of Isaiah, God says to his people through the prophet (49:6):

> It is too light a thing that you should be my servant to raise up the tribes of Jacob and to restore the preserved of Israel; I will give you as a light to the nations, that my salvation may reach to the end of the earth.[9]

In the Gospel of Matthew, Jesus turns this latent potential into a radically intrusive program for action. His final words to his apostles are

> Go therefore, and make disciplines of *all nations*, baptizing them in the name of the Father and of the Son and of the Holy Spirit, teaching them to observe all that I have commanded you; and, lo, I am with you always, even to the close of the age. (Matthew 28:19–20; emphasis added)

How ever did this instruction, as the first Christians put it into practice, lead to the secular study of "world religions" as we know it today?

The Social Oddity of the Early Church

In the earliest centuries of its long history, the Christian church defined its belief as different from the official polytheism of the Roman Empire, on the one hand, and from the monotheism of Rabbinic Judaism, on the other, inasmuch as the rabbinic Jews did not recognize Jesus as God incarnate. But if the church was thus, to borrow a convenient phrase from contemporary American life, a faith-based organization, it was not just a school of thought: it was also an *organization*. As faith-based, it undeniably placed unique and unprecedented stress on belief (and indeed set the pattern by which today all those religiously active in any way are routinely called *believers*, even when not all regard belief as central to their practice). Yet as an organization, the church depended not just on a distinct set of beliefs but also on a social identity separate, on the one hand, from that of the Roman Empire (or any other empire) and equally separate, on the other, from that of the Jewish nation (or any other nation). As a faith-based, voluntary, nonprofit, multiethnic, egalitarian, nongovernmental organization, the Christian church was a social novelty: nothing quite like it had ever been seen before. And as Christians, growing steadily in number, projected their novel collective self-understanding upon Roman and Jewish social reality alike, the effect was profoundly disruptive. Though many others would follow, these were the first two instances of Christian projection, and an analysis of how they worked is especially instructive.

By encouraging Roman polytheists to *convert* to Christianity while maintaining that they did not thereby cease to be Romans, the Christians implicitly invented religious conversion itself as an existential possibility. The term *religion* did not exist then in Greek, Latin, or Aramaic as a fully developed universal category containing both Roman polytheism and Christianity, but in the very action of conversion the future category was already implicit. By seeking to convert Roman polytheists to Christianity, the early Christians implied that Roman religiosity was a domain both separate from the rest of Roman life and replaceable. You could exchange your Roman religiosity for this modified Jewish religiosity, as the very act of conversion demonstrated, while bringing the rest of your Roman identity with you.

In the first century, conversion thus defined was an unprecedented and socially disruptive novelty. Until the destabilizing intrusion of Christianity, respect for the Roman gods had always been inseparable from simply being Roman: religious identity and civic identity had always constituted an unbroken whole. Christianity encouraged Romans to split that single identity into a double identity: religion, on the one hand; culture and ethnicity, on the other. In this sequestration of the religiously meaningful from the religiously neutral or meaningless was born the very possibility of secular culture, as well as religion as Western modernity has come to understand it—religion as involving some semblance of faith and some form of collective identity separable from ethnicity or culture.

In by far the most important instance of this division of social identity, the original Christian Jews, having adopted a minority understanding of Jewish tradition, denied that they were any less Jewish for that reason. Writing of his Jewish critics, St. Paul fumed (2 Corinthians 11:22): "Are they Israelites? So am I!" Much of first-century Jewry would not have disagreed with him had the matter stopped there, for there were many peacefully coexisting Jewish views about Jewish belief and practice. As no more than the latest variation on the old themes, the Christian Jews would not have created anything structurally new. But they did create something new by taking the further step of bringing themselves, with their recognizably Jewish religious views (views indeed unrecognizable as anything except Jewish), into an unprecedented social relationship with non-Jews—namely, into the Christian church. By linking themselves to non-Jews in this way, without renouncing their Jewish identity, the Christian Jews—enjoying particular success in the Roman Diaspora—demonstrated that as they conceived their own Jewish religiosity to be distinguishable from the rest of what was then the Jewish way of life, so they conceived the same two components of identity to be likewise distinguishable for all other Jews.

Rabbinic Judaism, dominant in Palestine and the Mesopotamian Diaspora, would eventually repudiate this Christian projection and reassert that Jewish religiosity and Jewish identity are one and indistinguishable. In the rabbinic view that became and has remained dominant in world Judaism, there are no "Judaists," only Jews. But this reassertion did not happen overnight: it took generations, even centuries. Neither the Romans nor the Jews nor the Christians themselves immediately understood the full novelty of what was coming into existence.

Through most of world history, in most parts of the world, what we are accustomed to call religion, ethnicity, culture, and way of life have been inextricable parts of a single whole. How did Christianity begin to become an exception to this general rule? On the one hand, it appropriated a set of Jewish religious ideas—including monotheism, revelation, covenant, scripture, sin, repentance, forgiveness, salvation, prophecy, messianism, and apocalypticism—without adopting the rest of the highly developed and richly nuanced Jewish way of life. On the other hand, it universalized these Jewish religious ideas, creating a new social entity, the church, through which non-Jews could be initiated into an enlarged version of the ancestral Jewish covenant with God. The Jews had believed for centuries God's declaration, "I am the LORD your God, who have separated you from the peoples" (Leviticus 20:24) and "you are a people holy to the LORD your God" (Deuteronomy 7:6). In effect, the Christian Jews split the idea of covenanted separateness and holiness from what consequently became the relatively secularized idea of nationality. The Jews were still a people, they maintained, but God had now revised and universalized the terms of his covenant. In the words of Jesus' apostle Peter, "Truly I perceive that God shows no partiality, but in every nation any one who fears him and does what is right is acceptable to him" (Acts 10:34–35).

The original Greek word for church, *ekklēsia*, suggests a collective understanding of church members as "called out" from other kinds of religious, ethnic, or political membership into this new—and now, in principle, universal—"people set apart as holy." The *ekklēsia* offered its members a sense of sacred peoplehood, but it tellingly lacked much else that ordinarily maintains a national identity. It had no ancestral land, no capital city, no language of its own, no literature at the start other than what it had inherited from the Jews, no distinct cuisine, no standard dress, and no political or governmental support beyond the organizational management of the church itself. Moreover, this ethnically mixed and socially unpromising group was atheist in its attitude toward all gods except the God of Israel as they had come to understand him—God as incarnate in Jesus the Messiah. Within the political culture of the Roman Empire, this rejection of the empire's gods was a seditious and rebellious rejection of Roman sovereignty itself. When, unsurprisingly, the empire recognized it as such and began intermittently to persecute the church, the Christian sense of separateness only grew.

In this form, and despite intermittent persecution, the church grew quietly but steadily for more than three centuries. At that point, with perhaps a fifth of the population of the Roman Empire enrolled in separate local Christian churches under relatively autonomous elected supervisors (bishops), the emperor Constantine (r. 312–37) first legalized Christianity and then stabilized its doctrine by requiring the Christian bishops—ordered to convene for the first time as a council at Nicaea, near his eventual capital city of Constantinople—to define it. In 381, the emperor Theodosius (r. 379–95) made this newly defined Christianity the official religion of the Roman Empire, and the new religion—no longer persecuted but now operating under a large measure of imperial control—began a fateful reversal of course. It began to fuse with the political governance and the Hellenistic culture of imperial Rome, compromising the character of the *ekklēsia* as a domain separate from nationality or culture. In a word, it began to normalize.

The establishment of Christianity as the state religion of the Roman Empire ushered in a period of rapid growth, pushed by the government, within the borders of the empire. Beyond them, however, most notably in the Persian Empire just to the east, its new status had the opposite effect.

Once relatively unhindered as a social movement taken to be as compatible with Persian rule as with Roman, Christianity now became suspect as the official religion of the enemy.

Meanwhile, in Rome itself—the "First Rome," as historically prior to the Eastern Empire's capital, Constantinople—and in the western European territories that it administered, a partial but significant return to the original separation of domains occurred just a century later. In 476, Odoacer, king of an invading Germanic tribe, deposed the last Roman emperor, Romulus Augustulus, without effectively assuming authority over the Christian church. Instead, the power of the bishop of Rome—the highest surviving official of the old imperial order—over the church in western Europe began to grow, while the power of kings and feudal lords over all that was not the church steadily grew as well. The nominally unified imperial authority over the empire and its established religion thus split apart. To be sure, for centuries the pope claimed the authority to anoint kings to their royal offices, and at certain moments this was a claim that could be sustained. But gradually, a sense that civilian and religious authority were different and separate began to set in. At the same time, the identity of the church as, once again, detached or disembedded from the state and from culture alike—the church as a potentially universal separate domain, a holy world unto itself—began to consolidate.

The Four-Cornered Medieval Map of Religion

Wealth, power, and population in the world west of India were concentrated during the sixth century in the Persian Empire and in the Eastern Roman or Byzantine Empire. Western Europe during the same century—all that had once been the Western Roman Empire—was far poorer, weaker, more sparsely populated, and culturally more isolated than the empires to its east. Then, during the seventh and eighth centuries, a third major power arose. Arabia had long provided mercenary soldiers to both of the then-dominant empires; but religiously inspired by the Islam newly preached by Muhammad (ca. 570–632) and militarily unified under his successors, it became a major world power in its own right with stunning speed. Arab armies conquered the entirety of the Persian Empire within a generation. Within a century, they had taken from the Eastern Roman Empire its Middle Eastern and North African possessions (half of its total territory) as well as the major Mediterranean islands. From what had been the Western Roman Empire, they had subtracted three-quarters of Spain and penetrated deep into France until driven back across the Pyrenees by the unprecedented European alliance that defeated them in the 732 Battle of Poitiers.

The political map of the world had been redrawn from India to the Atlantic, but what of the religious map? How did western European Christians now understand themselves among the religions of the world? The symbolic birth date of Europe as Christendom has long been taken to be Christmas Day of the year 800. On that date, Pope Leo III crowned Charles the Great, better known as Charlemagne—the grandson of Charles Martel, who had unified the European forces at Poitiers—as the first "Holy Roman Emperor." The Muslim invasion from distant Arabia had shocked an isolated and fragmented region into an early assertion of common religious and geographical identity. As a result, there was a readiness to give political expression to a dawning collective self-understanding. The lost Western Roman Empire was by no means reconstituted: Charlemagne was an emperor without much of an empire, his coronation expressing a vision more than a reality. But the vision itself mattered decisively in another way, for what came into existence at about this time was an understood quadripartite map of the world of religion that would remain standard in Europe for centuries.

There was, first and foremost for Christians, Christianity itself: the Christian church understood to be the same single, separate domain wherever it was found, with the same distinct relationship to national and cultural identity. To the extent that it rested on common faith, the church could be divided by heresy; but even heretical Christians, of whom there would be fewer in the early ninth century than there had been in earlier Christian centuries, were still understood to be Christians. They were practicing the right religion in a wrong way, but they were not practicing another religion altogether.

There was, second, Judaism: the Jews of Europe, a population living among Christians, disparaged but well known, whose relationship to Christianity was well remembered and whose religious authenticity rested on a recognized if more or less resented prior relationship with the same God that the Christians worshipped. Christian understanding of Jewish religious life as the Jews actually lived it was slender, and Christian knowledge of the vast rabbinic literature that had come into existence between the second and the ninth century, much of it in far-off Mesopotamia, was virtually nonexistent. Knowledge of Greek had been lost in Latin Europe, and knowledge of the Hebrew and Aramaic that the Jews of Europe had managed to preserve (despite recurrent persecution) was confined to them alone. Yet, this ignorance notwithstanding, Christian Europe was well aware that the Jews practiced a religion different from their own. And the implicit Christian understanding of religion as a separate domain of potentially universal extent was reinforced by the fact that from the outside, Jewish religious practice appeared to be at least as deeply divorced from national and cultural practices as was Christian religious practice: the Jews, who had lost their land and were dispersed around the world, lived in Europe much as Europe's Christians lived.

The third corner of Europe's four-cornered understanding of world religion was Islam, though the terms *Islam* and *Muslim* would not come into European usage until centuries later. Even the term *Arab* was not standard. The multinational religious commonwealth that we now call world Islam has been traditionally referred to by the Muslims themselves with the Arabic expression *dar al-islam*, the "House of Islam" or the "House of Submission" (because *islam* means "submission"—that is, submission to God). Whether it was *Saracen, Moor, Turk, or Arab*, the ethnic terms used by Christians to refer to the Muslims who faced them in the south and the east depended on time and place. Christendom as the Holy Roman Empire had become a domain geographically separate from the House of Islam. Similarly, Christianity as distinct from Christendom was evidently a domain of belief and practice separate from that of Islam. But among Christians, the further inference was that as Christian identity was separate from Bavarian or Florentine identity, so Muslim identity must be separate from Arab or Turkish identity. To some extent, this was a false inference, for obligatory Arabic in the Qur'an and obligatory pilgrimage to Mecca did much to preserve the originally Arab identity of Islam. Yet the tricontinental distribution and ethnic variability of the House of Islam fostered among Europeans an understanding of Islam as, like Christianity, a potentially universal religion separable from the ethnicity of any one of its component parts.

As Christian anxiety mounted that the year 1000 might mark the end of the world (an outcome that some Christians saw predicted in the New Testament book of Revelation), Muhammad came to be seen by some as the Antichrist, a destructive figure whose appearance during the last apocalyptic period before the end had been foretold (again in the book of Revelation). Yet gradually, albeit as "Mohammedanism," Islam came to be differentiated from Christianity in theological rather than in such floridly mythological terms. The Qur'an was translated into Latin in 1142. The High Middle Ages began to witness various forms of religious and cultural encounter—some as an unintended consequence of the Crusades; others through the influence of large Christian minorities living under Muslim rule and, over time, substantial Muslim minorities living under Christian rule, notably in Spain and Sicily. Finally, there was the mediating influence of a cross-culturally significant Jewish population residing on either side of the Muslim–Christian border and communicating across it. One result of these minglings was a gradually growing overlap in the techniques in use in all three communities for the exegesis of the sacred scriptures that for each mattered so much.

As Muslim monotheism came gradually into clearer focus, medieval Christianity came to recognize Muslims as worshippers of the same God that Jews and Christians worshipped. Meanwhile, Islam was, like Christianity, a religion that actively sought converts who were then made part of a separate quasi-national, quasi-familial, yet potentially universal social entity. The genesis of the Western understanding of religion as such—religion as a separate but expandable social category—was thus significantly advanced by Christianity's encounter with another social entity so like itself in its universalism and its relative independence from ethnic or cultural identity.

The fourth corner of the world religion square was occupied by a ghost—namely, the memory of long-dead Greco-Roman polytheism. Christianity was born among the urban Jews of the Roman Empire and spread gradually into the countryside. Even in largely rural Europe, monasteries functioned as surrogate cities and Christianity spread outward from these centers of structure and literacy. *Pagus* is the Latin word for "countryside," and in the countryside the old polytheisms lingered long after they had died out in the cities. Thus, a rural polytheist was a *paganus*, and *paganismus* (paganism) became synonymous with polytheism. In England, pre-Christian polytheism lingered in the inhospitable heath, and so *heathenism* became an English synonym for *paganism*. Though polytheism is not necessarily idolatrous (one may believe in many gods without making a single idol), polytheistic belief and idolatrous practice were generally conflated. More important for the centuries that lay ahead, the increasingly jumbled memory of what Greco-Roman polytheism—remembered as "paganism"—had been in the Christian past was projected upon the enormous and almost entirely unknown world beyond the realms occupied by Christians, Muslims, and Jews.

The quadripartite typology just sketched was only one long-lived stage in the development of the comparative study of religion in Christian Europe. We may pause to note, however, that as of the year 800 Judaism and Islam were operating under similar typologies. The Qur'an, definitive for all Islamic thought, takes frequent and explicit note of Judaism and Christianity, while the place occupied by the memory of Greco-Roman polytheism in Christianity is occupied in the Qur'an by the memory of polytheism as it existed in Arabia at the time when Muhammad began to receive his revelations. World Jewry, as a minority maintaining its identity and its religious practice in both Christendom and the House of Islam, had a richer experience of both Christians and Muslims than either of those two had of the other. Yet what functioned for Jews in the way that the memory of Greco-Roman polytheism functioned for Christians and the memory of Arabian polytheism functioned for Muslims was the memory of ancient Canaanite, Philistine, and Babylonian polytheism as recorded in the Bible and used thereafter as a template for understanding all those who were the enemies of God and the persecutors of his Chosen People.

Now, the comparison of two religions on terms set by one of them is like the similarly biased comparison of two nationalities: the outcome is a predictable victory for the side conducting the comparison. In fact, when religion and ethnicity are fused, religious comparison is commonly stated in ethnic terms rather than in what we would consider religious terms. Thus, in the Hebrew Bible, apostasy from the religion of Israel is called "foreign worship" ('avodah zarah) rather than simply false worship, though falsehood or worse is unmistakably implied. To the extent that ethnicity is taken to be a matter of brute fact, and therefore beyond negotiation, religion bound to ethnicity has seemed a nonnegotiable matter of fact as well.

In this regard, however, the condition of medieval Christian Europe was interestingly unstable. Demographically, the two largest religious realities it knew—Islam and Christianity itself—were consciously and ideologically multinational in character, and both actively sought converts from all nations. Judaism was not evangelistic in this way, but world Jewry was uniquely the world's first global nation: the bulk of its population was distributed internationally in such a way that Jews were accustomed in every place to distinguish their ethnicity from the ethnicity of the locale and their religion from its religion. Christian prejudice often prevented Jewish acculturation (not to suppose that Jews always wished to acculturate), but it did not always do so. And so during extended periods of Christian toleration, even the generally firm Jewish sense that religion, ethnicity, and culture were a seamless whole may have become more difficult to sustain. This three-sided—Christian, Muslim, and Jewish—embrace of the notion that religion was a separate domain set the stage in Europe for the comparison of the three on terms derived from a neutral fourth entity that was not to be equated with any one of them.

This fourth entity was Aristotelian philosophy as recovered in Europe during the eleventh and twelfth centuries. Of course, the philosophical discussions that began to be published—such as Abelard's mid-twelfth-century *Dialogue among a Philosopher, a Jew, and a Christian*, in which the philosopher of the title often appears to be a Muslim—always ended in victory for the imagined Christian. Yet Abelard (1079–1142) was eventually condemned by the church because his dialogue clearly recognized reason, mediated by philosophy, as independent of the religions being discussed and as capable of rendering judgments upon them all. Philosophy as that fourth, neutral party would be joined over time by psychology, sociology, anthropology, economics, evolutionary biology, cognitive science, and other analytical tools. But these enlargements lay centuries in the future. As the Middle Ages were succeeded by the Renaissance, philosophy had made a crucial start toward making neutral comparisons, even though Europe's quadripartite map of the world's religions was still quite firmly in place, with most comparisons still done on entirely Christian and theological terms.

The Renaissance Rehearsal of Comparative Religion

The Italian Renaissance—beginning in the fourteenth century and flourishing in the fifteenth and sixteenth—is commonly taken to be more important as a movement in art and literature than in philosophy or religion. To be sure, it did not attempt a transformation of European Christianity comparable to that of the Protestant Reformation of the sixteenth century. But the kind of religious comparison that began in the early eighteenth century, in the aftermath of Europe's devastating seventeenth-century Protestant–Catholic Wars of Religion, was foreshadowed during the Renaissance by the revival of classical Greek and Latin and by the recovery of masterpieces of world literature written in those languages.

First of all, perfected knowledge of Latin and the recovered knowledge of Greek enabled Italian scholars to publish critical editions of the texts of classical antiquity as well as philologically grounded historical criticism of such later Latin texts as the Donation of Constantine, exposed as a papal forgery by the Italian humanist Lorenzo Valla (1407–1457). It was in Renaissance Italy, too, that Christian Europe first recovered knowledge of biblical Hebrew. The earliest chair of Hebrew was established late in the fifteenth century at the University of Bologna. Despite repeated persecutions, ghettoizations, and expulsions, the Jewish population of Italy grew substantially during the Renaissance, enthusiastically embracing the then-new technology of printing with movable type. The first complete publication of the Hebrew Bible in the original, with Jewish commentaries, appeared in Venice in 1517 and proved highly instructive to Christian Europe; by the end of the following century, Italian scholars were even starting to read both the post-biblical rabbinic literature and the Kabbalah, writings in a later extra-rabbinic Jewish mystical tradition that fascinated some of them. Little by little, Christian Europe was beginning to learn from Europe's Jews.

As the Renaissance began to introduce Christian Europe by slow degrees to the critical examination of ancient texts as well as to the inner religious life of Judaism, it accomplished something similar in a more roundabout way for the lost religions of Greece and Rome. The humanists of the Renaissance did not believe in the gods and goddesses of Olympus as they believed in God the Almighty Father of Christianity, but even as they read the classical literature only as literature, they nonetheless were taken deep inside the creedal, ritual, imaginative, and literary life of another religion—namely, the lost Greco-Roman polytheism. During the Italian Renaissance, the term *humanist* (Italian *umanista*), we should recall, was not used polemically, as if in some sort of pointed contrast to *theist*. Rather, it was a declaration of allegiance to the humanizing, civilizing power of art and imaginative literature. Renaissance humanism's imaginative engagement with the religions of classical Greece and Rome thus constituted an unplanned rehearsal for the real-world, real-time imaginative engagements with non-Christian religions and cultures that lay immediately and explosively ahead for Europe. When the Spanish *conquistadores* encountered the living polytheism of Aztec Mexico, their first interpretive instinct was to translate the gods of Tenochtitlán into their nearest Greek and Roman equivalents. This was an intellectually clumsy move, to be sure, but less clumsy than interpreting them exclusively in mono-theist Christian terms would have been. Moreover, because neither classical paganism nor Aztec polytheism was taken to be true, the two could be com-pared objectively or, if you will, humanistically—and from that early and fumbling act of comparison many others would follow.

In the study of philosophy, the Renaissance added Plato and various ancient Neoplatonists to the Aristotle of the medieval universities. More important, perhaps, it began to read late-classical moral philosophies—notably Stoicism and Epicureanism—whose frequent references to the gods made them in effect lost religions. Sometimes inspiring, sometimes scandal-ous, these recovered moral philosophies introduced personality and inner complexity into the inherited category of paganism. Philosophical recover-ies of this sort could remain a purely academic exercise, but for that very reason their influence might be more subtly pervasive. Often, those who studied these texts professed to be seeking only their pro forma subordina-tion to the truth of Roman Catholic Christianity. Nonetheless, the ideas found their way into circulation. To be sure, the few who took the further step of propagating pagan worldviews as actual alternatives to Christian faith or Aristotelian cosmology could pay a high price. The wildly specula-tive Neoplatonist Giordano Bruno (1548–1600) was burned at the stake as a heretic. But others, scarcely less speculative, spread their ideas with little official interference and in response to widespread popular curiosity.

Comparative Christianity in the Protestant Reformation

Important as the Renaissance was to the development in Europe of a capac-ity for religious comparison, the Protestant Reformation was surely even more important, for it forced Europeans in one region after another to com-pare forms of Christianity, accept one, and reject the others. Frequently, this lacerating but formative experience required those who had rejected Catholi-cism to reject one or more contending forms of Protestantism as well. This was clearly the case during the English Civil War (1642–51), which forced English Christians to side either with the Anglican king or with the Puritan rebels who beheaded him; but there were other such choices, some of them much more complicated.

Tentative moves toward tolerance during these struggles were far less frequent than fierce mutual persecution and, on either side, the celebration of victims as martyrs. The Catholics tried to dismiss and suppress the Prot-estants as merely the latest crop of Christian heretics. The Protestants commonly mythologized Rome as Babylon and compared Catholics to the ancient Babylonians, viewing them as pagans who had taken the New Israel, the Christian church, into exile and captivity. The century and a half of the reformations and the Wars of Religion certainly did not seem to promise a future of sympathetic, mutually respectful religious comparison. And yet within the religious game of impassioned mutual rejection then being played, each side did develop formidable knowledge of the practices, beliefs, and arguments of the other. To the extent that the broader religious comparison initiated during the Enlightenment of the late seventeenth and the eighteenth centuries called for close observation, firsthand testimony, logical analysis, and preparatory study of all kinds, its debt to both the Protestant Reformation and the Catholic Counter-Reformation is enormous.

Particularly important was the historical awareness that the Protestant Reformation introduced into Christian thought. Protestantism took the New Testament to be a historically reliable presentation of earliest Christianity and, using that presentation as a criterion, proceeded to reject the many aspects of Roman Catholic practice that appeared to deviate from it. To be sure, the Roman church had been reading, copying, and devotedly commenting on the Bible for centuries, but it had not been reading it as history. Here the Renaissance paved the way for the Reformation, for the Bible that Rome read was the Bible in a Latin translation; and the Renaissance, as it recovered the knowledge of Hebrew and Greek, had recovered the ability to read the original texts from which that Latin translation had been made. In 1516, the Dutch humanist Desiderius Erasmus published a bilingual, Greek-Latin edition of the New Testament, correcting the received Latin to bring it into conformity with the newly recovered Greek. Armed with this new tool, the many educated Europeans who knew Latin but not Greek could immediately see that the Latin on which the church had relied for a thousand years was at many points unreliable and in need of revision. In this way, Erasmus, a child of the Renaissance, took a first, fateful step toward historicizing the Bible.

The Reformation, launched just a year later with the publication by Martin Luther of "Ninety-Five Theses on the Power and Efficacy of Indulgences," would take the further, explosive step of historicizing the church itself. To quote a famous line from Reformation polemics, Erasmus "laid the egg that Luther hatched." Thus, two epoch-making historical tools of Protestantism as it would dynamically take shape became integral parts of the later comparative study of non-Christian religions as undertaken by Christian scholars: first, the reconstruction of the composition history of the original texts themselves by scholars who had mastered the original languages; and second, the comparison of later religious practice to earlier through the study of the recovered and historically framed original texts.

In one regard, finally, Protestantism may have indirectly contributed to the comparative study of religion by setting in motion a gradual subversion of the very understanding of religion as a domain separate from ethnicity and culture that had been constitutive of Christian self-understanding almost from its start. Mark C. Taylor argues brilliantly in *After God* (2007) that what is often termed the disappearance of God or the disappearance of the sacred in modernity is actually the integration of that aspect of human experience with the rest of modern experience—a process whose onset he traces to Martin Luther's and John Calvin's sanctification of all aspects of human life as against medieval Christianity's division of the religious life of monks and nuns from the worldly (secular) life of laypeople.[10]

This progressive modern fusion of once separate domains would explain the spread in the West of the experience of the holy in ostensibly secular contexts and of the aesthetic in ostensibly religious contexts. Clearly the earlier Christian sense of religion as a separate domain has lingered powerfully in the West. Yet if Taylor is right, then post-Protestant religious modernity in the West, though deeply marked by Protestantism, may be a paradoxical correction of Christianity to the world norm. Or, to put the matter more modestly, the diffuse post-Christian religiosity of the modern West may bear a provocative similarity to the much older but equally diffuse religiosity of South and East Asia or indeed of pre-Christian world Jewry.

Toleration, Science, Exploration, and the Need for a New Map

After decades of controversy climaxing in all-out war, it became clear to exhausted Protestants and Catholics alike that neither could dictate the religious future of Europe. The Wars of Religion came to a close in 1648 with the Peace of Westphalia, which, though it by no means established individual freedom of religion, did end international religious war in Europe. Its key principle—*Cuius regio, eius religio* (literally, "Whose the rule, his the religion")—allowed the king or the government of each nation to establish a national religion, but effectively banned any one nation from attempting to impose its religion upon another. At the international level, in other words, there was agreement to disagree. Christian religious fervor itself—at least of the sort that had burned heretics, launched crusades, and so recently plunged Europe into civil war—fell into relative disrepute. The latter half of the seventeenth century saw what Herbert Butterfield (1900–1979), a major historian of Christianity in European history, once called "the Great Secularization."[11]

The old religious allegiances remained, but by slow degrees they began to matter less, even as national allegiance and national devotion—patriotism, as it came to be called—began to take on the moral gravity and ceremonial solemnity of religious commitment and the fallen soldier began to supplant the martyr. In 1689, John Locke published *A Letter Concerning Toleration*, in which he advanced the idea that a state would better guarantee peace within its borders by allowing many religions to flourish than by imposing any one of them. Locke favored a division of the affairs of religion as essentially private from the affairs of state as essentially public, capturing an attitudinal shift that was already in the air during the Enlightenment and would significantly mark the comparative study of religion as it took lastingly influential shape in the following century.

More intensely than by nascent toleration, the mood of the late seventeenth century was marked by wonder at the discoveries of natural science, above all those of Isaac Newton, whose major work establishing the laws of motion and universal gravitation was published in 1687. The poet Alexander Pope captured the popular mood in a famous couplet, written as Newton's epitaph (1730): "Nature, and Nature's Laws lay hid in Night. / God said, *Let Newton be!* and All was *Light*." Light was the master image of the Enlightenment—light, light, and "more light" (the legendary last words of Johann Wolfgang von Goethe [1749–1832]). Though the notion of natural law did not begin with Newton, his vision of the vast, calm, orderly, and implicitly benign operation of the laws of motion and gravity was unprecedented and gave new impetus to the search for comparable natural laws governing many other phenomena, including religion. Was there such a thing as a natural religion? If so, how did Christianity or any other actual religion relate to it? This idea, too, was pregnant with the promise of a future comparative study of religion.

While northern European Christianity was fighting the Wars of Religion, southern European Christianity had been transforming both the demography of Christendom and its understanding of the physical geography of the planet. The globe-spanning Portuguese and Spanish empires came into existence with speed comparable only to the Arab conquests of the seventh and eighth centuries. In evangelizing the Americas, the Portuguese and the Spaniards may have made Christianity for the first time the world's largest religion. In any case, their success in establishing colonial trading outposts along the African, Indian, Japanese, and Chinese coasts as well as founding the major Spanish colony of the Philippine Islands (named for the king of Spain) meant that European trade with India and China, above all the lucrative spice trade, no longer needed to pass through Muslim Central Asia or the Muslim Middle East.

Catholic missionaries did not have the success in Asia that they enjoyed in the Americas, yet the highly educated and culturally sophisticated Jesuit missionaries to Asia and the Americas became a significant factor in the evolving religious self-understanding of Europe itself. As extensive reports on the religions of Mexico, Peru, and above all India, China, and Japan reached Europe, they were published and read by many others besides the religious superiors for whom they had been written. Portugal and Spain had opened Europe's doors to a vastly enlarged world. The centuries-old quadripartite European division of the world's religions—Christianity, Judaism, Islam, and Paganism—was still generally in place in European minds. But from that point forward, as the sophistication of the religions of Asia and the Americas as well as the material and social brilliance of their civilizations came into focus, the inadequacy of *paganism* as a catchall term became evident, as did the need for new ways to speak of the newly recognized reality.

A New Reference Book Defines a New Field of Study

If any occasion can be singled out as the juncture when all these factors coalesced and produced a powerful new engagement with *world religions* in a way that approached the modern understanding of that phrase, it is the publication in Amsterdam between 1723 and 1737 of an epochal reference work, one that should indeed be seen as a direct ancestor of *The Norton Anthology of World Religions*. Appearing in seven sumptuous volumes comprising more than 3,000 pages with 250 pages of engravings, this encyclopedic production was *Religious Ceremonies and Customs of All the Peoples of the World* (*Cérémonies et coutumes religieuses de tous les peuples du monde*) by Jean-Frédéric Bernard and Bernard Picart. Here, for the first time, was a presentation in one large work of all the religions of the world then known to Europe. Here, for the first time, was an attempt to reckon with how Europe's religious self-understanding would have to change in light of the previous two centuries of exploration, far-flung evangelization, and colonization.

It is important to note that this work, which was an immediate success and went through many editions and translations (and plagiarizations and piracies) over the next two hundred years, did not begin in the academic world and spread outward to the general public. Its address was directly to the general literate public—to the French public first, but quickly to other publics reading other languages. Jean Frederic Bernard, brilliant but far from famous, was not just its behind-the-scenes research director, editor, and author: he was also its entrepreneurial publisher. It was a masterstroke on his part to secure the collaboration of Bernard Picart, already famous as an engraver producing reproductions of masterpiece paintings in an era before public art museums and long before photography, when what the public knew about art was limited to what they saw in church or what they acquired as engravings. By enabling the European public to see Picart's depictions of Aztec and Asian temples, costumes, and ceremonies, reconstructed from missionaries' descriptions, Bernard and Picart introduced the stimulating possibility of visual comparison. Where visual comparison led, philosophical and other critical comparison were intended to follow—and did.

As noted above, in the latter decades of the seventeenth century and the first of the eighteenth John Locke and a few other thinkers began to argue forcefully for religious toleration. Like Locke, Bernard and Picart were radical Calvinists as well as early "freethinkers," and the Netherlands was unique in their lifetimes as a haven for refugee dissidents and minorities of various kinds. Locke himself took refuge in the Netherlands during a turbulent and threatening period in England. Bernard's Huguenot (French Calvinist) family had fled to the Netherlands when Jean Frederic was a boy. Picart, having abandoned Catholicism, moved there permanently as an adult, joining a large émigré French or French-speaking population in Amsterdam. The Peace of Westphalia, though it had imposed mutual forbearance in religious matters at the international level, had not done so at the national level. Protestants were still severely persecuted in France, as were Catholics in England. In the Netherlands, by contrast, though Calvinists were overwhelmingly dominant in public life, the private practice of Catholicism was indulged, while Jews were allowed public worship, and even deists or atheists had little to fear from the government. So it happened that though their great work was written in French, Bernard and Picart had good reason to publish it in the Netherlands.

In their magisterial account of the making of this work, *The Book That Changed Europe: Picart and Bernard's "Religious Ceremonies of the World,"* the historians Lynn Hunt, Margaret C. Jacob, and Wijnand Mijnhardt speculate about another possible consequence of its publication in the Netherlands—namely, the relative oblivion that overtook it in the twentieth century. The most populous European nations have tended to understand the intellectual history of the West through the minds of their own most influential thinkers, then through those of their major rivals, and only then through authors, however important, whose works were written or published in the smaller nations. Be that as it may, "Picart," as the work was commonly called, had two lasting effects far beyond the borders of the Netherlands. First, by discussing and illustrating the religions of Asia and of the Americas at length, it ended forever the quadripartite division of the world's religions that had structured European thought for eight hundred years. Second, it further solidified the conception of religion as a domain separable from culture and ethnicity. To quote *The Book That Changed Europe*, "This global survey of religious practices effectively *disaggregated and delimited* the sacred, making it specific to time, place, and institutions."[12]

There was now a greatly enlarged universe of religions to reckon with, to be sure, and Christian "teach ye all nations" missionary universalism had already mobilized to engage it. But also now, more strongly than ever, there was "religion" as an incipiently secular category capable of growth: it had lately been expanded by several new members and conceivably could be expanded further as further reports came in. The universalism of this emergent understanding of religion explains in part why the French Revolution, at the end of the eighteenth century, could presume to declare the "Rights of Man" rather than merely "of the [French] Citizen."

Bernard's and Picart's personal libraries suggest two favorite areas of reading: the ancient classics and travel books. The three historians note that 456 travel books were published in Europe in the fifteenth century, 1,566 in the seventeenth, and 3,540 in the eighteenth.[13] The co-creators' reading in the classics put them in touch with that pluralism of the mind made possible by the Renaissance recovery of classical moral philosophy and by the humanists' imaginative participation in the beliefs that figure so largely in classical literature. Their avid reading of travel reports gave them the enlarged geographical awareness made possible by the age of exploration.

As an early theorist of religion in this transformed mise-en-scène, Bernard blended elements of deist "natural religion" with classic Protestantism. His discussion of the religious customs of the world was scholastically Protestant in its combination of meticulous footnotes and sometimes-strenuous argumentation. More important for its later influence, Bernard's discussion was structurally Protestant in that it cast contemporary religious practice, wherever it was observed around the world, as the corruption of an earlier purity. But where sixteenth-century Protestantism had seen the purity of primitive Christianity, Bernard, writing in the full flush of eighteenth-century enthusiasm for natural science, saw the purity of an early, universal, natural, and "true" religion corrupted by the variously scheming priests of the religions reviewed. Despite this structural Calvinism in their philosophy of religion, Bernard and Picard were indebted to John Locke as well as to John Calvin; and especially when the non-Christian religions were under discussion, their manner was more often expository than forensic.

There is no doubt that Bernard discusses and Picart illustrates the religious customs and ceremonies of the world on the assumption both that each religion is, like Christianity, a separate, practice-defined domain and that these domains are all comparable. For better and for worse, the two of them contributed massively to the establishment of "religion" as a category projecting elements of Christian identity upon the vast, newly discovered worlds that lay beyond Christendom. Discussing Bernard and Picart's treatment of indigenous American religion, Hunt, Jacobs, and Mijnhardt declare:

> In short, Picart's images, especially when read alongside Bernard's text, *essentially created the category "religion."* Whereas the text sometimes wandered off on tangents about the sources of particular ceremonies, the similarities between rituals across space (Jewish and Catholic) and time (Roman antiquity and American Indian), or the disputes between scholars on the origins of different peoples, the images kept the focus on the most commonly found religious ceremonies—birth, marriage, death rituals, and grand processions—or on the most strikingly different practices,

which could range from the arcane procedures for the election of popes in Rome to human sacrifice in Mexico. Implicitly, the images transformed religion from a question of truth revealed to a select few of God's peoples (the Jews, the Catholics, and then the Protestants) to an issue of comparative social practices.[14]

The charge of Christian projection can plausibly be lodged against Picart and Bernard's interpretation of particular non-Christian rituals through their nearest equivalents in Christianity or Western antiquity. And yet if such habits of mind were limiting, they were scarcely crippling; and for Picart and Bernard themselves, they were evidently enabling and energizing. Is it true to say that between them, these two "essentially created the category 'religion'"? If they did so, we would claim, they did so largely through the convergence in their work and in themselves of the complex heritage that we have tried to sketch above.

Picart and Bernard carry forward the age-old, often suppressed, but never entirely forgotten understanding of the church as a thing in itself, not to be confounded with any nation or any set of cultural habits or practices. They carry forward the relatively subversive late medieval assumption that philosophy provides a neutral standpoint from which all religious may be compared. When considering religions remote from them in space rather than in time, they carry forward the Renaissance habit of drawing freely on classical paganism interpreted with textual sophistication and literary sympathy. They collate, as no one before them had yet done, the reports streaming into Europe about the religions of Asia and the Americas and, in their most brilliant stroke, they make these the basis for a major artistic effort to *see* what had been reported. They apply to their undertaking a distinct blend of moral seriousness, commercial enterprise, and erudite documentary attention to the particulars of religious practice that is their legacy from French Calvinist Protestantism. Finally, as sons of the Enlightenment, they bring a pioneering openness and breadth of vision to what they study.

Bernard can seem genuinely and intentionally prophetic when he writes:

> All religions resemble each other in something. It is this resemblance that encourages minds of a certain boldness to risk the establishment of a project of universal syncretism. How beautiful it would be to arrive at that point and to be able to make people with an overly opinionated character understand that with the help of charity one finds everywhere *brothers*.[15]

The place of good will—the sheer *novelty* of good will—in the study of religion has received far less attention than it deserves. Bernard's dream may seem commonplace now, when courteous interfaith dialogue is familiar enough in much of the West, but it was far from commonplace when he dreamed it.

Like *The Norton Anthology of World Religions*, Bernard and Picart's great work attended first and foremost to rituals and practices, considering beliefs only as expressed or embedded in these. Their work was path-breaking not just as a summary of what was then known about the religions of the world but also as an early demonstration of what sympathetic, participative imagination would later attain in the study of religion.

In painting their portraits of the religions of the world and in dreaming Bernard's dream ("How beautiful it would be . . . !"), Bernard and Picart were at the same time painting their own intellectual self-portrait as representative Europeans—neither clerics nor philosophers but thoughtful professionals—avid to engage in the comparison of the religions of the world on the widest possible scale. Religious comparison did not begin with them, nor had they personally created the intellectual climate in Europe that welcomed religious comparison once they so grandly attempted it. But it is not too much to say that in their day and to some significant degree because of them, Christian Europe finally learned how to compare religions.

Broadening the Foundation, Raising the Roof: 1737–1893

In 1737, when Picart and Bernard completed their work, Europe had barely discovered Australia. The peoples of the Arctic and of Oceania were living in nearly unbroken isolation. And even among peoples well-known to Europe, Japan was a forbidden kingdom, while China's first engagement with the West had only recently come to a xenophobic close. India was becoming relatively familiar, yet the doors of many smaller nations or regions remained barred. Europe had not yet lost its North and South American colonies to revolution; its later, nineteenth-century colonialist "scramble for Africa" had not yet begun. Russia had not yet expanded eastward to the Pacific. The English colonies in North America had not yet become the United States or expanded westward to the Pacific. The enlarged world that Bernard and Picart had sought to encapsulate in their illustrated reference work had many enlargements ahead, with corresponding consequences for the study of religion.

Though the intellectual framework for a global and comparative study of religion was essentially in place among an intellectual elite in Europe by the middle of the eighteenth century, much of even the known religious world remained culturally unexplored because the local languages were not understood. The accepted chronology within which Europeans situated new cultural and religious discoveries did not extend to any point earlier than the earliest events spoken of in the Old Testament. All this was to change during the century and a half that separates the publication of Picart from the convocation of the first World's Parliament of Religions at the 1893 Columbian Exposition in Chicago. That date may serve to mark the entrance of the United States of America into the story we have been telling and will bring us to the more immediate antecedents of *The Norton Anthology of World Religions*.

Broadening the Textual Base

Of special relevance for our work as anthologists is the enormous broadening of the textual foundation for religious studies that occurred during this long period. To review that transformation, we will consider the pivotal roles played by four European linguistic prodigies: F. Max Müller (1823–1900), James Legge (1815–1897), Sir William Jones (1746–1794), and Eugène Burnouf (1801–1852). One may grasp at a glance the scope of the documentary change that took place during the 150 years that followed the publication of Bernard and Picart's *Religious Ceremonies and Customs of All the Peoples of the World* by looking forward to the London publication between 1879 and 1910 of *The Sacred Books of the East* in no fewer than fifty volumes.

This enormous reference work, a superlative and in some regards still unsurpassed academic achievement, was produced under the general editorship of F. Max Müller, a German expatriate long resident in England. Müller's role in the nineteenth-century evolution of the disciplines of both comparative linguistics and comparative religious studies is large, but for the moment what concerns us is the sheer scope of the landmark reference work that he edited: two dozen volumes on Hinduism and Jainism translated into English from Sanskrit; nine on Buddhism alike from Sanskrit, from Pali (the canonical language of Indian Buddhism), and from other Asian languages; seven from Chinese on Confucianism, Daoism, and Chinese Buddhism; eight from Persian on Zoroastrianism; and two from Arabic on Islam. The range is astonishing, given that at the time when Bernard and Picart were writing and engraving, knowledge of *any* of these languages, even Arabic, was rare to nonexistent in Europe. How did Europeans learn them over the intervening century and a half? What motivated them to do so? The story blends missionary daring, commercial ambition, and sheer linguistic prowess in different proportions at different times.

Let us begin with Chinese. The first two modern Europeans known to have mastered Chinese were the Italian Jesuit missionaries Michele Ruggieri (1543–1607) and the preternaturally gifted Matteo Ricci (1552–1610), who entered China from the Portuguese island colony of Macao. Over time, as French Jesuits largely succeeded their Italian brethren in the Jesuit mission to China, the reports that they sent back to France about Qing dynasty (1644–1912) culture and the Confucian scholars they encountered stimulated French and broader European curiosity both about China itself and about the Chinese language. Though the Vatican terminated the Jesuits' Chinese mission on doctrinal grounds and though the Qing dynasty suppressed further Christian missionary work and expelled the missionaries themselves in 1724, a seed had been planted. In retirement on Macao, the French Jesuit Joseph Henri Marie de Prémare would compose the first-ever Chinese grammar in 1729. Later, during the nineteenth century, as Britain forced a weakening Qing dynasty to sign a treaty establishing coastal enclaves or "treaty ports" under British control, British Protestants commenced a new round of missionary activity in China, including the first attempt to translate the Bible into Chinese.

James Legge, originally a Scottish missionary to China, building on de Prémare's grammar and working with the help of Chinese Christians, undertook a major effort to translate the principal Confucian, Daoist, and Chinese Buddhist classics into English, always with the ultimate intention of promoting Christianity. Meanwhile, in 1814, Europe's first chair of Chinese and Manchu was established at the Collège de France. In 1822, Jean-Pierre Abel-Rémusat published in France a formal grammar of Chinese intended not for missionaries alone but for all interested European students. Legge himself became Oxford University's first professor of Chinese in 1876, and near the end of his life he was F. Max Müller's principal collaborator for Chinese texts in *The Sacred Books of the East*.

European penetration into China proceeded almost entirely from off-shore islands or coastal enclaves under European colonial control; China as a whole never became a Western colony. India, by contrast, did indeed become a Western colony—specifically, a British colony—and the West's acquisition of the Indian languages and first encounter with the Indian religious classics is largely a British story. From the sixteenth through the early eighteenth century, Portuguese, Dutch, French, and British commercial interests vied for primacy in the lucrative Indian market. By late in the eighteenth century, however, Britain had overtaken all European rivals and established India, including what is now Pakistan, as its most important future colony—more lucrative at the time than the thirteen North American colonies that would become the United States of America. Britain's colonial motives were originally commercial rather than either evangelical or academic, but after British commercial and political control was firmly established in the Indian subcontinent, first cultural and linguistic explorations and then Christian missionary activity would follow.

In the launch of Sanskrit studies in the West, no figure looms larger than Sir William Jones, an Anglo-Welsh jurist in Calcutta who was at least as prodigiously gifted in language study as Matteo Ricci or James Legge. Fascinated by all things Indian, Jones founded an organization, the Asiatic Society, to foster Indian studies; and in 1786, on its third anniversary, he delivered a historic lecture on the history of language itself. In it, he expounded the thesis that Sanskrit, Greek, Latin, most of the European vernacular languages, and probably Persian were all descendants of a vanished common ancestor. Today, linguistic scholarship takes for granted the reality of "Proto-Indo-European" as a lost ancient language whose existence is the only conceivable explanation for the similarities that Jones may not have been the very first to chart but was certainly the first to bring to a large European public.

Jones's lecture detonated an explosion of European interest in studying Sanskrit and in tracing the family tree of the Indo-European, or "Aryan," languages, including all the languages mentioned in the previous paragraph but notably excluding Hebrew and Arabic—descendants of a different linguistic ancestor, later postulated as Proto-Semitic. (In the Bible, it is from Noah's son Shem—*Sēm* in Greek—that the peoples of the Middle East are descended—whence the term *Sem*-itic.) Now, the New Testament had been written in Greek rather than Hebrew or Aramaic, and Western Christianity had quickly left its Aramaic-speaking Palestinian antecedents behind and become a Greek-speaking Mediterranean religion. Did that mean that Christianity was actually Indo-European, or "Aryan," rather than Semitic, even though Jesus and Paul were Jews? This became one cultural strand within the European enthusiasm for Sanskrit studies, as further discussed below. Suffice it to say for now that it was during this period that *Semitic* and *Semitism* were coined as linguistic terms and the anti-Jewish *anti-Semitic* and *anti-Semitism* were coined as prejudicial, pseudo-anthropological counterterms.

Of greater immediate importance for the broadening of the study of religion was the window that Sanskrit opened on an almost unimaginably vast Indian literature whose most ancient and venerated texts, the Vedas, may be as old as, or even older than, the oldest strata of the Old Testament. Sanskrit is the classical language of India, no longer spoken and perhaps artificially perfected as a sacred language at some unrecoverable point in the past. But India has in addition a great many vernacular languages, more of them than Europe has, and in a number of these languages, other extensive Hindu literatures exist. These, too, gradually came to light in the nineteenth and the early twentieth century as knowledge of the relevant languages gradually spread to Europe.

India, for all its immense internal variety, did and does have a sense of itself as a single great place and of its gods as the gods of that place. Siddhartha Gautama, the Buddha, was born in India, and Indian Buddhism was the first Buddhism. Buddhist texts in Sanskrit are foundational for all students of Buddhism. But after some centuries had passed, Buddhism largely died out in India, living on in Sri Lanka, Southeast Asia, China, Korea, Japan, Mongolia, and Tibet. The linguistic and cultural variety of these countries was enormous. The Buddha was not called by the same name in all of them (in China, for example, he was called "Fo"). Western travelers, not knowing the languages of any of the countries where Buddhism was dominant, were slow to recognize even such basic facts as that the Buddha himself was a historical personage and not simply one among the many deities and demons whose statues they saw in their travels.

Donald S. Lopez, Jr., Buddhism editor for *The Norton Anthology of World Religions*, has written or edited several books telling the fascinating tale of how the puzzle of international Buddhism slowly yielded to the painstaking Western acquisition of several difficult languages and the related gradual recovery of a second, astoundingly large multilingual religious literature standing alongside that of Hinduism. In his *From Stone to Flesh: A Short History of the Buddha* (2013), Lopez allows what we might call the statue story—the gradual realization that sculptures of the Buddha represented a man, not a god—to become the human face on this much larger and less visible story of literary and historical recovery.[16]

In the story of how a broad textual foundation was laid for the study of Buddhism, a third linguistic genius stands between the Anglo-Welsh William Jones and the expatriate German F. Max Müller—namely, the French polymath Eugène Burnouf, the last of the four gifted linguists mentioned near the start of this section. Because of the enthusiasm for Sanskrit studies that Jones had touched off in Europe, copies of texts in Sanskrit began reaching European "orientalists" during the first decades of the nineteenth century. Those that arrived from India itself, as they were translated, would enable the assembly of the twenty-one volumes of Hindu texts that open Müller's *Sacred Books of the East*. Initially, however, no Sanskrit texts dealing with Buddhism were forthcoming from the Indian subcontinent. This situation would change, thanks to the fortuitous posting of an energetic and culturally alert English officer, Brian Houghton Hodgson (1801?–1894), to Nepal, where Buddhism thrived. Hodgson collected dozens of Nepalese Buddhist texts in Sanskrit, including the crucially important *Lotus Sutra*, and arranged for copies to be shipped to Europe.

Burnouf had been appointed to the Sanskrit chair at the Collège de France five years before the first shipment from Hodgson arrived. Thanks in part to earlier work he had done in the study of Pali, the Indian language in which the oldest Buddhist texts survive, Burnouf seems to have quickly grasped that what he had before him was the key to the historical roots of Buddhism in India. But this recognition was father to the further insight that Buddhism was the first true world religion (or, as he was inclined to think, the first internationally embraced moral philosophy) in human history. Burnouf was among the first, if not the very first, to see Buddhism whole. His 1844 *Introduction à l'histoire du Buddhisme indien* (*Introduction to the History of Indian Buddhism*) was the first of a projected four volumes that, had he lived to write them, would surely have been his greatest work. The one lengthy volume that he did bring to completion was already of epoch-making importance, particularly in light of his influence on his student F. Max Müller.

What the discovery and European importation of the classical religious literatures of India and China meant for the comparative study of religion in the West can be signaled concisely in the terms *Confucianism, Daoism* (earlier, *Taoism*), *Hinduism,* and *Buddhism*. They are all Western coinages, hybrids combining an Asian word at the front end and the Greek morpheme *–ism* at the back end, and each represents the abstraction of a separate domain of religious literature and religious practice from the cultural and ethnic contexts in which it originated. The coinage of these terms themselves may not coincide exactly with the recovery of the respective literatures; but to the extent that nineteenth-century Western scholarship viewed the texts as the East's equivalent of the Bible, it all but unavoidably engaged them on structurally Christian and even Protestant terms, thereby furthering the European conception of each related *–ism* as a religion in Europe's now consolidated and universalist sense of the word.

Structurally, Protestant influence was apparent again whenever, in the manner of Bernard and Picart, the great nineteenth-century linguist-historians judged the early texts to be superior to the later ones. Thus, in the interpretation of newly available Chinese texts, the earlier, more interior or "philosophical" versions of Daoism and Confucianism were often judged superior to the later, more ceremonial or "religious" versions, in which Laozi or Kongzi (Confucius) seemed to be deified or quasi-deified. Similarly, in the nineteenth-century interpretation of Hindu literature, India's British colonial rulers celebrated the supposed nobility and purity of the early Vedas and Upanishads while disparaging later Hindu religious texts and especially actual nineteenth-century Hindu practice. In the Buddhist instance, Eugène Burnouf set the early, human, historical Indian Buddha—whom he understood to have preached an ethics of simplicity and compassion—against the later, superhuman metaphysical Buddha. Consciously or unconsciously, Burnouf's contrast of the historical and the metaphysical Buddha coincided strikingly with the contrast then being drawn for a wide Christian audience between the historical Jesus of Nazareth and the divine God incarnate of Christian faith.

In short, as this new, broadened textual foundation was laid for the documentary study of Hinduism, Buddhism, and Daoism, a Christian theology of scripture and a post-Protestant philosophy of history were often projected upon it by the brilliant but Eurocentric scholars who were shaping the field. However, once primary texts are in hand, their intrinsic power can exert itself against any given school of interpretation. Thus, for example, late twentieth-century scholarship began to foreground and valorize the late and the popular over the early and the elite in several traditions, dignifying texts and practices once thought unworthy of serious scholarly attention.

Though nineteenth-century scholars might shudder at such a shift, it is essentially to them that we owe the availability of the key texts themselves. To be sure, the full recovery and the translation of these literatures are works in progress; nonetheless, knowledge of their great antiquity and their scope—barely even dreamed of by Picart and Bernard—was substantially complete by the end of the nineteenth century. The literary foundation had been put in place for an enormously enlarged effort at comparative study.

Enlarging the Chronological Frame

As already noted, Europeans as late as the early nineteenth century situated new cultural and religious discoveries, including all the texts whose recovery we have been discussing, in a chronology of religion understood to commence no earlier than the earliest events spoken of in the Old Testament. This framework led to efforts, comical in retrospect, to link newly discovered places and newly encountered legends or historical memories in Asia and the Americas to place-names in the book of Genesis, to the Noah story of Genesis 6–9, and to legends about the eastward travels of the apostles of Christ. All this would change with a discovery that might be described as blowing the roof off recorded history.

During Napoleon Bonaparte's occupation of Egypt in 1798–99, a French soldier stationed near the town of Rosetta in the Nile delta discovered a large stone bearing an inscription in three scripts: first, ancient Egyptian hieroglyphics, a script that no one then could read; second, another unknown script, which turned out to represent a later form of the Egyptian language; and finally, a third script, Greek. It took two decades of work, but in 1822, Jean-François Champollion deciphered this "Rosetta Stone." In the ensuing decades, his breakthrough enabled later scholars to translate hundreds of ancient Egyptian hieroglyphic inscriptions recovered from the ruins of ancient Egypt's immense tombs and temples and to discover, as they did so, that the Egyptians had maintained a remarkably complete chronology stretching back millennia before the oldest historical events recorded in the Bible. Decades of archaeological excavation in Egypt further enabled the construction of a chronological typology of Egyptian pottery. And then, since Egyptian pottery and pottery fragments are found all over the ancient Near East in mounds (tells) left by the repeated destruction and reconstruction of cities on the same sites, Egyptian pottery could be used to date sites far removed from Egypt. Over time, the Egyptian chronology would become the anchor for a chronological reconstruction of the entire lost history of the Near East, much of it written on thousands of archaeologically recovered clay tablets inscribed in the Mesopotamian cuneiform script that at the start of the eighteenth century was as undecipherable as Egyptian hieroglyphic.

The cuneiform (literally, "wedge-shaped") writing system was used as early as the late fourth millennium B.C.E. for the representation of Sumerian, a mysterious language without known antecedents or descendants. Sumeria, the oldest civilization of the ancient Near East—situated near the southern tip of Iraq, just north of the Persian Gulf—appears to have invented cuneiform writing. Most extant cuneiform texts, however, survive as small tablets representing several ancient Semitic languages rather than Sumerian. Starting in the mid-nineteenth century, hundreds of thousands of cuneiform tablets were recovered by archaeological excavations nearly as important as those in Egypt.

Cuneiform was deciphered thanks to the discovery in Persia in 1835 of a trilingual set of incised cuneiform wall inscriptions in Behistun (Bisitun, Iran) that, like the Rosetta Stone, included one already-known language—in this case ancient Persian—that scholars were eventually able to recognize behind the mysterious script. The challenge lay in going beyond the Persian of that inscription to decipher the language—now known to be the Mesopotamian Semitic language Akkadian—represented by one of the other two inscriptions. Though Eugène Burnouf played almost as important a role in this decipherment as he played in the recovery of Indian Buddhism, it is Henry Rawlinson, the British East India Company officer who first visited the Behistun inscriptions in 1835, whose name is usually linked to the recovery for European scholarship of the lost cuneiform literatures of Mesopotamia.

None of the now-extinct religions whose literatures survive in cuneiform is anthologized in *The Norton Anthology of World Religions*; we have chosen only major, living international religions. But the recovery of these lost literatures significantly affected the evolving historical context for all religious comparison. What these texts made clear was that recorded history had not dawned in Athens and Jerusalem. The religion of ancient Israel, in particular, was relocated from the dawn of history to a late morning hour, and thus could no longer be seen as in any sense the ancient ancestor of all the religions of the world. On the contrary, it now became possible to study the Bible itself comparatively, as a text contemporaneous with other texts, produced by a religion contemporaneous with and comparable to other ancient Semitic religions. And since the Bible is an anthology produced over a millennium, it became possible and even imperative to study each stratum within the Bible as contemporaneous with differing sets of non-Israelite religions and their respective texts.

European Protestantism, accustomed since the Reformation to employing the Bible as a historically reliable criterion for criticizing and revising the inherited practices of Christianity, was deeply affected by the discovery of both prebiblical and contemporaneous extrabiblical literatures, for they were clearly a way to deepen the historical understanding of the Bible. But the recovery of these literatures, set alongside related evidence from archaeological excavation, was a threat as well as an opportunity. It was an opportunity because it enabled illuminating comparisons of key motifs in Hebrew mythology with their counterparts in other ancient Near Eastern mythologies; it was a threat because though it corroborated the historicity of some biblical events, it undermined that of others.

Arguably, religious truth can be conveyed as well through fiction as through history. Patristic and medieval Christianity had been content for centuries to search the Bible for moral allegories rather than for historical evidence. Where history was not a central concern, comparative Semitic studies could and did enrich the linguistic and literary interpretation of the Bible without impugning its religious authority. But because Protestantism, rejecting allegorical interpretation, had consistently emphasized and valorized the historical content of the Bible, Protestant Christianity had particular trouble entertaining the notion that the Bible could be historically false in some regards and yet still religiously valid. A desire to defend the Old Testament as historically valid thus arose as a second motivation for Semitic studies. In the process, the prestige of the study of history itself as an intellectual discipline able to produce authoritative judgments about religion was significantly enhanced if not indeed somewhat inflated.

The discovery of the Rosetta Stone and the Behistun inscriptions affected the comparative study of Islam as well, though less directly. The recovery of lost Semitic languages and their lost literatures invited comparative linguistic study of the now-increased number of languages clearly related to Aramaic, Hebrew, and Arabic—the three principal languages of this family that were already known at the end of the eighteenth century. This study led to the postulated existence of a lost linguistic ancestor, Proto-Semitic, from which they were all plausibly descended. Proto-Semitic then began to play a role in the study of the religions practiced by the peoples who spoke these languages, somewhat like the role that Proto-Indo-European was playing in the study of the religions practiced by the peoples who spoke Sanskrit, Greek, Latin, German, and the other languages of that linguistic family.

As Proto-Semitic was reconstructed, moreover, it became clear to scholars that classical Arabic, the Arabic of the Qur'an, resembled it very closely and thus was an extremely ancient language that preserved almost the entire morphology of the lost ancestor of all the Semitic languages. Classical Hebrew, by contrast, was shown to be a much younger Semitic language. In an era of so much speculation about the relationship between ancient religions and ancient languages, the near-identity of classical Arabic and Proto-Semitic suggested to some that Islam might have preserved and carried forward ancient features of a Semitic proto-religion that was the lost ancestor of all the Semitic religions, just as Proto-Semitic was the lost ancestor of all the Semitic languages.

Orientalism, Neo-Hellenism, and the Quest for the Historical Jesus

The emergence of "Semitic languages" and "Semitic religions" as groups whose members were identifiable through comparison meant that biblical studies and Qur'anic studies—or more generally the study of ancient Israel and that of pre- and proto-Islamic Arabia—were more closely linked in the nineteenth century than they usually are in the twenty-first. Julius Wellhausen (1844–1918), a major German biblical scholar, reconstructed the formative stages of both. Historical linguists in Wellhausen's day who engaged in such comparative study of languages and history were called "orientalists." *Orientalism* is a term now associated with cultural condescension to the peoples of a region extending from Turkey through Persia to the borders of Afghanistan; but when first coined, it connoted primarily a stance of neutral comparison across that large cultural realm, a realm that the study of the languages, ancient and modern, had now thrown open for historical study as never before.

Interest in the language and history of classical Greece also grew enormously in nineteenth-century Europe, fed both by Hellenic revivalism and by Christian anxiety. The upper class generally celebrated Greek literature and thought as expressing a humane ideal distinct from and even superior to that of Christianity. In the late eighteenth century, in his *The History of the Decline and Fall of the Roman Empire* (1776–88), the English historian Edward Gibbon had already presented the emergence of Christianity as in itself the key factor in the decline of a superior classical civilization; Gibbon elevated the nobility and civic virtue of republican Rome above the faith, hope, and charity of Pauline Christianity as celebrated by classic Protestantism.

In the nineteenth century, it was Greece rather than Rome that defined the cultural beau ideal for an intellectual elite across western Europe. The German philosopher Friedrich Nietzsche (1844–1900), a classicist by training, was steeped in this philo-Hellenic tradition and drew heavily upon it for his well-known critique of Christianity. In its devout classicism, nineteenth-century European culture thus continued and intensified a celebration of an idealized and indeed a more or less mythologized Greece that had begun during the Renaissance and continued during the Enlightenment.

This European cultural identification with Greece, whether or not tinged with antipathy toward Christianity, sometimes worked symbiotically with a larger geographical/cultural identification already mentioned—namely, Europe's identification with the larger world of the Indo-European peoples as distinct from and superior to the disparaged Semitic peoples, most notably the Jews. Religiously motivated Christian prejudice against Jews had by no means disappeared, but it was now joined by a form of pseudo-scientific racism that made more of national than of religious difference. Because nationalist self-glorification linked to invidious anti-Semitism had a seriously distorting effect on the comparative study of religion in nineteenth-century Europe, the full enfranchisement of Europe's Jews as fellow scholars would have, as we will see, a comparably important corrective effect.

A second motivation for classical studies, especially in Lutheran Germany, was Christian: an urgently felt need to write the still-unwritten history of the New Testament in the context of first-century Hellenistic Judaism. The historical reliability of the New Testament had been the foundation of the Lutheran critique of sixteenth-century Catholicism. But nineteenth-century New Testament scholars now claimed to recognize adulterations by the church within the Gospels themselves. To exaggerate only slightly, the challenge that nineteenth-century Protestant scholars saw themselves facing was to recover the historical Jesus from the church-corrupted Gospels in the same way that they understood the sixteenth-century reformers to have recovered the historical practice of Christianity from the corrupted church practice of their day.

"Historical Jesus" scholarship of this sort grew enormously in scope and erudition during the first decades of the nineteenth century, fed by the growing prestige of history as a social science and climaxing with the publication in 1835–36 of David Friedrich Strauss's massive, learned, sensationally successful, but scandalously skeptical *Life of Jesus, Critically Examined*, a German work that appeared in English in 1846 in an anonymous translation by the aspiring English novelist George Eliot (Marian Evans). Decades of further scholarship followed, some of it indirectly stimulated once again by archaeology. As the excavations by Heinrich Schliemann (1822–1890) proved that there was a Troy and that a great war had occurred there, thus allegedly proving the historical reliability of the *Iliad*, so, it was hoped, further archaeological and historical research might yet demonstrate the historical reliability of the New Testament.

A denouement occurred in 1906 with the publication of the German first edition of Albert Schweitzer's epoch-making *The Quest of the Historical Jesus.*[17] Schweitzer believed that the quest for the historical Jesus had actually succeeded as history. Yet the recovered historical Jesus was more a problem for contemporary Christianity than a solution, the renowned scholar ruefully concluded. Schweitzer's work continues to haunt historical Jesus scholarship, even though fresh quests and fresh alleged recoveries of the lost historical Jesus, both learned and popular, have continued to appear.

In sum, narrowly Christian though the quest for the historical Jesus may seem, it did much to establish historical study as the default mode of religious study. Its shadow lies across studies of the historical Buddha, the historical Laozi, and the historical Muhammad, among others, stamping them all with the assumption that in the study of any religious tradition, historical truth will prove the indisputable form of truth.

The Haskalah and Its Impact on the Comparative Study of Religion

The character of the literature of religious studies is determined as much by who is writing as by what is written about. So far, we have concentrated on changes in what was available as subject matter to be written about, thanks to the recovery of religious literatures either lost in time or remote in place. We turn now to a new line of inquiry and a new question: Who was to be commissioned to conduct the study, to do the writing, to tell the story of the religions of the world? In the late eighteenth and the nineteenth centuries, above all in Germany, a Jewish religious, cultural, and intellectual movement called the *Haskalah* emerged, one of whose effects would be the historic enfranchisement of Jews as, for the first time, full participants in Europe's comparative study of religion. Before saying more about the impact of the Haskalah upon secular religious studies in Europe, we should briefly review its direct and complex impact upon the Jews of Europe themselves.

Religiously, thanks in good measure to the pathbreaking work of the Jewish-German philosopher Moses Mendelssohn (1729–1786), the Haskalah gave rise to Reform Judaism as a revised form of Jewish belief and practice more attentive to the Tanakh, or Hebrew Bible (Christianity's Old Testament), than to the Talmud. However uncontroversial it may seem in the twenty-first century for the reformers to honor the biblical prophets rather than the Talmudic sages as the ethical pinnacle of the Jewish tradition, the shift was highly disruptive in the late eighteenth and the nineteenth centuries, for the emphasis in Jewish religious practice until then had been squarely on the Talmud and on the rabbinical sages whose debates, preserved in the Talmud, had made the rabbinate the final authority in Jewish religious observance. In the rabbinic tradition, the Talmud is the heart of the "Oral Torah" that Moses, the original rabbi (teacher), received from God and conveyed in speech to his first (rabbinical) students, beginning a teacher-to-student chain that legitimated the rabbinate as authoritative. To undercut the Talmud, Rabbinic Judaism's foundational second scripture, was thus to undercut the rabbis themselves.

Reform Judaism was religiously unsettling in another way because by going back to the Bible, thereby setting aside centuries of venerable Jewish tradition and subverting established rabbinical religious authority, its founders, beginning with Moses Mendelssohn, delivered a critique that bore a striking structural resemblance to German Lutheranism's back-to-the-Bible critique of Roman Catholicism. The Jewish reformation looked rather like the Christian, to the exhilaration of many Jews at the time in Lutheran northern Germany but to the consternation of others.

Religiously disruptive in these ways, the Haskalah—often referred to as the Jewish Enlightenment—represented as well a major turning point in Jewish European cultural life, away from oppressive and once inescapable social restriction and confinement. The *Maskilim*, as the leaders of the Haskalah were called, recognized that the dawn of a culture of toleration in Christian Europe might just light the path to an escape for Jews who were willing to acculturate in certain manageable ways. Mendelssohn himself, for example, became an acknowledged master of literary German as written by the intellectual elite of Berlin. German culture was then entering its most brilliant century. In an earlier century, German Jews would have had to become Christians to exit the ghetto and take part. But absent the requirement to convert, perhaps German Jews could become Jewish Germans. Such was the tacit hope of the Haskalah.

As Reform Judaism grew in popularity, thousands of Jews gambled that the ghetto walls were indeed coming down, and ultimately they were not mistaken. Despite the murderous anti-Semitism that would rise in the later nineteenth century and the genocide that would so profoundly scar the twentieth, a page had been turned for good in Western academic life—not least in the comparative study of religion.

For this anthology, the Haskalah mattered in one further, only slightly narrower regard: while no longer deferring to the immense corpus of rabbinic literature as authoritative, the Maskilim did not ignore it. On the contrary, they began to apply to it the same techniques of critical scholarship that the Renaissance had pioneered and that Protestantism and the Enlightenment had further developed for the interpretation of the Bible and other classical texts. The process of critically editing and translating the rabbinic literature, which placed yet another major religious literature within the reach of secular study, began very slowly and approached completion only in the twentieth century. Yet were it not for the Maskilim, that great work would not have been undertaken.

Most important of all, however, was the inclusion of Christianity's original "other" in the corps of those attempting in the West to make comparative sense of the religions of the world. This inclusion was truly a watershed event, for it foreshadowed a long list of subsequent, cumulatively transformative inclusions of the previously excluded. Religious studies in the twenty-first century is open to all qualified participants, but such has not always been the case. Broadening the textual basis for religious studies and exploding the temporal frame around it were important nineteenth-century developments. Broadening the composition of the population that would engage in religious studies was even more important.

The gradual inclusion of non-Christian scholars in the Western discussion of world religions has not entailed retiring the historically Christian but now secularized concept of religion (or the related concept of world religions), but Christian or Western scholars have lost any presumptive right to serve as moderators or hosts of the discussion. The overcoming of insufferable condescension, not to speak of outright prejudice, has played a part, but so too, and more importantly, have matters of perception, perspective, and the "othering" of Christianity: the rest had long been accustomed to see themselves through the eyes of the West; now the West has begun to see itself through the eyes of the rest.

The dynamic entry of Europe's Jews not just into the European study of religion but also into many other areas of European life brought about a massive backlash in the late nineteenth century, then the Nazi genocide in the twentieth, the post–World War II triumph of Zionism, and belatedly, among other consequences, a distinct mood of remorse and repentance in late twentieth-century European Christianity.[18] Somewhat analogous emotions accompanied the end of European colonialism during the same late twentieth-century decades amid exposés of the exploitation and humiliation suffered by the colonized. The comparative study of religion has both influenced and been influenced by these ongoing revisionist shifts of mood and opinion, but, to repeat, the first steps down this long path were taken by and during the Haskalah.

Evolution and the Comparative Study of Religion

While the decipherment of Egyptian hieroglyphic and Mesopotamian cuneiform were still throwing new light on the earliest centuries of recorded history, Charles Darwin's *On the Origin of Species by Means of Natural Selection* in 1859 and *The Descent of Man, and Selection in Relation to Sex* in 1871 shone a beam into the deeper darkness of the unrecorded, biological prehistory of the human species. At the time, no one, including Darwin, knew just how old *Homo sapiens* was as a species; the technique of absolute dating by the measurement of radioactive decay would not be developed until the mid-twentieth century. What Darwin could already demonstrate from the fossil record, however, was that the human species had evolved from earlier species in a process that antedated recorded history. The implications of this discovery for all forms of scientific and historical investigation were enormous and are still being explored. For the study of religion, the discovery meant that behind the religions of recorded history, there now stood in principle all the religions of human prehistory. At what point in human evolution did religion first appear, or was that even the right question? Should the question rather be about precursors to religion—earlier behaviors that would evolve into what we now call religion? How, if at all, could the practitioners of these prehistoric proto-religions or precursors to religion be studied?

Answers to that question are still being devised, but none involves their texts, for they left none. Tempting as it would be to explore new work being done on the evolution of religion before the invention of writing, such work is not properly a part of the study of religion to which *The Norton Anthology of World Religions* contributes, for ours is, after all, a collection of texts. We know that the human species emerged some two hundred thousand years ago in southwest Africa and migrated from there eastward and then northward through the Great Rift Valley in what appear to be two noteworthy spikes. One spike proceeded by way of Lake Victoria up the Nile River to where its delta empties into the Mediterranean Sea. The other spike crossed from Africa to Arabia at the Strait of Bab el Mandeb and then proceeded along the southeast coast of Arabia to the Strait of Hormuz, where it crossed into Asia. From there, one stream of human migrants veered northward to the delta of the Tigris River at the upper end of the Persian Gulf, while the other moved southward to the delta of the Indus River. The Indus delta and the river system above it cradled the civilization that, as it moved south into the Indian subcontinent, would produce the Vedas, written in Sanskrit, the earliest scriptures of ancient India. The Nile and the Tigris deltas and the river systems that lay above them would together define the "Fertile Crescent" within which ancient Israel would produce the earliest Hebrew scriptures. The invention of writing in the Tigris delta (Sumer) and the Nile Valley (Egypt) does not antedate the late fourth millennium B.C.E. The oldest works honored as scripture by Hinduism or by Judaism may be a full millennium younger than that. As recoverable from surviving texts, the story of the world's major, living, international religions can reach no further back in time than this.

To concede this much is not to concede that the earlier evolution of religion cannot be reconstructed at all or indeed even reconstructed in a way that would link it to the story told here. It is to concede only that that reconstruction would call for another kind of book than this one, assembling very different kinds of evidence than are assembled here.

The First World's Parliament of Religions

We may close this review of the development of religious studies between 1737 and 1893 with a visit to the World's Parliament of Religions at the World's Columbian Exposition in Chicago in 1893. The vast exposition, which ran for six months and attracted millions of visitors, was a celebration of progress—scientific, political, and cultural—during the five hundred years since Columbus had discovered America. (The exposition missed its intended 1892 opening by a few months.) Though the organizers often seemed to tacitly assume that the latest and greatest chapter in world progress was the American chapter and that thriving, optimistic Chicago was the epitome of American progress, nonetheless an exuberant, generally benevolent and inclusive curiosity characterized much on display. And though there was condescension in the presentation of model villages from "primitive" societies as natural history exhibits, there was also an acknowledgment that many fascinating and once entirely unknown societies were now no longer unknown and could be presented for the instruction of the interested.

As for the World's Parliament of Religions, it seemed to reflect a contemporary, enlightened, Protestant American view that there existed—or there could come into existence—something like a generic religion whose truth all specific religions could acknowledge without renouncing their respective identities. This view may have owed something to the many translations and plagiarizations of *The Religious Ceremonies and Customs of All the Peoples of the World* that for a century and a half had been steadily propagating Bernard and Picart's confidence that a pure, "natural" religion underlay the variously corrupted historical religions of the world. It may have owed something as well to the 1890 publication of James Frazer's *The Golden Bough*, a romantic and enormously popular work that marshaled classical mythology and selected early anthropological studies of primitive tribes in a grand evolutionary march from magic to science.[19] It may have reflected in addition the gradual influence on American Protestants of the Enlightenment ideas underpinning the United States Constitution. Under the Constitution, since there was no "religious test" for public office, a Muslim or even an atheist could legally become president.[20] The legal leveling explicit in the Constitution implicitly encouraged a comparable leveling in American society, first among Protestants but later extended to Catholics and Jews, and gradually to the adherents of other religions. The process was slow, but its direction was unmistakable.

What is most remarkable about the Parliament, however, is the simple fact that when the organizers invited representatives of Hinduism, Buddhism, Daoism, Confucianism, Shinto, Jainism, Islam, and Zoroastrianism to come together and deliberate with Christians and Jews, everyone accepted the invitation. Swami Vivekananda (1863–1902) accepted both the invitation and the idea behind it—namely, that Hinduism was a world religion. He did not object that there was no such thing as "Hinduism," that the religious life of India was not a separate province within a postulated empire named "religion," that Indians who honored the Vedas did not see themselves as en route to any brighter collective religious future, and so forth and so on. Objections like this are legitimate, but Vivekananda agreed to attend anyway, gave a sensationally well-received speech, and went on to found the Vedanta Society as an American branch of Hinduism. Plainly enough, he had begun to construe Hinduism as potentially a global religion, separable from Indian ethnicity. The Sri Lankan Buddhist Anagarika Dharmapala (1864–1933) did something similar. In the real world of religious practice, these were important ratifying votes for a vision of world religious pluralism.

"How beautiful it would be," Jean Frederic Bernard had written, "to arrive at that point and to be able to make people with an overly opinionated character understand that with the help of charity one finds everywhere *brothers*." If the organizers of the World's Parliament of Religions thought that they had arrived at that blessed point when Swami Vivekananda thrilled his American audience with the opening words of his oration, "Sisters and Brothers of America," they were mistaken. And yet something was happening. A change was taking place. In various related European and American venues, a subtle but distinct shift of attitude was under way.

Is it possible to contemplate beliefs that one does not share and practices in which one does not engage and to recognize in them the shaping of a life that one can recognize as human and even good? When attitudes shift on a question as basic as that one, novelists and poets are often the first to notice. The novelist Marcel Proust wrote as follows about the Hindu and Buddhist concepts of *samsara* and *karma*—though without ever using those words—in his early twentieth-century masterpiece *In Search of Lost Time* (1913–27):

He was dead. Dead for ever? Who can say? . . . All that we can say is that everything is arranged in this life as though we entered it carrying a burden of obligations contracted in a former life; there is no reason inherent in the conditions of life on this earth that can make us consider ourselves obliged to do good, to be kind and thoughtful, even to be polite, nor for an atheist artist to consider himself obliged to begin over again a score of times a piece of work the admiration aroused by which will matter little to his worm-eaten body, like the patch of yellow wall painted with so much skill and refinement by an artist destined to be for ever unknown and barely identified under the name Vermeer. All these obligations, which have no sanction in our present life, seem to belong to a different world, a world based on kindness, scrupulousness, self-sacrifice, a world entirely different from this one and which we leave in order to be born on this earth, before perhaps returning there to live once again beneath the sway of those unknown laws which we obeyed because we bore their precepts in our hearts, not knowing whose hand had traced them there[.][21]

Marcel Proust was not a Hindu, he was a Frenchman of Jewish descent. Like not a few writers of his day, he may have been influenced by Frazer's *The Golden Bough*, but *In Search of Lost Time* is in any case a novel, not a work of science, philosophy, or theology. And yet we might say that in the words quoted, Proust is a Hindu by sympathetic, participative imagination and thus among the heirs of Jean Frederic Bernard and Bernard Picart. This kind of imaginatively participant sympathy was taking hold in a new way.

In the United States, the World's Parliament of Religions reflected the same *Zeitgeist* and heralded, moreover, an organizational change that would occur in the latter third of the following century, building on all that had transpired since Bernard dreamed his dream. That change—the decision of the National Association of Biblical Instructors to reincorporate in 1964 as the American Academy of Religion—reflected the emergent conviction that some knowledge of the world's religions was properly a part of every American's education.[22]

If American intellectual culture is distinctive in any regard, it is distinctive in its penchant for popularization or for the democratization of knowledge. The intellectual leadership of the country has generally assumed that the work of intellectual discovery is not complete until everybody has heard the news. But judgment about what constitutes "news"—that is, what subjects constitute the core of education for all people—has changed over time, and knowledge of the world's religions has not always been on the list. It was during the twentieth century that it made the list, and so for the study of religion we may regard the World's Parliament of Religions as opening the twentieth century.

In the comparative study of religion, Europe was America's teacher until the end of World War II. The secular, neutral comparative study of religion was a European inspiration. The heavy lifting necessary to assemble linguistic and archaeological documentary materials for such study—the story we have been reviewing here—was almost entirely a European achievement as well. But a distinctive aspect of the American contribution to the story has been the impulse to share inspirations, achievements, and knowledge gained in the study of religion with the general public. A work like *The Norton Anthology of World Religions*, intended for the college undergraduate or the willing general reader, is a work entirely in the American grain. If you find the texts assembled in the collection that now follows surprising, if you find the editorial frame around them instructive, please know that you are cordially invited to explore the remaining five anthologies that with this one constitute the full *Norton Anthology of World Religions*.

Notes

The intellectual debts incurred in the foregoing introduction are far greater than could be registered even in a far longer list of footnotes than appears here. The subject matter touched upon could obviously command a far longer exposition than even so lengthy an introduction as this one has allowed. I beg the indulgence alike of the students I may have overburdened and of the scholars I have failed to acknowledge. JM

1. Kevin Schilback, "Religions: Are There Any?" *Journal of the American Academy of Religion* 78.4 (December 2010): 1112–38.
2. Frans de Waal, *The Bonobo and the Atheist: In Search of Humanism among the Primates* (New York: Norton, 2013), p. 210.
3. Daniel L. Pals, *Eight Theories of Religion*, 2nd ed. (New York: Oxford University Press, 2006); Michael Stausberg, ed., *Contemporary Theories of Religion: A Critical Companion* (London: Routledge, 2009). Strikingly, they do not overlap on a single entry.
4. Feynman is quoted in Dennis Overbye, "Laws of Nature, Source Unknown," *New York Times*, December 18, 2007.
5. Clifford Geertz, "Religion as a Cultural System," in *The Interpretation of Cultures: Selected Essays* (New York: Basic Books, 1973), p. 90 (emphasis his).
6. Ibid., p. 125.
7. Ibid., pp. 193–233.
8. Tomoko Masuzawa, *The Invention of World Religions, Or, How European Universalism Was Preserved in the Language of Pluralism* (Chicago: University of Chicago Press, 2005).
9. All Bible quotations in this introduction are from *The Holy Bible, Revised Standard Version* (New York: Thomas Nelson & Sons, 1952).
10. Mark C. Taylor, *After God* (Chicago: University of Chicago Press, 2007).
11. Herbert Butterfield, *The Englishman and His History* (Cambridge: The University Press, 1944), p. 119.
12. Lynn Hunt, Margaret C. Jacob, and Wijnand Mijnhardt, *The Book That Changed Europe: Picart and Bernard's "Religious Ceremonies of the World"* (Cambridge, Mass.: Belknap Press of Harvard University Press, 2010), p. 2 (emphasis added).
13. Ibid., p. 5.
14. Ibid., pp. 155–57 (emphasis added).
15. Jean Frederic Bernard, quoted in ibid., p. 241 (emphasis in original).
16. Donald S. Lopez, Jr., *From Stone to Flesh: A Short History of the Buddha* (Chicago: University of Chicago Press, 2013).
17. *The Quest of the Historical Jesus* is the colorful title of the English translation first published in 1910; Schweitzer's sober German title was *Von Reimarus zu Wrede: Eine Geschichte der Leben-Jesu-Forschung* (From Reimarus to Wrede: A History of Research into the Life of Jesus). Hermann Reimarus and William Wrede were earlier scholars.
18. For the background in World War II and its aftermath, see John Connelly, *From Enemy to Brother: The Revolution in Catholic Teaching on the Jews, 1933–1965* (Cambridge, Mass.: Harvard University Press, 2012).
19. James Frazer, *The Golden Bough: A Study in Magic and Religion: A New Abridgment from the Second and Third Editions* (Oxford: Oxford University Press, 2009). Frazer's extravaganza eventually grew to twelve volumes, now out of print. For a more recent and more richly informed account of the evolution of religion, see Robert M. Bellah, *Religion in Human Evolution: From the Paleolithic to the Axial Age* (Cambridge, Mass.: Belknap Press of Harvard University Press, 2011).
20. See Denise A. Spellberg, *Thomas Jefferson's Qur'an: Islam and the Founders* (New York: Knopf, 2013).
21. Marcel Proust, *In Search of Lost Time*, vol. 5, *The Captive; The Fugitive*, trans. C. K. Scott Moncrieff and Terence Kilmartin, rev. D. J. Enright (New York: Random House, 1993), 5:245–46.
22. See Preface, above, p. xxiii.

Weigh the writer's intention rather than his work,

the meaning of his words rather than his uncultivated style,

truth rather than beauty,

the exercise of affection rather than erudition of the intellect.

To do this:

you should not run rapidly

over the development of these considerations,

but should mull them over slowly

with the greatest care.

—BONAVENTURE, *Itinerarium mentis in Deum*

CHRISTIANITY

EDITED BY

Lawrence S. Cunningham

INTRODUCTION

The Words and the Word Made Flesh

The phrase *People of the Book* has migrated from the Qur'an to contemporary English as a designation for Judaism, Christianity, and Islam. But while Judaism is rooted in the Torah and Islam holds the Qur'an sacred as the very word of Allah, Christianity does not place the Bible in a comparably central position. Christians venerate the Bible, but the center of their religious faith is a person and not a book. Judaism honors the Patriarchs, and Islam hails Muhammad as the "Seal of the Prophets," but neither Jews nor Muslims worship their foundational leaders. Instead, Jews see the Patriarchs and Muslims see Muhammad as exemplary men of faith who lead others to the worship of God. Christians, by contrast, adore Jesus as their Savior and Redeemer, who rescues them from slavery to sin and reconciles them with God the Father. Accordingly, Christianity's central focus is on Jesus and the words and deeds that testify to him. All three religions have many stories, themes, and heroes in common; all three also have differences, of which the most crucial for Christians concerns the person of Jesus. In the course of this anthology, then, Jesus—called by believers the Christ—will be seen as the key to Christian literature since it is from his character, his actions, and his message that the energy of the Christian tradition derives.

The Apostolic Era (4 B.C.E.–100 C.E.)

Jesus was a Jew who lived in the first century of the Common Era in an eastern part of the Roman Empire then known as Palestine. Much about his existence is obscure, beginning with his physical appearance. The Gospels—the first-century accounts of Jesus' life and work, included in the New Testament (Christian Scriptures)—do not say what Jesus looked like. Since artists have inevitably viewed the vanished world of ancient Israel through the lenses of their own places and times, they have depicted him in countless guises. Early Christian paintings depict him as a beardless youth wearing a toga. Mosaics from the Byzantine Empire (fifth century through the mid-fifteenth century) show a black-bearded man holding the globe in his hand.

Jesus' cultural life must be understood in the context of first-century Jewish Palestine. Jesus worshipped in local synagogues, but also, on the great holy days, at the Temple, a huge complex in Jerusalem. The Jerusalem Temple of Jesus' time was the second temple to have been built in that city. The first, built during the reign of King Solomon in the tenth century B.C.E, was destroyed by Babylonian conquerors in 586 B.C.E. During Jesus' lifetime, the Second Temple was at the center of Jewish life even for the majority of Jews who lived outside Palestine but came to Jerusalem as pilgrims for the great feasts. This Second Temple and the religious culture that depended on it were destroyed by the Romans during the First Jewish War (66–70 C.E.). The destruction of the Second Temple marked the start of a gradual split between Christian Jews (who by then had accepted claims for Jesus' divinity) and rabbinic Jews (who had not), but a few centuries would pass before the two Jewish groups were clearly and finally distinguishable as separate religions.

This 4th-century sculptural evocation of Christ as a young shepherd with a lamb draped around his shoulders is among the earliest major examples of Christian art. Rather than as a portrait, it is to be read as a symbol conceptually evoking the "Good Shepherd" of John 10:1–21, who lays down his life for his sheep.

Jesus' exact birth date is uncertain, but he was probably born in 4 B.C.E. in the village of Nazareth, in the northern Palestinian region of Galilee. He died around 30 C.E. in Jerusalem, crucified as a criminal by Roman authorities. The reported inscription on his cross, "This is the King of the Jews" (Luke 23:38), reads as a mocking reference to the crime of revolting against Roman political authority, but Jesus had not sought to take power as an ordinary king, however revolutionary his teaching may have been in other regards. The Gospel accounts (tentatively dated after 70 C.E.) depict him not as a political militant but as a wandering, radical preacher with a public career that lasted only one to three years. His native language was evidently Aramaic, but he may have known enough Hebrew to read the Torah (the most important Hebrew Scripture) and probably did know enough Koine, or common, Greek to communicate with Roman soldiers and colonial officials. (Koine, rather than Latin, was the lingua franca of the Roman Empire at that time.)

Jesus' earliest followers—the Apostles, for whom the founding era is named, and the more numerous disciples—sometimes address him in the Gospels as "rabbi" (Aramaic for "teacher" or "my teacher"). Jesus' position was not, however, that of a modern synagogue rabbi. Rabbinic Judaism, the ancestor religion of the Judaism of modern times, did not begin to take organizational shape until decades after Jesus' death. The Pharisees, who are mentioned in the Gospels, were forerunners of the group called the Tannaim, who founded rabbinic Judaism.

Jesus' disciples recognized him not just as a teacher but also, more daringly, as the "Messiah" promised by the prophets in the Hebrew Bible, especially the prophet Isaiah. The Hebrew word *mashiakh*, from which the English *messiah* is derived, means "anointed one." The English word *Christ* is derived from the Greek translation for *mashiakh*, *Khristós*. In Jewish tradition, anointing had profound significance because, until the suppression of the hereditary Davidic monarchy and the destruction of the First Temple, Israel's kings had been anointed as a sign of their election. Generations of Jews had lived in hope that a future anointed descendent of David, the greatest Israelite king, would arise to restore the sovereignty and glory of Israel. According to the Gospels, Jesus was that descendent. He was *Yeshua Mashiakh*—"Joshua the Messiah"—or, as he is known in English, Jesus Christ.

The basic beliefs of the early Christians could be summarized as follows:

Jesus, born miraculously to the virgin Mary of Nazareth, was called by God to proclaim the imminence of divine rule upon Earth (the coming "kingdom" of which Jesus repeatedly spoke). He preached always to Jewish crowds, but attracted a few Gentile (non-Jewish) listeners. In the manner of the earlier Israelite prophets, he demanded an intensified and spiritualized observance of Torah (referred to in the New Testament as "the Law" or "the Law of Moses"). He championed the poor, criticized the rich, praised humility, denounced pride, and above all celebrated generous, unlimited, forgiving love. With the Pharisees, he engaged in fierce disputes over his compassionate interpretation of the Law and over his occasionally startling claims of authority. Indeed, in pronouncing that "the Son of man is Lord also of the Sabbath" (Mark 2:27), Jesus identified himself as "the Son of Man," an exalted figure mentioned in the Book of Daniel 7:13, thus laying claim to divine authority. Jesus' miracles, often called "signs" in the Gospels, demonstrated that he exercised this authority even over nature.

Fearing that the crowds Jesus was attracting and the claims he was making would bring down the wrath of Rome, the Temple authorities in Jerusalem denounced him to the Roman procurator, Pontius Pilate, who ordered him put to death by crucifixion. Entombed on a Friday, he rose from among the dead, by the power of God, on the following Sunday. After appearing repeatedly and mysteriously to his disciples, he ascended into heaven, where he remains "seated at the right hand of the Father" (Psalms 110:1 and Mark 12:36). After Jesus' ascension, the Holy Spirit descended on his dozen closest disciples (known as the Twelve Apostles), inspiring them to serve as fearless emissaries (the meaning of the Greek word apostolos) of the "Good News" about how his life, death, and Resurrection would save the world. (The English word gospel translates the Greek eu-angelion, which literally means "good-news.") At the end of time, he will return in triumph, the dead will rise, and humankind will face him as their final judge.

The relationship of Christianity to the religion of ancient Israel is revealed clearly and intimately in the relationship of the Christian Scriptures, the New Testament, to the inherited Jewish Scriptures, Christianity's Old Testament. For the Christian Jews who wrote the New Testament, the basic beliefs summarized in the previous two paragraphs were not the abrogation but the fulfillment and extension of God's original covenant with the Chosen People of Israel. The hope for a covenant made new by enlargement or transformation had been a part of Israelite and Jewish thought since at least the sixth century B.C.E. The prophets Isaiah and Jeremiah had given eloquent expression to this hope. The inherited Jewish Scriptures expressed both the original covenant and the hope for a new covenant. The emerging Christian Scriptures, the written expression of the renewed and enlarged covenant, came to be called the New Testament (*testament* is an older English synonym for *covenant*), while the older Scriptures became for Christians the Old Testament.

For the first-century Christian Jews who wrote the New Testament, the older Scriptures were quite simply the Word of God. By finding in them repeated references to Jesus, the Evangelists (the authors of the four canonical Gospels) and Saint Paul (the rabbinically trained Jew who wrote the most important Letters of the New Testament) found divine, written confirmation of the Christian faith. For this reason and others, the Old Testament became no less a part of the emerging Christian Bible than the New Testament, though the terms *Old Testament* and *New Testament* would not be applied to the writings themselves for nearly a century after the last books of the New Testament had been written. In earliest Christian usage, the term *covenant* (Latin *testamentum,* Greek *diathēkē*) referred to the relationship between God and God's people, however defined, rather than to the Scriptures that expressed this relationship.

Jesus' very earliest followers met regularly in private homes to pray, to listen to the recitation of the remembered words of Jesus and the remembered accounts of his deeds (some of these remembered accounts would later constitute the Gospels). These meetings would conclude with a shared meal that they called the Eucharist (from the Greek word for thanksgiving). They believed that this meal recapitulated the Last Supper. According to the first three Gospels (those of Matthew, Mark, and Luke; called the Synoptic Gospels in Christian interpretation), Jesus shared this Passover meal, his last meal, with his Twelve Apostles on the night before his Crucifixion. (In the fourth Gospel, the Gospel of John, this meal is celebrated on the night before Passover. The Synoptic Gospels overlap more extensively—indeed sometimes verbatim—with one another than any one of them does with the Gospel of John.) During the Last Supper, Jesus gave the Apostles bread and wine and told them these were his body and blood. The early Christian communities performed thereafter a ritualized version of this meal in thanksgiving for his self-sacrificial death and his redemptive Resurrection. Just as the Passover meal celebrates ancient Israel's liberation from slavery to Egypt's pharaoh and the start of the Israelites' journey toward the promised land of Canaan, so the Eucharist—also known as the Mass, Holy Communion, or the Lord's Supper—celebrates humankind's liberation from slavery to sin and the start of its journey toward the paradise of eternal life.

The disciples also performed a ceremony called baptism, in which converts were initiated as members of the newborn Church by being immersed in water. This ritual was understood as a sharing in the death and Resurrection of Jesus, and it differed thereby from (though it also built on) the symbolic rite of repentance and purification carried out at the Jordan River by John the Baptist, a relative of Jesus, who preached repentance and conducted baptisms there even before Jesus began to preach in public. John's baptism of Jesus marked the beginning of Jesus' public life.

The early Christian communities were governed by elders (*presbuteroi*, the Greek word from which later terms such as *presbyter* and *priest* are derived) and by supervisors (*episkopoi*, from which *bishop* is derived). Few details about the appointment of these figures can be found in the New Testament or other sources from the Apostolic Era, but both democratic and charismatic elements appear to have been involved in their being chosen. Formal consecration in a leadership role came about through the laying on of hands, an act that symbolized conferring on the recipient both the power of the community and the blessing of God.

The growth of Christianity appears to have taken place by a process akin to cell division. When a Christian community attained a certain size, it split into two or more groups, which then kept in touch with other Christian communities through traveling preachers and circular letters. Early Christian communities spread throughout the Roman Empire with surprising speed, thanks to good roads, the relative safety of travel, and the widespread use of Koine as a second language that facilitated communication among peoples who did not share a first language. Nor was this expansion constrained by the boundaries of the Roman Empire. Three generations after the death of Jesus, Christian communities had spread not only as far west as present-day Spain but also as far east as the Persian Empire. There were similar Christian outposts around the Mediterranean and in North Africa.

Many of these early Christians lived alongside early rabbinic Jewish communities, especially in the large Jewish Diaspora outside Palestine. Since Christianity, beginning with Jesus, was a Jewish creation, the early Christians brought with them many aspects of Jewish law and custom as their movement spread. The question of whether to retain or reject given ancestral Jewish practices had been important for the Christian Jews. It became even more so for Gentiles who wished to join the culturally still quite Jewish community of Jesus' followers. Was it necessary for a Gentile to observe Jewish dietary laws? Did male Gentile converts have to be circumcised? As Christianity slowly distanced itself from ancestral Jewish rituals, there arose an inevitable tension between it and the Rabbinic Judaism that was evolving alongside it. Some of the anti-Jewish sentiments expressed in the Christian Gospels may reflect an early stage in these struggles, though the writers expressing the sentiments were Jews themselves.

The Patristic Era (100–600 C.E.)

From the middle of the first century till the beginning of the fourth, Christians were intermittently persecuted by Roman authorities. These persecutions varied in intensity from place to place. In the year 250, the emperor Decius issued an edict for the suppression of Christianity, triggering empire-wide persecution. In the last part of the third century and as late as 304, the emperor Diocletian led campaigns against his Christian subjects.

Believers fell afoul of Roman law for complicated reasons. Because the Christians denied the legitimacy—indeed, the existence—of the Roman pantheon (all the officially recognized gods), the Romans often called them atheists. Believing in just one God, the Christians refused to participate in the polytheistic Roman religious rites that functioned at the time as a pledge of allegiance to imperial authority. The Christian refusal to join in the festivals of the Roman gods, swear before their images, or offer gestures of worship to them made the Christians not merely dissidents but, by implication, subversives. The Jews made the same refusal, but the Romans granted them grudging tolerance for two reasons: They were a distinct nation in Roman eyes, and they had both an ancient literature and an established religious tradition. The Christians, by contrast, were not a distinct nation; to judge from the few Roman accounts that survive, their movement appeared to the Romans not as a venerable ancient religion but as a sinister new superstition whose practitioners were proselytizing vigorously, always seeking to lure new Romans into their fold. In sum, then, the Romans saw the Christians as a threat to the social harmony of the empire. Reverence not just toward the paterfamilias as head of the Roman family and toward the emperor as the head of the Roman state but also toward the Roman gods as the protectors of both was deemed essential for public welfare. Scorning this reverence, the Christians were scorned in turn and sometimes persecuted as a public menace.

The public image of early Christianity was undoubtedly affected by the fact that, in Roman eyes, the Christians worshipped a known criminal. Crucifixion was considered not just a terrible but also a shameful form of execution, one suitable above all for despised foreigners and treacherous slaves. Yet the crucified Jesus, who died for his beliefs, was a model for the early Christians. Martyrdom lay close to the heart of early Christianity; under persecution, many Christians were willing to die for their faith. Among the most popular kinds of early Christian literature were descriptions of the deaths of Christian martyrs, circulated for the edification of the faithful. In Rome, some of the many Christians buried in underground cemeteries, called catacombs, were martyrs. By the late second century, Christians had developed the custom of praying near these and other martyrs' tombs.

This form of veneration gave rise to a widespread cult of the martyrs, who were thought to have intercessory powers in heaven because they had sacrificed their lives on Earth. In time, churches were built over martyrs' tombs in widely scattered locations that then became destinations for pilgrims. Some of them, like the church of Santiago (Saint James) de Compostela, in Spain, attract pilgrims to this day. Where no martyr was entombed, the relic of a martyr would often be placed under the altar of a new church.

A good deal of early Christian literature argued apologetically—that is, defensively, as if in reply to early Roman suspicion—that it was not bizarre or irrational to admire Jesus even though he died on a cross. Christian writers would contrast the tree of the knowledge of good and evil, whose forbidden fruit (according to the Old Testament Book of Genesis) Adam and Eve ate in the Garden of Eden, thus bringing death into the world, with the "tree" of the cross, where Jesus' death paradoxically restored the immortality that the first couple had lost for themselves and their descendents through their sin. Essential to this defense, of course, as also to the conduct of the martyrs, was a firm belief in an afterlife of reward and punishment—a concept that for much of the Roman Empire was a disruptive novelty, attractive to some, outlandish to others.

By the early fourth century, it has been estimated, one out of every five persons in the Roman Empire was at least nominally Christian. Further persecution finally came to seem contrary to the public interest. In 313, through the Edict of Milan, the emperors Constantine and Licinius legalized Christianity throughout the empire. As Christianity, now legal, continued to expand, the Roman state soon took a more active role in its administration. An epochal moment in this shift occurred in 325, when Constantine convoked, at Nicaea (present-day İznik, near Istanbul), the first ecumenical (universal) council of bishops. Seeking to impose consensus within the religion he had endorsed, he directed the bishops to settle a raging debate about the equality of Jesus Christ with God.

The New Testament had spoken of the relationship of Jesus Christ to God and to the Holy Spirit in different and not easily reconcilable ways. Often Jesus had addressed God as his Father, implying that the two were distinct. Sometimes, however, and indeed at dramatic moments he had spoken of the two as a single being. Unsurprisingly, then, the theological status of Jesus became a vexing issue as Christianity grew. And there was a further complication: Although the phrase *Holy Spirit* appears a few times in the Hebrew Bible (Psalms 51:11; Isaiah 63:10), ancient Israel had generally seen that spirit as an attribute of God, not as a separate metaphysical entity. In Gospel usage, by contrast, the word seems at times to refer to a distinct person or reality. Recognizing the novelty of the New Testament usage, the late-second-century North African Christian writer Tertullian coined the word *trinitas* (English "trinity") to convey the uniquely Christian idea of three persons in one divine reality: Father, Son, and Holy Spirit. But this coinage more named the puzzle than solved it, and various schools of thought—drawing on Greek philosophical ideas as well as on Jewish Scripture—sought to cope intellectually with what Tertullian had named.

That Constantine's council was held in the city of Nicaea reflected a momentous eastward shift in Roman power. Barbarians from northern and eastern Europe were making incursions deep into the Italian peninsula. In reaction, Constantine was building a new, lavishly designed, and heavily fortified capital near the Greek town of Byzantium, where the Black Sea joins the Aegean. He named this capital New Rome, but in popular usage it became *Constantinopolis* ("Constantinesville"), Constantinople, present-day Istanbul. This shift of imperial authority to the Greek-speaking East eventually resulted in tensions between Rome and Constantinople and ultimately a division of the empire into the (Latin) Western Roman Empire and the (Greek) Eastern Roman Empire, later known as the Byzantine Empire. Already in Constantine's time, there were parallel bodies of Christian texts in Latin and in Greek as well as many related doctrinal disputes. Though the creed issued by the Council of Nicaea, the Nicene Creed, was promulgated as normative for the whole of the newly legalized and soon-to-be-official Christian Church, cultural and theological differences between West and East

Christ the Ruler of All (*Christos Pantocrator* in Greek) was one of Christianity's earliest large, public images. The painted panel shown here, from the 6th or 7th century, was preserved in Saint Catherine's Monastery in the remote Sinai desert from later outbreaks of iconoclasm. Two fingers held together symbolize Christ's simultaneous divinity and humanity. The two plus the uplifted thumb symbolize the Holy Trinity.

increased and worsened, notably with the rise of Arianism. This Christian movement was named for Arius, a priest and theologian in the early Church who taught that Jesus, though divine, was not uncreated—thus not quite equal with God. Heretical by the definitions of the Council of Nicaea, Arianism enjoyed widespread support and even intermittent imperial favor.

By this time, Christianity had taken the first steps in its distinct intellectual synthesis of the Jewish heritage and the classical Greek heritage. The writers who were most responsible for this foundational first theological and civilizational synthesis in Christian history are known as the Fathers of the Church, and the era in which they lived and wrote is called the Patristic Era. A number of these Church fathers were present at the Council of Nicaea, where they addressed a specific theological question. Subsequently, the Church fathers produced a broad cultural and philosophical synthesis that was carried forward by the Greek- and Latin-speaking European Christendoms of the Middle Ages and by the Arabic-speaking cultural world that Islam brought into existence starting late in the seventh century.

The Roman Empire's historic shift first to toleration of Christianity and then to outright patronage of it permitted the Church to continue its expansion within and beyond the borders of the Roman Empire. In the fourth century, Armenia was the first nation to become officially Christian, when its king was baptized. Christian missionaries followed the trade routes to the East, and Christian churches were established in the Syriac-, Arabic-, and Aramaic-speaking countries of the Middle East. In Jerusalem at the end of the fourth century (according to the writings of the pilgrim nun Egeria), Greek-, Syriac-, and Latin-speaking Christians attended services in the church built by Helena, the mother of Constantine.

Churches of the East and West continued to debate doctrinal issues about the person of Jesus. In 381 in Constantinople, the Second Ecumenical Council elaborated on the creed that had been formulated at Nicaea in 325. In that same year, Emperor Theodosius made Nicene Christianity the official religion of the Roman Empire. In 431 in the city of Ephesus (near present-day Selçuk, in Turkey), the Third Ecumenical Council affirmed that Mary was not just the mother of the human Jesus; she was also the *Theotókos*, or "God bearer." In 451 in the town of Chalcedon (now a district of Istanbul), the Fourth Ecumenical Council defined Jesus Christ as a single person with two natures, one human and the other divine. That formula derived from the thinking both of Latin-speaking theologians in the West and of Greek-speaking theologians in the center. The formula was not accepted, however, by certain Eastern Churches, such as those in Armenia, Egypt, Ethiopia, and parts of Mesopotamia (present-day Syria and Iraq). These Churches are known as the Oriental Christians or the Non-Chalcedonian Orthodox.

From that period on, the Christian world was divided politically, linguistically, and culturally into three large parts. First, there was the Latin-speaking West, centered in Rome and under the authority of the bishop of Rome (who later came to be known as the pope). Second, there was the Greek-speaking center, governed from Constantinople under the Byzantine emperor. Third, there was the East, speaking Syriac or any of several other languages and comprising a set of distinctive Churches and Church cultures, each under the autonomous authority of its respective patriarch. The latter Churches are sometimes called *autocephalous*, meaning that they have their own leaders, such as the pope of the large community of Coptic Christians, descendents of the ancient inhabitants of Egypt.

Between the legalization of Christianity in 313 and the establishment of newly clarified orthodox Christianity as the state religion of the Roman Empire in 381, Christian emperors aided the official, orthodox Church by funding and expanding its public buildings and monuments. In other ways as well, the ties between state and church became steadily closer, with consequences good and bad. Christianity's transformation from a once-persecuted sect into an imperially established religion brought with it many of the temptations that power and wealth can bring. One reaction to this transformation was the rise of the ascetic movement. The adjective *ascetic* derives from the ancient Greek term for practice, training, or exercise. Fervent Christians who found the distractions and temptations of urban life an impediment to practicing their piety fled the cities to take up a life of discipline, simplicity, prayer, and religious observance in more or less isolated rural areas. Thus was monasticism born. As persecution and physical martyrdom came to an end, the ascetic-as-martyr now replaced the classic martyr as the ideal Christian figure. An early biography of Saint Anthony of Egypt, often considered the founder of Christian monasticism, said that the saint was a "martyr every day of his life." Gradually institutionalized, monasticism spread far beyond the borders of Egypt to Europe, where it underwent a long and complex evolution.

By the end of the fifth century, the Western Roman Empire had disintegrated as a result of external military attacks and internal societal collapse. Some historians refer to the period between the empire's fall and the beginning of the High Middle Ages, in the eleventh century, as the Dark Ages. This term is meant to convey the relative breakdown of the Patristic Era's synthesis of Hellenic and Judaic culture. Yet during this period of relative cultural decline, Christianity nonetheless spread farther into Europe. By the beginning of the seventh century, the Western Church—now using only Latin and regional languages—encompassed most of the old Western Roman Empire, with outposts in Ireland and in most of Europe west of the Rhine and Danube Rivers. In Western Europe, which had few towns of any size, Christianity was anchored by monks, whose tradition had been rural from the outset and who created durably influential rural centers of learning, medicine, and culture in the absence of large cities. Monastic missionaries traveling south and east from Ireland and England proved particularly important: Germany, for example, was evangelized by a monk from England, Saint Boniface.

Meanwhile, robust Christian life radiated as well from Greek-speaking Constantinople into and beyond the Eastern Roman Empire. In the ninth century, two Greek-born brothers, Cyril and Methodius, trained in Constantinople, preached the Gospel in the southernmost Slavic-speaking countries (including parts of what is now Bulgaria, the Balkan peninsula, and regions as far north as Slovakia). They also translated the Gospels and the liturgy into the language of Slavs living in Macedonia, not far from Constantinople; that language survives in Orthodox Church usage as Old Church Slavonic. In making their translation, they employed an alphabet of their own invention (the immediate ancestor of what is now called the Cyrillic alphabet), basing it on the Greek alphabet. A major cultural turning point in the missionary effort that the brothers launched came about when the rulers of Kiev, Ukraine, adopted Christianity in 988. This conversion led in time to the Christianization of the Russians farther north and of adjacent Slavic peoples, although the Christianization of Scandinavia and the remaining northernmost reaches of Europe happened only later.

From the Christian East, the influence of the autocephalous Churches spread south along the southwest coast of India, east through Mesopotamia along trade routes reaching as far as western China, and to some extent west from Egypt and Libya along the North African coast. All of North Africa was Christian, if only sometimes orthodox, until the Arab conquests of the eighth century. Thereafter, Christian communities, sometimes quite sizable, lived on in the East under Muslim rule. Smaller communities survive in many areas to this day.

The Middle Ages (600–1300)

In the seventh century, the eastern and southern expansion of Christendom was checked by the rise of Islam. After the death in 632 of Muhammad, the prophet whose preaching launched the new faith, Islam spread outward from Arabia with stunning speed. Christian communities survived under Muslim rule; but within less than a century, Muslim Arabs had conquered all of the Middle East, including Jerusalem, as well as the southern coast of the Mediterranean as far as the Straits of Gibraltar and beyond. Most of Spain was conquered and would remain Islamic until its gradual reconquest by Catholic monarchs climaxed in 1492.

From the earliest days to the present, tensions and belligerence have marred relations between Christians and Muslims, although there have also been positive cultural exchanges of great significance. Medieval Christians initially viewed Islam not as a new religion but as a breakaway religious movement within Christianity. Indeed, this view survived as late as the early fourteenth century, when the Italian poet Dante Alighieri, in his *Divine Comedy* (1308–21), labeled Muhammad a "schismatic"—one whose secession introduced disunion and division into the universal Church.

Contemporary with the rise of Islam, there occurred a modest cultural revival in Western Europe known as the Carolingian Renaissance. This period is named for Charlemagne (in Latin, Carolus Magnus), the king of a western Germanic tribal people called the Franks, who was crowned as Holy Roman emperor by the pope in 800. In 732, at the battle of Poitiers in west central France, Charlemagne's grandfather, Charles Martel, had halted an invasion by Arabs advancing from Spain into the Frankish Kingdom. Perhaps inspired by his grandfather's example, Charlemagne defended and promoted his realm religiously and culturally as well as militarily. He established schools at monasteries and cathedrals, reformed education, and promoted the liberal arts through the work of scholars such as Alcuin of York, an Englishman who joined the Carolingian court.

During this period, most of the monasteries in the West adopted the Rule of Benedict, a set of precepts written around 550 by Saint Benedict for monks living communally under the authority of an abbot. During the late tenth and the eleventh centuries, the immense Benedictine monastery at Cluny, France, became a major center of learning, establishing affiliated centers, called priories, that operated with considerable independence from the local ecclesiastical authorities not just in France but also in Britain and elsewhere. Monastic culture may be said to have reached its pinnacle at and through Cluny.

Charlemagne died in 814. In the following century, dynastic squabbling led to the breakup of the Frankish Kingdom and the Holy Roman Empire, although the latter survived vestigially until 1806.

In 1054, the Roman and Byzantine Churches formally separated. Since that schism, formalized by decrees of mutual excommunication, the Churches that remained in communion with the See of Rome (the diocese of Rome and its bishop, the pope) have been known as Roman Catholic or simply Catholic, whereas those whose allegiance was to Byzantium have generally been known as Greek Catholic, Orthodox, Greek Orthodox, or Eastern Orthodox. The last term is somewhat misleading, because the autocephalous Churches to the east of Byzantium are the true Eastern Christianity.

Despite the estrangement of Greek from Latin Christendom, in 1095 the Byzantine emperor Alexos I Komnenos appealed to Pope Urban II for military assistance in repelling the encroachment of Seljuk Turks on his territory. Thus began the First Crusade. The purpose of this Crusade and the others like it that followed, at least as preached to the European Christians who took part, was not to rescue the Byzantine Empire but to retake the holy places in Jerusalem and maintain or restore Christendom there. Between 1095 and 1291, crusaders—so named because they wore a cross (Latin *crux*) emblazoned on their uniforms as a sign that they were to recapture the "true Cross," thought to be in Jerusalem—established European Christian rule over the major Mediterranean islands and much of the Levant (the eastern shore of the Mediterranean Sea). Over time, some of the crusader expeditions devolved into little more than raids in search of plunder. Infamously, for example, the Fourth Crusade (1202–04) included the sack of Christian Constantinople itself. By the end of the thirteenth century, the Levantine crusader states had all failed. In 1453, Muslim Turks of the ascendant Ottoman Turkish Empire, having conquered what remained of the Byzantine Empire, brought down Byzantium, the last bastion of what had been the Roman Empire.

In geopolitical terms, the only lasting effect of the Crusades was the reestablishment of Christian control over the major islands of the Mediterranean, which had been stepping-stones to the Middle East. Yet the memory of the Crusades casts a pall over relations between Islam and Christianity, especially between Arab Islam and western European Christianity. Today, *crusader* remains a pejorative word in most majority-Muslim countries, its reference now often transferred from the defeated medieval expeditions to modern forces of European and American imperialism and colonialism.

Far from the battlefields of the Crusades, life in Western Europe improved in various ways in the twelfth and especially the thirteenth centuries. Towns and cities thrived, and trade routes were extended. The urbanization of Western Europe partially explains the emergence of mendicant, or alms-supported (literally, "begging"), monastic orders as opposed to economically self-sufficient orders such as the Benedictines. Leading mendicant orders included the Franciscans, Dominicans, Carmelites, and Augustinians. Unlike Benedictine monks, who took a vow of stability that required them to stay (and work) in one, typically rural monastery for their whole lives, mendicant friars were mobile, eager to travel, and free to evangelize full-time in the growing towns and cities.

During the eleventh and twelfth centuries, while monasticism continued to flourish, a more town-centered intellectualism emerged alongside it. This new perspective is perhaps best exemplified by Saint Anselm of Canterbury, a twelfth-century monk who was born in Italy, trained in France, and eventually appointed archbishop of Canterbury, England. Anselm was a gifted theologian, and his writings are still read and discussed today. Meanwhile, Rome itself was showing new signs of life. A Church reform program enunciated by the eleventh-century pope Gregory VII, a former monk, bore fruit over the next century as the new religious orders were founded, older ones were reformed, and zealous clerics attempted to go back to biblical sources to reinvigorate the Church.

In this same period, the first universities emerged. They were located in towns or cities, among them Salerno and Bologna, Oxford and Cambridge, and Paris and Montpellier. The center of educational gravity was steadily shifting away from the monastic cloisters to the new universities. University scholars called scholastics (literally, "school men"), such as Albert the Great, Thomas Aquinas, and Bonaventure, reshaped the character of Catholic thought, retrieving and adapting elements of ancient Greek science and philosophy that had been neglected in Europe for hundreds of years.

This period—the so-called High Middle Ages (ca. 1000–1300)—also saw innovations in music, as polyphonic, or "many-voiced," singing became widespread; innovations in the visual arts, beginning with the Italians Cimabue and Giotto, who broke with the highly formal and stylized Byzantine

The first of the universities in Europe's Middle Ages was founded in Bologna in 1088. This illumination shows a University of Bologna lecture in progress.

manner of painting figures and reintroduced the classical technique of drawing from life; and innovations in architecture, such as a new supporting structure, the flying buttress, that made possible giant windows bringing light as well as height to the Gothic cathedrals far beyond what had been possible for the earlier Romanesque churches. Unlike even the largest monasteries, the greatest of the Gothic cathedrals—built first in France and later in the rest of Europe—combined all the newer arts in urban monuments whose size and grandeur vividly demonstrated the growing importance of town and city life. Fourteenth-century Gothic art has nothing to do with the Goths, a Germanic tribe famous for having sacked the city of Rome in the fourth and fifth centuries. Renaissance Italians attached the adjective *Gothic*—meaning barbaric—to northern European art as a term of disparagement, because the Italians were then reviving the very different styles of ancient Greece and Rome.

The Late Middle Ages and the Renaissance (1300–1517)

In the fourteenth century, Western Europe suffered through a series of natural, social, and political disasters. In the middle of the century, the Black Death—a pandemic of bubonic plague—killed 30 to 60 percent of the population. This mass death triggered an economic depression that in turn led to widespread peasant revolts in France and Italy. In 1309, a Frenchman was elected pope and chose to live in Avignon, France, rather than in Rome. Through a succession of French popes, the papacy remained in Avignon until 1376. After the papacy's return to Rome in 1377, intense political disputes resulted in the Western Schism, during which three men each claimed to be the true pope. By the time the dispute was resolved, the prestige of the papacy had suffered greatly. The second half of the fourteenth century saw the onset of a protracted conflict—the Hundred Years' War—between France and England, as well as devastation in Ukraine, Poland, and Hungary from the mid-century Mongol invasions.

Despite these hugely traumatic events, culture flourished in fourteenth-century Europe, above all in Italy. The Italian poet and humanist Petrarch (Francesco Petrarca) addressed the joy and grief of love in his *Canzoniere* (ca. 1327–68), a collection of poems written daringly in Italian rather than in the traditional Latin. In *The Divine Comedy*, Dante mapped out a trip through the confines of hell, the mountain of purgatory, and the celestial realm of heaven. Their countryman Giovanni Boccaccio created a sort of counter-Dantesque human comedy in *The Decameron* (ca. 1350–53), a collection of one hundred variously tragic, comic, and erotic tales told by ten friends in Florence during the Black Death. The Englishman Geoffrey Chaucer, partly inspired by *The Decameron*, wrote his *Canterbury Tales* (ca. 1387–1400), in which pilgrims—monks, nuns, and laypeople alike—tell tales while en route to the shrine city of Canterbury.

In fifteenth-century Italy, there was a spectacular flowering of painting, sculpture, and architecture. Much of this activity centered in and around Florence, in central Italy, radiating eastward to Venice and southward to Rome. The major artists of the era, such as Donatello and the young Michelangelo, produced works of astounding beauty and emotional richness. This art sprang from a renaissance of interest in classical antiquity, an interest stimulated in part by the arrival of Greek scholars fleeing west after the fall of Constantinople.

The writers and artists of the southern European Renaissance were not indifferent to Christianity, but they favored the pagan classics and Platonist philosophy as an alternative to what they viewed as the obscurity and pedantic argumentation of the neo-Aristotelian medieval schoolmen. Too, they favored the canons of classical art and architecture over the artistic styles of the late Middle Ages, which they disparaged as "Gothic." In private, many of the giants of the Renaissance were intensely and even quite traditionally religious (see Petrarch's "Ascent of Mount Ventoux"), but they were expressing their faith in new ways, with a greater attention to natural forms and to the body in particular. This artistic development coincided with the emergence of a broader cultural and educational reform movement centered in Florence and Naples. This movement—humanism, from the phrase *literae humaniores* ("humane literature")—promoted the study not only of Scripture and the writings of the Church fathers but also and especially of the poetic and dramatic masterpieces of ancient Greece and Rome. Christian humanists, such as the fifteenth-century Neoplatonist philosophers Marsilio Ficino and Pico della Mirandola, saw no essential barriers between theology and secular learning.

During the Late Middle Ages and the Renaissance, groups such as the Lollards, in England, and the Waldensians, in France, began to challenge the orthodoxy of medieval Catholicism as presided over by the papacy. Northern humanists—such as John Colet and Thomas More, in England, and Desiderius Erasmus, in the Netherlands—took a large step further. While they assumed that the Catholic Church would remain indispensable as an institution, they believed that the corruption and abuses of the Church needed to be reformed. Their reform movement was based not on such later radical measures as the dissolution of the monasteries but only on classical learning, especially philology (the study of languages) and textual studies. They viewed medieval scholastic theology as dry, inelegant, and overly technical, and, reaching back in Christian history, they undertook an intense exploration of the Greek and Latin Fathers of the Church.

The most lasting contribution of these northern humanists to the later course of Christian history resulted from their desire to read the Jewish Scriptures in the original Hebrew and the New Testament in the original Greek (the latter as an alternative to Saint Jerome's Latin version, the Vulgate, which had been used by the Western Church since its completion in 405). Erasmus collated three Greek manuscripts of the New Testament to create what he took to be a correct or at least a greatly improved source text. After producing this new edition of the original Greek, he produced a corrected Latin version that differed sharply from the Vulgate, which literate Europe knew well enough to immediately recognize the difference. The stage was now set for an explosive new development in which a new appropriation of the Bible would play a central role.

Reformations and the Wars of Religion (1517–1700)

No single cause triggered what would become known as the Protestant Reformation. The many factors included dissatisfaction with clerical misbehavior and ignorance, especially neglect of Holy Scripture; resistance to papal interference in national politics (e.g., the excommunication of England's King Henry VIII in 1533 and of its Queen Elizabeth I in 1570); and resentment of the burdensome financial demands of the Roman Curia ("court" in medieval Latin), which, under the pope, governed the entire Western Church. The Reformers called for a shift away from exclusive reliance on exterior devotional practices—such as pilgrimages, indulgences, and worship of the saints—to a more personal, interior form of piety. They promoted vernacular translations of Scripture with a revolutionary technology first developed in the mid-fifteenth century: the printing press with moveable type. Moveable type made it economically possible to disseminate new ideas, including and especially theological ones, to wide audiences with a speed hitherto unknown. With increasing literacy, Bible-reading became a widespread habit, and along with it came a host of new, often warring, interpretations.

In Germany, the priest and theology professor Martin Luther openly broke with the Roman Catholic Church. Luther's Reformation held to some old Catholic usages (baptism, the Eucharist) while reshaping both creed and worship to emphasize faith and grace over devotional practices that he regarded as mechanical, superstitious, and even idolatrous. In Switzerland, the French pastor and theologian John Calvin, originally trained as a humanist lawyer, led a far more radical Reformation. Calvin abandoned the traditional Catholic teaching that people were free to accept or reject God's saving grace. He believed such human freedom to be incompatible with divine omnipotence. Instead, he taught that the salvation of some and the damnation of all others was predestined. Luther and his followers called themselves *Evangelicals* ("Gospelers"), while the term *Reformed* was applied to Calvin's followers.

In England, the Reformation was initially occasioned by the issue of whether Henry VIII's marriage could be annulled, which was a jurisdictional rather than an essentially religious issue. When Pope Clement VII refused to grant the annulment, the king declared himself head of the Church of England, creating a new, prototypical national Church. Despite its separation from Roman authority, however, the Church of England retained many elements of Catholic worship.

The Anabaptist, or radically Reformist, Churches constituted a fourth Protestant stream, whose many descendents include the Mennonites and the Amish. Emphasizing simplicity, community, and often pacifism, the Anabaptist movement rejected the practice of infant baptism and reintroduced the ancient Christian practice of adult baptism after an experience of conversion. For the many already baptized as infants, this was a rebaptism; hence the term *Anabaptist*—literally, "rebaptizer."

The Protestant Reformation has given birth to a stunning variety of theologies and denominations, starting in the sixteenth century but continuing into the twenty-first. Broadly speaking, the many Protestant denominations have been united in rejecting Catholic practices such as the extreme veneration of Mary and the saints and the lavish use of religious iconography. They have insisted on the sufficiency of faith (as distinct from virtue and good works) and on the authority of Scripture (as opposed to tradition or ecclesiastical authority). In addition, by rejecting clerical celibacy, they have signaled their insistence on a clergy less separate from the world of family life and gainful occupation. During the Reformation, the Protestants dissolved the monasteries; abolished the monastic vows of poverty, chastity, and obedience; built churches that by Catholic standards were stark and bare; and concentrated on preaching the Word of God rather than conducting elaborate ceremonial liturgies.

In the aftermath of the Protestant Reformation, Western Christians who remained in full communion (complete dogmatic agreement) with the pope continued to use the term *Catholic* to refer to themselves. Thenceforth this term stood in audible distinction from *Protestant*, the term that became general for Christians of the newer reformist movements. Both sides adopted both halves of this nomenclature. Within three generations after Luther's break with Rome, the Protestant Reformation had spread through much of Europe. The Baltic and Scandinavian countries were Protestant, as were Britain, parts of France and Switzerland, and much of Germany. Catholicism maintained its presence in Portugal, Spain, Italy, Bavaria, and most of France as well as in some Middle European countries, including Austria, Hungary, and Poland.

The Catholic response to the challenges of the Protestant Reformation— a response sometimes called the Catholic Reformation or the Counter-Reformation—took various forms. To energize Catholic life and spirituality, new religious communities of men and women were established. Some of these orders, such as the Jesuits and Capuchin Franciscans, were militantly missionary in outlook. In addition, in twenty-five sessions for three periods between 1545 and 1563, the Catholic bishops met as an ecumenical council in the city of Trent, in northern Italy. One of the turning points in Church history, the Council of Trent was convened to carry out disciplinary reforms within the Catholic Church and to formally define certain Catholic beliefs and practices. The work of that council shaped the Catholic ethos until the twentieth century.

The period of the Protestant and Catholic Reformations was marked by sharp polemics. It was also characterized by voyages of discovery and by colonial enterprises based in Western Europe. Catholic missionaries, in tandem with Spanish and Portuguese explorers, brought Catholicism to the vast territories of South and Central America. Some English Protestants, unhappy with the Church of England, migrated as colonists to the wilderness of North America and eventually helped found the United States. Their French counterparts—some of them Catholics, some of them Huguenots (Calvinists)—settled farther north and west in what would eventually become French Canada.

In the aftermath of the Reformations, European countries had to deal with entrenched religious diversity. Would Catholics and Protestants who lived in the same area and spoke the same language tolerate each other? The answer at first was clearly no. In Germany, the Thirty Years' War (1618–48) began largely as a religious conflict between Protestants and Catholics in the Holy Roman Empire. By its end, the war had involved most countries in Europe. The Thirty Years' War was ended by the Peace of Westphalia, which settled the issue of religious identity on the Continent through the principle of *cujus regio, ejus religio*: Each nation would officially profess the religion of its leader. In England, from 1642 until 1651, the English Civil War—a series of armed conflicts and political machinations—resulted in part from differences of opinion about religious freedom and the relation-

ship between church and state. The Puritan installation of a commonwealth eventually gave way to the Anglican restoration of the monarchy but
with clear accommodation of the Puritans—Calvinist reformers who
rejected residual elements of Catholicism in the Church of England. The
terrible human costs of the Thirty Years' War, the English Civil War, and
Protestant/Catholic conflicts in France eventually helped inspire the
political and intellectual secularism of the Enlightenment as well as the
religious neutrality of the American Constitution. Yet Catholicism and
Protestantism became important elements of the respective national identities of Europe—a development that would foster over time the transformation of the empirical fact of nationality into the ideology of European
nationalism.

Despite the violence and terror of sectarian warfare, religious art continued to flourish in seventeenth- and early-eighteenth-century Europe,
through architectural masterpieces such as Saint Peter's Basilica, in Rome,
l'Église du Dôme, in Paris, and Saint Paul's Cathedral, in London; through
the religious painting of Michelangelo, Caravaggio, El Greco, and Rembrandt; in the sacred music of Claudio Monteverdi, Heinrich Schütz, Henry
Purcell, Antonio Vivaldi, Johann Sebastian Bach, and George Frideric Handel;
in the church oratory of John Donne, António Vieira, and Jacques Bénigne
Bossuet; and in the poetry of Théodore-Agrippa d'Aubigné, along with devout
English writers from George Herbert to John Milton.

The strictly religious writing of this period was characterized by its special passion and intensity. In France, the mathematician, physicist, and
philosopher Blaise Pascal wrote a defense of Christianity, published posthumously in 1669 as *Pensées* ("Thoughts"), that gave unforgettable expression to a modern skeptic's quest for faith. Across the Channel, the far less
sophisticated but oddly powerful work of the tinker John Bunyan, *Pilgrim's
Progress* (1678), presented a popular allegory of the Christian believer fleeing a doomed world. The ecstatic yet strictly orthodox devotions of the great
sixteenth-century Spanish mystics, Saint Teresa of Avila and Saint John of
the Cross, were imported into France, where they inspired the writers of
the French School of Spirituality. In Germany, a Protestant reform movement called Pietism, stressing religious feeling, represented a reaction
against the intellectualism of the so-called Lutheran scholastics. Like the
French School, Pietists emphasized the experiential dimensions of personal
faith over complex doctrine and theology. Their movement has had a continuing influence on other denominations, as seen in the founding of Methodism by the eighteenth-century Anglican clergyman John Wesley.

Other seventeenth-century thinkers dealt with ideas that eventually
posed major challenges to the Judeo-Christian understanding of the world,
its origins, and its significance. Galileo—an Italian physicist, mathematician,
astronomer, and philosopher—was found guilty of heresy for supporting the
heliocentric (sun-centered), rather than geocentric (Earth-centered), view of
the universe that had been presented by the Renaissance-era Polish astronomer Copernicus. The English mathematician and physicist Isaac Newton,
while maintaining an idiosyncratic religious faith, presented a purely empirical account of the physical world that dazzled his contemporaries.

Suddenly, the visible universe could be understood as a kind of mecha-
nism that functioned according to predictable laws. In philosophy, the
French thinker René Descartes introduced a new method of radical doubt in

Calvinists were violently hostile to "idolatrous" Catholic religious art. They eventually developed an austere religious aesthetic that profoundly influenced modern art and especially modern architecture. The new religious aesthetic is well illustrated by this Calvinist church interior, Utrecht, Netherlands, as painted in 1645 by Pieter Sanraeden.

his inquiry into how the mind can know anything about itself or the world around it. Baruch Spinoza, a Dutch Jew, rejected the traditional Jewish and Christian distinction between creation and Creator, regarding all things as part of God. The Englishman Thomas Hobbes directly challenged the idea that kings ruled by divine right. Kings were indispensable, he argued, yet their power derived from the consensual if implicit surrender of power by those they governed.

Encounters with Modernity (1700–1914)

The term *Enlightenment* applies to a complex movement that had roots in the seventeenth century but reached full flower in the eighteenth. Enlightenment thinkers downplayed the power of authority, instead prizing rigorous intellectual inquiry and the scientific method (observation and experimentation). The leading voices of the Enlightenment were also concerned with issues of justice, tolerance, and human rights. In general, these thinkers opposed any religious faith that went beyond what they saw as the universal dictates of reason. The leading religious theory among Enlightenment thinkers was Deism, the conception of God as a distant governor of the universe who guaranteed the basic order of nature but did not otherwise interfere with his creation.

Enlightenment thinkers were partly motivated by the dark memory of the Wars of Religion. In different ways, they sought to rescue ethics, politics, and even religion from the excesses of sectarian dogma and passion. Because they emphasized scientific objectivity over faith, they commonly denied the possibility of God's intervention in nature by miracles, and this denial entailed a new skepticism toward the Bible. The ideas of Enlightenment thinkers had their greatest theological impact on nineteenth-century liberal German Protestant philosophers and Bible scholars who accepted many of the conclusions of the newer, more skeptical biblical criticism and rejected what they saw as the rigid dogmatic thinking not just of Catholics but also of orthodox Protestants.

Yet alongside this continuation and further development of seventeenth-century rationalism, the eighteenth and nineteenth centuries witnessed an enormous flowering of romantic religious sentiment in continental Europe (where it included German Pietism), in Britain (where Methodism was its principal vehicle), and in Britain's North American colonies (where religious emotion was expressed in a movement called the Great Awakening).

Throughout the nineteenth century, the political power of the Roman Catholic Church declined. Republican forms of government or parliamentary monarchies arose in Europe's Catholic countries, producing spasms of revolution against the traditional bond between church and state. In Italy, the Papal States—areas controlled directly by the pope—disappeared with the country's unification in the middle of the century. Meanwhile, revolutions erupted against Spain and Portugal in Latin America, undermining the Catholic Church's power there. Yet Greece gained its freedom from the Ottoman Empire by reinvigorating Greek Orthodoxy as a key to the country's cultural and historical identity as well as by drawing on the memory of the Hellenic democracy of classical antiquity.

As the United States expanded to the west and south from its original thirteen colonies, religion continued to play a significant role in the country's governance and governing ideology. But despite the American Founders' emphasis on the equality and freedom of all (male) citizens, the ownership of black slaves remained legal. Indeed, slave labor was a major factor in the country's rapid economic growth. In the late seventeenth century, certain Christian groups—notably the Quakers and some Evangelicals—had denounced slavery as un-Christian. Eighteenth-century Enlightenment thinkers then condemned it for violating the inherent rights of humanity. By the mid-nineteenth century, abolitionism had triumphed in Britain and was spreading rapidly in the United States, relying in both countries on rhetoric and ideology heavily derived from Christian sources. African-American Christians, almost exclusively Protestant, found inspiration in the liberationist themes of the Bible through hymns known as spirituals. While the United States had banned the further importation of African slaves in 1808, the country's Civil War (1861–65) resulted mainly from the South's refusal to end—indeed, its determination to expand—the slavery of the actually or ethnically African people already in North America. With the North's victory in the war and the passage of the Thirteenth Amendment to the Constitution, slavery was abolished in the United States in 1865.

Elsewhere, in colonies controlled by European powers, both Protestant and Catholic missionaries from European countries found fertile ground for growth. This growth was especially strong in Africa. North Africa remained Muslim, but missionary expansion in sub-Saharan Africa laid a foundation for the flourishing and even explosive growth of Christianity there today. Toward the end of the nineteenth century, foreign missionaries had also cultivated small but vigorous Christian followings in China and India.

However, in the post-Enlightenment culture of Europe, many scientists and philosophers continued to challenge religious faith in general and Christianity in particular. For the followers of the eighteenth-century philosopher Immanuel Kant, religion had been largely reducible to morality, and morality had been reducible to a set of duties required by one's conscience. Prayer was not required, and miracles never happened. In the nineteenth century, the most vigorous critics of faith and especially Christianity were two Germans: the political philosopher and socialist Karl Marx and the philosopher Friedrich Nietzsche. Marx saw religion as "the opium of the people," a poor palliative to keep the workers of the world longing for the happiness of the afterlife and oblivious to the political remedy for their misery. Nietzsche excoriated Christianity and Judaism for making a virtue of weakness—for turning inferiority and infirmity into meekness and humility while condemning virile pagan magnanimity as pride. Nietzsche proposed a

This 1840 sketch of Søren Kierkegaard (1813–1855) is by Niels Christian. Kierkegaard offered a powerful double critique of religion: both of the domesticated, acculturated Christian practice of his native Denmark and of G. F. W. Hegel's then massively influential attempt to fit Christianity into a supposedly larger philosophical process.

"transvaluation of values" that would restore the honor of pagan vitality and expose the slave mentality behind Judeo-Christian ethics.

In England, the naturalist Charles Darwin triggered the greatest nineteenth-century debate about religion. In his *On the Origin of Species* (1859), Darwin drew evidence from living birds and animals as he attempted to explain both evolution within individual species and the emergence of new species. According to Darwin's theory, a process called natural selection led to the promotion ("selection"), over time, of traits favoring the survival of a species in its habitat. Natural selection likewise led to the extinction of unfavorable traits. In *The Descent of Man* (1871), Darwin applied his evolutionary theory to human origins. Darwin's ideas seemed to deal a lethal blow to the long-accepted biblical account of creation (and the Bible's whole vision of nature). According to the poetic story in Genesis 1:1–2:4, God created the world in six days. But the geologist Charles Lyell and others had already shown that the world was much older than the supposed biblical date of 4004 B.C.E. assigned to it in the seventeenth century by the Church of Ireland archbishop James Ussher. And Darwin's investigations showed similarly that species evolved over vast spans of time. As a result, nineteenth-century Christian polemicists who believed in biblical inerrancy resisted Darwin's theories (as do proponents of "creation science" today). If the Bible's account of creation had been superseded, did it follow that the Bible as a whole could have no authority?

The answer did not lie in a defense of the Bible's cosmology but in a deepened literary understanding of the Bible. This "higher criticism," though troubling in itself to many Christians, had a broadly apologetic rationale within it. Arguing that the Bible was a complex combination of numerous earlier sources and texts, the practitioners of higher criticism proposed to interpret them like any other ancient work of literature and yet, in the last analysis, to recover from their interpretation a new defense of the continuing viability of the Christian tradition.

For the Catholic Church, the intellectual trends of the nineteenth century were particularly disturbing. The Church took an aggressively defensive posture, condemning certain philosophical and theological ideas (often under the heading of "modernism," an amalgam of higher criticism, secularism, historicism, and other allegedly relativistic ways of thinking); forbidding their discussion in Catholic circles; and restricting books that promulgated them. The already strongly hierarchical Church further centralized authority in the hands of the antimodernist Pope Pius IX and his Curia. The apex of this centralizing tendency occurred at the First Vatican Council (1870), which proclaimed that the pope, when instructing the Church on matters of faith or morals, is guided by the Holy Spirit and thus infallible. Papal infallibility scandalized many outside the Catholic Church (and some inside it). Paradoxically, however, Catholicism experienced a revival in late-nineteenth-century Britain, where scientific discoveries allegedly had most undermined all forms of Christianity. Was the "sea of faith," as the nineteenth-century English poet Matthew Arnold famously described it, ebbing or flooding?

The Twentieth Century (1914–2001)

The first half of the twentieth century was marked by two catastrophic world wars. These wars exposed the extent to which European Christianity had merged and compromised with competing European nationalisms. In addition, these horrific conflicts squelched the heady Enlightenment optimism that scientific advances and rational politics heralded a new age of ongoing and irreversible progress. The tragic reality of World War I (1914–18), whose murderousness was multiplied by new scientific advances in military killing, spurred the rise of totalitarian regimes—Marxism-Leninism (Communism) in Russia and later in China, National Socialism (Nazism) in Germany, and Fascism in Italy, Spain, and Japan—that proved far more inhuman than the governments they replaced. Each of these ideologies played a role in World War II (1939–45), during which the National Socialists of Germany allied with the Fascists of Italy and Japan to conquer large swathes of Europe and Asia and mount a serious threat to dominate the planet. When World War II culminated with the astonishing and horrifying American explosion of two atomic bombs in Japan, postwar humanity suddenly confronted the possibility that it could destroy itself and much of life on its home planet, all in a paradoxical triumph for the science that once seemed to herald only bounty and beauty for the human race.

Even the period between the two world wars was characterized by appalling human suffering. In the 1930s, the Great Depression eroded faith in capitalism and left millions of people destitute in North America and Europe. In that same decade, the Soviet dictator Joseph Stalin ordered mass killings of his own people, while the German leader Adolf Hitler took the first steps in his genocidal campaign to rid Germany and then the world of Jews.

How were Christians, in particular, affected by this series of terrifying events? Since at the turn of the century the world's Christian population was still heavily European, wars that marked Europe so profoundly could not fail to mark Christianity as well. On the eve of World War I, despite the intellectual challenges that science and Enlightenment philosophy had posed to Christianity, there still existed a substantial liberal consensus, replicated similarly in each European nation, that a nation's national identity and its Christian religious identity were mutually reinforcing partners in world progress. This consensus provided some of the moral justification for European colonialism. The appalling slaughter of World War I, a war without a real victor, weakening and impoverishing nearly every nation that took part, shattered both the nationalist and the religious components of that consensus, at least for the thinkers and movements that loom largest in retrospect.

Even before World War I, a conservative Protestant reaction to liberal Christianity, especially to liberal biblical criticism as a part of it, had taken shape, paralleling earlier if differently configured Catholic resistance. Fundamentalism was named after a multivolume, multiauthored American essay collection, *The Fundamentals* (1910–16), which insisted on the literal truth of the Bible, especially regarding the virgin birth and the Resurrection of Jesus. But Fundamentalism entailed little critique of the repeated fusion of Christian faith with national pride.

This critique was most especially the achievement of a minority strand of Reformed German Christianity, which took shape in the teeth of a more total fusion of church and national state than the world had ever seen. Karl Barth may be regarded as the founding theologian of this movement, and Dietrich Bonhoeffer as its prophet and saint.

World War I coincided with another event of major consequence for world Christianity: the Russian Revolution (1917). When that revolution brought an atheist, Communist regime to power and turned the Russian Empire into the Soviet Union, the Russian Orthodox Church was effectively driven underground by merciless persecution. During the 1920s and 1930s, as the stage was set for World War II, some European Churches became instruments of Fascism and Nazism, while others offered quasi-clandestine resistance. A vocal pacifist movement included many Christians, but it diminished in numbers in the face of Fascist aggression. With Britain's ability to hold out against Germany in grave doubt, the question of American neutrality grew urgent. At a crucial moment, the American theologian Reinhold Niebuhr offered a reasoned case against Christian pacifism at such a juncture and in favor of American intervention.

In the wake of World War II, liberal Christian thinkers and activists viewed the official Churches as having failed in their duty as peacemakers. One fruit of this period of self-examination was a renewal of the ecumenical movement, an ongoing attempt on the part of different kinds of Christians to find their way back to the Christian unity that had disappeared in the centuries after the Christian Wars of Religion. Though the movement had been mainly Protestant when it began in the early twentieth century, it grew after World War II to include Greek Orthodox and Roman Catholics. The crossing of denominational lines was stimulated in part by the desire to address cooperatively the enormously pressing postwar problems of poverty and the mass dislocation of entire populations. Yet against the hope of the ecumenical movement for reconciliation and common cause, competing national or ethnic allegiances still sometimes set Christians at odds with one another. The conflict in Northern Ireland between Irish nationalist Catholics (favoring Irish independence from Britain) and British nationalist Protestants (loyalists, or unionists) was perhaps the best-known twentieth-century example, but the slaughter of the Tutsi by the Hutu in Uganda, both parties to the attempted genocide being Christian, was by far the bloodiest.

If the ecumenical movement represented the survival and continuation of late-nineteenth-century liberal Christianity, Evangelicalism may be said to represent the revival and rapid evolution of Fundamentalism as the conservative Protestant reaction to liberalism. The half-century after World War II was a period of unprecedented American influence around the world. The United States was the one major world power whose territory had been almost entirely untouched by the war. Militarily and economically, the country projected its power as never before and projected its Christianity to some extent as well. Before World War I and between the world wars, American Fundamentalism had tended more to withdraw from the larger society than to energetically evangelize it. Evangelicalism was different in just this regard. While sharing the Fundamentalist theology to a considerable degree, notably in the emphasis placed on the Crucifixion as an act of divine atonement for human sin, Evangelicals actively and effectively recruited for their form of Christianity through major revival meetings not just in North America but also in Africa, South America, and Asia. In the United States, nearly one in every four citizens is an Evangelical Christian.

Pentecostalism is a distinct modern Christian movement, also American in origin. Although Pentecostals may have broadly Fundamentalist or Evangelical views, their movement stresses religious experience over theological precision. The name refers to the descent of the Holy Spirit in the form of "tongues of fire" upon Jesus' Apostles at the Jewish feast of Pentecost (Hebrew *Shavuot*), seven weeks after the feast of Passover. The Book of Acts describes the Apostles as "all filled with the Holy Spirit" on that Pentecost, "and [they] began to speak in other tongues, as the Spirit gave them utterance." Pentecostals seek to be filled with the Holy Spirit as the Apostles were on that occasion. Thus the many Pentecostal denominations—including the Church of God, the General Council of Assemblies of God, and the United Pentecostal Church—emphasize transcendent experiences such as speaking in tongues. During and since the twentieth century, Pentecostalism, like Fundamentalism and Evangelicalism, has grown explosively outside the United States, principally in Africa and Latin America but also in China.

While liberal and conservative forms of Protestantism revived and evolved after World War II, ferment gradually grew within Roman Catholicism as well. For Catholics, this agitation culminated in the Second Vatican Council (1962–65), which replaced Latin with vernacular languages in the liturgy and significantly improved relations with other Christian Churches and other religions, especially Judaism. A postwar generation of Catholic theologians saw their faith as too little concerned with the plight of the poor and too identified with the ruling classes. From that analysis sprang a "theology of liberation"—an insistence that the message of Jesus was not only about the ultimate end of human beings in a salvation beyond history, but was also designed to free people and give them a just and dignified life in *this* world. Christianity, to use the best-known formulation of liberation theology, must offer "a preferential option for the poor."

The New Millennium (2001–the Present)

When one surveys the contemporary Christian world, it is difficult to find an overall trend within its astonishing variety. What is there in common between, say, an austere Quaker meeting, where people sit silently awaiting the Spirit to prompt them to speak, and the gorgeous panoply of a Russian Orthodox liturgy on a feast day? How is it that conservative Christians who seem most concerned with doctrinal purity can sometimes work with Christians on the left whose chief concern is social justice? What is the relationship between a transnational Church such as Roman Catholicism and a small independent "storefront" congregation? Despite often profound differences in belief and practice, the world's countless manifestations of Christianity share a relation to Jesus Christ. After all, the Christian Church began not with a creed but with the story of Jesus' life. Within Christianity as a world religion, each branch and denomination has its own emphases and practices. Yet each form of Christianity ultimately draws its identity from Jesus, who is proclaimed in the Gospels as Son of God and Anointed One.

The broad picture of world Christianity today reflects huge shifts in demographics. Europe, once accounting for the largest portion of world Christian population, is now both the most secular region of the world and home to a population steadily shrinking because of sub-replacement rates of

The first non-European pope in 1200 years, the first pope ever elected from the Southern Hemisphere, and the first pope ever elected from the Americas, Jorge Mario Bergoglio, of Argentina, was also the first Jesuit pope and the first pope to take Francis as his pontifical name. Seventy percent of the world's Roman Catholics now live outside Europe, including forty percent in South America. Bergoglio's election was seen as emblematic of a broad demographic shift toward the global South in world Christianity.

reproduction. Meanwhile, past missionary successes in areas that now have high birth rates have led to the emergence of a North/South division in Christendom, with the South more populous, less wealthy, and perhaps more fervent than the North. With the slow demise of colonial rule by the North over the South, national and regional Churches have arisen that are rooted in the experience of the formerly colonized people.

Christianity was also profoundly affected by the late-twentieth-century revolution in communications. Just as the invention in moveable type in the fifteenth century enormously hastened the exchange of ideas and thereby fueled the Protestant Reformation, so the electronic media made possible the rapid—even instantaneous—dissemination of Christian teaching throughout the world. As the century ended, the long-term impact of the communications revolution upon Christian practice was still difficult to predict.

In every age, culture has affected the way Christianity was preached and how it was received. The early Christians confronted the claims of the official Roman religion. Seventeenth-century Christians engaged with "the new philosophy" (science), which "call[ed] all in doubt," to quote the English poet and clergyman John Donne. Nineteenth-century Christians wrestled with the theories of Darwin and of Marx. In the twentieth century, as Christians examined their faith amid the ruins of war and genocide, two scientists further relativized humanity's position in the grand scheme of things. The German-born American physicist Albert Einstein introduced a new era in physics with his theory of relativity, which contradicted the Newtonian idea that time and space were absolute. The Austrian neurologist and psychoanalyst Sigmund Freud, with his many disciples and popularizers, assaulted the notion that humans were "rational" animals by arguing (rationally!) that they were driven by unconscious needs and desires. Both thinkers challenged Christianity even as they disturbed the serene Enlightenment picture of human consciousness situated in a harmonious, orderly world. Similarly, in the twenty-first century, when neuroscience and postmodern cultural philosophy present new alternatives to, or arguments against, Christian belief and practice, new Christian apologists have risen to the occasion.

Christian literature is undeniably mountainous. From that abundance, some works have become classics, and many of those classics are excerpted in this collection. What constitutes a classic? Such a work not only reflects the tenor of the times in which it was written but also somehow carries an abundance of meaning that wins a new readership in every subsequent age. Saint Augustine wrote in the fourth and fifth centuries, but Saint Thomas Aquinas read him in the thirteenth century; Martin Luther and John Calvin read him in the sixteenth century; Martin Luther King, Jr., read him in the twentieth century; contemporary theologians read him today.

All the same, while Augustine may epitomize the classic Christian author, there stands behind and beyond Augustine the figure of Jesus Christ as the classic of the Christian tradition in person. Jesus speaks for and to each age of Christianity, and each age must "relearn" him for his message to reach across history. When we read about Jesus, we are reading against the two-thousand-year background of meditation, discussion, argument, and formulation about him. As a historical tradition, Christianity accumulates and modifies the meaning of Jesus' words and deeds, his message and its significance. Thus, the Christian writing of every age can be understood as a commentary on, and an amplification of, the superabundance of Jesus Christ.

NOTE ON TRANSLITERATION

The *Norton Anthology of World Religions* rule for representing Hebrew, Aramaic, Greek, or other non-Roman (non-Latin) writing systems in Roman characters is to simplify as much as possible and aim for ease of recognition and pronunciation rather than for perfect consistency. Diacritics, including macrons (indicators of vowel length), are avoided. Thus, typically, *Christos Pantocrator* rather than *Khristós Pantokrátōr,* for the early Christian image of "Christ, Ruler of All." The governing criterion throughout is ease of usage for the general reader.

The Apostolic Era
4 B.C.E.–100 C.E.

"FOR, AS IT IS WRITTEN . . .": THE OLD TESTAMENT AS VALIDATION OF THE NEW, THE NEW TESTAMENT AS CULMINATION OF THE OLD

This period of the anthology is called "The Apostolic Era" because it is devoted to the teachings of Jesus' Apostles. Why, then, does this period begin with passages from the Old Testament? Christians have long believed that the Old Testament (the Jewish Bible, or Tanakh; also known as the Hebrew Bible) consists of sacred writings that prophesy the coming of the promised savior. Indeed, some of the New Testament writings presume the listener is aware of the Jewish sacred writings. In his Gospel, the Apostle Matthew cites them directly. In some of his letters, the Apostle Paul interprets them frequently.

In the second century, an influential Christian bishop named Marcion of Sinope split the nascent Christian community by attracting many to the view that Jesus' Heavenly Father and the Holy Warrior of the Hebrew Scriptures were not the same deity and that, accordingly, Christians were not to honor the Hebrew writings as Scripture. Of what would eventually become the New Testament canon, Marcion proposed to retain only the Gospel of Luke and the principal letters of Paul. In Marcion's day, however, the very notion of a canon—a fixed and final list of works regarded as scriptural—was novel and indeed was fostered by his radical

Saint Paul Preaching in Athens (1515–16): The Italian artist Raphael (1483–1520) created this image for one of the tapestries in the Sistine Chapel, Rome.

challenge. Ultimately, the community did not accept Marcion's dissident view. For even Jesus, in the Gospel of Luke, quotes Hebrew Scripture as part of his self-validation. In Luke 22:37, for example, Jesus says, "For I tell you that this scripture must be fulfilled in me, 'And he was reckoned with transgressors'; for what is written about me has its fulfillment" (Revised Standard Version). Jesus is quoting Isaiah 53:12.

The Christian majority insisted that the older Scriptures—which it eventually designated the Old Testament—had to be read in the nascent Church. Like a large majority of the Jews of the Roman Empire, the Christians read the older Scriptures in the Greek translation produced centuries earlier, initially for the émigré Jews of Egypt. Without those Scriptures, much of the language, many of the ideas, and the social milieu of the New Testament would be incomprehensible. In fact, some of the New Testament writers take pains to explain in their texts certain customs of the Jews.

The word *testament* in the phrase *New Testament* should be heard as an archaic synonym for the somewhat more transparent term *covenant*. Ancient Israel understood God to have created a covenant, or agreement, between his chosen people and himself: on his side, solemn promises; on their side, solemn commitments. Jesus had brought to the world an amplification and an extension to all humankind of the promises God first made to the Old Testament patriarch Abraham and his progeny. This amplification and extension constituted a New Covenant or New Testament, and the Greek writings that expressed it came to be called by just that title, with the older, Hebrew writings that expressed the original covenant then assigned the complementary title Old Covenant or Old Testament. Complementarity was indeed to be the understood and continuing relationship between the two, against Marcion's assertion of incompatibility. Neither covenant, in the developed view of the Christian Church, and therefore neither collection of texts could be fully understood without the other. An anonymous New Testament text known as Letter to the Hebrews makes that point explicitly: "Long ago God spoke to our ancestors in many and various ways by the prophets but in this last days he has spoken to us by a Son whom he appointed heir of all things, through whom he also created the world" (Letter to the Hebrews 1:1–2).

The New Testament consists of twenty-seven books written during the first and early second century in Koine. The Greek word *koine* means "common," and Koine was a simplified, international dialect of Greek common to millions in the Roman Empire whose first language was not Greek. The writers of the New Testament in the main were Christian Jews residing in the Empire's large Greek-speaking Jewish Diaspora. Together, the Old Testament and the New Testament make up the Christian Bible, and according to Christian tradition, no writings are comparable to the Bible in divine inspiration and authority. The Bible is uniquely valid as a textual basis for Christian doctrine, and for many centuries only the Bible was read aloud as part of worship.

The works of the New Testament belong to three genres. In order of appearance:

- narrative: the four Gospels—traditionally attributed to Matthew, Mark, Luke, and John—plus the Acts of the Apostles, which, though it follows John in the traditional ordering, continues the account given in Luke;

- epistolary: the thirteen letters, or epistles, traditionally attributed to Paul; the anonymous Letter to the Hebrews; and the seven letters addressed to all Christians and attributed, respectively, to James, Peter (two letters), John (three), and Jude; and finally
- apocalyptic: the Book of Revelation, the only work of the New Testament traditionally referred to as a Book.

NARRATIVE

The word *gospel* is a Middle English translation of the Greek word *euangelion,* adapted in Latin as *evangelium,* meaning "good announcement" or simply "good news." The authors of the Gospels are traditionally called by the related term *evangelist.* The core content of all four Gospels is the life, death, and Resurrection of Jesus, interpreted always in the light of the Hebrew Scriptures. Two of the four Gospels, Matthew and Luke, include an account of the birth (or birth and childhood) of Jesus. The Gospel of John begins with a prologue identifying Jesus as the eternal Word of God. The Word "became flesh and dwelt among us, full of grace and truth" (1:14). The Gospel of Mark, widely believed to be the first written, covers only Jesus' public life and begins with his baptism by John the Baptist. The Acts of the Apostles continues the narrative of the Gospel of Luke into the story of the founding of the Church. After Jesus' departure, his original disciples became his emissaries (the meaning of the Greek word *apostolos*). In this mission, they were hugely assisted by Paul, an early Jewish enemy of Christianity who became its most spectacularly colorful and influential Apostle during the course of a turbulent career. The Apostles' work and their adventures as they encountered opposition are the subject matter of Acts.

EPISTOLARY

The New Testament letters fall into three groups. The largest group consists of thirteen letters by or in the spirit of Paul. Though these letters refer to events occurring after those narrated in the Gospels, the oldest of them were written earlier than the earliest Gospel and are, in fact, the oldest writings in the New Testament. The seven surely written by Paul are addressed either to one of the newborn Churches—of Galatia, in Asia Minor (modern Turkey); of Corinth (two letters), Philippi, and Thessalonika, all in Greece; and of Rome (the longest and most theologically elaborate letter)—or to a Christian named Philemon (the shortest and most personal letter). Letters to the churches of Colossus and Ephesus as well as a second letter to Thessalonika are written in a Pauline spirit but are not, in the opinion of scholars, Paul's own work. Finally, two pastoral letters to Timothy and one to Titus are falsely or piously attributed to Paul but, again, not written by him.

The second-largest group of letters is attributed to James (one letter), Peter (two), John (three), and Jude (one). These letters are either more broadly addressed or unaddressed and by implication intended for the entirety of the early Christian movement. The letter known as 2 Peter, for example, is addressed to "those who have obtained a faith of equal standing with ours in the righteousness of our God and Savior Jesus Christ" (1:1).

When a Pauline letter is addressed to a "church"—as, for example, 1 Corinthians is addressed to "the church of God which is at Corinth," the reference is not to anything as large and public, much less architectural, as the word *church* now summons up. The Christian movement grew rapidly, however, and its component parts remained in touch with one another. These letters to all Christians are, by comparison with the Pauline letters, somewhat less theological and somewhat more hortatory and inspirational.

The final "group" has just one member—namely, the Letter to the Hebrews. Like the letters to all Christians, sometimes called the catholic (because universal) letters, this letter is not addressed to a Church in a particular location. Unlike the catholic letters, however, it is addressed not to all Christians but only to those of Jewish descent, celebrating their heritage and eloquently arguing for Christ as its culmination.

In broadest terms, the New Testament letters are the beginning of the unending process of Christian reflection upon the meaning of the life, work, teaching, and example of Christ.

APOCALYPTIC

Among the Jews of the time of Christ, a genre of writing arose that sought to "unveil" or "reveal"—from the Greek *apokalyptein*—a hidden meaning in the ancient Scriptures. This meaning typically provided a key to future events, sometimes to the end of time. Many apocalypses survive from roughly 200 B.C.E. to 150 C.E., but only one full-fledged example of this visionary genre has been incorporated into the New Testament: The Book of Revelation, the last-written work of the New Testament, a flamboyant, often confusing vision of great persecution yielding ultimately to the definitive victory of good over evil and the final triumph of Christ as the "Lamb of God."

Through a complex process, the Christian Church decided on its canon of texts. These twenty-seven books represented the consensus of various Christian communities, especially those of ancient background that had some connection to the Apostles—notably Jerusalem, Rome, and, in Syria, Antioch and Damascus, both mentioned prominently in the Acts of the Apostles. By the early second century, the four Gospels and a dozen of Paul's letters were read as authoritative in many of the early Christian communities. The oldest existing list that consists of today's twenty-seven books appears in an Easter letter written by Bishop Athanasius of Alexandria in 367. A Christian bishop often writes an open letter at Easter to the priests and laity of his diocese, and such letters are sometimes occasions for significant instruction. That Athanasius's letter included a list of the books of the New Testament signals clearly that in his day the question of which books were to be regarded as Christian Scripture was enough of an open question that it could command serious attention from an influential Christian bishop.

The Books of the New Testament were written for specific religious purposes. For example, the letters were most commonly written to specific early Christian communities about specific conditions in those communities. They were meant to be read aloud to the addressed communities and then to be circulated to other communities linked to the addressees. Because of their presumed Apostolic authority, they gained near universal respect and eventually made it into the canon of the New Testament. While they reveal little about the earthly life of Jesus, they are an invaluable resource for an understanding of Christianity in relation to Judaism and the predominant pagan culture. They describe early Christian practices, such as praying and teaching, and they explain how the early Christians understood the significance of Jesus the Christ.

While the four Gospels provide much information about the ministry of Jesus, they are not, in the modern sense of the term, biographies. The writers tell us that they wrote to strengthen the faith of the believing communities for which they were written. As John puts it: "Now Jesus did many other signs in the presence of his disciples, which are not written in this book. But these are written so that you may come to believe that Jesus is the Messiah, the Son of God, and that through believing you may have life in his name" (John 20:30–31).

The Gospels have complicated relationships with each other. Matthew, Mark, and Luke are called the Synoptic Gospels (Greek *syn*, "together," +*optic*, "seen") because they are visibly similar. That is, they include many of the same stories, often in the same order and sometimes with the same wording. Scholars believe that Mark is the earliest-written Gospel and that the Apostles Matthew and Luke were familiar with it. In addition, Matthew and Luke each include in their Gospels independent material about Jesus, presumably drawn from oral tradition about him. Many scholars believe that Matthew or Luke, or perhaps both independently, drew on a written source of sayings of Jesus, evidently unknown to Mark. John describes many of the same incidents as the other three, but the emphases are strikingly different. In the Synoptics, for example, John the Baptist actually baptizes Jesus. In the Gospel of John, the Baptist acclaims Jesus but does not subject him to Johannine baptism, which is actually a ritual of repentance. The effect, in John, is to emphasize the exalted holiness of Jesus. Too, in the Synoptics' account of the Last Supper, the climax comes at the moment when Jesus

> took bread, and blessed, and broke it, and gave it to them, and said, "Take; this is my body." And he took a cup, and when he had given thanks he gave it to them, and they all drank of it. And he said to them, "This is my blood of the covenant, which is poured out for many. (Mark 14:22–23)

John's account of the Last Supper does not refer to Jesus' dramatic bread-and-wine ritual. Instead, its high point comes early, when Jesus washes his disciples' feet before beginning a long and eloquent farewell discourse on love, unmatched in the Synoptics.

It is virtually certain that, in addition to these varied narratives, other contemporary written understandings (and misunderstandings) of Jesus once existed that are now lost to history. Luke tantalizingly hints in this direction when he notes in the preface to his Gospel that "*many* [emphasis added] have undertaken to set down an orderly account," but he, after "investigating everything carefully" (Luke 1:1–3), has now taken thought to write a truly ordered account. But his was not to be the last word. Surely nearer the mark are the last words of the Gospel of John: "There are also many other things which Jesus did; were every one of them to be written, I suppose that the world itself could not contain the books that would be written" (John 21:25).

Chronology

THE APOSTOLIC ERA (4 B.C.E.–100 C.E.)

ca. 4 B.C.E. Birth of Jesus

ca. 26 C.E. Beginning of John the Baptist's ministry

ca. 30 Crucifixion of Jesus

ca. 35 Conversion of the Apostle Paul

ca. 46–62 Paul's missionary journeys; Pauline Letters (Epistles) to early Christian churches written

ca. 50 Council of Jerusalem (Acts 15): Gentiles (pagan converts to Christianity) not required to observe all Jewish dietary laws or undergo circumcision

ca. 60 Paul under house arrest in Rome

64 Fire of Rome: massive conflagration blamed by Emperor Nero on the Christians

66–70 First Jewish War: crushing Roman victory

70 Fall of Jerusalem: destruction of Second Temple

ca. 70–100 Four canonical Gospels written

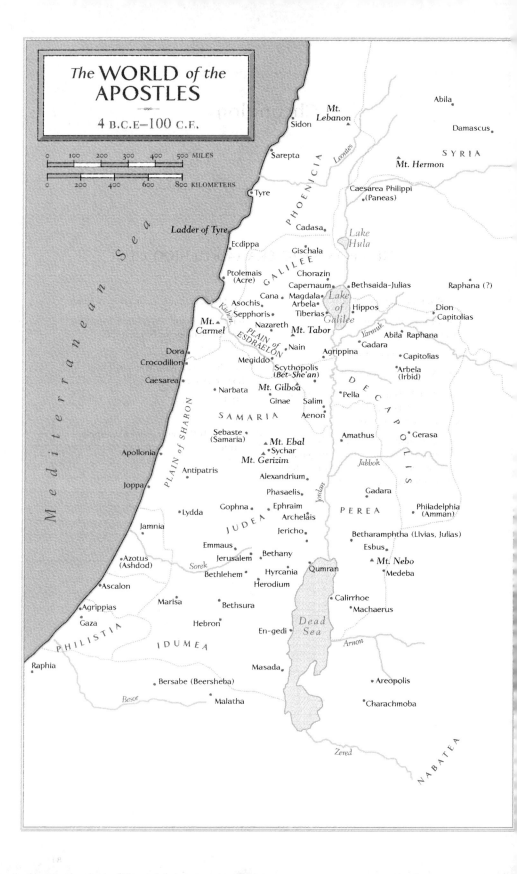

The WORLD of the APOSTLES

4 B.C.E–100 C.E.

0   100   200   300   400   500 MILES

0   200   400   600   800 KILOMETERS

Mediterranean Sea

Abila

Damascus

SYRIA

Mt. Lebanon

Sidon

Sarepta

PHOENICIA

Leontes

Mt. Hermon

Caesarea Philippi
(Paneas)

Tyre

Ladder of Tyre

Cadasa

Lake Hula

Ecdippa

Gischala

GALILEE

Ptolemais (Acre)

Chorazin

Capernaum

Bethsaida-Julias

Raphana (?)

Cana

Magdala

Lake of Galilee

Asochis

Arbela

Hippos

Dion

Capitolias

Sepphoris

Tiberias

Kishon

Nazareth

Mt. Carmel

Mt. Tabor

PLAIN of ESDRAELON

Nain

Yarmuk

Abila   Raphana

Agrippina

Gadara

Dora

Megiddo

Capitolias

Crocodilion

Scythopolis
(Bet-She'an)

DECAPOLIS

Arbela
(Irbid)

Caesarea

Narbata

Mt. Gilboa

Ginae

Salim

Pella

SAMARIA

Aenon

PLAIN of SHARON

Sebaste
(Samaria)

Amathus

Gerasa

Apollonia

Mt. Ebal

Sychar

Mt. Gerizim

Jabbok

Antipatris

Alexandrium

Joppa

Phasaelis

Gadara

Gophna

Ephraim

PEREA

Philadelphia
(Amman)

Lydda

Archelais

Jordan

JUDEA

Jamnia

Jericho

Betharamphtha (Livias, Julias)

Emmaus

Esbus

Azotus
(Ashdod)

Jerusalem

Bethany

Sorek

Bethlehem

Hyrcania

Qumran

Mt. Nebo

Medeba

Herodium

Ascalon

Calirrhoe

Marisa

Bethsura

Machaerus

Agrippias

Dead Sea

Gaza

Hebron

En-gedi

PHILISTIA

IDUMEA

Arnon

Raphia

Masada

Areopolis

Bersabe (Beersheba)

Besor

Malatha

Charachmoba

Zered

NABATEA

THE OLD TESTAMENT

GENESIS 1–3, 12:1–3, 15:1–6, 22:1–19

The word *genesis* is from the Greek for beginning or origin. The Book of Genesis begins the Bible and concerns the origin of the world, including all the creatures in the world. In other words, Genesis presents the Judeo-Christian creation story. Elements of this story, such as that water was the fundamental substance of everything, come from ancient Near Eastern myths. In those myths, however, multiple gods take part in creation. In Genesis, God alone creates everything in heaven and on Earth.

Chapter 1 presents the first of two accounts of creation. Here, God starts by forming the physical universe, then moves from lower forms of life to animals to humans (man and woman as equal, both in the image of God). The emphasis is on God's speaking: "God said, 'Let there be light.' . . . God called the light Day, and the darkness He called Night," and so on. Christians have read this calling of creation into being through speech as a dim revelation of Jesus Christ as the Word. As John puts it in the prologue to his Gospel: "In the beginning was the Word, and the Word was with God, and the Word was God. . . . And the Word was made flesh, and dwelt among us, (and we beheld his glory, the glory as of the only begotten of the Father,) full of grace and truth" (John 1:1, 1:14).

Chapter 2 presents the second account of creation. Here, humans are not created equal. Man, called Adam, is created first. Woman, Eve, is taken from Adam's rib to be his companion. Only then are plants and animals created. In chapter 3, Adam and Eve disobey a direct order from God. In the Garden of Eden, led astray by Satan in the form of a serpent, these first humans eat the fruit that God has forbidden to them. Thus, they introduce sin into the world. Christians have viewed Jesus as the second Adam, who brings not sin but redemption into the world.

The next eight chapters of Genesis continue to present the earliest history of humanity. In chapter 12, God calls upon a patriarch named Abram (renamed Abraham by God in Genesis 17:5), commanding him to migrate from his ancestral home to a new land, to which God will direct him. Because of God's promise to Abraham, this new home is commonly referred to as the "promised land" and Abraham's descendents are known as the "chosen people." And because God thus establishes a covenant, or contract, with Abraham—the physical ancestor of the Jews—Christians regard him, through their new covenant, as their spiritual ancestor. God called Abraham; the covenant begins with him. But Abraham trusted in God when he answered the call, and God "reckoned it to his merit" (Genesis 15:6). Thus, Abraham was saved—brought into a transformative relationship with God—by his faith. Christians—brought into a comparably transformative relationship by their faith—are his spiritual children.

Genesis 22 presents a story that has come to be called "the binding of Isaac." In the previous chapter, God promised that Abraham's legacy would carry on in the form of Abraham's son Isaac. Here, God orders Abraham to sacrifice Isaac. Why? According to the Letter of James, Abraham's willingness to sacrifice Isaac completes Abraham's faith by proving it genuine: "Was not Abraham our father justified by works, when he offered his son Isaac upon the altar? You see that faith was active along with his works, and faith was completed by works" (2:21–22). God's saving Isaac from death, according to the Letter to the Hebrews, prefigures Jesus' Resurrection: "[Abraham] was confident that God had the power even to raise the dead; and so, figuratively speaking, he was given back Isaac from the dead" (11:19). Christian commentators see the sacrifice of Isaac as a prophetic "type" of the sacrifice of Christ on the cross. They especially emphasize the elements that parallel the suffering of Jesus as presented in the four Gospels: the carrying of wood; the path up a hill; the willingness to be sacrificed.

PRONOUNCING GLOSSARY

Adonai-yireh: *a´-doh-nai yi-ray´* [*ai* rhyming with *rye*]
Asshur: *ah´-shur*
Beer-sheba: *behr-shee´-bah*
Cush: *kush*
Dammesek Eliezer: *dah-meh´-sek el-ee-ay´-zer*

Euphrates: *yoo-fray´-teez*
Gihon: *ghee-hohn´*
Havilah: *hah-vee´-lah*
Moriah: *moh-rai´-ah* [*ai* rhyming with *rye*]
Pishon: *pee-shohn´*
Tigris: *tai´-gris* [*ai* rhyming with *rye*]

GENESIS

I

(1) When God began to create heaven and earth—(2) the earth being unformed and void, with darkness over the surface of the deep and a wind from God sweeping over the water—(3) God said, "Let there be light"; and there was light. (4) God saw that the light was good, and God separated the light from the darkness. (5) God called the light Day, and the darkness He called Night. And there was evening and there was morning, a first day.

(6) God said, "Let there be an expanse in the midst of the water, that it may separate water from water." (7) God made the expanse, and it separated the water which was below the expanse from the water which was above the expanse. And it was so. (8) God called the expanse Sky. And there was evening and there was morning, a second day.

(9) God said, "Let the water below the sky be gathered into one area, that the dry land may appear." And it was so. (10) God called the dry land Earth, and the gathering of waters He called Seas. And God saw that this was good, (11) And God said, "Let the earth sprout vegetation: seed-bearing plants, fruit trees of every kind on earth that bear fruit with the seed in it." And it was so, (12) The earth brought forth vegetation: seed-bearing plants of every kind, and trees of every kind bearing fruit with the seed in it. And God saw that this was good. (13) And there was evening and there was morning, a third day.

(14) God said, "Let there be lights in the expanse of the sky to separate day from night; they shall serve as signs for the set times—the days and the years; (15) and they shall serve as lights in the expanse of the sky to shine upon the

FROM "Genesis" in *JPS Hebrew-English Tanakh: The Traditional Hebrew Text and The New JPS Translation*, 2nd Ed. Bracketed insertions are the translator's.

earth." And it was so. (16) God made the two great lights, the greater light to dominate the day and the lesser light to dominate the night, and the stars. (17) And God set them in the expanse of the sky to shine upon the earth, (18) to dominate the day and the night, and to separate light from darkness. And God saw that this was good. (19) And there was evening and there was morning, a fourth day.

(20) God said, "Let the waters bring forth swarms of living creatures, and birds that fly above the earth across the expanse of the sky." (21) God created the great sea monsters, and all the living creatures of every kind that creep, which the waters brought forth in swarms, and all the winged birds of every kind. And God saw that this was good. (22) God blessed them, saying, "Be fertile and increase, fill the waters in the seas, and let the birds increase on the earth." (23) And there was evening and there was morning, a fifth day.

(24) God said, "Let the earth bring forth every kind of living creature: cattle, creeping things, and wild beasts of every kind." And it was so. (25) God made wild beasts of every kind and cattle of every kind, and all kinds of creeping things of the earth. And God saw that this was good. (26) And God said, "Let us make man in our image, after our likeness. They shall rule the fish of the sea, the birds of the sky, the cattle, the whole earth, and all the creeping things that creep on earth." (27) And God created man in His image, in the image of God He created him; male and female He created them. (28) God blessed them and God said to them, "Be fertile and increase, fill the earth and master it; and rule the fish of the sea, the birds of the sky, and all the living things that creep on earth."

(29) God said, "See, I give you every seed-bearing plant that is upon all the earth, and every tree that has seed-bearing fruit; they shall be yours for food. (30) And to all the animals on land, to all the birds of the sky, and to everything that creeps on earth, in which there is the breath of life, [I give] all the green plants for food." And it was so. (31) And God saw all that He had made, and found it very good. And there was evening and there was morning, the sixth day.

2

(1) The heaven and the earth were finished, and all their array. (2) On the seventh day God finished the work that He had been doing, and He ceased[1] on the seventh day from all the work that He had done. (3) And God blessed the seventh day and declared it holy, because on it God ceased from all the work of creation that He had done. (4) Such is the story of heaven and earth when they were created.

When the Lord God made earth and heaven—(5) when no shrub of the field was yet on earth and no grasses of the field had yet sprouted, because the Lord God had not sent rain upon the earth and there was no man to till the soil, (6) but a flow would well up from the ground and water the whole surface of

---

1. I.e., "rested." God's resting on the seventh day is the source of the Sabbath, the day of rest.

the earth—(7) the Lord God formed man[2] from the dust of the earth.[3] He blew into his nostrils the breath of life, and man became a living being.

(8) The Lord God planted a garden in Eden, in the east, and placed there the man whom He had formed. (9) And from the ground the Lord God caused to grow every tree that was pleasing to the sight and good for food, with the tree of life in the middle of the garden, and the tree of knowledge of good and bad.

(10) A river issues from Eden to water the garden, and it then divides and becomes four branches. (11) The name of the first is Pishon, the one that winds through the whole land of Havilah, where the gold is. ([12] The gold of that land is good; bdellium is there, and lapis lazuli.[4]) (13) The name of the second river is Gihon, the one that winds through the whole land of Cush. (14) The name of the third river is Tigris, the one that flows east of Asshur. And the fourth river is the Euphrates.

(15) The Lord God took the man and placed him in the garden of Eden, to till it and tend it. (16) And the Lord God commanded the man, saying, "Of every tree of the garden you are free to eat; (17) but as for the tree of knowledge of good and bad, you must not eat of it; for as soon as you eat of it, you shall die."

(18) The Lord God said, "It is not good for man to be alone; I will make a fitting helper for him." (19) And the Lord God formed out of the earth all the wild beasts and all the birds of the sky, and brought them to the man to see what he would call them; and whatever the man called each living creature, that would be its name. (20) And the man gave names to all the cattle and to the birds of the sky and to all the wild beasts; but for Adam no fitting helper was found. (21) So the Lord God cast a deep sleep upon the man; and, while he slept, He took one of his ribs and closed up the flesh at that spot. (22) And the Lord God fashioned the rib that He had taken from the man into a woman; and He brought her to the man. (23) Then the man said,

> "This one at last
> Is bone of my bones
> And flesh of my flesh.
> This one shall be called Woman,[5]
> For from man[6] was she taken."

(24) Hence a man leaves his father and mother and clings to his wife, so that they become one flesh.

3

(25) The two of them were naked, the man and his wife, yet they felt no shame. (1) Now the serpent was the shrewdest of all the wild beasts that the

---

2. *Adam* (Hebrew).
3. Many Hebrew feminine nouns end in *-ah*. *Adamah*, the Hebrew word for "soil" or "ground," thus looks as if it ought to be the female counterpart to *adam*, meaning "man." Rabbinic interpretation would later interpret this wordplay to mean that man is made from the feminine version of his essence, just as woman is made from man's essence.

4. The meaning of the Hebrew is uncertain.
5. *Isha* (feminine of *ish*, "man"). *Ishsha*, with a doubling of the Hebrew letter for *sh*, means "her husband." The wordplay thus links the Hebrew word for "woman" to the man to whom she is sexually connected.
6. *Ish* (Hebrew).

Lord God had made. He said to the woman, "Did God really say: You shall not eat of any tree of the garden?" (2) The woman replied to the serpent. "We may eat of the fruit of the other trees of the garden. (3) It is only about fruit of the tree in the middle of the garden that God said: 'You shall not eat of it or touch it, lest you die.'" (4) And the serpent said to the woman, "You are not going to die, (5) but God knows that as soon as you eat of it your eyes will be opened and you will be like divine beings who know good and bad." (6) When the woman saw that the tree was good for eating and a delight to the eyes, and that the tree was desirable as a source of wisdom, she took of its fruit and ate. She also gave some to her husband, and he ate. (7) Then the eyes of both of them were opened and they perceived that they were naked; and they sewed together fig leaves and made themselves loincloths.

(8) They heard the sound of the Lord God moving about in the garden at the breezy time of day; and the man and his wife hid from the Lord God among the trees of the garden. (9) The Lord God called out to the man and said to him, "Where are you?" (10) He replied, "I heard the sound of You in the garden, and I was afraid because I was naked, so I hid." (11) Then He asked, "Who told you that you were naked? Did you eat of the tree from which I had forbidden you to eat?" (12) The man said, "The woman You put at my side—she gave me of the tree, and I ate." (13) And the Lord God said to the woman, "What is this you have done!" The woman replied, "The serpent duped me, and I ate." (14) Then the Lord God said to the serpent,

"Because you did this,
More cursed shall you be
Than all cattle
And all the wild beasts:
On your belly shall you crawl
And dirt shall you eat
All the days of your life.
(15) I will put enmity
Between you and the woman,
And between your offspring and hers;
They shall strike at your head,
And you shall strike at their heel."
(16) And to the woman He said,
"I will make most severe
Your pangs in childbearing;
In pain shall you bear children.
Yet your urge shall be for your husband,
And he shall rule over you."
(17) To Adam He said, "Because you did as your
    wife said and ate of the tree about which I
    commanded you, 'You shall not eat of it,'
Cursed be the ground because of you;
By toil shall you eat of it
All the days of your life:
(18) Thorns and thistles shall it sprout for you.
But your food shall be the grasses of the field;
(19) By the sweat of your brow

> Shall you get bread to eat,
> Until, you return to the ground—
> For from it you were taken.
> For dust you are,
> And to dust you shall return."

(20) The man named his wife Eve, because she was the mother of all the living. (21) And the Lord God made garments of skins for Adam and his wife, and clothed them.

(22) And the Lord God said, "Now that the man has become like one of us, knowing good and bad, what if he should stretch out his hand and take also from the tree of life and eat, and live forever!" (23) So the Lord God banished him from the garden of Eden, to till the soil from which he was taken. (24) He drove the man out, and stationed east of the garden of Eden the cherubim and the fiery ever-turning sword, to guard the way to the tree of life.

12:1–3

(1) The Lord said to Abram, "Go forth from your native land and from your father's house to the land that I will show you.

> (2) I will make of you a great nation,
> And I will bless you;
> I will make your name great,
> And you shall be a blessing.
> (3) I will bless those who bless you
> And curse him that curses you;
> And all the families of the earth
> Shall bless themselves by you."

15:1–6

(1) Some time later, the word of the Lord came to Abram in a vision. He said,

> "Fear not, Abram,
> I am a shield to you;
> Your reward shall be very great."

(2) But Abram said, "O Lord God, what can You give me, seeing that I shall die childless, and the one in charge of my household is Dammesek Eliezer!" (3) Abram said further, "Since You have granted me no offspring, my steward will be my heir." (4) The word of the Lord came to him in reply, "That one shall not be your heir; none but your very own issue shall be your heir." (5) He took him outside and said, "Look toward heaven and count the stars, if you are able to count them." And He added, "So shall your offspring be." (6) And because he put his trust in the Lord, He reckoned it to his merit.

22:1–19

(1) Some time afterward, God put Abraham to the test. He said to him, "Abraham," and he answered, "Here I am." (2) And He said, "Take your son,

your favored one, Isaac, whom you love, and go to the land of Moriah.[1] and offer him there as a burnt offering on one of the heights that I will point out to you." (3) So early next morning, Abraham saddled his ass and took with him two of his servants and his son Isaac. He split the wood for the burnt offering, and he set out for the place of which God had told him. (4) On the third day Abraham looked up and saw the place from afar. (5) Then Abraham said to his servants, "You stay here with the ass. The boy and I will go up there; we will worship and we will return to you."

(6) Abraham took the wood for the burnt offering and put it on his son Isaac. He himself took the firestone[2] and the knife; and the two walked off together. (7) Then Isaac said to his father Abraham, "Father!" And he answered, "Yes, my son." And he said, "Here are the firestone and the wood; but where is the sheep for the burnt offering?" (8) And Abraham said, "God will see to the sheep for His burnt offering, my son." And the two of them walked on together.

(9) They arrived at the place of which God had told him. Abraham built an altar there; he laid out the wood; he bound his son Isaac; he laid him on the altar, on top of the wood. (10) And Abraham picked up the knife to slay his son. (11) Then an angel of the Lord called to him from heaven: "Abraham! Abraham!" And he answered, "Here I am." (12) And he said, "Do not raise your hand against the boy, or do anything to him. For now I know that you fear God, since you have not withheld your son, your favored one, from Me." (13) When Abraham looked up, his eye fell upon a ram, caught in the thicket by its horns. So Abraham went and took the ram and offered it up as a burnt offering in place of his son. (14) And Abraham named that site Adonai-yireh,[3] whence the present saying, "On the mount of the Lord there is vision."

(15) The angel of the Lord called to Abraham a second time from heaven, (16) and said, "By Myself I swear, the Lord declares: Because you have done this and have not withheld your son, your favored one, (17) I will bestow My blessing upon you and make your descendants as numerous as the stars of heaven and the sands on the seashore; and your descendants shall seize the gates of their foes. (18) All the nations of the earth shall bless themselves by your descendants, because you have obeyed My command." (19) Abraham then returned to his servants, and they departed together for Beer-sheba; and Abraham stayed in Beer-sheba.

1. Associated by tradition with the site of the future Temple.

2. I.e., flint.
3. The Lord will see to it (Hebrew).

EXODUS 19–20:23

As recounted in Genesis, Abraham was the progenitor of a people. Abraham's line continued through his son Isaac, whose son Jacob received the name Israel from an angel. The Book of Exodus continues the story of Abraham's descendents, who have developed from small, seminomadic tribes into a nation-size population, the Israelites. Enslaved by the Egyptians, the Israelites are freed by the combined, miraculous efforts of God and Moses, an Israelite slave adopted into the household of Pharaoh, king of Egypt. The term *exodus*, from the Greek for "going out," refers to the Israelites' departure from Egypt. The Book of Exodus narrates not just that departure but also God's dramatic formation of a covenant with the Israelites. Three months after their exit from Egypt, the Israelites encamp near a mountain called Sinai, or Horeb. Moses mounts to the summit of Sinai, where he receives a series of messages from God. First, God offers the Israelites a covenant. Two days after the people have effectively accepted this covenant in advance, God delivers through Moses a code that has come to be known as the Ten Commandments or the Decalogue (from the Greek: *deka*, "ten," + *logos*, "word"). Moses eventually spends a mythical forty days and forty nights on Mount Sinai. His reception of the full Torah—encompassing much more than the Ten Commandments and commonly referred to in Christian tradition as the Law of Moses—is foundational for both traditions to the extent that an understood formal, or covenanted, relationship with God is foundational for both.

The Ten Commandments remain nonetheless the core of biblical morality. As reported in the New Testament, Jesus cited the commandments in his discourses. Christians continue to view these commandments as sacred words from God. However, most Christian observance deviates from the commandments in one important particular. With a few exceptions, Christians celebrate their Sabbath on the first day of the week, Sunday, when Christ rose, rather than on the last day of the week, Saturday, when God rested from his labor of creation. This change is understood as an external marker of Christianity's new covenant.

PRONOUNCING GLOSSARY

Rephidim: *re-fi-deem´*   Sinai: *sai´-nai* [*ai* rhyming with *rye*]

EXODUS

19

(1) On the third new moon after the Israelites had gone forth from the land of Egypt, on that very day, they entered the wilderness of Sinai. (2) Having journeyed from Rephidim, they entered the wilderness of Sinai and encamped in the wilderness. Israel encamped there in front of the mountain, (3) and Moses went up to God. The Lord called to him from the mountain, saying, "Thus shall you say to the house of Jacob and declare to the children of Israel: (4) 'You have seen what I did to the Egyptians, how I bore you on eagles' wings and brought you to Me. (5) Now then, if you will obey Me faithfully and keep My covenant, you shall be My treasured possession among all the peoples. Indeed, all the earth is Mine, (6) but you shall be to Me a kingdom of priests and a holy nation.' These are the words that you shall speak to the children of Israel."

(7) Moses came and summoned the elders of the people and put before them all that the Lord had commanded him. (8) All the people answered as one, saying, "All that the Lord has spoken we will do!" And Moses brought back the people's words to the Lord. (9) And the Lord said to Moses, "I will come to you in a thick cloud, in order that the people may

FROM "Exodus" in *JPS Hebrew-English Tanakh: The Traditional Hebrew Text and The New JPS Translation*, 2nd Ed.

hear when I speak with you and so trust you ever after." Then Moses reported the people's words to the Lord, (10) and the Lord said to Moses, "Go to the people and warn them to stay pure[1] today and tomorrow. Let them wash their clothes. (11) Let them be ready for the third day; for on the third day the Lord will come down, in the sight of all the people, on Mount Sinai. (12) You shall set bounds for the people round about, saying, 'Beware of going up the mountain or touching the border of it. Whoever touches the mountain shall be put to death: (13) no hand shall touch him, but he shall be either stoned or shot; beast or man, he shall not live,' When the ram's horn sounds a long blast, they may go up on the mountain."

(14) Moses came down from the mountain to the people and warned the people to stay pure, and they washed their clothes. (15) And he said to the people, "Be ready for the third day: do not go near a woman."

(16) On the third day, as morning dawned, there was thunder, and lightning, and a dense cloud upon the mountain, and a very loud blast of the horn; and all the people who were in the camp trembled. (17) Moses led the people out of the camp toward God, and they took their places at the foot of the mountain.

(18) Now Mount Sinai was all in smoke, for the Lord had come down upon it in fire; the smoke rose like the smoke of a kiln, and the whole mountain trembled violently. (19) The blare of the horn grew louder and louder. As Moses spoke, God answered him in thunder. (20) The Lord came down upon Mount Sinai, on the top of the mountain, and the Lord called Moses to the top of the mountain and Moses went up. (21) The Lord said to Moses, "Go down, warn the people not to break through to the Lord to gaze, lest many of them perish. (22) The priests also, who come near the Lord, must stay pure, lest the Lord break out against them." (23) But Moses said to the Lord, "The people cannot come up to Mount Sinai, for You warned us saying, 'Set bounds about the mountain and sanctify it.'" (24) So the Lord said to him, "Go down, and come back together with Aaron; but let not the priests or the people break through to come up to the Lord, lest He break out against them." (25) And Moses went down to the people and spoke to them.

20:1–23

(1) God spoke all these words, saying:

(2) I the Lord am your God who brought you out of the land of Egypt, the house of bondage: (3) You shall have no other gods besides Me.

(4) You shall not make for yourself a sculptured image, or any likeness of what is in the heavens above, or on the earth below, or in the waters under the earth. (5) You shall not bow down to them or serve them. For I the Lord your God am an impassioned God, visiting the guilt of the parents upon the children, upon the third and upon the fourth generations of those who reject Me, (6) but showing kindness to the thousandth generation of those who love Me and keep My commandments.

---

1. Refrain from sexual relations (see 19:15), which render both parties temporarily impure.

(7) You shall not swear falsely by the name of the Lord your God; for the Lord will not clear one who swears falsely by His name.

(8) Remember the sabbath day and keep it holy. (9) Six days you shall labor and do all your work, (10) but the seventh day is a sabbath of the Lord your God: you shall not do any work—you, your son or daughter, your male or female slave, or your cattle, or the stranger who is within your settlements. (11) For in six days the Lord made heaven and earth and sea, and all that is in them, and He rested on the seventh day; therefore the Lord blessed the sabbath day and hallowed it.

(12) Honor your father and your mother, that you may long endure on the land that the Lord your God is assigning to you.

(13) You shall not murder.

You shall not commit adultery.

You shall not steal.

You shall not bear false witness against your neighbor.

(14) You shall not covet your neighbor's house: you shall not covet your neighbor's wife, or his male or female slave, or his ox or his ass, or anything that is your neighbor's.

(15) All the people witnessed[1] the thunder and lightning, the blare of the horn and the mountain smoking; and when the people saw it, they fell back and stood at a distance. (16) "You speak to us," they said to Moses, "and we will obey; but let not God speak to us, lest we die." (17) Moses answered the people, "Be not afraid; for God has come only in order to test you, and in order that the fear of Him may be ever with you, so that you do not go astray." (18) So the people remained at a distance, while Moses approached the thick cloud where God was.

(19) The Lord said to Moses:

Thus shall you say to the Israelites: You yourselves saw that I spoke to you from the very heavens: (20) With Me, therefore, you shall not make any gods of silver, nor shall you make for yourselves any gods of gold. (21) Make for Me an altar of earth and sacrifice on it your burnt offerings and your sacrifices of well-being,[2] your sheep and your oxen; in every place where I cause My name to be mentioned I will come to you and bless you. (22) And if you make for Me an altar of stones, do not build it of hewn stones; for by wielding your tool upon them you have profaned them. (23) Do not ascend My altar by steps, that your nakedness may not be exposed upon it.

---

1. Literally, "saw the voices."　　　2. One type of sacrifice.

DEUTERONOMY 6:1–15

Whereas the first four Books of the Bible—Genesis, Exodus, Leviticus, and Numbers—narrate the early history of the Israelites, the Book of Deuteronomy takes the form of sermons or speeches spoken by Moses shortly before the entry of the Jews into Canaan.

In the Gospel of Mark 12:28–31, Jesus is asked to name the greatest commandment. His first answer is Deuteronomy 6:4: "Hear, O Israel! The Lord is our God, the Lord alone." Later, Jesus' unhesitant declaration of allegiance to this classic formulation of Jewish monotheism served as a brake on attempts to insinuate something like ditheism (belief in two gods) or some form of polytheism into Christian belief. Jesus goes on in the Gospel to complement the greatest commandment with the second-greatest, "You shall love your neighbor as yourself." In this universalized form, Christian tradition has remembered and celebrated the Book of Leviticus 19:18, which Jesus quotes.

DEUTERONOMY

6:1–15

(1) And this is the Instruction—the laws and the rules—that the Lord your God has commanded [me] to impart to you, to be observed in the land that you are about to cross into and occupy, (2) so that you, your children, and your children's children may revere the Lord your God and follow, as long as you live, all His laws and commandments that I enjoin upon you, to the end that you may long endure. (3) Obey, O Israel, willingly and faithfully, that it may go well with you and that you may increase greatly [in] a land flowing with milk and honey, as the Lord, the God of your fathers, spoke to you.

(4) Hear, O Israel! The Lord is our God, the Lord alone. (5) You shall love the Lord your God with all your heart and with all your soul and with all your might. (6) Take to heart these instructions with which I charge you this day. (7) Impress them upon your children. Recite them when you stay at home and when you are away, when you lie down and when you get up. (8) Bind them as a sign on your hand and let them serve as a symbol on your forehead; (9) inscribe them on the doorposts of your house and on your gates.

(10) When the Lord your God brings you into the land that He swore to your fathers, Abraham, Isaac, and Jacob, to assign to you—great and flourishing cities that you did not build, (11) houses full of all good things that you did not fill, hewn cisterns that you did not hew, vineyards and olive groves that you did not plant—and you eat your fill, (12) take heed that you do not forget the Lord who freed you from the land of Egypt, the house of bondage. (13) Revere only the Lord your God and worship Him alone, and swear only by His name. (14) Do not follow other gods, any gods of the peoples about you—(15) for the Lord your God in your midst is an impassioned God—lest

From "Deuteronomy" in *JPS Hebrew-English Tanakh: The Traditional Hebrew Text and The New JPS Translation*, 2nd Ed. Bracketed insertions are the translator's.

the anger of the Lord your God blaze forth against you and He wipe you off the face of the earth.

1 SAMUEL 2:1–10 AND 2 SAMUEL 7:8–17

In the New Testament, the Old Testament is not referred to as the Old Testament. Instead, it is called "the Law and the Prophets." The Law in that phrase is the Law of Moses—the first five Books of the Bible, always called Torah in Jewish tradition. "The Prophets" are not just the works that later Christian tradition understands by that term, such as the Book of Isaiah. "The Prophets" are also Joshua, Judges, Samuel, and Kings. These works may best be understood as history interpreted prophetically, victory being understood as the reward for loyalty to God and defeat the punishment for disloyalty. Thus, in the beginning, because of their covenant loyalty to God, the Twelve Tribes of Israel defeat their enemies and take possession of much of the land known as Canaan (Joshua, Judges). They achieve their greatest glory when they are united under King David (1 Samuel, 2 Samuel), who enormously extends their domain. In 1 Samuel 7:8–17, God, speaking through the prophet Nathan, promises David an eternal dynasty. At the end, however, because of their covenant disloyalty to God, they lose possession of their land and are carried into exile in Assyria and Babylon (1 Kings, 2 Kings).

Why are these events important for Christianity? After the bitter loss of national sovereignty and even its partial restoration (discussed in the Books of Ezra and Nehemiah), the Israelites take hope from God's promise. They await the appearance of an heir to David—a shoot from the root of Jesse, David's father—who will restore the remembered glory of the Davidic Era. According to genealogies in the Gospels of Matthew and Luke, Jesus is in fact a descendent of David. In Luke, Jesus is born in "the city of David, which is called Bethlehem," because his father, Joseph, who was "of the house and lineage of David," has been summoned there for a census (2:3). Thus, in Christian tradition, Jesus fulfills the ancient Davidic hope, albeit in a highly transformed and paradoxical way. In his preaching, Jesus often spoke of the "kingdom of God," the "kingdom of heaven," or simply "the kingdom." His parables, or comparison stories, frequently begin, "The kingdom of heaven is like. . . ." They aim to suggest what human life would be like if God were in charge. By implication, they turn the blessings promised to Israel through David into blessings promised to the whole world through Jesus.

The set of events that will culminate in the triumphs and then the tribulations of the House of David begins with the birth of Samuel to the long-barren Hannah. In 1 Samuel 2:1–10, Hannah utters a hymn of gratitude to the Lord for the birth of Samuel. This eloquent expression of compassion for the downtrodden is an early example of a motif in the historical Books of the Old Testament: God's predilection for the poor, humble, and weak against the rich, proud, and powerful. In the New Testament, Hannah's hymn is strongly echoed in Mary's hymn of gratitude (Luke 1:46–55) for the coming birth of the son whom the Angel of the Lord has told her to name Jesus. Indeed, Mary has been assured that Jesus "will reign over the house of Jacob for ever; and of his kingdom there will be no end," just as was promised to David (Luke 1:31, 33).

Sheol: *sheh-ohl´*

1 SAMUEL

2:1–10

(1) And Hannah prayed:

> My heart exults in the Lord;
> I have triumphed through the Lord.
> I gloat over my enemies;
> I rejoice in Your deliverance.
>
> (2) There is no holy one like the Lord,
> Truly, there is none beside You;
> There is no rock like our God.
>
> (3) Talk no more with lofty pride,
> Let no arrogance cross your lips!
> For the Lord is an all-knowing God;
> By Him actions are measured.
>
> (4) The bows of the mighty are broken,
> And the faltering are girded with strength.
> (5) Men once sated must hire out for bread;
> Men once hungry hunger no more.
> While the barren woman bears seven,
> The mother of many is forlorn.
> (6) The Lord deals death and gives life,
> Casts down into Sheol and raises up.
> (7) The Lord makes poor and makes rich;
> He casts down, He also lifts high.
> (8) He raises the poor from the dust,
> Lifts up the needy from the dunghill,
> Getting them with nobles,
> Granting them seats of honor.
> For the pillars of the earth are the Lord's;
> He has set the world upon them.
> (9) He guards the steps of His faithful,
> But the wicked perish in darkness—
> For not by strength shall man prevail.
>
> (10) The foes of the Lord shall be shattered;
> He will thunder against them in the heavens.

From "1 Samuel" in *JPS Hebrew-English Tanakh: The Traditional Hebrew Text and The New JPS Translation*, 2nd Ed. From "2 Samuel" in New Revised Standard Version Bible.

The Lord will judge the ends of the earth.
He will give power to His king,
And triumph to His anointed one.

2 SAMUEL

7:8–17

(8) Now therefore thus you shall say to my servant David: Thus says the Lord of hosts: I took you from the pasture, from following the sheep to be prince over my people Israel; (9) and I have been with you wherever you went, and have cut off all your enemies from before you; and I will make for you a great name, like the name of the great ones of the earth. (10) And I will appoint a place for my people Israel and will plant them, so that they may live in their own place, and be disturbed no more; and evildoers shall afflict them no more, as formerly, (11) from the time that I appointed judges over my people Israel; and I will give you rest from all your enemies. Moreover the Lord declares to you that the Lord will make you a house. (12) When your days are fulfilled and you lie down with your ancestors, I will raise up your off-spring after you, who shall come forth from your body, and I will establish his kingdom. (13) He shall build a house for my name, and I will estab-lish the throne of his kingdom forever. (14) I will be a father to him, and he shall be a son to me. When he commits ubiquity, I will punish him with a rod such as mortals use, with blows inflicted by human beings. (15) But I will not take my steadfast love from him. * * * (16) Your house and your kingdom shall be made sure forever before me; your throne shall be estab-lished forever. (17) In accordance with all these words and with all this vision, Nathan spoke to David.

PSALMS 22, 23, 110 AND PROVERBS 8:22–31

The Book of Psalms consists of 150 religious poems. Seventy-three of these poems traditionally are attributed to King David (ca. 1040–970 B.C.E.), second king of the United Kingdom of Israel (ca. 1003–970 B.C.E.) and, according to the Gospels of Matthew and Luke, an ancestor of Jesus Christ through both Joseph and Mary. Several of the psalms—notably, Psalm 110, which is quoted in the New Testament (Matthew 22:44 and elsewhere)—focus on God's anointed, his earthly king. Some praise God, whereas some beg for God's help.

According to the Christian tradition, Psalm 22 prophesies the sufferings of the coming savior. In two of the Gospels, Jesus utters the opening words of this psalm before he dies on the cross (Matthew 27:46 and Mark 15:34). Because this psalm progresses from agony to ecstatic triumph, however, he may have intended the bystanders to recall the closing triumph and not just the opening agony. The psalm's two final verses have been taken as a prophecy that the story of Jesus' death and Resurrection was destined to spread around the world.

Other psalms, such as Psalm 23, have been read as prophesying the coming of the Messiah. This connection is due to King David's prominence in the Book of

Psalms. As noted in 2 Samuel 8–16, David began as a shepherd and was made a king by God, who elsewhere refers to himself as the Shepherd of Israel: "As a shepherd seeks out his flock when some of his sheep have been scattered, so I will seek out my sheep" (Ezekiel 34:12). Jesus calls himself "the Good Shepherd" (John 10:14). While according to Christian tradition the opening of Psalm 23, "The Lord is my shepherd," is thus a reference to Jesus, the shepherd of the psalm may as easily be God protecting and shepherding Jesus, his Messiah, his anointed (verse 5: "thou anointest my head with oil"), even in the "valley of the shadow of death" (verse 4).

Proverbs 8:22–31 is an Old Testament poem whose place in Christian interpretive tradition involves an equation between the Wisdom of God and the Word of God. In the Book of Proverbs, the Wisdom of God is personified as female and said to have been created before the world was created and thereafter to have been involved with God as cocreator. When God created the world, step by step, "I was there" (8:27), and "I was by his side, * * * delighting him day after day" (8:30). This passage makes a striking comparison with the prologue to the Gospel of John: "In the beginning was the Word, and the Word was with God, and the Word was God. . . . All things were made by him, and without him was not any thing made that was made" (John 1:1, 3). Via this linkage to the Gospel of John, Proverbs 8:22–31 has been a passage of particular interest to feminist theologians as pointing, potentially, to a deep feminine dimension in the identity of Christ and even of God.

PRONOUNCING GLOSSARY

Bashan: *bah-shahn´*
Melchizedek: *mel-kee´-ze-dek*
Psalms: *sahlms*

Yahweh: *yah´-way*
Zion: *zai´-on* [*ai* rhyming with *rye*]

PSALMS

22

(1) My God, my God, why have you forsaken me?
    Why are you so far from saving me,
    so far from my cries of anguish?
(2) My God, I cry out by day, but you do not answer,
    by night, but I find no rest.

(3) Yet you are enthroned as the Holy One;
    you are the one Israel praises.
(4) In you our ancestors put their trust;
    they trusted and you delivered them.
(5) To you they cried out and were saved;
    in you they trusted and were not put to shame.

(6) But I am a worm and not a man,
    scorned by everyone, despised by the people.

FROM "Psalm 22" in *The Holy Bible, New International Version*. From "Psalm 23" in *The English Bible, King James Version, The Old Testament: A Norton Critical Edition*. From "Psalm 110" in *The Holy Bible, Containing the Old and New Testaments, Revised Standard Version: Catholic Edition*. From "Proverbs" in *The Jerusalem Bible*.

(7) All who see me mock me;
    they hurl insults, shaking their heads.
(8) "He trusts in the Lord," they say,
    "let the Lord rescue him.
Let him deliver him,
    since he delights in him."

(9) Yet you brought me out of the womb;
    you made me trust in you, even at my mother's breast.
(10) From birth I was cast on you;
    from my mother's womb you have been my God.

(11) Do not be far from me,
    for trouble is near
    and there is no one to help.

(12) Many bulls surround me;
    strong bulls of Bashan encircle me.
(13) Roaring lions that tear their prey
    open their mouths wide against me.
(14) I am poured out like water,
    and all my bones are out of joint.
My heart has turned to wax;
    it has melted within me.
(15) My mouth is dried up like a potsherd,
    and my tongue sticks to the roof of my mouth;
    you lay me in the dust of death.

(16) Dogs surround me,
    a pack of villains encircles me;
    they pierce my hands and my feet.
(17) All my bones are on display;
    people stare and gloat over me.
(18) They divide my clothes among them
    and cast lots for my garment.

(19) But you, Lord, do not be far from me.
    You are my strength; come quickly to help me.
(20) Deliver me from the sword,
    my precious life from the power of the dogs.
(21) Rescue me from the mouth of the lions;
    save me from the horns of the wild oxen.

(22) I will declare your name to my people;
    in the assembly I will praise you.
(23) You who fear the Lord, praise him!
    All you descendants of Jacob, honor him!
    Revere him, all you descendants of Israel!
(24) For he has not despised or scorned
    the suffering of the afflicted one;
he has not hidden his face from him
    but has listened to his cry for help.

(25) From you comes the theme of my praise in the great assembly;
    before those who fear you I will fulfill my vows.
(26) The poor will eat and be satisfied;
    those who seek the Lord will praise him—
    may your hearts live forever!

(27) All the ends of the earth
    will remember and turn to the Lord,
and all the families of the nations
    will bow down before him,
(28) for dominion belongs to the Lord
    and he rules over the nations.

(29) All the rich of the earth will feast and worship;
    all who go down to the dust will kneel before him—
    those who cannot keep themselves alive.
(30) Posterity will serve him;
    future generations will be told about the Lord.
(31) They will proclaim his righteousness,
    declaring to a people yet unborn:
    He has done it!

23

(1) The Lord is my shepherd; I shall not want.
(2) He maketh me to lie down in green pastures: he leadeth me beside
    the still waters.
(3) He restoreth my soul: he leadeth me in the paths of righteousness for
    his name's sake.
(4) Yea, though I walk through the valley of the shadow of death, I will
    fear no evil: for thou art with me; thy rod and thy staff they
    comfort me.
(5) Thou preparest a table before me in the presence of mine enemies:
    thou anointest my head with oil, my cup runneth over.
(6) Surely goodness and mercy shall follow me all the days of my life: and
    I will dwell in the house of the Lord for ever.

110

(1) The Lord says to my lord:
    "Sit at my right hand,
    till I make your enemies
    your footstool."

(2) The Lord sends forth from Zion
    your mighty scepter.
    Rule in the midst of your foes!
(3) Your people will offer themselves freely
    on the day you lead your host
    upon the holy mountains

From the womb of the morning
    like dew your youth will come to you.
(4) The Lord has sworn
    and will not change his mind,
"You are a priest for ever
    after the order of Melchizedek."[1]

(5) The Lord is at your right hand;
    he will shatter kings on the day of his wrath.
(6) He will execute judgment among the nations,
    filling them with corpses;
he will shatter chiefs
    over the wide earth.
(7) He will drink from the brook by the way;
    therefore he will lift up his head.

PROVERBS

8:22–31

(22) 'Yahweh created me when his purpose first unfolded,
    before the oldest of his works.
(23) From everlasting I was firmly set,
    from the beginning, before earth came into being.
(24) The deep was not, when I was born,
    there were no springs to gush with water.
(25) Before the mountains were settled,
    before the hills, I came to birth;
(26) before he made the earth, the countryside,
    or the first grains of the world's dust.
(27) When he fixed the heavens firm, I was there,
    when he drew a ring on the surface of the deep,
(28) when he thickened the clouds above,
    when he fixed fast the springs of the deep,
(29) when he assigned the sea its boundaries
    —and the waters will not invade the shore—
    when he laid down the foundations of the earth,
(30) I was by his side, a master craftsman,
    delighting him day after day,
    ever at play in his presence,
(31) at play everywhere in his world,
    delighting to be with the sons of men.'

---

1. See Genesis 14:18. Melchizedek, a priest of "God Most High," offered a sacrifice of bread and wine in thanksgiving for Abram's victory in battle.

ISAIAH 9:1–6, 11:1–9, 40:1–8, 52:13–53, 56:1–8

The prophet Isaiah (eighth century B.C.E.), a member of the court of King Heze-kiah of Judah, was one of the earliest prophets operating in a "literary" vein. The literary prophets opposed the "official" prophets, and they were the first biblical prophets whose pronouncements were written, collected, and preserved. Isaiah is the first of the three major literary prophets, the others being Jeremiah and Ezekiel; all are distinguished by the length of their books. The literary prophets spoke and wrote strongly worded pronouncements about moral behavior and social justice, predicting national catastrophes that would punish the Israelites for sin.

Historically, Isaiah received his prophetic call around 740 B.C.E. According to Isaiah 6, God touched Isaiah's mouth with a burning coal to purify it. In the Christian tradition, Isaiah is seen as foretelling the coming of the savior, and early passages in the Book of Isaiah, including chapter 9, appear to describe the person of Jesus. Thus, 9:1–6 is frequently read during the Christmas season. Isaiah 11:1–9 is seen as foretelling the essential message of the coming Messiah, and it is used frequently both in worship and biblical commentary as a reference to Jesus. Isaiah 40:3–4 is taken in the Gospels as a prophetic reference to the future desert ministry of John the Baptist. (See, for example, the Gospel of Mark 1:3.)

Isaiah became a monumental figure in Israelite religion. Partly as a result, an anonymous sixth-century-B.C.E. prophet took on the earlier Isaiah's identity in writing what became chapters 40–55 of the Book of Isaiah. These latter chapters, also called Second Isaiah or Deutero-Isaiah, include extended passages about a "suffering servant." According to the Christian tradition—for example, in the Gospel of Matthew—these passages apply to the sufferings of Jesus. Selections from the Deutero-Isaiah are read in worship during Holy Week and especially on Good Friday. Chapters 56–66, thought to have been written by a third writer in the Isaiah tradition, are sometimes referred to as Third Isaiah or Trito-Isaiah. Isaiah 56:1–8, welcoming eunuchs and foreigners into the "house" or temple of the Lord, is an exceptionally bold vision of the expansion of the ancestral Jewish covenant to include the once excluded. The end of verse 7—"my house shall be called a house of prayer for all peoples"—is quoted in the Gospels of Matthew (21:13), Mark (11:17), and Luke (19:46).

PRONOUNCING GLOSSARY

Midian: *mi´-dee-an*
Naphtali: *naf´-ta-lee*

Zebulun: *ze´-byoo-lun*

ISAIAH

9:1–6

(1) But there will be no gloom for those who were in anguish. In the former time he brought into contempt the land of Zebulun and the land of Naphtali,[1] but in the latter time he will make glorious the way of the sea, the land beyond the Jordan, Galilee of the nations.[2]

> (2) The people who walked in darkness
>   have seen a great light;
>   those who lived in a land of deep darkness—
>   on them light has shined.
> (3) You have multiplied the nation,
>   you have increased its joy;
>   they rejoice before you
>   as with joy at the harvest,
>   as people exult when dividing plunder.
> (4) For the yoke of their burden,
>   and the bar across their shoulders,
>   the rod of their oppressor,
>   you have broken as on the day of Midian.[3]
> (5) For all the boots of the tramping warriors
>   and all the garments rolled in blood
>   shall be burned as fuel for the fire.
> (6) For a child has been born for us,
>   a son given to us;
>   authority rests upon his shoulders;
>   and he is named
>   Wonderful Counselor, Mighty God,
>   Everlasting Father, Prince of Peace.

11:1–9

(1) There shall come forth a shoot from the stump of Jesse,[1]
    and a branch shall grow out of his roots.
(2) And the Spirit of the Lord shall rest upon him,
    the spirit of wisdom and understanding,
    the spirit of counsel and might,
    the spirit of knowledge and the fear of the Lord.
(3) And his delight shall be in the fear of the Lord.

FROM "Isaiah 9" in New Revised Standard Version Bible. From "Isaiah 11" and "Isaiah 56" in *The Holy Bible, Containing the Old and New Testaments, Revised Standard Version: Catholic Edition*. From "Isaiah 40" in *The English Bible, King James Version, The Old Testament: A Norton Critical Edition*. From "Isaiah 52–53" in New American Bible, Rev. Ed.

1. Far northern Israelite tribes, subjected early to foreign conquest.
2. David's kingdom extended well east of the Jordan. The prophecy envisions the recovery of lost territory and lost glory. "Galilee" refers generally to northernmost Israelite territory, already lost to Israel and settled by foreigners ("the nations") in Isaiah's day.
3. The day of a great victory over Midian, a foreign invader. See Judges 7–8.
1. A resident of Judah who became the father of David, king of the Israelites (see p. 94); also mentioned in the genealogy of Jesus.

He shall not judge by what his eyes see,
    or decide by what his ears hear;
(4) but with righteousness he shall judge the poor,
    and decide with equity for the meek of the earth;
  and he shall smite the earth with the rod of his mouth,
    and with the breath of his lips he shall slay the wicked.
(5) Righteousness shall be the girdle of his waist,
    and faithfulness the girdle of his loins.

(6) The wolf shall dwell with the lamb,
    and the leopard shall lie down with the kid,
  and the calf and the lion and the fatling together,
    and a little child shall lead them.
(7) The cow and the bear shall feed;
    their young shall lie down together;
    and the lion shall eat straw like the ox.
(8) The sucking child shall play over the hole of the asp,
    and the weaned child shall put his hand on the adder's den.
(9) They shall not hurt or destroy
    in all my holy mountain;
  for the earth shall be full of the knowledge of the Lord
    as the waters cover the sea.

40:1–8

(1) Comfort ye, comfort ye my people, saith your God.
(2) Speak ye comfortably to Jerusalem, and cry unto her, that her warfare
    is accomplished, that her iniquity is pardoned: for she hath
    received of the Lord's hand double for all her sins.
(3) The voice of him that crieth in the wilderness, Prepare ye the way of
    the Lord, make straight in the desert a highway for our God.
(4) Every valley shall be exalted, and every mountain and hill shall be
    made low: and the crooked shall be made straight, and the rough
    places plain:
(5) And the glory of the Lord shall be revealed, and all flesh shall see it
    together: for the mouth of the Lord hath spoken it.

(6) The voice said, Cry. And he said, What shall I cry? All flesh is grass,
    and all the goodliness thereof is as the flower of the field:
(7) The grass withereth, the flower fadeth: because the spirit of the Lord
    bloweth upon it: surely the people is grass.
(8) The grass withereth, the flower fadeth: but the word of our God shall
    stand for ever.

52

*   *   *

SUFFERING AND TRIUMPH OF THE SERVANT OF THE LORD

(13) See, my servant shall prosper,
    he shall be raised high and greatly exalted.

(14) Even as many were amazed at him—
    so marred were his features,
    beyond that of mortals
    his appearance, beyond that of human beings—
(15) So shall he startle many nations,
    kings shall stand speechless;
    For those who have not been told shall see,
    those who have not heard shall ponder it.

53

(1) Who would believe what we have heard?
    To whom has the arm of the LORD been revealed?
(2) He grew up like a sapling before him,
    like a shoot from the parched earth;
    He had no majestic bearing to catch our eye,
    no beauty to draw us to him.
(3) He was spurned and avoided by men,
    a man of suffering, knowing pain,
    Like one from whom you turn your face,
    spurned, and we held him in no esteem.
(4) Yet it was our pain that he bore,
    our sufferings he endured.
    We thought of him as stricken,
    struck down by God and afflicted,
(5) But he was pierced for our sins,
    crushed for our iniquity.
    He bore the punishment that makes us whole,
    by his wounds we were healed.
(6) We had all gone astray like sheep,
    all following our own way;
    But the LORD laid upon him
    the guilt of us all.
(7) Though harshly treated, he submitted
    and did not open his mouth;
    or a sheep silent before shearers,
    he did not open his mouth.
(8) Seized and condemned, he was taken away.
    Who would have thought any more of his destiny?
    For he was cut off from the land of the living,
    struck for the sins of his people.
(9) He was given a grave among the wicked,
    a burial place with evildoers,
    Though he had done no wrong,
    nor was deceit found in his mouth.
(10) But it was the LORD's will to crush him with pain.
    By making his life as a reparation offering,
    he shall see his offspring, shall lengthen his days,
    and the LORD's will shall be accomplished through him.
(11) Because of his anguish he shall see the light;
    because of his knowledge he shall be content;
    My servant, the just one, shall justify the many,
    their iniquity he shall bear.

(12) Therefore I will give him his portion among the many,
    and he shall divide the spoils with the mighty,
  Because he surrendered himself to death,
    was counted among the transgressors,
  Bore the sins of many,
    and interceded for the transgressors.

56:1–8

(1) Thus says the Lord:
    "Keep justice, and do righteousness,
  for soon my salvation will come,
    and my deliverance be revealed.
(2) Blessed is the man who does this,
    and the son of man who holds it fast,
  who keeps the sabbath, not profaning it,
    and keeps his hand from doing any evil."

(3) Let not the foreigner who has joined himself to the Lord say,
    "The Lord will surely separate me from his people";
  and let not the eunuch say,
    "Behold, I am a dry tree."
(4) For thus says the Lord:
  "To the eunuchs who keep my sabbaths,
  who choose the things that please me and hold fast my covenant,
(5) I will give in my house and within my walls
    a monument and a name
    better than sons and daughters;
  I will give them an everlasting name
    which shall not be cut off.

(6) "And the foreigners who join themselves to the Lord,
    to minister to him, to love the name of the Lord,
    and to be his servants,
  every one who keeps the sabbath, and does not profane it,
    and holds fast my covenant—
(7) these I will bring to my holy mountain,
    and make them joyful in my house of prayer;
  their burnt offerings and their sacrifices
    will be accepted on my altar;
  for my house shall be called a house of prayer
    for all peoples.
(8) Thus says the Lord God,
    who gathers the outcasts of Israel,
  I will gather yet others to him
    besides those already gathered."

JEREMIAH 31:31–34

Jeremiah, like Isaiah, was a literary prophet. Around 646 B.C.E., he was born to a priestly family, and he became a priest. Around 626 B.C.E., he began to prophesy, denouncing social ills and political misjudgments and warning that the "victory of Babylon" would be the judgment of God. After the Babylonians conquered Judah and destroyed the First Temple in 586 B.C.E., Jeremiah prophesied in the name of the Lord against the priests, aristocrats, and other Jews who planned to seek refuge in Egypt (Jeremiah 42–43). For this opposition, the refugees denounced Jeremiah as a false prophet. They forced him to accompany them to Egypt, where he continued his denunciations and where he presumably died. Against his will, Jeremiah was part of the first voluntary diaspora—that is, the first establishment of a substantial Jewish settlement outside Israel.

In the following passage, Jeremiah prophesies a "new covenant" (31:31). The "old" covenant was the Law of Moses, the contract established at Mount Sinai between God and the Jewish people. Jeremiah's new covenant would renew the original, but it would be written on the heart rather than on the stone tablets mentioned in Exodus 31–32—a sign of sincerity. God promised to place "My Teaching"—in the Hebrew, literally "My Torah"—in the heart of every Jew.

In Christian tradition, Jeremiah's reference to a new covenant meant much more than a renewal of the old covenant. According to the Christian interpretation—beginning with the Letter to the Hebrews 8:8–12, where this passage is quoted in full—the new covenant was not to "be like the covenant I made with their fathers, when I took them by the hand to lead them out of the land of Egypt" (verse 32). Moses was the mediator of that covenant. Jesus was the mediator of the new covenant, which was to expand the old by admitting to it all who are "called" (Letter to the Hebrews 8:15), promising them the forgiveness of the sins they may have committed under the terms of the old covenant and the boon not of a promised land but of eternal life.

Because Christian tradition sees the formation of this new covenant as the fruit of the death and Resurrection of Jesus, the Christian Scriptures that were assembled to provide an account of the new covenant were eventually called the New Testament, *testament* being simply an archaic English synonym for *covenant*.

JEREMIAH

31:31–34

(31) See, a time is coming—declares the Lord—when I will make a new covenant with the House of Israel and the House of Judah. (32) It will not be like the covenant I made with their fathers, when I took them by the hand to lead them out of the land of Egypt, a covenant which they broke, though I espoused[1] them—declares the Lord. (33) But such is the covenant I will make with the House of Israel after these days—declares the Lord: I will put My Teaching into their inmost being and inscribe it upon their hearts. Then I will be their God, and they shall be My people. (34) No longer

FROM "Jeremiah" in *JPS Hebrew-English Tanakh: The Traditional Hebrew Text and The New JPS Translation*, 2nd Ed.

1. The meaning of the Hebrew is uncertain.

will they need to teach one another and say to one another, "Heed the Lord"; for all of them, from the least of them to the greatest, shall heed Me—declares the Lord.

> For I will forgive their iniquities,
> And remember their sins no more.

EZEKIEL 37:1–14 AND DANIEL 7:1–14

Ezekiel, the third of the three major literary prophets of ancient Israel, lived and worked in the sixth century B.C.E. among the Jewish exiles in Babylon. His visionary oracles bespeak the psychological dislocation of national humiliation and exile but also an indomitable hope of national recovery. In one of these oracles, God promises to cleanse and profoundly transform Israel: "I will cleanse you from all your unclean-ness and from all your fetishes. And I will give you a new heart and put a new spirit into you: I will remove the heart of stone from your body and give you a heart of flesh" (Ezekiel 36:25–26). The image is clearly akin to Jeremiah's (31:33) of a new Torah written on the heart.

Of all Ezekiel's visions, however, none more deeply marked later Christian imagi-nation than his brilliant and haunting vision, in the first fourteen lines of Ezekiel 37, of being set down in a valley full of dead men's bones and being ordered by God to bring those dead back to life by the power of God's Word. For Ezekiel, this vision represented the collective resurrection back to independent national life of the defeated and, as it were, dead nation of Israel.

During this vision, God addresses Ezekiel three times as "son of man." In both the Hebrew of the Book of Ezekiel and the Aramaic of the portion of the Book of Daniel anthologized here, this phrase is an idiom for "human being." Modern translations often render the phrase as "human being" or "mortal." This anthology reproduces the seventeenth-century King James Version, because the KJV's literal translation "son of man" had great theological importance. In the Gospel of Mark, it received a momentous new interpretation, plausibly traceable to the historical Jesus.

This new interpretation is intimately linked to Daniel 7:13, for whose interpreta-tion a little historical background is essential. In 539 B.C.E., the Persians defeated the Babylonian Empire. Israel—now, essentially, Jerusalem and environs—became a small semiautonomous domain within the Persian Empire. In 333 B.C.E., Greek rule succeeded Persian, and it lasted until 168 B.C.E., when a century of indepen-dent Jewish rule began, preceding the takeover by the Roman Empire. Daniel 1–6 was written under Persian or early Greek rule; Daniel 7–12, the latter half of the book, was written just as newly oppressive Greek rule was yielding to Jewish independence.

In Daniel 7:1–14, the title figure experiences a vision in which the successive empires ruling over Israel are represented by monsters and in which Israel, victori-ous at last, is represented by "one like a son of man." During the years between 167 B.C.E. and the lifetime of Jesus, influential circles in Jewish tradition took what in the Book of Daniel is a mere symbol and reimagined it as an actual celestial being called the Son of Man. Daringly, Jesus identified himself as this heavenly figure come down to save the world (see p. 127).

In later centuries, Christians linked Ezekiel's vision of mass resurrection to one or another of the many Christian visions of a general resurrection before the Last

Judgment, when the dead from all past times will rise together at the Second Coming of the Son of Man (see Matthew 25:31–46 [p. 116] and Revelation 11).

PRONOUNCING GLOSSARY

Babylon: *Ba´-bi-lon*　　　　　　　　　Belshazzar: *Behl´-sha-zahr*

EZEKIEL

37:1–14

(1) The hand of the Lord was upon me, and carried me out in the spirit of the Lord, and set me down in the midst of the valley which was full of bones, (2) and caused me to pass by them round about: and, behold, there were very many in the open valley; and, lo, they were very dry. (3) And he said unto me, Son of man, can these bones live? And I answered, O Lord God, thou knowest. (4) Again he said unto me, Prophesy upon these bones, and say unto them, O ye dry bones, hear the word of the Lord. (5) Thus saith the Lord God unto these bones; Behold, I will cause breath to enter into you, and ye shall live: (6) and I will lay sinews upon you, and will bring up flesh upon you, and cover you with skin, and put breath in you, and ye shall live; and ye shall know that I am the Lord. (7) So I prophesied as I was commanded: and as I prophesied, there was a noise, and behold a shaking, and the bones came together, bone to his bone. (8) And when I beheld, lo, the sinews and the flesh came up upon them, and the skin covered them above: but there was no breath in them. (9) Then said he unto me, Prophesy unto the wind, prophesy, Son of man, and say to the wind, Thus saith the Lord God; Come from the four winds, O breath, and breathe upon these slain, that they may live. (10) So I prophesied as he commanded me, and the breath came into them, and they lived, and stood up upon their feet, an exceeding great army.

(11) Then he said unto me, Son of man, these bones are the whole house of Israel: behold, they say, Our bones are dried, and our hope is lost: we are cut off for our parts. (12) Therefore prophesy and say unto them, Thus saith the Lord God; Behold, O my people, I will open your graves, and cause you to come up out of your graves, and bring you into the land of Israel. (13) And ye shall know that I am the Lord, when I have opened your graves, O my people, and brought you up out of your graves, (14) and shall put my spirit in you, and ye shall live, and I shall place you in your own land: then shall ye know that I the Lord have spoken it, and performed it, saith the Lord.

DANIEL

7:1–14

(1) In the first year of Belshazzar king of Babylon[1] Daniel had a dream and visions of his head upon his bed: then he wrote the dream, and told the

From "Ezekiel" and "Daniel" in *The English Bible, King James Version, The Old Testament: A Norton Critical Edition.*

1. Or Balthazar (6th century B.C.E.); according to the Book of Daniel, the last king of Babylon.

sum of the matters. (2) Daniel spake and said, I saw in my vision by night, and, behold, the four winds of the heaven strove upon the great sea. (3) And four great beasts came up from the sea, diverse one from another. (4) The first was like a lion, and had eagle's wings: I beheld till the wings thereof were plucked, and it was lifted up from the earth, and made stand upon the feet as a man, and a man's heart was given to it. (5) And behold another beast, a second, like to a bear, and it raised up itself on one side, and it had three ribs in the mouth of it between the teeth of it: and they said thus unto it, Arise, devour much flesh. (6) After this I beheld, and lo another, like a leopard, which had upon the back of it four wings of a fowl; the beast had also four heads; and dominion was given to it. (7) After this I saw in the night visions, and behold a fourth beast, dreadful and terrible, and strong exceedingly; and it had great iron teeth: it devoured and brake in pieces, and stamped the residue with the feet of it; and it was diverse from all the beasts that were before it; and it had ten horns. (8) I considered the horns, and, behold, there came up among them another little horn, before whom there were three of the first horns plucked up by the roots: and, behold, in this horn were eyes like the eyes of man, and a mouth speaking great things.

(9) I beheld till the thrones were cast down, and the Ancient of days[2] did sit, whose garment was white as snow, and the hair of his head like the pure wool: his throne was like the fiery flame, and his wheels as burning fire. (10) A fiery stream issued and came forth from before him: thousand thousands ministered unto him, and ten thousand times ten thousand stood before him: the judgment was set, and the books were opened. (11) I beheld then because of the voice of the great words which the horn spake: I beheld even till the beast was slain, and his body destroyed, and given to the burning flame. (12) As concerning the rest of the beasts, they had their dominion taken away: yet their lives were prolonged for a season and time.

(13) I saw in the night visions, and, behold, one like the Son of man came with the clouds of heaven, and came to the Ancient of days, and they brought him near before him. (14) And there was given him dominion, and glory, and a kingdom, that all people, nations, and languages, should serve him: his dominion is an everlasting dominion, which shall not pass away, and his kingdom that which shall not be destroyed.

---

2. This phrase is a name for God in Aramaic.

THE NEW TESTAMENT

JOHN 1:1–18

"In the beginning God created the heaven and the earth": In the King James Version of the Old Testament, this sentence opens the Book of Genesis. "In the beginning was the Word, and the Word was with God, and the Word was God": In the King James Version of the New Testament, this sentence opens the Gospel of John. In other words, at the start of his Gospel, the Apostle John consciously alludes to the creation account in Genesis. One form of creation leads to another, for John argues that God's creative Word took on human flesh (1:14) and dwelt on Earth. As the Word, Jesus is also the "light of men" (1:4) and is associated with grace and truth (1:14).

John's text constitutes strong evidence for early Christian belief in the pre-existence with God of the historical figure known as Jesus. This hymn may well have been an ancient, independent text. If so, John simply adapted it as a prologue and as a solemn summary of his Gospel's main argument.

John (ca. 6 C.E.–ca. 100) was the brother of James, another of the Twelve Apostles, the two being known as the Sons of Zebedee. Five books of the New Testament have long been attributed to John: the Gospel of John, the three Letters of John, and the Book of Revelation. Modern scholars doubt that John, Son of Zebedee, wrote all five. Indeed, scholars regularly refer to the Gospel of John as simply "the Fourth Gospel." Nonetheless, the five books are still often described as stemming from "the Johannine School" on the basis of a common store of images, a similar and highly distinctive Greek style, a set of recurring emphases, and a common theology (or "Christology") attributing to Jesus an exalted divine or quasi-divine identity.

Salient among the common emphases is the theme of love as a distinctive quality of the community forming around Jesus. The famous sentence "God is love" occurs in the First Letter of John (1 John 4:8). In the Gospel of John, at the Last Supper, Jesus washes his Twelve Apostles' feet and tells them to serve one another as he has served them: "It is by your love for one another that everyone will recognize that you are my disciples" (John 13:35).

According to the Gospel of John 20, John—referred to obliquely as the disciple "whom Jesus loved" (20:2)—was the first of the Twelve Apostles to see the empty tomb of the risen Christ, just as he had been the only Apostle who remained at the foot of the cross during Jesus' Crucifixion. At Jesus' instruction, it was John who took Jesus' mother, Mary, into his care (19:25–27) after Jesus' death. John may then have lived for a long time among the Christian communities in Asia Minor, perhaps in Ephesus. According to Christian tradition, all of the other Apostles suffered martyrdom before John died, of natural causes, as a very old man.

In this anthology, the excerpts from the four canonical Gospels begin with the prologue to the Gospel of John and end (John 20) with that Gospel's account of Jesus' Resurrection. First, Mary of Magdala (Mary the Magdelene), then John, and finally Peter find Jesus' tomb empty. The assembled Twelve Apostles are then visited by the risen Christ, who breathes his spirit into them just as, in Genesis 2:7, God breathed his spirit into the first man, having fashioned him from the dust of the earth. The implication of the Gospel's opening, "In the beginning," is clear at its closing: The world is about to be created anew by the warm breath of the Lord.

JOHN

1:1–18

(1) In the beginning was the Word, and the Word was with God, and the Word was God. (2) The same was in the beginning with God. (3) All things were made by him; and without him was not any thing made that was made. (4) In him was life; and the life was the light of men. (5) And the light shineth in darkness; and the darkness comprehended it not.

(6) There was a man sent from God, whose name was John. (7) The same came for a witness, to bear witness of the Light, that all men through him might believe. (8) He was not that Light, but was sent to bear witness of that Light. (9) That was the true Light, which lighteth every man that cometh into the world.

(10) He was in the world, and the world was made by him, and the world knew him not. (11) He came unto his own, and his own received him not. (12) But as many as received him, to them gave he power to become the sons of God, even to them that believe on his name: (13) which were born, not of blood, nor of the will of the flesh, nor of the will of man, but of God.

(14) And the Word was made flesh, and dwelt among us, (and we beheld his glory, the glory as of the only begotten of the Father,) full of grace and truth. (15) John bare witness of him, and cried, saying, This was he of whom I spake, He that cometh after me is preferred before me: for he was before me. (16) And of his fulness have all we received, and grace for grace. (17) For the law was given by Moses, but grace and truth came by Jesus Christ. (18) No man hath seen God at any time; the only begotten Son, which is in the bosom of the Father, he hath declared him.

FROM "John" in *The English Bible, King James Version, The New Testament: A Norton Critical Edition.*

LUKE 1–2:14

The Gospel of Luke is a historical and theological account of Jesus' life and ministry. Luke the Evangelist wrote this account sometime between 59–60 C.E. and 80–90. Because Luke had not witnessed Jesus' actions, he based his Gospel on the best available sources (1:1–3), including the Gospel of Mark. However, he rearranged some events to suit his theological emphases. These were the emphases of a writer who was either 1) an assimilated Greek-speaking Jew at home in the culturally Hellenized world of the eastern Mediterranean; 2) a Gentile convert to Christianity; or, conceivably, 3) a Gentile convert to Judaism, later persuaded that Jesus was the Jewish Messiah. As any one of these, Luke—who may or may not have been the "beloved physician" mentioned by Paul at Colossians 4:14—would have wanted the generally peaceful relations that the Jewish Diaspora enjoyed with Roman imperial authority to continue and to be extended, if possible, to the new, heavily Jewish, and already suspect Christian movement spreading rapidly through the Diaspora. To be sure, relations among Jews and non-Jews outside Palestine were not always idyllic. Nonetheless, during the Jewish Wars—which began in 66 C.E. and ended in 135 C.E.—violent hostility existed between a powerful rebel party among the Jews of Palestine and the Roman Empire. Luke appears to be at pains to dissociate Christianity, still a largely Jewish movement, from anything remotely approaching sedition.

This goal explains, at least in part, why the Gospel of Luke begins with a beautifully idealized and appealing evocation of Jewish village life unfolding peacefully under Roman rule in Palestine. This serene nativity narrative, or "Christmas story," still much loved in Christian tradition, is unique to the Gospel of Luke. Equally unique to this Gospel is the line that Jesus speaks as the Roman soldiers nail him to the cross: "Father, forgive them, for they know not what they do" (23:34). In effect, the Gospel of Luke exonerates Rome in advance.

PRONOUNCING GLOSSARY

Abijah: *ah-bee´-jah*
Augustus: *a-gus´-tus*
Elijah: *e-lai´-jah* [*ai* rhyming with *rye*]
Herod: *heh´-rod*

Judea: *joo-dee´-a*
Quirinius: *kwir-in´-ee-oos*
Zechariah: *ze-kah-rai´-uh* [*ai* rhyming with *rye*]

LUKE

1:1–139

(1) Since many have undertaken to set down an orderly account of the events that have been fulfilled among us, (2) just as they were handed on to us by those who from the beginning were eyewitnesses and servants of the word, (3) I too decided, after investigating everything carefully from the very first, to write an orderly account for you, most excellent Theophilus,[1] (4) so that you may know the truth concerning the things about which you have been instructed.

(5) In the days of King Herod of Judea,[2] there was a priest named Zechariah, who belonged to the priestly order of Abijah. His wife was a descendant of Aaron, and her name was Elizabeth. (6) Both of them were righteous before God, living blamelessly according to all the commandments and regulations of the Lord. (7) But they had no children, because Elizabeth was barren, and both were getting on in years.

(8) Once when he was serving as priest before God and his section was on duty, (9) he was chosen by lot, according to the custom of the priesthood, to enter the sanctuary of the Lord and offer incense. (10) Now at the time of the incense offering, the whole assembly of the people was praying outside. (11) Then there appeared to him an angel of the Lord, standing at the right side of the altar of incense. (12) When Zechariah saw him, he was terrified; and fear overwhelmed him. (13) But the angel said to him, "Do not be afraid, Zechariah, for your prayer has been heard. Your wife Elizabeth will bear you a son, and you will name him John. (14) You will have

FROM "Luke" in New Revised Standard Version Bible.

1. Luke's Gentile auditor is possibly fictional.
2. Herod the Great, Roman king of Judaea (73–4 B.C.E.; reigned from 37 B.C.E. until his death).

joy and gladness, and many will rejoice at his birth, (15) for he will be great in the sight of the Lord. He must never drink wine or strong drink; even before his birth he will be filled with the Holy Spirit. (16) He will turn many of the people of Israel to the Lord their God.[3] (17) With the spirit and power of Elijah[4] he will go before him, to turn the hearts of parents to their children, and the disobedient to the wisdom of the righteous, to make ready a people prepared for the Lord." (18) Zechariah said to the angel, "How will I know that this is so? For I am an old man, and my wife is getting on in years." (19) The angel replied, "I am Gabriel. I stand in the presence of God, and I have been sent to speak to you and to bring you this good news. (20) But now, because you did not believe my words, which will be fulfilled in their time, you will become mute, unable to speak, until the day these things occur."

(21) Meanwhile the people were waiting for Zechariah, and wondered at his delay in the sanctuary. (22) When he did come out, he could not speak to them, and they realized that he had seen a vision in the sanctuary. He kept motioning to them and remained unable to speak. (23) When his time of service was ended, he went to his home.

(24) After those days his wife Elizabeth conceived, and for five months she remained in seclusion. She said, (25) "This is what the Lord has done for me when he looked favorably on me and took away the disgrace I have endured among my people."

(26) In the sixth month the angel Gabriel was sent by God to a town in Galilee called Nazareth, (27) to a virgin engaged to a man whose name was Joseph, of the house of David. The virgin's name was Mary. (28) And he came to her and said, "Greetings, favored one! The Lord is with you." (29) But she was much perplexed by his words and pondered what sort of greeting this might be. (30) The angel said to her, "Do not be afraid, Mary, for you have found favor with God. (31) And now, you will conceive in your womb and bear a son, and you will name him Jesus. (32) He will be great, and will be called the Son of the Most High, and the Lord God will give to him the throne of his ancestor David. (33) He will reign over the house of Jacob forever, and of his kingdom there will be no end." (34) Mary said to the angel, "How can this be, since I am a virgin?" (35) The angel said to her, "The Holy Spirit will come upon you, and the power of the Most High will overshadow you; therefore the child to be born will be holy; he will be called Son of God. (36) And now, your relative Elizabeth in her old age has also conceived a son; and this is the sixth month for her who was said to be barren. (37) For nothing will be impossible with God." (38) Then Mary said, "Here am I, the servant of the Lord; let it be with me according to your word." Then the angel departed from her.

(39) In those days Mary set out and went with haste to a Judean town in the hill country, (40) where she entered the house of Zechariah and greeted Elizabeth. (41) When Elizabeth heard Mary's greeting, the child leaped in her womb. And Elizabeth was filled with the Holy Spirit (42) and exclaimed with a loud cry, "Blessed are you among women, and blessed is the fruit of

---

3. The son of Zechariah and Elizabeth will be John the Baptist, Jesus' cousin.
4. According to Jewish tradition, the return of the Old Testament prophet Elijah would herald the coming of the Messiah. Zechariah equates his son with Elijah.

your womb. (43) And why has this happened to me, that the mother of my Lord comes to me? (44) For as soon as I heard the sound of your greeting, the child in my womb leaped for joy. (45) And blessed is she who believed that there would be a fulfillment of what was spoken to her by the Lord."

(46)   And Mary said,
　　"My soul magnifies the Lord,
(47)　and my spirit rejoices in God my Savior,
(48) for he has looked with favor on the lowliness of his servant.
　　Surely, from now on all generations will call me blessed;
(49) for the Mighty One has done great things for me,
　　and holy is his name.
(50) His mercy is for those who fear him
　　from generation to generation.
(51) He has shown strength with his arm;
　　he has scattered the proud in the thoughts of their hearts.
(52) He has brought down the powerful from their thrones,
　　and lifted up the lowly;
(53) he has filled the hungry with good things,
　　and sent the rich away empty.
(54) He has helped his servant Israel,
　　in remembrance of his mercy,
(55) according to the promise he made to our ancestors,
　　to Abraham and to his descendants forever."

(56) And Mary remained with her about three months and then returned to her home.

(57) Now the time came for Elizabeth to give birth, and she bore a son. (58) Her neighbors and relatives heard that the Lord had shown his great mercy to her and they rejoiced with her.

(59) On the eighth day they came to circumcise the child, and they were going to name him Zechariah after his father. (60) But his mother said; "No; he is to be called John." (61) They said to her, "None of your relatives has this name." (62) Then they began motioning to his father to find out what name he wanted to give him. (63) He asked for a writing tablet and wrote, "His name is John." And all of them were amazed. (64) Immediately his mouth was opened and his tongue freed, and he began to speak, praising God. (65) Fear came over all their neighbors, and all these things were talked about throughout the entire hill country of Judea. (66) All who heard them pondered them and said, "What then will this child become?" For, indeed, the hand of the Lord was with him.

(67) Then his father Zechariah was filled with the Holy Spirit and spoke this prophecy:

(68) "Blessed be the Lord God of Israel,
　　for he has looked favorably on his people and redeemed them.
(69) He has raised up a mighty savior for us
　　in the house of his servant David,
(70) as he spoke through the mouth of his holy prophets from of old,
(71)　that we would be saved from our enemies and from the hand of all
　　who hate us.
(72) Thus he has shown the mercy promised to our ancestors,
　　and has remembered his holy covenant,

(73) the oath that he swore to our ancestor Abraham,
> to grant us (74) that we, being rescued from the hands of our
> enemies,
> might serve him without fear, (75) in holiness and righteousness
> before him all our days.
(76) And you, child, will be called the prophet of the Most High,
> for you will go before the Lord to prepare his ways,
(77) to give knowledge of salvation to his people
> by the forgiveness of their sins.
(78) By the tender mercy of our God,
> the dawn from on high will break upon us,
(79) to give light to those who sit in darkness and in the shadow of death,
> to guide our feet into the way of peace."

(80) The child grew and became strong in spirit, and he was in the wilderness until the day he appeared publicly to Israel.

2:1–14

(1) In those days a decree went out from Emperor Augustus[5] that all the world should be registered. (2) This was the first registration and was taken while Quirinius[6] was governor of Syria. (3) All went to their own towns to be registered. (4) Joseph also went from the town of Nazareth in Galilee to Judea, to the city of David called Bethlehem, because he was descended from the house and family of David. (5) He went to be registered with Mary, to whom he was engaged and who was expecting a child. (6) While they were there the time came for her to deliver her child. (7) And she gave birth to her firstborn son and wrapped him in bands of cloth, and laid him in a manger, because there was no place for them in the inn.

(8) In that region there were shepherds living in the fields, keeping watch over their flock by night. (9) Then an angel of the Lord stood before them, and the glory of the Lord shone around them, and they were terrified. (10) But the angel said to them, "Do not be afraid, for see—I am bringing you good news of great joy for all the people: (11) to you is born this day in the city of David a Savior, who is the Messiah, the Lord. (12) This will be a sign for you: you will find a child wrapped in bands of cloth and lying in a manger." (13) And suddenly there was with the angel a multitude of the heavenly host, praising God and saying,

> (14) "Glory to God in the highest heaven,
> and on earth peace among those whom he favors!"

---

5. Augustus Caesar, first Roman emperor (27 B.C.E.–14 C.E.; reigned from 27 B.C.E. until his death).

6. Roman military legate, or governor (ca. 51 B.C.E.–21 C.E.), known to have served under Augustus Caesar in Syria.

MATTHEW 5–7, 19:16–26, 25:31–46

Like the Gospel of Luke, the Gospel of Matthew narrates the life, ministry, death, and Resurrection of Jesus. According to a broad consensus among New Testament scholars, Luke and Matthew drew their core narrative from the Gospel of Mark. According to a further, almost equally broad consensus, Luke and Matthew also drew on a second source—a now-lost written collection of Jesus' sayings. According to the two-source hypothesis, Luke and Matthew combined their sources differently, and each added further material of his own—Luke from other now-lost written accounts, Matthew perhaps from his own eyewitness recollections as well as from other oral or written accounts. The Gospel of John, strikingly different from these three Synoptic Gospels, as they are commonly called, had an independent origin.

Because Matthew 5 opens with a reference to Jesus going up a mountain before teaching his disciples, this section has sometimes been called the "Sermon on the Mount." But Matthew 5–7 is not a sermon. It is a collection of sayings, including short recitations such as the prayer now usually called the "Lord's Prayer" (6:6–10). Each saying is pregnant with meaning, each could have been the culmination of a longer discussion, and each may have been spoken for the first time in some highly particular set of circumstances.

Chapter 5 includes a string of assertions that begin "Blessed are." Called in Christian tradition the Beatitudes (from the Latin word *beati*, "blessed"), these assertions amount to a profile of a classic biblical prophet. Jesus is calling on all who hear him to consider themselves blessed by God should these prophetic traits be theirs and even if they should be abused for their beliefs: "'Rejoice and be glad, for your reward will be great in heaven. Thus they persecuted the prophets who were before you'" (5:12). These lay prophets should be exceptional, standing out as "'the light of the world'" (verse 14) and "'the salt of the earth'" (verse 13). Yet their prophetic message should not abolish the Law of Moses, which will never pass away (verses 18–19), but rather call for a fiery intensity in adhering to the Law: "'If your right eye causes you to sin, tear it out and throw it away'" (verse 29). Since there is little record of Jesus' disciples performing actions of this kind, Jesus may be issuing the string of extreme commands partly for rhetorical effect, to shock his hearers into an awareness of how very far they stand from true observance of the Law. And yet Jesus does not shock his listeners for shock's sake alone. He intends for them to implement an agenda, which is presented elsewhere in Matthew.

Together with many other sayings in these chapters, the sayings in chapter 6 form an extended and linked polemic against hypocrisy and a plea for humility, simplicity, and trust. According to these statements, prayers and good works are praiseworthy only when they are performed so quietly and privately that that they scarcely present an occasion for praise. The Lord's Prayer, coming midway in this chapter (verses 9–12), is spoken in this humble, trusting, and one-day-at-a-time mood, for the creation of which, Jesus says, there is one key condition: One must first forgive one's enemies and only then ask God's help in meeting one's everyday needs.

Chapter 7 includes the "Golden Rule" at verse 12 ("Do to others whatever you would have them do to you. This is the law and the prophets"), and it begins with an application of that rule: "Stop judging, that you may not be judged. For as you judge, so will you be judged, and the measure with which you measure will be measured out to you" (verses 1–2). This chapter concludes with a string of sayings that counterbalance those on trust at the end of chapter 6. In these verses, the emphasis falls on works as an indispensable complement to faith: "'Every tree that does not bear good fruit will be cut down and thrown into the fire. So by their fruits you will know them. Not everyone who says to me, 'Lord, Lord,' will enter the kingdom of heaven, but only the one who does the will of my Father in heaven" (19–21).

At Matthew 19:16–26, a wealthy young man asks Jesus, "'Teacher, what good must I do to gain eternal life?'" Jesus' reply culminates with a challenge: "'If you wish to be perfect, go, sell what you have and give to [the] poor, and you will have treasure in heaven. Then come, follow me.' When the young man heard this statement, he went away sad, for he had many possessions." Some of Jesus' followers evidently did give up everything to follow him. Such extreme actions were efforts to achieve the perfection of God (5:48 reads "So be perfect, just as your heavenly father is perfect").

Matthew 25:31–46 is a vision of the Last Judgment. Here, the righteous who enter eternal life, just as the wealthy young man in Matthew 19 hoped to do, are people who—without ever thinking of Jesus—have fed the hungry, clothed the naked, healed the sick, and visited those in prison. The inclusion of convicted criminals among those who must be served is surprising, even radical.

But in Matthew 5, Jesus has already offered his most radical and notorious teaching:

> "You have heard that it was said, 'An eye for an eye and a tooth for a tooth.' But I say to you, offer no resistance to one who is evil. When someone strikes you on (your) right cheek, turn the other one to him as well. . . . You have heard that it was said, 'You shall love your neighbor and hate your enemy.' But I say to you, love your enemies, and pray for those who persecute you, that you may be children of your heavenly Father, for he makes his sun rise on the bad and the good, and causes rain to fall on the just and the unjust. (verses 38–39, 42–45)

Is pacifism possible? During the Passion, Jesus enacts pacifism when violent hands are laid upon him (see Mark 14:49–50). The rhetorical Jesus may deal in mad impossibilities. The real Jesus deals in disturbing possibilities.

PRONOUNCING GLOSSARY

Gehenna: *ghe-hen´-uh*
Pharisees: *fair´-i-sees*

Raqa: *rah-kah´*
Sanhedrin: *san-hee´-drin*

MATTHEW

5

(1) When he saw the crowds, he went up the mountain, and after he had sat down, his disciples came to him.
(2) He began to teach them, saying:

(3) "Blessed are the poor in spirit,
    for theirs is the kingdom of heaven.
(4) Blessed are they who mourn,
    for they will be comforted.
(5) Blessed are the meek,
    for they will inherit the land.

From "Matthew" in New American Bible, Rev. Ed. Bracketed insertions are the original editors'.

(6) Blessed are they who hunger and thirst for righteousness,
   for they will be satisfied.
(7) Blessed are the merciful,
   for they will be shown mercy.
(8) Blessed are the clean of heart,
   for they will see God.
(9) Blessed are the peacemakers,
   for they will be called children of God.
(10) Blessed are they who are persecuted for the sake of righteousness, for theirs is the kingdom of heaven.
(11) Blessed are you when they insult you and persecute you and utter every kind of evil against you [falsely] because of me.
(12) Rejoice and be glad, for your reward will be great in heaven. Thus they persecuted the prophets who were before you.

(13) "You are the salt of the earth. But if salt loses its taste, with what can it be seasoned? It is no longer good for anything but to be thrown out and trampled underfoot.
(14) You are the light of the world. A city set on a mountain cannot be hidden.
(15) Nor do they light a lamp and then put it under a bushel basket; it is set on a lampstand, where it gives light to all in the house.
(16) Just so, your light must shine before others, that they may see your good deeds and glorify your heavenly Father.

(17) "Do not think that I have come to abolish the law or the prophets. I have come not to abolish but to fulfill.
(18) Amen, I say to you, until heaven and earth pass away, not the smallest letter or the smallest part of a letter will pass from the law, until all things have taken place.
(19) Therefore, whoever breaks one of the least of these commandments and teaches others to do so will be called least in the kingdom of heaven. But whoever obeys and teaches these commandments will be called greatest in the kingdom of heaven.
(20) I tell you, unless your righteousness surpasses that of the scribes and Pharisees,[1] you will not enter into the kingdom of heaven.

(21) "You have heard that it was said to your ancestors, 'You shall not kill; and whoever kills will be liable to judgment.'

(22) But I say to you, whoever is angry with his brother will be liable to judgment, and whoever says to his brother, 'Raqa,' will be answerable to the Sanhedrin, and whoever says, 'You fool,' will be liable to fiery Gehenna.[2]
(23) Therefore, if you bring your gift to the altar, and there recall that your brother has anything against you,

---

1. In the 1st century, the Pharisees were one of the three major sects in Judaism. They were known for strict observance of written law and for insistence on their own oral traditions regarding the law. They were distinct from scribes (lawyers and drafters of legal documents), though the two groups might have overlapped. Both groups bit-terly opposed Jesus for claiming autonomous authority as an interpreter of the law.
2. Literally, a valley near Jerusalem where an idolatrous cult sacrificed children. Figuratively, hell; a destination of the wicked. "Raqa": an Aramaic epithet, perhaps equivalent to *imbecile*. "Sanhedrin": the highest judicial body of Judaism.

(24) leave your gift there at the altar, go first and be reconciled with your brother, and then come and offer your gift.

(25) Settle with your opponent quickly while on the way to court with him. Otherwise your opponent will hand you over to the judge, and the judge will hand you over to the guard, and you will be thrown into prison. (26) Amen, I say to you, you will not be released until you have paid the last penny.

(27) "You have heard that it was said, 'You shall not commit adultery.' (28) But I say to you, everyone who looks at a woman with lust has already committed adultery with her in his heart.

(29) If your right eye causes you to sin, tear it out and throw it away. It is better for you to lose one of your members than to have your whole body thrown into Gehenna.

(30) And if your right hand causes you to sin, cut it off and throw it away. It is better for you to lose one of your members than to have your whole body go into Gehenna.

(31) "It was also said, 'Whoever divorces his wife must give her a bill of divorce.'

(32) But I say to you, whoever divorces his wife (unless the marriage is unlawful) causes her to commit adultery, and whoever marries a divorced woman commits adultery.

(33) "Again you have heard that it was said to your ancestors, 'Do not take a false oath, but make good to the LORD all that you vow.'

(34) But I say to you, do not swear at all; not by heaven, for it is God's throne;

(35) nor by the earth, for it is his footstool; nor by Jerusalem, for it is the city of the great King.

(36) Do not swear by your head, for you cannot make a single hair white or black.

(37) Let your 'Yes' mean 'Yes,' and your 'No' mean 'No.' Anything more is from the evil one.

(38) "You have heard that it was said, 'An eye for an eye and a tooth for a tooth.'

(39) But I say to you, offer no resistance to one who is evil. When someone strikes you on [your] right cheek, turn the other one to him as well.

(40) If anyone wants to go to law with you over your tunic, hand him your cloak as well.

(41) Should anyone press you into service for one mile, go with him for two miles.

(42) Give to the one who asks of you, and do not turn your back on one who wants to borrow.

(43) "You have heard that it was said, 'You shall love your neighbor and hate your enemy.'

(44) But I say to you, love your enemies, and pray for those who persecute you, (45) that you may be children of your heavenly Father, for he makes his sun rise on the bad and the good, and causes rain to fall on the just and the unjust.

(46) For if you love those who love you, what recompense will you have? Do not the tax collectors do the same?

(47) And if you greet your brothers only, what is unusual about that? Do not the pagans do the same?

(48) So be perfect, just as your heavenly Father is perfect.

6

(1) "[But] take care not to perform righteous deeds in order that people may see them; otherwise, you will have no recompense from your heavenly Father.

(2) When you give alms, do not blow a trumpet before you, as the hypocrites do in the synagogues and in the streets to win the praise of others. Amen, I say to you, they have received their reward.

(3) But when you give alms, do not let your left hand know what your right is doing,

(4) so that your almsgiving may be secret. And your Father who sees in secret will repay you.

(5) "When you pray, do not be like the hypocrites, who love to stand and pray in the synagogues and on street corners so that others may see them. Amen, I say to you, they have received their reward.

(6) But when you pray, go to your inner room, close the door, and pray to your Father in secret. And your Father who sees in secret will repay you.

(7) In praying, do not babble like the pagans, who think that they will be heard because of their many words.

(8) Do not be like them. Your Father knows what you need before you ask him.

(9) "This is how you are to pray:
　　Our Father in heaven,
　　hallowed be your name,
(10) your kingdom come,
　　your will be done,
　　on earth as in heaven.

(11) Give us today our daily bread;
(12) and forgive us our debts,
　　as we forgive our debtors;
(13) and do not subject us to the final test,
　　but deliver us from the evil one.

(14) If you forgive others their transgressions, your heavenly Father will forgive you.

(15) But if you do not forgive others, neither will your Father forgive your transgressions.

(16) "When you fast, do not look gloomy like the hypocrites. They neglect their appearance, so that they may appear to others to be fasting. Amen, I say to you, they have received their reward.

(17) But when you fast, anoint your head and wash your face,

(18) so that you may not appear to be fasting, except to your Father who is hidden. And your Father who sees what is hidden will repay you.

(19) "Do not store up for yourselves treasures on earth, where moth and decay destroy, and thieves break in and steal.

(20) But store up treasures in heaven, where neither moth nor decay destroys, nor thieves break in and steal.

(21) For where your treasure is, there also will your heart be.

(22) "The lamp of the body is the eye. If your eye is sound, your whole body will be filled with light;

(23) but if your eye is bad, your whole body will be in darkness. And if the light in you is darkness, how great will the darkness be.

(24) "No one can serve two masters. He will either hate one and love the other, or be devoted to one and despise the other. You cannot serve God and mammon.

(25) "Therefore I tell you, do not worry about your life, what you will eat [or drink], or about your body, what you will wear. Is not life more than food and the body more than clothing?

(26) Look at the birds in the sky; they do not sow or reap, they gather nothing into barns, yet your heavenly Father feeds them. Are not you more important than they?

(27) Can any of you by worrying add a single moment to your life-span?

(28) Why are you anxious about clothes? Learn from the way the wild flowers grow. They do not work or spin.

(29) But I tell you that not even Solomon[1] in all his splendor was clothed like one of them.

(30) If God so clothes the grass of the field, which grows today and is thrown into the oven tomorrow, will he not much more provide for you, O you of little faith?

(31) So do not worry and say, 'What are we to eat?' or 'What are we to drink?' or 'What are we to wear?'

(32) All these things the pagans seek. Your heavenly Father knows that you need them all.

(33) But seek first the kingdom [of God] and his righteousness, and all these things will be given you besides.

(34) Do not worry about tomorrow; tomorrow will take care of itself. Sufficient for a day is its own evil.

---

1. The king of Israel who built the First Temple, renowned for wisdom, wealth, and power.

7

(1) "Stop judging, that you may not be judged.

(2) For as you judge, so will you be judged, and the measure with which you measure will be measured out to you.

(3) Why do you notice the splinter in your brother's eye, but do not perceive the wooden beam in your own eye?

(4) How can you say to your brother, 'Let me remove that splinter from your eye,' while the wooden beam is in your eye?

(5) You hypocrite, remove the wooden beam from your eye first; then you will see clearly to remove the splinter from your brother's eye.

(6) "Do not give what is holy to dogs, or throw your pearls before swine, lest they trample them underfoot, and turn and tear you to pieces.

(7) "Ask and it will be given to you; seek and you will find; knock and the door will be opened to you.

(8) For everyone who asks, receives; and the one who seeks, finds; and to the one who knocks, the door will be opened.

(9) Which one of you would hand his son a stone when he asks for a loaf of bread,

(10) or a snake when he asks for a fish?

(11) If you then, who are wicked, know how to give good gifts to your children, how much more will your heavenly Father give good things to those who ask him.

(12) "Do to others whatever you would have them do to you. This is the law and the prophets.

(13) "Enter through the narrow gate; for the gate is wide and the road broad that leads to destruction, and those who enter through it are many.

(14) How narrow the gate and constricted the road that leads to life. And those who find it are few.

(15) "Beware of false prophets, who come to you in sheep's clothing, but underneath are ravenous wolves.

(16) By their fruits you will know them. Do people pick grapes from thornbushes, or figs from thistles?

(17) Just so, every good tree bears good fruit, and a rotten tree bears bad fruit.

(18) A good tree cannot bear bad fruit, nor can a rotten tree bear good fruit.

(19) Every tree that does not bear good fruit will be cut down and thrown into the fire.

(20) So by their fruits you will know them.

(21) "Not everyone who says to me, 'Lord, Lord,' will enter the kingdom of heaven, but only the one who does the will of my Father in heaven.

(22) Many will say to me on that day, 'Lord, Lord, did we not prophesy in your name? Did we not drive out demons in your name? Did we not do mighty deeds in your name?'

(23) Then I will declare to them solemnly, 'I never knew you. Depart from me, you evildoers.'

(24) "Everyone who listens to these words of mine and acts on them will be like a wise man who built his house on rock.

(25) The rain fell, the floods came, and the winds blew and buffeted the house. But it did not collapse; it had been set solidly on rock.

(26) And everyone who listens to these words of mine but does not act on them will be like a fool who built his house on sand.

(27) The rain fell, the floods came, and the winds blew and buffeted the house. And it collapsed and was completely ruined."

(28) When Jesus finished these words, the crowds were astonished at his teaching,

(29) for he taught them as one having authority, and not as their scribes.

19:16–26

(16) Now someone approached him and said, "Teacher, what good must I do to gain eternal life?" (17) He answered him, "Why do you ask me about the good? There is only One who is good. If you wish to enter into life, keep the commandments." (18) He asked him, "Which ones?" And Jesus replied, "'You shall not kill; you shall not commit adultery; you shall not steal; you shall not bear false witness; (19) honor your father and your mother'; and 'you shall love your neighbor as yourself.'" (20) The young man said to him, "All of these I have observed. What do I still lack?" (21) Jesus said to him, "If you wish to be perfect, go, sell what you have and give to [the] poor, and you will have treasure in heaven. Then come, follow me." (22) When the young man heard this statement, he went away sad, for he had many possessions. (23) Then Jesus said to his disciples, "Amen, I say to you, it will be hard for one who is rich to enter the kingdom of heaven. (24) Again I say to you, it is easier for a camel to pass through the eye of a needle than for one who is rich to enter the kingdom of God." (25) When the disciples heard this, they were greatly astonished and said, "Who then can be saved?" (26) Jesus looked at them and said, "For human beings this is impossible, but for God all things are possible." * * *

25:31–46

(31) "When the Son of Man comes in his glory, and all the angels with him, he will sit upon his glorious throne, (32) and all the nations will be assembled before him. And he will separate them one from another, as a shepherd separates the sheep from the goats. (33) He will place the sheep on his right and the goats on his left. (34) Then the king will say to those on his right, 'Come, you who are blessed by my Father. Inherit the kingdom prepared for you from the foundation of the world. (35) For I was hungry and you gave me food, I was thirsty and you gave me drink, a stranger and you welcomed me, (36) naked and you clothed me, ill and you cared for me, in prison and you visited me.' (37) Then the righteous will answer him and say, 'Lord, when did we see you hungry and feed you, or thirsty and give you drink? (38) When did we see you a stranger and welcome you, or naked and clothe you? (39) When did we see you ill or in prison, and visit you?' (40) And the

king will say to them in reply, 'Amen, I say to you, whatever you did for one of these least brothers of mine, you did for me.' (41) Then he will say to those on his left, 'Depart from me, you accursed, into the eternal fire prepared for the devil and his angels. (42) For I was hungry and you gave me no food, I was thirsty and you gave me no drink, (43) a stranger and you gave me no welcome, naked and you gave me no clothing, ill and in prison, and you did not care for me.' (44) Then they will answer and say, 'Lord, when did we see you hungry or thirsty or a stranger or naked or ill or in prison, and not minister to your needs?' (45) He will answer them, 'Amen, I say to you, what you did not do for one of these least ones, you did not do for me.' (46) And these will go off to eternal punishment, but the righteous to eternal life."

LUKE 10:21–37 AND 15:1–23

To preach his message and teach his disciples, Jesus most commonly told stories built around the details of everyday life. Jesus' stories are known as parables, and his parables represent approximately a third of his recorded teachings. The word *parable* comes from the Greek for "comparison" and "to throw"; in other words, the presenter of a parable throws out a set of presumably fictional events for the audience to catch. By comparing that set with a second set of events, presumably ones in real life, the audience grasps the moral attitude or religious principle being conveyed by the parable. As a translation of the corresponding Hebrew word, *parable* can also mean "riddle." The historicity, or factuality, of the parable is not important. The moral attitude or religious principle behind the parable is what matters. Fables, such as those attributed to the ancient Greek figure Aesop, can be parables. Analogies used by lawyers in court can also be parables. The Czech-born, Jewish, German-language writer Franz Kafka (1883–1924) famously used the parable form for some of his very short fiction.

If love is the signature theme of the Johannine literature, compassion and forgiveness are comparably signature themes in the Lucan literature. These sentiments are prominent in the parable of the Good Samaritan, a touching story intended to extend and universalize the injunction in Leviticus 19:18 to love one's fellow (country)man. Deep-rooted prejudice separated Jews and Samaritans, but in the parable a Samaritan overcomes that prejudice to rescue a Jew. In the parable of the Prodigal Son, the father's forgiveness matches the son's repentance.

His contemporaries would have found some of Jesus' stories odd or extravagant, but this effect was part of Jesus' teaching strategy. To make his profound points, he wanted to arrest the attention of his hearers. Because these rhetorical and pedagogical devices are the words of Jesus, Christians place high emphasis on the parables.

PRONOUNCING GLOSSARY

Jericho: *je´-ri-koh*

Levite: *lee´-vait* [*ai* rhyming with *rye*]

Pharisees: *fair´-i-sees*

Samaritan: *suh-ma´-ri-tan*

LUKE

10:21–37

[The Parable of the Good Samaritan]

(21) At that same hour Jesus rejoiced in the Holy Spirit and said, "I thank you, Father, Lord of heaven and earth, because you have hidden these things from the wise and the intelligent and have revealed them to infants; yes, Father, for such was your gracious will. (22) All things have been handed over to me by my Father; and no one knows who the Son is except the Father, or who the Father is except the Son and anyone to whom the Son chooses to reveal him." (23) Then turning to the disciples, Jesus said to them privately, "Blessed are the eyes that see what you see! (24) For I tell you that many prophets and kings desired to see what you see, but did not see it, and to hear what you hear, but did not hear it."

(25) Just then a lawyer stood up to test Jesus. "Teacher," he said, "what must I do to inherit eternal life?" (26) He said to him, "What is written in the law? What do you read there?" (27) He answered, "You shall love the Lord your God with all your heart, and with all your soul, and with all your strength, and with all your mind; and your neighbor as yourself." (28) And he said to him, "You have given the right answer; do this, and you will live."

(29) But wanting to justify himself, he asked Jesus, "And who is my neighbor?" (30) Jesus replied, "A man was going down from Jerusalem to Jericho, and fell into the hands of robbers, who stripped him, beat him, and went away, leaving him half dead. (31) Now by chance a priest was going down that road; and when he saw him, he passed by on the other side. (32) So likewise a Levite, when he came to the place and saw him, passed by on the other side. (33) But a Samaritan while traveling came near him; and when he saw him, he was moved with pity. (34) He went to him and bandaged his wounds, having poured oil and wine on them. Then he put him on his own animal, brought him to an inn, and took care of him. (35) The next day he took out two denarii, gave them to the innkeeper, and said, 'Take care of him; and when I come back, I will repay you whatever more you spend.' (36) Which of these three, do you think, was a neighbor to the man who fell into the hands of the robbers?" (37) He said, "The one who showed him mercy." Jesus said to him, "Go and do likewise."

15:1–32

[The Parable of the Prodigal Son]

(1) Now all the tax collectors and sinners were coming near to listen to him. (2) And the Pharisees and the scribes[1] were grumbling and saying, "This fellow welcomes sinners and eats with them."

(3) So he told them this parable: (4) "Which one of you, having a hundred sheep and losing one of them, does not leave the ninety-nine in the wilder-

FROM "Luke" in New Revised Standard Version Bible.

1. See note 1, p. 118.

ness and go after the one that is lost until he finds it? (5) When he has found it, he lays it on his shoulders and rejoices. (6) And when he comes home, he calls together his friends and neighbors, saying to them, 'Rejoice with me, for I have found my sheep that was lost.' (7) Just so, I tell you, there will be more joy in heaven over one sinner who repents than over ninety-nine righteous persons who need no repentance.

(8) "Or what woman having ten silver coins, if she loses one of them, does not light a lamp, sweep the house, and search carefully until she finds it? (9) When she has found it, she calls together her friends and neighbors, saying, 'Rejoice with me, for I have found the coin that I had lost.' (10) Just so, I tell you, there is joy in the presence of the angels of God over one sinner who repents."

(11) Then Jesus said, "There was a man who had two sons. (12) The younger of them said to his father, 'Father, give me the share of the property that will belong to me.' So he divided his property between them. (13) A few days later the younger son gathered all he had and traveled to a distant country, and there he squandered his property in dissolute living. (14) When he had spent everything, a severe famine took place throughout that country, and he began to be in need. (15) So he went and hired himself out to one of the citizens of that country, who sent him to his fields to feed the pigs. (16) He would gladly have filled himself with the pods that the pigs were eating; and no one gave him anything. (17) But when he came to himself he said, 'How many of my father's hired hands have bread enough and to spare, but here I am dying of hunger! (18) I will get up and go to my father, and I will say to him, "Father, I have sinned against heaven and before you; (19) I am no longer worthy to be called your son; treat me like one of your hired hands."' (20) So he set off and went to his father. But while he was still far off, his father saw him and was filled with compassion; he ran and put his arms around him and kissed him. (21) Then the son said to him, 'Father, I have sinned against heaven and before you; I am no longer worthy to be called your son.' (22) But the father said to his slaves, 'Quickly, bring out a robe—the best one—and put it on him, put a ring on his finger and sandals on his feet. (23) And get the fatted calf and kill it, and let us eat and celebrate; (24) for this son of mine was dead and is alive again; he was lost and is found!' And they began to celebrate.

(25) "Now his elder son was in the field; and when he came and approached the house, he heard music and dancing. (26) He called one of the slaves and asked what was going on. (27) He replied, 'Your brother has come, and your father has killed the fatted calf, because he has got him back safe and sound.' (28) Then he became angry and refused to go in. His father came out and began to plead with him. (29) But he answered his father, 'Listen! For all these years I have been working like a slave for you, and I have never disobeyed your command; yet you have never given me even a young goat so that I might celebrate with my friends. (30) But when this son of yours came back, who has devoured your property with prostitutes, you killed the fatted calf for him!' (31) Then the father said to him, 'Son, you are always with me, and all that is mine is yours. (32) But we had to celebrate and rejoice, because this brother of yours was dead and has come to life; he was lost and has been found.'"

MARK 1:1–13, 5:35–43, 6:45–52, 8:27–9:8, 14–16:8

As explained above, the Gospels of Luke, Matthew, and Mark share the core story of the life, works, death, and Resurrection of Jesus. That story comes from the account in the Gospel of Mark. In Mark's account, the story begins when Jesus' adult career is inaugurated with his baptism by John the Baptist. The events that lie between that beginning and his violent end include a great many miracles. Most of these miracles are cures for people's ailments, but some are "nature miracles," with or without human beneficiaries, that serve to demonstrate Jesus' divine power. The following selections include one miracle of each kind. Interspersed with these miracle stories are parables and instructions, but Mark includes many fewer of these than are found in Matthew and Luke.

Distinctive of Mark is a recurrent utter bafflement about Jesus on the part of people who are nonetheless drawn to him. Their bafflement is matched by the reader's as Jesus insists, while preaching and performing spectacular actions, that he wants no one to be told about what he is doing. Three times, moreover, he predicts to his incredulous disciples that as the "Son of Man," he must suffer, die, and then rise again.

"Son of Man"—so crucial to Jesus' self-understanding that he uses it of himself in virtually all of the most solemn moments of his turbulent career—is an allusion to the Book of Daniel. In chapter 7 of that Old Testament Book (see p. 107), the seer Daniel has a vision of the past oppression and future redemption of Israel. Each of Israel's past oppressors is represented by a different beast in the vision. Then, climactically, Daniel sees "one like the Son of man" (verse 13), a figure representing Israel. Israel's destined triumph becomes clear as God—"the Ancient of days" (verses 9, 13)—awards this figure "dominion, and glory, and a kingdom, that all people, nations, and languages, should serve him: his dominion is an everlasting dominion, which shall not pass away, and his kingdom one that which shall not be destroyed" (verse 14).

During the 175 years between the writing of Daniel and the time of Jesus, the view had taken hold in widely influential Jewish circles that the "Son of man" image in Daniel 7 referred to an actual celestial being, a heavenly Son of Man, whose descent from heaven would bring about at last the promised definitive triumph of the Lord God. Jesus' boldest claim, bolder even than his claim to be the Messiah, was his claim to be, in person, this celestial Son of Man. His was thus what is called an apocalyptic view, meaning a view that unveils a veiled reference in Scripture to the course of human events and to God's final plan for the world and for all who are in it (*apokalypsis* in Greek means "unveiling"). Some understood and were thrilled by his claim to be the Son of Man. Others understood and were scandalized by it. Still others quite possibly heard only a cryptic claim to be "the human being" and did not know what to make of him. All of this background lends the Gospel of Mark a sense of mystery and sometimes ominous suspense.

One such moment comes at Mark 8:31: "Then he began to teach them [his closest disciples] that the Son of Man must undergo great suffering . . . and after three days rise again." Another comes at 14:41, when the events that will lead to his agony are set in motion: "'Enough! The hour has come; the Son of Man is betrayed into the hands of sinners." Another comes quickly thereafter, at 14:61–62, when one of his accusers asks him pointedly, "'Are you the Messiah, the Son of the Blessed One?'" and he answers with an affirmation and then an escalation: "'I am'" and "you will see the Son of Man seated at the right hand of the Power" [alluding to Psalms 110:1] and "coming with the clouds of heaven" [alluding to Daniel 7:13].'"

The English word *passion* normally refers to any compelling emotion. When capitalized and used with the definite article as *the Passion*, the word refers to the climactic trial, torture, and crucifixion of Jesus in the Gospels. (Both senses derive ultimately from a Latin verb meaning "to undergo" or "to experience.") The Passion narrative first took shape in the Gospel of Mark. Mark's is the shortest account of the Passion. It lacks, for example, several moving statements that Jesus makes from the cross in the Gospel of Luke. Moreover, because Mark's account of Jesus' life before the Passion is also far shorter than those in the other Gospels, the Gospel of Mark can seem to be a Passion narrative merely preceded by a long introduction. Finally, though this Gospel includes a stunningly brief account of Jesus' Resurrection, it lacks the post-Resurrection appearances that conclude the other Gospels, and this lack makes the Passion loom all the larger in it.

Yet in its core structure, the Gospel of Mark has bequeathed a master plot to world literature. This story—of a man who loves and serves the poor; who speaks the truth that the civilian and religious authorities do not want to hear; who is ruthlessly repudiated, humiliatingly mocked, and brutally executed; who is abandoned at the end by his friends, comforted only by a handful of fearless women, but then achieves a spectacular final vindication—has been reborn again and again. Its countless realizations have appeared in the greatest Western fiction, drama, poetry, music, and visual art and in the humblest, most popular, and most accessible modern forms of all these. Few if any examples of intentionally religious art can claim so much.

PRONOUNCING GLOSSARY

Arimathea: *a-ri-mah-thee´-uh*
Barabbas: *bahr-ab´-bahs*
Bethany: *be´-thuh-nee*
Bethsaida: *beth-sai´-duh* [*ai* rhyming with *rye*]
Caesarea Philippi: *se-sah-ree´-uh fil-i´-pai* [*ai* rhyming with *rye*]
centurion: *sin-toor´-ee-uhn*
Cyrene: *sai-ree´-nee* [*ai* rhyming with *rye*]
Elijah: *e-lai´-jah* [*ai* rhyming with *rye*]
"Eloi, Eloi, lema sabachthani?": *e-loh-ee´ e-loh-ee´ le-mah´ se-bahk´-tah-nee?*

Galilean: *ga-li-lee´-uhn*
Gethsemane: *geth-se´-man-ee*
Golgotha: *gohl´-goh-thuh*
Isaiah: *ai-zay´-uh* [*ai* rhyming with *rye*]
Iscariot: *is-ca´-ree-oht*
Judean: *joo-dee´-an*
Magdalene: *mag´-duh-lin*
Pilate: *pai´-luht* [*ai* rhyming with *rye*]
Rabbi: *ra´-bai* [*ai* rhyming with *rye*]
Salome: *sahl-oh´-may*
"Talitha cum": *tah´-lee-thah koom*

MARK

1:1–13

(1) The beginning of the good news of Jesus Christ, the Son of God.
(2) As it is written in the prophet Isaiah,
  "See, I am sending my messenger ahead of you,
  who will prepare your way;

FROM "Mark" in New Revised Standard Version Bible.

(3) the voice of one crying out in the wilderness:
'Prepare the way of the Lord,
make his paths straight,'"[1]

(4) John the baptizer appeared in the wilderness, proclaiming a baptism of repentance for the forgiveness of sins. (5) And people from the whole Judean countryside and all the people of Jerusalem were going out to him, and were baptized by him in the river Jordan, confessing their sins. (6) Now John was clothed with camel's hair, with a leather belt around his waist, and he ate locusts and wild honey. (7) He proclaimed, "The one who is more powerful than I is coming after me; I am not worthy to stoop down and untie the thong of his sandals. (8) I have baptized you with water; but he will baptize you with the Holy Spirit."

(9) In those days Jesus came from Nazareth of Galilee and was baptized by John in the Jordan. (10) And just as he was coming up out of the water, he saw the heavens torn apart and the Spirit descending like a dove on him. (11) And a voice came from heaven, "You are my Son, the Beloved;[2] with you I am well pleased."

(12) And the Spirit immediately drove him out into the wilderness. (13) He was in the wilderness forty days, tempted by Satan; and he was with the wild beasts; and the angels waited on him.

5:35–43

(35) While he was still speaking, some people came from the leader's house to say, "Your daughter is dead. Why trouble the teacher any further?" (36) But overhearing what they said, Jesus said to the leader of the synagogue, "Do not fear, only believe." (37) He allowed no one to follow him except Peter, James, and John, the brother of James. (38) When they came to the house of the leader of the synagogue, he saw a commotion, people weeping and wailing loudly. (39) When he had entered, he said to them, "Why do you make a commotion and weep? The child is not dead but sleeping." (40) And they laughed at him. Then he put them all outside, and took the child's father and mother and those who were with him, and went in where the child was. (41) He took her by the hand and said to her, "Talitha cum,"[1] which means, "Little girl, get up!" (42) And immediately the girl got up and began to walk about (she was twelve years of age). At this they were overcome with amazement. (43) He strictly ordered them that no one should know this, and told them to give her something to eat.

6:45–52

(45) Immediately he made his disciples get into the boat and go on ahead to the other side,[1] to Bethsaida, while he dismissed the crowd. (46) After saying farewell to them, he went up on the mountain to pray.

---

1. Isaiah 40:1–8.
2. 2 Samuel 7:14.
1. Jesus addresses the girl in Aramaic.
1. Jesus has miraculously multiplied loaves and fishes to feed a throng, which is apparently on the west side of the Lake of Galilee. He orders his Apostles to depart by boat for Bethsaida, on the northeast side of the lake.

(47) When evening came, the boat was out on the sea,[2] and he was alone on the land. (48) When he saw that they were straining at the oars against an adverse wind, he came towards them early in the morning, walking on the sea. He intended to pass them by. (49) But when they saw him walking on the sea, they thought it was a ghost and cried out; (50) for they all saw him and were terrified. But immediately he spoke to them and said, "Take heart, it is I; do not be afraid." (51) Then he got into the boat with them and the wind ceased. And they were utterly astounded, (52) for they did not understand about the loaves, but their hearts were hardened.[3]

8:27–38

(27) Jesus went on with his disciples to the villages of Caesarea Philippi; and on the way he asked his disciples, "Who do people say that I am?" (28) And they answered him, "John the Baptist; and others, Elijah;[1] and still others, one of the prophets." (29) He asked them, "But who do you say that I am?" Peter answered him, "You are the Messiah." (30) And he sternly ordered them not to tell anyone about him.

(31) Then he began to teach them that the Son of Man must undergo great suffering, and be rejected by the elders, the chief priests, and the scribes,[2] and be killed, and after three days rise again. (32) He said all this quite openly. And Peter took him aside and began to rebuke him. (33) But turning and looking at his disciples, he rebuked Peter and said, "Get behind me, Satan! For you are setting your mind not on divine things but on human things."

(34) He called the crowd with his disciples, and said to them, "If any want to become my followers, let them deny themselves and take up their cross and follow me. (35) For those who want to save their life will lose it, and those who lose their life for my sake, and for the sake of the gospel, will save it. (36) For what will it profit them to gain the whole world and forfeit their life? (37) Indeed, what can they give in return for their life? (38) Those who are ashamed of me and of my words in this adulterous and sinful generation, of them the Son of Man will also be ashamed when he comes in the glory of his Father with the holy angels."

9:1–8

(1) And he said to them, "Truly I tell you, there are some standing here who will not taste death until they see that the kingdom of God has come with power."

(2) Six days later, Jesus took with him Peter and James and John, and led them up a high mountain apart, by themselves. And he was transfigured before them, (3) and his clothes became dazzling white, such as no one on earth could bleach them. (4) And there appeared to them Elijah with Moses,[1]

---

2. In the Gospels, the Lake of Galilee is repeatedly referred to as a sea.
3. Cruelty is not implied, only dullness of mind.
1. According to Jewish tradition, the return of the Old Testament prophet Elijah would herald the coming of the Messiah. John had recently been executed. Some thought Jesus was John brought back to life. They were, however, cousins close in age.

2. See note 1, p. 118.
1. Elijah personifies the prophets and Moses personifies the Law (see the discussions of these figures on, respectively, pp. 94 and 89). The meaning of this scene, called the Transfiguration, is that Jesus fulfills both of these figures.

In Jewish antiquity, the bones of prominent people were sometimes exhumed and reburied in stone boxes called ossuaries. In 1990, this ossuary, dating to the 1st century c.e., was discovered in a burial cave in south Jerusalem. Ornately carved on the facing side, it bears on two of its other sides the Aramaic inscription "Joseph son of Caiphas." The reference is plausibly to the high priest by that name mentioned in the passion narrative of the Gospels of Matthew and John.

who were talking with Jesus. (5) Then Peter said to Jesus, "Rabbi, it is good for us to be here; let us make three dwellings, one for you, one for Moses, and one for Elijah." (6) He did not know what to say, for they were terrified. (7) Then a cloud overshadowed them, and from the cloud there came a voice. "This is my Son, the Beloved; listen to him!" (8) Suddenly when they looked around, they saw no one with them any more, but only Jesus.

14

(1) It was two days before the Passover and the festival of Unleavened Bread.[1] The chief priests and the scribes[2] were looking for a way to arrest Jesus by stealth and kill him; (2) for they said, "Not during the festival, or there may be a riot among the people."

(3) While he was at Bethany in the house of Simon the leper, as he sat at the table, a woman came with an alabaster jar of very costly ointment of nard, and she broke open the jar and poured the ointment on his head. (4) But some were there who said to one another in anger, "Why was the ointment wasted in this way? (5) For this ointment could have been sold for more than three hundred denarii, and the money given to the poor." And they scolded her. (6) But Jesus said, "Let her alone; why do you trouble her? She has performed a good service for me. (7) For you always have the poor with

1. The Jewish holiday of Passover, also known as the Festival of Unleavened Bread, is a seven- or eight-day commemoration of the ancient Israelites' Exodus, or escape from slavery in Egypt. The first night of Passover involves a special meal called the seder.
2. See note 1, p. 118.

you, and you can show kindness to them whenever you wish; but you will not always have me. (8) She has done what she could; she has anointed my body beforehand for its burial. (9) Truly I tell you, wherever the good news is proclaimed in the whole world, what she has done will be told in remembrance of her."

(10) Then Judas Iscariot, who was one of the twelve,[3] went to the chief priests in order to betray him to them. (11) When they heard it, they were greatly pleased, and promised to give him money. So he began to look for an opportunity to betray him.

(12) On the first day of Unleavened Bread, when the Passover lamb is sacrificed, his disciples said to him, "Where do you want us to go and make the preparations for you to eat the Passover?" (13) So he sent two of his disciples, saying to them, "Go into the city, and a man carrying a jar of water will meet you; follow him, (14) and wherever he enters, say to the owner of the house, 'The Teacher asks, Where is my guest room where I may eat the Passover with my disciples?' (15) He will show you a large room upstairs, furnished and ready. Make preparations for us there." (16) So the disciples set out and went to the city, and found everything as he had told them; and they prepared the Passover meal.

(17) When it was evening, he came with the twelve. (18) And when they had taken their places and were eating, Jesus said, "Truly I tell you, one of you will betray me, one who is eating with me." (19) They began to be distressed and to say to him one after another, "Surely, not I?" (20) He said to them, "It is one of the twelve, one who is dipping bread into the bowl with me. (21) For the Son of Man goes as it is written of him, but woe to that one by whom the Son of Man is betrayed! It would have been better for that one not to have been born."

(22) While they were eating, he took a loaf of bread, and after blessing it he broke it, gave it to them and said, "Take; this is my body." (23) Then he took a cup, and after giving thanks he gave it to them, and all of them drank from it. (24) He said to them, "This is my blood of the covenant, which is poured out for many. (25) Truly I tell you, I will never again drink of the fruit of the vine until that day when I drink it new in the kingdom of God."

(26) When they had sung the hymn, they went out to the Mount of Olives.[4] (27) And Jesus said to them, "You will all become deserters; for it is written,

> 'I will strike the shepherd,
> and the sheep will be scattered.'[5]

(28) But after I am raised up, I will go before you to Galilee."[6] (29) Peter said to him, "Even though all become deserters, I will not." (30) Jesus said to him, "Truly I tell you, this day, this very night, before the cock crows twice, you will deny me three times." (31) But he said vehemently, "Even though I must die with you, I will not deny you." And all of them said the same.

(32) They went to a place called Gethsemane;[7] and he said to his disciples. "Sit here while I pray." (33) He took with him Peter and James and John, and

---

3. I.e., one of Jesus' Twelve Apostles.
4. A mountain ridge just east of the Jerusalem of Jesus' day.
5. See Zechariah 13:7.

6. A large region in northern Israel where Jesus conducted his ministry.
7. A garden on the lower slope of the Mount of Olives.

began to be distressed and agitated. (34) And he said to them, "I am deeply grieved, even to death; remain here, and keep awake." (35) And going a little farther, he threw himself on the ground and prayed that, if it were possible the hour might pass from him. (36) He said, "Abba,[8] Father, for you all things are possible; remove this cup from me; yet, not what I want, but what you want." (37) He came and found them sleeping; and he said to Peter, "Simon, are you asleep? Could you not keep awake one hour? (38) Keep awake and pray that you may not come into the time of trial; the spirit indeed is willing, but the flesh is weak." (39) And again he went away and prayed, saying the same words. (40) And once more he came and found them sleeping, for their eyes were very heavy; and they did not know what to say to him. (41) He came a third time and said to them, "Are you still sleeping and taking your rest? Enough! The hour has come; the Son of Man is betrayed into the hands of sinners. (42) Get up let us be going. See, my betrayer is at hand."

(43) Immediately, while he was still speaking, Judas, one of the twelve, arrived; and with him there was a crowd with swords and clubs, from the chief priests, the scribes, and the elders. (44) Now the betrayer had given them a sign, saying, "The one I will kiss is the man; arrest him and lead him away under guard." (45) So when he came, he went up to him at once and said, "Rabbi!" and kissed him. (46) Then they laid hands on him and arrested him. (47) But one of those who stood near drew his sword and struck the slave of the high priest, cutting off his ear. (48) Then Jesus said to them, "Have you come out with swords and clubs to arrest me as though I were a bandit? (49) Day after day I was with you in the temple teaching, and you did not arrest me. But let the scriptures be fulfilled." (50) All of them deserted him and fled.

(51) A certain young man was following him, wearing nothing but a linen cloth. They caught hold of him, (52) but he left the linen cloth and ran off naked.

(53) They took Jesus to the high priest; and all the chief priests, the elders, and the scribes were assembled. (54) Peter had followed him at a distance, right into the courtyard of the high priest; and he was sitting with the guards, warming himself at the fire. (55) Now the chief priests and the whole council were looking for testimony against Jesus to put him to death; but they found none. (56) For many gave false testimony against him, and their testimony did not agree. (57) Some stood up and gave false testimony against him, saying, (58) "We heard him say, 'I will destroy this temple that is made with hands, and in three days I will build another, not made with hands.'" (59) But even on this point their testimony did not agree. (60) Then the high priest stood up before them and asked Jesus, "Have you no answer? What is it that they testify against you?" (61) But he was silent and did not answer. Again the high priest asked him, "Are you the Messiah, the Son of the Blessed One?" (62) Jesus said, "I am; and

> 'you will see the Son of Man
> seated at the right hand of the Power,'
> and 'coming with the clouds of heaven.'"[9]

8. Father (Aramaic).
9. See Psalms 110:1 and Daniel 7:13.

(63) Then the high priest tore his clothes and said, "Why do we still need witnesses? (64) You have heard his blasphemy! What is your decision?" All of them condemned him as deserving death. (65) Some began to spit on him, to blindfold him, and to strike him, saying to him, "Prophesy!" The guards also took him over and beat him.

(66) While Peter was below in the courtyard, one of the servant-girls of the high priest came by. (67) When she saw Peter warming himself, she stared at him and said, "You also were with Jesus, the man from Nazareth." (68) But he denied it, saying, "I do not know or understand what you are talking about." And he went out into the forecourt. Then the cock crowed. (69) And the servant-girl, on seeing him, began again to say to the bystanders, "This man is one of them." (70) But again he denied it. Then after a little while the bystanders again said to Peter, "Certainly you are one of them; for you are a Galilean." (71) But he began to curse, and he swore an oath, "I do not know this man you are talking about." (72) At that moment the cock crowed for the second time. Then Peter remembered that Jesus had said to him, "Before the cock crows twice, you will deny me three times." And he broke down and wept.

15

(1) As soon as it was morning, the chief priests held a consultation with the elders and scribes and the whole council. They bound Jesus, led him away, and handed him over to Pilate.[1] (2) Pilate asked him, "Are you the King of the Jews?" He answered him, "You say so." (3) Then the chief priests accused him of many things. (4) Pilate asked him again, "Have you no answer? See how many charges they bring against you." (5) But Jesus made no further reply, so that Pilate was amazed.

(6) Now at the festival he used to release a prisoner for them, anyone for whom they asked. (7) Now a man called Barabbas was in prison with the rebels who had committed murder during the insurrection. (8) So the crowd came and began to ask Pilate to do for them according to his custom. (9) Then he answered them, "Do you want me to release for you the King of the Jews?" (10) For he realized that it was out of jealousy that the chief priests had handed him over. (11) But the chief priests stirred up the crowd to have him release Barabbas for them instead. (12) Pilate spoke to them again, "Then what do you wish me to do with the man you call the King of the Jews?" (13) They shouted back, "Crucify him!" (14) Pilate asked them, "Why, what evil has he done?" But they shouted all the more, "Crucify him!" (15) So Pilate, wishing to satisfy the crowd, released Barabbas for them; and after flogging Jesus, he handed him over to be crucified.

(16) Then the soldiers led him into the courtyard of the palace (that is, the governor's headquarters); and they called together the whole cohort. (17) And they clothed him in a purple cloak; and after twisting some thorns into a crown, they put it on him. (18) And they began saluting him, "Hail, King of the Jews!" (19) They struck his head with a reed, spat upon him, and knelt down in homage to him. (20) After mocking him, they stripped him of the

---

1. Pontius Pilate, prefect of the Roman province of Judaea from 26 to 36 C.E.

purple cloak and put his own clothes on him. Then they led him out to crucify him.

(21) They compelled a passer-by, who was coming in from the country, to carry his cross; it was Simon of Cyrene, the father of Alexander and Rufus. (22) Then they brought Jesus to the place called Golgotha (which means the place of a skull). (23) And they offered him wine mixed with myrrh; but he did not take it. (24) And they crucified him, and divided his clothes among them, casting lots to decide what each should take.

(25) It was nine o'clock in the morning when they crucified him. (26) The inscription of the charge against him read, "The King of the Jews." (27) And with him they crucified two bandits, one on his right and one on his left. (28) Those who passed by derided him, shaking their heads and saying, "Aha! You who would destroy the temple and build it in three days, (30) save yourself, and come down from the cross!" (31) In the same way the chief priests, along with the scribes, were also mocking him among themselves and saying, "He saved others; he cannot save himself. (32) Let the Messiah, the King of Israel, come down from the cross now, so that we may see and believe." Those who were crucified with him also taunted him.

(33) When it was noon, darkness came over the whole land until three in the afternoon. (34) At three o'clock Jesus cried out with a loud voice, "Eloi, Eloi, lema sabachthani?"[2] which means, "My God, my God, why have you forsaken me?" (35) When some of the bystanders heard it, they said, "Listen, he is calling for Elijah."[3] (36) And someone ran, filled a sponge with sour wine, put it on a stick, and gave it to him to drink, saying, "Wait, let us see whether Elijah will come to take him down." (37) Then Jesus gave a loud cry and breathed his last. (38) And the curtain of the temple was torn in two, from top to bottom. (39) Now when the centurion, who stood facing him, saw that in this way he breathed his last, he said, "Truly this man was God's Son!"

(40) There were also women looking on from a distance; among them were Mary Magdalene, and Mary the mother of James the younger and of Joses,[4] and Salome. (41) These used to follow him and provided for him when he was in Galilee; and there were many other women who had come up with him to Jerusalem.

(42) When evening had come, and since it was the day of Preparation, that is, the day before the sabbath, (43) Joseph of Arimathea, a respected member of the council, who was also himself waiting expectantly for the kingdom of God, went boldly to Pilate and asked for the body of Jesus. (44) Then Pilate wondered if he were already dead; and summoning the centurion, he asked him whether he had been dead for some time. (45) When he learned from the centurion that he was dead, he granted the body to Joseph. (46) Then Joseph bought a linen cloth, and taking down the body, wrapped it in the linen cloth, and laid it in a tomb that had been hewn out of the rock. He then rolled a stone against the door of the tomb. (47) Mary Magdalene and Mary the mother of Joses saw where the body was laid.

---

2. Jesus quotes Psalms 22:1 in Aramaic, correctly translated by Mark.
3. The bystanders are mistaken: Jesus is crying to God.
4. Possibly the wife of Zebedee and mother of the Apostles James and John. See Matthew 27:56. "Mary Magdalene": Mary of Magdala, a follower of Jesus known from elsewhere in the Gospels. "Mary the mother of James the younger and of Joses": a figure mentioned here for the first time.

16

(1) When the sabbath was over, Mary Magdalene, and Mary the mother of James, and Salome bought spices, so that they might go and anoint him. (2) And very early on the first day of the week, when the sun had risen, they went to the tomb. (3) They had been saying to one another, "Who will roll away the stone for us from the entrance to the tomb?" (4) When they looked up, they saw that the stone, which was very large, had already been rolled back. (5) As they entered the tomb, they saw a young man, dressed in a white robe, sitting on the right side; and they were alarmed. (6) But he said to them, "Do not be alarmed; you are looking for Jesus of Nazareth, who was crucified. He has been raised; he is not here. Look, there is the place they laid him. (7) But go tell his disciples and Peter that he is going ahead of you to Galilee; there you will see him, just as he told you." (8) So they went out and fled from the tomb, for terror and amazement had seized them; and they said nothing to anyone, for they were afraid.[1]

1. According to the best ancient manuscripts of this Gospel, Mark ends at 16:8. Mark 16:9–20 is an assemblage of verses from other Gospels and dealing with the Resurrection.

JOHN 20 AND ACTS 2:1–8, 12–46

Why has longstanding Christian tradition inserted the Gospel of John between the Gospel of Luke and its sequel, the Acts of the Apostles (both addressed to "Theophilus," the Greek name suggesting Luke's possibly imagined Gentile auditor)? The answer may be that John 14:25–29 seems to predict Acts 2, the most important chapter of Acts. In the Jerusalem Bible translation, this passage from John reads:

> I have said these things to you
> While still with you;
> But the Advocate, the Holy Spirit,
> Whom the Father will send in my name,
> Will teach you everything
> And remind you of all I have said to you.
> Peace I bequeath to you,
> My own peace I give you
> A peace the world cannot give, this is my gift to you.
> Do not let your hearts be troubled or afraid.
> You heard me say:
> I am going away, and shall return.
> If you loved me you would have been glad
> To know that I am going to the Father,
> For the Father is greater than I.
> I have told you this now before it happens,
> So that when it does happen you may believe.

John 20 presents an account of one return: Jesus' Resurrection. Since whatever else the Resurrection meant, it did not mean that Jesus would resume his life where it had left off, his disciples were faced with a towering question: "Now what?" In this passage from John, Jesus predicts, in broad terms, how that question will be answered: "the Advocate [Greek *parakletos*], the Holy Spirit" will be sent in his name.

And then it happens. In Acts 2, that promised Advocate, that very Holy Spirit, arrives in the form of "tongues, as of fire" (verse 3) hovering above the assembled Apostles' heads. What is the result? Peter bursts forth to preach an "inflamed" street sermon—the first public Christian sermon—to Jews from around the world who are visiting Jerusalem for the feast of Shavuot, called Pentecost in the Greek-speaking Diaspora. Three thousand are converted on the spot, and the Christian Church is born. The life of Christ and the lives of those who have received his Spirit are thus conjoined as a single, continuing life story. That continuity and that conjunction are the distinct emphasis and the distinct achievement of Luke the Evangelist.

PRONOUNCING GLOSSARY

Didymus: *di´-di-mus*
Galileans: *ga-li-lee´-uhns*
Hades: *hay´-dees*

Judea: *joo-dee´-a*
Magdalene: *mag´-duh-lin*
Rabboni: *rah-boh´-nee*

JOHN

20

(1) The first day of the week cometh Mary Magdalene early, when it was yet dark, unto the sepulchre, and seeth the stone taken away from the sepulchre. (2) Then she runneth, and cometh to Simon Peter, and to the other disciple, whom Jesus loved, and saith unto them, They have taken away the Lord out of the sepulchre, and we know not where they have laid him. (3) Peter therefore went forth, and that other disciple, and came to the sepulchre. (4) So they ran both together: and the other disciple did outrun Peter, and came first to the sepulchre. (5) And he stooping down, and looking in, saw the linen clothes lying; yet went he not in. (6) Then cometh Simon Peter following him, and went into the sepulchre, and seeth the linen clothes lie, (7) and the napkin, that was about his head, not lying with the linen clothes, but wrapped together in a place by itself. (8) Then went in also that other disciple, which came first to the sepulchre, and he saw, and believed. (9) For as yet they knew not the scripture, that he must rise again from the dead. (10) Then the disciples went away again unto their own home.

(11) But Mary stood without at the sepulchre weeping: and as she wept, she stooped down, and looked into the sepulchre, (12) and seeth two angels in white sitting, the one at the head, and the other at the feet, where the body of Jesus had lain. (13) And they say unto her, Woman, why weepest thou? She saith unto them, Because they have taken away my Lord, and I know not where they have laid him. (14) And when she had thus said, she turned herself back, and saw Jesus standing, and knew not that it was Jesus. (15) Jesus saith unto her, Woman, why weepest thou?

From "John" in *The English Bible, King James Version, The New Testament: A Norton Critical Edition*. From "Acts" in New Revised Standard Version Bible.

whom seekest thou? She, supposing him to be the gardener, saith unto him, Sir, if thou have borne him hence, tell me where thou hast laid him, and I will take him away. (16) Jesus saith unto her, Mary. She turned herself, and saith unto him, Rabboni; which is to say, Master. (17) Jesus saith unto her, Touch me not; for I am not yet ascended to my Father: but go to my brethren, and say unto them, I ascend unto my Father, and your Father; and to my God, and your God. (18) Mary Magdalene came and told the disciples that she had seen the Lord, and that he had spoken these things unto her.

(19) Then the same day at evening, being the first day of the week, when the doors were shut where the disciples were assembled for fear of the Jews, came Jesus and stood in the midst, and saith unto them, Peace be unto you. (20) And when he had so said, he shewed unto them his hands and his side. Then were the disciples glad, when they saw the Lord. (21) Then said Jesus to them again, Peace be unto you: as my Father hath sent me, even so send I you. (22) And when he had said this, he breathed on them, and saith unto them, Receive ye the Holy Ghost: (23) whose soever sins ye remit, they are remitted unto them; and whose soever sins ye retain, they are retained.

(24) But Thomas, one of the twelve, called Didymus, was not with them when Jesus came. (25) The other disciples therefore said unto him, We have seen the Lord. But he said unto them, Except I shall see in his hands the print of the nails, and put my finger into the print of the nails, and thrust my hand into his side, I will not believe. (26) And after eight days again his disciples were within, and Thomas with them: then came Jesus, the doors being shut, and stood in the midst, and said, Peace be unto you. (27) Then saith he to Thomas, Reach hither thy finger, and behold my hands; and reach hither thy hand, and thrust it into my side: and be not faithless, but believing. (28) And Thomas answered and said unto him, My Lord and my God. (29) Jesus saith unto him, Thomas, because thou hast seen me, thou hast believed: blessed are they that have not seen, and yet have believed.

(30) And many other signs truly did Jesus in the presence of his disciples, which are not written in this book: (31) but these are written, that ye might believe that Jesus is the Christ, the Son of God; and that believing ye might have life through his name.

ACTS

2

(1) When the day of Pentecost had come, they were all together in one place. (2) And suddenly from heaven there came a sound like the rush of a violent wind, and it filled the entire house where they were sitting. (3) Divided tongues, as of fire, appeared among them, and a tongue rested on each of them. (4) All of them were filled with the Holy Spirit and began to speak in other languages, as the Spirit gave them ability.

(5) Now there were devout Jews from every nation under heaven living in Jerusalem. (6) And at this sound the crowd gathered and was bewildered,

because each one heard them speaking in the native language of each. (7) Amazed and astonished, they asked, "Are not all these who are speaking Galileans?[1] (8) And how is it that we hear, each of us, in our own native language? * * * (12) All were amazed and perplexed, saying to one another, "What does this mean?" (13) But others sneered and said, "They are filled with new wine."

(14) But Peter, standing with the eleven raised his voice and addressed them, "Men of Judea and all who live in Jerusalem, let this be known to you, and listen to what say. (15) Indeed, these are not drunk, as you suppose, for it is only nine o'clock in the morning. (16) No, this is what was spoken through the prophet Joel:

(17) 'In the last days it will be, God declares,
      that I will pour out my Spirit upon all flesh,'
         and your sons and your daughters shall prophesy,
      and your young men shall see visions,
         and your old men shall dream dreams.
(18) Even upon my slaves, both men and women,
      in those days I will pour out my Spirit;
      and they shall prophesy.
(19) And I will show portents in the heaven above
      and signs on the earth below,
         blood, and fire, and smoky mist.
(20) The sun shall be turned to darkness
      and the moon to blood,
         before the coming of the Lord's great and glorious day.
(21) Then everyone who calls on the name of the Lord shall be saved.'[2]

(22) "You that are Israelites, listen to what I have to say: Jesus of Nazareth, a man attested to you by God with deeds of power, wonders, and signs that God did through him among you, as you yourselves know— (23) this man, handed over to you according to the definite plan and foreknowledge of God, you crucified and killed by the hands of those outside the law. (24) But God raised him up, having freed him from death, because it was impossible for him to be held in its power. (25) For David says concerning him,

            'I saw the Lord always before me,
                  for he is at my right hand so that I will not be shaken;
      (26) therefore my heart was glad, and my tongue rejoiced;
                  moreover my flesh will live in hope.
      (27) For you will not abandon my soul to Hades,
                  or let your Holy One experience corruption.
      (28) You have made known to me the ways of life;
                  you will make me full of gladness with your presence.'[3]

(29) "Fellow Israelites, I may say to you confidently of our ancestor David that he both died and was buried, and his tomb is with us to this day. (30) Since he was a prophet, he knew that God had sworn with an oath to

---

1. Jewish by religion, Galileans were ethnically distinguishable from the Jews of Judaea, where Jerusalem is located.

2. Joel 2:28–32.
3. Psalms 16:8–11. For background on David, see pp. 94–96.

him that he would put one of his descendants on his throne. (31) Foreseeing this, David spoke of the resurrection of the Messiah, saying,

> 'He was not abandoned to Hades,
> nor did his flesh experience corruption.'

(32) This Jesus God raised up, and of that all of us are witnesses. (33) Being therefore exalted at the right hand of God, and having received from the Father the promise of the Holy Spirit, he has poured out this that you both see and hear. (34) For David did not ascend into the heavens, but he himself says,

> 'The Lord said to my Lord,
> "Sit at my right hand,
> (35)   until I make your enemies your footstool." '[4]

(36) Therefore let the entire house of Israel know with certainty that God has made him both Lord and Messiah, this Jesus whom you crucified."

(37) Now when they heard this, they were cut to the heart and said to Peter and to the other apostles, "Brothers, what should we do?" (38) Peter said to them, "Repent, and be baptized every one of you in the name of Jesus Christ so that your sins may be forgiven; and you will receive the gift of the Holy Spirit. (39) For the promise is for you, for your children, and for all who are far away, everyone whom the Lord our God calls to him." (40) And he testified with many other arguments and exhorted them, saying, "Save yourselves from this corrupt generation." (41) So those who welcomed his message were baptized, and that day about three thousand persons were added. (42) They devoted themselves to the apostles' teaching and fellowship, to the breaking of bread and the prayers.

(43) Awe came upon everyone, because many wonders and signs were being done by the apostles. (44) All who believed were together and had all things in common; (45) they would sell their possessions and goods and distribute the proceeds to all, as any had need. (46) Day by day, as they spent much time together in the temple, they broke bread at home and ate their food with glad and generous hearts, praising God and having the goodwill of all the people. And day by day the Lord added to their number those who were being saved.

4. Psalms 110:1.

2 CORINTHIANS 10–11

What made the good news of the Gospel good? As newborn Christianity spread outward in all directions from Jerusalem and Galilee through the Roman Empire and beyond, Jesus' Apostles and other missionaries of the Gospel had to answer this question. In a culture in which books were rare and costly, the answer would usually have been given in preaching rather than in writing. Of the literature that resulted when the answer was given in writing, much has been lost, and most of what survived never achieved the status of Christian Scripture on a par with the Hebrew Scriptures or the Gospels. Of the writings that did achieve such status, almost all are letters, often densely argued and always ardently expressed. And within that body of scriptural letters, no letter-writer looms larger than Saul of Tarsus.

Saul, born a Jew in the Greek-speaking city of Tarsus (part of present-day Turkey), grew up in Jerusalem and studied Torah there with a teacher, Gamaliel, well known to later rabbinic tradition. Gamaliel was a Pharisee, and Saul, later Paul, counts himself one as well. In Philippians 3:5–6, he describes himself as "circumcised on the eighth day, a member of the people of Israel, of the tribe of Benjamin, a Hebrew born of Hebrews; as to the law, a Pharisee, as to zeal, a persecutor of the church; as to righteousness under the law, blameless." In his letters, Paul's way of debating the meaning of Torah with his fellow Jews owed much to his Jerusalem training. He was not one of Jesus' Twelve Apostles, but he may conceivably have seen Jesus at some point during Jesus' earthly life, and he certainly knew Jesus' leading Apostles as their lives lengthened and their following grew. As the story is told in the Acts of the Apostles 9:1–31 and 22:1–22, the risen Jesus called Saul to become uniquely an "Apostle to the Gentiles" (Romans 11:13), at which point Saul took the name Paul and began his career of travel and tireless evangelism.

The Roman Empire of the first century, though culturally brutal in many ways, preserved peace in and among its constituent parts with impressive effectiveness. This *Pax Romana,* "Roman Peace," enabled the construction of the best road system the world had yet seen and, though travel remained perilous, fostered a degree of commercial and cultural integration that was also virtually without parallel. And if the Empire was networked, the extensive Jewish Diaspora within it was doubly networked. Jewish communities in different parts of the Empire were in touch with one another, and all were in touch with Jerusalem as a spiritual capital standing alongside Rome as a military and commercial capital.

Paul first spread his message through this Jewish network: in Arabia, then Syria, through Anatolia and Asia Minor (modern Turkey), across the Bosporus and the Dardanelles into Macedonia, Greece, and Italy as far north as Rome, where Christian tradition says he was martyred. By his own report, some people found Paul's letters more impressive than they found him in person (2 Corinthians 10:10). Yet however physically unprepossessing he may have been (iconographic tradition portrays him bald and on the short side), he was evidently fearless and dogged in confronting one group of strangers after another and winning a hearing for his message. Preaching in a synagogue, he would sometimes be turned away angrily, but sometimes make converts. Preaching on the public square, he would sometimes be met by blank incomprehension and indifference, but again sometimes make converts.

In the following selections, Paul establishes his credentials to preach the Gospel to Jew and Gentile alike. The first excerpt is from his second letter to Christians in Corinth, a city in Greece. The second is his one letter to Christians in Galatia, in the highlands of central Anatolia. Because he was neither the first nor the last Christian evangelist in the field, Paul often needed to defend his unique status against other contenders. In an exuberant metaphor, he compares himself to a matchmaker presenting his new Christian community as a chaste virgin about to married to Christ and warns the community against dangerous dalliance with other supposed matchmakers (2 Corinthians 11:1–4).

Paul vociferously insists, however, that his embrace of Christ does not make him one whit less a Jew: "Are they Hebrews? So am I. Are they Israelites? So am I. Are they descendants of Abraham? So am I?" But he goes on: "Are they ministers of Christ? I am talking like a madman—I am a better one: with far greater labors, far more imprisonments, with countless floggings, and often near death" (2 Corinthians

11:22–23). It was evidently a well-established practice in the early Church of sending apostles or apostolic delegations—missionaries, to use the more usual modern term—from an established Christian community to some new region where the Church was unknown. Paul sets himself apart from this practice as one whose commission has come directly from God.

PRONOUNCING GLOSSARY

Achaia: *ah-kai´-uh* [*ai* rhyming with *rye*]   Macedonia: *ma-se-doh´-nee-uh*
Aretas: *ah-ray´-tahs*

2 CORINTHIANS

10

(1) I myself, Paul, appeal to you by the meekness and gentleness of Christ—I who am humble when face to face with you, but bold toward you when I am away!—(2) I ask that when I am present I need not show boldness by daring to oppose those who think we are acting according to human standards. (3) Indeed, we live as human beings, but we do not wage war according to human standards; (4) for the weapons of our warfare are not merely human, but they have divine power to destroy strongholds. We destroy arguments (5) and every proud obstacle raised up against the knowledge of God, and we take every thought captive to obey Christ. (6) We are ready to punish every disobedience when your obedience is complete.

(7) Look at what is before your eyes. If you are confident that you belong to Christ, remind yourself of this, that just as you belong to Christ, so also do we. (8) Now, even if I boast a little too much of our authority, which the Lord gave for building you up and not for tearing you down, I will not be ashamed of it. (9) I do not want to seem as though I am trying to frighten you with my letters. (10) For they say, "His letters are weighty and strong, but his bodily presence is weak, and his speech contemptible." (11) Let such people understand that what we say by letter when absent, we will also do when present.

(12) We do not dare to classify or compare ourselves with some of those who commend themselves. But when they measure themselves by one another, and compare themselves with one another they do not show good sense. (13) We, however, will not boast beyond limits, but will keep within the field that God has assigned to us, to reach out even as far as you. (14) For we were not overstepping our limits when we reached you; we were the first to come all the way to you with the good news of Christ. (15) We do not boast beyond limits, that is, in the labors of others, but our hope is that as your faith increases, our sphere of action among you may be greatly enlarged, (16) so that we may proclaim the good news in lands beyond you, without boasting of work already done in someone else's sphere of action. (17) "Let the one who boasts, boast in the Lord." (18) For it is not those who commend themselves that are approved, but those whom the Lord commends.

FROM "2 Corinthians" and "Galatians" in New Revised Standard Version Bible.

II

(1) I wish you would bear with me in a little foolishness. Do bear with me! (2) I feel a divine jealousy for you, for I promised you in marriage to one husband, to present you as a chaste virgin to Christ. (3) But I am afraid that as the serpent deceived Eve by its cunning,[1] your thoughts will be led astray from a sincere and pure devotion to Christ. (4) For if someone comes and proclaims another Jesus than the one we proclaimed, or if you receive a different spirit from the one you received, or a different gospel from the one you accepted, you submit to it readily enough. (5) I think that I am not in the least inferior to these super-apostles. (6) I may be untrained in speech, but not in knowledge; certainly in every way and in all things we have made this evident to you.

(7) Did I commit a sin by humbling myself so that you might be exalted, because I proclaimed God's good news to you free of charge? (8) I robbed other churches by accepting support from them in order to serve you. (9) And when I was with you and was in need, I did not burden anyone, for my needs were supplied by the friends who came from Macedonia. So I refrained and will continue to refrain from burdening you in any way. (10) As the truth of Christ is in me, this boast of mine will not be silenced in the regions of Achaia. (11) And why? Because I do not love you? God knows I do!

(12) And what I do I will also continue to do, in order to deny an opportunity to those who want an opportunity to be recognized as our equals in what they boast about. (13) For such boasters are false apostles, deceitful workers, disguising themselves as apostles of Christ. (14) And no wonder! Even Satan disguises himself as an angel of light. (15) So it is not strange if his ministers also disguise themselves as ministers of righteousness. Their end will match their deeds.

(16) I repeat, let no one think that I am a fool; but if you do, then accept me as a fool, so that I too may boast a little. (17) What I am saying in regard to this boastful confidence, I am saying not with the Lord's authority, but as a fool; (18) since many boast according to human standards, I will also boast. For you gladly put up with fools, being wise yourselves! (20) For you put up with it when someone makes slaves of you, or preys upon you, or takes advantage of you, or puts on airs, or gives you a slap in the face. (21) To my shame, I must say, we were too weak for that!

But whatever anyone dares to boast of—I am speaking as a fool—I also dare to boast of that. (22) Are they Hebrews? So am I. Are they Israelites? So am I. Are they descendants of Abraham? So am I. (23) Are they ministers of Christ? I am talking like a madman—I am a better one: with far greater labors, far more imprisonments, with countless floggings, and often near death. (24) Five times I have received from the Jews the forty lashes minus one. (25) Three times I was beaten with rods. Once I received a stoning. Three times I was shipwrecked; for a night and a day I was adrift at sea, (26) on frequent journeys, in danger from rivers, danger from bandits, danger from my own people, danger in the wilderness, danger at sea, danger from false brothers and sisters; (27) in toil and hardship, through many a sleepless

1. For the story of Eve's deception, see p. 83.

night, hungry and thirsty, often without food, cold and naked. (28) And, besides other things, I am under daily pressure because of my anxiety for all the churches. (29) Who is weak, and I am not weak? Who is made to stumble, and I am not indignant?

(30) If I must boast, I will boast of the things that show my weakness. (31) The God and Father of the Lord Jesus (blessed be he forever!) knows that I do not lie. (32) In Damascus, the governor under King Aretas guarded the city of Damascus in order to seize me, but I was let down in a basket through a window in the wall, and escaped from his hands.

ROMANS 7–9 AND GALATIANS 3:6–9, 23–29

What made the good news of the Gospel good? According to the Apostle Paul, the most influential of the early Christian missionaries, the good news is this: For those who enter an empowering new relationship with Christ through the spiritual state of faith and the ritual of baptism, immorality will yield to morality, and mortality will yield to immortality. This transformation is what it means to be "saved" (Romans 9:27). Accepting Jesus as Lord means being empowered to live as a Christian beyond any means you could manage on your own. Having thus been transformed, you had the supreme hope of rising after death as Christ rose and living in glory forever.

In Galatians 5:19–21, Paul notes that "the works of the flesh are obvious: fornication, impurity, licentiousness, idolatry, sorcery, enmities, strife, jealousy, anger, quarrels, dissensions, factions, envy, drunkenness, carousing, and things like these." He contrasts these failings with the works of the Spirit, the sanctified life made possible through the power of Christ:

> By contrast, the fruit of the Spirit is love, joy, peace, patience, kindness, generosity, faithfulness, gentleness, and self-control. There is no law against such things. And those who belong to Christ Jesus have crucified the flesh with its passions and desires. (5:22–24)

Paul recognized in the Torah of his rabbinical education (see p. 140) a superior moral instruction. The Hebrew word *torah*—commonly translated "law" in biblical Greek—means more properly "instruction." But in the following excerpt from the Letter to the Romans, Paul asks: What good is an instruction if I cannot follow it? What good is a law if I am powerless to obey it? For Paul, Torah—here, "the law"—is "spiritual," but he is "flesh," and his flesh is weak:

> For we know that the law is spiritual; but I am of the flesh, sold into slavery under sin. I do not understand my own actions. For I do not do what I want, but I do the very thing I hate. Now if I do what I do not want [i.e., what the law requires], I agree that the law is good. But in fact it is no longer I that do it, but sin that dwells within me. For I know that nothing good dwells within me, that is, in my flesh. I can will what is right, but I cannot do it. . . . For I delight in the law of God in my inmost self, but I see in my members another law at war with the law of my mind, making me captive to the law of sin that dwells in my members. Wretched man that I am! Who will rescue me from this body of death? (Romans 7:14–18, 22–24)

So, there is nothing amiss in the world around him that Paul does not find also amiss in himself. But he believes that what he cannot do alone he can accomplish with the grace—that is, with the more than natural assistance—of Christ. Thus, what is good news for him personally should be good news for the whole world as well. His wretchedness yields to a shout of thankfulness: "Thanks be to God through Jesus Christ our Lord!" (Romans 7:25).

Paul believes that he must free the world not so much from slavish observance of the law as from the self-punishing conviction that only by perfect adherence to the law can he or anyone escape the abyss of moral failure. It is not that he seeks liberation from Torah so as to live a free and natural or instinctive life. Far from it! For him, those who live in accord with nature are "slaves to the elemental spirits of the universe" (Galatians 4:3), and these "elements," far from being bold or noble, are "weak and beggarly" (Galatians 4:9). The law has been like a tutor for the world, showing it the distance that lies between its deprived and depraved natural state and the dignity and beauty of a truly moral life. But having now recognized that distance, the world must further recognize that only by trusting in the Lord and accepting both the grace and the forgiveness offered through Christ can it achieve true goodness. To do otherwise is to remain in captivity.

Through adoption by baptism, each person can become a brother or sister of Christ—a child of the Jewish God. Thus, Jesus, as the firstborn Son of God, is a sibling "within a large family" (Romans 8:29). In addition, according to Paul, those adopted into the family of God are a chosen people on a par with the Jews. They may not be physical descendants of the Old Testament patriarch Abraham, but they are his spiritual descendants. At Romans 9:25, Paul quotes the prophet Hosea (2:23): "Those who were not my people I will call 'my people,' and her who was not beloved I will call 'beloved.'"

In Galatians 3:6–9, which here follows the selections from Romans, Paul extends an argument about Abraham. When Abraham trusted in God's promise to make his offspring innumerable and to give him and them a land of their own, God gave Abraham credit for that act of trust. A large entry, in other words, was made on the credit side of Abraham's spiritual ledger. As the Jewish Publication Society translation renders Genesis 15:6, "He reckoned it to his merit." Paul argues, by analogy, that God will give Christians spiritual credit for believing that, thanks to Christ, they will live forever. When Paul speaks of justification, he does not mean self-defense or self-exoneration. Instead, he means reconciliation of the spiritual ledger, where "it is God who justifies" (Romans 8:33). In each Christian's reckoning of moral credit for good works and moral debit for evil ones, does everything come out even?

In this way, as accounts with the Lord are brought into balance, a further prophecy will come true: Abraham's spiritual descendents will be even more numerous than his physical ones, and all will be "brothers in Christ." As all are adopted into brotherhood with the same Christ, so all become fellow adoptees, one to another:

> As many of you as were baptized into Christ have clothed yourselves with Christ. There is no longer Jew or Greek, there is no longer slave or free, there is no longer male and female; for all of you are one in Christ Jesus. And if you belong to Christ, then you are Abraham's offspring, heirs according to the promise. (Galatians 3:27–29)

PRONOUNCING GLOSSARY

Esau: *ee´-saw*
Galatians: *guh-lay´-shuhnz*
Gomorrah: *go-mor´-ruh*
Hosea: *hoh-zay´-uh*

Isaiah: *ai-say´-uh* [*ai* rhyming with *rye*]
Pharaoh: *fa´-roh*
Sodom: *sah´-dom*
Zion: *zai´-uhn* [*ai* rhyming with *rye*]

ROMANS

7

(1) Do you not know, brothers and sisters—for I am speaking to those who know the law—that the law is binding on a person only during that person's lifetime? (2) Thus a married woman is bound by the law to her husband as long as he lives; but if her husband dies, she is discharged from the law concerning the husband. (3) Accordingly, she will be called an adulteress if she lives with another man while her husband is alive. But if her husband dies, she is free from that law, and if she marries another man, she is not an adulteress.

(4) In the same way, my friends, you have died to the law through the body of Christ, so that you may belong to another, to him who has been raised from the dead in order that we may bear fruit for God. (5) While we were living in the flesh, our sinful passions, aroused by the law, were at work in our members to bear fruit for death. (6) But now we are discharged from the law, dead to that which held us captive, so that we are slaves not under the old written code but in the new life of the Spirit.

(7) What then should we say? That the law is sin? By no means! Yet, if it had not been for the law, I would not have known sin. I would not have known what it is to covet if the law had not said, "You shall not covet." (8) But sin, seizing an opportunity in the commandment, produced in me all kinds of covetousness. Apart from the law sin lies dead. (9) I was once alive apart from the law, but when the commandment came, sin revived (10) and I died, and the very commandment that promised life proved to be death to me. (11) For sin, seizing an opportunity in the commandment, deceived me and through it killed me. So the law is holy, and the commandment is holy and just and good.

(13) Did what is good, then, bring death to me? By no means! It was sin, working death in me through what is good, in order that sin might be shown to be sin, and through the commandment might become sinful beyond measure.

(14) For we know that the law is spiritual; but I am of the flesh, sold into slavery under sin. (15) I do not understand my own actions. For I do not do what I want, but I do the very thing I hate. (16) Now if I do what I do not want, I agree that the law is good. (17) But in fact it is no longer I that do it, but sin that dwells within me. (18) For I know that nothing good dwells within me, that is, in my flesh. I can will what is right, but I cannot do it. (19) For I do not do the good I want, but the evil I do not want is what I do. (20) Now if I do what I do not want, it is no longer I that do it, but sin that dwells within me.

(21) So I find it to be a law that when I want to do what is good, evil lies close at hand. (22) For I delight in the law of God in my inmost self, (23) but I see in my members another law at war with the law of my mind, making me captive to the law of sin that dwells in my members. (24) Wretched man that I am! Who will rescue me from this body of death? (25) Thanks be to God through Jesus Christ our Lord!

FROM "Romans" and "Galatians" in New Revised Standard Version Bible.

So then, with my mind I am a slave to the law of God, but with my flesh I am a slave to the law of sin.

8

(1) There is therefore now no condemnation for those who are in Christ Jesus. (2) For the law of the Spirit of life in Christ Jesus has set you free from the law of sin and of death. (3) For God has done what the law, weakened by the flesh, could not do: by sending his own Son in the likeness of sinful flesh; and to deal with sin, he condemned sin in the flesh, (4) so that the just requirement of the law might be fulfilled in us, who walk not according to the flesh but according to the Spirit. (5) For those who live according to the flesh set their minds on the things of the flesh, but those who live according to the Spirit set their minds on the things of the Spirit. (6) To set the mind on the flesh is death, but to set the mind on the Spirit is life and peace. (7) For this reason the mind that is set on the flesh is hostile to God; it does not submit to God's law—indeed it cannot, (8) and those who are in the flesh cannot please God.

(9) But you are not in the flesh; you are in the Spirit, since the Spirit of God dwells in you. Anyone who does not have the Spirit of Christ does not belong to him. (10) But if Christ is in you, though the body is dead because of sin, the Spirit is life because of righteousness. (11) If the Spirit of him who raised Jesus from the dead dwells in you, he who raised Christ from the dead will give life to your mortal bodies also through his Spirit that dwells in you.

(12) So then, brothers and sisters, we are debtors, not to the flesh, to live according to the flesh— (13) for if you live according to the flesh, you will die; but if by the Spirit you put to death the deeds of the body, you will live. (14) For all who are led by the Spirit of God are children of God. (15) For you did not received a spirit of slavery to fall back into fear, but you have received a spirit of adoption. When we cry, "Abba!¹ Father!" (16) it is that very Spirit bearing witness with our spirit that we are children of God, (17) and if children, then heirs, heirs of God and joint heirs with Christ—if, in fact, we suffer with him so that we may also be glorified with him.

(18) I consider that the sufferings of this present time are not worth comparing with the glory about to be revealed to us. (19) For the creation waits with eager longing for the revealing of the children of God; (20) for the creation was subjected to futility, not of its own will but by the will of the one who subjected it, in hope (21) that the creation itself will be set free from its bondage to decay and will obtain the freedom of the glory of the children of God. (22) We know that the whole creation has been groaning in labor pains until now; (23) and not only the creation, but we ourselves, who have the first fruits of the Spirit, groan inwardly while we wait for adoption, the redemption of our bodies. (24) For in hope we were saved. Now hope that is seen is not hope. For who hopes for what is seen? (25) But if we hope for what we do not see, we wait for it with patience.

---

1. See note 8, p. 133.

(26) Likewise the Spirit helps us in our weakness; for we do not know how to pray as we ought, but that very Spirit intercedes with sighs too deep for words. (27) And God, who searches the heart, knows what is the mind of the Spirit, because the Spirit intercedes for the saints according to the will of God.

(28) We know that all things work together for good for those who love God, who are called according to his purpose. (29) For those whom he foreknew he also predestined to be conformed to the image of his Son, in order that he might be the firstborn within a large family. (30) And those whom he predestined he also called; and those whom he called he also justified; and those whom he justified he also glorified.

(31) What then are we to say about these things? If God is for us, who is against us? (32) He who did not withhold his own Son, but gave him up for all of us, will he not with him also give us everything else? (33) Who will bring any charge against God's elect? It is God who justifies. (34) Who is to condemn? It is Christ Jesus, who died, yes, who was raised, who is at the right hand of God, who indeed intercedes for us. (35) Who will separate us from the love of Christ? Will hardship, or distress, or persecution, or famine, or nakedness, or peril, or sword? (36) As it is written,

> "For your sake we are being killed all day long;
> we are accounted as sheep to be slaughtered."[2]

(37) No, in all these things we are more than conquerors through him who loved us. (38) For I am convinced that neither death, nor life, nor angels, nor rulers, nor things present, nor things to come, nor powers, (39) nor height, nor depth, nor anything else in all creation, will be able to separate us from the love of God in Christ Jesus our Lord.

9

(1) I am speaking the truth in Christ—I am not lying; my conscience confirms it by the Holy Spirit—(2) I have great sorrow and unceasing anguish in my heart. (3) For I could wish that I myself were accursed and cut off from Christ for the sake of my own people, my kindred according to the flesh. (4) They are Israelites, and to them belong the adoption, the glory, the covenants, the giving of the law, the worship, and the promises; (5) to them belong the patriarchs, and from them, according to the flesh, comes the Messiah, who is over all, God blessed forever. Amen.

(6) It is not as though the word of God had failed. For not all Israelites truly belong to Israel, (7) and not all of Abraham's children are his true descendants; but "It is through Isaac that descendants shall be named for you."[1] (8) This means that it is not the children of the flesh who are the children of God, but the children of the promise are counted as descendants. (9) For this is what the promise said, "About this time I will return and Sarah shall have a son."[2] (10) Nor is that all; something similar happened to Rebecca when

---

2. Psalms 44:22.
1. God had said to Abraham, "It is through [your son] Isaac that your offspring will be reckoned" (Hebrews 11:18). In other words, God designated that the chosen people would descend from Abraham's line through Isaac.
2. Genesis 18:14. Sarah was Abraham's wife. Their son was Isaac.

she had conceived children by one husband, our ancestor Isaac. (11) Even before they had been born or had done anything good or bad (so that God's purpose of election might continue, (12) not by works but by his call) she was told, "The elder shall serve the younger."[3] (13) As it is written,

> "I have loved Jacob,
> but I have hated Esau."[4]

(14) What then are we to say? Is there injustice on God's part? By no means! (15) For he says to Moses,

> "I will have mercy on whom I have mercy,
> and I will have compassion on whom I have compassion."[5]

(16) So it depends not on human will or exertion, but on God who shows mercy. (17) For the scripture says to Pharaoh, "I have raised you up for the very purpose of showing my power in you, so that my name may be proclaimed in all the earth."[6] (18) So then he has mercy on whomever he chooses, and he hardens the heart of whomever he chooses.

(19) You will say to me then, "Why then does he still find fault? For who can resist his will?" (20) But Who indeed are you, a human being, to argue with God? Will what is molded say to the one who molds it, "Why have you made me like this?" (21) Has the potter no right over the clay, to make out of the same lump one object for special use and another for ordinary use? (22) What if God, desiring to show his wrath and to make known his power, has endured with much patience the objects of wrath that are made for destruction; (23) and what if he has done so in order to make known the riches of his glory for the objects of mercy, which he has prepared beforehand for glory—(24) including us whom he has called, not from the Jews only but also from the Gentiles? (25) As indeed he says in Hosea,

> "Those who were not my people I will call 'my people,'
> and her who was not beloved I will call 'beloved.'"[7]
> (26) "And in the very place where it was said to them, 'You are not my
> people,'
> there they shall be called children of the living God."[8]

(27) And Isaiah cries out concerning Israel, "Though the number of the children of Israel were like the sand of the sea, only a remnant of them will be saved; (28) for the Lord will execute his sentence on the earth quickly and decisively."[9] (29) And as Isaiah predicted,

3. From Genesis 25:23.
4. From Malachi 1:2–3, where God says, "Yet I have loved Jacob, but Esau I have hated, and I have turned his mountains into a wasteland and left his inheritance to the desert jackals." Isaac and Rebecca had two sons, Jacob and Esau. God "loved" Jacob by continuing the line of the chosen people through him. Thus, Jacob received the name Israel, and his descendants became the Israelites. God "hated" Esau by not continuing the line through him. Paul's references to biblical lineage are a way of summarizing the spiritual benefits of God's grace, election (or selection), and promise of glory to come.
5. Exodus 33:19.
6. Exodus 9:16. "Scripture" here means the word of God as interpreted by Moses. In Exodus 9, God dictates what Moses should say to Pharaoh, the Egyptian ruler, to convince Pharaoh to free the enslaved Israelites.
7. Hosea 2:23.
8. Hosea 1:10.
9. Isaiah 10:22.

"If the Lord of hosts had not left survivors to us,
 we would have fared like Sodom
 and been made like Gomorrah."[1]

(30) What then are we to say? Gentiles, who did not strive for righteousness, have attained it, that is, righteousness through faith; (31) but Israel, who did strive for the righteousness that is based on the law, did not succeed in fulfilling that law. (32) Why not? Because they did not strive for it on the basis of faith, but as if it were based on works. They have stumbled over the stumbling stone, (33) as it is written,

"See, I am laying in Zion a stone that will make people stumble, a rock
    that will make them fall,
 and whoever believes in him will not be put to shame."[2]

GALATIANS

3:6–9, 23–29

(6) Just as Abraham "believed God, and it was reckoned to him as righteousness,"[1] (7) so, you see, those who believe are the descendants of Abraham. (8) And the scripture, foreseeing that God would justify the Gentiles by faith, declared the gospel beforehand to Abraham, saying, "All the Gentiles shall be blessed in you."[2] (9) For this reason, those who believe are blessed with Abraham who believed.

✳   ✳   ✳

(23) Now before faith came, we were imprisoned and guarded under the law until faith would be revealed. (24) Therefore the law was our disciplinarian until Christ came, so that we might be justified by faith. (25) But now that faith has come, we are no longer subject to a disciplinarian, (26) for in Christ Jesus you are all children of God through faith. (27) As many of you as were baptized into Christ have clothed yourselves with Christ. (28) There is no longer Jew or Greek, there is no longer slave or free, there is no longer male and female; for all of you are one in Christ Jesus. (29) And if you belong to Christ, then you are Abraham's offspring, heirs according to the promise.

1. Isaiah 1:9.
2. Isaiah 28:16; 1 Peter 2:6.

1. Genesis 15:6.
2. Genesis 12:3.

PHILIPPIANS 1:27–2:11 AND 1 CORINTHIANS 15:12–19, 35–44, 51–58

The Letter of Paul to the Philippians is one of the New Testament texts certain to have been written by the Apostle Paul. Sometime between 50 and 62 C.E., Paul wrote this letter to the Church at Philippi, an early center of Christianity in Greece with which Paul had a close relationship.

Philippians 2:5–11 may be a quotation of an ancient hymn. These verses are often called the "kenosis hymn." For Christians, *kenosis* (Greek for emptiness) means emptying oneself of one's will and becoming entirely receptive to God's will. The model for this process is Jesus Christ, who emptied himself in the service of divine will, becoming humbled to death on the cross. For this self-sacrifice, God exalted Jesus beyond everyone. In this way, the story of Jesus may be a reversal of the story of Adam. As recounted in Genesis, Adam was the first man, a creature who (by eating the fruit forbidden by God) attempted to become like God and was therefore humbled and driven from paradise. Thus was "paradise lost," to borrow the title of John Milton's seventeeth-century epic poem. And how was "paradise regained," to borrow the title of Milton's second epic? Romans 5:18 puts it in a sentence: "As one man's trespass led to condemnation for all men, so one man's act of righteousness leads to acquittal and life for all men."

To state the matter so symmetrically and logically, however, is to miss what may have been the key to Paul's historic success. What may matter most about the kenosis hymn is just that it is a hymn, already familiar to his hearers, and quite possibly summoning a melody into their minds. Paul, like many a modern preacher, borrows musical emotion at a peak moment in his oration.

Afterlife in some form was taken for granted in the Greco-Roman religious culture of the Mediterranean basin in the first century of the Common Era, but it was a realm neither of reward nor punishment, a state of being neither dead to the extinction of consciousness nor alive in any meaningful way. Whether one was a hero or a scoundrel, moreover, the same afterlife awaited one. By strongest contrast, in Jewish religious culture during the last centuries before the Common Era, the belief had arisen in an afterlife that was a reward for some and punishment for others. This view is vividly expressed in the Books of Maccabees and the Book of Wisdom. These Books became part of the Greco-Jewish biblical canon in the second century B.C.E., which later became the standard Christian canon of the Old Testament. Built into this theology of the afterlife was the assumption that if men and women could have moral debts to God, God could have moral debts to them and could discharge them after death or after death and resurrection.

Resurrection may have been Paul's most passionately held belief, and in this anthology's excerpts from 1 Corinthians 15, Paul infuses his expression of resurrection with rhetorical passion. When he writes, at 15:51–52,

> Behold, I show you a mystery; we shall not all sleep, but we shall all be changed. In a moment, in the twinkling of an eye, at the last trump: for the trumpet shall sound, and the dead shall be raised incorruptible, and we shall be changed,

he offers no logical or ethical argument but only shares an ecstatic vision. He quotes Hosea from memory and approximately: "O death, where is thy sting? O grave, where is thy victory?" For the millions in his world whose lives were lived in literal, lifelong slavery; for women who were regarded as chattel, the property of their husbands in a patriarchal society; for entire nations the flower of whose youth were harvested for servitude on Roman galleys or in the Roman legions, this vision may have mattered far more than his most dazzlingly astute theological or scriptural arguments.

This graffito depicts a man worshipping a crucified figure with the head of a donkey. The inscription scratched under the crucified figure reads, in Greek, "Alexamonos worships his god." This obvious jibe at a Christian dates from the early 3rd century and was found on a wall on the Palatine Hill, in Rome, in the 19th century.

PHILIPPIANS

1:27–30

(27) Whatever happens, conduct yourselves in a manner worthy of the gospel of Christ. Then, whether I come and see you or only hear about you in

FROM "Philippians" in The Holy Bible, New International Version. From "Corinthians" in The English Bible, King James Version, The New Testament: A Norton Critical Edition.

my absence, I will know that you stand firm in the one Spirit, striving together as one for the faith of the gospel (28) without being frightened in any way by those who oppose you. This is a sign to them that they will be destroyed, but that you will be saved—and that by God. (29) For it has been granted to you on behalf of Christ not only to believe in him, but also to suffer for him, (30) since you are going through the same struggle you saw I had, and now hear that I still have.

2:1–11

(1) Therefore if you have any encouragement from being united with Christ, if any comfort from his love, if any common sharing in the Spirit, if any tenderness and compassion, (2) then make my joy complete by being like-minded, having the same love, being one in spirit and of one mind. (3) Do nothing out of selfish ambition or vain conceit. Rather, in humility value others above yourselves, (4) not looking to your own interests but each of you to the interests of the others.

(5) In your relationships with one another, have the same mindset as Christ Jesus:

(6) Who, being in very nature God,
    did not consider equality with God something to be used to his own
        advantage;
(7) rather, he made himself nothing
    by taking the very nature of a servant,
    being made in human likeness.
(8) And being found in appearance as a man,
    he humbled himself
    by becoming obedient to death—
        even death on a cross!

(9) Therefore God exalted him to the highest place
    and gave him the name that is above every name,
(10) that at the name of Jesus every knee should bow,
    in heaven and on earth and under the earth,
(11) and every tongue acknowledge that Jesus Christ is Lord,
    to the glory of God the Father.

1 CORINTHIANS

15:12–19, 35–44, 51–58

(12) Now if Christ be preached that he rose from the dead, how say some among you that there is no resurrection of the dead? (13) But if there be no resurrection of the dead, then is Christ not risen: (14) and if Christ be not risen, then is our preaching vain, and your faith is also vain. (15) Yea, and we are found false witnesses of God; because we have testified of God that he raised up Christ: whom he raised not up, if so be that the dead rise not. (16) For if the dead rise not, then is not Christ raised: (17) and if Christ be not

raised, your faith is vain; ye are yet in your sins. (18) Then they also which are fallen asleep in Christ are perished. (19) If in this life only we have hope in Christ, we are of all men most miserable.

* * *

(35) But some man will say, How are the dead raised up? and with what body do they come? (36) Thou fool, that which thou sowest is not quickened, except it die: (37) and that which thou sowest, thou sowest not that body that shall be, but bare grain, it may chance of wheat, or of some other grain: (38) but God giveth it a body as it hath pleased him, and to every seed his own body. (39) All flesh is not the same flesh: but there is one kind of flesh of men, another flesh of beasts, another of fishes, and another of birds. (40) There are also celestial bodies, and bodies terrestrial: but the glory of the celestial is one, and the glory of the terrestrial is another. (41) There is one glory of the sun, and another glory of the moon, and another glory of the stars: for one star differeth from another star in glory.

(42) So also is the resurrection of the dead. It is sown in corruption; it is raised in incorruption: (43) it is sown in dishonour; it is raised in glory: it is sown in weakness; it is raised in power: (44) it is sown a natural body; it is raised a spiritual body. There is a natural body, and there is a spiritual body. * * *

(51) Behold, I shew you a mystery; We shall not all sleep, but we shall all be changed, (52) in a moment, in the twinkling of an eye, at the last trump: for the trumpet shall sound, and the dead shall be raised incorruptible, and we shall be changed. (53) For this corruptible must put on incorruption, and this mortal must put on immortality. (54) So when this corruptible shall have put on incorruption, and this mortal shall have put on immortality, then shall be brought to pass the saying that is written, Death is swallowed up in victory. (55) O death, where is thy sting? O grave, where is thy victory? (56) The sting of death is sin; and the strength of sin is the law. (57) But thanks be to God, which giveth us the victory through our Lord Jesus Christ. (58) Therefore, my beloved brethren, be ye stedfast, unmoveable, always abounding in the work of the Lord, forasmuch as ye know that your labour is not in vain in the Lord.

THE LETTER TO THE HEBREWS 11–12:2
AND JAMES 2:14–24

The Letter to the Hebrews is an anonymous letter written perhaps before the Romans' destruction of the Second Temple (70 C.E.). The Letter formally names neither its author nor its recipient community, though it is written as if by a Jew to his brother Jews: "Long ago God spoke to our ancestors in many and various ways by the prophets," etc. (Hebrews 1:1). In fact, the purpose of Hebrews is to encourage recent converts to Christianity to persevere in the face of persecution. The main idea of this text is that Jesus Christ is the mediator between God and humanity—he is a high priest celebrating the unique, unrepeatable, and never to be surpassed sacrifice of himself.

The following selection from Hebrews is a catalog of "witnesses in a great cloud" (12:1). They are the great figures of faith in ancient Israel. In addition to being models for Christians to follow, these exemplars represent the history of salvation before the coming of Christ. The Letter to the Hebrews thus presents faith in Christ not as a break with Jewish religion but as the religious culmination of a long history of Israelite and Jewish faith. Unique, however, among the New Testament letters, the Letter to the Hebrews also presents the self-oblation of Christ on the cross as the culmination of the long history of sacrifice throughout Israelite and Jewish history, up to the time of Christ.

During the life of Christ and through the first decades of the birth of Christianity, animal sacrifice continued in the Temple of Jerusalem; and though the Gospels present the high priest and Temple leadership as complicit in the condemnation and execution of Jesus, they offer no polemic against the Temple or against the animal sacrifices taking place there. Luke the Evangelist approvingly reports that Jesus' parents offered a Temple sacrifice after Jesus' birth (Luke 2:22–24). In the Acts of the Apostles 2:46–47, Luke reports that after Jesus' death and Resurrection, Jesus' leading followers continued to frequent the Temple. Animal sacrifice ended forcibly with the destruction of the Second Temple. To the extent that the founding generation of Christian Jews had devoutly participated in Temple sacrifice and had continued to embrace sacrifice as divinely mandated, the central argument of the Letter to the Hebrews may be directed to them, demonstrating how sacrifice within Judaism could live on in the ritually memorialized sacrifice of Christ (e.g., through the Lord's Supper, a ritual meal that symbolically reenacted the Last Supper and the self-sacrifice on the cross).

Like the Letter to the Hebrews, the Letter of James was probably written before the destruction of the Second Temple. It too may be implicitly addressed to a readership of Christian Jews in a time of trial. By being addressed to no one, "catholic" letters of this kind—like those of John and Jude—are addressed to the entire Christian universe (Greek *katholikos*, "universal"). Theological or pastoral letters of general Christian interest, they may be pseudepigraphical—that is, bearing a false epigraph or title and not actually written by the venerable figures to whom they are attributed.

In James, the emphasis is on moral living and good works. Whereas the Apostle Paul emphasized the merit that Abraham won through faith (see p. 150), James focuses on Abraham's good works.

PRONOUNCING GLOSSARY

Abel: *ay´-bell*
Barak: *buh-rahk´*
Cain: *kayn*
Enoch: *ee´-nok*

Esau: *ee´-saw*
Gideon: *gi´-dee-on*
Jephthah: *jef´-thah*
Jericho: *je´-ri-koh*

THE LETTER TO THE HEBREWS

11

The Exemplary Faith of Our Ancestors

(1) Only faith can guarantee the blessings that we hope for, or prove the existence of realities that are unseen. (2) It is for their faith that our ancestors are acknowledged.

(3) It is by faith that we understand that the ages were created by a word from God, so that from the invisible the visible world came to be.

(4) It was because of his faith that Abel offered God a better sacrifice than Cain,[1] and for that he was acknowledged as upright when *God* himself made acknowledgement of *his offerings*. Though he is dead, he still speaks by faith.

(5) It was because of his faith that Enoch[2] was taken up and did not experience death: *he was no more, because God took him*; because before his assumption he was acknowledged to *have pleased God*. (6) Now it is impossible to please God without faith, since anyone who comes to him must believe that he exists and rewards those who seek him.

(7) It was through his faith that Noah,[3] when he had been warned by God of something that had never been seen before, took care to build an ark to save his family. His faith was a judgement on the world, and he was able to claim the uprightness which comes from faith.

(8) It was by faith that Abraham obeyed the call to *set out* for a country that was the inheritance given to him and his descendants, and that *he set out* without knowing where he was going. (9) By faith he *sojourned* in the Promised Land as though it were not his, living in tents with Isaac and Jacob, who were heirs with him of the same promise. (10) He looked forward to the well-founded city, designed and built by God.

(11) It was equally by faith that Sarah, in spite of being past the age, was made able to conceive, because she believed that he who had made the promise was faithful to it. (12) Because of this, there came from one man, and one who already had the mark of death on him, descendants *as numerous as the stars of heaven and the grains of sand on the seashore which cannot be counted.*

(13) All these died in faith, before receiving any of the things that had been promised, but they saw them in the far distance and welcomed them, recognising that they were only *strangers and nomads on earth*. (14) People who use such terms about themselves make it quite plain that they are in search of a homeland. (15) If they had meant the country they came from, they would have had the opportunity to return to it; (16) but in fact they were longing for a better homeland, their heavenly homeland. That is why God is not ashamed to be called their God, since he has founded the city for them.

From "Hebrews" in *The Jerusalem Bible*. From "James" in *The Holy Bible, Containing the Old and New Testaments, Revised Standard Version: Catholic Edition.*

1. Abel and Cain were sons of Adam and Eve. Abel, a shepherd, offered God a sacrifice from his flock. Cain, a farmer, offered God produce. After God rejected Cain's offering, Cain killed Abel.

2. Adam's great-grandson

3. Enoch's great-grandson.

(17) It was by faith that Abraham, *when put to the test, offered up Isaac.* He offered to sacrifice *his only son* even though he had yet to receive what had been promised, (18) and he had been told: *Isaac is the one through whom your name will be carried on.* He was confident that God had the power even to raise the dead; and so, figuratively speaking, (19) he was given back Isaac from the dead.

(20) It was by faith that this same Isaac gave his blessing to Jacob and Esau for the still distant future. (21) By faith Jacob, when he was dying, blessed each of Joseph's sons, *bowed in reverence, as he leant on his staff.* (22) It was by faith that, when he was about to die, Joseph mentioned the Exodus of the Israelites and gave instructions about his own remains.[4]

(23) It was by faith that Moses, when he was born, *was kept hidden by his parents for three months;* because they *saw* that he was a *fine* child; they were not afraid of the royal edict. (24) It was by faith that, *when he was grown up,* Moses refused to be known as the son of Pharaoh's daughter (25) and chose to be ill-treated in company with God's people rather than to enjoy the transitory pleasures of sin. (26) He considered that the humiliations offered to the Anointed were something more precious than all the treasures of Egypt, because he had his eyes fixed on the reward. (27) It was by faith that he left Egypt without fear of the king's anger; he held to his purpose like someone who could see the Invisible. (28) It was by faith that he kept *the Passover* and sprinkled *the blood* to prevent *the Destroyer* from touching any of their first-born sons. (29) It was by faith they crossed the Red Sea as easily as dry land, while the Egyptians, trying to do the same, were drowned.[5]

(30) It was through faith that the walls of Jericho fell down when the people had marched round them for seven days. (31) It was by faith that Rahab the prostitute welcomed the spies and so was not killed with the unbelievers.[6]

(32) What more shall I say? There is not time for me to give an account of Gideon, Barak, Samson, Jephthah, or of David, Samuel and the prophets.[7] (33) These were men who through faith conquered kingdoms, did what was upright and earned the promises. They could keep a lion's mouth shut, (34) put out blazing fires and emerge unscathed from battle. They were weak people who were given strength to be brave in war and drive back

4. Joseph was the eleventh of Jacob's 12 sons. Sold by his brothers into slavery in Egypt, he rose to become the most powerful man in Egypt next to Pharoah. Before he died, Joseph asked that when the Israelites left Egypt, they would take his bones with them.
5. This paragraph recounts events in the life of Moses. During Moses' infancy, Pharoah ordered the execution of the Israelites' first-born sons. Moses' mother saved him from execution by hiding him for three months, then set him adrift in a basket. He was adopted as a foundling by the Egyptian royal family. Rebelling against the Egyptians' laws, he killed a slaveholder, then fled, eventually returning to Egypt after being instructed by God to emancipate the Israelites. To aid Moses' efforts, God brought 10 plagues upon the Egyptians. The tenth—the slaying of the Egyptians' first-born sons—convinced the Egyptians to order the Israelites to depart Egypt. The Passover festival commemorates the way the tenth plague "passed over"

the houses of the Israelites: Moses had instructed the Israelites to mark their doorposts with lambs' blood so that they would not "suffer the destroyer" (Exodus 12:23). Moses parted the Red Sea to lead his people out of Egypt, and the sea then closed over the Egyptian army, which was pursuing them.
6. According to the Book of Joshua, Rahab sheltered two Israelite spies who were gathering information about her hometown of Jericho after the Israelites' flight from Egypt. The Israelites destroyed the wall of Jericho by walking around it with the ark of the covenant—a chest containing the stone tablets on which the Ten Commandments were inscribed—for seven days.
7. Allusions to the lives and works of all these figures fill this paragraph. "Gideon, Barak, Samson, Jephthah": See the Book of Judges. "David, Samuel, and the prophets": See the Books of Samuel and Kings, plus narrative portions of the Book of Jeremiah.

foreign invaders. (35) Some returned to their wives from the dead by resurrection; and others submitted to torture, refusing release so that they would rise again to a better life. (36) Some had to bear being pilloried and (37) flogged, or even chained up in prison. They were stoned, or sawn in half, or killed by the sword; they were homeless, and wore only the skins of sheep and goats; they were in want and hardship, and maltreated. (38) They were too good for the world and they wandered in deserts and mountains and in caves and ravines. (39) These all won acknowledgement through their faith, but they did not receive (40) what was promised, since God had made provision for us to have something better, and they were not to reach perfection except with us.

12:1–2

The Example of Jesus Christ

(1) With so many witnesses in a great cloud all around us, we too, then, should throw off everything that weighs us down and the sin that clings so closely, and with perseverance keep running in the race which lies ahead of us. (2) Let us keep our eyes fixed on Jesus, who leads us in our faith and brings it to perfection: for the sake of the joy which lay ahead of him, he endured the cross, disregarding the shame of it, and *has taken his seat at the right* of God's throne. * * *

JAMES

2:14–24

(14) What does it profit, my brethren, if a man says he has faith but has not works? Can his faith save him? (15) If a brother or sister is ill-clad and in lack of daily food, (16) and one of you says to them, "Go in peace, be warmed and filled," without giving them the things needed for the body, what does it profit? (17) So faith by itself, if it has no works, is dead.

(18) But some one will say, "You have faith and I have works." Show me your faith apart from your works, and I by my works will show you my faith. (19) You believe that God is one; you do well. Even the demons believe—and shudder. (20) Do you want to be shown, you foolish fellow, that faith apart from works is barren? (21) Was not Abraham our father justified by works, when he offered his son Isaac upon the altar? (22) You see that faith was active along with his works, and faith was completed by works, (23) and the scripture was fulfilled which says, "Abraham believed God, and it was reckoned to him as righteousness";[1] and he was called the friend of God. (24) You see that a man is justified by works and not by faith alone. * * *

---

1. Genesis 15:6.

REVELATION 20–21:8

The Bible opens with the creation of the world in the Book of Genesis, and it closes with the end of the world in the Book of Revelation. As discussed in the period introduction, Revelation belongs to the genre known as apocalypse (from the Greek *apokalypsis*, "uncovering" or "unveiling"). This apocalypse purports to unveil a series of eschatological (from the Greek *eschatos*, "final") visions vouchsafed to a writer self-identified as John and living on the Greek island of Patmos. The subject of John's visions is how God will win his final victory over Satan and "the Beast" at the end of time.

Revelation combines a dense tissue of literally hundreds of biblical allusions, with actions swirling up from the writer's wildly kinetic and chaotic imagination. Scholars believe that the Beast, called "Babylon" in the text, is a symbol for the idolatrous and oppressive Roman Empire. At its core, Revelation may be a defiant and even violent act of faith on the part of an aggrieved and enraged Christian Jew fleeing the Roman destruction of the Temple, but possible references to later historical events hint at subsequent elaboration by a second or third writer. The work offers its readers or hearers on the one hand an acknowledgement of the tribulations they have undergone and on the other hand a resounding declaration that their final victory is assured.

The culminating passage, excerpted below, envisions a period known as the "millennium"—a thousand-year reign by the "priests of God and of Christ" (20:6), after which Satan is loosed for one last horrific rampage before being "thrown into the lake of fire and brimstone" to "be tormented day and night for ever and ever" (20:10). God's final triumph is presented as the creation of "a new heaven and a new earth" (21:1) in which "'he will wipe away every tear from their eyes, and death shall be no more, neither shall there be mourning nor crying nor pain any more, for the former things have passed away'" (20:4). The ravaged city of Jerusalem will be re-created in mythic splendor, a city arrayed as a bride for her marriage to the Lamb of God—that is, to Jesus, once the sacrificial victim led like a lamb to the slaughter, now enthroned forever in heaven.

The Book of Revelation makes a rather odd conclusion for the New Testament. Almost without exception, its allusions are to the Old Testament. It reads in some ways as the work of a Jew writing from within the long tradition of Jewish apocalyptic writing that came to a literally crashing end with the destruction of Jerusalem. The writer has clearly thrown in his lot with the Christians, but what he knows of Christianity he seems to know by hearsay or oral tradition. In its violence, too, the work might seem the very antithesis of "the peace of Christ" that had become the proto-Christian ideal. The unreal, phantasmagoric character of the work has circumscribed it in a world of its own, notwithstanding the fact that in every generation some Christians have labored to take it literally.

PRONOUNCING GLOSSARY

Alpha: *al´-fah*
Gog: *gohg*
Hades: *hay´-dees*

Magog: *mah-gohg´*
Omega: *oh-may´-gah*

REVELATION

20

(1) Then I saw an angel coming down from heaven, holding in his hand the key of the bottomless pit and a great chain. (2) And he seized the dragon, that ancient serpent, who is the Devil and Satan, and bound him for a thousand years, (3) and threw him into the pit, and shut it and sealed it over him, that he should deceive the nations no more, till the thousand years were ended. After that he must be loosed for a little while.

(4) Then I saw thrones, and seated on them were those to whom judgment was committed. Also I saw the souls of those who had been beheaded for their testimony to Jesus and for the word of God, and who had not worshiped the beast or its image and had not received its mark on their foreheads or their hands. They came to life, and reigned with Christ a thousand years.[1] (5) The rest of the dead did not come to life until the thousand years were ended. This is the first resurrection. (6) Blessed and holy is he who shares in the first resurrection! Over such the second death has no power, but they shall be priests of God and of Christ, and they shall reign with him a thousand years.

(7) And when the thousand years are ended, Satan will be loosed from his prison (8) and will come out to deceive the nations which are at the four corners of the earth, that is, Gog and Magog, to gather them for battle; their number is like the sand of the sea.[2] (9) And they marched up over the broad earth and surrounded the camp of the saints and the beloved city; but fire came down from heaven and consumed them,[3] (10) and the devil who had deceived them was thrown into the lake of fire and brimstone where the beast and the false prophet were, and they will be tormented day and night for ever and ever.

(11) Then I saw a great white throne and him who sat upon it; from his presence earth and sky fled away, and no place was found for them. (12) And I saw the dead, great and small, standing before the throne, and books were opened. Also another book was opened, which is the book of life. And the dead were judged by what was written in the books, by what they had done.[4] (13) And the sea gave up the dead in it, Death and Hades gave up the dead in them, and all were judged by what they had done. (14) Then Death and Hades were thrown into the lake of fire. This is the second death, the lake of fire; (15) and if any one's name was not found written in the book of life, he was thrown into the lake of fire.[5]

21:1–8

(1) Then I saw a new heaven and a new earth; for the first heaven and the first earth had passed away, and the sea was no more.[1] (2) And I saw the holy city, new Jerusalem, coming down out of heaven from God, prepared as a bride

FROM "Revelation" in *The Holy Bible, Containing the Old and New Testaments, Revised Standard Version: Catholic Edition.*

1. See Daniel 7:9, 22, 27.
2. See Ezekiel 38:2, 9, 15.
3. See 2 Kings 1:10–12.
4. See Daniel 7:9–10.
5. See Revelation 3:5.
1. See Isaiah 66:22.

adorned for her husband;[2] (3) and I heard a great voice from the throne saying, "Behold, the dwelling of God is with men. He will dwell with them, and they shall be his people, and God himself will be with them;[3] (4) he will wipe away every tear from their eyes, and death shall be no more, neither shall there be mourning nor crying nor pain any more, for the former things have passed away."[4]

(5) And he who sat upon the throne said, "Behold, I make all things new." Also he said, "Write this, for these words are trustworthy and true."[5] (6) And he said to me, "It is done! I am the Alpha and the Omega, the beginning and the end. To the thirsty I will give water without price from the fountain of the water of life.[6] (7) He who conquers shall have this heritage, and I will be his God and he shall be my son.[7] (8) But as for the cowardly, the faithless, the polluted, as for murderers, fornicators, sorcerers, idolaters, and all liars, their lot shall be in the lake that burns with fire and brimstone, which is the second death."

2. See Revelation 3:12.
3. See Ezekiel 37:27.
4. See Isaiah 25:8, 35:10.
5. See Isaiah 43:19.
6. See Isaiah 55:1.
7. See Psalms 89:27–28.

The Patristic Era
100–600 C.E.

THE BIRTH AND GROWTH OF THE FIRST CHRISTENDOM

The adjective *patristic* comes from the noun *patres*, Latin for "fathers." We think of the period of early Christianity as the Patristic Era, since the preponderant evidences of Christianity are found in the writings of the so-called fathers of the Church. In Greek, Latin, and Syriac, the fathers wrote works in an array of genres, from letters to technical theological treatises. Many of these writings were focused on the internal life of the Church. For example, literature of instruction was used to teach converts to the faith. With the rise of monasticism, a large body of writing was generated about how that form of Christianity should be practiced. Scribes recorded the sermons of some of the most important Church fathers, such as Saint John Chrysostom in the East and Saint Augustine in the West. In the mid-nineteenth century, the French priest Jacques-Paul Migne (1800–1875) edited a now-classic collection of some of the patristic literature: Migne compiled 221 volumes for the Latin fathers and 165 volumes for the Greek fathers. The Greek volumes include Latin translations, however, and so present much less original material than the Latin volumes do.

Understanding the nature and function of these various forms of early Christian literature helps

The Virgin Mary as the Mother of God: detail from southwestern entrance mosaic, Hagia Sophia, Istanbul. For the full image, see the color insert.

us understand the growth of Christianity in its cultural context, a context circumscribed by the Roman Empire.

Christianity was prohibited by the Roman authorities very early in its development. Christians reacted to this prohibition in two ways. When, beginning in the first century, Christians were martyred by the Romans, the communities saved testimonies of the martyrs in various forms. Subsequently, beginning in the second century, Christians wrote defenses of their own beliefs and practices. In rhetoric, such defenses are known as *apologies*, meaning "formal justifications." Over time, this Christian apologetic tradition yielded to polemics against pagan religion and against Jews who resisted the Christian claim that Jesus was the Messiah promised by the ancient Hebrew prophets.

Because not all Christian communities and individuals believed the same things about their faith, myriad schools of theological opinion produced a vast body of polemical literature. The early Church fathers struggled to sort out the authentic core of Christian belief, and their attempts led to the calling of ecumenical (general) councils of bishops, whose mission was to set out the rules of the faith. During the Patristic Era, several such councils were held. Their creedal statements—including the four excerpted here—summarize mountains of polemical literature.

In addition to these literary texts, the early Christian community created many liturgical texts. The word *liturgy* means public rite. As their worship became more public and more formalized, the Christians saw their liturgical language not just as pious words but as official statements of belief. An old saying has it that *lex orandi, lex credendi*, "the rule of worship is the rule of faith," and vice versa. Thus, to "excommunicate" Church members is to ban them from participating in the "members only" liturgy of the Eucharist.

Scripture was read in worship, but it was also studied as the basis for the claims and the worship practices of Christianity. In the late second century, such biblical study yielded a tradition of commentary on the Books of the Bible, a tradition that grew vast and has continued to this day. In both the Greek-speaking and Latin-speaking Churches, many of these commentaries were composed by bishops to be preached as sermons. In the early third century, Origen of Alexandria, a layman later ordained as a priest, worked diligently to establish a correct text of the Bible and wrote commentary on each Book. In this work, Origen was far ahead of his time. It has been said that he discussed every biblical textual crux (that is, difficult or unanswered question) ever known to scholars.

In addition to liturgical texts, hymns and poetry were composed for the edification of the faithful. Hymns and odes were, in fact, the chosen means of instruction in the Syriac-speaking Church. Saint Ephrem the Syrian and other theologians in the East wrote hymns that range over most of the themes of the Bible. In the West, Saint Ambrose of Milan wrote Latin hymns for his congregation that, in translation, may be found in Christian hymnals today.

During the Patristic Era, the vast majority of Christians did not own books, which were expensive and available only to an elite educated class. Thus, many of the works of the Patristic Era—especially sermons, commentaries on Scripture, and martyrdom stories—were *heard*, not read. That fact helps us appreciate the rhetorical character of so much of this literature, and it aids us in understanding the Apostle Paul's statement that "faith comes from hearing" (Romans 10:17).

Chronology

THE PATRISTIC ERA (100–600 C.E.)

ca. 80–120 *Didache*, earliest known Christian catechism/treatise

132–35 Second Jewish War; Jews again defeated by Romans and now banished from Jerusalem

ca. 155–56 Martyrdom of Polycarp

ca. 155–57 Justin Martyr writes *Apology*

ca. 160–75 *Diatessaron* (Greek, "[one] from the four"), first harmonization of the Gospels, by Assyrian-born Christian apologist Tatian

161–80 Persecution of Christians under Roman emperor Marcus Aurelius

ca. 150–200 Gnostic Gospel of Thomas written

203 Martyrdom of Felicity and Perpetua

235 Origen writes *Exhortation to Martyrdom*

249–51 Persecution of Christians under Roman emperor Decius

ca. 250 and after Eremetical monasticism well established in Egypt and Syria; Saint Anthony and desert fathers

284–305 Persecution of Christians under Roman emperor Diocletian

301 Armenia becomes first country to officially adopt Christianity

312 Roman emperor Constantine has vision of the cross at Battle of Milvian Bridge

313 Edict of Milan: Constantine legalizes Christianity

318–23 Saint Pachomius the Great founds first group-based Christian monastery in Egypt

ca. 324 Eusebius, bishop of Caesarea, writes *Church History*, first major history of Christianity

325 Council of Nicaea defines Jesus as "consubstantial" with God the Father

337 Death of Constantine the Great

361–63 Julian the Apostate, last pagan Roman emperor, tries and fails to revive paganism

367 Saint Athanasius of Alexandria lists all twenty-seven books of the New Testament

380 Emperor Theodosius makes Christianity the established religion of the Roman Empire

381 Council of Nicaea-Constantinople

383 Death of Ulfilas, who translated the Bible into Gothic

387 Baptism of Saint Augustine of Hippo

389–91 Roman emperor Theodosius bans paganism

ca. 400 Saint Jerome translates the Bible into Latin (Vulgate)

410 Rome sacked by the Visigoths; Saint Augustine writes *City of God*

431 Council of Ephesus: Mary declared *Theotokos*, the Mother of God

432? Saint Patrick leads mission to Ireland

451 Council of Chalcedon defines Jesus as having two natures, divine and human, in one person

476 Last Western Roman emperor, Romulus Augustus, deposed

496 Baptism of Clovis, king of the Franks and first Catholic king of France

525 Dionysius Exiguus, a monk, originates the custom of numbering years as before or after the birth of Christ

529 Saint Benedict of Nursia (Italy) founds Abbey of Monte Cassino; Rule of Saint Benedict written

537 Justinian inaugurates the Church of Hagia Sophia (Holy Wisdom), in Constantinople

589 Irish monk Columbanus leaves Ireland to found monasteries in France and Italy

ca. 589 Death of Saint David, bishop and patron saint of Wales

590–604 Pope Gregory the Great reforms liturgy, promotes missions

597 Saint Augustine of Canterbury begins mission to England

EARLY CHRISTIAN WORSHIP

As the New Testament makes clear, the early Christian communities gathered for prayer and worship (Acts 16:25). There is some evidence that the early Christian Jews maintained their ties to their local synagogues and, in Jerusalem, went to the great Temple. As tensions mounted between them and the rabbinical majority, these links to the ancestral faith slackened and then ruptured. Despite this break, Christians have always used the Book of Psalms as part of their prayer and Jewish Scriptures as part of their worship. In addition, some of the New Testament texts probably were shaped in part by their use in early Christian worship. For example, as discussed in "The Apostolic Era," the prologue of John's Gospel (John 1:1–18) and a hymn praising Jesus for "emptying himself" (Philippians 2:5–11) might have existed as hymns before being incorporated into the New Testament.

Christians have always seen worship as the symbolic expression of belief. As a consequence, they have always seen correct—"orthodox"—worship as inextricably tied to correct belief. However, the New Testament does not make clear how belief translated into worship for the earliest Christians—that is, we do not know how they performed their rites. Subsequent communities had three formal ceremonies: the ritual of initiation called baptism, the communal meal of bread and wine called the Eucharist, and the laying on of hands upon appointment to a spiritual office (i.e., a position of responsibility in the Church). In subsequent history, these rites became more formalized.

Who led early Christian worship? The New Testament mentions numerous ministries in a structured order (see 1 Corinthians 12:28–31). Governing the Church and providing liturgical leadership for its members, these ministers were the *bishop* (from the Greek for "superintendent"), who presided over a local church; his clergy, who were called *presbyters* (from the Greek for "elders"); and *deacons* (from the Greek for "servants"), who organized the charitable work of the church. This order, established by the first century, was clarified and solidified over time.

SAINT JUSTIN MARTYR
ca. 100–165

FROM THE APOLOGY

The man known as Justin Martyr was born in the city of Flavia Neapolis (today Nablus), in Palestine. His parents were pagans. After his conversion to Christianity, Justin became an itinerant philosopher, scholar, and teacher. In Rome, he started his own school. After a dispute with another philosopher, Justin was denounced to the Roman authorities as a Christian. He and several of his fellow Christians were tried and found guilty, flogged, and beheaded. Justin is considered a saint by the Roman Catholic Church and the Eastern Orthodox Church.

Of his works, only two Christian apologies and a dialogue survive. In these writings, Justin quotes or refers to numerous Books of the Bible. In his *Apology*, also known as the *First Apology*, written sometime between 150 and 155, Justin uses material from the three Synoptic Gospels (Matthew, Mark, and Luke). This long work argues for the value of Christianity and pleads with the Roman emperor Antoninus Pius (86–161; reigned from 138 until his death) to end the persecution of Christians.

The following selection describes early Christian baptism and Sunday worship in Rome. According to this text, those to be baptized were first instructed in what the community believed and then were asked for their assent to such belief. The Sunday worship consists of two parts: first, a proclamation of Scripture and reflections upon the scriptural passage in the form of a homily (sermon); second, the Eucharist. The Eucharistic minister was simply called the one "who presides." Justin also notes that the community contributed to a common purse to aid the needy. This purse is the source of the plate or basket still used for collection of donations in Christian churches.

PRONOUNCING GLOSSARY

Eucharist: *yoo´-kah-rist*   Pontius Pilate: *pon´-shus pai´-luht* [*ai* Mithraic: *mith-ray´-ic*   rhyming with *rye*]

FROM THE APOLOGY

CHAPTER 61

Those who are convinced and believe what we[1] say and teach is the truth, and pledge themselves to be able to live accordingly, are taught in prayer and fasting to ask God to forgive their past sins, while we pray and fast with them. Then we lead them to a place where there is water, and they are regenerated in the same manner in which we ourselves were regenerated. In the name of God, the Father and Lord of all, and of our Savior, Jesus Christ, and of the Holy Ghost, they then receive the washing with water. For Christ said: 'Unless you be born again, you shall not enter into the kingdom of heaven.'[2] Now, it is clear to everyone how impossible it is for those who have been born once to enter their mothers' wombs again. Isaias the Prophet[3] explained, as we already stated, how those who have sinned and then repented shall be freed of their sins. These are his words: 'Wash yourselves, be clean, banish sin from your souls; learn to do well: judge for the fatherless and defend the widow; and then come and let us reason together, saith the Lord. And if your sins be as scarlet, I will make them white as wool; and if they be red as crimson, I will make them white as snow. But if you will not hear me, the sword shall devour you: for the mouth of the Lord hath spoken it.'[4] And this is the reason, taught to us by the Apostles, why we baptize the way we do. We were totally unaware of our first birth, and were

TRANSLATED BY Thomas B. Falls. Bracketed insertions are the translator's.

1. The Christian community, with people such as Justin at its head. "Those who are convinced": new converts.
2. John 3:3.
3. Isaiah (active 742–701 B.C.E.), Old Testament

prophet regarded as a saint. Parts of the Book of Isaiah (see p. 101) are considered the prophet's own words, but the writings of later prophets have been attached to the Book.
4. Isaiah 1:16–29.

born of necessity from fluid seed through the mutual union of our parents, and were trained in wicked and sinful customs. In order that we do not continue as children of necessity and ignorance, but of deliberate choice and knowledge, and in order to obtain in the water the forgiveness of past sins, there is invoked over the one who wishes to be regenerated, and who is repentant of his sins, the name of God, the Father and Lord of all; he who leads the person to be baptized to the laver calls him by this name only. For, no one is permitted to utter the name of the ineffable God, and if any-one ventures to affirm that His name can be pronounced, such a person is hopelessly mad. This washing is called illumination, since they who learn these things become illuminated intellectually. Furthermore, the illuminated one is also baptized in the name of Jesus Christ, who was crucified under Pontius Pilate, and in the name of the Holy Spirit, who predicted through the Prophets everything concerning Jesus.

✻　　✻　　✻

CHAPTER 65

After thus baptizing the one who has believed and given his assent, we escort him to the place where are assembled those whom we call brethren, to offer up sincere prayers in common for ourselves, for the baptized person, and for all other persons wherever they may be, in order that, since we have found the truth, we may be deemed fit through our actions to be esteemed as good citizens and observers of the law, and thus attain eternal salvation. At the conclusion of the prayers we greet one another with a kiss. Then, bread and a chalice containing wine mixed with water are presented to the one presiding over the brethren. He takes them and offers praise and glory to the Father of all, through the name of the Son and of the Holy Spirit, and he recites lengthy prayers of thanksgiving to God in the name of those to whom He granted such favors. At the end of these prayers and thanksgiving, all present express their approval by saying 'Amen.' This Hebrew word, 'Amen,' means 'So be it.' And when he who presides has celebrated the Eucharist, they whom we call deacons permit each one present to partake of the Eucharistic bread, and wine and water; and they carry it also to the absentees.

CHAPTER 66

We call this food the Eucharist, of which only he can partake who has acknowledged the truth of our teachings, who has been cleansed by bap-tism for the remission of his sins and for his regeneration, and who regu-lates his life upon the principles laid down by Christ. Not as ordinary bread or as ordinary drink do we partake of them, but just as, through the word of God, our Savior Jesus Christ became Incarnate and took upon Himself flesh and blood for our salvation, so, we have been taught, the food which has been made the Eucharist by the prayer of His word,[5] and which nourishes our flesh and blood by assimilation, is both the flesh and blood of that

5. Not the Word of God but rather Jesus' words in consecrating the Host, or Eucharistic bread: "This is My Body; this is My Blood" (Luke 22:19; Matthew 26:26–27; Mark 14:22).

Jesus who was made flesh. The Apostles in their memoirs, which are called Gospels, have handed down what Jesus ordered them to do; that He took bread and, after giving thanks, said: 'Do this in remembrance of Me; this is My body.' In like manner, He took also the chalice, gave thanks, and said: 'This is My blood'; and to them only did He give it. The evil demons, in imitation of this, ordered the same thing to be performed in the Mithraic mysteries. For, as you know or may easily learn, bread and a cup of water, together with certain incantations, are used in their mystic initiation rites.[6]

CHAPTER 67

Henceforward, we constantly remind one another of these things. The rich among us come to the aid of the poor, and we always stay together. For all the favors we enjoy we bless the Creator of all, through His Son Jesus Christ and through the Holy Spirit. On the day which is called Sunday we have a common assembly of all who live in the cities or in the outlying districts, and the memoirs of the Apostles or the writings of the Prophets are read, as long as there is time. Then, when the reader has finished, the president of the assembly verbally admonishes and invites all to imitate such examples of virtue. Then we all stand up together and offer up our prayers, and, as we said before, after we finish our prayers, bread and wine and water are presented. He who presides likewise offers up prayers and thanksgivings, to the best of his ability, and the people express their approval by saying 'Amen.' The Eucharistic elements are distributed and consumed by those present, and to those who are absent they are sent through the deacons. The wealthy, if they wish, contribute whatever they desire, and the collection is placed in the custody of the president. [With it] he helps the orphans and widows, those who are needy because of sickness or any other reason, and the captives and strangers in our midst; in short, he takes care of all those in need. Sunday, indeed, is the day on which we all hold our common assembly because it is the first day on which God, transforming the darkness and [prime] matter, created the world; and our Savior Jesus Christ arose from the dead on the same day. For they crucified Him on the day before that of Saturn,[7] and on the day after, which is Sunday, He appeared to His Apostles and disciples, and taught them the things which we have passed on to you also for consideration.

---

6. Mithraism was a mystery cult (i.e., a cult devoted to mysteries, or secret religious rites) of Eastern origins, widespread in the Roman Empire. Its rites included a ceremonial meal. Its followers (exclusively male) worshipped the Persian sun god. *Mystery* has also come to mean a Christian sacrament, specifically the Eucharist.

7. Saturday, named for the Roman god Saturnus.

ANONYMOUS
early second century

THE DIDACHE

Didache is the Greek word for "teaching." The *Didache* is also known as the *Teaching of the Twelve Apostles*. This ancient handbook, in circulation possibly as early as 100 in Roman Syria, is a kind of instructional manual, or catechism, for use in a Christian community, many of whose members were recent or prospective converts from Greco-Roman polytheism. Its three main sections deal with Christian ethics, rites such as baptism and the Eucharist (including a very early Eucharistic prayer), and Church organization. Chapters 1–6, on the "Two Ways," are thought to be a sermon preached before a baptism. Chapters 7–10 present a ritual that includes baptism, fasting, and communion. Chapters 11–15 concern the ministry and dealing with traveling prophets. The final chapter, 16, is a brief apocalypse. With detailed information on many early Christian practices, the text provides a sense of how aspects of earlier Jewish belief and practice were transformed for the developing religion.

Considered but rejected as part of the New Testament canon, the *Didache* was lost for centuries. In the late nineteeth century, it was rediscovered and first translated into English.

PRONOUNCING GLOSSARY

Didache: *di´-dah-kay* Hosanna: *ho-sah´-nah*
Eucharist: *yoo´-kah-rist* Marana tha: *mah-rah´-nah thah*

THE DIDACHE
An Instruction of the Lord Given to the Heathen[1] by the Twelve Apostles

1. (1) Two Ways there are, one of Life and one of Death, and there is a great difference between the Two Ways.

(2) Now, the Way of Life is this: *first, love the God who made you; secondly, your neighbor as yourself*: do not do to another *what you do not wish to be done to yourself.*

(3) The lesson of these words is as follows: *bless those that curse you*, and *pray for your enemies*; besides, fast *for those that persecute you.* For *what thanks do you deserve when you love those that love you? Do not the heathen do as much?* For your part, *love those that hate you*; in fact, have no enemy. (4) *Abstain from gratifying the carnal* [and bodily] *impulses.* When anyone gives you a blow *on the right cheek, turn to him the other as well*, and *be*

TRANSLATED BY James A. Kleist. Bracketed insertions are the translator's; angle brackets have been converted to square brackets. The italicized words are Bible quotations.

1. Pagans (i.e., new converts).

perfect; when *anyone forces you to go one mile with him, go two with him;* when anyone takes *your cloak* away, give *him your coat also;* when anyone robs you of *your property, demand no return.* You really cannot do it. (5) *Give to anyone that asks you, and demand no return;* the Father wants His own bounties to be shared with all. Happy the giver who complies with the commandment, for he goes unpunished. Trouble is in store for the receiver: if someone who is in need receives, he will go unpunished; but he who is not in need will have to stand trial as to why and for what purpose he received; and, if he is thrown into prison, he will be questioned about his conduct, and *will not be released from that place until he has paid the last penny.* (6) However, in this regard, there is also a word of Scripture: *Let your alms sweat in your hands until you find out to whom to give.*

2. (1) A further commandment of the Teaching: (2) *Do not murder; do not commit adultery;* do not practice pederasty; do not fornicate; *do not steal;* do not deal in magic; do not practice sorcery; do not kill a fetus by abortion, or commit infanticide. *Do not covet your neighbor's goods.* (3) *Do not perjure yourself; do not bear false witness;* do not calumniate; do not bear malice. (4) Do not be double-minded or double-tongued, for a double tongue is *a deadly snare.* (5) Your speech must not be false or meaningless, but made good by action. (6) Do not be covetous, or rapacious, or hypocritical, or malicious, or arrogant. Do not have designs upon your neighbor. (7) Hate no man; but correct some, pray for others, for still others sacrifice your life as a proof of your love.

3. (1) My child, shun evil of any kind and everything resembling it. (2) Do not be prone to anger, for anger leads to murder. Do not be fanatical, not quarrelsome, not hot-tempered; for all these things beget murder. (3) My child, do not be lustful, for lust leads to fornication. Do not be foul-mouthed or give free rein to your eyes; for all these things beget adultery. (4) My child, do not be an augur, because it leads to idolatry. Do not be an enchanter, not an astrologer, not an expiator,[2] and do not wish to see [and hear] these things, for they all beget idolatry. (5) My child, do not be a liar, for lying leads to theft. Do not be a lover of money, or a vain pretender. All these things beget thievery. (6) My child, do not be a grumbler, because it leads to blasphemy; or self-willed, or evil-minded. All these things beget blasphemy.

(7) On the contrary, be gentle, for *the gentle will inherit the land.* (8) Be long-suffering, and merciful, and guileless, and quiet, and good, and *with trembling treasure* forever *the instructions* you have received. (9) Do not carry your head high, or open your heart to presumption. Do not be on intimate terms with the mighty, but associate with holy and lowly folk. (10) Accept as blessings the casualties that befall you, assured that nothing happens without God.

4. (1) My child, day and night *remember him who preaches God's word to you,* and honor him as the Lord, for where His lordship is spoken of, there

---

2. In this list of pagan religious functionaries, a priest who performed a spiritual cleansing after ritual or moral pollution.

is the Lord. (2) Seek daily contact with the saints to be refreshed by their discourses. (3) Do not start a schism, but pacify contending parties. *Be just in your judgment*: make no distinction between man and man when correcting transgressions. (4) Do not waver in your decision.

(5) Do not be one that opens his hands to receive, but shuts them when it comes to giving. (6) If you have means at your disposal, pay a ransom for your sins. (7) Do not hesitate to give, and do not give in a grumbling mood. You will find out who is the good Rewarder. (8) Do not turn away from the needy; rather, share everything with your brother, and do not say: "It is private property." If you are sharers in what is imperishable, how much more so in the things that perish!

(9) Do not withdraw your hand from your son or your daughter, but from their youth teach them the fear of God. (10) Do not, when embittered, give orders to your slave, male or female, for they hope in the same God; otherwise, they might lose the fear of God, who is the Master of both of you. He surely is not coming to call with an eye to rank and station in life; no, He comes to those whom the Spirit has prepared. (11) But you, slaves, be submissive to your masters as to God's image in reverence and fear.

(12) Abhor all sham and whatever is not pleasing to the Lord. (13) Do not by any means neglect the *commandments of the Lord*, but *hold fast* to the traditions, *neither adding nor subtracting anything*. (14) In church confess your sins, and do not come to your prayer with a guilty conscience.

Such is the Way of Life.

5. (1) The Way of Death is this. First of all, it is wicked and altogether accursed: *murders, adulteries*, lustful desires, *fornications, thefts, idolatries*, magical arts, *sorceries*, robberies, *false testimonies*, hypocrisy, duplicity, *fraud, pride, malice*, surliness, *covetousness*, foul talk, jealousy, rashness, haughtiness, *false pretensions*, [the lack of the fear of God]. (2) It is the way of persecutors of the good, haters of the truth, lovers of falsehood; of men ignorant of the reward for right living, not *devoted to what is good* or to just judgment, intent upon not what is good but what is evil; of strangers to gentleness and patient endurance; of *men who love vanities*, and *fee hunters*; of men that have no heart for the poor, are not concerned about the oppressed, do not know their Maker; *of murderers of children*, destroyers of God's image; of men that turn away from the needy, oppress the afflicted, act as counsels for the rich, are unjust judges of the poor—in a word, of men steeped in sin. Children, may you be preserved from all this!

6. (1) See *that no man leads you astray* from this Way of the Teaching, since any other teaching takes you away from God. (2) Surely, if you are able to bear the Lord's yoke in its entirety, you will be perfect; if you are not able, then do what you can. (3) And in the matter of food, do what you can stand; but be scrupulously on your guard against meat offered to idols; for that is a worship of dead gods.

7. (1) Regarding baptism. Baptize as follows: after first explaining all these points, *baptize in the name of the Father and of the Son and of the Holy Spirit*, in running water. (2) But if you have no running water, baptize in other water; and if you cannot in cold, then in warm. (3) But if you have neither,

pour water on the head three times *in the name of the Father and of the Son and of the Holy Spirit*. (4) Before the baptism, let the baptizer and the candidate for baptism fast, as well as any others that are able. Require the candidate to fast one or two days previously.

8. (1) Your *fasts* should not coincide with those of *the hypocrites*. They fast on Mondays and Tuesdays; you should fast on Wednesdays and Fridays. (2) And do not *pray as the hypocrites do*, but pray as the Lord has commanded in the Gospel:

> *Our Father, who art in heaven; hallowed be Thy name; Thy kingdom come; Thy will be done on earth as it is in heaven; give us this day our daily bread, and forgive us our debts as we also forgive our debtors; and lead us not into temptation, but deliver us from evil; for* Thine is the power and the glory for evermore.[3]

(3) Say this prayer three times a day.

9. (1) Regarding the Eucharist. Give thanks as follows: (2) First, concerning the cup:

> "We give Thee thanks, Our Father,
> for the Holy Vine of David[4] Thy servant,
> which Thou hast made known to us
> through Jesus, Thy Servant."

> "To Thee be the glory for evermore."

(3) Next, concerning the broken bread:

> "We give Thee thanks, Our Father,
> for the life and knowledge
> which Thou hast made known to us
> through Jesus, Thy Servant."

> "To Thee be the glory for evermore."

> (4) "As this broken bread was scattered over the hills
> and then, when gathered, became one mass,
> so may Thy Church be gathered
> from the ends of the earth into Thy Kingdom."

> "For Thine is the glory and the power
> through Jesus Christ for evermore."

(5) Let no one eat and drink of your Eucharist but those baptized in the name of the Lord; to this, too, the saying of the Lord is applicable: *Do not give to dogs what is sacred.*

---

3. This version of the Lord's Prayer differs from the version in Matthew (6:9–13) by adding the final verse after "deliver us from evil." Most Protestant Churches include another version of this verse, known as the doxology ("For thine is the kingdom and the power and the glory for ever and ever. Amen"), which derives from an inferior Byzantine manuscript of Matthew.

4. King David (ca. 1040–970 B.C.E.), second king of the United Kingdom of Israel (ca. 1003–970 B.C.E.). According to tradition, David was divinely elected; according to the Gospels of Matthew and Luke, he was an ancestor of Jesus Christ through Joseph.

10. (1) After you have taken your fill of food, give thanks as follows:

> (2) "We give Thee thanks, O Holy Father,
> for Thy holy name
> which Thou hast enshrined in our hearts,
> and for the knowledge and faith and immortality
> which Thou hast made known to us
> through Jesus, Thy Servant."

> "To Thee be the glory for evermore."

> (3) "Thou, Lord Almighty,
> *hast created all things* for the sake of Thy name
> and hast given food and drink for men to enjoy,
> that they may give thanks to Thee;
> but to us Thou hast vouchsafed spiritual food and
>   drink and eternal life
> through [Jesus], Thy Servant."

> (4) "Above all, we give Thee thanks
> because Thou art mighty."

> "To Thee be the glory for evermore."

> (5) "Remember, O Lord, Thy Church:
> deliver her from all evil,
> perfect her in Thy love,
> and *from the four winds assemble* her, the sanctified,
>   in Thy kingdom
> which Thou hast prepared for her."

> "For Thine is the power and the glory for evermore."

> (6) "May Grace come, and this world pass away!"
> "*Hosanna to the God of David!*"
> "If anyone is holy, let him advance; if anyone is
> not, let him be converted. *Marana tha!*"[5]
> "Amen."

(7) But permit the prophets[6] to give thanks as much as they desire.

11. (1) Accordingly, when an itinerant teaches you all that has just been said, welcome him. (2) But should the teacher himself be a turncoat and teach a different doctrine so as to undermine (this teaching), do not listen to him. But if he promotes holiness and knowledge of the Lord, welcome him as the Lord.

(3) Now, as regards the apostles and prophets, act strictly according to the precept of the Gospel. (4) Upon his arrival every apostle must be welcomed as the Lord; (5) but he must not stay except one day. In case of necessity, however, he may stay the next day also; but if he stays three days, he is a false

---

5. Come, Lord! (ancient Aramaic).
6. Evidently this ancient Christian community included "prophets" who prayed ecstatically under the impulse of the Holy Spirit.

prophet.[7] (6) At his departure the apostle must receive nothing except food to last till the next night's lodging; but if he asks for money, he is a false prophet.

(7) Moreover, if any prophet speaks in ecstasy, do not test him or entertain any doubts; for *any sin may be forgiven*, but this sin *cannot be forgiven*. (8) However, not everyone speaking in ecstasy is a prophet, except he has the ways of the Lord about him. So by their ways must the true and the false prophet be distinguished. (9) No prophet who in an ecstasy orders the table spread, must partake of it; otherwise, he is a false prophet. (10) Any prophet that teaches the truth, yet does not live up to his teaching, is a false prophet. (11) When a prophet, once approved as genuine, does something by way of symbolizing the Church in an earthly manner, yet does not instruct others to do all that he himself is doing, he is not liable to your judgment, for his judgment rests with God. After all, the Prophets of old acted in the same manner. (12) But if anyone says in ecstasy, "Give me money," or something else, you must not listen to him. However, should he tell you to give something for others who are in need, let no one condemn him.

12. (1) Anyone *coming in the name of the Lord* must be welcomed; but, after that, test him and find out—you will of course use your discretion either for or against him. (2) If the arrival is a transient visitor, assist him as much as you can, but he may not stay with you more than two days, or, if necessary, three. (3) But if he intends to settle among you, then, in case he is a craftsman, let him work for his living; (4) if he has no trade or craft, use your judgment in providing for him, so that a follower of Christ will not live idle in your midst. (5) But if he is not satisfied with this arrangement, he is a Christmonger.[8] Be on your guard against such people.

13. (1) Every genuine prophet who is willing to settle among you *is entitled to his support*. (2) Likewise, every genuine teacher is, like *a laborer, entitled to his support*. (3) Therefore, take all first fruits of vintage and harvest, of cattle and sheep, and give these first fruits to the prophets; for they are your high priests. (4) But if you have no prophet, give them to the poor. (5) When you bake bread, take the first loaf and give it according to the commandment. (6) Likewise, when you open a fresh jar of wine or oil, take the first draught and give it to the prophets. (7) Of money and cloth and any other possession, first set aside a portion according to your discretion and give it according to the commandment.

14. (1) On the Lord's own day,[9] assemble in common to break bread and offer thanks; but first confess your sins, so that your sacrifice may be pure. (2) However, no one quarreling with his brother may join your meeting until they are reconciled; your sacrifice must not be defiled. (3) For here we have the saying of the Lord: *In every place and time offer me a pure sacrifice; for I am a mighty King, says the Lord; and my name spreads terror among the nations.*

---

7. These apostles were not Jesus' Twelve Apostles. They were itinerant preachers who witnessed to the truth of the Christian message. This community desired that they not stay in one place but rather continue their journeys as missionaries.

8. A peddler of Christ; i.e., a preacher more interested in earning his living than in spreading the Gospel.
9. Sunday.

15. (1) Accordingly, elect for yourselves bishops and deacons, men who are an honor to the Lord, of gentle disposition, not attached to money, honest and well-tried; for they, too, render you the sacred service of the prophets and teachers. (2) Do not, then, despise them; after all, they are your dignitaries together with the prophets and teachers.

(3) Furthermore, correct one another, not in anger, but in composure, as you have it in the Gospel; and when anyone offends his neighbor, let no one speak with him—in fact, he should not even be talked about by you—until he has made amends. (4) As regards your prayers and alms and your whole conduct, do exactly as you have it in the Gospel of Our Lord.

16. (1) *Watch* over your life; *your lamps* must not go out, nor *your loins* be ungirded; on the contrary, *be ready. You do not know the hour in which Our Lord is coming.* (2) Assemble in great numbers, intent upon what concerns your souls. Surely, of no use will your lifelong faith be to you if you are not perfected at the end of time. (3) For in the last days[1] the false prophets and corrupters will come in swarms; the sheep will turn into wolves, and love will turn into hate. (4) When lawlessness is on the increase, men will hate and persecute and betray one another; and then the Deceiver of this world[2] will appear, claiming to be the Son of God, and give *striking exhibitions of power;* the earth will be given over into his hands, and he will perpetrate outrages such as have never taken place since the world began. (5) Then humankind will undergo the fiery test, and *many will lose their faith* and perish; but *those who stand firm* in their faith will be saved by none other than the Accursed.[3] (6) *And then the proofs* of the truth *will appear;* the first proof, an opening in the heavens; the next proof, *the sounding of the trumpet;* and the third, the resurrection of the dead—(7) not of all indeed, but in accordance with the saying: *The Lord will come and all the saints with Him.* (8) *Finally,* the world *will behold* the Lord *riding the clouds in the sky.*

---

1. "Last days": a Gospel phrase meaning the end of the world, just before Judgment.
2. The Deceiver is Satan (from Revelation 20:7–8).
3. Jesus; see Deuteronomy 21:22–23.

EGERIA
late fourth century

FROM THE TRAVELS OF EGERIA

By the mid-fourth century, Roman emperors had officially acknowledged Christianity. Indeed, they encouraged Christians—clergy and laypeople—to make pilgrimages to Jerusalem and the Holy Land around it. Probably in the early 380s, an educated woman named Egeria, Etheria, or even Sylvia made such a pilgrimage. She may have been a native of Galicia, in northwestern Spain. Her journey lasted over three years and took her through much of the eastern Roman Empire. We do not know if she ever returned home.

At some point, apparently after her return to Constantinople from Jerusalem, the woman generally known as Egeria wrote a letter in Vulgar (i.e., vernacular) Latin to a circle of women in her home region. In her letter, Egeria sought to describe exactly what she had seen and how those things differed from what she had previously known. She was not the first Christian pilgrim to describe such a trip, but Egeria's travel report may have been the first formal writing by a Christian woman in western Europe.

Perhaps as little as a third of her letter, covering about four months, has survived, and that is in a fragmentary later copy. The document is known as *Itinerarium Egeriae* (Travels of Egeria) or *Peregrinatio Aetheriae* (Pilgrimage of Aetheria) or *Peregrinatio ad Loca Sancta* (Pilgrimage to the Holy Places), and most of what we know about it comes from Valerio of Bierzo, also known as Valerius, a seventh-century Galician monk. In a letter to his fellow monks, Valerius described the work, including some of the parts that are lost. Different copies of his letter use the different names for the pilgrim, whom he identifies as a nun.

Egeria addresses her readers as *sorores* (Latin for "sisters") as a nun would, but at the time lay Christians commonly referred to their fellow believers as "sisters" and "brothers." She appears to have been financially self-sufficient and to have had more social freedom than most women of the time would have enjoyed, but lay women and nuns occasionally made lone pilgrimages.

The surviving part of her letter, the middle, begins after Egeria has traveled from Constantinople to Jerusalem, where she has stayed for three years. It ends during her description of the liturgical practices in the churches at Jerusalem. In the following selection, Egeria provides a first-hand account of how people were instructed during the Lenten season (the 40-day period of penitence and fasting between Ash Wednesday and Easter) before they were baptized by the presiding bishop on the eve of Easter Sunday. Egeria's description of these elaborate and formalized practices is invaluable because it helps document the development of the Christian liturgy. Annual Easter worship became universal among Christians at the end of the fourth century.

PRONOUNCING GLOSSARY

Anastasis: *ah-nah´-stah-sis*
catechesis: *ca-tuh-kee´-suhs*
catechumens: *ca-tuh-kyoo´-muhns*

Egeria: *e-gee´-ree-uh*
Martyrium: *mahr-tir´-ee-uhm*

FROM THE TRAVELS OF EGERIA

As they come in one by one,[1] the bishop asks their neighbours questions about them: "Is this person leading a good life? Does he respect his parents? Is he a drunkard or a boaster?" He asks about all the serious human vices. And if his inquiries show him that someone has not committed any of these misdeeds, he himself puts down his name; but if someone is guilty he is told to go away, and the bishop tells him that he is to amend his ways before he may come to the font. He asks the men and the women the same questions. But it is not too easy for a visitor to come to baptism if he has no witnesses who are acquainted with him.

Now, ladies and sisters, I want to write something which will save you from thinking all this is done without due explanation. They have here the

TRANSLATED BY John Wilkinson.

1. Egeria refers to those who, just before the Lenten season, have put their names on a list for baptism.

custom that those who are preparing for baptism during the season of the Lenten fast go to be exorcized by the clergy first thing in the morning, directly after the morning dismissal in the Anastasis.[2] As soon as that has taken place, the bishop's chair is placed in the Great Church, the Martyrium, and all those to be baptized, the men and the women, sit round him in a circle. There is a place where the fathers and mothers stand, and any of the people who want to listen (the faithful, of course) can come in and sit down, though not catechumens,[3] who do not come in while the bishop is teaching.

His subject is God's Law; during the forty days he goes through the whole Bible, beginning with Genesis, and first relating the literal meaning of each passage, then interpreting its spiritual meaning. He also teaches them at this time all about the resurrection and the faith. And this is called *catechesis*.[4] After five weeks' teaching they receive the Creed, whose content he explains article by article in the same way as he explained the Scriptures, first literally and then spiritually. Thus all the people in these parts are able to follow the Scriptures when they are read in church, since there has been teaching on all the Scriptures from six to nine in the morning all through Lent, three hours' catechesis a day. At ordinary services when the bishop sits and preaches, ladies and sisters, the faithful utter exclamations, but when they come and hear him explaining the catechesis, their exclamations are far louder, God is my witness; and when it is related and interpreted like this they ask questions on each point.

At nine o'clock they are dismissed from Catechesis, and the bishop is taken with singing straight to the Anastasis. So the dismissal is at nine, which makes three hours' teaching a day for seven weeks. But in the eighth, known as the Great Week, there is no time for them to have their teaching if they are to carry out all the services I have described. So when seven weeks have gone by, and only the week of Easter remains, the one which people here call the Great Week, the bishop comes early into the Great Church, the Martyrium. His chair is placed at the back of the apse, behind the altar, and one by one the candidates go up to the bishop, men with their fathers and women with their mothers, and repeat the Creed to him. When they have done so, the bishop speaks to them all as follows: "During these seven weeks you have received instruction in the whole biblical Law. You have heard about the faith, and the resurrection of the body. You have also learned all you can as catechumens of the content of the Creed. But the teaching about baptism itself is a deeper mystery, and you have not the right to hear it while you remain catechumens. Do not think it will never be explained; you will hear it all during the eight days of Easter after you have been baptized. But so long as you are catechumens you cannot be told God's deep mysteries."

Then Easter comes, and during the eight days from Easter Day to the eighth day, after the dismissal has taken place in the church and they have come with singing into the Anastasis, it does not take long to say the prayer

2. Greek for "resurrection"; a part of the Church of the Holy Sepulchre, the church complex honoring the Resurrection of Christ built by the emperor Constantine and his mother, Helena, early in the 4th century. The site is venerated as including both the place where Jesus was crucified and the place where he rose.
3. Christian converts receiving the catechism, or oral religious instruction, before being baptized.
4. The word *catechism* comes from the Greek word *katekhizen*, "to instruct orally" or "to teach by word of mouth."

and bless the faithful; then the bishop stands leaning against the inner screen in the cave of the Anastasis, and interprets all that takes place in Baptism. The newly-baptized come into the Anastasis, and any of the faithful who wish to hear the Mysteries; but, while the bishop is teaching, no catechumen comes in, and the doors are kept shut in case any try to enter. The bishop relates what has been done, and interprets it, and, as he does so, the applause is so loud that it can be heard outside the church. Indeed the way he expounds the mysteries and interprets them cannot fail to move his hearers.

In this province there are some people who know both Greek and Syriac,[5] but others know only one or the other. The bishop may know Syriac, but he never uses it. He always speaks in Greek, and has a presbyter beside him who translates the Greek into Syriac, so that everyone can understand what he means. Similarly the lessons read in church have to be read in Greek, but there is always someone in attendance to translate into Syriac so that the people understand. Of course there are also people here who speak neither Greek nor Syriac, but Latin. But there is no need for them to be discouraged, since some of the brothers or sisters who speak Latin as well as Greek will explain things to them. And what I admire and value most is that all the hymns and antiphons and readings they have, and all the prayers the bishop says, are always relevant to the day which is being observed and to the place in which they are used. They never fail to be appropriate.

5. An ancient Aramaic language once spoken by Syrian Christians.

SAINT JOHN CHRYSOSTOM
ca. 347–407

FROM THE EUCHARISTIC PRAYER
IN THE BYZANTINE LITURGY

Born in Antioch to Greco-Syrian parents, the man known as John Chrysostom became the archbishop of Constantinople (398–404), where he attempted to reform the clergy and was eventually banished for his challenges to authority. His surname is the Anglicized form of *Chrysostomos* ("golden-mouthed"), which he was given at some point during or after his life because of his eloquence. He is venerated as a saint by various Orthodox and Catholic Churches, including the Roman Catholic Church; some Anglican provinces; and parts of the Lutheran Church.

John's most famous writings include hundreds of homilies, or short sermons, on Books of the Old and New Testaments. In addition to treatises on theological topics such as monastic life, the instruction of catechumens, and the human inability to fully comprehend the divine, he wrote homilies denouncing Jews and so-called Judaizing Christians (i.e., ones who adhered to Mosaic Law).

The Byzantine Liturgy, also known as the Divine Liturgy of Saint John Chrysostom, is the most celebrated divine liturgy of the Byzantine Church. It was probably used originally by the School of Antioch, then revised in Constantinople under John's guidance (and thus is attributed to him). The following selection from the liturgy is the prayer at the heart of early Christian worship. It is used on most of the Sundays of the year in the Orthodox Church, commonly known as the Greek or Eastern

Orthodox Church. This prayer is strikingly more elaborate than both the restrained Eucharistic prayer found in the *Didache* and the sober Roman Catholic Mass. The italic "stage directions" are not part of the original text, but dialogue is built into the very nature of liturgy: The priest speaks to, as well as for, the people.

PRONOUNCING GLOSSARY

Anaphora: *an-a´-for-uh*   Hosanna: *ho-sah´-nah*
Cherubim: *chair´-oo-bim*   Sabaoth: *sah´-bah-ohth*
Chrysostom: *cris´-suhs-tuhm*   Seraphim: *sehr´-uh-fim*

FROM THE EUCHARISTIC PRAYER
IN THE BYZANTINE LITURGY
The Anaphora[1]

Deacon: Let us stand aright! Let us stand with fear! Let us attend, that we may offer the Holy Oblation in peace.

Choir: A mercy of peace! A sacrifice of praise!

The Deacon returns to the Altar. The Priest blesses the faithful:

Priest: The grace of our Lord Jesus Christ, the love of God the Father, and the communion of the Holy Spirit be with all of you.

Choir: And with your spirit.

Priest: Let us lift up our hearts.

Choir: We lift them up unto the Lord.

Priest: Let us give thanks unto the Lord.

Choir: It is meet and right to worship the Father, and the Son, and the Holy Spirit: the Trinity, one in essence, and undivided.

The Priest prays:

Priest: It is meet and right to hymn Thee, to bless Thee, to praise Thee, to give thanks to Thee, and to worship Thee in every place of Thy dominion: for Thou art God ineffable, inconceivable, invisible, incomprehensible, ever-existing and eternally the same. Thou and Thine only-begotten Son and Thy Holy Spirit. Thou it was who brought us from non-existence into being and, when

---

FROM *Service Books of the Orthodox Church*, vol. 1: *The Divine Liturgy of St. John Chrysostom.*

1. Offering (Greek); in Eastern Christianity, the term commonly applied to the central prayer of the Eucharistic liturgy.

we had fallen away, didst raise us up again, and didst not cease to do all things until Thou hadst brought us up to heaven, and hadst endowed us with Thy Kingdom which is to come. For all these things we give thanks to Thee, and to Thine only-begotten Son, and to Thy Holy Spirit; for all things of which we know and of which we know not, whether manifest or unseen; and we thank Thee for this Liturgy which Thou hast deigned to accept at our hands, though there stand by Thee thousands of arch-angels and hosts of angels, the Cherubim and the Seraphim,[2] six-winged, many-eyed, who soar aloft, borne on their pinions:

Singing the triumphant hymn, shouting, proclaiming and saying:

As the Priest chants the above, the Deacon touches the paten with each of the points of the star (making the sign of the Cross—east, west, north and south),[3] then kisses it and lays it aside; he goes to the right side of the Holy Table.

Choir: Holy! Holy! Holy! Lord of Sabaoth![4] Heaven and earth are full of Thy glory! Hosanna in the highest! Blessed is He that comes in the name of the Lord! Hosanna in the highest!

The Priest prays:

Priest: With these blessed powers, O Master who lovest mankind, we also cry aloud and say: Holy art Thou and all-holy, Thou and Thine only-begotten Son and Thy Holy Spirit! Holy art Thou and all-holy, and magnificent is Thy glory! Who hast so loved Thy world as to give Thine only-begotten Son, that whoever believes in Him should not perish but have everlasting life; who, when He had come and had fulfilled all the dispensation for us, in the night in which He was given up—or rather, gave Himself up for the life of the world—took bread in His holy, pure, and blameless hands; and when He had given thanks and blessed it, and hallowed it, and broken it, He gave it to His holy disciples and apostles, saying:

Take! Eat! This is My Body which is broken for you, for the remission of sins.

As the Priest says the above words, the Deacon points to the paten with his stole.[5]

2. In the traditional Christian celestial hierarchy of angels (spiritual beings), angels are the lowest order. Archangels are one step up from them. Cherubim are next-to-highest, and seraphim are highest.
3. The paten is a shallow dish used to hold the bread for the liturgy. In the Eastern Orthodox and Greek-Catholic Churches, the paten is called a *diskos*. Atop the *diskos* is a small frame called the asterisk or star-cover. Symbolizing the Star of Bethlehem (the star that signaled the birth of Jesus), the asterisk consists of two metal strips laid one on top of the other, joined in the center, and able to be turned perpendicular to each other and arched to form a standing cross. In the Greek-Catholic Church, a small star is suspended from the asterisk. In the Eastern Orthodox Church, the asterisk is considered a star. The sacred vessels for the Eucharist, such as the paten (*diskos*) and the asterisk, are usually kept on the Prothesis, or Table of Oblation, here called the Holy Table.
4. Hosts or Armies (Hebrew); used almost exclusively in titles of majesty for God (i.e., "Lord of [Heavenly] Hosts").
5. A liturgical vestment that consists of a narrow cloth band, often highly decorated; worn around the neck with the bands hanging down the chest.

Priest: And likewise, after supper, He took the cup, saying:

            Drink of it, all of you! This is My Blood of the New Testament, which is shed for you and for many, for the remission of sins!

Choir: Amen.

As the Priest says the above words, the Deacon points to the chalice with his stole.

Priest: Remembering this saving commandment and all those things which have come to pass for us: the Cross, the Tomb, the Resurrection on the third day, the Ascension into heaven, the Sitting at the right hand, and the second and glorious Coming.

The Deacon crosses his right hand over his left, and elevates the Holy Gifts.[6]

Priest: Thine own of Thine own we offer unto Thee, on behalf of all and for all.

Choir: We praise Thee. We bless Thee. We give thanks unto Thee, O Lord. And we pray unto Thee, O our God.

The Priest, bowing his head, prays:

Priest: Again we offer unto Thee this reasonable and bloodless worship, and ask Thee, and pray Thee, and supplicate Thee: Send down Thy Holy Spirit upon us and upon these Gifts here offered.

The Priest and the Deacon bow three times before the Holy Table as they say:

Priest: O Lord, who didst send down Thy Most Holy Spirit upon Thine apostles at the third hour:[7] Take Him not from us, O Good One, but renew Him in us who pray to Thee.

Deacon: Create in me a clean heart, O God, and put a new and right spirit within me.

Priest: O Lord, who didst send down Thy Most Holy Spirit upon Thine apostles at the third hour: Take Him not from us, O Good One, but renew Him in us who pray to Thee.

Deacon: Cast me not away from Thy presence, and take not Thy Holy Spirit from me.

---

6. In the Eastern Orthodox Church and the Eastern Catholic Churches, a term for the consecrated elements (i.e., the bread once it has been turned to flesh and the wine once it has been turned to blood).

7. In an event representing the birth of the Church, the Holy Spirit descended on and inspired Jesus' Twelve Apostles at "the third hour of the day" (Acts 2:15), i.e., at 9 A.M. This event is commemorated by the Christian feast day of Pentecost, the seventh Sunday after Easter.

Priest: O Lord, who didst send down Thy Most Holy Spirit upon Thine
            apostles at the third hour: Take Him not from us, O Good One,
            but renew Him in us who pray to Thee.

The Deacon points to the paten with his stole, saying:

Deacon: Bless, Master, the Holy Bread.

The Priest blesses the Holy Bread with the Sign of the Cross, saying:

Priest: And make this Bread the precious Body of Thy Christ.

Deacon: Amen.

The Deacon points to the chalice with his stole, saying:

Deacon: Bless, Master, the Holy Cup.

The Priest blesses the Holy Cup with the Sign of the Cross, saying:

Priest: And that which is in this Cup the precious Blood of Thy Christ.

Deacon: Amen.

The Deacon points to both, saying:

Deacon: Bless both, Master.

The Priest blesses the Holy Gifts, saying:

Priest: Making the change by Thy Holy Spirit.

Deacon: Amen. Amen. Amen.

The Deacon bows his head to the Priest and says:

Deacon: Remember me, a sinner, holy Master.

Priest: May the Lord God remember you in His Kingdom always, now
            and ever and unto ages of ages.

Deacon: Amen.

The Priest makes a low bow before the Holy Table and continues praying:

Priest: That they may be to those who partake for the purification of
            soul, for the remission of sins, for the communion of Thy Holy
            Spirit, for the fulfillment of the Kingdom of Heaven, for bold-
            ness towards Thee, and not for judgment or condemnation.

✻　✻　✻

The Priest prays:

Priest:[8]   [Unto Thee we commend our whole life and our hope, O Master who lovest mankind. We ask Thee, and pray Thee, and supplicate Thee: Make us worthy to partake of the heavenly and awesome Mysteries of this sacred and spiritual table with a pure conscience: for remission of sins, for forgiveness of transgressions, for the communion of the Holy Spirit, for the inheritance of the Kingdom of Heaven, for boldness towards Thee, but not for judgment or condemnation.]

---

8. The following prayer is bracketed because the priest says it in a low voice, inaudible to the congregation.

THE ROMAN PERSECUTIONS

From the middle of the first century until the early fourth century, the Roman government periodically persecuted the Christian Church as an outlawed movement. These persecutions began locally and became empire-wide. At their base was a Roman law, ascribed to the first-century emperor Nero, that forbade anyone to profess the name of Christian. When Christians brought before Roman courts were unwilling to renounce Christianity, they were found guilty and typically executed. Their executions were often—in the Roman manner—grisly.

Since the Romans generally tolerated religious beliefs that differed from their own, why did they treat Christianity with such hostility? At the heart of Roman civilization was the virtue of *pietas*—"duty" or "devotion." Children were expected to show this mixture of love and fear within the family, the family was expected to show it toward the state, and the state was expected to show it toward the pantheon of gods. The Romans believed that *pietas* produced societal harmony, "the peace of the gods." By contrast, they were ready to blame every major problem in the Empire on a lack of harmony with the gods. In refusing to honor the pantheon, Christians threatened the common good. They were considered treasonous enemies of the state. The persecution of Christians intensified in the late third and early fourth centuries, when the Empire suffered terrible internal problems (vast unemployment, civic unrest, inflation) and external ones (continuing barbarian invasions across the imperial boundaries).

The Christians viewed their persecution by the Romans as an extension of Jesus' arrest and execution by Roman authorities. By being persecuted, in other words, they were honoring the life and legacy of the Anointed One. The stories of Christian martyrs became central to Christian identity. The dates of martyrs' deaths were recorded, their burial places were honored, and their intercession on Earth was prayed for. Many later Christian practices—such as the keeping of shrines to the martyrs, the veneration of saints, and the honoring of relics—derive from this period of persecution. In turn, these later practices helped shape the designs of churches, the particular events of the liturgical calendar, and other aspects of Christianity.

TACITUS
ca. 56–ca. 120

FROM THE ANNALS

Not much is known about the life of Publius (or Gaius) Cornelius Tacitus. He was a Roman senator and is generally considered the Empire's greatest historian. His two major works—the *Histories* and the *Annals*—chronicle the reigns of many first-century Roman emperors. However, the *Annals* might have been unfinished at his death; and of the sixteen volumes Tacitus completed of the work, Books 7–10 and parts of Books 5, 6, 11 and 16 are lost. The existing volumes end with the year 66, during the reign of Nero (37–68; reigned from 54 until his death).

In 64, parts of Rome were devastated by a fire that spread quickly and burned for six days. The fire might have been accidental or the result of arson, and the few surviving accounts differ as to how much of the city it damaged or destroyed. In the *Annals*, written generations after the event, Tacitus claims that only four of Rome's fourteen districts escaped the fire. Seven districts suffered serious damage, and three were completely destroyed. According to Tacitus, Nero was away from the city when the fire started, but rushed back to organize a relief effort, paid for that effort from his own funds, opened his palaces to provide shelter for those left homeless, and arranged for the delivery of food to the survivors. After the destruction had been cleared away, Nero enacted a new urban development plan. He also built a new palace complex, the Domus Aurea, in an area affected by the fire.

In this selection from the *Annals*, Tacitus notes that some Romans blamed Nero for the fire (they accused him of having it set so as to clear the location of the Domus Aurea). To deflect the blame, Nero scapegoated the Christians, unleashing persecutions against them. In describing the persecutions, Tacitus does not call Christianity a religion. He calls it, in Latin, a *superstitio*—a "superstition" or something like an irrational fanatic belief.

PRONOUNCING GLOSSARY

Judaea: *joo-dee´-uh*

Pontius Pilatus: *pon´-shus pee-lah´-tus*

Tacitus: *ta´-si-tus*

Tiberius: *tai-bir´-ee-uhs* [*ai* rhyming with *rye*]

FROM THE ANNALS

But neither human resources, nor imperial munificence, nor appeasement of the gods, eliminated sinister suspicions that the fire had been instigated. To suppress this rumour, Nero fabricated scapegoats—and punished with every refinement the notoriously depraved Christians (as they were popularly called). Their originator, Christ, had been executed in Tiberius' reign by the governor of Judaea, Pontius Pilatus. But in spite of this temporary setback the deadly superstition had broken out afresh, not only in Judaea (where the mischief had started) but even in Rome. All degraded and shameful practices collect and flourish in the capital.

First, Nero had self-acknowledged Christians arrested. Then, on their information, large numbers of others were condemned—not so much for incendiarism as for their anti-social tendencies. Their deaths were made farcical. Dressed in wild animals' skins, they were torn to pieces by dogs, or crucified, or made into torches to be ignited after dark as substitutes for daylight. Nero provided his Gardens for the spectacle, and exhibited displays in the Circus,[1] at which he mingled with the crowd—or stood in a chariot, dressed as a charioteer. Despite their guilt as Christians, and the

---

TRANSLATED BY Michael Grant.

1. The largest stadium in Rome and in the Empire, used for chariot races and other forms of mass entertainment.

ruthless punishment it deserved, the victims were pitied. For it was felt that they were being sacrificed to one man's brutality rather than to the national interest.

PLINY THE YOUNGER   THE EMPEROR TRAJAN
ca. 61–ca. 113   53–117

LETTERS

The man now known as Pliny the Younger was actually named Gaius Plinius Caecilius Secundus. He was born in what is now northern Italy and was the nephew of the celebrated Roman scholar now known as Pliny the Elder. A lawyer, an author, and a government administrator, Pliny the Younger is known for his hundreds of surviving letters, many of them addressed to reigning emperors or to notables such as his friend Tacitus (see preceding selection).

Around 110, the emperor Trajan (53–117; reigned from 98 until his death) appointed Pliny the governor of the province of Bithynia and Pontus, in what is now Turkey. Pliny held this position until his death. In the following exchange of letters, the emperor and his provincial governor discuss Pliny's treatment of Christians in the province, and Pliny describes some practices of these early Christians. The new religion was spreading quickly, despite the Roman law against calling oneself a Christian. Like Tacitus, however, Pliny refers to Christianity not as a religion but as a superstition.

PRONOUNCING GLOSSARY

Pliny: *pli´-nee*   Trajan: *tray´-juhn*

LETTERS
[Pliny to Emperor Trajan]

(1) It is my custom, sir, to bring before you everything about which I am in doubt. For who can better guide my uncertainty or inform my ignorance? I have never been present at trials of Christians; for that reason I do not know what the charge usually is and to what extent it is usually punished. (2) I have been in no little uncertainty about whether any distinction should be made between different ages or whether, however young they may be, they should be treated no differently from the more mature ones; whether pardon should be granted for repentance or whether it is of no help to the man who has been a Christian at all to have given it up; whether it is the name itself, if it is free from crimes, or the crimes associated with the name which are being punished. Meanwhile, in the case of those who were prosecuted before me on the charge of being Christians, I followed this procedure. (3) I asked

Translated by Wynne Williams.

the people themselves whether they were Christians. Those who admitted that they were I asked a second and a third time, warning them of the punishment; those who persisted I ordered to be executed. For I was in no doubt that, whatever it might be that they were admitting to, their stubbornness and unyielding obstinacy certainly ought to be punished. (4) There were others of a similar madness whom I have listed as due to be sent on to the city, because they were Roman citizens.

Subsequently, through the very course of dealing with the matter, as usually happens, the charge spread widely and more forms of it turned up. (5) An anonymous pamphlet containing the names of many persons was posted up. Those who denied that they were or had been Christians, after they had called upon the gods when I dictated the formula, and after they had made offerings of incense and wine to your statue which I had ordered to be brought in along with the cult-images of the gods for this purpose, and had in addition cursed Christ, none of which acts, it is said, those who are truly Christians can be compelled to perform, I decided should be discharged. (6) Others, named by an informer, said that they were Christians and then denied it; they said that they had in fact been Christians but had given it up, some three years before, some more years earlier than that, and a few even twenty years ago. All these also both paid homage to your statue and to the cult-images of the gods and cursed Christ. (7) Moreover they maintained that this had been the sum of their guilt or error, that they had been in the habit of gathering together before dawn on a fixed day, and of singing antiphonally a hymn to Christ as if to a god, and of binding themselves by oath, not to some wickedness, but not to commit acts of theft or robbery or adultery, not to break faith, not to refuse to return money placed in their keeping when called upon to do so. When these ceremonies had been completed, they said it had been their custom to disperse and to meet again to take food, but food that was ordinary and harmless; they said that they had given up doing even this after my edict, in which, in accordance with your instructions, I had banned secret societies. (8) So I believed it to be all the more necessary to ascertain what the truth was from two slave women, who were called deaconesses, and under torture. I found nothing other than a depraved and extravagant superstition.

(9) Accordingly I postponed the hearing and hastened to consult you. For the matter seemed to me to be worthy of your consideration, especially on account of the number of people who are endangered. For many persons of every age, of every rank, of both sexes, are being brought and will be brought into danger. The infection of this superstition has spread, not only through the towns, but also through the villages and the countryside; it seems possible for it to be checked and put right. (10) At any rate it is well established that temples which just now were almost abandoned have begun to be thronged, and customary rites which had long been suspended to be renewed, and the flesh of sacrificial victims, for which until recently very few buyers were to be found, to be sold far and wide.[1] From this it is easy to conjecture what a host of people could be reformed, if room were given for repentance.

---

1. I.e., people who were calling themselves Christians are again frequenting Roman temples, taking part in Roman rites, and willing to eat the meat of animals sacrificed to the Roman gods.

[*Trajan to Pliny*]

(1) You followed the procedure which you ought to have followed, my dear Secundus, in examining the cases of those who were being prosecuted before you as Christians. For no rule with a universal application, such as would have, as it were, a fixed form, can be laid down. (2) They should not be sought out; if they are prosecuted and proved to be guilty, they should be punished, provided, however, that the man who denies that he is a Christian and makes this evident by his action, that is by offering prayers to our gods, shall obtain pardon for his repentance, however suspect he may be with regard to the past. However, pamphlets posted up without an author's name ought to have no place in any criminal charge. For they both set the worst precedent and are not in keeping with the spirit of our age.

ANONYMOUS
early second century

FROM THE MARTYRDOM OF POLYCARP

Polycarp (69 or 70–155), reportedly a disciple of the Apostle John, was a Christian bishop of Smyrna (present-day Izmir, Turkey). Shortly before his death, the city had suffered through a plague and an earthquake, and the Roman citizens had come to believe the gods were punishing them for harboring Christians. During the Roman festival of *Commune Asiae*, a major occasion of emperor worship and commemorative games, Polycarp was arrested and brought to the city stadium. Together with a number of his fellow Christians, he was given the opportunity to renounce his religion and publicly pay homage to the emperor (at that time, Antoninus Pius) as Lord. For refusing to do so, he was tortured to death. He is regarded as a saint in the Roman Catholic, Eastern Orthodox, Oriental Orthodox, Anglican, and Lutheran Churches.

Polycarp's death is reported in the following selection, a circular letter of the sort used to communicate among the early Christian communities. With the aim of instructing readers and listeners about Polycarp's virtues, the anonymous author amplifies the martyr's story by drawing parallels to the death of Jesus Christ. Also notable here are the use of the term *Catholic Church* and the increasing antagonism between Jews and Christians.

PRONOUNCING GLOSSARY

Herod: *he´-rud*

Nicetas: *nai-see´-tuhs* [*ai* rhyming with *rye*]

Polycarp: *pahl´-ee-cahrp*

proconsul: *proh-cahn´-suhl*

Smyrna: *smir´-nuh*

FROM THE MARTYRDOM OF POLYCARP

9. (1) As Polycarp entered the arena, a voice was heard from heaven: *Be strong,* Polycarp, *and act manfully.* Nobody saw the speaker, but those of our people who were present heard the voice. When he was finally led up to the tribunal, there was a terrific uproar among the people on hearing that Polycarp had been arrested.

(2) So when he had been led up, the proconsul questioned him whether he was Polycarp, and, when he admitted the fact, tried to persuade him to deny the faith.

He said to him, "Respect your age," and all the rest they were accustomed to say; "swear by the Fortune of Caesar; change your mind; say, 'Away with the atheists!'"

But Polycarp looked with a stern mien at the whole rabble of lawless heathen in the arena; he then groaned and, looking up to heaven, said, with a wave of his hand at them: "Away with the atheists!"

(3) When the proconsul insisted and said: "Take the oath and I will set you free; revile Christ," Polycarp replied: "For six and eighty years I have been serving Him, and He has done no wrong to me; how, then, dare I blaspheme my King who has saved me!"

10. (1) But he again insisted and said: "Swear by the Fortune of Caesar."

He answered: "If you flatter yourself that I shall swear by the Fortune of Caesar, as you suggest, and if you pretend not to know me, let me frankly tell you: I am a Christian! If you wish to learn the teaching of Christianity, fix a day and let me explain."

(2) "Talk to the crowd," the proconsul next said.

"You," replied Polycarp, "I indeed consider entitled to an explanation; for we have been trained to render honor, in so far as it does not harm us, to magistrates and authorities appointed by God; but as to that crowd, I do not think it proper to make an appeal to them."

11. (1) "Well," said the proconsul, "I have wild beasts, and shall have you thrown before them if you do not change your mind."

"Call for them," he replied; "to us a change from better to worse is impossible; but it is noble to change from what is evil to what is good."

(2) Again he said to him: "If you make little of the beasts, I shall have you consumed by fire unless you change your mind."

"The fire which you threaten," replied Polycarp, "is one that burns for a little while, and after a short time goes out. You evidently do not know the fire of the judgment to come and the eternal punishment, which awaits the wicked. But why do you delay? Go ahead; do what you want."

12. (1) As he said this and more besides, he was animated with courage and joy, and his countenance was suffused with beauty. As a result, he did not collapse from fright at what was being said to him; the proconsul, on the other hand, was astounded, and sent his herald to announce three times in the

---

Translated by James A. Kleist. The translator uses italic type wherever, invariably without citation, the ancient author echoes or quotes Scripture. The bracketed insertion is the translator's.

centre of the arena: "Polycarp has confessed to being a Christian." (2) Upon this announcement of the herald, the whole multitude of heathens and of Jews living at Smyrna shouted with uncontrolled anger and at the top of their voices: "This is the teacher of Asia, the father of the Christians, the destroyer of our gods! He teaches many not to sacrifice and not to worship!" Amid this noisy demonstration, they called upon Philip, the minister of public worship in Asia, to let loose a lion upon Polycarp. But he replied he had no authority to do so, since he had already closed the hunting sports. (3) Then they decided with one accord to demand that he should burn Polycarp alive. Of course, the vision that had appeared to him in connection with the pillow—when he saw it on fire during his prayer and then turned to his trusted friends with the prophetic remark: "I must be burnt alive"—had to be fulfilled!

13. (1) Then the thing was done more quickly than can be told, the crowds being in so great a hurry to gather logs and firewood from the shops and baths! And the Jews, too, as is their custom, were particularly zealous in lending a hand. (2) When the pyre was prepared, he laid aside all his clothes, unfastened the loin cloth, and prepared also to take off his shoes. He had not been in the habit of doing this, because the faithful always vied with each other to see which of them would be the first to touch his body. Even before his martyrdom, he had always been honored for holiness of life. (3) Without delay the material prepared for the pyre was piled up round him; but when they intended to nail him as well, he said: "Leave me just as I am. He who enables me to endure the fire will also enable me to remain on the pyre unbudging, without the security afforded by your nails."

14. (1) So they did not nail him, but just fastened him. And there he was, with his hands put behind him, and fastened, like a ram towering above a large flock, ready for sacrifice, a holocaust prepared and acceptable to God! And he looked up to heaven and said:

> "O Lord God, O Almighty, Father of Thy beloved and blessed Son Jesus Christ, through whom we have received the knowledge of you—*God of angels and hosts and all creation*—and of the whole race of saints who live under your eyes! (2) I bless Thee, because Thou hast seen fit to bestow upon me this day and this hour, that I may share, among the number of the martyrs, the cup of Thy Anointed and *rise to* eternal *life* both in soul and in body, in virtue of the immortality of the Holy Spirit. May I be accepted among them in Thy sight today as a rich and pleasing sacrifice, such as Thou, the true God that cannot utter a falsehood, hast prearranged, revealed in advance, and now consummated. (3) And therefore I praise Thee for everything; I bless Thee; I glorify Thee through the eternal and heavenly High Priest Jesus Christ, Thy beloved Son, through whom be glory to Thee together with Him and the Holy Spirit, both now and for the ages yet to come. Amen."

15. (1) When he had wafted up the *Amen* and finished the prayer, the men attending to the fire lit it; and when a mighty flame shot up, we, who were privileged to see it, saw a wonderful thing; and we have been spared to tell the tale to the rest. (2) The fire produced the likeness of a vaulted chamber,

like a ship's sail bellying to the breeze, and surrounded the martyr's body as with a wall; and he was in the centre of it, not as burning flesh, but as bread that is baking, or as gold and silver refined in a furnace! In fact, we even caught an aroma such as the scent of incense or of some other precious spice.

16. (1) At length, seeing that his body could not be consumed by fire, those impious people ordered an executioner to approach him and run a dagger into him. This done, there issued [a dove and] a great quantity of blood, with the result that the fire was quenched and the whole crowd was struck by the difference between unbelievers and elect. (2) And of the elect the most wonderful Polycarp was certainly one—an apostolic and prophetic teacher in our times, and a bishop of the Catholic Church at Smyrna. In fact, every word his lips have uttered has been, or will yet be, fulfilled.

17. (1) But the jealous and malicious rival,[1] the adversary of the race of saints, had witnessed the splendor of his martyrdom, had seen that his life was blameless from the beginning, and now saw him adorned with the crown of immortality and carrying off an incontestable prize. And so he busied himself preventing even his poor body from being laid hold of by us. Many, of course, were eager to do so and have a share in the possession of his holy remains. (2) He therefore instigated Nicetas, Herod's father and Alce's brother, to plead with the magistrate not to deliver up his body; "or else," he said, "they will abandon the Crucified and worship this man in good earnest." This he said at the urgent representations of the Jews, who were again on the alert when we intended to take him out of the fire. They did not realize that we shall never bring ourselves either to abandon Christ, who suffered for the salvation of all those that are saved in the whole world—*the Innocent for sinners!*—or to worship any other. (3) Him we worship as being the Son of God, the martyrs we love as being disciples and imitators of the Lord; and deservedly so, because of their unsurpassable devotion to their King and Teacher. May it be our good fortune, too, to be their companions and fellow disciples!

1. Satan.

ORIGEN
185–ca. 254

FROM AN EXHORTATION TO MARTYRDOM

Origen was born into a Christian family. He grew up in Greek-speaking Alexandria, Egypt, where he received an education that was both Hellenistic and Christian. Both sides of his education are so much in evidence in his voluminous theological writings that it remains a permanently open question whether he brought the thinking of the ancient Greek philosopher Plato to Christianity or brought Christianity to Platonic philosophy. Before he was a theologian, Origen was a Scripture scholar. Indeed, in the intensity and erudition of his engagement with Scripture, Origen may be regarded as the father of all Christian Scripture scholarship.

Origen's most remarkable work, which survives only in fragments, was a vast effort to establish the original text of the Jewish Bible, Christianity's Old Testament. Entitled the *Hexapla* (Greek, meaning "sixfold"), this work arranged the extant Hebrew, a Greek transliteration of the Hebrew, and four different Greek translations in parallel columns with coded, meticulously executed annotations indicating where the six texts coincided and where they differed. As a critical edition of Scripture, the *Hexapla* was intended for a learned minority. Origen's broader, more popular influence was felt through his inspirational Bible commentaries, notably on the Song of Songs (see p. 306) and on the Gospel of John.

Origen believed in a triple incarnation of God. There was God's physical Incarnation in the body of Jesus the Christ, born of the Virgin Mary, crucified under Pontius Pilate, then raised to glorious life and ascended to heaven. There was God's ecclesiastical incarnation as the Church, the mystical body of Christ made up of all Christians who had been born again through baptism. And finally there was God's scriptural incarnation in the Bible, God's infallible Word. The three were clearly and closely related. The struggle to understand the mysteries of the Word of God was for Origen just one form of the never-ending, highly Platonic (here meaning striving toward an ideal) struggle of the sincere Christian toward the spirit and away from the flesh. All moral striving, most especially against lust (Origen went so far as to castrate himself), was a part of that single spiritual struggle. It was less for this than for more theoretical Platonic excesses, at least perceived excesses, that Origen, like Tertullian (see p. 210), was eventually ruled to have fallen into heresy and that, under the later Christian emperor Justinian, his works were widely destroyed.

Origen's father, Leonidas, was martyred when Origen was seventeen. Origen was martyred late in life, during the persecution of the emperor Decius. Origen's influence lived on, as did the memory of his example. For him, even martyrdom was merely a final occasion to resist Satan, idolatry, sin, and the flesh. The excerpt below is from Origen's exhortation to his fellow Christians to accept martyrdom with courage and trust in God.

PRONOUNCING GLOSSARY

Ananias: *a-nuh-nai´-uhs* [*ai* rhyming with rye]
Azarias: *a-zuh-rai´-uhs*
Haman: *hah´-mahn*
Misael: *mee´-sah-el*

Mordecais: *mor´-de-kaiz* [*ai* rhyming with rye]
Nebuchadnezzar: *ne-buh-kuhd-ne´-zuhr*
Origen: *or´-i-jen*

FROM AN EXHORTATION TO MARTYRDOM

* * * We know that once we have been persuaded by Jesus to abandon idols and the atheism of worshiping many gods the Enemy[1] cannot persuade us to commit idolatry, though he tries to force us. That is why he[2] empowers those over whom he has authority to do such things, and he will make those who are tempted either martyrs or idolaters. And even now he says again and again, "All these I will give you, if you will fall down and worship me."[3]

TRANSLATED BY Rowan A. Greer. The section numbers and the translator's parenthetical Bible citations have been omitted.

1. Satan.
2. Satan.

3. Matthew 4:9.

Let us then take great care never to commit idolatry and subject ourselves to demons; for the idols of the Gentiles are demons.[4] What a state the person is in who has deserted the easy yoke and the light burden of Christ[5] to subject himself once again to the yoke of demons and to bear the burden of the heaviest sin! How can this be after we have known that the heart of those who worship idols is ashes[6] and their life more worthless than clay[7] and after we have said, "Our fathers possessed false idols, and none of them can bring rain"?[8]

It was not just of old that Nebuchadnezzar's image of gold was set up, nor only then that he threatened Ananias, Azarias, and Misael that he would throw them into the burning fiery furnace unless they worshiped it.[9] Even now Nebuchadnezzar says the same thing to us, the true Hebrews in exile from our homeland. But as for us, let us imitate those holy men so that we may experience the heavenly dew that quenches every fire that arises in us and cools our governing mind. Perhaps even now Haman wishes you Mordecais to bow down to him. But you must say, "I will not set the glory of men above the glory of the God of Israel."[1] Let us overturn Bel by the Word of God, and let us slay the dragon with Daniel, so that when we come near the lions' mouths, we may be able to suffer nothing from them, while only those to blame for our present contest will be devoured by the lions that cannot eat us up.[2] Let us endure because among the noble deeds of Job it is said, "If I put my hand to my mouth and kissed it, this would be reckoned the greatest iniquity for me."[3] And it is likely they will order us to put our hand to our mouth and kiss it.[4]

Let us also observe that it is not in His addresses to the many that prophecies of martyrdom are made, but in those to the apostles. For first it is said, "These twelve Jesus sent out, charging them, 'Go nowhere among the Gentiles,' and the rest."[5] Then there is added, "Beware of men; for they will deliver you up to councils, and flog you in their synagogues, and you will be dragged before governors and kings for my sake, to bear testimony before them and the Gentiles. When they deliver you up, do not be anxious how you are to speak or what you are to say; for what you are to say will be given to you in that hour; for it is not you who speak, but the Spirit of your Father speaking through you. Brother will deliver brother up to death, and the father his child, and children will rise against parents and have them put to death; and you will be hated by all for my name's sake. But he who endures to the end will be saved. When they persecute you in one town, flee to the next; for truly, I say to you, you will not have gone through all the towns of Israel, before the Son of Man comes."[6]

* * *

4. See Psalms 96:5 and 1 Chronicles 16:26. "Gentiles": heathens, pagans.
5. See Matthew 11:30.
6. See Wisdom 15:10.
7. See Jeremiah 16:19.
8. See Jeremiah 14:22.
9. Origen alludes to Daniel 3 in the Septuagint, the Greek form read in the early Christian Church.
1. Origen quotes Esther 4:17 in the Septuagint.
2. Origen quotes Bel and the Dragon, a narrative in the Septuagint that forms chapter 14 of the extended Book of Daniel. Catholics and Orthodox Christians consider the story canonical, but Protestants consider it apocryphal. In one episode, the prophet Daniel defeats the priests of Bel, then kills a dragon whom the Babylonians believe is a god, and finally is cast into a lions' den, from which he emerges unscathed.
3. Job 31:27–28.
4. Origen alludes to a gesture employed in the idol worship of his day.
5. Matthew 10:5.
6. Matthew 10:17–23.

Also the following exhortation to martyrdom, found in Matthew, was spoken to no others but the Twelve. We, too, should hear it, since by hearing it we shall be brothers of the apostles who heard it and shall be numbered with the apostles. This is the passage: "Do not fear those who kill the body but cannot kill the soul; rather fear Him who can destroy both soul and body in hell."[7] And in the verses that follow the Lord teaches us that no one comes to the contest of martyrdom without providence. For it is said, "Are not two sparrows sold for a penny? And not one of them will fall to the ground without your Father in heaven. But even the hairs of your head are all numbered. Fear not, therefore; you are of more value than many sparrows. So every one who confesses me before men, I also will confess before my Father who is in heaven; but whoever denies me before men, I also will deny before my Father who is in heaven."[8]

*   *   *

Therefore, those who destroy us kill the life of the body; for such is the meaning of "fear not those who kill the body," found in the same words in both Matthew and Luke.[9] And after killing the body, even if they wish, they cannot kill the soul; indeed, they have "no more than they can do."[1] For how could the soul that has been made alive by the confession itself be destroyed? And in Isaiah the One who exhorts us to martyrdom joins in bearing witness to this with His Son. The passage reads, "You are my witnesses, and I am a witness, says the Lord God, and the Son whom I have chosen."[2]

And notice that this commandment is given not to Jesus' servants but to His friends,[3] "Do not fear those who kill the body, and after that have no more that they can do."[4] Therefore, the One to be feared is "Him who can destroy both soul and body in hell."[5] For He alone "after He has killed" has "power to cast into hell."[6] Those He casts into hell are they who fear those who kill the body and do not fear "Him who, after He has killed, has power to cast into hell." We may suppose that no matter who else has the hairs of his head numbered, the verse is obviously true of those who are cut off for Jesus. Therefore, we shall confess the Son of God before men and not before gods, that He who is confessed may confess us in turn before God and His Father, and confess the one who confessed Him on earth Himself in heaven.

---

7. Matthew 10:28.
8. Matthew 10:29–33.
9. Matthew 10:28; Luke 12:4.
1. Luke 12:4.
2. Origen quotes Isaiah 43:10 in the Septuagint.

3. See John 15:15.
4. Luke 12:4.
5. Matthew 10:28.
6. Luke 12:5.

ANONYMOUS EDITOR
early third century

FROM THE PASSION OF PERPETUA AND FELICITY

The term *passion*, as applied to the sufferings of Jesus in the hours before and during his Crucifixion, first appears in second-century Christian texts. It subsequently has also been applied to the accounts of Christian martyrdoms.

Two Christian martyrs, Perpetua and Felicity, lived in the Roman province of Carthage (today part of Tunisia, in northern Africa). Vibia Perpetua was a noblewoman, and Felicity was her slave. Together with three fellow Christians, they were arrested and executed in 203, during the persecutions of the emperor Septimius Severus. Perpetua and Felicity are venerated as saints by the Roman Catholic, Lutheran, Episcopalian, and other Churches.

The full chronicle of their deaths may have been given its final form by the noted Roman writer and Church father Tertullian (see p. 210). However, parts of it are a first-person narrative by Perpetua. That narrative—part of which is included here—is the oldest Christian text known to have been written by a woman. Perpetua's emphasis on dreams and visions as well as her frequent allusions to the Holy Spirit have led some scholars to think her text may reflect Montanism, an ecstatic form of Christianity then common among Christians in northern Africa.

PRONOUNCING GLOSSARY

Felicitas: *fe-li´-see-tahs*

Hilarianus: *hi-lar-ee-ah´-nuhs*

Minucius Timinianus: *mi-noo´-shuhs ti-min-ee-ah´-nuhs*

Pomponius: *pohm-poh´-nee-uhs*

Revocatus: *re-voh-cah´-tuhs*

Saturninus: *sa-ter-nai´-nuhs* [*ai* rhyming with *rye*]

Secundulus: *se-cuhn´-duh-luhs*

Vibia Perpetua: *vi´-bee-uh per-pe´-too-uh*

FROM THE PASSION OF PERPETUA AND FELICITY

2. A number of young catechumens[1] were arrested, Revocatus and his fellow slave Felicitas, Saturninus and Secundulus, and with them Vibia Perpetua, a newly married woman of good family and upbringing. Her mother and father were still alive and one of her two brothers was a catechumen like herself. She was about twenty-two years old and had an infant son at the breast. (Now from this point on the entire account of her ordeal is her own, according to her own ideas and in the way that she herself wrote it down.)

✳   ✳   ✳

6. One day while we were eating breakfast we were suddenly hurried off for a hearing. We arrived at the forum, and straight away the story went about the neighbourhood near the forum and a huge crowd gathered. We walked up to

TRANSLATED BY Herbert Musurillo.

1. Christian converts receiving the catechism, or oral religious instruction, before being baptized.

the prisoner's dock. All the others when questioned admitted their guilt. Then, when it came my turn, my father appeared with my son, dragged me from the step, and said: 'Perform the sacrifice—have pity on your baby!'

Hilarianus the governor, who had received his judicial powers as the successor of the late proconsul Minucius Timinianus, said to me: 'Have pity on your father's grey head; have pity on your infant son. Offer the sacrifice for the welfare of the emperors.'

'I will not', I retorted.

'Are you a Christian?' said Hilarianus.

And I said: 'Yes, I am.'

When my father persisted in trying to dissuade me, Hilarianus ordered him to be thrown to the ground and beaten with a rod. I felt sorry for father, just as if I myself had been beaten. I felt sorry for his pathetic old age.

Then Hilarianus passed sentence on all of us: we were condemned to the beasts, and we returned to prison in high spirits. But my baby had got used to being nursed at the breast and to staying with me in prison. So I sent the deacon Pomponius straight away to my father to ask for the baby. But father refused to give him over. But as God willed, the baby had no further desire for the breast, nor did I suffer any inflammation; and so I was relieved of any anxiety for my child and of any discomfort in my breasts.

* * *

10. The day before we were to fight with the beasts I saw the following vision. Pomponius the deacon came to the prison gates and began to knock violently. I went out and opened the gate for him. He was dressed in an unbelted white tunic, wearing elaborate sandals. And he said to me: 'Perpetua, come; we are waiting for you.'

Then he took my hand and we began to walk through rough and broken country. At last we came to the amphitheatre out of breath, and he led me into the centre of the arena.

Then he told me: 'Do not be afraid. I am here, struggling with you.' Then he left.

I looked at the enormous crowd who watched in astonishment. I was surprised that no beasts were let loose on me; for I knew that I was condemned to die by the beasts. Then out came an Egyptian against me, of vicious appearance, together with his seconds, to fight with me. There also came up to me some handsome young men to be my seconds and assistants.

My clothes were stripped off, and suddenly I was a man. My seconds began to rub me down with oil (as they are wont to do before a contest). Then I saw the Egyptian on the other side rolling in the dust. Next there came forth a man of marvellous stature, such that he rose above the top of the amphitheatre. He was clad in a beltless purple tunic with two stripes (one on either side) running down the middle of his chest. He wore sandals that were wondrously made of gold and silver, and he carried a wand like an athletic trainer and a green branch on which there were golden apples.

And he asked for silence and said: 'If this Egyptian defeats her he will slay her with the sword. But if she defeats him, she will receive this branch.' Then he withdrew.

We drew close to one another and began to let our fists fly. My opponent tried to get hold of my feet, but I kept striking him in the face with the heels of my feet. Then I was raised up into the air and I began to pummel him without as it were touching the ground. Then when I noticed there was a lull, I put my two hands together linking the fingers of one hand with those of the other and thus I got hold of his head. He fell flat on his face and I stepped on his head.

The crowd began to shout and my assistants started to sing psalms. Then I walked up to the trainer and took the branch. He kissed me and said to me: 'Peace be with you, my daughter!' I began to walk in triumph towards the Gate of Life.[2] Then I awoke. I realized that it was not with wild animals that I would fight but with the Devil, but I knew that I would win the victory. So much for what I did up until the eve of the contest. About what happened at the contest itself, let him write of it who will.

✻   ✻   ✻

✻ ✻ ✻ And so the martyrs got up and went to the spot of their own accord as the people wanted them to, and kissing one another they sealed their martyrdom with the ritual kiss of peace. The others took the sword in silence and without moving, especially Saturninus, who being the first to climb the stairway was the first to die. For once again he was waiting for Perpetua. Perpetua, however, had yet to taste more pain. She screamed as she was struck on the bone; then she took the trembling hand of the young gladiator and guided it to her throat. It was as though so great a woman, feared as she was by the unclean spirit, could not be dispatched unless she herself were willing.

Ah, most valiant and blessed martyrs! Truly are you called and chosen for the glory of Christ Jesus our Lord! And any man who exalts, honours, and worships his glory should read for the consolation of the Church these new deeds of heroism which are no less significant than the tales of old. For these new manifestations of virtue will bear witness to one and the same Spirit who still operates, and to God the Father almighty, to his Son Jesus Christ our Lord, to whom is splendour and immeasurable power for all the ages. Amen.

---

2. "Porta Sanavivaria": the portal through which competing Roman gladiators entered the arena and triumphant gladiators exited.

OTHER CHRISTIAN GOSPELS

By the end of the second century, if not before, the Church accepted the Gospels of Matthew, Mark, Luke, and John as canonical. That is, they became part of the authorized list—the canon—of texts accepted as worthy of being read aloud in the Church's liturgy. Many other gospels that circulated within the early Christian communities did not enter the scriptural canon. These books are often called *apocrypha*, from the Greek word for "hidden away."

Scholars have not been able to determine how widely the apocryphal gospels were circulated, how large the audience was for them, and why they never gained wide acceptance. Some of these gospels were more connected with particular schools of esoteric philosophy than with Christianity. Some of them that have been lost are referred to, sometimes antagonistically, by early Christian writers. For example, some of them circulated widely enough that Irenaeus of Lyons, in the late second century (see p. 208), made the effort to refute them as heretical. Of the few that have survived the centuries, some—such as the Gospel of Thomas and the Gospel of Judas—were discovered in modern times.

Why were they written? Some of these gospels were meant to "fill in the blanks." For example, the canonical Gospels tell us a little about the birth and early life of Jesus, but a series of "infancy gospels" (such as the Protoevangelium of James) speculate about his life before age thirty, when he began his public ministry. Other gospels present an alternative version of Jesus' life. These gospels are often identified with an early Christian movement known as Gnosticism—from the Greek word *gnosis*, "knowledge." The many forms of Gnosticism shared certain elements: The Gnostics denied that Jesus was human, arguing that he only appeared to be human and only seemed to have died. They further stipulated that he revealed a secret wisdom only to a worthy group of initiates. Gnostics also proposed a complicated picture of the cosmos, emphasizing the radical separation of God from his creation. Between the spiritual divinity and fallen material humanity was an intervening series of angels, powers, and other celestial beings. In general, the Gnostics despised the flesh and subordinated it to the spirit. Until the recent discoveries of some ancient Gnostic texts at Nag Hammadi, Egypt, most of the available information about Gnosticism came from its opponents, most notably from Irenaeus.

ANONYMOUS
mid-to-late second century?

FROM THE GOSPEL OF THOMAS

The Gospel According to Thomas, commonly known as the Gospel of Thomas, was discovered in Egypt in December 1945; but since antiquity, it has been known to exist. Found with a collection of other writings, including other apocrypha, the manuscript was written in Coptic (an Afro-Asiatic language once spoken in Egypt) in the third century, and it is thought to be based on a mid-to-late-second-century Greek text.

Although it is called a gospel, this text has no narrative. Different in structure and tone from the canonical Gospels and from other New Testament apocrypha, it is a "sayings gospel," consisting of over a hundred sayings attributed to Jesus. Some of these sayings were most likely taken from the canonical Gospels; a few are original to this text. Some stand alone; some appear in parables; others appear in short dialogues with his disciples, including Apostles such as Simon Peter, Matthew, and Thomas. The Gospel of Thomas includes a possible allusion to Jesus' death, but it does not mention his Crucifixion, his Resurrection, or his delivery of final judgment on humanity. Indeed, this gospel does not consider Jesus the Messiah.

FROM THE GOSPEL OF THOMAS
Prologue

These are the hidden sayings that the living Jesus spoke and Judas Thomas the Twin[1] recorded.

(1) And he said, "Whoever discovers the interpretation of these sayings will not taste death."

(2) Jesus said, "Let one who seeks not stop seeking until one finds. When one finds, one will be troubled. When one is troubled, one will marvel and will rule over all."

(3) Jesus said, "If your leaders say to you, 'Look, the kingdom is in heaven,' then the birds of heaven will precede you. If they say to you, 'It is in the sea,' then the fish will precede you. Rather, the kingdom is inside you and it is outside you.

"When you know yourselves, then you will be known, and you will understand that you are children of the living father. But if you do not know yourselves, then you dwell in poverty, and you are poverty."

(4) Jesus said, "The person old in days will not hesitate to ask a little child seven days old about the place of life, and that person will live. For many of the first will be last and will become a single one."

(5) Jesus said, "Know what is in front of your face, and what is hidden from you will be disclosed to you. For there is nothing hidden that will not be revealed."

* * *

(10) Jesus said, "I have thrown fire upon the world, and look, I am watching it until it blazes."

(11) Jesus said, "This heaven will pass away, and the one above it will pass away.

"The dead are not alive, and the living will not die.

"During the days when you ate what is dead, you made it alive. When you are in the light, what will you do?

TRANSLATED BY Marvin Meyer. Bracketed insertions are the translator's.

1. The name *Thomas* is derived from an Aramaic word meaning "twin."

"On the day when you were one, you became two. But when you become two, what will you do?"

*   *   *

(13)   Jesus said to his followers, "Compare me to something and tell me what I am like."

     Simon Peter said to him, "You are like a just messenger."

     Matthew said to him, "You are like a wise philosopher."

     Thomas said to him, "Teacher, my mouth is utterly unable to say what you are like."

     Jesus said, "I am not your teacher. Because you have drunk, you have become intoxicated from the bubbling spring that I have tended."

     And he took him, and withdrew, and spoke three sayings to him.

     When Thomas came back to his friends, they asked him, "What did Jesus say to you?"

     Thomas said to them, "If I tell you one of the sayings he spoke to me, you will pick up rocks and stone me, and fire will come from the rocks and consume you."

*   *   *

(22)   Jesus saw some babies nursing. He said to his followers, "These nursing babies are like those who enter the kingdom."

     They said to him, "Then shall we enter the kingdom as babies?"

     Jesus said to them, "When you make the two into one, and when you make the inner like the outer and the outer like the inner, and the upper like the lower, and when you make male and female into a single one, so that the male will not be male nor the female be female, when you make eyes in place of an eye, a hand in place of a hand, a foot in place of a foot, an image in place of an image, then you will enter [the kingdom]."

(23)   Jesus said, "I shall choose you, one from a thousand and two from ten thousand, and they will stand as a single one."

(24)   His followers said, "Show us the place where you are, for we must seek it."

     He said to them, "Whoever has ears should hear. There is light within a person of light, and it shines on the whole world. If it does not shine, it is dark."

*   *   *

(37)   His followers said, "When will you appear to us and when shall we see you?"

     Jesus said, "When you strip without being ashamed and you take your clothes and put them under your feet like little children and trample them, then [you] will see the child of the living one and you will not be afraid."

(38)   Jesus said, "Often you have desired to hear these sayings that I am speaking to you, and you have no one else from whom to hear them. There will be days when you will seek me and you will not find me."

*   *   *

(42)   Jesus said, "Be passersby."

*   *   *

(50)   Jesus said, "If they say to you, 'Where have you come from?' say to
       them, 'We have come from the light, from the place where the
       light came into being by itself, established [itself], and appeared
       in their image.' If they say to you, 'Is it you?' say, 'We are its chil-
       dren, and we are the chosen of the living father.' If they ask you,
       'What is the evidence of your father in you?' say to them, 'It is
       motion and rest.'"

*   *   *

(77)   Jesus said, "I am the light that is over all things. I am all: From me
       all has come forth, and to me all has reached. Split a piece of
       wood; I am there. Lift up the stone, and you will find me there."

*   *   *

(82)   Jesus said, "Whoever is near me is near the fire, and whoever is
       far from me is far from the kingdom."
(83)   Jesus said, "Images are visible to people, but the light within them
       is hidden in the image of the father's light. He will be disclosed,
       but his image is hidden by his light."
(84)   Jesus said, "When you see your likeness, you are happy. But when
       you see your images that came into being before you and that
       neither die nor become visible, how much you will bear!"

*   *   *

(113) His followers said to him, "When will the kingdom come?"
       "It will not come by watching for it. It will not be said, 'Look,
       here it is,' or 'Look, there it is.' Rather, the father's kingdom is
       spread out upon the earth, and people do not see it."
(114) Simon Peter said to them, "Mary should leave us, for females are
       not worthy of life."
       Jesus said, "Look, I shall guide her to make her male, so that she
       too may become a living spirit resembling you males. For every
       female who makes herself male will enter heaven's kingdom."

ANONYMOUS
mid-to-late second century?

FROM THE PROTOEVANGELIUM OF JAMES

The Protoevangelium ("Pre-Gospel") of James, also known as the Gospel of James
and the Infancy Gospel of James, was written in Greek, probably about 145. The
earliest known manuscript, from the third or early fourth century, was found in
1958. However, the text was known in the West by the fifth century. While never

In this fresco, the Florentine painter, architect, and sculptor Giotto (Giotto di Bondone, ca. 1267–1337) depicts the first meeting of Mary's parents, Joachim and Anna, at the Golden Gate in Jerusalem. This image is part of a fresco cycle at the *Scrovegni Chapel*, also known as the *Arena Chapel*, in Padua, Italy. Completed in 1305, the cycle celebrates the life of the Virgin Mary and includes details about Mary's early life, such as her parents' names, found only in the Protoevangelium of James.

accepted as canonical, this gospel was read widely in the medieval period because it supplied details (however fanciful) about the infancy of Jesus that were not mentioned by Matthew and Luke. Purporting to have been written by James, Jesus' brother and Apostle, it takes dramatic license in two paragraphs by entering into the thoughts of Joseph, Jesus' adoptive father. It is also the oldest source asserting that Mary, mother of Jesus and James, was a virgin before, during, and after Jesus' birth.

The titles on the ancient manuscripts include "The Birth of Mary," "The Story of the Birth of Saint Mary, Mother of God," and "The Birth of Mary; The Revelation of James." The narrative names the parents (Joachim and Anna) of Mary, describes Mary's birth and upbringing, and speaks of her service in the temple at Jerusalem. These "facts" about Mary later appear in medieval and Renaissance art.

PRONOUNCING GLOSSARY

Augustus: *uh-guhs´-tuhs*
Bethlehem: *beth´-le-hem*
Judaea: *joo-dee´-uh*

Protoevangelium: *prohtoh-ee-vohn-gay´-lee-um*
Salome: *sah´-loh-may*

FROM THE PROTOEVANGELIUM OF JAMES

17. And there was an order from the Emperor Augustus, that all in Bethlehem of Judaea should be enrolled.[1] And Joseph said: I shall enrol my sons, but what shall I do with this maiden? How shall I enrol her? As my wife? I am ashamed. As my daughter then? But all the sons of Israel know that she is not my daughter. The day of the Lord shall itself bring it to pass as the Lord will. And he saddled the ass, and set her upon it; and his son led it, and Joseph followed. And when they had come within three miles, Joseph turned and saw her sorrowful; and he said to himself: Likely that which is in her distresses her. And again Joseph turned and saw her laughing. And he said to her: Mary, how is it that I see in thy face at one time laughter, at another sorrow? And Mary said to Joseph: Because I see two peoples with my eyes; the one weeping and lamenting, and the other rejoicing and exulting. And they came into the middle of the road, and Mary said to him: Take me down from off the ass, for that which is in me presses to come forth. And he took her down from off the ass, and said to her: Whither shall I lead thee, and cover thy disgrace? for the place is desert.

18. And he found a cave there, and led her into it; and leaving his two sons beside her, he went out to seek a midwife in the district of Bethlehem.

And I Joseph was walking, and was not walking; and I looked up into the sky, and saw the sky astonished; and I looked up to the pole of the heavens, and saw it standing, and the birds of the air keeping still. And I looked down upon the earth, and saw a trough lying, and work-people reclining: and their hands were in the trough. And those that were eating did not eat, and those that were rising did not carry it up, and those that were conveying anything to their mouths did not convey it; but the faces of all were looking upwards. And I saw the sheep walking, and the sheep stood still; and the shepherd raised his hand to strike them, and his hand remained up. And I looked upon the current of the river, and I saw the mouths of the kids resting on the water and not drinking, and all things in a moment were driven from their course.

19. And I saw a woman coming down from the hill-country, and she said to me: O man, whither art thou going? And I said: I am seeking an Hebrew midwife. And she answered and said unto me: Art thou of Israel? And I said to her: Yes. And she said: And who is it that is bringing forth in the cave? And I said: A woman betrothed to me. And she said to me: Is she not thy wife? And I said to her: It is Mary that was reared in the temple of the Lord, and I obtained her by lot as my wife. And yet she is not my wife, but has conceived of the Holy Spirit.

And the widwife said to him: Is this true? And Joseph said to her: Come and see. And the midwife went away with him. And they stood in the place of the cave, and behold a luminous cloud overshadowed the cave. And the midwife said: My soul has been magnified this day, because mine eyes have seen

TRANSLATED BY Alexander Walker.

1. Recorded in the census (for tax purposes). "Emperor Augustus": the first Roman emperor (Gaius Julius Caesar, 63 B.C.E.–14 C.E.; reigned from 27 B.C.E. until his death).

strange things—because salvation has been brought forth to Israel. And immediately the cloud disappeared out of the cave, and a great light shone in the cave, so that the eyes could not bear it. And in a little that light gradually decreased, until the infant appeared, and went and took the breast from His mother Mary. And the midwife cried out, and said: This is a great day to me, because I have seen this strange sight. And the midwife went forth out of the cave, and Salome[2] met her. And she said to her: Salome, Salome, I have a strange sight to relate to thee: a virgin has brought forth—a thing which her nature admits not of. Then said Salome: As the Lord my God liveth, unless I thrust in my finger, and search the parts, I will not believe that a virgin has brought forth.

20. And the midwife went in, and said to Mary: Show thyself; for no small controversy has arisen about thee. And Salome put in her finger, and cried out, and said: Woe is me for mine iniquity and mine unbelief, because I have tempted the living God; and, behold, my hand is dropping off as if burned with fire. And she bent her knees before the Lord, saying: O God of my fathers, remember that I am the seed of Abraham, and Isaac, and Jacob; do not make a show of me to the sons of Israel, but restore me to the poor; for Thou knowest, O Lord, that in Thy name I have performed my services, and that I have received my reward at Thy hand. And, behold, an angel of the Lord stood by her, saying to her: Salome, Salome, the Lord hath heard thee. Put thy hand to the infant, and carry it, and thou wilt have safety and joy. And Salome went and carried it, saying: I will worship Him, because a great King has been born to Israel. And, behold, Salome was immediately cured, and she went forth out of the cave justified. And behold a voice saying: Salome, Salome, tell not the strange things thou hast seen, until the child has come into Jerusalem.

---

2. In canonical and apocryphal accounts, identified variously as a follower of Jesus, mother of the Apostles James and John, or the sister of Mary; venerated as Mary Salome in some Churches.

ARTICULATIONS OF CHRISTIAN BELIEF

The creed—a formal, public statement of belief mingling theology and historical memory—is a distinctive and innovative feature of early Christianity. As a voluntary movement not confined to a single nationality, the new religion had no home territory, no sacred or native language, and no government sponsorship or regulation. Creeds provided for it what nationality, territory, language, and sponsorship provided for many other religions, especially in the first centuries of the Common Era—namely, internal coherence and a reliable criterion for membership and mutual recognition.

The earliest Christian creed seems to have originated at least as early as the second century, in a set of answers to questions that prospective converts taking instruction in Christianity had to answer correctly to be judged ready for Church membership. Baptism was the Church's initiation rite, and a question-and-answer session was regularly a part of the rite. Put together in a single statement, these baptismal answers eventually became the Apostles' Creed (which varies in its particulars from Church to Church but invariably begins "I believe in God"). Though never solemnly ratified, this shortest of the creeds has enjoyed exceptionally wide use in Christianity. The form in which it survives dates back, however, only to the reign of Charlemagne, who became Holy Roman Emperor in 800 and adopted it as his semi-official creed.

At various times, particularly during the Patristic Era, Christian leaders have gathered from all parts of the Christian world to collectively define and declare their faith. The creeds or declarations of faith that issued from these ecumenical (universal) councils have been of lasting importance in the history of Christianity. The first four ecumenical councils are recognized as authoritative by the Protestant, Roman Catholic, and Eastern (Greek) Orthodox Churches: Nicaea (325), Nicaea-Constantinople (381), Ephesus (431), and Chalcedon (451). The Eastern (Greek) Orthodox Church recognizes, in addition, three later councils: Constantinople II (553), Constantinople III (680), and Nicaea II (787). The Roman Catholic Church recognizes all seven of these plus fourteen later councils, culminating with the Second Vatican Council (1962–65). Greek was the language employed by all of the crucial first seven ecumenical councils, and participation in the early councils was principally from the Greek-speaking eastern half of the Roman Empire.

Note, however, that not all collective statements of faith emerge from ecumenical councils. During and just after the Protestant Reformation, there was an explosion of collective declarations of faith: the Confession of Augsburg (Lutheran, 1530), the Geneva Confession (Calvinist, 1536), and the Westminster Confession (Presbyterian, 1646), to name just three. None of these confessions (or "professions," in contemporary English) was the work of an ecumenical council.

In addition, not all forms of Christianity are creedal. Quakerism, stressing ongoing inspiration, has traditionally regarded creeds as impositions on the freedom of the Holy Spirit. Certain other Christian groups have insisted on the final and total authority of Scripture and have regarded creeds, perhaps especially the ancient imperial creeds, as infringing on that supreme authority.

IRENAEUS OF LYONS
130?–202

FROM AGAINST THE HERESIES

Very little is known about the life of the Church father Irenaeus. He was born in Smyrna, in Asia Minor (modern-day İzmir, Turkey), and served as bishop in Lugdunum, in Gaul (modern-day Lyon, or Lyons, France). He is recognized as a saint by the Eastern Orthodox, Roman Catholic, Lutheran, and Episcopal Churches.

His best-known work is *Against the Heresies* (ca. 185). In the following brief selection from this massive text, Irenaeus presents a statement of orthodox Christian belief. In this statement, which may be an expansion of the early Christians' interrogatory baptismal creed, Irenaeus contrasts orthodox belief with the errors of the Gnostics.

FROM AGAINST THE HERESIES

BOOK 1, CHAPTER 10

Unity of the Faith of the Church throughout the Whole World

1. The Church, though dispersed throughout the whole world, even to the ends of the earth, has received from the apostles and their disciples this faith: [She believes] in one God, the Father Almighty, Maker of heaven, and earth, and the sea, and all things that are in them; and in one Christ Jesus, the Son of God, who became incarnate for our salvation; and in the Holy Spirit, who proclaimed through the prophets the dispensations of God, and the advents, and the birth from a virgin, and the passion, and the resurrection from the dead, and the ascension into heaven in the flesh of the beloved Christ Jesus, our Lord, and His [future] manifestation from heaven in the glory of the Father "to gather all things in one,"[1] and to raise up anew all flesh of the whole human race, in order that to Christ Jesus, our Lord, and God, and Saviour, and King, according to the will of the invisible Father, "every knee should bow, of things in heaven, and things in earth, and things under the earth, and that every tongue should confess"[2] to Him, and that He should execute just judgment towards all; that He may send "spiritual wickednesses,"[3] and the angels who transgressed and became apostates, together with the ungodly, and unrighteous and wicked, and profane among men, into everlasting fire; but may, in the exercise of His grace, confer immortality on the righteous, and holy, and those who have kept His commandments, and have persevered in His love, some from the beginning [of their Christian course], and others from [the date of] their repentance, and may surround them with everlasting glory.

TRANSLATED BY Alexander Roberts and William Rambaut.

1. Ephesians 1:10.
2. Philippians 2:10–11.
3. Ephesians 6:12.

2. As I have already observed, the Church, having received this preaching and this faith, although scattered throughout the whole world, yet, as if occupying but one house, carefully preserves it. She also believes these points [of doctrine] just as if she had but one soul, and one and the same heart, and she proclaims them, and teaches them, and hands them down, with perfect harmony, as if she possessed only one mouth. For, although the languages of the world are dissimilar, yet the import of the tradition is one and the same. For the Churches which have been planted in Germany do not believe or hand down anything different, nor do those in Spain, nor those in Gaul, nor those in the East, nor those in Egypt, nor those in Libya, nor those which have been established in the central regions[4] of the world. But as the sun, that creature of God, is one and the same throughout the whole world, so also the preaching of the truth shineth everywhere, and enlightens all men that are willing to come to a knowledge of the truth. Nor will any one of the rulers in the Churches, however highly gifted he may be in point of eloquence, teach doctrines different from these (for no one is greater than the Master); nor, on the other hand, will he who is deficient in power of expression inflict injury on the tradition. For the faith being ever one and the same, neither does one who is able at great length to discourse regarding it, make any addition to it, nor does one, who can say but little, diminish it.

3. It does not follow because men are endowed with greater and less degrees of intelligence, that they should therefore change the subject-matter [of the faith] itself, and should conceive of some other God besides Him who is the Framer, Maker, and Preserver of this universe, (as if He were not sufficient for them), or of another Christ, or another Only-begotten. But the fact referred to simply implies this, that one may [more accurately than another] bring out the meaning of those things which have been spoken in parables, and accommodate them to the general scheme of the faith; and explain [with special clearness] the operation and dispensation of God connected with human salvation; and show that God manifested long suffering in regard to the apostasy of the angels who transgressed, as also with respect to the disobedience of men; and set forth why it is that one and the same God has made some things temporal and some eternal, some heavenly and others earthly; and understand for what reason God, though invisible, manifested Himself to the prophets not under one form, but differently to different individuals; and show why it was that more covenants than one were given to mankind; and teach what was the special character of each of these covenants; and search out for what reason "God hath concluded every man in unbelief, that He may have mercy upon all";[5] and gratefully describe on what account the Word of God became flesh and suffered; and relate why the advent of the Son of God took place in these last times, that is, in the end, rather than in the beginning [of the world]; and unfold what is contained in the Scriptures concerning the end [itself], and things to come; and not be silent as to how it is that God has made the Gentiles, whose salvation was despaired of, fellow-heirs, and of the same body, and partakers with the saints; and discourse how it is that "this mortal body shall put on immortality, and this corruptible shall put on incorruption";[6] and

4. Probably Palestine.
5. Romans 11:32.
6. 1 Corinthians 15:54.

proclaim in what sense [God] says, "That is a people who was not a people; and she is beloved who was not beloved";[7] and in what sense He says that "more are the children of her that was desolate, than of her who possessed a husband."[8] For in reference to these points, and others of a like nature, the apostle exclaims: "Oh! the depth of the riches both of the wisdom and knowledge of God; how unsearchable are His judgments, and His ways past finding out!"[9]

*　*　*

7. Hosea 2:23.　　　　　　　　　　　　　　9. Isaiah 14:1.
8. Romans 9:25.

TERTULLIAN
ca. 160–225

FROM DE SPECTACULIS

Quintus Septimus Florens Tertullianus, known to history as Tertullian, was born most likely in Roman North Africa and became a convert to Christianity at about age forty. Well-educated in Greco-Roman literature and philosophy, he was a forceful and influential apologist for the religious movement he had joined at a time when it was still a small minority in the Roman Empire. Though he wrote in Greek as well as in Latin, he was culturally more a pragmatic, moralistic Roman than an artistic, speculative Greek, and his influence was greatest in the Latin Church.

Tertullian is believed to have been the first to refer collectively to God the Father, Jesus Christ, and the Holy Spirit by the Latin term *Trinitas* (English, "Trinity"). For this and other reasons, he may rightly be reckoned a pathbreaking Christian theologian in an era before the first ecumenical councils had taken place and therefore before Christianity had an officially enforced orthodoxy. Late in life, Tertullian was associated with a charismatic Christian movement called by its adherents New Prophecy and by its detractors Montanism (for its founder, Montanus of Phrygia). Since this movement was eventually condemned as a heresy (it was not universally so condemned during his lifetime), Tertullian came to seem a heterodox thinker. Yet he did much to launch the process of philosophically shaped theological reflection on the Christian message that eventuated in orthodoxy and continued through the centuries as Christian theology.

As Christianity grew within the Roman Empire, it became a force affecting even those who were not Christian. One indication of this influence was the steady decline of the Roman gladiatorial games, in which combatants fought to the death for the entertainment of spectators. The more Christians there were in the Empire, the fewer were the spectators for these brutal spectacles. Though a few freedmen from the very lowest Roman classes became gladiators voluntarily and even, so long as they survived, could achieve fame and relative wealth, most gladiators were slaves, prisoners of war, or condemned criminals. Among the latter were sometimes Christians condemned for disloyalty to the Empire and forced to face lions and other beasts in the amphitheater. While this practice understandably fostered Christian antagonism toward the games, the new religion condemned gladiatorial combat in principle as no more than a form of licensed murder. In his *De Spectaculis* ("Concerning Public Shows"), Tertullian—a strict, ascetic, often censorious moralist—condemns Roman chariot races for their indecency and reckless violence as well as the Roman theater for its sometimes pornographic displays. As seen in the following excerpt, however, he reserves his most forceful condemnation for the savagery of the gladiatorial games.

FROM DE SPECTACULIS

[On Roman Circus, Theater, and Gladiatorial Games]

The Gentiles[1] have not truth in its completeness, because their teacher of truth is not God; so they construe evil and good to square with their own judgement and pleasure; sometimes a thing is good that at other times is bad, and the same with evil, now evil now good. So it comes about that a man who will scarcely lift his tunic in public for the necessities of nature, will take it off in the circus in such a way as to make a full display of himself before all; that a man who guards the ears of his maiden daughter from every smutty word, will himself take her to the theatre to hear words of that sort and to see gestures to match; that the man who when he sees a quarrel on the streets coming to blows will try to quiet it or expresses his strong disapproval, will in the stadium applaud fights far more dangerous; that he who shudders at the body of a man who died by nature's law the common death of all, will, in the amphitheatre, gaze down with most tolerant eyes on the bodies of men mangled, torn in pieces, defiled with their own blood; yes, and that he who comes to the spectacle to signify his approval of murder being punished, will have a reluctant gladiator hounded on with lash and rod to do murder; that the man who calls for the lion as the punishment for some notorious murderer, will call for the rod of discharge for a savage gladiator and give him the cap of liberty as a reward, yes! and the other man who was killed in the fight he will have fetched back to take a look at his face, with more delight inspecting under his eyes the man he wished killed at a distance; and, if he did not wish it, so much the crueller he!

* * *

It is our duty to hate these assemblies and gatherings of the heathen, were it only that there the name of God is blasphemed; that there, every day, the shout is raised to set the lion upon us; that from there persecution begins; that there temptation has its base. What will you do when you are caught in that heaving tide of guilty voices? I do not suggest that you can run any risk there of suffering from men—nobody recognizes you for a Christian; but think well over it, what it means for you in heaven. Do you doubt but that at that very moment when the devil is raging in his assembly, all the angels look forth from heaven, and mark down man by man, how this one has spoken blasphemy and that has listened, the one has lent his tongue, the other his ears, to the devil, against God? Will you not rather fly the chairs of the enemies of Christ, "the seat of the pestilences," the very overhanging air defiled with sinful cries? Granted that you have there something that is sweet, agreeable and innocent, some things that are excellent. No one mixes poison with gall and hellebore; no, it is into delicacies well

TRANSLATED BY T. R. Glover. The section numbers have been omitted.

1. Heathens, pagans.

made, well flavoured, and, for the most part, sweet things, that he drops the venom. So does the devil; the deadly draught he brews, he flavours with the most agreeable, the most welcome gifts of God. So count all you find there—brave and honest, resounding, musical, exquisite—as so much honey dropping from a poisoned bit of pastry; and do not count your appetite for the pleasure worth the risk in the sweetness.

Let his own guests batten on sweets of that sort. The place, the time, the host who invites, are theirs. Our feast, our marriage-festival, is not yet. We cannot take our place at table with them, because they cannot with us. It is a matter of turn and turn about. Now they are happy, and we are afflicted. "The world," it says, "will rejoice; you will be sad."[2] Then let us mourn while the heathen rejoice, that, when they have begun to mourn, we may rejoice; lest, if we share their joy now, then we may be sharing their mourning too. You are too dainty, O Christian, if you long for pleasure in this world as well as the other—a bit of a fool into the bargain, if you think *this* pleasure. Philosophers have given the name "pleasure" to quiet and tranquillity; in it they rejoice, take their ease in it, yes, glory in it. And you—why, I find you sighing for goal-posts, the stage, the dust, the arena. I wish you would tell me; cannot we live without pleasure, who must die with pleasure? For what else is our prayer but that of the apostle "to leave the world and be at home with the Lord"?[3] Our pleasure is where our prayer is.

But now, if you think we are to pass this interval of life here in delights, why are you so ungrateful as not to find enough in the great pleasures, the many pleasures, given you by God, and not to recognize them? What has more joy in it than reconciliation with God, the Father and Lord, than the revelation of truth, the recognition of error, and forgiveness for all the great sins of the past? What greater pleasure is there than disdain for pleasure, than contempt for the whole world, than true liberty, than a clean conscience, than life sufficient, than the absence of all fear of death? than to find yourself trampling underfoot the gods of the Gentiles, expelling demons, effecting cures, seeking revelations, living to God? These are the pleasures, the spectacles of Christians, holy, eternal, and free. Here find your games of the circus,—watch the race of time, the seasons slipping by, count the circuits,[4] look for the goal of the great consummation, battle for the companies of the churches, rouse up at the signal of God, stand erect at the angel's trump,[5] triumph in the palms[6] of martyrdom. If the literature of the stage delight you, we have sufficiency of books, of poems, of aphorisms, sufficiency of songs and voices, not fable, those of ours, but truth; not artifice but simplicity. Would you have fightings and wrestlings? Here they are—things of no small account and plenty of them. See impurity overthrown by chastity, perfidy slain by faith, cruelty crushed by pity, impudence thrown into the shade by modesty; and such are the contests among us, and in them we are crowned. Have you a mind for blood? You have the blood of Christ.

2. See John 16:20.
3. See Philippians 1:23.
4. Laps around the track; here, perhaps, years of life.
5. Trumpet.
6. Palm leaves were symbols of victory.

THE FIRST ECUMENICAL COUNCIL
325

THE NICENE CREED

Some would name as the earliest ecumenical council a historic meeting of Church leaders, including Saint Paul and Saint James, described in the Acts of the Apostles and sometimes called the Council of Jerusalem. The question at that gathering was whether circumcision was to be required for Church membership of gentile males or only of Jewish males. (The answer: only of Jews.) The first true ecumenical council, however—and, because pattern-setting, the most important of them—was a great gathering of bishops in 325. Like the subsequent early ecumenical councils, this council was convoked by a Roman emperor—in this case, Constantine. It took place in the small town of Nicaea (present day İznik), near what would become the emperor's fabled capital, Constantinople (Istanbul).

As the emperor who legalized Christianity by the Edict of Milan (313), Constantine may be regarded as both the Empire's last pagan emperor and its first Christian one, whether or not he ever truly converted. Constantine's private motives for desiring consensus among the Christians of his Empire undoubtedly owed a good deal to imperial expedience: The Empire had powerful external enemies and could ill afford deep religious division at home.

The Council of Nicaea had the profound effect of creating a Christian orthodoxy with tacit imperial backing. At the time, a Christian leader named Arius was promulgating an extremely popular heretical form of Christianity. Arianism regarded Jesus Christ as God's first creature rather than as coequal with God. At the conclusion of their council, the bishops in Nicaea formulated a creed to refute this teaching.

The Nicene Creed, also known as the Creed of Nicaea, was most likely based on a Trinitarian baptismal creed used in Jerusalem. However, in their version of the creed, the bishops incorporated the Greek term *homooúsios* to declare that the Son was of the "same substance" or "same being" as the Father. The English translation that follows reads "from the substance of the Father . . . consubstantial with the Father." The bishops probably learned about the term from Gnostic writings, where it first appeared.

The final, one-sentence paragraph of the Nicene Creed is a later addition.

PRONOUNCING GLOSSARY

homooúsious: *hoh-moh-oo´-zee-os*   Nicene: *nai-seen´* [*ai* rhyming with *rye*]

THE NICENE CREED

(1) We believe in one God the Father all-powerful, Maker of all things both seen and unseen. (2) And in one Lord Jesus Christ, the Son of God, the Only-begotten begotten from the Father, that is from the substance of the Father, God from God, light from light, true God from true God, begotten not made, consubstantial with the Father, through whom all things came to be, both those in heaven and those in earth; (3) for us humans and for our salvation he came down and became incarnate, became human, (4) suffered and (5) rose up on the third day, (6) went up into the heavens, (7) is coming to judge the living and the dead. (8) And in the Holy Spirit.

And those who say "there once was when he was not," and "before he was begotten he was not," and that he came to be from things that were not, or from another hypostasis or substance, affirming that the Son of God is subject to change or alteration—these the catholic and apostolic church anathematizes.

FROM Jaroslav Pelikan, *Credo: Historical and Theological Guide to Creeds and Confessions of Faith in the Christian Tradition.*

THE SECOND ECUMENICAL COUNCIL
381

THE CREED OF NICAEA-CONSTANTINOPLE

Many Christian Churches incorporate the Nicene Creed into their worship, but the form in which they most often recite it is not exactly the form adopted in 325 at Nicaea (see p. 213). It is rather a significant expansion of the original Nicene Creed, and it has commonly been attributed to the Second Ecumenical Council, which took place in 381 at the then-recently completed Constantinople. Both creeds begin, significantly, "*We* believe" (emphasis added), for a group identity, not an individual Christian profile, was being fashioned. The Creed of Nicaea-Constantinopole, however it came to formulation, reaffirms the equality of the Father and the Son. It expands the Nicene Creed most notably at the end, where "We believe . . . in the Spirit, the holy [i.e., the Holy Spirit]" is lengthened by the addition of

> the lordly, and life-giving one, proceeding forth from the Father, co-worshiped and co-glorified with Father and Son, the one who spoke through the prophets; in one, holy, catholic, and apostolic church. We confess one baptism for the forgiving of sins. We look forward to a resurrection of the dead and life in the age to come. Amen.

The Council of Constantinople occurred just a few years before Emperor Theodosius made Christianity the official and only religion of the Roman Empire. The bishops at Constantinople also stipulated that no other creed was to be adopted in the Christian Church, and this creed quickly acquired the uniquely authoritative status that it retains in much of modern Christianity. The following text is the "Nicene Creed" that is used today by all creedal Churches.

PRONOUNCING GLOSSARY

Nicaea: *nai-see´-uh* [*ai* rhyming with *rye*]

THE CREED OF NICAEA-CONSTANTINOPLE

(1) We believe in one God the Father all-powerful, Maker of heaven and of earth, and of all things both seen and unseen. (2) And in one Lord Jesus Christ, the only-begotten Son of God, begotten from the Father before all the ages, light from light, true God from true God, begotten not made, consubstantial with the Father, through whom all things came to be; (3) for us humans and for our salvation he came down from the heavens and became incarnate from the Holy Spirit and the Virgin Mary, became human (4) and was crucified on our behalf under Pontius Pilate; he suffered and was buried (5) and rose up on the third day in accordance with the Scriptures; (6) and he went up into the heavens and is seated at the Father's right hand; (7) he is coming again with glory to judge the living and the dead; his kingdom will have no end. (8) And in the Spirit, the holy, the lordly, and life-giving one, proceeding forth from the Father, co-worshiped and co-glorified with Father and Son, the one who spoke through the prophets; (9) in one, holy, catholic, and apostolic church. (10) We confess one baptism for the forgiving of sins. (11) We look forward to a resurrection of the dead (12) and life in the age to come. Amen.

FROM Jaroslav Pelikan, *Credo: Historical and Theological Guide to Creeds and Confessions of Faith in the Christian Tradition.*

THE THIRD ECUMENICAL COUNCIL
431

THE FORMULA OF UNION AT EPHESUS

By the fifth Christian century, the celebration of the Virgin Mary was growing rapidly, and its growth was surely accelerated by the influence of the newly promulgated creeds. For if Jesus, Mary's son, was "consubstantial" with his divine father (see pp. 213 and 214), then she was in that sense the august Mother of God. Celebrating her maternal identity became a way of reinforcing and underscoring Jesus' exalted but then-contested identity as truly divine. The one belief reinforced the other.

Popular devotion to Mary as the Mother of God acquired official endorsement at the Third Ecumenical Council. In our time, the common assumption about divinity is that it is an absolute: As one cannot be somewhat pregnant, one cannot be somewhat —or partly or almost—divine. So we assume, but this very assumption is a legacy of Christianity's first ecumenical councils.

What Arius had been to the Council of Nicaea, Nestorius was to this third council. It was held in 431 in Ephesus (near present-day Selçuk, in Turkey), a Greek city on the eastern shore of the Aegean Sea. The bishops in Ephesus issued a formula to refute the errors of the followers of Nestorius, then the archbishop of Constantinople, who maintained that the Son of God and Jesus Christ were two mystically linked persons, one divine and the other human—or, in any case, one more divine than the other. According to Nestorius, Mary was the mother of only the human Jesus of Nazareth, not the divine Christ. In saying that Mary was *Theotokos* (Greek) or *Deipara* (Latin)—the "God bearer"—the Council of Ephesus repudiated Nestorius by using a title that was already well known and hallowed in the Greek and Latin Churches.

Nestorius, though condemned by the Council as a heretic, maintained until his death that he was an orthodox Christian. And since the decrees of a council convoked by a Roman emperor could not be imposed beyond the boundaries of the Empire, Nestorianism lived on for centuries in Mesopotamia, Persia, and points east, all lying beyond the Empire's eastern border. The Assyrian Orthodox Church, surviving in modern Iraq, is Nestorian to this day.

PRONOUNCING GLOSSARY

Ephesus: *e´-phe-suhs*

THE FORMULA OF UNION AT EPHESUS

We will state briefly what we are convinced of and profess about the God-bearing Virgin and the manner of the incarnation of the only-begotten Son of God—not by way of addition but in the manner of a full statement, even as we have received and possess it from of old from the Holy Scriptures and from the tradition of the holy fathers, adding nothing at all to the creed put foward by the holy fathers at Nicaea. For, as we have just said, that creed is sufficient both for the knowledge of godliness and for the repudiation of all heretical false teaching. We shall speak not presuming to approach the unapproachable; but we confess our own weakness and so shut out those who would reproach us for investigating things beyond the human mind.

We confess, then, our Lord Jesus Christ, the only-begotten Son of God, perfect God and perfect man of a rational soul and a body, begotten before all ages from the Father in his Godhead, the same in the last days, for us and for our salvation, born of Mary the Virgin, according to his humanity, one and the same consubstantial with the Father in Godhead and consubstantial with us in humanity, for a union of two natures took place. Therefore we confess one Christ, one Son, one Lord. According to this understanding of the unconfused union, we confess the Holy Virgin to be the Mother of God

FROM Jaroslav Pelikan, *Credo: Historical and Theological Guide to Creeds and Confessions of Faith in the Christian Tradition*.

because God the Word took flesh and became man and from his very conception united to himself the temple he took from her. As to the evangelical and apostolic expressions about the Lord, we know that theologians treat some in common as of one person and distinguish others as of two natures, and interpret the God-befitting ones in connexion with the Godhead of Christ and the lowly ones with his humanity.

THE FOURTH ECUMENICAL COUNCIL
451

ON THE PERSON AND NATURES OF CHRIST

What Arius had been for the First Ecumenical Council (see p. 213) and Nestorius for the Third (see p. 215), the "monophysite" school of theological thought, centered in Alexandria, Egypt, was for the Fourth Ecumenical Council. This council was held in 451 in the town of Chalcedon (now a district of greater Istanbul).

According to monophysitism, God the Son and Jesus of Nazareth had only one (Greek *monos*) nature (Greek *physis*) between them, and that one divine. That is, Jesus' human nature was wholly dissolved in the divinity of God the Son. In Chalcedon, the bishops issued a decree saying that Jesus Christ was one person but possessed two natures, one human and the other divine. This decree was an attempt to strike a balance between two views: the emphasis on Christ's divinity at the expense of his humanity and the emphasis on his humanity over his divinity. To use the sometimes highly technical language of patristic theology: Chalcedonian or orthodox Christology (doctrine of Christ) is *dyophysite*, meaning that it views Christ as God Incarnate, one person, with two (Greek *dyo*) natures (Greek *physis*).

However, certain Eastern Churches (such as those of Armenia, Egypt, and Ethiopia) did not accept the bishops' formulation because of different understandings of person and nature. These forms of non-Chalcedonian Christology are termed *monophysite*, *miaphysite*, or *henophysite*. Nuances of terminology aside, all of these Churches assert that Christ has just one nature, and that one divine.

ON THE PERSON AND NATURES OF CHRIST

So, following the saintly fathers, we all with one voice teach the confession of one and the same Son, our Lord Jesus Christ: the same perfect in divinity and perfect in humanity, the same truly God and truly man, of a rational soul and a body; consubstantial with the Father as regards his divinity, and the same consubstantial with us as regards his humanity; like us in all respects except for sin; begotten before the ages from the Father as regards his divinity, and in the last days the same for us and for our salvation from Mary, the Virgin God-bearer as regards his humanity; one and the same Christ, Son, Lord, Only-begotten, acknowledged in two natures which undergo no confusion, no

FROM Jaroslav Pelikan, *Credo: Historical and Theological Guide to Creeds and Confessions of Faith in the Christian Tradition*. The translation's intertextual numbers have been omitted.

change, no division, no separation; at no point was the difference between the natures taken away through the union, but rather the property of both natures is preserved and comes together into a single person and a single subsistent being; he is not parted or divided into two persons, but is one and the same only-begotten Son, God, Word, Lord Jesus Christ, just as the prophets taught from the beginning about him, and as the Lord Jesus Christ himself instructed us, and as the creed of the fathers handed it down to us.

Since we have formulated these things with all possible accuracy and attention, the sacred and universal synod decreed that no one is permitted to produce, or even to write down or compose, any other creed or to think or teach otherwise. As for those who dare either to compose another creed or even to promulgate or teach or hand down another creed for those who wish to convert to a recognition of the truth from Hellenism or from Judaism, or from any kind of heresy at all: if they be bishops or clerics, the bishops are to be deposed from the episcopacy and the clerics from the clergy; if they be monks or layfolk, they are to be anathematized.

SAINT JOHN OF DAMASCUS
ca. 675–749

FROM THREE TREATISES ON IMAGES

The man known as John of Damascus or John Damascene was born Yuhanna (or Yanah) ibn Mansur ibn Sarjunin in Damascus. Sometime in the early 700s, he became a monk at Mar Saba, a Greek Orthodox monastery near Jerusalem. He was ordained as a priest and spent the rest of his life at Mar Saba, where his rhetorical skills earned him the nickname *Chrysorrhoas* (Greek for "the golden orator"; literally, "the golden stream"). He is venerated as a saint by the Eastern (Greek) Orthodox, Roman Catholic, Eastern (Syriac) Catholic, and Lutheran Churches and by the Anglican Communion.

Shortly before becoming a monk, John wrote three groundbreaking treatises on religious images. The following selection is from John's defense of the use of icons in Christian worship. He was responding to Christian iconoclasts ("image breakers"), who labeled the use of icons idolatrous, and particularly to the Byzantine emperor Leo III (ca. 685–741; reigned from 717 until his death), who in 726 issued his first edict against the veneration of images and their exhibition in public places. In 754, iconoclasts had John condemned at the Council of Hieria. However, John's defense was important for the life of the Orthodox Church, which still makes use of icons in its worship. John's condemnation was reversed, and the legitimacy of such icons was proclaimed, at the Second Council of Nicaea, in 787.

Born seventy-five years after the conventionally designated close of the Patristic Era, John of Damascus is a transitional figure between the Patristic Era and the Middle Ages. Damascus having fallen to the Arab armies in 634, the Christian community into which John was born had been under a Muslim regime for forty years. According to some reports, his family adjusted well to this regime. Culturally and religiously, however, he was in full continuity with the Greek Christianity of the Byzantine Roman Empire, much of which the Arabs now ruled. His defense of the Christian veneration of icons strikingly counters the Muslim prohibition of such veneration. The extent to which the Muslim prohibition may have influenced the Byzantine iconoclasm that John condemns remains an open question. In any case, Muslim influence did not inhibit John in his defense of iconodulia, the veneration of images. In the Christian world, John's view prevailed until the Calvinist Reformation, eight centuries later.

FROM THREE TREATISES ON IMAGES

From the Third Treatise

(26) Who first made images?

God himself first begat his Only-begotten Son and Word, his living and natural image, the exact imprint of his eternity; he then made human kind in accordance with the same image and likeness. And Adam saw God and heard the sound of his feet, as he walked in the evening, and he hid himself in paradise;[1] and Jacob saw and wrestled with God[2]—it is clear that God appeared to him as a man— and Moses saw him as a human back, and Isaias saw him as a man seated on a throne, and Daniel saw the likeness of a man, and as a son of man coming upon the ancient of days.[3] No one, however, saw the nature of God, but the figure and image of one who was yet to come. For the invisible Son and Word of God was about to become truly human, that he might be united to our nature and seen upon earth. All those, therefore, who saw the figure and image of the One who was to come venerated him, as Paul the Apostle says in the Epistle to the Hebrews, "All these died in faith, not having obtained the promises, but have seen and greeted them from afar."[4] Should I not, therefore, make an image of the one who appeared for my sake in the nature of flesh, and venerate and honor him with the honor and veneration offered to his image? Abraham did not see God's nature ("for no one has ever seen God"),[5] but the image of God and falling down he venerated him.[6] Jesus the son of Nave did not see the nature of an angel, but its image (for the angelic nature cannot be seen by bodily eyes) and falling down he venerated him,[7] likewise also Daniel (for an angel is not God, but God's creature and slave and attendant), he venerated him, not as God, but as God's attendant and servant.[8] And should I not make images of the friends of Christ, and should I not venerate them, not as gods, but as images of God's friends? For neither Jacob nor Daniel venerated the angels who appeared to them as gods, neither do I venerate the image as God, but through the images of his saints I offer veneration and honor to God, for whose sake I reverence his friends also, and this I do out of respect [for them]. God was not united to the angelic nature, but to human nature. God did not become an angel, but in nature and truth God

TRANSLATED BY Andrew Louth. Bracketed insertions are the translator's.

1. See Genesis 3:8.
2. See Genesis 32:25–31.
3. See Daniel 7:13. "Moses . . . back": See Exodus 33:18–23. "Isaiah . . . throne": See Isaiah 6:1.
4. Hebrews 11:13.
5. John 1:18.

6. See Genesis 18:1–3.
7. "Jesus . . . Nave": Greek *Iēsous* (Latin *Jesus*) is a translation of the Hebrew *Joshua*. The allusion here is to Joshua Son of Nun (Joshua 5:13–15). The intrusion of "Nave" remains unexplained.
8. See Daniel 8:15–17, 10:7–21.

became a human being. "For God did not take on him [the nature of] angels, but he took on him the seed of Abraham."[9] The Son of God did not become an angelic nature hypostatically;[1] the Son of God became hypostatically a human nature. Angels do not participate in, nor do they become sharers in, the divine nature, but in divine activity or grace; human beings, however, do participate in, and become sharers of, the divine nature, as many as partake of the holy Body of Christ and drink his precious Blood; for it is united to the divinity hypostatically, and the two natures are hypostatically and inseparably united in the Body of Christ of which we partake, and we share in the two natures, in the body in a bodily manner, and in the divinity spiritually, or rather in both in both ways, not that we have become identical [with God] hypostatically (for we first subsisted, and then we were united), but through assimilation with the Body and the Blood. And how are those who through the keeping of the commandments preserve their union pure not greater than the angels? Our nature is a little lower than the angels because of death and the grossness of the body, but through God's favor and union with him it has become greater than the angels. For the angels stand with fear and trembling before [that nature] seated on the throne of glory in Christ, and they will stand trembling at the judgment. It is not said of them in Scripture that they will be seated together with, or be partakers of, the divine glory ("for they are all ministering spirits sent forth to serve, for the sake of those who are to inherit salvation"),[2] not that they will reign together, nor that they will be glorified together, nor that they will sit at the Father's table, but the saints are sons of God, sons of the kingdom and heirs of God and fellow-heirs with Christ. Therefore, I honor the saints and I glorify them together with Christ as his slaves and friends and fellow-heirs: slaves by nature, friends by choice, and sons and heirs by divine grace, as the Lord said to the Father.

9. Hebrews 2:16.
1. Substantially or essentially.

2. Hebrews 1:14.

PSEUDO-DIONYSIUS THE AREOPAGITE
fl. ca. 500

FROM ON MYSTICAL THEOLOGY

According to the New Testament, Dionysius the Areopagite was converted to Christianity by the Apostle Paul (Acts 17:34). Historians have not been able to identify the sixth-century Syrian monk who adopted the pseudonym Dionysos and thus became mistaken for both the biblical convert and the third-century Christian martyr Saint Denis (also called Dionysius, Dennis, or Denys). "Dionysos" wrote a series of Greek treatises and letters that aimed to unite Neoplatonic philosophy with Christian theology. The major works of the so-called Pseudo-Dionysius the Areopagite are "On the Celestial Hierarchy," "On the Ecclesiastical Hierarchy," "On the Names of God," and the latter's companion piece, "On Mystical Theology."

Mystical theology, as Pseudo-Dionysius uses the phrase, discusses the mystery of God rather than, as a modern reader might expect, discussing human mystical or esoteric experience. Addressing "Timothy, my friend"—likely meaning the Apostle Paul's disciple of that name, but chosen to add some first-century atmosphere to the text—Pseudo-Dionysius argues that the nature of God is ineffable, is beyond all rational formulas, and can be described only with negatives, as in not-this and not-that. This brief treatise profoundly affected later theology in Greece and, after being translated into Latin in the ninth century, in the West. It was not until the Renaissance that the author was discovered to be pseudonymous.

PRONOUNCING GLOSSARY

Areopagite: *ehr-ree-ah´-pah-gait*

Dionysius: *dai-oh-nee´-see-uhs*

Dionysos: *dai-oh-nai´-sos* [*ai* ryhming with *rye*]

FROM ON MYSTICAL THEOLOGY

From CHAPTER ONE

What Is the Divine Darkness?

1. Trinity!! Higher than any being,
          any divinity, any goodness!
    Guide of Christians
        in the wisdom of heaven!
Lead us up beyond unknowing and light,
    up to the farthest, highest peak
        of mystic scripture,
    where the mysteries of God's Word
        lie simple, absolute and unchangeable
        in the brilliant darkness of a hidden silence.
    Amid the deepest shadow
        they pour overwhelming light
        on what is most manifest.
    Amid the wholly unsensed and unseen
        they completely fill our sightless minds
        with treasures beyond all beauty.

For this I pray; and, Timothy, my friend, my advice to you as you look for a sight of the mysterious things, is to leave behind you everything perceived and understood, everything perceptible and understandable, all that is not and all that is, and, with your understanding laid aside, to strive upward as much as you can toward union with him who is beyond all being and knowledge. By an undivided and absolute abandonment of yourself and everything, shedding all and freed from all, you will be uplifted to the ray of the divine shadow which is above everything that is.

                  ✳   ✳   ✳

TRANSLATED BY Evelyn Sire.

CHAPTER FOUR

That the Supreme Cause of Every Perceptible Thing Is Not Itself Perceptible

So this is what we say. The Cause of all is above all and is not inexistent, life-less, speechless, mindless. It is not a material body, and hence has neither shape nor form, quality, quantity, or weight. It is not in any place and can neither be seen nor be touched. It is neither perceived nor is it perceptible. It suffers neither disorder nor disturbance and is overwhelmed by no earthly passion. It is not powerless and subject to the disturbances caused by sense perception. It endures no deprivation of light. It passes through no change, decay, division, loss, no ebb and flow, nothing of which the senses may be aware. None of all this can either be identified with it nor attributed to it.

From CHAPTER FIVE

That the Supreme Cause of Every Conceptual Thing Is Not Itself Conceptual

Again, as we climb higher we say this. It is not soul or mind, nor does it pos-sess imagination, conviction, speech, or understanding. Nor is it speech per se, understanding per se. It cannot be spoken of and it cannot be grasped by understanding. It is not number or order, greatness or smallness, equal-ity or inequality, similarity or dissimilarity. It is not immovable, moving, or at rest. It has no power, it is not power, nor is it light. It does not live nor is it life. It is not a substance, nor is it eternity or time. It cannot be grasped by the understanding since it is neither knowledge nor truth. It is not kingship. It is not wisdom. It is neither one nor oneness, divinity nor goodness. Nor is it a spirit, in the sense in which we understand that term. It is not sonship or fatherhood and it is nothing known to us or to any other being. It falls neither within the predicate of nonbeing nor of being. Existing beings do not know it as it actually is and it does not know them as they are. There is no speaking of it, nor name nor knowledge of it. Darkness and light, error and truth—it is none of these. It is beyond assertion and denial. We make asser-tions and denials of what is next to it, but never of it, for it is both beyond every assertion, being the perfect and unique cause of all things, and, by virtue of its preeminently simple and absolute nature, free of every limita-tion, beyond every limitation; it is also beyond every denial.

* * *

BIOGRAPHICAL AND AUTOBIOGRAPHICAL TEXTS

Many Christian texts from antiquity include autobiographical reflections, first-person accounts of how individuals have been affected and transformed by religious faith. For example, in his letters, such as 2 Corinthians 11–12, Saint Paul reflects on his life in terms of his spirituality. Only in the very late fourth century, with his *Confessions*, did Saint Augustine of Hippo write what can be confidently called a full autobiography about Christian experience. Such introspective literature became widespread in the medieval and postmedieval world, so it is essential reading for the study of Christian spirituality or of the personal experience of religious faith.

SAINT JEROME
ca. 347–420

FROM LETTERS

Eusebius Sophronius Hieronymus—called in English Jerome or Saint Jerome and revered as a Doctor (from the Latin for "Teacher") of the Church—was a prodigiously prolific and notoriously opinionated writer. Indeed, among the fathers of the Church, he is second in his overall output only to Saint Augustine of Hippo, with whom he conducted a voluminous and sometimes stormy correspondence. Jerome is best remembered in Christian history for his epoch-making translation of the Bible from Hebrew, Aramaic, and Greek into Latin. Since the early Greek-speaking Church read the Old Testament in an ancient Greco-Jewish translation called the Septuagint and since the Latin-speaking Church knew the Jewish Scriptures only in translations made from that Greek, Jerome's insistence on the priority of the original Hebrew language was unprecedented in his day.

His translation—called the Vulgate because Latin was then the "vulgar," or common, language in the Western empire—eclipsed all other Latin translations and became over time so utterly identified with the Bible that medieval Europe forgot the great translator's insistence on the original. The early acceptance of the new translation had been far from automatic, however, and owed much to the blessing and backing of the pope who commissioned it, Damasus I (pope from 366 until his death, in 384).

Jerome was also a highly gifted letter-writer, one of the most dynamic and distinctive voices in Latin literature. In the passages that follow, from his famous letter to Eustochium (a young female disciple), which is mostly a treatise on the ascetic life, Jerome recounts his struggles to overcome both his sensual desires and his passion for the pagan classics. Though he stresses the need to vanquish the sinful self, he dramatizes that self and shows its persistent vitality.

Cicero: *sí´-se-roh*   Plautus: *plow´-tuhs*

FROM LETTERS

How often, when I was established in the desert[1] and in that vast solitude which is scorched by the sun's heat and affords a savage habitation
for monks, did I think myself amid the delights of Rome! I would sit
alone because I was filled with bitterness.[2] My limbs were roughly clad in
sackcloth—an unlovely sight. My neglected skin had taken on the appearance of an Ethiopian's body. Daily I wept, daily I groaned, and whenever
insistent slumber overcame my resistance, I bruised my awkward bones upon
the bare earth. Of food and drink I say nothing, since even the sick drink
only cold water, and to get any cooked food is a luxury. There was I, therefore,
who from fear of hell had condemned myself to such a prison, with only scor-
pions and wild beasts as companions. Yet I was often surrounded by dancing
girls. My face was pale from fasting, and my mind was hot with desire in a
body cold as ice. Though my flesh, before its tenant, was already as good as
dead, the fires of the passions kept boiling within me.

And so, destitute of all help, I used to lie at Jesus' feet. I bathed them with
my tears, I wiped them with my hair.[3] When my flesh rebelled, I subdued it
by weeks of fasting. I do not blush at my hapless state; nay rather, I lament
that I am not now what I was then. I remember that I often joined day to
night with my lamentation and did not cease beating my breast until peace
of mind returned with the Lord's rebuke. I was afraid even of my little
cell—as though it were conscious of my thoughts. Angry at myself and
tense, I used to go out alone into the desert. Whenever I saw some deep valley, some rugged mountain, some precipitous crags, it was this I made my
place of prayer, my place of punishment for the wretched flesh. And—as my
Lord Himself is witness—after many tears, after fixing my eyes on the heavens, I sometimes seemed to myself to be surrounded by companies of angels
and rejoiced, singing happily: *We run after thee to the odor of thy ointments.*[4]

*   *   *

It was many years ago when, for the sake of the kingdom of heaven, I had
cut myself off from my home, my parents, my sister, my kinsmen, and—
what was even more difficult—from an accustomed habit of good living.[5]
I was going to Jerusalem to be a soldier of Christ. But I could not do without the library which I had collected for myself at Rome by great care and
effort. And so, poor wretch that I was, I used to fast and then read Cicero.[6]
After frequent night vigils, after shedding tears which the remembrance of

TRANSLATED BY Charles Christopher Mierow. The translation's section and subsection numbers have been
omitted.

1. The desert of Chalcis, not far from ancient
Antioch, Syria.
2. See Ruth 1:20: "Call me Mara [Hebrew for
bitterness]."
3. See Luke 7:38.

4. See Song of Songs (Song of Solomon) 1:3.
5. See Mark 10:29.
6. Marcus Tullius Cicero (106–43 B.C.E.),
Roman statesman, orator, and author.

past sins brought forth from my inmost heart, I would take in my hands a volume of Plautus.[7] When I came to myself and began to read a prophet again, I rebelled at the uncouth style and—because with my blinded eyes I could not look upon the light—I thought this the fault not of my eyes but of the sun.

While the old serpent[8] was thus having sport with me, in about Mid-Lent a fever attacked my enfeebled body and spread to my very vitals, what I say is almost beyond belief, but without cessation it so wrought havoc upon my wretched limbs that my flesh could scarcely cling to my bones. Meanwhile preparations for my funeral were being made. My entire body was already cold. The vital warmth of life still throbbed feebly only in my poor breast. Suddenly I was caught up in the spirit and dragged before the tribunal of the Judge. Here there was so much light and such a glare from the brightness of those standing around that I cast myself on the ground and dared not look up. Upon being asked my status, I replied that I was a Christian. And He who sat upon the judgment seat said: "Thou liest. Thou art a Ciceronian, not a Christian. *Where thy treasure is, there is thy heart also.*"[9] I was struck dumb on the spot. Amid the blows—for He had ordered me to be beaten—I was tormented the more by the flame of conscience. I repeated to myself the verse: *And who shall confess thee in hell?*[1] However, I began to cry aloud and to say with lamentation: "Have mercy on me, Lord, have mercy upon me."[2] The petition re-echoed amid the lashes. Finally, casting themselves before the knees of Him who presided, the bystanders besought Him to have mercy on the young man, granting me opportunity to repent of my error and then to exact the penalty if I ever again read books of pagan literature. Being caught in such an extremity, I would have been willing to make even greater promises. I began to take an oath, swearing by His name, saying: "O Lord, if ever I possess or read secular writings, I have denied thee." After I had uttered the words of this oath, I was discharged and returned to the world above. To the surprise of all, I opened my eyes, which were suffused with such showers of tears that my grief produced belief in the incredulous. That had not been mere sleep or meaningless dreams, by which we are often deceived. As witness I have the tribunal before which I lay, as witness the judgment of which I was afraid. May it never be my fate to undergo such questioning! My shoulders were black and blue, and I felt the blows after I awoke from sleep. After that I read God's word with greater zeal than I had previously read the writings of mortals.

---

7. Titus Maccius Plautus (ca. 254–184 B.C.E), Roman dramatist.
8. Satan, who tempted Eve in the form of a serpent (see p. 83).
9. See Matthew 6:21.
1. See Psalm 6:6.
2. See Psalm 56:2.

SAINT AUGUSTINE OF HIPPO
354–430

FROM CONFESSIONS

Aurelius Augustinus, known to the world as Augustine, is one of the giants of Christian and world literature. He was born in Thagaste (now Souk Ahras, Algeria), in the Roman province of Numidia. His mother, Monica, was a devout Christian; his father, Patricius, was a pagan (who converted very late in life at his wife's urging). Monica wanted Augustine baptized as a child, but Patricius forbade it. Augustine's first language seems to have been Latin, and his education began in Thagaste and nearby Madaurus. At age seventeen, he moved to Carthage (now a suburb of modern-day Tunis) to study the art of rhetoric. He became attracted to the teachings of Manichaeism, a Gnostic religion (although he never became more than an auditor, the lowest class of membership), and he lived with a woman who gave birth to his son. After more than a decade of teaching grammar and then rhetoric, Augustine grew disgusted with the wild, undisciplined behavior of his students and emigrated to Italy. In late 384, in Milan, he accepted the highly respected professorship of rhetoric at the imperial court. Monica joined him in Milan and remained there until her death

By this time, Augustine had drifted from Manichaeism. He was drawn toward Christianity by his studies of Neoplatonism; by his association with Ambrose, the bishop of Milan and an accomplished scholar; and by his friendships with like-minded young spiritual "seekers," such as Alypius and Ponticianus, who were stirred by reports about a new monastic movement initiated in Egypt by the monk Anthony (ca. 250–355), now known as Anthony the Great or Saint Anthony (see p. 262). In the famous conversion scene recounted in his *Confessions*, Augustine was baptized by Ambrose at Easter in 387.

Augustine then committed himself to a celibate life and resigned his academic post. After the deaths of his mother and his son, he returned to Africa, where he sold his estate and distributed the proceeds to the poor. He turned his family house into a monastery, which went on to enormously influence the ecclesiastical life of North Africa and western Europe. In 391, Augustine was ordained a priest at Hippo Regius (Annaba, Algeria), and he was made a bishop five years after that. For the next quarter-century, he led his community, preached, taught, and wrote. He left behind over a hundred titles in theology, scriptural interpretation, sermons, and letters. Augustine died in 430, as a Vandal army tightened its grip on the city of Hippo Regius, most of which it would soon destroy. He is venerated as a Doctor (from the Latin for "Teacher") of the Church and as a saint in the Roman Catholic, Eastern Orthodox, Oriental Orthodox, and Lutheran Churches and by the Anglican Communion.

Between 397 and 398, Augustine wrote his thirteen-book *Confessions*, which is sometimes published as *The Confessions of St. Augustine*. This work may rightly be regarded as the fountainhead of Western autobiography or memoir. For Augustine, "confession" does not primarily mean the public admission of regrettable or shameful acts. It is rather the proclamation of one's faith in God. Addressing God, Augustine writes in the second person, but he intends his story to be "overheard" by his fellow Christians, who are called on to praise God for his rescue of Augustine the sinner. By building on the famed narrative of Saint Paul's response to the call of Christ (Acts 9:1–30) Augustine helped make conversion one of the central themes of Christian life. He concludes his *Confessions* with four books of nonautobiographical, deeply passionate meditations on the opening verses of Genesis, time, memory, and reading Scripture.

Alypius: *uh-li´-pee-uhs*

Cicero: *si´-se-roh*

Hortensius: *hor-ten´-see-uhs*

Manicheans: *ma-ni-kee´-uhns*

Nebridius: *ne-bree´-dee-uhs*

Ponticianus: *pon-tee-cee-ahn´-uhs*

FROM CONFESSIONS

From BOOK EIGHT

VI

* * *

(14) On a certain day—Nebridius[1] was away for some reason I cannot recall—there came to Alypius and me at our house one Ponticianus, a fellow countryman of ours, being from Africa, holder of an important post in the Emperor's court. There was something or other he wanted of us and we sat down to discuss the matter. As it happened he noticed a book on a gaming table by which we were sitting. He picked it up, opened it, and found that it was the Apostle Paul, which surprised him because he had expected that it would be one of the books I wore myself out teaching. Then he smiled a little and looked at me, and expressed pleasure but surprise too at having come suddenly upon that book, and only that book, lying before me. For he was a Christian and a devout Christian; he knelt before You in church, O our God, in daily prayer and many times daily. I told him that I had given much care to these writings. Whereupon he began to tell the story of the Egyptian monk Anthony, whose name was held in high honour among Your servants, although Alypius and I had never heard it before that time. When he learned this, he was the more intent upon telling the story, anxious to introduce so great a man to men ignorant of him, and very much marvelling at our ignorance. But Alypius and I stood amazed to hear of Your wonderful works, done in the true faith and in the Catholic Church so recently, practically in our own times, and with such numbers of witnesses. All three of us were filled with wonder, we because the deeds we were now hearing were so great, and he because we had never heard them before.

* * *

VII

(16) This was the story Ponticianus told. But You, Lord, while he was speaking, turned me back towards myself, taking me from behind my own back where I had put myself all the time that I preferred not to see myself. And You set

---

TRANSLATED BY F. J. Sheed. In the original translation, some Bible quotations, allusions, and echoes were signaled with italic type. The italics have been romanized, and Bible citations have been provided where pertinent. The bracketed insertion is in the original translation.

1. A close friend of Augustine.

me there before my own face that I might see how vile I was, how twisted and unclean and spotted and ulcerous. I saw myself and was horrified; but there was no way to flee from myself. If I tried to turn my gaze from myself, there was Ponticianus telling what he was telling; and again You were setting me face to face with myself, forcing me upon my own sight, that I might see my iniquity and loathe it. I had known it, but I had pretended not to see it, had deliberately looked the other way and let it go from my mind.

(17) But this time, the more ardently I approved those two[2] as I heard of their determination to win health for their souls by giving themselves up wholly to Your healing, the more detestable did I find myself in comparison with them. For many years had flowed by—a dozen or more—from the time when I was nineteen and was stirred by the reading of Cicero's *Hortensius*[3] to the study of wisdom; and here was I still postponing the giving up of this world's happiness to devote myself to the search for that of which not the finding only but the mere seeking is better than to find all the treasures and kingdoms of men, better than all the body's pleasures though they were to be had merely for a nod. But I in my great worthlessness—for it was greater thus early—had begged You for chastity, saying, "Grant me chastity and continence, but not yet." For I was afraid that You would hear my prayer too soon, and too soon would heal me from the disease of lust which I wanted satisfied rather than extinguished. So I had gone wandering in my sacrilegious superstition through the base ways [of the Manicheans]: not indeed that I was sure they were right but that I preferred them to the Christians, whom I did not inquire about in the spirit of religion but simply opposed through malice.

(18) I had thought that my reason for putting off from day to day the following of You alone to the contempt of earthly hopes was that I did not see any certain goal towards which to direct my course. But now the day was come when I stood naked in my own sight and my conscience accused me: "Why is my voice not heard? Surely you are the man who used to say that you could not cast off vanity's baggage for an uncertain truth. Very well: now the truth is certain, yet you are still carrying the load. Here are men who have been given wings to free their shoulders from the load, though they did not wear themselves out in searching nor spend ten years or more thinking about it."

Thus was I inwardly gnawed at. And I was in the grip of the most horrible and confounding shame, while Ponticianus was telling his story. He finished the tale and the business for which he had come; and he went his way, and I to myself. What did I not say against myself, with what lashes of condemnation did I not scourge my soul to make it follow me now that I wanted to follow You! My soul hung back. It would not follow, yet found no excuse for not following. All its arguments had already been used and refuted. There remained only trembling silence: for it feared as very death the cessation of that habit of which in truth it was dying.

✳   ✳   ✳

2. Alypius and Ponticianus.
3. Or "On the Philosophy," a dialogue (now lost)

written in 45 B.C.E. by the Roman statesman, orator, and author Marcus Tullius Cicero.

XII

(28) When my most searching scrutiny had drawn up all my vileness from the secret depths of my soul and heaped it in my heart's sight, a mighty storm arose in me, bringing a mighty rain of tears. That I might give way to my tears and lamentations, I rose from Alypius:[4] for it struck me that solitude was more suited to the business of weeping. I went far enough from him to prevent his presence from being an embarrassment to me. So I felt, and he realised it. I suppose I had said something and the sound of my voice was heavy with tears. I arose, but he remained where we had been sitting, still in utter amazement. I flung myself down somehow under a certain fig tree[5] and no longer tried to check my tears, which poured forth from my eyes in a flood, an acceptable sacrifice to Thee.[6] And much I said not in these words but to this effect: And Thou, O Lord, how long?[7] How long, Lord; wilt Thou be angry forever?[8] Remember not our former iniquities.[9] For I felt that I was still bound by them. And I continued my miserable complaining: "How long, how long shall I go on saying tomorrow and again tomorrow? Why not now, why not have an end to my uncleanness this very hour?"

(29) Such things I said, weeping in the most bitter sorrow of my heart. And suddenly I heard a voice from some nearby house, a boy's voice or a girl's voice, I do not know: but it was a sort of sing-song, repeated again and again, "Take and read, take and read." I ceased weeping and immediately began to search my mind most carefully as to whether children were accustomed to chant these words in any kind of game, and I could not remember that I had ever heard any such thing. Damming back the flood of my tears I arose, interpreting the incident as quite certainly a divine command to open my book of Scripture and read the passage at which I should open. For it was part of what I had been told about Anthony, that from the Gospel which he happened upon he had felt that he was being admonished, as though what was being read was being spoken directly to himself: Go, sell what thou hast and give to the poor, and thou shalt have treasure in heaven; and come follow Me.[1] By this experience he had been in that instant converted to You. So I was moved to return to the place where Alypius was sitting, for I had put down the Apostle's book there when I arose. I snatched it up, opened it and in silence read the passage upon which my eyes first fell: Not in rioting and drunkenness, not in chambering and impurities, not in contention and envy, but put ye on the Lord Jesus Christ and make not provision for the flesh in its concupiscences.[2] I had no wish to read further, and no need. For in that instant, with the very ending of the sentence, it was as though a light of utter confidence shone in all my heart, and all the darkness of uncertainty vanished away.

(30) Then leaving my finger in the place or marking it by some other sign, I closed the book and in complete calm told the whole thing to Alypius and

---

4. I.e., from where Alypius and Augustine were sitting.
5. See John 1:48.
6. Psalms 51:19.
7. Psalms 6:3.

8. Psalms 79:5.
9. Psalms 79:8.
1. Anthony walked into a church just as this passage—Matthew 19:21—was being read aloud.
2. Romans 13:13–14.

he similarly told me what had been going on in himself, of which I knew nothing. He asked to see what I had read. I showed him, and he looked further than I had read. I had not known what followed. And this is what followed: Now him that is weak in faith, take unto you.[3] He applied this to himself and told me so. And he was confirmed by this message, and with no troubled wavering gave himself to God's good will and purpose—a purpose indeed most suited to his character, for in these matters he had been immeasurably better than I.

Then we went in to my mother and told her, to her great joy. We related how it had come about: she was filled with triumphant exultation, and praised You who are mighty beyond what we ask or conceive: for she saw that You had given her more than with all her pitiful weeping she had ever asked. For You converted me to Yourself so that I no longer sought a wife nor any of this world's promises, but stood upon that same rule of faith in which You had shown me to her so many years before.[4] Thus You changed her mourning into joy,[5] a joy far richer than she had thought to wish, a joy much dearer and purer than she had thought to find in grandchildren of my flesh.

From BOOK TEN

* * *

XXVII

(38) Late have I loved Thee, O Beauty so ancient and so new; late have I loved Thee! For behold Thou wert within me, and I outside; and I sought Thee outside and in my unloveliness fell upon those lovely things that Thou hast made. Thou wert with me and I was not with Thee. I was kept from Thee by those things, yet had they not been in Thee, they would not have been at all. Thou didst call and cry to me and break open my deafness: and Thou didst send forth Thy beams and shine upon me and chase away my blindness: Thou didst breathe fragrance upon me, and I drew in my breath and do now pant for Thee: I tasted Thee,[6] and now hunger and thirst for Thee:[7] Thou didst touch me, and I have burned for Thy peace.

* * *

FROM THE CITY OF GOD

The City of God, also known in English as *The City of God against the Pagans*, is Augustine's greatest theological work. Running about twelve hundred pages in modern translations, this encyclopedic volume, written between 413 and 428, covers every characteristic feature of Christian life and thought up to its time. In the following excerpt, Augustine reveals the characteristic harshness of his position on

3. Romans 14:1.
4. In Book Three, Augustine recounts his mother's vision of the two of them standing on a wooden rule (i.e., belonging to the same faith).

5. See Psalms 30:11.
6. See Psalms 34:8.
7. See Matthew 5:6.

evil. In his view, the Fall—Adam and Eve's sin of disobedience in eating the forbidden fruit of the tree of the knowledge of good and evil (see p. 83)—is a monumental catastrophe. Because of this "original sin," the human condition, the state of the human heart and soul, descends into utter corruption. The soul's corruption infects the body (or "flesh") through physical lusts and other wickedness, suffering, and death. This state is universal, passed on to each child by his or her parents in the act of generation, and incurable except for the gift of God's special favor, or grace. But grace cannot be earned, and no one has a right to it. Redemption is granted to "some" persons, but not in ways that can be predicted or grasped by human intelligence.

This whole process is known as predestination, a concept that played an immense role in later Christian theology, most importantly in Calvinism and related schools of thought (e.g., Jansenism). Predestination can be traced back to the New Testament (e.g., Paul in Romans 9:13); but it can seem more than a little gloomy, especially when taken to indicate that the majority of the human race is condemned to hell. While the doctrine is still widely believed in Evangelical circles, it has been denied or softened by Roman Catholics, Eastern Orthodox Christians, and many "mainstream" Protestant denominations, such as Anglicans, Methodists, and some Lutherans.

PRONOUNCING GLOSSARY

Epicurean: *eh-pi-kyu-ree´-uhn*   Magdalene: *mag´-duh-lin*
Galatians: *guh-lay´-shuns*

This catacomb funerary tablet is for Atimetus, age eight; ca. 200 c.e., Catacomb of St. Sebastian, Rome. For Christians, as Augustine explains in *The City of God*, Jesus has redeemed humanity from death by his Resurrection. Two domestic slaves in Caesar's household expressed their hope for resurrection by adorning their young son's burial niche with an anchor—the symbol of that hope—and a fish. The Greek word for *fish* spells out an acronym for "Jesus Christ, God's Son, Savior."

FROM THE CITY OF GOD

BOOK XIV

1. That All Men Would Have Been Plunged into an Everlasting Second Death by the Sin of the First Man, Had Not God's Grace Redeemed Many

As I have already said in the preceding books,[1] God chose to create the human race from one single man. His purpose in doing this was not only that the human race should be united in fellowship by a natural likeness, but also that men should be bound together by kinship in the unity of concord, linked by the bond of peace. And the individual members of this race would not have been subject to death, had not the first two—one of whom was created from no one, and the other from him—merited it by their disobedience. So great was the sin of those two that human nature was changed by it for the worse; and so bondage to sin and the necessity of death were transmitted to their posterity.

Now the sway of the kingdom of death over men was so complete that all would have been driven headlong, as their due punishment, into that second death to which there is no end, had not some of them been redeemed by the unmerited grace of God. Thus it is that, though there are a great many nations throughout the world, living according to different rites and customs, and distinguished by many different forms of language, arms and dress, there nonetheless exist only two orders, as we may call them, of human society; and, following our Scriptures, we may rightly speak of these as two cities.[2] The one is made up of men who live according to the flesh, and the other of those who live according to the spirit. Each desires its own kind of peace, and, when they have found what they sought, each lives in its own kind of peace.

2. That Life According to the Flesh Is to Be Understood as Arising Not Only from the Faults of the Body, but Also from Those of the Mind

First, therefore, we must see what it is to live according to the flesh and according to the spirit. For anyone who takes what we have just said at face value may err, either because he does not remember how Holy Scripture uses this manner of speaking, or because he pays too little heed to it. On the one hand, he may certainly suppose that the Epicurean philosophers live according to the flesh; for they place man's highest good in the pleasure of the body.[3] And he may suppose that the same is true of the other philosophers who hold in some way that the good of the body is man's highest good. And he may also suppose that it is true of the common people: of

TRANSLATED BY R. W. Dyson. The bracketed insertions are the translator's.

1. See Book XII, sections 22 and 28.
2. See Ephesians 2:19 and Philippians 3:20.
3. Actually, the Epicureans—followers of the Greek philosopher Epicurus (341–270 B.C.E.)— emphasized the avoidance of pain rather than gross physical pleasures. They also advocated moderate living and thus the avoidance of pain from overindulgence.

those who subscribe to no doctrine, who do not practise any kind of philosophy, but who, having a leaning towards lust, know no delight except that derived from the pleasure which they receive through the senses. On the other hand, he may suppose that the Stoics, who place man's highest good in the mind,[4] live according to the spirit; for what is man's mind if not spirit? In fact, however, it is clear that all of these live according to the flesh in the sense intended by Divine Scripture when it uses the expression.

For Scripture does not use the term 'flesh' to mean only the body of an earthly and mortal creature, as when it says: 'All flesh is not the same flesh: but there is one kind of flesh of men, another flesh of beasts, another of fishes, and another of birds.'[5] On the contrary, there are many other ways in which it uses the term, to signify different things. And among these various usages is that by which man himself—that is, the nature of man—is designated by 'flesh': a manner of speaking in which the whole is represented by a part; for example, 'By the deeds of the Law there shall no flesh be justified.'[6] For what does the apostle wish us to understand by this if not 'no man'? This is made clearer a little later, where he says, 'No man is justified by the Law';[7] and, in the Epistle to the Galatians, he says: 'Knowing that a man is not justified by the works of the Law.'[8]

According to this, we interpret the words 'And the Word was made flesh'[9] to mean that Christ became man. Certain persons who have not rightly understood this passage have supposed that Christ was without a human soul. But just as, when we read in the Gospel the words of Mary Magdalene, 'They have taken away my Lord, and I know not where they have laid Him,'[1] the whole is signified by the part, for she spoke only of the flesh of Christ, which she thought had been taken away from the sepulchre in which it was buried; so too the whole is signified by the part when the word 'flesh' is used but 'man' is meant, as in the instances given above.

The ways in which the Divine Scriptures use the word 'flesh,' then, are very numerous, and it would take too long to examine and collect them all. Our present purpose is to discover the meaning of life 'according to the flesh,' which is clearly an evil, even though the nature of flesh is not evil in itself. Let us, then, diligently examine that passage in the epistle which the apostle Paul wrote to the Galatians, where he says:

> Now the works of the flesh are manifest, which are these; Adultery, fornication, uncleanness, lasciviousness, idolatry, witchcraft, hatred, variance, emulations,[2] wrath, strife, seditions, heresies, envying, murders, drunkenness, revellings, and such like: of the which I tell you before, as I have also told you in time past, that they which do such things shall not inherit the kingdom of God.[3]

If we give to the whole of this passage of the apostle's epistle as much consideration as our present question is found to require, we shall be able to solve the question of what it is to live according to the flesh. For among the

4. Stoicism—founded by the Greek philosopher Zeno of Citium (ca. 335–ca. 263 B.C.E.)—viewed the intellect and wisdom as ways of avoiding destructive emotions.
5. 1 Corinthians 15:39.
6. Romans 3:20. In the New Testament Books of Romans and Galatians, the Apostle Paul discusses "justification" as God's reconciliation of

each individual's spiritual ledger (see p. 144).
7. Galatians 3:11 (not Romans, as "a little later" seems to indicate).
8. Galatians 2:16
9. John 1:14.
1. John 20:13.
2. Rivalries. "Variance": dissension.
3. Galatians 5:19–21.

'works of the flesh' which he says are 'manifest,' and which he enumerates and condemns, we find not only those which pertain to the pleasures of the flesh, such as fornication, uncleanness, lasciviousness, drunkenness and revellings, but also those which demonstrate vices of the mind and which have nothing to do with fleshly pleasure. For when it comes to idolatry, witchcraft, hatred, variance, emulations, wrath, strife, seditions, heresies: who does not see that these are vices of the mind rather than of the body? It may be, indeed, that a man tempers his desire for bodily pleasure out of devotion to an idol, or because of some heretical error. Even such a man as this, though he is seen to restrain and suppress the lusts of the flesh, is still convicted, on the authority of the apostle, of living according to the flesh; yet it is his very abstinence from the pleasures of the flesh that demonstrates that he is engaged in the damnable works of the flesh.

Who can feel hatred except in the mind? Would anyone, speaking to an enemy, or to someone who he thinks is his enemy, say, 'Your flesh is ill disposed towards me,' rather than 'Your mind'? Finally, just as, if anyone heard of 'carnalities' (if there were such a word), he would undoubtedly attribute them to the flesh [caro], so no one doubts that 'animosities' pertain to the mind [animus]. Why, then, does the 'teacher of the Gentiles in faith and verity'[4] give the name 'works of the flesh' to all these and similar failings? Simply because, using that figure of speech by which the whole is signified by a part, he intends the word 'flesh' to be understood as meaning 'man.'

3. The Cause of Sin Proceeds from the Soul, Not the Flesh; and the Corruption Resulting from Sin Is Not Itself a Sin, but a Punishment

Now someone may say that the flesh is the cause of moral evils of every kind, because it is thanks to the influence of the flesh that the soul lives as it does. But he who says this has not considered the whole nature of man with sufficient care. For 'the corruptible body presseth down the soul.'[5] Hence also the apostle, speaking of this corruptible body, first says, 'Our outward man perisheth,'[6] and then goes on to say,

> For we know that if our earthly house of this tabernacle[7] were dissolved, we have a building of God, a house not made with hands, eternal in the heavens. For in this we groan, earnestly desiring to be clothed upon with our house which is from heaven: if so be that being clothed we shall not be found naked. For we that are in this tabernacle do groan, being burdened: not for that we would be unclothed, but clothed upon, that mortality might be swallowed up of life.[8]

We are pressed down by the corruptible body, therefore, yet we know that the cause of our being pressed down is not the nature and substance of the

---

4. 1 Timothy 2:7. The "teacher" is Paul, the author of the First Letter to Timothy; the "Gentiles" are heathens, pagans.
5. Wisdom 9:15.
6. 2 Corinthians 4:16.
7. "Our earthly house of this tabernacle": the body.

8. 2 Corinthians 5:1–4; i.e., as translated in the New International Version of the Bible: "because we do not wish to be unclothed but to be clothed with our heavenly dwelling, so that what is mortal may be swallowed up by life" (life in the fullest spiritual sense, as elaborated below).

body, but its corruption; and, knowing this, we do not wish to be divested of the body, but to be clothed with its immortality. For there will still be a body then; but, because it will not be corruptible, it will not be a burden. At the present time, therefore, 'the corruptible body presseth down the soul, and the earthly tabernacle weigheth down the mind that museth upon many things.'[9] Nonetheless, those who suppose that the ills of the soul derive from the body are in error.

Virgil, it is true, seems to be expounding Platonic teaching in his magnificent verse when he says, 'The force of those seeds is fiery, and their source is heavenly, to the extent that they are not impeded by harmful bodies nor enfeebled by earthly limbs and dying members.'[1] Also, he wishes us to understand that the body is the source of all four of the most notable disturbances of the mind: desire, fear, joy and grief, which are the origin, as it were, of all sins and vices. And so he adds: 'Hence come desire and fear, gladness and sorrow; nor do they look up to heaven, but are confined in a dark and sightless cave.' Our faith, however, is something very different. For the corruption of the body, which presseth down the soul, was not the cause of the first sin, but its punishment; nor was it corruptible flesh that made the soul sinful, but the sinful soul that made the flesh corruptible.

Thus, though this corruption of the flesh results in some incitements to sin and in sinful desires themselves, we still must not attribute to the flesh all the vices of a wicked life. Otherwise, we should absolve the devil from all such vices, since he has no flesh. Certainly, we cannot say that the devil is a fornicator or a drunkard, or that he commits any other such vice pertaining to the pleasures of the flesh, even though it is he who secretly tempts and incites us to such sins. He is, however, supremely proud and envious; and these vices of pride and envy have so possessed him that he is doomed by them to eternal punishment in the prison of this murky air of ours.

Now those vices which hold sway over the devil are attributed by the apostle to the flesh, even though it is certain that the devil does not have any flesh. For the apostle says that hatred, variance, jealousy, wrath and envy are works of the flesh; and the source and origin of all these evils is pride, which reigns in the devil even though he is without flesh. For who has more hatred for the saints than he? Who is found to be more at variance with them, or more wrathful towards them, or more jealous and envious of them? Yet he has all these faults without having flesh. How, then, can they be the 'works of the flesh' other than because they are the works of man, to whom, as I have said, the apostle applies the term 'flesh'?

It is not, then, by having flesh, which the devil does not have, that man has become like the devil. Rather, it is by living according to his own self; that is, according to man. For the devil chose to live according to self when he did not abide in the truth, so that the lie that he told was his own, and not God's. The devil is not only a liar; he is 'the father of lies': he was, indeed, the first to lie, and falsehood, like sin, began with him.

*   *   *

9. Wisdom 9:15.

1. In these verses (730ff) from Book 6 of his epic poem *Aeneid*, the Roman poet Virgil (70–19 B.C.E.) draws on ideas from the Greek philosopher Plato (ca. 428–348 or 347 B.C.E.) about the earthly being an imperfect copy of the heavenly ideal; hence, the souls of mortals are seeds from the divine spirit.

28. Of the Quality of the Two Cities, the Earthly and the Heavenly

Two cities, then, have been created by two loves: that is, the earthly by love of self extending even to contempt of God, and the heavenly by love of God extending to contempt of self. The one, therefore, glories in itself, the other in the Lord; the one seeks glory from men, the other finds its highest glory in God, the Witness of our conscience. The one lifts up its head in its own glory; the other says to its God, 'Thou art my glory, and the lifter up of mine head.'[2] In the Earthly City, princes are as much mastered by the lust for mastery as the nations which they subdue are by them; in the Heavenly, all serve one another in charity, rulers by their counsel and subjects by their obedience. The one city loves its own strength as displayed in its mighty men; the other says to its God, 'I will love Thee, O Lord, my strength.'[3]

Thus, in the Earthly City, its wise men, who live according to man, have pursued the goods of the body or of their own mind, or both. Some of them who were able to know God 'glorified Him not as God, neither were thankful; but became vain in their imagination, and their foolish heart was darkened. Professing themselves to be wise' (that is, exalting themselves in their wisdom, under the dominion of pride), 'they became fools, and changed the glory of the incorruptible God into an image made like to corruptible man, and to birds, and four-footed beasts, and creeping things' (for in adoring images of this kind they were either the leaders of the people or their followers); 'and they worshipped and served the creature more than the Creator, Who is blessed forever.'[4] In the Heavenly City, however, man has no wisdom beyond the piety which rightly worships the true God, and which looks for its reward in the fellowship not only of holy men, but of angels also, 'that God may be all in all.'[5]

2. Psalms 3:3.
3. Psalms 18:1.

4. Romans 1:21–25
5. 1 Corinthians 15:28.

SULPICIUS SEVERUS
ca. 360–ca. 420

FROM LIFE OF SAINT MARTIN

Not much is known about Sulpicius (or Sulpitius) Severus, who was born to a noble family in Aquitaine, in southwestern France. He received a classical education and became a lawyer, but upon the death of his young wife and after getting to know Martin of Tours (316–397), he increasingly devoted himself to monastic life and was ordained as a priest. Although his history of the world from the creation to the end of the fourth century, the *Chronicle* (ca. 403), was widely read, his most popular work was his *Life of Saint Martin* (composition date unknown), which helped to make his old friend one of the best-known Christian saints.

Martin was born to pagan parents in the city of Sabaria (modern-day Szombathely, in western Hungary). His father, an officer of the Imperial Horse Guard in the Roman army, was later transferred to Ticinum (now Pavia, in northern Italy).

Martin, as the son of a military father, was automatically drafted into the cavalry and wound up serving near what is now the city of Amiens, in far northern France. At age eighteen, after experiencing a vision of Christ, Martin was baptized. Two years later, he left the army. In 371, against his will, he was consecrated bishop of Tours, in central France. He subsequently built a monastery at Marmoutier, across the Loire river from Tours, and divided his time between zealous pastoral work and cloistered prayer. Much of the rural population was still pagan, adherents of druidic religion. Martin opposed their beliefs and practices with both sacred eloquence and old-fashioned violence, such as by destroying shrines.

Life of Saint Martin can be seen as a model of the immensely successful genre of lives of the saints, which was practiced in the Catholic and Eastern Orthodox Churches. Unconcerned with the strictures of what we would call history, Sulpicius Severus and countless other hagiographers describe Christian heroes who, once they have abandoned "the world," are more or less perfect beings, endowed with every conceivable virtue. Displaying incredible courage, they convert sinners, work endless miracles, endure ferocious persecution and strenuous ascetic exercises, survive assassination attempts, encounter and conquer Satan, and leave the masses, believing or otherwise, awestruck. Some of the saints undoubtedly engaged in activities that even their secular critics would consider admirable. Martin, for instance, despite his hatred of heretics, pleaded with the Roman emperor Maximus to spare the life of the heretical Spanish cleric Priscillian. (Maximus agreed, but later had Priscillian and his followers beheaded.)

Martinmas is celebrated on November 11. This feast day was long famous in England because it was when cattle would be slaughtered and salted for winter. In the Early Middle Ages, Martinmas was followed by forty days of fasting and preparation for Christmas. This period was later shortened to what is now known as Advent (from the fourth Sunday before Christmas to December 25). Saint Martin has also been particularly celebrated in northern France and the Low Countries.

PRONOUNCING GLOSSARY

Amiens: *am-mee-uhn´*
catechumen: *ca-tuh-kyoo´-muhn*
Loire: *luh-wahr´*
Pannonia: *pah-noh-nee´-uh*

Sabaria: *sah-bah´-ree-uh*
Sulpicius Severus: *sul-pee´-see-uhs*
   se-ver´-uhs
Ticinum: *tee´-chee-nuhm*

FROM LIFE OF SAINT MARTIN

CHAPTER II

Military Service of St. Martin

Martin, then, was born at Sabaria in Pannonia, but was brought up at Ticinum, which is situated in Italy. His parents were, according to the judgment of the world, of no mean rank, but were heathens. His father was at first simply a soldier, but afterwards a military tribune. He himself in his youth following military pursuits was enrolled in the imperial guard, first under king Constantine, and then under Julian Caesar.[1] This, however, was

---

Translated by Alexander Roberts. The bracketed insertion is the translator's.

1. Roman emperor (ca. 331–363; reigned from 361 until his death); also called Julian the Apostate. "Constantine": Roman emperor (died 337; reigned from 306 until his death).

not done of his own free will, for, almost from his earliest years, the holy infancy of the illustrious boy aspired rather to the service of God. For, when he was of the age of ten years, he betook himself, against the wish of his parents, to the Church, and begged that he might become a catechumen.[2] Soon afterwards, becoming in a wonderful manner completely devoted to the service of God, when he was twelve years old, he desired to enter on the life of a hermit; and he would have followed up that desire with the necessary vows, had not his as yet too youthful age prevented. His mind, however, being always engaged on matters pertaining to the monasteries or the Church, already meditated in his boyish years what he afterwards, as a professed servant of Christ, fulfilled. But when an edict was issued by the ruling powers in the state, that the sons of veterans should be enrolled for military service, and he, on the information furnished by his father, (who looked with an evil eye on his blessed actions) having been seized and put in chains, when he was fifteen years old, was compelled to take the military oath, then showed himself content with only one servant as his attendant. And even to him, changing places as it were, he often acted as though, while really master, he had been inferior; to such a degree that, for the most part, he drew off his [servant's] boots and cleaned them with his own hand; while they took their meals together, the real master, however, generally acting the part of servant. During nearly three years before his baptism, he was engaged in the profession of arms, but he kept completely free from those vices in which that class of men become too frequently involved. He showed exceeding kindness towards his fellow-soldiers, and held them in wonderful affection; while his patience and humility surpassed what seemed possible to human nature. There is no need to praise the self-denial which he displayed: it was so great that, even at that date, he was regarded not so much as being a soldier as a monk. By all these qualities he had so endeared himself to the whole body of his comrades, that they esteemed him while they marvelously loved him. Although not yet made a new creature in Christ, he, by his good works, acted the part of a candidate for baptism. This he did, for instance, by aiding those who were in trouble, by furnishing assistance to the wretched, by supporting the needy, by clothing the naked, while he reserved nothing for himself from his military pay except what was necessary for his daily sustenance. Even then, far from being a senseless hearer of the Gospel, he so far complied with its precepts as to take no thought about the morrow.

CHAPTER III

Christ Appears to St. Martin

Accordingly, at a certain period, when he had nothing except his arms and his simple military dress, in the middle of winter, a winter which had shown itself more severe than ordinary, so that the extreme cold was proving fatal to many, he happened to meet at the gate of the city of Amiens a poor man destitute of clothing. He was entreating those that passed by to have compas-

2. Might take instruction as a Christian convert.

sion upon him, but all passed the wretched man without notice, when Martin, that man full of God, recognized that a being to whom others showed no pity, was, in that respect, left to him. Yet, what should he do? He had nothing except the cloak in which he was clad, for he had already parted with the rest of his garments for similar purposes. Taking, therefore, his sword with which he was girt, he divided his cloak into two equal parts, and gave one part to the poor man, while he again clothed himself with the remainder. Upon this, some of the by-standers laughed, because he was now an unsightly object, and stood out as but partly dressed. Many, however, who were of sounder understanding, groaned deeply because they themselves had done nothing similar. They especially felt this, because, being possessed of more than Martin, they could have clothed the poor man without reducing themselves to nakedness. In the following night, when Martin had resigned himself to sleep, he had a vision of Christ arrayed in that part of his cloak with which he had clothed the poor man. He contemplated the Lord with the greatest attention, and was told to own as his the robe which he had given. Ere long, he heard Jesus saying with a clear voice to the multitude of angels standing round—"Martin, who is still but a catechumen, clothed me with this robe." The Lord, truly mindful of his own words (who had said when on earth—"Inasmuch as ye have done these things to one of the least of these, ye have done them unto me"[3]) declared that he himself had been clothed in that poor man; and to confirm the testimony he bore to so good a deed, he condescended to show him himself in that very dress which the poor man had received. After this vision the sainted man was not puffed up with human glory, but, acknowledging the goodness of God in what had been done, and being now of the age of twenty years, he hastened to receive baptism. He did not, however, all at once, retire from military service, yielding to the entreaties of his tribune, whom he admitted to be his familiar tent-companion. For the tribune promised that, after the period of his office had expired, he too would retire from the world. Martin, kept back by the expectation of this event, continued, although but in name, to act the part of a soldier, for nearly two years after he had received baptism.

*　　*　　*

CHAPTER X

Martin as Bishop of Tours

And now having entered on the episcopal office, it is beyond my power fully to set forth how Martin distinguished himself in the discharge of its duties. For he remained with the utmost constancy, the same as he had been before. There was the same humility in his heart, and the same homeliness in his garments. Full alike of dignity and courtesy, he kept up the position of a bishop properly, yet in such a way as not to lay aside the objects and virtues of a monk. Accordingly he made use, for some time, of the cell connected with the church; but afterwards, when he felt it impossible to tolerate the disturbance caused by the numbers of those visiting it, he established a monastery for himself about two miles outside the city. This spot was so secret and

---

3. Matthew 25:40.

retired that he enjoyed in it the solitude of a hermit. For, on one side, it was surrounded by a precipitous rock of a lofty mountain, while the river Loire had shut in the rest of the plain by a bay extending back for a little distance; and the place could be approached only by one, and that a very narrow passage. Here, then, he possessed a cell constructed of wood. Many also of the brethren had, in the same manner, fashioned retreats for themselves, but most of them had formed these out of the rock of the overhanging mountain, hollowed into caves. There were altogether eighty disciples, who were being disciplined after the example of the saintly master. No one there had anything which was called his own; all things were possessed in common. It was not allowed either to buy or to sell anything, as is the custom among most monks. No art was practiced there, except that of transcribers, and even this was assigned to the brethren of younger years, while the elders spent their time in prayer. Rarely did any one of them go beyond the cell, unless when they assembled at the place of prayer. They all took their food together, after the hour of fasting was past. No one used wine, except when illness compelled them to do so. Most of them were clothed in garments of camels' hair.[4] Any dress approaching to softness was there deemed criminal, and this must be thought the more remarkable, because many among them were such as are deemed of noble rank. These, though far differently brought up, had forced themselves down to this degree of humility and patient endurance, and we have seen numbers of these afterwards made bishops. For what city or church would there be that would not desire to have its priests from among those in the monastery of Martin?

4. See Matthew 3:4 and 1:8.

SAINT PATRICK
late fifth century

FROM CONFESSION

The few verifiable details of Saint Patrick's life appear in two letters he wrote in Latin: the first, his *Confessio* (known as the *Confession*, the *Confessions*, or the *Declaration*), and the second, his *Epistola* (known as the *Letter to the Soldiers of Coroticus*). Scholars have puzzled about many of the particular places Patrick mentions. It is safe to say that at about age sixteen, Irish raiders captured him in Wales and enslaved him in Ireland. After working as a herdsman for six years, he escaped and returned to his family. Eventually, he returned to Ireland as an ordained bishop. By the seventh century, he had come to be revered as the patron saint of Ireland, as he is today by the Roman Catholic, Eastern (Greek) Orthodox, and Lutheran Churches and by the Anglican Communion. Although the years of Patrick's life are uncertain, Saint Patrick's Day is observed on March 17, the presumed date of his death. This holiday is celebrated in many countries as a liturgical feast day, a celebration of Ireland, or both. The legend related to this holiday—that it celebrates Saint Patrick's chasing of the snakes out of Ireland—is entirely false. There were no snakes in Ireland for anyone to chase out.

In the following selections from the *Confession*, Patrick reports some details about his early life. Throughout the text, he seeks to justify his life as a missionary against (unknown) critics of his ministry.

Bannavem Taburniae: *bahn´-nah-vem Tah-ber´-nee-ay*
Calpornius: *cal-por´-nee-uhs*

Potitus: *poh-tai´-tuhs* [*ai* rhyming with *rye*]

FROM CONFESSION

I am Patrick, a sinner, most unlearned, the least of all the faithful, and utterly despised by many. My father was Calpornius, a deacon, son of Potitus, a priest, of the village Bannavem Taburniae; he had a country seat nearby, and there I was taken captive.

I was then about sixteen years of age. I did not know the true God. I was taken into captivity to Ireland with many thousands of people—and deservedly so, because we turned away from God, and did not keep His commandments, and did not obey our priests, who used to remind us of our salvation. And the Lord brought over us the wrath of His anger[1] and scattered us among many nations,[2] even unto the utmost part of the earth,[3] where now my littleness is placed among strangers.

2. And there the Lord opened the sense of my unbelief that I might at last remember my sins and be converted with all my heart to the Lord my God, who had regard for my abjection, and mercy on my youth and ignorance, and watched over me before I knew Him, and before I was able to distinguish between good and evil, and guarded me, and comforted me as would a father his son.

3. Hence I cannot be silent—nor, indeed, is it expedient—about the great benefits and the great grace which the Lord has deigned to bestow upon me in the land of my captivity;[4] for this we can give to God in return after having been chastened by Him, to exalt and praise His wonders[5] before every nation that is anywhere under the heaven.[6]

4. Because there is no other God, nor ever was, nor will be, than God the Father unbegotten, without beginning, from whom is all beginning, the Lord of the universe, as we have been taught; and His son Jesus Christ, whom we declare to have always been with the Father, spiritually and ineffably begotten by the Father before the beginning of the world, before all beginning; and by Him are made all things visible and invisible. He was made man, and, having defeated death, was received into heaven by the Father; and He hath given Him all power over all names in heaven, on earth, and under the earth, and every tongue shall confess to Him that Jesus Christ

---

TRANSLATED BY Ludwig Bieler. In the original translation, italic type signaled Bible quotations, allusions, and echoes. The italics have been romanized, and Bible citations have been provided where pertinent.

1. See Romans 1:18 and the Nicene Creed (p. 213).
2. See Psalms 44:11.
3. See Luke 11:31, Judith 2:9, Ecclesiasticus 44:21, and 1 Maccabees 3:9.
4. Tobit 13:6.
5. See Isaiah 25:1.
6. See Acts 2:5.

is Lord and God,[7] in whom we believe, and whose advent we expect soon to be, judge of the living and of the dead,[8] who will render to every man according to his deeds; and He has poured forth upon us abundantly the Holy Spirit,[9] the gift and pledge of immortality, who makes those who believe and obey sons of God and joint heirs with Christ;[1] and Him do we confess and adore, one God in the Trinity of the Holy Name.

5. For He Himself has said through the Prophet: Call upon me in the day of thy trouble, and I will deliver thee, and thou shalt glorify me.[2] And again He says: It is honourable to reveal and confess the works of God.[3]

* * *

9. For this reason I long had in mind to write, but hesitated until now; I was afraid of exposing myself to the talk of men, because I have not studied like the others, who thoroughly imbibed law and Sacred Scripture, and never had to change from the language of their childhood days, but were able to make it still more perfect. In our case, what I had to say had to be translated into a tongue foreign to me, as can be easily proved from the savour of my writing, which betrays how little instruction and training I have had in the art of words; for, so says Scripture, by the tongue will be discovered the wise man, and understanding, and knowledge, and the teaching of truth.[4]

* * *

As a youth, nay, almost as a boy not able to speak, I was taken captive, before I knew what to pursue and what to avoid. Hence to-day I blush and fear exceedingly to reveal my lack of education; for I am unable to tell my story to those versed in the art of concise writing—in such a way, I mean, as my spirit and mind long to do, and so that the sense of my words expresses what I feel.

11. But if indeed it had been given to me as it was given to others, then I would not be silent because of my desire of thanksgiving; and if perhaps some people think me arrogant for doing so in spite of my lack of knowledge and my slow tongue, it is, after all, written: The stammering tongues shall quickly learn to speak peace.[5]

* * *

13. Wherefore, then, be astonished, ye great and little that fear God,[6] and you men of letters on your estates, listen and pore over this. Who was it that roused up me, the fool that I am, from the midst of those who in the eyes of men are wise, and expert in law, and powerful in word and in everything? And He inspired me—me, the outcast of this world—before others, to be the man (if only I could!) who, with fear and reverence and without blame, should faithfully serve the people to whom the love of Christ conveyed and gave me for the duration of my life, if I should be worthy; yes indeed, to serve them humbly and sincerely.

14. In the light, therefore, of our faith in the Trinity I must make this choice, regardless of danger I must make known the gift of God and ever-

7. See Philippians 2:10–11.
8. See 1 Peter 4:5, 2 Timothy 4:1, and Acts 10:42.
9. See Titus 3:5.
1. See Romans 8:17.
2. Psalms 50:15.
3. Tobit 12:7.
4. See Proverbs 15:2.
5. Isaiah 32:4.
6. See Psalms 115:13.

lasting consolation, without fear and frankly I must spread everywhere the name of God so that after my decease I may leave a bequest to my brethren and sons whom I have baptised in the Lord—so many thousands of people.

* * *

62. I pray those who believe and fear God, whosoever deigns to look at or receive this writing which Patrick, a sinner, unlearned, has composed in Ireland, that no one should ever say that it was my ignorance if I did or showed forth anything however small according to God's good pleasure; but let this be your conclusion and let it so be thought, that—as is the perfect truth—it was the gift of God. This is my confession before I die.

ANONYMOUS
eighth century

SAINT PATRICK'S BREASTPLATE

In its original form, in Old Irish, this litany appears in the *Liber Hymnorum,* a two-manuscript collection of hymns that is kept in Dublin. The Old Irish lyrics were attributed to Saint Patrick (see previous headnote) and thus are known as "The Lorica of Saint Patrick." The Latin word *lorica* means a breastplate and, by extension, any kind of protection. This "breastplate" was probably composed in the eighth century, however, to be used as a talisman against danger or illness. An 1889 verse translation by Cecil Frances Alexander— known by its opening line, "I bind unto myself today"—is included in the hymnal of the Episcopal Church and is often sung on Saint Patrick's Day and on Trinity Sunday.

SAINT PATRICK'S BREASTPLATE

I arise to-day
    through a mighty strength, the invocation of the Trinity,
    through belief in the Threeness,
    through confession of the Oneness
    towards the Creator.   5

I arise to-day
    through the strength of Christ with His Baptism,
    though the strength of His Crucifixion with His Burial,
    through the strength of His Resurrection with His Ascension,
    through the strength of His descent for the Judgment of Doom.   10

I arise to-day
    through the strength of the love of Cherubim,

TRANSLATED BY Ludwig Bieler. The parenthetical and bracketed insertions are the original editors'; angle brackets have been converted to square ones.

in obedience of Angels,
in the service of the Archangels,
in hope of resurrection to meet with reward,   15
in prayers of Patriarchs,
in predictions of Prophets,
in preachings of Apostles,
in faiths of Confessors,
in innocence of Holy Virgins,   20
in deeds of righteous men.

I arise to-day
  through the strength of Heaven:
  light of Sun,
  brilliance of Moon,   25
  splendour of Fire,
  speed of Lightning,
  swiftness of Wind,
  depth of Sea,
  stability of Earth,   30
  firmness of Rock.

I arise to-day
  through God's strength to pilot me:
  God's might to uphold me,
  God's wisdom to guide me,   35
  God's eye to look before me,
  God's ear to hear me,
  God's word to speak for me,
  God's hand to guard me,
  God's way to lie before me,   40
  God's shield to protect me,
  God's host to secure me—
    against snares of devils,[1]
    against temptations of vices,
    against inclinations (?) of nature,   45
    against everyone who shall wish me ill,
    afar and anear,
    alone and in a crowd.

I summon to-day all these powers between me (and these evils)—
  against every cruel and merciless power that may oppose my body   50
    and my soul,
  against incantations of false prophets,
  against black laws of heathenry,
  against false laws of heretics,
  against craft (?) of idolatry,
  against spells of women and smiths and wizards,   55
  against every knowledge [that endangers] man's body and soul.

Christ to protect me to-day
  against poison, against burning,

1. See Ephesians 6:10–17.

against drowning, against wounding,
   so that there may come abundance of reward.   60
Christ with me, Christ before me, Christ behind me,
Christ in me, Christ beneath me, Christ above me,
Christ on my right, Christ on my left,
Christ where I lie, Christ where I sit, Christ where I arise,
Christ in the heart of every man who thinks of me,   65
Christ in the mouth of every man who speaks of me,
Christ in every eye that sees me,
Christ in every ear that hears me.

I arise to-day
   through a mighty strength, the invocation of the Trinity,   70
   through belief in the Threeness,
   through confession of the Oneness
   towards the Creator.

Salvation is of the Lord.
Salvation is of the Lord.   75
Salvation is of Christ.
May Thy salvation, O Lord, be ever with us.

EARLY CHRISTIAN HYMNODY

According to evidence in the New Testament, the early Christians sang hymns either in worship or as summaries of Christian belief. For the texts of these hymns, they most likely used the psalms and canticles from the Old Testament. We know nothing about their mode of singing or whether they accompanied their singing with musical instruments. We do know that slightly later, during the very early Middle Ages, church music was monophonic and unaccompanied.

Saint Augustine of Hippo (see p. 226) wrote sermons on all 150 psalms, and in them he frequently mentions that the particular psalm had been sung as a hymn before the delivery of a sermon. In the *Confessions*, Augustine notes that Saint Ambrose wrote original hymns for Ambrose's congregation in Milan. In fact, some of Ambrose's compositions are sung today in vernacular translations of his original Latin. In the West at least, Ambrose's use of nonscriptural hymns was an innovation. The Syriac-speaking Churches of the Middle East, by contrast, favored hymns and odes both for use in worship and as a vehicle for Christian instruction. From the fourth century on in the Greek- and Latin-speaking Churches, hymns greatly increased in number and importance.

Why did hymns become popular? In centuries past, books were rare, expensive, and available only to an educated few. Hymns became the vehicle of disseminating Christian culture to the masses due to their regular meters, repetition of sentiments, and singability. Believers in the educated class composed hymns in the meter and style of the Greek and Roman classical tradition, demonstrating that the ideas and sentiments of Christians could replace the ideas and sentiments of pagan antiquity.

PRUDENTIUS
348–411?

FROM ODE IN HONOR OF THE BLESSED MARTYR LAWRENCE

Aurelius Prudentius Clemens was born in the Roman province of Tarraconensis (now northern Spain) and probably died in approximately the same part of the world. A prolific poet with complete mastery of the classical ode, he frequently took Christian martyrs as his subject. His poems were meant for an aristocratic audience, however, not for liturgical use.

The subject of the following selection, Lawrence of Rome (ca. 225–258), was one of seven deacons killed in the persecution ordered by the emperor Valerian (died 260; reigned from 253 until his death). Lawrence is venerated as a saint by the Roman Catholic, Eastern Orthodox, and Lutheran Churches and by the Anglican Communion. In this ode, Prudentius proclaims that the deaths of the martyrs will conquer the powers of the ancient Roman gods. The theme of the martyr as spiritual warrior is common in early Christian literature. Less common, and much celebrated

This 5th-century mosaic—in the Mausoleum of Galla Placidia, Ravenna, Italy—depicts the martyrdom of Saint Lawrence. On the far left is a cupboard opened to reveal Gospel codices. To the right of that is the gridiron on which Lawrence was burned to death. Above the gridiron is a window made of alabaster.

in later centuries, is Lawrence's gallows humor as presented in the following excerpt from Prudentius's ode. The Roman prefect, enraged that Lawrence has brought him not gold but the poor and wretched of the city as the Church's treasure, sentences Lawrence to be roasted slowly to death. From the grill, Lawrence jests with the prefect that he is well done on one side and ready to be turned over (lines 401–02). This scene appears frequently in medieval Christian art.

PRONOUNCING GLOSSARY

Prudentius: *proo-den´-shuhs*   Remus: *ree´-mus*
Quirinus: *kwir-eye´-nus*

FROM ODE IN HONOR OF THE BLESSED MARTYR LAWRENCE

> When slow, consuming heat had seared
> The flesh of Lawrence for a space,
> He calmly from his gridiron made
> This terse proposal to the judge: 400
>
> 'Pray turn my body, on one side
> Already broiled sufficiently,
> And see how well your Vulcan's fire
> Has wrought its cruel punishment.'

Translated by Sister M. Clement Eagan.

The prefect bade him to be turned.   405
Then Lawrence spoke: 'I am well baked,
And whether better cooked or raw,
Make trial by a taste of me.'

He said these words in way of jest;
Then raising shining eyes to heaven   410
And sighing deeply, thus he prayed
With pity for unholy Rome:

'O Christ, O Name above all names,[1]
Of God the Father, Light and Power,[2]
O Maker of the earth and sky,   415
And Founder of this city's walls,

'Rome's sceptre Thou didst make supreme,
Subjecting to the conquering arms
Of togaed sons of Quirinus[3]
All nations of the universe,   420

'That one dominion might unite
The races of the world, diverse
In manners and observances,
In tongues and rites and inborn traits.

'Lo, all the human race has bowed   425
Beneath the rod of Remus' sons;[4]
Dissenting tribes one language speak
And live in peace and harmony.

'This sovereignty was foreordained
That all the world with greater ease,   430
Might by a single bond be linked
Beneath the power of Christian law.

'Grant to Thy Roman people, Christ,
That they may wear the Christian name,
For through their city Thou didst give   435
To others one religious faith.

'All members of this realm are joined
In fealty to this saving creed.
The conquered world has civil grown,
And may the head be tamed at last.'   440

                    *   *   *

Among these sons, O saint of Christ,
Give audience to a rustic poet

---

1. See Philippians 2:9.
2. See Hebrews 1:3.
3. In Roman mythology, an early god of the
Roman state; originally named Romulus, but

renamed from *quiris*, Latin for spear.
4. In some versions of the Roman myth, the
Roman state was founded by Romulus together
with his brother, Remus.

Who humbly bares his sinful heart   575
And owns his guilt and misery.

I am not worthy Christ Himself
Should hear me, this too well I know,
But martyr advocates can win
His salutary grace for me.   580

O kindly hear Prudentius,
A culprit at the bar of Christ,
And from the bondage of the flesh
And earthly fetters set him free.

SAINT EPHREM THE SYRIAN
306?–373

FROM HYMNS ON THE NATIVITY

The theologian and writer Ephrem the Syrian was born and died in what is now southeastern Turkey. Writing in Syriac, the Semitic language then spoken in that region, he composed hymns, poems, sermons in verse, and prose interpretations of Bible texts. He was so prolific and his works were so popular that, for centuries after he died, hundreds of Christian works were written under his name. He is venerated as a saint worldwide and especially by the Syriac Orthodox Church, in which he was one of the most important early fathers.

In the following hymn, also known as "Ode on the Nativity," Ephrem imaginatively expands Luke 2:8–20, the Gospel passage in which shepherds visit the newborn Jesus. In Ephrem's version, the shepherds bring a newborn lamb as a gift to Jesus, who will later be acclaimed by John the Baptist as the "Lamb of God which taketh away the sin of the world" (John 1:29). In seeing Jesus as a lamb, John the Baptist echoes the story of the Hebrew Passover, an Old Testament event in which the blood of sacrificial lambs saved the Israelite people from slaughter by the Angel of Death (Exodus 12). Likewise, the adult Jesus saves humankind from eternal death when he goes, like a lamb, to his Crucifixion during Passover. And since Jesus' sacrifice on the cross is to be the last sacrifice of history, the lamb in Ephrem's hymn thanks the infant Jesus for saving the sheep and oxen of the future as well. The shepherds then acclaim Jesus (Luke reports no such acclamation) with a theologically elaborate greeting in which their staff—poetically identified with the staff of the shepherd Moses (see p. 89)—acknowledges Jesus' metaphorical staff. The Son of God is thus the "'Shepherd of the universe'" (line 15).

The hymn then delivers a string of biblical allusions. It recalls that the Israelites, in their desert wanderings, turned repeatedly against Moses, becoming "like dragons" (line 18). It alludes to the Messianic vision of Isaiah in which wolf and lamb live together (Isaiah 11:6). It likens the newborn savior to Noah, who saved humankind through his ark (Genesis 6–9). It recalls that Jesus is descended from David (Luke 2:3) and that, by virtue of Jesus' birth, Satan—the "wolf" who attacked the "lamb" Adam in the Garden of Eden (see p. 83)—has been destroyed in principle. It then imagines a general rejoicing in Bethlehem (also unrecorded in the Gospels), in which virgins preserve their chastity, barren wives are made fertile by having caressed the newborn, and elderly people exult because Jesus will restore even ancient Adam and Eve to youth.

In literary terms, Ephrem's hymn owes less to Greek models than to Semitic and, above all, biblical ones. Its author, whose name is Jewish, reflects the diasporic Jewish culture that was the matrix for Christianity. He offers a virtuoso improvisation upon Jewish Scriptures and the Christian Scriptures appended to them.

FROM HYMNS ON THE NATIVITY

HYMN 7

They carried and offered to Him: suckling lamb
to the Paschal Lamb, the first-born to the First-born,
a sacrifice to the Sacrifice, a temporal lamb
to the True Lamb. A fitting sight
that a lamb to the Lamb should be offered.   5
The lamb bleated while being offered
to the First-born. He thanked the Lamb
that came to free sheep and oxen
from sacrifices, even the traditional
paschal lamb that served as a symbol of the Son.   10
The shepherds approached to worship Him.
With their staffs they greeted Him,
prophesying, "Peace, O Greatest
of shepherds! The staff of Moses
acknowledges Your staff, Shepherd of the universe."   15
For You [are the One] Moses acknowledged—he whose
lambs became wolves and whose sheep became
like dragons and his ewes [like]
savage beasts. In the fearful wasteland
his flock became rabid and attacked him.   20
You, then, the shepherds will acknowledge,
for You reconciled wolves and lambs
in the flock. You are the newborn
Who is older than Noah and younger than Noah,
Who pacified all in the ark.   25
For the sake of a lamb, David, Your father
killed a lion. O Son of David,
You have killed the hidden wolf
that killed Adam, the innocent lamb
who grazed and bleated in paradise.   30
By that song of praise brides awoke suddenly
and chose chastity, and virgins
preserved their chastity, and even young girls
were purified. They rose early and came
in throngs to worship the Son.   35
The old women of the town of David came
to the daughter of David, speaking blessings:
"Blessed is our native land whose streets are made light

TRANSLATED BY Kathleen E. McVey. Bracketed insertions are the translator's.

by the ray of Jesse! Today the throne of David
is established by You, the Son of David."   40
Old men cried out, "Blessed is the Babe
Who restored Adam's youth; he was displeased to see
that he grew old and wasted away, yet the serpent who killed him
shed [his skin] and recovered his youth. Blessed is the Babe
by whom Eve and Adam were restored to youth."   45
The chaste women said, "Blessed Fruit,
bless our fruits, given to You
as first fruits." Aglow, they prophesied
about their children, who, when they were killed,
would be plucked by Him as first fruits.   50
The barren women hovered over and held Him.
They caressed [Him] and said, "O Blessed Fruit [conceived]
without intercourse, bless our wombs
during intercourse. Have pity on our barrenness,
Miraculous Child of virginity."   55

SAINT ROMANOS THE MELODIST
early sixth century

THE STANDING HYMN

There are few sources of information about Romanos the Melodist or the Hymnographer (also known as Romanus or Roman). Born Jewish in what is now Syria, he was ordained a deacon in what is now the city of Beirut, and until his death he served at the Hagia Sophia, the Great Church in Constantinople. He is venerated as a saint by the Greek Orthodox and Roman Catholic Churches.

   In the Greek Orthodox and Greek Catholic tradition, an Akathistos Hymn is a hymn dedicated to a saint, to a holy event, or to one person of the Holy Trinity. *Akathistos* comes from the ancient Greek for "not sitting," because when the hymn is sung—and sometimes during the entire service—the congregation is expected to stand, except for the aged and the infirm. The following selection comes from a very long "standing" hymn—long credited to Romanos, now sometimes to the seventh-century Byzantine poet George Pisida—addressed to and exalting the Virgin Mary as Theotokos ("God-bearer"; see p. 215). This work, considered the ultimate Akathistos Hymn, is central to the Orthodox Church: sung during Lent services, often recited at home by families, and said daily in monasteries. It is the one complete *kontakion* (plural *kontakia*; Greek for a long, structured, responsorial sermon in verse) still in use in the Byzantine Rite. The hymn is sung in conjunction with the veneration of an icon of the Virgin Mary. The opening stanza is a *proemion* (prelude). The subsequent twenty-four stanzas alternate between long and short ones: The long ones, *oikos* (or *ikos*, to reflect modern Greek pronunciation; the term means "house"), include entreaties addressed to the Virgin ("Rejoice!"). Each entreaty is followed by one of the Virgin's glories—that is, by a reason for her to rejoice. The successive *kontakia* are about the Virgin Mary, but are spoken as if she is present. The initial letter of each stanza follows the sequence of the twenty-four-letter Greek alphabet; in this translation, the letters follow the sequence of the English alphabet, omitting (arbitrarily, according to the translator) *v* and *x*. The first twelve stanzas present a narrative of Christ's life, starting with the Annunciation to the Virgin and continuing through Jesus' presentation in the Temple. The remaining twelve stanzas concern theological matters related to God, the Virgin, and Christ.

PRONOUNCING GLOSSARY

Chaldaeans: *chal-day-ahns*   Stygian: *sti´-jee-uhn*
Cherubim: *chehr´-oo-bim*   Symeon: *si´-mee-uhn*
Seraphim: *sehr´-uh-fim*

THE STANDING HYMN

To you, my champion and general, the victory celebrations,
to you, God-bearer, saved from sufferings,
I, your city, ascribe the thanks.
As you have unassailable might,
deliver me from all manner of dangers,
that I may cry to you:
      'Rejoice, bride unbrided.'

A leader of the angels was sent from heaven
to announce to the God-bearer the 'Rejoice':[1]
and perceiving you, Lord, embodied
by means of his bodiless voice,
he was exalted and halted, crying out to her thus:
      'Rejoice, you through whom jubilation will shine:
rejoice, you through whom imprecation will decline.
      Rejoice, recalling of the fallen Adam:
rejoice, redemption of the tears of Eve.[2]
      Rejoice, height hard to climb by mortal surmise:
rejoice, depth hard to plumb even for angels' eyes.
      Rejoice, because you are the throne of the King:
rejoice, for you support him who supports everything.
      Rejoice, star making the Sun show his face:
rejoice, womb where divine incarnation takes place.
      Rejoice, you through whom creation is created afresh:
rejoice, you through whom the Creator as a babe becomes flesh.
      Rejoice, bride unbrided.'

Because the holy Woman perceived herself wholly pure,
she boldly addressed Gabriel:
'It seems hard to my spirit to give admittance
to the paradox of your utterance:
for you foretell pregnancy from a seedless conception, crying:
      "Alleluia".'

TRANSLATED BY Roger Green.

1. See Luke 1:26–38 and Matthew 1:18–21.
2. See p. 83.

Calling on God's minister,
the Virgin sought to know unknown knowledge:
'How is it possible for a son
out of chaste loins to be born? Tell me.'
He replied to her in awe, only crying thus:
  'Rejoice, confidante of God's secret deliberation:
 rejoice, confidence of men's silent supplication.
  Rejoice, preface to Christ's miracles:
 rejoice, paraphrase of his principles.
  Rejoice, ladder set in heaven whereby God has descended:
 rejoice, bridge conveying those from earth into heaven.
  Rejoice, wonder by angels widely broadcast:
 rejoice, wound making demons greatly downcast.
  Rejoice, who ineffably parturiate[3] the light of day:
 rejoice, who do not impart to anyone the way.
  Rejoice, who outdate the knowledge of the wise:
 rejoice, who illuminate the minds of the faithful.
  Rejoice, bride unbrided.'

Divine power of the Most High then overshadowed
her untried in marriage, making her conceive:
and her fruitful womb he revealed
as a pleasant field
for all wishing to harvest a yield of salvation through chanting thus:
  'Alleluia.'

Enclosing God within her womb,
the Virgin hurried to Elisabeth:[4]
the unborn child of the latter, at once
recognizing the greeting of the former, rejoiced,
and, springing as if singing, cried to the God-bearer:
  'Rejoice, vine with unwithering shoot:
 rejoice, farm with untainted fruit.
  Rejoice, you who cultivate the cultivator loving mankind:
 rejoice, you who grow in your garden the gardener of our life.
  Rejoice, arable yielding a bountiful stack of pity:
 rejoice, table wielding a plentiful stock of mercy.
  Rejoice, because you are furbishing a lush pasturage:
 rejoice, because you are furnishing for souls an anchorage.
  Rejoice, accepted incense of mediation:
 rejoice, the whole world's propitiation.
  Rejoice, goodwill of God towards mortals:
 rejoice, free speech of mortals towards God.
  Rejoice, bride unbrided.'

Feeling within himself a whirl of doubtful thoughts,
prudent Joseph was disturbed,[5]
seeing that you were unmated
and suspecting a secret coupling, O Blameless One:
but on ascertaining that your conceiving was from the Holy Spirit, he exclaimed:
  'Alleluia.'

---

3. Give birth to.
4. See Luke 1:41–45.

5. See Matthew 1:19–25.

God's incarnate presence the angels sang in hymns,[6]
the shepherds heard and, running as though towards a shepherd,
they saw him as a blameless lamb
pastured in the womb of Mary,
and hymning her they declaimed:
　　　'Rejoice, mother of lamb and shepherd:
　rejoice, fold of sensible sheep.
　　　Rejoice, buttress against invisible predators:
　rejoice, portress of the gates of paradise.
　　　Rejoice, because heaven exults with earth:
　rejoice, because earth dances with the heavens.
　　　Rejoice, loquacity of the apostles that cannot be struck dumb:
　rejoice, audacity of the victorious martyrs that cannot be overcome.
　　　Rejoice, solid fortification of faith:
　rejoice, lucid indication of grace.
　　　Rejoice, through whom Hades has been stripped bare:
　rejoice, through whom we have been clothed in glory.
　　　Rejoice, bride unbrided.'

Having seen a star leading to God,
wise men followed its brightness,
and retaining it as a torch
searched with its aid for a mighty king:
and when they attained the unattainable, they rejoiced, crying to him:
　　　'Alleluia.'

In the hands of the Virgin, sons of the Chaldaeans
saw him who with his hands made men:
and sensing him to be their Master,
even though he had taken on the form of a servant,
they hastened to honour him with their gifts and to cry to the Blessed
　　Woman:
　　　'Rejoice, mother of an unsetting star:
　rejoice, dawn of a mystic day.
　　　Rejoice, who extinguish the furnace of duplicity:
　rejoice, who illumine the initiates of the Trinity.
　　　Rejoice, who depose from rule an inhuman tyrant:
　rejoice, who expose to view Christ, a human-loving Lord.
　　　Rejoice, who liberate us from the religion of savages:
　rejoice, who extricate us from sin's Stygian ravages.
　　　Rejoice, who quench the worship of fire:
　rejoice, who deliver us from the flame of passions.
　　　Rejoice, leader of the faithful towards piety:
　rejoice, breeder, in all people, of gaiety.
　　　Rejoice, bride unbrided.'

Journeying back to Babylon,
having become god-bearing heralds,
the wise men fulfilled your oracle,

---

6. See Luke 2:1–20 and Matthew 2:1–12.

proclaiming you to everyone as the Christ,
abandoning Herod as horrid, for he did not know how to chant:
    'Alleluia.'

Kindling in Egypt the light of truth,[7]
you banished the darkness of falsehood:
for, Saviour, the idols of that land,
unable to withstand your strength, collapsed:
and those who were delivered from them cried to the God-bearer:
    'Rejoice, restitution of humans:
  rejoice, destitution of demons.
    Rejoice, who patrol the ambages of trickery:
  rejoice, who control the images' treachery.
    Rejoice, sea slaughtering the Pharaoh of the mind:
  rejoice, rock watering those thirsty for life.
    Rejoice, pillar of fire, guiding those in darkness:
  rejoice, canopy of the world, broader than a cloud.
    Rejoice, substitutor of Manna as food:
  rejoice, distributor of what is holy and good.
    Rejoice, promised land:
  rejoice, from whom flow honey and milk.
    Rejoice, bride unbrided.'

Lord, when Symeon was about to begone
from this present deceitful eon,[8]
you were given to him as an infant,
but you were recognized by him even as perfect God:
wherefore he was astonished at your ineffable wisdom, crying:
    'Alleluia.'

Manifesting himself to us his creatures,
the Creator displayed a new creation,
he sprang from an unsown womb,
preserving it, as it had been, uncorrupted,
that we, beholding the miracle, might hymn the Woman, exclaiming:
    'Rejoice, flower that does not faint:
  rejoice, crown of self-restraint.
    Rejoice, who project a foreshowing of resurrection glory:
  rejoice, who reflect the angels' life-story.
    Rejoice, tree laden with splendid fruit, which the faithful eat:
  rejoice, trunk shady with broad leaves, beneath which many retreat.
    Rejoice, who give birth to an indicator for those who have gone astray:
  rejoice, who are pregnant with a liberator for those under another's sway.
    Rejoice, petition to the just Assessor:[9]
  rejoice, remission for many a transgressor.
    Rejoice, splendid dress of those stripped of the courage to speak:
  rejoice, tenderness overcoming all passions.
    Rejoice, bride unbrided.'

7. See Matthew 2:13–23.
8. See Luke 2:25–35.

9. God, as the reckoner of each believer's spiritual account (see p. 144).

Now that we have seen a strange birth,
we are estranged from the earth,
transferring our minds to heaven:
for this is why God on high appeared as a humble mortal,
wishing to draw up to the height those who cry to him:
        'Alleluia.'

On earth below, the uncircumscribed Word was wholly present
and was in no way absent from heaven above:
for a divine condescension took place,
not a change of location,
and the bearing of a child by a Virgin filled with God, who heard these words:
        'Rejoice, monstrance of God unconfinable:
rejoice, entrance of hallowed mystery.
        Rejoice, for the faithless a doubtful story:
rejoice, for the faithful a doubtless glory.
        Rejoice, divinest transportation of him above the Cherubim:
rejoice, the finest habitation of him above the Seraphim.
        Rejoice, who align opposites in harmony:
rejoice, who combine virginity and maternity.
        Rejoice, through whom transgression is nullified:
rejoice, through whom Paradise is opened wide.
        Rejoice, the key to Christ's domain:
rejoice, guarantee of eternal gain.
        Rejoice, bride unbrided.'

Perceiving the mighty work of your being made man,
all angel-kind marvelled:
for they saw him, who as God is inaccessible,
a man accessible to all,
dwelling among us, yet hearing on all sides this:
        'Alleluia.'

Quailing before you, God-bearer, eloquent orators
we behold as dumb as fishes:
for they are at a loss to say
how you both remain a virgin and are capable of childbearing:
but we, marvelling at the mystery, with faith cry:
        'Rejoice, of God's wisdom a repository:
rejoice, of his providence a depository.
        Rejoice, who discover metaphysicians to be blind:
rejoice, who uncover rhetoricians as lacking in mind.
        Rejoice, because the smart debaters have been made to drivel:
rejoice, because the myth-creators have been made to shrivel.
        Rejoice, who divide the Athenians' tangled skeins:[1]
rejoice, who provide for fishermen full seines.[2]
        Rejoice, who draw us up from the depth of unknowing:
rejoice, who illumine many towards knowing.
        Rejoice, for those wishing to be saved a boat:

---

1. I.e., undo the entanglements of Greek mythology.   2. See Matthew 4:19.

rejoice, a port for those on the sea of life afloat.
      Rejoice, bride unbrided.'

Regulator of everything, wishing to save the world,
he came hither of his own accord,
and, as God, being a shepherd,
he appeared like us, for us:
and summoning like to like, as God he hears:
      'Alleluia.'

Shelter you are for virgins, Virgin God-bearer,
and for all those who have recourse to you:
for the Creator of heaven and earth
made you, Immaculate One,
dwelling in your womb and teaching all to address you thus:
      'Rejoice, mainstay of virgin continence:
rejoice, gateway to our deliverance.
      Rejoice, surveyor of reformed intelligence:
rejoice, purveyor of divine excellence.
      Rejoice, for you have revived those conceived in disgrace:
rejoice, for to those deprived of sense you have given advice.
      Rejoice, who destroy the overthrower of rationality:
rejoice, who bear the sower of purity.
      Rejoice, of a seedless wedding the bridal room:
rejoice, who betroth the faithful to the Lord as groom.
      Rejoice, good nursemaid of virgin girls:
rejoice, the bridesmaid of holy souls.
      Rejoice, bride unbrided.'

Trying to match in extent the multitude
of your many mercies, every hymn fails:
for though we offer to you, holy King,
as many strains of song as there are grains of sand,
we accomplish nothing worthy of your gifts to those who cry to you:
      'Alleluia.'

Unto those in darkness appearing
we behold the holy Virgin as a lambent torch:
for, kindling the insubstantial light,
she leads everyone towards divine knowledge,
illumining the mind with dawn's radiance, honoured with this utterance:
      'Rejoice, gleam of the thought-begetting sun:
rejoice, beam of the never-setting moon.
      Rejoice, lightning enlightening souls:
rejoice, thunder frightening foes.
      Rejoice, because you diffuse the light that broadly glows:
rejoice, because you effuse the river that broadly flows.
      Rejoice, who portray the font's prefigurement:
rejoice, who remove our sin's disfigurement.
      Rejoice, washing-bowl cleansing the conscience:
rejoice, mixing-bowl dispensing enjoyments.
      Rejoice, fragrance of Christ's sweet exhalation:

rejoice, existence of mystic exultation.
    Rejoice, bride unbrided.'

Wishing to grant grace in respect of ancient debts,
he who absolves all mankind
came, of his own will,
to reside with those residing outside his grace:
and tearing up the debit sheet he hears on all sides this:
    'Alleluia.'

Your offspring we sing, all praising you,
God-bearer, as a living church:
for, dwelling in your womb,
the Lord, who holds all things in his hand,
sanctified, glorified, and taught everyone to cry to you:
    'Rejoice, tent of God and Word:
rejoice, saint greater than saints.
    Rejoice, treasure-chest gilded by the Spirit:
rejoice, treasure-house of life inexhaustible.
    Rejoice, diadem prized of reverent monarchs:
rejoice, honoured pride of deferent hierarchs.
    Rejoice, fortification of the church never shaken:
rejoice, circumvallation of the kingdom never taken.
    Rejoice, through whom trophies are erected:
rejoice, through whom enemies are dejected.
    Rejoice, cure of my outer skin:
rejoice, care for my soul within.
    Rejoice, bride unbrided.'

Zealously hymned by all, Mother, who have given birth
to the most holy Word of all holy things,
accepting the present offering,
deliver from every calamity
and from future damnation all those who cry to you:
    'Alleluia.'

ANONYMOUS
eighth century?

FROM THE DREAM OF THE ROOD

This "vision" poem, one of the oldest in Old English alliterative verse, praises the Rood (i.e., Christ's cross; from the Old English *rōd*, meaning "pole") as the instrument of human salvation. In both its language and its forest imagery, this poem marks a transition from south to north and from the patristic era to the medieval.

FROM THE DREAM OF THE ROOD

Listen! Let me tell you about the best of dreams,
what I dreamed about at around midnight,
after the bearers of voices took their rest.
It seemed to me that I saw a most wondrous tree raised aloft,
enveloped in light, the brightest of beams.   5
All that beacon was encrusted with gold.
Gems stood out, beautiful at the earth's corners;
likewise there were five upon the shoulder-span.
All fair things throughout time and creation
beheld there the messenger of the Lord.   10
Indeed, that was not a criminal's gallows,
but holy spirits and men throughout the earth
and all this glorious creation beheld it there.
Splendid was that victory-tree,
and I was stained with sins, terribly wounded by evildoing.   15
I saw the tree of glory, honoured by its garments,
shining beautifully, clothed in gold;
gems had covered the Ruler's tree in splendour.
Yet through that gold I could perceive the ancient struggle of
    a wretched people,
in that it first began to sweat on the right side.   20
I was completely overcome by sorrows;
frightened I was by that fair sight.
I saw that restless beam and beacon ever-changing its garments
    and colours;
at times it was made wet with moisture, drenched with the
    flow of blood and sweat,
at times adorned with treasure.   25
Moreover, lying there for a long while,
I watched, troubled with sorrows, the Saviour's tree
until I heard its voice.
Then the best of woods began to speak in words:

'That was long ago.   30
I still remember that I was hewn down at the edge of a forest,
cut off from my roots.
Strong enemies seized me there,
made a show and mockery of me for themselves,
ordered me to raise their condemned men aloft.   35
Then men bore me on their shoulders
until they finally set me up on a hill.
Enemies enough fastened me there.
Then I saw the Lord of mankind hastening with great courage
in His urgent need to mount upon me.   40
Then I dared not there against the Lord's word bend or break
when I saw that the corners of the earth did shake.
I could have felled all enemies but I stood fast.
Then the young warrior stripped himself,

TRANSLATED BY Richard J. Kelly and Ciarán L. Quinn.

who was God Almighty, strong and resolute.   45
He mounted the high gallows,
brave in the sight of many,
since He wished to set mankind free.
I trembled when the man embraced me,
yet I dared not bow to earth, fall to the land's spread,   50
but had to stand fast.
A rood, I was lifted up.
I raised aloft a powerful king, Lord of the Heavens;
I dared not bow down.
They pierced me through with dark nails;   55
on me the cleaving wounds can be seen, these open wounds of malice.
I dared not injure any of them;
they reviled the two of us together.
I was all drenched with the blood shed from the man's side
after He had sent forth His Spirit.   60
On that hill I had to endure many dreadful things;
I saw the God of hosts direly stretched out.
The darkness had covered with clouds the Body of the Ruler,
the Illuminating Light.
His shadow went forth, dark under clouds.   65
All creation wept, lamented the King's death.'

THE ASCETIC TRADITION

The adjective *ascetic* derives from the ancient Greek term for "practice, "training," or exercise." *Asceticism* has come to mean any practice meant to aid in a more perfect religious observance. According to the Gospel of Matthew, Jesus emphasized three forms of asceticism: prayer, almsgiving, and fasting. In 1 Corinthians 7:8–9, Paul advises the unmarried, male or female, to stay that way. The author of 1 Timothy (probably not Paul) urges widows not to remarry unless young and unable to control their desires (verse 5).

During the Roman persecutions, Christians had looked to their martyrs as supreme examples of "giving all" for Jesus Christ. As the Roman persecutions came to an end in the early fourth century, however, the exemplars of the Christian faith were more commonly to be found among those people who devoted their lives to Christian practice. As a recognized form of religious observance—indeed, as what we now call a lifestyle—asceticism had roots in the third century, but flourished in the fourth century.

The ascetic life took many forms. In Jerusalem, individuals lived solitary lives devoted to prayer, others took up the practice of perpetual virginity, and others formed small communities devoted to prayer and good works. In Egypt, people fled what they saw as the corruption of the cities and moved to the desert, where they took up lives of simple work, prayer, and hospitality. During the first three centuries of the Common Era, Christianity had been an urban phenomenon; its bishops, significantly, were always the bishops of cities. Even under persecution, Christians did not flee to the countryside to escape. But as the Roman Empire first allowed, then espoused, and finally imposed Christianity, its embrace began to seem corrupting to some who recalled how the Empire had seemed the epitome of evil to earlier generations.

Those who moved to the desert, however—the "desert fathers" and a few "desert mothers"—were less conservative than socially and religiously innovative. The literature they produced was of two general kinds: "rules of life" and accounts of the lives and sayings of the more famous ascetics, to whom people went for spiritual guidance. By no means were all Christians expected to take up the ascetic life, but such a life was an honored option for those who chose it. Partly from the varied experiments in ascetic living that took place during this period, a less solitary monasticism (from the Greek *monos*, meaning "single") arose with long-term consequences for Christianity wherever it spread.

Such experiments in more organized communal asceticism were not unique to Christianity. The Essenes—a major religious movement in first-century Palestinian Jewry—formed at least one desert community of religious dissidents, the community that produced and/or preserved the texts we know as the Dead Sea Scrolls. The Athenian philosophers, too, and their descendents throughout the Greek-speaking Mediterranean world often formed communities that scorned luxury, honored celibacy, and took up a disciplined search for wisdom. Building on the Jewish tradition of Alexandria that had sought respect for Moses as a philosopher who had taught long before the rise of Athens, some fourth-century Christian ascetics claimed they were the true philosophers, the authentic lovers of wisdom. For them, wisdom was Jesus Christ, who had called himself the way, the truth, and the life (John 14:6).

SAINT ATHANASIUS OF ALEXANDRIA
ca. 296–373

FROM LIFE OF ANTHONY

Anthony (ca. 251–356), a Christian in Alexandria, Egypt, was the first ascetic known to have gone into the wilderness, specifically into the Scetis desert, toward the western outskirts of the Egyptian Delta. For this move (ca. 270–71), he has became known as Anthony the Great, Anthony the Abbot, Anthony of Egypt, Anthony of the Desert, Anthony the Anchorite, Abba (i.e., Father) Antonius, and Father of All Monks. He is venerated as a saint in Latin, Greek, and Eastern Christian Churches.

The following selection is from the biography of Anthony written by Athanasius of Alexandria. An archbishop and a theologian, Athanasius is also known as Athanasius the Great, Athanasius the Confessor, and Athanasius the Apostolic. He is venerated as a saint in many Churches. His *Life of Anthony* was one of the most popular and influential books for centuries after its appearance, helping spread the concept of monasticism, particularly in western Europe. According to Athanasius, Anthony was a "martyr every day of his life," a phrase that nicely signals how asceticism as a figurative martyrdom had succeeded literal martyrdom at the center of Christian devotion. The account of how Anthony gave up all his wealth to live a life of prayer strongly influenced Church fathers such as Saint Augustine of Hippo (see p. 226).

This excerpt begins with Anthony, talking to his fellow monks about how Satan once visited him in his cell—not a prison cell but either his small room in the monastery or, more likely for Anthony, his desert hut, his hermitage.

PRONOUNCING GLOSSARY

Athanasius: *a-thuh-nay´-zhus*
Job: *johb*

Nun: *noon*
Scetis: *skay´-tiss*

FROM LIFE OF ANTHONY

41. "And since I have become a fool in describing these events, receive this as well for your protection and fearlessness, and trust me, for I am not lying. Once someone knocked at the door of my cell. And when I went out, I saw someone who seemed massive and tall. When I asked, 'Who are you?' he said, 'I am Satan.' I said, 'What are you doing here?' And he asked, 'Why do the monks and all the other Christians censure me without cause? Why do they curse me every hour?' When I replied, 'Why do you torment them?' he said, 'I am not the one tormenting them, but they disturb themselves, for I have become weak. Haven't they read that *the swords of the enemy have failed utterly, and that you have destroyed their cities?*[1] I no longer have a place—no weapon, no city. There are Christians everywhere, and even the desert has filled with monks. Let them watch after themselves and stop

TRANSLATED BY Robert C. Gregg.

1. Psalms 8:6.

censuring me for no reason!' Marveling then at the grace of the Lord, I said to him: 'Even though you are always a liar, and never tell the truth, nevertheless this time, even if you did not intend to, you have spoken truly. For Christ in his coming reduced you to weakness, and after throwing you down he left you defenseless.' Upon hearing the Savior's name, and being unable to endure the scorching from it, he became invisible.

42. "Now if even the devil himself confesses that he is able to do nothing, then we ought to treat him and his demons with utter contempt. For his part, the enemy with his dogs has treacheries of the sort I have described, but we are able to scorn them, having learned of their weakness. Therefore let us not be plunged into despair in this way, nor contemplate horrors in the soul, nor invent fears for ourselves, saying, 'How I hope that when a demon comes, he will not overthrow me—or pick me up and throw me down—or suddenly set himself next to me and cast me into confusion!' We must not entertain these thoughts at all, nor grieve like those who are perishing. Instead, let us take courage and let us always rejoice, like those who are being redeemed. And let us consider in our soul that the Lord is with us, he who routed them and reduced them to idleness. Let us likewise always understand and take it to heart that while the Lord is with us, the enemies will do nothing to us. For when they come, their actions correspond to the condition in which they find us; they pattern their phantasms after our thoughts. Should they find us frightened and distressed, immediately they attack like robbers, having found the place unprotected. Whatever we are turning over in our minds, this—and more—is what they do. For if they see that we are fearful and terrified, they increase even more what is dreadful in the apparitions and threats, and the suffering soul is punished with these. However, should they discover us rejoicing in the Lord, thinking about the good things to come, contemplating things that have to do with the Lord, reflecting that all things are in the hand of the Lord, and that a demon has no strength against a Christian, nor has he any authority over anyone—then seeing the soul safeguarded by such thoughts, they are put to shame and turned away. It was for this reason that the enemy, seeing Job so defended, departed from him, but finding Judas unarmed with these, took him captive.[2] So if we wish to despise the enemy, let us always contemplate the things that have to do with the Lord, and let the soul always rejoice in hope. Then we shall see the antics of the demons to be like smoke, and we shall see them in flight rather than pursuit. For, as I said earlier, they are very cowardly, always expectant of the fire that has been prepared for them.

43. "For your fearlessness against them you have for yourselves also this sure sign. Whenever some apparition occurs, do not collapse in terror, but whatever it may be, ask first, bravely, 'Who are you and where do you come from?' And if it is a vision of holy ones, they will give you full assurance and transform your fear into joy. But if it is someone diabolical, it immediately is weakened, finding your spirit formidable. For simply by asking, 'Who are you and where do you come from?' you give evidence of your calmness. So

2. God hands Job over to Satan (Job 2:6). Though the Book of Job does not refer to Satan after chapter 2, Athanasius assumes that when God restores Job's fortunes, Satan is vanquished. On Judas, see John 14:27.

when the son of Nun asked, he learned; and the enemy did not go unseen when Daniel questioned him."[3]

44. All rejoiced while Anthony talked about these things. In some, the love of virtue increased, in others carelessness was discarded, and in still others conceit was brought to an end. And all were persuaded to hate the demonic conniving, marveling at the grace given by the Lord to Anthony for the discernment of spirits. So their cells in the hills were like tents filled with divine choirs—people chanting, studying, fasting, praying, rejoicing in the hope of future boons, working for the distribution of alms, and maintaining both love and harmony among themselves. It was as if one truly looked on a land all its own—a land of devotion and righteousness. For neither perpetrator nor victim of injustice was there, nor complaint of a tax collector.[4] And there was a multitude of ascetics, but among them all there was one mind, and it was set on virtue, so that when one saw the cells again, and such orderliness among the monks, he was moved to exclaim and say, *How lovely are your dwellings, Jacob, and your tents, Israel; like shady groves, and like a garden by a river, and like tents which the Lord pitched, and like cedars beside the waters.*[5]

3. The son of Nun is Joshua; see Joshua 5:13–15. Daniel questions Satan in the story of Susanna (see Daniel 13:51–52 in Roman Catholic and Eastern Orthodox Bibles; the story is not included in the Hebrew Bible and is considered apocryphal by Protestants).
4. There were no tax collectors to complain about (since the monks owned nothing of value to tax?).
5. Numbers 24:5–6.

SAINT GREGORY OF NYSSA
ca. 335–ca. 395

FROM LIFE OF MACRINA

Gregory of Nyssa, also known as Gregory Nyssen, lived in Cappadocia, a central region of what is now Turkey. A bishop and theologian, he is venerated as a saint by many Churches.

Gregory's family was aristocratic and, by the time of his birth, already celebrated for its piety. His grandmother, Macrina the Elder, was venerated as a saint, and the rest of the family could scarcely have been more prominent in church life than it was. Saint Gregory, however, especially revered his sister, Macrina the Younger (ca. 330–379). Thanks to her good works and asceticism, she was one of the most revered nuns of the Eastern Church and is venerated as a saint no less than her distinguished brother.

With the help of another brother, Peter, Macrina converted the family estate in Pontus (a northeastern region of Turkey) into a monastery and convent, where she remained for the rest of her life. After her death, at the request of the local governor, Gregory wrote a biography of his sister, much of which focuses on her pious death and its aftermath: her lengthy last words (reproduced in the following selection), her elaborate funeral, the mourning of both her extended family and the nuns of her community, remembrances by the mourners of her heroic purity of conduct, her wondrous miracles, and edifying instructions during her lifetime.

The *Life of Macrina* reflects an ideal of Christian piety that owes a great deal to Greek philosophical notions of the gulf between the purity of the soul and the corruption of the body as well as to a Greek aesthetic in which the good and the beautiful are fused. With the *Life of St. Martin* (see p. 236), it stands at the head of a long line of Christian "lives of the saints."

(see p. 236)

PRONOUNCING GLOSSARY

Macrina: *mah-kree´-nuh*   Nyssa: *ni´-suh*

FROM LIFE OF MACRINA
[*Saint Macrina's Last Words*]

When dawn came, it was clear to me that this day was to be the last for her in the life of the flesh, for the fever had consumed all her natural strength. When she saw our concern about her weakness, she tried to rouse us from our downcast hopes by dispersing again with her beautiful words the grief of our souls with her last slight and labored breathing. At this point, especially, my soul was in conflict because of what it was confronted by. My disposition was naturally made gloomy by the anticipation of never again hearing such a voice, but actually I had not yet accepted the idea that she was going to leave this mortal life, and my soul was so exalted by appearances that I secretly thought that she had transcended the common nature. For the fact was that, in her last breath, she experienced nothing strange in the expectation of the change and displayed no cowardice towards the departure from life. Instead, she philosophized with high intelligence on what had been decided upon by her about this life from the beginning up to her last breath, and this made her appear to belong no longer to the world of men. It was as if an angel had by some providence taken on human form, an angel who had no relation with or similarity to the life of the flesh and for whom it was not at all unreasonable to remain detached since the flesh was not part of her experience. For this reason, she seemed to me to be making clear to those present the divine and pure love of the unseen Bridegroom which she had secretly nourished in the depths of her soul, and she seemed to be communicating the disposition in her heart to go to the One she was longing for, so that, once loosed from the chains of the body, she might quickly be with Him. Truly, her race was towards the Beloved and nothing of the pleasure of life diverted her attention.

The day was almost over and the sun was beginning to set, but the zeal in her did not decline. Indeed, as she neared her end and saw the beauty of the Bridegroom more clearly, she rushed with greater impulse towards the One she desired, no longer speaking to those of us who were present, but to that very One toward whom she looked with steadfast eyes. Her couch was turned to the East and, stopping her conversation with us, for the rest of the time she addressed herself to God in prayer, beseeching Him with her hands and speaking in a low soft voice so that we barely heard what she said. This was her prayer and there is no doubt that it made its way to God and that it was heard by Him.

TRANSLATED BY Virginia Woods Callahan.

She said: 'O Lord, You have freed us from the fear of death;[1] You have made the end of life here the beginning of a true life for us. For a time, You give rest to our bodies in sleep and You awaken us again with the last trumpet.[2] The dust from which You fashioned us with Your hands You give back to the dust of the earth for safekeeping, and You who have relinquished it will recall it after reshaping with incorruptibility and grace our mortal and graceless substance. You redeemed us from the curse[3] and from sin, having taken both upon Yourself; You crushed the heads of the serpent[4] who had seized us with his jaws in the abyss of disobedience. Breaking down the gates of hell[5] and overcoming the one who had the empire of death,[6] You opened up for us a path to the resurrection. For those who fear You, You gave as a token the sign of the holy cross for the destruction of the Adversary and the salvation of our life. O God everlasting, towards whom I have directed myself from my mother's womb, whom my soul has loved[7] with all its strength, to whom I have dedicated my body and my soul from my infancy up to now, prepare for me a shining angel to lead me to the place of refreshment where is the water of relaxation[8] near the bosom of the holy Fathers. You who broke the flaming sword[9] and compassionately gave Paradise back to the man crucified with You,[1] remember me also in Your kingdom, for I, too, have been crucified with You, having nailed my flesh through fear of You and having feared Your judgments. Let the terrible abyss not separate me from Your chosen ones; let the Slanderer[2] not stand in my way or my sins be discovered before Your eyes if I have fallen and sinned in word or deed or thought because of the weakness of our nature. Do You who have power on earth to forgive sins forgive me so that I may be refreshed and may be found before You once I have put off my body, having no fault in the form of my soul, but blameless and spotless may my soul be taken into Your hands as an offering before Your face.' As she said this, she made the sign of the cross upon her eyes and mouth and heart, and little by little, as the fever dried up her tongue, she was no longer able to speak clearly; her voice gave out and only from the trembling of her lips and the motion of her hands did we know that she was continuing to pray.

Then, evening came on and the lamp was brought in. Macrina directed her eye toward the beam of light and made it clear that she was eager to say the nocturnal prayer and, although her voice failed her, with her heart and the movement of her hands, she fulfilled her desire and moved her lips in keeping with the impulse within her. When she had completed the thanksgiving and indicated that the prayer was over by making the sign of the cross, she breathed a deep breath and with the prayer her life came to an end. * * *

* * *

When the time came to cover the body with the robe, the injunction of the great lady made it necessary for me to perform this function. The woman

---

1. See Hebrews 2:15.
2. See 1 Corinthians 15:52.
3. See Genesis 3:19 and Galatians 3:13.
4. Macrina (or Gregory, in recounting her death-bed speech) quotes Psalms 74:13–14 from the ancient Greek translation (Septuagint) of the Old Testament (Septuagint numbering: Psalms 73).
5. See Matthew 16:18.
6. See Hebrews 2:14.
7. See Canticles 1:7; for information on Canticles, the Song of Songs, see p. 306.
8. See Psalms 23:2; Macrina quotes the Psalm in the Greek version (= Septuagint Psalms 22).
9. See Genesis 3:24.
1. See Luke 23:39–43.
2. The Devil.

who was present and sharing the great assignment with us said: 'Do not pass over the greatest of the miracles of the saint.' 'What is that?' I asked. She laid bare a part of the breast and said: 'Do you see this thin, almost imperceptible, scar below the neck?' It was like a mark made by a small needle. At the same time, she brought the lamp nearer to the place she was showing me. 'What is miraculous about that,' I said, 'if the body has a small mark here?' She said: 'This is left on the body as a reminder of the great help of God. At one time, there was a painful sore here and there was the risk that if it was not cut out it would develop into an irremediable illness if it should spread to places near the heart. Her mother begged her to accept the doctor's care and implored her many times saying that the art of medicine was given by God to man for his preservation. But Macrina considered worse than the disease laying bare part of the body to another's eyes, and one evening, after she had finished her usual tasks connected with her mother, she went inside the sanctuary and all night supplicated the God of healing, pouring out a stream from her eyes upon the ground, and she used the mud from her tears as a remedy for the disease. When her mother was earnestly distressed and asking her again to see the doctor, she said that there was a cure for her disease if her mother with her own hand would make the sign of the cross on the place. When the mother put her hand inside to make the sign of the cross on her breast, the sign of the cross worked and the sore disappeared. But this,' she said, 'is a small token and was seen then instead of the terrible sore, and remained to the end as a reminder, I suppose, of the divine consideration, a cause and reason for unceasing thanksgiving to God.'

* * *

I do not think it is wise to add to my story all the other details we heard from those who lived with her and knew her life accurately, for most men judge the credibility of what they hear according to the measure of their own experience, and what is beyond the power of the hearer they insult with the suspicion of falsehood as outside of the truth. Therefore, I pass over that incredible farming phenomenon at the time of the famine when, as the grain was given out in proportion to the need, the amount did not seem to grow smaller, but remained the same as it was before it was given to those asking for it. And after this, there were other events more surprising than these; the healing of disease, the casting out of devils, true prophecies of future events, all of which are believed to be true by those who knew the details accurately, amazing although they are. But for the material-minded, they are beyond what can be accepted. They do not know that the distribution of graces is in proportion to one's faith, meager for those of little faith,[3] great for those who have within themselves great room for faith. So, in order not to do harm to those who have no faith in the gifts of God, I have decided against enumerating the greater miracles, judging it sufficient to end my work about Macrina with what I have already related.

---

3. In several places in the Bible (e.g., Luke 12:28), the phrase "ye of little faith" describes people who doubt Jesus' power to perform miracles.

ANONYMOUS
fourth and fifth centuries

FROM SAYINGS OF THE DESERT FATHERS

During the decades after Anthony moved to the desert (see p. 262), thousands of ascetics, hermits, and monks and a handful of nuns followed his example. As a result, Anthony is considered the founder of desert monasticism. The men who joined this movement, most of them laypeople, became known as the Desert Fathers.

The desert settlements consisted of mud-brick dwellings, and the main collection of such dwellings came to be named Kellia, "The Cells." A smaller settlement, Pherme, was a satellite community to Kellia. At Kellia and Pherme, the monks lived in individual cells, sometimes in small clusters, and gathered weekly for worship.

People began going to the desert to ask for advice from the desert dwellers. Over time, the short wisdom sayings and short wisdom stories of the Desert Fathers became a recognized genre, beginning as an oral tradition in the Coptic language. In the fifth century, these sayings and stories were collected as Coptic, Syriac, Greek, and Latin texts. Consisting partly of descriptions of the desert dwellers' experiences and spiritual practices, they were extremely popular among early Christian monks and appeared in various forms. One Latin collection was *Apophthegmata Patrum*, known as *Sayings of the Desert Fathers*, the source of the following selection.

PRONOUNCING GLOSSARY

Ammonas: *am´-moh-nahs* Pherme: *fair´-may*
Bessarion: *be-sahr´-ee-uhn* Scete: *skay´-tay*

FROM SAYINGS OF THE DESERT FATHERS

XL

One of the brethren had sinned, and the priest told him to leave the community. So then Abbot Bessarion got up and walked out with him, saying: I too am a sinner!

XLI

A brother in Scete happened to commit a fault, and the elders assembled, and sent for Abbot Moses to join them. He, however, did not want to come. The priest sent him a message, saying: Come, the community of the brethren is waiting for you. So he arose and started off. And taking with him a very old basket full of holes, he filled it with sand, and carried it behind him. The elders came out to meet him, and said: What is this, Father? The elder replied: My sins are running out behind me, and I do not see them,

TRANSLATED BY Thomas Merton. The parenthetical Bible citations are the translator's.

and today I come to judge the sins of another! They, hearing this, said nothing to the brother but pardoned him.

XLII

A certain brother inquired of Abbot Pastor, saying: What shall I do? I lose my nerve when I am sitting alone at prayer in my cell. The elder said to him: Despise no one, condemn no one, rebuke no one, God will give you peace and your meditation will be undisturbed.

XLIII

An elder said: Do not judge a fornicator if you are chaste, for if you do, you too are violating the law as much as he is. For He who said thou shalt not fornicate also said thou shalt not judge.

XLIV

One of the Fathers told a story of a certain elder who was in his cell busily at work and wearing a hairshirt when Abbot Ammonas came to him. When Abbot Ammonas saw him wearing a hairshirt he said: That thing won't do you a bit of good. The elder said: Three thoughts are troubling me. The first impels me to withdraw somewhere into the wilderness. The second, to seek a foreign land where no one knows me. The third, to wall myself into this cell and see no one and eat only every second day. Abbot Ammonas said to him: None of these three will do you a bit of good. But rather sit in your cell, and eat a little every day, and have always in your heart the words which are read in the Gospel and were said by the Publican,[1] and thus you can be saved.

XLV

It was told of Abbot John the Dwarf that once he had said to his elder brother: I want to live in the same security as the angels have, doing no work, but serving God without intermission. And casting off everything he had on, he started out into the desert. When a week had gone by he returned to his brother. And while he was knocking on the door, his brother called out before opening, and asked: Who are you? He replied: I am John. Then his brother answered and said: John has become an angel and is no longer among men. But John kept on knocking and said: It is I. Still the brother did not open, but kept him waiting. Finally, opening the door, he said: If you are a man, you are going to have to start working again in order to live. But if you are an angel, why do you want to come into a cell? So John did penance and said: Forgive me, brother, for I have sinned.[2]

---

1. In Luke 18:10–14, the Publican is the public employee—a despised tax collector for the Romans—who stands far off in the Temple and Prays, "God be merciful to me, a sinner."
2. See Luke 23:34.

XLVI

Abbot Pastor said: If you have a chest full of clothing, and leave it for a long time, the clothing will rot inside it. It is the same with the thoughts in our heart. If we do not carry them out by physical action, after a long while they will spoil and turn bad.

XLVII

The same Father said: If there are three monks living together, of whom one remains silent in prayer at all times, and another is ailing and gives thanks for it, and the third waits on them both with sincere good will, these three are equal, as if they were performing the same work.

SAINT BENEDICT OF NURSIA
480?–543

FROM RULE OF SAINT BENEDICT

Benedict was born in Nursia (modern Norcia, in Umbria, northern Italy). He died at the monastery he founded at Monte Cassino, southeast of Rome, and is venerated as a saint by the Roman Catholic, Eastern (Greek) Orthodox, and Lutheran Churches and by the Anglican Communion.

In composing what he called his "little rule for beginners"—precepts for monks—Benedict drew on an earlier, anonymous document, *Rule of the Master.* Benedict envisioned a monastic community as like a family that lived a life of prayer, biblical study, and work. He discouraged the solitary life and disliked wandering ascetics. Intended for his own community in Italy, Benedict's rule was adopted in the ninth century as the standard monastic rule for men and women in the Western Church. It remains the standard Western monastic rule.

PRONOUNCING GLOSSARY

Eli: *ee´-lai* [*ai* rhyming with *rye*]   Shiloh: *shai´-loh* [*ai* rhyming with *rye*]

FROM RULE OF SAINT BENEDICT

Prologue

Listen carefully, my son, to the master's instructions, and attend to them with the ear of your heart. This is advice from a father who loves you; welcome it, and faithfully put it into practice. The labor of obedience will bring you back to him from whom you had drifted through the sloth of disobedience. This message of mine is for you, then, if you are ready to give up your own will, once and for all, and armed with the strong and noble weapons of obedience to do battle for the true King, Christ the Lord.

First of all, every time you begin a good work, you must pray to him most earnestly to bring it to perfection. In his goodness, he has already counted us as his sons, and therefore we should never grieve him by our evil actions. With his good gifts which are in us, we must obey him at all times that he may never become the angry father who disinherits his sons, nor the dread lord, enraged by our sins, who punishes us forever as worthless servants for refusing to follow him to glory.

*   *   *

Therefore we intend to establish a school for the Lord's service. In drawing up its regulations, we hope to set down nothing harsh, nothing burdensome. The good of all concerned, however, may prompt us to a little strictness in order to amend faults and to safeguard love. Do not be daunted immediately by fear and run away from the road that leads to salvation. It is bound to be narrow at the outset. But as we progress in this way of life and in faith, we shall run on the path of God's commandments, our hearts overflowing with the inexpressible delight of love. Never swerving from his instructions, then, but faithfully observing his teaching in the monastery until death, we shall through patience share in the sufferings of Christ that we may deserve also to share in his kingdom. Amen.

*   *   *

CHAPTER 2

Qualities of the Abbot

To be worthy of the task of governing a monastery, the abbot must always remember what his title signifies and act as a superior should. He is believed to hold the place of Christ in the monastery, since he is addressed by a title of Christ, as the Apostle indicates: *You have received the spirit of adoption of sons by which we exclaim, abba, father.*[1] Therefore, the abbot must never teach or decree or command anything that would deviate from the Lord's instructions. On the contrary, everything he teaches and commands should, like the leaven of divine justice, permeate the minds of his disciples. Let the abbot always remember that at the fearful judgment of God, not only

---

FROM *The Rule of St. Benedict in English*, ed. Timothy Fry. The translation's "verse numbers" and parenthetical Bible references have been omitted.

1. Romans 8:15. "Abba": father (Aramaic).

his teaching but also his disciples' obedience will come under scrutiny. The abbot must, therefore, be aware that the shepherd will bear the blame wherever the father of the household finds that the sheep have yielded no profit. Still, if he has faithfully shepherded a restive and disobedient flock, always striving to cure their unhealthy ways, it will be otherwise: the shepherd will be acquitted at the Lord's judgment. Then, like the Prophet, he may say to the Lord: *I have not hidden your justice in my heart; I have proclaimed your truth and your salvation,*[2] *but they spurned and rejected me.*[3] Then at last the sheep that have rebelled against his care will be punished by the overwhelming power of death.

Furthermore, anyone who receives the name of abbot is to lead his disciples by a twofold teaching: he must point out to them all that is good and holy more by example than by words, proposing the commandments of the Lord to receptive disciples with words, but demonstrating God's instructions to the stubborn and the dull by a living example. Again, if he teaches his disciples that something is not to be done, then neither must he do it, *lest after preaching to others, he himself be found reprobate*[4] and God some day call to him in his sin: *How is it that you repeat my just commands and mouth my covenant when you hate discipline and toss my words behind you?*[5] And also this: *How is it that you can see a splinter in your brother's eye, and never notice the plank in your own?*[6]

The abbot should avoid all favoritism in the monastery. He is not to love one more than another unless he finds someone better in good actions and obedience. A man born free is not to be given higher rank than a slave who becomes a monk, except for some other good reason. But the abbot is free, if he sees fit, to change anyone's rank as justice demands. Ordinarily, everyone is to keep to his regular place, because *whether slave or free, we are all one in Christ*[7] and share alike in bearing arms in the service of the one Lord, for *God shows no partiality among persons.*[8] Only in this are we distinguished in his sight: if we are found better than others in good works and in humility. Therefore, the abbot is to show equal love to everyone and apply the same discipline to all according to their merits.

In his teaching, the abbot should always observe the Apostle's recommendation, in which he says: *Use argument, appeal, reproof.*[9] This means that he must vary with circumstances, threatening and coaxing by turns, stern as a taskmaster, devoted and tender as only a father can be. With the undisciplined and restless, he will use firm argument; with the obedient and docile and patient, he will appeal for greater virtue; but as for the negligent and disdainful, we charge him to use reproof and rebuke. He should not gloss over the sins of those who err, but cut them out while he can, as soon as they begin to sprout, remembering the fate of Eli, priest of Shiloh.[1] For upright and perceptive men, his first and second warnings should be verbal; but those who are evil or stubborn, arrogant or disobedient, he can curb only by blows or some other physical punishment at the first offense.

2. Psalms 4:11.
3. Isaiah 1:2; Ezekiel 20:27.
4. 1 Corinthians 9:27.
5. Psalms 50:16–17.
6. Matthew 7:3.

7. Galatians 3:28; Ephesians 6:8.
8. Romans 2:11.
9. 2 Timothy 4:2. "The Apostle": Saint Paul.
1. 1 Samuel 2:11–4:18.

It is written, *The fool cannot be corrected with words;*[2] and again, *Strike your son with a rod and you will free his soul from death.*[3]

The abbot must always remember what he is and remember what he is called, aware that more will be expected of a man to whom more has been entrusted. He must know what a difficult and demanding burden he has undertaken: directing souls and serving a variety of temperaments, coaxing, reproving and encouraging them as appropriate. He must so accommodate and adapt himself to each one's character and intelligence that he will not only keep the flock entrusted to his care from dwindling, but will rejoice in the increase of a good flock. Above all, he must not show too great concern for the fleeting and temporal things of this world, neglecting or treating lightly the welfare of those entrusted to him. Rather, he should keep in mind that he has undertaken the care of souls for whom he must give an account. That he may not plead lack of resources as an excuse, he is to remember what is written: *Seek first the kingdom of God and his justice, and all these things will be given you as well,*[4] and again, *Those who fear him lack nothing.*[5]

The abbot must know that anyone undertaking the charge of souls must be ready to account for them. Whatever the number of brothers he has in his care, let him realize that on judgment day he will surely have to submit a reckoning to the Lord for all their souls—and indeed for his own as well. In this way, while always fearful of the future examination of the shepherd about the sheep entrusted to him and careful about the state of others' accounts, he becomes concerned also about his own, and while helping others to amend by his warnings, he achieves the amendment of his own faults.

CHAPTER 3

Summoning the Brothers for Counsel

As often as anything important is to be done in the monastery, the abbot shall call the whole community together and himself explain what the business is; and after hearing the advice of the brothers, let him ponder it and follow what he judges the wiser course. The reason why we have said all should be called for counsel is that the Lord often reveals what is better to the younger. The brothers, for their part, are to express their opinions with all humility, and not presume to defend their own views obstinately. The decision is rather the abbot's to make, so that when he has determined what is more prudent, all may obey. Nevertheless, just as it is proper for disciples to obey their master, so it is becoming for the master on his part to settle everything with foresight and fairness.

Accordingly in every instance, all are to follow the teaching of the rule, and no one shall rashly deviate from it. In the monastery no one is to follow his own heart's desire, nor shall anyone presume to contend with his abbot defiantly, or outside the monastery. Should anyone presume to do so, let him be subjected to the discipline of the rule. Moreover, the abbot himself must fear God and keep the rule in everything he does; he can be sure

2. Proverbs 29:19.
3. Proverbs 23:14.

4. Matthew 6:33.
5. Psalms 34:10.

beyond any doubt that he will have to give an account of all his judgments to God, the most just of judges.

If less important business of the monastery is to be transacted, he shall take counsel with the seniors only, as it is written: *Do everything with counsel and you will not be sorry afterward.*[6]

* * *

6. Sirach 32:24. Sirach, a Book of the Greek Bible and one of the apocryphal Books of the English Bible, is also referred to as Ben Sirach, Ben Sira, Siracides, and Ecclesiasticus.

The Middle Ages
600–1300

THE BIRTH AND GROWTH OF A EUROPEAN CHRISTENDOM

Though Jesus may have spoken Greek only as a second language, Paul spoke Greek as his native tongue. All the Scriptures of the New Testament were written in Greek and were first published for Greek-speaking Christian communities around the eastern Mediterranean. It is scarcely an exaggeration to say that Christianity was born speaking Greek.

From Italy west, the Roman Empire spoke Latin rather than Greek; from Palestine east, it spoke Aramaic. Yet the educated Roman elite in both regions knew the Greek classics, even when, like Augustine, they read them in translation. It is no surprise, then, that the intellectual leaders of the new religion—Origen, Tertullian, Jerome, Augustine, Ambrose, and others—interpreted their own as well as the inherited Jewish Scriptures in ways deeply marked by Greek thought, especially Platonic thought. Christianity had become a cultural synthesis by the time it became the state religion of the Roman Empire in 381.

After the fourth century and through the end of the late antique period, however, the old Roman Empire in the West was under siege by the so-called barbarians from the North. These migrating Germanic tribes breached Roman frontiers,

In this illumination, the 12th-century Benedictine abbess Hildegard of Bingen is seated within her monastery's cloister, reading or dictating one of her visions to a male visitor or perhaps a secretary. The flames above her head represent her divine inspiration.

moving into western Europe, then into the Balkans, Spain, and Italy and across the Mediterranean into Roman North Africa. In the Latin-speaking western half of the Roman Empire, the cultural synthesis broke down beginning roughly in the 500s, after the imperial administration there succumbed to the successive waves of Germanic invasion. Though these tribes were often culturally Romanized and knew Latin, they did not know or learn Greek, and what ensued after "the fall of Rome in the West" was cultural decline and the disappearance of Greek learning under the feudal and ecclesiastical rule that now replaced imperial government. The life of Christendom in Europe was then further darkened by later waves of debilitating invasion: the Arabs in the seventh and eighth centuries, the Vikings in the eighth and ninth centuries, and the Mongols in the thirteenth century. While Rome declined as a city, Constantinople, in the East, emerged as the new center of Christian identity. Though the Crusades of the eleventh and twelfth centuries were begun at the request of the Byzantine Emperor, who was also the head of the Greek Orthodox Church, Crusader looting of Constantinople deepened an East/West estrangement in Christendom commonly dated to mutual excommunications issued in 1054.

Through all of these changes, knowledge of Latin and of Roman culture survived in the European monasteries of the early Middle Ages. Monasteries became social, cultural, and educational centers. In hitherto unevangelized areas, new monasteries became missionary extensions of the Christian Church. The early Middle Ages have been called the "Benedictine Centuries" in the West because of the influence of the monasteries where the Rule of Saint Benedict became the standard. Monastery schools taught Latin, and monastic scriptoria painstakingly copied and distributed Latin works—mainly, of course, the Bible in Latin. By the ninth century, communities of nuns following the Rule of Saint Benedict were widespread. Few women in medieval Europe were better educated or more influential than the abbesses of the largest and wealthiest Benedictine nunneries.

In the eleventh and twelfth centuries, the period sometimes called the High Middle Ages, a cultural innovation took hold that would eventually sweep the world: the historic organization of the university as a relatively independent community of scholars, albeit initially clerics. The emergence of the university from the all-male, cathedral-based, cleric-run schools sharply accelerated the process by which Europe would begin to rediscover and then enthusiastically embrace the forgotten cultural wealth of its past. In the twelfth and thirteenth centuries, university learning—now in the newly important university towns rather than in the rural locations favored by monasteries—was further stimulated by the recovery in translation of major works by the great Greek philosopher Aristotle. By an unlikely roundabout path, these works had been translated from Greek into Aramaic in Roman-ruled Damascus and adjacent areas. After the Arab conquests of the seventh and eighth centuries, they were further translated from Aramaic into Arabic in Damascus and Baghdad. Still later, in the eleventh century, they were translated again from Arabic into Latin in culturally mixed, Muslim-Christian Spain. Finally, moving especially from the Cathedral School at Toledo, Spain, Aristotle in Latin translation spread to the curriculum of all the new, Latin-speaking universities.

By the early twelfth century, European urban centers had begun to flourish. Groups of mendicant, or begging, friars ("brothers") developed into the Franciscans, Dominicans, Carmelites, and Augustinians, major orders that contributed vigorously to the new university life. By the thirteenth century, the great cathedrals had been built, medieval university life thrived, and a cosmopolitan commercial order came into being, based especially on textile manufacture and the wool trade.

Chronology

THE MIDDLE AGES (600–1300)

638 Arabs conquer Jerusalem

711 Arab conquest of Spain begins

716 Saint Boniface leaves England on mission to Germany

early 700s Iconoclasm grows in Central and Eastern Christianity; John of Damascus defends use of icons

731 Saint Bede the Venerable completes *Ecclesiastical History of the English People*

732 Charles Martel (grandfather of eventual Holy Roman emperor Charlemagne) wins Battle of Poitiers, blocking Muslim expansion into France

787 Second Council of Nicaea condemns iconoclasm

863 Saints Cyril and Methodius sent from Constantinople to evangelize the Slavs

910 Influential Abbey of Cluny founded, in Burgundy

945? Princess Olga of Ukraine converts to Christianity

963 Athanasius the Athonite founds monastery on Mount Athos, a major spiritual center of the Greek Orthodox Church

988 Mass baptism at Kiev under Vladimir, Princess Olga's grandson, inaugurates Christianization of Ukraine, Russia, and adjacent regions

1054 Great Schism marks permanent split between Church of Rome (Western Europe) and Church of Constantinople (Eastern Europe, Turkey, and parts of Eastern Mediterranean)

1075 Construction begins on Cathedral of Santiago de Compostela, Spain, most popular Christian pilgrimage site after Jerusalem and Rome

1075–1122 Investiture controversy, over the right of kings to appoint bishops and abbots, results in decline of royal power

1093 Theologian Saint Anselm becomes archbishop of Canterbury

1095 Council of Clermont: Pope Urban II proclaims First Crusade

1098 Founding of monastery at Cîteaux, France, by Cistercian monks favoring strict interpretation of Saint Benedict's Rule

1099 Crusaders capture Antioch and Jerusalem

11th century European universities founded

1204 Fourth Crusade; Crusaders plunder Constantinople

1209–29 Albigensian (neo-Gnostic) heresy suppressed in southern France

1265–74 Saint Thomas Aquinas writes major works of theology

MISSIONARY EXPANSION

Even though the Christian Church was illegal in the Roman Empire until the early fourth century, Christians grew in number. By the time Christianity was officially tolerated by law—with the Edict of Milan, a letter signed by the emperors Constantine and Licinius in 313—an estimated fifth of the empire was Christian. Scholars have long argued about the reasons for such growth. It could be explained partly by conditions within the empire: political stability, good roads, a single language for communication. It could also be explained partly by structural features of Christianity: the Church's practice of offering practical help to its members and others, as well as the openness of the Christian community to all classes of society and to women.

Christianity grew through a process analogous to cell division. When a community grew too large to fit in the house that served as its church, another "house church" was founded for worship. Most of this earliest growth occurred in towns and cities. The countryside was slow to feel the presence of the Christian Church; indeed, the Latin word for the countryside, *pagus*, is the source of the English word *pagan*.

Christianity also grew through the work of the preachers and evangelists who carried the faith through and beyond the empire. For example, monks often formed settlements whose influence radiated out from those monastic bases. Such settlements were particularly powerful in thinly populated areas where city life did not exist. The monastic center could provide both the resources (grain storage, medicine, education, shelter, etc.) and the workers needed to extend Christianity and civilized life into the countryside.

From the fourth century on, Christian communities sprang up as missionaries followed the empire's trade routes, such as those for spices and silk. Missionaries pushed beyond the old Roman frontier, to the British Isles in the north and beyond the Rhine River in the east. There is fair evidence from the seventh century of Christian communities as far away as China and India. The first country to declare itself Christian before the end of the Roman persecutions was Armenia, which was converted by traveling Christians early in the fourth century. Ukraine, however, was not evangelized until just before 1000; Scandinavia, not until after that year.

SAINT BEDE THE VENERABLE
673?–735

FROM ECCLESIASTICAL HISTORY OF THE ENGLISH PEOPLE

Bede was a monk, scholar, writer, linguist, and translator. He lived in the medieval kingdom of Northumbria (modern-day northern England and southeast Scotland). Venerated as a saint by the Roman Catholic, Eastern Orthodox, and Lutheran Churches and by the Anglican Communion, he is the only native of Great Britain to have been made (in 1899) a Doctor (from the Latin for "Teacher") of the Church.

This title recognizes individuals as having been of major importance to the Church, particularly in contributing to theology or doctrine.

Bede was at once a serious historian and a devout monk, living in a God-haunted and miracle-filled world. While modern readers are likely to find his obsession with the correct date for Easter off-putting, there are memorable moments in his account of the growth and consolidation of Christianity in Britain. In Book Two, chapter 1, Bede presents the fateful encounter between the future pope Gregory the Great (pope from 590 until his death, in 604) and a group of pagan British slave boys. Upon learning that the handsome slaves are Angles (Latin *Angli*), members of a Germanic tribe that had migrated from coastal northern Germany to England in the fifth century C.E., Gregory jests that they are like angels (*angeli*). Then he puns on the names of their native region and its king. After becoming pope, Gregory sent a successful mission to evangelize the Angles and the closely related Saxons.

In Book Two, chapters 12–14, Bede depicts the pagan king Edwin of Northumbria (585?–633; reigned from 616 until his death) in the process of converting to Christianity, thanks to the efforts of a missionary, Paulinus of York (d. 644), who had previously saved Edwin from his mortal enemies. Edwin is already convinced of the truth of Christianity, but he summons his royal council to debate whether they should accept the new religion. At the council meeting, somewhat improbably but also somewhat self serving, Coifi, the king's leading priest, admits the uselessness of his own gods. An unnamed nobleman makes a now-famous remark about the brevity and precariousness of human life, a remark that wins over everyone else, though his powerful insight is not actually religious.

PRONOUNCING GLOSSARY

Aelle: *a´-luh* [rhymes with *calla*]
Bede: *beed*
Coifi: *coh-ee´-fee*

Deira: *de-ee´-ruh*
Paulinus: *pow-lye´-nuhs*
Phocas: *foh´-kuhs*

FROM ECCLESIASTICAL HISTORY OF THE ENGLISH PEOPLE

From BOOK TWO

[From *Chapter 1*]

About this time, in the year of our Lord 605, having ruled the apostolic Roman Church most illustriously for thirteen years, six months, and ten days, the blessed Pope Gregory died and was taken up to his eternal home in heaven. And it is fitting that he should receive fuller mention in this history, since it was through his zeal that our English nation was brought from the bondage of Satan to the Faith of Christ, and we may rightly term him our own apostle. For during his pontificate, while he exercised supreme authority over all the churches of Christendom that had already long since been converted, he transformed our still idolatrous nation into a church of Christ. So, we may rightly describe him by the term apostle; for if he is not an apostle to others, yet doubtless he is to us, and we are *the seal of his apostleship in the Lord.*[1]

TRANSLATED BY Leo Sherley-Price.

1. See 1 Corinthians 9:2.

Among the early inhabitants of Britain was a Germanic tribe called the Angles. According to a legend recounted in Bede's *Ecclesiastical History*, Pope Gregory I saw captured Angles in a Roman slave market; remarked on their beauty, saying, *"Non Angli sed angeli"* ("Not Angles but angels"); and dispatched a missionary to their country. The visionary English artist William Blake captured the scene in this 1793 watercolor, *Non Angli sed Angeli*.

*   *   *

Gregory ruled the Church during the reigns of the Emperors Maurice and Phocas,[2] and in the second year of the latter's reign he passed from this life and entered the true life of heaven. His body was laid to rest on March the twelfth in the church of Saint Peter the Apostle before the sanctuary, whence he will one day rise in glory with other shepherds of Holy Church. On his tomb was inscribed this epitaph:

> Receive, O earth, the body that you gave,
> Till God's lifegiving power destroy the grave.
> Over his heaven-bound soul death holds no sway
> Who steps through death into a fairer day.
> The life of this high Pontiff, here at rest,
> With good deeds past all reckoning was blest.
> He fed the hungry, and he clothed the chill,
> And by his teaching shielded souls from ill.
> Wisdom was in his words, and all he wrought
> Was as a pattern, acting what he taught.
> To Christ he led the Angles, by God's grace
> Swelling Faith's armies with a new-won race.
> O holy pastor, all your work and prayer
> To God you offered with a shepherd's care.
> Triumphant now you reap your just reward,
> Raised to high place, the consul of the Lord.

---

2. The Byzantine emperor Maurice reigned from 582 until 602; Phocas then took the throne and reigned until 610.

I must here relate a story, handed down to us by the tradition of our fore-bears, which explains Gregory's deep desire for the salvation of our nation. We are told that one day some merchants who had recently arrived in Rome displayed their many wares in the market-place. Among the crowd who thronged to buy was Gregory, who saw among other merchandise some boys exposed for sale. These had fair complexions, fine-cut features, and beauti-ful hair. Looking at them with interest, he enquired from what country and what part of the world they came. 'They come from the island of Britain,' he was told, 'where all the people have this appearance.' He then asked whether the islanders were Christians, or whether they were still ignorant heathens. 'They are pagans,' he was informed. 'Alas!' said Gregory with a heartfelt sigh: 'how sad that such bright-faced folk are still in the grasp of the author of dark-ness, and that such graceful features conceal minds void of God's grace! What is the name of this race?' 'They are called Angles,' he was told. 'That is appro-priate,' he said, 'for they have angelic faces, and it is right that they should become joint-heirs with the angels in heaven. And what is the name of the province from which they have been brought?' 'Deira,' was the answer. 'Good. They shall indeed be rescued *de ira*—from wrath—and called to the mercy of Christ. And what is the name of their king?' 'Aelle,' he was told. 'Then,' said Gregory, making play on the name, 'it is right that their land should echo the praise of God our Creator in the word *Alleluia*.'

Approaching the Pope of the apostolic Roman see—for he was not yet Pope himself—Gregory begged him to send preachers of the word to the English people in Britain to convert them to Christ, and declared his own eagerness to attempt the task should the Pope see fit to direct it. This per-mission was not forthcoming, for although the Pope himself was willing, the citizens of Rome would not allow Gregory to go so far away from the city. But directly Gregory succeeded to the Papacy himself, he put in hand this long cherished project. He sent other missionaries in his place; but it was his prayers and encouragement that made their mission fruitful. And I have thought it fitting to include this traditional story in the history of our Church.

[From *Chapter 12*]

While King Edwin hesitated to accept the word of God at Paulinus' preach-ing, he used to sit alone for hours, as I have said, earnestly deliberating what he should do and what religion he should follow. On one of these occasions, the man of God came to him and, laying his right hand on his head, enquired whether he remembered this sign.[3] The king trembled and would have fallen at his feet; but Paulinus raised him and said in a friendly voice: 'God has helped you to escape from the hands of the enemies whom you feared, and it is through His bounty that you have received the king-dom that you desired. Remember the third promise that you made, and hesitate no longer. Accept the Faith and keep the commands of Him who has delivered you from all your earthly troubles and raised you to the glory of an earthly kingdom. If you will henceforward obey His will, which he reveals to you through me, he will save you likewise from the everlasting doom of the wicked and give you a place in His eternal kingdom in heaven.'

---

3. Paulinus alludes to a disturbing dream vision that he knows God has sent to King Edwin.

[From *Chapter 13*]

When he heard this, the king answered that it was his will as well as his duty to accept the Faith that Paulinus taught, but said that he must still discuss the matter with his principal advisers and friends, so that, if they were in agreement with him, they might all be cleansed together in Christ the Fount of Life. Paulinus agreed, and the king kept his promise. He summoned a council of the wise men, and asked each in turn his opinion of this strange doctrine and this new way of worshipping the godhead that was being proclaimed to them.

Coifi, the chief Priest, replied without hesitation: 'Your Majesty, let us give careful consideration to this new teaching; for I frankly admit that, in my experience, the religion that we have hitherto professed seems valueless and powerless. None of your subjects has been more devoted to the service of our gods than myself; yet there are many to whom you show greater favour, who receive greater honours, and who are more successful in all their undertakings. Now, if the gods had any power, they would surely have favoured myself, who have been more zealous in their service. Therefore, if on examination you perceive that these new teachings are better and more effectual, let us not hesitate to accept them.'

Another of the king's chief men signified his agreement with this prudent argument, and went on to say: 'Your Majesty, when we compare the present life of man on earth with that time of which we have no knowledge, it seems to me like the swift flight of a single sparrow through the banqueting-hall where you are sitting at dinner on a winter's day with your thegns[4] and counsellors. In the midst there is a comforting fire to warm the hall; outside, the storms of winter rain or snow are raging. This sparrow flies swiftly in through one door of the hall, and out through another. While he is inside, he is safe from the winter storms; but after a few moments of comfort, he vanishes from sight into the wintry world from which he came. Even so, man appears on earth for a little while; but of what went before this life or of what follows, we know nothing. Therefore, if this new teaching has brought any more certain knowledge, it seems only right that we should follow it.' The other elders and counsellors of the king, under God's guidance, gave similar advice.

[*From Chapter 14*]

So King Edwin, with all the nobility of his kingdom and a large number of humbler folk, accepted the Faith and were washed in the cleansing waters of Baptism in the eleventh year of his reign, which was the year of our Lord 627, and about one hundred and eighty years after the first arrival of the English in Britain. * * *

---

4. Nobles, courtiers.

RUDOLF OF FULDA
800?–ca. 862–65

FROM THE LIFE OF ABBESS LEOBA

Rudolf was a monk of the Benedictine monastery of Fulda, Germany. In 822, he became head of the monastery school. In addition to being a theologian and teacher, he wrote some of the most important works of his time. Rudolf's *Vita Leobae Abbatissae Biscofesheimensis*—most likely written in 836, translated here as *The Life of Abbess Leona*—is the first known Saxon biography of a woman.

Leoba of Tauberbischofsheim (ca. 710–ca. 781–82) was born in Wessex, England. Her cousin, born Winfrid or Wynfrid or Wynfrith but known as Boniface (ca. 675–754), traveled as a missionary from England to Germany and is considered the founder of the German Church. At Boniface's invitation, Leoba went to Germany to found a monastery and help Christianize the area. She died of natural causes in Schornsheim, Germany, and is venerated as a saint by the Roman Catholic and Eastern Orthodox Churches. Leoba is an excellent early example of the influence and social prominence enjoyed by the (well-born) abbesses of the great monasteries for women. In this regard, only wealthy widows bore comparison with abbesses. Boniface was killed in Frisia (along the southeastern corner of the North Sea) by inhabitants who were resisting his conversion attempts. He is venerated by the Roman Catholic, Eastern Orthodox, and Lutheran Churches and by the Anglican Communion.

FROM THE LIFE OF ABBESS LEOBA
[From *Prologue*]

There was a certain poor little crippled girl, who sat near the gate of the monastery begging alms. Every day she received her food from the abbess's table, her clothing from the nuns and all other necessities from them; these were given to her from divine charity. It happened that after some time, deceived by the suggestions of the devil, she committed fornication, and when her appearance made it impossible for her to conceal that she had conceived a child she covered up her guilt by pretending to be ill. When her time came, she wrapped the child in swaddling clothes and cast it at night into a pool by the river which flowed through that place. In this way she added crime to crime, for she not only followed fleshly sin by murder, but also combined murder with the poisoning of the water. When day dawned, another woman came to draw water and, seeing the corpse of the child, was struck with horror. Burning with womanly rage, she filled the whole village with her uncontrollable cries and reproached the holy nuns with these

TRANSLATED BY C. H. Talbot.

indignant words: "Oh, what a chaste community! How admirable is the life of nuns, who beneath their veils give birth to children and exercise at one and the same time the function of mothers and priests, baptising those to whom they have given birth. For, fellow-citizens, you have drawn off this water to make a pool, not merely for the purpose of grinding corn,[1] but unwittingly for a new and unheard-of kind of Baptism. Now go and ask those women, whom you compliment by calling them virgins, to remove this corpse from the river and make it fit for us to use again. Look for the one who is missing from the monastery and then you will find out who is responsible for this crime." At these words all the crowd was set in uproar and everybody, of whatever age or sex, ran in one great mass to see what had happened. As soon as they saw the corpse they denounced the crime and reviled the nuns. When the abbess heard the uproar and learned what was afoot she called the nuns together, told them the reason, and discovered that no one was absent except Agatha, who a few days before had been summoned to her parents' house on urgent business: but she had gone with full permission. A messenger was sent to her without delay to recall her to the monastery, as Leoba could not endure the accusation of so great a crime to hang over them. When Agatha returned and heard of the deed that was charged against her she fell on her knees and gazed up to heaven, crying: "Almighty God, who knowest all things before they come to pass, from whom nothing is hid and who hast delivered Susanna from false accusations when she trusted in Thee,[2] show Thy mercy to this community gathered together in Thy name and let it not be besmirched by filthy rumours on account of my sins; but do Thou deign to unmask and make known for the praise and glory of Thy name the person who has committed this misdeed."

On hearing this, the venerable superior, being assured of her innocence, ordered them all to go to the chapel and to stand with their arms extended in the form of a cross until each one of them had sung through the whole psalter, then three times each day, at Tierce, Sext and None,[3] to go round the monastic buildings in procession with the crucifix at their head, calling upon God to free them, in His mercy, from this accusation. When they had done this and they were going into the church at None, having completed two rounds, the blessed Leoba went straight to the altar and, standing before the cross, which was being prepared for the third procession, stretched out her hands towards heaven, and with tears and groans prayed, saying: "O Lord Jesus Christ, King of virgins, Lover of chastity, unconquerable God, manifest Thy power and deliver us from this charge, because the reproaches of those who reproached Thee have fallen upon us." Immediately after she had said this, that wretched little woman, the dupe and the tool of the devil, seemed to be surrounded by flames, and, calling out the name of the abbess, confessed to the crime she had committed. Then a great shout rose to heaven: the vast crowd was astounded at the miracle, the nuns began to weep with joy, and all of them with one voice gave expression to the merits of Leoba and of Christ our Saviour.

---

1. The citizens have dammed a stream to create a waterfall, which turns a water wheel, which turns a millstone, which grinds wheat (here "corn") into flour.
2. This story appears in a part of the Book of Daniel that, during the Reformation, was deleted from the Protestant canon.
3. Monks and nuns sang prayers and Scriptures at fixed hours each day, including Tierce (the third hour), Sext (the sixth), and None (the ninth), counting from about 6 A.M.

So it came about that the reputation of the nuns, which the devil had tried to ruin by his sinister rumour, was greatly enhanced, and praise was showered on them in every place. But the wretched woman did not deserve to escape scot-free and for the rest of her life she remained in the power of the devil. * * *

ANONYMOUS
early twelfth century

FROM THE RUSSIAN PRIMARY CHRONICLE

Sometime in the early twelfth century, possibly about 1113, an anonymous compiler at the Monastery of the Caves in Kiev created a history of Kievan Rus'—a medieval polity also known as the "land of the Rus"—from about the late ninth century to 1110. Kievan Rus' was centered on Kiev, in present-day Ukraine, but its territory included parts of present-day Belarus and western Russia. (For reasons connected with transliteration from the Cyrillic alphabet, the place name is written with a final apostrophe [Rus'], while the name of the people is written without one [Rus].) Traditionally, the chronicle has been attributed to a monk named Nestor. However, Nestor may have simply edited earlier works. Other versions followed but no longer exist. The earliest extant version, dating from 1377, was compiled by a monk named Laurentius. Although the Russian Empire and the modern state of Russia came centuries after this chronicle, the *Primary Chronicle* is most commonly known in English as the *Russian Primary Chronicle*. It is also named for its opening words, *Tale of Bygone Years*.

This compilation of writings is the principal source of the history of the eastern Slavs up to that point. It is also the oldest source of history concerning the conversion of the Rus under Prince Vladimir. Around 1000, according to this chronicle, emissaries of the prince rejected Islam, Roman Catholicism, and Judaism, but were impressed enough by the beauty of the Byzantine culture of Constantinople to bring Orthodox Christianity to the land of the Rus.

PRONOUNCING GLOSSARY

Gomorrah: *go-mor´-ruh*
Khazars: *kah´-zahrs*
Russes: *roos´-ehz*

Sodom: *so´-dom*
Tsargrad: *zahr´-grad*

FROM THE RUSSIAN PRIMARY CHRONICLE

For at this time the Russes were ignorant pagans. The devil rejoiced thereat, for he did not know that his ruin was approaching. He was so eager to destroy the Christian people, yet he was expelled by the true cross even from these very lands. The accursed one thought to himself, "This is my

TRANSLATED BY Samuel H. Cross. The translator's parenthetical Bible citations have been omitted.

habitation, a land where the apostles have not taught nor the prophets prophesied." He knew not that the Prophet had said, "I will call those my people who are not my people."[1] Likewise it is written of the Apostles, "Their message has gone out into all the earth and their words to the end of the world."[2] Though the Apostles have not been there in person, their teachings resound like trumpets in the churches throughout the world. Through their instruction we overcome the hostile adversary, and trample him under our feet. For likewise did the Holy Fathers trample upon him, and they have received the heavenly crown in company with the holy martyrs and the righteous.

* * *

* * * Vladimir was visited by Bulgarians of Mohammedan faith, who said, "Though you are a wise and prudent prince, you have no religion. Adopt our faith, and revere Mahomet." Vladimir inquired what was the nature of their religion. They replied that they believed in God, and that Mahomet instructed them to practice circumcision, to eat no pork, to drink no wine, and, after death, promised them complete fulfillment of their carnal desires. "Mahomet," they asserted, "will give each man seventy fair women. He may choose one fair one, and upon that woman will Mahomet confer the charms of them all, and she shall be his wife. Mahomet promises that one may then satisfy every desire, but whoever is poor in this world will be no different in the next." They also spoke other false things which out of modesty may not be written down. Vladimir listened to them, for he was fond of women and indulgence, regarding which he heard with pleasure. But circumcision and abstinence from pork and wine were disagreeable to him. "Drinking," said he, "is the joy of the Russes. We cannot exist without that pleasure."

Then came the Germans, asserting that they were come as emissaries of the Pope. They added, "Thus says the Pope: 'Your country is like our country, but your faith is not as ours. For our faith is the light. We worship God, who has made heaven and earth, the stars, the moon, and every creature, while your gods are only wood.'" Vladimir inquired what their teaching was. They replied, "Fasting according to one's strength. But whatever one eats or drinks is all to the glory of God, as our teacher Paul[3] has said." Then Vladimir answered, "Depart hence; our fathers accepted no such principle."

The Jewish Khazars[4] heard of these missions, and came themselves saying, "We have learned that Bulgarians and Christians came hither to instruct you in their faiths. The Christians believe in him whom we crucified, but we believe in the one God of Abraham, Isaac, and Jacob."[5] Then Vladimir inquired what their religion was. They replied that its tenets included circumcision, not eating pork or hare, and observing the Sabbath. The Prince then asked where their native land was, and they replied that it was in Jerusalem. When Vladimir inquired where that was, they made answer, "God was angry at our forefathers, and scattered us among the gentiles on account

---

1. Hosea 2:23. "The Prophet": Hosea.
2. Psalms 19:4.
3. The Apostle Paul.
4. A Turkish-speaking people who were converted to Judaism in the 7th century. Part of a

widespread seminomadic people, they settled in an area between modern-day western Russia and eastern Ukraine.
5. See the headnote for Genesis 1–2, 12:1–3, 22 (p. 83).

of our sins. Our land was then given to the Christians." The Prince then demanded, "How can you hope to teach others while you yourselves are cast out and scattered abroad by the hand of God? If God loved you and your faith, you would not be thus dispersed in foreign lands. Do you expect us to accept that fate also?"

Then the Greeks[6] sent to Vladimir a scholar, who spoke thus: "We have heard that the Bulgarians came and urged you to adopt their faith, which pollutes heaven and earth. They are accursed above all men, like Sodom and Gomorrah, upon which the Lord let fall burning stones, and which he buried and submerged.[7] The day of destruction likewise awaits these men, on which the Lord will come to judge the earth, and to destroy all those who do evil and abomination. * * *

Then the scholar said, "We have likewise heard how men came from Rome to convert you to the Roman faith. It differs but little from ours, for they commune with wafers, called oblates, which God did not give them, for he ordained that we should commune with bread. For when he had taken bread, the Lord gave it to his disciples, saying, 'This is my body broken for you.' Likewise he took the cup, and said, 'This is my blood of the New Testament.'[8] They do not so act, for they have modified the faith." Then Vladimir remarked that the Jews had come into his presence and had stated that the Germans and the Greeks believe in him whom they had crucified. To this the scholar replied, "Of a truth we believe in him. For some of the prophets foretold that God should be incarnate, and others that he should be crucified and buried, but arise on the third day and ascend into heaven. For the Jews killed the prophets, and still others they persecuted. When their prophecy was fulfilled, our Lord came down to earth, was crucified, arose again, and ascended into heaven. He awaited their repentance for forty-six years, but they did not repent, so that the Lord let loose the Romans upon them. Their cities were destroyed, and they were scattered among the gentiles, under whom they are now in servitude."

Vladimir then inquired why God should have descended to earth and should have endured such pain. The scholar then answered and said, "If you are desirous of hearing the story, I shall tell you from the beginning why God descended to earth." Vladimir replied, "Gladly would I hear it." Whereupon the scholar thus began his narrative:

* * *

"When they took him from the Cross, they laid him in a tomb, and the Jews sealed the tomb with a seal, and stationed guards there, saying, 'Perhaps his disciples will steal him away.' Then, upon the third day, he arose, and having arisen from the dead, he appeared to his disciples, saying to them, 'Go among all the nations, and teach all peoples baptism in the name of the Father and the Son and the Holy Ghost.' He remained with them forty days, appearing to them after the Resurrection. When the forty days had elapsed, he bade them go to the Mount of Olives, and there he appeared to them and blessed them, saying, 'Remain in the city of Jerusalem until I send the promise of my Father.' Having thus spoken, he ascended into heaven. They worshipped him, and returned to Jerusalem, where they

6. Greek Orthodox Christians from Constantinople.

7. See Genesis 19:1–25.
8. See Luke 22:19–20.

gathered together in the Temple. When fifty days were passed, the Holy Spirit descended upon the Apostles. After they had received the promise of the Holy Spirit, they separated throughout the world, teaching and baptizing with water."

Then Vladimir said, "Wherefore was he born of woman, and crucified on the tree, and baptized with water?" The scholar answered:

"Since the human race first sinned through woman, when the devil misled Adam through the agency of Eve so that he was deprived of Paradise, God for this reason avenged himself on the devil. Because of the first woman, victory fell to the devil's lot, for it was through woman that Adam fell from Paradise. But after being incarnate by a woman, God made the faithful enter into Paradise. God suffered pain upon the tree in order that the devil might be conquered by the tree, and that the righteous might taste of the tree of life." * * *

* * *

As he spoke thus, he exhibited to Vladimir a canvas on which was depicted the Judgment Day of the Lord, and showed him, on the right, the righteous going to their bliss in Paradise, and on the left, the sinners on their way to torment. Then Vladimir sighed and said, "Happy are they upon the right, but woe to those upon the left!" The scholar replied, "If you desire to take your place upon the right with the just, then accept baptism." Vladimir took this counsel to heart, saying "I shall wait yet a little longer," for he wished to inquire about all the faiths. Vladimir then gave the scholar many gifts, and dismissed him with great honor.

* * * Vladimir summoned together his vassals and the city-elders, and said to them, "Behold, the Bulgarians came before me urging me to accept their religion. Then came the Germans and praised their own faith; and after them came the Jews. Finally the Greeks appeared, criticizing all other faiths but commending their own, and they spoke at length, telling the history of the whole world from its beginning. Their words were artful, and it was wondrous to listen and pleasant to hear them. They preach the existence of another world. 'Whoever adopts our religion and then dies shall arise and live forever. But whosoever embraces another faith, shall be consumed with fire in the next world.' What is your opinion on this subject, and what do you answer?" The vassals and the elders replied, "You know, oh Prince, that no man condemns his own possessions, but praises them instead. If you desire to make certain, you have servants at your disposal. Send them to inquire about the ritual of each and how he worships God."

Their counsel pleased the prince and all the people, so that they chose good and wise men to the number of ten, and directed them to go first among the Bulgarians and inspect their faith. The emissaries went their way, and when they arrived at their destination they beheld the disgraceful actions of the Bulgarians and their worship in the mosque; then they returned to their own country. Vladimir then instructed them to go likewise among the Germans, and examine their faith, and finally to visit the Greeks. They thus went into Germany, and after viewing the German ceremonial, they proceeded to Tsargrad, where they appeared before the Emperor. He inquired on what mission they had come, and they reported to him all that had occurred. When the Emperor heard their words, he rejoiced, and did them great honor on that very day.

On the morrow, the Emperor sent a message to the Patriarch to inform him that a Russian delegation had arrived to examine the Greek faith, and directed him to prepare the church and the clergy, and to array himself in his sacerdotal robes, so that the Russes might behold the glory of the God of the Greeks. When the Patriarch received these commands, he bade the clergy assemble, and they performed the customary rites. They burned incense, and the choirs sang hymns. The Emperor accompanied the Russes to the church, and placed them in a wide space, calling their attention to the beauty of the edifice, the chanting, and the offices of the archpriest and the ministry of the deacons, while he explained to them the worship of his God. The Russes were astonished, and in their wonder praised the Greek ceremonial. * * *

Thus they returned to their own country, and the Prince called together his vassals and the elders. Vladimir then announced the return of the envoys who had been sent out, and suggested that their report be heard. He thus commanded them to speak out before his vassals. The envoys reported, "When we journeyed among the Bulgarians, we beheld how they worship in their temple, called a mosque, while they stand ungirt. The Bulgarian bows, sits down, looks hither and thither like one possessed, and there is no happiness among them, but instead only sorrow and a dreadful stench. Their religion is not good. Then we went among the Germans, and saw them performing many ceremonies in their temples; but we beheld no glory there. Then we went on to Greece, and the Greeks led us to the edifices where they worship their God, and we knew not whether we were in heaven or on earth. For on earth there is no such splendor or such beauty, and we are at a loss how to describe it. We only know that God dwells there among men, and their service is fairer than the ceremonies of other nations. For we cannot forget that beauty. Every man, after tasting something sweet, is afterward unwilling to accept that which is bitter, and therefore we cannot dwell longer here." Then the vassals spoke and said, "If the Greek faith were evil, it would not have been adopted by your grandmother Olga,[8] who was wiser than all other men." Vladimir then inquired whether they should all accept baptism, and they replied that the decision rested with him.

---

8. Or Helga (ca. 890–969), wife of Prince Igor (died 945); a convert to Orthodox Christianity who visited Constantinople in 957, she influenced the conversion of her grandson Vladimir.

MEDIEVAL MONASTICISM

By the eleventh century, the great monastic centers had developed from outposts for missionary purposes into stable institutions of learning and culture. Attached to these centers were schools for the education of young men who aspired to the monastic life or who would take up careers in civic or economic life. Instruction was based on the classical liberal arts curriculum but oriented toward the study of Scripture. The instructors also copied manuscripts; corrected mistakes in existing manuscripts; served in the monastic libraries, where manuscripts were stored; and wrote treatises.

During the Middle Ages, women generally did not receive much formal education unless they had aristocratic parents who arranged for home instruction. Monasteries for women provided the exception to this general neglect. Nuns were taught to read and write because they had to read Scripture during formal worship in church and to write and copy liturgical manuscripts. In addition, nuns learned the fine arts of calligraphy, manuscript illumination, and music along with practical arts, such as general medicine and agriculture. Indeed, the most emancipated women of the period were nuns, especially the abbesses, of large monasteries. Some abbesses headed monasteries for men and women, and they were frequently depicted as wearing the ring of a bishop and carrying a crosier, or pastoral staff.

Medieval monastic literature was generally about matters of concern to a monastic audience, such as collections of sermons, commentaries on Scripture and on earlier Christian writings, treatises on spiritual life, and chronicles of history. Ancillary to such topics were skills derived from the liberal arts, such as astronomy, arithmetic, and music. The audience for this literature consisted of monks, who could read or have books read to them, and educated laypeople. Nine out of ten people were functionally illiterate, so their main means of learning was listening. Ordinary people learned about biblical narratives from sermons or illustrations, such as murals. Indeed, stained glass windows in churches were known as "the Bible of the poor."

SAINT ANSELM OF CANTERBURY
1033–1109

FROM MEDITATIONS

The man known as Anselm has also been called Aosta (for his birthplace, a city in what are now the Italian Alps) and Bec (for his home monastery, in a village of what is now northern France). Born into a noble family, he was a Benedictine monk, a philosopher, and—from 1093 to 1109 except for periods of exile from England—the archbishop of Canterbury. He died in Canterbury, and in 1720 he was proclaimed a Doctor (from the Latin for "Teacher") of the Church. This title recognizes individuals as having been of major importance to the Church, particularly in contributing to theology or doctrine.

The following selection includes an abbreviated version of the explanation of the Incarnation that he offers in his book *Cur Deus Homo* ("Why God Became Man"). The Incarnation was the act by which God chose to be born and to die as the human being Jesus of Nazareth, Jesus the Messiah, Jesus Christ. Anselm considers why this act, this change, was necessary or even desirable.

FROM MEDITATIONS

Meditation on Human Redemption

Christian soul, brought to life again out of the heaviness of death, redeemed and set free from wretched servitude by the blood of God, rouse yourself and remember that you are risen, realize that you have been redeemed and set free. Consider again the strength of your salvation and where it is found. Meditate upon it, delight in the contemplation of it. Shake off your lethargy and set your mind to thinking over these things. Taste the goodness of your Redeemer, be on fire with love for your Saviour. Chew the honeycomb of his words, suck their flavour which is sweeter than sap, swallow their wholesome sweetness. Chew by thinking, suck by understanding, swallow by loving and rejoicing. Be glad to chew, be thankful to suck, rejoice to swallow.

What then is the strength and power of your salvation and where is it found? Christ has brought you back to life. He is the good Samaritan[1] who healed you. He is the good friend who redeemed you and set you free by laying down his life for you. Christ did all this. So the strength of your salvation is the strength of Christ.

Where is the strength of Christ? 'Horns are in his hands, there is his strength hid.'[2] Indeed horns are in his hands, because his hands were nailed to the arms of the cross. But what strength is there in such weakness, what height in such lowliness? What is there to be venerated in such abjection? Surely something is hidden by this weakness, something is concealed by this humility. There is something mysterious in this abjection. O hidden strength: a man hangs on a cross and lifts the load of eternal death from the human race; a man nailed to wood looses the bonds of everlasting death that hold fast the world. O hidden power: a man condemned with thieves saves men condemned with devils, a man stretched out on the gibbet draws all men to himself. O mysterious strength: one soul coming forth from torment draws countless souls with him out of hell, a man submits to the death of the body and destroys the death of souls.

Good Lord, living Redeemer, mighty Saviour, why did you conceal such power under such humility? Was it that you might deceive the devil, who by deceiving man had thrown him out of paradise?[3] But truth deceives no one. He who is ignorant or does not believe the truth, deceives himself, and

TRANSLATED BY Benedicta Ward.

1. See Luke 10:30–37.
2. Habakkuk 3:4.

3. See the headnote for Genesis 1–2, 12:1–3, 22 (p. 83).

whoever sees the truth and hates or despises it, deceives himself. But truth itself deceives no one. Or was it so that the devil might deceive himself? No, even as truth deceives no one, so it does not mean anyone to deceive himself, although when it permits this it might be said to do so. You did not assume human nature to conceal what was known of yourself, but to reveal what was not known. You declared yourself to be true God; by what you did you showed yourself to be true man. The thing was itself a mystery, not made mysterious. It was not done like this so that it might be hidden, but so that it might be accomplished in the way ordained. It was not secret to deceive anyone, but secret so that it might be carried out. If it is said to be mysterious, this is only to say that it was not revealed to everyone. The truth does not show itself to all, but it refuses itself to no one. So, Lord, you did not do this to deceive anyone, or so that anyone might deceive himself, but only so that you might carry out your work, in all things established in the truth. So let anyone who is deceived about your truth complain of his own falsehood, not of yours.

Or has the devil in justice anything against either God or man, that God had to act in this secret way for man, rather than openly by strength? Was it so that by unjustly killing a just man the devil should justly lose the power he had over the unjust? But clearly God owes nothing to the devil except punishment, nor does man owe him anything except to reverse the defeat which in some way he allowed himself to suffer by sinning; and this he does by preserving his integrity intact even through the hardness of death. But that also man owed to God alone, for he had not sinned against the devil but against God, and man was not of the devil, but both man and devil were of God. When the devil vexed man, he did it with the zeal of wickedness not of justice, and God did not order him to do it, but only permitted it; the justice of God not of the devil exacted this. So then there is nothing on the side of the devil to cause God to hide or dissemble his strength in saving mankind.

Was it then another kind of necessity that made the highest humble himself so, and the mighty one labour so much to do this work? But all necessities and impossibilities are subject to his will. What he wills, must be; what he wills not, cannot be. Therefore this was done by his will alone. And because his will is always good, he did this solely out of goodness.

God was not obliged to save mankind in this way, but human nature needed to make amends to God like this. God had no need to suffer so laboriously, but man needed to be reconciled thus. God did not need to humble himself, but man needed this, so that he might be raised from the depths of hell. The divine nature did not need nor was it able to be humiliated and to labour. It was for the sake of human nature that all these things needed to be done, so that it might be restored to that for which it was made. But neither human nature nor anything that was not God could suffice for this. For man cannot be restored to that state in which he was first established unless he is made like the angels in whom there is no sin. And that could not be done unless he received forgiveness for all his sins, and that could not be unless he first made entire satisfaction.

To make such satisfaction it was necessary that the sinner, or someone for him, should give to God of his own something that he does not owe him, and something more valuable than all that is not God. For to sin is to dishonour God, and this no man ought to do, even if it means that all that is other than God should perish. Immutable truth and plain reason then demand that whoever sins should give something better to God in return for the honour of which he has deprived him, that is more than the supposed good for the sake of which he dishonoured him.

Human nature alone could not do this, nor could it be reconciled without the satisfaction of the debt, nor could the justice of God pass over the disorder of sin in his kingdom. The goodness of God came to help, and the Son of God assumed manhood in his own person, so that God and man should be one and the same person. He had what was above all beings that are other than God, and he took on himself all the debt that sinners ought to pay, and this when he himself owed nothing, so that he could pay the debt for the others who owed it and could not pay.

More precious is the life of that man than all that is not God, and it is more than all the debt that sinners owe in order to make satisfaction for their sins. For his death was more than all that can be thought outside the person of God. It is clear that such a life is more good than all sins are bad. This man, who was not obliged to die for a debt, because he was not a sinner, gave his life of his own accord to the Father, when he allowed his life to be taken from him, for the sake of righteousness. This gave an example to others not to reject the righteousness of God because of death, which of necessity they would all at some time have to undergo, for he who was not obliged to suffer death and could have avoided it with justice, willed to give himself up to death and underwent it for the sake of righteousness. Thus in him human nature gave to God something it had of its own, willingly, and not because it was owed. So through him human nature might be redeemed in the other men who had not got that which would pay the debt that they owed.

In all this, divine nature was not humbled but human nature was exalted. God was not made any less, but mankind was mercifully helped. In that man, human nature did not suffer anything as of necessity, but solely of free will. He did not submit to violence, but freely embraced it out of goodness, to the honour of God and the benefit of other men. For praise and mercy he bore what evil brought upon him, and he was not coerced by obedience, but he ordained it to be so by the power of his wisdom.

For the Father did not order that man to die and compel him to do so, but what Christ understood would please the Father and benefit man, that he did of his own free will. In this matter the Father could not force him, for it was something that he had no right to exact from him. Such honour could not but please the Father, when the Son freely offered it with such good will. So the Son freely obeyed the Father, when he willed freely to do what he knew would please him. But since the Father gave him that good will (which nevertheless was free), it is not undeservedly said that he received it as a command of the Father. In this way he was made 'obedient to the Father,' 'even unto death,' and 'as the Father gave him commandment, even so he did,' and 'the cup that the Father gave him, he drank.'[4] This is the perfect and free obedience of human nature, in that Christ freely submitted his

4. See Matthew 26:42.

own free will to God, and perfectly used in liberty the good will he had
received, without any compulsion.

So that man redeemed all others in that what he freely gave to God paid
for the debtors what they owed. By this price man was not only redeemed
from blame but whenever he returns with genuine penitence he is received,
though that penitence is not promised to sinners. Because of that which was
done on the cross, by the cross our Christ has redeemed us. Then whosoever wills to come to this grace with the love it deserves, will be saved. And
those who despise it are justly damned, because they do not pay the debt
they owe.

See, Christian soul, here is the strength of your salvation, here is the cause
of your freedom, here is the price of your redemption. You were a bond-slave
and by this man you are free. By him you are brought back from exile, lost,
you are restored, dead, you are raised. Chew this, bite it, suck it, let your
heart swallow it, when your mouth receives the body and blood of your
Redeemer. Make it in this life your daily bread, your food, your way-bread,
for through this and not otherwise than through this, will you remain in
Christ and Christ in you, and your joy will be full.

But, Lord, you gave yourself up to death that I might live; how can I be
happy about a freedom which is not wrought without your chains? How can
I rejoice in my salvation, which would not be without your sorrows? How
can I enjoy a life which meant your death? Shall I rejoice with those who by
their cruelty made you suffer? For unless they had done it you would not
have suffered, and if you had not suffered these good things would not have
been mine. But if I grieve because of their cruelty, how can I also rejoice in
the benefits that I only possess because of your sufferings? Their wickedness
could have done nothing unless you freely permitted it, nor did you suffer
except because in love you willed it. Thus I must condemn their cruelty,
imitate your death and sufferings, and share them with you, giving thanks
for the goodness of your love. And thus may I safely rejoice in the good that
thereby comes to me.

Now, little man, leave their cruelties to the justice of God, and think of
what you owe your Saviour. Consider what he was to you, what he did for you,
and think that for what he did for you he is the more worthy to be loved. Look
into your need and his goodness, and see what thanks you should render
him, and how much love you owe him. You were in darkness, on uncertain
ground, descending into the chaos of hell that is beyond redemption. A
huge leaden weight hung round your neck, dragging you downwards, an
unbearable burden pressed upon you, invisible enemies were striking at you
with all their might. You were without any help and you did not know it, for
you were conceived and born in that state. What was happening to you, to
what place were you rushing away? Remember and tremble; think and be
afraid.

Good Lord Jesus Christ, thus was I placed, neither asking nor conjectur-
ing, when as the sun you gave me light, and showed me what a state I was
in. You threw away the leaden weight which was dragging me down, you
took off the burden that pressed upon me, you drove off those who were
attacking me, and opposed them on my behalf. You called me by a new
name, which you gave me from your name. And I who was bent down, you
made upright in your sight, saying, 'Be of good cheer. I have redeemed you.
I have given my life for you. You shall leave the evil you were in, and not fall

into the pit to which you were going, if you cleave to me. I will lead you into my kingdom and make you an heir of God and co-heir with me.'[5] From then on you accepted me into your care so that nothing could harm my soul against my will. And lo, even before I cleaved to you as you counselled, you did not let me fall into hell, but looked forward to when I should cleave to you; even then you were keeping your promises.

Lord, it was so with me, and this is what you have done for me. I was in darkness, knowing nothing of myself, in a slippery place, for I was weak and prone to fall into sin, I was descending into the chaos of hell, for in my first parents I had fallen from righteousness into wickedness, which is the way to hell, and from blessedness to temporal misery for ever. The weight of original sin dragged me downwards, and the unbearable burden of the judgement of God pressed upon me; my demon enemies thrust vehemently against me to make me do other damnable sins.

When I was destitute of all help, you illuminated me, and showed me what I was, for when I was still unable to see this, you taught others the truth on my behalf and you showed it to me before I asked it. The load that dragged at me, the burden that weighed me down, the enemies that opposed me—you cast them all back when you removed the sin in which I was conceived and born and its condemnation. You forbade evil spirits to attack my soul. You made me a Christian, called by your own name, by which I confessed you, and you acknowledged me to be among your redeemed. You have set me upright and raised me to the knowledge and love of yourself. You have made me sure of the salvation of my soul, for you have given your life for it, and you have promised me your glory if I follow you. And when I was not following you, but was still committing many sins which you had forbidden, you waited for me to follow you till you could give me what you promised.

Consider, O my soul, and hear, all that is within me, how much my whole being owes to him! Lord, because you have made me, I owe you the whole of my love; because you have redeemed me, I owe you the whole of myself; because you have promised so much, I owe you all my being. Moreover, I owe you as much more love than myself as you are greater than I, for whom you gave yourself and to whom you promised yourself. I pray you, Lord, make me taste by love what I taste by knowledge; let me know by love what I know by understanding. I owe you more than my whole self, but I have no more, and by myself I cannot render the whole of it to you. Draw me to you, Lord, in the fullness of love. I am wholly yours by creation; make me all yours, too, in love.

Lord, my heart is before you. I try, but by myself I can do nothing; do what I cannot. Admit me into the inner room of your love. I ask, I seek, I knock. You who made me seek, make me receive; you who gave the seeking, give the finding; you who taught the knocking, open to my knock.[6] To whom will you give, if you refuse my petition? Who finds, if this seeking is in vain? To whom is it opened, if to this knocking it is closed? What do you give to those who do not pray if you deny your love to those who do? By you I have desire; by you let me have fulfilment. Cleave to him, my soul, and never leave off. Good Lord, do not reject me; I faint with hunger for your love;

refresh me with it. Let me be filled with your love, rich in your affection, completely held in your care. Take me and possess me wholly, who with the Father and the Holy Spirit are alone blessed to ages of ages. Amen.

SAINT HILDEGARD OF BINGEN
1098–1179

FROM SCIVIAS

Hildegard belonged to a noble family of the Rhineland, in southwest Germany. Sometime before she reached adulthood, Hildegard's parents placed her in a convent, where in 1136 the nuns elected her their *magistra* ("mistress"). She founded two monasteries, went on preaching tours, and corresponded regularly with everyone from local bishops to the pope. Hildegard is venerated as a saint by the Lutheran Church, the Anglican Communion, and the Roman Catholic Church, which also honors her as a Doctor (from the Latin for "Teacher") of the Church.

A polymath, Hildegard wrote texts on natural history, medicine, and obstetrics; theological treatises; autobiographical accounts of her visionary experiences; plays; and poetry. Her music has received particular attention, from recording artists as well as historians and musicologists.

PRONOUNCING GLOSSARY

Bingen: *bing'-en*   Scivias: *shee-vee'-ahss*

FROM SCIVIAS

VISION TWELVE

The New Heaven and the New Earth

After this I looked, and behold, all the elements and creatures were shaken by dire convulsions; fire and air and water burst forth, and the earth was made to move, lightning and thunder crashed and mountains and forests fell, and all that was mortal expired. And all the elements were purified, and whatever had been foul in them vanished and was no more seen. And I heard a voice resounding in a great cry throughout the world, saying, "O ye children of men who are lying in the earth, rise up one and all!"

And behold, all the human bones in whatever place in the earth they lay were brought together in one moment and covered with their flesh; and they all rose up with limbs and bodies intact, each in his or her gender, with the good glowing brightly and the bad manifest in blackness so that each one's deeds were openly seen. And some of them had been sealed with the

---

TRANSLATED BY Mother Columbia Hart and Jane Bishop. Parts of the translation set in italics have been made roman.

sign of faith, but some had not; and some of those signed had a gold radiance about their faces, but others a shadow, which was their sign.

And suddenly from the East a great brilliance shone forth; and there, in a cloud, I saw the Son of Man, with the same appearance He had had in the world and with His wounds still open, coming with the angelic choirs. He sat upon a throne of flame, glowing but not burning, which floated on the great tempest which was purifying the world. And those who had been signed were taken up into the air to join Him as if by a whirlwind, to where I had previously seen that radiance which signifies the secrets of the Supernal Creator; and thus the good were separated from the bad. And, as the Gospel indicates, He blessed the just in a gentle voice and pointed them to the heavenly kingdom, and with a terrible voice condemned the unjust to the pains of Hell, as is written in the same place.[1] Yet He made no inquiry or statement about their works except the words the Gospel declares would be made there; for each person's work, whether good or bad, showed clearly in him. But those who were not signed stood afar off in the northern region, with the Devil's band; and they did not come to this judgment, but saw all these things in the whirlwind, and awaited the end of the judgment while uttering bitter groans.

And when the judgment was ended, the lightnings and thunders and winds and tempests ceased, and the fleeting components of the elements vanished all at once, and there came an exceedingly great calm. And then the elect became more splendid than the splendor of the sun; and with great joy they made their way toward Heaven with the Son of God and the blessed armies of the angels. And at the same time the reprobate were forced with great howling toward the infernal regions with the Devil and his angels; and so Heaven received the elect, and Hell swallowed up the reprobate. And at once such great joy and praise arose in Heaven, and such great misery and howling in Hell, as were beyond human power to utter. And all the elements shone calm and resplendent, as if a black skin had been taken from them; so that fire no longer had its raging heat, or air density, or water turbulence, or earth shakiness. And the sun, moon and stars sparkled in the firmament like great ornaments, remaining fixed and not moving in orbit, so that they no longer distinguished day from night. And so there was no night, but day. And it was finished.

And again I heard the voice from Heaven, saying to me:

1. IN THE LAST DAYS THE WORLD WILL BE DISSOLVED IN DISASTERS LIKE A DYING MAN

These mysteries manifest the last days, in which time will be transmuted into the eternity of perpetual light. For the last days will be troubled by many dangers, and the end of the world will be prefigured by many signs. For, as you see, on that last day the whole world will be agitated by terrors and shaken by tempests, so that whatever is fleeting and mortal in it will be ended. For the course of the world is now complete, and it cannot last longer, but will be consummated as God wills. For as a person who is to die is captured and laid low by many infirmities, and in the hour of his death suffers great pain in his dissolution, so too the greatest adversities will precede the

1. See Matthew 25:31–46.

end of the world and at last dissolve it in terror. For the elements will then display their terrors, because they will not be able to do so afterward.

2. ALL CREATION WILL BE MOVED AND PURIFIED OF ALL THAT IS MORTAL IN IT

And so, at this consummation, the elements are unloosed by a sudden and unexpected movement: all creatures are set into violent motion, fire bursts out, the air dissolves, water runs off, the earth is shaken, lightnings burn, thunders crash, mountains are broken, forests fall, and whatever in air or water or earth is mortal gives up its life. For the fire displaces all the air, and the water engulfs all the earth; and thus all things are purified, and whatever was foul in the world vanishes as if it had never been, as salt disappears when it is put into water.

3. THE BODIES OF THE DEAD WILL RISE AGAIN IN THEIR WHOLENESS AND GENDER

And when, as you saw, the divine command to rise again resounds, the bones of the dead, wherever they may be, are brought together in one moment and covered with their flesh. They will not be hindered by anything; but if they were consumed by fire or water, or eaten by birds or beasts, they will be speedily restored. And so the earth will yield them up as salt is extracted from water; for My eye knows all things, and nothing can be hidden from Me. And so all people will rise again in the twinkling of an eye,[2] in soul and body, with no deformity or mutilation but intact in body and in gender; and the elect will shine with the brightness of their good works, but the reprobate will bear the blackness of their deeds of misery. Thus their works will not there be concealed, but will appear in them openly.

4. THE RISEN WHO ARE SIGNED AND UNSIGNED

And some of them are sealed with the sign of faith, but some are not; and the consciences of some who have faith shine with the radiance of wisdom, but the consciences of others are murky from their neglect. And thus they are clearly distinguished; for the former have done the works of faith, but the latter have extinguished it in themselves. And those who do not have the sign of faith are those who chose not to know the living and true God either in the old Law or in the new Grace.

5. THE SON WILL COME TO THE JUDGMENT IN HUMAN FORM

And then the Son of God, in the human form He had at His Passion when He suffered by the will of the Father to save the human race, will come to judge it, surrounded by the celestial army; He will be in the brightness of eternal life, but in the cloud that hides celestial glory from the reprobate. For the Father vouchsafed to Him the judging of the visible things of the world, because He had lived visibly in the world; as He Himself shows in the Gospel, saying:

---

2. See 1 Corinthians 15:52.

6. THE GOSPEL ON THIS SUBJECT

"And He has given Him power to judge, because He is the Son of Man."[3] Which is to say:

The Father has borne witness to His Son. What does this mean? The Father gave power to the Son, because He remained with the Father in divinity but received humanity from a mother; and, because He is human, He received also from the Father that every creature should feel Him as the Son of God, for all creatures were created and formed by God. And therefore all deeds will be judged by the Son, whatever their nobility or baseness, and He will put them in their proper order. For, as He was a man palpable and visible in the world, He can justly distinguish all that is visible in the world. And He will appear in His power of judging terrible to the unjust but gentle to the just, and judge them so that the very elements will feel the purgation.

7. THE SIGNED WILL BE TAKEN UP EASILY TO MEET THEIR JUDGE

And those who are signed are taken up to meet the Just Judge not with difficulty but with great speed, so that in them, who had faith in God, the works of faith may clearly be seen. And, as was shown you, the good are separated from the bad, for their works are dissimilar. For here it is apparent how both the bad and the good have sought God, in infancy and childhood and youth and old age.

8. ALL GOD'S FLOWERS, THE GREAT HEROES OF THE CHURCH, WILL APPEAR RADIANT

And here all the flowers of My Son will shine out in radiance; that is to say, the patriarchs and prophets who lived before His Incarnation, the apostles who lived with Him in the world, the martyrs, confessors, virgins and widows who have faithfully imitated Him, the holders of high office, both secular and spiritual, in My Church, and the anchorites and monks who chastised and mortified their flesh and imitated the humility and charity of the angels in their garments, thus belittling themselves for My Son's name. Those who seek Me in the contemplative life because they think that life is more glorious than another are as nothing to Me; but any who seek Me in humility in that life because the Holy Spirit inspired them to do so, I will put in the first ranks in the celestial homeland.

9. AMID THE SILENCE OF HEAVEN, THE SON WILL GIVE SENTENCE ON ALL

Then the heavens will subdue their praises and remain awhile in silence, while the Son of God pronounces judicial sentence both on the just and on the unjust. And they will give ear with reverence and honor to how He decides; and He will gently grant supernal joys to the just, and terribly consign the unjust to the pains of Hell. And there will be no further excuses or questions about human works, for here the consciences of both the good and the bad are naked and revealed.

---

3. John 5:27.

10. WHY THE GOOD AND THE BAD NEED TO BE JUDGED

Now the just, who will receive the words of the most equitable Judge, have indeed done many good works, but while they lived in the world they did not act with fullness of perfection, and therefore their deeds must now be judged. And the unjust, who will suffer a severe judgment against them, have indeed done much evil; but they did not act in ignorance of the Divine Majesty, in the wicked unbelief that would damn them without judgment. And so they will not escape the Judge's sentence, for all things must be weighed equitably.

11. UNBELIEVERS ARE ALREADY JUDGED AND SO WILL NOT COME TO THE JUDGMENT

But those who are not signed in faith, because they did not believe in God, will tarry in the North, the region of perdition, with the Devil's band, and not come to this judgment. But they will see it all in obscurity and await its end, groaning deeply within themselves because they persevered in unbelief and did not know the true God. For they neither worshipped the living God in the Old Testament before the institution of baptism, nor received the remedy of baptism in the Gospel, but continued under the curse of Adam's fall,[4] with its penalty of damnation. And therefore they are already judged, for the crime of infidelity.

12. WHEN THE JUDGMENT IS FINISHED, A GREAT CALM WILL ARISE

And when the judgment is ended, the terrors of the elements, the lightnings and thunders and winds and tempests, will cease, and all that is fleeting and transitory will melt away and no longer be, like snow melted by the heat of the sun. And so, by God's dispensation, an exceedingly great calm will arise.

13. GLORY WILL RECEIVE THE ELECT AND HELL SWALLOW UP THE DAMNED

And thus the elect will become splendid with the splendor of eternity, and with My Son their Head and the glorious celestial army will embrace glory and the heavenly joys; while the reprobate, together with the Devil and his angels, will wretchedly direct their course toward eternal punishment, where eternal death awaits them for following their lusts instead of My commands. And so Heaven will receive the elect into the glory of eternity, because they have loved the Ruler of the heavens; and Hell will swallow up the reprobate, because they did not renounce the Devil. And then such great joy and praise will resound in the glory of Heaven and such great groaning and howling will arise in Hell as to exceed the grasp of the human understanding. For the first have eternal life and the second eternal death, as My Son declares in the Gospel, saying:

---

4. Adam and Eve's, and thus humanity's, fall from divine grace; see the headnote for Genesis 1–2, 12:1–3, 22 (p. 83).

14. THE GOSPEL ON THIS SUBJECT

"And these shall go into everlasting punishment; but the just into life everlasting."[5] Which is to say: Those who befoul themselves in the house of evil passions, and do not thirst to drink justice from the Supreme Goodness, will come in the course of their infidelity and wickedness to submersion in the pains of eternal perdition, and according to their deeds will receive the torments of Hell. But the builders of the heavenly Jerusalem, who faithfully stand in the gates of the daughter of Zion,[6] will be radiant in the eternal life, which the fruitfulness of the chaste Virgin miraculously gave to all believers.

15. HOW THE ELEMENTS AND HEAVENLY BODIES WILL BE CHANGED, AND NIGHT ENDED

And, as you see, when all these things are over the elements will shine out with the greatest brightness and beauty, and all blackness and filth will be removed from them. And fire, without its raging heat, will blaze like the dawn; air without density will be completely limpid; water without its power to flood or drown will stand transparent and calm, and earth without shakiness or roughness will be firm and level. And so all these will be transformed into great calm and beauty.

And the sun and moon and stars will sparkle in the firmament like precious stones set in gold, with great glory and brilliance; and they will no longer restlessly revolve in orbit so as to distinguish day from night. For the world will have ended and they will have become immutable; and from that time on there will be no darkness, and day will be perpetual. As My beloved John witnesses, when he says:

16. WORDS OF JOHN

"And there shall be no more night, and they will not need the light of the lamp or the light of the sun; for the Lord God will illumine them."[7] Which is to say: One who possesses a treasure sometimes hides it and at other times shows it, and even so night conceals the light, and day drives out the darkness and brings light to humanity. But it will not be so when time is transformed; for then the shade of night will be put to flight and its darkness will not appear from that time on. For in this transmutation the light people now light to dispel the darkness will not be needed; and the sun will not move and by its motion bring times of darkness. For then the day will be without end; for the Ruler of all, in the immutable glory of His Divinity, will illumine those who in the world have by His grace escaped the darkness.

But let the one who has ears sharp to hear inner meanings ardently love My reflection and pant after My words, and inscribe them in his soul and conscience.

5. Matthew 25:46.
6. See Psalms 9:14.

7. Revelation 22:5.

SAINT BERNARD OF CLAIRVAUX
1090–1153

FROM SERMONS ON THE SONG OF SONGS

The Song of Songs is also known as the Song of Solomon, the Canticle of Canticles, and simply Canticles. A 117-verse Book of the Old Testament, it is one of the shortest but also one of most frequently analyzed texts in the Bible. Commentaries on it exist from as far back as the third century.

Though attributed to Solomon (968–928 B.C.E.), king of Israel, the Song of Songs was composed six or so centuries later by an unknown author. It is a mysterious collection of love poems that have no explicitly religious content. In these poems, a man and a woman (identified in one verse as "the Shulamite") progress from courtship to consummation. The Song of Songs also includes a chorus, the "daughters of Jerusalem." The romantic content of these poems has often been interpreted as symbolizing either the relationship between God and Israel or the relationship between Christ and the Church.

In the following sermon on the Song of Songs—one of the eighty he wrote—Saint Bernard of Clairvaux presents this text as an allegory of the relationship between Christ and the human soul, with Christ playing the role of the male lover and Bernard (or any other believer) playing the female beloved. Bernard correlates this Book of Scripture with what he calls "the book of our own experience." He intended such sermons, conspicuous for their affective piety, to help monks deepen their contemplative life.

Bernard lived in northeastern France. A famous monastic reformer, he founded Clairvaux Abbey, a Cistercian monastery. He is venerated as a saint by the Anglican Communion, the Lutheran Church, and the Roman Catholic Church, which also honors him as a Doctor (from the Latin for "Teacher") of the Church.

PRONOUNCING GLOSSARY

Clairvaux: *clehr-voh´*

FROM SERMONS ON THE SONG OF SONGS

SERMON 3

The Kiss of the Lord's Feet, Hands and Mouth

1. Today the text we are to study is the book of our own experience. You must therefore turn your attention inwards, each one must take note of his own particular awareness of the things I am about to discuss. I am attempting to discover if any of you has been privileged to say from his heart: "Let him kiss me with the kiss of his mouth."[1] Those to whom it is given to utter these words sincerely are comparatively few, but any one who has received this mystical

---

TRANSLATED BY Kilian Walsh.

1. Song of Songs 1:2.

kiss from the mouth of Christ at least once, seeks again that intimate experience, and eagerly looks for its frequent renewal. I think that nobody can grasp what it is except the one who receives it. For it is "a hidden manna,"[2] and only he who eats it still hungers for more.[3] It is "a sealed fountain"[4] to which no stranger has access; only he who drinks still thirsts for more.[5] Listen to one who has had the experience, how urgently he demands: "Be my savior again, renew my joy."[6] But a soul like mine, burdened with sins, still subject to carnal passions,[7] devoid of any knowledge of spiritual delights, may not presume to make such a request, almost totally unacquainted as it is with the joys of the supernatural life.

2. I should like however to point out to persons like this that there is an appropriate place for them on the way of salvation. They may not rashly aspire to the lips of a most benign Bridegroom, but let them prostrate with me in fear at the feet of a most severe Lord. Like the publican full of misgiving,[8] they must turn their eyes to the earth rather than up to heaven. Eyes that are accustomed only to darkness will be dazzled by the brightness of the spiritual world,[9] overpowered by its splendor, repulsed by its peerless radiance and whelmed again in a gloom more dense than before. All you who are conscious of sin, do not regard as unworthy and despicable that position where the holy sinner laid down her sins, and put on the garment of holiness. There the Ethiopian changed her skin,[1] and, cleansed to a new brightness, could confidently and legitimately respond to those who insulted her:[2] "I am black but lovely, daughters of Jerusalem."[3] You may ask what skill enabled her to accomplish this change, or on what grounds did she merit it? I can tell you in a few words. She wept bitterly,[4] she sighed deeply from her heart, she sobbed with a repentance that shook her very being, till the evil that inflamed her passions was cleansed away. The heavenly physician came with speed to her aid, because "his word runs swiftly."[5] Perhaps you think the Word of God is not a medicine? Surely it is, a medicine strong and pungent, testing the mind and the heart.[6] "The Word of God is something alive and active. It cuts like any double-edged sword but more finely. It can slip through the place where the soul is divided from the spirit, or the joints from the marrow: it can judge the secret thoughts."[7] It is up to you, wretched sinner, to humble yourself as this happy penitent did so that you may be rid of your wretchedness.[8] Prostrate yourself on the ground, take hold of his feet, soothe them with kisses, sprinkle them with your tears and so wash not them but yourself. Thus you will become one of the "flock of shorn ewes as they come up from the washing."[9] But even then you may not dare to lift up a face suffused with shame and grief, until you hear the sentence: "Your sins are forgiven,"[1] to be followed by the summons: "Awake, awake, captive daughter of Sion, awake, shake off the dust."[2]

2. Revelation 2:17.
3. See Sirach 24:29.
4. Song of Songs 4:12.
5. See Sirach 24:29.
6. See Psalms 51:14.
7. See 2 Timothy 3:6.
8. See Luke 18:9–14.
9. See Proverbs 4:18–19.
1. See Jeremiah 13:23.
2. See Psalms 119:42.

3. Song of Songs 1:5.
4. See Luke 22:62.
5. Psalms 147:15.
6. See Psalms 7:10.
7. Hebrews 4:12.
8. See Luke 7:37–50.
9. Song of Songs 4:2.
1. Luke 7:48.
2. Isaiah 52:1–2.

II

3. Though you have made a beginning by kissing the feet, you may not presume to rise at once by impulse to the kiss of the mouth; there is a step to be surmounted in between, an intervening kiss on the hand for which I offer the following explanation. If Jesus says to me: "Your sins are forgiven," what will it profit me if I do not cease from sinning? I have taken off my tunic, am I to put it on again?[3] And if I do, what have I gained? If I soil my feet again after washing them, is the washing of any benefit? Long did I lie in the slough of the marsh,[4] filthy with all kinds of vices; if I return to it again I shall be worse than when I first wallowed in it. On top of that I recall that he who healed me said to me as he exercised his mercy: "Now you are well again, be sure not to sin any more, or something worse may happen to you."[5] He, however, who gave me the grace to repent, must also give me the power to persevere, lest by repeating my sins I should end up by being worse than I was before.[6] Woe to me then, repentant though I be, if he without whom I can do nothing[7] should suddenly withdraw his supporting hand. I really mean nothing; of myself I can achieve neither repentance nor perseverance, and for that reason I pay heed to the Wise Man's advice: "Do not repeat yourself at your prayers."[8] The Judge's threat to the tree that did not yield good fruit is another thing that makes me fearful.[9] For these various reasons I must confess that I am not entirely satisfied with the first grace by which I am enabled to repent of my sins; I must have the second as well, and so bear fruits that befit repentance,[1] that I may not return like the dog to its vomit.[2]

4. I am now able to see what I must seek for and receive before I may hope to attain to a higher and holier state.[3] I do not wish to be suddenly on the heights, my desire is to advance by degrees. The impudence of the sinner displeases God as much as the modesty of the penitent gives him pleasure. You will please him more readily if you live within the limits proper to you, and do not set your sights at things beyond you.[4] It is a long and formidable leap from the foot to the mouth, a manner of approach that is not commendable. Consider for a moment: still tarnished as you are with the dust of sin, would you dare touch those sacred lips? Yesterday you were lifted from the mud, today you wish to encounter the glory of his face? No, his hand must be your guide to that end. First it must cleanse your stains, then it must raise you up. How raise you? By giving you the grace to dare to aspire. You wonder what this may be. I see it as the grace of the beauty of temperance and the fruits that befit repentance,[5] the works of the religious man. These are the instruments that will lift you from the dunghill[6] and cause your hopes to soar. On receiving such a grace then, you must kiss his hand, that is, you must give glory to his name, not to yourself.[7] First of all you must glorify him because he has forgiven your sins, secondly because

---

3. See Song of Songs 5:3.
4. See Psalms 40:3.
5. John 5:14.
6. See Luke 11:26.
7. See John 15:5.
8. Sirach 7:15. "The Wise Man": the author of the Book of Sirach, Jesus the son of Sirach of Jerusalem, who flourished about two hundred years before Jesus Christ.

9. See Matthew 3:7–10.
1. See Luke 3:8.
2. See Proverbs 26:11.
3. See Matthew 7:8.
4. See Sirach 3:22.
5. See Luke 3:8.
6. See Psalms 113:7.
7. See Psalms 114:9.

he has adorned you with virtues. Otherwise you will need a bold front to face reproaches such as these: "What do you have that was not given to you? And if it was given, how can you boast as though it were not?"[8]

III

5. Once you have had this twofold experience of God's benevolence in these two kisses, you need no longer feel abashed in aspiring to a holier intimacy. Growth in grace brings expansion of confidence. You will love with greater ardor, and knock on the door with greater assurance, in order to gain what you perceive to be still wanting to you. "The one who knocks will always have the door opened to him."[9] It is my belief that to a person so disposed, God will not refuse that most intimate kiss of all, a mystery of supreme generosity and ineffable sweetness. You have seen the way that we must follow, the order of procedure: first, we cast ourselves at his feet, we weep before the Lord who made us,[1] deploring the evil we have done. Then we reach out for the hand that will lift us up, that will steady our trembling knees.[2] And finally, when we shall have obtained these favors through many prayers and tears, we humbly dare to raise our eyes to his mouth, so divinely beautiful, not merely to gaze upon it, but— I say it with fear and trembling—to receive its kiss. "Christ the Lord is a Spirit before our face,"[3] and he who is joined to him in a holy kiss[4] becomes through his good pleasure, one spirit with him.[5]

6. To you, Lord Jesus, how truly my heart has said: "My face looks to you. Lord, I do seek your face."[6] In the dawn you brought me proof of your love,[7] in my first approach to kiss your revered feet you forgave my evil ways as I lay in the dust. With the advancement of the day you gave your servant reason to rejoice[8] when, in the kiss of the hand, you imparted the grace to live rightly. And now what remains, O good Jesus, except that suffused as I am with the fullness of your light, and while my spirit is fervent, you would graciously bestow on me the kiss of your mouth, and give me unbounded joy in your presence.[9] Serenely lovable above all others, tell me where will you lead your flock to graze, where will you rest it at noon?[1] Dear brothers, surely it is wonderful for us to be here,[2] but the burden of the day calls us elsewhere. These guests, whose arrival has just now been announced to us, compel me to break off rather than to conclude a talk that I enjoy so much. So I go to meet the guests, to make sure that the duty of charity, of which we have been speaking, may not suffer neglect, that we may not hear it said of us: "They do not practice what they preach."[3] Do you pray in the meantime that God may accept the homage of my lips[4] for your spiritual welfare, and for the praise and glory of his name.[5]

8. 1 Corinthians 4:7.
9. Luke 11:10.
1. See Psalms 95:6.
2. See Isaiah 35:3.
3. Bernard is quoting from the Vulgate (Latin Bible), Lamentions 4:20.
4. See 1 Corinthians 16:20.
5. See 1 Corinthians 6:17.
6. Psalms 27:8.

7. See Psalms 143:8.
8. See Psalms 86:4.
9. See Psalms 16:11.
1. See Song of Songs 1:6.
2. See Luke 9:33.
3. Matthew 23:3.
4. See Psalms 119:108.
5. See 1 Peter 1:7.

THE MENDICANT TRADITION

During the eleventh and twelfth centuries, various attempts were made to renew Christianity in the West. Monasticism gained vigor through movements such as the one in Cluny, France. Pope Gregory VII (pope from 1073 until his death, in 1085) determinedly led reform efforts. New and old religious orders underwent structural and liturgical experiments in an effort to answer this question: What is the best way to live the Gospel? Some saw the monastic life of prayer as the optimal mode. Others favored preaching as a way to imitate the lives of the Apostles. Still others thought poverty best constituted the evangelical life. As the parochial clergy sought to raise the level of Christian practice in their communities, laypeople—critical of the laxity within the Church orders—followed movements aimed at bringing their own lives closer to the Gospel.

For centuries, monastic institutions typically had been established in rural agricultural areas, and monks were expected to lead stable, withdrawn lives. Beginning in the twelfth century, there was much more mobility in European culture generally, especially with the growth of cities. But even as urbanization led to a burst of cathedral-building, and as the schools associated with the cathedrals gained importance, a new type of religious life emerged: the so-called mendicant orders.

The word *mendicant* means beggar. While historically monks had lived off the revenues from their holdings, which they shared as a community, the mendicants gained their sustenance by begging for alms. In living on only what was given to them, their goal was not to avoid work but to forgo the sometimes scandalously comfortable livelihoods enjoyed by the monks and the parish clergy. In addition, they moved—as individuals and in groups—from town to town, city to city, as they preached to the people. Mendicants shared some characteristics with monks— such as the vows of poverty, of chastity, and of obedience (the so-called evangelical counsels)—but they were more urban, more mobile, and more focused on preaching. The four major mendicant orders that emerged in this period were the Augustinians, the Carmelites, the Dominicans, and the Franciscans. The Dominicans and the Franciscans were far more numerous and more important than the Augustinians and the Carmelites.

The Dominicans were founded by the Spanish-born cleric Dominic of Osma (1170–1221), also known as Dominic de Guzmán, Domingo Félix de Guzmán, and Saint Dominic. Their official name was the Friars Preachers (*friar* meaning "brother"), but they are popularly called the Dominicans or the Order of Preachers. They adopted their Rule of life from the ancient Rule of Saint Augustine of Hippo (see p. 226), but they especially emphasized learning for the sake of preaching and teaching. In the thirteenth century, they produced some of the most famous scholars in Europe, such as the German philosopher and theologian Albertus Magnus (also known as Saint Albert the Great; ca. 1200–1280) and his student Saint Thomas Aquinas (see p. 317). By the end of the thirteenth century, most major cities in western Europe had a Dominican church, with long naves designed to accommodate large crowds to hear preaching.

The Franciscans were founded by the Italian cleric Francis of Assisi (see p. 311). After adopting a simple life of poverty and prayer around 1209, Francis attracted huge numbers of followers. He founded his order in 1210, and by 1218, it is estimated, the order had over 3,000 members. Francis also founded a community of cloistered nuns under the direction of his friend Clare (1194–1253), now known as

Saint Clare of Assisi, and he wrote a Rule of life for laypeople who wished to follow his spiritual way of living. Like the Dominicans, the Franciscans founded preaching churches throughout western Europe in the thirteenth century. Francis also desired to send missionaries to Muslim lands. He was reluctant to encourage his followers to pursue higher studies because he feared they would thus gain positions of power and not be able to live a life of poverty as he envisioned it. That resistance to learning would not hold after the death of the saint.

The mendicants, particularly the Franciscans, had an enormous impact on the religious culture of the High Middle Ages. They emphasized the goodness of God's creation, a love for the poor, and the humanity of Christ. The emphasis that mendicant piety laid on the humanity of Christ and the saints was vividly reflected in early Renaissance Italian art.

In addition to preaching in Europe, the mendicants accompanied Crusaders on the various campaigns to the Middle East. On their own, they followed the trade routes. For example, Franciscan friars followed the spice trade as far as China to the east and California to the west.

Monastic life of course continued in rural Europe after the twelfth century, but the mendicant tradition had a larger role to play in European cities and, through missionaries, outside of Europe.

SAINT FRANCIS OF ASSISI
1181 or 1182–1226

THE TESTAMENT

Francis was born Francesco di Pietro di Bernardone and belonged to a wealthy family. He fought as a soldier for Assisi, but in 1204, while preparing to go off to war, he had a vision that inspired him to return to Assisi and dedicate his life to Christianity. Twenty years later, having founded orders of monks and nuns, Francis reportedly experienced religious ecstasy that resulted in his receiving stigmata: five marks resembling the wounds that Jesus Christ received during his Passion. He is, along with Saint Catherine of Siena (see p. 310), one of Italy's two patron saints.

Francis wrote the following document, his only autobiographical composition, at different times during his final year. In this testament, he pleads for his followers to remain true to his ideal of poverty, to his desire that they not try to rise in the Church, and to the Gospel as he read it. He celebrates the desire to do "honest work": hard work, physical work. Francis saw his turn to lepers, described at the opening of this piece, as the beginning of his life of faith.

PRONOUNCING GLOSSARY

Ostia: *oh´-stee-uh*   Paraclete: *par´-uh-kleet*

THE TESTAMENT

The Lord gave me, Brother Francis, thus to begin doing penance in this way: for when I was in sin, it seemed too bitter for me to see lepers. And the Lord Himself led me among them and I showed mercy to them. And when I left them, what had seemed bitter to me was turned into sweetness of soul and body. And afterwards I delayed a little and left the world.[1]

And the Lord gave me such faith in churches that I would pray with simplicity in this way and say: "We adore You, Lord Jesus Christ, in all Your churches throughout the whole world and we bless You because by Your holy cross You have redeemed the world."

Afterwards the Lord gave me, and gives me still, such faith in priests who live according to the rite of the holy Roman Church because of their orders that, were they to persecute me, I would still want to have recourse to them. And if I had as much wisdom as Solomon[2] and found impoverished priests of this world, I would not preach in their parishes against their will. And I desire to respect, love and honor them and all others as my lords. And I do not want to consider any sin in them because I discern the Son of God in them and they are my lords. And I act in this way because, in this world, I see nothing corporally of the most high Son of God except His most holy Body and Blood which they receive and they alone administer to others. I want to have these most holy mysteries honored and venerated above all things and I want to reserve them in precious places. Wherever I find our Lord's most holy names and written words in unbecoming places, I want to gather them up and I beg that they be gathered up and placed in a becoming place. And we must honor all theologians and those who minister the most holy divine words and respect them as those who minister to us spirit and life.[3]

And after the Lord gave me some brothers, no one showed me what I had to do, but the Most High Himself revealed to me that I should live according to the pattern of the Holy Gospel. And I had this written down simply and in a few words and the Lord Pope confirmed it for me. And those who came to receive life gave whatever they had to the poor and were content with one tunic, patched inside and out, with a cord and short trousers. We desired nothing more. We clerical [brothers] said the Office as other clerics did; the lay brothers said the Our Father; and we quite willingly remained in churches. And we were simple and subject to all.

And I worked with my hands, and I still desire to work; and I earnestly desire all brothers to give themselves to honest work. Let those who do not know how to work learn, not from desire to receive wages, but for example and to avoid idleness. And when we are not paid for our work, let us have recourse to the table of the Lord, begging alms from door to door. The Lord revealed a greeting to me that we should say: "May the Lord give you peace."[4]

FROM Francis of Assisi, *Early Documents*, vol. 1: *The Saint*, ed. Regis J. Armstrong, J. A. Wayne Helman, and William J. Short. The translation's verse numbers and Bible citations have been omitted. Italicized type corresponding to the citations has been made roman. Bracketed insertions are the translator's.

1. I.e., after a little while, Francis left secular life and dedicated himself full-time to religion.
2. An ancient king of Israel; see 1 Kings 4:30–31.
3. See John 6:63.
4. See 2 Thessalonians 3:16.

Let the brothers be careful not to receive in any way churches or poor dwellings or anything else built for them unless they are according to the holy poverty we have promised in the Rule. As pilgrims and strangers,[5] let them always be guests there.

I strictly command all the brothers through obedience, wherever they may be, not to dare to ask any letter from the Roman Curia,[6] either personally or through an intermediary, whether for a church or another place or under the pretext of preaching or the persecution of their bodies. But, wherever they have not been received, let them flee into another country[7] to do penance with the blessing of God.

And I firmly wish to obey the general minister of this fraternity and the other guardian whom it pleases him to give me. And I so wish to be a captive in his hands that I cannot go anywhere or do anything beyond obedience and his will, for he is my master.

And although I may be simple and infirm, I nevertheless want to have a cleric always with me who will celebrate the Office for me as it is prescribed in the Rule.

And let all the brothers be bound to obey their guardians and to recite the Office according to the Rule.[8] And if some might have been found who are not reciting the Office according to the Rule and want to change it in some way, or who are not Catholics, let all the brothers, wherever they may have found one of them, be bound through obedience to bring him before the custodian of that place nearest to where they found him. And let the custodian be strictly bound through obedience to keep him securely day and night as a man in chains, so that he cannot be taken from his hands until he can personally deliver him into the hands of his minister. And let the minister be bound through obedience to send him with such brothers who would guard him as a prisoner until they deliver him to the Lord of Ostia, who is the Lord, the Protector and the Corrector of this fraternity.[9]

And the brothers may not say: "This is another rule." Because this is a remembrance, admonition, exhortation, and my testament, which I, little brother Francis, make for you, my blessed brothers, that we might observe the Rule we have promised in a more Catholic way.

And let the general minister and all the other ministers and custodians be bound through obedience not to add to or take away from these words. And let them always have this writing with them together with the Rule. And in all the chapters which they hold, when they read the Rule, let them also read these words. And I strictly command all my cleric and lay brothers, through obedience, not to place any gloss upon the Rule or upon these words saying: "They should be understood in this way." But as the Lord has given me to speak and write the Rule and these words simply and purely, may you understand them simply and without gloss and observe them with a holy activity until the end.

And whoever observes these things, let him be blessed in heaven with the blessing of the Most High Father, and on earth with the blessing of His

5. See 1 Peter 2:11, especially in the King James Version.
6. The central administrative office of the Roman Catholic Church.
7. See Matthew 10:23.
8. Those who enter the clerical state with a view to ordination to the priesthood are obliged to recite the liturgical prayers that make up what is called the Divine Office.
9. The Lord of Ostia, a Roman Catholic cardinal, served as the head of the Franciscan Order.

Beloved Son with the Most Holy Spirit, the Paraclete, and all the powers of heaven and with all the saints. And, as far as I can, I, little brother Francis, your servant, confirm for you, both within and without, this most holy blessing.

THE CANTICLE OF BROTHER SUN

Francis worked on this hymn at various times in his life and completed it on his deathbed. Originally composed in his Umbrian dialect, it may be the first recorded piece of Italian literature. Its roots are in Psalms 148 and, especially, the *Benedicite* (Latin for "Bless!"), verses 35–68 of the Song of the Three Young Men, an Apocryphal addition to chapter 3 of the Book of Daniel from the first or second century B.C.E.

As in the *Benedicite*, all creatures are called on to bless the Lord. Each force of nature—air (sun, moon, stars, wind, clouds, and weather), water, fire, and earth—is greeted as a "brother" or "sister," depending on the term's grammatical gender in Italian. Though the piece ends with a warning about "the second death" (hell), it displays Francis's characteristic childlike wonder and joy, emphasizing how creation praises God in its very being. Francis hoped his friars would recite or sing "The Canticle of Brother Sun" in the city squares as a prelude to preaching.

THE CANTICLE OF BROTHER SUN

Most High, all-powerful, good Lord,
   Yours are the praises, the glory, and the honor, and all blessing,[1]
To You alone, Most High, do they belong,
   and no human is worthy to mention Your name.
Praised be You, my Lord, with all Your creatures,   5
   especially Sir Brother Sun,
   Who is the day and through whom You give us light.
And he is beautiful and radiant with great splendor;
   and bears a likeness of You, Most High One.
Praised be You, my Lord, through Sister Moon and the stars,[2]   10
   in heaven You formed them clear and precious and beautiful.
Praised be You, my Lord, through Brother Wind,
   and through the air, cloudy and serene, and every kind of weather,
   through whom You give sustenance to Your creatures.
Praised be You, my Lord, through Sister Water,[3]   15
   who is very useful and humble and precious and chaste.
Praised be You, my Lord, through Brother Fire,[4]
   through whom You light the night,[5]

FROM Francis of Assisi, *Early Documents*, vol. 1: *The Saint*, ed. Regis J. Armstrong, J. A. Wayne Helman, and William J. Short. The translation's verse numbers and Bible citations have been omitted. Italicized type corresponding to the citations has been made roman.

1. See Revelation 4:9, 11.
2. See Psalms 148:3. "Through": Here, Francis used the Italian preposition *per*, which could also mean "for." Thus, the line could be giving thanks "for Sister Moon and the stars." Some translators use "through" to reflect the biblical idea that all creation praises God.
3. See Psalms 148:4.
4. See the Song of the Three Young Men, verse 44.
5. See Psalms 78:14.

and he is beautiful and playful and robust and strong.
Praised be You, my Lord, through our Sister Mother Earth,[6]   20
    who sustains and governs us,
    and who produces various fruit with colored flowers and herbs.[7]

Praised be You, my Lord, through those who give pardon for Your love,
    and bear infirmity and tribulation.
    Blessed are those who endure in peace   25
        for by You, Most High, shall they be crowned.

Praised be You, my Lord, through our Sister Bodily Death,
    from whom no one living can escape.
    Woe to those who die in mortal sin.
    Blessed are those whom death will find in Your most holy will,   30
        for the second death shall do them no harm.[8]

Praise and bless my Lord and give Him thanks[9]
and serve Him with great humility.

FROM LITTLE FLOWERS

This enormously popular collection of anecdotes and legends dates from a late-fourteenth-century Latin manuscript, *Actus beati Francisci et sociorum eius* ("The Acts of Blessed Francis and his Companions"), which was translated into Italian as *Fioretti* ("Little Flowers"). In 58 brief, loosely-strung-together chapters, this work depicts the teaching, preaching, miracles, and adventures of Francis and his early followers in a (mostly) idyllic atmosphere of evangelical poverty and simplicity.

In chapter 16, Francis, a tenderhearted lover of animals, delivers a sermon to a huge flock of birds. Citing Jesus in the Sermon on the Mount ("Look at the birds of the air: they neither sow nor reap nor gather into barns, and yet your heavenly Father feeds them"; Matthew 7:26), Francis praises and congratulates the birds, welcoming them into the community of creation. (Later he rescues some wild doves and tames a ferocious, human-eating wolf.) This now-famous scene has often been celebrated in art and music, as in Franz Liszt's piano piece *Legend: St. Francis Preaching to the Birds* (1862–63).

Christian thinkers, like the practitioners of monotheistic religions generally, have had difficulty deciding what to make of nonhuman animals. The often-cited text of Genesis 1:28, "[Let humans] have dominion over the fish of the sea, and over the birds of the air, and every living thing that lives upon the earth," seems to present animals as divine gifts for human use. But Job 38–41, Psalm 104, and other Bible passages express awe at the majesty, mystery, and power of animals. Francis shares this latter sentiment, but is he suggesting that animals are conscious of God and part of his plan of salvation? In any event, Pope John Paul II (pope from 1978 until his death, in 2005) declared Francis the patron saint of ecology, and his successor, Cardinal Jorge Mario Bergoglio, took office as Pope Francis in 2013.

6. See Daniel 3:74.
7. See Psalms 104:13–14.

8. See Revelation 2:11, 20:6.
9. See Daniel 3:85.

PRONOUNCING GLOSSARY

Bevagna: *be-vah´-nyuh*   Cannara: *cahn-nahr´-uh*

FROM LITTLE FLOWERS

[*Saint Francis Preaches to the Birds*]

And leaving them much consoled and disposed to do penance, he left there and came between Cannara and Bevagna.[1] And while going with the same fervor through that district with his companions, he looked up and saw near the road some trees on which there was such a countless throng of different birds as had never been seen before in that area. And also a very great crowd of birds was in a field near those trees. While he gazed and marveled at the multitude of birds, the Spirit of God came over him and he said to his companions: "Wait for me here on the road. I am going to preach to our sisters, the birds."

And he went into the field toward the birds that were on the ground. And as soon as he began to preach, all the birds that were on the trees came down toward him. And all of them stayed motionless with the others in the field, even though he went among them, touching many of them with his habit. But not a single one of them made the slightest move, and later they did not leave until he had given them his blessing, as Brother James of Massa, a holy man, said, and he had all the above facts from Brother Masseo, who was one of those who were the companions of the holy Father at that time.

The substance of St. Francis' sermon to those birds was this: "My little bird sisters, you owe much to God your Creator, and you must always and everywhere praise Him, because He has given you freedom to fly anywhere— also He has given you a double and triple covering, and your colorful and pretty clothing, and your food is ready without your working for it, and your singing that was taught to you by the Creator, and your numbers that have been multiplied by the blessing of God—and because He preserved your species in Noah's ark so that your race should not disappear from the earth.[2] And you are also indebted to Him for the realm of the air which He assigned to you. Moreover, you neither sow nor reap, yet God nourishes you, and He gives you the rivers and springs to drink from. He gives you high mountains and hills, rocks and crags as refuges, and lofty trees in which to make your nests. And although you do not know how to spin or sew, God gives you and your little ones the clothing which you need. So the Creator loves you very much, since He gives you so many good things. Therefore, my little bird sisters, be careful not to be ungrateful, but strive always to praise God."

Now at these words of St. Francis, all those birds began to open their beaks, stretch out their necks, spread their wings, and reverently bow their heads to the ground, showing by their movements and their songs that

TRANSLATED BY Raphael Brown.

1. Two towns in central Italy.   2. See Genesis 6–8.

the words which St. Francis was saying gave them great pleasure. And when St. Francis noticed this, he likewise rejoiced greatly in spirit with them, and he marveled at such a great throng of birds and at their very beautiful variety and also at their attention and familiarity and affection. And therefore he devoutly praised the wonderful Creator in them and gently urged them to praise the Creator.

Finally, when he had finished preaching to them and urging them to praise God, St. Francis made the Sign of the Cross over all those birds and gave them permission to leave. Then all the birds rose up into the air simultaneously, and in the air they sang a wonderful song. And when they had finished singing, according to the form of the Cross which St. Francis had made over them, they separated in an orderly way and formed four groups. And each group rose high into the air and flew off in a different direction: one toward the east, another toward the west, the third toward the south, and the fourth toward the north. And each group sang marvelously as it flew away.

Thereby they signified that, just as St. Francis—who was to bear the marks of Christ's Cross—had preached to them and made the Sign of the Cross over them, so they had separated in the form of a cross and had flown away, singing, toward the four quarters of the world, thus suggesting that the preaching of the Cross of Christ, which had been renewed by St. Francis, was to be carried throughout the world by him and by his friars, who, like birds, possess nothing of their own in this world and commit themselves entirely to the Providence of God.

And so they were called eagles by Christ when He said, "Wherever the body shall be, there the eagles will gather."[3] For the saints who place their hope in the Lord will take on wings like eagles and will fly up to the Lord and will not die for all eternity.

To the praise of Christ. Amen.

3. Matthew 24:28. Francis conflates eagles and vultures.

SAINT THOMAS AQUINAS
1225–1274

FROM ON THE LORD'S PRAYER

Thomas Aquinas was born in Aquino, present-day Lazio, in the Kingdom of Sicily. A hugely influential philosopher and theologian, he is a Doctor (from the Latin for "Teacher") of the Roman Catholic Church. This title recognizes individuals as having been of major importance to the Church, particularly in contributing to theology or doctrine. Thomas's best-known works are the *Summa Theologica* (1265–74), a theological manual, and the *Summa contra Gentiles* (1264 or 1270–73), a collection of scriptural commentaries and syntheses. He is venerated by the Roman Catholic and Lutheran Churches and by the Anglican Communion.

Thomas studied at the University of Paris and subsequently was a teacher and administrator there. He wrote "On the Lord's Prayer" as part of his duty as a "master of the sacred page" (commentator on Scripture), as theology professors at the university were known. The Christian tradition of commenting on the Lord's Prayer goes back as far as the second century, but the structure of the argument in this work and the citations from the Church fathers were typical of the new, highly rationalized "scholastic" style of commentary. This selection comes from Thomas's commentary on Matthew 6:9–15; for background on Matthew 5–7, see p. 116.

PRONOUNCING GLOSSARY

Damascene: *da´-muh-seen*

Saint Thomas Aquinas—commonly portrayed as bald and portly— appears as a pensive young monk in this painting by his fellow Dominican Fra Bartolomeo (1472–1517).

FROM ON THE LORD'S PRAYER

This prayer has three qualities: brevity, completeness and effectiveness. There are two reasons for its brevity: it means that everyone can easily learn it, both great and small, learned and unlearned, because he is "the same Lord of all, who is rich toward all who call on him" (Romans 10:12). Secondly, it is to give us confidence that we shall easily obtain what we are asking for. "The Lord will make a shortened word upon the earth" (Isaiah 10:23).

It is also complete. As Augustine[1] says, anything that can be contained in other prayers is contained in this one. So he says that if we are praying appropriately and correctly, then whatever words we may be using we are not saying anything other than what is laid down in the Lord's Prayer. God himself gave us this prayer and "God's works are complete" (Deuteronomy 32:4).

It is effective because, according to Damascene,[2] prayer is a petition made to God for things that are fitting. "You ask and you do not receive because you ask badly" (James 4:3). But knowing what we ought to ask for is extremely difficult, as is knowing what we ought to desire. "We do not know what we ought to pray for, but the Spirit himself entreats for us" (Romans 8:26). Because the Lord himself taught us this prayer, it is particularly effective. This is why it says in Luke 11:1–2, "Lord, teach us to pray . . . and he said to them, 'When you pray, say "Our Father."'"

In this prayer the Lord does two things: first, he gives us the prayer, then he indicates a reason for it ("if you forgive . . .").

TRANSLATED BY Simon Tugwell. The parenthetical citations are Thomas's, sometimes adjusted by the translator.

1. Saint Augustine of Hippo (see p. 226). 2. Saint John of Damascus (see p. 218).

You must realize that in all speeches (*oratio*), including those of orators, the good will of the addressee is won first before any petition is made. So this should be done in a speech addressed to God, just as it is in a speech addressed to human beings. But the purpose is not the same in each case. In the case of human beings we win their good will inasmuch as we influence their minds, but in the case of God it is a matter of our raising our minds to him.

Accordingly the Lord specifies two things which we need when we pray in order to win good will: we must believe that the one we are praying to is willing to give and that he is able to give. So he says, "Father," because if he is a Father he wills what is best for his children, and "who art in the heavens" because if he is in heaven he can do whatever he wills.

Five things are achieved by saying "Father." First, it instructs us in our faith, and faith is necessary for people who pray. There have been three errors which preclude prayer, two entirely destroy prayer and the third concedes more than it should, and they are all eliminated by the Lord's saying "Our Father." Some people have said that God is not concerned about human affairs. "They have said, 'The Lord has abandoned the earth'" (Ezekiel 9:9). On this view it is a waste of time asking God for anything. Other people have said that there is a divine providence and that it does make provision for everything, but it subjects everything to the constraint of necessity, so there is no need to pray because, if God is making provision, then it will happen just so. The third error concedes too much, saying that God arranges everything by his providence, but his divine plan is changed by prayer.

All these errors are eliminated by the Lord saying, "Our Father who art in the heavens." If he is a Father, then he does exercise providence over his children: "Your providence, Father, guides it" (Wisdom 14:3). And the second error is also eliminated: "father" is relative to "children," as "master" is to "servant," so in calling God "Father" we are calling ourselves his children (*liberi*). Almost nowhere in scripture do we find God called the Father of inanimate creatures, though there is an exception in Job 38:28, "Who is the rain's father?" So "Father" is relative to "son" and "son" implies freedom. So we are not subjected to the constraint of necessity. And by saying, "Who art in the heavens," he excludes any mutability from God's plan, showing that everything is unchanging because he is unchanging. So the prayer makes us believe that God arranges everything in accordance with the nature of things, so that effects follow from causes. It is by providence that human beings achieve their goals by their own activity. So prayer does not alter providence nor will it be outside providence, it falls within providence: God's providence arranges for such and such a boon to be granted to us by means of such and such a prayer. So we are, first of all, instructed in our faith by the words "Our Father."

Secondly, these words raise our hopes. If God is our Father, he is willing to give us things. As it says below (Matthew 7:11), "If you who are evil know how to give good things to your children, how much more will your Father who is in heaven give good things to those who ask him?"

Thirdly, they serve to stimulate charity. It is natural for children to love their father and vice versa. "Children, obey your parents in the Lord" (Ephesians 6:1).

Fourthly, we are invited to imitate God. "Be imitators of God, like dearest children" (Ephesians 5:1). "So that you may be children of your Father" (Matthew 5:45). Children ought to imitate their father as far as they can. "You will call me 'Father' and you will not cease to come after me" (Jeremiah 3:19).

Fifthly, we are called to humility. "If I am your Father, where is my honor?" (Malachi 1:6).

In saying "Our Father" our feelings for our neighbors are set in order. "Is there not one Father of us all?" (Malachi 2:10). If we all have one Father, none of us ought to despise any of our neighbors on the grounds of birth.

But why do we not say, "My Father"? There are two reasons. First, Christ wanted to reserve that to himself as his own, because he is God's Son by nature, whereas we are his children by adoption[3] and that is common to all of us. "I am ascending to my Father and to your Father" (John 20:17), because he is "mine" in a different sense from that in which he is "yours." Secondly, as Chrysostom[4] says, the Lord is teaching us not to make private prayers, but to pray generally for the whole people; this kind of prayer is more acceptable to God. In Chrysostom's words, "In God's eyes a prayer is more pleasing if it comes from fraternal love rather than from need." "Pray for one another" (James 5:16).

The second thing belonging to the winning of good will is "Who art in the heavens," and this is interpreted in two ways. First, literally, with reference to the bodily heavens. Not that he is confined there. "'Do I not fill heaven and earth?' says the Lord" (Jeremiah 23:24). The reason for saying, "Who art in the heavens," is that the heavens are the highest part of creation. "Heaven is my seat" (Isaiah 66:1). This makes provision for the weak who are unable to rise above bodily things. Augustine says that this is the reason why we pray toward the East, because the movement of the sky is from the East, and God is above our spirit just as the sky is above our body. So we are given to understand that our spirit ought to turn to God, just as we turn our bodies to the sky when we pray. So he says "Who art in the heavens" to raise our attention away from the things of earth "to an incorruptible inheritance . . . preserved in heaven" (1 Peter 1:4).

Alternatively, the heavens can be taken to mean the saints, as in Isaiah 1:2, "Hear, you heavens." "You dwell in your holy one" (Psalms 21:4). And he says this to give us a greater confidence in obtaining what we pray for, because he is not far from us. "You are in us, Lord" (Jeremiah 14:9).

* * *

"As we too forgive our debtors." People can be debtors in two senses: either because they have sinned against us, or because they owe us money or something of the kind. We are not being urged to forgive the second sort of debt, but to forgive any sin whatsoever, even with the loss of our temporal goods. It would be outrageous for me to ask God for mercy and not grant mercy to my fellow servant. "One human being cherishes wrath against another and then asks for help from God" (Ecclesiasticus 28:3). "Forgive your neighbor who harms you."

___

3. I.e., through baptism; see the headnote for Romans 7–9 and Galatians 3:6–9, 23–29 (p. 144).
4. Here, not Saint John Chrysostom (see p. 180) but the 5th-century figure known as Pseudo-

Chrysostom, author of *Opus Imperfectum in Mattheum,* a Latin commentary on the Gospel of Matthew.

But what are we to say of those who refuse to forgive, but still say the Our Father? It looks as if they ought never to say it, because they are lying. So it is reported that some people used to miss out the clause, "As we forgive our debtors." But this is faulted by Chrysostom on two grounds: first, because it does not respect the church's pattern in praying, and secondly, because no prayer is acceptable to God if it does not retain what Christ composed. So we must maintain that people do not sin if they say the Our Father, whatever state of ill will and grave sin they may be in, because people in that situation should do whatever good they can, like almsgiving and prayers, which do not merit eternal life, but do prepare the way for the recovery of grace. Nor is someone in this position lying, because the prayer is pronounced, not in the name of the individual, but in the name of the whole church, and there is no doubt that the church forgives the debts of all those who are in the church. But a person in such a position loses the benefit of it, because only people who forgive gain the benefit.

Augustine raises the question whether it is only those who forgive offenses who are forgiven by the Lord. It looks as if this benefit is gained only by people who forgive offenses. But Augustine answers the question * * * by saying that God wants us to forgive offenses in the same way that he forgives our guilt, and he does not forgive us unless we ask. So anyone who is so disposed as to be ready to forgive anyone who asks pardon does not lose the benefit, so long as in general he does not hate anyone * * *.

※　※　※

"But deliver us from evil." This is the last petition. "Deliver us" from past, present and future evil, from the evil of guilt, of punishment and of all ill. As Augustine says, every Christian in any kind of trouble pours out tears at these words and utters groans. "Rescue me from my enemies, my God" (Psalms 58:2). "I myself will comfort you, who are you that you should be afraid?" (Isaiah 51:12).

"Amen," that is, "So be it" in Hebrew. Nobody has been willing to translate it, out of reverence, because the Lord frequently used the word. By it we are given confidence that we shall obtain what we pray for, provided we observe all that has been said and are the kind of people who forgive and so on.

In the Greek three more phrases are added, on which Chrysostom comments: first, "For thine is the kingdom," then "and the power and the glory, Amen."[5] And these correspond to three earlier phrases: "Thine is the kingdom" to "Thy kingdom come," "the power" to "Thy will be done" and "the glory" to "Our Father" and to everything else which relates to God's honor. Alternatively, it is tantamount to: "You can do these elevated things because you are a king, and so no one can hinder you; yours is the power, so you can give a kingdom, and yours is the glory, so 'Not to us, Lord, not to us, but to your name give the glory'" (Psalms 113:9).

"For if you forgive. . . ." The Lord attached a condition in his prayer, "Forgive us as we too forgive," and this condition might seem burdensome to people, so the Lord explains the reason for it. And in this connection he

5. These very ancient phrases, from the Christian East, are commonly in Protestant versions of the Lord's Prayer, though they do not appear in the Gospel text of the Lord's Prayer (Matthew 6:9–15). They are recited in the Roman Catholic liturgy but not as part of the Lord's Prayer.

does two things: first, he shows that this condition is profitable, then secondly, he shows that it is necessary. It is profitable because by it we obtain the forgiveness of our sins: "If you forgive other people their sins," by which they have sinned against you, "then your heavenly Father will also forgive you your trespasses," which you have committed against him. "Forgive your neighbor who harms you and then when you pray your sins will be forgiven" (Ecclesiasticus 28:2).

But notice that he says, "If you forgive. . . ." As long as human beings live innocently they are gods, but when they sin they fall into the human condition: "I said to you, 'You are gods' . . . but you will die like human beings" (Psalms 81:6–7). So you, who are gods and spiritual people, are to forgive sinful human beings. Again, notice that he says, "Our Father who art in the heavens." The cause of the offenses which occur among people is always to do with something earthly, so heavenly people who have a Father in heaven ought to be free of all quarrels over earthly things. "Be merciful as your Father is merciful . . ." (Luke 6:36).

This condition is also necessary, because without it there is no forgiveness of sins, because "if you do not forgive. . . ." And this is not surprising, because no sin can ever be forgiven without charity. "Charity covers all faults" (Proverbs 10:12). If you have hatred for your brethren, you are not in charity and so your sin is not forgiven. "One human being cherishes wrath against another and then asks for help from God" (Ecclesiasticus 28:3). "There is judgment without mercy for anyone who does not practice mercy" (James 2:13).

But one might think, if this is so and offenses are to be forgiven, that the church sins when she does not forgive. We must say that she would sin if she did not forgive a sinner who asked for pardon. If the sinner does not ask for pardon and she does not forgive because of hatred, then she sins, but if it is for the good of the sinner or of other people, to avoid encouraging them to evil ways, that is, then she does not sin.

FROM SUMMA CONTRA GENTILES

Thomas Aquinas likely wrote this comprehensive treatise against the Gentiles (i.e., nonbelievers or pagans) between 1270 and 1273. In three of its four books, he deals with "natural theology," or what can be known about God from reason and natural observation alone, without appeal to faith or the Bible. In the following four chapters from Book 2, Thomas makes the case for what is known today as intelligent design. Every being, the argument goes, is known by its internal activity and its related external artifacts. Thus, the wisdom, knowledge, goodness, beauty, and so on, of the Creator shine forth in his creatures. Beyond that, Christianity makes believers see God's presence in the universe; and, by contemplating that divine image, they are spiritually transformed into better images of their creator.

Thomas warns Christians not to stop short at creatures themselves, such as through idolatry (mistaking God's handiwork for God himself) or by maintaining that God can work only through nature (thus denying miracles). Finally, Aquinas distinguishes between philosophy and theology: Philosophy, which includes what we would call science, deals with the phenomenal world as philosophers find it. Theology views reality as shaped by the divine First Cause, and therefore its subject matter is intrinsically superior to all others.

As traditional Jewish and Christian theologians generally do, Aquinas continuously quotes Scripture (even where the verses cited are not quite pertinent), which he takes to be the supreme, unquestionable repository of truth. The position he presents here, still popular today, came under skeptical fire during the Enlightenment, when it was argued that if the logic of creationism is true, then God must also be responsible for all the evil, disorder, and pain caused by flaws in his divine design.

FROM SUMMA CONTRA GENTILES

[On Knowing the Creator through His Creatures]

From BOOK 2

Chapter 1

THE CONNECTION BETWEEN THE FOLLOWING CONSIDERATIONS AND THE PRECEDING ONES

"I meditated upon all Thy works:
I meditated upon the works of Thy hands"
(Psalms 142:5)

[1] Of no thing whatever can a perfect knowledge be obtained unless its operation is known, because the measure and quality of a thing's power is judged from the manner and type of its operation, and its power, in turn, manifests its nature; for a thing's natural aptitude for operation follows upon its actual possession of a certain kind of nature.

[2] There are, however, two sorts of operation, as Aristotle[1] teaches in *Metaphysics* IX: one that remains in the agent and is a perfection of it, as the act of sensing, understanding, and willing; another that passes over into an external thing, and is a perfection of the thing made as a result of that operation, the acts of heating, cutting and building, for example.

[3] Now, both kinds of operation belong to God: the former, in that He understands, wills, rejoices, and loves; the latter, in that He brings things into being, preserves them, and governs them. But, since the former operation is a perfection of the operator, the latter a perfection of the thing made, and since the agent is naturally prior to the thing made and is the cause of it, it follows that the first of these types of operation is the ground of the second, and naturally precedes it, as a cause precedes its effect. Clear evidence of this fact, indeed, is found in human affairs; for in the thought and will of the craftsman lie the principle and plan of the work of building.

[4] Therefore, as a simple perfection of the operator, the first type of operation claims for itself the name of *operation*, or, again, of *action*; the second, as being a perfection of the thing made, is called *making* so that the things which a craftsman produces by action of this kind are said to be his *handiwork*.

[5] Of the first type of operation in God we have already spoken in the preceding Book of this work, where we treated of the divine knowledge

TRANSLATED BY James F. Anderson. The bracketed paragraph numbers and insertions are the translator's.

1. Greek philosopher (384–322 B.C.E.).

and will. Hence, for a complete study of the divine truth, the second operation, whereby things are made and governed by God, remains to be dealt with.

[6] In fact, this order we can gather from the words quoted above. For the Psalmist first speaks of meditation upon the first type of operation, when he says: "I have meditated on all Thy operations"; thus, *operation* is here referred to the divine act of understanding and will. Then he refers to meditation on God's works: "and I meditated on the works of Thy hands"; so that by "the works of Thy hands" we understand heaven and earth, and all that is brought into being by God, as the handiwork produced by a craftsman.

Chapter 2

THAT THE CONSIDERATION OF CREATURES IS USEFUL FOR INSTRUCTION OF FAITH

[1] This sort of meditation on the divine works is indeed necessary for instruction of faith in God.

[2] First, because meditation on His works enables us in some measure to admire and reflect upon His wisdom. For things made by art are representative of the art itself, being made in likeness to the art. Now, God brought things into being by His wisdom; wherefore the Psalm (103:24) declares: "Thou hast made all things in wisdom." Hence, from reflection upon God's works we are able to infer His wisdom, since, by a certain communication of His likeness, it is spread abroad in the things He has made. For it is written: "He poured her out," namely, wisdom, "upon all His works" (Ecclesiastes 1:10). Therefore, the Psalmist, after saying: "Thy knowledge is become wonderful to me: it is high, and I cannot reach it," and after referring to the aid of the divine illumination, when he says: "Night shall be my light," etc., confesses that he was aided in knowing the divine wisdom by reflection upon God's works, saying: "Wonderful are Thy works, and my soul knoweth right well" (Psalms 138:6, 11, 14).

[3] Secondly, this consideration [of God's works] leads to admiration of God's sublime power, and consequently inspires in men's hearts reverence for God. For the power of the worker is necessarily understood to transcend the things made. And so it is said: "If they," namely, the philosophers, "admired their power and effects," namely of the heavens, stars, and elements of the world, "let them understand that He that made them is mightier than they" (Wisdom 13:4). Also it is written: "The invisible things of God are clearly seen, being understood by the things that are made: His eternal power also and divinity" (Romans 1:20). Now, the fear and reverence of God result from this admiration. Hence, it is said: "Great is Thy name in might. Who shall not fear Thee, O King of Nations?" (Jeremiah 10:6–7).

[4] Thirdly, this consideration incites the souls of men to the love of God's goodness. For whatever goodness and perfection is distributed to the various creatures, in partial or particular measure, is united together in Him universally, as in the source of all goodness, as we proved in Book I. If, therefore, the goodness, beauty, and delightfulness of creatures are so alluring to the minds of men, the fountainhead of God's own goodness, compared with the rivulets of goodness found in creatures, will draw

the enkindled minds of men wholly to Itself. Hence it is said in the Psalm (91:5): "Thou hast given me, O Lord, a delight in Thy doings, and in the works of Thy hands I shall rejoice." And elsewhere it is written concerning the children of men: "They shall be inebriated with the plenty of Thy house," that is, of all creatures, "and Thou shalt make them drink of the torrent of Thy pleasure: for with Thee is the fountain of life" (Psalms 35:9–10). And, against certain men, it is said: "By these good things that are seen," namely, creatures, which are good by a kind of participation, "they could not understand Him that is" (Wisdom 13:1), namely, truly good; indeed, is goodness itself, as was shown in Book I.

[5] Fourthly, this consideration endows men with a certain likeness to God's perfection. For it was shown in Book I that, by knowing Himself, God beholds all other things in Himself. Since, then, the Christian faith teaches man principally about God, and makes him know creatures by the light of divine revelation, there arises in man a certain likeness of God's wisdom. So it is said: "But we all beholding the glory of the Lord with open face, are transformed into the same image" (II Corinthians 3:18).

[6] It is therefore evident that the consideration of creatures has its part to play in building the Christian faith. And for this reason it is said: "I will remember the works of the Lord, and I will declare the things I have seen: by the words of the Lord are His works" (Ecclesiasticus 42:15).

Chapter 3

THAT KNOWLEDGE OF THE NATURE OF CREATURES SERVES TO DESTROY ERRORS CONCERNING GOD

[1] The consideration of creatures is further necessary, not only for the building up of truth, but also for the destruction of errors. For errors about creatures sometimes lead one astray from the truth of faith, so far as the errors are inconsistent with true knowledge of God. Now, this happens in many ways.

[2] First, because through ignorance of the nature of creatures men are sometimes so far perverted as to set up as the first cause and as God that which can only receive its being from something else; for they think that nothing exists beyond the realm of visible creatures. Such were those who identified God with this, that, and the other kind of body; and of these it is said: "Who have imagined either the fire, or the wind, or the swift air, or the circle of the stars, or the great water, or the sun and moon to be the gods" (Wisdom 13:2).

[3] Secondly, because they attribute to certain creatures that which belongs only to God. This also results from error concerning creatures. For what is incompatible with a thing's nature is not ascribed to it except through ignorance of its nature—as if man were said to have three feet. Now, what belongs solely to God is incompatible with the nature of a created thing, just as that which is exclusively man's is incompatible with another thing's nature. Thus, it is from ignorance of the creature's nature that the aforesaid error arises. And against this error it is said: "They gave the incommunicable name to stones and wood" (Wisdom 14:21). Into this error fell those who attribute the creation of things, or knowledge of the future, or the working of miracles to causes other than God.

[4] Thirdly, because through ignorance of the creature's nature something is subtracted from God's power in its working upon creatures. This is evidenced in the case of those who set up two principles of reality; in those who assert that things proceed from God, not by the divine will, but by natural necessity; and again, in those who withdraw either all or some things from the divine providence, or who deny that it can work outside the ordinary course of things. For all these notions are derogatory to God's power. Against such persons it is said: "Who looked upon the Almighty as if He could do nothing" (Job 22:17), and: "Thou showest Thy power, when men will not believe Thee to be absolute in power" (Wisdom 12:17).

[5] Fourthly, through ignorance of the nature of things, and, consequently, of his own place in the order of the universe, this rational creature, man, who by faith is led to God as his last end, believes that he is subject to other creatures to which he is in fact superior. Such is evidently the case with those who subject human wills to the stars, and against these it is said: "Be not afraid of the signs of heaven, which the heathens fear" (Jeremiah 10:2); and this is likewise true of those who think that angels are the creators of souls, that human souls are mortal, and, generally, of persons who hold any similar views derogatory to the dignity of man.

[6] It is, therefore, evident that the opinion is false of those who asserted that it made no difference to the truth of the faith what anyone holds about creatures, so long as one thinks rightly about God, as Augustine[2] tells us in his book *On the Origin of the Soul*. For error concerning creatures, by subjecting them to causes other than God, spills over into false opinion about God, and takes men's minds away from Him, to whom faith seeks to lead them.

[7] For this reason Scripture threatens punishment to those who err about creatures, as to unbelievers, in the words of the Psalm (27:5): "Because they have not understood the works of the Lord and the operations of His hands, Thou shalt destroy them, and shalt not build them up"; and: "These things they thought and were deceived," and further on: "They esteemed not the honor of holy souls" (Wisdom 2:21–22).

Chapter 4

THAT THE PHILOSOPHER AND THE THEOLOGIAN CONSIDER CREATURES IN DIFFERENT WAYS

[1] Now, from what has been said it is evident that the teaching of the Christian faith deals with creatures so far as they reflect a certain likeness of God, and so far as error concerning them leads to error about God. And so they are viewed in a different light by that doctrine and by human philosophy. For human philosophy considers them as they are, so that the different parts of philosophy are found to correspond to the different genera of things. The Christian faith, however, does not consider them as such; thus, it regards fire not as fire, but as representing the sublimity of God, and as being directed to Him in any way at all. For as it is said: "Full of the glory of the Lord is His work. Hath not the Lord made the saints to declare all His wonderful works?" (Ecclesiasticus 42:16–17).

---

2. Saint Augustine of Hippo (see p. 226).

[2] For this reason, also, the philosopher and the believer consider different matters about creatures. The philosopher considers such things as belong to them by nature—the upward tendency of fire, for example; the believer, only such things as belong to them according as they are related to God—the fact, for instance, that they are created by God, are subject to Him, and so on.

[3] Hence, imperfection is not to be imputed to the teaching of the faith if it omits many properties of things, such as the figure of the heaven and the quality of its motion. For neither does the natural philosopher consider the same characters of a line as the geometrician, but only those that accrue to it as terminus of a natural body.

[4] But any things concerning creatures that are considered in common by the philosopher and the believer are conveyed through different principles in each case. For the philosopher takes his argument from the proper causes of things; the believer, from the first cause—for such reasons as that a thing has been handed down in this manner by God, or that this conduces to God's glory, or that God's power is infinite. Hence, also, [the doctrine of the faith] ought to be called the highest wisdom, since it treats of the highest cause; as we read in Deuteronomy (4:6): "For this is your wisdom and understanding in the sight of nations." And, therefore, human philosophy serves her as the first wisdom. Accordingly, divine wisdom sometimes argues from principles of human philosophy. For among philosophers, too, the first philosophy utilizes the teachings of all the sciences in order to realize its objectives.

[5] Hence again, the two kinds of teaching do not follow the same order. For in the teaching of philosophy, which considers creatures in themselves and leads us from them to the knowledge of God, the first consideration is about creatures; the last, of God. But in the teaching of faith, which considers creatures only in their relation to God, the consideration of God comes first, that of creatures afterwards. And thus the doctrine of faith is more perfect, as being more like the knowledge possessed by God, who, in knowing Himself, immediately knows other things.

MEDIEVAL LATIN HYMNODY

From Saint Ambrose of Milan (died 397) to Richard Rolle of Hampole (died 1349), the Middle Ages witnessed a vast flowering of religious poetry and hymnody, written naturally in Latin, the language of the Western Church. Such verse based its meter, for the most part, on the words' accents rather than on the length (or "quantity") of the syllables, as in classical poetry; and it introduced the novel feature of rhyme. Though these works play a diminished role in today's Roman Catholic liturgy (the Second Vatican Council, 1963–65, largely replaced Latin with the various modern vernaculars), a number of them remain noteworthy as masterpieces of popular religious art, marked by a simple theology, vivid images, and bold, direct language.

Ave Maris Stella ("Hail, O Star of the Ocean"), an anonymous hymn from around the ninth century, is a tribute to Mary and a vivid example of the distinctly non-Scriptural cult of the Virgin, who is seen as playing a crucial role in the redemption of humanity. The second stanza depicts her as the "anti-Eve." Throughout the hymn, Mary is celebrated for her quasi-divine power to set sinners free, hear their prayers, and lead them to heaven. The poem ends, as many such hymns do, with a doxology, or formulaic praise of the Trinity.

Salve Regina ("Hail, Holy Queen") is one of the most popular Marian hymns. From summer to winter, it is sung at compline, the evening monastic service. It is also used to end the recitation of the rosary. The poem dates perhaps from the late eleventh century, and it has been attributed to Bishop Aimar of Le Puy; to a German monk, Hermann of Reichenau; and to others. Its ecstatic language seems to verge on Mariolatry. The Virgin Mother is hailed as the believer's "life," "sweetness," and "hope," as "clement," "loving," and, once again, "sweet." Christ is mentioned as Mary's child, whom she will show to her followers after the woes of earthly life are over. Two familiar, and correlated, medieval themes are invoked: life as a journey through a "valley of tears" (a phrase possibly first seen in this hymn) and human existence as wretched exile from the true homeland of heaven.

Victimae Paschali Laudes ("Christians, to the Paschal Victim") is commonly ascribed to Wipo (died 1050), chaplain to the Holy Roman Emperors Conrad II and Henry III. It is a sequence, or hymn sung at Mass between the Gradual and the Gospel, in this case on Easter Sunday. Its spare language celebrates the paradox of Christ's victory over death by dying ("Life's own Champion, slain, / yet lives to reign"). The hymn concludes with a dialogue between the choir and the figure of Mary Magdalene, who is identified in John 20:1–18 as the first person to have seen and spoken with the risen Jesus.

Pange, Lingua, Gloriosi ("Sing, My Tongue, the Savior's Glory") was written by Saint Thomas Aquinas (see p. 317) for the feast of Corpus Christi, which was observed ten days after Pentecost. It is also sung on Maundy Thursday, in Passion Week. The hymn elegantly glorifies the Eucharist and in particular the Catholic doctrine of transubstantiation, according to which the sacrament transforms the essences of the bread and of the wine into Christ's real presence, while leaving the bread and wine's physical "accidents" (elements) and appearance untouched.

In the third stanza, Aquinas cites the ancient Christian theme of the Last Supper (a Passover seder, according to the Synoptic Gospels) as a revolutionary *new* Passover. That is, just as the blood of the sacrificial lambs (or goats) was smeared on the lintel and doorposts of the Israelites' houses in Egypt (Exodus 12:5–7) to ward off the Angel of Death (or "destroyer," Exodus 12:23), so Jesus' blood rescues Christians from lethal punishment for their sins. The last two stanzas of the hymn are sung as part of the once widespread Catholic devotional service called Benediction of the Blessed Sacrament.

Like the *Pange, Lingua, Gloriosi*, the *Dies Irae* ("Day of Wrath") is written in the forceful rhythm of trochaic tetrameter. Once credited to Thomas of Celano—a Franciscan friar who died around 1255—but now considered anonymous, the *Dies Irae* is probably the most familiar of all medieval hymns. It was originally sung as a sequence at funeral Masses, and in this way it came to be set to music in the famous Requiem Masses of Mozart (1791) and Verdi (1874). Hector Berlioz also used the Gregorian chant of the *Dies Irae* in his *Symphonie Fantastique* (1830). Building on the apocalyptic tradition of both the Hebrew Bible (Isaiah 24–27, Zephaniah 1:14–16, etc.) and the New Testament (Matthew 25, Revelation 6–18, etc.), the hymn emphasizes less the grandeur of universal judgment at the end of time and more the terror felt by the guilty individual Christian sinner (the poem's male narrator) facing his divine judge, Jesus.

In 1970, the Vatican removed this hymn from the Catholic Mass for the Dead, no doubt because the hymn's dark, threatening tone is at odds with the positive teaching of ultimate divine triumph and everlasting bliss for the faithful. But the tone is precisely what gives the poem its eerie, haunting power.

PRONOUNCING GLOSSARY

Ave Maris Stella: *ah´-vay mah´-rees stell´-ah*
Dies Irae: *dee´-ace ee´-ray*
Pange, Lingua, Gloriosi: *pahn´-jay, lin´-gwah, glor´-ee-oh-see*
Salve Regina: *sahl´-vay ray-jee´-nah*
Victimae Paschali Laudes: *vic´-tee-may pahss-cahl´-lee lahw´-dace*

ANONYMOUS
ca. ninth century

AVE MARIS STELLA

Hail, O Star of the ocean,
God's own Mother blest,
ever sinless Virgin,
gate of heav'nly rest.

Taking that sweet Ave,
which from Gabriel came,
peace confirm within us,
changing Eve's name.[1]

5

FROM the *Liturgia Horarum*. Translation based on a cento from the Roman Breviary. "Thesaurus Precum Latinarum: Treasury of Latin Prayers," © Michael W. Martin, 1998–2011.

1. "Ave"—the first word of the angel Gabriel's greeting to Mary in the Vulgate translation of Luke 1:28—is *Eva*, the Latin for "Eve," spelled backwards.

Break the sinners' fetters,
make our blindness day,   10
chase all evils from us,
for all blessings pray.

Show thyself a Mother,
may the Word divine
born for us thine Infant   15
hear our prayers through thine.

Virgin all excelling,
mildest of the mild,
free from guilt preserve us
meek and undefiled.   20

Keep our life all spotless,
make our way secure
till we find in Jesus,
joy for evermore.

Praise to God the Father,   25
honor to the Son,
in the Holy Spirit,
be the glory one. Amen.

ANONYMOUS
late eleventh century?

SALVE REGINA

Hail, holy Queen, Mother of Mercy,
our life, our sweetness, and our hope.
To thee do we cry,
poor banished children of Eve.[1]
To thee do we send up our sighs,   5
mourning and weeping in this valley of tears.
Turn then, most gracious advocate,
thine eyes of mercy toward us;
and after this our exile,
show unto us the blessed fruit of thy womb, Jesus.   10
O clement, O loving, O sweet Virgin Mary.

FROM Richard J. Breyer, *Blessed Art Thou: A Treasury of Marian Prayers and Devotions.*

1. See the headnote for Genesis 1–3, 12:1–3, 15:1–6, 22:1–19 (p. 83).

Pray for us, O holy Mother of God,
that we may be made worthy of the promises of Christ.
Amen.

WIPO
died 1050

VICTIMAE PASCHALI LAUDES

Christians, to the Paschal Victim
offer sacrifice and praise.

The sheep are ransomed by the Lamb;
and Christ, the undefiled,
hath sinners   5
to his Father reconciled.

Death with life contended:
combat strangely ended!
Life's own Champion, slain,
yet lives to reign.   10

Tell us, Mary:
say what thou didst see upon the way.

The tomb the Living did enclose;
I saw Christ's glory as He rose!

The angels there attesting;   15
shroud with grave-clothes resting.

Christ, my hope, has risen:
He goes before you into Galilee.[1]

That Christ is truly risen
from the dead we know.   20
Victorious King, Thy mercy show!
Amen, Alleluia.

FROM the Roman Missal. "Thesaurus Precum Latinarum: Treasury of Latin Prayers," © Michael W. Martin, 1998–2011.

1. See Matthew 28:7.

SAINT THOMAS AQUINAS
1225–1274

PANGE, LINGUA, GLORIOSI

Sing, my tongue, the Savior's glory,
of His flesh the mystery sing;
of the Blood, all price exceeding,
shed by our immortal King,
destined, for the world's redemption,   5
from a noble womb to spring.

Of a pure and spotless Virgin
born for us on earth below,
He, as Man, with man conversing,
stayed, the seeds of truth to sow;   10
then He closed in solemn order
wondrously His life of woe.

On the night of that Last Supper,
seated with His chosen band,
He the Pascal victim eating,   15
first fulfills the Law's command;
then as Food to His Apostles
gives Himself with His own hand.

Word-made-Flesh, the bread of nature
by His word to Flesh He turns;   20
wine into His Blood He changes;—
what though sense no change discerns?
Only be the heart in earnest,
faith her lesson quickly learns.

Down in adoration falling,   25
Lo! the sacred Host we hail;
Lo! o'er ancient forms departing,
newer rites of grace prevail;
faith for all defects supplying,
where the feeble sense fail.   30

To the everlasting Father,
and the Son who reigns on high,
with the Holy Ghost proceeding
forth from Each eternally,

FROM *Liturgia Horarum and Latin Hymns* by F. A. March, LL.D., 1894. Trans. Fr. Edward Caswall. "Thesaurus Precum Latinarum: Treasury of Latin Prayers," © Michael W. Martin, 1998–2011.

be salvation, honor, blessing,   35
might and endless majesty.
Amen. Alleluia.

ANONYMOUS
thirteenth century

DIES IRAE

Day of wrath and terror looming,
Heaven and earth to ash consuming—
Seer's and Psalmist's true foredooming![1]

Ah, what agony of trembling,
When the Judge, mankind assembling,   5
Probeth all beyond dissembling!

Hear the trumpet-blast resounding,
Through all tombs of earth rebounding,
Summons to the judgement sounding.

Life and death will stand confounded,   10
Seeing man, of clay compounded,
Rise to hear his doom propounded.

Open then, with all recorded,
Lies the book, from whence awarded
Doom shall pass, with deed accorded.   15

Then the Judge will sit, revealing
Every hidden thought and feeling,
Unto each requital dealing.

What shall wretched I be crying,
To what friend for succour flying,   20
When the just in fear are sighing?

Ruler dread, thy proclamation
Frees the chosen from damnation;
Fount of love, grant me salvation.

FROM *The Missal in Latin and English*.

1. Two visions of judgment. "Seer": in classical literature, the Sibyl, a pagan female prophetess. "Psalmist": in the Old Testament, David, the second king of Israel; see the headnote for Psalms 22, 23, 110 and Proverbs 8:22–31 (p. 96).

Remember that my lost condition   25
Caused, dear Lord, thy mortal mission;
Spare my soul that day's perdition.

Thou with weary steps hast sought me,
Crucified hast dearly bought me;
Have thy pains no profit brought me?   30

Righteous judge of retribution,
Grant the gift of absolution
Ere the day of restitution.

Shame and grief my soul oppressing,
I bewail my life's transgressing,   35
Hear me, Lord, my sins confessing.

Thou didst heed the thief's petition,
And the Magdalene's contrition—[2]
Hope for me, too, of remission!

Though my prayers deserve thy spurning,   40
Yet, thy eyes of pity turning,
Save me from eternal burning.

With the sheep of thy salvation
On thy right hand be my station[3]
At that awful separation.   45

When the heavy malediction
Smites the damned with hell's affliction,
Call me to thy benediction.

Crushed to dust, I, suppliant bending,
(All my heart contrition rending)   50
Crave thy care when life is ending.

On that day of tearful wonder,
When the tomb is rent asunder,
Guilty man to doom shall waken;
Leave him not, dear God, forsaken.   55

Lord of mercy, Jesus blest,
Grant them everlasting rest. Amen.

2. As often happens, Jesus' disciple Mary Magdalene is here mistakenly conflated with the "woman of the city, who was a sinner" (Luke 7:36–50). "Thief": the criminal who was crucified alongside Jesus, begged Jesus to remember him when he came into Jesus' kingdom, and was told, "Today you will be with me in Paradise" (Luke 23:39–43); in Christian lore, he is known as the Good Thief or St. Dismas.
3. See Psalms 110:1.

The Late Middle Ages and the Renaissance

1300–1517

EUROPEAN CHRISTENDOM IN FULL FLOWER

The European Crusaders of the 1100s and 1200s failed in their signature attempt to permanently reestablish Christian control over the Holy Land. However, they reestablished permanent European control over the major Mediterranean islands. Starting around 1300, the onset of the period often called the Late Middle Ages, western Europe began to enjoy a period of internal peace and relative security from disruption by foreign conquest, notwithstanding the expansion of the Ottoman (Turkish) Empire into southeastern Europe. The four great cataclysmic events of the fourteenth century—the Black Death, an outbreak of bubonic plague that decimated European cities; the Hundred Years' War, which consisted of terrible clashes between France and England; the Mongol invasion of eastern and central Europe; and the internal schism of the papacy—brought institutional tragedy and economic disruption to the West. Yet cultural development with transformative religious consequences continued. In the Christian East, the Byzantine Empire was tottering, and after the

Dante Alighieri (1265–1321): Dante wrote his Christian epic poem *The Divine Comedy* in homage to Virgil's *Aeneid*. Emilio Demi's nineteenth-century sculpture of the Renaissance poet stands in the facade of the Uffizi Gallery, in Florence.

fall of Constantinople to the Ottoman Turks in 1453, Greek scholars fled to Italy, bringing with them Greek classics long lost to western Europe.

During this period, the technology of book production—including paper manufacture, printing from woodblocks, and book binding—developed rapidly as did the "software" of book culture: chapter divisions, indexes, concordances, and the like. In and around the new universities, large, one-volume Bibles were first produced, their books finally fixed in the order that survives to this day and with much the same appearance. These often magnificently illuminated Bibles modeled not just the modern Bible but also the modern book itself. In effect, movable type was the one element lacking, and this came in 1455, when Johannes Gutenberg published his handsome first edition of a Latin Bible printed with movable type. The Gutenberg Revolution advanced the Renaissance, as Venice quickly became a publishing capital.

The story of the Renaissance is more than a story of lost literature recovered. It is also a story of new literature and, crucially, of new literary languages. It was in the late thirteenth and the fourteenth centuries, in Italy, that major literature consciously invoking classical Roman or Greek models was first written in a European vernacular. Works of great intrinsic literary merit had been written earlier in European vernaculars—notably in Old Irish, Old Norse, Old French, and Old English. But the authors of those works had not consciously built on revived pagan classical models as did the Italian masters of the 1300s.

Among these masters, the first and greatest was Dante Alighieri, whose masterpiece, the epic poem *The Divine Comedy*, includes as a major character the ancient Roman epic poet Virgil. Virgil's work, the *Aeneid*, follows its title character, the Trojan warrior Aeneas, from the defeat of Troy through a long voyage to the future Rome, whose greatness a god summons up before him in a vision. Borrowing this model, Dante portrays himself voyaging, initially with Virgil's help, from Earth to hell, through purgatory, and finally to heaven, thus fusing Christian revelation (and a good bit of the philosophical culture of the medieval university) with a pagan literary model, all in stunningly beautiful Italian.

Dante and, just after him, Giovanni Boccaccio and Francesco Petrarca (Petrarch) implanted the revolutionary idea that anything said in Latin could be said in a modern language such as Italian. Latin lived on for centuries as the common language of high culture in Europe, but vernacular sermons began to be published in the 1300s that drew with daring speculation on the philosophical and theological learning of the universities. Striking among these sermons are those preached in German by the Dominican theologian and mystic Meister Eckhart.

Meanwhile, in plazas outside the major cathedrals and churches of Europe, a far less clerical form of vernacular Christian literature was coming into being: free public religious dramas, performed and then published in the various vernacular languages of Europe. These were "miracle plays" on biblical themes and "morality plays" exhorting the audience to good Christian conduct. Among the surviving "morality plays," the anonymous Dutch work known in its English translation as *Everyman* or *The Summoning of Everyman* is undoubtedly the most famous.

These broad cultural developments led to a gradual shift of emphasis away from the group and toward a novel fusion of private reading with

Christian devotion. During the decades that preceded the Protestant Reformation, the most widely translated and printed single religious book (after the Bible) was the intensely private, intensely personal *Imitation of Christ* by Thomas à Kempis, a practitioner of what was called, notably, the *Devotio Moderna*.

Modern devotion? No, the Latin word *moderna* did not yet mean what the English word *modern* means. Scholars translate *Devotio Moderna* as "New Devotion," and the nuance of "new" for *moderna* is "of *this* time" rather than of any earlier time. Times were changing. The nun Catherine of Siena, in Italy; the anonymous nun known to history as Julian of Norwich, in England; and the itinerant preacher Margery Kempe, also in England, surprised their contemporaries with the theological originality of their views. In Geoffrey Chaucer's *Canterbury Tales*, where biblical and classical allusion mingle as freely as they do in *The Divine Comedy*, the Wife of Bath is clearly modeled on such independent and outspoken women. Times were changing partly because women were beginning to raise their voices.

Chronology

THE LATE MIDDLE AGES AND THE
RENAISSANCE (1300–1517)

1309–77 Babylonian Captivity of the papacy: popes reside in Avignon

1321 Dante Alighieri completes *Divine Comedy*

1345 Founding of greatest Russian monastery, Holy Trinity, at Sergiev Posad, near Moscow

1351 Hesychasm—internal prayer, especially Jesus Prayer, as a quest for union with God—confirmed as official doctrine of Eastern Orthodox Church

1381 Peasants Revolt in England begins, with renegade Lollard priest John Ball playing a major role

1378–1417 Great Western Schism, with popes and antipopes dueling for power

1421 Thomas á Kempis completes *The Imitation of Christ*

1453 Fall of Constantinople to Turks; Greek-speaking refugees flee to Italy, bring manuscripts with them; knowledge of Greek revives in Western Europe

1480 Spanish Inquisition founded

1492 Fall of Granada, last Muslim fortress in Spain; expulsion of the Jews from Spain; discovery of the Americas; Iberian colonialism and massive growth of world Christian population begins

1516 Erasmus publishes first printed Greek New Testament

VISIONS OF HELL AND HEAVEN, CREATION AND CREATOR

In the Late Middle Ages and the Renaissance, European Christendom was under revision: Things already envisioned were being seen anew. The world was changing, partly by looking back, partly by looking forward, and Christianity was changing with it. For Dante, the first great author in the Italian language, artistic energy from the rebirth of the Latin classics enabled a renewal of the inherited Christian vision of Earth, hell, purgatory, and heaven. For the Dominican priest Meister Eckhart, an inherited vision of the relationship between creator and creation was made new through an engagement with the philosophical speculations of the late medieval universities. Catherine of Siena and Julian of Norwich presented their ecstatic and mystical visions in vernacular language. Literary use of the vernacular was as much a sign of changing times as was Thomas à Kempis's use, in *The Imitation of Christ*, of a simple, almost conversational form of late Latin.

DANTE ALIGHIERI
1265–1321

FROM THE DIVINE COMEDY

Dante, the greatest of Italian poets, was born Durante Alighieri in the Republic, or city-state, of Florence. At his christening, his first name was changed to Dante. In some ways, we know more about Dante's political life than about his personal life. His family belonged to the Guelphs, the papal party, as opposed to the Ghibellines, who supported the Holy Roman emperor. At the time, the papacy ruled the so-called Papal States (large contiguous regions of central and northeastern Italy), and Dante was a member of the White Guelphs, a faction of the papal party that wanted to limit the power of the pope as a secular monarch. Dante particularly opposed the power-hungry Pope Boniface VIII (pope from 1294 until his death, in 1303), whose eternal damnation he confidently predicted in verse (*Inferno* XIX, 52–54). Dante played an active role in the Florentine government; but Boniface, favoring the Black Guelphs, had him exiled from Florence in 1301. Dante never returned, feeling both love and hate for the city. He died in Ravenna, where his remains are buried.

Dante is best known for the epic poem *La Commedia* (1308–21), later named *La Divina Commedia* ("The Divine Comedy") by the fourteen-century Italian writer Giovanni Boccaccio, who consolidated the poet's classic status by writing his biography and lecturing about him. In imaginatively and allegorically depicting hell, purgatory, and the soul's journey toward God in the afterlife, the poem's three parts—*Inferno*, *Purgatorio*, and *Paradiso*—encapsulate the medieval Christian worldview. In addition to *The Divine Comedy*, Dante wrote the *Vita Nuova* ("The New Life," 1290–94), a cycle of poems posthumously celebrating Beatrice Portinari, whom he had loved since boyhood and whom he chose to be his figurative guide through *Paradiso*. He also wrote *Convivio* ("Banquet," 1304–07), an incomplete series of philosophical essays; *De Vulgari Eloquentia* ("On Eloquence in the Vernacular," ca. 1302–05), a Latin essay on vernacular poetry; and *De Monarchia* ("On Monarchy"), a treatise on imperial and papal politics from 1309 to 1312, concluded just before his death.

Dante's epic is a visionary journey. There is one introductory canto, and each of the three parts consists of thirty-three cantos, for a total of one hundred. The poem is written in hendecasyllabic lines (eleven beats, in varying rhythms) of terza rima (from the Italian for "third rhyme"). This rhyme scheme consists of three-line stanzas in which the first and third lines of the first stanza rhyme, the first and third lines of the second stanza rhyme with the second line of the first stanza, and so on. The pattern is thus a-b-a, b-c-b, c-d-c, and so on. There is no limit on the number of stanzas, but at the end of each stanza chain is a four- or five-line stanza in which the final line or couplet rhymes with the second line. Thus, c-d-c-d or c-d-c dd. Dante's native Tuscan dialect became the national language of Italy thanks, in part, to his use of it as the language of this work.

By "comedy," Dante meant not a work of humor (though there are some diabolical hijinks in the *Inferno*) but a story that progresses from trouble to eventual happiness. The epic's protagonist is both the historical Dante and an ideal Christian Everyman, who is informed and transformed by his dream travels through the next world. His adventures begin on the night of Holy Thursday and end on Easter Sunday, and they take place in the year 1300, when Dante was thirty-five, or halfway through his biblically assigned lifespan of seventy years (Psalms 90:10—but Dante wound up dying at around fifty-six). At this crucial juncture, the morally confused and "lost" Dante is assailed by lethal danger in the forms of three allegorical beasts: a leopard, a lion, and a she-wolf (generally taken to symbolize lust, pride, and greed, respectively). He cries for help from a ghostly figure, who turns out to be Virgil (70–19 B.C.E.), the great Roman epic poet, Dante's supreme artistic model, and—for medieval Christians generally and Dante specifically—the epitome of goodness in the natural realm. Medieval writers also thought of Virgil as a magician, and his Fourth Eclogue was believed to prophesy the birth of Christ. Virgil serves as Dante's guide as far as the Earthly Paradise atop Mount Purgatory, into which, as an unbaptized pagan, he cannot go.

In Canto III, Virgil and Dante encounter the famous inscription on the gates of Hell. Just as Dante's Hell is a vile caricature of Heaven, the three tercets of this inscription are a parody of the Trinity. The "Power," "Wisdom," and "Love" that built Hell are coded language for the Father, Son, and Holy Spirit, since the name of God cannot be pronounced in Hell. The first denizens whom Virgil and Dante meet in Satan's kingdom are a group traditionally called the Trimmers: morally uncommitted persons and the angels who remained neutral in the epoch-making heavenly battle between the good and evil spirits. They lived without infamy or praise, and now they receive only Virgil's and Dante's silence.

In the final canto of *Paradiso*, Saint Bernard of Clairvaux (see p. 306) prays aloud. A leading promoter of the Marian cult (see "Medieval Latin Hymnody," p. 328), Bernard intones a hymn to the Virgin, calling her *figlia del tuo figlio*, "daughter of your son," since Jesus was both (as God) her father and (as man) her son. Like many other medieval writers, Dante treats Mary as an all-but-divine queen. Encouraged by Bernard, Dante follows the glance of the Virgin toward God.

Dante emphasizes the incommunicable nature of this beatific vision. It is a "Living Radiance," three circles of light that are yet one light (the Trinity). He fixes his eyes on the "second aureole," which is God the Son, "painted with man's image" (because of the Incarnation). He falls silent in ecstasy, and the poem concludes.

PRONOUNCING GLOSSARY

Alighieri: *ah-lih-gyehr´-ee*   Mantuans: *man´-too-uhns*
Beatrice: *bay-ah-tree´-chay*   Sibyl: *si´-buhl*
Lombardy: *lom´-buhr-dee*   *sub Julio: soob yoo´-lee-oh*

FROM INFERNO

From CANTO I

Midway on our life's journey, I found myself
  In dark woods, the right road lost. To tell
  About those woods is hard—so tangled and rough

And savage that thinking of it now, I feel
  The old fear stirring: death is hardly more bitter.   5
  And yet, to treat the good I found there as well

I'll tell what I saw, though how I came to enter
  I cannot well say, being so full of sleep
  Whatever moment it was I began to blunder

Off the true path. But when I came to stop   10
  Below a hill that marked one end of the valley
  That had pierced my heart with terror, I looked up

Toward the crest and saw its shoulders already
  Mantled in rays of that bright planet that shows
  The road to everyone, whatever our journey.   15

Then I could feel the terror begin to ease
  That churned in my heart's lake all through the night.
  As one still panting, ashore from dangerous seas,

Looks back at the deep he has escaped, my thought
  Returned, still fleeing, to regard that grim defile   20
  That never left any alive who stayed in it.

After I had rested my weary body awhile
  I started again across the wilderness,
  My left foot always lower on the hill,

And suddenly—a leopard, near the place   25
  The way grew steep: lithe, spotted, quick of foot.
  Blocking the path, she stayed before my face

And more than once she made me turn about
  To go back down. It was early morning still,
  The fair sun rising with the stars attending it   30

As when Divine Love set those beautiful
  Lights into motion at creation's dawn,
  And the time of day and season combined to fill

TRANSLATED BY Robert Pinsky.

My heart with hope of that beast with festive skin—
    But not so much that the next sight wasn't fearful: 35
    A lion came at me, his head high as he ran,

Roaring with hunger so the air appeared to tremble.
    Then, a grim she-wolf—whose leanness seemed to compress
    All the world's cravings, that had made miserable

Such multitudes; she put such heaviness   40
    Into my spirit, I lost hope of the crest.
    Like someone eager to win, who tested by loss

Surrenders to gloom and weeps, so did that beast
    Make me feel, as harrying toward me at a lope
    She forced me back toward where the sun is lost.   45

While I was ruining myself back down to the deep,
    Someone appeared—one who seemed nearly to fade
    As though from long silence. I cried to his human shape

In that great wasteland: "Living man or shade,
    Have pity and help me, whichever you may be!"   50
    "No living man, though once I was," he replied.

"My parents both were Mantuans from Lombardy,
    And I was born *sub Julio*, the latter end.
    I lived in good Augustus's Rome,[1] in the day

Of the false gods who lied. A poet, I hymned   55
    Anchises' noble son, who came from Troy
    When superb Ilium in its pride was burned.[2]

But you—why go back down to such misery?
    Why not ascend the delightful mountain, source
    And principle that causes every joy?"   60

"Then are you Virgil? Are you the font that pours
    So overwhelming a river of human speech?"
    I answered, shamefaced. "The glory and light are yours,

That poets follow—may the love that made me search
    Your book in patient study avail me, Master!   65
    You are my guide and author, whose verses teach

The graceful style whose model has done me honor.
    See this beast driving me backward—help me resist,
    For she makes all my veins and pulses shudder."

---

1. During the reign of Augustus (63 B.C.E.–14 C.E.), the 1st Roman emperor (from 27 B.C.E. until his death). "Mantuans from Lombardy": hailing from the capital of the region of Lombardy, in what is now Italy. "*Sub Julio*": during the reign of Julius Caesar (100–44 B.C.E.), Roman general and statesman.

2. In Virgil's epic poem *Aeneid*, the hero Aeneas escapes (with his son and with his father, Anchises) from his home city, Troy (in Latin, *Ilium*), after it is burned by Greek warriors.

"A different path from this one would be best 70
   For you to find your way from this feral place,"
   He answered, seeing how I wept. "This beast,

The cause of your complaint, lets no one pass
   Her way—but harries all to death. Her nature
   Is so malign and vicious she cannot appease 75

Her voracity, for feeding makes her hungrier.

* * *

Therefore I judge it best that you should choose
   To follow me, and I will be your guide
   Away from here and through an eternal place: 90

To hear the cries of despair, and to behold
   Ancient tormented spirits as they lament
   In chorus the second death they must abide.

Then you shall see those souls who are content
   To dwell in fire because they hope some day 95
   To join the blessed: toward whom, if your ascent

Continues, your guide will be one worthier than I—
   When I must leave you, you will be with her.
   For the Emperor who governs from on high

Wills I not enter His city, where none may appear 100
   Who lived like me in rebellion to His law.
   His empire is everything and everywhere,

But that is His kingdom, His city, His seat of awe.
   Happy is the soul He chooses for that place!"
   I: "Poet, please—by the God you did not know— 105

Help me escape this evil that I face,
   And worse. Lead me to witness what you have said,
   Saint Peter's gate,[3] and the multitude of woes—"

Then he set out, and I followed where he led.

From CANTO III

THROUGH ME YOU ENTER INTO THE CITY OF WOES,
THROUGH ME YOU ENTER INTO ETERNAL PAIN,
THROUGH ME YOU ENTER THE POPULATION OF LOSS.

JUSTICE MOVED MY HIGH MAKER, IN POWER DIVINE,
WISDOM SUPREME, LOVE PRIMAL. NO THINGS WERE 5
BEFORE ME NOT ETERNAL; ETERNAL I REMAIN.

3. The entrance to Heaven.

ABANDON ALL HOPE, YOU WHO ENTER HERE.
   These words I saw inscribed in some dark color
   Over a portal. "Master," I said, "make clear

Their meaning, which I find too hard to gather."   10
   Then he, as one who understands: "All fear
   Must be left here, and cowardice die. Together,

We have arrived where I have told you: here
   You will behold the wretched souls who've lost
   The good of intellect." Then, with good cheer   15

In his expression to encourage me, he placed
   His hand on mine: so, trusting to my guide,
   I followed him among things undisclosed.

The sighs, groans and laments at first were so loud,
   Resounding through starless air, I began to weep: 20
   Strange languages, horrible screams, words imbued

With rage or despair, cries as of troubled sleep
   Or of a tortured shrillness—they rose in a coil
   Of tumult, along with noises like the slap

Of beating hands, all fused in a ceaseless flail   25
   That churns and frenzies that dark and timeless air
   Like sand in a whirlwind. And I, my head in a swirl

Of error, cried: "Master, what is this I hear?
   What people are these, whom pain has overcome?"
   He: "This is the sorrowful state of souls unsure,   30

Whose lives earned neither honor nor bad fame.
   And they are mingled with angels of that base sort
   Who, neither rebellious to God nor faithful to Him,

Chose neither side, but kept themselves apart—
   Now Heaven expels them, not to mar its splendor,   35
   And Hell rejects them, lest the wicked of heart

Take glory over them." And then I: "Master,
   What agony is it, that makes them keen their grief
   With so much force?" He: "I will make brief answer:

They have no hope of death, but a blind life   40
   So abject, they envy any other fate.
   To all memory of them, the world is deaf.

Mercy and justice disdain them. Let us not
   Speak of them: look and pass on." * * *

FROM PARADISO

CANTO XXXIII

"Virgin Mother, daughter of thy son;
   humble beyond all creatures and more exalted;
   predestined turning point of God's intention;

thy merit so ennobled human nature
   that its divine Creator did not scorn   5
   to make Himself the creature of His creature.

The Love that was rekindled in Thy womb
   sends forth the warmth of the eternal peace
   within whose ray this flower has come to bloom.

Here, to us, thou art the noon and scope   10
   of Love revealed; and among mortal men,
   the living fountain of eternal hope.

Lady, thou art so near God's reckonings
   that who seeks grace and does not first seek thee
   would have his wish fly upward without wings.   15

Not only does thy sweet benignity
   flow out to all who beg, but oftentimes
   thy charity arrives before the plea.

In thee is pity, in thee munificence,
   in thee the tenderest heart, in thee unites   20
   all that creation knows of excellence!

Now comes this man who from the final pit
   of the universe up to this height has seen,
   one by one, the three lives of the spirit.

He prays to thee in fervent supplication   25
   for grace and strength, that he may raise his eyes
   to the all-healing final revelation.

And I, who never more desired to see
   the vision myself than I do that he may see It,
   add my own prayer, and pray that it may be   30

enough to move you to dispel the trace
   of every mortal shadow by thy prayers
   and let him see revealed the Sum of Grace.

I pray thee further, all-persuading Queen,
   keep whole the natural bent of his affections   35
   and of his powers after his eyes have seen.

TRANSLATED BY John Ciardi.

CHRISTIANITY

Hagia Sophia mosaic, Istanbul, Turkey, 6th–9th century

The place of the empire in the emergent Orthodox Church is well illustrated in this mosaic. Mary sits enthroned as an empress with the infant Jesus seated on her lap as a prince. Reflecting Orthodox doctrine, the two medallions flanking her head include Greek abbreviations for "Mother" and "of God." To her left, Emperor Constantine (d. 337) holds a model of Constantinople. To her right, Emperor Justinian (d. 565) holds a model of the Basilica of Hagia Sophia ("holy wisdom" in Greek). © GAVIN HELLIER / ROBERT HARDING WORLD IMAGERY / CORBIS

Detail from the Crucifixion (above) and Resurrection (right), from the Isenheim Altarpiece, Matthias Grünewald, ca. 1515

No artist has captured Jesus' abject humiliation and glorious triumph more compellingly than the German painter Matthias Grünewald (ca. 1455–1528). Grünewald painted with the virtuosity of the Renaissance but with a Catholic sensibility beholden to the Middle Ages. He lived into the first decade of the Protestant Reformation and is honored as a saint by the Lutheran Church.

Saint Peter's Basilica, the Vatican, begun 1506, completed 1626

In the interior view shown here, TV ES PETRUS, Latin for "Thou art Peter," can be seen in the golden frieze at upper right. These words begin the Gospel passage (Matthew 16:18) that continues "and upon this rock I will build my church." For the papacy, Roman Catholicism claimed an authority older than the New Testament—namely, the "apostolic succession," reaching back to when Peter and the other Apostles took instruction from Jesus.

ERICH LESSING / ART RESOURCE, NY / © ARTRES

Madonna of the Book, Sandro Botticelli, ca. 1479

In the *Madonna of the Book*, the Italian Renaissance master Sandro Botticelli (1445–1510) presents Jesus' suffering on the cross—a motif absent from earliest Christian art but dominant during the Middle Ages—by suggestion: A delicate crown of thorns encircles the baby's left wrist, and he holds three tiny nails between finger and thumb. The thorns and nails suggest that the Bible—perhaps the most jarring feature in this tranquil vision—lies open to an Old Testament prophecy of the suffering and death that await. When Botticelli was painting, the Reformation lay just over the horizon. When it arrived, the Protestant Reformers would use the Bible to condemn many practices of the Renaissance Roman Catholic Church.

The Holy Communion of the Protestants and Ride to Hell of the Catholics, Lucas Cranach the Younger

In this woodcut, the great Lutheran artist Lucas Cranach the Younger (1515–1586) polemically depicts differences between Lutheranism and Catholicism. Before the Lutheran Communion table on the left, the pious receive the sacrament in the form of wine and bread (Catholics then received only bread). The pope ("Antichrist") presides over the Catholic altar on the right, which is piled with bags of money and flanked by a coffer, as a fat monk delivers a rooster for the pope's next banquet. In the pulpit to the left of the dividing pillar, Martin Luther preaches from the open Bible. In the pulpit to the right, a devil pumps poison into the ear of a laughing monk. KUPFERSTICHKABINETT, STAATLICHE MUSEEN, BERLIN, GERMANY / ART RESOURCE, NY

Head of Christ, Rembrandt van Rijn, late 1640s

The Dutch painter Rembrandt van Rijn (1606–1669)—possibly using a young Amsterdam Jew as model—depicted the head of Christ many times. The later popularity of one of these images in particular suggests that the introspective artist anticipated a change ahead. For in the eighteenth century, many Christians—Protestants and Catholics alike—turned their piety inward to the quiet memory of Jesus defined during his lifetime by his forgiving compassion.

JOERG P. ANDERS / ART RESOURCE, NY

The battle standard of Miguel Hidalgo, 1810

According to a Mexican legend of the mid-seventeenth century, the Blessed Virgin Mary, calling herself *Nuestra Señora de Guadalupe* ("Our Lady of Guadalupe"), had appeared during the sixteenth century before a humble Indian, Juan Diego. On Diego's *tilma*, or cloak, the Virgin had imprinted an image of herself with Indian features. In time, the miraculous image of Our Lady of Guadalupe came to be particularly cherished by the Indian (indigenous) and large *mestizo* (mixed) populations of Mexico. In the early nineteenth century, rallying this mixed population to the cause of independence from Spain, the ex-priest and revolutionary Miguel Hidalgo depicted the *Virgen de Guadalupe* on his battle banner.

THE GRANGER COLLECTION, NY

Saint Basil's Cathedral, Red Square, Moscow

Communist rule has had a large impact on contemporary Christianity. In particular, decades of oppressively institutionalized atheism in the Soviet Union have left their mark on Russian Orthodox Christianity. In 1929, Saint Basil's Cathedral was forcibly turned into a Russian state museum.

Protect him from the stirrings of man's clay;
 see how Beatrice and the blessed host
 clasp reverent hands to join me as I pray."

The eyes that God reveres and loves the best   40
 glowed on the speaker, making clear the joy
 with which true prayer is heard by the most blest.

Those eyes turned then to the Eternal Ray,
 through which, we must indeed believe, the eyes
 of others do not find such ready way.   45

And I, who neared the goal of all my nature,
 felt my soul, at the climax of its yearning,
 suddenly, as it ought, grow calm with rapture.

Bernard then, smiling sweetly, gestured to me
 to look up, but I had already become   50
 within myself all he would have me be.

Little by little as my vision grew
 it penetrated further through the aura
 of the high lamp which in Itself is true.

What then I saw is more than tongue can say.   55
 Our human speech is dark before the vision.
 The ravished memory swoons and falls away.

As one who sees in dreams and wakes to find
 the emotional impression of his vision
 still powerful while its parts fade from his mind—   60

just such am I, having lost nearly all
 the vision itself, while in my heart I feel
 the sweetness of it yet distill and fall.

So, in the sun, the footprints fade from snow.
 On the wild wind that bore the tumbling leaves   65
 the Sibyl's oracles[1] were scattered so.

O Light Supreme who doth Thyself withdraw
 so far above man's mortal understanding,
 lend me again some glimpse of what I saw;

make Thou my tongue so eloquent it may   70
 of all Thy glory speak a single clue
 to those who follow me in the world's day;

for by returning to my memory
 somewhat, and somewhat sounding in these verses,
 Thou shalt show man more of Thy victory.   75

---

1. Pagan prophecies.

So dazzling was the splendor of that Ray,
   that I must certainly have lost my senses
   had I, but for an instant, turned away.

And so it was, as I recall, I could
   the better bear to look, until at last   80
   my vision made one with the Eternal Good.

Oh grace abounding that had made me fit
   to fix my eyes on the eternal light
   until my vision was consumed in it!

I saw within Its depth how It conceives   85
   all things in a single volume bound by Love,
   of which the universe is the scattered leaves;

substance, accident, and their relation
   so fused that all I say could do no more
   than yield a glimpse of that bright revelation.   90

I think I saw the universal form
   that binds these things, for as I speak these words
   I feel my joy swell and my spirits warm.

Twenty-five centuries since Neptune saw
   the Argo's keel[2] have not moved all mankind,   95
   recalling that adventure, to such awe

as I felt in an instant. My tranced being
   stared fixed and motionless upon that vision,
   ever more fervent to see in the act of seeing.

Experiencing that Radiance, the spirit   100
   is so indrawn it is impossible
   even to think of ever turning from It.

For the good which is the will's ultimate object
   is all subsumed in It; and, being removed,
   all is defective which in It is perfect.   105

Now in my recollection of the rest
   I have less power to speak than any infant
   wetting its tongue yet at its mother's breast;

and not because that Living Radiance bore
   more than one semblance, for It is unchanging   110
   and is forever as it was before;

2. Since Neptune, the ancient Greek god of the sea, saw the Argo, the first sailing vessel able to hold fifty men.

rather, as I grew worthier to see,
    the more I looked, the more unchanging semblance
    appeared to change with every change in me

Within the depthless deep and clear existence   115
    of that abyss of light three circles shown—
    three in color, one in circumference:

the second from the first, rainbow from rainbow;
    the third, an exhalation of pure fire
    equally breathed forth by the other two.   120

But oh how much my words miss my conception,
    which is itself so far from what I saw
    that to call it feeble would be rank deception!

O Light Eternal fixed in Itself alone,
    by Itself alone understood, which from Itself   125
    loves and glows, self-knowing and self-known;

that second aureole which shone forth in Thee,
    conceived as a reflection of the first—
    or which appeared so to my scrutiny—

seemed in Itself of Its own coloration   130
    to be painted with man's image. I fixed my eyes
    on that alone in rapturous contemplation.

Like a geometer wholly dedicated
    to squaring the circle,[3] but who cannot find,
    think as he may, the principle indicated—   135

so did I study the supernal face.
    I yearned to know just how our image merges
    into that circle, and how it there finds place;

but mine were not the wings for such a flight.
    Yet, as I wished, the truth I wished for came   140
    cleaving my mind in a great flash of light.

Here my powers rest from their high fantasy,
    but already I could feel my being turned—
    instinct and intellect balanced equally

as in a wheel whose motion nothing jars—   145
by the Love that moves the Sun and the other stars.

---

3. The challenge, proposed by ancient geometers and since proven impossible, of constructing a square with the same areas as a given circle, in a limited number of steps, using only a compass and a straightedge.

MEISTER ECKHART
ca. 1260–1327

[SERMON 15: ON POVERTY OF SPIRIT]

We have only spotty knowledge about the life of Eckhart von Hochheim, who was born near Gotha, in Thuringia (part of central Germany). At age fifteen, he joined the Dominicans (see p. 310) at Erfurt, the capital of Thuringia. After completing his novitiate in 1280, Eckhart studied further at the famed Dominican house of study in Cologne. His German title, "Meister," refers to the master's degree in theology that he earned in Paris when he was about forty. He spent his life as a professor (in Paris, Strasbourg, Cologne, and possibly Frankfurt), but he also served as an administrator (prior and provincial) for the Dominicans. The extreme novelty of Eckhart's teachings and writings stirred suspicion, leading to charges of heresy by the archbishop of Cologne and a trial before the Inquisition in Venice (1327). Eckhart protested his innocence, but in 1329 he was excommunicated by Pope John XXII (pope from 1316 until his death, in 1334). By that time, he had vanished. He is thought to have died in Avignon, where the papacy was then located. Eckhart's work remained under a cloud of official disapproval, and much of it was unpublished until the late nineteenth century.

Eckhart's thought is hard to categorize. He belongs to a distinct minority of Christian theologians who concentrate on creation (divine goodness) rather than redemption (sin and forgiveness). He has been called a Neoplatonist because he stresses God as the source from which all being emanates and with which the individual can become spiritually united. In denying any ultimate distinction between God and the self, Eckhart may veer into pantheism (the universe is divine) or panentheism (roughly, nature is the body, and God is the soul), both of which defy Christian orthodoxy. While Eckhart's abstruse doctrine had limited popular appeal, it has influenced a diverse group of mystics, theologians, and philosophers, from his younger German Dominican colleagues to Martin Luther (see p. 399) to the current generation of Catholic intellectuals.

Eckhart's Sermon 15, delivered in German, must have puzzled its original audience. Indeed, he begins by warning of its difficulty and ends by suggesting that his listeners should not be troubled if they do not understand. It purports to be a meditation on a statement from Jesus' Sermon on the Mount (Matthew 5–7). But if, according to Matthew, Jesus praises detachment from material goods without demanding actual poverty, Eckhart carries detachment to a level never mentioned in the New Testament. After abruptly dismissing as "asses" all those who understand Matthew 5:3 as a call for ascetic renunciation, Eckhart treats the verse as a mystical formula for self-annihilation. In this radical sense of emptiness, the very act of striving for greater selflessness would be evidence of ongoing self-centeredness. Instead, Eckhart wants people to be as free of their "created will" as when they did not exist, that is, when they were still undifferentiated "parts" of God. In that imagined condition, Eckhart says, "I desired nothing, for I was a pure being and a knower of myself in delight of the truth. There I willed myself and nothing else." He says nothing specific about how to get back, while on Earth, to this blissful state of affairs. He boldly asserts, however, that all attempts to describe God go wrong because they all imply limitation: "God is neither being nor intelligent nor does he know this or that. Thus God is free of all things, and therefore he is all things."

[SERMON 15: ON POVERTY OF SPIRIT]

"Blessed are the poor in spirit, for theirs is
the kingdom of heaven." (Matthew 5:3)

Blessedness opened its mouth of wisdom and spoke: "Blessed are the poor in spirit, for theirs is the kingdom of heaven." Every angel and every saint and everything that was ever born must remain silent when the wisdom of the Father speaks; for all the wisdom of the angels and of all creatures is sheer nothingness before the groundless wisdom of God. And this wisdom has declared that the poor are blessed.

Now there exist two kinds of poverty: an *external* poverty, which is good and is praiseworthy in a person willing to take it upon himself or herself through the love of our Lord Jesus Christ, because he was himself poor on earth. Of this poverty I do not want to speak any further. For there is still another kind of poverty, an *inner* poverty, by which our Lord's word is to be understood when he says: "Blessed are the poor in spirit."

Now I beg you to be just so poor as to understand this speech. For I tell you by the eternal truth, if you are not equal to this truth of which we now want to speak, then you cannot understand me.

Various people have questioned me about what poverty is in itself and what a poor person is. That is what we want to answer.

Bishop Albrecht[1] says that a poor person is one who takes no satisfaction in any of the things that God ever created—and that is well said. But we say it better still and take poverty in a yet higher understanding: he is a poor person who wills nothing and knows nothing and has nothing. Of these three points we are going to speak and I beseech you for the love of God that you understand this truth if you can. But if you do not understand it, do not worry yourselves because of it, for the truth I want to talk about is of such a kind that only a few good people will understand it.

First, we say that one is a poor person who wills nothing. What this means, many people do not correctly understand. These are the people who in penitential exercise and external practices, of which they make a great deal, cling to their selfish I. The Lord have pity upon such people who know so little of the divine truth! Such people are called holy on account of external appearance, but inwardly they are asses, for they do not grasp the real meaning of divine truth. Indeed, these individuals too say that one is a poor person who wills nothing. However, they interpret this to mean that one should so live as to never fulfill one's own will in any way, but rather strive to fulfill the ever-beloved will of God. These people are right in their way, for their intention is good and for that we want to praise them. May God in his mercy grant them the kingdom of heaven. But in all divine truth, I say that these people are not poor people, nor do they resemble poor people. They are highly considered only in the eyes of those who know no better. I, however, say that they are asses who understand nothing of divine truth. Because of their good intentions,

TRANSLATED BY Matthew Fox. The bracketed insertions are the translator's.

1. Or Albertus Magnus (ca. 1200–1280), founder of the Dominican house of study in Cologne. He and Eckhart seem to have met upon Eckhart's arrival, but the bishop died that year, so Eckhart would have been taught by some of his disciples.

they may receive the kingdom of heaven. But of that poverty of which I now want to speak, they know nothing.

These days, if someone asks me what a poor person is who wills nothing, I answer and say: So long as a person has his own wish in him to fulfill even the ever-beloved will of God, if that is still a matter of his will, then this person does not yet possess the poverty of which we want to speak. Indeed, this person then still has a will with which he or she wants to satisfy God's will, and that is not the right poverty. For a human being to possess true poverty, he or she must be as free of his or her created will as they were when they did not yet exist. Thus I say to you in the name of divine truth, as long as you have the will, even the will to fulfill God's will, and as long as you have the desire for eternity and for God, to this very extent you are not properly poor, for the only one who is a poor person is one who wills nothing and desires nothing.

When I still stood in my first cause, there I had no God and was cause of myself. There I willed nothing, I desired nothing, for I was a pure being and a knower of myself in delight of the truth. There I willed myself and nothing else. What I willed, that I was; and what I was, that I willed. There I stood, free of God and of all things. But when I took leave from this state of free will and received my created being, then I had a God. Indeed, before creatures were, God was not yet "God"; rather, he was what he was. But when creatures came to be and when they received their created being, then God was no longer "God" in himself; rather, he was "God" in the creatures.

Now we say that God, insofar as he is "God," is not a perfect goal for creatures. Indeed, even the lowliest creature *in* God possesses as high a rank. And if a fly possessed reason and could consciously seek the eternal abyss of divine being out of which it has come, then we would say that God, with all he is as God would still be incapable of fulfilling and satisfying this fly. Therefore we pray God to rid us of "God" so that we may grasp and eternally enjoy the truth where the highest angel and the fly and the soul are equal. There is where I stood and willed what I was, and I was what I willed. So then we say, if people are to be poor in will, they must will and desire as little as they willed and desired when they were not yet. And in this way is a person poor who wills nothing.

Second, a poor person is one who knows nothing. We have said on other occasions that a person should live a life neither for himself, nor for the truth, nor for God. But now we say it differently and want to go further and say: Whoever achieves this poverty must so live that they not even know themselves to live, either for oneself or for truth or for God. One must be so free of all knowledge that he or she does not know or recognize or perceive that God lives in him or her; even more, one should be free of all knowledge that lives in him or her. For, when people still stood in God's eternal being, nothing else lived in them. What lived there was themselves. Hence we say that people should be as free of their own knowledge as when they were not yet, letting God accomplish whatever God wills. People should stand empty.

Everything that ever came out of God once stood in pure activity. But the activity proper to people is to love and to know. It is a moot question, though, in which of these happiness primarily consists. Some authorities have said that it lies in knowing, some say it lies in loving, still others say that it lies in knowing and in loving. These are closer to the truth. We say, however, that it lies neither in knowing nor in loving. Rather, there is a something in the soul from which knowing and loving flow. It does not itself know and love as do the forces of the soul. Whoever comes to know this something knows what happiness consists in. It has neither before nor after, and it is in need of nothing additional, for it can neither gain nor lose. For this very reason it is deprived of understanding that God is acting within it. Moreover, it is that identical self which enjoys itself just as God does. Thus we say that people shall keep themselves free and void so that they neither understand nor know that God works in them. Only thus can people possess poverty. The masters say that God is a being, an intelligent being, and that he knows all things. We say, however: God is neither being nor intelligent nor does he know this or that. Thus God is free of all things, and therefore he is all things. Whoever is to be poor in spirit, then, must be poor of all his own understanding so that he knows nothing about God or creatures or himself. Therefore it is necessary that people desire not to understand or know anything at all of the works of God. In this way is a person able to be poor of one's own understanding.

Third, one is a poor person who has nothing. Many people have said that perfection consists in people possessing none of the material things of the earth. And indeed, that is certainly true in one sense: when one holds to it intentionally. But this is not the sense that I mean.

I have said before that one is a poor person who does not even will to fulfill God's will, that is, who so lives that he or she is empty both of his own will and of God's will, just as they were when they were not yet. About this poverty we say that it is the highest poverty. Second, we have said one is a poor person who himself understands nothing of God's activity in him or her. When one stands as free of understanding and knowing [as God stands void of all things], then that is the purest poverty. But the third kind of poverty of which we are now going to speak is the most difficult: that people have nothing.

Now give me your undivided attention. I have often said, and great masters say this too: People must be so empty of all things and all works, whether inward or outward, that they can become a proper home for God, wherein God may operate. But now we say it differently. If people stand free of all things, of all creatures, of God and of themselves, but if it still happens that God can find a place for acting in them, then we say: So long as that is so, these persons are not poor in the strictest poverty. For God does not desire that people reserve a place for him to work in. Rather, true poverty of spirit consists in keeping oneself so free of God and of all one's works that if God wants to act in the soul, God himself becomes the place wherein he wants to act—and this God likes to do. For when God finds a person as poor as this, God operates his own work and a person sustains God in him, and God is himself the place of his operation, since God is an agent who acts within himself. Here, in this poverty, people attain the eternal being that they once were, now are, and will eternally remain.

*　*　*

If anyone cannot understand this discourse, let them not trouble their hearts about it. For, as long as people do not equal this truth, they will not understand this speech. For this is an unveiled truth that has come immediately from the heart of God.

That we may so live as to experience it eternally, so help us God. Amen.

ANONYMOUS
late fifteenth century

FROM THE SUMMONING OF EVERYMAN

The Summoning of Everyman is either an English translation of a Dutch original (*Elckerlijc*) or the English original of a Dutch translation. This drama is the best-known example of a morality play, a popular allegory designed to teach a straightforward Christian lesson in how to live. According to the lesson, we are all doomed to die, and when we come to the grave's edge, any wealth or strength or beauty or intellectual gifts, any friends or relations or talents we may have acquired, are guaranteed to abandon us. The only thing dying persons can count on are their good deeds and the knowledge that they need to confess their sins and be absolved in the sacrament of confession. With the character of Good Deeds at his side, Everyman descends to his death, where he joins Jesus.

The theme of an ordinary person encountering the ultimate "moment of truth" has enjoyed continuous popularity. In 1911, the Austrian poet Hugo von Hofmannsthal adapted the play into German, and since 1920 it has been performed every year at the Salzburg Festival. The Swedish filmmaker Ingmar Bergman borrowed from it for his movie *The Seventh Seal* (1957), and the American novelist Philip Roth (born 1933) incorporated it into his novel *Everyman* (2006).

FROM THE SUMMONING OF EVERYMAN

[*Enter*] DEATH.

DEATH
　Almighty God, I am here at your will,
　Your commandment to fulfil.　　　　　　　　　　65
GOD
　Go thou to Everyman
　And show him, in my name,
　A pilgrimage he must on him take,
　Which he in no wise may escape,
　And that he bring with him a sure reckoning　　70
　Without delay or any tarrying.
DEATH
　Lord, I will in the world go run over all
　And truly outsearch both great and small.
　Every man will I beset that liveth beastly,

FROM *Everyman and Mankind*, eds. Douglas Bruster and Eric Rasmussen. Bracketed insertions are the original editors'.

Out of God's laws, and dreadeth not folly.   75
He that loveth richesse I will strike with my dart,
His sight to blind, and from heaven to depart—
Except that alms be his good friend—
In hell for to dwell, world without end.   [*Exit God.*]
Lo, yonder I see Everyman walking.   80
Full little he thinketh on my coming.
His mind is on fleshly lusts and his treasure,
And great pain it shall cause him to endure
Before the Lord heaven king.—
Everyman, stand still! Whither art thou going   85
Thus gaily? Hast thou thy maker forget?

                    [*Enter*] EVERYMAN.

EVERYMAN
    Why askest thou?
    Wouldst thou wit?[1]
DEATH
    Yea, sir, I will show you.
    In great haste I am sent to thee   90
    From God, out of his majesty.
EVERYMAN
    What? Sent to me?
DEATH
    Yea, certainly.
    Though thou have forgot Him here,
    He thinketh on thee in the heavenly sphere,   95
    As, ere we depart, thou shalt know.
EVERYMAN
    What desireth God of me?
DEATH
    That shall I show thee:
    A reckoning he will needs have,
    Without any longer respite.   100
EVERYMAN
    To give a reckoning longer leisure I crave;
    This blind matter troubleth my wit.[2]
DEATH
    On thee thou must take a long journey.
    Therefore thy book of count with thee thou bring,
    For turn again thou cannot by no way.   105
    And look thou be sure of thy reckoning,[3]
    For before God thou shalt answer and show
    Thy many bad deeds and good but a few,
    How thou hast spent thy life and in what wise,
    Before the chief Lord of paradise.   110
    Have ado that we were in that way,
    For, wit thou well, thou shalt make none attorney.[4]

---

1. Would you know the answer?
2. Mind.
3. On God's reckoning of each individual's spiritual ledger, see p. 144.

4. "Have . . . attorney": Bestir yourself so we can get moving, because, understand well, you will not be able to appoint a representative.

EVERYMAN

Full unready I am such reckoning to give.
I know thee not. What messenger art thou?

DEATH

I am Death, that no man dreadeth,[5]   115
For every man I 'rest,[6] and no man spareth,
For it is God's commandment
That all to me should be obedient.

EVERYMAN

O Death, thou comest when I had thee least in mind!
In thy power it lieth me to save;   120
Yet of my good will I give[7] thee if thou will be kind—
Yea, a thousand pound shalt thou have—
And defer this matter till another day.

DEATH

Everyman, it may not be, by no way.
I set not by gold, silver nor richesse,   125
Ne by pope, emperor, king, duke ne princes;
For, an[8] I would receive gifts great,
All the world I might get,
But my custom is clean contrary:
I give thee no respite. Come hence and not tarry.   130

EVERYMAN

Alas! Shall I have no longer respite?
I may say Death giveth no warning!
To think on thee it maketh my heart sick,
For all unready is my book of reckoning.
But twelve year and I might have abiding,[9]   135
My counting book I would make so clear
That my reckoning I should not need to fear.
Wherefore Death, I pray thee, for God's mercy,
Spare me till I be provided of remedy.

DEATH

Thee availeth not to cry, weep and pray,   140
But haste thee lightly that thou were gone that journey,[1]
And prove thy friends if thou can;
For, wit thou well, the tide abideth no man,
And in the world each living creature
For Adam's sin must die of nature.[2]   145

EVERYMAN

Death, if I should this pilgrimage take
And my reckoning surely make,
Show me, for saint charity,
Should I not come again[3] shortly?

DEATH

No, Everyman: an thou be once there,   150
Thou mayst never more come here,
Trust me verily.

---

5. That fears no man.
6. Arrest.
7. Either "out of my good will I will give" or "of my goods I will give."
8. If.

9. But if I could have a delay of twelve years.
1. But go quickly on your way.
2. By its nature; on "Adam's sin," see p. 83.
3. Return. "Saint charity": out of charitable compassion.

EVERYMAN

> O gracious God in the high seat celestial,
> Have mercy on me in this most need![4]
> Shall I have no company from this vale terrestrial   155
> Of mine acquaintance that way me to lead?

DEATH

> Yea, if any be so hardy
> That would go with thee and bear thee company.
> Hie thee that thou were gone to God's magnificence,
> Thy reckoning to give before his presence.   160
> What, weenest thou thy life is given thee,
> And thy worldly goods also?

EVERYMAN

> I had weened so, verily.

DEATH

> Nay, nay, it was but lent thee;
> For as soon as thou art go,   165
> Another a while shall have it and then go therefro,
> Even as thou hast done.
> Everyman, thou art mad. Thou hast thy wits[5] five
> And here on earth will not amend thy life;
> For suddenly I do come.   170

EVERYMAN

> O wretched caitiff,[6] whither shall I flee,
> That I might scape this endless sorrow?
> Now, gentle Death, spare me till tomorrow,
> That I may amend me
> With good advisement.   175

DEATH

> Nay, thereto I will not consent,
> Nor no man will I respite;
> But to the heart suddenly I shall smite
> Without any advisement.
> And now out of thy sight I will me hie.   180
> See thou make thee ready shortly,
> For thou mayst say this is the day
> That no man living may scape away.   [*Exit.*]

---

4. I.e., in my hour of greatest need!
5. Senses.

6. Everyman is addressing himself.

SAINT CATHERINE OF SIENA
1347–1380

FROM THE DIALOGUE

The woman known as Saint Catherine was born Caterina Benincasa in Siena, Italy, and died in Rome. She was a mystic, reformer, spiritual advisor, tertiary (member of a monastic third order) of the Dominican Order, scholastic philosopher, and theologian. Fearlessly outspoken, she worked to bring the papacy of Gregory XI (pope from 1370 until his death, in 1378) from exile in Avignon, France, to then strife-torn Rome. She also worked to establish peace among the Italian city-states and between them and the papacy. She is venerated in the Roman Catholic and Lutheran Churches and the Anglican Communion; and she is, along with Saint Francis of Assisi (see p. 311), one of Italy's two patron saints. In 1970, she was proclaimed a Doctor (from the Latin for "Teacher") of the Roman Catholic Church. This title recognizes individuals as having been of major importance to the Church, particularly in contributing to theology or doctrine.

Because Catherine dictated all of her writing, she is often assumed to have been illiterate or barely literate. She may have been able to read Latin and Italian, however. Over 300 of her letters have survived—including personal letters to the pope—and as a body they are considered one of the great works of early Tuscan literature. In addition to the letters, she wrote twenty-six prayers and the *Dialogue* (1377–78). This four-treatise work is a dialogue between God and a soul that is rising up to God. In the prologue, the first of the following two selections, Catherine provides personal reflections, which she dictated to her confessor and friend, the Dominican friar Raymond of Capua. While she uses the first person ("I remember"), she also refers to herself in the third person ("a certain servant of God"). In "The Bridge," the second selection, she describes the Christian life through a rather original metaphor.

FROM THE DIALOGUE
Prologue

IN THE NAME OF CHRIST CRUCIFIED AND OF GENTLE MARY

1

A soul rises up, restless with tremendous desire for God's honor and the salvation of souls. She has for some time exercised herself in virtue and has become accustomed to dwelling in the cell of self-knowledge in order to know better God's goodness toward her, since upon knowledge follows love. And loving, she seeks to pursue truth and clothe herself in it.

But there is no way she can so savor and be enlightened by this truth as in continual humble prayer, grounded in the knowledge of herself and of God. For by such prayer the soul is united with God, following in the footsteps of Christ crucified, and through desire and affection and the union of

TRANSLATED BY Suzanne Noffke.

In *The Mystic Marriage of Catherine of Siena* (c. 1490), by Ambrogio Bergognone, Catherine (right) holds the hand of the Virgin Mary. The depiction of Christ as a little boy and of Catherine holding a lily, symbolizing virginity, signals the spiritual nature of the marriage.

love he makes of her another himself. So Christ seems to have meant when he said, "If you will love me and keep my word, I will show myself to you, and you will be one thing with me and I with you."[1] And we find similar words in other places from which we can see it is the truth that by love's affection the soul becomes another himself.

✻   ✻   ✻

The Bridge

26

Then God eternal, to stir up even more that soul's love for the salvation of souls, responded to her:

Before I show you what I want to show you, and what you asked to see, I want to describe the bridge for you. I have told you that it stretches from heaven to earth by reason of my having joined myself with your humanity, which I formed from the earth's clay.

This bridge, my only-begotten Son, has three stairs. Two of them he built on the wood of the most holy cross, and the third even as he tasted the great bitterness of the gall and vinegar they gave him to drink. You will recognize in these three stairs three spiritual stages.

The first stair is the feet, which symbolize the affections. For just as the feet carry the body, the affections carry the soul. My Son's nailed feet are a stair by which you can climb to his side, where you will see revealed his inmost heart. For when the soul has climbed up on the feet of affection and looked with her mind's eye into my Son's opened heart, she begins to feel the love of her own heart in his consummate and unspeakable love. (I say consummate because it is not for his own good that he loves you; you cannot do him any good, since he is one with me.) Then the soul, seeing how tremendously she is loved, is herself filled to overflowing with love. So,

---

1. See John 14:21–23.

having climbed the second stair, she reaches the third. This is his mouth, where she finds peace from the terrible war she has had to wage because of her sins.

At the first stair, lifting the feet of her affections from the earth, she stripped herself of sin. At the second she dressed herself in love for virtue. And at the third she tasted peace.

So the bridge has three stairs, and you can reach the last by climbing the first two. The last stair is so high that the flooding waters cannot strike it— for the venom of sin never touched my Son.[1]

But though this bridge has been raised so high, it still is joined to the earth. Do you know when it was raised up? When my Son was lifted up on the wood of the most holy cross he did not cut off his divinity from the lowly earth of your humanity. So though he was raised so high he was not raised off the earth. In fact, his divinity is kneaded into the clay of your humanity like one bread. Nor could anyone walk on that bridge until my Son was raised up. This is why he said, "If I am lifted up high I will draw everything to myself."[2]

When my goodness saw that you could be drawn in no other way, I sent him to be lifted onto the wood of the cross. I made of that cross an anvil where this child of humankind could be hammered into an instrument to release humankind from death and restore it to the life of grace. In this way he drew everything to himself: for he proved his unspeakable love, and the human heart is always drawn by love. He could not have shown you greater love than by giving his life for you.[3] You can hardly resist being drawn by love, then, unless you foolishly refuse to be drawn.

I said that, having been raised up, he would draw everything to himself. This is true in two ways: First, the human heart is drawn by love, as I said, and with all its powers: memory, understanding, and will. If these three powers are harmoniously united in my name, everything else you do, in fact or in intention, will be drawn to union with me in peace through the movement of love, because all will be lifted up in the pursuit of crucified love. So my Truth indeed spoke truly when he said, "If I am lifted up high, I will draw everything to myself." For everything you do will be drawn to him when he draws your heart and its powers.

What he said is true also in the sense that everything was created for your use, to serve your needs. But you who have the gift of reason were made not for yourselves but for me, to serve me with all your heart and all your love. So when you are drawn to me, everything is drawn with you, because everything was made for you.

It was necessary, then, that this bridge be raised high. And it had to have stairs so that you would be able to mount it more easily.

1. See Hebrews 4:15.
2. See John 12:32.

3. See John 15:13.

27

This bridge has walls of stone so that travelers will not be hindered when it rains. Do you know what stones these are? They are the stones of true solid virtue. These stones were not, however, built into walls before my Son's passion. So no one could get to the final destination, even though they walked along the pathway of virtue. For heaven had not yet been unlocked with the key of my Son's blood, and the rain of justice kept anyone from crossing over.

But after these stones were hewn on the body of the Word, my gentle Son[4] (I have told you that he is the bridge), he built them into walls, tempering the mortar with his own blood. That is, his blood was mixed into the mortar of his divinity with the strong heat of burning love.

By my power the stones of virtue were built into walls on no less a foundation than himself, for all virtue draws life from him, nor is there any virtue that has not been tested in him. So no one can have any life-giving virtue but from him, that is, by following his example and his teaching. He perfected the virtues and planted them as living stones built into walls with his blood. So now all the faithful can walk without hindrance and with no cringing fear of the rain of divine justice, because they are sheltered by the mercy that came down from heaven through the incarnation of this Son of mine.

And how was heaven opened? With the key of his blood. So, you see, the bridge has walls and a roof of mercy. And the hostelry of holy Church is there to serve the bread of life and the blood, lest the journeying pilgrims, my creatures, grow weary and faint on the way. So has my love ordained that the blood and body of my only-begotten Son, wholly God and wholly human, be administered.

At the end of the bridge is the gate (which is, in fact, one with the bridge), which is the only way you can enter. This is why he said, "I am the Way and Truth and Life; whoever walks with me walks not in darkness but in light."[5] And in another place my Truth said that no one could come to me except through him,[6] and such is the truth.

I explained all this to you, you will recall, because I wanted to let you see the way. So when he says that he is the Way he is speaking the truth. And I have already shown you that he is the Way, in the image of a bridge. He says he is Truth, and so he is, and whoever follows him goes the way of truth. And he is Life. If you follow this truth you will have the life of grace and never die of hunger, for the Word has himself become your food. Nor will you ever fall into darkness, for he is the light undimmed by any falsehood. Indeed, with his truth he confounds and destroys the lie with which the devil deceived Eve.[7] That lie broke up the road to heaven, but Truth repaired it and walled it up with his blood.

Those who follow this way are children of the truth because they follow the truth. They pass through the gate of truth and find themselves in me. And I am one with the gate and the way that is my Son, eternal Truth, a sea of peace.

4. See 1 Corinthians 3:11.
5. See John 14:6, 8:12.

6. See John 14:6.
7. See the discussion of Eve on p. 83.

But those who do not keep to this way travel below through the river—a way not of stones but of water. And since there is no restraining the water, no one can cross through it without drowning.

Such are the pleasures and conditions of the world. Those whose love and desire are not grounded on the rock but are set without order on created persons and things apart from me (and these, like water, are continually running on) run on just as they do. Though it seems to them that it is the created things they love that are running on by while they themselves remain firm, they are in fact continually running on to their end in death. They would like to preserve themselves (that is, their lives and the things they love) and not run away to nothingness. But they cannot. Either death makes them leave all behind, or by my decree these created things are taken away from them.

Such as these are following a lie by going the way of falsehood. They are children of the devil, who is the father of lies.[8] And because they pass through the gate of falsehood they are eternally damned.

28

So you see, I have shown you truth and falsehood, that is, my way, which is truth, and the devil's way, which is falsehood. These are the two ways, and both are difficult.

How foolish and blind are those who choose to cross through the water when the road has been built for them! This road is such a joy for those who travel on it that it makes every bitterness sweet for them, and every burden light.[9] Though they are in the darkness of the body they find light, and though they are mortal they find life without death. For through love and the light of faith they taste eternal Truth, with the promise of refreshment in return for the weariness they have borne for me. For I am grateful and sensitive. And I am just, giving each of you what you have earned: reward for good and punishment for sin.

Your tongue could never tell, nor your ears hear, nor your eyes see the joy they have who travel on this road,[1] for even in this life they have some foretaste of the good prepared for them in everlasting life.

They are fools indeed who scorn such a good and choose instead to taste even in this life the guarantee of hell by keeping to the way beneath the bridge. For there the going is most wearisome and there is neither refreshment nor any benefit at all, because by their sinfulness they have lost me, the supreme and eternal Good. So there is good reason—and it is my will— that you and my other servants should feel continual distress that I am so offended, as well as compassion for the harm that comes to those who so foolishly offend me.

Now you have heard and seen what this bridge is like. I have told you all this to explain what I meant when I said that my only-begotten Son is a bridge, as you see he is, joining the most high with the most lowly.

8. See John 8:44.
9. See Matthew 11:30.

1. See 1 Corinthians 2:9.

JULIAN OF NORWICH
1342–ca. 1416

FROM SHOWINGS

In the Late Middle Ages, prosperous churches sometimes supported women who lived in solitary seclusion on the church premises. Withdrawing from ordinary pursuits and devoting themselves to prayer and meditation, these women were called *anchoresses* or *anchorites*, from an ancient Greek word for "withdrawal." The best-known anchoress of the Late Middle Ages was an anonymous woman, known as Julian of Norwich because the Church of St. Julian, in Norwich, England, supported her. During her lifetime, Julian became well known throughout England as a mystic and spiritual authority. The mystic Margery Kempe (see p. 379), in her autobiography, mentions visiting Julian for spiritual advice.

In a narrative known variously as *Revelations of Divine Love*, *Revelations*, or *Showings*, Julian reports a series of intense visions she had of Jesus Christ and the Virgin Mary while she was suffering from a severe illness. Written very soon after Julian's visions, a shorter version of this narrative well expresses her early humility, touched with something approaching timidity, and so has its distinct appeal. The following selections include chapters 4 and 8 from *The Short Text*. Chapter 8 is striking for its counsel that God wants us to laugh and for its apparent, enormously optimistic assumption of universal salvation, all Satan's efforts to populate hell having proven vain. Fifteen or more years later, Julian produced a more pondered, more theological version known as *The Long Text*. In the following selections, chapters 58–60 are from this longer text. Chapter 60 highlights God's "courtesy," another theme in Julian.

Julian's *Long Text* is believed to be the first published book written in English by a woman. It is also among the most powerful Christian writings in English. Again exploring her visions, Julian records the deep intuitions she had in prayer, fearlessly using maternal imagery to describe God and Christ. She distinguishes three kinds of "revelations" or "showings": those she saw bodily, insights in her mind, and spiritual visions in her imagination. These distinctions were a commonplace derived from the biblical commentaries of Saint Augustine of Hippo (see p. 226). When the poet T. S. Eliot (see p. 574) based three lines of his poem *Little Gidding* (1942) on a quotation from Julian, he contributed to a distinct twentieth-century revival of interest in her. Eliot quoted from chapter 27 of *The Long Text*: "Sin is behovely [necessary], but all will be well, and all will be well, and all manner of thing will be well."

PRONOUNCING GLOSSARY

Norwich: *nor´-itch*

FROM SHOWINGS

THE FOURTH CHAPTER

And at the same time as I saw this corporeal sight,[1] our Lord showed me a spiritual sight of his familiar love. I saw that he is to us everything which is good and comforting for our help. He is our clothing, for he is that love which wraps and enfolds us, embraces us and guides us, surrounds us for his love, which is so tender that he may never desert us. And so in this sight I saw truly that he is everything which is good, as I understand.

And in this he showed me something small, no bigger than a hazelnut, lying in the palm of my hand, and I perceived that it was as round as any ball. I looked at it and thought: What can this be? And I was given this general answer: It is everything which is made. I was amazed that it could last, for I thought that it was so little that it could suddenly fall into nothing. And I was answered in my understanding: It lasts and always will, because God loves it; and thus everything has being through the love of God.

In this little thing I saw three properties. The first is that God made it, the second is that he loves it, the third is that God preserves it. But what is that to me? It is that God is the Creator and the lover and the protector. For until I am substantially united to him, I can never have love or rest or true happiness; until, that is, I am so attached to him that there can be no created thing between my God and me. And who will do this deed? Truly, he himself, by his mercy and his grace, for he has made me for this and has blessedly restored me.

In this God brought our Lady to my understanding. I saw her spiritually in her bodily likeness, a simple, humble maiden, young in years, of the stature which she had when she conceived. Also God showed me part of the wisdom and truth of her soul, and in this I understood the reverent contemplation with which she beheld her God, marvelling with great reverence that he was willing to be born of her who was a simple creature created by him. And this wisdom and truth, this knowledge of her creator's greatness and of her own created littleness, made her say meekly to the angel Gabriel: Behold me here, God's handmaiden.[2] In this sight I saw truly that she is greater, more worthy and more fulfilled, than everything else which God has created, and which is inferior to her. Above her is no created thing, except the blessed humanity of Christ. This little thing which is created and is inferior to our Lady, St. Mary—God showed it to me as if it had been a hazelnut—seemed to me as if it could have perished because it is so little.

In this blessed revelation God showed me three nothings, of which nothings this is the first that was shown to me. Every man and woman who wishes to live contemplatively needs to know of this, so that it may be pleasing to them to despise as nothing everything created, so as to have the love of uncreated God. For this is the reason why those who deliberately occupy themselves with earthly business, constantly seeking worldly well-being, have not God's rest in their hearts and souls; for they love and seek their

---

TRANSLATED BY Edmund Colledge and James Walsh.

1. Julian has experienced a vision of Jesus' grace: blood flowing from beneath the crown of thorns atop a crucifix.
2. See Luke 1:38.

rest in this thing which is so little and in which there is no rest, and do not know God who is almighty, all wise and all good, for he is true rest. God wishes to be known, and it pleases him that we should rest in him; for all things which are beneath him are not sufficient for us. And this is the reason why no soul has rest until it has despised as nothing all which is created. When the soul has become nothing for love, so as to have him who is all that is good, then is it able to receive spiritual rest.

THE EIGHTH CHAPTER

And after this I saw God in an instant of time, that is, in my understanding, and by this vision I saw that he is present in all things. I contemplated it carefully, knowing and perceiving through it that he does everything which is done. I marvelled at this vision with a gentle fear, and I thought: What is sin? For I saw truly that God does everything, however small it may be, and that nothing is done by chance, but it is of the endless providence of God's wisdom. Therefore I was compelled to admit that everything which is done is well done, and I was certain that God does no sin. Therefore it seemed to me that sin is nothing, for in all this sin was not shown to me. And I did not wish to go on feeling surprise at this, but I contemplated our Lord and waited for what he would show me. And on another occasion God did show me, nakedly in itself, what sin is, as I shall tell afterwards.

And after this as I watched I saw the body bleeding copiously, the blood hot, flowing freely, a living stream, just as I had before seen the head bleed. And I saw this in the furrows made by the scourging, and I saw this blood run so plentifully that it seemed to me that if it had in fact been happening there, the bed and everything around it would have been soaked in blood.

God has created bountiful waters on the earth for our use and our bodily comfort, out of the tender love he has for us. But it is more pleasing to him that we accept freely his blessed blood to wash us of our sins, for there is no drink that is made which it pleases him so well to give us; for it is so plentiful, and it is of our own nature.

And after this, before God revealed any words to me, he allowed me to contemplate longer all that I had seen and all that was contained in it. And then there was formed in my soul this saying, without voice and without opening of lips: With this the fiend is overcome. Our Lord said this to me with reference to his Passion, as he had shown it to me before; and in this he brought into my mind and showed me a part of the devil's malice and all of his impotence, and this by showing me that his Passion is the overcoming of the fiend. God showed me that he still has the same malice as he had before the Incarnation, and he works as hard, and he sees as constantly as he did before that all chosen souls escape him to God's glory. And in that is all the devil's sorrow; for everything which God permits him to do turns to joy for us and to pain and shame for him, and he has as much sorrow when God permits him to work as when he is not working. And that is because he can never do as much evil as he would wish, for his power is all locked in God's hands. Also I saw our Lord scorning his malice and despising him as nothing, and he wants us to do the same. Because of this sight I laughed greatly, and that made those around me to laugh as well; and their laughter was pleasing to me. I thought that I wished that all my fellow Christians had seen what I saw. Then they would all have laughed with me. But I did not see Christ laugh; nevertheless, it is pleasing to him that we laugh to comfort ourselves, and that we rejoice in God because the devil is overcome. And after that I became serious again, and said: I see. I see three things: sport and scorn and seriousness. I see sport, that the devil is overcome; and I see scorn, that God scorns him and he will be scorned; and I see seriousness, that he is overcome by the Passion of our Lord Jesus Christ and by his death, which was accomplished in great earnest and with heavy labour.

After this our Lord said: I thank you for your service and your labour, and especially in your youth.

✻ ✻ ✻

THE FIFTY-EIGHTH CHAPTER

God the blessed Trinity, who is everlasting being, just as he is eternal from without beginning, just so was it in his eternal purpose to create human nature, which fair nature was first prepared for his own Son, the second person; and when he wished, by full agreement of the whole Trinity he created us all once. And in our creating he joined and united us to himself, and through this union we are kept as pure and as noble as we were created. By the power of that same precious union we love our Creator and delight in him, praise him and thank him and endlessly rejoice in him. And this is the work which is constantly performed in every soul which will be saved, and this is the godly will mentioned before.

And so in our making, God almighty is our loving Father, and God all wisdom is our loving Mother, with the love and the goodness of the Holy Spirit, which is all one God, one Lord. And in the joining and the union he is our very true spouse and we his beloved wife and his fair maiden, with which wife he was never displeased; for he says: I love you and you love me, and our love will never divide in two.

I contemplated the work of all the blessed Trinity, in which contemplation I saw and understood these three properties: the property of the fatherhood, and the property of the motherhood, and the property of the lordship in one God. In our almighty Father we have our protection and our bliss, as regards our natural substance, which is ours by our creation from without beginning; and in the second person, in knowledge and wisdom we have our perfection, as regards our sensuality, our restoration and our salvation, for he is our Mother, brother and saviour; and in our good Lord the Holy Spirit we have our reward and our gift for our living and our labour, endlessly surpassing all that we desire in his marvellous courtesy, out of his great plentiful grace. For all our life consists of three: In the first we have our being, and in the second we have our increasing, and in the third we have our fulfillment. The first is nature, the second is mercy, the third is grace.

As to the first, I saw and understood that the high might of the Trinity is our Father, and the deep wisdom of the Trinity is our Mother, and the great love of the Trinity is our Lord; and all these we have in nature and in our substantial creation. And furthermore I saw that the second person, who is our Mother, substantially the same beloved person, has now become our mother sensually, because we are double by God's creating, that is to say substantial and sensual. Our substance is the higher part, which we have in our Father, God almighty;

and the second person of the Trinity is our Mother in nature in our substantial creation, in whom we are founded and rooted, and he is our Mother of mercy in taking our sensuality. And so our Mother is working on us in various ways, in whom our parts are kept undivided; for in our Mother Christ we profit and increase, and in mercy he reforms and restores us, and by the power of his Passion, his death and his Resurrection he unites us to our substance. So our Mother works in mercy on all his beloved children who are docile and obedient to him, and grace works with mercy, and especially in two properties, as it was shown, which working belongs to the third person, the Holy Spirit. He works, rewarding and giving. Rewarding is a gift for our confidence which the Lord makes to those who have laboured; and giving is a courteous act which he does freely, by grace, fulfilling and surpassing all that creatures deserve.

Thus in our Father, God almighty, we have our being, and in our Mother of mercy we have our reforming and our restoring, in whom our parts are united and all made perfect man, and through the rewards and the gifts of grace of the Holy Spirit we are fulfilled. And our substance is in our Father, God almighty, and our substance is in our Mother, God all wisdom, and our substance is in our Lord God, the Holy Spirit, all goodness, for our substance is whole in each person of the Trinity, who is one God. And our sensuality is only in the second person, Christ Jesus, in whom is the Father and the Holy Spirit; and in him and by him we are powerfully taken out of hell and out of the wretchedness on earth, and gloriously brought up into heaven, and blessedly united to our substance, increased in riches and nobility by all the power of Christ and by the grace and operation of the Holy Spirit.

THE FIFTY-NINTH CHAPTER

And we have all this bliss by mercy and grace, and this kind of bliss we never could have had and known, unless that property of goodness which is in God had been opposed, through which we have this bliss. For wickedness has been suffered to rise in opposition to that goodness; and the goodness of mercy and grace opposed that wickedness, and turned everything to goodness and honour for all who will be saved. For this is that property in God which opposes good to evil. So Jesus Christ, who opposes good to evil, is our true Mother. We have our being from him, where the foundation of motherhood begins, with all the sweet protection of love which endlessly follows.

As truly as God is our Father, so truly is God our Mother, and he revealed that in everything, and especially in these sweet words where he says: I am he; that is to say: I am he, the power and goodness of fatherhood; I am he, the wisdom and the lovingness of motherhood; I am he, the light and the grace which is all blessed love; I am he, the Trinity; I am he, the unity; I am he, the great supreme goodness of every kind of thing; I am he who makes you to love; I am he who makes you to long; I am he, the endless fulfilling of all true desires. For where the soul is highest, noblest, most honourable, still it is lowest, meekest and mildest.

And from this foundation in substance we have all the powers of our sensuality by the gift of nature, and by the help and the furthering of mercy and grace, without which we cannot profit. Our great Father, almighty God, who is being, knows us and loved us before time began. Out of this knowledge, in his most wonderful deep love, by the prescient eternal counsel of all the blessed Trinity, he wanted the second person to become our Mother, our brother and our saviour. From this it follows that as truly as God is our Father, so truly is God our Mother. Our Father wills, our Mother works, our good Lord the Holy Spirit confirms. And therefore it is our part to love our God in whom we have our being, reverently thanking and praising him for our creation, mightily praying to our Mother for mercy and pity, and to our Lord the Holy Spirit for help and grace. For in these three is all our life: nature, mercy and grace, of which we have mildness, patience and pity, and hatred of sin and wickedness; for the virtues must of themselves hate sin and wickedness.

And so Jesus is our true Mother in nature by our first creation, and he is our true Mother in grace by his taking our created nature. All the lovely works and all the sweet loving offices of beloved motherhood are appropriated to the second person, for in him we have this godly will, whole and safe forever, both in nature and in grace, from his own goodness proper to him.

I understand three ways of contemplating motherhood in God. The first is the foundation of our nature's creation; the second is his taking of our nature, where the motherhood of grace begins; the third is the motherhood at work. And in that, by the same grace, everything is penetrated, in length and in breadth, in height and in depth without end; and it is all one love.

THE SIXTIETH CHAPTER

But now I should say a little more about this penetration, as I understood our Lord to mean: How we are brought back by the motherhood of mercy and grace into our natural place, in which we were created by the motherhood of love, a mother's love which never leaves us.

Our Mother in nature, our Mother in grace, because he wanted altogether to become our Mother in all things, made the foundation of his work most humbly and most mildly in the maiden's womb. And he revealed that in the first revelation, when he brought that meek maiden before the eye of my understanding in the simple stature which she had when she conceived; that is to say that our great God, the supreme wisdom of all things, arrayed and prepared himself in this humble place, all ready in our poor flesh, himself to do the service and the office of motherhood in everything. The mother's service is nearest, readiest and surest: nearest because it is most natural, readiest because it is most loving, and surest because it is truest. No one ever might or could perform this office fully, except only him. We know that all our mothers bear us for pain and for death. O, what is that? But our true Mother Jesus, he alone bears us for joy and for endless life, blessed may he be. So he carries us within him in love and travail, until the full time when he wanted to suffer the sharpest thorns and cruel pains that ever were or will be, and at the last he died. And when he had finished, and had borne us so for bliss, still all this could not satisfy his wonderful love. And he revealed this in these great surpassing words of love: If I could suffer more, I would suffer more. He could not die any more, but he did not want to cease working; therefore he must needs nourish us, for the precious love of motherhood has made him our debtor.

The mother can give her child to suck of her milk, but our precious Mother Jesus can feed us with himself, and does, most courteously and most tenderly, with the blessed sacrament, which is the precious food of true life; and with all the sweet sacraments he sustains us most mercifully and graciously, and so he meant in these blessed words, where he said: I am he whom Holy Church preaches and teaches to you. That is to say: All the health and the life of the sacraments, all the power and the grace of my word, all the goodness which is ordained in Holy Church for you, I am he.

The mother can lay her child tenderly to her breast, but our tender Mother Jesus can lead us easily into his blessed breast through his sweet open side, and show us there a part of the godhead and of the joys of heaven, with inner certainty of endless bliss. And that he revealed in the tenth revelation, giving us the same understanding in these sweet words which he says: See, how I love you, looking into his blessed side, rejoicing.

This fair lovely word 'mother' is so sweet and so kind in itself that it cannot truly be said of anyone or to anyone except of him and to him who is the true Mother of life and of all things. To the property of motherhood belong nature, love, wisdom and knowledge, and this is God. For though it may be so that our bodily bringing to birth is only little, humble and simple in comparison with our spiritual bringing to birth, still it is he who does it in the creatures by whom it is done. The kind, loving mother who knows and sees the need of her child guards it very tenderly, as the nature and condition of motherhood will have. And always as the child grows in age and in stature, she acts differently, but she does not change her love. And when it is even older, she allows it to be chastised to destroy its faults, so as to make the child receive virtues and grace. This work, with everything which is lovely and good, our Lord performs in those by whom it is done. So he is our Mother in nature by the operation of grace in the lower part, for love of the higher part. And he wants us to know it, for he wants to have all our love attached to him; and in this I saw that every debt which we owe by God's command to fatherhood and motherhood is fulfilled in truly loving God, which blessed love Christ works in us. And this was revealed in everything, and especially in the great bounteous words when he says: I am he whom you love.

THOMAS À KEMPIS
ca. 1380–1471

FROM THE IMITATION OF CHRIST

Thomas Hemerken was born in Kempen, Germany. The name *Thomas à Kempis* means "Thomas of Kempen"; indeed, in German he is known as Thomas von Kempen. He was educated in the Netherlands, where he became a Roman Catholic monk and remained until his death. A prolific writer, he was also a prolific copyist of the Bible in the era before the invention of printing. His important works include a series of sermons, and he is the probable author of *The Imitation of Christ*, first composed in Latin around 1418–27.

One of the best-known books on Christian devotion, this work exemplifies what later scholars have called the "New Devotion" (*Devotio Moderna*)—a form of spirituality that resists external observances, prizes interior religious sentiments, and focuses on the humanity of Jesus Christ. Originating in the Low Countries, the movement had an enormous impact on late medieval piety.

The Imitation of Christ continues to be popular among Christian readers. In this work, Thomas à Kempis comes across as calm and meditative, earnest and encouraging, much in the manner of a spiritual director counseling a seeker. Rather than presenting miracle or martyrdom stories, flights of ardent oratory, or polemics against civil or ecclesiastical authority, this work anticipates the gradual, quiet privatization of religion in the Modern Era.

FROM THE IMITATION OF CHRIST

BOOK ONE

Chapter I

OF THE IMITATION OR FOLLOWING OF CHRIST AND OF THE DESPISING OF ALL VANITIES OF THE WORLD

He that followeth me, saith Christ our Saviour, walketh not in darkness, for he shall have the light of life.[1] These be the words of our Lord Jesus Christ, whereby we be admonished to follow his teachings and his manner of living, if we will truly be illumined and delivered from all blindness of heart.

Let all the study of our heart from henceforth be to have our meditation wholly fixed in the life of Christ. His teachings are of more virtue and of more strength than are the words of all angels and saints; and he that through grace hath the inner eye of his soul opened to the soothfast[2] beholding of the Gospels of Christ shall find in them hidden manna. But it is oft times seen that some who hear the Gospels have little sweetness therein, and that is because they have not the spirit of Christ. Wherefore if we desire to have the true understanding of his Gospels we must study to conform our life to his life as nigh as we can.

What availeth it to reason high secret mysteries of the Trinity if a man lack meekness, whereby he displeaseth the Trinity? Truly nothing. For high curious reasons make not a man holy nor rightwise, but a good life maketh him beloved with God. I had rather feel compunction of heart for my sins than only to know the definition of compunction. If thou knewest all the Bible without the book, and the sayings of all philosophers by heart, what should it profit thee without grace and charity?[3]

All that is in this world is vanity, but to love God and only to serve him. This is the most noble and the most excellent wisdom that may be in any creature, by despising of this world to draw daily nearer and nearer to the kingdom of heaven.

It is therefore a great vanity to labour inordinately for worldly riches that shortly shall perish, and to covet honour or any other inordinate pleasures or fleshly delights in this world, whereby a man after this life shall be sore and grievously punished. How great a vanity is it also to desire a long life, and little to care for a good life; to heed things present, and not to provide for things that are to come; to love things that shortly shall pass away, and not to haste thither where is joy everlasting.

TRANSLATED BY Richard Whitford.

1. See John 8:12.
2. Honest, fair-minded.

3. See 1 Corinthians 13:2.

Have this common proverb oft in thy mind: the eye is not satisfied nor fully pleased with the sight of any bodily thing, nor the ear with hearing. Therefore study to withdraw the love of thy soul from all things that be visible and turn it to things that be invisible; for they that follow their sensuality hurt their own conscience and lose the grace of God.

Chapter XIV

THAT WE SHALL NOT JUDGE LIGHTLY OTHER MEN'S DEEDS NOR CLEAVE MUCH TO OUR OWN WILL

Have always a good eye to thyself and be ware thou judge not lightly other men. In judging others a man oft laboureth in vain, oft erreth, and lightly offendeth God; but in judging himself and his own deeds he always laboureth fruitfully and to his ghostly profit.

We judge oft times after our heart and our own affections and not after the truth, for we lose the true judgement through our private love. If God were always the whole intent of our desire we should not so lightly err in our judgements nor so lightly be troubled because we be resisted of our will; but commonly there is in us some inward inclination or some outward affection that draweth our heart with them from the true judgement.

Many persons, through a secret love that they have to themselves, work indiscreetly after their own will and not after the will of God, and yet they know it not. They seem to stand in great inward peace when things follow after their mind, but if it follow otherwise than they would, anon they be moved with impatience and be right heavy and pensive.

By diversity of opinions be sprung many times dissension between friends and neighbours, and also between religious and devout persons. An old custom is not easily broken, and no man will lightly be moved from his own will; but if thou cleave more to thine own will or to thine own reason than to the meek obedience of Jesus Christ, it will be long before thou be a man illumined with grace. For almighty God willeth that we be perfectly subject and obedient to him and that we rise high above our own will and above our own reason by a great burning love and a whole desire to him.

Chapter XV

OF WORKS DONE IN CHARITY

For nothing in the world, nor for the love of any created thing, is evil to be done. But sometimes for the need and comfort of our neighbour a good deed may be deferred, or be turned into another good deed; for thereby the good deed is not destroyed but is changed into better.

Without charity the outward deed is little to be praised; but whatsoever is done of charity, be it never so little or never so despisable in sight of the world, it is right profitable before God, who judgeth all things after the intent of the doer and not after the greatness or worthiness of the deed. He doth much that much loveth God; and he doth much that doth his deed well; and he doth his deed well that doth it rather for the commonalty than for his own will. A deed sometimes seemeth to be done of charity and of love to God when it is rather done of a carnality, and of a fleshly love, than of a charitable love. For commonly some carnal inclination to our friends, some inordinate love to ourselves, some hope of a temporal reward or desire of some other profit, moveth us to do the deed, and not the pure love of charity.

Charity seeketh not himself in that he doth, but he desireth to do only that which shall be honour and praising to God. He envieth no man, for he loveth no private love. He will not joy in himself but he coveteth above all things to be blessed in God. He knoweth well that no goodness beginneth originally of man, and therefore he referreth all goodness to God, of whom all things proceed and in whom all blessed saints do rest in everlasting fruition. O he that had a little sparkle of this perfect charity should feel soothfastly in his soul that all earthly things be full of vanity.

Chapter XVI

OF THE SUFFERING OF OTHER MEN'S DEFAULTS

Such defaults as we cannot amend in ourselves or in others we must patiently suffer till our Lord of his goodness will otherwise dispose. And we shall think that haply it is so best to be, for the proving of our patience, without which our merits are but little to be pondered. Nevertheless thou shalt pray heartily that our Lord of his great mercy and goodness vouchsafe to help us that we may patiently bear such impediments.

If thou admonish any person once or twice and he will not take it, strive not overmuch with him but commit all to God, that his will be done and his honour acknowledged in all his servants; for he can well by his goodness turn evil into good. Study always that thou be patient in suffering of other men's defaults, for thou hast many things in thyself that others do suffer of thee, and if thou cannot make thyself to be as thou wouldst, how mayst thou then look to have another to be ordered in all things after thy will?

We would gladly have others perfect, but we will not amend our own defaults. We would that others should be straitly corrected for their offences, but we will not be corrected. It misliketh us that others have liberty, but we will not be denied of that we ask. We would that others should be restrained according to the statutes, but we in no wise will be restrained. Thus it appeareth evident that we seldom ponder our neighbour as we do ourselves.

If all men were perfect, what had we then to suffer of our neighbours for God? Therefore God hath so ordained that each one of us shall learn to bear another's burden; for in this world no man is without default, no man without burden, no man sufficient to himself, and no man wise enough of himself. Wherefore it behoveth each one of us to bear the burden of others, to comfort others, to help others, to counsel others, and to instruct and admonish others in all charity. Who is of most virtue appeareth best in time of adversity. Occasions make not a man frail, but they show openly what he is.

OUTSPOKEN WOMEN AND THE FIRST
STIRRINGS OF REFORM

The ascetic impulse in Christianity has always been to some degree corrective. The desire for ascetic correction first appeared during the fourth century, when Christianity became the established religion of the Roman Empire, the Christian Church began to grow wealthy, and some churchmen began to grow self-indulgent. Over the centuries, the Church retained an ideal of simplicity, with the periodic need for reform. For example, the coarse cloth habit of the Franciscans stems from the goal of Saint Francis, in the thirteenth century, to dress as simply as Christ and thus to set an example for the clergy no less than for the laity.

In the late Middle Ages and the Renaissance, churchmen were sometimes undone by their very success. As writers began to express themselves in the popular languages of Europe and women began to join the Christian conversation, the all too comfortable churchmen (or churchwomen) became a newly prominent target for indignant and sometimes humorous mockery.

WILLIAM LANGLAND
ca. 1330–1387

FROM PIERS PLOWMAN

Only a few biographical details are known about William Langland, and scholars have gleaned these items from Langland's *Piers Plowman*, a long, unrhymed allegorical poem with a tangled textual history. The work is a dream vision about the quest for salvation amid the bad behavior of Christians, especially the clergy, during the fourteenth century.

In the fifth section (or Passus) of the poem, the figure of Reason appears, introducing personified versions of the Seven Deadly Sins, so called because they pose a mortal threat to the soul. The list, which goes back in its best-known form to Pope Gregory I (pope from 590 until his death, in 604), is cited by Langland as follows: Pride, Lechery, Envy, Wrath, Avarice, Gluttony, and Sloth.

In *Piers Plowman*, Sloth is personified as a degenerate middle-aged priest, a negligent, idle, wasteful, dishonest lout who keeps a concubine. He is ignorant, but he is educated enough to end his confession by exclaiming in Latin, "Alas for me, for I have led a barren life in my youth!" Pressed by Repentance, Sloth vows to mend his ways.

At this point, the poet shifts the emphasis from sloth as laziness to sloth as "Wanhope," Langland's term for personified *acedia,* the apathy or inward laziness that was known as a frequent affliction of monks and other religious people. Personified wakefulness arrives as a character named *Vigilate* (Latin for "Wake Up!") to sprinkle water on drowsy Sloth's face and cry, "Beware of Wanhope who wants to betray you!" Sloth's hope, his only hope, is to wake up, straighten out, and repent.

PRONOUNCING GLOSSARY

Benedicite: be-ne-dee´-chee-tay
Cato: *kay´-toh*
Heu michi quod sterilem duxi vitam iuuenilem: ay´-oo mee´-kee kwohd ste-ree-lem dooks´-see vee´-tahm yoo-ven-ee-lem
Vigilate: vee-gee-lah´-tay

FROM PIERS PLOWMAN

From PASSUS VII

[On Sloth and a Slothful Monk]

Then Sloth came all beslobbered with two slimy eyes.
"I must sit to be shriven or else shall nap;
I cannot stand well or stop or kneel without a stool.
Once I'm in my bed, unless my bottom demands it,
No ringing shall make me rise until I'm ready to dine."   5
He began *benedicite*[1] with a burp and knocked his breast,
Stretched and roared and finally snored.
"What! Awake, man!" said Repentance, "and rush to your confession!"
        "If I should die today I'd dread it terribly;
I don't know my *pater noster* perfectly as the priest says it.   10
I do know rhymes about Robin Hood and Randolph Earl of Chester,[2]
But not of our Lord nor of our Lady the least that was ever made.
I have vowed forty vows and forgotten them by morning,
I never performed penances that the priest ordered
Nor was really sorry for my sins, I never took the time.   15
And if I pray any prayers, unless it be in anger,
What I tell with my tongue is ten miles from my heart.
I'm occupied every day, holidays and otherwise,
With idle tales at the ale-house and other times in churches.
God's pain and passion is very seldom in my mind.   20
    I never visited a feeble man or one fettered in prison.
I'd rather hear a dirty joke or a lie to laugh at
Or to slander men or compare them unfairly
Than all that Mark ever wrote, Matthew, John, or Luke.
Vigils and fasting days I can forget them all   25
And lie abed in Lent with my lover in my arms
Till matins and mass are done, then I'm mentioned by the friars.
I'm not shriven sometime, unless frightened by illness,
Twice in ten years and then I don't tell the half of it.
    I've been priest and parson passing thirty winters   30

TRANSLATED BY George Economou. Some italicized, unnumbered lines—interpolations from another version of the text—have been made roman and numbered.

1. Blessing (Latin).
2. Ranulf de Blondeville, 6th Earl of Chester, also known as the 4th Earl of Chester (1172– 1232), an Anglo-Norman baron. "Robin Hood": This reference is the earliest written mention of the legendary outlaw.

Yet I can neither chant notes nor sing nor read a saint's life.
But I can spot a hare in a field or furlong
And hold court for knights and account with the reeve.
But I cannot construe Cato[3] or read like a scholar.
    And if I beg or borrow anything, unless it's recorded,   35
I forget it immediately, if any man asks for it
Six times or seven I forswear it with oaths,
And thus have I vexed true men ten hundred times.
And sometimes my servants' salaries fall behind:
It's pitiful to hear the reckoning when we read the accounts,   40
So with wicked will I pay my workmen.
If any man does me a good deed or helps me at need
I return unkindness for courtesy, I can't understand it,
For I have and have had something like a hawk's manners,
I'm not lured with love unless there's a morsel under thumb.   45
The kindness my fellow Christians showed me formerly,
Sixty times I, Sloth, have since forgotten it
In speech and in sparing speech, many times I've spoiled
Both flesh and fish, and kept provisions so long
Till everybody hated to look upon or smell it;   50
Both bread and ale, butter, milk, and cheese
Were wasted under my care, and the house set on fire,
And went about in my youth without any industry,
And ever since I've been a beggar because of foul sloth.
Heu michi quod sterilem duxi vitam iuuenilem."[4]   55
    "And you don't repent?" asked Repentance, and right at
        that he fainted,
Till *Vigilate*[5] the watchful drew water from his eyes
And sprinkled it on his face and cried fast to him
And said, "Beware of Wanhope who wants to betray you!
'I'm sorry for my sins,' say to yourself   60
And beat yourself on the breast and beg of God grace,
For there is no guilt so great that his goodness is not greater."
    Then Sloth sat up and crossed himself often
And made a vow before God for his foul sloth:
"On no Sunday for the next seven years, unless sickness prevent me,   65
Shall I fail to go before daybreak to the dear church
And hear matins and mass as if I were a monk.
No ale after eating shall hold me back
Till I have heard evensong, I swear on the cross."
    But what are the branches that bring men to sloth?   70
It's when a man does not mourn for his misdeeds,
Badly performs the penances the priest has imposed,
Does no almsdeeds, dreads not sin,
Lives against the faith and keeps no law
And has no desire to learn about or hear of our Lord   75

---

3. "Construe Cato": parse the nouns, verbs, and other parts of speech in the usual Latin textbook. During the Middle Ages, the *Distichs of Cato* (generally known as *Cato*), a 3rd- or 4th-century Latin collection of proverbial wisdom and morality by an unknown author, Dionysius Cato, was the most popular Latin textbook.

4. Alas for me, because I led a fruitless [i.e., sterile] life as a young man (Latin).
5. A character whose Latin name means "watch," "wake up," or "stay awake"; see, e.g., Matthew 26:41, Mark 13:33–37, 1 Corinthians 16:13, and 1 Peter 5:8.

But does to hear of rogues, whores, and somebody's profits.
When men speak of Christ or cleanness of soul
He becomes angry and will hear only words of mirth.
Penance and poor men and the passion of saints
He hates to hear about and all who speak of them.   80
These are the branches, beware, that bring a man to wanhope.
    You lords and ladies and legates of Holy Church
Who feed wise-fools, flatterers and liars,
And like to listen to them to get your laughs—
    Woe to you that now laugh—   85
And give such as them food and favors and refuse poor men,
In the hour of your death I'm very much afraid
Lest that manner of men bring you into great sorrow.
    Both those who consent to a deed and those who do it will
      be punished equally.

*   *   *

    Clerks and knights welcome king's minstrels   100
And for love of their lord listen to them at feasts;
Much more, it seems to me, rich men should
Have beggars before them, for such men are God's minstrels,
As he says himself, Saint John bears witness:
    He that despiseth you, despiseth me.[6]   105
Therefore I counsel you rich men, when you make revels,
For the solace of your souls have such minstrels:
The poor for a wise-fool sitting at your table,
With a learned man to teach you what our Lord suffered
To save your soul from Satan your enemy   110
And to fiddle for you without flattery the tale of Good Friday,
And a blind man for a jester or a bedridden woman
To cry for largess before our Lord, to show your good praise.

*   *   *

    Then Repentance was ready and advised them all to kneel: 125
"I shall beseech in behalf of all sinners our Savior's grace,
To amend us of our misdeeds, to grant mercy to us all."

6. Luke 10:16.

MARGERY KEMPE
ca. 1373–1438

FROM THE BOOK OF MARGERY KEMPE

Margery Burnham was born into a solidly bourgeois family in what is now King's Lynn, Norfolk, England. Her father was a five-time mayor of the town and a member of Parliament. At age twenty, she married John Kempe, by whom she eventually had fourteen children. After a difficult first pregnancy, she suffered a complete mental collapse, with frequent hallucinations. Until she recovered after being reassured by a vision of Jesus, she was kept in chains for six months. Around age forty, Kempe was released from her marriage through a vow of celibacy. She began a career of pilgrimage to the Holy Land and many European shrines that seems to have continued for the rest of her life. Unlettered at least in Latin, she dictated her autobiography (completed the year of her death), perhaps the first in English, to two scribes.

As is often the case, religious authorities took a dim view of Kempe's mystic revelations. She was suspected of membership in the Lollards, an early group of English reformers who were often subject to fierce persecution. In the following dramatic scene, some of which is surely invented, Kempe ("the said creature," as she calls herself) bravely tangles with, refutes, and wins applause from Thomas Arundel, the archbishop of York (1354–1414) and his subordinates. Catholic tradition had always followed Paul's mandate that "women should keep silence in church" (1 Corinthians 14:34). When attacked for breaking this rule, Margery cites the unnamed woman who publicly hails Jesus in Luke 11:27. Kempe does not, she says, preach from a pulpit, but she claims the freedom to speak her mind. Unflappably contradicting the archbishop at every turn, she calls upon the Church hierarchy to abide by the morality of the Gospel. Throughout this scene, Kempe echoes and revives celebrated moments in which the Apostles Peter, Paul, John, Stephen, and others proclaim their faith before Jewish or Roman authorities or hostile crowds, sometimes at the risk of death (e.g., Acts of the Apostles 2:14–40, 3:11–26, and 4:5–22).

FROM THE BOOK OF MARGERY KEMPE
[Examination before the Archbishop of York]

* * * There was a monk who should preach in York, who had heard much slander and much evil language of the said creature. And, when he should preach, there was a great multitude of people to hear him, and she was present with them. And so, when he was in his sermon, he rehearsed many matters so openly that the people conceived well it was because of her, wherefore her friends that loved her well were full sorry and heavy thereof, and she was much the more merry, for she had matter to prove her patience and her charity wherethrough she trusted to please our Lord Christ Jesus. When the sermon was done, a doctor of divinity who loved her well, with many others also, came to her and said, "Margery, how have you done this day?"

Translated by Lynn Staley.

"Sir," she said, "right well, blessed be God. I have cause to be right merry and glad in my soul that I may suffer anything for his love, for he suffered much more for me."

Anon after came a man of good will who loved her right well, with his wife and others, and led her seven miles thence to the Archbishop of York, and brought her into a fair chamber, where came a good clerk, saying to the good man who had brought her thither, "Sir, why have you and your wife brought this woman hither? She shall steal away from you, and then shall you have shame of her."

The good man said, "I dare well say she will abide and be at her answering with good will."

On the next day she was brought into the Archbishop's chapel, and there came many of the Archbishop's household, despising her, calling her "lollard" and "heretic," and swearing many a horrible oath that she should be burnt. And she, through the strength of Jesus, said again to them, "Sirs, I fear you shall be burnt in hell without end unless you amend yourselves of your swearing of oaths, for you keep not the commandments of God. I would not swear as you do for all the good of this world."

Then they went away as if they were ashamed. She then, making her prayer in her mind, asked grace so to conduct herself that day as was most pleasant to God and profit to her own soul and good example to her fellow Christians. Our Lord, answering her, said it should be right well. At the last, the said Archbishop came into the chapel with his clerks, and sharply he said to her, "Why go you in white? Are you a maiden?"

She, kneeling on her knees before him, said, "No, sir, I am no maiden; I am a wife."

He commanded his household to fetch a pair of fetters and said she should be fettered, for she was a false heretic. And then she said, "I am no heretic, nor shall you prove me one."

The Archbishop went away and let her stand alone. Then she made her prayers to our Lord God almighty to help her and succor her against all her enemies, ghostly and bodily, a long while, and her flesh trembled and quaked wonderfully so that she was fain to put her hands under her clothes so that it should not be espied.

Afterward the Archbishop came again into the chapel with many worthy clerks, among which was the same doctor who had examined her before and the monk who had preached against her a little time before in York. Some of the people asked whether she were a Christian woman or a Jew; some said she was a good woman, and some said no. Then the Archbishop took his seat, and his clerks also, each of them in his degree, many people being present. And in the time while the people were gathering together and the Archbishop taking his seat, the said creature stood all behind, making her prayers for help and succor against her enemies with high devotion, so long that she melted all into tears. And at the last she cried loudly therewith, so that the Archbishop and his clerks and many people had great wonder of her, for they had not heard such crying before. When her crying was passed, she came before the Archbishop and fell down on her knees, the Archbishop saying full roughly unto her, "Why weep you so, woman?"

She, answering, said, "Sir, you shall wish some day that you had wept as sorely as I."

And then anon, after the Archbishop put to her the Articles of our Faith, to which God gave her grace to answer well and truly and readily without any great study so that he might not blame her, then he said to the clerks, "She knows her faith well enough. What shall I do with her?"

The clerks said, "We know well that she knows the Articles of the Faith, but we will not suffer her to dwell among us, for the people have great faith in her dalliance, and perhaps she might pervert some of them."

Then the Archbishop said unto her, "I am badly informed of you; I hear said you are a right wicked woman."

And she said again, "Sir, so I hear said that you are a wicked man. And, if you are as wicked as men say, you shall never come into heaven unless you amend yourself while you are here."

Then he said full roughly, "Why, you, what say men of me?"

She answered, "Other men, sir, can tell you well enough."

Then said a great clerk with a furred hood, "Peace, you speak of yourself and let him be."

Afterward said the Archbishop to her, "Lay your hand on the book here before me and swear that you shall go out of my diocese as soon as you may."

"No, sir," she said. "I pray you, give me leave to go again into York to take my leave of my friends."

Then he gave her leave for one day or two. She thought it was too short a time, wherefore she said again, "Sir, I may not go out of this diocese so hastily, for I must tarry and speak with good men before I go, and I must, sir, with your leave, go to Bridlington and speak with my confessor, a good man, who was the good prior's confessor, who is now canonized."

Then said the Archbishop to her, "You shall swear that you shall neither teach nor challenge the people in my diocese."

"No, sir, I shall not swear," she said, "for I shall speak of God and reprove those who swear great oaths wheresoever I go, unto the time that the pope and holy church have ordained that no man shall be so hardy to speak of God, for God almighty forbids not, sir, that we shall speak of him. And also the gospel makes mention that, when the woman had heard our Lord preach, she came before him with a loud voice and said, 'Blessed be the womb that bore you and the teats that gave you suck.' Then our Lord said again to her, 'Forsooth so are they blessed that hear the word of God and keep it.' And therefore, sir, I think that the gospel gives me leave to speak of God."

"A, sir," said the clerks, "here know we well that she has a devil within her, for she speaks of the gospel."

Immediately a great clerk brought forth a book and laid Saint Paul for his part against her that no woman should preach.

She, answering thereto, said, "I preach not, sir, I go in no pulpit. I use but communication and good words, and that will I do while I live."

Then said a doctor who had examined her beforetime, "Sir, she told me the worst tales of priests that ever I heard."

The bishop commanded her to tell that tale.

"Sir, by your reverence, I spoke but of one priest by way of example, who as I have learned went wayward in a wood through the sufferance of God for the profit of his soul until the night came upon him. He, destitute of his lodging, found a fair garden, in which he rested that night, having a fair pear tree in the midst all flourished with flowers and embellished, and blooms full delectable to his sight, where came a bear, great and violent, ugly to behold, shaking the pear tree and knocking down the flowers. Greedily this grievous beast ate and devoured those fair flowers. And, when he had eaten them, turning his tail end in the priest's presence, voided them out again at the shameful part.

"The priest, having great abomination of that loathly sight, conceiving great heaviness for doubt of what it might mean, on the next day wandered forth on his way all heavy and pensive and fortuned to meet with a seemly aged man, like a palmer or a pilgrim, who inquired of the priest the cause of his heaviness. The priest, rehearsing the matter before written, said he conceived great dread and heaviness when he beheld that loathly beast befoul and devour such fair flowers and blooms and afterward so horribly devoid them before him at his tail end, and he not understanding what this might mean.

"Then the palmer, showing himself the messenger of God, thus addressed him, 'Priest, you yourself are the pear tree, somewhat flourishing and flowering through saying your service and administering the sacraments, though you do so undevotedly, for you take full little heed how you say your matins and your service, just so it is blabbered to an end. Then go you to your mass without devotion, and for your sin have you full little contrition. You receive there the fruit of everlasting life, the sacrament of the altar, in full feeble disposition. Afterward all the day after you mis-spend your time, you give yourself to buying and selling, chopping and changing, as if you were a man of the world. You sit at the ale, giving yourself to gluttony and excess, to lust of your body, through lechery and uncleanness. You break the commandments of God through swearing, lying, detraction, and backbiting, and the use of other such sins. Thus by your misgovernance, like the loathly bear, you devour and destroy the flowers and blooms of virtuous living to your endless damnation and many men's hindering unless you have grace from repentance and amending.'"

Then the Archbishop liked well the tale and commended it, saying it was a good tale. And the clerk who had examined her beforetime, in the absence of the Archbishop, said, "Sir, this tale smites me to the heart."

The foresaid creature said to the clerk, "A worshipful doctor, sir, in the place where my dwelling is mostly, is a worthy clerk, a good preacher, who boldly speaks against the misgovernance of the people and will flatter no man. He says many times in the pulpit, 'If any man is evil pleased with my preaching, note him well, for he is guilty.' And right so, sir," said she to the clerk, "fare you by me, God forgive it you."

The clerk knew not well what he might say to her. Afterward the same clerk came to her and prayed her for forgiveness that he had been so against her. Also he prayed her specially to pray for him. And then anon after, the Archbishop said, "Where shall I find a man who might lead this woman from me?"

Quickly many young men started up, and every man said, "My Lord, I will go with her."

The Archbishop answered, "You are too young; I will not have you."

Then a good sober man from the Archbishop's household asked his Lord what he would give him if he should lead her. The Archbishop offered him five shillings, and the man asked for a noble.[1] The Archbishop, answering, said, "I will not spend so much on her body."

"Yes, good sir," said the said creature, "our Lord shall reward you right well again."

---

1. A coin of greater value.

Then the Archbishop said to the man, "See, here is five shillings, and lead her fast out of this country."

She, kneeling down on her knees, asked his blessing. He, praying her to pray for him, blessed her and let her go.

Then she, going again to York, was received by many people and by full worthy clerks, who delighted in our Lord who had given her, not lettered, wit and wisdom to answer so many learned men without villainy or blame. Thanks be to God.

GEOFFREY CHAUCER

ca. 1343–1400

FROM THE CANTERBURY TALES

Geoffrey Chaucer was born in London and died there, becoming the first poet to be buried in Poet's Corner of Westminster Abbey. In addition to being the greatest English poet of his day, he was a bureaucrat, courtier, diplomat, philosopher, scientist, and astronomer. His best-known work is the *Canterbury Tales*, a series of linked narrative poems that describe Christians on a pilgrimage from London to the shrine of Saint Thomas Becket at Canterbury Cathedral. Each pilgrim tells a tale, and each tale begins with a prologue. At the time, the dominant literary languages in England were French and Latin. Chaucer pioneered the poetic use of the vernacular, Middle English.

In lines 447–78 of the General Prologue of the *Canterbury Tales*, Chaucer presents one of the great characters in English literature, the Wife of Bath. Her name is Alisoun, and she is good-looking, broad-hipped, gap-toothed—a sign of amorousness—and slightly deaf. A "worthy woman," a skilled clothier and well-dressed, she is an inveterate pilgrim, having been to Jerusalem three times. In her own Prologue, Alisoun discusses marriage, in which she is a serious expert. Her five marriages can be seen as a reference to the Samaritan woman in John 4, who has had five husbands and is living with a lover. Alisoun, however, is strictly monogamous and has remarried each time after being widowed.

Although the Wife of Bath begins by saying that she bases her comments not on authority but on personal experience, she turns out to have considerable, if amateurish, familiarity with the Bible. She cites Jesus' presence at the wedding in Cana (John 2:1) and the divine command to increase and multiply (Genesis

This image of the Wife of Bath comes from the Ellesmere Chaucer, an illuminated manuscript from the early 1400s of Geoffrey Chaucer's *The Canterbury Tales*. Earthy as well as learned, the Wife of Bath is one of the more memorable of Chaucer's famous pilgrims.

1:28). She speaks with zest of the polygamous Solomon (who, according to 1 Kings 11:23, had 700 wives and 300 concubines), and echoes Saint Paul's begrudging concession, "It is better to marry than to burn [with desire]" (1 Corinthians 7:9).

According to the Wife of Bath's Tale (not included here), women want dominion over their husbands, and they lure and badger their mates into granting them that dominion. In her Prologue, however, the presenter of that old misogynistic cliché is proto-feminist: forthright, independent, unabashed, and resistant to clerical and masculine hegemony. Virginity, she argues, is noble but not required. She is lustily comfortable in her own skin and eager to be paid her "debt" (conjugal rights, from 1 Corinthians 7:2) by her husband.

FROM THE CANTERBURY TALES

From The Wife of Bath's Prologue

"Experience, no other authority,
Is good enough ground to stand on, and enough for me
To speak of marriage, its sorrows and its woes.
For, gentlemen, since I was twelve years old
I've walked away from church with five good husbands—   5
If five times married is legal, by the law of this land—
And each were worthy men, all things considered.
But I've been told that Jesus attended only
A single wedding, up in Galilee,
And this example, it's said, should truly teach me   10
That I should not be married more than once.
And here are biting words that Christ pronounced
Beside a well—Jesus, both God and man,
Speaking to a woman, a Samaritan:
'You've had five husbands,' he said, scolding the lady,   15
'So the man who has you today, I tell you, is surely
Not your husband.' And that's what he said, truly.
Yet exactly what he meant, I cannot say,
Except to ask just why the fifth of her men
Was not, in fact and law, an honest husband   20
For this Samaritan? For just how many
Men was she entitled to take in marriage?
Numbers have never been counted: people have managed
To marry without arithmetic. I've never
Heard of such a definition. Whatever   25
Learnèd men may guess, and interpret, down
And up and all around, here's what counts
For me: God has ordered us to wax
And multiply. That is a noble text
I perfectly understand. And he also said   30
My husband should leave his mother and father for me.
He didn't talk about numbers, that I can see,
Or bigamy—or even octógamy!
Why should men speak of this as villainy?

TRANSLATED BY Burton Raffel.

"Hear the wise old king named Solomon.   35
I guess he married a lot more times than once!
I wish our God would make it legal for me
To have my fun half as often as he!
O, the gifts of God he had for his wives!
No living man could try it and hope to survive.   40
God knows, and the Bible says, the very first night
He slept with every single one of his wives.
God be blessed that I have married five!
I welcome the sixth, whenever he arrives.
Frankly, I have no use for chastity.   45
Whenever my husband leaves this world behind,
Some other Christian man will make me his wife,
Without any need for delay or silly waiting.
The apostle says so himself: a wife with no mate
Is free to marry wherever she thinks it's best,   50
Marriage, he said quite clearly, is not sinning,
For marrying, he stressed, is better than burning.
Why should it matter to me if people curse
Old Lamech, who had two wives? Is that bigamy?
Now Abraham seems holy enough to me,   55
And also Jacob, as far as I can see,
Yet both of them had many more wives than two,
And other holy men, they did it too.
Look in the Bible. Where do you see the word
Of God, in clear and unmistakable terms,   60
Forbidding marriage at any age? Where?
And where does God command virginity?
I know as well as you, without a doubt,
That when the apostle talked of maidenhood
He said that God did not command it. Men do,   65
And they can advise it, but then it's up to you:
Advice about something is not what you have to do,
But what you choose for yourself, using your judgment.
If God had commanded virginity for women,
He would have denied all marriage—and you know he didn't.   70
Remember, too: if seed is never sown,
Where could virginity be ever grown?
Paul knew very well he could not command
Something his master had clearly never demanded.
Announce a contest, and a prize, for virginity: 75
All women can run, but who runs the best? We'll see.
        "But Paul is not addressing the entire world:
Those inspired by God will hear his words.
And of course the apostle himself was surely a virgin.
But yet, although he said in the clearest words   80
He wished all men would share his virginity,
His preference is not a command, nor should it be.
And those who prefer to be married can never be
Condemned as sinners, which is good enough for me.
If my husband dies, I marry again, free   85
Of sin, exempt from charges of bigamy.
Paul's wish that good men's hands would keep from touching

Apply to women in bed or lying on couches,
Since fire's not dangerous unless there's tinder.
This is a scene that most of you remember.   90
In short, Paul says that good virginity
Surpasses a thing of impossibilities—
Impossible, that is, unless he
And she agree to live in chastity.
     "That's fine with me, I've no desire for a life   95
Like that—though abstinence is better than outright
bigamy: body and spirit unstained.
I make no boast, my life has been open and plain.
You're all aware that a lord's expensive household
Contains some cups and spoons not made of gold.   100
Some are plain wood, and the lord is satisfied.
God calls our spirits to him in different styles,
But all these differences are put inside us
By God, a little of this and of that, as he likes
     "For sure, virginity is a great perfection,   105
As continence can come from great devotion.
But we know the source of all perfection is Christ,
Who told the people who heard him to change their lives,
Sell everything they owned and give it to the poor,
And then they could follow him, be perfect and pure.   110
But gentlemen, excuse me, I couldn't endure it.
At whatever age I am, I want to bestow
The flower of my body in the acts and fruits of love.
     "Tell me, indeed, why are our bodies shaped
With parts and places made for procreation,   115
And made so by God, the perfect body maker?
Believe me, they're not made *not* to be used.
Interpret things as you like, and say what you choose,
Declare one part was made for urine excretion
And that, and our female parts, are an explanation   120
And guide for telling one sex from the other,
And say it, both up and down, as a source for that knowledge,
And nothing more. Do you think that stands for the truth?
Experience tells you it's certainly not true.
To keep religious folk well satisfied,   125
I say all uses are good, and all have been tried—
That is, our natural parts are good, and they work.
And whatever they do, God's pleased (if not his church).
Why else should wise men write in their holy texts
That a man is bound to pay his marriage debt   130
To his wife? How could he possibly make that payment
If he never used his God-given implement?
God gave his creatures these tools for urine excretion,
And also for making new lives in God's creation.
     "But no one, I say, should think themselves compelled   135
To use this equipment, given by God himself:
No one must be obliged to populate
The earth. Chastity is too little too late.
Christ was a virgin, but shaped like any man,
And so were many saints, since the world began.   140

They chose the road of chastity for themselves.
But I will not, I tell you that myself.
Let them be seen as bread whiter than snow,   .
And call we women loaves of the darkest brown.
And yet, with good brown bread, as Mark has written,   145
Our good Lord, Jesus, fed a host of men.
However God himself has made us, there
I'll stay; brown bread or black, I do not care.
When I'm a wife, I'll use his gifts to me
As he has given them, all generously.   150
If I am ever reluctant, God send me sorrow!
My husband will have it at night, and in the morning,
Whenever he wishes to come and pay his debt.
And I want a husband, the youngest one I can get,
And he will owe me my debt, and serve me, too,   155
For I will make my pound of his flesh a duty
He must fulfill, as long as I'm his wife."

Reformations and the Wars of Religion
1517–1700

DESTRUCTION AND CREATION AT THE HIGH TIDE OF RELIGIOUS PASSION

The causes of the Protestant Reformation included the rising tide of nationalism, the inability of the Catholic Church to reform itself adequately, and the new humanist scholars, who studied the Bible with an emphasis on the original languages. Another cause may have been the invention, in the fifteenth century, of moveable type, which made books more easily available and facilitated a more interior piety.

After Martin Luther's break with Rome in the second decade of the sixteenth century, reform ideas with quite different emphases sprang up across Europe, from the Switzerland of John Calvin to the England of Henry VIII. By mid-century, the map of the continent was already being redrawn along religious lines. From its first days, too, the Reformation had its radical side, as in the diffuse but durably influential Anabaptist movement. The Anabaptists (from the Greek *anabaptisma*, "rebaptism"), so called from their practice of requiring an adult baptism of recruits to their movement, sought to live in radical conformity to

In this detail from *The Holy Communion of the Protestants and Ride to Hell of the Catholics* by Lucas Cranach the Younger (1515–1586), a devil pours his message into the ear of a monk preaching to a group of Catholic clerics. For the full image, see the color insert.

the way of life of the earliest Christian communities as they found it described in parts of the New Testament. Depending on their locations, groups descended from the sixteenth-century Anabaptists overlapped and interacted in the seventeenth century and later with German and Czech Lutherans, with Swiss and French Calvinists, and with English Anglicans and later Quakers and Methodists.

The Catholic Church responded to the profound divisions of the sixteenth century in two ways, sometimes collectively known as the Counter-Reformation. First, at a council in the northern Italian city of Trent between 1545 and 1563, the Church hierarchy initiated a wide range of institutional reforms and more clearly defined what was basic to Catholic belief and practice. Second, new religious orders, most conspicuously the Society of Jesus (Jesuits), became centers of renewed Catholic piety. These new orders, some of men and some of women, actively countered Protestant preaching and evangelism in Europe with preaching and evangelism aimed at retaining popular loyalty to the Catholic Church.

During the sixteenth century, Spain and Portugal colonized all of South and Central America as well as much of North America, hugely increasingly the Christian population of the world. Both the new religious orders and older orders, such as the Franciscans and the Dominicans, played prominent missionary roles in this effort. During the seventeenth century, English and French colonies in North America brought French Catholicism as well as Anglicanism and dissident strands of English Christianity to North America.

From the late sixteenth century to the mid-seventeenth century, central and western Europe and the British Isles were embroiled in the savage religious conflicts known as the Wars of Religion. During the Thirty Years' War (1618–48), largely between Lutherans and Catholics, wartime deaths reduced the population of Germany by a third. During the English Civil War (1642–51), between the Anglicans and the (Calvinist) Puritans, more British and Irish lives were lost than in World War I. In France, loss of life was also heavy at times as the officially Catholic monarchy persecuted, then tolerated, then again persecuted its sizable (Calvinist) Huguenot minority.

During the latter decades of the seventeenth century, a militarily exhausted Christian Europe retreated from religious war and the more inflammatory kinds of polemical theology that had accompanied it. The advent of Deism, a self-conscious philosophical alternative to traditional Christianity, began a distinct shift toward spiritualities that underscored experience and personal emotion. Despite the great violence of the Wars of Religion, artistic creativity flourished throughout this period. Alongside the German Lutheran organist and composer Johann Sebastian Bach (1685–1750) and the Italian Catholic sculptor and architect Gianlorenzo Bernini (1598–1680), there stands in literature John Milton (see p. 454), a convert to Puritanism from Anglicanism, who wrote his epic poem *Paradise Lost* in the thick of Britain's bloody religious conflict. This period also includes Spain's *Siglo de Oro*, or Golden Age, which provided many examples of Baroque literature mingling classical subject matter with Christianity.

The period of the Reformations and the Wars of Religion overlapped with developments in the history of science. The Italian astronomer and physicist Galileo Galilei (1564–1642) was born at the start of the era, and the English mathematician and physicist Isaac Newton (1642–1727) died at its end. Among educated Christians, the scientific discoveries of these giants and their colleagues created a new cultural ideal. The idealization of reason, of reasonability, and of universally valid, unchanging truth in all domains would greatly influence the character of Christianity in western Europe after 1700.

Chronology

REFORMATIONS AND THE WARS
OF RELIGION (1517–1700)

1517 In Wittenberg, Martin Luther posts his ninety-five theses on indulgences

1521 Luther excommunicated

1525 Puritan William Tyndale's English translation of the New Testament smuggled into England

1531 In Mexico, beginning of the legend of the appearance of Our Lady of Guadalupe

1534 In England, King Henry VIII's Act of Supremacy establishes Church of England; Luther's complete German Bible published

1536 King Christian III makes Lutheranism state religion of Denmark and Norway; John Calvin's *Institutes of the Christian Religion*, a classic of systematic theology, published

1536–40 Henry VIII dissolves monasteries in England, Wales, and Ireland

1540 Pope Paul III approves founding of Society of Jesus (Jesuits)

1545–63 Council of Trent: major effort of Catholic reform and reorganization

1549 In England, Thomas Cranmer writes and edits *The Book of Common Prayer*

1555 Peace of Augsburg, between Emperor Charles V and alliance of Lutheran princes, introduces principle *Cuius regio, eius religio*, whereby ruler determines religion of his or her realm (but of no other)

1559 Pope Paul IV issues Index of Prohibited Books

1560 Geneva Bible, important Protestant translation with Calvinist annotations and (for first time) verse numbers

1562–98 French wars of religion, ended by Edict of Nantes, establishing religious tolerance for Protestants

1563 Thirty-Nine Articles, official creed of Church of England; *Foxe's Book of Martyrs*, perennial Protestant classic, published

1571 Battle of Lepanto, crucial defeat of Ottoman navy by Catholic forces off coast of western Greece

1572 Saint Bartholomew's Day massacre, of Protestants by Catholics, in France

1582 Introduction of Gregorian calendar (named after Pope Gregory XIII)

1600 Giordano Bruno, Dominican priest, burned at stake for heresy

1601 Jesuit missionary Matteo Ricci appointed advisor at the Chinese imperial court, in Beijing

1609 Founding of Baptist Church, in Amsterdam, by John Smyth

1611 Publication of King James Version of the Bible

1616 Galileo condemned by Roman Inquisition for supporting heliocentrism

1618 Thirty Years' War begins, initially driven by religious conflicts between Catholics and Protestants, later engulfing much of Central and Western Europe

1620 English and Dutch "Pilgrims" (Calvinist Separatists) arrive in Plymouth, Massachusetts

1636 Roger Williams establishes Providence Plantation, with unprecedented freedom of conscience, prototype of later American religious pluralism

1642–51 Parliamentarian Puritans battle royalist Anglicans in English Civil War

1647 George Fox founds Quakers (Society of Friends)

1648 Peace of Westphalia ends Thirty Years' War; principle of *Cuius regio, eius religio* grounds Westphalian system of modern nation-states

1650 Archbishop James Ussher concludes Creation began on night before Sunday, October 23, 4004 B.C.E.

1667 John Milton publishes *Paradise Lost*

1669 Blaise Pascal's *Pensées* published posthumously

1675 Philipp Jakob Spener's *Pia Desideria* ("Pious Desires"), a foundational document of Pietism, published

1682 Martyrdom of Father Avvakum Petrov, leader of Russian Old Believers rebelling against the liturgical reforms of Patriarch Nikon

1685 Louis XIV revokes Edict of Nantes, making Protestantism again illegal in France; mass emigration of Huguenots

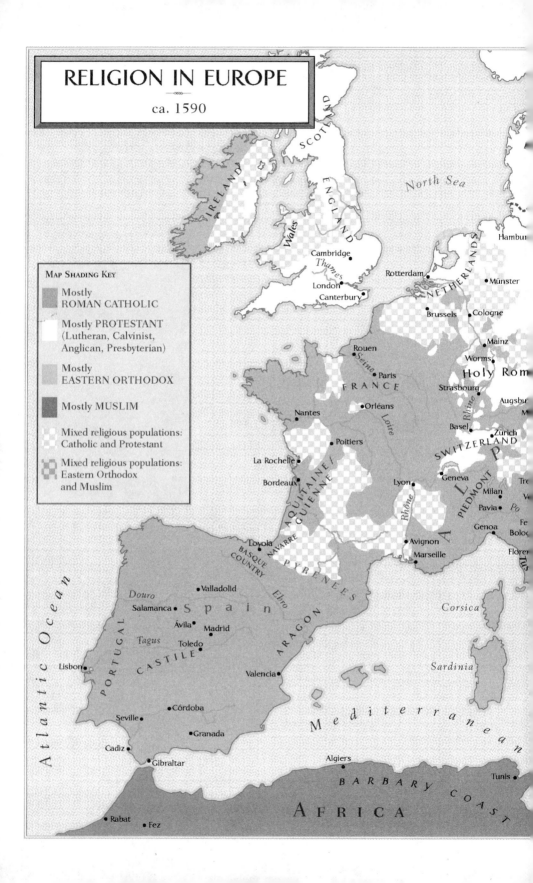

RELIGION IN EUROPE

ca. 1590

MAP SHADING KEY

Mostly
ROMAN CATHOLIC

Mostly PROTESTANT
(Lutheran, Calvinist,
Anglican, Presbyterian)

Mostly
EASTERN ORTHODOX

Mostly MUSLIM

Mixed religious populations:
Catholic and Protestant

Mixed religious populations:
Eastern Orthodox
and Muslim

North Sea

SCOTLAND

IRELAND

ENGLAND

Wales

Cambridge
Thames
London
Canterbury

NETHERLANDS

Hambur

Rotterdam

Münster

Brussels

Cologne

Mainz

Worms

Holy Rom

Rouen

Seine

Paris

FRANCE

Strasbourg

Augsbu

Orléans

Rhine

Loire

Basel

Zürich

Nantes

M

SWITZERLAND

Poitiers

A

La Rochelle

Geneva

Tre

Bordeaux

Lyon

Milan

AQUITAINE/
GUIENNE

Rhône

PIEDMONT

Pavia

Po

Ve

Genoa

Fe

Bolog

Loyola

NAVARRE

Avignon

Florer

BASQUE
COUNTRY

Marseille

Tus

PYRENEES

Valladolid

Corsica

Douro

Salamanca

S p a i n

ARAGON

Ebro

Ávila

Madrid

Tagus

Toledo

CASTILE

Sardinia

Lisbon

PORTUGAL

Valencia

Córdoba

M e d i t e r r a n e a n

Seville

Granada

Cadiz

Algiers

Gibraltar

Tunis

A t l a n t i c   O c e a n

B A R B A R Y   C O A S T

A F R I C A

Rabat

Fez

Stockholm

SWEDEN

RK

Copenhagen

Baltic Sea

Courland

Novgorod

RUSSIA

Berlin

Vittenberg

Elbe

Bohemia

Prague

pire

ria

ice

TEUTONIC ORDER

Vistula

KINGDOM OF POLAND

Silesia

Oder

Moravia

Danube

Austria Vienna

Sava

ROYAL HUNGARY

Warsaw

Cracow

Buda

Belgrade CARPATHIAN MOUNTAINS

Dnieper

Kiev

Dneister

Prut

Danube

0   100   200   300   400   500 MILES

0   200   400   600   800 KILOMETERS

Approximate line
of division between
Roman Catholics and
Eastern Orthodox
Christians

Black Sea

Adriatic Sea

I t a l y

ome

Naples

Tyrrhenian Sea

Palermo

Sicily

S e a

Malta

O   T   T   O   M   A   N

Constantinople

E   M   P   I   R   E

A S I A   M I N O R

Chios

Thebes

Aegean Sea

Smyrna (Izmir)

Athens

Morea

Crete

Rhodes

Cyprus

PILLARS OF THE PROTESTANT
REFORMATION IN GERMANY, FRANCE,
AND ENGLAND

Martin Luther and John Calvin are the best-remembered Protestant Reformers because they left so many spiritual and intellectual heirs. All the Reformers, however, can be thought of as variations on the theme of Christian prophecy, which is ultimately rooted in Jesus and the biblical prophets before him. A prophet is primarily not a predictor of the future, but a spokesman for God, a messenger who is at once an adversary of and an advocate for his people.

Prophets are given to extravagant rhetoric, splendid visions, and moral rigor. To religious traditionalists, they inevitably look like "loose cannons"; and until their messages take hold (if they take hold), prophets often live dangerously. Without the protection of Frederick III, elector of Saxony, Luther would have suffered the death of an excommunicated heretic. Calvin fled Catholic France to Switzerland in 1534 to escape a similar fate and lived on to reform (and largely rule) Geneva as a Protestant city-state that became a refuge for like-minded dissidents from as far away as England.

Luther and Calvin and the many followers they soon won over called for a return to the "primitive" (meaning "early") Christianity of the New Testament, which they saw as more egalitarian and less hierarchical than the debased Roman Catholic Church. The erudite Reformers needed to challenge and refute the vast body of medieval scholastic theology (see the headnote for Thomas Aquinas, p. 317), to reeducate their congregations, and to attack the equally erudite Catholic controversialists who engaged them in furious wars of words. The new technology of mass publication made the conflict more intense. Popular interest in religion and theology was much stronger than it is now—indeed, it would be some three centuries before the majority of printed books dealt with anything else.

As humanists, trained in Greek and Latin, the Reformers read their sacred texts with a more critical eye than their predecessors had. They noted, for example, that the different European words for "priest" all come from the Greek word *presbyteros*, which actually means "elder," while the word *episkopos*, usually translated as "bishop," means "overseer." In other words, they saw the clergy less as privileged performers of rituals, especially the "sacrifice" of the mass, and more as guides and guardians. They were not convinced when Catholic apologists quoted Matthew 16:18, "You are Peter [*Petros*], and on this rock [*petra*] I will build my church," as an authorization of papal supremacy. Because some of Jesus' first disciples, including Peter, were married men, Luther and Calvin attacked clerical celibacy and made a point of taking wives.

Luther and Calvin were redoubtable authors. Despite the legend, Luther almost certainly never nailed his ninety-five theses against indulgences to the door of the All Saints Church in Wittenberg; but he did translate the theses into German and quickly disseminate them across Germany and Europe. His polemical essays, such as "The Freedom of a Christian" (1520) and "On the Bondage of the Will" (1525), stirred countless readers. His *Small Catechism* (1529) and his translation of the Bible (1522, 1534) are still very much in use today. As Luther's teaching spread through German-speaking countries and Scandinavia, so Calvin's spread to France, the Netherlands, England, and the English-speaking world. Millions of believers found Calvin's vision of unknowable divine omnipotence, as expressed in his *Institutes of the Christian Religion* (1536), mysteriously compelling.

Unlike Luther and Calvin, Thomas Cranmer—England's pillar of the Reformation—was martyred for his Protestantism. Yet while history recognizes Lutheranism and Calvinism, there is no Cranmerism, nor is there any Henricianism in honor of King Henry VIII, whose Act of Supremacy brought the independent Church of England into existence in 1534. As the archbishop of Canterbury, Cranmer became in that year something like the king's prime minister for religion in Britain and Ireland. With Henry, he created a political structure that proved important far beyond the British Isles. England has never honored Henry VIII as a great Christian, but his elevation of English royal authority over papal authority—the king determining the very religion of the nation—modeled the religious compromise that much of Europe at length imposed upon itself as the 1648 Peace of Westphalia.

Cranmer's more lasting personal contribution to the Anglican strand of the Protestant Reformation was literary and conservative rather than political. Largely by the power of his language, he created for England a Protestant version of the Christian sacramental tradition whose hold on much of the English population was too powerful ever to be overthrown.

MARTIN LUTHER
1483–1546

FROM THE FREEDOM OF A CHRISTIAN, *FROM* LARGE CATECHISM, AND *FROM* SMALL CATECHISM FOR ORDINARY PASTORS AND PREACHERS

Martin Luther lived in Saxony, a state of the Holy Roman Empire, now part of Germany. As a Roman Catholic monk, priest, and professor of theology, he disputed many of the Church's practices, particularly the selling of pardons, or indulgences, for sins. In 1517, he officially questioned the practice, writing a "Disputation on the Power and Efficacy of Indulgences," a series of questions that has come to be known as *The Ninety-Five Theses*. Three years later, Pope Leo X (pope from 1513 until his death, in 1521) ordered Luther to retract his writings, as did the Holy Roman emperor Charles V (reigned 1519–56) the next year. Luther's refusal caused the pope to excommunicate him and the emperor to declare him an outlaw.

As a result, Luther's radicalism increased. He rejected the authority of the pope, arguing that all baptized Christians were united in a common priesthood. He considered the Bible to be the only source of divinely revealed knowledge. He translated the Bible into vernacular German, making it more accessible to the masses. He emphasized that faith in Jesus Christ, not good deeds or personal merit, earned a person salvation through God's grace. He married, setting a precedent for Protestant clerics. Those who follow his teachings are part of the Lutheran Church.

Luther's 1520 essay "The Freedom of a Christian," which he sent to Pope Leo X with an open letter, presents something like the distilled essence of Luther's thought—and the thought of countless later Protestants. As an Augustinian monk unable to keep all the rules and regulations of the Catholic Church, Luther felt tormented. He found

The German artist Lucas Cranach painted this portrait of Martin Luther around 1526. By the time it was done, Luther had definitively broken with the Roman Catholic Church and had married Katharina von Bora, a former nun.

deliverance in the writings of the Apostle Paul, especially the Letter to the Romans. Paul, who had endured similar agonies with the Torah, argues that Christ has redeemed his followers from the Law. Our degenerate human nature, in fact, makes it impossible for us to realize our own good intentions:

> So I find it to be a law that when I want to do right, evil lies close at hand. For I delight in the law of God, in my inmost self, but I see in my members another law at war with the law of my mind and making me captive to the law of sin which dwells in my members. Wretched man that I am! Who will deliver me from this body of death? Thanks be to God through Jesus Christ our Lord! So then, I of myself serve the law of God with my mind, but with my flesh I serve the law of sin. There is therefore now no condemnation for those who are in Christ Jesus. For the law of the Spirit of life in Christ Jesus has set me free from the law of sin and death. (Romans 7:21–8:2, Revised Standard Version; see p. 144).

By the force of his clearly charismatic personality and by his prodigious output as a writer, Martin Luther undertook a virtual second foundation of Christianity. His immensely influential *Large Catechism* (1529), though written as simply a manual for pastors and teachers, was in fact a summation of what he believed to be the core teachings and practices of Christianity. Its discussion of the sixth commandment ("Thou shalt not commit adultery," Exodus 20:14; see p. 89) launched the Reformation's celebration of marriage as a sacred covenant and its condemnation of religious celibacy as unnatural and a breeding ground for sin. Luther's *Small Catechism for Ordinary Pastors and Preachers* (1529) remains in use to this day, its question-and-answer form enabling easy understanding and memorization. Yet more foundational than either of these, not just for Luther but for all of Protestantism and indirectly for all of Christianity, was his engagement with the Letter to the Romans. Saint Paul had translated the Gospel into a message of solace and liberation for the trapped and anguished individual soul. Luther embraced that translation with passionate urgency. Commentaries on Romans had been written before Luther's, of course, and others would be written after his. In the twentieth century, Karl Barth (see p. 579) would launch a major movement in Christianity with his commentary on Romans. Yet Luther's reading of Romans, informing all his work, remains historic.

PRONOUNCING GLOSSARY

Baal: *bay´-uhl*   Job: *johb*
Hosea: *hoh-zay´-uh*

FROM THE FREEDOM OF A CHRISTIAN

To make the way smoother for the unlearned—for only them do I serve—I shall set down the following two propositions concerning the freedom and the bondage of the spirit:

A Christian is a perfectly free lord of all, subject to none.

A Christian is a perfectly dutiful servant of all, subject to all.

These two theses seem to contradict each other. If, however, they should be found to fit together they would serve our purpose beautifully. Both are Paul's own statements, who says in I Cor. 9, "For though I am free from all men, I have made myself a slave to all,"[1] and in Rom. 13, "Owe no one anything, except to love one another."[2] Love by its very nature is ready to serve and be subject to him who is loved. So Christ, although he was Lord of all, was "born of woman, born under the law,"[3] and therefore was at the same time a free man and a servant, "in the form of God" and "of a servant."[4]

Let us start, however, with something more remote from our subject, but more obvious. Man has a twofold nature, a spiritual and a bodily one. According to the spiritual nature, which men refer to as the soul, he is called a spiritual, inner, or new man. According to the bodily nature, which men refer to as flesh, he is called a carnal, outward, or old man, of whom the Apostle writes in II Cor. 4, "Though our outer nature is wasting away our inner nature is being renewed every day."[5] Because of this diversity of nature the Scriptures assert contradictory things concerning the same man, since these two men in the same man contradict each other, "for the desires of the flesh are against the Spirit, and the desires of the Spirit are against the flesh," according to Gal. 5.[6]

First, let us consider the inner man to see how a righteous, free, and pious Christian, that is, a spiritual, new, and inner man, becomes what he is. It is evident that no external thing has any influence in producing Christian righteousness or freedom, or in producing unrighteousness or servitude. A simple argument will furnish the proof of this statement. What can it profit the soul if the body is well, free, and active, and eats, drinks, and does as it pleases? For in these respects even the most godless slaves of vice may prosper. On the other hand, how will poor health or imprisonment or hunger or thirst or any other external misfortune harm the soul? Even the most godly men, and those who are free because of clear consciences, are afflicted with these things. None of these things touch either the freedom or the servitude

TRANSLATED BY W. A. Lambert, revised by Harold J. Grimm. The translators' bracketed insertions have been omitted.

1. 1 Corinthians 9:19.
2. Romans 13:8.
3. Galatians 4:4.
4. Philippians 2:6–7.
5. 2 Corinthians 4:16.
6. Galatians 5:17.

of the soul. It does not help the soul if the body is adorned with the sacred robes of priests or dwells in sacred places or is occupied with sacred duties or prays, fasts, abstains from certain kinds of food, or does any work that can be done by the body and in the body. The righteousness and the freedom of the soul require something far different since the things which have been mentioned could be done by any wicked person. Such works produce nothing but hypocrites. On the other hand, it will not harm the soul if the body is clothed in secular dress, dwells in unconsecrated places, eats and drinks as others do, does not pray aloud, and neglects to do all the above-mentioned things which hypocrites can do.

Furthermore, to put aside all kinds of works, even contemplation, meditation, and all that the soul can do, does not help. One thing, and only one thing, is necessary for Christian life, righteousness, and freedom. That one thing is the most holy Word of God, the gospel of Christ, as Christ says, John 11, "I am the resurrection and the life; he who believes in me, though he die, yet shall he live";[7] and John 8, "So if the Son makes you free, you will be free indeed";[8] and Matt. 4, "Man shall not live by bread alone, but by every word that proceeds from the mouth of God."[9] Let us then consider it certain and firmly established that the soul can do without anything except the Word of God and that where the Word of God is missing there is no help at all for the soul. If it has the Word of God it is rich and lacks nothing since it is the Word of life, truth, light, peace, righteousness, salvation, joy, liberty, wisdom, power, grace, glory, and every incalculable blessing. This is why the prophet in the entire Psalm[1] and in many other places yearns and sighs for the Word of God and uses so many names to describe it.

On the other hand, there is no more terrible disaster with which the wrath of God can afflict men than a famine of the hearing of his Word, as he says in Amos.[2] Likewise there is no greater mercy than when he sends forth his Word, as we read in Psalm 107: "He sent forth his word, and healed them, and delivered them from destruction."[3] Nor was Christ sent into the world for any other ministry except that of the Word. Moreover, the entire spiritual estate—all the apostles, bishops, and priests—has been called and instituted only for the ministry of the Word.

You may ask, "What then is the Word of God, and how shall it be used, since there are so many words of God?" I answer: The Apostle explains this in Romans 1. The Word is the gospel of God concerning his Son, who was made flesh, suffered, rose from the dead, and was glorified through the Spirit who sanctifies. To preach Christ means to feed the soul, make it righteous, set it free, and save it, provided it believes the preaching. Faith alone is the saving and efficacious use of the Word of God, according to Rom. 10: "If you confess with your lips that Jesus is Lord and believe in your heart that God raised him from the dead, you will be saved."[4] Furthermore, "Christ is the end of the law, that every one who has faith may be justified."[5] Again, in Rom. 1, "He who through faith is righteous shall live."[6] The Word of God cannot be received and cherished by any works whatever but only by faith. Therefore it is clear that, as the soul needs only the Word of

7. John 11:25.
8. John 8:36.
9. Matthew 4:4.
1. Psalms 119.
2. Amos 8:11.

3. Psalms 107:20.
4. Romans 10:9.
5. Romans 10:4. See the discussion of moral "justification" on p. 144.
6. Romans 1:17.

God for its life and righteousness, so it is justified by faith alone and not any works; for if it could be justified by anything else, it would not need the Word, and consequently it would not need faith.

This faith cannot exist in connection with works—that is to say, if you at the same time claim to be justified by works, whatever their character—for that would be the same as "limping with two different opinions,"[7] as worshiping Baal and kissing one's own hand, which, as Job says, is a very great iniquity.[8] Therefore the moment you begin to have faith you learn that all things in you are altogether blameworthy, sinful, and damnable, as the Apostle says in Rom. 3, "Since all have sinned and fall short of the glory of God,"[9] and, "None is righteous, no, not one; . . . all have turned aside, together they have gone wrong" * * *.[1] When you have learned this you will know that you need Christ, who suffered and rose again for you so that, if you believe in him, you may through this faith become a new man in so far as your sins are forgiven and you are justified by the merits of another, namely, of Christ alone.

Since, therefore, this faith can rule only in the inner man, as Rom. 10 says, "For man believes with his heart and so is justified,"[2] and since faith alone justifies, it is clear that the inner man cannot be justified, freed, or saved by any outer work or action at all, and that these works, whatever their character, have nothing to do with this inner man. On the other hand, only ungodliness and unbelief of heart, and no outer work, make him guilty and a damnable servant of sin. Wherefore it ought to be the first concern of every Christian to lay aside all confidence in works and increasingly to strengthen faith alone and through faith to grow in the knowledge, not of works, but of Christ Jesus, who suffered and rose for him, as Peter teaches in the last chapter of his first Epistle * * *.[3] No other work makes a Christian. Thus when the Jews asked Christ, as related in John 6, what they must do "to be doing the work of God,"[4] he brushed aside the multitude of works which he saw they did in great profusion and suggested one work, saying, "This is the work of God, that you believe in him whom he has sent";[5] "for on him has God the Father set his seal."[6]

Therefore true faith in Christ is a treasure beyond comparison which brings with it complete salvation and saves man from every evil, as Christ says in the last chapter of Mark: "He who believes and is baptized will be saved; but he who does not believe will be condemned."[7] Isaiah contemplated this treasure and foretold it in chapter 10: "The Lord will make a small and consuming word upon the land, and it will overflow with righteousness."[8] This is as though he said, "Faith, which is a small and perfect fulfilment of the law, will fill believers with so great a righteousness that they will need nothing more to become righteous." So Paul says, Rom. 10, "For man believes with his heart and so is justified."[9]

Should you ask how it happens that faith alone justifies and offers us such a treasure of great benefits without works in view of the fact that so many works, ceremonies, and laws are prescribed in the Scriptures, I

7. 1 Kings 18:21.
8. See Job 31:27–28.
9. Romans 3:23.
1. Romans 3:10–12.
2. Romans 10:10.
3. 1 Peter 5:10.

4. John 6:28.
5. John 6:29.
6. John 6:27.
7. Mark 16:16.
8. Isaiah 10:22, paraphrased.
9. Romans 10:10.

answer: First of all, remember what has been said, namely, that faith alone, without works, justifies, frees, and saves; we shall make this clearer later on. Here we must point out that the entire Scripture of God is divided into two parts: commandments and promises. Although the commandments teach things that are good, the things taught are not done as soon as they are taught, for the commandments show us what we ought to do but do not give us the power to do it. They are intended to teach man to know himself, that through them he may recognize his inability to do good and may despair of his own ability. That is why they are called the Old Testament and constitute the Old Testament. For example, the commandment "You shall not covet"[1] is a command which proves us all to be sinners, for no one can avoid coveting no matter how much he may struggle against it. Therefore, in order not to covet and to fulfil the commandment, a man is compelled to despair of himself, to seek the help which he does not find in himself elsewhere and from someone else, as stated in Hosea: "Destruction is your own, O Israel: your help is only in me."[2] As we fare with respect to one commandment, so we fare with all, for it is equally impossible for us to keep any one of them.

Now when a man has learned through the commandments to recognize his helplessness and is distressed about how he might satisfy the law— since the law must be fulfilled so that not a jot or tittle shall be lost, otherwise man will be condemned without hope—then, being truly humbled and reduced to nothing in his own eyes, he finds in himself nothing whereby he may be justified and saved. Here the second part of Scripture comes to our aid, namely, the promises of God which declare the glory of God, saying, "If you wish to fulfil the law and not covet, as the law demands, come, believe in Christ in whom grace, righteousness, peace, liberty, and all things are promised you. If you believe, you shall have all things; if you do not believe, you shall lack all things." That which is impossible for you to accomplish by trying to fulfil all the works of the law—many and useless as they all are— you will accomplish quickly and easily through faith. God our Father has made all things depend on faith so that whoever has faith will have everything, and whoever does not have faith will have nothing. "For God has consigned all men to disobedience, that he may have mercy upon all," as it is stated in Rom. 11.[3] Thus the promises of God give what the commandments of God demand and fulfil what the law prescribes so that all things may be God's alone, both the commandments and the fulfilling of the commandments. He alone commands, he alone fulfils. Therefore the promises of God belong to the New Testament. Indeed, they are the New Testament.

Since these promises of God are holy, true, righteous, free, and peaceful words, full of goodness, the soul which clings to them with a firm faith will be so closely united with them and altogether absorbed by them that it not only will share in all their power but will be saturated and intoxicated by them. If a touch of Christ healed, how much more will this most tender spiritual touch, this absorbing of the Word, communicate to the soul all things that belong to the Word. This, then, is how through faith alone without works the soul is justified by the Word of God, sanctified, made true, peaceful, and free, filled

---

1. Exodus 20:17.
2. Hosea 13:9.

3. Romans 11:32.

with every blessing and truly made a child of God, as John 1 says: "But to all who . . . believed in his name, he gave power to become children of God."[4]

From what has been said it is easy to see from what source faith derives such great power and why a good work or all good works together cannot equal it. No good work can rely upon the Word of God or live in the soul, for faith alone and the Word of God rule in the soul. Just as the heated iron glows like fire because of the union of fire with it, so the Word imparts its qualities to the soul. It is clear, then, that a Christian has all that he needs in faith and needs no works to justify him; and if he has no need of works, he has no need of the law; and if he has no need of the law, surely he is free from the law. It is true that "the law is not laid down for the just."[5] This is that Christian liberty, our faith, which does not induce us to live in idleness or wickedness but makes the law and works unnecessary for any man's righteousness and salvation.

* * *

Let this suffice concerning the inner man, his liberty, and the source of his liberty, the righteousness of faith. He needs neither laws nor good works but, on the contrary, is injured by them if he believes that he is justified by them.

Now let us turn to the second part, the outer man. Here we shall answer all those who, offended by the word "faith" and by all that has been said, now ask, "If faith does all things and is alone sufficient unto righteousness, why then are good works commanded? We will take our ease and do no works and be content with faith." I answer: not so, you wicked men, not so. That would indeed be proper if we were wholly inner and perfectly spiritual men. But such we shall be only at the last day, the day of the resurrection of the dead. As long as we live in the flesh we only begin to make some progress in that which shall be perfected in the future life. For this reason the Apostle in Rom. 8 calls all that we attain in this life "the first fruits of the Spirit"[6] because we shall indeed receive the greater portion, even the fulness of the Spirit, in the future. This is the place to assert that which was said above, namely, that a Christian is the servant of all and made subject to all. Insofar as he is free he does no works, but insofar as he is a servant he does all kinds of works. How this is possible we shall see.

Although, as I have said, a man is abundantly and sufficiently justified by faith inwardly, in his spirit, and so has all that he needs, except insofar as this faith and these riches must grow from day to day even to the future life; yet he remains in this mortal life on earth. In this life he must control his own body and have dealings with men. Here the works begin; here a man cannot enjoy leisure; here he must indeed take care to discipline his body by fastings, watchings, labors, and other reasonable discipline and to subject it to the Spirit so that it will obey and conform to the inner man and faith and not revolt against faith and hinder the inner man, as it is the nature of the body to do if it is not held in check. The inner man, who by faith is created in the image of God, is both joyful and happy because of Christ in whom so many benefits are conferred upon him; and therefore it is his one occupation to serve God joyfully and without thought of gain, in love that is not constrained.

4. John 1:12.
5. 1 Timothy 1:9.

6. Romans 8:23.

FROM LARGE CATECHISM

The Sixth Commandment

"You shall not commit adultery."

The following commandments are easily understood from the preceding one. They all teach us to guard against harming our neighbor in any way. They are admirably arranged. First they deal with our neighbor's person. Then they proceed to the person nearest and dearest to him, namely, his wife, who is one flesh and blood with him.[1] In no possession of his can we inflict a greater injury upon him. Therefore, it is explicitly forbidden here to dishonor his wife. Adultery is particularly mentioned because among the Jewish people marriage was obligatory. Youths were married at the earliest age possible. The state of virginity was not commended, neither were public prostitution and lewdness tolerated as they are now. Accordingly adultery was the most common form of unchastity among them.

Inasmuch as there is a shameful mess and cesspool of all kinds of vice and lewdness among us, this commandment applies to every form of unchastity, however it is called. Not only is the external act forbidden, but also every kind of cause, motive, and means. Your heart, your lips, and your whole body are to be chaste and to afford no occasion, aid, or encouragement to unchastity. Moreover, you are to defend, protect, and rescue your neighbor whenever he is in danger or need, and on the contrary to aid and assist him so that he may retain his honor. Whenever you fail to do this (though you could prevent a wrong) or wink at it as if it were no concern of yours, you are just as guilty as the culprit himself. In short, everyone is required both to live chastely himself and to help his neighbor do the same. Thus God by his commandment wants every husband or wife guarded and protected from any trespass.

Inasmuch as this commandment is concerned specifically with the estate of marriage and gives occasion to speak of it, let us carefully note, first, how highly God honors and glorifies the married life, sanctioning and protecting it by his commandment. He sanctioned it above in the fourth commandment, "You shall honor father and mother"; but here, as I said, he has secured it and protected it. Therefore he also wishes us to honor, maintain, and cherish it as a divine and blessed estate. Significantly he established it as the first of all institutions, and he created man and woman differently (as is evident) not for lewdness but to be true to each other, be fruitful, beget children, and support and bring them up to the glory of God.

God has therefore most richly blessed this estate above all others and, in addition, has supplied and endowed it with everything in the world in order that this estate might be provided for richly and adequately. Married life is no matter for jest or idle curiosity, but it is a glorious institution and an object of God's serious concern. For it is of the highest importance to him that persons be brought up to serve the world, promote knowledge of God, godly living, and all virtues, and fight against wickedness and the devil.

TRANSLATED BY Theodore G. Tappert. The translation's section numbers have been omitted.

1. See Genesis 2:24.

Therefore I have always taught that we should not despise or disdain marriage, as the blind world and the false clergy do, but view it in the light of God's Word, by which it is adorned and sanctified. It is not an estate to be placed on a level with the others; it precedes and surpasses them all, whether those of emperor, princes, bishops, or anyone else. Important as the spiritual and civil estates are, these must humble themselves and allow all people to enter the estate of marriage, as we shall hear. It is not an exceptional estate, but the most universal and the noblest, pervading all Christendom and even extending throughout all the world.

In the second place, remember that it is not only an honorable estate but also a necessary one, and it is solemnly commanded by God that in general men and women in all conditions, who have been created for it, shall be found in this estate. Yet there are some (although few) exceptions whom God has especially exempted—some who are unsuited for married life and others whom he has released by a high supernatural gift so that they can maintain chastity outside of marriage. Where nature has its way, as God implanted it, it is not possible to remain chaste outside of marriage; for flesh and blood remain flesh and blood, and the natural inclinations and stimulations have their way without let or hindrance, as everyone's observation and experience testify. Therefore, to make it easier for man to avoid unchastity in some measure, God has established marriage, so that everyone may have his allotted portion and be satisfied with it—although here, too, God's grace is still required to keep the heart pure.

From this you see how the papal rabble, priests, monks, and nuns resist God's order and commandment when they despise and forbid marriage, and boast and vow that they will maintain perpetual chastity while they deceive the common people with lying words and wrong impressions. For no one has so little love and inclination for chastity as those who under the guise of great sanctity avoid marriage and either indulge in open and shameless fornication or secretly do even worse—things too evil to mention, as unfortunately has been only too well proved. In short, even though they abstain from the act, yet their hearts remain so full of unchaste thoughts and evil desires that they suffer incessant ragings of secret passion, which can be avoided in married life. Therefore all vows of chastity apart from marriage are condemned and annulled by this commandment; indeed, all poor, captive consciences deceived by their monastic vows are even commanded to forsake their unchaste existence and enter the married life. Even granting that the monastic life is godly, yet it is not in their power to maintain chastity, and if they remain they will inevitably sin more and more against this commandment.

I say these things in order that our young people may be led to acquire a love for married life and know that it is a blessed and God-pleasing estate. Thus it may in due time regain its proper honor, and there may be less of the filthy, dissolute, disorderly conduct which now is so rampant everywhere in public prostitution and other shameful vices resulting from contempt of married life. Therefore parents and magistrates have the duty of so supervising youth that they will be brought up to decency and respect for authority and, when they are grown, will be married honorably in the fear of God. Then God will add his blessing and grace so that men may have joy and happiness in their married life.

Let it be said in conclusion that this commandment requires everyone not only to live chastely in thought, word, and deed in his particular situation (that is, especially in the estate of marriage), but also to love and cherish the wife or husband whom God has given. For marital chastity it is above all things essential that husband and wife live together in love and harmony, cherishing each other wholeheartedly and with perfect fidelity. This is one of the chief ways to make chastity attractive and desirable. Under such conditions chastity always follows spontaneously without any command. This is why St. Paul so urgently admonishes husbands and wives to love and honor each other.[2] Here you have another precious good work—indeed, many and great works—which you can joyfully set over against all "spiritual estates" that are chosen without God's Word and commandment.

SMALL CATECHISM FOR ORDINARY PASTORS AND PREACHERS

[Preface]

Martin Luther,
To all faithful and upright pastors and preachers.
Grace, mercy, and peace in Jesus Christ our Lord.

The deplorable, wretched deprivation that I recently encountered while I was a visitor has constrained and compelled me to prepare this catechism, or Christian instruction, in such a brief, plain, and simple version.

Dear God, what misery I beheld! The ordinary person, especially in the villages, knows absolutely nothing about the Christian faith, and unfortunately many pastors are completely unskilled and incompetent teachers. Yet supposedly they all bear the name Christian, are baptized, and receive the holy sacrament, even though they do not know the Lord's Prayer, the Creed, or the Ten Commandments! As a result they live like simple cattle or irrational pigs and, despite the fact that the gospel has returned,[1] have mastered the fine art of misusing all their freedom.

O you bishops! How are you going to answer to Christ, now that you have so shamefully neglected the people and have not exercised your office for even a single second? May you escape punishment for this! You forbid the cup in the Lord's Supper[2] and insist on observance of your human laws, while never even bothering to ask whether the people know the Lord's Prayer, the Creed, the Ten Commandments, or a single section of God's Word. Shame on you forever!

Therefore, my dear sirs and brothers, who are either pastors or preachers, I beg all of you for God's sake to take up your office boldly, to have pity on your people who are entrusted to you, and to help us bring the catechism to the people, especially to the young. Moreover, I ask that those unable to do

TRANSLATED BY Timothy H. Lull. The translator's bracketed insertions have been omitted.

2. See Ephesians 5:22, 25 and Colossians 3:18–25.
1. I.e., the Lutherans have restored the authentic message of Jesus.
2. By the Middle Ages, the Catholic Church administered communion only through consumption of the consecrated host (except for the priest celebrating the Mass). After the Second Vatican Council (see p. 628), the use of wine became common again.

any better take up these charts and versions and read them to the people word for word in the following manner:

In the first place, the preacher should above all take care to avoid changes or variations in the text and version of the Ten Commandments, the Lord's Prayer, the Creed, the sacraments, etc., but instead adopt a single version, stick with it, and always use the same one year after year. For the young and the unlettered people must be taught with a single, fixed text and version. Otherwise, if someone teaches one way now and another way next year— even for the sake of making improvements—the people become quite easily confused, and all the time and effort will go for naught.

The dear church Fathers also understood this well. They used one form for the Lord's Prayer, the Creed, and the Ten Commandments. Therefore, we, too, should teach these parts to the young and to people who cannot read in such a way that we neither change a single syllable nor present or recite it differently from one year to the next. Therefore, choose for yourself whatever version you want and stick with it for good. To be sure, when you preach to educated and intelligent people, then you may demonstrate your erudition and discuss these parts with as much complexity and from as many different angles as you can. But with the young people, stick with a fixed, unchanging version and form. To begin with, teach them these parts: the Ten Commandments, the Creed, the Lord's Prayer, etc., following the text word for word, so that they can also repeat it back to you and learn it by heart.

Those who do not want to learn these things—who must be told how they deny Christ and are not Christians—should also not be admitted to the sacrament, should not be sponsors for children at baptism, and should not exercise any aspect of Christian freedom, but instead should simply be sent back home to the pope and his officials and, along with them, to the devil himself. Moreover, their parents and employers ought to deny them food and drink and advise them that the prince[3] is disposed to drive such coarse people out of the country.

Although no one can or should force another person to believe, nevertheless one should insist upon and hold the masses to this: that they know what is right and wrong among those with whom they wish to reside, eat, and earn a living. For example, if people want to live in a particular city, they ought to know and abide by the laws of the city whose protection they enjoy, no matter whether they believe or are at heart scoundrels and villains.

In the second place, once the people have learned the text well, then teach them to understand it, too, so that they know what it means. Take up again the form offered in these charts or some other short form that you may prefer. Then adhere to it without changing a single syllable, just as was stated above regarding the text. Moreover, allow yourself ample time for it, because you need not take up all the parts at once but may instead handle them one at a time. After the people understand the First Commandment well, then take up the Second, and so on. Otherwise they will be so overwhelmed that they will hardly remember a single thing.

In the third place, after you have taught the people a short catechism like this one, then take up a longer catechism and impart to them a richer and fuller understanding. Using such a catechism, explain each individual

3. John of Saxony (1468–1532), elector of Saxony from 1525 until his death.

commandment, petition, or part with its various works, benefits, and blessings, harm and danger, as you find treated at length in so many booklets. In particular, put the greatest stress on that commandment or part where your people experience the greatest need. For example, you must strongly emphasize the Seventh Commandment, dealing with stealing, to artisans and shopkeepers and even to farmers and household workers, because rampant among such people are all kinds of dishonesty and thievery. Likewise, you must emphasize the Fourth Commandment to children and the common people, so that they are orderly, faithful, obedient, and peaceful. Always adduce many examples from the Scriptures where God either punished or blessed such people.

In particular, at this point also urge governing authorities and parents to rule well and to send their children to school. Point out how they are obliged to do so and what a damnable sin they commit if they do not, for thereby, as the worst enemies of God and humanity, they overthrow and lay waste both the kingdom of God and the kingdom of the world. Explain very clearly what kind of horrible damage they do when they do not help to train children as pastors, preachers, civil servants, etc., and tell them that God will punish them dreadfully for this. For in our day and age it is necessary to preach about these things. The extent to which parents and governing authorities are now sinning in these matters defies description. The devil, too, intends to do something horrible in all this.

Finally, because the tyranny of the pope has been abolished, people no longer want to receive the sacrament, and they treat it with contempt. This, too, needs to be stressed, while keeping in mind that we should not compel anyone to believe or to receive the sacrament and should not fix any law or time or place for it. Instead, we should preach in such a way that the people make themselves come without our law and just plain compel us pastors to administer the sacrament to them. This can be done by telling them: You have to worry that whoever does not desire or receive the sacrament at the very least around four times a year despises the sacrament and is no Christian, just as anyone who does not listen to or believe the gospel is no Christian. For Christ did not say, "Omit this," or "Despise this," but instead, "Do this, as often as you drink it . . ."[4] He really wants it to be done and not completely omitted or despised. "Do this," he says.

Those who do not hold the sacrament in high esteem indicate that they have no sin, no flesh, no devil, no world, no death, no dangers, no hell. That is, they *believe* they have none of these things, although they are up to their neck in them and belong to the devil twice over. On the other hand, they indicate that they need no grace, no life, no paradise, no heaven, no Christ, no God, nor any other good thing. For if they believed that they had so much evil and needed so much good, they would not neglect the sacrament, in which help against such evil is provided and in which so much good is given. It would not be necessary to compel them with any law to receive the sacrament. Instead, they would come on their own, rushing and running to it; they would compel themselves to come and would insist that you give them the sacrament.

For these reasons you do not have to make any law concerning this, as the pope did. Only emphasize clearly the benefit and the harm, the need

4. See 1 Corinthians 11:25.

and the blessing, the danger and the salvation in this sacrament. Then they will doubtless come on their own without any compulsion. If they do not come, give up on them and tell them that those who do not pay attention to or feel their great need and God's gracious help belong to the devil. However, if you either do not urge such participation or make it into a law or poison, then it is your fault if they despise the sacrament. How can they help but neglect it, if you sleep and remain silent?

Therefore, pastors and preachers, take note! Our office has now become a completely different one than it was under the pope. It has now become serious and salutary. Thus, it now involves much toil and work, many dangers and attacks, and in addition little reward or gratitude in the world. But Christ himself will be our reward, so long as we labor faithfully. May the Father of all grace grant it, to whom be praise and thanks in eternity through Christ, our Lord. Amen.

A MIGHTY FORTRESS IS OUR GOD

Martin Luther wrote both the words and the melody to this most stirring anthem of the Protestant Reformation barely ten years after publishing his famous ninety-five theses, supposedly by posting them on the door of Wittenberg Cathedral. Translated many times, "A Mighty Fortress Is Our God" appears here in a long-established American translation first published in 1853 by Frederick H. Hedge, a Unitarian professor of German at Harvard University. Though Luther evokes a battle not with demonized human opponents but with actual demons, whose existence and power he never doubted, over time the hymn became something of a sectarian battle hymn during Europe's Wars of Religion. Today it is sung by Christians of every stripe.

A MIGHTY FORTRESS IS OUR GOD

A mighty fortress is our God,
a bulwark never failing;
our helper he amid the flood
of mortal ills prevaling.
For still our ancient foe   5
doth seek to work us woe;
his craft and power are great,
and armed with cruel hate,
on earth is not his equal.

Did we in our own strength confide,   10
our striving would be losing,
were not the right man on our side,
the man of God's own choosing.
Dost ask who that may be?
Christ Jesus, it is he;   15

TRANSLATED BY Frederic H. Hedge.

Lord Sabaoth, his name,
from age to age the same,
and he must win the battle.

And though this world, with devils filled,
should threaten to undo us,   20
we will not fear, for God hath willed
his truth to triumph through us.
The Prince of Darkness grim,
we tremble not for him;
his rage we can endure,   25
for lo, his doom is sure;
one little word shall fell him.

That word above all earthly powers,
no thanks to them, abideth;
the Spirit and the gifts are ours,   30
thru him who with us sideth.
Let goods and kindred go,
this mortal life also;
the body they may kill;
God's truth abideth still;   35
his kingdom is forever.

JOHN CALVIN
1504–1565

FROM THE INSTITUTES OF THE CHRISTIAN RELIGION

John Calvin was born Jean Chauvin in Noyon, Picardy, Kingdom of France. A law-yer trained in classical literature who became a pastor and theologian, Calvin broke from the Roman Catholic Church around 1530. Fleeing violence against Protes-tants in France, he moved to Switzerland, where he became involved in the Church reform movement in Geneva. Local authorities expelled him from Geneva, but eventually he returned as the head of the reform movement. Calvin introduced new forms of Church government and liturgy, and he promoted the Reformation throughout Europe. As a writer and preacher, he argued that God, an absolute sov-ereign, predestined the eternal fates of certain human souls: The chosen would be saved, and the damned would be sent to hell. Calvin's theological system later became known as Calvinism and became the foundation of the Reformed and Pres-byterian Churches.

In the following selection—from chapter 21 of Calvin's *Institutes of the Chris-tian Religion* (1536), a grand, systematic presentation of Protestant thought—Calvin addresses predestination. One of the great abysses of Christian theology, the idea of predestination stems from the Apostle Paul's doctrine of grace. In Romans 11:6, a passage that Calvin quotes, Paul wrestles with Jews' largely having rejected Christ. This fact—devastating for him, a devout Jew—leads Paul to reflect, as he often does, on the freedom and unpredictability of God's grace. Because it is a gift to us, that grace cannot be earned; it is gratuitous. So—contrary to believers' expectations—the "godless," ignorant pagans, by doing nothing, have embraced the Gospel, while the godly Jews, by immersing themselves in the Torah, have lost the opportunity for grace. Paul can only hope that the Jews will see the error of their ways.

If, however, we cannot win God's favor through "works" (virtuous behavior), and if God's judgments are "unsearchable" and his ways "inscrutable" (Romans 11:33), how can we tell where we stand with God? If we cannot know, might we then swing in a void between the two classic sins against hope: presumption and despair?

Paul also mentions the important biblical theme of the "remnant" (Romans 11:5), the small group of survivors from the various divinely sent catastrophes, such as the Flood (Genesis 8–11) and the death in the wilderness of the Exodus generation (see p. 89). Will those who survive their earthly trials and enter heaven, likewise, make up a small minority of all people? Jesus seems to imply as much when he says in the Sermon on the Mount, "Enter by the narrow gate; for the gate is wide and the way is easy, that leads to destruction, and those who enter by it are many. For the gate is narrow and the way is hard, that leads to life, and those who find it are few" (Matthew 7:13).

Gulia non alio tantum se Flamine fscta,
Nec se alio tollit Scotia Vate magis.

According to the Latin caption at the bottom of this 1597 engraving of John Calvin by Janus-Jacobus Boissard, France boasts of no religious leader so much (as of Calvin), nor does Scotland honor any prophet more. In Geneva, the Scottish clergyman John Knox (ca. 1514–1572) met Calvin and learned about Reformed theology from him. Knox eventually returned to his native land and helped reform its Church along Calvinist lines. After Paul, Augustine, Thomas, and Martin Luther, Calvin was perhaps the most influential theologian in all of Christian history. The caption arcing over his head reads simply but rather proudly: "John Calvin, Theologian."

Undeterred by the apparent severity and rigidity of Jesus' doctrine, Calvin argues that Christians can have confidence in God's loving mercy. God's mercy has been shown in various ways: by Jesus' sacrifice; by the gift of faith that so many Christians have received; and by their perseverance in private prayer, in public worship, and in righteous behavior (a *sign* of their "election," not the price they pay to attain it). Christians know that God is both infinitely just and infinitely compassionate, even if they cannot penetrate the mystery of how the two qualities are compatible in him.

Believers, then, should neither arrogantly "pry" into nor lazily ignore "useful, necessary, and sweet" predestination. In this powerfully radical interpretation of Scripture, the mind-boggling grandeur and uncanny otherness of God remains paramount. Theologians, meanwhile, continue to debate whether predestination is compatible with free will, whether God's foreknowledge of our actions amounts to causing them, and why God would create humans who are doomed before they are born.

FROM THE INSTITUTES OF THE CHRISTIAN RELIGION
[On Predestination]

1. The covenant of life is not preached equally to all, and among those to whom it is preached, does not always meet with the same reception. This diversity displays the unsearchable depth of the divine judgment, and is without doubt subordinate to God's purpose of eternal election. But if it is plainly owing to the mere pleasure of God that salvation is spontaneously offered to some, while others have no access to it, great and difficult questions immediately arise, questions which are inexplicable, when just views are not entertained concerning election and predestination. To many this seems a perplexing subject, because they deem it most incongruous that of the great body of mankind some should be predestinated to salvation, and others to destruction. How ceaselessly they entangle themselves will appear as we proceed. We may add, that in the very obscurity which deters them, we may see not only the utility of this doctrine, but also its most pleasant fruits. We shall never feel persuaded as we ought that our salvation flows from the free mercy of God as its fountain, until we are made acquainted with his eternal election, the grace of God being illustrated by the contrast—viz. that he does not adopt all promiscuously to the hope of salvation, but gives to some what he denies to others. It is plain how greatly ignorance of this principle detracts from the glory of God, and impairs true humility. * * * Those who preclude access, and would not have any one to obtain a taste of this doctrine, are equally unjust to God and men, there being no other means of humbling us as we ought, or making us feel how much we are bound to him. Nor, indeed, have we elsewhere any sure ground of confidence. This we say on the authority of Christ, who, to deliver us from all fear, and render us invincible amid our many dangers, snares and mortal conflicts, promises safety to all that the Father has taken under his protection (John 10:26). From this we infer, that all who know not that they are the peculiar people of God, must be wretched from perpetual trepidation, and that those therefore, who, by overlooking the three advantages which we have noted,[1] would destroy the very foundation of our safety, consult ill for themselves and for all the faithful. What? Do we not here find the very origin of the Church, which, as Bernard rightly teaches (Serm. in Cantic),[2] could not be found or recognized among the creatures, because it lies hid (in both cases wondrously) within the lap of blessed predestination, and the mass of wretched condemnation?

But before I enter on the subject, I have some remarks to address to two classes of men. The subject of predestination, which in itself is attended with considerable difficulty, is rendered very perplexed and hence perilous by human curiosity, which cannot be restrained from wandering into forbidden paths and climbing to the clouds determined * * * that none of the secret things of God shall remain unexplored [if human curiosity can explore them]. When we see many, some of them in other respects not bad men, everywhere

TRANSLATED BY Henry Beveridge.

1. According to Calvin, predestination magnifies God's mercy, God's glory, and believers' humility.

2. I.e., in the Sermons on the Song of Songs (see p. 306).

rushing into this audacity and wickedness, it is necessary to remind them of the course of duty in this matter. First, then, when they inquire into predestination, let them remember that they are penetrating into the recesses of the divine wisdom, where he who rushes forward securely and confidently, instead of satisfying his curiosity will enter an inextricable labyrinth. For it is not right that man should with impunity pry into things which the Lord has been pleased to conceal within himself, and scan that sublime eternal wisdom which it is his pleasure that we should not apprehend but adore, that therein also his perfections may appear. Those secrets of his will, which he has seen it meet to manifest, are revealed in his word—revealed in so far as he knew to be conducive to our interest and welfare.

*   *   *

3. There are others who, when they would cure this disease, recommend that the subject of predestination should scarcely if ever be mentioned, and tell us to shun every question concerning it as we would a rock. Although their moderation is justly commendable in thinking that such mysteries should be treated with moderation, yet because they keep too far within the proper measure, they have little influence over the human mind, which does not readily allow itself to be curbed. Therefore, in order to keep the legitimate course in this matter, we must return to the word of God, in which we are furnished with the right rule of understanding. For Scripture is the school of the Holy Spirit, in which as nothing useful and necessary to be known has been omitted, so nothing is taught but what it is of importance to know. Everything, therefore, delivered in Scripture on the subject of predestination we must beware of keeping from the faithful, lest we seem either maliciously to deprive them of the blessing of God, or to accuse and scoff at the Spirit, as having divulged what ought on any account to be suppressed. * * * We say, then, that Scripture clearly proves this much, that God by his eternal and immutable counsel determined once for all those whom it was his pleasure one day to admit to salvation, and those whom, on the other hand, it was his pleasure to doom to destruction. We maintain that this counsel, as regards the elect, is founded on his free mercy, without any respect to human worth, while those whom he dooms to destruction are excluded from access to life by a just and blameless, but at the same time incomprehensible, judgment. In regard to the elect, we regard calling as the evidence of election, and justification as another symbol of its manifestation, until it is fully accomplished by the attainment of glory. But as the Lord seals his elect by calling and justification, so by excluding the reprobate either from the knowledge of his name or the sanctification of his Spirit, he by these marks in a manner discloses the judgment which awaits them. * * *

THOMAS CRANMER
1489–1556

FROM THE BOOK OF COMMON PRAYER

Thomas Cranmer, a leading light of the English Reformation, was born into a middle-class family in Nottinghamshire. He earned his M.A. from Cambridge in 1515 and his doctorate eleven years later. By 1520, he had been ordained as a priest. He supported King Henry VIII's effort to get a papal annulment of his marriage to Catherine of Aragon so as to be free to marry Anne Boleyn; he baptized Elizabeth, the daughter of Anne and Henry who would become Queen Elizabeth I; and he heard the last confession of Anne—whom he thought innocent of Henry's charges, including high treason, adultery, and incest—before she was beheaded. In 1533, Henry appointed Cranmer the archbishop of Canterbury, that is, clerical head of the English Church, which by then was independent of the Roman Catholic Church. Cranmer edited and contributed significantly to *The Book of Common Prayer* (1549, 1552), a major document of Christian piety and a masterpiece of English literature. In 1553, when Catherine and Henry's daughter Mary Tudor, a Catholic, became queen, Cranmer's Protestant sympathies put him in peril. He was condemned for heresy in a Vatican-controlled trial, recanted, then withdrew his recantation and was burned at the stake. Cranmer made a point of thrusting his right hand, which had written his earlier disavowal of his beliefs, into the fire first.

The Book of Common Prayer underwent several minor revisions during the century after Cranmer's death. The 1662 edition is still in use—in various slightly or significantly modernized versions—among the 80 million or so Anglicans in Britain and around the world. Although Elizabeth I was long deceased in 1662, the edition retains her name at the place where the English monarch is to be prayed for in the liturgy.

In the following selection from the 1662 edition, Cranmer outlines the service called the Lord's Supper, Holy Communion, or the Eucharist, a sacrament that derives from the Roman Catholic Mass. During the Reformation, Catholic and Protestant theologians went through long, complex, and bitter struggles over the precise meaning of the sacrament. Catholics believed that, once consecrated, the "accidents" (elements) of bread and wine maintained their physical qualities but nonetheless were transformed into the actual body and blood of Christ. Protestants generally wanted to understand the Eucharist as a memorial of the Last Supper, with the bread and wine serving as mere symbols of Jesus.

With his solemn and sonorous language, Cranmer finesses the question. Christians, he says, "spiritually eat the flesh of Christ, and drink his blood." He warns communicants not to take the sacrament if they are unreconciled with God or their neighbor because of serious sin. And he alludes to an ominous biblical passage: "For anyone who eats [the bread] and drinks [the cup] without discerning the body eats and drinks judgment [or damnation] upon himself. That is why many of you are weak and ill, and some have died" (1 Corinthians 11:29–30). But the prevailing note in Cranmer's description of the service is noble decorum, combining humility, gratitude (the root meaning of the word *Eucharist*), and festivity.

FROM THE BOOK OF COMMON PRAYER

From *The Order for the Administration of the Lord's Supper or Holy Communion*

So many as intend to be partakers of the holy Communion shall signify their names to the Curate, at least some time the day before.

✻   ✻   ✻

The Table at the Communion time having a fair white linen cloth upon it, shall stand in the body of the Church, or in the Chancel, where Morning and Evening Prayer are appointed to be said. And the Priest standing at the north side of the Table shall say the Lord's Prayer with the Collect following, the people kneeling.

Our Father which art in heaven, Hallowed be thy Name, Thy kingdom come, Thy will be done, in earth as it is in heaven. Give us this day our daily bread; And forgive us our trespasses, As we forgive them that trespass against us; And lead us not into temptation, But deliver us from evil. AMEN.

THE COLLECT

Almighty God, unto whom all hearts be open, all desires known, and from whom no secrets are hid: Cleanse the thoughts of our hearts by the inspiration of thy Holy Spirit, that we may perfectly love thee, and worthily magnify thy holy Name; through Christ our Lord. AMEN.

✻   ✻   ✻

Let us pray for the whole state of Christ's Church militant here in earth.[1]

Almighty and everliving God, who by thy holy Apostle[2] hast taught us to make prayers and supplications, and to give thanks, for all men: We humbly beseech thee most mercifully to receive these our prayers, which we offer unto thy Divine Majesty; beseeching thee to inspire continually the universal Church with the spirit of truth, unity, and concord: And grant, that all they that do confess thy holy Name may agree in the truth of thy holy Word, and live in unity, and godly love. We beseech thee also to save and defend all Christian Kings, Princes, and Governors; and specially thy servant ELIZABETH our Queen; that under her we may be godly and quietly governed: And grant unto her whole Council, and to all that are put in authority under her, that they may truly and indifferently minister justice, to the punishment of wickedness and vice, and to the maintenance of thy true religion, and virtue. Give grace, O heavenly Father, to all Bishops and Curates, that they may both by their life and doctrine set forth thy true and lively Word, and rightly and duly administer thy holy Sacraments: And to all thy people give

---

1. According to Christian theology, the Church Militant (living believers on Earth) is one division of the Church; the other two divisions are the Church Triumphant (those in heaven) and, in Roman Catholic theology, the Church Suffering or Church Expectant (those in purgatory).
2. Saint Paul.

thy heavenly grace; and specially to this congregation here present; that, with meek heart and due reverence, they may hear, and receive thy holy Word; truly serving thee in holiness and righteousness all the days of their life. And we most humbly beseech thee of thy goodness, O Lord, to comfort and succour all them, who in this transitory life are in trouble, sorrow, need, sickness, or any other adversity. And we also bless thy holy Name for all thy servants departed this life in thy faith and fear; beseeching thee to give us grace so to follow their good examples, that with them we may be partakers of thy heavenly kingdom: Grant this, O Father, for Jesus Christ's sake, our only Mediator and Advocate. AMEN.

※　※　※

At the time of the Celebration of the Communion, the Communicants being conveniently placed for the receiving of the holy Sacrament, the Priest shall say this Exhortation.

Dearly beloved in the Lord, ye that mind to come to the holy Communion of the Body and Blood of our Saviour Christ, must consider how Saint Paul exhorteth all persons diligently to try and examine themselves, before they presume to eat of that Bread, and drink of that Cup. For as the benefit is great, if with a true penitent heart and lively faith we receive that holy Sacrament; (for then we spiritually eat the flesh of Christ, and drink his blood; then we dwell in Christ, and Christ in us; we are one with Christ, and Christ with us;) so is the danger great, if we receive the same unworthily. For then we are guilty of the Body and Blood of Christ our Saviour; we eat and drink our own damnation, not considering the Lord's Body; we kindle God's wrath against us; we provoke him to plague us with divers diseases, and sundry kinds of death. Judge therefore yourselves, brethren, that ye be not judged of the Lord;[3] repent you truly for your sins past; have a lively and stedfast faith in Christ our Saviour; amend your lives, and be in perfect charity with all men; so shall ye be meet partakers of those holy mysteries. And above all things ye must give most humble and hearty thanks to God, the Father, the Son, and the Holy Ghost, for the redemption of the world by the death and passion of our Saviour Christ, both God and man; who did humble himself, even to the death upon the Cross, for us miserable sinners, who lay in darkness and the shadow of death; that he might make us the children of God, and exalt us to everlasting life. And to the end that we should alway remember the exceeding great love of our Master and only Saviour Jesus Christ, thus dying for us, and the innumerable benefits which by his precious blood-shedding he hath obtained to us; he hath instituted and ordained holy mysteries, as pledges of his love, and for a continual remembrance of his death, to our great and endless comfort. To him therefore, with the Father and the Holy Ghost, let us give (as we are most bounden) continual thanks; submitting ourselves wholly to his holy will and pleasure, and studying to serve him in true holiness and righteousness all the days of our life. AMEN.

Then shall the Priest say to them that come to receive the holy Communion,

---

3. Compare Matthew 7:1–2.

Ye that do truly and earnestly repent you of your sins, and are in love and charity with your neighbours, and intend to lead a new life, following the commandments of God, and walking from henceforth in his holy ways: Draw near with faith, and take this holy Sacrament to your comfort; and make your humble confession to Almighty God, meekly kneeling upon your knees.

Then shall this general Confession be made, in the name of all those that are minded to receive the holy Communion, by one of the Ministers: both he and all the people kneeling humbly upon their knees and saying,

Almighty God, Father of our Lord Jesus Christ, Maker of all things, Judge of all men: We acknowledge and bewail our manifold sins and wickedness, Which we from time to time most grievously have committed, By thought, word, and deed, Against thy Divine Majesty, Provoking most justly thy wrath and indignation against us. We do earnestly repent, And are heartily sorry for these our misdoings; The remembrance of them is grievous unto us; The burden of them is intolerable. Have mercy upon us, Have mercy upon us, most merciful Father; For thy Son our Lord Jesus Christ's sake, Forgive us all that is past; And grant that we may ever hereafter Serve and please thee in newness of life, To the honour and glory of thy Name; Through Jesus Christ our Lord. AMEN.

Then shall the Priest (or the Bishop, being present,) stand up, and turning himself to the people, pronounce this Absolution,

Almighty God, our heavenly Father, who of his great mercy hath promised forgiveness of sins to all them that with hearty repentance and true faith turn unto him; Have mercy upon you; pardon and deliver you from all your sins; confirm and strengthen you in all goodness; and bring you to everlasting life; through Jesus Christ our Lord. AMEN.

Then shall the Priest say,

Hear what comfortable words our Saviour Christ saith unto all that truly turn to him.

Come unto me all that travail and are heavy laden, and I will refresh you. *St. Matthew 11.28*

So God loved the world, that he gave his only-begotten Son, to the end that all that believe in him should not perish, but have everlasting life. *St. John 3.16*

Hear also what Saint Paul saith.

This is a true saying, and worthy of all men to be received, that Christ Jesus came into the world to save sinners. *1 St. Timothy 1.15*

Hear also what Saint John saith.

If any man sin, we have an Advocate with the Father, Jesus Christ the righteous; and he is the propitiation for our sins. *1 St. John 2.1*

After which the Priest shall proceed, saying,

Priest.   Lift up your hearts.
Answer.   We lift them up unto the Lord.
Priest.   Let us give thanks unto our Lord God.
Answer.   It is meet and right so to do.

✻   ✻   ✻

Then shall the Priest, kneeling down at the Lord's Table, say in the name of all them that shall receive the Communion this Prayer following.

We do not presume to come to this thy Table, O merciful Lord, trusting in our own righteousness, But in thy manifold and great mercies. We are not worthy so much as to gather up the crumbs under thy Table. But thou art the same Lord, whose property is always to have mercy: Grant us therefore, gracious Lord, so to eat the flesh of thy dear Son Jesus Christ, and to drink his blood, that our sinful bodies may be made clean by his body, and our souls washed through his most precious blood, and that we may evermore dwell in him, and he in us. AMEN.

When the Priest, standing before the Table, hath so ordered the Bread and Wine, that he may with the more readiness and decency break the Bread before the people, and take the Cup into his hands, he shall say the Prayer of Consecration, as followeth.

Almighty God, our heavenly Father, who of thy tender mercy didst give thine only Son Jesus Christ to suffer death upon the Cross for our redemption; who made there (by his one oblation of himself once offered) a full, perfect, and sufficient sacrifice, oblation, and satisfaction, for the sins of the whole world; and did institute, and in his holy Gospel command us to continue, a perpetual memory of that his precious death, until his coming again: Hear us, O merciful Father, we most humbly beseech thee; and grant that we receiving these thy creatures of bread and wine, according to thy Son our Saviour Jesus Christ's holy institution, in remembrance of his death and passion, may be partakers of his most blessed Body and Blood: who, in the same night that he was betrayed, [a] took Bread; and, when he had given thanks, [b] he brake it, and gave it to his disciples, saying, Take, eat; [c] this is my Body which is given for you: Do this in remembrance of me. Likewise after supper [d] he took the Cup; and, when he had given thanks, he gave it to them, saying, Drink ye all of this; for [e] this is my Blood of the New Testament, which is shed for you and for many for the remission of sins: Do this, as oft as ye shall drink it, in remembrance of me. AMEN.
[a] *Here the Priest is to take the Paten into his hands:*
[b] *And here to break the Bread:*
[c] *And here to lay his hand upon all the Bread.*
[d] *Here he is to take the Cup into his hand:*

[e] *And here to lay his hand upon every vessel (be it Chalice or Flagon) in which there is any Wine to be consecrated.*

Then shall the Minister first receive the Communion in both kinds himself, and then proceed to deliver the same to the Bishops, Priests, and Deacons, in like manner, (if any be present,) and after that to the people also in order, into their hands, all meekly kneeling. And, when he delivereth the Bread to any one, he shall say,

The Body of our Lord Jesus Christ, which was given for thee, preserve thy body and soul unto everlasting life: Take and eat this in remembrance that Christ died for thee, and feed on him in thy heart by faith with thanksgiving.

And the Minister that delivereth the Cup to any one shall say,

The Blood of our Lord Jesus Christ, which was shed for thee, preserve thy body and soul unto everlasting life: Drink this in remembrance that Christ's Blood was shed for thee, and be thankful.

* * *

After shall be said as followeth.

* * *

Almighty and everliving God, we most heartily thank thee, for that thou dost vouchsafe to feed us, who have duly received these holy mysteries, with the spiritual food of the most precious Body and Blood of thy Son our Saviour Jesus Christ; and dost assure us thereby of thy favour and goodness towards us; and that we are very members incorporate in the mystical body of thy Son, which is the blessed company of all faithful people; and are also heirs through hope of thy everlasting kingdom, by the merits of the most precious death and passion of thy dear Son. And we most humbly beseech thee, O heavenly Father, so to assist us with thy grace, that we may continue in that holy fellowship, and do all such good works as thou hast prepared for us to walk in; through Jesus Christ our Lord, to whom, with thee and the Holy Ghost, be all honour and glory, world without end. AMEN.

* * *

Then the Priest (or Bishop if he be present) shall let them depart with this Blessing.

The peace of God, which passeth all understanding, keep your hearts and minds in the knowledge and love of God, and of his Son Jesus Christ our Lord: And the blessing of God Almighty, the Father, the Son, and the Holy Ghost, be amongst you and remain with you always. AMEN.

DUELING MARTYROLOGIES:
CHRISTIAN CONTRA CHRISTIAN

With the Edict of Milan (313), which granted Christians the right to practice their religion in peace, and with the adoption of Christianity as the official state religion by Emperor Theodosius I (reigned 379–95) in 381, orthodox Christians no longer faced the threat of martyrdom. Then, however, began the persecution and sometimes the execution by the imperial and ecclesiastical authorities of heterodox (heretical) Christians, such as the fourth- and fifth-century Donatists in Roman-ruled North Africa. The numbers involved were often small; much later, they grew, with the emergence in twelfth-century France of the Cathars, who were brutally suppressed in the Albigensian Crusade (1209–55), and the Waldensians, who were persecuted in Germany and northern Italy as well as in France. These movements were of significant size and impressive internal organization. For the established Christian Church of the sixteenth century, the nascent Protestant movements were simply so many latter-day Donatists or Albigensians. In a word, they were heretics.

The Church—now for the first time beginning to be called, restrictively, "the Catholic Church" or "the Roman Church" or "the Roman Catholic Church"—fought heresy through its various Inquisitions, the first of which was founded in southern France in 1184. As members of a besieged minority, Protestants were initially on the receiving end of religious persecution. With the spread and consolidation of their political power in Switzerland and northern Europe, however, they vigorously meted out punishments, against both Catholics and dissident Protestant sects, especially the Anabaptists. As mutual persecution escalated toward outright religious warfare, Protestants and Catholics alike, invoking the martyrologies of the first Christian centuries (see p. 186), celebrated their fallen as martyrs. No martyrology from this period is better known or has been more influential than *Acts and Monuments* (1563–83), better known as *Foxe's Martyrs*, by John Foxe (1516–1587). This enormous two-volume work, almost four times longer than the Bible and typically placed next to the Bible in English Protestant homes, glorified the men and women persecuted by the Catholic Church. Although Foxe's narratives were sometimes inaccurate or distorted, their vast array of damaging facts helped to imprint fiercely negative images of "papism" in the minds of Protestants in Britain and beyond, into the twentieth century. Catholic martyrologies were scarcely less voluminous than their Protestant counterparts, even if no single Catholic work achieved the semi-Scriptural status of *Foxe's Martyrs*.

From today's vantage point, torturing and killing people for their beliefs looks like the height of perverse injustice. During the Middle Ages and in early modern times, both secular and sacred authorities saw heretical teachings as so many threats to eternal truth and public order. Heretics were often allowed to save their lives by recanting, but those who persevered in their errors faced execution. The latter category included the figures represented in the following selections: a Dutch Anabaptist named Elizabeth and the Jesuit priest Robert Southwell.

ELIZABETH, A DUTCH ANABAPTIST
sixteenth century

FROM THE MIRROR OF MARTYRS

The Anabaptist movement began during the Reformation in sixteenth-century Europe. Some consider it distinct from Protestantism; as many consider it a diffuse but crucial fourth strand of Protestantism, alongside Lutheranism, Calvinism, and Anglicanism. The name comes from the ancient Greek for "baptizing again," and it refers to the practice of rebaptizing converts who were baptized as infants. In fact, the Anabaptists considered a confession of faith vital for baptism, so they rejected the value of infant baptism. For their beliefs—in their view, attempts to live in accord with the Gospel—the Anabaptists suffered terribly during the sixteenth and early seventeenth centuries at the hands of Protestants and Roman Catholics.

The stories of those who suffered were anonymously compiled in *The Mirror of Martyrs* (a book still read in Amish Churches, the Amish being one offshoot of the Anabaptists). A young mother, on the eve of her execution by Catholic authorities in Belgium, wrote the following letter to her daughter.

PRONOUNCING GLOSSARY

Janneken Munstdorp: *yahn´-ne-ken munst´-dorp*

FROM THE MIRROR OF MARTYRS
Letter
*[Testament] written to Janneken my
own dearest daughter, while I was
(unworthily) confined for the
Lord's sake, in prison, at
Antwerp, A.D. 1573*

The true love of God and wisdom of the Father strengthen you in virtue, my dearest child; the Lord of heaven and earth, the God of Abraham, the God of Isaac, and the God of Jacob, the Lord in Israel,[1] keep you in His virtue, and strengthen and confirm your understanding in His truth. My dear little child, I commend you to the almighty, great and terrible God, who only is wise, that He will keep you, and let you grow up in His fear, or that He will take you home in your youth, this is my heart's request of the Lord: you who are yet so young, and whom I must leave here in this wicked, evil, perverse world.

Since, then, the Lord has so ordered and foreordained it, that I must leave you here, and you are here deprived of father and mother, I will commend you to the Lord; let Him do with you according to His holy will. He will

---

FROM *The Protestant Reformation*, ed. Hans J. Hillerbrand.

1. As recounted in Genesis and Exodus, Abraham was the progenitor of the Israelites. Abraham's line continued through his son Isaac, whose son Jacob received the name Israel from an angel.

govern you, and be a Father to you, so that you shall have no lack here, if you only fear God; for He will be the Father of the orphans and the Protector of the widows.

Hence, my dear lamb, I who am imprisoned and bound here for the Lord's sake, can help you in no other way; I had to leave your father for the Lord's sake, and could keep him only a short time. We were permitted to live together only half a year, after which we were apprehended, because we sought the salvation of our souls. They took him from me, not knowing my condition, and I had to remain in imprisonment, and see him go before me; and it was a great grief to him, that I had to remain here in prison. And now that I have abided the time, and borne you under my heart with great sorrow for nine months, and given birth to you here in prison, in great pain, they have taken you from me. Here I lie, expecting death every morning, and shall now soon follow your dear father. And I, your dear mother, write you, my dearest child, something for a remembrance, that you will thereby remember your dear father and your dear mother.

Since I am now delivered up to death, and must leave you here alone, I must through these lines cause you to remember, that when you have attained your understanding, you endeavor to fear God, and see and examine why and for whose name we both died; and be not ashamed to confess us before the world, for you must know that it is not for the sake of any evil. Hence be not ashamed of us; it is the way which the prophets and the apostles went, and the narrow way which leads into eternal life, for there shall no other way be found by which to be saved.

Hence, my young lamb, for whose sake I still have, and have had, great sorrow, seek, when you have attained your understanding, this narrow way, though there is sometimes much danger in it according to the flesh, as we may see and read, if we diligently examine and read the Scriptures, that much is said concerning the cross of Christ. And there are many in this world who are enemies of the cross, who seek to be free from it among the world, and to escape it. But, my dear child, if we would with Christ seek and inherit salvation, we must also help bear His cross; and this is the cross which He would have us bear: to follow His footsteps, and to help bear His reproach; for Christ Himself says: "Ye shall be persecuted, killed, and dispersed for my name's sake." Yea, He Himself went before us in this way of reproach, and left us an example, that we should follow His steps; for, for His sake all must be forsaken, father, mother, sister, brother, husband, child, yea, one's own life. * * *

Thus, my dear child, it is now fulfilled in your dear father and mother. It was indeed prophesied to us beforehand, that this was awaiting us; but not everyone is chosen hereunto, nor expects it; the Lord has chosen us hereunto. Hence, when you have attained your understanding, follow this example of your father and mother. And, my dear child, this is my request of you, since you are still very little and young; I wrote this when you were but one month old. As I am soon now to offer up my sacrifice, by the help of the Lord, I leave you this: "That you fulfil my request, always uniting with them that fear God; and do not regard the pomp and boasting of the world, nor the great multitude, whose way leads to the abyss of hell, but look at the little flock of Israelites, who have no freedom anywhere, and must always flee from one land to the other, as Abraham did; that you may hereafter obtain your fatherland; for if you seek your salvation, it is easy to perceive which is the way that leads to life, or the way that leads into hell. Above all things, seek the kingdom of heaven and His righteousness; and whatever you need besides shall be added unto you. Matt. 6:33."

* * *

I leave you here; oh, that it had pleased the Lord, that I might have brought you up; I should so gladly have done my best with respect to it; but it seems that it is not the Lord's will. And though it had not come thus, and I had remained with you for a time, the Lord could still take me from you, and then, too, you should have to be without me, even as it has now gone with your father and myself, that we could live together but so short a time, when we were so well joined since the Lord had so well mated us, that we would not have forsaken each other for the whole world, and yet we had to leave each other for the Lord's sake. So I must also leave you here, my dearest lamb; the Lord that created and made you now takes me from you, it is His holy will. I must now pass through this narrow way which the prophets and martyrs of Christ passed through, and many thousands who put off the mortal clothing, who died here for Christ, and now they wait under the altar till their number shall be fulfilled, of which number your dear father is one. And I am now on the point of following him, for I am delivered up to death, as it appears in the eyes of man; but if it were not the will of the Lord (though it seems that I am delivered up to death), He could yet easily deliver me out of their hands and give me back to you, my child. Even as the Lord returned to Abraham his son Isaac, so He could still easily do it; He is still the same God that delivered Daniel out of the lion's den, and the three young men out of the fiery furnace;[2] He could still easily deliver me out of the hands of man. * * *

* * *

And now, Janneken, my dear lamb, who are yet very little and young, I leave you this letter, together with a gold real, which I had with me in prison, and this I leave you for a perpetual adieu, and for a testament; that you may remember me by it, as also by this letter. Read it, when you have understanding, and keep it as long as you live in remembrance of me and of your father, if peradventure you might be edified by it. And I herewith bid you adieu, my dear Janneken Munstdorp, and kiss you heartily, my dear lamb, with a perpetual kiss of peace. Follow me and your father, and be not ashamed to confess us before the world, for we were not ashamed to confess our faith before the world, and this adulterous generation; hence I pray you, that you be not ashamed to confess our faith, since it is the true evangelical faith, another than which shall never be found.

2. An apocryphal addition to chapter 3 of the Old Testament Book of Daniel, known by names such as the Prayer of Azariah and the Song of the Three Young Men, consists of the prayers of Hananiah, Mishael, and Azariah, three young men who praise God after being placed in a fiery furnace during a persecution of Jews in Babylon. "Abraham . . . Isaac": the binding of Isaac (see the headnote for Genesis 1–3, 12:1–3, 15:1–6, 22:1–19, p. 83). "Daniel . . . lion's den": see Daniel 6.

Let it be your glory, that we did not die for any evil doing, and strive to do likewise, though they should also seek to kill you. And on no account cease to love God above all, for no one can prevent you from fearing God. If you follow that which is good, and seek peace, and ensue it, you shall receive the crown of eternal life; this crown I wish you and the crucified, bleeding, naked, despised, rejected and slain Jesus Christ for your bridegroom.

HENRY MORE
1586–1661

FROM THE ELIZABETHAN JESUITS

Queen Elizabeth I of England (reigned from 1558 until her death, in 1603) saw the papacy and the Catholic states of Europe as a single, lethal military and political threat to her officially Anglican realm, especially after the failed assault by the Grand Armada of Spain in 1588. Most of Protestant England joined the queen in seeing English Catholic priests as foreign agents subject to execution for treason. The condemned were hanged, taken down while still alive, drawn (castrated and disemboweled), and finally quartered (cut in four pieces, which were then put on display).

This sentence was imposed on the English Jesuit Robert Southwell (ca. 1561–1595), who was also a devotional poet (see p. 450). Southwell's martyrdom was chronicled by another English Jesuit, Henry More (1586–1661), a great-grandson of the martyred English statesman and author Sir Thomas More. Henry portrays the young priest as both lionhearted and golden-tongued in facing his accusers. Southwell defends the use of equivocation to protect the lives of outlawed priests, such as himself, hiding in the houses of Catholic laypeople. After all, he argues, anyone would and should lie if the queen's mortal enemies demanded to know her whereabouts. For him, a lie told to save a life is not a sin, much less an act of treason.

FROM THE ELIZABETHAN JESUITS
[The Trial and Execution of Robert Southwell]

'You, Southwell, were among the first to teach that if a man were asked if he had seen you at someone's house, he could reply on oath that he had not, even when he most certainly had. If you deny that, there is someone here to affirm it. In truth, what is that if not lying, perjury, deception, and holding

---

Translated by Francis Edwards. The text's section numbers have been omitted. The text's ellipses may represent editorial omissions; Norton editorial asterisks represent editorial omissions for this anthology. The bracketed insertion is the translator's.

open the door to evil cunning, so that nothing in law or in justice, or any-thing else henceforth may be done according to the usage of our forebears? All must be liable to fraud and deception. How in the last resort will you deal with such men? It is altogether obvious what punishments, what condign penalties they merit who go about to confuse, pervert and overthrow the kingdom, its religion, peace, life and the customs of its people with their loathsome principles and practice.'

Before this onslaught, Southwell stood his ground like an athlete unwinded, his mind unbowed and alert. * * *

                         *   *   *

    * * * I ask you, Mr. Attorney, to consider the case of a King of France tak-ing up arms against us, invading the kingdom, and seizing the realm. He then looks for the Queen, who has retreated to some hiding-place in the palace of which you are aware. Suppose you were taken in the court, and the king asked you where she was hiding, and refused to believe you until you were sworn. What would you do? To hesitate would be to reveal; not to swear, to betray. What would you reply? I suppose you would point out the place. But who of all people here present would declare you to be a good man and faithful subject of the Queen, and not rather a traitor? You would swear, therefore, even if you knew, that you did not know; or say that you had no idea where in the palace the Queen could be hidden so as not to use your knowledge for a frightful crime. * * * And this is precisely our predicament. Catholics are endangered as to their liberty, property and lives if they keep a priest in the house. Who would forbid them to avoid such a calamity by an equivocal reply? * * *

                         *   *   *

    The judge addressed a few words to the jury, and ordered them to retire once more to deliberate. They returned after a short interval, and declared Southwell guilty. He was asked, according to custom, if he had anything further to say in his defence. 'Only this', he replied, 'I ask God from my heart to forgive, in His great mercy, all those who have conspired in any way for my killing.' Sentence was then pronounced in the prescribed form. He was led away to execution two days later.

It was 3 March [1595] * * *. The day had scarcely dawned when the gaoler came to warn him, after he had been awakened, that this was the day he must die. Southwell embraced him warmly. 'Truly, you bring me most wel-come news,' he said, 'I am sorry there is nothing much left for me to give you. But take this nightcap of mine as a token of gratitude.' The gaoler trea-sured the cap as long as he lived, and refused to part with it at any price. Southwell was now stretched on a hurdle. His mind leapt for joy even more than his body jumped about during the unusual horse-ride. Frequently he cried out, 'Christ, my God, you give your unworthy servant too much honour. You allow him too much glory.' When he reached the death-dealing scaffold, he raised himself up as far as he could. He greeted the final cross which he had longed for even as a boy . . . As he was led under the scaffold on the cart, he made the sign of the cross, and addressed the crowd on a text of the Apostle.

They waited tense and silent for God. 'If we die, we die in the Lord. Whether we live or die, therefore, we are the Lord's . . . [1]

* * *

He made his speech, directed with much fervour to fervent spirits, in a way that moved his listeners to considerable sympathy. Even the Protestant divines, who interrupted from time to time, were eventually reduced to silence. Southwell, himself protesting, strove in a loud voice to cope with their importunity. 'Whatever these men say or do,' said he, pointing at the ministers, 'I live and die a Catholic. All of you here who are Catholics bear witness to me in this; and pray for me!' Then recollecting himself, he got ready for imminent departure, praying in Latin with the utmost concentration of mind and body . . . After this, they drove the horses and cart away from the place, and once again he fortified himself with the sign of the cross . . . He hung still living for quite some time, beating his breast with his hand . . . In the end, the executioner, who had not adjusted the rope properly, clung to his feet and killed him. Some wanted him cut down still breathing, which would have been in strict accordance with the sentence. But the people prevented it. So did the magistrate who presided over the execution . . . Eternal happiness already seemed to shine in the dead man's face. Neither the pallor of death nor the bruising compression of the rope disfigured his countenance. His heart slipped from the hand of the blood-bespattered executioner; nor did it prove easy to burn . . .

Some considered it proper to mourn after his death the man whom living they tried to destroy. They even thought this a service of God. Baron Mountjoy[2] certainly admired the steadfastness of the innocent victim. 'May my soul,' he said, 'be with the soul of this man.' On two or three occasions, he forestalled some who tried to cut the rope while Southwell was still alive. And the bystanders admired Southwell as much as he did. No one smeared him after his death. None, contrary to usual custom, wronged him by word or deed. But the butchery now followed its normal course. His body was cut into four sections, and his head stuck on a pike. No one made a sound while it was done. So ended his drama. * * *

1. See Romans 14:8.
2. Charles Blount, 8th Baron Mountjoy, a spectator at the execution.

SPANISH MYSTICS OF THE CATHOLIC REFORMATION

The word *mystic* is cognate with *mystery* and derives originally from the Greek word for an initiate in one of the many ancient Greek cults. The root meaning is connected with the closing of the eyes that was required of neophytes in the course of their initiation: As the eyes close, the initiate is drawn inward into the privacy of the mind. In Christian usage, *mystic* still connotes inwardness. A mystic has received an intimate, interior, emotionally powerful communication or revelation from God, often one that transcends reason or language.

Mystic revelation differs from prophecy in that the message or experience is not initially meant to be proclaimed to others. Rather, this personal gift from God is to be savored with gratitude. The bold public engagement that often follows yields some of the adventure of mysticism, for established religious authority is ever suspicious of mysticism. However inward mysticism may seem, after all, it places the mystic beyond received legal norms and administrative control. Thus, the great Spanish poet and mystic Fray Luís de León (1527–1591) was jailed by the Spanish Inquisition for nearly five years for authorizing himself to translate into Spanish the Song of Songs (see p. 306). (Legend has it that shortly after his release, he walked into his university lecture hall and dryly began the class, "As we were saying yesterday. . . .") The mystic Saint John of the Cross (1542–1591), one of Spain's greatest poets, was imprisoned in a tiny cell for his spiritually emboldened efforts to reform the Carmelite Order.

The core of the Spanish Catholic mysticism of Saint Teresa of Avila and Saint Ignatius Loyola—the figures presented in this section—is progressive surrender to the love of God. The practitioner of mental prayer tries to shake off the distractions and demands of the busy, discursive ego, and achieve union with God. Ultimately, this practice results in a state of blissful passivity and ecstasy, where one is entirely carried out of oneself.

The sixteenth-century Spanish mystics deeply marked the practice of all Catholic mysticism through the next four centuries, perhaps most especially through the many schools of the Jesuit Order, which was founded by Ignatius Loyola. Though not confined to the physical cloister, Catholic mysticism has been the lay Catholic's retreat into a spiritual cloister, a cloister of inwardness confining to some but to others a liberation.

Protestantism has also had its mystics. George Fox (1624–1691), the founder of the Quakers, lived his entire life under the direction of an "inner voice." The English artist and poet William Blake (1757–1827) and the Swedish philosopher Emanual Swedenborg (1688–1772) made similar claims for their visions. Joseph Smith (see p. 505) was seen as a prophet by his Mormon followers, but might as easily be characterized as a Protestant mystic.

SAINT IGNATIUS OF LOYOLA
1491–1556

FROM THE SPIRITUAL EXERCISES

Iñigo López was born in Loyola, in the Basque Country of Spain. At some point early in life, he began calling himself Ignacio (Ignatius). A knight from a noble family, he experienced a spiritual conversion while recovering from battle wounds and abandoned his military career. After a brief period as a hermit, he began studying theology in Spain and France. He attempted to settle in the Holy Land in 1523, but was sent back to Europe by the Franciscans. Fourteen years later, he founded the Society of Jesus—the Jesuit Order, characterized by a quasi-military mystique of obedience and by a wide-ranging commitment to education, to preaching, and to missionary work—and he became the Society's first superior general. Ignatius died in Rome and is venerated by the Roman Catholic and Anglican Churches.

The Society of Jesus was an important part of the Catholic Reformation, and Ignatius's devotion to the Catholic Church is reflected in his *Spiritual Exercises.* Composed from 1522 to 1524, this handbook is a set of meditations, prayers, and mental exercises. The course is divided into four weeklong sessions and is designed to be carried out over a period of 28–30 days, though it is often undertaken for a far shorter period. Critical to the process is Ignatius's notion of "discernment." By focusing on Jesus' life, the retreatant can discern Jesus' will for his or her own life. The person can then make decisions about how to live. Formally approved by the pope in 1548, the exercises are also performed by non-Catholics.

The key to Jesuit spirituality, *The Spiritual Exercises* is not a book to be read but rather a manual to be worked with, like a modern how-to guide. In its full form, the course consists of a month of intense reflection, self-examination, and prayer, under the supervision of a trained expert, generally a priest. The goal is to transform the mind and heart and, ideally, prompt the individual to dedicate himself to a life in religion, perhaps even as a Jesuit. (The inclusive language of these translated excerpts is out of line with Ignatius's habit of referring only to male exercitants.) Exercitants are motivated to volunteer for heroic service in the army of Jesus (Ignatius called his order a "company," in the military sense); to accept a life of poverty ("spiritual," physical, or both); and to endure verbal and physical abuse intended to give rise to a Christ-like humility, as opposed to the Satanic traps of riches, honor, and pride. The ideal state is of devout indifference to wordly goods, a detachment that enables the person to use, or refrain from using, external things with only one end in mind: the advancement of the kingdom of God. Ignatius calls indifference the "Principle and Foundation" of the *Exercises*; together with obedience, indifference helps make the Jesuit a flexible, efficient tool in the hands of his superiors, who are to be likewise intent on promoting God's work.

Throughout the *Exercises*, the method of meditation is highly visual. Whatever the topic, be it a scene from the Gospels or the pains of hell, the person is asked to imagine a concrete location, specific figures (e.g., Jesus and Mary, "Our Lady"), and other physical effects to create a sense of being there. In the famous "Meditation on the Two Standards" (excerpted here), from the first week, the figures are warring forces, led by Christ and Satan, in a sort of Crusader setting. Jesus, "the supreme commander of the good people," is outside Jerusalem; Satan, "the leader of the enemy," is in Babylon.

PRONOUNCING GLOSSARY

Ignatius of Loyola: *ig-nay´-shus* of *loy-oh´-lah*

FROM THE SPIRITUAL EXERCISES

[From *A Meditation on the Two Standards*]

THE FIRST EXERCISE

IS A MEDITATION BY USING THE THREE POWERS OF THE SOUL ABOUT THE FIRST, SECOND, AND THIRD SINS.

It contains, after a preparatory prayer and two preludes,
three main points and a colloquy.

The Preparatory Prayer is to ask God our Lord for the grace that all my intentions, actions, and operations may be ordered purely to the service and praise of his Divine Majesty.

The First Prelude is a composition made by imagining the place. Here we should take notice of the following. When a contemplation or meditation is about something that can be gazed on, for example, a contemplation of Christ our Lord, who is visible, the composition consists of seeing in imagination the physical place where that which I want to contemplate is taking place. By physical place I mean, for instance, a temple or a mountain where Jesus Christ or Our Lady happens to be, in accordance with the topic I desire to contemplate.

When a contemplation or meditation is about something abstract and invisible, as in the present case about the sins, the composition will be to see in imagination and to consider my soul as imprisoned in this corruptible body, and my whole compound self as an exile in this valley [of tears][1] among brute animals. I mean, my whole self as composed of soul and body.

The Second Prelude is to ask God our Lord for what I want and desire. What I ask for should be in accordance with the subject matter. For example, in a contemplation on the Resurrection, I will ask for joy with Christ in joy; in a contemplation on the Passion, I will ask for pain, tears, and suffering with Christ suffering.

* * *

Note. All the contemplations or meditations ought to be preceded by this same preparatory prayer, which is never changed, and also by the two preludes, which are sometimes changed in accordance with the subject matter.

* * *

TRANSLATED BY George E. Ganss. The translation's section numbers have been omitted. The bracketed insertions are the translator's.

1. See the discussion of *Salve Regina* on p. 328.

INTRODUCTION TO THE CONSIDERATION ON STATES OF LIFE

We have already considered the example which Christ our Lord gave us for the first state of life, which consists in the observance of the commandments. He gave this example when he lived in obedience to his parents.

We have also considered the example he gave us for the second state, that of evangelical perfection, when he remained in the temple, separating himself from his adoptive father and human mother in order to devote himself solely to the service of his eternal Father.

While continuing our contemplations of his life, we now begin simultaneously to explore and inquire: In which life or state does his Divine Majesty wish us to serve him?

Therefore to gain some introduction to this matter, we shall in our next exercise observe the intention of Christ our Lord, and in contrast, that of the enemy of human nature. We shall also think about how we ought to dispose ourselves in order to come to perfection in whatsoever state of life God our Lord may grant us to elect.

THE FOURTH DAY
A MEDITATION ON TWO STANDARDS, THE ONE OF CHRIST, OUR SUPREME COMMANDER AND LORD, THE OTHER OF LUCIFER, THE MORTAL ENEMY OF OUR HUMAN NATURE

The Preparatory Prayer will be as usual.

The First Prelude. This is the history. Here it will be to consider how Christ calls and desires all persons to come under his standard, and how Lucifer in opposition calls them under his.

The Second Prelude. A composition, by imagining the place. Here it will be to imagine a great plain in the region of Jerusalem, where the supreme commander of the good people is Christ our Lord; then another plain in the region of Babylon, where the leader of the enemy is Lucifer.

The Third Prelude. It is to ask for what I desire. Here it will be to ask for insight into the deceits of the evil leader, and for help to guard myself against them; and further, for insight into the genuine life which the supreme and truthful commander sets forth, and grace to imitate him.

PART I. THE STANDARD OF SATAN

The First Point. Imagine the leader of all the enemy in that great plain of Babylon. He is seated on a throne of fire and smoke, in aspect horrible and terrifying.

The Second Point. Consider how he summons uncountable devils, disperses some to one city and others to another, and thus reaches into the whole world, without missing any provinces, places, states, or individual persons.

The Third Point. Consider the address he makes to them: How he admonishes them to set up snares and chains; how first they should tempt people to covet riches (as he usually does, at least in most cases), so that they may more easily come to vain honor from the world, and finally to surging pride. In this way, the first step is riches, the second is honor, and the third is pride; and from these three steps the enemy entices them to any other vices.

PART II. THE STANDARD OF CHRIST

Similarly, in contrast, gaze in imagination on the supreme and true leader, who is Christ our Lord.

The First Point. Consider how Christ our Lord takes his place in that great plain near Jerusalem, in an area which is lowly, beautiful, and attractive.

The Second Point. Consider how the Lord of all the world chooses so many persons, apostles, disciples, and the like. He sends them throughout the whole world, to spread his doctrine among people of every state and condition.

The Third Point. Consider the address which Christ our Lord makes to all his servants and friends whom he is sending on this expedition. He recommends that they endeavor to aid all persons, by attracting them, first, to the highest degree of spiritual poverty and also, if his Divine Majesty would be served and pleased to choose them for it, to no less a degree of actual poverty; second, by attracting them to a desire of reproaches and contempt, since from these results humility.

In this way there will be three steps: the first, poverty in opposition to riches; the second, reproaches or contempt in opposition to honor from the world; and the third, humility in opposition to pride. Then from these three steps they should induce people to all the other virtues.

The First Colloquy should be with Our Lady. I beg her to obtain for me grace to be received under the standard of her Son and Lord; that is, to be received, first, in the highest degree of spiritual poverty and also, if his Divine Majesty would be served and if he should wish to choose me for it, to no less a degree of actual poverty; and second, in bearing reproaches and injuries, that through them I may imitate him more, if only I can do this without sin on anyone's part and without displeasure to his Divine Majesty. Then I will say a Hail Mary.

The Second Colloquy. It will be to ask the same grace from the Son, that he may obtain it for me from the Father. Then I will say the Soul of Christ.

The Third Colloquy will be to ask the same grace from the Father, that he may grant it to me. Then I will say an Our Father.

Note. This exercise will be made at midnight and again after arising. There will also be two repetitions of it, one near the hour of Mass and one near that of Vespers. Each of these exercises will close with the three colloquies: one with Our Lady, one with the Son, and one with the Father. * * *

SAINT TERESA OF ÁVILA
1515–1582

FROM THE BOOK OF HER LIFE

Teresa Sánchez de Cepeda y Ahumada was born into a noble family (though her paternal grandfather was a converted Jew [*marrano*] and her father purchased his title) in the province of Ávila, Spain, and died in the Salamanca province. Also known as Teresa of Jesus, she was a nun, a noted mystic, a theologian, a writer, and a reformer of the Carmelite Order. Together with Saint John of the Cross (see p. 429), she founded the Discalced (from the Latin for "barefoot") Carmelite Order, bare feet standing, so to speak, for a determination to live a more ascetic and devout life in common. Though a cloistered sister, she took repeated journeys across Spain, establishing and organizing convents. She is one of the few women who bear the title Doctor (from the Latin for "Teacher") of the Church.

Despite her lack of formal education, Teresa wrote masterpieces of contemplative and mystical writing. Her books *The Interior Castle* and *The Way of Perfection* are major testimonies to the meditative and mystical practices of the Spanish Counter-Reformation. She wrote her autobiography at the suggestion of her confessor, as a way to forestall accusations of heresy or lack of orthodoxy. Under the Spanish Inquisition, anyone, and especially a woman attempting to be a theologian, was liable to be accused of such deviance.

Ávila: *ah´-vee-lah*

The Italian sculptor, architect, and painter Gian or Giovanni Lorenzo Bernini created this white marble sculpture of Saint Teresa of Ávila in 1647–52. Known as *Saint Teresa in Ecstasy*, the *Ecstasy of Saint Teresa*, and the *Transverberation of Saint Teresa*, it is the central sculptural group in the Cornaro Chapel, in the church of Santa Maria della Vittoria, Rome. (Bernini also designed the setting of the chapel in marble, stucco, and paint.) In her autobiography, Saint Teresa describes undergoing such a *transverberation*—literally, a "piercing" of the heart by a dart of divine love.

FROM THE BOOK OF HER LIFE

CHAPTER I

Childhood and Early Impressions. The Blessing of Pious Parents.
Desire of Martyrdom. Death of the Saint's Mother.

1. I had a father and mother, who were devout and feared God. Our Lord also helped me with His grace. All this would have been enough to make me good, if I had not been so wicked. My father was very much given to the reading of good books; and so he had them in Spanish, that his children might read them. These books, with my mother's carefulness to make us say our prayers, and to bring us up devout to our Lady and to certain Saints, began to make me think seriously when I was, I believe, six or seven years old. It helped me, too, that I never saw my father and mother respect anything but goodness. They were very good themselves. My father was a man of great charity towards the poor, and compassion for the sick, and also for servants; so much so, that he never could be persuaded to keep slaves, for he pitied them so much: and a slave belonging to one of his brothers being once in his house, was treated by him with as much tenderness as his own children. He used to say that he could not endure the pain of seeing that she was not free. He was a man of great truthfulness; nobody ever heard him swear or speak ill of any one; his life was most pure.

2. My mother also was a woman of great goodness, and her life was spent in great infirmities. She was singularly pure in all her ways. Though possessing great beauty, yet was it never known that she gave reason to suspect that she made any account whatever of it; for, though she was only three-and-thirty years of age when she died, her apparel was already that of a woman advanced in years. She was very calm, and had great sense. The sufferings she went through during her life were grievous, her death most Christian.

3. We were three sisters and nine brothers. All, by the mercy of God, resembled their parents in goodness except myself, though I was the most cherished of my father. And, before I began to offend God, I think he had some reason—for I am filled with sorrow whenever I think of the good desires with which our Lord inspired me, and what a wretched use I made of them. Besides, my brothers never in any way hindered me in the service of God.

4. One of my brothers was nearly of my own age; and he it was whom I most loved, though I was very fond of them all, and they of me. He and I used to read Lives of Saints together. When I read of martyrdom undergone by the Saints for the love of God, it struck me that the vision of God was very cheaply purchased; and I had a great desire to die a martyr's death—not out of any love of Him of which I was conscious, but that I might most quickly attain to the fruition of those great joys of which I read that they were reserved in Heaven; and I used to discuss with my brother how we could become martyrs. We settled to go together to the country of the Moors, begging our way for the love of God, that we might be there beheaded; and our Lord, I believe, had given us courage enough, even at so tender an age, if we

FROM *St. Teresa of Jesus of the Order of Our Lady of Carmel: Embracing the Life, Relations, Maxims, and Foundations Written by the Saint; Also, a History of St. Teresa's Journeys and Foundations*, ed. John J. Burke.

could have found the means to proceed; but our greatest difficulty seemed to be our father and mother.

5. It astonished us greatly to find it said in what we were reading that pain and bliss were everlasting. We happened very often to talk about this; and we had a pleasure in repeating frequently, "For ever, ever, ever." Through the constant uttering of these words, our Lord was pleased that I should receive an abiding impression of the way of truth when I was yet a child.

6. As soon as I saw it was impossible to go to any place where people would put me to death for the sake of God, my brother and I set about becoming hermits; and in an orchard belonging to the house we contrived, as well as we could, to build hermitages, by piling up small stones one on the other, which fell down immediately; and so it came to pass that we found no means of accomplishing our wish. Even now, I have a feeling of devotion when I consider how God gave me in my early youth what I lost by my own fault. I gave alms as I could—and I could but little. I contrived to be alone, for the sake of saying my prayers—and they were many—especially the Rosary, to which my mother had a great devotion, and had made us also in this like herself. I used to delight exceedingly, when playing with other children, in the building of monasteries, as if we were nuns; and I think I wished to be a nun, though not so much as I did to be a martyr or a hermit.

7. I remember that, when my mother died, I was about twelve years old—a little less. When I began to understand my loss, I went in my affliction to an image of our Lady, and with many tears implored her to be my mother. I did this in my simplicity, and I believe that it was of service to me; for I have by experience found the royal Virgin helped me whenever I recommended myself to her; and at last she has brought me back to herself. It distresses me now, when I think of, and reflect on, that which kept me from being earnest in the good desires with which I began.

8. O my Lord, since Thou art determined to save me—may it be the pleasure of Thy Majesty to effect it!—and to bestow upon me so many graces, why has it not been Thy pleasure also—not for my advantage, but for Thy greater honour—that this habitation, wherein Thou hast continually to dwell, should not have contracted so much defilement? It distresses me even to say this, O my Lord, because I know the fault is all my own, seeing that Thou hast left nothing undone to make me, even from my youth, wholly Thine. When I would complain of my parents, I cannot do it; for I saw nothing in them but all good, and carefulness for my welfare. Then, growing up, I began to discover the natural gifts which our Lord had given me—they were said to be many; and, when I should have given Him thanks for them, I made use of every one of them, as I shall now explain, to offend Him.

CHRISTIANITY REACHES THE
NEW WORLD AND CHINA

The centuries of the Reformations and the Christian Wars of Religion, when Christians were at each others' throats in so much of the Christian heartland, were also the centuries when, for the first time, Christianity overtook Islam in sheer size and became what it has remained: the largest religion in the world.

Catholic Christian missionaries accompanied or soon followed in the wake of the historic sixteenth-century commercial and military explorations by Portugal and Spain, great powers then at the pinnacle of their world influence. Dominicans, Franciscans, and Jesuits were among the leading religious orders dedicated to this global missionary work. Not until the eighteenth and nineteenth centuries did Protestant Christian missionaries become as active.

The Catholic missions were hugely successful in the Americas; most of the indigenous inhabitants of the Americas converted to Catholic Christianity. In Asia, the Philippine Islands were also almost entirely Christianized. Contemporaneous Catholic missions to India, China, and Japan were another story. In the Far East, the Western evangelizers were few in number and ever vulnerable to suppression amid a large, dense population hostile to outside ideas.

The Jesuits in India made a promising start under the gifted Italian Roberto de Nobili (1588–1656). An intellectually even more far-sighted effort by the Jesuits in China, above all through the work of Matteo Ricci (1552–1610), achieved much greater success. These efforts, however, were suppressed by the Vatican. Though the sort of cultural adaptation achieved by the Jesuits was opposed by other religious orders and Rome in the seventeenth century, all eventually accepted such accommodation.

Along with their religion, the Catholic missionaries brought Western languages and cultures as well as diseases and sometimes brutal oppression to the Americas. Yet in many cases the missionaries tried to protect the natives against the Iberian colonizers. The best exemplar of this latter effort is the Dominican friar Bartolomé de las Casas, included in this section, who lobbied the Spanish government on behalf of the Indians. Las Casas originally proposed importing African slaves to replace the enslaved Indians, but he changed his mind and defended the Africans as well. His vivid reports on the abuses of Spanish rule, especially in his scathing *Short Account of the Destruction of the Indies* (1552), contributed paradoxically to what is sometimes called the Black Legend of Spanish Catholic colonialism as a saga of unmitigated barbaric cruelty. At the time, Spain's Protestant enemies consumed this legend eagerly. However, their eventual colonial record would prove no better.

BARTOLOMÉ DE LAS CASAS
1484–1556

FROM RULES FOR CONFESSORS

Bartolomé de las Casas was born in Seville, Spain, and died in Madrid. In 1502, he became one of the first settlers in the New World colonies. During the following decades, he advocated for the rights of the natives and protested vigorously against their enslavement by the Spanish colonizers, especially by appealing to the Spanish court. After a failed attempt to establish a peaceful colony on the coast of Venezuela, Las Casas became a Dominican monk, and his continued work on behalf of indigenous peoples took him to Central America, then to Mexico, and back to Spain. For a brief time, he served as bishop of Chiapas, Mexico.

A pioneering theorist and activist in the field of human rights, Las Casas chronicled the first decades of the colonization of the West Indies. His most famous works, *The Destruction of the Indies* (1552) and *Historia de Las Indias* (unfinished but published in three volumes in 1875), focus particularly on the atrocities committed by the colonizers. As bishop of Chiapas, Las Casas wrote the following selection, a manual for the administration of the sacrament of confession in his diocese. In these rules, he stipulated that colonial overlords could not receive the sacraments if they enslaved native peoples. While all Roman Catholic priests can exercise the sacrament of penance and hear confessions, their right to exercise these powers is granted by the local bishop, precisely to ensure that the priests live up to their responsibilities.

PRONOUNCING GLOSSARY

Bartolomé de las Casas: *bar-toh-loh-may´ day lahs cah´-sahs*
Castile: *cah-steel´*

comenderos: *coh-men-de´-rohs*
conquistadors: *cohn-kees´-tah-dors*
encomiendas: *en-coh-mee-en´-dahs*

FROM RULES FOR CONFESSORS
Prologue

Confessors should keep to and judge by the following twelve rules when they hear confessions of penitents in the Indies, or elsewhere of penitents from the Indies, those who have been conquistadors overseas, who have held or now hold natives by allotment, or had a share in the wealth made from natives or through natives.

The first rule, for present purposes, deals with three kinds of penitents who come to confession: 1) conquistadors, 2) settlers who have allotments of natives, those otherwise called *comenderos*, or those who control *encomiendas*,[1] 3) merchants, not every one, but those who transported arms and

---

Translated by Patrick Francis Sullivan. Bracketed insertions are the translator's.

1. As legally defined in 1503, the Spanish crown's entrustment to a conquistador, soldier, official, or other Spaniard of a specified number of natives in a particular area. "*Comenderos*" (or *encomenderos*): the receivers of such grants, who were required to protect the indigenous people entrusted to them and instruct them in Christianity. The *encomiendas* did not include land, but the *encomenderos* tended to gain control of land as they abused the people living on it.

provisions to the ones doing the conquering, the ones making war on the natives, merchants warlike themselves in their cooperation. If it is a conquistador, one who, close to death, wants to go to confession, call a notary public or an official of the King before the penitent begins. The confessor should make the conquistador declare, ordain, and grant the following things: First, he is to agree and say that he chooses so-and-so for his confessor, a secular priest or religious priest of x order. Then that the conquistador is a believing Christian and wants to depart this life free of offense to God and with clear conscience, thus to stand before the judgment seat of God in a state of innocence. He gives his confessor complete power over all those matters the confessor judges to pertain to his salvation—insofar as the penitent is able and is obliged to by divine and human law in the discharge of his conscience. If the confessor should think, should judge it necessary for the man to give back all he owns in the manner the confessor judges best, leaving nothing at all to his heirs, the confessor is free to do so. It is what the sick man, penitent man should do, would do freely, if he were still alive, for the safety of his soul. As a dying man, he submits all he owns to his confessor's best judgment, without condition, without limit of any kind.

Second, the writer declares, admits he took part in this or that conquest or those wars against the natives in the Indies, was responsible himself or helped commit the robberies, the violences, the devastations, the murders, the enslavements of natives, and that the destruction of many cities and towns was done for that express purpose.

Third, the writer declares, admits that he brought no wealth from Castile.[2] Everything he owns he owns from the natives, or through them, though some possessions come from his own labor. He admits how much the wealth is that he has from the natives, how much he owes them, what the damages are he has done them, or cooperated in doing since he came out to the Indies, and that far greater wealth than his would not suffice to pay them back. And therefore it is his wish, his final wish that the confessor he named should give it all back, should make total satisfaction, at least insofar as all his holdings could do it, as the confessor shall see fit for the man's soul, and to that end he binds the confessor in strict conscience.

Fourth, if the penitent should hold any Indians enslaved, whatever the way or the title by which he got them or keeps them, he is to give them their freedom instantaneously, and irrevocably, no ifs, ands, or buts. He is to beg pardon from them for the harm he did in making them slaves, in taking their freedom from them, or helping to do so, or in being an accomplice in the slave making, and if not in the slave making, pardon for having in bad faith purchased them, held them, used them as slaves. * * *

Fifth, that the penitent revoke any other will he has made, or codicil to a will, affirming this will to be the only one he wants to have stand as valid and sound, and that it be obeyed as his last. * * *

Sixth, the penitent is to make a solemn oath, in legal and binding form, an oath he will keep and fulfill, concerning all his goods, furnishings, holdings, that he consents to the disposition his confessor shall command to be made of all his material goods, nothing at all excepted. Should it happen that the penitent recovers from his illness, he will not revoke this will, in whole or in part, while he lives, nor at the end when he dies. * * *

2. North-central province of Spain that includes the capital, Madrid.

* * * After the penitent makes and signs the will as described above, the confessor then hears the confession. The confessor urges the penitent to have a deep, deep sorrow and regret for his enormous sins. They are the sins he committed, doing terrible damages and evils himself, or aiding them to be done, harrassing the natives, robbing them, killing them, depriving them of their freedom, of their authority, of their womenfolk, of their children, of their living, making countless widows, countless orphans of them, blackening their name by calling them beasts, extremes of cruelty committed or promoted against the natives. * * *

The penitent must regret not only what he committed with his own hands, he must be sorry as well for all the evils, all the harm done by those others he came out with. Each of them is responsible for the whole. The reasoning is this: every one of them who came out knew well why they came—to conquer, they all had exactly that purpose. And they brought no authorization from the King to do the evils they did. And even if they had such authorization, it would have been worthless as an excuse, no reason could justify the horrible wars they waged against the natives. The only reason they had was their own ambition, their insatiable greed. And therefore each one of them is obliged to have remorse for the offenses all committed. * * * Each one is required to make restitution for what everyone stole, what everyone acquired so wickedly, for the damages all did, even though a particular person did not gain or spend a cent of the fortune made. Each one is obliged to restore the fortune.

Third rule: the confessor, once he has a reckoning of all the goods of the penitent, should learn broadly which were the places where the penitent did the harm, the evil to the natives, he and his accomplices. And if the injured parties are alive still, or their offspring are, the confessor shall order them paid what he thinks just, and shall make known in a public way what he has worked out and made mandatory. If there are no survivors among said natives, restitution shall be made for the good of their villages, if the villages were not entirely destroyed. Natives from other areas nearby may be brought in to restore said villages. They are to be given their livelihood, or sources of livelihood, or provisions to start them off. Or restitution may be made by freeing natives who were enslaved during the time when tyranny reigned and fear of the Lord and of eternal damnation impelled no one who held slaves to set them free. * * *

Fourth rule: Even if the dead man has a hundred legitimate sons, he may not leave them a cent, nothing is owed them by law, nothing by way of inheritance, they have no right to that estate. Out of charity he may leave them what the confessor thinks is enough to feed them. Though he can give enough of a livelihood so they can become settlers. * * * He can even give them preference over strangers, all other things being equal, but beyond that nothing. The explanation for the first part of the rule is this: Not a one of those conquistadors has a single cent that is really his. * * *

*   *   *

Eleventh rule: Those merchants sinned mortally who imported war matériel such as firearms, gunpowder, bullets, lances, swords, and the worst weapon of all, horses, while the Spaniards were in the act of conquering and subjugating the natives—as they are now doing in Peru, have been doing all along, as they did in New Spain and Guatemala, Santa Marta, Venezuela, and other places. They are guilty of all the evils, of all the damage done by those things, they are bound to restitution for whatever they stole, for whomever they terrorized, killed, destroyed.

The reason for the rule is this: They were participants, causes along with the actual doers of the evils, the plunderers, the devastators, because of the aid they gave them through the matériel of war. They knew, more or less, those wars, those conquests, were unjust. At the very least they were in doubt or were obliged to doubt the justice of them. And that is quite enough to put them in bad faith. They are guilty of the whole thing. So, in like manner, they are obliged to make restitution of the money they made selling arms to the conquistador, though they wielded no weapon themselves. Since the robbers, the thugs, had nothing they had not stolen, they paid the merchants in stolen gold and silver, so were unable to give the least bit of that back, while the wine and clothing they had were luxury items and useless for other than gifts. What we say supposes the merchants were not in good faith. * * *

Twelfth rule: The confessor must dispose the penitent to keep a firm purpose, in the future, about two things. First, that he never again participate in a conquest or war against the natives. Spaniards will never have a just cause for war against the peoples of the Indies of the Ocean Sea,[3] no matter the passage of time or years. Second, he will not go to Peru while the thugs there are in rebellion against the King. And even if they should return to obedience, he will not go while they continue to slaughter natives and make our faith a thing of mockery to them.

"These are hard words and who can take them? The one who would follow the straight and narrow path that leads to eternal life."[4]

---

3. I.e., the Caribbean Sea. 4. See John 6:60.

SOR JUANA INÉS DE LA CRUZ
1651–1695

FROM REPLY TO SISTER PHILOTHEA

Juana Inés de Asbaje y Ramírez de Santillana was born in San Miguel Nepantla, New Spain (modern-day Mexico), and died in Mexico City. Self-educated, she became a scholar, theologian, poet, and playwright. Although she lived as a subject of colonial Spain, she is considered one of the first Mexican writers to produce literature in Spanish.

It has often been remarked that in socioeconomic terms, the freest women in male-dominated European and colonial societies were wealthy, childless widows. In Catholic countries, well-born, well-educated nuns, living in convents maintained effectively for women of their class, could approximate the freedom of such widows. Juana became just such a nun, taking the title Sor (Sister) Juana de la Cruz in the convent of the small, well-provided Order of St. Jerome in Mexico City.

Sor Juana's voluminous writings, many of which were published after her death, are in various genres. They reflect the eclectic but independent mind of a brilliant woman who had enjoyed neither the benefits nor the restrictions of extensive formal schooling but could read whatever she wanted and buy whatever she needed.

At the request and for the private purposes of an eminent friend, the bishop of Puebla, Manuel Fernandez de Santa Cruz, Sor Juana wrote a critique of a published sermon by the then-eminent Portuguese-Brazilian Jesuit António de Vieira (1608–1697). Clearly impressed by the learnedness, stylishness, clarity, and cogency of the exposition, Bishop Fernandez published Sor Juana's critique. He gave it the arcane title *Athenagoric Letter* (Letter in the Manner of Athenagoras) and framed it as a letter from Sor Juana to a fictitious Sor Filotea. The title is apparently an allusion to the famous letter that Athenagoras, a Greek convert to early Christianity, wrote in 177 to Emperor Marcus Aurelius, urging toleration for oppressed Christians. Thereupon, writing in the name of Filotea, the bishop wrote a response to Sor Juana, lavishing praise on her yet urging that she devote her talents to the exposition of the Bible rather than the writing of secular literature. At times, he bluntly exhorts Sor Juana to give up higher learning altogether: "Other religious women sacrifice their will in the name of obedience; yours it is to imprison the understanding, which is the most difficult but the most pleasing holocaust that can be offered on the altar of religion."

Sor Juana was beginning to acquire fame for her poetry and drama at the time she wrote her response: *Reply to Sister Philothea* (Latin form of the Spanish *Filotea*), often called, in Spanish, simply *La Respuesta*. No work of Sor Juana's—and few works in her time—had a sharper feminist edge than this letter. Displaying rhetorical indignation and playful irreverence, Sor Juana addresses her correspondent with studied familiarity as her dear sister in religion, knowing, of course, that she is addressing a powerful bishop as "my Lady." She adroitly urges toleration for teachers, scholars, and oppressed intellectual women, poets in the lead.

The 18th-century painter Miguel Cabrera, a member of the indigenous Zapotec people of New Spain (modern-day Mexico), painted this portrait of Sor Juana in 1750. Oil on canvas, it hangs in the National Museum of History, Chapultepec Castle, Mexico City. (Detail shown here.)

Sor Juana died a few years later, and during those years she seems to have been forced to call her writing career to a halt. Her reply was published post-humously.

PRONOUNCING GLOSSARY

Pharisee: *fair´-i-see* Salome: *sahl-oh´-may*
Philothea: *fee-loh-tay´-ah* Vieira: *vee-ay´-rah*
Pliny: *pli´-nee*

FROM REPLY TO SISTER PHILOTHEA

There is no doubt that much knowledge of history, customs, ceremonies, proverbs, and idioms of the times in which they were written is necessary in order to know the nature of the references and allusions in many passages in holy scripture. *Scindite corda vestra, et non vestimenta vestra* [Rend your heart and not your garments—Joel 2:13]. Is this not an allusion to the ceremony in which the Hebrews had to rend their garments as a sign of grief, as did the evil high priest when he said that Christ had blasphemed? (Matthew 26:65). Do not the many passages of the apostle Paul concerning the help for widows also reflect the customs of those times? The passage about the valiant woman, *Nobilis in portis vir eius* [Her husband is praised at the gates—Proverbs 31:23], does that not allude to the custom of the courts sitting in judgment at the city gates? The *dare terram Deo* [give the land to God], does it not mean to make some kind of vow? *Hiemantes* [those wintering], is not this what they called public sinners who did penance in the open air, as distinguished from those who did penance in the doorway of the churches? The reproach that Christ made to the Pharisee for his failing to kiss him in greeting and to wash his feet, was it not based on the custom among the Jews to do these things? * * *

All this requires more study than some think, who, remaining at the level of grammar, or at most using the four basic principles of formal logic, think they can interpret scripture and cling doggedly to *Mulieres in Ecclesiis taceant*,[1] without knowing how it should be understood. As to the other passage, *Mulier in silentio discat* [Woman shall learn in silence—I Timothy 2:11], this passage is more in favor than against women, since it requires them to study, and while they study it is clear that they need to be silent. We also read: *Audi Israel, et tace* [Hear, Israel, and be silent].[2] There, the whole assembly of men and women is addressed, and all are commanded to be silent, because for those hearing and learning it is only right for them to be attentive and silent. If this is not the case, I would like those interpreters and exegetes of St. Paul to explain to me how they understand *Mulieres in Ecclesia taceant*, based on their conception of church, which in the material sense can be pulpits and lecterns, or in the formal sense the universality of the faithful. If they understand it in the first sense, which is, in my opinion,

TRANSLATED BY Pamela Kirk Rappaport. Bracketed insertions are the translator's.

1. Let women be silent in the church (Latin); 1 Corinthians 14:34–35.

2. Deuteronomy 27:9 but with the key terms reversed: "Be attentive, Israel, and hear."

its true meaning in this instance, because we see that in effect it is not permitted that women teach publicly or preach, why should those women who study in private be reprimanded? If church is understood in the second sense, and the prohibition of the Apostle applied in the most far-reaching sense so that women are not allowed even in secret to write or study, how can it be that the church has permitted women like Gertrude, Teresa, Bridget, the nun of Ágreda,[3] and many others to do so? And if they tell me that these were saints, though that is true, it does not nullify my argument. In the first place, because St. Paul's proposition is absolute, including all women without excepting holy ones, because in his time there were holy women such as Martha and Mary, Marcela, Mary, the mother of Jacob and Salome,[4] and many others who participated with fervor in the primitive church, and Paul did not exclude them in his statement. Today we see that the church permits both women saints and those who are not to write, since the nun of Ágreda and María de la Antigua[5] are not canonized and their writings circulate. Neither were St. Teresa and the others canonized at the time they were writing. Therefore St. Paul's prohibition aims only at the public nature of the pulpit, because if the Apostle had prohibited all writing to women, the church would also not permit it as it does today.

✻   ✻   ✻

If there were a crime associated with the *Athenagoric Letter*, was it more than simply to report my opinion with all the permissions I owe to our Holy Mother Church? Because if she, with her most holy authority, does not forbid me doing so, why should others prohibit me? It was impudence on my part to develop an opinion contrary to Vieira's, but it was not impudence on the part of Father Vieira to contradict three holy fathers of the church?[6] Is my mind, such as it is, not as free as his, since it is descended from the same source? Is his opinion one of the revealed truths of our holy faith that we are required to believe blindly? Furthermore, I never failed to give what respect is due to a man such as he, as his defender has failed to do when he forgot the words of Titus Livius:[7] *Artes committatur decor* [The arts are to be respected]. Nor did I lay a finger on the Society of Jesus.[8] Nor did I write anything that went beyond the judgment of the one who suggested it to me. And according to Pliny,[9] *non similis est conditio publicantis, et nominatim dicentis* [It is one thing to say something, another to have it published]. Had I believed it would be published, it would not have been as slipshod as it was.

3. Gertrude of Helfta (1256–1302), in Saxony, celebrated in 17th-century Spain; Teresa of Ávila (see p. 434); Bridget of Sweden (1303–1373), whose dictated religious visions were published in a Latin translation; and María de Jesús de Ágreda (1602–1665), of Spain, were nuns admired for their learning and their sanctity. The last named was the object of widespread devotion in the Mexico (then including modern Arizona and New Mexico) of Sor Juana's day.
4. Martha and Mary were two sisters who were friends of Jesus; see John 11. There is no Marcela in the New Testament (though there was a Saint Marcella of Rome, 325–410); this name might be Sor Juana's mistake for Mary, the mother of John Mark (Acts 12:12), since Marcella is the feminine form of Mark. Mary, the mother of Jacob (i.e., the Apostle James the Less,

brother of Jesus), and Salome (the wife of Zebedee and mother of the Apostles James the Greater and John) are mentioned in Mark 16:1.
5. Spanish nun and devotional writer (1566–1611).
6. Vieira contradicted Saints Augustine (see p. 226), John Chrysostom (see p. 180), and Thomas Aquinas (see p. 317) on the question of what constituted the essence of Christ's love for humanity.
7. Roman historian (59 B.C.E.–17 C.E.), known in English as Livy.
8. The Jesuit order (see p. 430). Sor Juana writes with droll irony, for though she had dared to criticize the thinking of one famous Jesuit, "laying a finger on" the powerful order was quite beyond her.
9. Pliny the Elder (23–79 C.E.), Roman scholar.

If it were heretical in the opinion of my critic, why did he not denounce it? In that case he would remain avenged, and I would be happier to be appreciated as I ought with the name of Catholic and obedient daughter of my Holy Mother Church than with many accolades as a learned woman. If the letter is rough, as you rightly point out, you may laugh, although it will be a forced laugh. I'm not asking for your approval, since I was free to disagree with Vieira, just as anyone is free to disagree with my findings.

*   *   *

If I turn my eyes again to that much maligned facility for composing poetry—which for me is so natural that I do violence to myself not to write this letter in verse—I could say, *Quidquid conabar dicere, versus erat* [When I tried to say something, poetry resulted]. Seeing this facility condemned and blamed so much by so many, I searched very deliberately for the harm it could cause, without being able to find it. Rather, I have seen poetry applauded in the mouths of the sibyls and sanctified through the writing of the prophets, especially King David.[1] * * *

If the evil consists in women writing poetry, we have already seen that many women have used poetry in a praiseworthy fashion. What then is the harm in my doing so? Of course, I admit I am base and vile, but I do not believe that anyone has seen a single indecent couplet of mine. Moreover, I have never written anything of my own free will, but rather because of the entreaties and commands of others, so that I cannot recall having written anything for my own pleasure except a little scrap of a thing they call *El Sueño* [The Dream].[2] The letter that you, my Lady, have so honored, I wrote with greater reluctance than any other, as much because it concerned sacred matters for which (as I have said) I have reverence and awe, as because it might have the appearance of intending to spark controversy, something for which I have a natural aversion. I believe, had I been able to anticipate the fortunate destiny for which it was born—like another Moses, after I had thrown it out to be exposed to the waters of the Nile of silence, where it would be found and cherished by a princess such as you[3]—I believe, I repeat, that if I had understood this would be its fate, I would have strangled it with my own hands at the moment of birth, for fear that my clumsy, ignorant scribbling would appear before the light of your wisdom. The magnitude of your kindness is revealed since your will praises precisely what must be repugnant to your enlightened mind. But since destiny cast it on your doorstep, a foundling and an orphan, so that you even gave it a name, it grieves me that among all its shortcomings, it also bears the defects of hasty composition. * * *

* * * Although my nature is such that most often I ruin the opportunities or mix it with such defects and imperfections that I spoil what by itself would have been good. Thus in the little I have published, not only my name, but not even the permission for publication has been a decision of my own, but the decision of others beyond my control, such as happened

---

1. Second king of the United Kingdom of Israel (ca. 1040–970 B.C.E.; reigned from ca. 1002 until his death); traditionally considered the author of nearly half of the Book of Psalms (see p. 96).
2. Sor Juana writes with mock modesty, for this work is in fact her longest, most ambitious, and most admired poem.
3. In Exodus 2, Pharaoh's daughter, an Egyptian princess, rescues the infant Moses from the Nile. Sor Juana addresses the bishop playfully as "a princess such as you."

with the *Athenagoric Letter*. As a result, only the *Exercises for the Incarnation* and the *Offerings for the Sorrows* were printed with my permission for public devotion, but without my name. I will send you some copies of them so that, if it seems good to you, you can distribute them among our sisters, the religious of your holy community, and moreover of your city. I can only send you one copy of *Sorrows* because the rest have been used up and no more can be made. I only wrote them for the devotion of my sisters many years ago, and afterward they were published. Their subjects are so disproportionate to my tepid heart and to my ignorance that it was only their subject, our great Queen, that helped me. There is something about the consideration of most holy Mary that is bound to inflame the coldest heart. * * *

* * *

Venerable Lady, if the style of this letter has not been to your liking, I beg pardon for its homely familiarity or less than due respect since, while I have been treating you as a veiled religious, my sister, I have forgotten the distance between myself and your illustrious person. If I were to see you without the veil, that would not happen. But you, with your common sense and your kindness, will make up for and correct the terms in question. If the *Vos*[4] seems incongruous to you, I used it because it seemed to me that out of the reverence that I owe you it would be irreverent to address you as *Your Reverence*. Change it from what appeared appropriate to what you deserve. I dared not exceed the limits of your style or violate the margin of your modesty.

Keep me in your good graces in order to beseech divine favors for me. May the Lord grant you much increase and keep you safe, as I beg of him and need.

From the convent of our father St. Jerome in Mexico City, the first day of March sixteen hundred and ninety one.

Your most favored servant, Juana Inés de la Cruz

4. A third-person locution such as "your grace" would be more appropriate for a bishop than the second-person *vos*—"you" in regional Spanish. In addressing the bishop as a fellow nun, Sor Juana teases him for hiding behind the pseudonym Sor Filotea.

NICHOLAS TRIGAULT
1577–1628

[A SEVENTEENTH-CENTURY JESUIT MISSIONARY IN CHINA]

Born in Douai, France (then part of the Spanish Netherlands), Nicholas Trigault played a major role in bringing news of Chinese civilization to the West. A Jesuit priest and scholar, he volunteered for the Jesuit missions in China and arrived in Nanjing in 1611. By 1563, the Jesuits had established a permanent station in the Portuguese colony of Macao, whence they launched a unique cultural, scientific, and religious embassy to the mainland. Priests such as Matteo Ricci (1552–1610), an Italian—who were skilled in mathematics, astronomy, physics, and engineering—made a powerful impression on the Chinese intellectual elite, especially when they introduced unfamiliar technology, such as clocks, and did so in fluent Chinese.

In 1613, Trigault left Macao for Rome to promote and raise money for the mission. During his twenty-one-month journey, he translated Ricci's China journal into Latin and supplied it with a book-length introduction to Chinese society, from which the following excerpt is taken. When published in 1615 as *De Christiana Expeditione apud Sinas Suscepta ab Societate Jesu* ("About the Christian Expedition to China Undertaken by the Society of Jesus"), Trigault's work caused a sensation, and Trigault became enough of a celebrity to have his portrait sketched by the Flemish artist Peter Paul Rubens (1577–1640) in 1617. The next year, he returned to China with another band of missionaries. Ten years later, however, Trigault hanged himself, possibly while depressed over his failure to convince the Jesuits in China to use the Chinese term *shang-di* ("High Sovereign") for God.

Cosmopolitans such as Ricci and Trigault tried to find as many points of agreement as possible between Christianity and Chinese culture. They praised the Chinese "Prince of Philosophers," K'ung-Fu-tzu (551–479 B.C.E.), and awarded him the Latin name Confucius. They noted Chinese respect for the Golden Rule, which was memorably cited, in different versions, by the eminent Jewish teacher Rabbi Hillel (1st century B.C.E.–1st century C.E.) and by Jesus (Matthew 7:12). They defended the custom of venerating dead ancestors and placing food on their graves as mere familial piety and not pagan superstition. They presented Chinese culture as highly spiritual, moral, and untainted by the "monsters of vice" found in the Egyptian and Greco-Roman religions. They felt sure that if Christian missionaries avoided European arrogance and dressed and acted like the supremely influential "Litterati" (a class of scholarly civil servants, also known as mandarins), the door would be thrown open to what we now call ecumenism, which would lead to waves of conversion. "The teachings of this academy," Trigault writes, "are so far from being contrary to Christian principles, that such an institution could derive great benefit from Christianity and might be developed and perfected by it." The way had been paved by the ancient traditional belief in "one supreme being whom they called the King of Heaven, or designated by some other name indicating his rule over heaven and earth."

The liberal Jesuit strategy of cultural assimilation was stoutly resisted by the Spanish Franciscans and other conservative Catholic groups influential in the Vatican. The "Chinese rites controversy" raged for more than a century until, in 1742, Pope Benedict XIV condemned the Jesuit approach. In 1778, after being condemned in, and exiled from, many parts of Europe and Latin America, the Jesuits were suppressed altogether by Pope Clement XIV, not to be restored until 1814. In 1939, Pope Pius XII lifted the ban on the Chinese veneration of the dead. By the late twentieth century, "inculturation" had become official Catholic missionary policy, and Matteo Ricci was being considered for sainthood.

PRONOUNCING GLOSSARY

Confucius: *kun-fyoo´-shus*　　　　　Nicholas Trigault: *nee-coh-lah´ tree-goh´*

[A SEVENTEENTH-CENTURY JESUIT MISSIONARY IN CHINA]

Of all the pagan sects known to Europe, I know of no people who fell into fewer errors in the early ages of their antiquity than did the Chinese. From the very beginning of their history it is recorded in their writings that they recognized and worshiped one supreme being whom they called the King of Heaven, or designated by some other name indicating his rule over heaven

TRANSLATED BY L. J. Gallagher.

and earth. It would appear that the ancient Chinese considered heaven and earth to be animated things and that their common soul was worshiped as a supreme deity. As subject to this spirit, they also worshiped the different spirits of the mountains and rivers, and of the four corners of the earth. They also taught that the light of reason came from heaven and that the dictates of reason should be hearkened to in every human action. Nowhere do we read that the Chinese created monsters of vice out of this supreme being or from his ministering deities, such as the Romans, the Greeks, and the Egyptians evolved into gods or patrons of the vices.

*   *   *

* * * The sect of the Litterati is proper to China and is the most ancient in the kingdom. They rule the Republic, have an extensive literature, and are far more celebrated than the others. Individually, the Chinese do not choose this sect; they rather imbibe the doctrine of it in the study of letters. No one who attains honors in the study of letters or who even undertakes the study would belong to any other sect. Confucius is their Prince of Philosophers, and according to them, it was he who discovered the art of philosophy. They do not believe in idol worship. In fact they have no idols. They do, however, believe in one deity who preserves and governs all things on earth. Other spirits they admit, but these are of less restricted domination and receive only minor honors. The real Litterati teach nothing relative to the time, the manner, or the author of the creation of the world. * * *

*   *   *

Although the Litterati, as they are called, do recognize one supreme deity, they erect no special temple in his honor. No special place is assigned for his worship, consequently no priests or ministers are designated to direct that worship. We do not find any special rites to be observed by all or precepts to be followed, nor any supreme authority to explain or promulgate laws or to punish violations of laws pertaining to a supreme being. Neither are there any public or private prayers or hymns to be said or sung in honor of a supreme deity. The duty of sacrifice and the rites of worship for this supreme being belong to the imperial majesty alone. This is so true that if anyone else should offer such a sacrifice in usurpation of this right, he would be punished as an intruder upon the duty of the king and as a public enemy. * * *

The most common ceremony practiced by all the Litterati, from the king down to the very lowest of them, is that of the annual funeral rites * * *. As they themselves say, they consider this ceremony as an honor bestowed upon their departed ancestors, just as they might honor them if they were living. They do not really believe that the dead actually need the victuals which are placed upon their graves, but they say that they observe the custom of placing them there because it seems to be the best way of testifying their love for their dear departed. Indeed, it is asserted by many that this particular rite was first instituted for the benefit of the living rather than for that of the dead. In this way it was hoped that children, and unlearned adults as well, might learn how to respect and to support their parents who were living, when they saw that parents departed were so highly honored by those who were educated and prominent. This practice of placing food upon the graves of the dead seems to be beyond any charge of sacrilege and perhaps also free from any taint of superstition, because they do not in any respect consider their ancestors to be gods, nor do they petition them for anything or hope for anything from them. However, for those who have accepted the teachings of Christianity, it would seem much better to replace this custom with alms for the poor and for the salvation of souls.

The Temple of Confucius is really the cathedral of the upper lettered and exclusive class of the Litterati. The law demands that a temple be built to the Prince of Chinese Philosophers in every city, and in that particular part of the city which has been described as the center of learning. These temples are sumptuously built and adjoining them is the palace of the magistrate who presides over those who have acquired their first literary degree. In the most conspicuous place in the temple there will be a statue of Confucius, or if not a statue, a plaque with his name carved in large letters of gold. Near to this are placed the statues of certain of his disciples whom the Chinese revere as saints, but of an inferior order.

BAROQUE DEVOTION IN A CENTURY OF CONVERSION AND COUNTERCONVERSION

In the sixteenth and especially the seventeenth centuries, Christian fervor was disconcertingly indifferent to doctrine and to the creedal boundaries between the now proliferating denominations. There is, proverbially, no fervor like first fervor and no first fervor like the fervor of a convert. Since this was an era of frequent conversion, it was an era of ardent poetry as well, often poetry with the distinct late Renaissance or post-Renaissance theatricality we call baroque. Christians who might even go to war over their theological differences could pour forth their sincere religious emotion in surprisingly similar language.

The examples here, all English, should not be taken to suggest that England alone produced Christian lyric poetry during this period. With many local variations, the same sort of work was being produced in other European language communities. But England may have presented a particularly dynamic arena of religious conversion and counterconversion. The martyr Robert Southwell (see p. 426) began and remained a Catholic, just as the priest George Herbert began and remained an Anglican. However, John Donne began as a Catholic but became an Anglican, and Richard Crashaw began as an Anglican but became a Catholic. Theologically at odds, these four poets are akin in their depth of religious feeling, foreshadowing the priority that religious feeling acquired a century or two later.

ROBERT SOUTHWELL
1561–1595

THE BURNING BABE[1]

As I in hoary winter's night stood shivering in the snow,
Surprised I was with sudden heat which made my heart to glow;
And lifting up a fearful eye to view what fire was near,
A pretty babe all burning bright did in the air appear;
Who, scorchèd with excessive heat, such floods of tears did shed   5
As though his floods should quench his flames which with
    his tears were fed.
"Alas," quoth he, "but newly born in fiery heats I fry,

---

1. Published in 1602.

Yet none approach to warm their hearts or feel my fire but I!
My faultless breast the furnace is, the fuel wounding thorns,
Love is the fire, and sighs the smoke, the ashes shame and scorns; 10
The fuel justice layeth on, and mercy blows the coals,
The metal in this furnace wrought are men's defilèd souls,
For which, as now on fire I am to work them to their good,
So will I melt into a bath to wash them in my blood."
With this he vanished out of sight and swiftly shrunk away, 15
And straight[2] I callèd unto mind that it was Christmas day.

2. Straightaway: immediately.

JOHN DONNE
1572–1631

DEATH, BE NOT PROUD[1]

Death, be not proud, though some have callèd thee
Mighty and dreadful, for thou art not so;
For those whom thou think'st thou dost overthrow
Die not, poor Death, nor yet canst thou kill me.
From rest and sleep, which but thy pictures be, 5
Much pleasure; then from thee much more must flow,
And soonest our best men with thee do go,
Rest of their bones, and soul's delivery.[2]
Thou art slave to fate, chance, kings, and desperate men,
And dost with poison, war, and sickness dwell, 10
And poppy or charms can make us sleep as well
And better than thy stroke; why swell'st[3] thou then?
One short sleep past, we wake eternally
And death shall be no more; Death, thou shalt die.[4]

1. Written between 1601 and 1610; published
posthumously.
2. I.e., to find rest for their bones and delivery for
their souls.
3. Puff yourself up.
4. See 1 Corinthians 15:26.

GEORGE HERBERT
1593–1633

THE HOLDFAST[1]

I threatened to observe the strict decree
    Of my dear God with all my power and might.
    But I was told by one, it could not be;
Yet I might trust in God to be my light.

Then will I trust, said I, in him alone.   5
    Nay, ev'n to trust in him, was also his;
    We must confess, that nothing is our own.
Then I confess that he my succor is.

But to have nought is ours, not to confess
    That we have nought. I stood amazed at this,   10
    Much troubled, till I heard a friend express,
That all things were more ours by being his.

What Adam had, and forfeited for all,[2]
Christ keepeth now, who cannot fail or fall.

1. Published in 1633. The title is inspired by Psalms 73:27 in *The Book of Common Prayer*: "It is good for me to hold me fast by God."

2. On Adam and Eve's, and thus humanity's, fall from divine grace, see p. 83.

RICHARD CRASHAW
ca. 1613–1649

FROM TO THE NOBLEST AND BEST OF LADIES, THE COUNTESS OF DENBIGH[1]

Persuading Her to Resolution in Religion, and to Render Herself without Further Delay into the Communion of the Catholic Church.

What heaven-entreated heart is this,
Stands trembling at the gate of bliss,
Holds fast the door, yet dares not venture
Fairly to open it, and enter?
Whose definition is a doubt   5
'Twixt life and death, 'twixt in and out.

1. Published in 1652.

Say, lingering fair! why comes the birth
Of your brave soul so slowly forth?
Plead your pretenses (O you strong
In weakness!) why you choose so long   10
In labor of your self to lie,
Not daring quite to live nor die.
Ah, linger not, loved soul! a slow
And late consent was a long no;
Who grants at last, long time tried   15
And did his best to have denied.
What magic bolts, what mystic bars,
Maintain the will in these strange wars!
What fatal yet fantastic bands
Keep the free heart from its own hands!   20
So when the year takes cold, we see
Poor waters their own prisoners be;
Fettered and locked up fast they lie
In a sad self-captivity,
Th' astonished nymphs their flood's strange fate deplore,   25
To see themselves their own severer shore.
　Thou that alone canst thaw this cold,
And fetch the heart from its stronghold,
Almighty Love! end this long war,
And of a meteor make a star.[2]   30
O fix this fair Indefinite;
And 'mongst thy shafts of sovereign light
Choose out that sure decisive dart
Which has the key of this close heart,
Knows all the corners of 't, and can control   35
The self-shut cabinet of an unsearched soul.
O let it be at last love's hour!
Raise this tall trophy of thy power;
Come once the conquering way, not to confute,
But kill this rebel-word, *irresolute*,   40
That so, in spite of all this peevish strength
Of weakness, she may write, *resolved at length*.

　　　　　*　*　*

Disband dull fears; give faith the day.
To save your life, kill your delay.
It is love's siege, and sure to be
Your triumph, though his victory.   60
'Tis cowardice that keeps this field,
And want of courage not to yield.
Yield, then, O yield, that love may win
The fort at last, and let life in.
Yield quickly, lest perhaps you prove   65
Death's prey before the prize of love.
This fort of your fair self, if 't be not won,
He is repulsed indeed; but you are undone.

2. I.e., turn something transient into something permanent.

EPICS OF SALVATION

Dante Alighieri's epic poem *The Divine Comedy* (see p. 342) is not truly based on the Bible. Dante's cosmology—its division into the realms of Inferno, Purgatorio, and Paradiso—derives from medieval speculation and is thus abstract, not directed toward a mass audience. Like Dante, the English poet John Milton wrote intellectually demanding poetry. In effect, Milton wrote for the growing but still relatively limited readership of educated Christian humanists. Meanwhile, a much larger popular audience awaited a writer who could write on an epic scale, expressing the same widely shared Calvinist vision (see p. 412) but in a simpler and more emotional language. The self-taught English writer John Bunyan achieved large and durable success with his *Pilgrim's Progress,* a prose epic (occasionally interrupted by simple poetry) in which the hero is the ordinary Protestant wending his humble path toward the promise of salvation. Bunyan's good-hearted hero, allegorically named Christian, is the allegorical Everyman of two centuries earlier (see p. 356) brought back to literary life and converted to the embattled theology of a new era.

JOHN MILTON
1608–1674

FROM PARADISE LOST

John Milton was born in the Cheapside area of London and died in the Bunhill area. Internationally famous during his lifetime, he was a poet; a scholarly man of letters who wrote in English, Latin, and Italian; and a civil servant during a time of religious and political turmoil. Milton's first poems, written at age fifteen, were paraphrases of biblical Psalms. His most famous works are the religious epic poem *Paradise Lost* (1667, 1674) and its sequel, *Paradise Regained* (1671). His polemical text *Areopagitica* (1644) is an impassioned defense of free speech and freedom of the press.

The theology of Milton's *Paradise Lost* elaborates immensely on just the first three chapters of the Book of Genesis. When Milton sets out in his famous prologue (excerpted here), to "justify the ways of God to men," his understanding of the ways of God owes much to the theology of John Calvin. In Calvin's vision of salvation, the most vivid tenet is the "total depravity" of human nature: Thanks to the heritability of Adam and Eve's sin (see p. 83), humankind is born not just guilty but also spiritually ruined and so incapable of knowing anything about God unless God takes the initiative.

In Milton's epic translation of this vision, God does take the initiative. In the end, in Book XII (also excerpted here), Adam is shown the future that awaits his offspring in God's providential plan, a plan evoked more fully in *Paradise Regained*. He then comes to recognize that his painful expulsion from the Garden of Paradise has been turned to immense good by the benevolence of the deity he offended.

Aonian: *ay-oh´-nee-an*   Siloa: *si´-loh-ah*
Oreb: *or´-eb*   Sinai: *sai´-nai* [*ai* rhyming with *rye*]

FROM PARADISE LOST

From BOOK I

Of man's first disobedience, and the fruit
Of that forbidden tree, whose mortal taste
Brought death into the world, and all our woe,
With loss of Eden, till one greater man
Restore us, and regain the blissful seat,   5
Sing heavenly Muse, that on the secret top
Of Oreb, or of Sinai, didst inspire
That shepherd, who first taught the chosen seed,[1]
In the beginning how the heavens and earth
Rose out of chaos: or if Sion hill   10
Delight thee more, and Siloa's brook that flowed
Fast by the oracle of God[,][2] I thence
Invoke thy aid to my advent'rous song,
That with no middle flight intends to soar
Above the Aonian mount,[3] while it pursues   15
Things unattempted yet in prose or rhyme.
And chiefly thou O Spirit, that dost prefer
Before all temples the upright heart and pure,
Instruct me, for thou knowst; thou from the first
Wast present, and with mighty wings outspread   20
Dovelike satst brooding on the vast abyss
And mad'st it pregnant: what in me is dark
Illumine, what is low raise and support;
That to the height of this great argument
I may assert the eternal providence,   25
And justify the ways of God to men.

* * *

From BOOK XII

* * *

He ended; and thus Adam last replied.[1]
How soon hath thy prediction, seer blest,

---

1. Israel. "That shepherd": Moses, who received prophecies from God on Mount Horeb, also called Oreb or Sinai (see p. 89).
2. The Temple of Mount Sion. At the original site of Jerusalem, Siloah—also known as Siloa, Siloam, and Shiloah and referred to variously as a pool or stream—flowed below Mount Sion.
3. Mount Helicon, in Greece; one haunt of the classical Muses to whom Milton is comparing his Muse, the eternal Spirit of God.

1. "He" is the Archangel Michael, who has just presented to Adam a vision, following Christ's Second Coming, of "respiration to the just, / And vengeance to the wicked" and of "new heavens, new earth, ages of endless date / Founded in righteousness and peace and love."

Measured this transient world, the race of time,
Till time stand fixed: beyond is all abyss,   555
Eternity, whose end no eye can reach.
Greatly instructed I shall hence depart,
Greatly in peace of thought, and have my fill
Of knowledge, what this vessel can contain;
Beyond which was my folly to aspire.   560
Henceforth I learn that to obey is best,
And love with fear the only God, to walk
As in his presence, ever to observe
His providence, and on him sole depend,
Merciful over all his works, with good   565
Still overcoming evil, and by small
Accomplishing great things, by things deemed weak
Subverting worldly strong, and worldly wise
By simply meek; that suffering for truth's sake
Is fortitude to highest victory,   570
And to the faithful death the gate of life;
Taught this by his example whom I now
Acknowledge my redeemer ever blest.
      To whom thus also the angel last replied:
This having learned, thou hast attained the sum   575
Of wisdom; hope no higher, though all the stars
Thou knewst by name, and all the ethereal powers,
All secrets of the deep, all nature's works,
Or works of God in heaven, air, earth, or sea,
And all the riches of this world enjoyedst,   580
And all the rule, one empire; only add
Deeds to thy knowledge answerable, add faith,
Add virtue, patience, temperance, add love,
By name to come called charity, the soul
Of all the rest: then wilt thou not be loath   585
To leave this Paradise, but shalt possess
A paradise within thee, happier far.
Let us descend now therefore from this top
Of speculation; for the hour precise
Exacts our parting hence; and see the guards,   590
By me encamped on yonder hill, expect
Their motion, at whose front a flaming sword,
In signal of remove, waves fiercely round;
We may no longer stay: go, waken Eve;
Her also I with gentle dreams have calmed   595
Portending good, and all her spirits composed
To meek submission: thou at season fit
Let her with thee partake what thou hast heard,
Chiefly what may concern her faith to know,
The great deliverance by her seed to come   600
(For by the woman's seed) on all mankind,
That ye may live, which will be many days,
Both in one faith unanimous though sad,
With cause for evils past, yet much more cheered
With meditation on the happy end.   605
      He ended, and they both descend the hill;

Descended, Adam to the bower where Eve
Lay sleeping ran before, but found her waked;
And thus with words not sad she him received.
    Whence thou returnst, and whither wentst, I know;   610
For God is also in sleep, and dreams advise,
Which he hath sent propitious, some great good
Presaging, since with sorrow and heart's distress
Wearied I fell asleep; but now lead on;
In me is no delay; with thee to go,   615
Is to stay here; without thee here to stay,
Is to go hence unwilling; thou to me
Art all things under heaven, all places thou,
Who for my wilful crime art banished hence.
This further consolation yet secure   620
I carry hence; though all by me is lost,
Such favour I unworthy am vouchsafed,
By me the promised seed shall all restore.
    So spake our mother Eve, and Adam heard
Well pleased, but answered not; for now too nigh   625
The archangel stood, and from the other hill
To their fixed station, all in bright array
The cherubim descended; on the ground
Gliding metéorous, as evening mist
Ris'n from a river o'er the marish glides,   630
And gathers ground fast at the labourer's heel
Homeward returning. High in front advanced,
The brandished sword of God before them blazed
Fierce as a comet; which with torrid heat,
And vapour as the Libyan air adust,   635
Began to parch that temperate clime; whereat
In either hand the hastening angel caught
Our lingering parents, and to the eastern gate
Led them direct, and down the cliff as fast
To the subjected plain; then disappeared.   640
They looking back, all the eastern side beheld
Of Paradise, so late their happy seat,
Waved over by that flaming brand, the gate
With dreadful faces thronged and fiery arms:
Some natural tears they dropped, but wiped them soon;   645
The world was all before them, where to choose
Their place of rest, and providence their guide:
They hand in hand with wandering steps and slow,
Through Eden took their solitary way.

JOHN BUNYAN
1628–1688

FROM THE PILGRIM'S PROGRESS

Born into the very lowest stratum of English society and with little formal education, John Bunyan was a near contemporary of John Milton (see p. 454). The two shared broadly Puritan views, which put them at odds with the Church of England and with the monarchical government during the English Civil War (1642–51). Written most likely during a six-month period in 1675 when Bunyan was jailed as a dissident, and published in 1678, *The Pilgrim's Progress* is a theological allegory of the Christian soul's passage from the burden of sin and the threat of hell to the relief of grace and the joy of heaven. It is a monument of English popular culture and devotional imagination.

A kind of fairy tale filled with close calls, hideous enemies, brave and beauteous allies, and interludes of tender serenity, *The Pilgrim's Progress* can be seen as an ancestor of much English fantasy literature, most especially such twentieth-century works as J. R. R. Tolkien's *Lord of the Rings* (1954–55), which many enthusiasts have read as a political or spiritual allegory. In Bunyan's tale, abstract nouns become characters through lively talk and vivid action, as awe-inspiring figures such as Christ and Satan tower in the background. The landscape of perils includes the colorfully named features Doubting Castle, the Slough of Despond, the Hill of Difficulty, and—in one of Bunyan's innumerable echoes of the King James Version of the Bible—the Valley of the Shadow of Death.

The work, whose fuller title is *The Pilgrim's Progress from This World to That Which Is to Come*, consists of two parts. In the first part, Christian, the pilgrim of the title, sets out alone on the "straight and narrow path," having failed to persuade his wife and children to join him. In the second part, with Christian now safely in heaven, his wife, Christiana, belatedly and penitently sets out on the same arduous journey. In the following excerpt from the second part, Christiana and her companion, Mercy, having witnessed the slaying of a giant ("the sight of the Fight") and escaped from lions ("Lyons," in the period spelling preserved here), sojourn in blessed security in a refuge for wayfaring pilgrims operated by a family of personified virtues whose feminine members include Prudence, Piety, and Charity. This selection's charming details include Mercy's laughing girlishly in her sleep and dreaming that Christ, when he comes for her, will bring her a necklace and earrings as well as celestial transport.

FROM THE PILGRIM'S PROGRESS

From THE SECOND PART

Now because it was somewhat late, and because the Pilgrims were weary with their Journey, and also made faint with the sight of the Fight, and of the terrible Lyons: Therefore they desired as soon as might be, to prepare to go to Rest. Nay, said those of the Family, refresh your selves first with a morsel of Meat. For they had prepared for them a Lamb, with the accustomed Sauce belonging thereto. For the Porter had heard before of their coming, and had told it to them within. So when they had Supped, and ended their Prayer with a Psalm, they desired they might go to rest. But let us, said

Christiana, if we may be so bold as to chuse, be in that Chamber that was my Husbands, when he was here. So they had them up thither, and they lay all in a Room. When they were at Rest, *Christiana* and *Mercy* entred into discourse about things that were convenient.

Chris. Little did I think once, that when my Husband went on Pilgrimage I should ever a followed.

Mercy. And you as little thought of lying in his Bed, and in his Chamber to Rest, as you do now.

Chris. And much less did I ever think of seeing his Face with Comfort, and of Worshipping the Lord the King with him, and yet now I believe I shall.

Mercy. Hark, don't you hear a Noise?

Christiana. Yes, 'tis as I believe, a Noise of Musick, for joy that we are here.

Mer. Wonderful! Musick in the House, Musick in the Heart, and Musick also in Heaven, for joy that we are here.

Thus they talked a while, and then betook themselves to sleep; so in the Morning, when they were awake *Christiana* said to *Mercy*.

Chris. What was the matter that you did laugh in your sleep to Night? I suppose you was in a Dream?

Mercy. So I was, and a sweet Dream it was; but are you sure I laughed?

Christiana. Yes, you laughed heartily; But prethee Mercy tell me thy Dream?

Mercy. I was a Dreamed that I sat all alone in a solitary place, and was bemoaning of the hardness of my Heart. Now I had not sat there long, but methought many were gathered about me, to see me, and to hear what it was that I said. So they harkened, and I went on bemoaning the hardness of my Heart. At this, some of them laughed at me, some called me Fool, and some began to thrust me about. With that, methought I looked up, and saw one coming with Wings towards me. So he came directly to me, and said, *Mercy*, what aileth thee? Now when he had heard me make my complaint, he said, *Peace be to thee*: he also wiped mine Eyes with his Hanker-chief, and *clad* me in *Silver* and *Gold*; he put a Chain about my Neck, and Ear-rings in mine Ears, and a beautiful Crown upon my Head. Then he took me by my Hand, and said, *Mercy*, come after me. So he went up, and I followed, till we came at a Golden Gate. Then he knocked, and when they within had opened, the man went in and I followed him up to a Throne, upon which one sat, and he said to me, *welcome Daughter*. The place looked bright, and twinkling like the Stars, or rather like the *Sun*, and I thought that I saw your Husband there, so I awoke from my Dream. But did I laugh?

Christiana. Laugh! Ay, and well you might to see your self so well. For you must give me leave to tell you, that I believe it was a good Dream, and that as you have begun to find the first part true, so you shall find the second at last. God speaks once, yea twice, yet Man perceiveth it not. In a Dream, in a Vision of the Night, when deep sleep falleth upon men, in slumbering upon the Bed. We need not, when a-Bed, lie awake to talk with God; he can visit us while we sleep, and cause us then to hear his Voice. Our Heart oft times wakes when we sleep, and God can speak to that, either by Words, by Proverbs, by Signs, and Similitudes, as well as if one was awake.

Mercy. Well, I am glad of my Dream, for I hope ere long to see it fulfilled, to the making of me laugh again.

Christiana. I think it is now time to rise, and to know what we must do?

Mercy. Pray, if they invite us to stay a while, let us willingly accept of the proffer. I am the willinger to stay awhile here, to grow better acquainted with these Maids; methinks *Prudence, Piety,* and *Charity,* have very comly and sober Countenances.

Chris. We shall see what they will do. So when they were up and ready, they came down. And they asked one another of their rest, and if it was Comfortable, or not?

Mer. Very good, said Mercy. *It was one of the best Nights Lodging that ever I had in my Life.*

Then said *Prudence,* and *Piety,* If you will be perswaded to stay here awhile, you shall have what the House will afford.

Charity. Ay, and that with a very good will, said Charity. So they consented, and stayed there about a Month or above: And became very Profitable one to another. * * *

PROTESTANT CATHOLICS, CATHOLIC PROTESTANTS, AND BEYOND

"Catholic" and "Protestant" are indispensable labels for real-world conditions, but they cover a broad spectrum of internal differences—and external similarities—that are frequently ignored. Catholic thinkers—such as the doomed Dominican friar Girolamo Savonarola (1452–1498), who became the secular and spiritual ruler of Florence in the 1490s—have condemned clerical corruption with the force of rather severe Protestants. Protestant thinkers—such as Philipp Melanchthon (1497–1560), a German theologian and key supporter of Martin Luther—have taken conciliatory approaches toward Catholic doctrine and practice. Such deliberate blurring of sharp definitions can also be found in certain large groups of believers. For example, the Church of England is often seen (and often sees itself) as a bridge, or middle way, between Roman Catholicism and both Lutheranism and the Reformed Churches.

There are few more distinguished representatives of the English "straddling" impulse than the priest-poet John Donne. Donne was born into a solidly Catholic family, but for political and professional reasons he joined the Church of England. Eventually ordained a priest of that Church, he rose to great prominence not just as a poet, but also as a court preacher and as the author of simultaneously prayerful and provocative theological essays. In one of these essays, "Expostulation 19," Donne celebrates God as "metaphorical"—that is, as speaking in the Bible through a wild plethora of images, figures, allegories, and hyperboles. In celebrating God for such verbal acrobatics, Donne could well have been celebrating his own manner on the page. In so doing, he would have been celebrating himself as a recalcitrantly Catholic kind of Protestant, since the burgeoning Puritan movement in England self-consciously cultivated plain speech and an understanding of the Bible as literally rather than figuratively true.

If Donne could be called a Catholic Protestant, seventeenth-century French Catholic adherents of an originally Dutch school of theology called Jansenism might be regarded as Calvinist Catholics. Jansenism stressed the intrinsic sinfulness of human beings, their utter helplessness without grace, their predestination to heaven or hell, and the supreme power of divine forgiveness. The movement was condemned by the Church in 1713, but in France and Quebec its spirit lingered well into the nineteenth century. One exponent of Jansenist ideas was the mathematical and scientific genius Blaise Pascal, who fervently advocated a position sometimes called fideism, an awareness that religious faith, unlike science, could not be grounded on reason. He argued for the living, accessible-but-impenetrable God of the Bible and against God as a philosophical abstraction needed to get the world started but of little interest after that. For Pascal, a God who could be measured and explained with merely human concepts would be a very minor deity. In pleading the case for Christianity to skeptical secularists, Pascal avoids the usual theological arguments, stressing the terror and confusion of living in a universe without God and claiming that the seemingly irrational doctrine of original (i.e., inherited) sin helps explain the incredible profusion of evils afflicting the world.

Many theologians, of course, would stop far short of such a radical stance. But as Christianity of any kind, Catholic or Protestant, came under heavier fire from secular critics, the once disputed doctrinal issues separating sects and denominations appeared less crucial. For twentieth-century Christians who wish to see themselves as belonging to an ecumenical family, the colonial-era Anglo-American thinker Roger Williams is a prophet of pluralism. The term *pluralism* did not even exist in Williams's day, however, so novel was the notion of religious toleration, especially as extended not just to all Christians but to all without qualification. Williams observed the persecution of English Puritans by the established Anglican Church, then witnessed oppression of Baptists and other dissenters by the American Puritans. Providence Plantation, which he founded with the support of the Narragansett Indians after fleeing Massachusetts and which later became Rhode Island, modeled religious toleration for what would later become the United States of America. For Williams, freedom of worship was not what the Enlightenment required but what Jesus required. He was horrified by the blood shed on both sides during Britain's savage religious Civil War. "Forc'd worship," his term for religious conformity enforced by the state, was not just a crime against conscience. It was also a violent betrayal of Christian truth.

BLAISE PASCAL
1623–1662

FROM PENSÉES

Blaise Pascal was born in Clermont-Ferrand, France, and died in Paris. He was a child prodigy, educated by his father, and early in life he did important work in the natural and applied sciences. While still a teenager, he invented the mechanical calculator. At sixteen, he wrote a significant treatise about projective geometry. His many other significant contributions include work in mathematics, physics, philosophy, and theology, and his influence has extended to economics and social science.

While still in his twenties, Pascal affiliated with a group of Catholic intellectuals at the Convent of Port-Royal, in Paris, who were profoundly marked by Calvinist theology and piety. Much of the Calvinist influence on the Port-Royal group stemmed from the work of the Dutch Catholic theologian by whom they were particularly instructed, Cornelius Jansenius (1585–1638). Jansenism, as their movement came to be called, generally to its disparagement, would eventually be condemned as heretical by Rome. Pascal, however, like Jansenius, intended only to defend the legitimacy of Christianity. By assembling sketches, sayings, and interpretations of the New Testament as the fulfillment of the prophecies of the Old Testament, Pascal apparently intended to prove the divinity of Jesus. Discovered after his death, these *Pensées* ("thoughts" or, better, "reflections"), as they have come to be called, have been assembled by various editors in different orders, Pascal having left no outline for the work. The writing is characterized by Pascal's aphoristic style, with emotional expressions that sink to near despair and climb toward mysticism. Pascal's now-famous "wager," presented here, is the work of a very Protestant kind of Catholic and remains a starting point for discussions of the viability of religious faith in a scientific age.

PRONOUNCING GLOSSARY

Blaise Pascal: *blays pahs-cahl´*   stultitiam: *stool-tee´-tsee-yahm*
Pensées: *pohn´-say*

FROM PENSÉES

From 233

Let us now speak according to natural lights.[1]

If there is a God, He is infinitely incomprehensible, since, having neither parts nor limits, He has no affinity to us. We are then incapable of knowing either what He is or if He is. This being so, who will dare to undertake the decision of the question? Not we, who have no affinity to Him.

Who then will blame Christians for not being able to give a reason for their belief, since they profess a religion for which they cannot give a reason? They declare, in expounding it to the world, that it is a foolishness, *stultitiam*;[2] and then you complain that they do not prove it! If they proved it, they would not keep their word; it is in lacking proofs, that they are not lacking in sense. "Yes, but although this excuses those who offer it as such, and takes away from them the blame of putting it forward without reason, it does not excuse those who receive it." Let us then examine this point, and say, "God is, or He is not." But to which side shall we incline? Reason can decide nothing here. There is an infinite chaos which separated us. A game is being played at the extremity of this infinite distance where heads or tails will turn up. What will you wager? According to reason, you can do neither the one thing nor the other; according to reason, you can defend neither of the propositions.

Do not then reprove for error those who have made a choice; for you know nothing about it. "No, but I blame them for having made, not this choice, but a choice; for again both he who chooses heads and he who chooses tails are equally at fault, they are both in the wrong. The true course is not to wager at all."

Yes; but you must wager. It is not optional. You are embarked. Which will you choose then? Let us see. Since you must choose, let us see which interests you least. You have two things to lose, the true and the good; and two things to stake, your reason and your will, your knowledge and your happiness; and your nature has two things to shun, error and misery. Your reason is no more shocked in choosing one rather than the other, since you must of necessity choose. This is one point settled. But your happiness? Let us weigh the gain and the loss in wagering that God is. Let us estimate these two chances. If you gain, you gain all; if you lose, you lose nothing. Wager, then, without hesitation that He is.—"That is very fine. Yes, I must wager; but I may perhaps wager too much."—Let us see. Since there is an equal risk of gain and of loss, if you had only to gain two lives, instead of one, you

---

TRANSLATED BY W. F. Trotter.

1. I.e., according to unaided human reason.   2. Folly (Latin).

might still wager. But if there were three lives to gain, you would have to play (since you are under the necessity of playing), and you would be imprudent, when you are forced to play, not to chance your life to gain three at a game where there is an equal risk of loss and gain. But there is an eternity of life and happiness. And this being so, if there were an infinity of chances, of which one only would be for you, you would still be right in wagering one to win two, and you would act stupidly, being obliged to play, by refusing to stake one life against three at a game in which out of an infinity of chances there is one for you, if there were an infinity of an infinitely happy life to gain. But there is here an infinity of an infinitely happy life to gain, a chance of gain against a finite number of chances of loss, and what you stake is finite. It is all divided; wherever the infinite is and there is not an infinity of chances of loss against that of gain, there is no time to hesitate, you must give all. And thus, when one is forced to play, he must renounce reason to preserve his life, rather than risk it for infinite gain, as likely to happen as the loss of nothingness.

For it is no use to say it is uncertain if we will gain, and it is certain that we risk, and that the infinite distance between the *certainty* of what is staked and the *uncertainty* of what will be gained, equals the finite good which is certainly staked against the uncertain infinite. It is not so, as every player stakes a certainty to gain an uncertainty, and yet he stakes a finite certainty to gain a finite uncertainty, without transgressing against reason. There is not an infinite distance between the certainty staked and the uncertainty of the gain; that is untrue. In truth, there is an infinity between the certainty of gain and the certainty of loss. But the uncertainty of the gain is proportioned to the certainty of the stake according to the proportion of the chances of gain and loss. Hence it comes that, if there are as many risks on one side as on the other, the course is to play even; and then the certainty of the stake is equal to the uncertainty of the gain, so far is it from fact that there is an infinite distance between them. And so our proposition is of infinite force, when there is the finite to stake in a game where there are equal risks of gain and of loss, and the infinite to gain. This is demonstrable; and if men are capable of any truths, this is one.

"I confess it, I admit it. But, still, is there no means of seeing the faces of the cards?"—Yes, Scripture and the rest, etc. "Yes, but I have my hands tied and my mouth closed; I am forced to wager, and am not free. I am not released, and am so made that I cannot believe. What, then, would you have me do?"

True. But at least learn your inability to believe, since reason brings you to this, and yet you cannot believe. Endeavour then to convince yourself, not by increase of proofs of God, but by the abatement of your passions. You would like to attain faith, and do not know the way; you would like to cure yourself of unbelief, and ask the remedy for it. Learn of those who have been bound like you, and who now stake all their possessions. These are people who know the way which you would follow, and who are cured of an ill of which you would be cured. Follow the way by which they began; by acting as if they believed, taking the holy water, having masses said, etc. Even this will naturally make you believe, and deaden your acuteness.—"But this is what I am afraid of."—And why? What have you to lose?

But to show you that this leads you there, it is this which will lessen the passions, which are your stumbling-blocks.

The end of this discourse.—Now, what harm will befall you in taking this side? You will be faithful, honest, humble, grateful, generous, a sincere friend, truthful. Certainly you will not have those poisonous pleasures, glory and luxury; but will you not have others? I will tell you that you will thereby gain in this life, and that, at each step you take on this road, you will see so great certainty of gain, so much nothingness in what you risk, that you will at last recognise that you have wagered for something certain and infinite, for which you have given nothing.

ROGER WILLIAMS
1603–1683

FROM THE BLOODY TENET OF PERSECUTION, FOR CAUSE OF CONSCIENCE, IN A CONFERENCE BETWEEN TRUTH AND PEACE

"If one of the several sorts [of Christian] should by major vote attain the sword of steel: what weapons doth Christ Jesus authorize them to fight with in His cause?" Roger Williams, a dissident Christian in colonial America, asked this bold question in "The Bloody Tenet of Persecution," a 1643 essay penned shortly after religious civil war had broken out in the British Isles. With this question, Williams silently invokes the example of Jesus' pacifism in a Gospel passage familiar to his Christian readers:

> Then they came and laid hands on Jesus and arrested him. Suddenly, one of those with Jesus put his hand on his sword, drew it, and struck the slave of the high priest, cutting off his ear. Then Jesus said to him, "Put your sword back into its place; for all who take the sword will perish by the sword." (Matthew 26:50–52)

In the aftermath of the Christian Wars of Religion, a good many—especially in England and in Germany, the two countries where those wars had led to the greatest slaughter—began to ask questions about religion, violence, and government. Among such people were Deists, believers in a deity and a universal, innate morality but not in a savior, sacred scripture, or miracles. Deism was a first step in the secularization that began to take root in Christian Europe starting in the late seventeenth century. Deists were increasingly drawn to the idea that those of different religious persuasions could better cooperate if all were willing to surrender certain key functions to a secular state.

Roger Williams supported such ideas on explicitly Christian grounds. In an open letter, he once compared members of different religions living in a single state to passengers of different religions sailing on a single ship and prepared to leave the actual sailing to the captain. The opposite view—namely, that no ship could be seaworthy unless the passengers were religiously united—was by far more common in his day. By dissenting from that view in fervently Puritan Massachusetts, Williams shocked his contemporaries and incurred a sentence of banishment back to England. Before the sentence could be carried out, however, he fled to the company and protection of the Narragansett Indians in what would later become the colony and then the American federal state of Rhode Island. Under his leadership, Rhode

Island became a refuge for members of minority Christian religions as well as for Jews.

Well over a century later, the Constitution of the United States stipulated in Article 6 and later in the First Amendment that the United States would have no religious test for public office and no national religion. Though the American state became in this way a secular or at least religiously neutral state, it also became the kind of state that, in Roger Williams's opinion, Jesus would favor. Williams, in so many ways a son of the Calvinist Reformation, was also a prophet of the Enlightenment.

PRONOUNCING GLOSSARY

liberavi animam meam: *lee-behr-ah´-vee ah´-nee-mahm may´-ahm*

FROM THE BLOODY TENET OF PERSECUTION, FOR CAUSE OF CONSCIENCE, IN A CONFERENCE BETWEEN TRUTH AND PEACE

To every Courteous Reader.

While I plead the cause of *truth* and *innocency* against the bloody *doctrine* of *persecution* for cause of *conscience*, I judge it not unfit to give *alarm* to myself, and all men to prepare to be *persecuted* or hunted for cause of *conscience*.

Whether thou standest charged with ten or but two talents,[1] if thou huntest any for cause of *conscience*, how canst thou say thou followest the *Lamb of God* who so abhorred that practice?

If Paul, if Jesus Christ, were present here at London, and the question were proposed what religion would they approve of: the Papists, Prelatists,[2] Presbyterians, Independents, etc. would each say, "Of mine, of mine."

But put the second question, if one of the several sorts should by major vote attain the sword of steel: what weapons doth Christ Jesus authorize them to fight with in His cause? Do not all men hate the persecutor, and every conscience true or false complain of cruelty, tyranny? etc.

Two mountains of crying guilt lie heavy upon the backs of all that name the name of Christ in the eyes of Jews, Turks and Pagans.

First, the blasphemies of their idolatrous inventions, superstitions, and most unchristian conversations.

Secondly, the bloody, irreligious and inhumane oppressions and destructions under the mask or veil of the name of Christ, etc.

O how like is the jealous Jehovah, the consuming fire to end these present slaughters in a greater slaughter of the holy witnesses? Revelation 11.

Six years preaching of so much truth of Christ (as that time afforded in King Edward's days) kindles the flames of Queen Mary's bloody persecutions.[3]

Who can now but expect that after so many scores of years preaching and professing of more truth, and amongst so many great contentions amongst the very best of Protestants, a fiery furnace should be heat, and who sees not now the fires kindling?

1. Individuals.
2. Episcopalians.
3. So many Protestants were burned at the stake during the reign of Mary Tudor (1516–1558; reigned from 1553 until her death) that she was nicknamed Bloody Mary. "King Edward's days": Edward VI (1537–1553) reigned from 1547 until his death.

I confess I have little hopes till those flames are over, that this discourse against the doctrine of persecution for cause of conscience should pass current (I say not amongst the wolves and lions, but even amongst the sheep of Christ themselves) yet *liberavi animam meam*,[4] I have not hid within my breast my soul's belief; and although sleeping on the bed either of the pleasures or profits of sin thou thinkest thy conscience bound to smite at him that dares to waken thee? Yet in the midst of all these civil and spiritual wars I hope we shall agree in these particulars.

First, however, the proud (upon the advantage of an higher earth or ground) overlook the poor and cry out schismatics, heretics, etc. shall blasphemers and seducers escape unpunished, etc. Yet there is a sorer punishment in the Gospel for despising of Christ than Moses, even when the despiser of Moses was put to death without mercy, Hebrews 10.28–29. "He that believeth not shall be damned," Mark 16.16.

Secondly, whatever worship, ministry, ministration, the best and purest are practiced without faith and true persuasion that they are the true institutions of God, they are sin, sinful worships, ministries, etc. And however in civil things we may be servants unto men, yet in divine and spiritual things the poorest peasant must disdain the service of the highest prince: "Be ye not the servants of men," I Corinthians 14.

Thirdly, without search and trial no man attains this faith and right persuasion, I Thessalonians 5. "Try all things."

In vain have English Parliaments permitted English Bibles in the poorest English houses, and the simplest man or woman to search the Scriptures, if yet against their soul's persuasion from the Scripture, they should be forced (as if they lived in Spain or Rome itself without the sight of a Bible) to believe as the Church believes.

Fourthly, having tried, we must hold fast, I Thessalonians 5. upon the loss of a crown, Revelation 13. we must not let go for all the flea bitings of the present afflictions, etc. having bought truth dear, we must not sell it cheap, not the least grain of it for the whole world, no not for the saving of souls, though our own most precious; least of all for the bitter sweetening of a little vanishing pleasure.

For a little puff of credit and reputation from the changeable breath of uncertain sons of men.

For the broken bags of riches on eagles' wings: For a dream of these, any or all of these which on our deathbed vanish and leave tormenting stings behind them: Oh, how much better is it from the love of truth, from the love of the Father of Lights, from whence it comes, from the love of the Son of God, who is the way and the truth, to say as He, John 18.37: "For this end was I born, and for this end came I into the world that I might bear witness to the truth."

4. I have freed my soul (Latin).

Encounters with Modernity
1700–1914

CHRISTIANITY CHALLENGED AND ENLARGED

What was the state of the western European Christian mind circa 1700? How did that mind develop over the ensuing two centuries? One way to answer these difficult questions is to consider western European Christian focal points during the modern period. Each of the following "awarenesses" contributed to modernity and to modern Christianity:

- A *new awareness of history.* During the Renaissance, Europeans looked back to classical pagan antiquity and, as a result, brought about transformations in the arts, letters, and political thought. During the Reformations, they looked back to classical Christian antiquity and, as a result, brought about transformations in religious practices and theological self-understandings. During each of these periods, a look backward prompted a look forward. For the moderns, then, history mattered, it had made them what they were, and it was not over. Where was history going? What would the Christianity of the future look like?

This illustration—*Profession of Faith of the Savoyard Vicar,* by the French engraver Jean-Baptiste Simonet—appeared in the 1778 edition of *Emile,* by Jean-Jacques Rousseau (see p. 478).

- *A new awareness of geography.* Colonialism was not a religious exercise per se. For example, the British East India Company, a trading enterprise that eventually came to rule large areas of India, excluded British missionaries from India until 1815. But colonialism and growing European and then Euro-American power had many implications for Christianity. The Iberian colonization of the Americas, beginning in the fifteenth century and accompanied from the start by missionary activity, more than doubled the size of Christendom. In the sixteenth and seventeenth centuries, Catholic missionaries in Asia sent reports to Europe that radically complicated the world religious picture. Christianity was growing larger and stronger, but where did it fit in a world that was larger and more complex than Europeans had imagined?

- *A new awareness of nature.* The moderns came to understand nature as autonomously lawful—operating by its own "natural" laws. This image was fostered by, above all, the epoch-making discoveries of the mathematician and physicist Isaac Newton (1642–1727). Newton's laws of motion, published just forty years after the Wars of Religion, became emblematic of what reason (or Reason)—as opposed to religious passion—could accomplish. Such discoveries engendered a dream of nature as a realm of both peaceful order and mutual tolerance. Could reason discern a natural and therefore universal religion, one older and more truthful than the historical Christianities so recently and so dismayingly embroiled in blood? In the eighteenth century, the new philosophical creed of Deism became widely popular among European and American elites (e.g., the Founding Fathers). Deists advocated a natural religion and denied the interference of a Creator with the laws of the universe.

- *A new, skeptical attitude toward miracles.* Intimately connected with the new awareness of nature was a skepticism concerning miracles. Natural laws existed; how could God, Jesus, Mary, or a patron saint have broken those laws at will? If the natural laws were unbreakable, and if miracles therefore never happened, how true were the biblical accounts of miraculous events? If any biblical accounts were questionable, how true was the Bible as a whole?

- *A new and progressively more intense attachment to nationality.* Patriotism, love of country, began to replace piety, love of God. The tears of reverence once reserved for those who died for the faith began to be shed for those who died for their country. And the same veil, of devotion transcending reason, that once swathed the memory of the martyr began now to swathe that of the "fallen" soldier. Like the new skepticism toward miracles, this new ardor for the nation was part of the broad transformation of Christendom into a secular, multinational Europe with a Christian heritage and a nationally divided Christian constituency of fluctuating size.

- *A new and countervailing awareness of emotion.* A sense of the irreplaceable importance of emotion in human life was perhaps the most pervasive new awareness. The cult of sublime emotion began, most likely, as a reaction to the cult of reason. For Evangelical Christianity, during and long after the American "Great Awakening" of the first half of the nineteenth century, this reaction often took the form of a blessed but entirely interior assurance of salvation. For Christians generally, emotionally exalted religious experience—as distinct from polemical argumentation—had a new legitimation. A more emotionally charged sense of God's presence in nature was joined by the kindred movements of literary and musical Romanticism. In addition, adjacent to the legitimation of emotion but finally quite distinct from it was an intellectual and artistic acknowledgment of mystery, paradox, and the sublime.

- A *new awareness of individual rights.* In emphasizing the emotional dimension of their faith, Christians focused on an essentially private experience. While argumentation must be shared to qualify as argumentation, there is literally no arguing with emotional experience. Yet because it can be contagious, emotional experience can build community just as powerfully as argumentation can. Rational argumentation—regardless of the social class, property, or inherited influence of any given speaker or writer—was crucial to the birth of democracy. But are people equal only if and when they can argue as equals? What if they lack the education to do that? Do they not also have *feelings*, and do those feelings count for nothing? In his epoch-making novel *Julie, or the New Heloise* (1761), Jean-Jacques Rousseau dignified the feeling subject, even if that subject happened to be a servant with little education. Whether the shift in social sensibility that made *Julie* such a sensation preceded or followed the rise of the "religion of the heart" in Christianity is secondary. What is primary is that as European democracy broadened, modern European Christianity participated in the broadening.

- A *nascent new awareness of rights transcending gender and race.* As individualism took hold in modernity, the practice of considering each person in his own right ought logically to have included men and women alike and all people regardless of race or ethnicity, but it did not. Individual rights remained largely the rights of men—indeed, of white Christian men. But change was coming, and different forms of liberation were discernibly linked. In 1792, the Romantic radical Mary Wollstonecraft (1759–1797) wrote *A Vindication of the Rights of Woman.* This bold comment on what the French Revolution's famous *Declaration of the Rights of Man* (1789) was *not* doing to educate and liberate French women was a step toward what is now called feminism. The end of the American Civil War led, in 1868, to the ratification of the Fourteenth Amendment to the Constitution, which guaranteed equal protection of the laws to all people born on the territory of the United States. The Fourteenth Amendment indirectly protected Jews and other ethnic or religious minorities no less than it protected the emancipated slaves now turned, overnight, into voting citizens.

"Encounters with Modernity" is divided into four subsections that individually reflect these modernist "awarenesses": "The Bible within the Limits of Reason Alone" shows the refraction of history, geography, nature, and miracles through reference to the Bible or to the Church. "Romanticism, Nature, and the Christianity of the Heart" foregrounds nature, but also discusses nationality, emotional experience, individual rights, and the dignity of women and blacks. "Scandal and Paradox, Fear and Faith" examines the impact of mystery, paradox, and the limits of reason, even on minds immune to the appeal of secular or religious emotion. Finally, "The Sea of Faith: Ebb or Flood?" presents contrasting late-nineteenth-century views on the question of whether Christianity was thriving or failing, growing or shrinking.

Chronology

ENCOUNTERS WITH MODERNITY (1700–1914)

1715 Pope Clement XI condemns the Chinese (Confucian) rites, declaring them incompatible with Christianity and ending Jesuit mission to China

ca. 1730–40 First Great Awakening, in Europe and America

1738 In England, Charles and John Wesley found Methodism

1741 Jonathan Edwards delivers his sermon "Sinners in the Hands of an Angry God"

1767–1814 Suppression of Jesuit order (protected in Russia)

1769 Founding of San Diego de Alcalá, first Franciscan mission in what will later be California

1774–78 Gotthold Ephraim Lessing publishes Samuel Reimarus's pathbreaking "higher criticism" of the Bible

ca. 1780 Sunday school movement (instruction in Christian doctrine) launched by Anglican philanthropist Robert Raikes

1787 U.S. Constitution establishes separation of Church and state

1789–99 French Revolution disestablishes (Roman Catholic) Christianity in France

1790–1830 Clapham (London) Sect, Anglican group, actively opposes African slave trade

ca. 1800–40 Second Great Awakening, in America

1801 Concordat between Napoléon Bonaparte, as "first consul" of the French Republic, and Pope Pius VII formally recognizes Catholicism as the majority but not official religion of France, while preserving rights of Protestants and Jews and subordinating Church to state; the Concordat remains in effect until 1905

1816 The Reverend Richard Allen founds African Methodist Episcopal Church, in Philadelphia, uniting black Methodists

1830 Publication of the Book of Mormon

1833 John Keble's sermon "National Apostasy" launches Oxford Movement, a revival of Anglican interest in Roman Catholic traditions

1841 David Livingstone, Scottish missionary-explorer, arrives in South Africa

1861–65 American Civil War

1863 Founding of Seventh Day Adventist Church, in Battle Creek, Michigan; Emancipation Proclamation frees American slaves

1865 William and Catherine Booth found Salvation Army, in London

1870–71 First Vatican Council: dogma of papal infallibility

1871–78 *Kulturkampf* (German, "Culture Struggle"): Prussian prime minister Bismarck attempts to weaken Catholic Church

1879 Mary Baker Eddy founds Church of Christ, Scientist, in Boston

1885–87 Mwanga II, king of Buganda (Uganda), martyrs forty-five Catholic and Anglican converts

1897 Queen Victoria's "diamond jubilee": high tide of European colonial power and cultural confidence

1905 Official separation of Church and state in France

1906 Azusa Street revival, birth of Pentecostalism, in Los Angeles; Albert Schweitzer publishes *The Quest of the Historical Jesus*

THE BIBLE WITHIN THE LIMITS
OF REASON ALONE

The six writers represented here, spanning from the late seventeenth through the late nineteenth century, are presided over by the spirit of a writer who does not appear among them. The title "The Bible within the Limits of Reason Alone" deliberately echoes *Religion within the Limits of Reason Alone*, the title of a 1792 work by the Prussian philosopher Immanuel Kant (1724–1804). Kant's work brought a sharp reprimand from the king of Prussia, who was also the head of the Prussian state Church. In defending the work as philosophy of religion rather than theology, Kant successfully argued that he wrote it outside the jurisdiction of religious authority, under the auspices of the university rather than those of the Church.

The moment became crucially important in establishing the independence of philosophy, and indeed of the university, from the Church. It also contributed significantly to the disentanglement of philosophy from Christianity and vice versa. In the sixteenth century, philosophically mediated dogmatic distinctions had been matters of life and death, meaning that making the wrong distinction in the wrong place could cost you your property, your privilege, and even your life. By the eighteenth century, precise dogmatic distinctions mattered much less, and the respective histories of philosophy and Christianity now converged only to the degree that individual philosophers, Christian or not, brought them together. But while philosophy had shifted to the campus with some theologians in tow, highly theoretical discussions of Christianity shifted to the field of biblical criticism. Through biblical criticism, theologians were able to present learned subjects and radical new ideas to the Christians in the pews. It was not until the middle of the nineteenth century, if even then, that biblical criticism became as independent of church involvement as philosophy became after Kant. During the nineteenth century, academic philosophers of religion said much about Christianity, but did so largely to an audience outside the churches.

The general modern skepticism about miracles informs the first selection below, in which Hermann Samuel Reimarus unhesitatingly exposes contradictions in the Gospel accounts of Jesus' Resurrection. Reimarus believed in a God worthy of worship. But he gave early expression to a sensibility that led biblical critics to prefer subjects other than miracles when making cases for the Bible's continuing religious centrality. Such critics remained loyal to Christianity, but they also promoted Reason.

The philosopher Jean-Jacques Rousseau believed that all human institutions corrupt the natural goodness of the human being. In his philosophical novel *Emile*, Rousseau presents a vision of Christianity based on the modern dream of a natural religion, even a natural Gospel: Sincerity, authenticity, and the heart matter more than dogma, authority, and the mind.

Friedrich Schleiermacher, in writing the work excerpted here, wanted to dignify interiority and feeling no less than Rousseau did. But the "personal consciousness" in question was, for him, consciousness *of God*. Rather than an innate or natural religiosity, it was a personal consciousness based on Christian memory—that is, modeled first by Jesus for his disciples, who modeled it for theirs, and so forth down through the centuries. Significantly, however, Schleiermacher lingered little over the events of Jesus' life, much less over what had long been taken as the founding miracles of Christianity.

More than a century later, Adolf von Harnack, in the work excerpted here, maintains—very much as Schleiermacher had done—that the essence of Christianity is a distinctive personal consciousness of the Kingdom of God within. The Church should be fearlessly dispensed with, along with whatever parts of the Gospel (including, for him, the entire Gospel of John) that could be proven unhistorical. The historical kernel (an image that Harnack favored) could be recovered, and modernity required that it be revived.

Alfred Loisy's great work, recapitulated here in excerpts from a public lecture of his, was *The Gospel and the Church*. For Loisy, the essence of the Gospel *was* the Church; for had there been no Church, the Gospel would have been lost. And had the Gospel not changed, it would have died. Harnack's kernel, for Loisy, was a seed that had to germinate, grow into a plant, and survive as a living thing. Thus, over time, the Church evolved by discovering new aspects of the Gospel truth. Christianity existed in neither the mind nor the heart of the individual, but only in the community as what Christians collectively made of it.

HERMANN SAMUEL REIMARUS
1694–1768

FROM APOLOGY FOR RATIONAL WORSHIPPERS OF GOD

Hermann Samuel Reimarus, who was born and died in Hamburg, Germany, was one of the great pioneers of modern Scriptural studies. A professor of Hebrew and an erudite classicist, he became famous after his death for the so-called *Wolfenbüttel Fragments*, a collection of critical pieces on the Bible, published—anonymously because of their radical content—by his friend Gotthold Ephraim Lessing (died 1781). Lessing drew these fragments from Reimarus's unpublished treatise, *Apology for Rational Worshippers of God*.

As a Deist, Reimarus believed in God and immortality, but he refused to accept anything miraculous. He thought that Jewish tradition and Christian tradition deserved the same kind of rigorous, impartial scrutiny as any other ancient cultural material. Thus, in the following selection, Reimarus demonstrates that the Evangelists' four accounts of Jesus' Resurrection are incompatible. In addition, practically all the "evidence" cited in the stories is hearsay, and the texts often admit that the disciples reacted to the news of Jesus' rising with doubt and confusion. The conflicting reportage raises serious questions about the historicity of what is, doctrinally, the most important event in the life of the Messiah. In the following generations, Reimarus's once hugely controversial views about the investigation of doctrine would become standard operating procedure in much of the academic world.

PRONOUNCING GLOSSARY

Magdalene: *mag'-duh-lin*

Salome: *sahl-oh'-may*

Reimarus: *rai'-mahr-oos* [*ai* rhyming with *rye*]

FROM APOLOGY FOR RATIONAL WORSHIPPERS OF GOD
[*Contradictions in the Gospels' Resurrection Accounts*]

The first thing that we notice concerning the consistency of the four evangelists is that their stories diverge from each other in almost each and every point of the affair, and each one reads differently. Although this does not straightway show a contradiction, still it certainly does not make a unanimous story, especially since the difference is expressed in the most important elements of the event. And I am definitely assured that if today in court four witnesses were heard in a case and their testimony was as different in all respects as is that of our four evangelists, the conclusion would at least have to be made that no case could be constructed on such conflicting testimony. Here it is a question of the truth of Jesus' resurrection, and insofar as it is to be judged by the mere testimony of witnesses, a unanimity of their testimony is necessary as to who saw him, where and how often, what he said and did in the meantime, and finally, what became of him. But how does the testimony read among the four evangelists? (1) In John's story Mary Magdalene goes alone to the tomb; in Matthew, Mary Magdalene and the other Mary; in Mark, Mary Magdalene, Mary the mother of James, and Salome; in Luke, Mary Magdalene, Johanna, and Mary the mother of James, and others with them. (2) Matthew merely says that Mary went out to inspect the tomb; Mark, that they might come out and embalm him; Luke, that they carried the spices which they had prepared; John says nothing at all about why Mary went out. (3) According to Matthew, Mark, and Luke this Mary had gone only once to the tomb and had straightway seen an angel; but in John's story she goes out twice, the first time without having seen an angel, since she runs back and tells Peter, "They have taken away the Lord,"[1] and the second time when she returns and then sees the angel. (4) Peter and John are also supposed to have run out early to the tomb, as John reports; but the other evangelists do not say a word about it. (5) The angel's words in Matthew and Mark tell them not to be afraid, Jesus had risen, they should announce it to the disciples, he would precede them into Galilee.[2] But in Luke there is none of this; instead, "Remember how he told you while he was still in Galilee, that the Son of man must be delivered into the hands of sinful men, and be crucified, and on the third day rise."[3] In John the angel says nothing at all except this to Mary: "Woman, why are you weeping?"[4] (6) Jesus' words to Mary Magdalene on the road read this way in Matthew, "Hail! . . . Do not be afraid; go and tell my brethren to go to Galilee, and there they will see me."[5] In contrast, John says he told Mary Magdalene, "Woman, why are you weeping? . . . Mary . . . Do not hold me, for I have not yet ascended to the Father; but go to my brethren and say to them, I am ascending to my Father and your Father, to my God and your God."[6] (7) Matthew and John make no mention of Jesus' appearing to the

TRANSLATED BY Ralph S. Fraser.

1. John 20:13.
2. A region in northern Israel where Jesus conducted his ministry.
3. Luke 24:6–7.

4. John 20:13.
5. Matthew 28:9–10.
6. John 20:15, 16, 17.

two disciples on the road to Emmaus, as Mark and Luke do.[7] (8) Matthew does not say anything about Jesus' appearing to his disciples in Jerusalem, merely that this had happened once in Galilee and that some of the disciples doubted it was he.[8] On the other hand, Mark and Luke know nothing of the manifestation in Galilee, merely of the one in Jerusalem.[9] But John remembers two appearances in Jerusalem, a week apart; he relates the one in Galilee as the third, with completely different circumstances.[1] (9) The speeches that Jesus is supposed to have made to the disciples vary greatly among the evangelists, but it would be too lengthy to demonstrate this in all its details. Still, it is especially to be noted that in Luke's story Jesus does not say that they should baptize the converted as Matthew and Mark report,[2] but simply that they should preach repentance and the forgiveness of sins. However, in John Jesus tells the disciples nothing at all about either preaching or baptism. Rather, he says to Peter alone, "If you love me, feed my sheep."[3] (10) Mark and Luke, who themselves did not see Jesus, report his ascension.[4] But John and Matthew, disciples who claim to have seen Jesus themselves, are utterly silent on this important point. In their reports Jesus speaks with his disciples, then nothing more is said about where he was, and their story is at an end. To be sure, John still has so much on his heart to tell concerning things that Jesus did that there would not be enough room in all the world if these things would be written in books;[5] but I think that the few lines about his ascension would have found their bit of space and could have served a better purpose than all the monstrous hyperbole.

---

7. Mark 16:12–13 and Luke 24:213–53. Present-day scholars—centuries after Reimarus—regard Mark 16:9–19 as an epilogue added to the Gospel by a different writer; some editions print these verses in small type for that reason.
8. Matthew 28:16, 17.

9. Luke 24:36–49 and Mark 16:14ff.
1. John 20:19ff, 26ff.; John 21.
2. Matthew 28:19 and Mark 16:16.
3. John 21:17.
4. Mark 16:19 and Luke 24:50–53.
5. John 21:25.

JEAN-JACQUES ROUSSEAU
1712–1778

FROM EMILE, OR ON EDUCATION

Jean-Jacques Rousseau was a prodigiously gifted, often eccentric philosopher: a novelist, a social-political theorist, an opera composer, and the author of what may be the most important modern autobiography, his *Confessions* (1781–88). He was born and raised a Calvinist in Geneva, Switzerland; converted, somewhat by force, to Catholicism in Turin, Italy; and reconverted to Calvinism while in fact becoming a Deist. Rousseau's *Emile* (1762), a philosophical novel that doubles as a treatise on education, was publicly burned in both Calvinist Geneva and Catholic Paris because of the heretical views expressed in it.

The following selection, "Profession of Faith of the Savoyard Vicar," is a monologue from this provocative work. *Savoyard* means "from Savoy," a territory once comprising parts of southeastern France, western Switzerland, and northwestern

Italy; Rousseau's vicar is a Catholic priest. Outwardly orthodox and conscientious, no troublemaker, the vicar maintains a quiet agnosticism, secretly subscribing to a minimalist creed that rejects or ignores basic features of Christianity such as original sin (the Fall), redemption through Jesus' death and Resurrection, the sacramental system, miracles, and the clerical hierarchy. For Rousseau, the great source of evil in the world is not the sins (whether inherited from Adam and Eve or personally committed) of human individuals, but corrupt and vicious social institutions, including Churches. Like many Enlightenment thinkers, Rousseau was eager to reform religion by stripping it of irrational, parochial, superstitious accretions and setting free its "pure," always-and-everywhere-valid natural core.

In "Profession of Faith," the vicar is talking to the young Rousseau. Noting that much of the world has never heard of or does not much care for Christianity, Rousseau's priest offers his own radically simple, universal, and unbiased belief system. For example, he attacks the worship of frequently contradictory "holy books"; he notes that some great cultures have done without books altogether; and he argues that the vast mass of believers are cut off from the original languages of their Scriptures. The only book that matters is the "book of nature," along the lines of Saint Paul's sermon on the Areopagus (Acts 17:22–28): "The God who made the world and everything in it, being Lord of heaven and earth, does not live in shrines made by man." But the splendors of Creation are a text, the vicar says, that "speaks to all men a language that is intelligible to all minds." Humans, as Immanuel Kant would later argue, intuitively know what is right and wrong; and so they can serve God in the simplicity of their hearts, without any externally imposed religious code of law.

PRONOUNCING GLOSSARY

Jean-Jacques Rousseau: *zhahn-zhahk roo-soh´*

FROM EMILE, OR ON EDUCATION

From *Profession of Faith of the Savoyard Vicar*

You see, my son, to what absurdity pride and intolerance lead, when each man is so sure of his position and believes he is right to the exclusion of the rest of mankind. All my researches have been sincere—I take as my witness that God of peace Whom I adore and Whom I proclaim to you. But when I saw that these researches were and always would be unsuccessful, and that I was being swallowed up in an ocean without shores, I retraced my steps and restricted my faith to my primary notions. I have never been able to believe that God commanded me, under penalty of going to hell, to be so learned. I therefore closed all the books. There is one open to all eyes: it is the book of nature. It is from this great and sublime book that I learn to serve and worship its divine Author. No one can be excused for not reading it, because it speaks to all men a language that is intelligible to all minds. Let us assume that I was born on a desert island, that I have not seen any man other than myself, that I have never learned what took place in olden times in some corner of the world; nonetheless, if I exercise my reason, if I cultivate it, if I make good use of my God-given faculties which require no

Translated by Allan Bloom.

intermediary, I would learn of myself to know Him, to love Him, to love His works, to want the good that He wants, and to fulfill all my duties on earth in order to please Him. What more will all the learning of men teach me?

If I were a better reasoner or better educated, perhaps I would sense the truth of revelation, its utility for those who are fortunate enough to acknowledge it. But if I see in its favor proofs I cannot combat, I also see against it objections I cannot resolve. There are so many solid reasons for and against that I do not know what to decide, and I neither accept nor reject it. I reject only the obligation to acknowledge it, because this alleged obligation is incompatible with God's justice and because, far from removing the obstacles to salvation, it would have multiplied them and made them insurmountable for the greater part of mankind. With this exception I remain in respectful doubt about this point. I am not so presumptuous as to believe myself infallible. Other men have been able to achieve certainty about what seems uncertain to me. I reason for myself and not for them. I neither blame them nor imitate them. Their judgment may be better than mine, but it is not my fault that it is not mine.

* * *

This is the involuntary skepticism in which I have remained. But this skepticism is in no way painful for me, because it does not extend to the points essential to practice and because I am quite decided on the principles of all my duties. I serve God in the simplicity of my heart. I seek to know only what is important for my conduct. As for the dogmas which have an influence neither on actions nor on morality, and about which so many men torment themselves, I do not trouble myself about them at all. I regard all the particular religions as so many salutary institutions which prescribe in each country a uniform manner of honoring God by public worship. These religions can all have their justifications in the climate, the government, the genius of the people, or some other local cause which makes one preferable to another according to the time and place. I believe them all to be right as long as one serves God suitably. The essential worship is that of the heart. God does not reject its homage, if it is sincere, in whatever form it is offered to Him. I have been called—in the form of worship which I profess—to the service of the Church, and I perform with all possible exactness the tasks prescribed to me. My conscience would reproach me for voluntarily failing to do so on any point. You know that after a long interdict I obtained, through M. de Mellarède's[1] influence, permission to resume my functions in order to help me to live. Formerly I said the Mass with the lightness with which one eventually treats the most serious things when one does them too often. But since adopting my new principles, I celebrate it with more veneration. I am filled with the majesty of the Supreme Being, with His presence, and with the insufficiency of the human mind, which has so little conception of what relates to its Author. Bearing in mind that I bring to Him the prayers of the people in a prescribed form, I carefully follow all the rites, I recite attentively, I take care never to omit either the least word or the least ceremony. When I approach the moment of the consecration, I collect myself so as to perform it in the frame of mind that the

1. The father of the family for whom the vicar worked as a tutor.

Church and the grandeur of the sacrament demand. I try to annihilate my reason before the supreme intelligence. I say to myself: "Who are you to measure infinite power?" I pronounce the sacramental words with respect, and I put into them all the faith within my power. Whatever may be the case in regard to this inconceivable mystery, I have no fear that I shall be punished on Judgment Day for having profaned it in my heart.

FRIEDRICH SCHLEIERMACHER
1768–1834

FROM ON RELIGION: SPEECHES TO ITS CULTURED DESPISERS

Friedrich Schleiermacher, a Prussian academic theologian, was a key figure in the development of liberal Christianity. This movement is not related to liberalism in the contemporary social or political sense of the word. Rather than a specified set of beliefs, liberal Christianity represents a willingness to interpret Scripture apart from the conviction that Scripture or Church dogma is always correct. The movement began in the late eighteenth century as an attempt to rethink Christian faith after the assaults of higher criticism (secular biblical scholarship) and Enlightenment philosophy. In his best-known work, *On Religion: Speeches to Its Cultured Despisers* (1806, 1821, 1831), from which the following excerpts are taken, Schleiermacher locates the essence of religion not in doctrine, worship, or morality, but in what he calls "personal consciousness." This phrase, however, does not refer simply to feeling or thinking. Mere human awareness reveals that we are tiny blips in an infinitely vast universe—perhaps awed by the deity and full of compassion for our fellow wretches, but guilty and helpless. Fortunately, Schleiermacher argues, there is a bridge between us and God: Jesus.

Schleiermacher claims not to be impressed by Jesus' sublime ethical teachings or his unique character (because "these are all merely human things"). Instead, the scholar exalts the idea that Jesus incarnates, namely the idea "that everything finite requires higher mediation in order to be connected with the divine." But Jesus is not the only possible mediator; Christianity is not a "closed code," since there is no predicting what the Holy Spirit may yet reveal to humanity. And in an ecumenical embrace of people whom the German Jesuit theologian Karl Rahner (1904–1984) later called "anonymous Christians," Schleiermacher says that all those "who make the same intuition [i.e., of a Christ-like mediator] the basis of their religion are Christians."

In attempting to do justice to both rationalist critics of Scripture and heartfelt believers in Jesus, Schleiermacher antagonized both camps. Nonetheless, Schleiermacher's "existentialist" liberal Christianity, stressing the lost, bewildered condition of the would-be believer, has had a rich intellectual legacy in modern theology, notably in branches such as process theology and liberation theology.

PRONOUNCING GLOSSARY

Friedrich Schleiermacher: *freed´-rik shlai´-er-mah-ker* [*ai* rhyming with *rye*]

FROM ON RELIGION: SPEECHES TO ITS CULTURED DESPISERS

From *On the Religions* [from *Fifth Speech*]

* * * Religion is never supposed to rest, and nothing is to be so absolutely opposed to it that it cannot also exist with it concurrently. From everything finite we are to look upon the infinite; we are supposed to be capable of associating religious feelings and views with all sentiments of the mind, wherever they may have originated, and with all actions, whatever may be the objects to which they are related. That is the actual and highest goal of virtuosity in Christianity.

You will now easily discover how the original intuition of Christianity from which all these views derive determines the character of its feelings. What do you call the feeling of an unsatisfied longing that is directed toward a great object and of whose infinity you are conscious? What seizes you when you find the holy most intimately mixed with the profane, the sublime with the lowly and transitory? And what do you call the mood that sometimes forces you to presuppose the universality of this mixture and to search for it everywhere? This mood does not seize Christians now and then but is, rather, the dominant tone of all their religious feeling; this holy sadness—for that is the only name language affords me—accompanies every joy and every pain; every love and every fear accompanies it. Indeed, in Christians' pride as well as in their humility, it is the undertone to which all is related. If you know how to reproduce the interior of a mind from individual traits and do not allow yourself to be disturbed by the oddness that is intermixed with them from God knows where, you will find this feeling wholly dominant in the founder of Christianity. If a writer who has left behind only a few pages in a simple language is not too unimportant for you to turn your attention to him, then this undertone will speak to you from every word that is left to us by his bosom friend.[1] And if ever a Christian has permitted you to look into the holiest depth of his heart, it has certainly been just this one.

Thus is Christianity. I do not wish to gloss over its distortions and its manifold corruptions, for the corruptibility of everything holy, as soon as it becomes human, is a part of its original worldview. Nor do I wish to lead you further into its particulars; its proceedings lie before you, and I believe I have given you the thread that will lead you through all anomalies and, without being concerned for the outcome, will make the most precise overview possible for you. Only hold it fast, and from the very first look to nothing else than the clarity, variety, and richness with which that first basic idea developed. When I consider the holy image in the mutilated descriptions of the life of him who is the sublime originator of what has been the most majestic in religion even to now, I do not admire the purity of his ethical teaching, which only expressed what all persons who have become aware of their spiritual nature have in common with him, and which can have a greater value neither because of its utterance nor because of its being first. I do not admire

TRANSLATED BY Richard Crouter.

1. I.e., "the disciple whom Jesus loved" (John 21:20): the Apostle John, traditionally (but no longer) considered the author of the Gospel of John.

the uniqueness of his character, the intimate marriage of higher power with touching gentleness—every noble, simple heart in a special situation must exhibit a great character in certain respects; these are all merely human things. But the truly divine is the splendid clarity with which the great idea he had come to exhibit was formed in his soul, the idea that everything finite requires higher mediation in order to be connected with the divine. It is vain insolence to want to remove the veil that conceals and should conceal this idea's origin in him, because all beginning in religion is mysterious. The impertinent outrage that has dared to do this was able only to disfigure the divine, as if he had proceeded from the ancient idea of his people, whose annihilation he only wanted to express and in fact had expressed in too glorious a form when he claimed to be the one whom they awaited.[2]

Let us consider the living intuition of the universe that filled his soul only as we find it developed to perfection in him. If everything finite requires higher mediation in order not to stray even farther from the universe and become dispersed into emptiness and nothingness, in order to retain its connection with the universe and come to conscious awareness of it, then indeed what mediates cannot possibly be something merely finite that, in turn, itself requires mediation. It must belong to both; it must be a part of the divine nature just as much as and in the same sense in which it is part of the finite. But what did he see around himself except what was finite and in need of mediation, and where was there something better able to mediate than he himself? "No one knows the Father but the Son and any one to whom he chooses to reveal it."[3] This consciousness of the uniqueness of his religiousness, of the originality of his view, and of its power to communicate itself and arouse religion was at the same time the consciousness of his office as mediator and of his divinity. To say that he was confronted by the raw power of his enemy without hope of being able to live longer is unspeakably petty; but when he, forsaken, was at the point of becoming silent forever, without seeing any sort of institution really erected for community among his own people, facing the imposing ostentation of the old, corrupt religion that seemed strong and powerful, surrounded by everything that can instill awe and demand subjection, by everything he himself had been taught to honor from childhood on, he alone, supported by nothing but this feeling and without hesitation uttered that "yes" that is the greatest word a mortal has ever spoken.[4] This was thus the most glorious apotheosis, and no deity can be more certain than what thus posits itself. With this faith in himself, who can wonder that he was certain not only to be mediator for many but also to leave behind a great school that would derive its identical religion from his own; he was so certain that he instituted symbols for it before it yet existed[5] in the conviction that this would suffice to bring it into existence and that he had spoken even earlier with prophetic enthusiasm about the perpetuation in this school of his personal memorable occurrences.

2. The "impertinent outrage" is perpetrated not by ancient Israel, but by modern Bible critics who reduce all personal originality to historical process.
3. Matthew 11:27.
4. See Matthew 26:63–75, Mark 14:61–72, and Luke 22:70–71. The text might also be referring generally to Jesus' acceptance of his divinely willed Crucifixion, as in Matthew 26:39.
5. See, e.g., 1 Corinthians 11:23–26, Matthew 26:26–29, Mark 14:22–25, and Luke 22:14–20.

ADOLF VON HARNACK
1851–1930

FROM WHAT IS CHRISTIANITY?

Adolf von Harnack was born in a German-speaking region of Estonia, then a province of the Russian Empire, and died in Heidelberg, Germany. As a professor of towering reputation at Germany's University of Geissen and then at the University of Berlin, he was one of the best-known and most broadly influential academics of his day. He was what might now be called a public intellectual. As a historian, however, and one specializing in the Apostolic Era (he was a noted New Testament scholar) and the Patristic Era, Harnack sought to prioritize historical evidence over philosophical theory or theological dogma. Building on the work of other eminent German historians and theologians, most notably including David Friedrich Strauss (1808–1874), Harnack did not, in the classic Protestant manner, simply take the New Testament at its historical face value and then employ it to critique the Church. Instead, he subjected the New Testament to rigorous historical critique. The results of this critique—a kind of Gospel within the Gospel—were, for him, an essential part of the blueprint that liberal Christianity required (see the headnote for Friedrich Schleiermacher, p. 481).

For Harnack, liberal Christianity, fusing modernity and a Christianity now better aware of its own origins and its own essence, was destined to assimilate modernity without superseding it. Liberal Christianity of the sort that he energetically championed combined a radical reading of early Church history with a great confidence that modernity is so much the child of German Lutheran Protestantism that, far from being irreconcilable, the two are inseparable.

This liberal Christianity has three key parts. The first is that the Kingdom of God, about which Jesus told so many parables, has its true location in the hearts of individuals. The second is an intimate and transformative experience of the fatherhood of God. The third, closely related to the first two, is the "more excellent way" (1 Corinthians 12:31) of brotherly love beneath the fatherhood of God. The full, lived reality of historical Christianity, even German Protestant Christianity, had come to include much more, of course, than just these three simple features; but for Harnack, these features defined the essence, and the essence, he argued, would define the future.

Later in his life, Harnack became controversial for his German nationalism. In his prime, however, he was controversial instead for his willingness to extend the critical spirit of the Reformation to the New Testament itself. From within the received Gospels, he excavated a historically corrected Gospel on the basis of which, he argued, liberal Christianity could move confidently forward. Such was his thinking when he demoted one entire Gospel, the Gospel of John, for addressing the agenda of the early Church rather than the agenda of Jesus. Such was his thinking, again, when he wrote that the Bible, "the thing itself . . . alone is to be authority" in the Protestant Reformation as he hoped to see it properly carried through. In *What Is Christianity?* (1900), Harnack aims to be clear where the Reformers were unclear, to draw the conclusions that they failed to draw, and so to deliver at last the "fundamentals" that their insight demanded.

The career of Adolf von Harnack marked perhaps the apex of German higher criticism of the New Testament. Harnack was a German nationalist, and his uncritical patriotism at the start of World War I scandalized his influential twentieth-century student Karl Barth (see p. 579).

FROM WHAT IS CHRISTIANITY?

Protestantism was not only a Reformation but also a *revolution*. From the legal point of view the whole Church system against which Luther[1] revolted could lay claim to full obedience. It had just as much legal validity in Western Europe as the laws of the state themselves. When Luther burnt the papal bull[2] he undoubtedly performed a revolutionary act—revolutionary, not in the bad sense of a revolt against legal ordinance which is also moral ordinance as well, but certainly in the sense of a violent breach with a given legal condition. It was against this state of things that the new movement was directed, and it was to the following chief points that its protest in word and deed extended. Firstly: It protested against the entire hierarchical and priestly system in the Church, demanded that it should be abolished, and abolished it in favor of a common priesthood and an established order formed on the basis of the congregation. . . .

Secondly: It protested against all formal, external authority in religion; against the authority, therefore, of councils, priests, and the whole tradition of the Church. That alone is to be authority which shows itself to be such within and effects a deliverance; the thing itself, therefore, the gospel. Thus Luther also protested against the authority of the letter of the Bible; but this was a point on which neither he nor the rest of the Reformers were quite clear, and where they failed to draw the conclusions which their insight into fundamentals demanded.

Thirdly: It protested against all the traditional arrangements for public worship, all ritualism, and every sort of "holy work." As it neither knows nor tolerates, as we have seen, any specific form of worship, any material sacrifice

From *Adolf von Harnack: Liberal Theology at Its Height*, ed. Martin Rumscheidt.

1. Martin Luther (see p. 399).
2. In December 1520, Luther publicly burned a copy of a bull (letter, edict) sent to him six months earlier by Pope Leo X (pope from 1513 until his death, in 1521). The papal bull threatened Luther with excommunication unless he recanted various propositions that opposed Roman Catholic doctrine.

and service to God, any mass and any works done for God and with a view to salvation, the whole traditional system of public worship, with its pomp, its holy and semi-holy articles, its gestures and processions, came to the ground. How much could be retained in the way of form for *aesthetic* or *educational* reasons was, in comparison with this, a question of entirely secondary importance.

Fourthly: It protested against sacramentalism. Baptism and the Lord's Supper it left standing, as institutions of the primitive Church, or, as it might be, of the Lord himself; but it desired that they should be regarded either as symbols and marks by which the Christian is known, or as acts deriving their value exclusively from that message of the forgiveness of sins which is bound up with them. All other sacraments it abolished, and with them the whole notion of God's grace and help being accessible in bits, and fused in some mysterious way with definite corporeal things. To sacramentalism it opposed the *Word*, and to the notion that grace was given by bits, the conviction that there is only one grace, namely, to possess *God himself* as the source of grace. It was not because Luther was so very enlightened that in his tract "On the Babylonian Captivity" he rejected the whole system of sacramentalism—he had enough superstition left in him to enable him to advance some very shocking contentions—but because he had had inner experience of the fact that where "grace" does not endow the soul with the living God himself it is an illusion. Hence for him the whole doctrine of sacramentalism was an infringement of God's majesty and an enslavement of the soul.

Fifthly: It protested against the double form of morality, and accordingly against the higher form;[3] against the contention that it is particularly well-pleasing to God to make no use of the powers and gifts which are part of creation. The Reformers had a strong sense of the fact that the world passes away with the lusts thereof; we must certainly not represent Luther as the modern man cheerfully standing with his feet firmly planted on the earth; on the contrary, like the men of the Middle Ages he had a strong yearning to be rid of this world and to depart from the "vale of tears."[4] But because he was convinced that we neither can nor ought to offer God anything but trust in him, he arrived, in regard to the Christian's position in the world, at quite different theses from those which were advanced by the grave monks of previous centuries. As fastings and ascetic practices had no value before God, and were of no advantage to one's fellowmen, and as God is the Creator of all things, the most useful thing that a man can do is to remain in the position in which God has placed him. This conviction gave Luther a cheerful and confident view of earthly ordinances, which contrasts with and actually got the upperhand of his inclination to turn his back upon the world.

He advanced the definite thesis that all positions in life—constituted authority, the married state, and so on, down to domestic service—existed by the will of God, and were therefore genuinely spiritual positions in which

3. According to the pre-Reformation Christian understanding, priests and nuns, especially those living in monastic communities, practiced a higher form of morality, whereas laypeople practiced a lower form. The Lutheran Reformation (or revolution) recognized only the morality of the layperson and denied that any higher form existed.

4. A Christian phrase meaning the world, the sorrows of life, as opposed to the perfect afterlife; possibly derived from the Catholic hymn *Salve Regina* (see p. 330).

we are to serve God; a faithful maidservant stands higher, with him, than a contemplative monk. Christians are not to be always devising how they may find some new paths of their own, but to show patience and love of neighbor within the sphere of their given vocation. Out of this there grew up in his mind the notion that all worldly laws and spheres of activity have an independent title. It is not that they are to be merely tolerated, and have no right to exist until they receive it from the Church. No! they have rights of their own, and they form the vast domain in which the Christian is to give proof of his faith and love; nay, they are even to be respected in places which are as yet ignorant of God's revelation in the gospel.

It was thus that the same man who asked nothing of the world, so far as his own personal feelings were concerned, and whose soul was troubled only by thought for the Eternal, delivered mankind from the ban of asceticism. He was thereby really and truly the life and origin of a new epoch, and he gave it back a simple and unconstrained attitude towards the world, and a good conscience in all earthly labor. This fruitful work fell to his share, not because he secularized religion, but because he took it so seriously and so profoundly that, while in his view it was to pervade all things, it was itself to be freed from everything external to it.

ALFRED FIRMIN LOISY
1857- 1940

FROM THE FIRMIN LECTURES

Alfred Firmin Loisy was born in Ambrières, France, and died in Paris. A Scripture expert who was ordained a Roman Catholic priest in 1879, Loisy taught Hebrew at the Institut Catholique, in Paris, until he was dismissed in 1892. Charged with the heresy of "modernism," he was excommunicated in 1908. He finished his career as chair of the history of religions at the prestigious Collège de France.

Loisy's "sin" was to treat the Bible as a purely human, historically unreliable, and seriously flawed work. This method was inspired by the rationalistic secularism of Enlightenment philosophers such as David Hume and Immanuel Kant. The Vatican took an unyieldingly negative view of Loisy's approach. Biblical critics had divided views, however, and engaged in a steady stream of often heated disputes. In the following selection, one of six articles published between 1898 and 1900 under the pseudonym "A. Firmin," Loisy criticizes the great German scholar Adolf von Harnack (see p. 484), who was as much hated by orthodox Lutherans as Loisy was by orthodox Catholics.

In *What Is Christianity?* (1900), Harnack tries to identify the essence of the religion. He regards Christ apart from the local, limited, time-bound elements in Jesus' environment; ignores the Church in its ancient and modern forms; and stresses the relationship between the individual and God. Loisy argues that Christianity has no essence. "Pure Christianity" never existed, because, like any religion, Christianity is not a fixed form. It is a living, constantly evolving reality that carries all sorts of cultural "baggage" with it. The "alien" influences on Christianity have included Jewish messianic thinking, Greek philosophy, Roman law, and the Protestant Reformation. Furthermore, Loisy argues, individualism is "a partial, incomplete, and insufficient definition of the Christian religious consciousness." Religion is a social phenomenon; it requires an interacting community. Therefore a Church, not Jesus alone, embodies the perfect Christian ideal.

PRONOUNCING GLOSSARY

Alfred Firmin Loisy: *al´-fred feer-mang´ lwah-zee´*
Renan: *reh-nah´*

Sabatier: *sah-bah-tee-ay´*
Voltaire: *vohl-tehr´*

FROM THE FIRMIN LECTURES
From *The Individualist Theory of Religion*

Whether it be represented by Voltaire or Renan,[1] French rationalism finally comes down to the cult of pure reason or the religion of science. Rather different from this superficial rationalism is the religious concept, largely

---

TRANSLATED BY Christine E. Thirlway.

1. Ernest Renan (1823–1892), French philologist and historian. "Voltaire": pen name of the French writer François-Marie Arouet (1694–1778).

Germanic in origin and character, which we find professed by a large number of Protestant scholars who, having broken with the dogmatic tradition, claim to retain religion if not as a visible, social institution then at least as a real and necessary part of man's spiritual activity, a part which is distinct from philosophy and from science and which has been displayed in its highest form on earth, its unique and salvific model, in a word its revelation, in the Christ.

I

These scholars—let us simply mention Mr. A. Harnack in Germany and in France Mr. A. Sabatier[2]—criticize all beliefs not excepting the beliefs of Christianity; they do not accept miracles in the ordinary theological sense; on issues of biblical literature and history they are more or less in agreement with unbelieving rationalists; but they affirm God, religion, and faith as realities of the moral order. It is hard to be certain precisely what they mean by these three moral entities. Their creed appears to consist of a single article whose significance is not otherwise defined: man is saved, which is to say morally regenerated, by faith in God the Father revealed to him in Jesus. This formula for religion and Christianity would seem to be the final, legitimate, and logically inevitable expression of the true principle of the Reformation which excludes all external authority, the Church, tradition, the letter of the Scriptures, and recognizes no rule of faith other than the interior light of the spirit discerning God's word in the Scriptures. The Bible is not an authority for faith: this comes to birth spontaneously in the soul through contact with the divine word contained in the Bible. For the Bible, as a book, is not in itself that word but only inasmuch as it awakens, in human souls, faith in God the Father revealed by Jesus. The authority of the Scriptures is therefore less than relative; it consists simply in the fact that the Sacred Books are the ordinary source of the purest religious impressions and the most complete religious experience. This is proposed as the essential doctrine of the Reformation and also as pure Christianity. In this fashion it is intended that religion should escape the control of tradition and science, the tyranny of authority, and the indiscreet curiosity of criticism.

It is certainly true that this pure Christianity is pure Protestantism. The idea of it seems at first to be quite positive, but it has negative implications. Mr. Harnack and Mr. Sabatier are right to consider themselves heirs to the true spirit of Luther;[3] like him they teach salvation by faith alone, even though on the subject of God, Jesus, faith, and salvation, Luther held doctrines less distant than theirs from traditional teaching; and they agree once again with him in their exclusion of all that is not purely evangelical, all that was not formally taught, organized, or instituted by Jesus, although Luther thought the Gospel contained a great many things which these modern disciples claim not to see in it. If to be Protestant is to lay down the rules of one's religion oneself with the help of the Gospel, and not to be Catholic, then these theologians are the most perfect Protestants ever seen.

2. Auguste Sabatier (1839–1901), French Protestant theologian and educator who employed methods of historical criticism in biblical scholarship, promoted the development of liberal Protestant theology, and interpreted Christian doctrine as symbolizing religious feeling.
3. Martin Luther (see p. 399).

But is it not an abuse of language, a philosophical error, and a complete misunderstanding of history to present in the name of religion and Christianity something which is in itself, leaving aside the essential negation attached to the positive part of the doctrine, no more than a partial, incomplete, and insufficient definition of the Christian religious consciousness? Religion has never been conceived as something entirely personal to the individual, a mere psychological operation of which each person is both subject and judge. The direct and constant relationship religion establishes between man and God has always been regarded as implying at the same time an effective bond between man and his own kind. To say religion is to say the opposite of individualism. Religion, in all its forms, even the most imperfect, has always sought the union of men in God, not merely the union of man with God. And what may be said of all religion must also be said of Christianity above all. This is why, in history, everything that has borne the name of religion has been, in one way or another, an institution. This is why Christianity as well, when it ceased to be the hope of Israel, when by the death and the resurrection of the Savior it became a religion distinct from the Jewish religion, was also an institution. This is why the Reformers of the sixteenth century, while proposing the principle of individualism so as to be able to evade the Church's authority, felt obliged, in order to preserve something of the religion and the Christianity they did not want to abandon, to make Protestantism itself an institution and to provide their individual Christianity with a social form. This is why the new Doctors feel bound to recognize that it is "in organized religious societies, in their institutions, common worship, liturgy and rules of faith and of discipline that religion brings its fundamental principle to objective realisation, shows forth the soul within it and develops all its power."[4]

Now if religion, rather than being uniquely the religious consciousness of so many individuals, is the living institution in which this consciousness finds the nourishment and direction it needs, Christianity, which undoubtedly is and intends to be a religion, must of necessity be a religious institution; if it is bound to be a religious institution, it can be neither summed up in a sentiment nor defined in a single formula; even though it draws all its energies from its originator, and was to all intents and purposes realized in Jesus, it could not be wholly realized, factually and historically, in an individual conscience, even though this conscience should be that of Christ, nor confine itself to the communication of the sentiment which came to birth in that conscience. Apart from the fact that such communication cannot be conceived without reference to the exterior means which procures it and which, being indispensable, must form part of the true notion of religion, it is evident that a religious institution cannot remain static, because it is alive, that all movement implies change, and that no change which constitutes progress in the development of the institution should be considered as a departure from its principle; as long as the Christian institution continues to perform the work of the Gospel, as long as it transforms itself solely in the interests of performing this task better, it will remain within the spirit and intentions of Jesus, it will be true Christianity, and to undertake its destruction in the cause of a better restoration of the Gospel will be to pur-

---

4. From Sabatier's *Outlines of a Philosophy of Religion* (1897).

sue a dangerous illusion, since the Gospel could exist only once in its native form, and this form, with the best will in the world, cannot be restored.

II

*   *   *

The Church may be even more readily excused for not having managed to preach pure religion, in that the Gospel itself, according to the learned advocates of individualist Christianity, does not contain it unmixed. In the same way as Christianity, they tell us, received Greek and pagan forms in the Church, in the Gospel it had a specifically Jewish form: for the Savior did not find it sufficient simply to feel within himself the "consummation of the religious union of the divine and the human,"[5] he believed himself to be, he said he was, the Messiah, and this is a Jewish concept, not a religious idea of universal validity; he proclaimed the final judgment, the resurrection of the dead, all Jewish beliefs which our learned critics consider immaterial to religion and faith; he spoke of the Pentateuch as a historical book written by Moses, and the Psalms as the work of David;[6] in brief, on many occasions he showed himself Jewish in spirit and in practice, even though he is supposed not to have been so at heart; if therefore one wants to arrive at pure Christianity, one must divest it of its first wrapping, which is Jewish, as Jesus was by the fact of his birth and education; just as, if the Church of Rome were the only Christian confession and the Gospels had disappeared, and if true Christianity had not have been discovered half by Luther, and wholly by the modern heirs to his thought, one would still be able to retrieve it by divesting it of its Catholic wrapping.

That, however, would be a delicate operation, and, without wishing to offend the eminent men who engage in it in good faith, one may be permitted to think them incapable of succeeding. For what is involved is not really an individual task or particular work which has to be done once and for all thereafter never to require attention again. Let us not discuss the appreciation of the Jewish elements claimed to be present in the Savior's preaching, or of what may be taken to be purely Israelite in his mode of existence during his ministry; let us say rather, without going into these details, that the whole Gospel is Jewish in the sense that it was conditioned by Judaism and adapted to the circles in which it was preached. It could have been no other on pain of failing to be alive, nor could it stay as it was on pain of dying in the very place where it had been born. But for its life to continue, was it necessary for ingenious philosophers to examine the Gospels for what was purely universal and what purely Jewish, reject the latter and retain the former, and draw up for the apostles a short creed to include only the essence of what seems to our critics to be the perfect religion? It hardly needs saying that on this hypothesis, Christianity would have expired even more surely and promptly than if it had kept the whole of its Jewish form, and that it would have disconcerted its preachers before disheartening its hearers. The living Gospel was neither usefully able nor in duty bound to transform itself in the external forms it took, in the way it treated the Gentiles and organized and interpreted itself, other than in accordance with the new circumstances

5. Loisy paraphrases a central contention in Harnack's Christology—namely, Harnack's understanding of Jesus' identity as Jesus understood it and as it has subsequently been understood in Christian history.
6. "David": See p. 96. "Moses": See p. 89.

imposed upon it by events and by its own expansion; it adapted itself to those circumstances bit by bit as they arose, not through human, political reflection, but through a kind of intimate necessity, more or less felt, which made it develop whatever, in its current state of being, favored its progress, and correct anything through which it would have been hindered or compromised. The life of a religion never consists in seeking to discover a quintessence, but in its action on souls; and everything which advances this action, everything which religion draws into its orbit and uses for its own ends, participates in its life insofar as it serves that end. The question therefore is not to discover how to define the essence of Christianity or of the Gospel, for no absolute definition is possible, since Christianity is a living reality and not a concept of the mind; it is communicated by being described such as it is; if one insists on giving it a scientific form, one creates an abstract symbol which has in itself no religious effect, because such is not the property of abstractions. The question is to discover where the living Gospel is, where it has been ever since it began, where it continues to be today. It is a question of fact, not one of logical subtleties. In any case, one should not talk about a return to pure Christianity in the sense in which pure is used by our learned critics because, on their own admission, such a Christianity has never existed. Is one then to create it today by scientific means, and if one were to do so would this intellectual product be a living religion? This we are entitled to doubt, given that no religion ever has been founded in this manner.

ROMANTICISM, NATURE, AND THE CHRISTIANITY OF THE HEART

During the eighteenth and especially the nineteenth centuries, the Christianity of dogma and argument began to yield, for many, to a Christianity of simplicity and the heart. The emergence of what we might call Romantic Christianity was one paradoxical but unmistakable component of Christianity's encounter with modernity.

As nothing goes more directly to the heart than music, emotional hymnody assumed an unprecedented new importance in this period, especially in Protestant Christianity—Methodism in Britain, Pietism in Germany, and kindred developments elsewhere. Just as the previous section focused on France and Germany, this section focuses on Britain and the United States, and it includes an enduringly popular hymn by the eighteenth-century Methodist church-music composer Charles Wesley; a strikingly simple nineteenth-century hymn by Charlotte Elliot that would live on to become a classic of mid-twentieth-century Evangelical revivalism; an early published account for white America of the haunting hymnody of the nation's black slaves; and Julia Ward Howe's rhetorically biblical abolitionist anthem, "Battle Hymn of the Republic."

Hymnody was not, however, the only vehicle for Romantically emotional religiosity during these two centuries. Recollections by the American theologian Jonathan Edwards present Romantic Christianity inspired by nature. An account of an interior struggle by John Wesley, honored as a cofounder of Methodism, delivers a similar emotionality but with even greater urgency and a cathartic end that resonated with Protestants on both sides of the Atlantic.

After the Wars of Religion, Christians shared the Deist concern that all-out religious war never again be waged. Unlike Deists, however, Christians did not seek peace in a "natural" religion. Instead, they developed internal resources. For example, in the German Pietist community of Herrnhut, Nicolas von Zinzendorf developed rules filled with forbearance across dogmatic lines, a principled refusal to impose faith by force. That attitude initiated a trend that strengthened steadily with time. The emotional, if not exactly the logical, accompaniment of that attitude was a desire for a Christianity of simple practice rather than of complex and arcane theory. The conclusion in the anonymous *Way of the Pilgrim*, which ends this section, is that the "Jesus Prayer" sums up the entirety of the Bible and the Christian creed; the subtext is that a humble pilgrim may be holier than the learned officials to whom he brings an earnest question.

In nineteenth-century America, the constitutionally established free market in religion combined with self-reliance to produce an unparalleled burst of Church-founding. Many new Protestant denominations came into existence during the Second Great Awakening of the first half of that century. A good many of these denominations were "Restorationist." That is, they sought to restore the received, imported forms of American Christianity to a lost biblical purity just as classic European Protestantism had sought to do for the Catholic Christianity of the sixteenth century.

Not all of the new Churches achieved or even aspired to great size or institutional permanence. The largest, most durable, and perhaps most radical of them has been Mormonism. The prophetic vision of the Mormon Church's founder, Joseph Smith, was boldly individualist and self-reliant in the American vein, but it was also nationalist: Mormonism caught up the entire biblical story, including the whole of the European Christian story, in a new Restorationist vision, going back to the Bible but adding new Scriptures that assigned North America, its native inhabitants, and its American prophet a central role. Perhaps the antithesis of modernity in its faith in a founding prophetic revelation, Mormonism was surprisingly modern in these other regards.

Smith's near-contemporary Jarena Lee was a humble black freewoman of little education, working as a maidservant in New Jersey. In her lively and influential *Religious Experience and Journal*, Lee boldly defends her prophetic call to preach in the African Methodist Episcopal Church. Like the "Negro spirituals" that found a wide hearing for the first time during her lifetime, Lee's book opened American eyes and ears to Christian variety at home as well as to Christian sexual and racial potential that in the long run would not and could not be denied.

NICOLAS VON ZINZENDORF
1700–1760

FROM THE BROTHERLY AGREEMENT AT HERRNHUT

Pietism was an important seventeenth- and eighteenth-century reform movement within German Lutheranism, emphasizing orderly and decorous conduct, frequent prayer, generous charitable practice, and the free expression of religious emotion. With one important exception, institutional Lutheranism succeeded in containing and assimilating the new energies released by Pietism. The exception was the Moravian Church.

The Moravian Church was the surviving remnant of *Unitas Fratrum* ("The Union of Brothers"), a pre-Lutheran reform movement in Moravia and Bohemia, regions now part of the Czech Republic. The *Unitas Fratrum* movement had been inspired by Jan Hus, a Czech priest burned at the stake in Prague in 1415 for his proto-Protestant views. Hus's martyrdom sparked a devastating religious civil war that ended with a surprising degree of accommodation of the reformist movement by the Catholic Church. By the 1700s, however, in the wake of the broader Protestant Reformation, Moravia and Bohemia had been incorporated into the Holy Roman Empire, which was ruled by the Roman Catholic Habsburg dynasty, and the members of the already splintered Moravian Church came under severe external pressure as the Habsburgs initiated a policy of re-Catholicization.

Nicolas Ludwig von Zinzendorf, a count of the Prussian Empire who had acquired estates in Berthelsdorf near the Moravian border but beyond the reach of the Habsburgs, invited members of the Moravian Church to create a community there, which he called Herrnhut—"The Lord's Asylum." Though a Lutheran, Zinzendorf became a bishop in the Moravian Church; and over time, Herrnhut became a magnet for dissidents of Pietist inclination at odds with several different forms of Protestantism. Tensions arose among this disparate group, but the discipline of the "Brotherly Agreement" (1727) fostered mutual forbearance in matters of doctrine, while highly emotional prayer and hymnody, monastic in their frequency, helped to hold the community together in spirit. Though never large, the Moravian Church remained distinct from the Lutheran Church and became the first Protestant Church to seriously commit itself to foreign missions. The Moravian missions began, crucially, just as the northern European Protestant powers were beginning to establish overseas empires, and the Moravians set a pattern for others that followed.

Zinzendorf died at Herrnhut. In the United States today, the congregations of the Moravian Church and the Church of the Brethren preserve the memory and ideals of the "Brotherly Agreement" under the title "The Covenant for Christian Living."

PRONOUNCING GLOSSARY

Berthelsdorf: *behr´-tuls-dorf*   Herrnhut: *hehrn´-hoot*

FROM THE BROTHERLY AGREEMENT AT HERRNHUT

1. It shall be forever remembered by the inhabitants of Herrnhut, that it was built on the grace of the living God, that it is a work of his own hand, yet not properly intended to be a new town, but only an establishment erected for Brethren and for the Brethren's sake.

2. Herrnhut and its original old inhabitants must remain in a constant bond of love with all children of God belonging to the different religious persuasions—they must judge none, enter into no disputes with any, nor behave themselves unseemly toward any, but rather seek to maintain among themselves the pure evangelical doctrine, simplicity, and grace.

3. The following are the characteristics of a true member of Christ's body, and these we, the inhabitants of Herrnhut, who simply adhere to the foundation built on the Word of God, deem to be the most sure. Whosoever does not confess that he owes his awakening and salvation exclusively to the mercy of God in Christ Jesus, and that he cannot exist without it for one moment of his life, that the greatest perfection in life (were it possible to attain to it, without the intercession of the Mediator, urged by the plea of his blood and merit) would be of no avail in the sight of God, while it is made acceptable in the beloved; and whoever does not daily prove it by his whole conversation, that it is his full determination to be delivered from sin, through the merits of Jesus, and to follow daily more after holiness, to grow in the likeness of his Lord, to be cleansed from all spiritual idolatry, vanity, and self-will, to walk as Jesus did, and to bear his reproach and shame: such a one is not a genuine brother. But whosoever has this disposition of heart, though he maintain sectarian, fanatical, or at least defective opinions, shall not on that account be despised among us, nor in case of his even separating himself from us will we immediately forsake him, but we will rather follow him in his wanderings, and spare him, and bear with him in the spirit of love, patience, and meekness. But whosoever is not fully established on the above-named fundamental principles, though he do not wholly forsake them, shall be considered as a halting and wavering brother, and be reclaimed in the spirit of meekness.

❊   ❊   ❊

FROM *Pietists: Selected Writings*, ed. Peter C. Erb.

5. Those who, with an unfettered conscience, acquiesce in the present external regulations of the church will not hesitate to declare the ground of their acquiescence, to wit, that they do not consider human regulations and customs as an unalterable part of divine worship, but make use of them, agreeably to the dictates of Christian liberty, in a spirit of meekness, love, and obedience, till the Lord himself brings about a change. Should in aftertimes any particular order of things be introduced among us, in respect to the outward form of devotional rites, simplicity and edification must be aimed at exclusively.

6. Whoever has not been used to auricular confession, or has conscientious objections in his mind against it, shall not be forced to submit to it at Berthelsdorf; yet no one shall be permitted to go to the Holy Communion without the previous knowledge of the minister at Berthelsdorf, in order that all confusion and levity[1] may be prevented.

7. No one is to enter into confidential intercourse[2] with people that are notoriously wicked, or altogether worldly minded, lest offense should thereby be given; yet it is proper that such people should be treated as much as possible in an equitable and unassuming manner, and none should allow themselves in any vehemences against them.

* * *

10. In general, we consider it an abominable practice for anyone to judge and condemn his neighbor rashly, and without clear and full evidence, and without previously using all the acknowledged and scriptural degrees of brotherly correction. Whoever, therefore, is guilty of this unjustifiable proceeding subjects himself to well-merited censure.

11. Ministers, laborers, and all whose official incumbency it is to care for and watch over the souls of others must be at full liberty to hold frequent and full intercourse with one or the other, and no suspicion is to be cast on them on that account.

12. As the conversion of souls is the chief object of most of the present inhabitants of Herrnhut, everyone must be permitted to choose those with whom he would, for the time being, be more intimately connected, than he could be with others; and to alter his choice according to circumstances without fearing to give offense.

The intercourse between single persons of both sexes must have its restrictions, and the elders are empowered to prevent it whenever in any case scruples arise in their minds against such intercourse, though the apparent aim of it might be ever so laudable.

13. Envy, suspicion, and unfounded prejudice against the brethren must be most carefully guarded against. As everyone is at liberty to cultivate an intercourse with others, no one ought to take it amiss if another should appear more familiarly acquainted with the elders than he.

* * *

15. Agreeably to the practice of the primitive church, the Brethren are called upon to exert themselves in every possible way for the benefit of those

---

1. Unseemly frivolity.   2. Social contact, interaction.

who are of the same household of faith; and to all others they are to do as they would wish that others should do unto them.[3]

16. Whosoever has received the needful gift for it is to speak, the others to judge.[4]

17. Those who seem to be best suited one to the other may, without hesitation, live in the habit of close familiarity, join in prayer, and act in all respects as intimate friendship requires; yet such preference given to any individual must by no means be to the prejudice of cordial brotherly love toward all others; and it becomes the duty of those who are particularly acquainted one with the other to lend each other a helping hand as it regards doctrine, admonition, reproof, direction, yea, their whole spiritual course.

* * *

24. If anyone should be overtaken in a fault, he must not consider it disgraceful to be spoken to on the subject, or to receive admonition or reproof. He ought to take it in good part, and not allow himself to retort, much less think himself warranted on that account to withdraw from the fellowship of the Brethren. All matters of this kind should be judged and decided exclusively by those whose official incumbency requires their interference.

25. Whosoever spreads any unfounded report against another is bound to declare to the elders the reason of his allegations, and afterward to recant the report, whether required to do so in consequence of the complaint of the person injured thereby or not.

26. Whenever in public companies anything is said to the disadvantage of anyone not then present, everyone is authorized to acquaint the person alluded to of it, yet without naming the offender.

* * *

29. Everyone must conscientiously keep to himself what has been confidently, and as a secret, entrusted to him.

30. No one is to harbor anything in his mind against another, but rather immediately, and in a friendly and becoming manner, mention what may have offended him, without respect of persons. Complaints which have been purposely suffered to accumulate must not even be listened to, but quarrels, envy, and willful dissensions ought to be abominated by all, and those who are guilty of these things be looked upon as unbelievers.

* * *

33. Every effort shall be made to reclaim the erring by friendly reproof and discipline, but should this fail the offender is expected and required to leave the place.

34. The elders shall hold a conference every Saturday, and if any be cited to appear before that conference he is to obey the summons, and in case of reiterated and obstinate refusal he must leave the place.

---

3. Luke 6:31.
4. The gifts of the Holy Spirit are understood to be various, some given to one, some to another. See 1 Corinthians 12:4–11.

35. The watchers[5] are to sing a verse from a suitable hymn, at the change of the successive hours in the night, with a view to encourage and edify the Congregation.

36. The doctrine and example of Jesus and his apostles shall be the general and special rule of all our ministry and instruction.

37. Whosoever perseveres in an open course of levity and sin, though often before warned and admonished, shall be excluded from our brotherly fellowship, nor can he be readmitted till he has given sufficient proof of his being an altered character.

38. All the young people at Herrnhut who shall confess their faith in Christ are to be confirmed, after which these statutes are to be given them for their consideration.

* * *

41. Everyone shall be at liberty in love to admonish and rebuke his brother, whether there be ground for it or not. But this must be done with great modesty, and all vehemence on either side be carefully avoided. If an explanation or exculpation be offered, the person who gave the admonition ought either to be satisfied with it or refer the case to other Brethren.

42. Should we be called to suffer persecutions, everyone should consider them precious and most useful exercises; love those that persecute us, treat them respectfully, answer their questions with modesty and simplicity, and cheerfully submit to what may befall us, according to the confession we make before God and man.

5. In a quasi-monastic manner, different members of the community kept a watch or vigil for successive periods of the night, singing a hymn verse as each watch was followed by the next.

JONATHAN EDWARDS
1703–1758

FROM PERSONAL NARRATIVE

Jonathan Edwards is often regarded as North America's premier religious thinker. He was born in Connecticut, graduated from Yale College (now University), was a pastor in Massachusetts, and died in New Jersey, where he briefly served as the president of the College of New Jersey (now Princeton University). Influenced by Calvinist theology and Enlightenment thinking, Edwards helped shape the First Great Awakening. During a wave of reform in 1741, Edwards delivered the now-classic sermon "Sinners in the Hands of an Angry God." His many other writings include the books *Religious Affections* (1746), a treatise on conversion to Christianity, and *The Life of David Brainerd* (1749), a biography of an eighteenth-century missionary.

Edwards was the grandfather of Aaron Burr, the third vice president of the United States. He wrote his *Personal Narrative* around 1740, probably at the request of Burr's father, a minister. Including entries from his diary, the narrative can be seen as a mini-autobiography—an accounting of his activities, thoughts, religious experiences, and spiritual states. Above all, it expresses Edwards's obedience and dedication to God.

FROM PERSONAL NARRATIVE

The first instance that I remember of that sort of inward, sweet delight in God and divine things that I have lived much in since, was on reading those words, 1 Timothy 1:17. *Now unto the King eternal, immortal, invisible, the only wise God, be honor and glory for ever and ever, Amen.* As I read the words, there came into my soul, and was as it were diffused through it, a sense of the glory of the Divine Being; a new sense, quite different from any thing I ever experienced before. Never any words of scripture seemed to me as these words did. I thought with myself, how excellent a Being that was, and how happy I should be, if I might enjoy that God, and be rapt up to him in heaven, and be as it were swallowed up in him for ever! I kept saying, and as it were singing over these words of scripture to myself; and went to pray to God that I might enjoy him, and prayed in a manner quite different from what I used to do; with a new sort of affection. But it never came into my thought, that there was any thing spiritual, or of a saving nature in this.

From about that time, I began to have a new kind of apprehensions and ideas of Christ, and the work of redemption, and the glorious way of salvation by him. An inward, sweet sense of these things, at times, came into my heart; and my soul was led away in pleasant views and contemplations of them. And my mind was greatly engaged to spend my time in reading and meditating on Christ, on the beauty and excellency of his person, and the lovely way of salvation by free grace in him. I found no books so delightful to me, as those that treated of these subjects. Those words Canticles 2:1,[1] used to be abundantly with me, *I am the Rose of Sharon, and the Lily of the valleys.* The words seemed to me, sweetly to represent the loveliness and beauty of Jesus Christ. The whole book of Canticles used to be pleasant to me, and I used to be much in reading it, about that time; and found, from time to time, an inward sweetness, that would carry me away, in my contemplations. This I know not how to express otherwise, than by a calm, sweet abstraction of soul from all the concerns of this world; and sometimes a kind of vision, or fixed ideas and imaginations, of being alone in the mountains, or some solitary wilderness, far from all mankind, sweetly conversing with Christ, and wrapt and swallowed up in God. The sense I had of divine things, would often of a sudden kindle up, as it were, a sweet burning in my heart; an ardor of soul, that I know not how to express.

Not long after I first began to experience these things, I gave an account to my father of some things that had passed in my mind. I was pretty much affected by the discourse we had together; and when the discourse was ended, I walked abroad alone, in a solitary place in my father's pasture, for contemplation. And as I was walking there, and looking up on the sky and

1. Another name for the biblical Song of Songs (see p. 306).

clouds, there came into my mind so sweet a sense of the glorious *majesty* and *grace* of God, that I know not how to express. I seemed to see them both in a sweet conjunction; majesty and meekness joined together; it was a sweet, and gentle, and holy majesty; and also a majestic meekness; an awful sweetness; a high, and great, and holy gentleness.

After this my sense of divine things gradually increased, and became more and more lively, and had more of that inward sweetness. The appearance of every thing was altered; there seemed to be, as it were, a calm, sweet cast, or appearance of divine glory, in almost every thing. God's excellency, his wisdom, his purity and love, seemed to appear in every thing; in the sun, moon, and stars; in the clouds, and blue sky; in the grass, flowers, trees; in the water, and all nature; which used greatly to fix my mind. I often used to sit and view the moon for continuance; and in the day, spent much time in viewing the clouds and sky, to behold the sweet glory of God in these things; in the mean time, singing forth, with a low voice my contemplations of the Creator and Redeemer. And scarce any thing, among all the works of nature, was so sweet to me as thunder and lightning; formerly, nothing had been so terrible to me. Before, I used to be uncommonly terrified with thunder, and to be struck with terror when I saw a thunder storm rising; but now, on the contrary, it rejoiced me. I felt God, so to speak, at the first appearance of a thunder storm; and used to take the opportunity, at such times, to fix myself in order to view the clouds, and see the lightnings play, and hear the majestic and awful voice of God's thunder, which oftentimes was exceedingly entertaining, leading me to sweet contemplations of my great and glorious God. While thus engaged, it always seemed natural to me to sing, or chant for my meditations; or, to speak my thoughts in soliloquies with a singing voice.

✳   ✳   ✳

I remember, about that time, I used greatly to long for the conversion of some, that I was concerned with; I could gladly honour them, and with delight be a servant to them, and lie at their feet, if they were but truly holy. But some time after this, I was again greatly diverted with some temporal concerns, that exceedingly took up my thoughts, greatly to the wounding of my soul; and went on, through various exercises, that it would be tedious to relate, which gave me much more experience of my own heart, than I ever had before.

Since I came to this town [Northampton, Massachusetts], I have often had sweet complacency in God, in views of his glorious perfections and the excellency of Jesus Christ. God has appeared to me a glorious and lovely Being, chiefly on account of his holiness. The holiness of God has always appeared to me the most lovely of all his attributes. The doctrines of God's absolute sovereignty, and free grace, in shewing mercy to whom he would shew mercy; and man's absolute dependence on the operations of God's Holy Spirit, have very often appeared to me as sweet and glorious doctrines. These doctrines have been much my delight. God's sovereignty has ever appeared to me, great part of his glory. It has often been my delight to approach God, and adore him as a sovereign God, and ask sovereign mercy of him.

I have loved the doctrines of the gospel; they have been to my soul like green pastures. The gospel has seemed to me the richest treasure; the treasure that I have most desired, and longed that it might dwell richly in me. The way of salvation by Christ has appeared, in a general way, glorious and excellent, most pleasant and most beautiful. It has often seemed to me, that it would in a great measure spoil heaven, to receive it in any other way. That text has often been affecting and delightful to me, Isaiah 32:2. *A man shall be an hiding place from the wind, and a covert from the tempest, &c.*

* * *

JOHN WESLEY
1703–1791

FROM JOURNAL

John Wesley was born in Epworth, Lincolnshire, England, and died in London. As a young Anglican priest in London, he met and was impressed by the German-born Moravian missionary bishop Peter Böhler (1712–1775). Böhler had been sent as a missionary to Savannah, Georgia, by Nicolas von Zinzendorf (see p. 494). Wesley and his brother Charles (see p. 504) also traveled as missionaries to Savannah, but they quickly returned to London. Under von Zinzendorf's guidance, John and Charles Wesley then organized a small community that brought to Anglicanism what Pietism had brought to Lutheranism: decorous self-control in daily life, combined with emotion in worship and in religious experience. For

The Irish-born artist Nathaniel Hone painted this portrait of John Wesley in 1766. Wesley wears the gown and bands of an Anglican priest.

their orderly—methodical—habits, the Wesleys and their early followers were nicknamed "Methodists." They embraced the nickname and began to attract large crowds with their preaching, yet only after John Wesley's death did Methodism became a denomination distinct from Anglicanism. Emphasizing the individual's personal experience of Jesus Christ, the Wesleyan/Methodist movement inspired more than just the modern Methodist Church. All branches of the Evangelical movement—including Holiness Churches, Charismatic Churches, and Pentecostal Churches—are significantly indebted to what the Methodist movement began.

John Wesley's journal was originally published in twenty volumes from 1740 through 1789. The following excerpt, from May 1738, ends with his now-famous conversion, in London. The story of how Wesley's heart was "strangely warmed" by his faith in Christ became virtually paradigmatic for revival movements deep into the twentieth century.

FROM JOURNAL

11. In my return to England, January, 1738, being in imminent danger of death, and very uneasy on that account, I was strongly convinced that the cause of that uneasiness was unbelief; and that the gaining [of] a true, living faith was the 'one thing needful'[1] for me. But still I fixed not this faith on its right object: I meant only faith in God, not faith in or through Christ. Again, I knew not that I was wholly void of this faith; but only thought, I had not enough of it. So that when Peter Böhler, whom God prepared for me as soon as I came to London, affirmed of true faith in Christ (which is but one), that it had those two fruits inseparably attending it, 'Dominion over sin, and constant Peace from a sense of forgiveness,'[2] I was quite amazed, and looked upon it as a new Gospel. If this was so, it was clear I had not faith. But I was not willing to be convinced of this. Therefore, I disputed with all my might, and laboured to prove that faith might be where these were not; especially where the sense of forgiveness was not: For all the Scriptures relating to this I had been long since taught to construe away; and to call all Presbyterians who spoke otherwise.[3] Besides, I well saw, no one could, in the nature of things, have such a sense of forgiveness, and not *feel* it. But I felt it not. If then there was no faith without this, all my pretensions to faith dropped at once.

12. When I met Peter Böhler again, he consented to put the dispute upon the issue which I desired, namely, Scripture and experience. I first consulted the Scripture. But when I set aside the glosses of men, and simply considered the words of God, comparing them together, endeavouring to illustrate the obscure by the plainer passages; I found they all made against me, and was forced to retreat to my last hold, 'that experience would never

---

1. In Wesley's day, all trans-Atlantic crossings were mortally perilous. As he sets out, the "one needful thing," should he die, is faith. See Luke 10:42, where Martha is busy doing many things. Her sister, Mary, sits and listens to Jesus with faith. Mary, Jesus says, has done the "needful thing."
2. Wesley quotes Peter Böhler's words from memory.
3. Anglicans believed in the possibility of one's

having genuine faith *without* perfect confidence that one could control one's sinful inclinations ("Dominion over sin") or perfect certainty that one was forgiven ("constant Peace from a sense of forgiveness"). Some Presbyterians "spoke otherwise"; Böhler, too, "spoke otherwise." Wesley, who had been raised Anglican, had been trained to call anyone who "spoke otherwise" a Presbyterian. But Wesley came to adopt Böhler's belief.

agree with the *literal interpretation* of those scriptures. Nor could I therefore allow it to be true, till I found some living witnesses of it.'[4] He replied, he could show me such at any time; if I desired it, the next day. And accordingly, the next day he came again with three others, all of whom testified, of their own personal experience, that a true living faith in Christ is inseparable from a sense of pardon for all past, and freedom from all present, sins. They added with one mouth, that this faith was the gift, the free gift of God; and that he would surely bestow it upon every soul who earnestly and perseveringly sought it. I was now throughly convinced; and, by the grace of God, I resolved to seek it unto the end, 1. By absolutely renouncing all dependence, in whole or in part, upon *my own* works or righteousness; on which I had really grounded my hope of salvation, though I knew it not, from my youth up. 2. By adding to the constant use of all the other means of grace, continual prayer for this very thing, justifying, saving faith, a full reliance on the blood of Christ shed for *me*; a trust in Him, as *my* Christ, as *my* sole justification, sanctification, and redemption.

13. I continued thus to seek it (though with strange indifference, dulness, and coldness, and unusually frequent relapses into sin), till Wednesday, May 24. I think it was about five this morning, that I opened my Testament on those words, Τα μεγιστα ημιν και τιμια επαγγελματα δεδωρηται, ινα γενησθε θειας κοινωνοι φυσεως.[5] 'There are given unto us exceeding great and precious promises, even that ye should be partakers of the divine nature.' (2 Peter 2:4.) Just as I went out, I opened it again on those words, 'Thou art not far from the kingdom of God.'[6] In the afternoon I was asked to go to St. Paul's.[7] The anthem was, 'Out of the deep have I called unto thee, O Lord: Lord, hear my voice. O let thine ears consider well the voice of my complaint. If thou, Lord, wilt be extreme to mark what is done amiss, O Lord, who may abide it? For there is mercy with thee; therefore shalt thou be feared. O Israel, trust in the Lord: For with the Lord there is mercy, and with him is plenteous redemption. And He shall redeem Israel from all his sins.'[8]

14. In the evening I went very unwillingly to a society in Aldersgate Street, where one was reading Luther's[9] preface to the Epistle to the Romans. About a quarter before nine, while he was describing the change which God works in the heart through faith in Christ, I felt my heart strangely warmed. I felt I did trust in Christ, Christ alone for salvation: And an assurance was given me, that he had taken away *my* sins, even *mine*, and saved *me* from the law of sin and death. * * *

4. Wesley is quoting his own words to Böhler.
5. Wesley quotes the New Testament Greek from memory, leaving two words out. Verbatim, the text reads: τὰ μέγιστα ἡμῖν καὶ τίμια ἐπαγγέλματα δεδώρηται, ἵνα διὰ τούτων γένησθε θείας κοινωνοὶ φύσεως.
6. Mark 12:34.
7. St Paul's Cathedral, in London.

8. Psalm 130 in almost its entirety.
9. Martin Luther's (see p. 399). "A society in Aldersgate Street": In Methodist tradition, Wesley's experience is celebrated as his "Aldersgate Experience." This event occurred while he attended a worship service at the Moravian church on Aldersgate Street, before the separate life of organized Methodism had begun.

CHARLES WESLEY
1707–1788

LOVE DIVINE, ALL LOVES EXCELLING

Along with his brother John (see p. 501) and the Anglican priest George Whitfield, Charles Wesley is largely credited with founding the Methodist Evangelical movement in the United Kingdom. After the brothers returned to England from the colony of Georgia, Charles served as a preacher. He also wrote hymns, perhaps as many as eight thousand. His works are included in Christian hymn books across many denominations, and "Love Divine, All Loves Excelling" is one of his best-known. In the second stanza, "that second rest" refers to the same experience that John Wesley, in his journal, calls "constant Peace from a sense of forgiveness," while "Take away our power of sinning" refers to what, again in the journal, John calls "Dominion over sin." Because these notions were theologically controversial (Was the first one necessary? Was the second one possible?), Presbyterians and Anglicans often omitted or edited this verse in their hymnals. However, both denominations increasingly came to share the principal goal of the hymn—namely, to kindle a warmth of religious feeling—and so they retained the shortened or edited form.

LOVE DIVINE, ALL LOVES EXCELLING

'Love Divine, all loves excelling,
   Joy of heaven, to earth come down,
Fix in us thy humble dwelling,[1]
   All thy faithful mercies crown.[2]
Jesu, thou art all compassion,   5
   Pure unbounded love thou art;
Visit us with thy salvation,
   Enter every trembling heart.

Breathe, O breathe thy loving Spirit
   Into every troubled breast,   10
Let us all in thee inherit,
   Let us find that second rest:
Take away our power of sinning,
   Alpha and Omega be,[3]
End of faith as its beginning,   15
   Set our hearts at liberty.

Come, almighty to deliver,
   Let us all thy life receive;

---

1. Make our humble selves your home, your "fixed address."
2. A "mercy" is a gracious favor, a kindness not required by justice. This line urges Jesus to "crown"—add one more—mercy to all he has performed.
3. "Alpha and omega" (Revelation 21:6 and 22:13) are the first and last letters of the Greek alphabet; thus, they represent the beginning, the end, and everything in between.

Suddenly return, and never,
   Never more thy temples leave.   20
Thee we would be always blessing,
   Serve thee as thy hosts above,[4]
Pray, and praise thee without ceasing,
   Glory in thy perfect love.

Finish then thy New Creation,   25
   Pure and spotless let us be;
Let us see thy great salvation
   Perfectly restored in thee,
Changed from glory into glory[5]
   Till in heaven we take our place,   30
Till we cast our crowns before thee,[6]
   Lost in wonder, love, and praise!

4. As your armies of angels ("hosts" being a synonym for "armies").
5. From the glory of humanity into the reflected glory of divinity. Compare 2 Corinthians 3:18.
6. Compare Revelation 4:9–11; in the final ecstatic meeting with God, time and human distinctions, such as royalty and nobility, will end.

JOSEPH SMITH
1805–1844

FROM PEARL OF GREAT PRICE

The Constitution of the United States, ratified in 1787, stipulated that the country would have no religious requirement or "test" for federal office-holders and no established national religion. On the one hand, as restrictions, these rules deprived all of the new nation's religions of direct federal sponsorship or subsidy. On the other hand, as opportunities, these rules afforded protection to the irreligious as well as to those who might wish to change their religion, and they created a market free of government regulation for all who might wish to promote their religion or even found a new religion. This free market of religion had by far a larger and more immediate impact on American life than disestablishment did.

Within President George Washington's first term in office (1789–92), a religious revival called the Second Great Awakening began. (There had been a smaller, briefer Great Awakening in the earlier 1700s.) Continuing until the middle of the following century, the Second Great Awakening achieved its major impact in the territories west of the Allegheny Mountains that were settled as the new republic expanded. Here, where the long-established Episcopal, Congregationalist (Puritan), and Presbyterian Churches of the original thirteen colonies had no monopoly, where the only inhabitants were indigenous tribes, and where there were typically no church buildings, Methodist and Baptist missionaries led the way in staging great outdoor "revival meetings." These events took place in campgrounds to which settlers would travel from considerable distances and stay for days on end, hearing hours of emotional preaching and engaging in prolonged, sometimes ecstatic hymn-singing, all aimed at repentance and conversion.

The older denominations, notably the Presbyterians, took part in this Evangelical (Gospel-preaching, Gospel-spreading) exercise, but much of the preaching applied the logic or structure of Protestantism *to* the established Protestant denominations. That is, just as the dynamic and historic figures of the Protestant Reformation had looked back past Roman Catholicism, which they saw as riddled with adulterations, to the pure Christianity they saw in the Gospel, so the "Restorationist" preachers of the Second Great Awakening commonly looked back past the various forms of organized Protestantism then on offer to the lost but spiritually recoverable Christianity of the biblical past. Thus came into existence American-born denominations: those, such as the Millerites (later, Seventh-Day Adventists) and the Shakers, who believed that a Second Coming of Christ was near; those, such as the Disciples of Christ and the Church of Christ, that favored a consciously simplified Christianity; and many others, often loosely organized or not organized beyond an individual, local congregation.

The most radical and the most durable of these new movements was the Church of Jesus Christ of Latter-Day Saints, founded by Joseph Smith, a farmer in upstate New York. The following selection comes from a history of the Church that Smith wrote in 1838 (posthumously included in *Pearl of Great Price*, a collection of writings he published in Church periodicals). In this history, Smith describes how a miraculous vision brought him to believe that all the vigorously competing Christian denominations of his day were mistaken. God had led him, Smith later reported, to golden plates written (in "reformed Egyptian") or collated by an ancient scribe and prophet named Mormon, whose name was in time attached to Smith's followers, the Mormons. Smith translated the plates with the help of seer stones, Urim and Thummim (compare Exodus 28:30 and Leviticus 8:8), bound into a pair of spectacles.

The Book of Mormon, completed in 1830, tells the story of the Native Americans, who are identified with the ten lost tribes of northern Israel (2 Kings 17:1–41), from the Tower of Babel (Genesis 11:1–9) more than two millennia before Christ to the early fifth century of the Common Era. For example, in 3 Nephi 11, the recently risen Jesus appears to the Americans, the "other sheep that are not of this fold" whom he mentions in John 10:16.

Smith quickly attracted followers—and persecutors. The Mormons were forced to move from New York to Ohio to Missouri to Illinois, where a mob in blackface murdered Smith and his brother Hyrum. Smith's place was taken by Brigham Young (1801–1877), who in 1846–47 led the Mormons' "great migration" from Nauvoo, Illinois, to Salt Lake City, Utah. There are now about 14 million Mormons worldwide. While the Church achieved notoriety for the 1843 revelation that allowed polygamy, a Church manifesto banned the practice in 1890 after the U.S. government used military force to register an objection on legal grounds.

FROM PEARL OF GREAT PRICE

From *The History of Joseph Smith, the Prophet*

1. Owing to the many reports which have been put in circulation by evil-disposed and designing persons, in relation to the rise and progress of The Church of Jesus Christ of Latter-day Saints,[1] all of which have been designed by the authors thereof to militate against its character as a Church and its progress in the world—I have been induced to write this history, to

---

1. In the New Testament, the earliest Christians are sometimes referred to as "saints." In Romans 15:25, for example, Saint Paul writes: "At present, however, I am going to Jerusalem in a ministry to the saints." The "latter-day" Christians of the Mormon Church see themselves as the modern counterparts of such "former-day" Christians.

disabuse the public mind, and put all inquirers after truth in possession of the facts, as they have transpired, in relation both to myself and the Church, so far as I have such facts in my possession.

2. In this history I shall present the various events in relation to this Church, in truth and righteousness, as they have transpired, or as they at present exist, being now the eighth year since the organization of the said Church.

3. I was born in the year of our Lord one thousand eight hundred and five, on the twenty-third day of December, in the town of Sharon, Windsor county, State of Vermont . . . My father, Joseph Smith, Sen., left the State of Vermont, and moved to Palmyra, Ontario (now Wayne) county, in the State of New York, when I was in my tenth year, or thereabouts. In about four years after my father's arrival in Palmyra, he moved with his family into Manchester in the same county of Ontario—

* * *

5. Some time in the second year after our removal to Manchester, there was in the place where we lived an unusual excitement on the subject of religion. It commenced with the Methodists, but soon became general among all the sects in that region of country. Indeed, the whole district of country seemed affected by it, and great multitudes united themselves to the different religious parties, which created no small stir and division amongst the people, some crying, "Lo, here!" and others, "Lo, there!"[2] Some were contending for the Methodist faith, some for the Presbyterian, and some for the Baptist.

6. For, notwithstanding the great love which the converts to these different faiths expressed at the time of their conversion, and the great zeal manifested by the respective clergy, who were active in getting up and promoting this extraordinary scene of religious feeling, in order to have everybody converted, as they were pleased to call it, let them join what sect they pleased; yet when the converts began to file off, some to one party and some to another, it was seen that the seemingly good feelings of both the priests and the converts were more pretended than real; for a scene of great confusion and bad feeling ensued—priest contending against priest, and convert against convert; so that all their good feelings one for another, if they ever had any, were entirely lost in a strife of words and a contest about opinions.

7. I was at this time in my fifteenth year. My father's family was proselyted to the Presbyterian faith, and four of them joined that church, namely, my mother, Lucy; my brothers Hyrum and Samuel Harrison; and my sister Sophronia.

8. During this time of great excitement my mind was called up to serious reflection and great uneasiness; but though my feelings were deep and often poignant, still I kept myself aloof from all these parties, though I attended their several meetings as often as occasion would permit. In process of time my mind became somewhat partial to the Methodist sect, and I felt some desire to be united with them; but so great were the confusion and

2. An allusion to Luke 17:22–23, in which Jesus warns his followers against religious deceivers.

strife among the different denominations, that it was impossible for a person young as I was, and so unacquainted with men and things, to come to any certain conclusion who was right and who was wrong.

9. My mind at times was greatly excited, the cry and tumult were so great and incessant. The Presbyterians were most decided against the Baptists and Methodists, and used all the powers of both reason and sophistry to prove their errors, or, at least, to make the people think they were in error. On the other hand, the Baptists and Methodists in their turn were equally zealous in endeavoring to establish their own tenets and disprove all others.

10. In the midst of this war of words and tumult of opinions, I often said to myself: What is to be done? Who of all these parties are right; or, are they all wrong together? If any one of them be right, which is it, and how shall I know it?

11. While I was laboring under the extreme difficulties caused by the contests of these parties of religionists, I was one day reading the Epistle of James, first chapter and fifth verse, which reads: *If any of you lack wisdom, let him ask of God, that giveth to all men liberally, and upbraideth not; and it shall be given him.*

12. Never did any passage of scripture come with more power to the heart of man than this did at this time to mine. It seemed to enter with great force into every feeling of my heart. I reflected on it again and again, knowing that if any person needed wisdom from God, I did; for how to act I did not know, and unless I could get more wisdom than I then had, I would never know; for the teachers of religion of the different sects understood the same passages of scripture so differently as to destroy all confidence in settling the question by an appeal to the Bible.

13. At length I came to the conclusion that I must either remain in darkness and confusion, or else I must do as James directs, that is, ask of God. I at length came to the determination to "ask of God," concluding that if he gave wisdom to them that lacked wisdom, and would give liberally, and not upbraid, I might venture.

14. So, in accordance with this, my determination to ask of God, I retired to the woods to make the attempt. It was on the morning of a beautiful, clear day, early in the spring of eighteen hundred and twenty. It was the first time in my life that I had made such an attempt, for amidst all my anxieties I had never as yet made the attempt to pray vocally.

15. After I had retired to the place where I had previously designed to go, having looked around me, and finding myself alone, I kneeled down and began to offer up the desires of my heart to God. I had scarcely done so, when immediately I was seized upon by some power which entirely overcame me, and had such an astonishing influence over me as to bind my tongue so that I could not speak. Thick darkness gathered around me, and it seemed to me for a time as if I were doomed to sudden destruction.

16. But, exerting all my powers to call upon God to deliver me out of the power of this enemy which had seized upon me, and at the very moment when I was ready to sink into despair and abandon myself to destruction—not to an imaginary ruin, but to the power of some actual being from the unseen world, who had such marvelous power as I had never before felt in any being—just at this moment of great alarm, I saw a pillar of light exactly over my head, above the brightness of the sun,[3] which descended gradually until it fell upon me.

17. It no sooner appeared than I found myself delivered from the enemy which held me bound. When the light rested upon me I saw two Personages, whose brightness and glory defy all description, standing above me in the air. One of them spake unto me, calling me by name and said, pointing to the other—*This is My Beloved Son. Hear Him!*[4]

18. My object in going to inquire of the Lord was to know which of all the sects was right, that I might know which to join. No sooner, therefore, did I get possession of myself, so as to be able to speak, than I asked the Personages who stood above me in the light, which of all the sects was right (for at this time it had never entered into my heart that all were wrong)—and which I should join.

19. I was answered that I must join none of them, for they were all wrong; and the Personage who addressed me said that all their creeds were an abomination in his sight;[5] that those professors were all corrupt; that: "they draw near to me with their lips, but their hearts are far from me, they teach for doctrines the commandments of men, having a form of godliness, but they deny the power thereof."[6]

20. He again forbade me to join with any of them; and many other things did he say unto me, which I cannot write at this time. When I came to myself again, I found myself lying on my back, looking up into heaven. When the light had departed, I had no strength; but soon recovering in some degree, I went home. And as I leaned up to the fireplace, mother inquired what the matter was. I replied, "Never mind, all is well—I am well enough off." I then said to my mother, "I have learned for myself that Presbyterianism is not true." It seems as though the adversary[7] was aware, at a very early period of my life, that I was destined to prove a disturber and an annoyer of his kingdom;[8] else why should the powers of darkness[9] combine against me? Why the opposition and persecution that arose against me, almost in my infancy?

---

3. Jesus appeared to Saint Paul (then called Saul) in a light from heaven brighter than the sun (Acts 26:13). A pillar of light led the Israelites through the wilderness at night (Exodus 13:21).
4. This phrase evokes the "Transfiguration" episode of the Gospels (see, e.g., Mark 9:7).
5. The language here echoes that of the King James Version in references to whatever is forbidden to Israel. Compare, e.g., Leviticus 11:12.
6. Matthew 15:8–9, quoting Isaiah 29:13. The Gospel quotes the Greek version, not the Hebrew.
7. Satan.
8. Compare the incident in Matthew 8:28–33.
9. See Luke 22:53.

CHARLOTTE ELLIOTT
1789–1871

JUST AS I AM

Charlotte Elliott was born in Clapham, England, and died in Brighton. Her maternal grandfather, the Evangelical minister Henry Venn (1725–1797), had worked with John and Charles Wesley (see pp. 501 and 504), and he headed the Clapham Sect, a small group of social reformers within the Anglican Church. Throughout her life, Charlotte Elliott suffered from poor health, and illness-related fatigue eventually left her an invalid. For the personal use of fellow sufferers (rather than for congregational use), she wrote many hymns and religious poems. Probably her best-known work is the following hymn, which speaks of total reliance on the grace of Christ. Elliott first published "Just as I Am" in the *Invalid's Hymn Book* (1834)—which she coedited with a fellow invalid, a Miss Kiernan of Dublin—and in a pamphlet to raise money for a secondary school for the daughters of clergymen. It was later reprinted in almost every Protestant hymnal published in English. In a slightly shortened form, this conversion hymn achieved its greatest fame in the mid-twentieth century, when the American Evangelist Billy Graham (born 1918) used it as theme music for the "altar call" climax of his revivals.

JUST AS I AM

"Him that cometh unto me, I will in no wise cast out."
John 6:37.

I

Just as I am—without one plea,
But that thy blood was shed for me,
And that thou bid'st me come to thee,
    O Lamb of God, I come!

2

Just as I am—and waiting not
To rid my soul of one dark blot,
To thee, whose blood can cleanse each spot,
    O Lamb of God, I come!

5

3

Just as I am—though tossed about
With many a conflict—many a doubt,
"Fightings and fears within, without,"
    O Lamb of God, I come.

10

4

Just as I am—poor, wretched, blind,
Sight, riches, healing of the mind,
Yea, all I need, in thee to find,
    O Lamb of God, I come!   15

5

Just as I am—thou wilt receive,
Wilt welcome, pardon, cleanse, relieve,
Because thy promise I believe,
    O Lamb of God, I come!   20

6

Just as I am—thy love unknown
Has broken every barrier down,
Now, to be thine, yea, thine alone,
    O Lamb of God, I come!

JARENA LEE
1783–ca. 1849

FROM THE LIFE AND RELIGIOUS
EXPERIENCE OF JARENA LEE

In the United States, the story of the black Church and the story of black liberation have repeatedly intertwined, most famously in the work of the Reverend Dr. Martin Luther King, Jr. (see p. 624). In that double story of religion and freedom, Jarena Lee quite literally wrote one of the earliest chapters.

Lee (her surname by marriage) was born in Cape May, New Jersey. Her family was free but extremely poor, and Jarena had to leave home at age seven to work as a resident domestic servant. Little is known of her later childhood, but by twenty-one she was living in Philadelphia and, after a religious conversion, had joined the Bethel African Methodist Episcopal (A.M.E.) Church in that city. Five years later, Jarena married the Reverend Joseph Lee, the A.M.E. pastor of another church in the Philadelphia area. After her husband's early death, however, Lee returned to the Bethel A.M.E. Church with their two small children. There, during a sermon by the influential Reverend Richard Allen, a former slave, she first felt called by God to preach. Allen initially doubted Lee's calling, the ministry then being normally confined to men and to people with rather more education than hers. Later, after she rose during a sermon by a visiting preacher and eloquently exhorted the congregation from the text the preacher had chosen, Allen concluded that her call was genuine.

"Exhorter" was then a recognized position in the A.M.E. Church, separate from that of preacher and open to women. Arguing from Scripture, Lee rejected the distinction between exhorter and preacher. Though she was formally licensed by the

This portrait of Jarena Lee was painted from life in 1844. Depicting Lee as literate and religious, the image was used as the frontispiece for her book.

A.M.E. Church only to become an itinerant exhorter, the work she did traveling from town to town, speaking to racially mixed as well as black audiences, was preaching as far as she was concerned. True to Methodist tradition, she exhorted her hearers not just to repent of their sins and accept justification (forgiveness, salvation) from the Lord but also to seek "sanctification." This experience was the "second rest" that Charles Wesley had written of in "Love Divine, All Loves Excelling" (see p. 504) and John Wesley, in his journal, had called "Dominion over sin" (see p. 501). The phenomenon came more commonly to be called "Holiness" and to constitute a distinct strand within the broad American Calvinist/Methodist/Evangelical tradition.

In addition to being the first female preacher in the history of the A.M.E. Church, Lee wrote the first autobiography by a black American woman. And in self-publishing her autobiography, she became America's first black publisher. *The Life and Religious Experience of Jarena Lee, A Coloured Lady, Giving an Account of Her Call to Preach the Gospel, Written by Herself* (1836) sold out its first printing of one thousand copies, had a second printing of another thousand in 1839, and went into an enlarged and corrected second edition in 1849. In her memoir of her work as a preacher, Lee alludes only occasionally and with resigned patience to the sometimes brutal discrimination meted out to black travelers in the American North (travel in the South was out of the question). However, her opposition to slavery is never in doubt; in a section not included here, she calls it "that wretched system that emigrated from the bottomless pit . . . one of the greatest curses to any Nation." Upon the publication of the second printing of the first edition, Lee joined the American Anti-Slavery Society, an early abolitionist organization.

FROM THE LIFE AND RELIGIOUS EXPERIENCE OF JARENA LEE

My Call to Preach the Gospel

Between four and five years after my sanctification, on a certain time, an impressive silence fell upon me, and I stood as if some one was about to speak to me, yet I had no such thought in my heart. —But to my utter surprise there seemed to sound a voice which I thought I distinctly heard, and most certainly understood, which said to me, "Go preach the Gospel!" I immediately replied aloud, "No one will believe me." Again I listened, and again the same voice seemed to say—"Preach the Gospel; I will put words in your mouth, and will turn your enemies to become your friends."

At first I supposed that Satan had spoken to me, for I had read that he could transform himself into an angel of light for the purpose of deception.

Immediately I went into a secret place, and called upon the Lord to know if he had called me to preach, and whether I was deceived or not; when there appeared to my view the form and figure of a pulpit, with a Bible lying thereon, the back of which was presented to me as plainly as if it had been a literal fact.

In consequence of this, my mind became so exercised, that during the night following, I took a text and preached in my sleep. I thought there stood before me a great multitude, while I expounded to them the things of religion. So violent were my exertions and so loud were my exclamations, that I awoke from the sound of my own voice, which also awoke the family of the house where I resided. Two days after I went to see the preacher in charge of the African Society,[1] who was the Rev. Richard Allen, the same before named in these pages, to tell him that I felt it my duty to preach the gospel. But as I drew near the street in which his house was, which was in the city of Philadelphia, my courage began to fail me; so terrible did the cross appear, it seemed that I should not be able to bear it. Previous to my setting out to go to see him, so agitated was my mind, that my appetite for my daily food failed me entirely. Several times on my way there, I turned back again; but as often I felt my strength again renewed, and I soon found that the nearer I approached to the house of the minister, the less was my fear. Accordingly, as soon as I came to the door, my fears subsided, the cross was removed, all things appeared pleasant—I was tranquil.

I now told him, that the Lord had revealed it to me, that I must preach the gospel. He replied, by asking, in what sphere I wished to move in? I said, among the Methodists. He then replied, that a Mrs. Cook, a Methodist lady, had also some time before requested the same privilege; who, it was believed, had done much good in the way of exhortation, and holding prayer meetings; and who had been permitted to do so by the verbal license of the preacher in charge at the time. But as to women preaching, he said that our Discipline knew nothing at all about it—that it did not call for women preachers. This I was glad to hear, because it removed the fear of the cross—but no sooner did this feeling cross my mind, than I found that a love of souls had in a measure departed from me; that holy energy which burned within me, as a fire, began to be smothered. This I soon perceived.

O how careful ought we to be, lest through our by-laws of church government and discipline, we bring into disrepute even the word of life. For as unseemly as it may appear now-a-days for a woman to preach, it should be remembered that nothing is impossible with God. And why should it be thought impossible, heterodox, or improper for a woman to preach? seeing the Saviour died for the woman as well as for the man.

If the man may preach, because the Saviour died for him, why not the woman? seeing he died for her also. Is he not a whole Saviour, instead of a half one? as those who hold it wrong for a woman to preach, would seem to make it appear.

Did not Mary *first* preach the risen Saviour,[2] and is not the doctrine of the resurrection the very climax of Christianity—hangs not all our hope on

1. The original name of the African Methodist Episcopal Church.　　2. See John 20:1–18.

this, as argued by St. Paul?[3] Then did not Mary, a woman, preach the gospel? for she preached the resurrection of the crucified Son of God.

But some will say that Mary did not expound the Scripture, therefore, she did not preach, in the proper sense of the term. To this I reply, it may be that the term *preach* in those primitive times, did not mean exactly what it is now *made* to mean; perhaps it was a great deal more simple then, than it is now—if it were not, the unlearned fishermen could not have preached the gospel at all, as they had no learning.

To this it may be replied, by those who are determined not to believe that it is right for a woman to preach, that the disciples, though they were fishermen and ignorant of letters too, were inspired so to do. To which I would reply, that though they were inspired, yet that inspiration did not save them from showing their ignorance of letters, and of man's wisdom; this the multitude soon found out, by listening to the remarks of the envious Jewish priests. If then, to preach the gospel, by the gift of heaven, comes by inspiration solely, is God straitened: must he take the man exclusively? May he not, did he not, and can he not inspire a female to preach the simple story of the birth, life, death, and resurrection of our Lord, and accompany it too with power to the sinner's heart? As for me, I am fully persuaded that the Lord called me to labor according to what I have received, in his vineyard.[4] If he has not, how could he consistently bear testimony in favor of my poor labors, in awakening and converting sinners?

In my wanderings up and down among men, preaching according to my ability, I have frequently found families who told me that they had not for several years been to a meeting, and yet, while listening to hear what God would say by his poor female instrument, have believed with trembling— tears rolling down their cheeks, the signs of contrition and repentance towards God. I firmly believe that I have sown seed, in the name of the Lord, which shall appear with its increase at the great day of accounts, when Christ shall come to take up his jewels.

At a certain time, I was beset with the idea, that soon or late I should fall from grace and lose my soul at last. I was frequently called to the throne of grace[5] about this matter, but found no relief; the temptation pursued me still. Being more and more afflicted with it, till at a certain time, when the spirit strongly impressed it on my mind to enter into my closet[6] and carry my case once more to the Lord; the Lord enabled me to draw nigh to him, and to his mercy seat[7] at this time, in an extraordinary manner; for while I wrestled with him for the victory over this disposition to doubt whether I should persevere, there appeared a form of fire, about the size of a man's hand,[8] as I was on my knees; at the same moment there appeared to the eye of faith a man robed in a white garment, from the shoulders down to the feet; from him a voice proceeded, saying: "Thou shalt never return from the cross." Since that time I have never doubted, but believe that God will keep me until the day of redemption. Now I could adopt the very language of St. Paul, and say that nothing could have separated me from the

---

3. See 1 Corinthians 15:14.
4. See Matthew 20.
5. Called in conscience before the throne of God. Compare Hebrews 4:16.
6. Private room.

7. His throne. In Exodus 25, the mercy seat evokes the presence of the Lord.
8. Apparently an allusion to Acts 2:3, but see also 1 Kings 18:44.

love of God, which is in Christ Jesus.[9] Since that time, 1807, until the present, 1833, I have not ever doubted the power and goodness of God to keep me from falling, through the sanctification of the spirit and belief of the truth.

9. See Romans 8:39.

THOMAS WENTWORTH HIGGINSON
1823–1911

FROM NEGRO SPIRITUALS

Thomas Wentworth Higginson (a friend of the poet Emily Dickinson; see p. 552) was a Unitarian minister in Cambridge, Massachusetts. During the 1840s and 1850s, he was active in the abolitionism movement. In the Civil War, he served for several years as colonel of the 1st South Carolina Volunteers, the first federally authorized regiment of African-Americans. Higginson recognized the beauty of the spirituals sung by African-American slaves and handed down orally, viewing them as testaments of moral courage and wellsprings of religious faith. In June 1867, he published the following article in *The Atlantic Monthly* (in places, punctuation has been modernized). Some of the now-famous spirituals collected in Higginson's article—for example, "Blow Your Trumpet, Gabriel"—have had huge impacts on subsequent forms of music, including blues and jazz. Later generations have detected in many of the lyrics both coded messages of resistance and hidden hints of escape through the so-called underground railroad, a clandestine route to the nonslaveholding states.

FROM NEGRO SPIRITUALS

The war brought to some of us, besides its direct experiences, many a strange fulfillment of dreams of other days. For instance, the present writer had been a faithful student of the Scottish ballads, and had always envied Sir Walter[1] the delight of tracing them out amid their own heather, and of writing them down piecemeal from the lips of aged crones. It was a strange enjoyment, therefore, to be suddenly brought into the midst of a kindred world of unwritten songs, as simple and indigenous as the Border Minstrelsy, more uniformly plaintive, almost always more quaint, and often as essentially poetic.

This interest was rather increased by the fact that I had for many years heard of this class of songs under the name of "Negro Spirituals," and had even heard some of them sung by friends from South Carolina. I could now gather on their own soil these strange plants which I had before seen as in museums alone. True, the individual songs rarely coincided; there was a line here, a

1. Sir Walter Scott (1771–1832), Scottish poet and novelist, editor of a hugely popular and influential collection of Scottish border ballads.

chorus there—just enough to fix the class, but this was unmistakable. It was not strange that they differed, for the range seemed almost endless, and South Carolina, Georgia, and Florida seemed to have nothing but the generic character in common, until all were mingled in the united stock of camp melodies.

Often in the starlit evening I have returned from some lonely ride by the swift river, or on the plover-haunted barrens, and, entering the camp, have silently approached some glimmering fire, round which the dusky figures moved in the rhythmical barbaric dance the negroes call a "shout," chanting, often harshly, but always in the most perfect time, some monotonous refrain. Writing down in the darkness, as I best could—perhaps with my hand in the safe covert of my pocket—the words of the song, I have afterwards carried it to my tent, like some captured bird or insect, and then, after examination, put it by. Or, summoning one of the men at some period of leisure—Corporal Robert Sutton, for instance, whose iron memory held all the details of a song as if it were a ford or a forest—I have completed the new specimen by supplying the absent parts. The music I could only retain by ear, and though the more common strains were repeated often enough to fix their impression, there were others that occurred only once or twice.

The words will be here given, as nearly as possible, in the original dialect; and if the spelling seems sometimes inconsistent, or the misspelling insufficient, it is because I could get no nearer. I wished to avoid what seems to me the only error of Lowell's "Biglow Papers"[2] in respect to dialect—the occasional use of an extreme misspelling, which merely confuses the eye, without taking us any closer to the peculiarity of sound.

The favorite song in camp[3] was the following—sung with no accompaniment but the measured clapping of hands and the clatter of many feet. It was sung perhaps twice as often as any other. This was partly due to the fact that it properly consisted of a chorus alone, with which the verses of other songs might be combined at random.

I. HOLD YOUR LIGHT

Hold your light, Brudder Robert, —
    Hold your light,
Hold your light on Canaan's[4] shore.

What make ole Satan for follow me so?
Satan ain't got notin' for do wid me.
    Hold your light,
    Hold your light,
Hold your light on Canaan's shore.

2. An 1848 poetry collection by the American writer and editor James Russell Lowell (1819–1891).
3. A U.S. Army camp.

4. The Promised Land: the land that God promised to the Israelites, whom he liberated from bondage in Egypt.

This would be sung for half an hour at a time, perhaps, each person present being named in turn. It seemed the simplest primitive type of "spiritual." The next in popularity was almost as elementary, and, like this, named successively each one of the circle. It was, however, much more resounding and convivial in its music.

II. BOUND TO GO

Jordan River,[5] I'm bound to go,
Bound to go, bound to go—

Jordan River, I'm bound to go,
And bid 'em fare ye well.

My Brudder Robert, I'm bound to go,
Bound to go, &c.

My Sister Lucy, I'm bound to go,
Bound to go, &c.

Sometimes it was "tink 'em" (think them) "fare ye well." The ye was so detached, that I thought at first it was "very" or "vary well."

Another picturesque song, which seemed immensely popular, was at first very bewildering to me. I could not make out the first words of the chorus, and called it the "Romandar," being reminded of some Romaic song which I had formerly heard. That association quite fell in with the Orientalism of the new tent-life.[6]

III. ROOM IN THERE

O, my mudder is gone! my mudder is gone!
My mudder is gone into heaven, my Lord!
I can't stay behind!
Dere's room in dar, room in dar,
Room in dar, in de heaven, my Lord!
I can't stay behind,
Can't stay behind, my dear,
I can't stay behind!

O, my fader is gone! &c.

O, de angels are gone! &c.

O, I'se been on de road! I'se been on de road!
I'se been on de road into heaven, my Lord!

5. The waters of which parted so the Israelites could enter the Promised Land.
6. The Greek-speaking people of Byzantium thought of themselves politically, and quite correctly, as the continuation of the Roman Empire. Accordingly, they called themselves Romans and their language Roman; Romaikos in demotic, or vernacular, Greek refers to the Greek language.

The "Romaic" song that Higginson recalls is thus a Greek folk song. Because Greece had only recently become independent from the Ottoman (Turkish) Empire, it was commonly included as part of the study of the Middle East—the realm of the tent-dwellers, in many American imaginations. What is now called Near Eastern or Middle Eastern studies was then called Orientalism.

I can't stay behind!
O, room in dar, room in dar,
Room in dar, in de heaven, my Lord!
I can't stay behind!

By this time every man within hearing, from oldest to youngest, would be wriggling and shuffling, as if through some magic piper's bewitchment; for even those who at first affected contemptuous indifference would be drawn into the vortex erelong.

Next to these in popularity ranked a class of songs belonging emphatically to the Church Militant,[7] and available for camp purposes with very little strain upon their symbolism. This, for instance, had a true companion-in-arms heartiness about it, not impaired by the feminine invocation at the end.

IV. HAIL MARY

One more valiant soldier here,
    One more valiant soldier here,
One more valiant soldier here,
    To help me bear de cross.
O hail, Mary, hail!
    Hail, Mary, hail!
Hail, Mary, hail!
    To help me bear de cross.

I fancied that the original reading might have been "soul," instead of "soldier" —with some other syllable inserted, to fill out the metre—and that the "Hail, Mary," might denote a Roman Catholic origin, as I had several men from St. Augustine[8] who held in a dim way to that faith. It was a very ringing song, though not so grandly jubilant as the next, which was really impressive as the singers pealed it out, when marching or rowing or embarking.

V. MY ARMY CROSS OVER

My army cross over,
My army cross over.
O, Pharaoh's army drownded![9]
My army cross over.

We'll cross de mighty river,
    My army cross over,
We'll cross de river Jordan,
    My army cross over,
We'll cross de danger water,
    My army cross over,

---

7. According to Christian theology, living believers on Earth, one division of the Church; the other two divisions are the Church Triumphant (those in heaven) and, in Roman Catholic theology, the Church Suffering or Church Expectant (those in purgatory).
8. City in northeast Florida.
9. See Exodus 14:26–29.

> We'll cross de mighty Myo,
> > My army cross over. (*Thrice.*)
> O, Pharaoh's army drownded!
> > My army cross over.

I could get no explanation of the "mighty Myo," except that one of the old men thought it meant the river of death. Perhaps it is an African word. In the Cameroon dialect, "Mawa" signifies "to die."

JULIA WARD HOWE
1819–1910

THE BATTLE HYMN OF THE REPUBLIC

From the sixteenth through the mid nineteenth century, European and American Christians participated fully—as capturers, transporters, and owners—in the enslavement of Africans. During the same period, however, Christians took the lead in the slowly strengthening movement to abolish the savagery of the African slave trade and then of slavery itself. This movement came to a peak early in the nineteenth century in Britain and toward the end of that century in the United States.

In the U.S., the Christian abolitionist movement was strengthened because many of the American slaves had become Christians. The 1852 abolitionist novel *Uncle Tom's Cabin*, by the American writer Harriet Beecher Stowe (1811–1896), became a popular sensation partly because Uncle Tom is a saintly Bible-reading Christian slave who, at a moment of humiliation and despair, consoles himself by singing verses from "Amazing Grace." That hymn is itself the work of a well-known repentant slave-trader, the English clergyman and poet John Newton (1725–1807).

For Christian abolitionists such as Stowe and Julia Ward Howe, the American Civil War (1861–65) was a sacred cause because they saw in it the promise of liberation for the slaves. Howe published her "Battle Hymn of the Republic" in *The Atlantic Monthly* during the first year of the war. She intended it to be sung to the tune of an existing abolitionist song, "John Brown's Body," which is sung to an earlier hymn tune and celebrates an abolitionist martyr slain in his attempt to foment a slave uprising.

Howe's hopes for her poem were abundantly realized. With the verse "Glory, glory, hallelujah!" inserted twice before the final half-line of each of its five original stanzas, "Battle Hymn of the Republic" quickly became the sacred anthem of the Union Army. For Howe, the army of the Republic was the instrument of God's judgment on slaveholders of the Confederacy. Those who died in the process of imposing God's judgment on these sinners were, accordingly, like Christ himself: "As He died to make men holy, let us die to make men free." Writing in an era when the biblical allusions that echo in her verses would be readily heard as such, Howe helped make her understanding of the nobility of the war, and her justification for its violence, the general American understanding.

Howe's moment may mark a theological watershed, however. In later decades, Christians grew steadily less willing to imagine a God as warlike and wrathful as hers. In addition, her moment may mark a never-to-be-matched fusion of patriotism and piety. Later Christian generations grew steadily more reluctant to believe that God is ever wholly on one side in a war. Still, in her "Battle Hymn," Howe made the most of the rich rhetorical resources the Bible offered for expressing her militancy.

THE BATTLE HYMN OF THE REPUBLIC

Mine eyes have seen the glory of the coming of the Lord:[1]
He is trampling out the vintage where the grapes of wrath are stored;[2]
He hath loosed the fateful lightning of His terrible swift sword:[3]
           His truth is marching on.

I have seen Him in the watch-fires of a hundred circling camps,   5
They have builded Him an altar in the evening dews and damps;
I can read His righteous sentence[4] by the dim and flaring lamps:
           His day is marching on

I have read a fiery gospel writ in burnished rows of steel:[5]
"As ye deal with my contemners, so with you my grace shall deal;[6]   10
Let the Hero, born of woman, crush the serpent with his heel,[7]
           Since God is marching on."

He has sounded forth the trumpet that shall never call retreat;[8]
He is sifting out the hearts of men[9] before His judgment-seat:
Oh, be swift, my soul, to answer Him! be jubilant, my feet![1]   15
           Our God is marching on.

In the beauty of the lilies[2] Christ was born across the sea,
With a glory in His bosom that transfigures you and me:
As He died to make men holy, let us die to make men free,
           While God is marching on.   20

1. The Second Coming; see Mark 13:26.
2. As trodden grapes yield wine, so sinners shed blood when God tramples them in righteous wrath; see Revelation 14:19.
3. See Deuteronomy 32:41.
4. An allusion to the handwriting on the wall in Daniel 5:5.
5. Jesus came "to cast fire on the earth" (Luke 12:49).
6. God will deal well with those who fight his enemies; see 1 Samuel 2:30–31.
7. See Genesis 3:15.
8. The trumpet that proclaims both the day of judgment and the day of God's final march to victory; see 1 Thessalonians 4:16.
9. Separating sinners from the righteous is like sifting grain from chaff; see Matthew 3:12.
1. Compare Isaiah 52:17 and Romans 10:15.
2. Perhaps an allusion to Song of Solomon 6:2–3.

ANONYMOUS
mid-nineteenth century

FROM THE WAY OF A PILGRIM

The Way of a Pilgrim is a popular devotional work written by an anonymous Russian Orthodox Christian. Whereas pilgrims normally have a geographical destination—a shrine, a church, a monastery, or, classically, the Holy Land—the pilgrim of this work is not en route to a place. Instead, he is searching for an answer to the question posed on the first page of the work: How can a Christian obey the injunctions of Saint Paul to pray continuously, on every possible occasion, and in every place?

Eventually, the pilgrim finds his way to the sage he needs, a monastery elder who teaches him "the ceaseless Jesus Prayer." The pilgrim recites the prayer until it becomes part of him, at which point he experiences deep inner tranquillity.

The linkage between very frequent prayer and inner joy is distinctly Pietist, and the similar linkage in *The Way of a Pilgrim* may reflect religious contact between German Lutherans and Russian Orthodox. Catherine the Great (1729–1796; empress of Russia from 1762 until her death) encouraged Europeans to settle in Russia as a way of fostering technological progress and economic development. Such settlement was very largely German, and German Pietism had traveled east with the large community of "Volga Germans" that grew up along the Volga River.

More likely, however, this inspirational tale celebrates Hesychasm, a centuries-old Greek and Russian Orthodox ascetical and mystical tradition. Devotees of Hesychasm (from a Greek root meaning "stillness") cultivated solitude, prayer, and certain kinds of mind/body discipline as a path to inner peace and union with God. The *Philokalia,* mentioned in the selection below, was a compilation of sometimes very ancient texts in this tradition. The "Jesus Prayer" has its most certain root in that tradition.

PRONOUNCING GLOSSARY

Nicephorus: *ni-se´-fohr-uhs*   Philokalia: *fil-oh-kahl´-ee-uh*

FROM THE WAY OF A PILGRIM

From CHAPTER I

By the grace of God I am a Christian, by my deeds a great sinner, and by my calling a homeless wanderer of humblest origin, roaming from place to place. My possessions consist of a knapsack with dry crusts of bread on my back and in my bosom the Holy Bible. This is all!

On the twenty-fourth Sunday after Pentecost I came to church to attend the Liturgy and entered just as the epistle was being read. The reading was from Paul's First Letter to the Thessalonians, which says in part, "Pray constantly." These words made a deep impression on me and I started thinking of how it could be possible for a man to pray without ceasing when the practical necessities of life demand so much attention. I checked my Bible and saw with my own eyes exactly what I had heard, that it is necessary to pray continuously (1 Thessalonians 5:17); to pray in the Spirit on every possible occasion (Ephesians 6:18); in every place to lift your hands reverently in prayer (1 Timothy 2:8). I thought and thought about these words, but no understanding came to me.

What shall I do? I thought. Where can I find a person who will explain this mystery to me? I will go to the various churches where there are good preachers and perhaps I will obtain an explanation from them. And so I

TRANSLATED BY Helen Bacovin. The parenthetical Bible citations are the translator's.

went. I heard many very good homilies on prayer, but they were all instructions about prayer in general: what is prayer, the necessity of prayer, and the fruits of prayer, but no one spoke of the way to succeed in prayer. I did hear a sermon on interior prayer and ceaseless prayer but nothing about attaining that form of prayer. Inasmuch as listening to public sermons had not given me any satisfaction, I stopped attending them and decided, with the grace of God, to look for an experienced and learned person who would satisfy my ardent desire and explain ceaseless prayer to me.

* * *

* * * For five days I traveled in this manner on a long and wide road, and toward the evening of the fifth day an old man caught up with me who looked like a member of some religious community.

To my question he answered that he was a monk and that his hermitage was about ten versts from the main road, and he invited me to visit the hermitage. "We receive pilgrims and strangers and give them food and lodging in our guesthouse," he said.

Since I had no inclination to stop there, I replied, "My peace does not depend on a place to stay but on spiritual direction. I am not looking for food, as I have enough bread in my knapsack."

"And what manner of direction are you looking for; what seems to be puzzling you? Come, come dear brother, visit us; we have experienced elders[1] who can give spiritual nourishment and direct one on the path of truth according to the word of God and the writings of the holy Fathers."

"You see, Father, about a year ago while I was at a Liturgy I heard the following admonition from the Apostle Paul: 'Pray constantly.' Not being able to understand this I began to read the Bible, where in many places I found God's precept that it is necessary to pray continuously, to pray always, at all times and in all places, not only while working, not only when awake but also in one's sleep. 'I sleep but my heart is awake' (Song of Songs 5:2). I was very surprised by this and could not understand how this could be possible and by what means it could be accomplished. * * *

* * *

The course of this conversation brought us close to the hermitage. In order not to let this wise man go, and to quickly receive my heart's desire, I hurried to ask him, "Please, be gracious, Reverend Father, and explain the meaning of ceaseless mental prayer to me and show me how I can learn to practice it. I can see that you are both well versed and experienced in this matter."

The elder received my plea lovingly and invited me to visit him in his cell: "Come, stop by and I will give you a book of the holy Fathers from which, with the help of God, you can learn all about prayer and understand it clearly and in detail." When we entered his cell, the elder said, "The ceaseless Jesus Prayer is a continuous, uninterrupted call on the holy name of Jesus Christ with the lips, mind, and heart; and in the awareness of His abiding presence it is a plea for His blessing in all undertakings, in all

---

1. In Russia, monks who advanced through asceticism and withdrawal to become available for spiritual direction, blessing, and healing.

places, at all times, even in sleep. The words of the Prayer are: 'Lord Jesus Christ, have mercy on me!' Anyone who becomes accustomed to this Prayer will experience great comfort as well as the need to say it continuously. He will become accustomed to it to such a degree that he will not be able to do without it and eventually the Prayer will of itself flow in him.

"Now do you understand what ceaseless prayer is?" he asked me.

"Very clearly, dear Father. For the love of God please teach me how to make it my own," I exclaimed in joy.

"To learn about this prayer, we will read from a book called the *Philokalia*. This book, which was compiled by twenty-five holy Fathers, contains complete and detailed instructions about ceaseless prayer. The content of this book is of such depth and usefulness that it is considered to be the primary teacher of contemplative life, and as the Venerable Nicephorus[2] says, 'It leads one to salvation without labor and sweat.'"

"Is it then more important than the Holy Bible?" I asked.

"No, it is neither more important nor holier than the Bible, but it contains clear exposition of the ideas that are mysteriously presented in the Bible and are not easy for our finite mind to understand. I will give you an illustration. The sun—a great, shining, and magnificent light—cannot be contemplated and looked at directly with the naked eye. An artificial glass, a million times smaller and dimmer than the sun, is needed to look at the great king of lights to be enraptured by its fiery rays. In a similar way the Holy Bible is a shining light and the *Philokalia* is the necessary glass.

"Now if you will listen, I will read how you can learn ceaseless interior prayer." The elder opened the *Philokalia* to the account of St. Simeon the New Theologian[3] and began reading: "'Sit alone and in silence; bow your head and close your eyes; relax your breathing and with your imagination look into your heart; direct your thoughts from your head into your heart. And while inhaling say, "Lord Jesus Christ, have mercy on me," either softly with your lips or in your mind. Endeavor to fight distractions but be patient and peaceful and repeat this process frequently.'"

* * *

For a whole week I stayed alone in my hut and recited the Jesus Prayer six thousand times every day, neither worrying about anything nor paying attention to the distracting thoughts, no matter how severe they became. My main concern was to carry out the advice of my director as accurately as possible. And do you know what happened? I became so accustomed to the Prayer that if for a short while I stopped reciting it I felt as if I were missing something, as though I had lost something. When I would begin reciting the Prayer again, I would immediately feel great joy and delight. If I happened to meet someone then, I did not feel like talking. My only desire was to be alone and to recite the Prayer. I had become so accustomed to it in a week.

---

2. Saint Nicephorus the Solitary (14th century), venerated as the teacher of Saint Gregory Palamas, a celebrated mystic in the hesychastic tradition.

3. Byzantine monk and poet (10th–11th century), author of theological treatises that were controversial in their day.

As the elder had not seen me for ten days, he came to visit me. He listened as I gave him an account of my progress and then said, "You are now accustomed to the Prayer, so continue with this good habit and strengthen it. Do not waste any time but decide, with the help of God, to recite the Prayer twelve thousand times a day. Rise earlier and retire later; stay alone, and every two weeks come to me for direction."

SCANDAL AND PARADOX,
FEAR AND FAITH

The profoundly influential German philosopher Georg Wilhelm Friedrich Hegel (1770–1831) argued that the religions and the philosophies of the past had all been part of a predetermined evolutionary process. That process culminated, as its semifinal stage, in Christianity and then, as its final stage, in Hegel's idealist philosophy.

As applied to Hegelian philosophy, *idealist* does not mean the opposite of *materialist* or *selfish*. The term refers rather to the *idea* of God, in two senses: the idea of God that mankind might have and God's idea of himself. Over thousands of years, Hegel maintained, these ideas had come together under the controlling direction of the divine "Architect": "the one living Mind whose nature is to think, to bring to self-consciousness what it is, and with its being thus set as object before it, to be at the same time raised above it, and so to reach a higher stage of its own being." According to Hegelian philosophy, God's mind had become more godlike—it had reached "a higher stage of its own being"—when mankind's thought of God became identical with God's. Since mankind was now thinking God's thoughts, there was no God: There was only mankind. Alternatively, since humans were no longer thinking merely human thoughts, there was no mankind: There was only God.

Though Hegel's vast philosophical system could scarcely be proven or disproven, his narrative vision—of history marching forward from its origins to the present in accord with discernible, unvarying laws—proved contagious and intellectually intoxicating. Atheistically, Hegel's vision was applied in Marxism and then Communism, as a version of the economic future, in which bosses would cease to exist because the workers would become the bosses. Theistically, Hegel's vision was applied in theologies in which Christians would become indistinguishable from God.

But what if Christianity was not merely a phase in humanity's march through history, leading up to modernity? What if Christianity was about how, whatever awaits *Homo sapiens*, each individual human's lifespan must command that person's attention here and now? In short, what if Christianity was not a theory, not even a theory of morality, but rather a practice related to the choices that must inevitably shape an individual life?

In secular form in the mid-twentieth century, this personally challenging stance came to be called existentialism. Søren Kierkegaard, a Danish theologian whose writing is excerpted below, is among the most important forerunners of existentialism. In artfully ironic prose that dares the reader to take its verbal winking seriously, Kierkegaard attacks Hegelianism very powerfully. Kierkegaard shifts the philosophical focus from large processes that no one (apart, perhaps, from the Hegelian Architect) can control to small but compelling private decisions. Such unavoidable, terrifying decisions, according to Kierkegaard, must be made through either leaps of faith or plunges into despair.

In a style utterly unlike Kierkegaard's, John Henry Newman also connected Christianity with the lived life and the decisions that shape each life. Newman was an Anglican priest led by his study of the history of the Christian Church to become a Roman Catholic. In the work excerpted here, he offers an autobiographical, existential defense of his difficult and costly decision to convert.

As a young atheist, G. K. Chesterton found himself darkly fascinated by charges against Christianity. Later, as a playwright, journalist, popular theologian, and convert to Roman Catholicism (from a much greater distance than Newman had converted from), Chesterton became famous for exploring just such paradoxes.

JOHN HENRY NEWMAN
1801–1890

FROM APOLOGIA PRO VITA SUA

John Henry Newman was born in London and died in Birmingham, England. After a brilliant career as an Oxford University academic and Anglican priest, Newman became a leader in the Oxford Movement. This group of Anglicans aimed to restore many traditional forms of worship to the Church of England. In 1845, Newman left the Church of England and joined the Roman Catholic Church. In 1879, he became a cardinal-deacon of the Church.

Among Newman's major literary works is his spiritual autobiography, *Apologia pro Vita Sua* (1865–66). The title is Latin for "Defense of One's Life." Newman is not defending his life so much as defending his integrity in converting to Catholicism—with particular respect, in the passage quoted here (where some of the punctuation has been modernized), to papal infallibility, the Catholic doctrine that most scandalized his family and his Anglican colleagues. He is also responding to the charge that Catholics who can accept such a doctrine do not honor truth. After narrating the honest search that led him to enter the Catholic Church, Newman argues that the answers to some questions cannot be reached through logical or scientific reasoning.

PRONOUNCING GLOSSARY

Apologia Pro Vita Sua: *ah-poh-loh-gee´-uh proh vee´-tah soo´-ah*

Athanasius: *a-thuh-nay´-zhus*
ipse dixit: *ip´-say deeks´-eet*

FROM APOLOGIA PRO VITA SUA
From CHAPTER V
Position of My Mind since 1845

* * *

Starting then with the being of a God (which, as I have said, is as certain to me as the certainty of my own existence, though when I try to put the grounds of that certainty into logical shape I find a difficulty in doing so in mood and figure to my satisfaction), I look out of myself into the world of men, and there I see a sight which fills me with unspeakable distress. The world seems simply to give the lie to that great truth, of which my whole being is so full; and the effect upon me is, in consequence, as a matter of necessity, as confusing as if it denied that I am in existence myself. If I looked into a mirror, and did not see my face, I should have the sort of feeling which actually comes upon me, when I look into this living busy world, and see no reflexion of its Creator. This is, to me, one of those great difficulties of this absolute primary truth, to which I referred just now. Were it not for this voice, speaking so clearly in my conscience and my heart, I should be an atheist, or a pantheist, or a polytheist when I looked into the world. I am speaking for myself only; and I am far from denying the real force of the arguments in proof of a God, drawn from the general facts of human society and the course of history, but these do not warm me or enlighten me; they do not take away the winter of my desolation, or make the buds unfold and the leaves grow within me, and my moral being rejoice. The sight of the world is nothing else than the prophet's scroll, full of 'lamentations, and mourning, and woe.'[1]

To consider the world in its length and breadth, its various history, the many races of man, their starts, their fortunes, their mutual alienation, their conflicts; and then their ways, habits, governments, forms of worship; their enterprises, their aimless courses, their random achievements and acquirements, the impotent conclusion of long-standing facts, the tokens so faint and broken of a superintending design, the blind evolution of what turn out to be great powers or truths, the progress of things, as if from unreasoning elements, not towards final causes, the greatness and littleness of man, his far-reaching aims, his short duration, the curtain hung over his futurity, the disappointments of life, the defeat of good, the success of evil, physical pain, mental anguish, the prevalence and intensity of sin, the pervading idolatries, the corruptions, the dreary hopeless irreligion, that condition of the whole race, so fearfully yet exactly described in the Apostle's words, 'having no hope and without God in the world'[2]—all this is a vision to dizzy and appal; and inflicts upon the mind the sense of a profound mystery, which is absolutely beyond human solution.

What shall be said to this heart-piercing, reason-bewildering fact? I can only answer, that either there is no Creator, or this living society of men is in a true sense discarded from His presence. Did I see a boy of good make and mind, with the tokens on him of a refined nature, cast upon the world without provision, unable to say whence he came, his birth-place or his family connexions, I should conclude that there was some mystery connected with his history, and that he was one, of whom, from one cause or other, his parents were ashamed. Thus only should I be able to account for the contrast between the promise and the condition of his being. And so I argue about the world: *if* there be a God, *since* there is a God, the human race is implicated in some terrible aboriginal calamity. It is out of joint with the purposes of its Creator. This is a fact, a fact as true as the fact of its existence; and thus the doctrine of what is theologically called original sin becomes to me almost as certain as that the world exists, and as the existence of God.

1. Compare Ezekiel 2:10.
2. Compare Ephesians 2:12. "The Apostle": Saint Paul.

And now, supposing it were the blessed and loving will of the Creator to interfere in this anarchical condition of things, what are we to suppose would be the methods which might be necessarily or naturally involved in His purpose of mercy? Since the world is in so abnormal a state, surely it would be no surprise to me, if the interposition were of necessity equally extraordinary—or what is called miraculous. But that subject does not directly come into the scope of my present remarks. Miracles as evidence, involve a process of reason, or an argument; and of course I am thinking of some mode of interference which does not immediately run into argument. I am rather asking what must be the face-to-face antagonist, by which to withstand and baffle the fierce energy of passion and the all-corroding, all-dissolving scepticism of the intellect in religious inquiries? I have no intention at all of denying, that truth is the real object of our reason, and that, if it does not attain to truth, either the premiss or the process is in fault; but I am not speaking here of right reason, but of reason as it acts in fact and concretely in fallen man. I know that even the unaided reason, when correctly exercised, leads to a belief in God, in the immortality of the soul, and in a future retribution; but I am considering the faculty of reason actually and historically; and in this point of view, I do not think I am wrong in saying that its tendency is towards a simple unbelief in matters of religion. No truth, however sacred, can stand against it, in the long run; and hence it is that in the pagan world, when our Lord came, the last traces of the religious knowledge of former times were all but disappearing from those portions of the world in which the intellect had been active and had had a career.

And in these latter days, in like manner, outside the Catholic Church things are tending—with far greater rapidity than in that old time from the circumstance of the age—to atheism in one shape or other. What a scene, what a prospect, does the whole of Europe present at this day! and not only Europe, but every government and every civilization through the world, which is under the influence of the European mind! Especially, for it most concerns us, how sorrowful, in the view of religion, even taken in its most elementary, most attenuated form, is the spectacle presented to us by the educated intellect of England, France, and Germany! Lovers of their country and of their race, religious men, external to the Catholic Church, have attempted various expedients to arrest fierce wilful human nature in its onward course, and to bring it into subjection. The necessity of some form of religion for the interests of humanity, has been generally acknowledged: but where was the concrete representative of things invisible, which would have the force and the toughness necessary to be a breakwater against the deluge? * * *

The judgment, which experience passes whether on establishments or on education, as a means of maintaining religious truth in this anarchical world, must be extended even to Scripture, though Scripture be divine. Experience proves surely that the Bible does not answer a purpose for which it was never intended. It may be accidentally the means of the conversion of individuals; but a book, after all, cannot make a stand against the wild living intellect of man, and in this day it begins to testify, as regards its own structure and contents, to the power of that universal solvent, which is so successfully acting upon religious establishments.

Supposing then it to be the Will of the Creator to interfere in human affairs, and to make provisions for retaining in the world a knowledge of Himself, so definite and distinct as to be proof against the energy of human scepticism, in such a case—I am far from saying that there was no other way—but there is nothing to surprise the mind, if He should think fit to introduce a power into the world invested with the prerogative of infallibility in religious matters. Such a provision would be a direct, immediate, active, and prompt means of withstanding the difficulty; it would be an instrument suited to the need; and, when I find that this is the very claim of the Catholic Church, not only do I feel no difficulty in admitting the idea, but there is a fitness in it, which recommends it to my mind. And thus I am brought to speak of the Church's infallibility, as a provision, adapted by the mercy of the Creator, to preserve religion in the world, and to restrain that freedom of thought, which of course in itself is one of the greatest of our natural gifts, and to rescue it from its own suicidal excesses. And let it be observed that, neither here nor in what follows, shall I have occasion to speak directly of Revelation in its subject-matter, but in reference to the sanction which it gives to truths which may be known independently of it— as it bears upon the defence of natural religion. I say, that a power, possessed of infallibility in religious teaching, is happily adapted to be a working instrument, in the course of human affairs, for smiting hard and throwing back the immense energy of the aggressive, capricious, untrustworthy intellect—and in saying this, as in the other things that I have to say, it must still be recollected that I am all along bearing in mind my main purpose, which is a defence of myself.

I am defending myself here from a plausible charge brought against Catholics, as will be seen better as I proceed. The charge is this: —that I, as a Catholic, not only make profession to hold doctrines which I cannot possibly believe in my heart, but that I also believe in the existence of a power on earth, which at its own will imposes upon men any new set of *credenda*,[3] when it pleases, by a claim to infallibility; in consequence, that my own thoughts are not my own property; that I cannot tell that tomorrow I may not have to give up what I hold today, and that the necessary effect of such a condition of mind must be a degrading bondage, or a bitter inward rebellion relieving itself in secret infidelity, or the necessity of ignoring the whole subject of religion in a sort of disgust, and of mechanically saying every thing that the Church says, and leaving to others the defence of it. As then I have above spoken of the relation of my mind towards the Catholic Creed, so now I shall speak of the attitude which it takes up in the view of the Church's infallibility.

* * * I think the principle here enunciated to be the mere preamble in the formal credentials of the Catholic Church, as an Act of Parliament might begin with a 'Whereas.' It is because of the intensity of the evil which has possession of mankind, that a suitable antagonist has been provided against it; and the initial act of that divinely-commissioned power is of course to deliver her challenge and to defy the enemy. Such a preamble then gives a

3. Doctrines to be believed (Latin).

meaning to her position in the world, and an interpretation to her whole course of teaching and action.

*   *   *

Passing now from what I have called the preamble of that grant of power, which is made to the Church, to that power itself, Infallibility, I premise two brief remarks: 1. on the one hand, I am not here determining any thing about the essential seat of that power, because that is a question doctrinal, not historical and practical; 2. nor, on the other hand, am I extending the direct subject-matter, over which that power of Infallibility has jurisdiction, beyond religious opinion—and now as to the power itself.

This power, viewed in its fulness, is as tremendous as the giant evil which has called for it. It claims, when brought into exercise but in the legitimate manner, for otherwise of course it is but quiescent, to know for certain the very meaning of every portion of that Divine Message in detail, which was committed by our Lord to His Apostles. It claims to know its own limits, and to decide what it can determine absolutely and what it cannot. It claims, moreover, to have a hold upon statements not directly religious, so far as this—to determine whether they indirectly relate to religion, and, according to its own definitive judgment, to pronounce whether or not, in a particular case, they are simply consistent with revealed truth. It claims to decide magisterially, whether as within its own province or not, that such and such statements are or are not prejudicial to the *Depositum*[4] of faith, in their spirit or in their consequences, and to allow them, or condemn and forbid them, accordingly. It claims to impose silence at will on any matters, or controversies, of doctrine, which on its own *ipse dixit*,[5] it pronounces to be dangerous, or inexpedient, or inopportune. It claims that, whatever may be the judgment of Catholics upon such acts, these acts should be received by them with those outward marks of reverence, submission, and loyalty, which Englishmen, for instance, pay to the presence of their sovereign, without expressing any criticism on them on the ground that in their matter they are inexpedient, or in their manner violent or harsh. And lastly, it claims to have the right of inflicting spiritual punishment, of cutting off from the ordinary channels of the divine life, and of simply excommunicating, those who refuse to submit themselves to its formal declarations. Such is the infallibility lodged in the Catholic Church, viewed in the concrete, as clothed and surrounded by the appendages of its high sovereignty: it is, to repeat what I said above, a supereminent prodigious power sent upon earth to encounter and master a giant evil.

And now, having thus described it, I profess my own absolute submission to its claim. I believe the whole revealed dogma as taught by the Apostles, as committed by the Apostles to the Church, and as declared by the Church to me. I receive it, as it is infallibly interpreted by the authority to whom it is thus committed, and (implicitly) as it shall be, in like manner, further interpreted by that same authority till the end of time. I submit, moreover, to the universally received traditions of the Church, in which lies the

---

4. Deposit (Latin). Newman refers to the teachings entrusted by Jesus to his Twelve Apostles, who were the first Church, for safekeeping and transmission to their successors.
5. He himself said it (Latin); i.e., its own authority, without other argumentation or proof.

matter of those new dogmatic definitions which are from time to time made, and which in all times are the clothing and the illustration of the Catholic dogma as already defined. And I submit myself to those other decisions of the Holy See, theological or not, through the organs which it has itself appointed, which, waiving the question of their infallibility, on the lowest ground come to me with a claim to be accepted and obeyed. Also, I consider that, gradually and in the course of ages, Catholic inquiry has taken certain definite shapes, and has thrown itself into the form of a science, with a method and a phraseology of its own, under the intellectual handling of great minds, such as St. Athanasius, St. Augustine, and St. Thomas;[6] and I feel no temptation at all to break in pieces the great legacy of thought thus committed to us for these latter days.

* * *

6. Saints Athanasius of Alexandria (see p. 262), Augustine of Hippo (see p. 226), and Thomas Aquinas (see p. 317).

SØREN KIERKEGAARD
1813–1855

FROM FEAR AND TREMBLING

Søren Aabye Kierkegaard lived in Copenhagen. In his profoundly original philosophy and theology, he prized concrete reality over abstract thought. Advocating an individual, costly engagement with the demands of Christianity, he rejected the quasi-Hegelian notion that his homeland's apparent somnolence represented the human race's outgrowing Christianity. In his view, the Danes thought that simply being born in Denmark made them Christians. He mercilessly criticized the Lutheran State Church of Denmark for complacency and its clergy as sleepy, self-serving political appointees. His emphasis on individual responsibility, personal choice, and the emotions that arise from choices has led to his being called the first existentialist philosopher.

For Kierkegaard, each believer in Jesus Christ has a subjective relationship with the God-Man. Individual faith comes in a profound leap beyond ethics, "a teleological suspension of the ethical." Kierkegaard coined this phrase in *Fear and Trembling*, which he published in 1843 under the pseudonym Johannes de silentio (John of Silence). Through this invented character (*character* in both the theatrical and the popular senses of the word), Kierkegaard experimented with opinions not always entirely his own.

The work's title is a quote from Philippians 2:12: "Wherefore, my beloved, as ye have always obeyed, not as in my presence only, but now much more in my absence, work out your own salvation with fear and trembling." For Kierkegaard, "fear and trembling" refer to existential consequences: One cannot avoid the fearful decisions before which one might tremble. For him, the decision to be or not be a Christian was such a decision. And for him as for Saint Paul, salvation results from faith, the overcoming of skepticism and caution. The biblical patriarch Abraham made such a leap in trusting God when God told him to sacrifice his son Isaac (see p. 83).

In *Fear and Trembling*, Kierkegaard reckons with this paradigmatic "knight of faith," whose willingness to follow God's request was a nonheroic act of faith that surpassed natural ethical demands.

PRONOUNCING GLOSSARY

Ararat: *ah´-rah-raht*

Eliezer: *el-ee-ay´-zer*

Hagar: *ha´-gar*

Moriah: *moh-rye´-ah*

Søren Kierkegaard: *soh´-ren keer´-ke-gohr*

FROM FEAR AND TREMBLING

From *Preface*

In our age nobody stops at faith but goes further. To ask where they are going would perhaps be foolhardy; however, it is surely a sign of courtesy and good breeding for me to assume that everyone has faith, since otherwise it would be peculiar to talk of going further. In those olden days it was different; then faith was a lifelong task because it was assumed that proficiency in believing is not achieved in either days or weeks. When the tried and tested oldster drew near to his end, having fought the good fight and kept the faith,[1] his heart was still young enough not to have forgotten that fear and trembling which disciplined the youth and was well-controlled by the man but is not entirely outgrown by any person—except insofar as one succeeds in going further as soon as possible. Where those venerable figures arrived, there everyone in our age begins in order to go further.

The present writer is not at all a philosopher; he has not understood the System,[2] whether it exists or whether it is finished. He already has enough for his weak head in the thought of what huge heads everyone in our age must have since everyone has such huge thoughts. Even if one were able to convert the whole content of faith into conceptual form, it does not follow that one has comprehended faith, comprehended how one entered into it or how it entered into one. The present writer is not at all a philosopher; he is, poetically and tastefully expressed, a free-lancer who neither writes the System nor makes *promises* about the System, who neither swears by the System nor pledges himself *to* the System. He writes because for him it is a luxury that becomes all the more enjoyable and conspicuous the fewer who buy and read what he writes. He easily foresees his fate in an age when passion has been abandoned in order to serve scholarship, in an age when an author who wants readers must take care to write in such a way that his work can be conveniently skimmed through during the after-dinner nap, and take care to fashion his outer appearance in likeness to that polite garden apprentice in *The Advertiser*,[3] who with hat in hand and good refer-

---

TRANSLATED BY Sylvia Walsh. The translator's bracketed insertions have been omitted.

1. Compare 2 Timothy 4:7. "Tried . . . oldster": Saint Paul.

2. That of G. W. F. Hegel and his many followers

3. A Danish newspaper.

(see p. 525).

ences from the place where he was last employed recommends himself to an esteemed public. He foresees his fate of being totally ignored; he has a frightful presentiment that zealous criticism will put him through the mill many times. He dreads what is even more frightful, that one or another enterprising summarizer * * * will cut him up into paragraphs and do it with the same inflexibility as the man who, in service to the system of punctuation, divided his discourse by counting the words so that there were exactly 50 words to a period and 35 to a semicolon.[4] —I prostrate myself in deepest deference before every systematic snooper: "This is not the System, it does not have the least thing to do with the System. I invoke all the best upon the System and upon the Danish investors in this omnibus, for it is not likely to become a tower.[5] I wish them one and all good luck and prosperity."

Respectfully,
Johannes de silentio

Tuning Up

There was once a man who as a child had heard that beautiful story about how God tested Abraham and how he withstood the test, kept the faith, and received a son a second time contrary to expectation. When the man became older, he read the same story with even greater admiration, for life had separated what had been united in the child's pious simplicity. Indeed, the older he became, the more often his thoughts turned to that story; his enthusiasm became stronger and stronger, and yet he could understand the story less and less. Finally he forgot everything else because of it; his soul had only one wish, to see Abraham, one longing, to have been a witness to that event. His desire was not to see the beautiful regions of the Far East, not the earthly splendor of the Promised Land,[6] not that god-fearing married couple whose old age God had blessed[7] not the venerable figure of the aged patriarch, not the vigorous youth of Isaac bestowed by God—it would not have mattered to him if the same thing had taken place on a barren heath. His longing was to accompany them on the three day journey when Abraham rode with sorrow before him and Isaac by his side. His wish was to be present at the hour when Abraham lifted up his eyes and saw Mount Moriah in the distance, the hour he left the asses behind and went up the mountain alone with Isaac, for what engrossed him was not the artistic weave of the imagination but the shudder of the thought.

That man was not a thinker, he felt no need to go beyond faith; it seemed to him that it must be the greatest glory to be remembered as its father and an enviable lot to possess faith, even if no one knew it.

That man was not a learned exegete, he did not know Hebrew; had he known Hebrew, then perhaps he would easily have understood the story and Abraham.

---

4. Fifty words before every period, thirty-five words before every semicolon.
5. Compare Luke 14:28–30. "Danish . . . omnibus": Danish followers of Hegel. Kierkegaard believed the system would never reach completion.
6. See Genesis 12:1–2 and 17:8.
7. See Genesis 18:1–15 and 21:1–3.

I

"And God tested Abraham and said to him, take Isaac, your only son,
whom you love, and go to the land of Moriah and offer him there
as a burnt offering upon a mountain that I will show you."[8]

It was an early morning; Abraham rose early, had the asses saddled, and left
his tent, taking Isaac with him, but Sarah looked out the window after
them as they went down through the valley[9] until she could see them no
more. They rode silently for three days. On the morning of the fourth day
Abraham still did not say a word but lifted up his eyes and saw Mount
Moriah in the distance. He left the servant boys behind and went up to the
mountain alone, leading Isaac by the hand. But Abraham said to himself: "I
will not conceal from Isaac where this path is taking him." He stood still
and laid his hand upon Isaac's head for a blessing, and Isaac bowed to
receive it. And Abraham's countenance was paternal, his gaze was gentle,
his speech exhortatory. But Isaac could not understand him, his soul
could not be uplifted; he embraced Abraham's knees, he pleaded at his
feet, he begged for his young life, for his fair hopes, he recalled the joy in
Abraham's house, he recalled the sorrow and the solitude. Then Abraham
raised the boy up and walked along holding his hand, and his words were
full of comfort and exhortation. But Isaac could not understand him. He
climbed Mount Moriah, but Isaac understood him not. Then he turned
away from Isaac a moment, but when Isaac saw Abraham's countenance
again it was changed, his eyes were wild, his appearance a fright to
behold. He seized Isaac by the chest, threw him to the ground, and said:
"Foolish boy, do you believe that I am your father? I am an idolater. Do
you believe this is God's command? No, it is my desire." Then Isaac trembled and cried out in his anguish: "God in heaven have mercy on me, God
of Abraham have mercy on me; if I have no father on earth, then you be
my father!" But Abraham murmured under his breath to himself: "Lord in
heaven, I thank you; it is surely better for him to believe I am a monster
than to lose faith in you."

When the child is to be weaned, the mother blackens her breast, for it
would indeed be a shame for the breast to look delightful when the child
must not have it. So the child believes that the breast has changed, but the
mother is the same, her gaze is loving and tender as always. Fortunate the
one who did not need more frightful measures to wean the child![1]

II

It was an early morning; Abraham rose early, he embraced Sarah, the bride
of his old age, and Sarah kissed Isaac, who took away her disgrace,[2] who
was her pride, her hope for all generations. Then they rode silently along
the way, and Abraham's eyes were fastened upon the ground until the

---

8. A combination of paraphrase from and direct
quotation from Genesis 22.
9. Judith 10:10. (In the 16th century, the Protestant Reformers excised the Book of Judith from
the Bible.)

1. In Kierkegaard's day, children nursed for as
long as two years, and weaning sometimes
required measures like the one he describes.
2. Her barrenness; Isaac was her first child, born
in her old age.

fourth day when he lifted up his eyes and saw Mount Moriah far away, but his eyes turned again towards the ground. Silently he arranged the firewood and bound Isaac, silently he drew the knife; then he saw the ram that God had chosen. He sacrificed it and went home. ——— From that day on Abraham became old; he could not forget that God had demanded this of him. Isaac flourished as before, but Abraham's eyes were darkened, he saw joy no more.

When the child has grown larger and is to be weaned, the mother covers her breast in a maidenly manner so the child no longer has a mother. Fortunate the child who did not lose its mother in some other way!

III

It was an early morning; Abraham rose early, he kissed Sarah, the young mother, and Sarah kissed Isaac, her delight, her joy at all times. And Abraham rode pensively along the way; he thought of Hagar and the son whom he turned out into the desert.[3] He climbed Mount Moriah, he drew the knife.

It was a quiet evening when Abraham rode out alone, and he rode to Mount Moriah. He threw himself upon his face, he begged God to forgive his sin, that he had been willing to sacrifice Isaac, that the father had forgotten his duty toward the son. More than once he rode his lonely trail but found no peace of mind. He could not comprehend that it was a sin to have been willing to sacrifice to God the best he owned, that for which he himself would gladly have laid down his life many times. And if it were a sin, if he had not loved Isaac in this way, then he could not understand how it could be forgiven, for what sin was more grievous?

When the child is to be weaned, the mother too is not without sorrow that she and the child are more and more to be parted, that the child who first lay beneath her heart yet later reposed upon her breast will not be so close any more. Thus together they mourn this brief sorrow. Fortunate the one who kept the child so close and did not need to sorrow more!

IV

It was an early morning; everything was ready for the journey in Abraham's house. He took leave of Sarah, and the faithful servant Eliezer[4] saw him out along the road until he turned back again. They rode together in harmony, Abraham and Isaac, until they came to Mount Moriah. Yet Abraham calmly and gently prepared everything for the sacrifice, but as he turned away and drew the knife, Isaac saw that Abraham's left hand was clenched in despair, that a shudder went through his body—but Abraham drew the knife.

Then they returned home again and Sarah hurried to meet them, but Isaac had lost the faith. Never a word is spoken about this in the world;

3. At Sarah's request, Abraham drove his elder son, Ishmael, and Ishmael's mother, Sarah's slave Hagar, into the desert to die. Abraham knew—as Sarah did not—that God would res- cue them.

4. Who, before the birth of Ishmael and then Isaac, Abraham had feared would be his heir by default.

Isaac never spoke to any person about what he had seen, and Abraham did not suspect that anyone had seen it.

When the child is to be weaned, the mother has more solid food on hand so the child will not perish. Fortunate the one who has this stronger nourishment handy!

In these and many similar ways that man of whom we speak pondered over this event. Every time he returned home from a pilgrimage to Mount Moriah he collapsed from fatigue, clasped his hands, and said: "Surely no one was as great as Abraham. Who is able to understand him?"

From *Eulogy on Abraham*

* * * No one who was great in the world will be forgotten, but everyone was great in his own way, and everyone in proportion to the greatness of that which *he loved*. He who loved himself became great by virtue of himself, and he who loved other men became great by his devotedness, but he who loved God became the greatest of all. Everyone shall be remembered, but everyone became great in proportion to his *expectancy*. One became great by expecting the possible, another by expecting the eternal; but he who expected the impossible became the greatest of all. Everyone shall be remembered, but everyone was great wholly in proportion to the magnitude of that with which he *struggled*. For he who struggled with the world became great by conquering the world, and he who struggled with himself became great by conquering himself, but he who struggled with God became the greatest of all. Thus did they struggle in the world, man against man, one against thousands, but he who struggled with God was the greatest of all. Thus did they struggle on earth: there was one who conquered everything by his power, and there was one who conquered God by his powerlessness. There was one who relied upon himself and gained everything; there was one who in the security of his own strength sacrificed everything; but the one who believed God was the greatest of all. There was one who was great by virtue of his power, and one who was great by virtue of his wisdom, and one who was great by virtue of his hope, and one who was great by virtue of his love, but Abraham was the greatest of all, great by that power whose strength is powerlessness, great by that wisdom whose secret is foolishness, great by that hope whose form is madness, great by the love that is hatred to oneself.

* * *

By faith Abraham received the promise that in his seed all the generations of the earth would be blessed.[5] Time passed, the possibility was there, Abraham had faith; time passed, it became unreasonable, Abraham had faith. There was one in the world who also had an expectancy.[6] Time passed, evening drew near; he was not so contemptible as to forget his expectancy,

5. See Genesis 12:1–3.
6. Unclear reference. Possibly the exiled Roman poet Ovid (43 B.C.E.–?17 C.E.), who died hoping to be recalled from exile; perhaps Kierkegaard, alluding to a personal disappointment through the veil of his pseudonym.

and therefore he will not be forgotten, either. Then he sorrowed, and his sorrow did not disappoint him as life had done, it did everything it could for him; in the sweetness of his sorrow he possessed his disappointed expectancy. It is human to sorrow, human to sorrow with the sorrowing, but it is greater to have faith, more blessed to contemplate the man of faith. We have no dirge of sorrow by Abraham. As time passed, he did not gloomily count the days; he did not look suspiciously at Sarah, wondering if she was not getting old; he did not stop the course of the sun so she would not become old and along with her his expectancy; he did not soothingly sing his mournful lay for Sarah. Abraham became old, Sarah the object of mockery in the land, and yet he was God's chosen one and heir to the promise that in his seed all the generations of the earth would be blessed. Would it not have been better, after all, if he were not God's chosen? What does it mean to be God's chosen? Is it to be denied in youth one's youthful desire in order to have it fulfilled with great difficulty in one's old age? But Abraham believed and held to the promise. If Abraham had wavered, he would have given it up. He would have said to God, "So maybe it is not your will that this should be; then I will give up my wish. It was my one and only wish, it was my blessedness. My soul is open and sincere; I am hiding no secret resentment because you denied me this." He would not have been forgotten, he would have saved many by his example, but he still would not have become the father of faith, for it is great to give up one's desire, but it is greater to hold fast to it after having given it up; it is great to lay hold of the eternal, but it is greater to hold fast to the temporal after having given it up.

Then came the fullness of time. If Abraham had not had faith, then Sarah would surely have died of sorrow, and Abraham, dulled by grief, would not have understood the fulfillment but would have smiled at it as at a youthful dream. But Abraham had faith, and therefore he was young, for he who always hopes for the best grows old and is deceived by life, and he who is always prepared for the worst grows old prematurely, but he who has faith—he preserves an eternal youth. So let us praise and honor that story! For Sarah, although well advanced in years, was young enough to desire the pleasure of motherhood, and Abraham with his gray hairs was young enough to wish to be a father. Outwardly, the wonder of it is that it happened according to their expectancy; in the more profound sense, the wonder of faith is that Abraham and Sarah were young enough to desire and that faith had preserved their desire and thereby their youth. He accepted the fulfillment of the promise, he accepted it in faith, and it happened according to the promise and according to his faith. Moses struck the rock with his staff, but he did not have faith.[7]

So there was joy in Abraham's house when Sarah stood as bride on their golden wedding day.

But it was not to remain that way; once again Abraham was to be tried. He had fought with that crafty power that devises all things, with that vigilant enemy who never dozes, with that old man who outlives everything—he had fought with time and kept his faith. Now all the frightfulness of the struggle was concentrated in one moment. "And God tempted Abraham

7. See Numbers 20:9–13.

and said to him, take Isaac, your only son, whom you love, and go to the land of Moriah and offer him as a burnt offering on a mountain that I shall show you."[8]

So everything was lost, even more appallingly than if it had never happened! So the Lord was only mocking Abraham! He wondrously made the preposterous come true; now he wanted to see it annihilated. This was indeed a piece of folly, but Abraham did not laugh at it as Sarah did when the promise was announced. All was lost! Seventy years of trusting expectancy,[9] the brief joy over the fulfillment of faith. Who is this who seizes the staff from the old man, who is this who demands that he himself shall break it! Who is this who makes a man's gray hairs disconsolate, who is this who demands that he himself shall do it! Is there no sympathy for this venerable old man, none for the innocent child? And yet Abraham was God's chosen one, and it was the Lord who imposed the ordeal. Now everything would be lost! All the glorious remembrance of his posterity, the promise in Abraham's seed—it was nothing but a whim, a fleeting thought that the Lord had had and that Abraham was now supposed to obliterate. That glorious treasure,[1] which was just as old as the faith in Abraham's heart and many, many years older than Isaac, the fruit of Abraham's life, sanctified by prayer, matured in battle, the blessing on Abraham's lips—this fruit was now to be torn off prematurely and rendered meaningless, for what meaning would it have if Isaac should be sacrificed! That sad but nevertheless blessed hour when Abraham was to take leave of everything he held dear, when he once more would raise his venerable head, when his face would shine as the Lord's, when he would concentrate all his soul upon a blessing that would be so powerful it would bless Isaac all his days—this hour was not to come! For Abraham would indeed take leave of Isaac, but in such a way that he himself would remain behind; death would separate them, but in such a way that Isaac would become its booty. The old man would not, rejoicing in death, lay his hand in blessing on Isaac, but, weary of life, he would lay a violent hand upon Isaac. And it was God who tested him! * * *

* * *

We read in sacred scripture: "And God tempted Abraham and said: Abraham, Abraham, where are you? But Abraham answered: Here am I."[2] You to whom these words are addressed, was this the case with you? When in the far distance you saw overwhelming vicissitudes approaching, did you not say to the mountains, "Hide me," and to the hills, "Fall on me"?[3] Or, if you were stronger, did your feet nevertheless not drag along the way, did they not long, so to speak, for the old trails? And when your name was called, did you answer, perhaps answer softly, in a whisper? Not so with Abraham. Cheerfully, freely, confidently, loudly he answered: Here am I. We read on: "And Abraham arose early in the morning."[4] He hurried as if to a celebration, and early in the morning he was at the appointed place on Mount

8. Paraphrase and partial quotation of Genesis 22:1–3.
9. According to a careful reading of Genesis, Abraham was then a hundred years old and seventy years had passed since God's promise to him of offspring. See Genesis 21:5.
1. God's promise.
2. Genesis 22:1–2.
3. Luke 12:30; compare Hosea 10:8.
4. Genesis 22:3.

Moriah. He said nothing to Sarah, nothing to Eliezer—who, after all, could understand him, for did not the nature of the temptation extract from him the pledge of silence? "He split the firewood, he bound Isaac, he lit the fire, he drew the knife."[5] My listener! Many a father has thought himself deprived of every hope for the future when he lost his child, the dearest thing in the world to him; nevertheless, no one was the child of promise in the sense in which Isaac was that to Abraham. Many a father has lost his child, but then it was God, the unchangeable, inscrutable will of the Almighty, it was his hand that took it. Not so with Abraham! A harder test was reserved for him, and Isaac's fate was placed, along with the knife, in Abraham's hand. And there he stood, the old man with his solitary hope. But he did not doubt, he did not look in anguish to the left and to the right, he did not challenge heaven with his prayers. He knew it was God the Almighty who was testing him; he knew it was the hardest sacrifice that could be demanded of him; but he knew also that no sacrifice is too severe when God demands it—and he drew the knife.

Who strengthened Abraham's arm, who braced up his right arm so that it did not sink down powerless! Anyone who looks upon this scene is paralyzed. Who strengthened Abraham's soul lest everything go black for him and he see neither Isaac nor the ram! Anyone who looks upon this scene is blinded. And yet it perhaps rarely happens that anyone is paralyzed or blinded, and still more rarely does anyone tell what happened as it deserves to be told. We know it all—it was only an ordeal.

If Abraham had doubted as he stood there on Mount Moriah, if irresolute he had looked around, if he had happened to spot the ram before drawing the knife, if God had allowed him to sacrifice it instead of Isaac—then he would have gone home, everything would have been the same, he would have had Sarah, he would have kept Isaac, and yet how changed! For his return would have been a flight, his deliverance an accident, his reward disgrace, his future perhaps perdition. Then he would have witnessed neither to his faith nor to God's grace but would have witnessed to how appalling it is to go to Mount Moriah. Then Abraham would not be forgotten, nor would Mount Moriah. Then it would not be mentioned in the way Ararat, where the ark landed,[6] is mentioned, but it would be called a place of terror, for it was here that Abraham doubted.

Venerable Father Abraham! When you went home from Mount Moriah, you did not need a eulogy to comfort you for what was lost, for you gained everything and kept Isaac—was it not so? The Lord did not take him away from you again, but you sat happily together at the dinner table in your tent, as you do in the next world for all eternity. Venerable Father Abraham! Centuries have passed since those days, but you have no need of a late lover to snatch your memory from the power of oblivion, for every language calls you to mind—and yet you reward your lover more gloriously than anyone else. In the life to come you make him eternally happy in your bosom; here in this life you captivate his eyes and his heart with the wonder of your act. Venerable Father Abraham! Second Father of the race! You who were the

5. Paraphrase of Genesis 22:9–10.
6. See Genesis 8:4.

first to feel and to bear witness to that prodigious passion that disdains the terrifying battle with the raging elements and the forces of creation in order to contend with God, you who were the first to know that supreme passion, the holy, pure, and humble expression for the divine madness that was admired by the pagans—forgive the one who aspired to speak your praise if he has not done it properly. He spoke humbly, as his heart demanded; he spoke briefly, as is seemly. But he will never forget that you needed 100 years to get the son of your old age against all expectancy, that you had to draw the knife before you kept Isaac; he will never forget that in 130 years you got no further than faith.[7]

7. According to Genesis 25:7, Abraham died at the age of 175. Kierkegaard apparently reckons his age to have been forty-five when God commanded him to sacrifice Isaac.

G. K. CHESTERTON
1874–1936

FROM ORTHODOXY

Gilbert Keith Chesterton was born in London and died in Beaconsfield, Buckinghamshire, England. As a critic, an essayist, a poet, a detective novelist, and a swashbuckling defender of Christianity, he published some eighty books. In 1922—at a time when later modernity's fusion of nationality and religion had made religious conversion in England seem close to political treason—Chesteron converted from Anglicanism to Roman Catholicism, cheerfully opening a path for apostasy.

Known for jousting publicly and ebulliently with the leading intellectuals of his day, Chesteron delighted in paradoxical, whimsical, and counterintuitive points of view. In the following selection—the chapter "Paradoxes of Christianity," from his volume *Orthodoxy* (1908)—he combines autobiography and argument, making his case more brassily than logically or historically. Though he boasts of having had little exposure to Christian apologetics, he was a full-time apologist for much of his life. Starting out as a "pagan" and then a "complete agnostic," he was drawn to Christianity by reading atheists. Contradictory attacks on Christianity—say, that the religion is at once too focused on hell and too focused on heaven, too austere and too full of majesty, promoting virginity and promoting married life—convince him that the fault lies not in the Church, but in its enemies. Finally, Chesteron celebrates orthodox Christianity's monopoly on theological truth, "the wild truth reeling but erect."

PRONOUNCING GLOSSARY

Gnosticism: *nah´-sti-sizm*   Malthusian: *mal-thoo´-zhun*

FROM ORTHODOXY

From *Paradoxes of Christianity*

* * * I was a pagan at the age of twelve, and a complete agnostic by the age of sixteen; and I cannot understand any one passing the age of seventeen without having asked himself so simple a question. I did, indeed, retain a cloudy reverence for a cosmic deity and a great historical interest in the Founder of Christianity. But I certainly regarded Him as a man; though perhaps I thought that, even in that point, He had an advantage over some of His modern critics. I read the scientific and sceptical literature of my time—all of it, at least, that I could find written in English and lying about; and I read nothing else; I mean I read nothing else on any other note of philosophy. The penny dreadfuls which I also read were indeed in a healthy and heroic tradition of Christianity; but I did not know this at the time. I never read a line of Christian apologetics. I read as little as I can of them now. It was Huxley and Herbert Spencer and Bradlaugh[1] who brought me back to orthodox theology. They sowed in my mind my first wild doubts of doubt. Our grandmothers were quite right when they said that Tom Paine[2] and the free-thinkers unsettled the mind. They do. They unsettled mine horribly. The rationalist made me question whether reason was of any use whatever; and when I had finished Herbert Spencer I had got as far as doubting (for the first time) whether evolution had occurred at all. As I laid down the last of Colonel Ingersoll's atheistic lectures the dreadful thought broke across my mind, "Almost thou persuadest me to be a Christian."[3] I was in a desperate way.

This odd effect of the great agnostics in arousing doubts deeper than their own might be illustrated in many ways. I take only one. As I read and re-read all the non-Christian or anti-Christian accounts of the faith, from Huxley to Bradlaugh, a slow and awful impression grew gradually but graphically upon my mind—the impression that Christianity must be a most extraordinary thing. For not only (as I understood) had Christianity the most flaming vices, but it had apparently a mystical talent for combining vices which seemed inconsistent with each other. It was attacked on all sides and for all contradictory reasons. No sooner had one rationalist demonstrated that it was too far to the east than another demonstrated with equal clearness that it was much too far to the west. No sooner had my indignation died down at its angular and aggressive squareness than I was called up again to notice and condemn its enervating and sensual roundness. In case any reader has not come across the thing I mean, I will give such instances as I remember at random of this self-contradiction in the sceptical attack. I give four or five of them; there are fifty more.

Thus, for instance, I was much moved by the eloquent attack on Christianity as a thing of inhuman gloom; for I thought (and still think) sincere pessimism the unpardonable sin. Insincere pessimism is a social accomplishment,

---

1. Charles Bradlaugh (1833–1891), English reformer, atheist, and liberal member of Parliament. "Huxley": Thomas Henry Huxley (see p. 546). "Herbert Spencer": English philosopher and proponent of social Darwinism (1820–1903).
2. Thomas Paine (1737–1809), English-born American radical pamphleteer and philosopher.
3. Acts 26:28 (King James Version). "Colonel Ingersoll": Robert Green "Bob" Ingersoll (1833–1899), American Civil War veteran, political leader, and orator, known as "The Great Agnostic."

rather agreeable than otherwise; and fortunately nearly all pessimism is insincere. But if Christianity was, as these people said, a thing purely pessimistic and opposed to life, then I was quite prepared to blow up St. Paul's Cathedral.[4] But the extraordinary thing is this. They did prove to me in Chapter I (to my complete satisfaction) that Christianity was too pessimistic; and then, in Chapter II, they began to prove to me that it was a great deal too optimistic. One accusation against Christianity was that it prevented men, by morbid tears and terrors, from seeking joy and liberty in the bosom of Nature. But another accusation was that it comforted men with a fictitious providence, and put them in a pink-and-white nursery. One great agnostic asked why Nature was not beautiful enough, and why it was hard to be free. Another great agnostic objected that Christian optimism, "the garment of make-believe woven by pious hands,"[5] hid from us the fact that Nature was ugly, and that it was impossible to be free. One rationalist had hardly done calling Christianity a nightmare before another began to call it a fool's paradise. This puzzled me; the charges seemed inconsistent. Christianity could not at once be the black mask on a white world, and also the white mask on a black world. The state of the Christian could not be at once so comfortable that he was a coward to cling to it, and so uncomfortable that he was a fool to stand it. If it falsified human vision it must falsify it one way or another; it could not wear both green and rose-coloured spectacles. I rolled on my tongue with a terrible joy, as did all young men of that time, the taunts which Swinburne hurled at the dreariness of the creed—

"Thou hast conquered, O pale Galilaean, the world has grown gray with Thy breath."[6]

But when I read the same poet's accounts of paganism (as in "Atalanta"), I gathered that the world was, if possible, more gray before the Galilaean breathed on it than afterwards. The poet maintained, indeed, in the abstract, that life itself was pitch dark. And yet, somehow, Christianity had darkened it. The very man who denounced Christianity for pessimism was himself a pessimist. I thought there must be something wrong. And it did for one wild moment cross my mind that, perhaps, those might not be the very best judges of the relation of religion to happiness who, by their own account, had neither one nor the other.

It must be understood that I did not conclude hastily that the accusations were false or the accusers fools. I simply deduced that Christianity must be something even weirder and wickeder than they made out. A thing might have these two opposite vices; but it must be a rather queer thing if it did. A man might be too fat in one place and too thin in another; but he would be an odd shape. At this point my thoughts were only of the odd shape of the Christian religion; I did not allege any odd shape in the rationalistic mind.

* * *

And then in a quiet hour a strange thought struck me like a still thunderbolt. There had suddenly come into my mind another explanation. Suppose we heard an unknown man spoken of by many men. Suppose we were

4. In London.
5. An approximate quotation from Huxley's *Autobiography* (1889).
6. Line 35 from "Hymn to Proserpine," by the English poet Algernon Charles Swinburne (1837–1909).

puzzled to hear that some men said he was too tall and some too short; some objected to his fatness, some lamented his leanness; some thought him too dark, and some too fair. One explanation (as has been already admitted) would be that he might be an odd shape. But there is another explanation. He might be the right shape. Outrageously tall men might feel him to be short. Very short men might feel him to be tall. Old bucks who are growing stout might consider him insufficiently filled out; old beaux who were growing thin might feel that he expanded beyond the narrow lines of elegance. Perhaps Swedes (who have pale hair like tow) called him a dark man, while negroes considered him distinctly blonde. Perhaps (in short) this extraordinary thing is really the ordinary thing; at least the normal thing, the centre. Perhaps, after all, it is Christianity that is sane and all its critics that are mad—in various ways. I tested this idea by asking myself whether there was about any of the accusers anything morbid that might explain the accusation. I was startled to find that this key fitted a lock. For instance, it was certainly odd that the modern world charged Christianity at once with bodily austerity and with artistic pomp. But then it was also odd, very odd, that the modern world itself combined extreme bodily luxury with an extreme absence of artistic pomp. The modern man thought Becket's[7] robes too rich and his meals too poor. But then the modern man was really exceptional in history; no man before ever ate such elaborate dinners in such ugly clothes. The modern man found the church too simple exactly where modern life is too complex; he found the church too gorgeous exactly where modern life is too dingy. The man who disliked the plain fasts and feasts was mad on *entrées*. The man who disliked vestments wore a pair of preposterous trousers. And surely if there was any insanity involved in the matter at all it was in the trousers, not in the simply falling robe. If there was any insanity at all, it was in the extravagant *entrées*, not in the bread and wine.

I went over all the cases, and I found the key fitted so far. The fact that Swinburne was irritated at the unhappiness of Christians and yet more irritated at their happiness was easily explained. It was no longer a complication of diseases in Christianity, but a complication of diseases in Swinburne. The restraints of Christians saddened him simply because he was more hedonist than a healthy man should be. The faith of Christians angered him because he was more pessimist than a healthy man should be. In the same way the Malthusians[8] by instinct attacked Christianity; not because there is anything especially anti-Malthusian about Christianity, but because there is something a little anti-human about Malthusianism.

✳ ✳ ✳

✳ ✳ ✳ It *is* true that the historic Church has at once emphasized celibacy and emphasized the family; has at once (if one may put it so) been fiercely for having children and fiercely for not having children. It has kept them side by side like two strong colours, red and white, like the red and white

---

7. Saint Thomas à Becket (ca. 1118–1170), archbishop of Canterbury from 1162 until his death.
8. Malthusians, followers of the English political economist Thomas Malthus (1766–1834), believed that human population would inevitably grow faster than human agricultural production, resulting in famine unless other disasters reduced population first.

upon the shield of St. George.[9] It has always had a healthy hatred of pink. It hates that combination of two colours which is the feeble expedient of the philosophers. It hates that evolution of black into white which is tantamount to a dirty grey. In fact, the whole theory of the Church on virginity might be symbolized in the statement that white is a colour: not merely the absence of a colour. All that I am urging here can be expressed by saying that Christianity sought in most of these cases to keep two colours coexistent but pure. It is not a mixture like russet or purple; it is rather like a shot silk,[1] for a shot silk is always at right angles, and is in the pattern of the cross.

✳ ✳ ✳

This is the thrilling romance of Orthodoxy. People have fallen into a foolish habit of speaking of orthodoxy as something heavy, humdrum, and safe. There never was anything so perilous or so exciting as orthodoxy. It was sanity: and to be sane is more dramatic than to be mad. It was the equilibrium of a man behind madly rushing horses, seeming to stoop this way and to sway that, yet in every attitude having the grace of statuary and the accuracy of arithmetic. The Church in its early days went fierce and fast with any warhorse; yet it is utterly unhistoric to say that she merely went mad along one idea, like a vulgar fanaticism. She swerved to left and right, so as exactly to avoid enormous obstacles. She left on one hand the huge bulk of Arianism, buttressed by all the worldly powers to make Christianity too worldly. The next instant she was swerving to avoid an orientalism, which would have made it too unworldly. The orthodox Church never took the tame course or accepted the conventions; the orthodox Church was never respectable. It would have been easier to have accepted the earthly power of the Arians. It would have been easy, in the Calvinistic seventeenth century, to fall into the bottomless pit of predestination.[2] It is easy to be a madman: it is easy to be a heretic. It is always easy to let the age have its head; the difficult thing is to keep one's own. It is always easy to be a modernist; as it is easy to be a snob. To have fallen into any of those open traps of error and exaggeration which fashion after fashion and sect after sect set along the historic path of Christendom—that would indeed have been simple. It is always simple to fall; there are an infinity of angles at which one falls, only one at which one stands. To have fallen into any one of the fads from Gnosticism to Christian Science would indeed have been obvious and tame. But to have avoided them all has been one whirling adventure; and in my vision the heavenly chariot flies thundering through the ages, the dull heresies sprawling and prostrate, the wild truth reeling but erect.

---

9. Third-century Christian martyr; the patron saint of England.
1. A fabric made of silk that is woven from crossed yarns of two or more colors.
2. See the headnote for John Calvin (p. 412).

THE SEA OF FAITH: EBB OR FLOOD?

In the later nineteenth century, Europe—intellectually and demographically the capital of the Christian world—was at the peak of its material wealth, its political power, and, to all appearances, its self-confidence. The industrial revolution had produced a huge aggregate increase in wealth, whatever the inequities in the distribution of that wealth. Colonialism had spread European power and cultural influence around the globe. Confidence in the European secular order, in scientific progress, and even in European painting, music, and literature was so great that it seemed to promise the emergence of a new secular faith.

And yet Matthew Arnold—English cultural critic, educator, and poet—was worried about the course of European civilization. To his sadness, the power of Christianity appeared to be ebbing. Arnold hoped that the arts, especially poetry, could step in as a refiner of feeling and of intellect. "The best that has been thought and said in the world"—his phrase, in the 1882 essay "Literature and Science"—might make up for the inadequacies of its spiritual cousin, the Christianity of the heart. This hope provides glimmers of light on the dark waves rolling in Arnold's poem "Dover Beach," included here.

Was Christianity's demise a fact or an opinion? Arnold's contemporary the English biologist Thomas Henry Huxley coined the word *agnosticism* to convey his doubt regarding the existence of God. Huxley's thought, represented here by an excerpt from his essay "Agnosticism and Christianity," epitomizes the view that the only true proof is scientific proof. Huxley did not linger over arguments (aesthetic, forensic, political, or philosophical) that were not scientifically demonstrable, nor did he engage in a cultural war against Christianity.

And yet, of course, tides not only ebb; they also flood. Matthew Arnold's vision of the future hardly predicted the late-nineteenth-century resurgence of Roman Catholicism in Germany and Britain. Arnold's contemporary Gerard Manley Hopkins, a convert from Anglicanism to Catholicism, wrote poetry both religiously Romantic and stylistically unprecedented. Hopkins's work is represented here by his poem "The Windhover."

Arnold's and Hopkins's contemporary the poet Emily Dickinson lived in Massachusetts, where she literally stayed home. Her poetry, represented here by two selections, offers multiple interpretive possibilities while circling the Christian tradition, which she kept at a formal distance. Even when Dickinson does not attend a religious service, that service claims a place in her mind; she writes a poem about the mental and spiritual encounter. Rather than expressing simple faith or simple doubt, Dickinson lingers over quandary.

No less improbable and far more important than the resurgence of Roman Catholicism in the nineteenth century was the extraordinary success enjoyed in that century by Protestant missionaries in Africa. Today the black population of central Africa is heavily Christian. Though much of the Christian growth can be traced to a twentieth-century demographic explosion, there would have been no such explosion without the work of pioneering explorer-missionaries such as the famous Englishman David Livingstone, here represented by a memoir excerpt. In a sense, nineteenth-century Christianity, shaken at home by serious intellectual challenges, awoke to find that a new continent had been added to its world map.

At the start of the twentieth century, the New Testament scholar Albert Schweitzer published a book whose English title gave a long-lasting scholarly movement its name: *The Quest of the Historical Jesus.* In this work, Schweitzer concluded that the quest was over, its historical objective having essentially been achieved. As Schweitzer gravely explained, however, the quest had established that *Jesus had been mistaken* in some of his core beliefs. God's definitive intervention in human history, and with it the end of the world, had not come as the culmination of Jesus' life. Schweitzer maintained that Christianity could not be renewed—rebuilt—on the basis of a mistake, not even a mistake made by Jesus. Schweitzer remained intensely committed to Christianity, however. Astonishing his contemporaries, he earned a medical degree and began a long career as a medical missionary in Africa. The story of German historical criticism of the Bible and the story of the implantation of Christianity in black Africa converged in Schweitzer's career. Christianity was being transformed demographically on one continent even as Christians on another continent continued to ponder what was happening conceptually to their religion.

THOMAS HENRY HUXLEY
1825–1895

FROM AGNOSTICISM AND CHRISTIANITY

Thomas Henry Huxley was born in Ealing, Middlesex, England, and died in Eastbourne, Sussex. A self-taught biologist and distinguished comparative anatomist, he is remembered largely for championing Darwinism, such as in his legendary clash with Bishop Samuel Wilberforce at a debate on evolution held at Oxford University in 1860. Huxley is also famous for coining and personifying the term *agnosticism* ("unknowerism," from the Greek *a* [un] + *gnostikos* [knower]). In "Agnosticism and Christianity" (1889), Huxley argues that the agnostic is neither a coward nor an atheist in disguise, but simply a person who refuses to believe anything without strong, preferably scientific evidence. And since, as 2,500 years of philosophy have illustrated, there is no irrefutable proof for any statement about the soul or the supernatural or immortality, Huxley finds it not just permissible, but morally imperative, to stay within the bounds of reason and experience and suspend his judgment on all "metaphysical" questions. In addition to bolstering his own stance, Huxley attacks what he calls "Ecclesiasticism": excessive devotion to the Church. He has no problem with "scientific" (i.e., scholarly) theology as long as it stays in its own disciplinary territory and leaves doubters alone. With a final jab at any hostile Christians in his audience, Huxley notes that the bulk of modern culture is derived not from Christianity, but from "Greek science, Greek art, the ethics of old Israel, [and] the social organization of old Rome." In his lectures, essays, and books, Huxley drew on his broad humanistic background to allude, sometimes impishly, to a vast assortment of topics and authors. Here, he quotes Jesus to suggest that Jesus was far more Jewish than is often thought.

Athanasian: *a-thuh-nay´-zhuhn*

Beelzebub: *bee-el´-zuh-bub*

gnostics: *nah´-stics*

Hume: *hyoom*

Kant: *kahnt*

Nifelheim: *ni´-fel-haim* [*ai* rhyming with *rye*]

Tertullian: *ter-tul´-ee-uhn*

FROM AGNOSTICISM AND CHRISTIANITY

[*Agnosticism Defined*]

Nemo ergo ex me scire quaerat, quod me nescire scio,
nisi forte ut nescire discat.
—AUGUSTINUS, *De Civ. Dei*, XII.7.[1]

The present discussion has arisen out of the use, which has become general in the last few years, of the terms "Agnostic" and "Agnosticism."

The people who call themselves "Agnostics" have been charged with doing so because they have not the courage to declare themselves "Infidels." It has been insinuated that they have adopted a new name in order to escape the unpleasantness which attaches to their proper denomination. To this wholly erroneous imputation I have replied by showing that the term "Agnostic" did, as a matter of fact, arise in a manner which negatives it; and my statement has not been, and cannot be, refuted. Moreover, speaking for myself, and without impugning the right of any other person to use the term in another sense, I further say that Agnosticism is not properly described as a "negative" creed, nor indeed as a creed of any kind, except in so far as it expresses absolute faith in the validity of a principle, which is as much ethical as intellectual. This principle may be stated in various ways, but they all amount to this: that it is wrong for a man to say that he is certain of the objective truth of any proposition unless he can produce evidence which logically justifies that certainty. This is what Agnosticism asserts; and, in my opinion, it is all that is essential to Agnosticism. That which Agnostics deny and repudiate, as immoral, is the contrary doctrine, that there are propositions which men ought to believe, without logically satisfactory evidence; and that reprobation ought to attach to the profession of disbelief in such inadequately supported propositions. The justification of the Agnostic principles lies in the success which follows upon its application, whether in the field of natural, or in that of civil, history; and in the fact that, so far as these topics are concerned, no sane man thinks of denying its validity.

Still speaking for myself, I add that though Agnosticism is not, and cannot be, a creed, except in so far as its general principle is concerned; yet that the application of that principle results in the denial of, or the suspension of judgment concerning, a number of propositions respecting which our contemporary ecclesiastical "gnostics"[2] profess entire certainty. And, in

---

1. "Let no one, then, seek to know from me what I know that I do not know, unless perchance so that he may learn not to know," a statement from *The City of God*, by Saint Augustine of Hippo (see p. 226).

2. In the early Church, Gnostics (see p. 200) were Christian heretics who claimed an exalted mystical knowledge above mere faith. Huxley equates his Church critics, who also claim higher knowledge, with the ancient heretics.

so far as these ecclesiastical persons can be justified in their old-established custom (which many nowadays think more honored in the breach than the observance)[3] of using opprobrious names to those who differ from them, I fully admit their right to call me and those who think with me "Infidels"; all I have ventured to urge is that they must not expect us to speak of ourselves by that title.

The extent of the region of the uncertain, the number of the problems the investigation of which ends in a verdict of not proven, will vary according to the knowledge and the intellectual habits of the individual Agnostic. I do not very much care to speak of anything as "unknowable." What I am sure about is that there are many topics about which I know nothing and which, so far as I can see, are out of reach of my faculties. But whether these things are knowable by anyone else is exactly one of those matters which is beyond my knowledge, though I may have a tolerably strong opinion as to the probabilities of the case. Relatively to myself, I am quite sure that the region of uncertainty—the nebulous country in which words play the part of realities—is far more extensive than I could wish. Materialism and Idealism; Theism and Atheism; the doctrine of the soul and its mortality or immortality—appear in the history of philosophy like the shades of Scandinavian heroes, eternally slaying one another and eternally coming to life again in a metaphysical "Nifelheim."[4] It is getting on for twenty-five centuries, at least, since mankind began seriously to give their minds to these topics. Generation after generation, philosophy has been doomed to roll the stone uphill; and, just as all the world swore it was at the top, down it has rolled to the bottom again.[5] All this is written in innumerable books; and he who will toil through them will discover that the stone is just where it was when the work began. Hume saw this: Kant saw it;[6] since their time, more and more eyes have been cleansed of the films which prevented them from seeing it; until now the weight and number of those who refuse to be the prey of verbal mystifications has begun to tell in practical life.

It was inevitable that a conflict should arise between Agnosticism and Theology; or rather, I ought to say, between Agnosticism and Ecclesiasticism. For Theology, the science, is one thing; and Ecclesiasticism, the championship of a foregone conclusion as to the truth of a particular form of Theology, is another. With scientific Theology, Agnosticism has no quarrel. On the contrary, the Agnostic, knowing too well the influence of prejudice and idiosyncrasy, even on those who desire most earnestly to be impartial, can wish for nothing more urgently than that the scientific theologian should not only be at perfect liberty to thresh out the matter in his own fashion; but that he should, if he can, find flaws in the Agnostic position; and, even if demonstration is not to be had, that he should put, in their full force, the grounds of the conclusions he thinks probable. The scientific theologian admits the Agnostic principle, however widely his results may differ from those reached by the majority of Agnostics.

3. Compare Shakespeare's *Hamlet* 1.4.18.
4. The "abode of mist" of Norse mythology.
5. In Greek mythology, the gods punished Sisyphus by making him roll to the top of a hill a great stone that would always roll back to the bottom just before he reached the top.
6. The Scottish philosopher David Hume (1711–

1776), the author of *Dialogues Concerning Natural Religion* (1779), and the German philosopher Immanuel Kant (1724–1804), the author of *Religion within the Limits of Reason Alone* (1793), agreed that certain questions were unanswerable.

But, as between Agnosticism and Ecclesiasticism, or, as our neighbors across the Channel call it, Clericalism,[7] there can be neither peace nor truce. The Cleric[8] asserts that it is morally wrong not to believe certain propositions, whatever the results of a strict scientific investigation of the evidence of these propositions. He tells us "that religious error is, in itself, of an immoral nature."[9] He declares that he has prejudged certain conclusions, and looks upon those who show cause for arrest of judgment as emissaries of Satan. It necessarily follows that, for him, the attainment of faith, not the ascertainment of truth, is the highest aim of mental life. And, on careful analysis of the nature of this faith, it will too often be found to be, not the mystic process of unity with the Divine, understood by the religious enthusiast; but that which the candid simplicity of a Sunday scholar once defined it to be. "Faith," said this unconscious plagiarist of Tertullian, "is the power of saying you believe things which are incredible."[1]

Now I, and many other Agnostics, believe that faith, in this sense, is an abomination; and though we do not indulge in the luxury of self-righteousness so far as to call those who are not of our way of thinking hard names, we do feel that the disagreement between ourselves and those who hold this doctrine is even more moral than intellectual. It is desirable there should be an end of any mistakes on this topic. If our clerical opponents were clearly aware of the real state of the case, there would be an end of the curious delusion, which often appears between the lines of their writings, that those whom they are so fond of calling "Infidels" are people who not only ought to be, but in their hearts are, ashamed of themselves. It would be discourteous to do more than hint the antipodal opposition of this pleasant dream of theirs to facts.

The clerics and their lay allies commonly tell us that if we refuse to admit that there is good ground for expressing definite convictions about certain topics, the bonds of human society will dissolve and mankind lapse into savagery. There are several answers to this assertion. One is that the bonds of human society were formed without the aid of their theology; and, in the opinion of not a few competent judges, have been weakened rather than strengthened by a good deal of it. Greek science, Greek art, the ethics of old Israel, the social organization of old Rome, contrived to come into being, without the help of anyone who believed in a single distinctive article of the simplest of the Christian creeds. The science, the art, the jurisprudence, the chief political and social theories, of the modern world have grown out of those of Greece and Rome—not by favor of, but in the teeth of, the fundamental teachings of early Christianity, to which science, art, and any serious occupation with the things of this world, were alike despicable.

Again, all that is best in the ethics of the modern world, in so far as it has not grown out of Greek thought, or Barbarian manhood, is the direct development of the ethics of old Israel. There is no code of legislation, ancient or

7. In France—"across the [English] Channel"— *cléricalisme* meant excessive influence of the Church on government. For Huxley, the English equivalent means unwelcome Church influence more generally.
8. Huxley refers to John Henry Newman (see p. 526).

9. Newman, *Essay on the Development of Christian Doctrine,* chapter 6, section 2.
1. The Church father Tertullian (see p. 210) was often credited with the actually unattested saying *Credo quia absurdum,* "I believe it because it is absurd."

modern, at once so just and so merciful, so tender to the weak and poor, as the Jewish law; and, if the Gospels are to be trusted, Jesus of Nazareth himself declared that he taught nothing but that which lay implicitly, or explicitly, in the religious and ethical system of his people.

> And the scribe said unto him, Of a truth, Teacher, thou hast well said that he is one; and there is none other but he and to love him with all the heart, and with all the understanding, and with all the strength, and to love his neighbour as himself, is much more than all whole burnt offerings and sacrifices. (Mark 12:32–33)

Here is the briefest of summaries of the teaching of the prophets of Israel of the eighth century; does the Teacher, whose doctrine is thus set forth in his presence, repudiate the exposition? Nay; we are told, on the contrary, that Jesus saw that he "answered discreetly," and replied, "Thou are not far from the kingdom of God."

So that I think that even if the creeds, from the so-called "Apostles'" to the so-called "Athanasian,"[2] were swept into oblivion; and even if the human race should arrive at the conclusion that, whether a bishop washes a cup or leaves it unwashed, is not a matter of the least consequence, it will get on very well. The causes which have led to the development of morality in mankind, which have guided or impelled us all the way from the savage to the civilized state, will not cease to operate because a number of ecclesiastical hypotheses turn out to be baseless. And, even if the absurd notion that morality is more the child of speculation than of practical necessity and inherited instinct, had any foundation; if all the world is going to thieve, murder, and otherwise misconduct itself as soon as it discovers that certain portions of ancient history are mythical; what is the relevance of such arguments to any one who holds by the Agnostic principle?

Surely, the attempt to cast out Beelzebub by the aid of Beelzebub[3] is a hopeful procedure as compared to that of preserving morality by the aid of immorality. For I suppose it is admitted that an Agnostic may be perfectly sincere, may be competent, and may have studied the question at issue with as much care as his clerical opponents. But, if the Agnostic really believes what he says, the "dreadful consequence" argufier (consistently, I admit, with his own principles) virtually asks him to abstain from telling the truth, or to say what he believes to be untrue, because of the supposed injurious consequences to morality. "Beloved brethren, that we may be spotlessly moral, before all things let us lie," is the sum total of many an exhortation addressed to the "Infidel." * * *

I trust that I have now made amends for any ambiguity, or want of fullness, in my previous exposition of that which I hold to be the essence of the Agnostic doctrine. Henceforward, I might hope to hear no more of the assertion that we are necessarily Materialists, Idealists, Atheists, Theists, or any other -ists, if experience had led me to think that the proved falsity

---

2. Athanasius of Alexandria (ca. 298–ca. 373) was the author of a widely used early Church creed that had, however, no official status. The anonymous Apostles' Creed is attested much later, but may have been in use long before its first attestation. For other, more definitive early creeds, see p. 207.

3. In the New Testament, one name for a devil. Jesus was accused of casting out demons by the power of this demon; see Luke 11:15.

of a statement was any guarantee against its repetition. And those who appreciate the nature of our position will see, at once, that when Ecclesiasticism declares that we ought to believe this, that, and the other, and are very wicked if we don't, it is impossible for us to give any answer but this: We have not the slightest objection to believe anything you like, if you will give us good grounds for belief; but, if you cannot, we must respectfully refuse, even if that refusal should wreck morality and insure our own damnation several times over. We are quite content to leave that to the decision of the future. The course of the past has impressed us with the firm conviction that no good ever comes of falsehood, and we feel warranted in refusing even to experiment in that direction. * * *

MATTHEW ARNOLD
1822–1888

DOVER BEACH

Matthew Arnold was born in Laleham-on-Thames, England, and died in Liverpool. In 1851, he married and began a thirty-five-year career as an inspector of schools. Arnold was elected professor of poetry at Oxford University in 1857, and he held that part-time position for ten years, after which he published only prose, such as critical essays on aesthetics and culture. His volume *New Poems* (1867) included "Dover Beach," which was written around 1851 and is considered the classic expression of the erosion of faith in the face of late-modern doubt. The poem's speaker draws a thematic thread from the ancient Greek playwright Sophocles looking at the Aegean Sea to the medieval "Sea of Faith" to himself in the nineteenth century.

PRONOUNCING GLOSSARY

Aegean: *ay-gee´-un*   Sophocles: *so´-foh-klees*

DOVER BEACH

The sea is calm tonight.
The tide is full, the moon lies fair
Upon the straits—on the French coast the light
Gleams and is gone; the cliffs of England stand,
Glimmering and vast, out in the tranquil bay.   5
Come to the window, sweet is the night air!
Only, from the long line of spray
Where the sea meets the moon-blanched land,
Listen! you hear the grating roar
Of pebbles which the waves draw back, and fling,   10
At their return, up the high strand,

Begin, and cease, and then again begin,
With tremulous cadence slow, and bring
The eternal note of sadness in.

Sophocles long ago   15
Heard it on the Aegean, and it brought
Into his mind the turbid ebb and flow
Of human misery;[1] we
Find also in the sound a thought,
Hearing it by this distant northern sea.   20

The Sea of Faith
Was once, too, at the full, and round earth's shore
Lay like the folds of a bright girdle furled.
But now I only hear
Its melancholy, long, withdrawing roar,   25
Retreating, to the breath
Of the night wind, down the vast edges drear
And naked shingles of the world.

Ah, love, let us be true
To one another! for the world, which seems   30
To lie before us like a land of dreams,
So various, so beautiful, so new,
Hath really neither joy, nor love, nor light,
Nor certitude, nor peace, nor help for pain;
And we are here as on a darkling plain   35
Swept with confused alarms of struggle and flight,
Where ignorant armies clash by night.

1. An allusion to Sophocles' *Antigone*, lines 585–91.

EMILY DICKINSON
1830–1886

[HE FUMBLES AT YOUR SOUL] *AND* [SOME KEEP
THE SABBATH GOING TO CHURCH—]

Emily Dickinson was born into a financially secure, politically and educationally
ambitious, and religiously engaged family in Amherst, Massachusetts. Her father, a
Calvinist politically prominent in the town, cofounded Amherst College as an institution dedicated to reinvigorating the conservative Calvinist tradition against Unitarian
innovations then spreading from Harvard University and elsewhere in the Boston
area. Unitarianism, which began as a school of theology and became an organized
American Church in the late eighteenth century, rejected belief in both the Trinity
(and therefore in the divinity of Jesus) and original sin (and therefore in inherited,
incorrigible sinfulness).

Original sin was a familiar feature of Calvinism. Calvinists in the United States, however, under the influence of Methodism, had begun to speak more often of faith and of the intense, interior conviction that, thanks to one's faith, one's salvation was assured. The Second Great Awakening sought to kindle this consoling experience in the thousands who gathered at the Awakening's revival meetings in the first half of the nineteenth century. In 1845, the Second Great Awakening took hold of Amherst. While many of her friends and classmates underwent the transformative experience, which culminated in a cathartic confession of faith, Dickinson was deeply moved, but held back. Indeed, that year she began to retreat from formal religious involvement. After 1852, she all but never attended church services.

While rarely leaving Amherst and, late in life, rarely leaving her home, Dickinson actively followed literary, intellectual, and social developments in Europe. She was well aware of the Unitarian intellectual ferment at Harvard and eagerly read the works of Henry David Thoreau, Ralph Waldo Emerson, and other American writers of their generation. She might be called tacitly Unitarian, for in her poetry she refers frequently to God and seldom to Jesus. But while Dickinson engages with the subject matter of Christianity, Christianity is not Dickinson's principal subject. If Matthew Arnold (see p. 551) is the canonical poet of doubt and Gerard Manley Hopkins (see p. 554) is the canonical poet of faith, Dickinson is a poet of both at once—the soft but subtle voice of quandary and of multiple alternatives entertained without resolution. She wrote the following two poems around the 1860s, leaving them untitled, as was her custom.

[HE FUMBLES AT YOUR SOUL]

He fumbles at your Soul
As Players at the Keys
Before they drop full Music on—
He stuns you by degrees—
Prepares your brittle Nature   5
For the Ethereal Blow
By fainter Hammers[1]—further heard—
Then nearer—Then so slow
Your Breath has time to straighten—
Your Brain—to bubble Cool—   10
Deals—One—imperial—Thunderbolt—
That scalps your naked Soul—

When Winds take Forests in their Paws—
The Universe—is still—

[SOME KEEP THE SABBATH GOING TO CHURCH—]

Some keep the Sabbath going to Church—
I keep it, staying at Home—

---

1. The keys of a piano activate felt hammers that strike metal cords. Dickinson owned and played a fine piano.

With a Bobolink for a Chorister—
And an Orchard, for a Dome—

Some keep the Sabbath in Surplice—   5
I just wear my Wings—
And instead of tolling the Bell, for Church,
Our little Sexton—sings.

God preaches, a noted Clergyman—
And the sermon is never long,   10
So instead of getting to Heaven, at last—
I'm going, all along.

GERARD MANLEY HOPKINS
1844–1889

THE WINDHOVER

Gerard Manley Hopkins was born in Stratford, Essex, England. In 1866, he felt the urge to convert from Anglicanism to Roman Catholicism, and he did so under the guidance of Cardinal John Henry Newman (see p. 526). In 1877, he was ordained as a Jesuit priest. After his ordination, Hopkins served as a parish priest in London, Liverpool, Glasgow, and other places, before being appointed chair of Greek and Latin at University College, Dublin, in 1884. He had an enormous workload and died of typhoid, probably exacerbated by exhaustion, five years later.

From 1868 until 1875, Hopkins wrote no poetry, convinced that it interfered with his religious practice. Church authorities convinced him to resume, but most of Hopkins's poetry remained unpublished during his lifetime; his work caused a sensation when it was brought to the public's attention in the early twentieth century. He is now considered one of the greatest Victorian poets and one of England's most gifted writers of sonnets. The following sonnet, written in 1877, exemplifies both Romantic poetry and Romantic Christianity. The speaker exults in the sheer natural "mastery" of a windhover, a small falcon named for its way of hovering, seemingly motionless, on the wind. Here, the windhover rides the mighty wind as a bold prince ("dauphin") or knight ("chevalier") might ride a great stallion. But while nature is typically the final destination for thought in Romantic poetry, here the thought extends "To Christ our Lord." Christ, too, was a prince, the son of the greatest king of all, and he, too, mastered great powers. The speaker's ecstatic "O my chevalier!" has a double address.

PRONOUNCING GLOSSARY

chevalier: *sheh-vah-leer´*   dauphin: *daw´-fin*

THE WINDHOVER

To Christ our Lord

I caught this morning morning's minion,[1] king-
   dom of daylight's dauphin, dapple-dawn-drawn Falcon, in his riding
   Of the rolling level underneath him steady air, and striding
High there, how he rung upon the rein of a wimpling[2] wing
In his ecstasy! then off, off forth on swing,   5
   As a skate's heel sweeps smooth on a bow-bend: the hurl and gliding
   Rebuffed the big wind. My heart in hiding
Stirred for a bird,—the achieve of, the mastery of the thing!

Brute beauty and valour and act, oh, air, pride, plume, here
   Buckle![3] AND the fire that breaks from thee then, a billion   10
Times told lovelier, more dangerous, O my chevalier!

   No wonder of it: shéer plód makes plough down sillion[4]
Shine, and blue-bleak embers, ah my dear,
   Fall, gall themselves,[5] and gash gold-vermilion.

1. Favorite.
2. Ruffling. "Rung": circled.
3. This verb may be a command, an entreaty, an exhortation, or a statement of fact; it means prepare for action, fasten together, collapse.
4. The moist, sometimes iridescent ridge between freshly ploughed furrows.
5. Break themselves open.

DAVID LIVINGSTONE
1813–1873

FROM MISSIONARY TRAVELS AND RESEARCHES IN SOUTH AFRICA

In the popular imagination, David Livingstone's life has been reduced to a one-liner: "Dr. Livingstone, I presume?" This apocryphal question was supposedly uttered in October 1871 by the Welsh-American journalist Henry Morton Stanley (1841–1904), who did actually meet Livingstone near Lake Tanganyika, in what is now Tanzania. By that time, Livingstone, a Scottish-born Congregationalist missionary-turned-explorer, had become an international celebrity, an iconic figure, mostly thanks to his book *Missionary Travels and Researches in South Africa* (1857). He had also not been heard from for six years.

Livingstone's career illustrates many facets and ironies of the nineteenth-century Christian missions. From boyhood to his mid-twenties, Livingstone did backbreaking work in cotton mills. After earning degrees in medicine and theology, he undertook to evangelize and map central and southern Africa, in the process enduring great privations and pains (among them, once being mauled by a lion). One of the many members of his expeditionary parties who did not return was his wife, Mary, who died of malaria during their 1858–64 exploration of the Zambezi River. Brave, stalwart, sincere, and fair-minded, Livingstone was the first European to see (and name) Victoria Falls, between southwest Zambia and northwest Zimbabwe, and one of the first Europeans to cross southern Africa from the Atlantic to the Indian Ocean. However, Livingstone's journeys often came to naught, as when he failed to "open up" the Zambezi or to find the source of the Nile. Although he vehemently protested the slave trade (which Britain had banned in 1807), his geographical discoveries and the publicity they attracted helped promote European colonialism in Africa. His heart was, fittingly, buried in Zambia.

PRONOUNCING GLOSSARY

Bakuena: *bah-kweh´-nah*

Bakwains: *bah-kwainz´*

Chonuane: *choh-nwah´-nay*

Kolobeng: *koh´-loh-beng*

Kuruman: *koo´-roo-mahn*

Mabotsa: *mah-boht´-sah*

Sechele: *say-chay´-leh*

Shokuane: *shoh-kwah´-nay*

FROM MISSIONARY TRAVELS AND RESEARCHES IN SOUTH AFRICA

[Livingstone Makes His First Convert]

From 1840 to 1845 I was employed in preparatory labours, and associated with other missionaries at Kuruman[1] and Mabotsa. From 1845 to 1849 I worked at Chonuane and Kolobeng, aided only by Mrs. Livingstone and two native teachers. I attached myself to the tribe called Bakuena, or Bakwains,[2] the chief of which, named Sechele, was then living with his subjects at a place called Shokuane. I was from the first struck by his intelligence, and by the especial manner in which we felt drawn to each other. * * *

* * *

On the first occasion in which I ever attempted to hold a public religious service, Sechele remarked that it was the custom of his nation to put questions when any new subject was brought before them. He then inquired if my forefathers knew of a future judgment. I replied in the affirmative, and began to describe the scene of the "great white throne, and Him who shall sit on it, from whose face the heaven and earth shall flee away," &c. "You startle me," he replied; "these words make all my bones to shake; I have no more strength in me: but my forefathers were living at the same time yours were, and how is it that they did not send them word about these terrible things sooner? They all passed away into darkness without knowing whither they were going." I explained the geographical barriers in the North, and the gradual spread of knowledge from the South, to which we first had access by means of ships; adding my belief that, as Christ had declared, the whole world would be enlightened by the Gospel. Pointing to the great Kalahári desert,[3] he replied, "You never can cross that country to the tribes beyond;

---

1. A town in what is now the Northern Cape province of the Republic of South Africa. Note that some of the place-names mentioned in Livingstone's account cannot be easily identified today.
2. A tribe of the Tswana people. Though many ethnic Tswana live in South Africa, Botswana is named after them. Livingstone worked along what is now part of the border between the two countries, partly coinciding with the Limpopo River.
3. Located largely in Botswana.

it is utterly impossible even for us black men, except in certain seasons, when more than the usual supply of rain falls, and an extraordinary growth of water-melons follows."

As soon as he had an opportunity of learning, he set himself to read with such close application that, from being comparatively thin, the effect of being addicted to the chase, he became corpulent from want of exercise. He acquired the alphabet on the first day of my residence at Chonuane, and I never went into the town but I was pressed to hear him read some chapters of the Bible. Isaiah was a great favourite with him; and he was wont to exclaim, "He was a fine man, that Isaiah; he knew how to speak."

He seconded my anxiety that his subjects should become converts to Christianity, and said, "Do you imagine these people will ever believe by your merely talking to them? I can make them do nothing except by thrashing them; and if you like, I shall call my head-men, and with our whips of rhinoceros-hide we will soon make them all believe together." The idea of using persuasion to subjects, whose opinion he would not have condescended to ask on any other matter, was especially surprising to him. He considered that they ought to be happy to embrace Christianity at his command. During the space of two years and a half he continued to profess to his people his full conviction of its truth, and acted uprightly in all the relations of life. He felt the difficulties of his situation, and often said, "O, I wish you had come to this country before I was entangled in the meshes of our customs!" In fact, he could not get rid of his superfluous wives without appearing to be ungrateful to their parents, who had done so much for him in his adversity.

In the hope of inducing others to accept his new faith, he asked me to have family worship in his house. This I did, and by-and-by I was surprised to hear how well he conducted the prayer in his own simple and beautiful style, for he was a thorough master of his language. At this time we were suffering from the effects of a drought, which was ascribed by the natives to Christianity, and none except his family, whom he ordered to attend, came near his meeting. "In former times," said he, "when a chief was fond of hunting, all his people got dogs and became fond of hunting too. If he was fond of dancing or music, all showed a liking to those amusements too. If the chief loved beer, they all rejoiced in strong drink. But in this case it is different. I love the Word of God, and not one of my brethren will join me."

He continued to make a consistent profession for about three years. Perceiving the difficulties of his case, and feeling compassion for the poor women, who were by far the best of our scholars, I had no desire that he should be in a hurry to make a full profession by baptism, and put away all his wives but one. His principal wife, too, was the most unlikely person in the tribe to partake his views. I have seen him again and again send her out of church to put on her gown, and she walked away with her lips shot out, the very picture of unutterable disgust at his new-fangled notions.

When he at last applied for baptism, I asked him how, being acquainted with the Bible, he thought he ought to act. He went home, and gave each of his supernumerary wives new clothing, together with all the goods they had been accustomed to keep in their huts for him. He then sent them to their parents with an intimation that he had no fault to find with them, but that he wished to follow the will of God. When he and his children were baptized, great numbers came to see the ceremony. Some thought, from a stupid story which had been circulated by the enemies to Christianity in the south, that the converts would be made to drink an infusion of "dead men's brains," and were astonished to find that only water was used. Seeing several old men in tears during the service, I afterwards asked them the cause of their weeping. They were crying to see their father, as the Scotch remark of a case of suicide, "so far left to himself." They seemed to think that I had thrown the glamour[4] over him and that he had become mine. All the friends of the divorced wives now became the opponents of our religion. The attendance at school and church dwindled down to very few besides the family of the chief. They all continued to treat us with respectful kindness, but to Sechele himself they uttered things which, had they ventured on in former times, would, as he often remarked, have cost them their lives.

I pass from the chief to give a rapid sketch of our dealing with his people, the Bakuena, or Bakwains. When first we went to reside at Chonuane about £1 worth of goods were given for a small piece of land sufficient for a garden. This purchase seemed strange to a tribe with whom the idea of buying land was entirely new; but we explained to them that we wished to avoid any cause of future dispute when ground had become more valuable. They readily acquiesced, and agreed that a similar piece should be allotted to any other missionary, at any other place to which the tribe might remove.

In our relations with this people we exercised no authority whatever. Our control depended entirely on persuasion; and, having taught them by kind conversation as well as by public instruction, I expected them to do what their own sense of right and wrong dictated. Five instances are known to me in which by our influence on public opinion war was prevented; and where, in individual cases, we failed to do good, the people at least behaved no worse than before. In general they were slow, like all the African people, in coming to a decision on religious subjects; but in questions affecting their worldly affairs they were keenly alive to their own interests. They were stupid in matters which had not come within the sphere of their observation, but in other things they showed more intelligence than our own uneducated peasantry. They are knowing in cattle, sheep, and goats, and can tell exactly the kind of pasturage suited to each. They distinguish with equal judgment the varieties of soil which are best suited to different kinds of grain. They are familiar with the habits of wild animals, and are well up in the maxims which embody their ideas of political wisdom.

During the first year of our residence at Chonuane we were visited by one of those droughts which occur from time to time in even the most favoured districts of Africa. The belief in the power of rain-making is one of the most deeply-rooted articles of faith in this country. The chief Sechele was himself a noted rain-doctor, and he often assured me that he found it more difficult to give up this superstition than anything else which Christianity required him to abjure. I pointed out to him that the only way to water the gardens was to select some never-failing river, make a canal, and irrigate the adjacent lands. The whole tribe moved accordingly to the Kolobeng, a

---

4. An archaic synonym for enchantment. Sechele's people think Livingstone's enchantment has driven their leader mad.

stream about forty miles distant. The Bakwains made the canal and dam in exchange for my labour in assisting to build a square house for their chief. They also erected their school under my superintendence. Our house at the river Kolobeng, which gave a name to the settlement, was the third I had reared with my own hands. A native smith taught me to weld iron; and having acquired some further information in this art as well as in carpentering and gardening * * *, I was becoming handy at most mechanical employments in addition to medicine and preaching. My wife could make candles, soap, and clothes; and thus we had nearly attained to the indispensable accomplishments of a missionary family in Central Africa—the husband to be a jack-of-all-trades without doors, and the wife a maid-of-all-work within.

ALBERT SCHWEITZER
1875–1965

FROM CHRISTIANITY AND THE RELIGIONS OF THE WORLD

Albert Schweitzer was born in Kaysersberg, a city in German-occupied Alsace-Lorraine, and died in Lambaréné, Gabon, on the west coast of Central Africa. After groundbreaking work as a theologian and as an organist-musicologist (he was a recognized expert on J. S. Bach), he went through a seven-year course of medical studies. In fact, Schweitzer's New Testament studies had led him to turn from religious teaching to missionary work. In 1913, as a medical doctor, Schweitzer headed off to a remote site in what was then French Equatorial Africa, where he spent much of the rest of his life. He won the Nobel Peace Prize in 1952.

In his lecture "Christianity and the Religions of the World," one of a series he delivered in February 1922, Schweitzer critiques ideas of human action and the perfectibility of the world. Modern Protestants, he explains, often have the mistaken notion that Jesus' Kingdom of God is an ethical utopia, made better by personal human striving. But for Jesus, human efforts are not pragmatic steps toward a more perfect world. Rather, the secular world is a more or less lost cause, hopelessly sinful. Christians thus need to strive for the good out of "inward necessity," by surrendering to God's absolute moral demands and not seeking measurable progress.

Jesus, at once pessimistic and optimistic (see the headnote for G. K. Chesterton, p. 540), believed that soon, at Jesus' Second Coming, God would intervene and transform the world (see Matthew 10:23, 16:28, and 24:34). "Soon" is relative, of course. For Schweitzer, the "interim ethic" that Jesus taught—how to conduct oneself in the brief interval between Jesus' lifetime and the coming "last days" (a Gospel phrase meaning the end of the world, just before judgment)—was inadequate for the twentieth century. World War I (1914–18), "a time of appalling and meaningless events," had just illustrated that history was going nowhere fast; and Christianity, however noble it was, could no longer be "a formula for explaining everything." The Christian had to cling to Christ, but the grand cosmic certainty of previous generations was gone forever.

FROM CHRISTIANITY AND THE RELIGIONS OF THE WORLD

All profound religion is mystical. To be freed from the world by being in God: that is the longing we have within us, so long as we do not numb ourselves in thoughtlessness. A union with God, however, which is realized through the intellectual act of "knowing," as conceived in the Eastern religions, must always remain a dead spirituality. It does not effect a re-birth, in God, into living spirituality. Living spirituality, real redemption from the world, cannot come but from that union with God which is ethically determined. The religions of the East are logical mysticism, Christianity alone is ethical mysticism.

Thus we go on our way through the world, not troubled about knowledge, but committing to God what we hope for, for ourselves and the world, and possessing all in all through being apprehended by the living, ethical God.

The first Christians expected the Kingdom of God to come speedily, as a complete transformation of the natural world into a perfect one. We have become more moderate in our expectations. We no longer think of the Kingdom of God as extending over the universe. We limit it to mankind and look forward to it as to the miracle of God's spirit bringing all human spirits into subjection.

The generations preceding ours wanted to believe, and were able to believe, that the miracle would be performed in a steady, slow development. We, however, having lived through, and still living in, a time of appalling and meaningless events, feel as if a terrible tidal wave had flung us back, far away from the harbour of the Kingdom of God, towards which we now have to start out afresh, rowing hard against storm and tide, without being certain of really making headway. Thus we, too, like the early Christians, are taught by God the awful discipline of the word: "My thoughts are not your thoughts."[1] He sets before us the difficult task of being faithful to the Kingdom of God as those who do not see and yet believe. We are able to accomplish that task, if we have been apprehended by Him.

When you preach the Gospel, beware of preaching it as the religion which explains everything. I suppose that in England, as on the Continent, thousands and thousands of men have despaired of Christianity, because they have seen and experienced the atrocities of the War. Confronted with the inexplicable, the religion in which they believed to have an explanation for every thing has collapsed.

For ten years, before I left for Africa, I prepared boys in the parish of St. Nicolai, in Strasbourg, for confirmation. After the war some of them came to see me and thanked me for having taught them so definitely that religion was not a formula for explaining everything. They said it had been that teaching which had kept them from discarding Christianity, whereas so many others in the trenches discarded it, not being prepared to meet the inexplicable.

When you preach, you must lead men out of the desire to know everything to the knowledge of the one thing that is needful, to the desire to be

TRANSLATED BY Johanna Powers.

1. Isaiah 55:8.

in God, and thus no more to conform to the world but to rise above all mysteries as those who are redeemed from the world. "If only I have Thee, I care nothing for heaven and earth."[2] "All things work together for good to them that love God."[3] Point men to these words as to the peaks of Ararat,[4] where they may take refuge when the flood of the inexplicable overwhelms all around.

2. Psalm 72:35 (as translated by Martin Luther; on Luther, see p. 399).

3. Romans 8:28.

4. Mountain in eastern Turkey; see Genesis 8:4.

The Twentieth Century

1914–2001

SIEGE AND SURVIVAL THROUGH A CENTURY OF WORLD WAR

The twentieth century was exceptionally violent. Of the many wars that occurred during its span, three stand out for their importance to Christianity: World War I (1914–18), World War II (1939–45), and the Cold War (the latter half of the century).

World War I yielded complex consequences for Christianity. Because of the massive casualties of Europe's first industrialized war, citizens of many nations repudiated the fusions of nationality and Christianity that had hardened over the course of the nineteenth century. Some who did so indicted the state more than they did the Church. Consider, for example, the English poet Wilfred Owen's "The Parable of the Old Man and the Young," included in this section. Others drew the lesson that the Church needed to reconstitute itself and reassert its spiritual autonomy. Consider the Anglo-American poet T. S. Eliot's "Journey of the Magi," also included here, which evokes Eliot's experience as an alienated ex-Christian returning to the faith.

The most extreme result of World War I was the rise, in Europe, of a fearsomely self-confident

This photograph shows Dresden, Germany, after it was firebombed by Britain and the United States weeks before the end of World War II in Europe. Ninety percent of the city center was destroyed. Many thousands of people burned to death.

and single-minded movement, Fascism, hungering for a deeper and more militarized absorption of all aspects of national life, Christianity included, into an apotheosized nation-state. The appeal of the Fascist movement was strongest in Germany, the country that had lost most in the war, though Fascist regimes also came to power in Italy and Spain. The most extreme form of twentieth-century Fascism was German National Socialism, usually called Nazism. The Swiss theologian Karl Barth reacted sharply against the absorption, envisioned by Nazism, of Christian identity by German national identity. Similarly, the theologians Dietrich Bonhoeffer and Reinhold Niebuhr—German and American, respectively—were prepared to take up arms to halt the colossal crimes of this fanatic hypernationalism.

The aftermath of World War II, like that of World War I, brought mixed consequences for Christians. Many Christians and non-Christians indicted the Churches for complicity with or inadequate resistance to moral outrage, especially with regard to the Nazis' attempted genocide of the Jews. Many Christians and non-Christians likewise viewed secular humanism as vacuous, discredited for failing to inspire moral decision or concerted action. Still, during the first postwar years, church attendance was strong. Among the previously disengaged who underwent conversions to or reengagements with Christianity were the English poet W. H. Auden, the American memoirist (and later monk) Thomas Merton, and the English writer C. S. Lewis. After the watershed 1960s, however, church attendance and Church affiliation steadily declined in Europe and North America.

For Christianity, the most consequential twentieth-century war might have been the Cold War, which effectively began with the Russian Revolution and the ensuing Russian Civil War (1917–22) and ended with the symbolic moments when Karol Wojtiła became the first Polish pope (John Paul II, 1978) and when the Berlin Wall was torn down (1989). Before the Communist (Russian) Revolution, Russian Orthodox Christianity had been the established religion of the Russian Empire, but other forms of Christianity as well as Judaism and Islam had been practiced throughout the Russian territories. After the revolution, the Communist ideology of the newly established Soviet Union—equivalently, its religion—was atheism imposed more aggressively than Russian Orthodoxy ever had been. After World War II, the expansion of Soviet domination into eastern and central Europe imposed the same regime on new Christian populations. Systematic Soviet hostility to all forms of Christianity eventually returned a quarter of the world's Christian population to a form of ongoing underground or semi-underground practice unseen in the West since the first centuries of the Christian Era.

The 1949 Chinese Revolution established atheism of the same sort in China, with comparable consequences for China's Christian minority. Similar regimes were established in North Korea, North Vietnam (and, after 1975, all of Vietnam), and Cuba, with similar consequences for their relatively larger Christian minorities (or, in Cuba, the Christian majority). Other instances could be added to this abbreviated list. Near the end of the century, however, central and eastern Europe, beginning with Poland, broke free from Soviet control. The Soviet Union dissolved in 1991, as federated Soviet republics declared their independence. Churches breathed more easily and operated more openly, but it is hard to measure the consequences of decades of actively propagated atheism. Christians "behind the Iron

Curtain"—cut off from the rest of the Christian world; generally barred on political grounds from creating or maintaining libraries, institutions of learning, or publishing houses—had written little that made lasting marks on the world Christian mind. In China, a sharp turn toward full engagement with world capitalism brought with it a relative liberalization in the state's treatment of the officially recognized religions, alongside active persecution of those not recognized; the state recognized Protestantism and Catholicism as separate religions, but it carefully policed both.

The Cold War did not come to a clear conclusion. Instead, a so-called Cold Peace ensued. During this relatively peaceful period, racial, ethnic, or colonized indigenous populations long submerged in the titanic military struggles of the first half of the century began to make their presences felt and win consideration for their human rights. In this process, there was at times a degree of continuity with a strand of pre–World War I Christian culture—namely, an insistence that social welfare was a responsibility shared by the Church and the state.

To some extent, the German theologian Paul Tillich offered a theological rationale for this broad movement of Christian activism. Four women—the Americans Jane Addams and Dorothy Day, the Russian Mother Maria Skobtsova, and the Guatemalan Rigoberta Menchú—were among those determinedly carrying forward this element in Christian tradition.

Of all submerged groups around the world, none was quite so submerged as black, sub-Saharan Africans and their descendents in the Americas. Having been preyed upon for centuries by Arab and Euro-American slave-traders, these people were still waiting to assume full membership in the emerging world community. Two black Christian churchmen played major leadership roles in beginning a transformation that has helped erode institutionalized discrimination: In the United States, the Reverend Dr. Martin Luther King, Jr., was a pivotal figure in the ending of segregation and discrimination. In South Africa, Bishop Desmond Tutu was instrumental in ending apartheid. The United States and South Africa had been established at about the same time by émigré European Protestants imposing their rule upon native populations in other continents. Rather than simply as struggles for racial justice, then, both the antisegregation campaign in the United States and the antiapartheid campaign in South Africa might also be construed as belated postcolonial rebellions.

By the end of the twentieth century, the United States, with a military establishment greater than that of the rest of the industrialized world combined, had divided the entire planet into contiguous American military commands, all officially construed as necessary for national defense. More pervasive still in the everyday lives of literally billions of people around the world was the power of capital. Accumulated wealth, and the power it brought, enabled a kind of internal colonization of nominally independent countries by a small ruling class of their own citizens. It was to this kind of neocolonialism—prevalent especially though not exclusively outside Europe and North America—that the theology of Gustavo Gutiérrez and other exponents of liberation theology, as it came to be called, arrived as a response. For Gutiérrez, like Menchú and other anticolonialist defenders of the rights of oppressed indigenous South Americans, Christianity did not represent an alienation to be overcome. Rather, it was an authentication to be reclaimed from its usurpers.

A different state of psychological and theological affairs obtained in post-colonial Muslim countries, including the de facto Russian colonies that emerged near the end of the century as post-Soviet states. For them, the "international community" brought into existence through the United Nations and other post–World War II cultural and, especially, fiscal institutions created by the victorious, historically Christian powers looked suspiciously Christian and colonial. In other words, this new world order was clearly not designed to Muslim specifications. The result late in the century, especially when governments in Muslim countries were both autocratic and beholden to this new international establishment, was rising tension between Muslims and Christians. By the end of the twentieth century, Christian minorities had sharply diminished in several Muslim-majority Arab countries; large and sometimes restive Muslim minorities resided in every European country as well as in the United States and faced secular as well as Christian prejudice; and violence was prevalent in postcolonial countries, such as Kenya and Nigeria, where large, approximately equal Christian and Muslim populations contended under weak or corrupt central governments.

On September 11, 2001, Al-Qaeda, a nongovernmental, paramilitary syndicate claiming Islamic authorization, launched devastating suicide bombing attacks on the East Coast of the United States. The American response to these attacks was invasion and governmental overthrow in two Muslim-majority countries: Afghanistan and Iraq. Afghanistan had negligibly few Christian citizens; Iraq's ancient Christian minority was largely eliminated by death or flight as an unintended consequence of the American invasion and occupation. At or after each of these flashpoints, intense interreligious debate took place in several forms: Muslims with or against other Muslims; Christians with or against other Christians; Muslims and Christians with or against one another. Yet what promised to be a startling, semipermanent feature of world Christian life in the twenty-first century had been in gestation for decades in the twentieth.

Throughout the twentieth century, technology repeatedly transformed social, religious, military, and scientific practice. In the first half of the century, the English philosopher Bertrand Russell took the view that science had provided a vision of the human future superior to Christianity's and, moreover, that Christianity, or religion in general, had become an obstruction to human welfare. By the end of the century, relations between science and Christianity—between actual scientists and actual Christians—were usually indifferent, sometimes hostile, occasionally quite friendly, and in a few cases, such as that of the French theologian and scientist Pierre Teilhard de Chardin, mystically ecstatic.

In all likelihood, the Christianity of the twentieth century is simply too close to be seen with any real clarity by a viewer in the early twenty-first century. Adequate narrative summary of so many overlapping stories being thus out of the question, this set of twentieth-century selections ends with a trio of poems. In quite a personal way, the postnationalist, post-Fascist, post-Communist, postcapitalist, posthumanist, Christian poet Czeslaw Milosz faced—and survived—the full siege of the twentieth century.

Chronology

THE TWENTIETH CENTURY (1914–2001)

1914–18 World War I, called at the time "The Great War"

1915 Beginning of Armenian genocide, in Turkey

1917 Russian Revolution: Persecution of Christians, especially bishops and clergy, begins under Communism in U.S.S.R.

1925 Scopes "monkey trial" in Dayton, Tennessee, on teaching evolution

1926–29 "Cristero" war in Mexico, between anticlerical government forces and Catholic rebels

1932 Karl Barth begins publication of *Church Dogmatics*

1930s Christian Churches mostly passive as Nazis consolidate power in Germany

1934 Barmen Declaration of Reformed German churchmen against subordination of churches to Nazi regime

1935 Germany passes anti-Semitic "Nuremberg Laws," signaling onset of genocide that eventually kills two-thirds of Europe's nine million Jews by end of World War II

1937 Pope Pius XI publishes encyclical condemning certain features of Nazism; anti-Nazi Dietrich Bonhoeffer publishes *Nachfolge* ("Discipleship"), in Germany

1937–45 World War II, in Europe, Africa, and Asia

1945–91 Cold War

1945 Nag Hammadi library, including texts of "Gnostic Gospels," discovered in Egypt

1946 Discovery of Dead Sea Scrolls

1948 Foundation of World Council of Churches, ecumenical group of 349 Christian Churches

1949 Chinese Civil War ends with establishment of People's Republic of China (Communist China); persecution of religions begins. Evangelist Billy Graham preaches his first major revival meeting, in Los Angeles

1950 Pope Pius XII promulgates dogma of Virgin Mary's Assumption into heaven

1950–53 Korean War

1953 Czeslaw Milosz publishes *The Captive Mind*

1955 CELAM (Latin American Episcopal Conference) founded, in Rio de Janeiro; originally a force promoting liberation theology, the group is taken over by conservative clerics in 1970s

1955–75 Vietnamese War

1962–65 Second Vatican Council

1962–63 United States Supreme Court rules against Bible readings and prayer in public schools

1963 Martin Luther King, Jr., delivers his "I Have a Dream" speech in Washington, D.C.

1965 *Nostra Aetate* (from Vatican II) cancels Catholic charge of deicide against the Jews

1979 Pope John Paul II visits Poland and encourages anticommunist forces

1989 Fall of Berlin Wall

1990 Reunification of Germany

1991 Dissolution of Soviet Union signals end of Cold War

1997 Death of Mother Teresa of Calcutta

2001 Al-Qaeda terrorists attack U.S.; U.S. invades Afghanistan; world Muslim-Christian relations worsen

JANE ADDAMS
1860–1935

FROM A NEW IMPULSE TO AN OLD GOSPEL

The Social Gospel movement, a development within liberal Protestantism, began in Britain in the latter half of the nineteenth century and peaked, at least under that name, in the United States and Canada in the early twentieth century. The movement's adherents believed that modernity and Christianity, properly understood and idealistically implemented, could be fruitfully symbiotic. After all, the Gospel repeatedly stresses the spiritual dignity and material needs of the poor. Western democracy is by definition the rule of all the people, not merely the rich or powerful. Could the Gospel, then, inspire a more perfect democracy?

Such was the optimistic hope, and one of its expressions was the Settlement House movement. This broadly Christian charitable movement was meant to replace the "Lady Bountiful" form of charity, in which the wealthy dropped in on the poor to bestow gifts. Seeking a deeper, more lasting form of engagement, groups of young, unmarried, well-to-do men or women would "settle" in the "foreign" territory of the poor, to provide cultural and educational betterment without an overt religious program.

The first settlement house was established in London in 1884. In the following decades, hundreds of settlement houses were established in England, the United States, and Canada. The North American settlement houses were typically located in communities of impoverished immigrants. Thus the word *settlement* took on a double meaning: Inspired by the Social Gospel, the houses' inhabitants would help the immigrants, often Catholic or Jewish, settle in their new homeland.

Perhaps the most famous of all settlement houses is Hull House, founded in 1889 by the activists Jane Addams and Ellen Gates Starr on Chicago's Near West Side, in the heart of a heavily Italian-immigrant neighborhood. Operating initially in the donated former residence of a real estate investor, Hull House grew steadily to become, by the start of World War I, a complex of thirteen buildings. Among the many consequences of World War I (1914–18), however, was decreased immigration from Europe to the United States. Another was a lessening of the cultural optimism that had fostered the Social Gospel movement.

Hull House was to some extent slowed by its own success, as its initial immigrant clientele acculturated into American life. Later clienteles replaced the first, however, including notably black immigrants from the American South. Hull House lived on through social and demographic changes, finally closing its doors only in 2012. Jane Addams and Ellen Gates Starr's larger achievement was in setting the stage for later, state-sponsored efforts at social welfare as well as for other religiously inspired movements for social change.

Though admired for her work on behalf of the poor, Addams was reviled in her time for campaigning at home and abroad against World War I. In retrospect, many came to view the "Great War" as tragically unnecessary. In 1931, for her charitable work, her antiwar activism, and her equally energetic support of women's suffrage, Addams became the first American woman to win the Nobel Peace Prize.

In the September 1892–February 1893 issue of the magazine *The Forum*, Addams published the following selection. Explaining the "subjective necessity" for Hull House, she presents democracy as a great project that Christianity motivates some people to perfect.

FROM A NEW IMPULSE TO AN OLD GOSPEL

"Hull House, which was Chicago's first Settlement, was established in September, 1889. It represented no association, but was opened by two women, backed by many friends, in the belief that the mere foothold of a house, easily accessible, ample in space, hospitable and tolerant in spirit, situated in the midst of the large foreign colonies which so easily isolate themselves in American cities, would be in itself a serviceable thing for Chicago. It was opened on general Settlement lines, in the conviction that along those lines many educated young people could find the best outlet for a certain sort of unexpressed activity. Hull House is neither a University Settlement nor a College Settlement: it calls itself a Social Settlement, an attempt to make social intercourse express the growing sense of the economic unity of society. It is an attempt to add the social function to democracy. It was opened on the theory that the dependence of classes on each other is reciprocal and that as the social relation is essentially a reciprocal relation, it gave a form of expression that has peculiar value." This I wrote in the *Forum* for October.

I attempt in this paper to treat of the subjective necessity for a Social Settlement, to analyze, as nearly as I can, the motives that underlie a movement which I believe to be based not only on conviction, but on genuine emotion. I have divided the motives which constitute the subjective pressure toward Social Settlements into three great lines: the first contains the desire to make the entire social organism democratic, to extend democracy beyond its political expression; the second is the impulse to share the race life, to bring as much as possible of social energy and the accumulation of civilization to those portions of the race which have little; the third springs from a certain *renaissance* of Christianity, a movement toward its early humanitarian aspects.

*   *   *

The third division of motives which I believe make toward the Settlement is the result of a certain *renaissance* going forward in Christianity. The impulse to share the lives of the poor, the desire to make social service, irrespective of propaganda, express the spirit of Christ, is as old as Christianity itself. We have no proof from the records themselves that the early Roman Christians, who strained their simple art to the point of grotesqueness in their eagerness to record a "good news" on the walls of the catacombs, considered this "good news" a religion. Jesus had imposed no cult nor rites. He had no set of truths labelled "Religious." On the contrary, his doctrine was that all truth was one, that the appropriation of it was freedom. His teaching had no dogma of its own to mark it off from truth and action in general. The very universality of it precluded its being a religion. He himself called it a revelation—a life. These early Roman Christians received the Gospel message, a command to love all men, with a certain joyous simplicity. The image of the Good Shepherd is blithe and gay beyond the gentlest shepherd of Greek mythology; the hart no longer pants, but rushes to the water brooks. The Christians looked for the continuous revelation, but believed what Jesus said, that this revelation to be held and made manifest must be put into terms of action; that action is the only organ man has for receiving and appropriating truth. "If any man will do His will, he shall know of the doctrine."[1]

That Christianity would have to be revealed and embodied in the line of social progress is a corollary to the simple proposition that man's action is found in his social relationships in the way in which he connects with his fellows, that his motives for action are the zeal and affection with which he regards his fellows. By this simple process was created a deep enthusiasm for humanity, which regarded man as at once the organ and object of revelation; and by this process came about that wonderful fellowship, that true democracy of the early Church, that so captivates the imagination. The early Christians were pre-eminently non-resistant. They believed in love as a cosmic force. There was no iconoclasm during the minor peace of the Church.[2] They did not yet denounce, nor tear down temples, nor preach the end of the world. They grew to a mighty number, but it never occurred to them, either in their weakness or in their strength, to regard other men for an instant as their foes or aliens. The spectacle of the Christians loving all men was the most astounding Rome had ever seen. They were eager to sacrifice themselves for the weak, for children and the aged. They identified themselves with slaves and did not avoid the plague.[3] They longed to share the common lot that they might receive the constant revelation. It was a new treasure which the early Christians added to the sum of all treasures, a joy hitherto unknown in the world—the joy of finding the Christ which Beth in each man,[4] but which no man can unfold save in fellowship. A happiness ranging from the heroic to the pastoral enveloped them. They were to possess a revelation as long as life had new meaning to unfold, new action to propose.

I believe that there is a distinct turning among many young men and women toward this simple acceptance of Christ's message. They resent the assumption that Christianity is a set of ideas which belong to the religious consciousness, whatever that may be, that it is a thing to be proclaimed and instituted apart from the social life of the community. They insist that it shall seek a simple and natural expression in the social organism itself. The Settlement movement is only one manifestation of that wider humanitarian movement which throughout Christendom, but pre-eminently in England, is endeavoring to embody itself, not in a sect, but in society itself. Tolstoi has reminded us all very forcibly of Christ's principle of non-resistance.[5] His formulation has been startling and his expression has deviated from the general movement, but there is little doubt that he has many adherents, men and women who are philosophically convinced of the futility of opposition, who believe that evil can be overcome only with good and cannot be opposed by evil. If love is the creative force of the universe, the principle

---

1. John 7:17.
2. "The minor peace of the Church": a phrase sometimes applied to the period after the legalization of Christianity by the Roman emperor Constantine, in the early fourth century, and before its imposition as the official religion of the empire by Emperor Theodosius, later in that century.
3. The early Christians aroused amazement by caring for plague victims rather than shunning them.
4. "The Christ which [be-eth] in each man": the Christ who is in each person. George Fox (1624–

1691), the founder of the Quakers, spoke of an "inner light" that is the "Christ within." The Quakers were prominent in the Social Gospel movement, but Addams appears to allude here rather than quote.
5. Around this time, the Russian novelist, philospher, and mystic Leo Tolstoy (1828–1910) was creating controversy in Russia with pacifist articles that would culminate in his book *The Kingdom of God Is within You*, first published in Germany in 1894.

which binds men together, and by their interdependence on each other makes them human, just so surely is anger the destructive principle of the universe, that which tears down, thrusts men apart, and makes them isolated and brutal.

WILFRED OWEN
1893–1918

THE PARABLE OF THE OLD MAN AND THE YOUNG

The Wars of Religion that had wracked Europe in the first half of the seventeenth century were ended by the Peace of Westphalia, which established not a common religion but a common principle of religion for all the signatories: *Cuius regio, eius religio*—literally, "Whose the rule, his the religion." The meaning of the principle was that the government of a state, however established, would determine the religion of the state. The narrower effect of the principle was the exclusive establishment of different Christian Churches in different European states. The broader effect was the creation over time of the "Westphalian System," by which states generally refrain from intervening in the internal affairs of other states in any regard.

For Christianity, through the eighteenth and nineteenth centuries, the effect of this new European order was mixed. The established Church of a given state would receive significant public support, but its influence would shrink by comparison with the spiritualized influence of the state itself as a new quasi-Church. In a sense, piety was transferred from one account to the other. As men once died nobly for their faith, now they were expected to die nobly for their nation.

Then, in the early twentieth century, Europe went just as savagely to nation-on-nation war as it had gone to religion-on-religion war in the early seventeenth century. And in the aftermath of World War I, a war that no one seemed truly to win, both the confident fusion of nationalism, patriotism, and optimism about the industrial progress that lay ahead and the pride in Western civilization that had characterized the late nineteenth century were as grievously wounded as Christianity had been in the aftermath of the Wars of Religion.

Christianity per se did not benefit from this postwar disillusionment, for in the various European nations Christianity was fused with nationalism to different degrees. The sense was at least blunted, however, that something civilized and superior had replaced Christianity for good.

Few poems capture the postwar, postpatriotic bitterness of European youth better than Wilfred Owen's "The Parable of the Old Man and the Young"—written, significantly, from the nominally winning side. Owen, an English soldier, died in battle at age 25, just a week before the end of the "Great War" (as it was then called). He left behind a small body of work, only some of which is religious. His best-known poem, "Dulce et Decorum Est," indicts the ruling class of Europe by quoting, in its final sentence, a familiar patriotic motto in Latin (Horace, *Odes* 3.2.13):

> If in some smothering dreams you too could pace
> Behind the wagon that we flung him in,
> And watch the white eyes writhing in his face,
> His hanging face, like a devil's sick of sin;

If you could hear, at every jolt, the blood
Come gargling from the froth-corrupted lungs,
Obscene as cancer, bitter as the cud
Of vile, incurable sores on innocent tongues,—
My friend, you would not tell with such high zest
To children ardent for some desperate glory,
The old Lie: Dulce et decorum est
Pro patria mori.

"Sweet and right it is to die for country"? Owen begged scathingly to differ. In "The Parable of the Old Man and the Young," he rewrites the conclusion of Genesis 22, in which Abraham is ordered by God not to sacrifice his son but to sacrifice a ram instead. In the Bible, Abraham obeys. In Owen's rewrite, the "old men" of Europe choose mass human slaughter rather than sacrifice their pride.

THE PARABLE OF THE OLD MAN AND THE YOUNG

So Abram rose, and clave the wood, and went,
And took the fire with him, and a knife.
And as they sojourned both of them together,
Isaac the first-born spake and said, My Father,
Behold the preparations, fire and iron, 5
But where the lamb, for this burnt-offering?
Then Abram bound the youth with belts and straps,
And builded parapets and trenches there,
And stretchèd forth the knife to slay his son.
When lo! an Angel called him out of heaven, 10
Saying, Lay not thy hand upon the lad,
Neither do anything to him, thy son.
Behold! Caught in a thicket by its horns,
A Ram. Offer the Ram of Pride instead.

But the old man would not so, but slew his son, 15
And half the seed of Europe, one by one.

T. S. ELIOT
1888–1965

JOURNEY OF THE MAGI

Thomas Stearns Eliot, the most celebrated and arguably the most influential twentieth-century poet writing in English, occupies a distinct if smaller position in the history of twentieth-century Christianity. Born in St. Louis into a family with deep roots in Unitarianism and New England, Eliot was educated at Harvard University; Oxford University; and the Sorbonne, in Paris. In England, he first taught school, then worked in the British banking industry, and finally became a literature editor at the publishing house Faber and Faber. In 1917, Eliot published his first poetry volume, which included his landmark dramatic monologue "The Love Song of J. Alfred Prufrock." Having made an early mark as something close to the poet laureate of post–World War I disillusionment and despair, Eliot published *The Waste Land* (1922), a monumental construction in verse, in which the title subject seemed to be the West in a state of bleakly ironic, learned but despairing decline. The poem became one of the major texts of modernist literature.

In 1927, Eliot shocked his family by becoming a British subject and his modernist admirers by becoming an Anglo-Catholic—that is, an Anglican drawn aesthetically and theologically toward earlier English Catholic culture. After his conversion, Eliot did not cease to be modern or modernist. But while his existential move was not widely copied, it came to represent the option—among Christians and non-Christians—of refusing or revising modernity as a collective choice. As a religious thinker, Eliot has had little impact in comparison with celebrated theologians of his time. He remains emblematic, however, of a new Christian option: spiritually defecting from the liberal, secular, militarized, industrialized, democratic, scientific, but repeatedly self-destructive consensus that is Western modernity to a recovery and re-espousal of the Christian past.

The poem "Journey of the Magi" (1927) opens with five lines from a Christmas sermon by the Anglican scholar-bishop Lancelot Andrewes (1555–1626), who oversaw the large team of translators that produced the King James Version of the Bible. The King James Version is recognized today no less than in Eliot's day as equaled only by the works of William Shakespeare in its impact on English literature. By building Andrewes into his poem, Eliot thus comments obliquely on the place of English Christianity within English letters. For readers who do not recognize an unattributed quotation from the forgotten Andrewes, "Journey of the Magi" is a poem about a difficult journey to witness a birth that has deeply marked its witness.

The title alludes to a story told in the second chapter of the Gospel of Matthew. Three wise men (*magoi* in Greek; *magi* in Latin), led by a star, journey from a distant unnamed land in the East to give gifts and pay homage to the newborn Jesus as the king of the Jews. Then they simply return home. Years later, how do they feel about their trip, the world, and themselves?

PRONOUNCING GLOSSARY

Magi: *may´-jai* [*ai* rhyming with *rye*]

JOURNEY OF THE MAGI

"A cold coming we had of it,
Just the worst time of the year
For a journey, and such a long journey:
The ways deep and the weather sharp,
The very dead of winter." 5
And the camels galled, sore-footed, refractory,
Lying down in the melting snow.
There were times we regretted
The summer palaces on slopes, the terraces,
And the silken girls bringing sherbet. 10
Then the camel men cursing and grumbling
And running away, and wanting their liquor and women,
And the night fires going out, and the lack of shelters,
And the cities hostile and the towns unfriendly
And the villages dirty and charging high prices: 15
A hard time we had of it.
At the end we preferred to travel all night,
Sleeping in snatches,
With the voices singing in our ears, saying
That this was all folly. 20

Then at dawn we came down to a temperate valley,
Wet, below the snow line, smelling of vegetation,
With a running stream and a water mill beating the darkness,
And three trees on the low sky.
And an old white horse galloped away in the meadow. 25
Then we came to a tavern with vine leaves over the lintel,
Six hands at an open door dicing for pieces of silver,
And feet kicking the empty wine skins.
But there was no information, and so we continued
And arrived at evening, not a moment too soon 30
Finding the place; it was (you may say) satisfactory.

All this was a long time ago, I remember,
And I would do it again, but set down
This set down
This: were we led all that way for 35
Birth or Death? There was a Birth, certainly,
We had evidence and no doubt. I had seen birth and death,
But had thought they were different; this Birth was
Hard and bitter agony for us, like Death, our death.
We returned to our places, these Kingdoms, 40
But no longer at ease here, in the old dispensation,
With an alien people clutching their gods.
I should be glad of another death.

BERTRAND RUSSELL
1872–1970

FROM WHY I AM NOT A CHRISTIAN

Bertrand Arthur William Russell, the Third Earl Russell, was born into a well-to-do aristocratic family in Wales. After graduating from Trinity College, Cambridge University, he taught political and social theory at the London School of Economics, then became a lecturer at Trinity. He made a brilliant early mark in mathematical logic with the three-volume *Principia Mathematica* (1910–13), coauthored with his former teacher Alfred North Whitehead. On the strength of the *Principia* alone, Russell is recognized as one of the founding thinkers of analytic philosophy—the philosophical tradition dominant since his day in Britain and the United States—and a seminal figure in the philosophy of science. Russell was also one of the most prominent public intellectuals of the twentieth century. In 1920, he traveled to Russia; soon after, he lectured in China on philosophy. In 1927, having returned to England, he founded an experimental school, with which he was associated for five years. Before the advent of World War II, Russell moved to the United States, where he taught at various universities before returning to England and Trinity. His voluminous publications—books, pamphlets, and essays—include high-level treatises and popular treatments. In 1950, he received the Nobel Prize in Literature.

Russell wrote until the end of his long life, and his positions changed and evolved over time. Resolutely contrarian; semisocialist in the home country of capitalism; pacifist and imprisoned for it in World War I; imprisoned again for opposing the American intervention in World War II; daringly progressive on matters such as abortion, contraception, extra- and premarital sexual relations, divorce, and homosexuality, Russell—self-described as yearningly religious in his youth—became eloquently antireligious and specifically anti-Christian in his adulthood. For the new and growing constituency of thoughtful people disdainful of Christianity, Russell provided a warmly welcome and enduringly popular voice in his essays "A Free Man's Worship" and "Why I Am Not a Christian."

In the following selection, the conclusion to "Why I Am Not a Christian," Russell argues that Christianity is "the principal enemy of moral progress in the world." He offers an imagined example of Roman Catholic sexual morality yielding emotionally painful, even physically harmful consequences. As sexual mores in cases like this one changed—and they changed radically—during the course of the twentieth century, Christian sexual teaching diverged ever more widely from popular sexual practice. The changing sexual mores may well have contributed, meanwhile, to the popular appeal in the West of Russell's Christianity-as-enemy-of-progress thesis. By the end of the century, however, many Churches found their own convergent paths to his conclusions.

Ultimately, Russell trusted science, and the word *science* as he used it often seemed to mean *scientists*: "Science can teach us, and I think our own hearts can teach us, no longer to look around for imaginary supports, no longer to invent allies in the sky." While emphasizing the personal experience of Romantic faith (see p. 493), Russell added and greatly helped popularize the premise that religion began in early observation of and theorization about the natural world. Religion therefore would or at least should fade away now that science had provided clearly superior observations and theories. Russell implied that science was capable of providing an emotional as well as an intellectual substitute for religion, a new and differently supportive "elder brother." He examined that issue very lightly, however, and for philosophers the science/religion question has remained very nearly where Russell left it.

Erewhon: *air´-eh-whon*

FROM WHY I AM NOT A CHRISTIAN
The Emotional Factor

* * * I do not think that the real reason why people accept religion has anything to do with argumentation. They accept religion on emotional grounds. One is often told that it is a very wrong thing to attack religion, because religion makes men virtuous. So I am told; I have not noticed it. You know, of course, the parody of that argument in Samuel Butler's book, *Erewhon Revisited*.[1] You will remember that in *Erewhon* there is a certain Higgs who arrives in a remote country, and after spending some time there he escapes from that country in a balloon. Twenty years later he comes back to that country and finds a new religion in which he is worshiped under the name of the "Sun Child," and it is said that he ascended into heaven. He finds that the Feast of the Ascension is about to be celebrated, and he hears Professors Hanky and Panky say to each other that they never set eyes on the man Higgs, and they hope they never will; but they are the high priests of the religion of the Sun Child. He is very indignant, and he comes up to them, and he says, "I am going to expose all this humbug and tell the people of Erewhon that it was only I, the man Higgs, and I went up in a balloon." He was told, "You must not do that, because all the morals of this country are bound round this myth, and if they once know that you did not ascend into heaven they will all become wicked"; and so he is persuaded of that and he goes quietly away.

That is the idea—that we should all be wicked if we did not hold to the Christian religion. It seems to me that the people who have held to it have been for the most part extremely wicked. You find this curious fact, that the more intense has been the religion of any period and the more profound has been the dogmatic belief, the greater has been the cruelty and the worse has been the state of affairs. In the so-called ages of faith, when men really did believe the Christian religion in all its completeness, there was the Inquisition, with its tortures;[2] there were millions of unfortunate women burned as witches; and there was every kind of cruelty practiced upon all sorts of people in the name of religion.

You find as you look around the world that every single bit of progress in humane feeling, every improvement in the criminal law, every step toward the diminution of war, every step toward better treatment of the colored races, or every mitigation of slavery, every moral progress that there has been in the world, has been consistently opposed by the organized churches of the world. I say quite deliberately that the Christian religion, as organized

---

1. The satirical novel *Erewhon Revisited Twenty Years Later, Both by the Original Discoverer of the Country and by His Son* (1901), by the English writer Samuel Butler (1835–1902), is a sequel to Butler's satirical novel *Erewhon* (1872).
2. The term *Inquisition* refers to any of several tribunals established by the Roman Catholic Church or by the government of an official Catholic state to enforce orthodoxy in belief and practice. The Spanish Inquisition was notorious for its use of trial by violent ordeal.

in its churches, has been and still is the principal enemy of moral progress in the world.

How the Churches Have Retarded Progress

You may think that I am going too far when I say that that is still so. I do not think that I am. Take one fact. You will bear with me if I mention it. It is not a pleasant fact, but the churches compel one to mention facts that are not pleasant. Supposing that in this world that we live in today an inexperienced girl is married to a syphilitic man; in that case the Catholic Church says, "This is an indissoluble sacrament. You must endure celibacy or stay together. And if you stay together, you must not use birth control to prevent the birth of syphilitic children." Nobody whose natural sympathies have not been warped by dogma, or whose moral nature was not absolutely dead to all sense of suffering, could maintain that it is right and proper that that state of things should continue.

That is only an example. There are a great many ways in which, at the present moment, the church, by its insistence upon what it chooses to call morality, inflicts upon all sorts of people undeserved and unnecessary suffering. And of course, as we know, it is in its major part an opponent still of progress and of improvement in all the ways that diminish suffering in the world, because it has chosen to label as morality a certain narrow set of rules of conduct which have nothing to do with human happiness; and when you say that this or that ought to be done because it would make for human happiness, they think that has nothing to do with the matter at all. "What has human happiness to do with morals? The object of morals is not to make people happy."

Fear, the Foundation of Religion

Religion is based, I think, primarily and mainly upon fear. It is partly the terror of the unknown and partly, as I have said, the wish to feel that you have a kind of elder brother who will stand by you in all your troubles and disputes. Fear is the basis of the whole thing—fear of the mysterious, fear of defeat, fear of death. Fear is the parent of cruelty, and therefore it is no wonder if cruelty and religion have gone hand in hand. It is because fear is at the basis of those two things. In this world we can now begin a little to understand things, and a little to master them by help of science, which has forced its way step by step against the Christian religion, against the churches, and against the opposition of all the old precepts. Science can help us to get over this craven fear in which mankind has lived for so many generations. Science can teach us, and I think our own hearts can teach us, no longer to look around for imaginary supports, no longer to invent allies in the sky, but rather to look to our own efforts here below to make this world a fit place to live in, instead of the sort of place that the churches in all these centuries have made it.

What We Must Do

We want to stand upon our own feet and look fair and square at the world— its good facts, its bad facts, its beauties, and its ugliness; see the world as it is and be not afraid of it. Conquer the world by intelligence and not merely by being slavishly subdued by the terror that comes from it. The whole conception of God is a conception derived from the ancient Oriental despotisms. It is a conception quite unworthy of free men. When you hear people in church debasing themselves and saying that they are miserable sinners, and all the rest of it, it seems contemptible and not worthy of self-respecting human beings. We ought to stand up and look the world frankly in the face. We ought to make the best we can of the world, and if it is not so good as we wish, after all it will still be better than what these others have made of it in all these ages. A good world needs knowledge, kindliness, and courage; it does not need a regretful hankering after the past or a fettering of the free intelligence by the words uttered long ago by ignorant men. It needs a fearless outlook and a free intelligence. It needs hope for the future, not looking back all the time toward a past that is dead, which we trust will be far surpassed by the future that our intelligence can create.

KARL BARTH
1886–1968

OUR ANXIETY AND GOD

Karl Barth was born in Basel, Switzerland, and died there. In the early 1930s, he was a professor of theology at German universities. A Calvinist pastor (see p. 412), Barth was trained in the liberal Protestant tradition, developed in stages by thinkers such as Friedrich Schleiermacher (see p. 481) and Adolf von Harnack (see p. 484), that predominated in nineteen-century Europe. According to liberal Christianity, especially in the work of these thinkers, Christianity was one realization of a universal natural religion. In the aftermath of World War I (1914–18), however, Barth became part of a powerful Protestant movement known as dialectical theology (later, often, neo-orthodoxy). According to dialectical theology, natural religion might or might not exist, but Christianity was not an instance of it. Christianity was something quite other, as its God was also quite other than whatever was acknowledged or worshipped in the postulated natural religion. Most important, Christianity could never fuse with a state or rely on enlightened good will to accomplish its purposes. Human nature was fallen, broken, inclined past all natural recovery to do the wrong thing rather than the right, and never entirely to be trusted. The only way to look at modernity, or anything else of human making, was askance.

Barth broke with Adolf von Harnack during the first weeks of World War I, when Harnack signed the aggressively nationalist "Manifesto of the Ninety-Three German Intellectuals to the Civilized World." The proper role for Christianity at a moment like that, to Barth's way of thinking, was not to join the parade but to cry, "Stop in the name of the Lord!"

Barth did not back Germany's enemies or espouse pacifism, but by the 1930s he was religiously and perhaps psychologically predisposed to believe the worst not just about the Nazi Party, but also, and more so, about the Nazi-approved and Nazi-supporting "German Christian" movement then taking shape. As German Christianity broke into factions during that turbulent time, a group called the Confessing

Church, counting many Lutherans among its members but with strong Calvinist influence, met in 1934 in the town of Barmen and issued a declaration, primarily written by Barth, insisting that the Church was and must ever remain distinct from the state. The point was explosive at the time. Though the Church had been subordinate to the state throughout Europe and the Americas since the Peace of Westphalia in 1648, and even though the two had grown ominously closer in the late nineteenth century, the total disappearance of the Church into the state had never before threatened as it did in the 1930s. To that prospect, the Barmen Declaration spoke a passionate "*Nein!*" Not long after its issuance, the Gestapo, the Nazi secret police, personally escorted Barth to the border: He was no longer welcome in Germany.

The work that made Barth's reputation and did most to launch dialectical theology was his commentary on Saint Paul's Letter to the Romans. Barth drew on that commentary in the following sermon, which he preached in Germany at Christmas 1932, near the end of a year in which the Nazis had consolidated their power. In simple, even consoling language, this piece touches on many of the central themes in Barth's voluminous body of work.

PRONOUNCING GLOSSARY

Barth: *bart*   Kyrie eleison: *kir´-ee-ay e-lay´-ee-suhn*

OUR ANXIETY AND GOD

This time I should like to explain what Christmas really means, by quoting the Apostle Paul. He once wrote: "Have no anxiety about anything, but in everything by prayer and supplication with thanksgiving let your requests be made known to God" (Philippians 4.6). Right away one can see that it is taken for granted that not only most but all people are anxious. It is not specially mentioned that many people exert themselves to dispel their anxieties with all sorts of excitement, distractions, and hullabaloo. This used to be tried out in the past even more often and with greater zeal than it is today, when for various reasons it is not quite so simple. What is supposed to banish anxieties is or was a special and not even a particularly wise form of making oneself anxious; for a while one tries to get round the anxiety in this way, but it only makes it worse. What does it mean, to be anxious? Obviously it means taking pains to master the great and the little sins, the needs, cares and tribulations of life. These pains already anticipate torment, in fact the torment of hell, and a needless torment too. Let it be understood that this torment lies not in the sins, needs, cares and tribulations of our life but in the pains we take to master them and in the anxieties we bear for them. Here we attempt something that is in itself an impossibility. Man cannot help himself. That he wants to help himself is his "sin," in the only serious sense of the word. As he tears at his chain, he makes all his limbs sore, but nobody has ever broken the chain. Our text takes it for granted that all men are anxious.

Over against it stands the direct and simple statement: "Have no anxiety about anything." This is not like so many fine words of consolation spoken

TRANSLATED BY Bernhard Citron.

by a man who is well off and for whom it is therefore easy to say them. When Paul wrote these words, he was engaged in a trial which was to end with his execution. What he expressed by these words was certainly not a statement that things are not so bad and that with a little patience they can be borne. The heavy chain of sins, needs, cares and tribulations by which man is fettered, with everything that this implies, is taken for granted. Everyone who reads this is asked to understand that in those words of Scripture his particular sorrow, his special depression and cheerlessness which may overshadow this year's Christmas celebration, is seen, considered and understood. It is understood not as something which is not really so bad, but rather as something whose badness should neither be denied nor glossed over, but is considered sympathetically. The reader should further notice that this man who is like the rest of us and who is in a very bad position himself, as bad in fact as any person can be in, says here quite clearly: "Have no anxiety about anything." Do not exert yourselves by wanting to help yourselves!

One can understand the meaning of this saying when it is first understood that he is talking of the thing that happened at Christmas. The Feast of Christmas reminds us of the fact that according to Holy Scripture God made Himself what we are. He assumed our humanity from His birth to His terrible death, together with all the dark sides and all the burden of human existence. He assumed all this when He became man Himself—tried, tempted, suffering, condemned, dying man. What does this mean? It means that our human existence ceased to be our own. Certainly we have it and live it, each one in his time and as long as his time lasts. But we have it and live it as something which is no longer our own, as a humanity which is kept by God, in God. Paul wrote on another occasion: "Your life is hid with Christ in God" (Colossians 3:3). This is the secret of Christmas; that God in Christ lived our life, bore its chain, suffered its grief, and died its death, so that all things that must be done to us are already done by Him; all tribulation is over, already done with, already transcended into resurrection, ascension and eternal triumph; all seeking, striving, desiring, and hurrying has already reached the goal, is already crowned and made perfect. Thus the anxiety which we suffer is already superseded and made superfluous. If the Feast of Christmas had the power to remind us of this secret of Christmas that *all is done already*, then we would immediately understand what this means: "Have no anxiety about anything." Why is it that in that case we just could not be anxious? We could not because we would fix our eyes steadfastly on God who became man and thus once for all bore our anxiety. We could not because we would then realise that it is ridiculous to try to help ourselves again, after we have already been helped. We could not because then for once we would be worried to death about the foolishness, wickedness and rebellion which lies in this fatal struggle of man and is nothing but a repetition of the sin that has been long forgiven. We could not because we would be infinitely grateful for not having to take such senseless trouble.

Paul's saying about anxiety and God is immediately followed by the other, better known one about the "peace of God which passes all understanding." If we let the Feast of Christmas tell us what it has to say to us about the child in the manger at Bethlehem by whom all human matters are kept and cared for, then the peace of God would indeed keep our hearts and minds so that we could not be anxious about anything.

One might express it also in this way: we would have *one thing only* to care about. This thing can and should involve trouble, for so it is ordained. But these are not the senseless troubles of those who want to help themselves. What is this ultimate care, left for us, permitted to us, imposed on us? Luther[1] had a very beautiful answer to this question: "We must be careful not to care for anything, but to be joyful before God and kind to our fellow man." Paul does not say that we should fold our arms and be idle: He knew that man must act and move as long as he lives. But there would not be that haunting anxiety, nor the mad drive to chase anxious thoughts away which is also a form of anxiety. If we would only understand the meaning of Christmas and confine our care to the one thing for which we really ought to care! Paul calls it the care of letting our requests be made known unto God.

Now we have our requests, our wishes, our aspirations and our hopes. We have just been told that we have and live our human existence within the time given to us. Our requests belong to it. But because our human existence is no longer our own (Christmas reminds us of that!) we cannot keep our requests to ourselves nor try to fulfil them by ourselves. We must leave them where Jesus Christ has taken them with our whole human existence; there they are—before God. We must allow ourselves to be helped in Jesus Christ, in his birth, death and resurrection. To allow ourselves to be helped, that is the care laid upon us, and the prayers of adoration and supplication needed for this is the trouble we have to take. In order for it to be true that all our requests lie before God, adoration and supplication are needed. We may and must move and act as befits people whose time is not yet at an end, but always in such a way that the motive and power of our movements and actions are our prayer and supplication by which our requests may be made known to God. In other words, we should let ourselves be helped definitely and thoroughly, as in fact we are already helped by the Child in the manger. Therefore thanksgiving is specially emphasised in this context. Not only our movements and actions but even our prayer and supplication might turn again into that foolish and prohibited self-help unless it really starts with our thanksgiving and joyful admission that self-help does not exist, it is entirely superfluous, for we are helped already. Anything in our movements and actions, and even in our most sincere prayers, which smells of self-help is forgiven in advance, simply and unconditionally.

> All this for us He did prepare
> And His great love to us declare.
> Therefore all Christians glad shall be
> And thank Him in eternity.
> *Kyrie eleison.*[2]

Kyrie eleison means "Lord have mercy upon us." There we are again at the only true carefulness which is preserved and wrapped in thanksgiving. "All this for us He did prepare." That is the only thing we have to worry about—no harassment, no hubbub, no self-help, but the cry for God's help which only they utter who are helped already. Why can't we do it? Why should not this

1. Martin Luther (see p. 399).
2. Barth quotes the final stanza of a piece well loved by his congregation, Luther's Christmas hymn "Gelobet seist du, Jesu Christ" (1524).

year of disgrace 1932[3] become a year of grace for us if we receive the simple message Christmas conveys to us, with the same simplicity?

3. In Germany in 1932, the Nazi Party forced Chancellor Franz von Papen, its last major and still effective political opponent, into retirement. The stage was now set, as all of Barth's hearers realized, for Adolf Hitler's appointment as chancellor in January 1933.

REINHOLD NIEBUHR
1892–1971

WHY THE CHRISTIAN CHURCH IS NOT PACIFIST

Karl Paul Reinhold Niebuhr was born in Missouri into a family of German Evangelical immigrants. He died in Massachusetts, having served as a pastor in Michigan, a professor of theology in New York, and a commentator on public affairs. Ultimately, he was perhaps the most widely read and admired American Protestant theologian of the twentieth century, at least in regard to American political life. Niebuhr's fluency in German and his relative familiarity with German religious culture meant that, though thoroughly American in his education, he was easily able to follow theological as well as political developments in Germany. Like Karl Barth (see p. 579), Niebuhr broke sharply with liberal Christianity. The climactic moment came when he lent his support to the entry of the United States into World War II. In the following selection, first published in 1940, he defends theologically the position that Christianity cannot be equated with pacifism.

In the postwar period (1945 and after), Niebuhr became known for Christian Realism. According to this form of dialectical theology, human nature is fallen, so all human ventures—even those with the greatest prima facie claim to moral rectitude—are subject to self-delusion, self-interest, and corruption. This emphasis grounds skepticism, to say the least, toward religious leaders who enter close relationships with political leaders, from whom Niebuhr kept his distance. Niebuhr's Christian Realism grounds caution even toward humanitarian causes. However, Niebuhr warmly supported the Social Gospel movement (see p. 569) and, later, the civil rights movement (see p. 624).

Niebuhr wrote prolifically, yet by far his best-known work is his shortest: the "Serenity Prayer," as it has come to be called. In his original formulation, it reads: "God, give us grace to accept with serenity the things that cannot be changed, courage to change the things which should be changed, and the wisdom to distinguish the one from the other."

PRONOUNCING GLOSSARY

Reinhold Niebuhr: *rain´-hold nee´-boor*

WHY THE CHRISTIAN CHURCH IS NOT PACIFIST

Whenever the actual historical situation sharpens the issue, the debate whether the Christian church is, or ought to be, pacifist is carried on with fresh vigor both inside and outside the Christian community. Those who are

584 | REINHOLD NIEBUHR

not pacifists seek to prove that pacifism is a heresy; while the pacifists contend, or at least imply, that the church's failure to espouse pacifism unanimously can be interpreted only as apostasy, and must be attributed to its lack of courage or to its want of faith.

There may be an advantage in stating the thesis, with which we enter this debate, immediately. The thesis is, that the failure of the church to espouse pacifism is not apostasy, but is derived from an understanding of the Christian gospel which refuses simply to equate the Gospel with the "law of love."[1] Christianity is not simply a new law, namely, the law of love. The finality of Christianity cannot be proved by analyses which seek to reveal that the law of love is stated more unambiguously and perfectly in the life and teachings of Christ than anywhere else. Christianity is a religion which measures the total dimension of human existence not only in terms of the final norm of human conduct, which is expressed in the law of love, but also in terms of the fact of sin. It recognizes that the same man who can become his true self only by striving infinitely for self-realization beyond himself is also inevitably involved in the sin of infinitely making his partial and narrow self the true end of existence. It believes, in other words, that though Christ is the true norm (the "second Adam") for every man, every man is also in some sense a crucifier of Christ.[2]

The good news of the gospel is not the law that we ought to love one another. The good news of the gospel is that there is a resource of divine mercy which is able to overcome a contradiction within our souls, which we cannot ourselves overcome. This contradiction is that, though we know we ought to love our neighbor as ourself, there is a "law in our members which wars against the law that is in our mind" (Romans 7:23), so that, in fact, we love ourselves more than our neighbor.

The grace of God which is revealed in Christ is regarded by Christian faith as, on the one hand, an actual "power of righteousness" which heals the contradiction within our hearts. In that sense Christ defines the actual possibilities of human existence. On the other hand, this grace is conceived as "justification," as pardon rather than power, as the forgiveness of God, which is vouchsafed to man despite the fact that he never achieves the full measure of Christ. In that sense Christ is the "impossible possibility." Loyalty to him means realization in intention, but does not actually mean the full realization of the measure of Christ. In this doctrine of forgiveness and justification, Christianity measures the full seriousness of sin as a permanent factor in human history. Naturally, the doctrine has no meaning for modern secular civilization, nor for the secularized and moralistic versions of Christianity. They cannot understand the doctrine precisely because they believe there is some fairly simple way out of the sinfulness of human history.

It is rather remarkable that so many modern Christians should believe that Christianity is primarily a "challenge" to man to obey the law of Christ; whereas it is, as a matter of fact, a religion which deals realistically with the problem presented by the violation of this law. Far from believing that the ills of the world could be set right "if only" men obeyed the law of Christ, it has always regarded the problem of achieving justice in a sinful world as a

---

1. See Luke 10:27 and many similar New Testament formulations.　　2. See 1 Corinthians 15:45–49.

very difficult task. In the profounder versions of the Christian faith the very utopian illusions, which are currently equated with Christianity, have been rigorously disavowed.

The Truth and Heresy of Pacifism

Nevertheless, it is not possible to regard pacifism simply as a heresy. In one of its aspects modern Christian pacifism is simply a version of Christian perfectionism. It expresses a genuine impulse in the heart of Christianity, the impulse to take the law of Christ seriously and not to allow the political strategies, which the sinful character of man makes necessary, to become final norms. In its profounder forms, this Christian perfectionism did not proceed from a simple faith that the "law of love" could be regarded as an alternative to the political strategies by which the world achieves a precarious justice. These strategies invariably involve the balancing of power with power; and they never completely escape the peril of tyranny on the one hand, and the peril of anarchy and warfare on the other.

In medieval ascetic perfectionism and in Protestant sectarian perfectionism (of the type of Menno Simons,[3] for instance) the effort to achieve a standard of perfect love in individual life was not presented as a political alternative. On the contrary, the political problem and task were specifically disavowed. This perfectionism did not give itself to the illusion that it had discovered a method for eliminating the element of conflict from political strategies. On the contrary, it regarded the mystery of evil as beyond its power of solution. It was content to set up the most perfect and unselfish individual life as a symbol of the Kingdom of God. It knew that this could be done only by disavowing the political task and by freeing the individual of all responsibility for social justice.

It is this kind of pacifism which is not a heresy. It is rather a valuable asset for the Christian faith. It is a reminder to the Christian community that the relative norms of social justice, which justify both coercion and resistance to coercion, are not final norms, and that Christians are in constant peril of forgetting their relative and tentative character and of making them too completely normative.

There is thus a Christian pacifism which is not a heresy. Yet most modern forms of Christian pacifism are heretical. Presumably inspired by the Christian gospel, they have really absorbed the Renaissance faith in the goodness of man, have rejected the Christian doctrine of original sin as an outmoded bit of pessimism, have reinterpreted the cross so that it is made to stand for the absurd idea that perfect love is guaranteed a simple victory over the world, and have rejected all other profound elements of the Christian gospel as "Pauline" accretions which must be stripped from the "simple gospel of Jesus." This form of pacifism is not only heretical when judged by the standards of the total gospel. It is equally heretical when judged by the facts of human existence. There are no historical realities which remotely conform to it. It is important to recognize this lack of conformity to the facts of experience as a criterion of heresy.

---

3. 1496–1561; an Anabaptist (see p. 423) whose followers were known as Mennonites. The Mennonite Church later adopted pacifism as part of its creed.

All forms of religious faith are principles of interpretation which we use to organize our experience. Some religions may be adequate principles of interpretation at certain levels of experience, but they break down at deeper levels. No religious faith can maintain itself in defiance of the experience which it supposedly interprets. A religious faith which substitutes faith in man for faith in God cannot finally validate itself in experience. If we believe that the only reason men do not love each other perfectly is because the law of love has not been preached persuasively enough, we believe something to which experience does not conform. If we believe that if Britain had only been fortunate enough to have produced 30 percent instead of 2 percent of conscientious objectors to military service, Hitler's heart would have been softened and he would not have dared to attack Poland,[4] we hold a faith which no historic reality justifies.

Such a belief has no more justification in the facts of experience than the communist belief that the sole cause of man's sin is the class organization of society and the corollary faith that a "classless" society will be essentially free of human sinfulness. All of these beliefs are pathetic alternatives to the Christian faith. They all come finally to the same thing. They do not believe that man remains a tragic creature who needs the divine mercy as much at the end as at the beginning of his moral endeavors. They believe rather that there is some fairly easy way out of the human situation of "self-alienation." In this connection it is significant that Christian pacifists, rationalists like Bertrand Russell, and mystics like Aldous Huxley[5] believe essentially the same thing. The Christians make Christ into the symbol of their faith in man. But their faith is really identical with that of Russell or Huxley.

The common element in these various expressions of faith in man is the belief that man is essentially good at some level of his being. They believe that if you can abstract the rational-universal man from what is finite and contingent in human nature, or if you can only cultivate some mystic-universal element in the deeper levels of man's consciousness, you will be able to eliminate human selfishness and the consequent conflict of life with life. These rational or mystical views of man conform neither to the New Testament's view of human nature nor yet to the complex facts of human experience.

The Contribution of a True Pacifism

Despite our conviction that most modern pacifism is too filled with secular and moralistic illusions to be of the highest value to the Christian community, we may be grateful for the fact that the Christian church has learned, since the last war, to protect its pacifists and to appreciate their testimony. Even when this testimony is marred by self-righteousness, because it does not proceed from a sufficiently profound understanding of the tragedy of human history, it has its value.

It is a terrible thing to take human life. The conflict between man and man and nation and nation is tragic. If there are men who declare that, no matter what the consequences, they cannot bring themselves to participate in this

---

4. World War II began with Nazi Germany's invasion of Poland on September 1, 1939.

5. English novelist and critic (1894–1963). For Bertrand Russell, see p. 576.

slaughter, the church ought to be able to say to the general community: We quite understand this scruple and we respect it. It proceeds from the conviction that the true end of man is brotherhood, and that love is the law of life. We who allow ourselves to become engaged in war need this testimony of the absolutist against us, lest we accept the warfare of the world as normative, lest we become callous to the horror of war, and lest we forget the ambiguity of our own actions and motives and the risk we run of achieving no permanent good from this momentary anarchy in which we are involved.

But we have a right to remind the absolutists that their testimony against us would be more effective if it were not corrupted by self-righteousness and were not accompanied by the implicit or explicit accusation of apostasy. A pacifism which really springs from the Christian faith, without secular accretions and corruptions, could not be as certain as modern pacifism is that it possesses an alternative for the conflicts and tensions from which and through which the world must rescue a precarious justice.

A truly Christian pacifism would set each heart under the judgment of God to such a degree that even the pacifist idealist would know that knowledge of the will of God is no guarantee of his ability or willingness to obey it. The idealist would recognize to what degree he is himself involved in rebellion against God, and would know that this rebellion is too serious to be overcome by just one more sermon on love, and one more challenge to man to obey the law of Christ.

DIETRICH BONHOEFFER
1906–1945

FROM THE COST OF DISCIPLESHIP

Dietrich Bonhoeffer was born into a Lutheran family in Breslau, Germany. As a teenager, he decided to become a pastor. At the University of Berlin, he studied under liberal theologians such as Adolf von Harnack (see p. 484). However, impressed by the dialectical theology of Karl Barth (see p. 579), Bonhoeffer began to think through a difficult synthesis of the liberal and dialectical theologies. As a postdoctoral student in New York, Bonhoeffer worked with Reinhold Niebuhr (see p. 583) and became interested in the practical, rather than purely intellectual, applications of faith. In 1931, he returned to Germany as a lecturer on theology and was ordained as a minister in the Old-Prussian Union Evangelical Church.

From the very start of the Nazi Party's ascension to power in the early 1930s, Bonhoeffer vocally opposed its activities. In 1934, he cofounded the Confessing Church, an alternative to the prevailing German Churches, which at best remained complacent and at worst collaborated with the Nazi government. Even while serving as a pastor to two German-speaking Protestant churches in London, Bonhoeffer helped organize underground training sessions for pastors in the Confessing Church. In 1939, as World War II ravaged Europe and the Nazis carried out their campaign to exterminate Jews and other "undesirables," Bonhoeffer returned to

New York. He considered remaining there as a refugee, but returned home and spent years engaging in dangerous, roving Resistance activity, including efforts to smuggle Jews out of Germany and one of several unsuccessful conspiracies to assassinate Adolf Hitler. In April 1943, he was arrested by the Gestapo, the Nazi secret police. The full extent of his Resistance involvement did not come immediately to the regime's attention, however, and so he was not executed until two years later—hanged naked, in the Flossenbürg concentration camp, just two weeks before the end of World War II.

Bonhoeffer's resistance to National Socialism derived from two sources: his conviction that the movement was pagan and his theological understanding of the demands of the Gospel. A disciple of Jesus, he argued, could not settle for "cheap grace." In his best-known book, *Nachfolge* (1937), translated in 1948 as *The Cost of Discipleship*, Bonhoeffer discusses Jesus' Sermon on the Mount as an inspiration for ethical rigor, or "costly grace." According to the Lutheran and Calvinist traditions to which Bonhoeffer was heir, salvation could not be earned by human good works, which were accepted only by the grace, or graciousness, of God. The risk in the Social Gospel (see p. 569)

This photo shows Dietrich Bonhoeffer at the Tegel Military Prison, in Berlin, not long before his execution.

was that humanitarian service—good works, social causes, and, worst of all, pride in their accomplishment—could make salvation seem no more than payment for human service rendered. But in the following selection, Bonhoeffer inveighs with prophetic rage against the opposite risk: that having accepted salvation as a gift from God, German Christians would retreat to their private lives, regardless of what was happening in the world around them. He saw such complacency as a betrayal of the heritage of the Protestant Reformation.

When *Nachfolge* was first published, Adolf Hitler's power was at its zenith. Just months later, on Hitler's fiftieth birthday, all German pastors were required to sign an oath of allegiance to the Führer. Terrified, most did so, even most of those who as members of the dissident Confessing Church had earlier offered public resistance. Bonhoeffer refused to sign, just as he later refused the asylum he could easily have procured in the United States or England.

Not until the 1950s did *The Cost of Discipleship* and, with it, Bonhoeffer's story win widespread recognition outside Germany. For example, the English poet W. H. Auden paid tribute to Bonhoeffer around 1958 (see p. 593). Bonhoeffer's collected works are surprisingly voluminous, and letters smuggled out from Nazi imprisonment during the last months of his life, quite apart from their emotional impact, have had a noteworthy intellectual impact on other theologians, particularly through his provocative vision of a "religionless Christianity."

PRONOUNCING GLOSSARY

Caesarea Philippi: *se-zuh-ree´-uh fi-li´-pai* [*ai* rhyming with *rye*]

catechumenate: *ca-tuh-kyoo´-men-uht*

Dietrich Bonhoeffer: *dee´-trik bahn´-hoh-fur*

Gennesareth: *gen-ne´-sah-ret*

FROM THE COST OF DISCIPLESHIP

Cheap grace is the preaching of forgiveness without requiring repentance, baptism without church discipline, communion without confession, absolution without personal confession. Cheap grace is grace without discipleship, grace without the cross, grace without Jesus Christ, living and incarnate.

* * *

Costly grace is the gospel which must be *sought* again and again, the gift which must be *asked* for, the door at which a man must *knock*.

Such grace is *costly* because it calls us to follow, and it is *grace* because it calls us to follow *Jesus Christ*. It is costly because it costs a man his life, and it is grace because it gives a man the only true life. It is costly because it condemns sin, and grace because it justifies the sinner. Above all, it is *costly* because it cost God the life of his Son: 'ye were bought at a price,'[1] and what has cost God much cannot be cheap for us. Above all, it is *grace* because God did not reckon his Son too dear a price to pay for our life, but delivered him up for us. Costly grace is the Incarnation of God.

Costly grace is the sanctuary of God; it has to be protected from the world, and not thrown to the dogs. It is therefore the living word, the Word of God, which he speaks as it pleases him. Costly grace confronts us as a gracious call to follow Jesus, it comes as a word of forgiveness to the broken spirit and the contrite heart. Grace is costly because it compels a man to submit to the yoke of Christ and follow him; it is grace because Jesus says: 'My yoke is easy and my burden is light.'[2]

On two separate occasions Peter received the call, 'Follow me.' It was the first and last word Jesus spoke to his disciple (Mark 1:17; John 21:22). A whole life lies between these two calls. The first occasion was by the lake of Gennesareth, when Peter left his nets and his craft and followed Jesus at his word. The second occasion is when the Risen Lord finds him back again at his old trade. Once again it is by the lake of Gennesareth, and once again the call is: 'Follow me.'[3] Between the two calls lay a whole life of discipleship in the following of Christ. Half-way between them comes Peter's confession, when he acknowledged Jesus as the Christ of God. Three times Peter hears the same proclamation that Christ is his Lord and God—at the beginning, at the end, and at Caesarea Philippi. Each time it is the same grace of Christ which calls to him 'Follow me' and which reveals itself to him in his confession of the Son of God. Three times on Peter's way did grace arrest him, the one grace proclaimed in three different ways.

This grace was certainly not self-bestowed. It was the grace of Christ himself, now prevailing upon the disciple to leave all and follow him, now working in him that confession which to the world must sound like the ultimate blasphemy, now inviting Peter to the supreme fellowship of martyrdom for the Lord he had denied, and thereby forgiving him all his sins. In

FROM *Dietrich Bonhoeffer: Witness to Jesus Christ*, ed. John de Gruchy.

1. 1 Corinthians 6:20.
2. Matthew 11:30.
3. The second "follow me" is heard at Mark 10:34: "If any man would come after me, let him deny himself and take up his cross and follow me." This invitation to take up the cross is what Bonhoeffer means in the next paragraph by "the ultimate blasphemy."

the life of Peter grace and discipleship are inseparable. He had received the grace which costs.

At Christianity spread, and the church became more secularized, this realization of the costliness of grace gradually faded. The world was christianized, and grace became its common property. It was to be had at low cost. Yet the church of Rome did not altogether lose the earlier vision. It is highly significant that the church was astute enough to find room for the monastic movement, and to prevent it from lapsing into schism. Here on the outer fringe of the church was a place where the older vision was kept alive. Here men still remembered that grace costs, that grace means following Christ. Here they left all they had for Christ's sake, and endeavoured daily to practise his rigorous commands. Thus monasticism became a living protest against the secularization of Christianity and the cheapening of grace. But the church was wise enough to tolerate this protest, and to prevent it from developing to its logical conclusion. It thus succeeded in relativizing it, even using it in order to justify the secularization of its own life. Monasticism was represented as an individual achievement which the mass of the laity could not be expected to emulate. By thus limiting the application of the commandments of Jesus to a restricted group of specialists, the church evolved the fatal conception of the double standard—a maximum and a minimum standard of Christian obedience. Whenever the church was accused of being too secularized, it could always point to monasticism as an opportunity of living a higher life within the fold, and thus justify the other possibility of a lower standard of life for others. And so we get the paradoxical result that monasticism, whose mission was to preserve in the church of Rome the primitive Christian realization of the costliness of grace, afforded conclusive justification for the secularization of the church. By and large, the fatal error of monasticism lay not so much in its rigorism (though even here there was a good deal of misunderstanding of the precise content of the will of Jesus) as in the extent to which it departed from genuine Christianity by setting up itself as the individual achievement of a select few, and so claiming a special merit of its own.

When the Reformation came, the providence of God raised Martin Luther to restore the gospel of pure, costly grace. Luther passed through the cloister; he was a monk, and all this was part of the divine plan. Luther had left all to follow Christ on the path of absolute obedience. He had renounced the world in order to live the Christian life. He had learnt obedience to Christ and to his church, because only he who is obedient can believe. The call to the cloister demanded of Luther the complete surrender of his life. But God shattered all his hopes. He showed him through the Scriptures that the following of Christ is not the achievement or merit of a select few, but the divine command to all Christians without distinction. Monasticism had transformed the humble work of discipleship into the meritorious activity of the saints, and the self-renunciation of discipleship into the flagrant spiritual self-assertion of the 'religious'. The world had crept into the very heart of the monastic life, and was once more making havoc. The monk's attempt to flee from the world turned out to be a subtle form of love for the world. The bottom having thus been knocked out of the religious life, Luther laid hold upon grace. Just as the whole world of monasticism was crashing about him in ruins, he saw God in Christ stretching forth his hand to save. He grasped that hand in faith, believing that 'after all, nothing we can do is of any avail, however good a life we live.' The grace which gave itself to him was a costly grace, and it shattered his whole existence. Once more he must leave his nets and follow. The first time was when he entered the monastery, when he had left everything behind except his pious self. This time even that was taken from him. He obeyed the call, not through any merit of his own, but simply through the grace of God. Luther did not hear the word: 'Of course you have sinned, but now everything is forgiven, so you can stay as you are and enjoy the consolations of forgiveness.' No, Luther had to leave the cloister and go back to the world, not because the world in itself was good and holy, but because even the cloister was only a part of the world.

Luther's return from the cloister to the world was the worst blow the world had suffered since the days of early Christianity. The renunciation he made when he became a monk was child's play compared with that which he had to make when he returned to the world. Now came the frontal assault. The only way to follow Jesus was by living in the world. Hitherto the Christian life had been the achievement of a few choice spirits under the exceptionally favourable conditions of monasticism; now it is a duty laid on every Christian living in the world. The commandment of Jesus must be accorded perfect obedience in one's daily vocation of life. The conflict between the life of the Christian and the life of the world was thus thrown into the sharpest possible relief. It was a hand-to-hand conflict between the Christian and the world.

✻ ✻ ✻

We Lutherans have gathered like eagles round the carcase of cheap grace, and there we have drunk of the poison which has killed the life of following Christ. It is true, of course, that we have paid the doctrine of pure grace divine honours unparalleled in Christendom, in fact we have exalted that doctrine to the position of God himself. Everywhere Luther's formula has been repeated, but its truth perverted into self-deception. So long as our church holds the correct doctrine of justification, there is no doubt whatever that she is a justified church! So they said, thinking that we must vindicate our Lutheran heritage by making this grace available on the cheapest and easiest terms. To be 'Lutheran' must mean that we leave the following of Christ to legalists, Calvinists and enthusiasts[4]—and all this for the sake of grace. We justified the world, and condemned as heretics those who tried to follow Christ. The result was that a nation became Christian and Lutheran, but at the cost of true discipleship. The price it was called upon to pay was all too cheap. Cheap grace had won the day.

But do we realize that this cheap grace has turned back upon us like a boomerang? The price we are having to pay today in the shape of the collapse of the organized church is only the inevitable consequence of our policy of making grace available to all at too low a cost. We gave away the word and sacraments wholesale, we baptized, confirmed, and absolved a whole nation unasked and without condition. Our humanitarian sentiment made us give that which was holy to the scornful and unbelieving. We poured forth unending streams of grace. But the call to follow Jesus in the narrow way was hardly ever heard.

4. Bonhoeffer speaks sardonically as a German Lutheran to his fellow German Lutherans, indicting them for leaving the costly, even dangerous, "following of Christ" to other kinds of Christians, to whom they condescend as "legalists, Calvinists and enthusiasts."

Where were those truths which impelled the early church to institute the cat-echumenate,[5] which enabled a strict watch to be kept over the frontier between the church and the world, and afforded adequate protection for costly grace? What had happened to all those warnings of Luther's against preaching the gospel in such a manner as to make men rest secure in their ungodly living? Was there ever a more terrible or disastrous instance of the Christianizing of the world than this? What are those three thousand Saxons put to death by Charlemagne compared with the millions of spiritual corpses in our country today?[6] With us it has been abundantly proved that the sins of the fathers are visited upon the children unto the third and fourth generations. Cheap grace has turned out to be utterly merciless to our Evangelical Church.

This cheap grace has been no less disastrous to our own spiritual lives. Instead of opening up the way to Christ it has closed it. Instead of calling us to follow Christ, it has hardened us in our disobedience. Perhaps we had once heard the gracious call to follow him, and had at this command even taken the first few steps along the path of discipleship in the discipline of obedience, only to find ourselves confronted by the word of cheap grace. Was that not merciless and hard? The only effect that such a word could have on us was to bar our way to progress, and seduce us to the mediocre level of the world, quenching the joy of discipleship by telling us that we were following a way of our own choosing, that we were spending our strength and disci-plining ourselves in vain—all of which was not merely useless, but extremely dangerous. After all, we were told, our salvation had already been accom-plished by the grace of God. The smoking flax was mercilessly extinguished.[7] It was unkind to speak to men like this, for such a cheap offer could only leave them bewildered and tempt them from the way to which they had been called by Christ. Having laid hold on cheap grace, they were barred for ever from the knowledge of costly grace. Deceived and weakened, men felt that they were strong now that they were in possession of this cheap grace—whereas they had in fact lost the power to live the life of discipleship and obedience. The word of cheap grace has been the ruin of more Christians than any commandment of works.

<hr>

5. In the early Church, "catechumens" were those who aspired to become Christians but were judged to need further instruction (sometimes through the "catechism") or other preparation before they could be admitted. Bonhoeffer's point is that membership in the Church was then not bestowed as lightly as it came to be in the virtu-ally "automatic" state Lutheranism of Prussia.
6. For Bonhoeffer, the disappearance of German Protestant Christendom into the Nazi state was an act of mass spiritual suicide, alongside which the famous, possibly fictional slaughter of pagan Saxons by the Christian emperor Charlemagne (742–814) paled into insignificance.
7. According to Matthew 12:20, a "smoking flax shall he not quench, till he send forth judgment to victory." Bonhoeffer sarcastically faults his fellow German Lutherans for acting as if, because the flax has already been quenched by Jesus and the victory won, they need do nothing.

W. H. AUDEN
1907–1973

FRIDAY'S CHILD

Wystan Hugh Auden was born in York, England, and educated at Christ Church College, Oxford. T. S. Eliot (see p. 574), as an editor at Faber & Faber, published Auden's first book of poety, and in broad outline Auden's story was a mirror image of Eliot's: Eliot was an American who became a British subject. Auden was an Englishman who, in 1946, became an American citizen. Eliot converted to Anglo-Catholicism on a specific day, publicly. Auden wandered from the same faith, then returned to belief in Christianity through a private, gradual evolution that was clearest in retrospect. Eliot's literary style was oracular and remote, whereas Auden's was vernacular and accessible. Eliot's poetic output is august but sparing—a pure and hard but small body of work. Auden's is relaxed but prodigal—an immense body of work, sometimes untidy on the page.

Around 1958, Auden wrote the poem "Friday's Child." He dedicated it to Dietrich Bonhoeffer (see p. 587). By then, Auden had left behind his youthful atheism and rejoined, as an American citizen and an Episcopalian, his family's religion. He had lived in Germany and had a summer home in Austria. He was well read in German theology. Like Bonhoeffer, he was drawn to the Christian existentialism of Søren Kierkegaard (see p. 531), with its stress on the ordeal of human choosing. Still, in "Friday's Child" Auden does not tell Bonhoeffer's story. The poem takes the same form as a children's verse that all English-speakers once grew up with:

> Monday's child is fair of face,
> Tuesday's child is full of grace,
> Wednesday's child is full of woe,
> Thursday's child has far to go,
> Friday's child is loving and giving,
> Saturday's child works hard for a living,
> But the child who is born on the Sabbath day
> Is bonny and blithe and good and gay.

In the poem, Friday's child appears as the capitalized "He." Auden evidently counts on his readers to recall not just the verse, but also the fact that Jesus Christ died on Good Friday, crucified naked. The poem is about the gift that Christ, as God Incarnate, gives from the cross. The relationship between the poem's ironic, at times opaque particulars and Bonhoeffer's life and work are left for the reader to interpet.

FRIDAY'S CHILD

(In Memory of Dietrich Bonhoeffer, Martyred at Flossenburg, April 9th, 1945)

> He told us we were free to choose
> But, children as we were, we thought—
> "Paternal Love will only use
>   Force in the last resort

On those too bumptious to repent."—   5
Accustomed to religious dread,
It never crossed our minds He meant
    Exactly what He said.

Perhaps He frowns, perhaps He grieves,
But it seems idle to discuss   10
If anger or compassion leaves
    The bigger bangs[1] to us.

What reverence is rightly paid
To a Divinity so odd
He lets the Adam whom He made   15
    Perform the Acts of God?[2]

It might be jolly if we felt
Awe at this Universal Man[3]
(When kings were local, people knelt);
    Some try to, but who can?   20

The self-observed observing Mind[4]
We meet when we observe at all
Is not alarming or unkind
    But utterly banal.

Though instruments at Its command   25
Make wish and counterwish come true,
It clearly cannot understand
    What It can clearly do.

Since the analogies are rot
Our senses based belief upon,   30
We have no means of learning what
    Is really going on,

And must put up with having learned
All proofs or disproofs that we tender
Of His existence are returned   35
    Unopened to the sender.

Now, did He really break the seal
And rise again?[5] We dare not say;
But conscious unbelievers feel
    Quite sure of Judgement Day.[6]   40

---

1. Perhaps a reference to the cosmological phrase *big bang*, coined in 1948.
2. See the discussion of Adam and Eve's transgression on p. 83.
3. A man who knows everything and can do everything, similar to a Renaissance man.
4. Mind as a replacement for God.
5. See Matthew 27:66. Pontius Pilate ordered the tomb of Jesus sealed. Rising, Jesus would have broken the seal.
6. I.e., quite sure that there will be no such day.

Meanwhile, a silence on the cross,
As dead as we shall ever be,
Speaks of some total gain or loss,
  And you and I are free

To guess from the insulted face   45
Just what Appearances He saves[7]
By suffering in a public place
  A death reserved for slaves.

7. Perhaps a reference to *Saving the Appearances: A Study in Idolatry* (1957), a literary sensation by the
English philosopher-critic Owen Barfield (1898–1997).

WILLIAM TEMPLE
1881–1944

FROM GERMAN ATROCITIES: AID FOR REFUGEES
[RESOLUTION ON BEHALF OF THE JEWS OF EUROPE]

William Temple was born in Exeter, in southwest England. His father, an archbishop, became the archbishop of Canterbury, the spiritual head of the Church of
England, in 1897. Temple was a star debater at Oxford (1900–04), where he also
taught philosophy (1904–10). After his ordination to the priesthood in 1909, he
became a celebrated preacher and wrote books of theology. An energetic Christian
leftist, he was the first president of the Workers' Educational Association (1908–24)
and a successful mediator in the 1926 general strike, a nine-day nationwide walk-
out called in support of locked-out coal miners. He was deeply involved in the ecumenical movement, and to counter anti-Semitism he founded the Council of
Christians and Jews. In 1942, he became the archbishop of Canterbury. Two years
later, he died from gout, after suffering from the disease all his life.

  On March 23, 1943, Temple addressed the House of Lords about the Holocaust,
reports of which had been belatedly trickling into the news. Few Christian voices
were speaking on behalf of the Jews when Temple challenged Britain to do all that
it could to save them. With controlled emotion, he lists horrors (many omitted in
our excerpt, most unknown to his audience) that the Nazis were inflicting on the
Jews. Initially his plea is nonreligious, as he points out that he and his peers are
"so wonderfully fed" that they could surely share their surplus with starving refugees. But Temple refers to the parable of the Good Samaritan (Luke 10:30–37),
where a priest and a Levite ignore a robbed and wounded Jew, whereas a Samaritan, a despised, semipagan outsider, comes to the Jew's aid at some cost to himself.
Since the great majority of Temple's listeners were professed Christians (and more
than two dozen were Anglican bishops), he could not have chosen a more cutting
text. Temple is saying, in effect: Unless we do something to help, we are all hypocrites. Unfortunately, his speech had no measurable result.

  After World War II, such moments would become a subject of great controversy,
as historians argued over the few and largely fruitless efforts by both secular governments and religious bodies (e.g., the Vatican) to help the Jews. The standard defense
of the Allied nations is that their priority was to defeat Germany militarily and thus
they could not afford special efforts for the Jewish masses under Nazi control.

FROM GERMAN ATROCITIES: AID FOR REFUGEES
[RESOLUTION ON BEHALF OF THE JEWS OF EUROPE]

* * * My Lords, I beg leave to move the Resolution standing in my name on the Order Paper. We are confronted, as all your Lordships know, with an evil the magnitude and horror of which it is impossible to describe in words. There has, I suppose, never been so great a manifestation of the power of sheer cruelty and of the determination to wreak upon a helpless people what is not vengeance, for there is no offence, but the satisfaction of a mere delight in power such as is to be witnessed on the continent of Europe at the present time. We are wisely advised not to limit our attention in this connexion to the sufferers of any one race, and we must remember that there are citizens of many countries who are subject to just the same kind of monstrous persecution, and even massacre. None the less, there has been a concentration of this fury against the Jews, and it is inevitable that we should give special attention to what is being carried through, and still further plotted against them.

We know that Hitler near the beginning of the war declared that this war must lead to the extermination of either the Jewish or the German people, and it should not be the Germans. He is now putting that threat into effect, and no doubt we are to a very large extent at present powerless to stop him. We are told that the only real solution is rapid victory. No doubt it is true that if we could win the war in the course of a few weeks we could still deliver multitudes of those who are now doomed to death. But we dare not look for such a result, and we know that what we can do will be but little in comparison with the need. My whole plea on behalf of those for whom I am speaking is that whether what we do be large or little it should at least be all we can do.

＊　　＊　　＊

I have myself lately received this information through the Board of Deputies of British Jews: "A message has been received from a Jewish member of the National Council of Poland who writes: 'Yesterday I received via Istanbul news from responsible sources about the situation of the Jews in Poland. The news relates to the beginning of February. The informants say—the information comes straight from Poland—that during January a new slaughter of Jews in Warsaw took place. The Jews defended themselves actively; over fifty Germans were killed. After this heroic defence a new slaughter of Jews followed. Over 5,000 were immediately deported. The complete extermination of the ghettos in Poland is going on. * * *

＊　　＊　　＊

The whole matter is so big and other claims are so urgent that we want further to make the proposition that there shall be appointed someone of high standing for whom this should be a primary responsibility. If we speak with impatience of what has been done or has not been done it is not, as I have tried already to show, from any lack of sympathy with the Government in the immense complexity of the tasks that they are carrying through, but just because of that complexity it seems to us more than can reasonably be asked of human beings that they should alongside of other responsibilities also undertake this on our behalf. For this reason I suggest appointing someone who should have real authority in the matter and should feel responsibility for this matter alone. So it is urged that there should be appointed someone of high standing, either within the Government or, if not that, from the Civil Service, to make it his first concern, and if the United Nations are ready to act together they should appoint a High Commissioner or else instruct the High Commissioner for Refugees, already active under the League of Nations,[1] who has at present only limited authority in relation to the Jews for whom we are seeking relief at present.

My chief protest is against procrastination of any kind. It was three months ago that the solemn declaration of the United Nations was made and now we are confronted with a proposal for an exploratory Conference at Ottawa. That sounds as if it involves much more delay. It took five weeks from December 17 for our Government to approach the United States, and then six weeks for the Government of the United States to reply, and when they did reply they suggested a meeting of representatives of the Government for preliminary exploration. The Jews are being slaughtered at the rate of tens of thousands a day on many days, but there is a proposal for a preliminary exploration to be made with a view to referring the whole matter after that to the Inter-Governmental Committee on Refugees. My Lords, let us at least urge that when that Conference meets it should meet not only for exploration but for decision. We know that what we can do is small compared with the magnitude of the problem, but we cannot rest so long as there is any sense among us that we are not doing all that might be done. We have discussed the matter on the footing that we are not responsible for this great evil, that the burden lies on others, but it is always true that the obligations of decent men are decided for them by contingencies which they did not themselves create and very largely by the action of wicked men. The priest and the Levite in the parable were not in the least responsible for the traveller's wounds as he lay there by the roadside and no doubt they had many other pressing things to attend to, but they stand as the picture of those who are condemned for neglecting the opportunity of showing mercy. We at this moment have upon us a tremendous responsibility. We stand at the bar of history, of humanity and of God. I beg leave to move.

Moved to resolve, That, in view of the massacres and starvation of Jews and others in enemy and enemy-occupied countries, this House desires to assure His Majesty's Government of its fullest support for immediate measures, on the largest and most generous scale compatible with the requirements of military operations and security, for providing help and temporary asylum to persons in danger of massacre who are able to leave enemy and enemy-occupied countries.

---

1. A multinational organization devoted to achieving world peace, founded after the end of World War I and thus preceding the United Nations, which was founded after World War II.

SIMONE WEIL
1909–1943

FROM REFLECTIONS ON THE RIGHT USE OF SCHOOL STUDIES WITH A VIEW TO THE LOVE OF GOD

Simone Weil was born in Paris to agnostic Jewish parents originally from Alsace. At age six, she refused to eat sugar on the grounds that soldiers fighting in World War I had to go without it. A precociously brilliant student, Weil received her degree in philosophy (1931) from the prestigious École Normale Supérieure, in Paris. She then taught philosophy at a secondary school for girls, in Le Puy-en-Velay, south-central France. An unorthodox Marxist, pacifist, and trade unionist, Weil was active in many social and political protests. Despite her pacifism, she fought—briefly and ineptly— for the Republican (anti-Fascist) side in the Spanish Civil War (1936–39). In Assisi, Italy, while recovering from a burn she suffered over a cooking fire in the war, Weil prayed for the first time. Though she never formally became a Christian, she was deeply influenced by her experiences during prayer and by a mystical sense of the presence of Christ. She was interested in other religions as well, including Hinduism and Buddhism. During World War II, Weil lived briefly in Marseille, France; briefly in New York City; and briefly in London, where she joined the French Resistance. She died in England from tuberculosis, weakened by refusing to eat more than what she thought people in occupied France were allowed to. Weil wrote many books, all published posthumously. A complex and sometimes contradictory thinker, she wrote with purity, clarity, and unrelenting force. Her best-known work is *The Need for Roots* (English translation, 1952), a political, cultural, and spiritual program for transforming postwar France and, by implication, all of Western society.

Weil wrote the following essay in 1942 for a Dominican priest and educator in Montpellier, France. Later published in *Waiting for God* (English edition 1959), the piece is a fair sample of Weil's intense spirituality, outlining a theology of schoolwork as prayer. Weil's account of the intellectual life is so passionately idealistic that it comes across more as a self-portrait than as usable advice for adolescents. According to Weil, the key to studying any subject is attention. Attention is likewise the essential prerequisite for becoming aware of God's presence, and it must be fueled not by dogged application, but by desire and hence joy. So joy makes studies "a preparation for spiritual life," since "desire alone draws God down." Merely solving a geometry problem, she argues, can give students a glimpse into "the unique, eternal, and living Truth"—Truth that Christians identify with Jesus (see John 14:6).

PRONOUNCING GLOSSARY

Curé d'Ars: *kyoor-ay´ dahrs*   Simone Weil: *si-mohn´ vay*
Racine: *rah-seen´*

FROM REFLECTIONS ON THE RIGHT USE OF SCHOOL STUDIES WITH A VIEW TO THE LOVE OF GOD

The key to a Christian conception of studies is the realization that prayer consists of attention. It is the orientation of all the attention of which the soul is capable toward God. The quality of the attention counts for much in the quality of the prayer. Warmth of heart cannot make up for it.

The highest part of the attention only makes contact with God, when prayer is intense and pure enough for such a contact to be established; but the whole attention is turned toward God.

Of course school exercises only develop a lower kind of attention. Nevertheless, they are extremely effective in increasing the power of attention that will be available at the time of prayer, on condition that they are carried out with a view to this purpose and this purpose alone.

Although people seem to be unaware of it today, the development of the faculty of attention forms the real object and almost the sole interest of studies. Most school tasks have a certain intrinsic interest as well, but such an interest is secondary. All tasks that really call upon the power of attention are interesting for the same reason and to an almost equal degree.

School children and students who love God should never say: "For my part I like mathematics"; "I like French"; "I like Greek." They should learn to like all these subjects, because all of them develop that faculty of attention which, directed toward God, is the very substance of prayer.

If we have no aptitude or natural taste for geometry, this does not mean that our faculty for attention will not be developed by wrestling with a problem or studying a theorem. On the contrary it is almost an advantage.

It does not even matter much whether we succeed in finding the solution or understanding the proof, although it is important to try really hard to do so. Never in any case whatever is a genuine effort of the attention wasted. It always has its effect on the spiritual plane and in consequence on the lower one of the intelligence, for all spiritual light lightens the mind.

If we concentrate our attention on trying to solve a problem of geometry, and if at the end of an hour we are no nearer to doing so than at the beginning, we have nevertheless been making progress each minute of that hour in another more mysterious dimension. Without our knowing or feeling it, this apparently barren effort has brought more light into the soul. The result will one day be discovered in prayer. Moreover, it may very likely be felt in some department of the intelligence in no way connected with mathematics. Perhaps he who made the unsuccessful effort will one day be able to grasp the beauty of a line of Racine[1] more vividly on account of it. But it is certain that this effort will bear its fruit in prayer. There is no doubt whatever about that.

Certainties of this kind are experimental. But if we do not believe in them before experiencing them, if at least we do not behave as though we believed in them, we shall never have the experience that leads to such certainties.

TRANSLATED BY Emma Craufurd.

1. Jean Racine (1639–1699), French dramatist.

There is a kind of contradiction here. Above a given level this is the case with all useful knowledge concerning spiritual progress. If we do not regulate our conduct by it before having proved it, if we do not hold on to it for a long time by faith alone, a faith at first stormy and without light, we shall never transform it into certainty. Faith is the indispensable condition.

The best support for faith is the guarantee that if we ask our Father for bread, he does not give us a stone. Quite apart from explicit religious belief, every time that a human being succeeds in making an effort of attention with the sole idea of increasing his grasp of truth, he acquires a greater aptitude for grasping it, even if his effort produces no visible fruit. An Eskimo story explains the origin of light as follows: "In the eternal darkness, the crow, unable to find any food, longed for light, and the earth was illumined." If there is a real desire, if the thing desired is really light, the desire for light produces it. There is a real desire when there is an effort of attention. It is really light that is desired if all other incentives are absent. Even if our efforts of attention seem for years to be producing no result, one day a light that is in exact proportion to them will flood the soul. Every effort adds a little gold to a treasure no power on earth can take away. The useless efforts made by the Curé d'Ars,[2] for long and painful years, in his attempt to learn Latin bore fruit in the marvelous discernment that enabled him to see the very soul of his penitents behind their words and even their silences.

*   *   *

Most often attention is confused with a kind of muscular effort. If one says to one's pupils: "Now you must pay attention," one sees them contracting their brows, holding their breath, stiffening their muscles. If after two minutes they are asked what they have been paying attention to, they cannot reply. They have been concentrating on nothing. They have not been paying attention. They have been contracting their muscles.

We often expend this kind of muscular effort on our studies. As it ends by making us tired, we have the impression that we have been working. That is an illusion. Tiredness has nothing to do with work. Work itself is the useful effort, whether it is tiring or not. This kind of muscular effort in work is entirely barren, even if it is made with the best of intentions. Good intentions in such cases are among those that pave the way to hell. Studies conducted in such a way can sometimes succeed academically from the point of view of gaining marks and passing examinations, but that is in spite of the effort and thanks to natural gifts; moreover such studies are never of any use.

Will power, the kind that, if need be, makes us set our teeth and endure suffering, is the principal weapon of the apprentice engaged in manual work. But, contrary to the usual belief, it has practically no place in study. The intelligence can only be led by desire. For there to be desire, there must be pleasure and joy in the work. The intelligence only grows and bears fruit in joy. The joy of learning is as indispensable in study as breathing is in running. Where it is lacking there are no real students, but only poor caricatures of apprentices who, at the end of their apprenticeship, will not even have a trade.

2. Jean-Baptiste-Marie Vianney (1786–1859), commonly known in English as Saint John Vianney, French priest venerated by the Catholic Church as the patron saint of parish priests.

It is the part played by joy in our studies that makes of them a preparation for spiritual life, for desire directed toward God is the only power capable of raising the soul. Or rather, it is God alone who comes down and possesses the soul, but desire alone draws God down. He only comes to those who ask him to come; and he cannot refuse to come to those who implore him long, often, and ardently.

Attention is an effort, the greatest of all efforts perhaps, but it is a negative effort. Of itself, it does not involve tiredness. When we become tired, attention is scarcely possible any more, unless we have already had a good deal of practice. It is better to stop working altogether, to seek some relaxation, and then a little later to return to the task; we have to press on and loosen up alternately, just as we breathe in and out.

Twenty minutes of concentrated, untired attention is infinitely better than three hours of the kind of frowning application that leads us to say with a sense of duty done: "I have worked well!"

But, in spite of all appearances, it is also far more difficult. Something in our soul has a far more violent repugnance for true attention than the flesh has for bodily fatigue. This something is much more closely connected with evil than is the flesh. That is why every time that we really concentrate our attention, we destroy the evil in ourselves. If we concentrate with this intention, a quarter of an hour of attention is better than a great many good works.

✻   ✻   ✻

The solution of a geometry problem does not in itself constitute a precious gift, but the same law applies to it because it is the image of something precious. Being a little fragment of particular truth, it is a pure image of the unique, eternal, and living Truth, the very Truth that once in a human voice declared: "I am the Truth."

Every school exercise, thought of in this way, is like a sacrament.

In every school exercise there is a special way of waiting upon truth, setting our hearts upon it, yet not allowing ourselves to go out in search of it. There is a way of giving our attention to the data of a problem in geometry without trying to find the solution or to the words of a Latin or Greek text without trying to arrive at the meaning, a way of waiting, when we are writing, for the right word to come of itself at the end of our pen, while we merely reject all inadequate words.

Our first duty toward school children and students is to make known this method to them, not only in a general way but in the particular form that bears on each exercise. It is not only the duty of those who teach them but also of their spiritual guides. Moreover the latter should bring out in a brilliantly clear light the correspondence between the attitude of the intelligence in each one of these exercises and the position of the soul, which, with its lamp well filled with oil, awaits the Bridegroom's coming with confidence and desire.[3] May each loving adolescent, as he works at his Latin prose, hope through this prose to come a little nearer to the instant when he will really be the slave—faithfully waiting while the master is absent, watching and listening—ready to open the door to him as soon as

---

3. See Matthew 25 and John 3:27–30.

he knocks. The master will then make his slave sit down and himself serve him with meat.

✢   ✢   ✢

So it comes about that, paradoxical as it may seem, a Latin prose or a geometry problem, even though they are done wrong, may be of great service one day, provided we devote the right kind of effort to them. Should the occasion arise, they can one day make us better able to give someone in affliction exactly the help required to save him, at the supreme moment of his need.

For an adolescent, capable of grasping this truth and generous enough to desire this fruit above all others, studies could have their fullest spiritual effect, quite apart from any particular religious belief.

Academic work is one of those fields containing a pearl so precious[4] that it is worth while to sell all our possessions, keeping nothing for ourselves, in order to be able to acquire it.

4. See Matthew 13:45–46.

MOTHER MARIA SKOBTSOVA
1891–1945

FROM THE SECOND GOSPEL COMMANDMENT

Mother Maria Skobtsova was born Elizaveta Pilenko to an upper-class family in Riga, Latvia, then part of the Russian Empire. As a teenager, she became an atheist, possibly in response to the death of her father. In 1906, she moved with her mother to St. Petersburg, where she married, bore a daughter, and, in 1913, divorced. In 1918, fleeing the turmoil that followed the Bolshevik Revolution, she moved to Anapa, a town on the Black Sea. While serving as mayor there, she was arrested and tried by the Whites, the anti-Communist army. However, the judge, Daniel Skobtsov, was a former teacher of hers, and she was acquitted. The pair married, had two children, and eventually relocated to Georgia, Yugoslavia, and Paris, where Skobtsova studied theology. In 1932, with her husband's permission, she was granted an ecclesiastical divorce and became a Russian Orthodox nun, taking the religious name of Maria. Determined to remain connected with the everyday world, Mother Maria Skobtsova turned her rented house into a convent, a refuge for the poor and disenfranchised, and a center for theological discussion. With the Nazi takeover of Paris in World War II, the house also began sheltering Jews. For crimes such as helping Jews get baptismal certificates, and arranging with garbage collectors to smuggle out Jewish children hidden in trash cans, Skobtsova was sent in 1943 to the notorious women's concentration camp in Ravensbrück, Germany, where two years later she was killed in the gas chamber. She was canonized as a saint by the Eastern Orthodox Church and is sometimes known as Saint Mary of Paris.

The title of the following selection comes from a crucial moment in the Synoptic Gospels. In Mark 12:28–34, Matthew 22:36–40, and Luke 10:25–28, a scribe, or expert in Jewish law, attempts to trip up Jesus by asking him what the greatest commandment is. Jesus replies:

You shall love the Lord your God with all your heart, and with all your soul, and with all your mind. This is the first and greatest commandment. And a second is like it, You shall love your neighbor as yourself. On these two commandments depend all the law and the prophets. (Matthew 37–40)

The "first" commandment quotes Deuteronomy 6:5; the "second" is from Leviticus 19:18. In her essay, Skobtsova attacks the Christian tendency to ignore the "second" commandment and see the world as an "evil phantom" in which "the only reality is God and my solitary soul trembling before Him." Many Christian groups have been marked to some extent by this imbalance, including the Russian Orthodox Church, which has always revered monks and solitary ascetics. As a corrective, Skobtsova offers the perennial Christian ideal of love and service for others, as denoted by the Russian concept of *sobornost*. The term, which literally means "conciliarism," was coined by nineteenth-century Slavophiles and later defined by the philosopher Nikolai Lossky (1875–1965) as "the combination of freedom and unity of many persons on the basis of their common love for the same absolute values." This concept is clearly intended as an antidote to Marxism and soulless modern individualism. For Skobtsova, it sums up the Gospels' message about self-sacrificing love as contrasted with the mere quest for "self-salvation" that sometimes occupies ascetics. In her life, Skobtsova seems to have practiced the theoretically simple message she preaches here.

PRONOUNCING GLOSSARY

Dostoevsky: *dos-tuh-yev´-skee*
Golgotha: *gohl´-goh-thah*
Khomiakov: *koh-mee-ah´-kohv*

Skobtsova: *skohbt-soh´-vah*
sobornost: *soh-bohr´-nohst*
Soloviev: *soh-loh´-vee-ev*

FROM THE SECOND GOSPEL COMMANDMENT

There exists in the Christian world a constant tendency, in moments of various historical catastrophes, to preach with great intensity an immersion in oneself, a withdrawal from life, a standing of the solitary human soul before God.

It appears to me that now, too, this tendency is beginning to show itself very strongly, producing a strange picture of the world: on one side all the diverse forces of evil, united and affirming the power of the collective, of the masses, and the worthlessness and insignificance of each separate human soul; and on the other side—dispersed and disunited Christian souls, affirming themselves in this dispersion and disunity, for whom the world becomes a sort of evil phantom, and the only reality is God and my solitary soul trembling before Him.

It seems to me that this state of mind is definitely a temptation, is definitely as terrible for each person as it is for the destiny of the Church of Christ, and I would like to rise against it with all my strength and call people to each other, to stand together before God, to suffer sorrows together, to resist temptations together. And I can find an enormous number of indisputable reasons for this call, in all areas of Christian life.

TRANSLATED BY Richard Pevear and Larissa Volokhonsky. The bracketed insertions are the translators'.

I will begin with what is perceived as most personal and intimate, the area which everyone knows to be precisely the one where the soul stands alone before God—with Orthodox prayers and, to limit myself still further, not with the prayers of the Church, uttered during church services, where their non-personal character goes without saying, but precisely with the personal prayers, known to everyone, which are said at home behind closed doors. I am thinking of the usual order of morning and evening prayers, which can be found in any prayer book and to which we have been accustomed since childhood. The important thing for me is to establish that an absolute majority of them are addressed to God from *us* and not from *me*. I want to look at them from that point of view.

They begin like this: "Glory to Thee, *our* God, glory to Thee." The prayer "O Heavenly King" ends with the words: "Come and abide in *us*, cleanse *us* from every impurity, and save *our* souls, O Good One." The Trisagion[1] ends: "have mercy on *us*." Then: "Lord, cleanse *us* from *our* sins, Master, pardon *our* transgressions, Holy One, visit *us* and heal us of *our* infirmities for Thy name's sake." Further on comes the Lord's Prayer, beginning with the address: "*Our* Father. . . . Give *us* this day *our* daily bread; and forgive *us* our debts, as *we* forgive *our* debtors. And lead *us* not into temptation, but deliver *us* from the evil one."

In the morning prayers, the plural is used as definitely and as clearly. "*We* fall down before Thee, *we* sing unto Thee . . . have mercy on *us*. . . . O come, let *us* worship God, *our* King . . . receive *our* prayer . . . cleanse *us* and heal *us* . . . that *we* may be found ready . . . for Thou hast borne the savior of *our* souls. . . ."

Further on come prayers for the living and the departed, that is, for others, not for oneself. Exactly the same thing is repeated in the evening prayers. Thus what is most personal, what is most intimate in an Orthodox person's life, is thoroughly pervaded by this sense of being united with everyone, the sense of the principle of *sobornost*, characteristic of the Orthodox Church. This is a fact of great significance; this forces us to reflect.

If this is so in a person's private prayer, there is no need to speak of prayer in the church. A priest cannot even celebrate the liturgy if he is alone; for that he must have at least one person who symbolizes the people. And the eucharistic mystery itself is precisely the common work of the Church, accomplished on behalf of all and for all.

It would be an unseemly protestantizing on the part of Orthodox people if they forgot these central and most characteristic particularities of their Orthodox truth. In the Orthodox Church man is not alone and his path to salvation is not solitary; he is a member of the Body of Christ, he shares the fate of his brothers in Christ, he is justified by the righteous and bears responsibility for the sins of the sinners. The Orthodox Church is not a solitary standing before God, but *sobornost*, which binds everyone with the bonds of Christ's love and the love for one another. And that is not something invented by theologians and philosophers, but a precise teaching of the Gospel, brought to life through the centuries of existence of the Church's body. Khomiakov, Dostoevsky, and

---

1. A standard liturgical hymn in most of the Eastern Orthodox, Oriental Orthodox, and Eastern Catholic Churches.

Soloviev,[2] who did much to explain these truths to broad segments of Russian educated society, were able to confirm it by references to the Word of God, to precise teachings from the Savior. The Orthodox man only fulfills the precepts of his faith when he takes them as a certain bi-une[3] commandment of love for God and love for one's neighbor.

There occur, of course, whole epochs of deviation from the right attitude toward this bi-unity. And it is especially characteristic of periods of catastrophe and general instability, when man in his pusillanimity tries to hide, to take cover, and not deal with anyone who belongs to this tottering world. It seems to him that if he remembers God alone, and stands before Him in his soul in order to save it, he will thereby be delivered from all calamity and remain clean in a time of universal defilement. Such a man should tirelessly repeat to himself the words of St. John the Theologian about hypocrites who say they love God without loving man [1 John 4:20]. How can they love God, whom they do not see, and hate their brother, who is near them? For the fulfillment of love for one's neighbor, Christ demanded that we lay down our soul for our friends. Here there is no sense in paraphrasing this demand and saying that it has to do not with the soul but with life, because when the apostle Paul says, about the fulfilling of Christ's demand, that he could wish he were separated from Christ, so long as he could see his brothers saved [Romans 9:3]—it is clear that he is speaking of the state of his soul, and not only his life.

Equally irrefutable is Christ's teaching about how we should deal with our neighbor, in His words about the Last Judgment [Matthew 25:31–45], when man will be asked not how he saved his soul by solitary endeavor but precisely how he dealt with his neighbor, whether he visited him in prison, whether he fed him when he was hungry, comforted him—in short, whether he loved his fellow man, whether this love stood before him as an immutable commandment of Christ. And here we cannot excuse ourselves from active love, from the selfless giving of our soul for our friends.

But even if we set aside the separate and particular Gospel teachings in this regard and turn to the whole activity of Christ on earth, it is here that we find the highest degree of the laying down of one's soul for others, the highest measure of sacrificial love and self-giving that mankind has known. "For God so loved the world that He gave His only-begotten Son" [John 3:16], calling us, too, to the same love. There is not and there cannot be any following in the steps of Christ without taking upon ourselves a certain share, small as it may be, of participation in this sacrificial deed of love. Anyone who loves the world, anyone who lays down his soul for others, anyone who is ready, at the price of being separated from Christ, to gain salvation for his brothers—is a disciple and follower of Christ. And inversely, anyone who abides in the temptation of self-salvation alone, anyone who does not take upon himself the responsibility for the pain and sin of the world, anyone who follows the path of "egoism," be it even "holy" egoism, simply does not hear what Christ says, and does not see what His sacrifice on Golgotha[4] was offered for.

Here it is important to stress once more that quite often various exercises in external virtue—feeding vagabonds, sheltering beggars, and so on—are also

2. Aleksey Stepanovich Khomyakov (1804–1860), Russian philosopher, theologian, and religious poet; Fyodor Mikhaylovich Dostoyevsky (1821–1881), Russian novelist; and Vladimir Sergeyevich Salavyov (1853–1900), Russian philosopher, theologian, poet, pamphleteer, and literary critic.
3. Combining two in one.
4. Or Calvary, the site at which Jesus was crucified.

accepted, as it were, by those who follow the path of self-salvation. But they are accepted as ascetic exercises useful for the soul. Of course, this is not the love that the Gospel teaches us, and it was not for this kind of love that Christ was crucified. His love, given to us in inheritance, is true sacrificial love, the giving of the soul not in order to receive it back with interest, so to speak, not as an act in its own name, but as an act in the name of a neighbor, and only in his name, our love for whom reveals to us the image of God in him. Here we cannot reason like this: Christ gave us the firm and true teaching that we meet Him in every poor and unhappy man. Let us take that into consideration and give this poor and unhappy man our love, because he only seems poor and unhappy to us, but in fact he is the King of Heaven, and with Him our gifts will not go for nothing, but will return to us a hundredfold. No, the poor and unhappy man is indeed poor and unhappy, and in him Christ is indeed present in a humiliated way, and we receive him in the name of the love of Christ, not because we will be rewarded, but because we are aflame with this sacrificial love of Christ and in it we are united with Him, with His suffering on the Cross, and we suffer not for the sake of our purification and salvation, but for the sake of this poor and unhappy man whose suffering is alleviated by ours. One cannot love sacrificially in one's own name, but only in the name of Christ, in the name of the image of God that is revealed to us in man.

✼   ✼   ✼

It can be said that for more than a century now Russian thought has been repeating with all its voices and in all possible ways that it has understood what it means to give one's soul for one's neighbors, that it wants to follow the path of love, the path of authentic mystical human communion, which is thereby also true communion with God. It has often happened in the history of thought that theoretical, philosophical, and theological presuppositions emerge first, but after that a certain idea strives to embody itself in life. All Russian spiritual works of the nineteenth century were filled with theoretical suppositions, the whole world heard them, they proved to be humanly brilliant, they determined the highest point of tension of the Russian spirit, its main characteristic. No wars or revolutions can destroy what has been done by Russian religious and philosophical genius over the course of the previous period in the history of Russian thought. Dostoevsky remains forever, and not only he. We can draw from these works, we can get from them an inestimable amount of data, answers to the most terrible questions, the posing of the most insoluble problems. One may boldly say that the main theme of nineteenth-century Russian thought had to do with the second commandment, with its dogmatic, moral, philosophical, social, and other aspects.

For us, for Orthodox people who are in the Church, and who were brought up on this Orthodox philosophy of the Russian people, our duty reveals itself with the utmost clarity: we must turn these theoretical presuppositions, these philosophical systems, these theological theories, these words *sobornost* and *Godmanhood*, which have recently become sacred, into so many practical landmarks both for our personal spiritual paths, the most cherished, most inward ones, and for any of our external endeavors.

We are called to embody in life the principles of *sobornost* and *Godmanhood*, which are at the foundation of our Orthodox Church; we are called to oppose the mystery of authentic human communion to all false relations among people. This is the only path on which Christ's love can live; moreover, this is the only path of life—outside it is death. Death in the fire and ashes of various hatreds that corrode modern mankind, class, national, and race hatreds, the godless and giftless death of cool, uncreative, imitative, essentially secular democracy. To all forms of mystical totalitarianism we oppose only one thing: the person, the image of God in man. And to all forms of passively collectivist mentality in democracy we oppose *sobornost*.

But we do not even oppose. We simply want to live as we are taught by the second commandment of Christ, which determines everything in man's relation to this earthly life, and we want to live this life in such a way that all those who are outside it can see and feel the unique, saving, unsurpassable beauty, the indisputable truth of precisely this Christian path.

We do not know whether we will be able to realize our hopes. It is basically a matter of God's will. But apart from God's will, God's help and grace, each of us is faced with the demand to strain all our forces, not fearing the most difficult endeavor, in ascetic self-restraint, giving our souls for others sacrificially and lovingly, to follow in Christ's footsteps to our appointed Golgotha.

DOROTHY DAY
1897–1980

FROM THE DUTY OF DELIGHT

Dorothy Day was born in New York City and raised in San Francisco and Chicago. Her family was nominally Episcopalian, but rarely attended church. Day began attending church by herself at age ten and was baptized and confirmed, but she considered herself an agnostic. After attending the University of Chicago at Urbana-Champaign for two years and traveling to various parts of the United States, Day returned to New York, where she worked for socialist publications and took part in antiwar and women's suffrage protests. She began to attend Roman Catholic Mass, and in 1927 she converted to Catholicism.

Five years later, with the French immigrant intellectual and former Christian Brother Peter Maurin, Day founded the Catholic Worker Movement. Beginning with the newspaper *The Catholic Worker* (which sold for a symbolic penny and which Day edited), the movement promoted—and still promotes—pacifism and Catholic-identified social teaching, aid to the poor and homeless and direct nonviolent action on their behalf, and communal living. Day was a prolific journalist and novelist, and in her later years she lectured around the world on grass-roots charity and pacifism. She died, after suffering a heart attack, in New York.

Day kept diaries from 1934 until her death. In the following selection from a late-1960s entry, Day is meditating on the role of money in American culture. Her thoughts are prompted in particular by the Catholic Worker's having to pay taxes on a $55,000 bequest because the group was not registered as a charitable organization. (Day and her colleagues wanted to stress that the gifts they channeled to the poor were single-minded offerings, not just ways to earn income tax deductions.) She weaves together Gospel verses and reflections on the contemporary scene by way of presenting the ideal of Christian poverty. This ideal is at once her own and thoroughly traditional: the radical cutting back on personal expense in favor of "the man on the Bowery, Skid Row, or prison, or prison camp, or battlefield." Day's approach is heroic and utopian, calling for structural changes in government and society but not waiting for the state to meet the needs of suffering people.

FROM THE DUTY OF DELIGHT

Money, a topic of vital interest to man. Like sex or food, it can be made subject of intense interest. How to get it, how to spend it. Men at highest level—enormous salary, enormous expenses. Tales of corruption in high places always involve money. [Abe] Fortas takes retaining fees to protect a client and is disgraced publicly. Disgraced and discredited.[1]

Dwight Macdonald[2] wrote once that a foundation was a large body of money surrounded by people, all of whom were trying to get some of it.

Foundations are tax-free, and the less powerful are now being investigated.

When gangsters, now called Mafiosi, are being convicted it is often on charge of evading income tax—not on charge of extortion, murder, blackmail, drug trafficking, white slave traffic.

The love of money is the root of all evil.[3]

Whence come wars among you? Each one seeking his own.[4]

People are secretive about money—how much they have, where it came from, inherited, earned? How closely it is tied up to work—hard work, work that is for the common good.

What are students learning in colleges and universities? To work for the common good, to contribute to the common good, or to get the degrees which will entitle them to enter ever-higher fields of learning and recompense.

What vast fields of knowledge there are which relate to man's need for a good life, for the food, clothing, and shelter man needs to lead a good life.

"A certain amount of goods is necessary to lead a good life," St. Thomas Aquinas[5] writes. How much goods? How much land does a man need? What do men live for?

These are questions which preoccupied Tolstoy[6] and about which he wrote so much.

What was the attitude of Jesus toward money? (Judas was the one who held the purse, who betrayed him for money and then threw the money away.[7] He was playing for greater stakes—power, world domination perhaps.)

---

1. In 1968, U.S. Supreme Court justice Abe Fortas (1910–1982) resigned from the bench due to ethical issues. The bracketed insertion is the original editor's.
2. American journalist, editor, and critic (1906–1982).
3. 1 Timothy 6:10.
4. See James 4:1 and 1 Corinthians 10:24.

5. See p. 317.
6. Leo Tolstoy (1828–1910), Russian novelist, philosopher, and mystic. "How Much Land Does a Man Need?" is the title of Tolstoy's 1886 short story/parable about the lethal power of greed.
7. See John 16:6 and Matthew 27:3–6.

"Take no thought for what ye shall eat or drink or wear. Your Father knows you have need of these things. Be like little children. Trust. Ask and you shall receive. If a child ask for bread will his father give him a stone? If he ask for fish, will he hand him a scorpion? Take no money on your journey. Do not lay up for yourselves treasures on earth."[8] Do you need money for paying taxes? And here Jesus does something fantastic, like something out of a fairytale. He doesn't tell Peter to go to Judas to get the money. He tells him to go fishing and open the mouth of the first fish he catches and take out the coin he will find there and pay the tribute "lest thou should offend them."[9]

Render to Caesar the things that are Caesar's[1] but the less you have of Caesar the less you have to give him. Jesus was living in an occupied country. At the moment it was peacetime, a Pax Romana.[2] It was Law and Order, Roman law and order, with a standing army to keep the peace. Jesus was not concerned with joining the resistance. He was laying down principles that made for true peace. They could take it or leave it. He forced no man. But he did try to arouse in man that hunger and thirst for "living water,"[3] for the abundant life, for the joy that no man can take from you, for the "unspeakable gift"[4] which so many have caught a vision of and have tried to communicate to others.

All this ruminating is because the Catholic Worker has been left $55,000 in a will. People are so cautious and secretive about money that I cannot write about the other legatees, just about ourselves. There were many claims to the will. Servants, friends, isolated missionaries were all left gifts, furniture was given to museums, pets were give to friends to care for, together with money to support them, and the residue of the estate was to be divided between 5 Catholic institutions, charitable institutions, of which we are one.

And now it is a question of taxes to be paid on this inheritance. Are we, or are we not a charitable institution? There was no question about the 4 others. They were accredited institutions, money that came to them could not be taxed. Accredited by the State. The State agreed that money for the poor was exempt from taxation. It was holy. It was on another plane, another level, on another dimension. You entered another realm when you dealt with this money. You dealt with a fairyland. You had gone thru the looking glass like Alice, or thru the wardrobe like the children in the C.S. Lewis stories.[5]

But we—the lawyers of the State decided—were living in *this world* as well as in the next. When we acted as tho all men were really brothers, as though "all the way to heaven is heaven"[6] because Jesus Christ had said "I am the Way"[7] and we were trying to "put on Christ"[8] as St. Paul advised,

---

8. This quotation combines, conflates, and paraphrases statements of Jesus from the Gospels, e.g., respectively: Matthew 6:25, 31; Matthew 6:32; Matthew 18:3; Luke 11:9 and Matthew 7:7–8; Matthew 7:9; Luke 11:12 and Matthew 7:10; Luke 9:3, Matthew 10:10, and Mark 6:8; and Matthew 6:19.
9. See Matthew 17:27.
1. Matthew 22:21.
2. Roman Peace (Latin), a term for the 1st-and-2nd-century period of the Roman Empire.
3. John 4:10–14.
4. 2 Corinthians 9:15.
5. In Lewis's *Chronicles of Narnia* (see p. 621)—

starting with the first novel, *The Lion, the Witch and the Wardrobe* (1950)—four children travel to a fantasyland through a wardrobe. The wardrobe is reminiscent of the looking glass, a mirror that serves as a portal, in *Through the Looking-Glass, and What Alice Found There* (1871), by the English writer Lewis Carroll (Charles Lutwidge Dodgson; 1832–1898).
6. A phrase attributed to Saint Catherine of Siena (see p. 360), used as the title of a June 1948 article by Day in *The Catholic Worker.*
7. John 14:6.
8. Romans 13:14.

and "put off the old man,"[9] and really act "as if we loved one another,"[1] "as if" our brother, our loved one, was the man on the Bowery, Skid Row, or prison, or prison camp, or battlefield; "as if" the Chinese, Soviets, North and South Vietnamese, Cubans, are truly our brothers, children of one Father, one Creator, maker of Heaven and earth, the moon and stars which we are exploring now—Oh God how wonderful are all Thy works.

9. Ephesians 4:22.   1. See John 4:7–21.

PAUL TILLICH
1886–1965

FROM DYNAMICS OF FAITH

Paul Tillich was born into a Lutheran family in the village of Starzeddel, Germany (present-day Starosiedle, Poland). He received his doctorate in philosophy in 1911 and was ordained as a Lutheran minister (like his father) the following year. After serving as a chaplain in the German army during World War I, Tillich taught theology at several German universities. In the early 1930s, he spoke out vigorously against Nazism. Following Adolf Hitler's election as chancellor of Germany, Tillich was dismissed in 1933 from his position at the University of Frankfurt. At the urging of Reinhold Niebuhr (see p. 583), he moved to New York and joined the faculty at Union Theological Seminary. For the rest of his life, Tillich remained in the United States, teaching at Union, then Harvard University, and finally at the University of Chicago.

Tillich was famous for conducting a dialogue between Christianity and contemporary secular culture, most notably existentialism. In books such as *The Shaking of the Foundations* (a collection of sermons, 1948), *The Courage to Be* (1952), and *Dynamics of Faith* (1957), he presented Christian theology in a dramatically different guise, as a universal quest that could be pursued with equal legitimacy by the believer and the atheist. Both faced a world fraught with anxiety, which demanded a bold and authentic self-affirmation.

In *Dynamics of Faith*, Tillich deviates from the traditional understanding of faith as an intellectual assent to truths that cannot be known by the senses. Traditional faith, according to Tillich, is just another form of "ultimate concern." Forget the old icons; one must search for a "God beyond god," "the Ground of Being." Requiring "total surrender," be it to the idol of success or the God of justice, faith is an act of "the total personality" (conscious and unconscious). Including and transcending rationality and emotion, thought and will, faith leads to a kind of ecstasy. This radical, highly psychological account of faith might apply just as well to artistic and sexual experiences as to religious ones, and Tillich's religion might resemble pantheism or even atheism as much as it does Christianity. Yet as a personal response to the threats and conundrums of the world, Tillich's thinking taps into a broad and deep vein of modern religious sensibility.

PRONOUNCING GLOSSARY

Jahweh: *yah´-way*   Tillich: *til´-ik*

FROM DYNAMICS OF FAITH

From *What Faith Is*

I. FAITH AS ULTIMATE CONCERN

Faith is the state of being ultimately concerned: the dynamics of faith are the dynamics of man's ultimate concern. Man, like every living being, is concerned about many things, above all about those which condition his very existence, such as food and shelter. But man, in contrast to other living beings, has spiritual concerns—cognitive, aesthetic, social, political. Some of them are urgent, often extremely urgent, and each of them as well as the vital concerns can claim ultimacy for a human life or the life of a social group. If it claims ultimacy it demands the total surrender of him who accepts this claim, and it promises total fulfillment even if all other claims have to be subjected to it or rejected in its name. If a national group makes the life and growth of the nation its ultimate concern, it demands that all other concerns, economic well-being, health and life, family, aesthetic and cognitive truth, justice and humanity, be sacrificed. The extreme nationalisms of our century are laboratories for the study of what ultimate concern means in all aspects of human existence, including the smallest concern of one's daily life. Everything is centered in the only god, the nation—a god who certainly proves to be a demon, but who shows clearly the unconditional character of an ultimate concern.

But it is not only the unconditional demand made by that which is one's ultimate concern, it is also the promise of ultimate fulfillment which is accepted in the act of faith. The content of this promise is not necessarily defined. It can be expressed in indefinite symbols or in concrete symbols which cannot be taken literally, like the "greatness" of one's nation in which one participates even if one has died for it, or the conquest of mankind by the "saving race," etc. In each of these cases it is "ultimate fulfillment" that is promised, and it is exclusion from such fulfillment which is threatened if the unconditional demand is not obeyed.

An example—and more than an example—is the faith manifest in the religion of the Old Testament. It also has the character of ultimate concern in demand, threat and promise. The content of this concern is not the nation—although Jewish nationalism has sometimes tried to distort it into that—but the content is the God of justice, who, because he represents justice for everybody and every nation, is called the universal God, the God of the universe. He is the ultimate concern of every pious Jew, and therefore in his name the great commandment is given: "You shall love the Lord your God with all your heart, and with all your soul, and with all your might" (Deuteronomy 6:5). This is what ultimate concern means and from these words the term "ultimate concern" is derived. They state unambiguously the character of genuine faith, the demand of total surrender to the subject of ultimate concern. The Old Testament is full of commands which make the nature of this surrender concrete, and it is full of promises and threats in relation to it. Here also are the promises of symbolic indefiniteness, although they center around fulfillment of the national and individual life, and the threat is the exclusion from such fulfillment through national extinction and individual catastrophe. Faith, for the men of the Old Testament, is the state of being ultimately and unconditionally concerned about Jahweh and about what he represents in demand, threat and promise.

Another example—almost a counter-example, yet nevertheless equally revealing—is the ultimate concern with "success" and with social standing and economic power. It is the god of many people in the highly competitive Western culture and it does what every ultimate concern must do: it demands unconditional surrender to its laws even if the price is the sacrifice of genuine human relations, personal conviction, and creative *eros*.[1] Its threat is social and economic defeat, and its promise—indefinite as all such promises—the fulfillment of one's being. It is the breakdown of this kind of faith which characterizes and makes religiously important most contemporary literature. Not false calculations but a misplaced faith is revealed in novels like *Point of No Return*.[2] When fulfilled, the promise of this faith proves to be empty.

Faith is the state of being ultimately concerned. The content matters infinitely for the life of the believer, but it does not matter for the formal definition of faith. And this is the first step we have to make in order to understand the dynamics of faith.

2. FAITH AS A CENTERED ACT

Faith as ultimate concern is an act of the total personality. It happens in the center of the personal life and includes all its elements. Faith is the most centered act of the human mind. It is not a movement of a special section or a special function of man's total being. They all are united in the act of faith. But faith is not the sum total of their impacts. It transcends every special impact as well as the totality of them and it has itself a decisive impact on each of them.

Since faith is an act of the personality as a whole, it participates in the dynamics of personal life. These dynamics have been described in many ways, especially in the recent developments of analytic psychology. Thinking in polarities, their tensions and their possible conflicts, is a common characteristic of most of them. This makes the psychology of personality highly dynamic and requires a dynamic theory of faith as the most personal of all personal acts. The first and decisive polarity in analytic psychology is that between the so-called unconscious and the conscious. Faith as an act of the total personality is not imaginable without the participation of the unconscious elements in the personality structure. They are always present and decide largely about the content of faith. But, on the other hand, faith is a conscious act and the unconscious elements participate in the creation of faith only if they are taken into the personal center which transcends each of them. If this does not happen, if unconscious forces determine the mental status without a centered act, faith does not occur, and compulsions take its place. For faith is a matter of freedom. Freedom is nothing more than the possibility of centered personal acts. The frequent discussion in which faith and freedom are contrasted could be helped by the insight that faith is a free, namely, centered act of the personality. In this respect freedom and faith are identical.

1. Passion, from the Greek for "sexual love."
2. A 1949 novel, by the American writer John P. Marquand (1893–1960), about an ambitious middle-class banker in New York City and his upbringing in small-town New England.

Also important for the understanding of faith is the polarity between what Freud and his school call ego and superego. The concept of the superego is quite ambiguous. On the one hand, it is the basis of all cultural life because it restricts the uninhibited actualization of the always-driving libido; on the other hand, it cuts off man's vital forces, and produces disgust about the whole system of cultural restrictions, and brings about a neurotic state of mind. From this point of view, the symbols of faith are considered to be expressions of the superego or, more concretely, to be an expression of the father image which gives content to the superego. Responsible for this inadequate theory of the superego is Freud's naturalistic negation of norms and principles. If the superego is not established through valid principles, it becomes a suppressive tyrant. But real faith, even if it uses the father image for its expression, transforms this image into a principle of truth and justice to be defended even against the "father." Faith and culture can be affirmed only if the superego represents the norms and principles of reality.

This leads to the question of how faith as a personal, centered act is related to the rational structure of man's personality which is manifest in his meaningful language, in his ability to know the true and to do the good, in his sense of beauty and justice. All this, and not only his possibility to analyze, to calculate and to argue, makes him a rational being. But in spite of this larger concept of reason we must deny that man's essential nature is identical with the rational character of his mind. Man is able to decide for or against reason, he is able to create beyond reason or to destroy below reason. This power is the power of his self, the center of self-relatedness in which all elements of his being are united. Faith is not an act of any of his rational functions, as it is not an act of the unconscious, but it is an act in which both the rational and the nonrational elements of his being are transcended.

Faith as the embracing and centered act of the personality is "ecstatic." It transcends both the drives of the nonrational unconscious and the structures of the rational conscious. It transcends them, but it does not destroy them. The ecstatic character of faith does not exclude its rational character although it is not identical with it, and it includes nonrational strivings without being identical with them. In the ecstasy of faith there is an awareness of truth and of ethical value; there are also past loves and hates, conflicts and reunions, individual and collective influences. "Ecstasy" means "standing outside of oneself"—without ceasing to be oneself—with all the elements which are united in the personal center.

A further polarity in these elements, relevant for the understanding of faith, is the tension between the cognitive function of man's personal life, on the one hand, and emotion and will, on the other hand. In a later discussion I will try to show that many distortions of the meaning of faith are rooted in the attempt to subsume faith to the one or the other of these functions. At this point it must be stated as sharply and insistently as possible that in every act of faith there is cognitive affirmation, not as the result of an independent process of inquiry but as an inseparable element in a total act of acceptance and surrender. This also excludes the idea that faith is the result of an independent act of "will to believe." There is certainly affirmation by the will of what concerns one ultimately, but faith is not a creation of the will. In the ecstasy of faith the will to accept and to surrender is an element, but not the cause. And this is true also of feeling. Faith is not an emotional outburst: this is not the meaning of ecstasy. Certainly, emotion is in it, as in every act of man's spiritual life. But emotion does not produce faith. Faith has a cognitive content and is an act of the will. It is the unity of every element in the centered self. Of course, the unity of all elements in the act of faith does not prevent one or the other element from dominating in a special form of faith. It dominates the character of faith but it does not create the act of faith.

This also answers the question of a possible psychology of faith. Everything that happens in man's personal being can become an object of psychology. And it is rather important for both the philosopher of religion and the practical minister to know how the act of faith is embedded in the totality of psychological processes. But in contrast to this justified and desirable form of a psychology of faith there is another one which tries to derive faith from something that is not faith but is most frequently fear. The presupposition of this method is that fear or something else from which faith is derived is more original and basic than faith. But this presupposition cannot be proved. On the contrary, one can prove that in the scientific method which leads to such consequences faith is already effective. Faith precedes all attempts to derive it from something else, because these attempts are themselves based on faith.

PIERRE TEILHARD DE CHARDIN
1881–1955

FROM THE MASS ON THE WORLD

Pierre Teilhard de Chardin, the scion of two old and distinguished French families, was born in the Château de Sarcenat, near Clermont-Ferrand. After receiving a Jesuit education that included a degree in mathematics and philosophy, he entered the Jesuit novitiate at Aix-en-Provence in 1899. From 1905 to 1908, he taught physics and chemistry at the Jesuit College in Cairo, and for the next three years he studied theology in England, synthesizing his multidisciplinary training with evolutionary theory. He was ordained a priest in 1911. The next year, he began work as a paleontologist at the Musée National d'Histoire Naturelle, in Paris. Following courageous service as a stretcher-bearer in World War I (he was awarded the Legion of Honor), Teilhard returned to Paris, where he first studied geology, botany, and zoology at the Sorbonne and then became an assistant professor at the Institut Catholique, receiving his doctorate in science in 1922. He then went to China, where he did pioneering work in paleontology and geology. He remained in that country for more than two decades, with time off for travels all over the world. Meanwhile, the Vatican forbade him to teach and refused permission to print any of his books. He returned to France in 1946 and was elected to the French Academy of Sciences in 1950, but spent the last years of his life in New York, associated with a private foundation that enabled him to continue his scientific research. He died on Easter Sunday.

Teilhard's best-known works, *The Phenomenon of Man* (1955) and *The Divine Milieu* (1957), were published posthumously. Despite his lifelong membership in the

Jesuit Order, Teilhard was a controversial figure within the Roman Catholic Church, whose ban on his work was never publicly lifted. Essentially, his cosmic optimism clashed with the doctrine of original sin. In Teilhard's view, an evolutionary process was transforming matter into spirit (consciousness), and humanity would ultimately fuse with God (the "Omega Point"). In *The Phenomenon of Man*, he offered an evolution-based sense of creation that differed from the account in the Book of Genesis (see p. 83).

In the following selection, written in 1923, Teilhard is on expedition in China. Though lacking the physical necessities (bread and wine) to celebrate Mass, he engages in the priestly act of offering "all the labors and sufferings of the world" to God, seeing Earth as his altar. From the perspective of dogmatic Catholic theology, this prayer is literally too good to be true, because it fails to acknowledge the pivotal roles of human evil and Jesus' redemptive agony. Teilhard's grand vision of "Light eliminating our darkness" sounds inevitable, universal, and blissful. Differences between believers and unbelievers, along with present-day conflicts and the violence of history, melt away in the glow of "Blazing Spirit." With its rapturous language, sweeping planetary perspective, and mental toughness, the piece provides a glimpse of Teilhard in his characteristic posture of hopeful adoration. "The Mass on the World" was published in Teilhard's *Hymn of the Universe* (1961), a volume that collected writings from 1916 to 1955.

PRONOUNCING GLOSSARY

Aisne: *eyn*   Pierre Teilhard de Chardin: *pyehr te-yahr duh shahr-dahn´*

FROM THE MASS ON THE WORLD

Since once again, Lord—though this time not in the forests of the Aisne[1] but in the steppes of Asia—I have neither bread, nor wine, nor altar, I will raise myself beyond these symbols, up to the pure majesty of the real itself; I, your priest, will make the whole earth my altar and on it will offer you all the labours and sufferings of the world.

Over there, on the horizon, the sun has just touched with light the outermost fringe of the eastern sky. Once again, beneath this moving sheet of fire, the living surface of the earth wakes and trembles, and once again begins its fearful travail. I will place on my paten, O God, the harvest to be won by this renewal of labour. Into my chalice I shall pour all the sap which is to be pressed out this day from the earth's fruits.

My paten and my chalice are the depths of a soul laid widely open to all the forces which in a moment will rise up from every corner of the earth and converge upon the Spirit. Grant me the remembrance and the mystic presence of all those whom the light is now awakening to the new day.

One by one, Lord, I see and I love all those whom you have given me to sustain and charm my life. One by one also I number all those who make up that other beloved family which has gradually surrounded me, its unity

1. The region in northern France associated with the Aisne River. Here, in 1918, prevented by his military service from celebrating the Eucharist, Teilhard wrote "The Priest," an essay that later became the basis for "The Mass on the World."

fashioned out of the most disparate elements, with affinities of the heart, of scientific research and of thought. And again one by one—more vaguely it is true, yet all-inclusively—I call before me the whole vast anonymous army of living humanity; those who surround me and support me though I do not know them; those who come, and those who go; above all, those who in office, laboratory and factory, through their vision of truth or despite their error, truly believe in the progress of earthly reality and who today will take up again their impassioned pursuit of the light.

This restless multitude, confused or orderly, the immensity of which terrifies us; this ocean of humanity whose slow, monotonous wave-flows trouble the hearts even of those whose faith is most firm: it is to this deep that I thus desire all the fibres of my being should respond. All the things in the world to which this day will bring increase; all those that will diminish; all those too that will die: all of them, Lord, I try to gather into my arms, so as to hold them out to you in offering. This is the material of my sacrifice; the only material you desire.

Once upon a time men took into your temple the first fruits of their harvests, the flower of their flocks. But the offering you really want, the offering you mysteriously need every day to appease your hunger, to slake your thirst is nothing less than the growth of the world borne ever onwards in the stream of universal becoming.

Receive, O Lord, this all-embracing host which your whole creation, moved by your magnetism, offers you at this dawn of a new day.

This bread, our toil, is of itself, I know, but an immense fragmentation; this wine, our pain, is no more, I know, than a draught that dissolves. Yet in the very depths of this formless mass you have implanted—and this I am sure of, for I sense it—a desire, irresistible, hallowing, which makes us cry out, believer and unbeliever alike: 'Lord, make us *one*.'

Because, my God, though I lack the soul-zeal and the sublime integrity of your saints, I yet have received from you an overwhelming sympathy for all that stirs within the dark mass of matter; because I know myself to be irremediably less a child of heaven than a son of earth; therefore I will this morning climb up in spirit to the high places, bearing with me the hopes and the miseries of my mother;[2] and there—empowered by that priesthood which you alone (as I firmly believe) have bestowed on me—upon all that in the world of human flesh is now about to be born or to die beneath the rising sun I will call down the Fire.

✳ ✳ ✳

Fire, the source of being: we cling so tenaciously to the illusion that fire comes forth from the depths of the earth and that its flames grow progressively brighter as it pours along the radiant furrows of life's tillage. Lord, in your mercy you gave me to see that this idea is false, and that I must overthrow it if I were ever to have sight of you.

In the beginning was *Power*, intelligent, loving, energizing. In the beginning was the *Word*, supremely capable of mastering and moulding whatever might come into being in the world of matter. In the beginning there were not coldness and darkness: there was the *Fire*. This is the truth.

---

2. I.e., Earth.

So, far from light emerging gradually out of the womb of our darkness, it is the Light, existing before all else was made which, patiently, surely, eliminates our darkness. As for us creatures, of ourselves we are but emptiness and obscurity. But you, my God, are the inmost depths, the stability of that eternal *milieu*, without duration or space, in which our cosmos emerges gradually into being and grows gradually to its final completeness, as it loses those boundaries which to our eyes seem so immense. Everything is being; everywhere there is being and nothing but being, save in the fragmentation of creatures and the clash of their atoms.

Blazing Spirit, Fire, personal, super-substantial, the consummation of a union so immeasurably more lovely and more desirable than that destructive fusion of which all the pantheists dream: be pleased yet once again to come down and breathe a soul into the newly formed, fragile film of matter with which this day the world is to be freshly clothed.

I know we cannot forestall, still less dictate to you, even the smallest of your actions; from you alone comes all initiative—and this applies in the first place to my prayer.

Radiant Word, blazing Power, you who mould the manifold so as to breathe your life into it; I pray you, lay on us those your hands—powerful, considerate, omnipresent, those hands which do not (like our human hands) touch now here, now there, but which plunge into the depths and the totality, present and past, of things so as to reach us simultaneously through all that is most immense and most inward within us and around us.

May the might of those invincible hands direct and transfigure for the great world you have in mind that earthly travail which I have gathered into my heart and now offer you in its entirety. Remould it, rectify it, recast it down to the depths from whence it springs. You know how your creatures can come into being only, like shoot from stem, as part of an endlessly renewed process of evolution.

Do you now therefore, speaking through my lips, pronounce over this earthly travail your twofold efficacious word: the word without which all that our wisdom and our experience have built up must totter and crumble—the word through which all our most far-reaching speculations and our encounter with the universe are come together into a unity. Over every living thing which is to spring up, to grow, to flower, to ripen during this day say again the words: This is my Body. And over every death-force which waits in readiness to corrode, to wither, to cut down, speak again your commanding words which express the supreme mystery of faith: This is my Blood.[3]

3. See Matthew 26:26–28, Mark 14:22–25, and Luke 22:15–20.

THOMAS MERTON
1915–1968

FROM NO MAN IS AN ISLAND

Thomas Merton was born in Prades, Pyrénées-Orientales, France, to an American mother and a father from New Zealand. The family relocated to New York City shortly afterward. Merton's mother died in 1921, and he returned to France with his father in 1925, then moved to England in 1928. After studying at Cambridge University, he moved back to New York, where he received bachelor's and master's degrees in English from Columbia University. In 1938, Merton converted from his baptismal religion, Anglicanism, to Roman Catholicism. In 1942, he became a Trappist monk (Order of the Cistercians of the Strict Observance) at the Abbey of Our Lady of Gethsemani, near Bardstown, Kentucky. Seven years later, he was ordained as a priest and received the name Father Louis. Twenty-seven years to the day after entering the monastery, while at an interfaith conference in Bangkok, Thailand, Merton died by accidental electrocution.

Between the publication of his first book of poetry, in 1944, and his death, Merton wrote over seventy books. His major topics were spirituality, social justice, and pacifism. He gained international fame and cultural influence with a best-selling memoir, *The Seven Storey Mountain* (1948). In the following selection from *No Man Is an Island* (1955), whose title comes from a poem by John Donne (p. 451), Merton addresses the life of the "spiritual man." His tone is impersonal, dispassionate, severe, and restrained, generalizing and omitting concrete details about the contemporary world and himself (the "my flesh" in the opening lines refers to no one in particular). In laying down what he sees as universal rules of spirituality, Merton warns about the pitfalls of Christian asceticism: "bitterness and bad temper," hatred of material things, and self-centeredness (such as the Pharisee's in Luke 18:4–9). Like a spiritual director, he dispenses traditional wisdom about the quest to control wayward human impulses en route to union with God. Finding different sorts of drama in the ways the search unfolds, Merton writes a latter-day *Imitation of Christ* (p. 371).

FROM NO MAN IS AN ISLAND

From *Asceticism and Sacrifice*

1. If my soul silences my flesh by an act of violence, my flesh will take revenge on the soul, secretly infecting it with a spirit of revenge. Bitterness and bad temper are the flowers of an asceticism that has punished only the body. For the spirit is above the flesh, but not completely independent of the flesh. It reaps in itself what it sows in its own flesh. If the spirit is weak with the flesh, it will find in the flesh the image and accusation of its own weakness.[1] But if the spirit is violent with the flesh it will suffer, from the flesh, the rebound of its own violence. The false ascetic begins by being cruel to everybody because he is cruel to himself. But he ends by being cruel to everybody but himself.

---

1. Compare Matthew 26:41.

NO MAN IS AN ISLAND | 619

2. There is only one true asceticism: that which is guided not by our own spirit but by the Spirit of God. The spirit of man must first subject itself to grace and then it can bring the flesh in subjection both to grace and to itself. "If by the Spirit you mortify the deeds of the flesh, you shall live" (Romans 8:13).

But grace is charitable, merciful, kind, does not seek its own interests. Grace inspires us with no desire except to do the will of God, no matter what His will may be, no matter whether it be pleasing or unpleasant to our own nature.

Those, then, who put their passions to death not with the poison of their own ambition but with the clean blade of the will of God will live in the silence of true interior peace, for their lives are hidden with Christ in God. Such is the meek "violence" of those who take Heaven by storm.

3. The spiritual life is not a mere negation of matter. When the New Testament speaks of "the flesh" as our enemy, it takes the flesh in a special sense. When Christ said: "The flesh profiteth nothing" (John 6:64), he was speaking of flesh without spirit, flesh living for its own ends, not only in sensual but even in spiritual things.

It is one thing to live *in* the flesh, and quite another to live *according to* the flesh. In the second case, one acquires that "prudence of the flesh which is opposed to God" because it makes the flesh an end in itself. But as long as we are on this earth our vocation demands that we live spiritually while still "in the flesh."

Our whole being, both body and soul, is to be spiritualized and elevated by grace. The Word Who was made flesh and dwelt among us, Who gave us His flesh to be our spiritual food, Who sits at the right hand of God in a body full of divine glory, and Who will one day raise our bodies also from the dead, did not mean us to despise the body or take it lightly when He told us to deny ourselves. We must indeed control the flesh, we must "chastise it and bring it into subjection," but this chastisement is as much for the body's benefit as for the soul's. For the good of the body is not found in the body alone but in the good of the whole person.

4. The spiritual man, who lives as a son of God, seeks the principle of his life above the flesh and above human nature itself. "As many as received Him, He gave them the power to become the sons of God, to them that believe in His name. Who are born not of blood, nor of the will of the flesh, nor of the will of man, but of God" (John 1:12–13). God Himself, then, is the source of the spiritual life. But He communicates His life and His Spirit to men, made of body and soul. It is not His plan to lure the soul out of the body, but to sanctify the two together, divinizing the whole man so that the Christian can say: "I live, now not I but Christ liveth in me. And that I live now in the flesh, I live in the faith of the Son of God Who loved me" (Galatians 2:20). "That the justification of the law might be fulfilled in us who walk not according to the flesh but according to the spirit . . . You are not in the flesh but in the Spirit if so be that the Spirit of God dwell in you" (Romans 8:4, 9).

5. We cannot become saints merely by trying to run away from material things. To have a spiritual life is to have a life that is spiritual in all its

wholeness—a life in which the actions of the body are holy because of the soul, and the soul is holy because of God dwelling and acting in it. When we live such a life, the actions of our body are directed to God by God Himself and give Him glory, and at the same time they help to sanctify the soul.

The saint, therefore, is sanctified not only by fasting when he should fast but also by eating when he should eat. He is not only sanctified by his prayers in the darkness of the night, but by the sleep that he takes in obedience to God, Who made us what we are. Not only His solitude contributes to his union with God, but also his supernatural love for his friends and his relatives and those with whom he lives and works.

God, in the same infinite act of will, wills the good of all beings and the good of each individual thing: for all lesser goods coincide in the one perfect good which is His love for them. Consequently it is clear that some men will become saints by a celibate life, but many more will become saints as married men, since it is necessary that there be more married men than celibates in the world. How then can we imagine that the cloister is the only place in which men can become saints? Now the life of the body seems to receive less consideration in the cloister than it does in secular life. But it is clear that married life, for its success, presupposes the capacity for a deeply human love which ought to be spiritual and physical at the same time. The existence of a sacrament of matrimony shows that the Church considers the body neither evil nor repugnant, but that the "flesh" spiritualized by prayer and the Holy Ghost, yet remaining completely physical, can come to play an important part in our sanctification.

6. It gives great glory to God for a person to live in this world using and appreciating the good things of life without care, without anxiety, and without inordinate passion. In order to know and love God through His gifts, we have to use them as if we used them not (1 Corinthians 7:31)—and yet we have to *use* them. For to use things as if we used them not means to use them without selfishness, without fear, without afterthought, and with perfect gratitude and confidence and love of God. All inordinate concern over the material side of life was reproved by Christ when He said: "What one of you, by taking thought, can add to his stature one cubit?" (Matthew 6:27). But we cannot use created things without anxiety unless we are detached from them. At the same time, we become detached from them by using them sparingly—and yet without anxiety.

The tremulous scrupulosity of those who are obsessed with pleasures they love and fear narrows their souls and makes it impossible for them to get away from their own flesh. They have tried to become spiritual by worrying about the flesh, and as a result they are haunted by it. They have ended in the flesh because they began in it, and the fruit of their anxious asceticism is that they "use things not," but do so as if they used them. In their very self-denial they defile themselves with what they pretend to avoid. They do not have the pleasure they seek, but they taste the bitter discouragement, the feeling of guilt which they would like to escape. This is not the way of the spirit. For when our intention is directed to God, our very use of material things sanctifies both them and us, provided we use them without selfishness and without presumption, glad to receive them from Him Who loves us and Whose love is all we desire.

C. S. LEWIS
1898–1963

FROM THE FOUR LOVES

Clive Staples Lewis was born in Belfast, Ireland, and died in Oxford, England. At age fifteen, he became an atheist and left the Church of Ireland (part of the Anglican Communion). He received a scholarship to University College, Oxford, in 1916, but left the next year to serve in the British Army during World War I. Once back at Oxford, Lewis had a brilliant record, with "Firsts" in classics, philosophy, ancient history, and English. In 1931, Lewis returned to Christianity, in large part thanks to his persuasive friend the English writer J. R. R. Tolkien (1892–1973). For the rest of his life, Lewis was a committed Anglican.

In addition to teaching English—at Oxford for nearly thirty years and then as the first professor of medieval and Renaissance English at Cambridge University—Lewis was a public intellectual; a prolific writer of fiction, science fiction, fantasy, poetry, and scholarly nonfiction; and one of the most celebrated twentieth-century apologists for Christianity. His most popular work, *The Chronicles of Narnia* (1950–56), is a series of seven fantasy novels for children. *The Screwtape Letters* (1942) consists of fictional letters from a senior devil, Screwtape, offering advice to his inexperienced nephew, Wormwood, on how to deceive and damn a Christian man whom he calls "the patient." For all of Screwtape's cleverness, the demons' targeted victim escapes, dies, and goes to heaven.

In *The Four Loves* (1960), Lewis meditates on the differences and similarities between friendship, affection, eros, and charity. In regard to this last and highest kind of love, he considers the dilemma of human attachment: to love is to become vulnerable; worse, it is inevitably to lose what one loves. Faced with this quandary, Saint Augustine (see p. 226), in the *Confessions*, argues that the only way out is to love God alone, the divine Lover who never fails or disappoints. Lewis disagrees. To love is to embrace tragedy (in 1960, his beloved wife died of bone cancer after four years of late marriage). The sole way to avoid such tragedy is to take refuge in frozen isolation (a form of hell). But if one gives oneself to God in a love that takes precedence over all others—Lewis quotes Jesus' fierce demand that his disciples "hate" their parents, spouses, and own lives—one paradoxically recovers all lost loves in Love itself.

PRONOUNCING GLOSSARY

Augustine: *uh-guhs´-tin*

Epaphroditus: *ep-af-ro-dai´-tus* [*ai* rhyming with *rye*]

Lazarus: *la´-zuh-rus*

Nebridius: *neh-bri´-dee-uhs*

FROM THE FOUR LOVES
From *Charity*

In words which can still bring tears to the eyes, St. Augustine describes the desolation in which the death of his friend Nebridius plunged him (*Confessions* IV, 10). Then he draws a moral. This is what comes, he says, of giving one's heart to anything but God. All human beings pass away. Do not let your happiness depend on something you may lose. If love is to be a blessing, not a misery, it must be for the only Beloved who will never pass away.

Of course this is excellent sense. Don't put your goods in a leaky vessel. Don't spend too much on a house you may be turned out of. And there is no man alive who responds more naturally than I to such canny maxims. I am a safety-first creature. Of all arguments against love none makes so strong an appeal to my nature as "Careful! This might lead you to suffering."

To my nature, my temperament, yes. Not to my conscience. When I respond to that appeal I seem to myself to be a thousand miles away from Christ. If I am sure of anything I am sure that His teaching was never meant to confirm my congenital preference for safe investments and limited liabilities. I doubt whether there is anything in me that pleases Him less. And who could conceivably begin to love God on such a prudential ground—because the security (so to speak) is better? Who could even include it among the grounds for loving? Would you choose a wife or a Friend—if it comes to that, would you choose a dog—in this spirit? One must be outside the world of love, of all loves, before one thus calculates. Eros, lawless Eros, preferring the Beloved to happiness, is more like Love himself than this.

I think that this passage in the *Confessions* is less a part of St. Augustine's Christendom than a hangover from the high-minded Pagan philosophies in which he grew up. It is closer to Stoic "apathy" or neo-Platonic mysticism than to charity. We follow One who wept over Jerusalem and at the grave of Lazarus, and, loving all, yet had one disciple whom, in a special sense, he "loved."[1] St. Paul has a higher authority with us than St. Augustine—St. Paul who shows no sign that he would not have suffered like a man, and no feeling that he ought not so to have suffered, if Epaphroditus had died (Philemon 2:27).

Even if it were granted that insurances against heartbreak were our highest wisdom, does God Himself offer them? Apparently not. Christ comes at last to say "Why hast thou forsaken me?"[2]

There is no escape along the lines St. Augustine suggests. Nor along any other lines. There is no safe investment. To love at all is to be vulnerable. Love anything, and your heart will certainly be wrung and possibly be broken. If you want to make sure of keeping it intact, you must give your heart to no one, not even to an animal. Wrap it carefully round with hobbies and little luxuries; avoid all entanglements; lock it up safe in the casket or coffin of your selfishness. But in that casket—safe, dark, motionless, airless—it will change. It will not be broken; it will become unbreakable, impenetrable, irredeemable. The alternative to tragedy, or at least to the risk of tragedy, is damnation. The only place outside Heaven where you can be perfectly safe from all the dangers and perturbations of love is Hell.

I believe that the most lawless and inordinate loves are less contrary to God's will than a self-invited and self-protective lovelessness. It is like hiding the talent in a napkin[3] and for much the same reason. "I knew thee

---

1. See Luke 19:41–44; John 11:33–35; and John 13:23–25, 19:26–27, 20:1–10, 21:1–25, and 21:20–23.

2. Matthew 27:46, where Jesus quotes Psalms 22:1.

3. See Luke 19:20.

that thou wert a hard man."[4] Christ did not teach and suffer that we might become, even in the natural loves, more careful of our own happiness. If a man is not uncalculating towards the earthly beloveds whom he has seen, he is none the more likely to be so towards God whom he has not. We shall draw nearer to God, not by trying to avoid the sufferings inherent in all loves, but by accepting them and offering them to Him; throwing away all defensive armour. If our hearts need to be broken, and if He chooses this as the way in which they should break, so be it.

It remains certainly true that all natural loves can be inordinate. *Inordinate* does not mean "insufficiently cautious." Nor does it mean "too big." It is not a quantitative term. It is probably impossible to love any human being simply "too much." We may love him too much *in proportion* to our love for God; but it is the smallness of our love for God, not the greatness of our love for the man, that constitutes the inordinacy. But even this must be refined upon. Otherwise we shall trouble some who are very much on the right road but alarmed because they cannot feel towards God so warm a sensible emotion as they feel for the earthly Beloved. It is much to be wished—at least I think so—that we all, at all times, could. We must pray that this gift should be given us. But the question whether we are loving God or the earthly Beloved "more" is not, so far as concerns our Christian duty, a question about the comparative intensity of two feelings. The real question is, which (when the alternative comes) do you serve, or choose, or put first? To which claim does your will, in the last resort, yield?

As so often, Our Lord's own words are both far fiercer and far more tolerable than those of the theologians. He says nothing about guarding against earthly loves for fear we might be hurt; He says something that cracks like a whip about trampling them all under foot the moment they hold us back from following Him. "If any man come to me and hate not his father and mother and wife . . . and his own life also, he cannot be my disciple" (Luke 14:26).

* * *

I will not say that this duty is hard; some find it too easy; some, hard almost beyond endurance. What is hard for all is to know when the occasion for such "hating" has arisen. Our temperaments deceive us. The meek and tender—uxorious husbands, submissive wives, doting parents, dutiful children—will not easily believe that it has ever arrived. Self-assertive people, with a dash of the bully in them, will believe it too soon. That is why it is of such extreme importance so to order our loves that it is unlikely to arrive at all.

* * *

For the dream of finding our end, the thing we were made for, in a Heaven of purely human love could not be true unless our whole Faith were wrong. We were made for God. Only by being in some respect like Him, only by being a manifestation of His beauty, lovingkindness, wisdom or goodness, has any earthly Beloved excited our love. It is not that we have loved them too much, but that we did not quite understand what we were loving. It is not that we

4. Matthew 25:24.

shall be asked to turn from them, so dearly familiar, to a Stranger. When we see the face of God we shall know that we have always known it. He has been a party to, has made, sustained and moved moment by moment within, all our earthly experiences of innocent love. All that was true love in them was, even on earth, far more His than ours, and ours only because His. In Heaven there will be no anguish and no duty of turning away from our earthly Beloveds. First, because we shall have turned already; from the portraits to the Original, from the rivulets to the Fountain, from the creatures He made lovable to Love Himself. But secondly, because we shall find them all in Him. By loving Him more than them we shall love them more than we now do.

MARTIN LUTHER KING, JR.
1929–1968

I HAVE A DREAM

Martin Luther King, Jr., was born Michael Luther King, Jr., in Atlanta, Georgia, and later changed his name to Martin. He received his B.A. from Morehouse College, in Atlanta; his B.D. from Crozer Theological Seminary, near Chester, Pennsylvania; and, in 1955, his Ph.D. in systematic theology from Boston University. In 1954, he became pastor of Dexter Avenue Baptist Church, in Montgomery, Alabama. From 1960 until his death, King served as copastor, with his father, of Ebenezer Baptist Church, in Atlanta; his grandfather had also served as pastor at the church. A member of the executive committee of the National Association for the Advancement of Colored People (NAACP), King led the nonviolent, 382-day Montgomery Bus Boycott, the first major African-American civil rights demonstration, in 1955. Two years later, King became president of the Southern Christian Leadership Conference, meant to provide leadership for the growing civil rights movement. During the massive protest he led in Birmingham, Alabama, in 1963, King wrote his electrifying manifesto "Letter from Birmingham Jail."

In August 1963, he directed between 200,000 and 300,000 people in a peaceful march on Washington, D.C., organized by a group of civil rights, labor, and religious organizations. At the end of the march, standing in front of the Lincoln Memorial and facing the Washington Monument, King delivered his now-famous "I Have a Dream" address. For his lifelong commitment to nonviolent protest, at age thirty-five, King became the youngest man to receive the Nobel Peace Prize. He was assassinated in Memphis, Tennessee, where he was to lead a protest march in sympathy with striking sanitation workers.

While "I Have a Dream" is first and foremost a political statement, it includes a number of important biblical references. In the sixth paragraph, "dark and desolate valley of segregation" echoes Psalms 23:4, as does "valley of despair" in the sixteenth paragraph. In the fourteenth paragraph, "until justice rolls down like waters and righteousness like a mighty stream" is a quotation from Amos (5:24), an angry prophet much given to attacking the forces of oppression and complacent corruption in the society of his day. The prediction that makes up the twenty-second paragraph—"I have a dream that one day every valley shall be exalted . . ."—comes from Isaiah 40:4–5, which celebrates Israel's return from exile in Babylon; it would also have been familiar to many listeners as a line from the opening section of Handel's *Mes-*

siah (1742). The final quotation, from the Negro spiritual "Free at Last," turns a reference to "Goin' meet King Jesus in the air" into a moment of explosive political hope.

But King is not simply framing a set of secular hopes and demands in pious language. The biblical images evoke the only coherent conceptual world that enslaved blacks, deprived of their homeland culture and their freedom, had access to. The Bible, like the many songs based on it (see p. 515), spoke to them of liberation, comfort after suffering, and long overdue reward. A century after U.S. president Abraham Lincoln (1809–1865; in office from 1861 until his death) signed the Emancipation Proclamation and subsequently helped pass the Thirteenth Amendment to the Constitution, segregation prolonged the oppression of bondage. The Bible's unchallenged place in American life added a dimension of sacred seriousness that lifted the civil rights movement beyond the usual political calculations of who-gets-what. Insofar as whites were sincere about their religion, they had to acknowledge King's explicit appeal to them as morally binding—which is why, in the wake of his still unrealized dream, the speech continues to resonate.

I HAVE A DREAM

I am happy to join with you today in what will go down in history as the greatest demonstration for freedom in the history of our nation.

Fivescore years ago, a great American, in whose symbolic shadow we stand today, signed the Emancipation Proclamation. This momentous decree came as a great beacon light of hope to millions of Negro slaves who had been seared in the flames of withering injustice. It came as a joyous daybreak to end the long night of their captivity.

But one hundred years later, the Negro still is not free; one hundred years later, the life of the Negro is still sadly crippled by the manacles of segregation and the chains of discrimination; one hundred years later, the Negro lives on a lonely island of poverty in the midst of a vast ocean of material prosperity; one hundred years later, the Negro is still languished in the corners of American society and finds himself in exile in his own land.

So we've come here today to dramatize a shameful condition. In a sense we've come to our nation's capital to cash a check. When the architects of our republic wrote the magnificent words of the Constitution and the Declaration of Independence, they were signing a promissory note to which every American was to fall heir. This note was the promise that all men, yes, black men as well as white men, would be guaranteed the unalienable rights of life, liberty, and the pursuit of happiness.

It is obvious today that America has defaulted on this promissory note in so far as her citizens of color are concerned. Instead of honoring this sacred obligation, America has given the Negro people a bad check; a check which has come back marked "insufficient funds." We refuse to believe that there are insufficient funds in the great vaults of opportunity of this nation. And so we've come to cash this check, a check that will give us upon demand the riches of freedom and the security of justice.

We have also come to this hallowed spot to remind America of the fierce urgency of now. This is no time to engage in the luxury of cooling off or to take the tranquilizing drug of gradualism. Now is the time to make real the promises of democracy; now is the time to rise from the dark and desolate valley of segregation to the sunlit path of racial justice; now is the time to

At the March on Washington for Jobs and Freedom, following a series of speeches and musical performances, Martin Luther King, Jr., delivered his "I Have a Dream" speech.

lift our nation from the quicksands of racial injustice to the solid rock of brotherhood; now is the time to make justice a reality for all God's children. It would be fatal for the nation to overlook the urgency of the moment. This sweltering summer of the Negro's legitimate discontent will not pass until there is an invigorating autumn of freedom and equality.

Nineteen sixty-three is not an end, but a beginning. And those who hope that the Negro needed to blow off steam and will now be content, will have a rude awakening if the nation returns to business as usual.

There will be neither rest nor tranquility in America until the Negro is granted his citizenship rights. The whirlwinds of revolt will continue to shake the foundations of our nation until the bright day of justice emerges.

But there is something that I must say to my people who stand on the warm threshold which leads into the palace of justice. In the process of gaining our rightful place we must not be guilty of wrongful deeds.

Let us not seek to satisfy our thirst for freedom by drinking from the cup of bitterness and hatred. We must forever conduct our struggle on the high plane of dignity and discipline. We must not allow our creative protest to degenerate into physical violence. Again and again we must rise to the majestic heights of meeting physical force with soul force.

The marvelous new militancy which has engulfed the Negro community must not lead us to a distrust of all white people, for many of our white brothers, as evidenced by their presence here today, have come to realize that their destiny is tied up with our destiny and they have come to realize that their freedom is inextricably bound to our freedom. This offense we share mounted to storm the battlements of injustice must be carried forth by a biracial army. We cannot walk alone.

And as we walk, we must make the pledge that we shall always march ahead. We cannot turn back. There are those who are asking the devotees of civil rights, "When will you be satisfied?" We can never be satisfied as long as the Negro is the victim of the unspeakable horrors of police brutality.

We can never be satisfied as long as our bodies, heavy with fatigue of travel, cannot gain lodging in the motels of the highways and the hotels of the cities. We cannot be satisfied as long as the Negro's basic mobility is from a smaller ghetto to a larger one.

We can never be satisfied as long as our children are stripped of their selfhood and robbed of their dignity by signs stating "for whites only." We cannot be satisfied as long as a Negro in Mississippi cannot vote and a Negro in New York believes he has nothing for which to vote. No, we are not satisfied, and we will not be satisfied until justice rolls down like waters and righteousness like a mighty stream.

I am not unmindful that some of you come here out of excessive trials and tribulation. Some of you have come fresh from narrow jail cells. Some of you have come from areas where your quest for freedom left you battered by the storms of persecution and staggered by the winds of police brutality. You have been the veterans of creative suffering. Continue to work with the faith that unearned suffering is redemptive.

Go back to Mississippi; go back to Alabama; go back to South Carolina; go back to Georgia; go back to Louisiana; go back to the slums and ghettos of the northern cities, knowing that somehow this situation can, and will be changed. Let us not wallow in the valley of despair.

So I say to you, my friends, that even though we must face the difficulties of today and tomorrow, I still have a dream. It is a dream deeply rooted in the American dream that one day this nation will rise up and live out the true meaning of its creed—we hold these truths to be self-evident, that all men are created equal.

I have a dream that one day on the red hills of Georgia, sons of former slaves and sons of former slave-owners will be able to sit down together at the table of brotherhood.

I have a dream that one day, even the state of Mississippi, a state sweltering with the heat of injustice, sweltering with the heat of oppression, will be transformed into an oasis of freedom and justice.

I have a dream my four little children will one day live in a nation where they will not be judged by the color of their skin but by the content of their character. I have a dream today!

I have a dream that one day, down in Alabama, with its vicious racists, with its governor having his lips dripping with the words of interposition and nullification, that one day, right there in Alabama, little black boys and black girls will be able to join hands with little white boys and white girls as sisters and brothers. I have a dream today!

I have a dream that one day every valley shall be exalted, every hill and mountain shall be made low, the rough places shall be made plain, and the crooked places shall be made straight and the glory of the Lord will be revealed and all flesh shall see it together.

This is our hope. This is the faith that I go back to the South with.

With this faith we will be able to hew out of the mountain of despair a stone of hope. With this faith we will be able to transform the jangling discords of our nation into a beautiful symphony of brotherhood.

With this faith we will be able to work together, to pray together, to struggle together, to go to jail together, to stand up for freedom together, knowing that we will be free one day. This will be the day when all of God's children will be able to sing with new meaning—"my country 'tis of thee; sweet land of liberty; of thee I sing; land where my fathers died, land of the pilgrim's pride; from every mountain side, let freedom ring"—and if America is to be a great nation, this must become true.

So let freedom ring from the prodigious hilltops of New Hampshire.

Let freedom ring from the mighty mountains of New York.

Let freedom ring from the heightening Alleghenies of Pennsylvania.

Let freedom ring from the snow-capped Rockies of Colorado.

Let freedom ring from the curvaceous slopes of California.

But not only that.

Let freedom ring from Stone Mountain of Georgia.

Let freedom ring from Lookout Mountain of Tennessee.

Let freedom ring from every hill and molehill of Mississippi, from every mountainside, let freedom ring.

And when we allow freedom to ring, when we let it ring from every village and hamlet, from every state and city, we will be able to speed up that day when all of God's children—black men and white men, Jews and Gentiles, Catholics and Protestants—will be able to join hands and to sing in the words of the old Negro spiritual, "Free at last, free at last; thank God Almighty, we are free at last."

THE SECOND VATICAN COUNCIL
1965

NOSTRA AETATE

The Second Vatican Council (also known as Vatican II) was the twenty-first ecumenical council of the Roman Catholic Church. (For information on ecumenical councils generally, see pp. 163 and 207.) It was the second such council held at St. Peter's Basilica, in the Vatican.

Pope Pius IX (1792–1878; pope from 1846 until his death) convoked the First Vatican Council in 1868. The mood at this council and the pope's intent were strongly defensive. Militarily, the Papal States—approximately the middle third of the Italian peninsula—were besieged by the forces battling for a united Italy under Giuseppe Garibaldi (1807–1882). Spiritually, the bishops who attended the council understood Roman Catholicism to be under threat from modernity. In 1864, Pius IX had issued a much-noticed "Syllabus of Errors," in which many of the assumptions of modernity (see pp. 469–72) were condemned as heretical. By far the most consequential and lastingly controversial action taken by the First Vatican Council, before it was abruptly cut short in 1870 when Rome fell to Garibaldi's forces, was its formal definition of papal infallibility as a part of Roman Catholic dogma.

Such was the troubled memory of the most recent ecumenical council when Pope John XXIII (1881–1963; pope from 1958 until his death) startled the world by convoking the Second Vatican Council, in 1962. More than the mere fact of the gathering, what startled was the unprecedented tone the amiable pope set—captured in an Italian word that became a byword for the council: *aggiornamento*, "updating." Rather than closed or anxiously defensive, the council, especially in certain historic declarations, seemed to strike a new tone of openness to modernity, to other Christian communions, and—in the following document—even to non-Christian religions.

The Greek term *oikouménē*, from which *ecumenical* is derived, originally referred to the entire inhabited world. For the first ecumenical council, the Council of Nicaea (see p. 213), bishops came from everywhere within the Roman Empire. Over time, in Church usage *ecumenical* came to refer to the entire Church, wherever located. In other words, the term describes efforts to improve relations among the many Christian Churches en route to some semblance of world Christian unity. Ecumenism, then, does not properly apply to relations between Christianity and the non-Christian religions. Nonetheless, the late twentieth and the twenty-first centuries have seen unprecedented efforts to foster inter-religious dialogue across even the deepest divisions.

On October 28, 1965, the bishops assembled at Vatican II issued the declaration *Nostra Aetate*, a revolutionary statement by the Catholic Church on the relationship of Catholic Christianity to the other religions of the world. The Latin title (its first words, as Vatican documents are commonly titled) means "In Our Time." Four non-Christian religious traditions—Hinduism, Buddhism, Judaism, and Islam—are referred to in the declaration, each in a few sentences. For its forthright condemnation of anti-Semitism, *Nostra Aetate* has had its largest impact on Catholic/Jewish relations.

John XXIII died before Vatican II had completed its work. He was succeeded by Paul VI (1897–1978), who oversaw the council until its close, in 1965. Paul VI is best remembered for issuing a 1968 letter to the Catholic Church: *Humanae Vitae,* "Of Human Life." This encyclical, by reasserting the Roman Catholic prohibition on all forms of artificial birth control, has been seen as marking the true close of Vatican II and the start of a gradual retreat from *aggiornamento*. Nonetheless, certain Vatican II declarations, especially *Nostra Aetate*, continue to have clear effects.

PRONOUNCING GLOSSARY

Nostra Aetate: *noh´-struh ay-tah´-tay*

NOSTRA AETATE

1. In our day, when people are drawing more closely together and the bonds of friendship between different peoples are being strengthened, the church examines more carefully its relations with non-christian religions. Ever aware of its duty to foster unity and charity among individuals, and even among nations, it reflects at the outset on what people have in common and what tends to bring them together.

Humanity forms but one community. This is so because all stem from the one stock which God created to people the entire earth (see Acts 17:26), and also because all share a common destiny, namely God. His providence, evident goodness, and saving designs extend to all humankind (see Wisdom 8:1; Acts 14:17; Romans 2:6–7; 1 Timothy 2:4) against the day when the elect are

---

FROM *Vatican Council II: The Basic Sixteen Documents*, ed. Austin Flannery. Some of the parenthetical Bible citations are from the Latin document, and some were supplied by the original editor of this English-language source.

gathered together in the holy city which is illumined by the glory of God, and in whose splendor all peoples will walk (see Apocalypse 21:23 ff.).

People look to their different religions for an answer to the unsolved riddles of human existence. The problems that weigh heavily on people's hearts are the same today as in past ages. What is humanity? What is the meaning and purpose of life? What is upright behavior, and what is sinful? Where does suffering originate, and what end does it serve? How can genuine happiness be found? What happens at death? What is judgment? What reward follows death? And finally, what is the ultimate mystery, beyond human explanation, which embraces our entire existence, from which we take our origin and towards which we tend?

2. Throughout history, to the present day, there is found among different peoples a certain awareness of a hidden power, which lies behind the course of nature and the events of human life. At times, there is present even a recognition of a supreme being, or still more of a Father. This awareness and recognition results in a way of life that is imbued with a deep religious sense. The religions which are found in more advanced civilizations endeavor by way of well-defined concepts and exact language to answer these questions. Thus, in Hinduism people explore the divine mystery and express it in both the limitless riches of myth and the accurately defined insights of philosophy. They seek release from the trials of the present life by ascetical practices, profound meditation and recourse to God in confidence and love. Buddhism in its various forms testifies to the essential inadequacy of this changing world. It proposes a way of life by which people can, with confidence and trust, attain a state of perfect liberation and reach supreme illumination either through their own efforts or with divine help. So, too, other religions which are found throughout the world attempt in different ways to overcome the restlessness of people's hearts by outlining a program of life covering doctrine, moral precepts and sacred rites.

The Catholic Church rejects nothing of what is true and holy in these religions. It has a high regard for the manner of life and conduct, the precepts and doctrines which, although differing in many ways from its own teaching, nevertheless often reflect a ray of that truth which enlightens all men and women. Yet it proclaims and is in duty bound to proclaim without fail, Christ who is the way, the truth and the life (John 1:6). In him, in whom God reconciled all things to himself (see 2 Corinthians 5:18–19), people find the fullness of their religious life.

The church, therefore, urges its sons and daughters to enter with prudence and charity into discussion and collaboration with members of other religions. Let Christians, while witnessing to their own faith and way of life, acknowledge, preserve and encourage the spiritual and moral truths found among non-Christians, together with their social life and culture.

3. The church has also a high regard for the Muslims. They worship God, who is one, living and subsistent, merciful and almighty, the Creator of heaven and earth, who has also spoken to humanity. They endeavor to submit themselves without reserve to the hidden decrees of God, just as Abraham submitted himself to God's plan,[1] to whose faith Muslims eagerly link their own. Although not acknowledging him as God, they venerate Jesus as a

---

1. For information on Abraham, other biblical figures mentioned in the following paragraphs, and concepts such as the New Covenant, see pp. 75, 83, and 89.

prophet; his virgin Mother they also honor, and even at times devoutly invoke. Further, they await the day of judgment and the reward of God following the resurrection of the dead. For this reason they highly esteem an upright life and worship God, especially by way of prayer, alms-deeds and fasting.

Over the centuries many quarrels and dissensions have arisen between Christians and Muslims. The sacred council now pleads with all to forget the past, and urges that a sincere effort be made to achieve mutual understanding; for the benefit of all, let them together preserve and promote peace, liberty, social justice and moral values.

4. Sounding the depths of the mystery which is the church, this sacred council remembers the spiritual ties which link the people of the new covenant to the stock of Abraham.

The church of Christ acknowledges that in God's plan of salvation the beginnings of its faith and election are to be found in the patriarchs, Moses and the prophets. It professes that all Christ's faithful, who as people of faith are daughters and sons of Abraham (see Galatians 3:7), are included in the same patriarch's call and that the salvation of the church is mystically prefigured in the exodus of God's chosen people from the land of bondage. On this account the church cannot forget that it received the revelation of the Old Testament by way of that people with whom God in his inexpressible mercy established the ancient covenant. Nor can it forget that it draws nourishment from that good olive tree onto which the wild olive branches of the Gentiles have been grafted (see Romans 11:17–24). The church believes that Christ who is our peace has through his cross reconciled Jews and Gentiles and made them one in himself (see Ephesians 2:14–16).

Likewise, the church keeps ever before its mind the words of the apostle Paul about his kin: "they are Israelites, and it is for them to be sons and daughters, to them belong the glory, the covenants, the giving of the law, the worship, and the promises; to them belong the patriarchs, and of their race according to the flesh, is the Christ" (Romans 9:4–5), the Son of the Virgin Mary. It is mindful, moreover, that the apostles, the pillars on which the church stands, are of Jewish descent, as are many of those early disciples who proclaimed the Gospel of Christ to the world.

As holy scripture testifies, Jerusalem did not recognize God's moment when it came (see Luke 19:42). Jews for the most part did not accept the Gospel; on the contrary, many opposed its spread (see Romans 11:28). Even so, the apostle Paul maintains that the Jews remain very dear to God, for the sake of the patriarchs, since God does not take back the gifts he bestowed or the choice he made. Together with the prophets and that same apostle, the church awaits the day, known to God alone, when all peoples will call on God with one voice and "serve him shoulder to shoulder" (Sophia [Wisdom] 3:9; see Isaiah 66:23; Psalms 65:4; Romans 11:11–32).

Since Christians and Jews have such a common spiritual heritage, this sacred council wishes to encourage and further mutual understanding and appreciation. This can be achieved, especially, by way of biblical and theological enquiry and through friendly discussions.

Even though the Jewish authorities and those who followed their lead pressed for the death of Christ (see John 19:6), neither all Jews indiscriminately at that time, nor Jews today, can be charged with the crimes committed during his passion. It is true that the church is the new people of God, yet the Jews should not be spoken of as rejected or accursed as if this followed from holy scripture. Consequently, all must take care, lest in catechizing or in preaching the word of God, they teach anything which is not in accord with the truth of the Gospel message or the spirit of Christ.

Indeed, the church reproves every form of persecution against whomsoever it may be directed. Remembering, then, its common heritage with the Jews and moved not by any political consideration, but solely by the religious motivation of christian charity, it deplores all hatreds, persecutions, displays of antisemitism levelled at any time or from any source against the Jews.

The church always held and continues to hold that Christ out of infinite love freely underwent suffering and death because of the sins of all, so that all might attain salvation. It is the duty of the church, therefore, in its preaching to proclaim the cross of Christ as the sign of God's universal love and the source of all grace.

5. We cannot truly pray to God the Father of all if we treat any people as other than sisters and brothers, for all are created in God's image. People's relation to God the Father and their relation to other women and men are so dependent on each other that the Scripture says "they who do not love, do not know God" (1 John 4:8).

There is no basis therefore, either in theory or in practice for any discrimination between individual and individual, or between people and people arising either from human dignity or from the rights which flow from it.

Therefore, the church reproves, as foreign to the mind of Christ, any discrimination against people or any harassment of them on the basis of their race, color, condition in life or religion. Accordingly, following the footsteps of the holy apostles Peter and Paul, the sacred council earnestly begs the christian faithful to "conduct themselves well among the Gentiles"[2] (1 Peter 2:12) and if possible, as far as depends on them, to be at peace with all people (see Romans 12:18) and in that way to be true daughters and sons of the Father who is in heaven (see Matthew 5:45).

2. I.e., in this sense, among the non-Christians.

GUSTAVO GUTIÉRREZ
born 1928

FROM THE TASK AND CONTENT OF LIBERATION THEOLOGY

Gustavo Gutiérrez Merino was born in Lima, Peru, of mixed Spanish and Quechuan ancestry. He studied medicine and humanities at the National University of San Marcos; psychology and philosophy at the University of Leuven (Louvain), Belgium; and theology at the Institut Pastoral d'Études Religieuses (IPER), Université Catholique, in Lyons, France. In 1959, he was ordained as a Roman Catholic priest in the Dominican Order. He has been a professor or visiting professor at universities in Peru, North America, and Europe and is currently a professor of theology at the University of Notre Dame, in Indiana. In 1993, he was awarded the Legion of Honor by the French government for his work among the poor and the oppressed. He is widely considered to be the father of liberation theology.

In "The Task and Content of Liberation Theology," Gutiérrez contrasts modern Western theology, which mostly confronts the problem of unbelief in a post-Christian world, with the theological discourses of places such as Latin America and the Caribbean, where religious belief is still the norm and the key figure is not the unbeliever, but the "nonperson," the downtrodden masses whose very existence calls into question "our economic, social, political, and cultural order." Liberation theology is less concerned with finding new answers than with changing the world. It sees the only authentic path to God as passing through commitment to the poor.

Gutiérrez notes that Christianity was first known as "the way" (Acts 9:2), namely both a way of thinking and a way of acting (or "lifestyle"), and so liberation theology is as much traditional as it is revolutionary. Nevertheless, from the outset, the Roman Catholic hierarchy has often accused this school of being Marxism in a Christian disguise, and of sacrificing orthodoxy to "orthopraxis" (doing justice). Gutiérrez, however, insists that liberation theology is based on spiritual insight, even though it is also committed to a "structural analysis" of the many forms of oppression (colonialist, capitalist, racist, sexist, etc.) that Latin American societies are laboring under. Its approach is "communitarian," in that centuries of abuse (sometimes aided and abetted by the Church) have coalesced into powerful institutional forces that must be opposed and transformed, for example through the founding of "Base Ecclesial Communities." Rather than the old-fashioned clerical hierarchies (pyramids of power with laypeople on the bottom), these groups are actively egalitarian. They embody Jesus' radical ideals, in that he called the poor "blessed" (Luke 6:20) and took their side (see the parable of Lazarus and the rich man in Luke 16:19–30). Still, it remains to be seen exactly what role liberation theology will play inside and outside the Catholic Church.

PRONOUNCING GLOSSARY

Arguedas: *ahr-ge´-dahs*

Bartolomé de Las Casas: *bar-toh-loh-may´ day lahs cah´-sahs*

credo ut intelligam: *cray´-doh oot in-tell´-ee-gahm*

derek: *de´-rek*

Gustavo Gutiérrez: *goo-stah´-voh goo-tee-ehr´-ez*

hodos: *haw´-doss*

Kunas: *koo´-nahs*

Mapuche: *mah-poo´-chay*

Medellín: *me-de-yeen´*

mündig: *moon´-dig*

raison d'être: *re´-zohn de´-truh*

FROM THE TASK AND CONTENT OF LIBERATION THEOLOGY

Theology as Critical Reflection

The theology of liberation is reflection on practice in the light of faith. In order to understand the scope of such an affirmation, it is helpful to examine the question posed at the outset of this discourse on faith, to see how in this perspective theological method and spirituality interrelate closely; and finally we can set out the present challenges.

TRANSLATED BY Judith Condor.

A POINT OF DEPARTURE

A good part of contemporary theology, since the Age of Enlightenment, appears to take as a point of departure the challenge raised by the (often unbelieving) modern spirit. The modern mentality questions the religious world and demands of it a purification and renewal. Bonhoeffer[1] takes up this challenge and incisively formulates the question that lies at the roots of much contemporary theology: 'how to announce God in a world that has come of age (mündig)?'

But in a continent like Latin America and the Caribbean, the challenge comes not in the first instance from the non-believer, but from the 'non-persons,' those who are not recognised as people by the existing social order: the poor, the exploited, those systematically and legally deprived of their status as human beings, those who barely realise what it is to be a human being. The 'non-person' questions not so much our religious universe but above all our economic, social, political and cultural order, calling for a transformation of the very foundations of a dehumanising society.

The question we face, therefore, is not so much how to talk of God in a world come of age, but how to proclaim God as Father in an inhuman world? How do we tell the 'non-persons' that they are the sons and daughters of God? These are the key questions for a theology that emerges from Latin America, and doubtless for other parts of the world in similar situations. These were the questions which, in a way, Bartolomé de Las Casas[2] and many others posed in the sixteenth century following their encounter with the indigenous population of America.

This does not mean that the questions posed by modernity are irrelevant for us. It is a question of emphasis, and in this light, poverty without doubt is the most important challenge.

REFLECTION ON PRAXIS

How to find a way to talk about a God who reveals Himself to us as love in a reality characterised by poverty and oppression? From the perspective of the theology of liberation, it is argued that the first step is to contemplate God and put God's will into practice; and only in a second moment can we think about God. What we mean to say by this is that the veneration of God and the doing of God's will are the necessary conditions for reflection on Him. In fact, only as a consequence of prayer and commitment is it possible to work out an authentic and respectful discourse about God. Through commitment, concretely commitment towards the poor, do we find the Lord (cf. Matthew 25:31–46); but at the same time this discovery deepens and renders more genuine our solidarity with the poor. Contemplation and commitment in human history are fundamental dimensions of Christian existence; in consequence, they cannot be avoided in the understanding of faith. The mystery is revealed through contemplation and solidarity with the poor; it is what we call the first act, Christian life, practice. Only thereafter can this life inspire reasoning: that is the second act.

---

1. Dietrich Bonhoeffer (see p. 587); imprisoned by the Nazis, he wrote speculatively about religion's role in the modern world. What, he asked, would a "religionless" Christianity look like?

2. See p. 438; Gutiérrez's book Diós o el Oro en las Indias (1989) is an important study of this groundbreaking figure.

Theology, as a critical reflection in the light of the Word adopted through faith on the presence of Christians in a tumultuous world, should help us to understand the relationship between the life of faith and the urgent need to build a society that is humane and just. It is called upon to make explicit the values of faith, hope and charity that that commitment involves. But it also helps to correct possible deviations, as well as to recall some aspects of the Christian life which risk being forgotten in view of immediate political priorities, however charitable those may be. This is the function of critical reflection which, by definition, should not be a Christian justification *a posteriori*. In essence, theology helps the commitment to liberation to be more evangelical, more concrete, more effective. Theology is at the service of the Church's task of evangelisation; it arises out of it as an ecclesial function.

The starting point for all theology is to be found in the act of faith. However, rather than being an intellectual adherence to the message, it should be a vital embracing of the gift of the Word as heard in the ecclesial community, as an encounter with God, and as love of one's brother and sister. It is about existence in its totality. To receive the Word, to give it life, to make it a concrete gesture; this is where understanding of faith begins. This is the meaning of Saint Anselm's *credo ut intelligam*.[3] The primacy of the love of God and the grace of faith give theology its *raison d'être*. Authentic theology is always spiritual, as was understood by the Fathers of the Church. All this means that the life of faith is not only a starting point, it is also the goal of theological reflection. To believe (life) and to understand (reflection) are therefore always part of a circular relationship.

A WAY OF LIVING AND THINKING

The distinction between the two moments (first and second acts) is a crucial point in the method of liberation theology; in other words, the process (method, *hodos*, the way) that should be followed for reflection in the light of the faith. This is indeed more traditional than many think, but what we need to underline here is that it is not only a question of theological methodology, rather it implies a lifestyle, a way of being, and of becoming a disciple of Jesus.

In the book which tells of the Acts of the first Christian communities, this is given a particular and original name: 'the way.' The term is used frequently in an absolute way without qualification. To follow the Way implies a pattern of conduct; the Hebrew word *derek*, which translates into Greek as *hodos*, in fact means both things at the same time: the way and conduct. Christians were characterised by their conduct and by their lifestyle. This is what distinguished the Christian communities in their early years in the Jewish and pagan world in which they lived and bore witness. Such conduct is a way of thinking and behaving, 'of walking according to the Holy Spirit' (Romans 8:4).

Following Jesus defines the Christian. It is a journey which, according to biblical sources, is a communitarian experience, because it is indeed a people that is on the move. The poor in Latin America have started to move in the struggle to affirm their human dignity and their status as sons and daughters of God. This movement embodies a spiritual experience. In other words, this is the place and the moment of an encounter with the Lord; it represents a way of following Jesus Christ.

---

3. I believe so that I may know (Latin); a phrase made famous by both Saint Anselm of Canterbury (see p. 294) and Saint Augustine of Hippo (see p. 226).

This is a fundamental point of reference for the theological reflection taking place in Latin America. It is aware that it is preceded by the spiritual experience of Christians committed to the process of liberation. This encounter with God and the discipleship of the Lord—sometimes extending to surrendering one's life, to martyrdom—has been made more urgent and fruitful by the events of recent years. In the context of the struggle for liberation motivated by love and justice for all, there has possibly opened up a new way of following Jesus in Latin America. There is a new spirituality which, for this very reason, resists clear definition and any attempt to imprison it in description, but which nevertheless is no less real or full of potential.

Following Jesus Christ is the basis of the direction that is adopted for doing theology. For this reason, it could be said that our methodology is our spirituality (in other words, a way of being Christian). Reflection on the mystery of God can be undertaken only if we follow in the steps of Jesus. Only if we walk in the way of the Spirit is it possible to understand and announce the gratuitous love of the Father for all people. Perhaps it is because of this relationship between Christian life and theological method that the Base Ecclesial Communities in Latin America[4] are becoming ever more the agents of such theological reflection.

A CONTINENT OF ALL BLOODS

From the outset, Latin American theological reflection raised the question of the 'other' in our society. The inadequacy, and indeed the errors, in the concentration on the reality of poverty adopted at that time made it necessary to analyse first the social and economic reasons for the marginalisation suffered by different categories of the poor (social class, culture, ethnicity and gender). Indeed, although a description of poverty is important, so long as its causes are not identified we are unable to do anything about it, or we are limited to trying to heal social rifts that require much deeper and broader solutions. Many of those causes—although not all—are social and economic. These are most unsettling for the power groups within Latin America and beyond, because they remind them of their responsibility for the conditions in which the majorities live. For this reason, they continually try to ascribe the differences to factors that mask the degree of social injustice. We should not forget this when with the best will in the world—and to some extent correctly—we are sensitive to certain aspects such as the race, culture and gender of the heterogeneous population of Latin America. We need to be clear about the different facets of the problem.

To adopt this perspective, to embark on a structural analysis, was one of the novelties of Medellín.[5] Many of the positions taken in recent years reveal the extent to which this approach has been engraved on the Latin American mind, and has been constantly reworked. At the same time, these positions show with great clarity the need to immerse ourselves in the multifaceted world of the poor, remaining attentive to its cultural and racial dimensions.

---

4. Christian communities that emerged in the late 1960s in Brazil and the Philippines and later spread to Africa, Asia, Australia, and North America. Derived from or inspired by liberation theology, these local groups perhaps realize the communitarian model of the Church proposed at the Second Vatican Council (see p. 628).

5. In Medellín, Colombia, in 1968, the Latin American Episcopal Conference (CELAM) held a conference to determine how to apply the teachings of the Second Vatican Council to Latin America. This conference helped determine the future of liberation theology.

Although a longstanding concern, the last few decades have allowed us to become more deeply involved in this complexity. The year 1992 stimulated the need to undertake a critical evaluation of the last 500 years of the continent's history,[6] and helped give more attention to the predicament of the various indigenous nations and to the black population which have been violently incorporated into our world. In many ways we have been witnesses over this period to the force given by the voices of these peoples; they remind us that the expression used by the Peruvian writer José María Arguedas [1911–1969] to describe Peru as a country 'of all bloods' can be applied to the whole continent.

All this affects the way of living and announcing the gospel, and certainly the theological reflection that accompanies it. The emphasis that these types of theology adopt, depending on which angle of poverty is the starting point, should not make us lose sight of the global dimension of the issue, nor to forget the horizon of understanding of our languages about God: the language of the marginalised and oppressed, the language of their liberation and the language of the gospel of Jesus.

It is necessary to avoid the possibility that the deepening of reflection on the suffering of the poor in Latin America transforms itself into fruitless searches for theological spaces, anguishing priorities and misunderstandings—with undisguised (in spite of appearances) intellectualist features—that in the long run only undermine the effort of the 'little ones'[7] of history in their struggle for life, justice and the right to be different. We also observe the existence of indigenous groups that are particularly forgotten and excluded. We refer to the aborigines of the Amazon, a region where—as pointed out in one of the texts of the bishops and missionaries—governments are more interested in natural resources than in the inhabitants. This is also the case of the Kunas of Panama and the Mapuche in Chile,[8] amongst others. The distance we need to cover in order to understand these peoples and to express solidarity with them is still long. Nevertheless, these peoples are beginning to make it clear that they live in lands that have always been theirs. This fact is partly a result of the liberating dimension of the gospel. However, it also constitutes a challenge to Christian faith.

What we have just mentioned continues to provide colour and flavour to the new role of the poor we referred to earlier. It too forms part of the—prolonged and stormy—search for identity in a continent of many colours which still finds difficulty in knowing what it is. For this very reason, the state and values of the poor in general, and of indigenous and black people in particular (and among them the women), constitute a challenge for evangelisation in our countries and a stimulus for different types of theological reflection. We face a real upsurge in fruitful understanding of faith, coming from cultural and human backgrounds of great importance. The initial perception of the other thus turns into a much more precise image, providing invaluable enrichment for the theology of liberation. However, much still needs to be done in this area.

---

6. I.e., because it was the 500th anniversary of the arrival to the Americas of Christopher Columbus (1451–1506), Genoese navigator and explorer for Spain.

7. See Matthew 18:1–6.
8. The Kunas and the Mapuche are indigenous minority groups.

Announcing the Gospel of Liberation

To know that the Lord loves us, to accept the gratuitous gift of his love, is the profound source of happiness of those who live according to the Word. To communicate this happiness is to evangelise. Such communication is the purpose of the reflection we call liberation theology. It concerns itself with a proclamation which is, in a way, gratuitous, just as the love which motivates it is gratuitous. What is received free, should be given freely, as the Gospel says. In the starting point for evangelisation there is always the experience of the Lord, a living out of the love of the Father that makes us His sons and daughters, transforming us, making us ever more fully brothers and sisters.

For us, all of this comes together—as we have pointed out—in the question: how to proclaim a God who is revealed as love in a world of poverty and exclusion? How to proclaim the God of life to people who suffer premature and unjust death? How to proclaim the 'Gospel of liberation'?

DESMOND TUTU
born 1931

FROM THE RAINBOW PEOPLE OF GOD

Desmond Tutu was born to a Xhosa family in a small town in Western Transvaal, South Africa. At age twelve, he moved with his family to Johannesburg. After graduating from Pretoria Bantu Normal College, he taught at high schools in Johannesburg and Mogale City, but resigned to protest the poor educational prospects for black South Africans. After studying at St. Peter's Theology College, in Johannesburg, he was ordained an Anglican priest in 1960, after which he earned bachelor's and master's degrees in theology from King's College London. For the next two decades, Tutu alternated between England and South Africa, serving at various points as a curate, a lecturer, an administrator, and a bishop. By the mid-1970s, he had become the first black Anglican dean of Johannesburg and a prominent political and social activist. During the 1980s, he became the archbishop of Cape Town, General Secretary of the South African Council of Churches, and thus the first black head of the Anglican Church in South Africa. He also became famous as an opponent of apartheid, and in December 1984—during a year that included both South Africa's largest-ever political strike and violence, sometimes deadly, between protesters and government forces—he received the Nobel Peace Prize. Tutu was a central figure in the reconciliation process between blacks and whites after the end of apartheid. Now retired, he remains a public commentator on political situations, especially those involving his country.

The following selection is from Tutu's Nobel Laureate speech. Tutu especially condemns the forced movement of blacks into settlements (called Bantustans, *Bantu* referring to a group of African peoples who speak Bantu languages) and the lack of civil and criminal justice afforded to both blacks and "mixed races" in South Africa.

PRONOUNCING GLOSSARY

bantustan: *ban´-too-stan*
shalom: *shah-lohm´*
Tutu: *too´-too*

Witwatersrand: *wit´-wah-ters-rand*
(English) or *vit´-vaw-ters-rahnt*
(Afrikaans)

FROM THE RAINBOW PEOPLE OF GOD

Your Majesty, members of the Royal Family, Mr. Chairman,[1] ladies and gentlemen:

Before I left South Africa, a land I love passionately, we had an emergency meeting of the executive committee of the South African Council of Churches with the leaders of our member churches. We called the meeting because of the deepening crisis in our land, which has claimed nearly two hundred lives this year alone. We visited some of the trouble spots on the Witwatersrand. I went with others to the East Rand.[2] We visited the home of an old lady. She told us that she looked after her grandson and the children of neighbors while their parents were at work. One day the police chased some pupils who had been boycotting classes, but they disappeared between the township houses. The police drove down the old lady's street. She was sitting at the back of the house in her kitchen, while her charges were playing in the yard in front of the house. Her daughter rushed into the house, calling out to her to come quickly. The old lady dashed out of the kitchen into the living room. Her grandson had fallen just inside the door, dead. He had been shot in the back by the police. He was six years old. A few weeks later, a white mother, trying to register her black servant for work, drove through a black township. Black rioters stoned her car and killed her baby of a few months old, the first white casualty of the current unrest in South Africa. Such deaths are two too many. These are part of the high cost of apartheid.

Every day in a squatter camp near Cape Town called KTC, the authorities have been demolishing flimsy plastic shelters which black mothers have erected because they were taking their marriage vows seriously. They have been reduced to sitting on soaking mattresses, with their household effects strewn round their feet, and whimpering babies on their laps, in the cold Cape winter rain. Every day the authorities have carried out these callous demolitions. What heinous crime have these women committed, to be hounded like criminals in this manner? All they have wanted is to be with their husbands, the fathers of their children. Everywhere else in the world they would be highly commended, but in South Africa, a land which claims to be Christian and which boasts a public holiday called Family Day, these gallant women are treated so inhumanely. Yet all they want is to have a decent and stable family life. Unfortunately, in the land of their

---

1. Egil Aarvik (1912–1990), chairman of the Norwegian Nobel Committee from 1982 until his death. "Your Majesty": the king of Norway, Olav V (1903–1991; reigned from 1957 until his death).
2. The eastern part of the Witwatersrand, which is the greater metropolitan area of Johannesburg.

Desmond Tutu, left, receives the Nobel Peace Prize in 1984 from Egil Aarvik, chairman of the Norwegian Nobel Committee.

birth it is a criminal offense for them to live happily with their husbands and the fathers of their children. Black family life is thus being undermined, not accidentally but by deliberate government policy. It is part of the price human beings, God's children, are called to pay for apartheid. An unacceptable price.

I come from a beautiful land, richly endowed by God with wonderful natural resources, wide expanses, rolling mountains, singing birds, bright shining stars out of blue skies, with radiant sunshine, golden sunshine. There is enough of the good things that come from God's bounty, there is enough for everyone, but apartheid has confirmed some in their selfishness, causing them to grasp greedily a disproportionate share, the lion's share, because of their power. They have taken 87 percent of the land, though being only about 20 percent of our population. The rest have had to make do with the remaining 13 percent. Apartheid has decreed the politics of exclusion: 73 percent of the population is excluded from any meaningful participation in the political decision-making processes of the land of their birth. The new constitution, making provision for three chambers, for whites, Coloreds and Indians, mentions blacks only once and thereafter ignores them completely. Thus this new constitution, lauded in parts of the West as a step in the right direction, entrenches racism and ethnicity. The constitutional committees are composed in the ratio of four whites to two Coloreds to one Indian—zero black . . . Hence this constitution perpetuates by law and entrenches white minority rule.

Blacks are expected to exercise their political ambitions in unviable, poverty-stricken, and bantustan homelands, ghettos of misery, inexhaustible reservoirs of cheap black labor, bantustans into which South Africa is being balkanized. Blacks are systematically being stripped of their South African citizenship and being turned into aliens in the land of their birth. This is apartheid's final solution, just as Nazism had its final solution for the Jews in Hitler's Aryan madness. The South African government is smart. Aliens can claim but very few rights, least of all political rights.

In pursuance of apartheid's ideological racist dream, over three million of God's children have been uprooted from their homes, which have been demolished, while they have been dumped in the bantustan homeland resettlement camps. I say dumped advisedly: only rubbish or things are dumped, not human beings. Apartheid has, however, ensured that God's children, just because they are black, should be treated as if they were things and not as of infinite value as being created in the image of God. These dumping grounds are far from where work and food can be procured easily. Children starve, suffer from the often irreversible consequences of malnutrition. This happens to them not accidentally but by deliberate government policy. They starve in a land that could be the bread basket of Africa, a land that normally is a net exporter of food.

The father leaves his family in the bantustan homeland, there eking out a miserable existence, while he, if he is lucky, goes to the so-called white man's town as a migrant, to live an unnatural life in a single-sex hostel for eleven months, being prey there to drunkenness, prostitution and worse. This migratory labor policy is declared government policy and has been condemned as a cancer in our society even by the white Dutch Reformed Church—not noted for being quick to criticize the government. This cancer, eating away at the vitals of black family life, is deliberate government policy. It is part of the cost of apartheid, exorbitant in terms of human suffering.

*　*　*

Once a Zambian and a South African, it is said, were talking. The Zambian boasted about their Minister of Naval Affairs. The South African asked, "But you have no navy, no access to the sea. How then can you have a Minister of Naval Affairs?" The Zambian retorted: "Well, in South Africa you have a Minister of Justice, don't you?"

It is against this system that our people have sought to protest peacefully since 1912 at least, with the founding of the African National Congress.[3] They have used the conventional methods of peaceful protest—petitions, demonstrations, deputations and even a passive resistance campaign. A tribute to our people's commitment to peaceful change is the fact that the only South Africans to win the Nobel Peace Prize are both black.[4] Our people are peace-loving to a fault. The response of the authorities has been an escalating intransigence and violence, the violence of police dogs, tear gas, detention without trial, exile, and even death. Our people protested peacefully against the pass laws in 1960 and 69 of them were killed on March 21, 1960, at Sharpeville, many shot in the back running away. Our children protested against inferior education, singing songs and displaying placards and marching peacefully. Many in 1976, on June 16 and subsequent times, were killed or imprisoned. Over 500 people died in that uprising. Many children went into exile. The whereabouts of many are unknown to their parents. At present, to protest that selfsame discriminatory education and the exclusion of

---

3. A South African liberation movement; now the country's governing political party.
4. In 1960, Chief Albert Luthuli, president-

general of the African National Congress (ANC), received the prize.

blacks from the new constitutional dispensation, the sham local black government, rising unemployment, increased rents and General Sales Tax, our people have boycotted and demonstrated. They have staged a successful two-day stay-away. Over 150 people have been killed. It is far too high a price to pay. There has been little revulsion or outrage in the West at this wanton destruction of human life.

✻   ✻   ✻

There is no peace in Southern Africa. There is no peace because there is no justice. There can be no real peace and security until there be first justice enjoyed by all the inhabitants of that beautiful land. The Bible knows nothing about peace without justice, for that would be crying, "Peace, peace, where there is no peace."[5] God's shalom, peace, involves inevitably righteousness, justice, wholeness, fullness of life, participation in decision making, goodness, laughter, joy, compassion, sharing and reconciliation.

I have spoken extensively about South Africa, first because it is the land I know best, but because it is also a microcosm of the world and an example of what is to be found in other lands in differing degree—when there is injustice, invariably peace becomes a casualty. In El Salvador, in Nicaragua and elsewhere in Latin America, there have been repressive regimes which have aroused opposition in those countries. Fellow citizens are pitted against one another, sometimes attracting the unhelpful attention and interest of outside powers, who want to extend their spheres of influence. We see this in the Middle East, in Korea, in the Philippines, in Kampuchea, in Vietnam, in Ulster, in Afghanistan, in Mozambique, in Angola, in Zimbabwe, behind the Iron Curtain.

Because there is global insecurity, nations are engaged in a mad arms race, spending billions of dollars wastefully on instruments of destruction, when millions are starving. And yet, just a fraction of what is expended so obscenely on defense budgets would make the difference in enabling God's children to fill their stomachs, be educated and given the chance to lead fulfilled and happy lives. We have the capacity to feed ourselves several times over but we are daily haunted by the spectacle of the gaunt dregs of humanity shuffling along in endless queues, with bowls to collect what the charity of the world has provided, too little too late. When will we learn, when will the people of the world get up and say, enough is enough? God created us for fellowship. God created us so that we should form the human family, existing together because we were made for one another. We are not made for an exclusive self-sufficiency but for interdependence, and we break that law of our being at our peril. When will we learn that an escalating arms race merely escalates global insecurity? We are now much closer to a nuclear holocaust than when our technology and our spending were less.

Unless we work assiduously so that all of God's children, our brothers and sisters, members of our one human family, enjoy the basic human rights, the right to a fulfilled life, the right of movement, the freedom to be fully human within a humanity measured by nothing less than the humanity of Jesus Christ himself, then we are on the road inexorably to self-destruction, we are not far from global suicide. And yet it could be so different.

---

5. See Jeremiah 6:14.

When will we learn that human beings are of infinite value because they have been created in the image of God, that it is blasphemy to treat them as if they were less than this, and to do so ultimately recoils on those who do this? In dehumanizing others, they are themselves dehumanized. Perhaps oppression dehumanizes the oppressor as much as, if not more than, the oppressed. They need each other to become truly free, to become human. We can be human only in fellowship, in community, in *koinonia*,[6] in peace.

Let us work to be peacemakers, those given a wonderful share in our Lord's ministry of reconciliation. If we want peace, so we have been told, let us work for justice. Let us beat our swords into plowshares.[7]

God calls us to be fellow workers with him so that we can extend his kingdom of shalom, of justice, of goodness, of compassion, of caring, of sharing, of laughter, joy and reconciliation, so that the kingdoms of this world will become the Kingdom of our God and of his Christ, and he shall reign for ever and ever. Amen. Then there will be fulfillment of the wonderful vision in the Revelation of St. John the Divine (Revelation 7:9ff).

6. Communion by intimate participation (ancient Greek).

7. See Isaiah 2:4.

RIGOBERTA MENCHÚ
born 1959

FROM I, RIGOBERTA MENCHÚ

Spain and Portugal were the first great European powers to establish colonial empires. During the nineteenth century, however, their empires became the first among the colonial European powers to succumb to national independence movements, specifically in South and Central America. Yet throughout the various empires, the new nation-states that then came into being often consisted of, de facto, more than one nation. Often, a small, relatively Westernized ruling class of one ethnicity dominated a large lower class made up of other ethnicities. As the submerged groups began to assert themselves in the later twentieth century, they often characterized themselves as the true, indigenous peoples of their home countries, denigrating their economic or political oppressors as culturally alien neocolonists.

The role of religion varied over the course of these independence movements. The movements that immediately followed the two world wars were typically secular or even anticlerical. Movements overthrowing European colonial rule not only disparaged Christianity as the religion of the European oppressor, but also often regarded even indigenous non-Christian religions as backward and therefore an obstacle to the modern states they sought to create. By the late twentieth century, however, human rights activism on behalf of indigenous peoples sometimes did not reject religion, but rather reappropriated it and turned it to humanitarian purposes in unprecedented ways. Consider Gustavo Gutiérrez (see p. 632), a Peruvian Catholic of mixed Spanish and Quechua ancestry, and Desmond Tutu (see p. 638), a South African of Xhosa descent. The work of such activists has differed from earlier nationalist movements in that they have not sought to overthrow a government or establish a separate state and that they typically have defended the oppressed in the name of a religion that the oppressor to some degree shares.

In Guatemala, by the late twentieth century, Evangelical Protestant missionaries had made a great many converts, but Roman Catholicism remained the major form of Christianity. Meanwhile, important elements of the native, pre-Columbian Mayan religion lived on among the Mayan Indians, through various customs and rituals. For Guatemalan women, one important remnant of the religion was the colorful Mayan native costume. That costume became a signature part of Rigoberta Menchú's public persona.

Menchú is a Guatemalan Catholic of Mayan (K'iche') descent. As an activist on behalf of the cultural as well as the political and economic rights of minority peoples, she embraced the Mayan elements in her religious heritage as much as she did the Catholic elements, while her political activism freely employed Evangelical as well as Catholic motifs. In the following selection from her memoir as told to Elisabeth Burgos-Debray, Menchú recounts how she invoked the examples of embattled figures from the Old Testament in motivating her oppressed fellow Mayans to confront their Ladino landlords. *Ladino* refers to the exclusively Spanish-speaking, usually urbanized, historically Westernized, and culturally dominant portion of Guatemala's population. The portrayal of Ladinos in *I, Rigoberta Menchú* stands in sharp contrast to the portrayal of Mayans, including Menchú, who learned Spanish only as a young adult.

In 1992, Menchú was awarded the Nobel Peace Prize for her work during the decades-long Guatemalan Civil War, in which both her parents lost their lives. Years later, the accuracy of some episodes in *I, Rigoberta Menchú* was challenged by an American reseacher, but the challenge was itself challenged by further American research and did not, in any case, compromise the central political/religious thrust of the book. Toward the end of the century, Menchú joined the Nobel Women's Initiative, an effort launched by six female winners of the Nobel Peace Prize to defend women's rights around the world.

PRONOUNCING GLOSSARY

fincas: *feen´-cahs*
Rigoberta Menchú: *ree-goh-behr´-tah men-choo´*

FROM I, RIGOBERTA MENCHÚ

From *The Bible and Self-Defence: The Examples of Judith, Moses, and David*

We began to study the Bible as our main text. Many relationships in the Bible are like those we have with our ancestors, our ancestors whose lives were very much like our own. The important thing for us is that we started to identify that reality with our own. That's how we began studying the Bible. It's not something you memorize, it's not just to be talked about and prayed about, and nothing more. It also helped to change the image we had, as Catholics and Christians: that God is up there and that God has a great kingdom for we the poor, yet never thinking of our own reality as a reality that we were actually living. But by studying the scriptures, we did. Take 'Exodus' for example, that's one we studied and analysed. It talks a lot about the life of

TRANSLATED BY Ann Wright.

Moses who tried to lead his people from oppression, and did all he could to free his people. We compare the Moses of those days with ourselves, the 'Moses' of today. 'Exodus' is about the life of a man, the life of Moses.

We began looking for texts which represented each one of us. We tried to relate them to our Indian culture. We took the example of Moses for the men, and we have the example of Judith, who was a very famous woman in her time and appears in the Bible.[1] She fought very hard for her people and made many attacks against the king they had then, until she finally had his head. She held her victory in her hand, the head of the King. This gave us a vision, a stronger idea of how we Christians must defend ourselves. It made us think that a people could not be victorious without a just war. We Indians do not dream of great riches, we want only enough to live on. There is also the story of David, a little shepherd boy who appears in the Bible, who was able to defeat the king of those days, King Goliath. This story is the example for the children. This is how we look for stories and psalms which teach us how to defend ourselves from our enemies. I remember taking examples from all the texts which helped the community to understand their situation better. It's not only now that there are great kings, powerful men, people who hold power in their hands. Our ancestors suffered under them too. This is how we identify with the lives of our ancestors who were conquered by a great desire for power— our ancestors were murdered and tortured because they were Indians. We began studying more deeply and, well, we came to a conclusion. That being a Christian means thinking of our brothers around us, and that every one of our Indian race has the right to eat. This reflects what God himself said, that on this earth we have a right to what we need. The Bible was our principal text for study as Christians and it showed us what the role of a Christian is. I became a catechist as a little girl and I studied the Bible, hymns, the scriptures, but only very superficially. One of the things Catholic Action[2] put in our heads is that everything is sinful. But we came round to asking ourselves: 'If everything is sinful, why is it that the landowner kills humble peasants who don't even harm the natural world? Why do they take our lives?' When I first became a catechist, I thought that there was a God and that we had to serve him. I thought God was up there and that he had a kingdom for the poor. But we realized that it is not God's will that we should live in suffering, that God did not give us that destiny, but that men on earth have imposed this suffering, poverty, misery and discrimination on us. We even got the idea of using our own everyday weapons, as the only solution left to us.

I am a Christian and I participate in this struggle as a Christian. For me, as a Christian, there is one important thing. That is the life of Christ. Throughout his life Christ was humble. History tells us he was born in a little hut. He was persecuted and had to form a band of men so that his seed would not disappear. They were his disciples, his apostles. In those days, there was no other way of defending himself or Christ would have used it against his oppressors,

1. In the Book of Judith, written in the second century B.C.E., the heroine, a brave Jew, rallies her people to defend themselves by beheading Holofernes, commander of the invading Assyrians. Part of the Christian Old Testament until the Reformation, when it was deleted from Protestant canons, the Book of Judith is retained in the Roman Catholic edition that Menchú cites.
2. A post–World War II movement founded in Europe in response to movements, especially Communism, that combined atheism and the defense of workers' interests. Originally, Catholic Action sought to combine Catholic faith with the defense of workers' interests. Later, especially in certain Spanish-speaking countries, it sometimes subsided into moralistic defense of the economic status quo.

against his enemies. He even gave his life. But Christ did not die, because generations and generations have followed him. And that's exactly what we understood when our first catechists fell.[3] They're dead but our people keep their memory alive through our struggle against the government, against an enemy who oppresses us. We don't need very much advice, or theories, or documents: life has been our teacher. For my part, the horrors I have suffered are enough for me. And I've also felt in the deepest part of me what discrimination is, what exploitation is. It is the story of my life. In my work I've often gone hungry. If I tried to recount the number of times I'd gone hungry in my life, it would take a very long time. When you understand this, when you see your own reality, a hatred grows inside you for those oppressors that make the people suffer so. As I said, and I say it again, it is not fate which makes us poor. It's not because we don't work, as the rich say. They say: 'Indians are poor because they don't work, because they're always asleep.' But I know from experience that we're outside ready for work at three in the morning. It was this that made us decide to fight. This is what motivated me, and also motivated many others. Above all the mothers and fathers. They remember their children. They remember the ones they would like to have with them now but who died of malnutrition, or intoxication in the *fincas*,[4] or had to be given away because they had no way of looking after them. It has a long history. And it's precisely when we look at the lives of Christians in the past that we see what our role as Christians should be today. I must say, however, that I think even religions are manipulated by the system, by those same governments you find everywhere. They use them through their ideas or through their methods. I mean, it's clear that a priest never works in the *fincas*, picking cotton or coffee. He wouldn't know what picking cotton was. Many priests don't even know what cotton is. But our reality teaches us that, as Christians, we must create a Church of the poor, that we don't need a Church imposed from outside which knows nothing of hunger. We recognize that the system has wanted to impose on us: to divide us and keep the poor dormant. So we take some things and not others. As far as sins go, it seems to me that the concept of the Catholic religion, or any other more conservative religion than Catholicism, is that God loves the poor and has a wonderful paradise in Heaven for the poor, so the poor must accept the life they have on Earth. But as Christians, we have understood that being a Christian means refusing to accept all the injustices which are committed against our people, refusing to accept the discrimination committed against a humble people who barely know what eating meat is but who are treated worse than horses. We've learned all this by watching what has happened in our lives. This awakening of the Indians didn't come, of course, from one day to the next, because Catholic Action and other religions and the system itself have all tried to keep us where we were. But I think that unless a religion springs from within the people themselves, it is a weapon of the system. So, naturally, it wasn't at all difficult for our community to understand all this and the reasons for us to defend ourselves, because this is the reality we live.

---

3. Menchú alludes to an atrocity described earlier in her book.
4. Plantations; in Guatemala, typically coffee plantations. For years during her middle childhood, Menchú worked picking coffee on a *finca*.

CZESLAW MILOSZ
1911–2004

CAMPO DEI FIORI, YOU WHO WRONGED, *AND* READINGS

Czeslaw Milosz was born in Lithuania when that country was ruled by imperial Russia. He knew Lithuanian, Russian, French, and English, but his first language was Polish—a reflection of Poland's then longstanding cultural hegemony over Lithuania. Milosz is accurately referred to as a Polish poet, yet he remained affectionately devoted to Lithuania. Poland's fusion of nationalism and Christianity in the late 1920s and the 1930s revolted him; partly as a result, he was an atheist as a young man. In the 1940s, however—partly in consequence of witnessing in Poland the horrors perpetrated by Nazi Germany, Nazism's absorption of the Church, and Nazism's glorification of nationality above all other values—he began to circle back toward the Catholic faith of his youth. Throughout his work, Milosz drew on Christian tradition, including the Bible. At the peak of his literary fame and political influence, he took up the study of Hebrew so as to translate the Psalms from the original into Polish. His identity as a poet and a public intellectual was as complex as his religious identity.

Milosz places and dates his poem "Campo dei Fiori" to Warsaw in 1943. That year, Polish Jews being herded together for Nazi butchery launched what is now known as the Warsaw Ghetto Uprising, a last desperate bid for liberation. The uprising ended in a mass slaughter of Jews by Nazis. Milosz addresses not that atrocity, however, but Polish Christian indifference to it. "Dark kites" of ash drift from the burning ghetto, a hot wind blows from it, but the amusements of a carnival day go forward nonchalantly.

After World War II, Milosz scandalized some émigré Polish intellectuals by entering the employ of Poland's Communist government at the peak of the Soviet Union's expansionist power. Ironically, Milosz was about to become Communism's most trenchant critic. In 1951, in Paris as cultural attaché for the People's Republic of Poland, he defected to France; two years later, he published his epoch-making exposé, *The Captive Mind*, whose analysis of the self-delusion of Communist intellectuals did not spare those intellectuals who sought to combine Communism and Catholicism.

Thirty years after *The Captive Mind*, with a Polish pope (John Paul II, elected in 1978) stirring unrest in his Catholic homeland (see p. 673) and with Milosz's work circulating there in underground editions, a new, independent, non-Communist labor movement, Solidarity, emerged in the shipyards of the Polish seaport Gdańsk. The Communist régime imposed martial law in a protracted but finally failed attempt to suppress Solidarity, which evolved rapidly into a broad social movement. Lines from Milosz's poem "You Who Wronged"—written in the United States some thirty years before—are engraved on a memorial at Gdańsk to workers slain in the Communist attempt to suppress their uprising. Within the decade, to the astonishment of the world, the Soviet empire of satellite states in Central and Eastern Europe broke apart, and the Soviet Union itself collapsed. Communism, launched in Poland as a movement on behalf of workers, was brought down by workers, some of them consciously drawing on Roman Catholic social teaching. The betrayed workers had overthrown their betrayer, whom Milosz here compares to Judas, the betrayer of Jesus, hanging himself for his crime.

In 1960, Milosz emigrated to the United States to accept a professorial appointment at the University of California, Berkeley. He published much of his poetry—including his poem "Readings"—after this move. In a chapter of *The Captive*

Czeslaw Milosz won the Nobel Prize in Literature in 1980 and is among the major poets of the twentieth century.

Mind, Milosz had brilliantly dissected the Soviet strategy of undermining Christianity without immediately and completely suppressing it. But he observed that "the masses in highly industrialized countries like England, the United States, or France are largely de-Christianized. Technology, and the way of life it produces, undermines Christianity far more effectively than do violent measures." In "Readings," Milosz considers the question "What is the good of reading the Gospels in Greek?" from his adopted vantage point: the de-Christianized, technologized, late-twentieth-century West.

Campo dei Fiori: *cahm´-poh day´-ee fee-ohr´-ee*
Czeslaw Milosz: *chess´-lahv mee´-wosh*

daimonizomenoi: *dai-moh-ni-dzo´-men-oy*
Giordano: *johr-dah´-noh*

CAMPO DEI FIORI

In Rome on the Campo dei Fiori[1]
baskets of olives and lemons,
cobbles spattered with wine
and the wreckage of flowers.
Vendors cover the trestles   5
with rose-pink fish;
armfuls of dark grapes
heaped on peach-down.

On this same square
they burned Giordano Bruno.[2]   10
Henchmen kindled the pyre
close-pressed by the mob.
Before the flames had died
the taverns were full again,
baskets of olives and lemons   15
again on the vendors' shoulders.

1. Italian for "Field of Flowers," a large plaza in Rome that hosts a daily open-air produce-and-flower market.
2. A Dominican friar burned at the stake for his heretical views (1548–1600). Visually, Campo dei Fiori is dominated by a large statue of Bruno erected in the early years of the united Italian republic.

I thought of the Campo dei Fiori
in Warsaw by the sky-carousel[3]
one clear spring evening
to the strains of a carnival tune.   20
The bright melody drowned
the salvos from the ghetto wall,
and couples were flying
high in the cloudless sky.

At times wind from the burning   25
would drift dark kites along
and riders on the carousel
caught petals in midair.
That same hot wind
blew open the skirts of the girls   30
and the crowds were laughing
on that beautiful Warsaw Sunday.

Someone will read as moral
that the people of Rome or Warsaw
haggle, laugh, make love   35
as they pass by martyrs' pyres.
Someone else will read
of the passing of things human,
of the oblivion
born before the flames have died.   40

But that day I thought only
of the loneliness of the dying,
of how, when Giordano
climbed to his burning
he could not find   45
in any human tongue
words for mankind,
mankind who live on.

Already they were back at their wine
or peddled their white starfish,   50
baskets of olives and lemons
they had shouldered to the fair,
and he already distanced
as if centuries had passed
while they paused just a moment   55
for his flying in the fire.

Those dying here, the lonely
forgotten by the world,
our tongue becomes for them
the language of an ancient planet.   60
Until, when all is legend
and many years have passed,

3. Ferris wheel.

on a new Campo dei Fiori
rage will kindle at a poet's word.

Warsaw, 1943

YOU WHO WRONGED

You who wronged a simple man
Bursting into laughter at the crime,
And kept a pack of fools around you
To mix good and evil, to blur the line,

Though everyone bowed down before you,   5
Saying virtue and wisdom lit your way,
Striking gold medals in your honor,
Glad to have survived another day,

Do not feel safe. The poet remembers.
You can kill one, but another is born.   10
The words are written down, the deed, the date.

And you'd have done better with a winter dawn,
A rope, and a branch bowed beneath your weight.

Washington, D.C., 1950

READINGS

You asked me what is the good of reading the Gospels in Greek.
I answer that it is proper that we move our finger
Along letters more enduring than those carved in stone,
And that, slowly pronouncing each syllable,
We discover the true dignity of speech.   5
Compelled to be attentive we shall think of that epoch
No more distant than yesterday, though the heads of caesars
On coins[1] are different today. Yet still it is the same eon.
Fear and desire are the same, oil and wine
And bread mean the same. So does the fickleness of the throng   10
Avid for miracles as in the past. Even mores,
Wedding festivities, drugs, laments for the dead
Only seem to differ. Then, too, for example,
There were plenty of persons whom the text calls
Daimonizomenoi,[2] that is, the demonized   15
Or, if you prefer, the bedeviled (as for "the possessed"

---

1. In the first century, when the Gospels were written and Rome ruled the Mediterranean world, coins bore the image of the Roman emperor, or caesar.

2. A Greek past participle, which Milosz proceeds to translate literally.

It's no more than the whim of a dictionary).
Convulsions, foam at the mouth, the gnashing of teeth
Were not considered signs of talent.[3]
The demonized had no access to print and screens,   20
Rarely engaging in arts and literature.
But the Gospel parable remains in force:
That the spirit mastering them may enter swine,[4]
Which, exasperated by such a sudden clash
Between two natures, theirs and the Luciferic,   25
Jump into water and drown (which occurs repeatedly).
And thus on every page a persistent reader
Sees twenty centuries as twenty days
In a world which one day will come to its end.

Berkeley, 1969

---

3. In various eras, frenzy was seen as a sign of artistic creation (e.g., Shakespeare's *A Midsummer Night's Dream* 5.1.12–13: "The poet's eye, in a fine frenzy rolling, / Doth glance from heaven to earth, from earth to heaven").
4. Compare Mark 5:1–13.

The New Millennium

2001–the Present

THE HOST RELIGION BECOMES
A FELLOW GUEST

At the end of the first decade of the twenty-first century, Christianity was demographically the world's largest religion, with 2.18 billion adherents, nearly a third of the world's 6.9 billion people. Centuries of dedicated missionary efforts, much of them in tandem with European colonization, had clearly been successful. Yet even at the end of its centuries-long expansion, Christianity was not the world's *majority* religion. That is, considered in global context, in terms of influence over the international community, all the world's religions were minority religions. As a voice contributing to "world culture"—much of that culture secular—how important would Christianity be in the future?

The five selections gathered in "The New Millennium" do not answer that question. Nor are they "Christian classics." However, they point toward possible growth areas, or "response areas," within Christianity. They signal developments that, at the end of the twenty-first century, may prove to have mattered more than they first appeared to.

Yeong Mee Lee is a Korean Bible scholar. In the essay included here, Lee presents *"minjung* theology," present-day Korea's indigenization of the centuries-old Western tradition of biblical interpretation. This appropriation may be a Christian

Pentecostal worship is in progress at the Yoido "Full Gospel" church in Seoul, Republic of Korea. Pentecostalism experienced enormous growth in the late twentieth and early twenty-first centuries, mostly outside Europe and North America.

analog to Korea's embrace of Western computer technology. Consider that the Republic of Korea is more fully "wired" than the United States. Which country provides a better clue to the Christian future?

Liu Zhenying, known as Brother Yun, is a Chinese Pentecostal Evangelist. As recounted partly in his memoir excerpt below, Brother Yun has become famous among East Asian Christians for spreading the Word through a network of Chinese home churches. The highly emotive, charismatic, or spirit-filled Pentecostal tradition originated in the United States, but its greatest growth has occurred in South America, Africa, and parts of Asia. Some substantial part of the Christian future may belong to such forms of Christianity, which escape the normative, hierarchical, highly doctrinal, administratively "managed" Christianity of the West.

When economies collapse and governments fall, religions sometimes live on to pick up the pieces. In the future, as everyday life is disrupted by environmental shock, religions may play important roles as societal buffers. With their 2002 "Declaration on the Environment," Patriarch Bartholomew I of Constantinople and the late Pope John Paul II spoke for a small, growing, and perhaps eventually significant wave of Christian activism on behalf of the environment.

For historical and ideological reasons, residents of Muslim-majority countries have been more suspicious than others of the allegedly post-Christian character of the "international community." Against this background, what is or should be the role of Christians from the former colonial powers working in or with their former Muslim colonies? Christian de Chergé, represented here by his "Spiritual Testament," devoted and finally lost his life to his attempt to offer a French Christian answer to that question. In the twenty-first century, relations between Muslims and Christians may prove to be one of the most powerful forces worldwide.

Finally, within the historic homelands of Christianity, in an inscrutably postmodern world where "none" may become the majority "religious preference," what will Christian faith and practice mean? How, personally, will they be experienced? In the excerpt below from his book of meditations, Christian Wiman, an American poet and an adult convert to Christian religious practice, discusses his own Christian experience. His thoughts suggest a range of possible answers about the shape of postmodern Christianity in the West.

Chronology

THE NEW MILLENNIUM (2001–THE PRESENT)

2001 Salafi Muslim terrorists attack U.S., which counterattacks by invading Afghanistan

2002 U.S. invades Iraq

2003 Openly gay priest Gene Robinson elected Episcopal bishop in Diocese of New Hampshire

2009 Copenhagen Climate Change Conference fails, even as global warming accelerates

2010 Human Rights Watch notes "growing religious intolerance" against Copts in Egypt

2011 Pew Forum *Global Christianity* report surveys historic demographic shift: 1.3 billion Christians in Global South, 860 million in Global North

2012 Roman Catholic pope Benedict XVI sends his first Twitter message

2013 Pope Benedict XVI retires, is succeeded by Jorge Mario Bergoglio of Argentina, the first Jesuit pope, the first non-European pope in many centuries, the first-ever pope from the southern hemisphere, and the first pope to take Francis (for Francis of Assisi) as his papal name

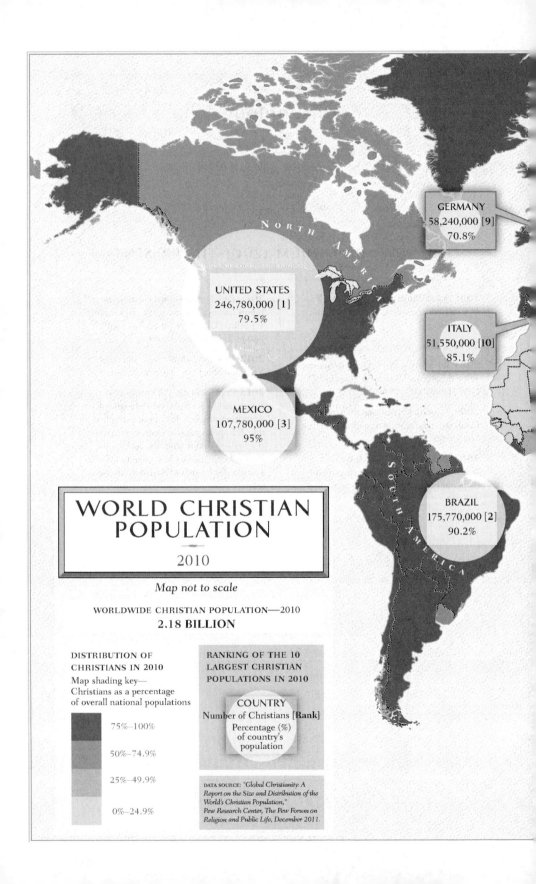

GERMANY
58,240,000 [9]
70.8%

UNITED STATES
246,780,000 [1]
79.5%

ITALY
51,550,000 [10]
85.1%

MEXICO
107,780,000 [3]
95%

BRAZIL
175,770,000 [2]
90.2%

WORLD CHRISTIAN POPULATION

2010

Map not to scale

WORLDWIDE CHRISTIAN POPULATION—2010
2.18 BILLION

DISTRIBUTION OF
CHRISTIANS IN 2010
Map shading key—
Christians as a percentage
of overall national populations

- 75%–100%
- 50%–74.9%
- 25%–49.9%
- 0%–24.9%

RANKING OF THE 10
LARGEST CHRISTIAN
POPULATIONS IN 2010

COUNTRY
Number of Christians [**Rank**]
Percentage (%)
of country's
population

DATA SOURCE: *"Global Christianity: A
Report on the Size and Distribution of the
World's Christian Population,"
Pew Research Center, The Pew Forum on
Religion and Public Life, December 2011.*

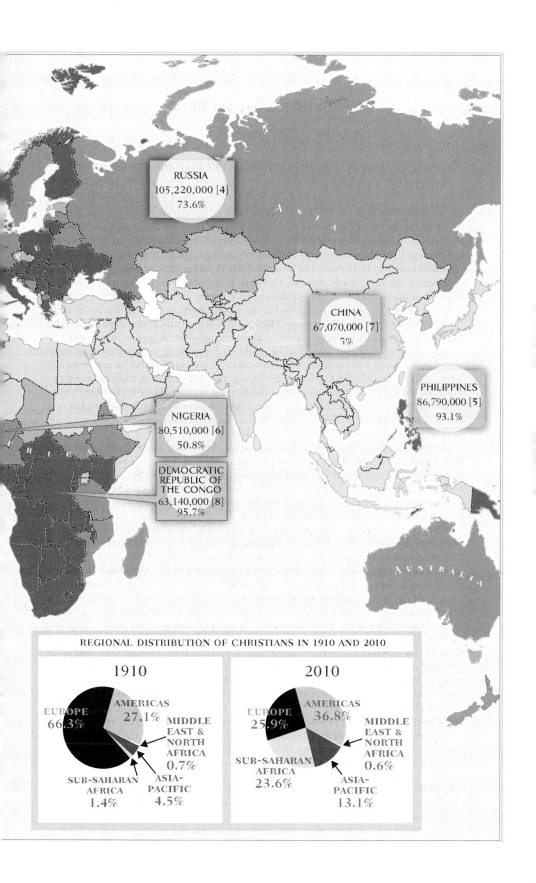

RUSSIA
105,220,000 [4]
73.6%

CHINA
67,070,000 [7]
7%

PHILIPPINES
86,790,000 [5]
93.1%

NIGERIA
80,510,000 [6]
50.8%

DEMOCRATIC
REPUBLIC OF
THE CONGO
63,140,000 [8]
95.7%

ASIA

AFRICA

AUSTRALIA

REGIONAL DISTRIBUTION OF CHRISTIANS IN 1910 AND 2010

1910

EUROPE
66.3%
AMERICAS
27.1%
MIDDLE EAST & NORTH AFRICA
0.7%
SUB-SAHARAN AFRICA
1.4%
ASIA-PACIFIC
4.5%

2010

EUROPE
25.9%
AMERICAS
36.8%
MIDDLE EAST & NORTH AFRICA
0.6%
SUB-SAHARAN AFRICA
23.6%
ASIA-PACIFIC
13.1%

YEONG MEE LEE
born 1966

FROM A POLITICAL RECEPTION OF THE BIBLE: KOREAN MINJUNG THEOLOGICAL INTERPRETATION OF THE BIBLE

Christianity first took hold in Korea in the late eighteenth century, through Korean neo-Confucians who learned of the faith through their Chinese counterparts. By the middle of the nineteenth century, despite intermittent persecutions, a substantial Roman Catholic community had been established in Korea. The first Presbyterian missionaries, from Scotland and the United States, reached Korea in the late nineteenth century. Early Korean converts to Presbyterianism quickly assumed leadership positions in the newly established Church.

Between 1910 and 1945, Korea was a Japanese colony, the first of the many colonies established in imperial Japan's twentieth-century militaristic expansion. The Japanese attempted to impose Shinto, a Japanese religion, on Korea, but Christianity was already too deeply rooted to be eradicated. Christian resistance to the Japanese consolidated a sense among Koreans that Christianity could be authentically Korean. Yet many Christians were developing a tacitly dissident stance toward the more authoritarian features of traditional Korean culture. They looked forward to establishing an independent Korea with a new emphasis on individual rights and democracy for all and with material as well as spiritual redemption for the *minjung*, or marginalized, impoverished mass of society.

When Japan was defeated in the Asian half of World War II (1937–45), the Soviet Union and the United States partitioned Korea, establishing the Communist Democratic People's Republic of Korea north of the thirty-eighth parallel and the capitalist Republic of Korea to its south. Despite North Korea's invasion of South Korea in 1950 and the resulting war between the two sides, the de facto border between the Koreas has remained essentially unchanged.

North Korea, a police state headed by a dictatorial dynasty, has descended into chronic, extreme poverty. The state atheism promoted in all Communist states has been imposed with exceptional rigor, especially in regard to Christianity. Largely for that reason, Christians constitute less than 2 percent of North Korea's population (though demographic estimates in a country where no independent research is permitted can be only rough approximations).

In South Korea, where freedom of religion is the rule, Christians constitute about 30 percent of the population, the second-highest percentage (after the Philippines) in Asia. By the early twenty-first century, there were more Presbyterians in South Korea than in Scotland or the United States. Korean Presbyterian churches were establishing branches in the United States. The flow of missionary traffic was running in both directions. South Korea was at first ruled by a series of American-backed dictators, but a popular democratic movement helped bring about both free elections and an economy that radically raised the national standard of living. Despite such societal achievements, however, a marginalized, impoverished class remained. Through a distinctive new form of biblical interpretation, South Korean practitioners of *minjung* theology sought to begin at the societal margin and proceed to the center. The influence of such thinking reached high and deep into the society. Kim Young Sam (born 1927; president 1993–98) acknowledged its impact on him. So did Kim Dae Jung (1925–2009; president 1998–2003), a long-time opponent of authoritarian rule and winner, in 2000, of the Nobel Peace Prize. But the influence of *minjung* theology is not confined to Korea. Like liberation theology (see p. 632), this movement has attracted international attention, notably through the work of the eminent German theologian Jürgen Moltmann (born 1926).

The following selection, an introduction to Korean *minjung* theology by the Presbyterian scholar Yeong Mee Lee, began as a paper presented at a 2005 international meeting in Singapore of the Society of Biblical Literature, a learned society of biblical interpreters and scholars of Semitic and Greco-Roman antiquity. The SBL later published Lee's remarks online (here, except as indicated, Lee's endnotes have been omitted). Lee is a professor of religion, theology, and women's studies at Hanshin University (in Osan City, South Korea), the institutional arm of the liberal Kijang branch of Korean Presbyterianism. She is part of the transformation of world biblical scholarship from a male pursuit to a male-and-female pursuit that is sensitive—as in the conclusion of this piece—to the occasional presence of feminine imagery in the Bible's presentation of God. As a Korean who earned her Ph.D. from New York's Union Theological Seminary, she is part of an ever-greater internationalization of biblical scholarship. As a radical Korean Presbyterian, she takes perhaps startling positions. For example, in this article Lee quotes with approval a *minjung* theologian's statement that "history itself is God."

PRONOUNCING GLOSSARY

Gerhard von Rad: *gehr´-hahrt von raht*
Habiru: *ha-bee´-roo*
hyl: [unpronounced]
Job: *johb*

Naboth: *nay´-bohth*
Ochios: *ok´-ee-ohs*
yld: [unpronounced]
Zarephath: *zahr-eh-fahth´*

FROM A POLITICAL RECEPTION OF THE BIBLE: KOREAN *MINJUNG* THEOLOGICAL INTERPRETATION OF THE BIBLE

This presentation is an introduction to the interpretation of the Bible among *minjung* biblical scholars, focusing in the area of Old Testament studies. While there have been quite a number of studies on *minjung* theology in general, few have called special attention to the method(s) of biblical interpretation of *minjung* biblical scholars. I will begin with a brief historical review of *minjung* theology and then continue the discussion to include hermeneutical principles used by *minjung* biblical scholars. Finally, I will suggest from a Korean woman's perspective that *minjung* biblical interpretation needs to provide a life-affirming biblical metaphor in the construction of a *minjung* theology of liberation. A life-affirming theology would enrich and empower the *minjung* people, offering a creative and holistic reconstruction of faith and life within the globalization of the world community.

Introduction to Minjung *Theology: A Historical Overview*

Minjung theology is a contextual theology that was born in response to the suffering of *minjung* under Park Chung Hee's regime in the 1960–70s.[1] *Minjung* theology was developed and refined even further during the 1980s

---

1. Park Chung-hee (1917–1979), South Korean army general, was president of South Korea from 1961 to 1979.

in the midst of the struggle for democracy under Jeon Du Whan's regime.[2] General Jeon became the President of Korea in 1980, suppressing the *min-jung*'s demonstration for democracy in Kwang Ju.[3] At its inception, *minjung* theology focused on the deplorable economic and cultural conditions of *minjung*. As it developed, and as the context changed, later *minjung* theology expanded to address political and social concerns that emerged from the *minjung* movement for democracy in the early 1980s. During that time, *minjung* theology addressed political issues that concern democracy, using a material and social revolutionary approach in the construction of *minjung* theology for the new millennium.

The Korean political environment has been subject to rapidly changing principles during the past decade. Korean society suffers from new economic, social, and cultural crises, resulting from financial crisis and the ensuing intervention of the International Monetary Fund (IMF)[4] in 1997–98. The pressure of the IMF on the Korean government for structural reform in the financial and corporate sectors caused President Kim Dae-jung to conform to its demands, which resulted in a sharp rise in the unemployment rate. Because of this imposed structural reform, many workers, both blue and white collar, lost their jobs; today they remain either unemployed or have had to survive through cobbling together part-time employment.

Korea jumped into the global market as well. Globalization can be defined as a process of integrating all peoples and nations into one global market, driven by global capital. In the process of a globalization that dominates all aspects of life, the traditional understanding of *minjung* is no longer evident, despite the fact that the majority of jobless and contingent laborers can certainly be considered as the *minjung* of the globalized world. Therefore, the task of *minjung* theology expands even further, to include theological insight that informs the meaning of life in this globalized world.

The "Minjung" as a Hermeneutical Key of Minjung Theology

THE MEANING OF "*MINJUNG*" AS A HERMENEUTICAL KEY FOR BIBLICAL INTERPRETATION

The term *minjung* was first used in academic discourse by two scholars, Ahn Byung Mu and Suh Nam Dong, in 1975. The term is used to refer to those who are marginalized from the center of society because of economic, cultural, social, and gender discrimination. *Minjung* theology explores the social reality of the *minjung* as the starting point for the formulation of Christian theology. The *minjung* reality does not refer to an individualistic existential framework for what describes human existence. It is a sociopolitical or socioeconomic framework. The reality of oppressive and miserable social existence creates a certain primacy over other realities, thus necessitating the act of interpretation. The collective experience of *min-*

---

2. Chun Doo-hwan (born 1931), South Korean army general, was president of South Korea from 1980 to 1988.
3. In May 1980, in the South Korean city of Gwangju, unarmed civilians demonstrated against the newly installed military government. Military

forces suppressed the demonstrations, killing hundreds. Because of this incident Gwangju is sometimes called "the shrine of Korean democracy."
4. An international organization that works to improve the economies of its member countries.

jung, or rather the "social biography of the *minjung*," serves as the hermeneutical basis of *minjung* theology for interpreting the resources of *minjung* theology, such as the Bible, tradition, and history.

THE BIBLE AS A REFERENCE FOR *MINJUNG* THEOLOGY

Minjung theology does not start from doctrines or the Bible itself but from the very life of *minjung*, sharing their struggles, pains, sufferings, aspirations, successes, and failures and envisioning hope for a new heaven and earth. Therefore, the sources for *minjung* theology are not limited to the Bible or to Church doctrine. The *minjung*'s life story, tradition, and history are also included. This is because Korean *minjung* history and traditions are rooted in the *minjung* understanding of God throughout history. In fact, *minjung* theologians consider God as a correlative term with history. Suh Nam Dong states that God is self-actualized in and through the historical process and historical events. For him, "God works through history. . . . History itself is God."[5] Here, history is not limited to Christian history, but includes all human history. For this reason, *minjung* theology discovered the presence of God within Korean history even before Christianity was introduced to Korea. The Bible is used as a reference, not as the norm, of *minjung* theology. And so, the hermeneutics of biblical interpretation of *minjung* theology begins with the *minjung* social context rather than the biblical texts themselves. *Minjung* theology is confessional in this matter.

Political Use of the Bible: Minjung *Theological Interpretation of the Bible*

The Bible is used to seek the meaning of *minjung*'s life and struggle. *Minjung* theologians employ a sociopolitical method of reading biblical texts, examining the social reality of *minjung* behind particular texts. Another method is to create a confluence of a biblical text with a *minjung* experience of history, crafting a source for *minjung* theological construction. Using these methods, *minjung* biblical interpretation comprises three stages of interpretation. The first stage is to review the background of the Korean *minjung* using the Old Testament as a historical basis. The similarities between biblical history and Korean history are clearly made evident. The second stage purports to clarify the position of today's *minjung* by using the insight that Old Testament history provides. The third stage works to suggest the hermeneutical and practical task for *minjung* and their supporters.

Minjung theological interpretation of the Bible travels in three directions that overlap, but are distinct in their destinations. The first is to seek the presence of *minjung* in the Bible. This is focused on the study of the social reality of *Habiru* in Exodus and *Ochios*[6] in Mark. The second direction highlights a biblical paradigm of *minjung* movement in the Bible. Liberation

---

5. Suh Nam Dong, *In Search of Minjung Theology* (Seoul: Hangilsa, 1983), 171 [Lee's note].
6. The common people (ancient Greek). "Habiru": a marginalized, sometimes nomadic, sometimes oppressed or enslaved population of indeterminate ethnicity at the margins of Egypt and other ancient Semitic societies. The "mixed multitude" (Exodus 12:38) that escaped Egypt under Moses may have included Habiru.

events such as the Exodus, the Crucifixion, and the Resurrection imply the significance of theological interpretation of liberation for the oppressed, the poor, or the dominated. The third avenue focuses on reading the whole Bible from *minjung* perspective, rather than finding a "canon within the canon."[7]

THE PRESENCE OF *MINJUNG* IN THE BIBLE

Minjung biblical scholars look for the voice and story of the *minjung* in the Bible. Immediately, the idea of the "Habiru" or Hebrew in the Exodus, the outcasts from the dominant social system, rises to the surface. These *Habiru* or Hebrews are identified with Korean *minjung* because, like the Hebrews, *minjung* suffered for years under the domination of ruthless governments and foreign oppressors.

The distinct contribution of the *minjung* biblical theologian is to highlight the subjectivity of Hebrews in the text as it is clear in Korean history. In Exodus 3, God commands Moses to confront the Pharaoh with God's will to bring God's people to the mountain of God. In other words, before God offers deliverance, the Hebrew people had to confront the pharaohs of the world. In confrontation with the oppressor, they would realize that it was Pharaoh who had infringed upon their rights. In this biblical story, *minjung* theologians see Moses not as a hero but as a representative of *minjung*. In this construct, God is considered as "an immanent force." In other words, God "lives along with *minjung*, is immanent within *minjung*, and is equal to *minjung*."[8]

God in Exodus is also a political force. God in the Exodus narrative stands on the side of the oppressed and downtrodden and will fight for them. Yet God is not the sole actor in the movement of liberation; he is the principal actor who invites the oppressed to be a partner in the process of liberation. People are offered the opportunity to assist in the restoration of their own rights, which have been infringed upon.

The emphasis of *minjung*'s subjectivity should not overlook the passivity of *minjung* at the same time because *minjung* can be the obstacles of their own liberation. In the Exodus narrative, distrust in the God of liberation is stated not only by Pharaoh but also by the majority of Hebrew *minjung*. In addition, the motif of complaining/murmuring in the wilderness demonstrates the passivity of *minjung*, highlighting their weakness in a crisis. The awakened *minjung* who actually responded to the call of God show the subjectivity of history.

THE EXODUS: A BIBLICAL PARADIGM OF
THE *MINJUNG* MOVEMENT OF LIBERATION

One of the tasks of the *minjung* biblical scholar is to find ample evidence of the *minjung* movement of liberation in the Bible. Moon Hee-suk and others offer the Exodus narrative as the primary example of the *minjung* movement of liberation. The Exodus is the paradigm of the *minjung* movement that most closely parallels the current Korean *minjung*'s context. *Minjung* theology highlights the sociopolitical or socioeconomic dimension of the Exodus narrative, rather than abstracting it to a spiritual and personal dimension.

---

7. Examples here are provided exclusively from Old Testament studies [Lee's note].

8. Suh-Nam Dong, 79 [Lee's note]; see note 5 above.

Biblical stories have their full meaning when they are re-embodied in and through the *minjung*'s own praxis of current sociopolitical liberation. *Minjung* themselves become the bridge connecting the hermeneutical gap between the liberating events of the Bible and events of today. The context or the nature of *minjung*'s social reality is different from what is perceived as the norm. However, the *minjung* experience or belief in a God who delivered the oppressed from social and political bondage in biblical times will inform and invite the Korean *minjung* into the Bible, believing the same God will deliver the oppressed in the present as well. The confession and belief that God who stands on the side of Hebrew slaves will stand on the side of the oppressed *minjung* fills a special gap between the Bible and the life of today's *minjung*. The story of Hebrew *minjung*'s experience in Exodus provides insight and hope to Korean *minjung* who are suffering. It is not the situation or the reality of *minjung* that compares two different groups of *minjung* in two different times and cultures. Rather, it is God who delivers the oppressed in the past and present and *minjung*'s experience that encounters God in history as the liberator. The past experience provides hope for the present; the present experience confirms the God of the past, creating a unity of past and present, history and reality. Thus, in a socioeconomic or sociopolitical sense, the biblical liberating events are clear paradigms for God's intervention in history, and such intervention takes place in the socioeconomic arena today.

INTERPRETATION OF THE BIBLE AS A WHOLE FROM THE *MINJUNG* PERSPECTIVE

While other biblical scholars find paradigms of the *minjung* movement of liberation in the Bible, Kim Jeong Joon reads the whole Old Testament from a *minjung* perspective.[9] He sees the Bible as a book of the Israelites' confession of God, who saves them throughout history. Under the great influence of a German scholar, Gerhard von Rad,[1] Kim starts his interpretation with the ancient Credo (Deuteronomy 26:5–9) which at its core is the Exodus event. From the Exodus event, he examines Deuteronomist history, the Prophets, and Psalms and Wisdom literature.

Kim criticizes Gerhard von Rad for the fact that while von Rad revealed the tradition and nature of the Israelites' ancient confession, he did not pay attention to *who* confessed the Credo. The confession cannot exist without a confessor. Thus, Kim Jeong Joon emphasizes the social reality of those who confess the credo in Deuteronomy 26:5–9. They are those who "wander," "are politically oppressed," and "suffered with overloaded labor" and thus "cried out." The motivation of God's salvation history is, in fact, the social reality of *minjung*, the outcasts, the oppressed, and the exploited.

Despite the fact that it is a history of powerful Israelite Kings, the Deuteronomist history connects with the social reality of *minjung* as seen in the story of the Widow of Zarephath (1 Kings 17:12–16) and in the story of Naboth's vineyard.[2] These stories emphasize the fulfillment of justice in the life of the *minjung*. Kim identifies the social reality of *minjung* by using terms that refer to the people who are the main concern of the Hebrew

9. Kim Jeong Joon, "References of Old Testament for Minjung Theology," *Theological Thought* 21 (1979): 5–32 [Lee's note].

1. Lutheran pastor and Old Testament scholar (1901–1971).
2. 1 Kings 21.

prophets. Terms such as the "needy" (*'ebony*; Amos 2:6, 4:1, 5:12, 8:4, and elsewhere), the "poor" (*dalim*; Amos 2:7, 4:1, 5:11, 8:6), and the "afflicted" (*'anawim*; 2:7, 8:4) in Amos are examples. Kim interprets the prophet Amos as the advocate for *minjung*'s human rights and for economic justice.

Kim also purports that the Psalms are songs and poems that originally emerged from the life of *minjung* or people from the grass roots, which were later adapted to worship. For example, he sees the Psalms of lamentation as the exclamation of *minjung* that expresses their sorrow, agony, and grief. In examining the Psalms of lamentation, he demonstrates that the categories of suffering fall into four areas: poverty, political oppression, victims of social sin, and physical and psychological pain.

Finally, Kim Jeong Joon suggests reading the book of Job as *minjung* literature rather than as a book of the rich or book of theodicy. For him, Job represents those who are entirely and suddenly deprived of their life without reason. Job's suffering is the suffering of *minjung*. Kim perceives that Proverbs includes not only the life wisdom and morals of the rulers, but also sayings, riddles, and proverbs that have been derived from *minjung*'s daily life. He also points out that the book of Proverbs considers poverty not simply as a result of oppression, but also as a result of laziness or foolishness. Kim also sees the possibilities of using the book of Proverbs as a guide book for the life of *minjung* after they are able to recover their human rights. Thus, he concludes that Wisdom literature can be a positive biblical resource for *minjung* life, expanding the concerns of *minjung* theology.

Kim Jeong Joon's view on Wisdom literature is distinctive and insightful in explaining the life of *minjung* in the era of globalization that experiences sudden financial collapse and abandonment by the family. One must note that, even more than ever, transnational capital, in the form of transnational corporations and speculative financial capital, has seeped and encroached into the life of the people, causing impoverishment at unprecedented levels. The suffering of *minjung* is now multi-dimensional.

Conclusion: Minjung *Theological Interpretation* of the Bible in the Era of Globalization

CHALLENGES OF GLOBALIZATION

Globalization and the global market drive people against life, causing them to live in despair. Traditional contradictions between classes, races, genders, and other conflicts are not only intensified but become violent. National social welfare and security systems are being dismantled in the process of the global marketization, and they are being integrated into the market. If *minjung* movements have been struggling for social justice, they now struggle for social rights and life at all levels and in all places. The task of liberation movements is how to strive for peace and security for life in the cosmos.

In seeking peace and security in life, we must search for authentic religious teachings for life that is just and peaceful. The search for the meaning of life becomes the central focus of theology in the era of globalization. The vision of a good and full life, the transformation of the conditions of life, or rather of death, for a new, just, and peaceful life, and the ways to celebrate the feast of life together are the concerns of biblical *minjung* hermeneutics. I believe that the task of biblical interpretation in *minjung* theology is to find biblical references for articulating a vision of life, analyzing the conditions of life, and developing praxis for life. In other words, the focus needs to be to liberate life from the forces of death and the forces of destruction in the context of globalization. Theology involves the vision and imagination of life.

FINDING A LIFE-AFFIRMING AND EMPOWERING THEOLOGICAL MOTIF IN THE BIBLE

The social reality of *minjung* in the era of globalization requires biblical studies of *minjung* theology to seek biblical metaphors or motifs that affirm life. The emphasis of the liberating forces of God as a warrior or a revolutionary figure who delivers the oppressed from trouble is powerful and dynamic. Yet the understanding is also destructive and violent.

I believe that the presentation of God as creator is an alternative and more fitting image of God in the era of globalization. The motif of creation should be seen not as ancillary to redemption or the backdrop for redemption, but rather as a motif in its own right, as exhibited particularly by Second Isaiah and the Priestly Writer.[3]

For example, the creation motif in Second Isaiah is introduced through birth imagery. The figure of a travailing woman is used to describe divine creative action in the book. Also, Isaiah 45:9–10 utilizes the figures of a potter and a begetting father to illustrate the creating action of God.

Deuteronomy 32:18 employs the image of a travailing woman to refer to the first formation of Israel as the people of God:

> You were unmindful of the Rock that bore you
> You forgot the God who gave you birth

In each line, the words of birth, *yld* and *hyl*, describe the divine action of creation or salvation as giving birth to Israel. God's action in the parallel line is exclusively maternal because the verb *hyl* elsewhere in the Bible takes only a feminine subject. As the childbirth imagery here refers to the first formation of Israel as the people of God, the same imagery is used to describe the restoration of the people of God in Isaiah 66:7–9. Isaiah 66:7–9 is more radical than the previous presentation of the first birth of Israel because it is not God but Zion who gives birth to the people; radically, God simply and strongly plays a midwife. At the same time, the text clarifies that it is God who ultimately makes the birth possible.

The description of creation through the birth metaphor is insightful to the construction of *minjung* theology. First, the creator God, like a woman in labor, does not appear as a removed, omniscient, all-controlling super power, but as a creative source of life. God endures labor pains in order to bring forth a new people,[4] rather than supervising the life of people from above. Here, God is seen as the imminent force in the life of *minjung*, a creative, present power. Second, the understanding of creation through a birth metaphor is related to salvation, a labor of new life. The divine behavior of creation "like a woman in labor" indicates neither panic nor fear, but

3. One of the contributors to a body of texts (called the Priestly Source) in the Pentateuch, the first five Books of the Bible, that focus on ritual and other matters of interest to ancient Israelite priests.

4. L. L. Bronner, "Gynomorphic Imagery in Exilic Isaiah (40–66)," *Dor le Dor* 12 (1983–84): 77 [Lee's note].

rather God's powerful behavior and its awesome effects. God endures birthpangs in order to bring forth new hope and life.[5] Third, the understanding of creation through the birth metaphor does not present the suffering of *minjung* as miserable or hopeless, but it perceives the suffering of *minjung* as hopeful, connecting to a creative power within it. The suffering will eventually be transformed into joy because God who suffers with the people is the God of new creation. Fourth, the understanding of creation through the birth metaphor depicts salvation and creation not as a one-time event, but as a continual process of which the goal is to create a new heaven and earth in the present reality. As a mother continues nurturing her just-born baby until she grows up and knows how to share that love with others, God and humans continue to take care of the new creation until humanity is able to recover wholeness and mutuality in this world. God is the meaning of life when God is encountered in the midst of the life and suffering of *minjung*, as seen in the whirlwind of Job 38.

5. Ibid [Lee's note].

CHRISTIAN DE CHERGÉ
1937–1996

SPIRITUAL TESTAMENT

Through European colonialism, Christianity expanded, and many of the areas it advanced into had, religiously and politically, been Muslim. Nowhere was this encroachment felt more acutely than around the Mediterranean, where Arab or Turkish Muslims faced Europeans of various nationalities. In centuries past, Muslims and Christians had battled, with gains and losses, dominance and submission, on both sides. By the early twentieth century, however, with the dismantlement of the Ottoman Empire after World War I, Muslim sovereignty effectively survived only in Turkey. Along the North African littoral, in Egypt, in the Middle East and Arabia, even in Persia, Europe seemed invincible. Muslims felt humiliated, and they perceived European power less in terms of nationality than in terms of religion.

Then, after World War II, Europe's onetime Arab or Muslim colonies all became independent states. What was to be the relationship between those states and the European states that had once ruled them? What was to be the relationship between Islam and Christianity in this postcolonial world? These questions remained unanswered and pressing in the early years of the twenty-first century, and it is with them as background that the following selection must be read.

Christian de Chergé was born in Colmar (Haut-Rhin), France. His father was a French general, and the family lived in Algeria for several years during World War II. France and Algeria face each across the Mediterranean. At the high tide of colonialism, France had incorporated Algeria as a province, yet without granting the Arab population, overwhelmingly Muslim, the rights of French citizens. After World War II, Algeria entered into a protracted civil war, which led to its independence from France in 1962. During the war of independence, de Chergé was sent to Algeria as a French soldier. While there, he befriended an Algerian Muslim with whom he had long, searching discussions about their respective religions. When this friend intervened to save de Chergé from armed rebels threatening to kill him and when, days later, the same man was killed in retaliation, the effect upon de Chergé was life-changing. Upon his return to France, he began studies for the Roman Catholic priesthood, determined to return to Algeria and resume somehow the interreligious, cross-cultural conversation that a murder had interrupted.

In 1964, de Chergé was ordained as a priest. Five years later, he joined a small Cistercian monastery, Notre-Dame de l'Atlas (Our Lady of the Atlas Mountains), in Tibhirine, Algeria. In 1984, having learned Arabic and studied the Qur'an, he became the prior (abbot or father superior) of Notre-Dame de l'Atlas. The monastery understood its mission to be, first, adoration of God and, second, reconciliation with rather than conversion of Algerian Muslims.

In 1991, after decades of one-party dictatorial rule, Algeria held its first free election. When electoral victory went to a Muslim party, however, the regime nullified the result, and civil war broke out. The defeated party, seeing the regime as French-influenced and, by implication, tainted with Christianity, demanded that all foreigners leave the country and imposed a reign of rural terror even on Muslims who deviated from their severe views. Many urged the monks of Atlas to flee, but after painful deliberation they chose to stay.

In 1993, de Chergé sent a letter to his family, to be opened only in the case of his violent death. In March 1996, he and six other monks from his monastery were kidnapped and, two months later, killed. Suspicion immediately fell on the Front Islamique de Salvation (Islamic Salvation Front), the Muslim party then waging war against the state. Though it may never be known who really killed the monks, deliberate provocation by the ruling party cannot be ruled out.

The atrocity created enormous revulsion in France. A predictably powerful second reaction followed when de Chergé's open letter was published on Pentecost Sunday in 1996. In his "Spiritual Testament," after pleading that his readers not stereotype the Muslims of Algeria, de Chergé movingly addresses his future killer. In 2011, a film based on the episode—*Des hommes and des dieux* ("Of Gods and Men"), directed by Xavier Beauvois—won the Grand Prix at Cannes.

PRONOUNCING GLOSSARY

Christian de Chergé: *kris-tyen´ duh shehr-zhay´*

SPIRITUAL TESTAMENT

If the day comes, and it could be today, that I am a victim of the terrorism that seems to be engulfing all foreigners living in Algeria, I would like my community, my Church, and my family to remember that I have dedicated my life to God and Algeria.

That they accept that the Lord of all life was not a stranger to this savage kind of departure; that they pray for me, wondering how I found myself worthy of such a sacrifice; that they link in their memory this death of mine with all the other deaths equally violent but forgotten in their anonymity.

My life is not worth more than any other—not less, not more. Nor am I an innocent child. I have lived long enough to know that I, too, am an

FROM John W. Kiser, *The Monks of Tibhirine: Faith, Love, and Terror in Algeria.*

accomplice of the evil that seems to prevail in the world around, even that which might lash out blindly at me. If the moment comes, I would hope to have the presence of mind, and the time, to ask for God's pardon and for that of my fellowman, and, at the same time, to pardon in all sincerity he who would attack me.

I would not welcome such a death. It is important for me to say this. I do not see how I could rejoice when this people whom I love will be accused, indiscriminately, of my death. The price is too high, this so-called grace of the martyr, if I owe it to an Algerian who kills me in the name of what he thinks is Islam.

I know the contempt that some people have for Algerians as a whole. I also know the caricatures of Islam that a certain (Islamist) ideology promotes. It is too easy for such people to dismiss, in good conscience, this religion as something hateful by associating it with violent extremists. For me, Algeria and Islam are quite different from the commonly held opinion. They are body and soul. I have said enough, I believe, about all the good things I have received here, finding so often the meaning of the Gospels, running like some gold thread through my life, and which began first at my mother's knee, my very first church, here in Algeria, where I learned respect for the Muslims.

Obviously, my death will justify the opinion of all those who dismissed me as naïve or idealistic: "Let him tell us what he thinks now." But such people should know my death will satisfy my most burning curiosity. At last, I will be able—if God pleases—to see the children of Islam as He sees them, illuminated in the glory of Christ, sharing in the gift of God's Passion and of the Spirit, whose secret joy will always be to bring forth our common humanity amidst our differences.

I give thanks to God for this life, completely mine yet completely theirs, too, to God, who wanted it for joy against, and in spite of, all odds. In this Thank You—which says everything about my life—I include you, my friends past and present, and those friends who will be here at the side of my mother and father, of my sisters and brothers—thank you a thousandfold.

And to you, too, my friend of the last moment, who will not know what you are doing. Yes, for you, too, I wish this thank-you, this "A-Dieu," whose image is in you also, that we may meet in heaven, like happy thieves,[1] if it pleases God, our common Father. Amen! Insha Allah!"[2]

1. According to the Gospels, two men were crucified with Jesus Christ, one on his right and one on his left. Neither of these men is named. According to Matthew, Mark, and John, both men mocked Jesus. According to Luke 23:39–43, however, only one of the men mocked Jesus. The other one—known as the Good Thief—asked Jesus to remember him in his kingdom. "A-Dieu": De Chergé is playing on the French word *merci*, "thank you." He speaks his *merci* to friends and family as well as to God. But the phrase *merci à dieu* ("thank you to God") is phonetically identical to *merci, adieu* ("thank you, goodbye"), which he imagines himself saying to his "friend of the last moment," his killer.
2. "Insha Allah": May God will it (Arabic); a familiar Muslim expression for "God willing."

LIU ZHENYING (BROTHER YUN)
born 1958

FROM THE HEAVENLY MAN

The People's Republic of China (PRC) formally recognizes Roman Catholicism and Protestantism as two religions. In the familiar Communist manner, however, the regime incorporates each religion as fully as possible into the state. All church officials are paid by the government and subject to government supervision. Alongside these state churches, there are unlicensed Catholic, Protestant, and Pentecostal churches, which are sometimes persecuted by the state.

The term *Pentecostal*, from a Greek word meaning fiftieth, alludes to the fiftieth day after the Resurrection of Christ. On this day, according to Acts of the Apostles 2 (see p. 136), the Holy Spirit descended on Christ's dispirited Apostles and inflamed them with zeal to spread the Gospel. In the early twentieth century, Pentecostalism—a Christian revival movement seeking to duplicate the disciples' overwhelmingly emotional experience and then imitate their fearless enthusiasm—began in Los Angeles. The movement has subsequently experienced explosive growth in Asia, South America, and, most of all, Africa. Indeed, the expansion of Pentecostalism represents a defining characteristic of the Christian world today. The simplicity and directness of the movement's emotional appeal has made it accessible to large numbers of poor, often illiterate people, unreachable by more sedate or complex strands of Christianity. However, the movement's emphasis on prosperity through Christianity—the "prosperity Gospel"—has attracted Christian criticism. Some Pentecostal leaders have turned to Korean *minjung* theology (see p. 658) for a corrective.

Liu Zhenying, famous as Brother Yun, is a Chinese Pentecostal Christian born, like a good many Pentecostals, in poverty. According to his memoir *The Heavenly Man* (2002), cowritten with and translated into English by Paul Hattaway, Brother Yun was instrumental in the 1980s and 1990s in the development of Chinese Pentecostal Christian house-church networks. For not joining the Communist-government-controlled Christian organization, he was jailed and tortured. After many years in a maximum security prison, he escaped—reportedly the only person to ever do so, and reportedly without human help—and eventually fled China. In 2001, he gained asylum in Germany. It is uncertain whether he will ever return to China.

In the following fervent manifesto, a chapter from *The Heavenly Man*, Brother Yun outlines his dream of a Spirit-filled missionary enterprise, the "Back to Jerusalem" movement, meant to evangelize Asia with missionaries from China. Brother Yun understands Christianity to have spread west: from

Brother Yun

Jerusalem to Europe to the Americas and then across the Pacific to China. In embracing persecution and possible martyrdom as the price of missionary expansion, he seeks to bring the journey of Christianity full circle: from China westward across Asia, all the way "back to Jerusalem."

Brother Yun's dream may be wildly unrealistic. Some of his claims for the movement's accomplishments may seem exaggerated. Not even all Chinese Pentecostals or house-church Christians agree with him. Yet his book has been embraced warmly by East Asian Christians who identify with his story of courage under persecution and, to some degree, share his dream.

FROM THE HEAVENLY MAN
From *Back to Jerusalem*

The Back to Jerusalem missionary movement is not an army with guns or human weapons. It isn't a group of well-dressed, slick professionals. It's an army of broken-hearted Chinese men and women whom God has cleansed with a mighty fire, and who have already been through years of hardship and deprivation for the sake of the gospel. In worldly terms they have nothing and appear unimpressive, but in the spiritual realm they are mighty warriors for Jesus Christ! We thank God that he *"chose the foolish things of the world to shame the wise; God chose the weak things of the world to shame the strong. He chose the lowly things of this world and the despised things— and the things that are not—to nullify the things that are, so that no one may boast before him."* 1 Corinthians 1:27–29.

God is calling thousands of house church warriors to write their testimonies with their own blood. We will walk across the borders of China, carrying the Word of God into the Muslim, Buddhist and Hindu worlds. Thousands will be willing to die for the Lord. They will see multitudes of souls saved, as well as awaken many sleeping churches in the West.

Hundreds of Western missionaries spilled their blood on Chinese soil in the past. Their example has inspired us to be willing also to die for the Lord wherever he leads us with his message. Many of our missionaries will be captured, tortured, and martyred for the sake of the gospel, but that will not stop us.

God has not only refined *us* in the fire of affliction for the past thirty years, he has also refined our methods. For example, we're totally committed to planting groups of local believers who meet in homes. We have no desire to build a single church building anywhere! This allows the gospel to spread rapidly, is harder for the authorities to detect, and allows us to channel all our resources directly into gospel ministry.

Some people have challenged the fact that we are sending missionaries outside China. They say we should stay in China and win our own country before we go out. To this illogical argument I respond with a simple question, "Then why does your country send missionaries? Is everyone in your country saved?"

If we stay in one place and refuse to advance until we've completely finished the job there, we'll never be able to impact the world with the gospel. Surely God's way is for us to be winning our home at the same time as we're sending new workers to the ends of the earth! Believe me, our vision to reach the world does not mean we'll stop or slow down our efforts to reach all of China with the gospel!

The two will take place hand-in-hand.

In fact, I believe the best way for the Chinese church to remain strong is to keep it motivated to reach out to the nations of the world. When believers focus on serving the Lord and reaching the lost, God blesses them and the church remains sharp. When we become self-centred and critical of each other, Satan has won already and the church will become a blunt, useless instrument.

We knew from the beginning that there is a high price to pay for this Back to Jerusalem mission. I'm not just talking about money! I'm talking about the many Chinese who will be martyred and suffer as this vision unfolds. Many will go on one-way tickets, realizing they'll never return to China to see their loved ones again.

We also realize Back to Jerusalem will cost a lot of money, but even though our churches are so poor, we have already collected tens of thousands of dollars to support our missionaries. Like the Macedonian church, many Chinese believers have given literally all they own. *"Out of the most severe trial, their overflowing joy and their extreme poverty welled up in rich generosity. For I testify that they gave as much as they were able, and even beyond their ability."* 2 Corinthians 8:2–3.[1]

The Chinese church is willing to pay the price.

Since my escape from China in 1997, I've been responsible for the training and implementation of the Back to Jerusalem missionaries.

When the first batch of thirty-nine missionaries left China in March 2000, thirty-six of them were arrested. They didn't lose their vision however. They went back home, prayed, and found another way to get across the border.

Little more than a year later, the number of Chinese house church missionaries outside China already exceeded four hundred, serving in more than ten countries. The floodgates are beginning to open.

Each Back to Jerusalem missionary receives training in several main subjects. These include:

1. How to suffer and die for the Lord. We examine what the Bible says about suffering, and look at how the Lord's people have laid down their lives for the advance of the gospel throughout history.
2. How to witness for the Lord. We teach how to witness for the Lord under any circumstance, on trains or buses, or even in the back of a police van on our way to the execution ground.
3. How to escape for the Lord. We know that sometimes it is the Lord who sends us to prison to witness for him, but we also believe the devil sometimes wants us to go to prison to stop the ministry God has called us to do. We teach the missionaries special skills such as how to free themselves from handcuffs, and how to jump from second-storey windows without injuring themselves.

---

1. Writing to the church in Corinth, the Apostle Paul commends the generosity of the church in Macedonia.

This is not a "normal" seminary or Bible College!

If you ever visit one of the places where we are training our Back to Jerusalem missionaries, you will see how serious we are to fulfil our destiny in God. You may see people with their hands handcuffed behind their backs, leaping from second-storey windows!

Nothing less is required if we are to break down the walls that separate Muslims, Hindus and Buddhists from knowing the sweet presence of Jesus.

• • •

When the elders of the Sinim Fellowship[2] heard how God had miraculously allowed me to escape from China, they appointed me as their "Authorized Representative," to speak for the house churches around the world.

The elders of the Sinim Fellowship drafted the following letter for me:

> To Brother Yun, our holy brother who is a close comrade of Christ the Lord and who is filled with the Spirit of the Power of God:
>
> You are the "chariots and horsemen of Israel"[3] of God! You carry the victorious message of the expansion of the kingdom of Christ in you!
>
> Dear Brother, you are sent by God from the Sinim Elders' Committee of the Chinese house churches as our authorized representative overseas!
>
> God has shown you, according to his guidance and Lordship, that life is the foundation, building up the church is the centre, and the training of workers is the point of breakthrough—the strategic place from where expansion can be carried out in all directions, radiating to every nation and people in the world, so that the ground that the sole of your foot walks on will become your inheritance!
>
> March forward towards the Muslims, the Hindus and the Buddhists in Europe, America, Africa, Australasia and Asia!
>
> We pray the Lord will give you wisdom and power from above, so that your message is filled with heavenly authority. Like the fire Samson tied to the foxes' tails,[4] it will burn wherever you go.
>
> May you accomplish the holy mission God has given you, to take the gospel back to Jerusalem, until the last holy disciple is added to the church and the bride is prepared to welcome the return of our Saviour Lord Jesus Christ,[5] so that the kingdoms of the world become the possession of our King! Our holy goal is that he will be King forever and ever.[6]
>
> We are ready to work hard with servants of the Lord all over the world, who are members of his body, serving one another with the spiritual gifts we have received, so that the holy mission of God can be fulfilled!

2. A network of Chinese house churches. According to Isaiah 49:12, Sinim is a place located far away, to the east or south or southeast of Jerusalem. *Sinim* is the modern Hebrew word for China.
3. In 2 Kings 2:12, the prophet Elijah speaks these words in religious ecstasy.
4. See Judges 15:4.
5. In Revelation 21:2, the "new Jerusalem" comes down from heaven "prepared as a bride adorned for her husband." In the Old Testament, Israel is the bride of God. In the New Testament, the Church—the new Jerusalem—becomes the bride of Christ at the end of time, here taken to be when the last convert has been made and the Church is complete.
6. See Revelation 11:15.

Dear Brother Yun, this is the conviction of all the servants of God in the Sinim Elders' Fellowship. May the Lord strengthen the task entrusted to you, lead you, and open the way ahead. We and all our co-workers are your solid shields. May the will of the Lord be done quickly, on earth as in heaven.[7] Amen!

Your co-workers in Christ and Elders of the Sinim Fellowship.

7. An allusion to the Lord's Prayer. See Matthew 6:10.

POPE JOHN PAUL II
1920–2005

ECUMENICAL PATRIARCH BARTHOLOMEW I
born 1940

COMMON DECLARATION ON ENVIRONMENTAL ETHICS

Pope John Paul II was born Karol Józef Wojtiła in Wadowice, Poland; pursued theological studies in his homeland; and, having survived the Nazi occupation of that country during World War II, earned advanced degrees in Rome. Ordained in succession priest, bishop, archbishop, and cardinal, he became in 1978 the first non-Italian to be elected pope, supreme pontiff of the Roman Catholic Church, in 455 years. In the following year, a trip he made to Poland attracted crowds of such unprecedented size and enthusiasm that he was widely credited with creating the political mood that made possible the epoch-making Solidarity movement (see p. 647)

Ecumenical Patriarch Bartholomew I was born Dimitrios Arhondonis in the ethnically Greek village of Zeytinli, on the island of Gökceada (Greek Imvros), Turkey. He pursued theological studies in a now closed Christian seminary in Turkey; did advanced work at several universities in Europe; was ordained a priest, then a bishop; and in 1991 became ecumenical patriarch of Constantinople, traditionally honored as first among equals in the bishoprics of the Eastern Orthodox Church. Concern for the environment became one of his signature concerns, involving him in various international environmental organizations and earning him the nickname "the Green Patriarch."

Early in the twentieth century, the conservation movement began as the desire to preserve places of natural beauty or renewable but not indestructible natural resources, such as forests. Late in the century, this movement started to shift from the local to the global: from the creation and protection of national parks and national seashores to planetary issues, such as the depletion of the ozone layer, the death of ocean fisheries, the erosion of arable land, desertification, the perilous scarcity of potable water, and the global consequences of toxic waste disposal.

Among all such challenges, none loomed larger at the turn of the century than climate change. In 1997, the United Nations Framework Convention on Climate Change held a conference in Kyoto, Japan. The protocols that resulted set voluntary but serious national targets for the reduction of so-called "greenhouse emissions": carbon emissions that when trapped by Earth's atmosphere contribute to the warming of its climate, as if Earth were a giant greenhouse.

Despite some promising early initiatives, global warming continued apace, leading to the sense of emergency that preceded a second conference, more than decade later, that many hoped would produce drastic, coordinated, international action. However, the Copenhagen (Denmark) Climate Change Conference of 2009 was an all but complete failure. A wan follow-up conference a year later, in Cancún, Mexico, merely confirmed a growing sense that the world's political leadership was incapable of addressing the looming threat.

As the Intergovernment Panel on Climate Change gathered data, the data grew more ominous. Some experts voiced the opinion that the point had passed when concerted action might have reversed or slowed global climate change. But environmental activism and related theological reflection had begun to gather momentum in the world's religions, perhaps particularly in Christianity. Though on various occasions science and Christianity had been famously at odds, on this occasion they were unexpectedly in unison.

"Common Declaration on Environmental Ethics," issued jointly in 2002 by Pope John Paul II and Ecumenical Patriarch Bartholomew I, accepts without demurral the key findings of environmental science. But then, invoking aspects of Christian tradition, this document exhorts Christians—indeed, "all men and women of good will"—to take responsible action. Early in the twenty-first century, most of the historical divisions in Christianity still existed in principle, but many of them no longer divided as seriously or bitterly as they once had. Would peril to the common human habitat bring all Christians together? Further, would the environmental threat foster new relations between Christianity and other religions?

PRONOUNCING GLOSSARY

Dimitrios Arhondonis: *duh-mee´-tree-ohs ar-hohn-doh´-nees*

Karol Józef Woytila: *kah´-rohl yoh´-zef voy-tee´-wah*

COMMON DECLARATION ON ENVIRONMENTAL ETHICS

We are gathered here today in the spirit of peace for the good of all human beings and for the care of creation. At this moment in history, at the beginning of the third millennium, we are saddened to see the daily suffering of a great number of people from violence, starvation, poverty and disease. We are also concerned about the negative consequences for humanity and for all creation resulting from the degradation of some basic natural resources such as water, air and land, brought about by an economic and technological progress which does not recognize and take into account its limits.

Almighty God envisioned a world of beauty and harmony, and He created it, making every part an expression of His freedom, wisdom and love (cf. Genesis 1:1–25).

At the centre of the whole of creation, He placed us, human beings, with our inalienable human dignity. Although we share many features with the rest of the living beings, Almighty God went further with us and gave us an immortal soul, the source of self-awareness and freedom, endowments that make us in His image and likeness (cf. Genesis 1:26–31; 2:7). Marked with that resemblance, we have been placed by God in the world in order to cooperate with Him in realizing more and more fully the divine purpose for creation.

At the beginning of history, man and woman sinned by disobeying God and rejecting His design for creation. Among the results of this first sin was the destruction of the original harmony of creation. If we examine carefully the social and environmental crisis which the world community is facing, we must conclude that we are still betraying the mandate God has given us: to be stewards called to collaborate with God in watching over creation in holiness and wisdom.

God has not abandoned the world. It is His will that His design and our hope for it will be realized through our co-operation in restoring its original harmony. In our own time we are witnessing a growth of an *ecological awareness* which needs to be encouraged, so that it will lead to practical programmes and initiatives. An awareness of the relationship between God and humankind brings a fuller sense of the importance of the relationship between human beings and the natural environment, which is God's creation and which God entrusted to us to guard with wisdom and love (cf. Genesis 1:28).

Respect for creation stems from respect for human life and dignity. It is on the basis of our recognition that the world is created by God that we can discern an objective moral order within which to articulate a code of environmental ethics. In this perspective, Christians and all other believers have a specific role to play in proclaiming moral values and in educating people in *ecological awareness*, which is none other than responsibility towards self, towards others, towards creation.

What is required is an act of repentance on our part and a renewed attempt to view ourselves, one another, and the world around us within the perspective of the divine design for creation. The problem is not simply economic and technological; it is moral and spiritual. A solution at the economic and technological level can be found only if we undergo, in the most radical way, an inner change of heart, which can lead to a change in lifestyle and of unsustainable patterns of consumption and production. A genuine *conversion* in Christ will enable us to change the way we think and act.

First, we must regain humility and recognize the limits of our powers, and most importantly, the limits of our knowledge and judgement. We have been making decisions, taking actions and assigning values that are leading us away from the world as it should be, away from the design of God for creation, away from all that is essential for a healthy planet and a healthy commonwealth of people. A new approach and a new culture are needed, based on the centrality of the human person within creation and inspired by environmentally ethical behavior stemming from our triple relationship to God, to self and to creation. Such an ethics fosters interdependence and stresses the principles of universal solidarity, social justice and responsibility, in order to promote a true culture of life.

Secondly, we must frankly admit that humankind is entitled to something better than what we see around us. We and, much more, our children and future generations are entitled to a better world, a world free from degradation, violence and bloodshed, a world of generosity and love.

Thirdly, aware of the value of prayer, we must implore God the Creator to enlighten people everywhere regarding the duty to respect and carefully guard creation.

We therefore invite all men and women of good will to ponder the importance of the following ethical goals:

1. To think of the world's children when we reflect on and evaluate our options for action.

2. To be open to study the true values based on the natural law that sustain every human culture.

3. To use science and technology in a full and constructive way, while recognizing that the findings of science have always to be evaluated in the light of the centrality of the human person, of the common good and of the inner purpose of creation. Science may help us to correct the mistakes of the past, in order to enhance the spiritual and material wellbeing of the present and future generations. It is love for our children that will show us the path that we must follow into the future.

4. To be humble regarding the idea of ownership and to be open to the demands of solidarity. Our mortality and our weakness of judgement together warn us not to take irreversible actions with what we choose to regard as our property during our brief stay on this earth. We have not been entrusted with unlimited power over creation, we are only stewards of the common heritage.

5. To acknowledge the diversity of situations and responsibilities in the work for a better world environment. We do not expect every person and every institution to assume the same burden. Everyone has a part to play, but for the demands of justice and charity to be respected the most affluent societies must carry the greater burden, and from them is demanded a sacrifice greater than can be offered by the poor. Religions, governments and institutions are faced by many different situations; but on the basis of the principle of subsidiarity all of them can take on some tasks, some part of the shared effort.

6. To promote a peaceful approach to disagreement about how to live on this earth, about how to share it and use it, about what to change and what to leave unchanged. It is not our desire to evade controversy about the environment, for we trust in the capacity of human reason and the path of dialogue to reach agreement. We commit ourselves to respect the views of all who disagree with us, seeking solutions through open exchange, without resorting to oppression and domination.

It is not too late. God's world has incredible healing powers. Within a single generation, we could steer the earth toward our children's future. Let that generation start now, with God's help and blessing.

CHRISTIAN WIMAN
born 1966

FROM MY BRIGHT ABYSS

Christian Wiman grew up in the arid flatlands of West Texas. After leaving home and making a substantial mark as a poet, he became in 2003 editor of the eminent literary magazine *Poetry*. In that position, with his acclaim as a poet now crowned with an assured income, he was on top of his chosen world. But in 2005, as he recounts in the essay "Love Bade Me Welcome" (2006), three things happened to him in close succession. First, he stopped writing poetry. It was as if the world had stopped speaking to him. Second, he suddenly fell in love. But though he was suffused with undreamed-of joy, "There were still no poems, and this ate at me constantly." Third, he learned that "I have an incurable cancer in my blood. The disease is as rare as it is mysterious, killing some people quickly and sparing others for decades, afflicting some with all manner of miseries and disabilities and leaving others relatively healthy until the end."

And then one morning, Wiman and his love found themselves going to church: "*Found ourselves.* That's exactly what it felt like." They were not seeking a miracle cure, but there they were. And finally "out of all these efforts at faith and love, out of my own inevitable failures at both, I have begun to write poems again." Seven years after all this happened, Wiman, a late convert from atheism to Christianity, published a book of prose, *My Bright Abyss: Meditation of a Modern Believer* (2013). The following excerpt does not represent—no excerpt could—postmodern Christianity. Still, only a postmodern Christian could have produced it.

Modernity had much to be proud of. It had delivered improved health and steadily lengthening life; sexual liberation; steadily dropping crime rates; and despite economic inequality, the greatest material wealth for the greatest number that the planet had ever seen. What more could anyone want? But some did want more. In postmodernity, some were prepared without reserve or apology to look backward as well as forward, to pick and choose in a mood of undisguised ambivalence, of yes-and-no, of engagement without commitment. Modernity—as a forward-looking but vague fusion of science, literature, art, and politics—no longer commanded the allegiance it had enjoyed a century earlier. And in just this open but guarded mood, Christianity became for some a newly available option.

Here, Wiman does not speak first of his new faith. Rather, he introduces the grave bravery of his old atheism, a bravery he is dubious about. To his new belief, he consistently brings the same suspicion he brings to his old unbelief. Though such relentless interrogation may sound dry, Wiman's subject, finally, is deliverance.

PRONOUNCING GLOSSARY

Camus: *ca-moo'*
Christian Wiman: *kris'-chun wai'-mun*
  [*ai* rhyming with *rye*]
Emmaus: *e-may'-uhs*

Giacometti: *jah-coh-met'-tee*
Kafka: *kahf'-kah*
Tillich: *til'-ik*

FROM MY BRIGHT ABYSS

Be careful. Be certain that your expressions of regret about your inability to rest in God do not have a tinge of self-satisfaction, even self-exaltation to them, that your complaints about your anxieties are not merely a manifestation of your dependence on them. There is nothing more difficult to outgrow than anxieties that have become useful to us, whether as explanations for a life that never quite finds its true force or direction, or as fuel for ambition, or as a kind of reflexive secular religion that, paradoxically, unites us with others in a shared sense of complete isolation: you feel at home in the world only by never feeling at home in the world.

• • •

It is this last complacency to which artists of our time are especially susceptible, precisely because it comes disguised as a lonely, heroic strength. Sometimes it truly is a strength: Giacometti, Beckett, Camus, Kafka.[1] Yet it is a deep truth of being human—and, I would argue, a hint at the immortal Spirit who is forever tugging us toward him—that even our most imaginative discoveries are doomed to become mere stances and attitudes. In this sense, art does advance over time, though usually this advance involves a recovery of elements and ideas we thought we had left behind for good. This is true not only for those who follow in the wake of great accomplishments but also for those who themselves did the accomplishing. What belief could be more self-annihilating, could more effectively articulate its own insufficiency and thereby prophesy its own demise, than twentieth-century existentialism? To say that there is nothing beyond this world that we see, to make death the final authority of our lives, is to sow a seed of meaninglessness into that very insight. The four artists above all knew that, and made of that fatal knowledge a fierce, new, and necessary faith: the austere, "absurd" persistence of spirit in both Camus and Beckett; the terrible, disfiguring contingency that, in Giacometti's sculptures, takes on the look of fate. There is genuine heroism here, but there is also—faintly at first, but then more persistently, more damagingly—an awareness of heroism. (Only Kafka seems to fully feel his defeat: he is perhaps the most "spiritual" artist among this group, though he treasures his misery too much ever to be released from it.) This flaw—the artist's pride—is what made the achievement possible, but it is also the crack that slowly widens over time, not lessening the achievement, but humanizing it, relativizing it. Insights that once seemed immutable and universal begin to look a little more like temporal, individual visions—visions from which, inevitably, there comes a time to move forward.

• • •

Christianity itself is this—temporal, relative—to some extent. To every age Christ dies anew and is resurrected within the imagination of man. This is

---

1. Franz Kafka (1883–1924), Czech-born, Jewish, German-language writer of absurdist novels and short stories. "Giacometti": Alberto Giacometti (1901–1966), Swiss sculptor of unnaturally elongated and emaciated human and animal figures. "Beckett": Samuel Beckett (1906–1989), Irish playwright, fiction writer, poet, and essayist whose works tend to focus on isolation, repetition, despair, and dark humor. "Camus": Albert Camus (1913–1960), French existentialist novelist, essayist, and playwright who explored the emptiness of modern life and the search for meaning.

why he could be a paragon of rationality for eighteenth-century England, a heroic figure of the imagination for the Romantics, an exemplar of existential courage for writers like Paul Tillich and Rudolf Bultmann.[2] One truth, then, is that Christ is always being remade in the image of man, which means that his reality is always being deformed to fit human needs, or what humans perceive to be their needs. A deeper truth, though, one that scripture suggests when it speaks of the eternal Word being made specific flesh, is that there is no permutation of humanity in which Christ is not present. If every Bible is lost, if every church crumbles to dust, if the last believer in the last prayer opens her eyes and lets it all finally go, Christ will appear on this earth as calmly and casually as he appeared to the disciples walking to Emmaus after his death, who did not recognize this man to whom they had pledged their very lives; this man whom they had seen beaten, crucified, abandoned by God; this man who, after walking the dusty road with them, after sharing an ordinary meal and discussing the scriptures, had to vanish once more in order to make them see.[3]

• • •

When I think of the years when I had no faith, what I am struck by, first of all, is how little this lack disrupted my conscious life. I lived not with God, nor with his absence, but in a mild abeyance of belief, drifting through the days on a tide of tiny vanities—a publication, a flirtation, a strong case made for some weak nihilism—nights all adagios and alcohol as my mind tore luxuriously into itself. I can see now how deeply God's absence affected my unconscious life, how under me always there was this long fall that pride and fear and self-love at once protected me from and subjected me to. Was the fall into belief or into unbelief? Both. For if grace woke me to God's presence in the world and in my heart, it also woke me to his absence. I never truly felt the pain of unbelief until I began to believe.

• • •

When I assented to the faith that was latent within me—and I phrase it carefully, deliberately, for there was no white light, no ministering or avenging angel that tore my life in two; rather it seemed as if the tiniest seed of belief had finally flowered in me, or, more accurately, as if I had happened upon some rare flower deep in the desert and had known, though I was just then discovering it, that it had been blooming impossibly year after parched year in me, surviving all the seasons of my unbelief. *When I assented to the faith that was latent within me,* what struck me were the ways in which my evasions and confusions, which I had mistaken for a strong sense of purpose, had expressed themselves in my life: poem after poem about unnamed and unnameable absences, relationships so transparently perishable they practically came with expiration dates on them, city after city sacked of impressions and peremptorily abandoned, as if I were some conquering army of insight seeing, I now see, nothing. Perhaps it is never disbelief, which at least is active and conscious, that destroys a person, but unacknowledged belief, or a need for

2. 1884–1976; German Bible scholar and theologian. For Paul Tillich, see p. 610.   3. See Luke 14:13–35.

belief so strong that it is continually and silently crucified on the crosses of science, humanism, art, or (to name the thing that poisons all these gifts of God) the overweening self.

• • •

They do not happen now, the sandstorms of my childhood, when the western distance ochred and the square emptied, and long before the big wind hit, you could taste the dust on your tongue, could feel the earth under you—and even something in you—seem to loosen slightly. Soon tumbleweeds began to skip and nimble by, a dust devil flickered firelessly in the vacant lot across the street from our house, and birds began rocketing past with their wings shut as if they'd been flung. Worse than snow, worse than ice, a bad sandstorm shrinks the world to the slit of your eyes, lifting from the fields an inchoate, creaturely mass that claws at any exposed skin as if the dust remembered what it was, which is what you are—alive, alive— and sought return. They do not happen now, whether because of what we've learned or because the earth itself has changed. Yet I can close my eyes and see all the trees tugging at their roots as if to unfasten themselves from the earth. I can hear the long-gone howl, more awful for its being mute.

• • •

Lord, I can approach you only by means of my consciousness, but consciousness can only approach you as an object, which you are not. I have no hope of experiencing you as I experience the world—directly, immediately— yet I want nothing more. Indeed, so great is my hunger for you—or is this evidence of your hunger for me?—that I seem to see you in the black flower mourners make beside a grave I do not know, in the embers' innards like a shining hive, in the bare abundance of a winter tree whose every limb is lit and fraught with snow. Lord, Lord, how bright the abyss inside that "seem."

APPENDICES

Glossary

Words in SMALL CAPS are defined in their own entries.

abbot (from Aramaic *abba*, "father"). The head of a monastery.

Acts of the Apostles. The fifth Book of THE NEW TESTAMENT, generally referred to as Acts. Telling the story of the growth of the Christian community under the impulse of THE HOLY SPIRIT (the APOSTLES of the title being not just THE TWELVE but also other disciples of Jesus, especially Paul), Acts begins with the ascension of Jesus into heaven and the descent of the Spirit, and it concludes with the arrival of Paul in Rome.

Advent. The period of four weeks (forty days in the Eastern Church) of prayer, fasting, and preparation for the feast of Jesus' nativity (Christmas).

Adventists. Members of a Christian movement, founded in the nineteenth century, who believe in the imminent SECOND COMING of Jesus. See MILLERITES and SEVENTH DAY ADVENTISTS.

aggiornamento (Italian, "updating"). The adaptation of the Catholic Church to the contemporary world, called for by Pope John XXIII (pope 1958–63).

agnosticism. Noun derived from *agnostic*, a term coined by Thomas Henry Huxley (1825–1895) to describe a person who believes that the existence of God cannot be rationally proved or disproved and that hence one must suspend judgment on the issue.

Albigensians. CATHARIST sect in twelfth- and thirteenth-century France, exterminated during the Albigensian Crusade (1209–55).

Amish. The members of an ANABAPTIST Church marked by strict, simple living and rejection of modern technology, now concentrated in Ohio, Pennsylvania, Indiana, and Ontario.

Anabaptists. Radical sixteenth-century Protestants from Germany, Switzerland, the Netherlands, and Moravia, who disapproved of infant BAPTISM, the swearing of oaths, participation in secular government, and the waging of war.

anchoress, anchorite (from Greek *anchoreta*, "a person who withdraws"). A hermit: a person who lives in seclusion for religious reasons; typically, in the MIDDLE AGES, one supported by a church.

Anglican Church, the. The established Church of England, founded by King Henry VIII (reigned 1509–47) through the Act of Supremacy (1534). See THE ANGLICAN COMMUNION.

Anglican Communion, the. A loose association of separately governed national churches that are linked theologically and liturgically to THE ANGLICAN CHURCH and THE BOOK OF COMMON PRAYER.

apocalypse (Greek, "revelation"). A biblical genre that envisions a violent end of the world, with punishment for evildoers and blissful rewards for God's faithful. See Isaiah 24–27, Daniel 7–12, and Revelation.

Apocrypha (Greek, "hidden things"). Writings, such as the Book of Judith, the Book of Tobit, or the Book of Ecclesiasticus, accepted in the Roman Catholic and Orthodox CANON but not in the Protestant CANON (because they are not in the TANAKH). Also called Deutero-Canonical Books.

apophatic theology. "Negative" discourse about God, stressing what God is not (e.g., immaterial, immutable, ineffable).

apostles. Jesus' disciples, including THE TWELVE.

Apostles' Creed, the. One of the oldest summaries of Christian faith, with links to the early Church. In its first known version, from around the middle of the second century, it reads: "I believe in God the Father Almighty. And in Jesus Christ his only begotten Son our Lord, who was born of the Holy Ghost and the Virgin Mary; crucified under Pontius Pilate, and buried; the third day he arose from the dead. He ascended into heaven, and sits at the right hand of the Father, whence he shall come to judge the living and the dead; and in the HOLY SPIRIT; the holy Church; the forgiveness of sins; the RESURRECTION of the body; life everlasting."

Apostolic Era, the. The period from roughly 30 to 100 C.E., comprising the careers of THE TWELVE.

Arianism. The Christian HERESY, from the teaching of Arius (256?–336), that Jesus was not equal to God.

Arminianism. The teaching of the Dutch REFORMED theologian Jacobus Arminius (1560–1609), denying CALVINIST PREDESTINATION and stressing the freedom of the will to respond to God's GRACE.

asceticism (Greek *askesis*, "training"). A variety of religious practices by Christians (among others)—including fasting, sexual abstinence, sensory deprivation, and self-inflicted pain—intended to overcome physical desires and lead individuals to increased spirituality.

Ash Wednesday. The first day of LENT, on which Catholics and other Christians are marked on the forehead with ashes as a reminder of mortality (see Genesis 3:19) and a sign of repentance.

Assumption, the. The Roman Catholic belief that after her death the Virgin Mary was taken up bodily into heaven.

baptism. The ritual of initiation into Christianity, with a symbolic death to one's old self (immersion in water) and rising to a new life in Christ.

Baptists. Members of a varied group of Protestant Churches in the English-speaking countries, rejecting infant BAPTISM and holding to a REFORMED theology that stresses personal salvation and the unassisted access of each individual Christian to God.

Beatitude (Latin, "blessedness"). A formula beginning "Blessed is" or "Blessed are," found in Matthew 5:3–11 and in many parts of the Hebrew Bible (Psalms, Proverbs, Deuteronomy, etc.).

Benedictines. Members of a religious order based on the model of the monastery founded in 529 at Monte Cassino, Italy, by Saint Benedict of Nursia (ca. 480–543) and governed by his Rule. Benedictine monks follow a highly structured daily order and, unlike the MENDICANT orders, take a vow of stability, to remain in the same community. The Rule of Benedict spells out these practices in considerable detail.

binding of Isaac, the (Hebrew *aqedah*). The account in Genesis 22 of how God told Abraham to offer his son Isaac as a sacrifice on Mount Moriah, but then relented and bade him offer a ram instead.

Book of Common Prayer, the. The abbreviated title for a series of prayer books, originally written and edited by Thomas Cranmer (1489–1556) for the Church of England and frequently revised since then. This literary masterpiece is the source of many familiar English sayings, such as "With this ring I thee wed."

Byzantine Empire, the. The Eastern Roman Empire, from 330, when Constantine established his capital in Constantinople, until the Turkish conquest in 1453.

Calvinism. The teaching of the Protestant Reformer John Calvin (1509–1564; see THE REFORMATION), stressing intrinsic human depravity, the omnipotence of divine GRACE, and PREDESTINATION to heaven and hell.

canon. In organized religion, any authoritative rule. With reference to scripture, the collection of writings deemed authoritative—that is, sacred—by a religious body. For example, THE NEW TESTAMENT is part of the Christian canon but not of the Jewish canon.

canonical hours. In Christian communities of the Western Church, such as monasteries, seven mandatory periods of daily prayer (matins/lauds, prime, terce, sext, nones, vespers, and compline) with Scripture readings and hymns.

Carmelites. Monks, nuns, and friars of the order of Our Lady of Mount Carmel (in northwest Israel). Founded in the twelfth century, the group moved to Cyprus and Sicily in 1238 and thence to western Europe.

catechism (from Greek *katekhizein*, "to teach by word of mouth"). A booklet of Christian religious instruction in question-and-answer form.

catechumen. A person being instructed in Christianity, especially during the early centuries of the Church.

Catharists (from Greek *katharos*, "pure"). Members of Christian sects, especially of the late MIDDLE AGES, who had a dualistic view of the world, as in MANICHAEISM; they rejected the Catholic Church and the priesthood.

Catholic Epistles, the. Seven NEW TESTAMENT Letters—the Letter of James, the two Letters of Peter, the three Letters of John, and the Letter of Jude—called "Catholic" (from the Greek word for "universal") because they seem to be addressed to Christians in general and to be discourses or sermons rather than personal communications.

Catholic worship. The Church distinguishes three levels: 1) *dulia* (veneration), given to saints and angels; 2) *hyperdulia* (extreme veneration), given to the Virgin Mary; and 3) *latria* (adoration), given to God alone.

charisma (Greek, "grace or favor"). Any of a number of divinely bestowed gifts or abilities. A *charismatic* was originally the "gifted" recipient of such divine favor; compare CHARISMATICS. An example of charisma is GLOSSOLALIA, as poured out on the APOSTLES on PENTECOST.

charismatics. In contemporary usage, members of various Christian denominations that focus on individual religious experience, receiving THE HOLY SPIRIT, faith healing, and GLOSSOLALIA.

Chinese Rites controversy, the. A conflict within the Roman Catholic Church, from about 1630 to 1715, over whether emperor worship, reverence for ancestors, and other aspects of traditional Chinese religion were compatible with Christianity. Jesuit missionaries claimed they were, but Pope Clement XI (pope 1700–21) ruled they were not.

Christ. Anglicization of the Greek *khristós*, "anointed one." As spoken of Jesus, the Greek word was originally a title rather than a name: "Jesus the Anointed One." This title itself was, in turn, a translation from the Hebrew MESSIAH.

Christendom. The Christian world as a political and cultural, rather than a spiritual, entity.

Christian humanism. The attempt—as in the writings of Petrarch (died 1374), Pico della Mirandola (died 1494), or Erasmus (died 1536)—to synthesize Christianity with the best of classical Greek and Latin culture.

Christology. The field of Christian theology concerned with articulating the nature and person of Jesus.

Cistercians. Members of a reformed monastic order started at Cîteaux, France, in the early 1100s. The most famous Cistercian was the theologian and poet Saint Bernard of Clairvaux (1090–1153).

clerical celibacy. The obligation of Catholic priests to remain unmarried. Though an early ascetic ideal, celibacy was not officially required until the First Lateran Council (1123).

Confessing Church, the (German *die Bekennende Kirche*). A movement within the German LUTHERAN and REFORMED Churches, founded in 1933, to counter the Nazi-approved German Christian Church.

Congregational Church, the. A group of independent Protestant Churches descended from the Puritan REFORMATION in England.

Conversos. Spanish and Portuguese Jews who converted to Catholicism, usually under pressure.

Council of Trent, the. An important Catholic Council (1545–63), which spelled out Catholic doctrine, condemned Protestantism, and reformed, clarified, and enforced Church discipline.

Counter-Reformation. The effort by the Catholic Church in the sixteenth century to resist and respond to the Protestant REFORMATION. See THE COUNCIL OF TRENT.

covenant. A pact or treaty; a crucial Jewish and Christian metaphor for the relationship between God and the community of believers (Hebrew *B'rit*, Greek *Diatheke*, Latin *Testamentum*).

crucifixion. A form of execution by slow torture, widely used in the Roman Empire against defeated enemies, rebellious slaves, and other alleged criminals. The victim was tied to a cross-shaped structure of wood, then his hands and feet were nailed to the wood so as to cause excruciating pain while he slowly died of dehydration and suffocation, a process that could take hours or even days. "The" Crucifixion is the execution of Jesus Christ by this means.

Crusades. A series of military invasions, usually divided into nine separate campaigns from 1085 to 1272, of the Holy Land and adjacent regions by Western Christian armies. Crusades were also launched at different times against the ALBIGENSIANS, the Tatars, the Muslim rulers of Spain, and others.

deacon. A church minister inferior to a priest.

Decalogue, the (Greek, "ten words"). The Ten Commandments, cited in two forms (Exodus 20:2–17 and Deuteronomy 5:6–21) and often taken to be the core of biblical law.

Deism. A "philosophical religion," popular in the eighteenth century, that accepts God as creator but otherwise ignores the supernatural, miracles, and Christian doctrines, such as redemption through Jesus' death on the cross.

desert fathers. The (mostly male) monks and hermits, at first inspired by Saint Anthony (250?–350?), who left the cities of Egypt for the desert in the northwestern Nile delta.

Deutero-Canonical Books. See APOCRYPHA.

Devotio Moderna (Latin, "new devotion"). A popular late-MEDIEVAL religious movement calling for personal piety, associated with the Dutch preacher Gerard Groote (1340–1384) and influential among Catholics and Protestants. Its best-known monument is Thomas à Kempis's *The Imitation of Christ* (1412 27).

dialectical theology. See NEO-ORTHODOXY.

Diaspora. Dispersal of the Jews outside Judah, beginning with the fall of Jerusalem in 586 B.C.E.

Diet of Worms. General assembly of the Holy Roman Empire in 1521, which ended by condemning the Protestant Reformer Martin Luther (1483–1546; see THE REFORMATION) and calling for his capture and punishment as a heretic (see HERESY).

Discalced (Barefoot) Carmelites. Members of a religious order founded in 1593 on the basis of reforms carried out by Saint Teresa of Ávila (1515–1582) and Saint John of the Cross (1542–1591). The men are active and contemplative, whereas the women are cloistered contemplatives.

Dominicans. Also known as the Order of Preachers (O.P.); a religious order founded by Saint Dominic de Guzman (1170?–1221), dedicated to preaching, teaching, and the fight against HERESY.

Easter. The Christian feast of the RESURRECTION of Jesus, celebrated in the Western Church on the first Sunday after the first full moon after March 21.

Eastern Orthodox Church, the. The body of Catholic Christians, perhaps 300 million in number, from many cultures, that has been formally separated from Rome since the GREAT SCHISM of 1054. This Church's members can be found in a great many countries, including Russia, Ukraine, Ethiopia, Egypt, Greece, Serbia, the United States, and Canada.

ecumenism. A series of efforts, mostly since the end of World War II, to promote dialogue, understanding, and reconciliation among the various Christian Churches and their members.

Episcopalian (from Latin *episcopus*, "bishop"). Referring to the Episcopal Church, the American Church in communion with the Church of England.

Erastianism. Belief of the right of the state to control ecclesiastical affairs, named (incorrectly) after the Swiss theologian Thomas Erastus (1524–1583).

eschatology. Branch of theology dealing with the end of the world, final judgment, and the afterlife.

Eucharist, the (Greek, "thanksgiving"). A SACRAMENTAL celebration and memorial service centered around Jesus' blessing and distribution of bread and wine. Also called the Mass, Holy Communion, and the Lord's Supper.

evangelical counsels. In Catholic theology, the vows of poverty, chastity, and obedience, seen as not required for salvation, but "counseled" by Jesus for those who wish to lead a "perfect" life (see Matthew 19:31).

Evangelicals. An umbrella term, derived from the Greek word for "gospel," for many contemporary Protestants, especially but not exclusively American Protestants (perhaps a quarter of the total U.S. population), who consciously strive to spread the "Good News" (Greek *eu-angelion*) of Christianity and are known for their often theologically, culturally, and politically conservative views. Evangelicals believe in biblical inerrancy and the need for personal regeneration.

evangelism. The promotion, winning, or revival of personal commitment to Jesus Christ.

excommunication. An ecclesiastical decree banning a person or persons from taking part in the SACRAMENTS (and receiving a Christian burial).

Fall, the. The Christian doctrine that the ORIGINAL SIN (Genesis 3) created a curse, inherited by all humans, that can be lifted only by Jesus' sacrificial death and RESURRECTION.

fathers of the Church. Major theologians writing in Greek and Latin from the late first century until the early MIDDLE AGES.

fideism. Pure faith independent of reason; reason is seen as incapable of reaching religious truth.

First Great Awakening, the. See GREAT AWAKENING.

Franciscans. Members of various religious orders, founded or inspired by Saint Francis of Assisi (1182?–1226), that stress preaching, missionary work, and a life of poverty.

friar (Latin *frater*, "brother"). A member of a Catholic MENDICANT order.

Fundamentalism. A conservative American theological movement that cites biblical inerrancy, the virgin birth of Jesus, the SUBSTITUTIONARY ATONEMENT, and the bodily RESURRECTION and physical return of Christ as nonnegotiable articles of faith.

glossolalia. The power to "speak in tongues," a gift to believers from THE HOLY SPIRIT (see Acts 2:4–11 and 1 Corinthians 14:5–19). In the early Church, the tongues in question were apparently some form of inspired ecstatic speech rather than foreign languages.

Gnosticism. Pagan, Jewish, and Christian school of thought that sees matter as evil and looks to advanced knowledge (Greek *gnosis*) of God for salvation.

Golden Rule, the. Widely acknowledged ethical principle that one should treat others as one wishes to be treated by them (or, negatively, one should not do to others what one would not want done to oneself); expressed in Leviticus 19:18 and Matthew 7:12.

Good Friday. The Friday on which Jesus was put to death, called "good" because his death was redemptive. Good Friday is followed by HOLY SATURDAY and EASTER.

Good Shepherd, the. A highly popular image of Jesus found in John 10:11–18 and derived from Psalms 23 and Ezekiel 34:11–16.

Gospel (from Old English *god-spel*, "good news," translating Greek *eu-angelion* and Latin *evangelium*). A narrative of the life and teachings of Jesus aimed at convincing readers that he is the MESSIAH. See SYNOPTIC GOSPELS.

grace. The free, unearned gift of God's favor and power.

Great Awakening. 1) The First: a wave of religious revivals in England and the American colonies around the mid-1700s. 2) The Second: a wave of religious revivals in the United States that peaked around 1800–30 before gradually fading; marked by camp meetings and mass conversions.

Great Schism. The fundamental split, dating from 1054, between the Roman Catholic Church and the Eastern Orthodox Church. The issues behind the break included the pope's assertion of supreme jurisdiction over all Christians, the dispute over whether THE HOLY SPIRIT "proceeds" from both the Father and the Son or only the Father, and many other longstanding cultural and theological differences.

Greek Orthodox Church, the. A body of Eastern Orthodox Churches originally located in the Byzantine Empire, still using Koine Greek as their language of worship, and now found in Greece and throughout the Hellenic Diaspora (Europe, America, Australia, etc.)

heresy (Greek, "faction"). A denial or rejection of traditional Christian dogma.

Hesychasm. The practice of inner prayer, especially THE JESUS PRAYER in the Eastern Orthodox Church. The term comes from the Greek *hesychia* ("stillness," "quietude") and refers to a "passive" spirituality with the aim of detaching the believer from the senses for an absorption in God.

heterodoxy. Any teaching that contradicts officially accepted Christian dogma.

higher criticism. Scholarly analysis and historical criticism of biblical texts, beginning in the seventeenth century.

historical Jesus, the. Jesus Christ as a person in history, sometimes contrasted with the "Christ of faith." Since the eighteenth century, attempts have been made to present the historical Jesus, stripped of supernatural or mythic features.

Holocaust, the (Greek, "whole burnt offering"). Metaphoric term, taken from Leviticus 1, for the Nazis' attempted genocide of the Jews during World War II. Some critics, questioning the appropriateness of using religious language for unspeakable crimes by a secular state, prefer the term *Shoah* (Hebrew, "calamity").

Holy Communion. See EUCHARIST, THE.

Holy Orders. In the Catholic Church, a SACRAMENT consisting of minor orders (originally porter, lector, exorcist, and acolyte) and major orders (subdeacon, deacon, and priest).

Holy Roman emperor. The title of the papally appointed (from 962 to 1806) Germanic ruler of a fluctuating group of states in central Europe. Some historians apply the title to Charlemagne (emperor 800–14) and his heirs.

Holy Saturday. The day before EASTER.

Holy Spirit, the. The divine Third Person of the TRINITY.

homoousious (Greek, "of the same substance"). An adjective used to declare Christ's equality with God, as defined by the Council of Nicaea in 325.

Huguenots. Sixteenth- and seventeenth-century French Protestants, many of whom fled France on account of Catholic persecutions.

Hutterites. ANABAPTIST sect named after Jacob Hutter (ca. 1500–1536). Originating in the South Tyrol (now part of Italy), Hutterites fled persecution to North America.

iconoclasm. Attacks—theological, physical, or both—on sacred images, a recurrent movement in Christianity and Islam. Among the most notable examples was the iconoclasm in the Byzantine Church (730–87 and 814–42).

Ignatian indifference. A principle of the spirituality of Saint Ignatius Loyola (1491–1556), according to which a Christian should not become attached to any created thing, but should use all things to promote the greater glory of God.

Immaculate Conception. Catholic dogma, promulgated by Pope Pius IX (pope 1846–78) in 1854, that the Virgin Mary was conceived without ORIGINAL SIN (see THE FALL).

inculturation. An approach to spreading the Gospel, increasingly favored by the Catholic Church since the time of Pope Pius XII (pope 1939–58), that involves positive adaptations to non-Christian cultural and religious practices.

indulgence. According to Catholic doctrine, partial or complete remission of temporal punishment (suffering in this world or in PURGATORY) due for sins that have been SACRAMENTALLY forgiven. Indulgences are obtained by reciting prayers or performing various religious activities.

Inquisition, the. A system of Roman Catholic tribunals, established in the late twelfth century and lasting until the nineteeth, to combat HERESY in various parts of Europe, India, and Latin America. Victims of the Inquisition often included Jews.

Jansenism. CALVINISTIC French Catholic movement, based on the work of the Dutch theologian Cornelius Jansen (1585–1638), with a pessimistic view of inborn human wickedness.

Jesuits. Members of a religious order founded in 1540 by Saint Ignatius Loyola (1491–1556), suppressed by the Church in 1773 but restored in 1814, and noted for their work in education and missions.

Jesus. The Latin form, imported into English, of the Greek name, *Iēsous*, used in the GOSPELS for the central figure in Christianity. In the ancient Greek translation of the TANAKH, *Iēsous* translates the name *Joshua*.

Jesus Prayer, the. The repeated recitation of the formula "Lord Jesus Christ, the Son of God, have mercy on me, a sinner."

Johannine. Referring to Saint John as the supposed author of the Gospel according to John, the Three Epistles of John, and the Book of Revelation.

Judaizers. Jewish Christians who insisted that Gentile converts were obliged to observe the Mosaic Law. They were attacked by the Apostle Paul in his Letter to the Galatians and elsewhere.

Judges. Charismatic warrior-chieftains, whose adventures are chronicled in the Book of Judges, from the period when Israel was a tribal confederation (ca. 1290–1040 B.C.E.). See CHARISMA.

Kenosis (Greek, "emptying"; see Philippians 2:5–10). Jesus' abandonment of his privileged divine status to take on human form.

King James Version, the. Also called the Authorized Version; an English translation of the Bible ordered in 1604 by King James I of England (reigned 1603–25) and first published in 1611. Composed by six separate committees and drawing freely on earlier translations, such as William Tyndale's (sixteenth century), the KJV is widely considered to be a timeless literary achievement.

kontakion. A Byzantine hymn, most notably one written by the Jewish-born poet and singer Saint Romanos the Melodist (ca. 490–ca. 556).

Lamb of God. A title applied to Jesus by John the Baptist (John 1:29, 36) and in many passages of the Book of Revelation; the phrase suggests that, like the sacrificial lamb whose blood was to be smeared on the doorposts and lintels of Israelite homes in Egypt (Exodus 12:7) to ward off the Angel of death (the Lord), Jesus' bloody self-sacrifice on the cross saves Christians from doom.

Last Judgment. The final act of human history, when God will gather all the humans who have ever lived and consign them individually to heaven or hell.

Last Supper, the. According to THE SYNOPTIC GOSPELS (see Matthew 26:26–29, Mark 14:22–25, and Luke 22:15–20), the PASSOVER SEDER at which Jesus founded and celebrated THE EUCHARIST. In John 13–17, the Last Supper is not a SEDER, and Jesus does not institute THE EUCHARIST at it.

laypeople (from Greek *laos*, "people"). Nonclerical members of a Church.

Lent. The forty-day period (not counting Sundays) of prayer and fasting from ASH WEDNESDAY to HOLY SATURDAY, in preparation for EASTER.

Letter of James, the. One of the "Catholic" Letters in THE NEW TESTAMENT, traditionally attributed to "the brother of the Lord" (Mark 6:3), a prominent figure in Acts but probably not the actual author. The Letter attacks faith without works (2:14–26).

lex orandi lex credendi (Latin, "the law of praying [is] the law of believing"). The doctrine that the formulas used in liturgical prayer reflect and consecrate theological beliefs.

liberation theology. A politically liberal or radical movement, named by the Peruvian writer Gustavo Gutiérrez (born 1928), that began in Latin America in the 1960s. Liberation theology presents Christianity as a call to relieve poverty and oppression through the Christian principles of love, equality, and service to others.

literary prophets. Biblical characters who wrote down and preserved their oracles (as opposed, for example, to the thaumaturgic, or wonder-working, prophets, such as Elijah and Elisha). The most important literary prophets are the major prophets: Isaiah, Jeremiah, and Ezekiel.

liturgy. Public worship of any kind, especially the Catholic MASS and other EUCHARISTIC services.

Lollards. The followers of John Wycliffe (ca. 1320–1394); this early Protestant movement criticized the corruption of the Catholic Church and supported a Scripture-based renewal.

Lord's Supper, the. See EUCHARIST, THE.

Lutherans. Originally, followers of the Protestant Reformer Martin Luther (1483–1546; see THE REFORMATION) and especially of his key teaching of justification by faith alone (see *SOLA FIDE*); subsequently, members of the Lutheran Church.

Manichaeism. Religious teaching based on the thinking of the Persian prophet Manes, or Mani (216?–276?), which saw the world as a battleground between the forces of good (identified with spirit) and those of evil (identified with matter).

Marranos (Spanish, "pigs"). Disparaging term for CONVERSOS.

Mass, the. See EUCHARIST, THE.

medieval. Referring to THE MIDDLE AGES.

mendicant (Latin, "begging"). Refers to Catholic religious orders, such as the DOMINICANS and the FRANCISCANS, whose members depend on charitable giving (as opposed to monks in self-sufficient monasteries), take vows of poverty, and engage in activities such as preaching, teaching, and missionary work.

Mennonites. Members of an ANABAPTIST group named after Menno Simons (1496–1561), a Dutch Reformer (see THE REFORMATION) and ex-Catholic priest; mennonites believe in EVANGELICAL simplicity and pacifism.

messiah (Hebrew *mashiach*, "anointed one"). In the Hebrew Bible, this term refers variously to a king of Israel—classically, to King David—or, later, to someone else chosen by God (e.g., King Cyrus of Persia in Isaiah 45:1–2) or, still later, to a kind of national savior whose arrival ushers in the end of the world. When used with a proper name, such as Jesus Messiah (Jesus CHRIST), the term is capitalized.

Methodists. Originally mocking term for the followers of John Wesley (1703–1791), a Protestant theologian who rejected CALVINIST PREDESTINATION and emphasized personal piety and social activism.

Middle Ages, the. A term coined during the RENAISSANCE (fourteenth and fifteenth centuries) for the centuries lying between classical Greco-Roman antiquity and the Renaissance revival of art, architecture, literature, and philosophy inspired by classical models.

Millerites. Followers of William Miller (1782–1849), American BAPTIST preacher best known for his role in founding the SEVENTH DAY ADVENTIST Church and in predicting that Jesus would return to Earth in 1844.

***minjung* theology.** A South Korean variety of LIBERATION THEOLOGY, originating in the 1970s (*minjung* is Korean for "masses").

miracle plays. See MYSTERY PLAYS.

Mishna (Hebrew, "oral instruction"). Body of the ORAL LAW that dates from around 200 C.E. and provided the foundation of the TALMUD.

monophysitism. The Christian HERESY that Jesus has only one (divine) nature.

modernism. The broad label for liberal theological trends condemned by Pope (now Saint) Pius X (pope 1903–14) in the encyclical *Pascendi Dominici Gregis* (1907). These tendencies included historical criticism of the Bible, secular rationalism, and the view of Church doctrine as perpetually evolving.

Montanism. A somewhat obscure Christian SCHISM characterized by ecstatic prophesying and moral severity. Montanism originated in second-century Asia Minor (present-day western Turkey), spread to North Africa, and lasted into the sixth century. The movement is named for Montanus, its founder, about whom little is known.

morality plays. Late MEDIEVAL Christian allegorical dramas (such as *Everyman*), designed to teach the dangers of sin and the need for repentance, beginning in the thirteenth century and popular until the sixteenth.

Moravian Brethren. A Protestant movement going back to Jan Hus (ca. 1389–1415); in 1772, driven out of Czech-speaking territory, the group took refuge in Saxony, where they built the village Herrnhut on the estate of Nicolas von Zinzendorf (1700–1760).

Moriscos. Spanish and Portuguese Muslims who converted to Christianity to avoid expulsion during the Christian reconquest of the Iberian peninsula; by 1614, after a series of expulsions, few of them remained.

Mormonism. The Church of Jesus Christ of Latter-Day Saints, founded by Joseph Smith in 1830. The Church's sacred scripture is the Book of Mormon, a collection of writings purportedly by American prophets who lived from around 2000 B.C.E. to 400 C.E.

mystery plays. Also called miracle plays; MEDIEVAL vernacular religious dramas, put on from the tenth century until THE REFORMATION, representing popular versions of episodes from the Bible and the lives of the saints.

mysticism. Direct personal consciousness of God's presence, usually in ways that defy description except metaphorically.

natural theology. The body of statements that can be made about God, not on the basis of revelation (such as in Scripture) but on the basis of unaided reason and observation. See Acts 17:22–31 and Romans 18–20.

Neo-Orthodoxy. Also known as dialectical theology; chiefly led by Karl Barth (1886–1968), a turning away from nineteenth-century liberal Protestant theology—which, in the wake of World War I, struck some observers as shallowly optimistic and complacent—and toward a classic sense of the transcendent otherness of God.

Nestorianism. The HERESY, of Nestorius (died 451), that Jesus was two distinct persons, divine and human, with two distinct natures, and that Mary was the mother of the human Jesus only.

New Testament, the. The Christian Scriptures, in twenty-seven books, consisting of four GOSPELS, the ACTS OF THE APOSTLES, the Letters of Paul and others, and the Book of Revelation.

Nicene Creed, the. The official formula of the Christian faith adopted by the Council of Nicaea in 325, emphasizing the divinity of Christ.

ninety-five theses, the. A series of theological propositions by the Protestant Reformer Martin Luther (1483–1546; see THE REFORMATION) against the sale of indulgences to finance the rebuilding of Saint Peter's Basilica, in Rome.

nun. A woman who belongs to a Catholic (or Eastern Orthodox, Anglican, or Lutheran) religious order or congregation and has taken vows of poverty, chastity, and obedience.

Old Testament, the. The Christian term for the inherited Jewish Scriptures that would become the Hebrew Bible, or TANAKH.

oral law, the. In Rabbinic Judaism, the body of sacred legislations given by Moses along with the written law of the TORAH (Deuteronomy 31:19) and later codified in the TALMUD.

original sin. The Christian theological notion that the disobedience of Adam and Eve (see Genesis 3) was a catastrophic event that resulted in the passing down through all human generations of a state of alienation from God, until the atonement of Jesus' sacrificial death.

pantheon, the (Greek, "all the gods") The Greek or Roman gods collectively.

Pantocrator (Greek, "all-powerful"). A depiction of Christ in the Greek Orthodox Church as a majestic, sometimes severe-looking Lord.

parable. A sometimes puzzling story or comparison presented by Jesus in the GOSPELS, often with a moral lesson that poses a challenge to the audience.

Parousia (Greek, "presence"). THE SECOND COMING of Jesus.

Passion, the. The trial, torture, and execution of Jesus, seen by Christians as the key to redemption.

Passover (Hebrew *pesach*). Jewish feast memorializing God's liberation of Israel from bondage in Egypt. Christians understand EASTER as their "paschal" (from *pesach*) feast; but in this feast, the blood of the Paschal Lamb (Christ) is understood to liberate not from slavery to an earthly power such as Egypt (or Rome) but from sin and death.

Pastoral Letters. The two Letters to Timothy and the Letter to Titus, attributed to Paul but now believed to be by later authors because their style (bland rather than bold and dramatic) and content (problems of Church administration rather than religious doctrine and controversies) differ markedly from Paul's.

patriarchs, the. Leading figures in the Book of Genesis, from Adam to Joseph.

patristic. Relating to the fathers of the Church and their writings.

Pelagianism. HERESY associated with the British monk Pelagius (354–430?), which denies that human nature was mortally wounded by ORIGINAL SIN and affirms that believers can achieve RIGHTEOUSNESS through their own free choices.

Pentecost (from the Greek for "fiftieth day"). Christian festival celebrating the descent of THE HOLY SPIRIT on Jesus' disciples (see Acts 2), seven weeks after EASTER. Related to the Jewish feast of SHAVUOT, celebrated seven weeks after PASSOVER.

Pentecostalism. CHARISMATIC twentieth-century Protestant movement, often traced back to the Azusa Street revival in Los Angeles (1906), that arose out of a post-BAPTISMAL experience of THE HOLY SPIRIT akin to that of the first PENTECOST; now a worldwide phenomenon.

Pharisees (Hebrew, "Separatists"). A major Jewish sect in the time of Jesus, often seen as the ancestors of later rabbinical Judaism. They believed in THE ORAL LAW and the afterlife, unlike the more aristocratic SADDUCEES. The hostile portrayal of the Pharisees in THE NEW TESTAMENT may reflect Christian bias.

Pietism. LUTHERAN movement, founded by Philipp Jacob Spener (1635–1705), that emphasized personal devotion, the necessity of being "born again," group Bible study, and a more democratic Church structure.

predestination. The belief that God has determined in advance the eternal salvation or damnation of human beings.

Presbyterians (from Greek *presbyteros*, "elder"). Members of a group of Protestant Churches, based on Scottish CALVINISM, that typically have no bishops.

prophet (Greek, "speaker," "spokesperson"). A messenger, claiming to be sent by God, who reports and interprets the divine will.

pseudepigrapha (Greek, "with false titles"). Writings incorrectly titled or attributed; for example, the First Letter of Peter shows a mastery of Greek prose style that belies the notion that its author was a onetime fisherman from Galilee.

purgatory. According to Roman Catholicism, the state after death where persons who have died in the state of GRACE but with unexpiated sins must suffer before being admitted to heaven.

Q (from German *Quelle*, "source"). A supposed collection of Jesus' sayings used by the authors of the GOSPELS of Matthew and Luke but not Mark.

Quakers. Members of the Society of Friends, founded in 1647–48 by George Fox (1624–1691), a radical Christian organization that has no official creed, ministers, or SACRAMENTS and stresses complete equality among its members.

Reformation, the. Various movements in sixteenth-century Europe, opposing doctrinal, structural, and moral abuses in the Catholic Church, that coalesced into the Protestant Churches. In its broadest sense, the term can include movements, such as the COUNTER-REFORMATION, that originated within Catholicism.

Reformed. While the term REFORMATION, as used in Christian history, is broad enough to comprise all of the sixteenth-century Protestant movements and resultant Churches, the adjective *Reformed* usually refers only to the many denominations that derive from CALVINISM, including notably METHODISTS and BAPTISTS.

religious (noun). A Catholic man or woman who has taken a vow of poverty, chastity, and obedience and lives in a religious community under a specific Rule.

Renaissance. The revival of classic Greek and Roman literature, art, and thought in Europe, beginning in Italy, during the fourteenth and fifteenth centuries.

resurrection. Lowercase: The Christian belief that at the LAST JUDGMENT the souls of the dead will be joined forever to their ("glorified," or transformed) bodies, as opposed to having immortal but purely "spiritual" souls. Capitalized: Christianity's foundational belief that on the Sunday following the Friday of his execution by CRUCIFIXION, Jesus was raised back to life by divine intervention.

Revised Standard Version, the. Corrected and modernized American edition (1946–52) of THE KING JAMES VERSION.

righteousness. In the theology of Saint Paul, the state of persons found just, or acceptable, in God's eyes; a pure gift, obtainable only through faith and not from an individual's virtuous endeavors.

Sabbath, the. A day of rest and worship; for Jews, Saturday; for most Christians, Sunday. But see SEVENTH DAY ADVENTISTS.

sacraments. In Catholic theology, ritual actions and signs of GRACE that effect what they symbolize: BAPTISM, confirmation, penance, THE EUCHARIST, final anointing, HOLY ORDERS, and matrimony. Many Protestant Churches accept only BAPTISM and THE EUCHARIST as SACRAMENTS.

Sadducees. Jewish priestly sect in the time of Jesus that rejected THE ORAL LAW and did not believe in life after death. Compare PHARISEES.

Saint Bartholomew's Day massacre, the. A wave of planned assassinations and mob violence directed at French Protestants in Paris and the provinces, beginning on August 23, 1572, and resulting in thousands of deaths (no precise figure is available).

Satan (Hebrew, "accuser"). In Christianity, the evil spirit who, disguised as a serpent, tricked Eve into eating the fruit of the tree of knowledge of good and evil (Genesis 3:1–7) and who continues to tempt human beings, including Jesus (see Matthew 4:1–11), to sin.

schism (Greek, "split"). The breaking apart of one Christian Church or community from another over disciplinary or theological issues; for example, of the ANGLICAN CHURCH from the Roman Catholic Church. Members of a church in schism are referred to, always pejoratively, as *schismatics*.

Second Coming, the. At the end of the world, when all the dead will rise, the reappearance of Jesus, who will judge all who have ever lived, sending the good to their eternal reward and the evil to their eternal punishment.

Second Great Awakening, the. See GREAT AWAKENING.

secular arm. Civil authority, especially as used in carrying out sentences passed by an established Church.

seder (Hebrew, "order"). The Jewish feast, celebrated at home, of the first night (or, in the Diaspora, first two nights) of PASSOVER.

seven deadly sins, the. A Catholic list of "mortal" (because they lead to eternal damnation) moral behaviors, often cited as anger, greed, sloth, pride, lust, envy, and gluttony.

Seventh Day Adventists. An ADVENTIST group that celebrates the Christian SABBATH on Saturday.

Shakers. The United Society of Believers in Christ's Second Appearing; followers of Ann Lee (1736–1784), an Englishwoman who emigrated to America in 1774. Shakers practiced gender equality, celibacy, and an intense common life.

Shavuot (Hebrew, "weeks"). Jewish festival celebrating the giving of the Law to Moses. In Christianity, this feast, reinterpreted, lives on as PENTECOST.

Social Gospel. An early-twentieth-century liberal Protestant movement, often associated with the BAPTIST minister and theologian Walter Rauschenbusch (1861–1918) and particularly concerned with social justice and the condition of the poor; it faded in the 1920s, but was revived by the civil rights movement.

Sola Fide (Latin, "by faith alone"). The Protestant theological position that no human actions, however laudable, can "earn" salvation because of the corruption of human nature.

Sola Scriptura (Latin, "by Scripture alone"). The characteristic Protestant belief that the Bible supplies all the knowledge needed for salvation.

Son of Man. Jesus' title for himself in THE NEW TESTAMENT, alluding to the Book of Daniel 7:13–14 and used in an extravagantly Messianic sense (see MESSIAH).

Song of Songs, the. Also known as the Song of Solomon; a biblical book of erotic poetry, attributed to King Solomon (tenth century B.C.E.), about a girl (the Shulamite) and her lover. God is never mentioned, but the book has often been interpreted allegorically to refer to the love between God and Israel or God and the individual soul.

Spiritual Exercises. Month-long program of meditation and prayers designed by Saint Ignatius of Loyola (1491–1556) to prompt a commitment to Jesus (and possibly to life as a Catholic RELIGIOUS).

stigmata (Greek, "tattoo marks"). Jesus' wounds from the Crucifixion—in his hands, feet, and side— when transferred, by a miracle or autosuggestion, to the body of a believer, such as Saint Francis of Assisi (1181 or 1182–1226).

substitutionary atonement. One of various theological schemes for explaining Jesus' mission; for example, according to Saint Anselm (1033–1109), the ORIGINAL SIN was at once infinite (because committed against an infinite God) and able to be expiated only by a human being (because committed by humans). Hence only Jesus, the God-man, was capable of expiating the sins of the human race (by his death) and thus saving it from divine punishment.

Synoptic Gospels, the. The three NEW TESTAMENT GOSPELS (Matthew, Mark, and Luke) whose texts resemble each other and often overlap. The fourth GOSPEL, John, differs the most from the other three and is thus not called Synoptic.

Synoptic Problem, the. Determining the relationships between THE SYNOPTIC GOS-PELS. Scholars now generally agree that Mark is the oldest of the GOSPELS and that Matthew and Luke borrow from Mark and from Q.

Syriac. The group of Aramaic dialects spoken in Syria, now used only as a liturgical language.

Talmud (Hebrew, teaching). Two large collections of rabbinical teachings (the Jerusalem or Palestinian Talmud and the larger and more important Babylonian Talmud), dating from ca. 200–500 C.E.

Tanakh. Acronym for the Hebrew Bible: T (Torah) = N (Nevi'im, "Prophets") + K (Ketuvim, "Writings").

teleological suspension of the ethical. According to the Danish philosopher Søren Kierkegaard (1813–1855), the process by which Abraham had to "transcend" the realm of ethics (e.g., "Thou shalt not kill") to reach the higher realm of faith (teleological = referring to an ultimate goal).

Ten Commandments, the. See DECALOGUE, THE.

theology. Discourse about God; the intellectual endeavor to explain and codify religious beliefs.

Theotokos (Greek, "God-bearer"). The doctrine, proclaimed by the Council of Ephesus in 431, that Mary was the mother of God and not just of the human Jesus.

Third Order. An association of (usually) Catholic LAYPEOPLE who live in accordance with the spirit of a religious order such as the FRANCISCANS, DOMINICANS, or CARMELITES without taking any of the formal vows of the "first" order (male RELIGIOUS) or "second" order (consecrated nuns).

Torah (Hebrew, "instruction"). The first five Books of the Hebrew Bible, usually referred to in Christian discourse as the Pentateuch.

Transfiguration. A scene in the GOSPELS (Matthew 17:1–9, Mark 9:2–8, and Luke 9:18–36) where Jesus appears—to the APOSTLES Peter, James, and John—on a high mountain (traditionally identified as Mount Tabor) and is accompanied by Moses (symbolizing the Law) and Elijah (symbolizing the prophets).

transubstantiation. The Roman Catholic belief that in the SACRAMENT of THE EUCHARIST the inner essence ("substance") of the bread and wine being offered is transformed into Jesus' body and blood while all their physical components ("accidents") remain the same.

Trinity, the. The Christian mystery that God is "one in three persons": a single divine nature that encompasses the Father, the Son (Christ), and THE HOLY SPIRIT. This doctrine does not appear as such in THE NEW TESTAMENT (where, among other things, it is not always clear that THE HOLY SPIRIT is to be understood as a separate person) and was not defined until around the year 400.

Twelve, the. Jesus' first Apostles, cited in Mark 3:16–19 as (Simon) Peter, James and John (the sons of Zebedee), Andrew, Philip, Bartholomew, Matthew, Thomas, James the son of Alpheus, Thaddeus, Simon the Canaanite, and Judas Iscariot (who was replaced after his death by Matthias).

Unitarianism. An unorthodox theological movement that denies THE TRINITY, the divinity of Jesus, and familiar Christian teachings such as THE FALL and redemption. After beginning in Poland and Transylvania in the sixteenth century, Unitarianism spread to England and America in the eighteenth century.

Vatican, the. A section of Rome, the remnant of the Papal States (a region of central Italy governed by the popes from 754 until 1870), established by the Lateran Treaty of 1929.

Vulgate, the (Latin, "[popular] edition"). The translation of the Hebrew, Aramaic, and Greek Scriptures into Latin by Saint Jerome (340?–420?). Completed in 405, the Vulgate was the standard Bible text for western European Christians until THE REFORMATION.

Wager, Pascal's (French, *le pari*). A thought experiment found in the *Pensées* by Blaise Pascal (1623–1662), proposing that since there is at least a small possibility that Christianity is true, it makes sense to "bet" on it. That way, if one lives as a good Christian, one loses nothing if there is no life after death but gains eternal happiness if there is.

Waldensians. Members of a Christian reform movement named after its French leader, Peter Waldo (twelfth century). Persecution in the seventeenth century led to their flight to Italy and elsewhere.

Western Schism, the. The period, from 1378 to 1417, when two men simultaneously claimed to be the pope; this conflict was resolved by the Council of Constance (1414–18).

World Council of Churches, the. An ecumenical organization, founded in 1948, of 349 Protestant Churches seeking to promote Christian unity.

Selected Bibliography

Overviews

The most recent attempt to provide a comprehensive history of Christianity is Diarmaid MacCulloch's *Christianity: The First Three Thousand Years* (New York: Penguin, 2009). Less thorough but highly readable and lavishly illustrated is Owen Chadwick's magisterial *A History of Christianity* (New York: Saint Martin's, 1995). A concise popular history and an accessible starting point is Robert Bruce Mullin's *A Short World History of Christianity* (Louisville, Ky.: Westminster John Knox Press, 2008). Douglas Jacobsen's *The World's Christians* (Oxford, Eng.: Blackwell, 2011) is a contemporary profile of Christians around the world. Martin Marty's *The Christian World: A Global History* (New York: Modern Library, 2007) is a brief overview—especially interesting in the current demographic context—that pays particular attention to African and Asian Christianity, past and present. A gracefully written invitation to the subject is Rowland Williams's *Why Study the Past?: The Quest for the Historical Church* (Grand Rapids, Mich.: William B. Eerdmans, 2005).

The Oxford Dictionary of the Christian Church, 3rd Ed., edited by F. L. Cross and E. A. Livingstone (New York: Oxford University Press, 2005), provides indispensable capsule summaries of Christian personages, practices, and movements. *The Cambridge Dictionary of Christianity*, edited by Daniel Patte (New York: Cambridge University Press, 2010), by some eight hundred scholars, stresses the inner pluralism of Christianity, past and present, around the world. Jaroslav Pelikan's five-volume *The Christian Tradition: A History of the Development of Doctrine* (Chicago: University of Chicago Press, 1971–89) is a compendious survey of Christian beliefs over the centuries. *The Oxford Companion to Christian Thought*, edited by Adrian Hastings et al. (New York: Oxford University Press, 2000), lacks the narrative quality of Pelikan's work, but is valuable for summarizing the main elements of Christian belief. *The Oxford History of Christian Worship*, edited by Geoffrey Wainwright and Karen Westerfield-Tucker (New York: Oxford University Press, 2005), is a comprehensive resource for the Christian liturgy. Concise studies of individual mystics and spiritual writers can be found in the ongoing Paulist Press series Classics of Western Spirituality.

The following books are useful surveys of the four major historical branches of Christianity. On Byzantine (Greek Orthodox) Catholicism and its descendants: Timothy Ware's *The Orthodox Church* (New York: Penguin, 1997), John Anthony McGuckin's *The Orthodox Church* (Oxford, Eng.: Blackwell, 2008), and Tibor Szamuely's *The Russian Tradition* (New York: McGraw-Hill, 1974) provide well-grounded overviews. On Alexandrian (monophysite) and Antiochian (Nestorian) Catholicism and their respective African and Asian descendants: *The Blackwell Companion to Eastern Christianity*, edited by Ken Parry (Oxford, Eng.: Oxford University Press, 2007), offers learned, state-of-the-question essays. For Roman Catholicism: Gerald O'Collins and Mario Ferrugia's *Catholicism* (New York: Oxford University Press, 2003) and Lawrence S. Cunningham's *Introduction to Catholicism* (New York: Cambridge University Press, 2005) are basic syntheses. For foundational Protestantism: George Forell's *The Protestant Faith* (Philadelphia: Fortress, 1960) and John Leith's *Introduction to the Reformed Tradition* (Atlanta: John Knox, 1981) are solid introductions to the Lutheran and Calvinist traditions, respectively, while Stephen Neill's *Anglicanism*, 4th Ed. (New York: Oxford University Press, 1977), is equally well established on its title subject. See also D. W. Bebbington's *Baptists through the Centuries: A History of a Global People* (Waco, Tex.: Baylor University Press, 2010), William J. Abraham and James E. Kirby's *The Oxford Handbook of Methodist Studies* (New York: Oxford University Press, 2009), and David Hempton's *Methodism: Empire of the Spirit* (New Haven: Yale University Press, 2005).

In the twentieth century, Christianity experienced explosive growth in Africa and Asia. In *The Church in Africa 1450–1950* (New York: Oxford University Press, 1988), Adrian Hastings surveys the last several centuries of African Christianity. *A World History of Christianity*, edited by Hastings (Grand Rapids, Mich.: William B. Eerdmans, 1999), traces the history of Christianity in every place on Earth where it has had a home. See also Hugh McLeod's edited volume *World Christianities, c. 1914–c. 2000* (New York: Cambridge University Press, 2006) and Philip Jenkins's *The Next Christendom: The Coming of Global Christianity* (New York: Oxford University Press, 2002).

The Apostolic Era (4 B.C.E.–100 C.E.)
Christopher de Hamel's *The Book: A History of the Bible* (New York: Phaidon, 2001) is a lavishly illustrated history of the Bible as a book. The history of the Bible, as a religious classic read overwhelmingly in translation, is largely the history of its translations. Of these, the first and most important was the Septuagint, the pre-Christian Jewish translation of the Hebrew Scriptures into Greek. The Vulgate, the earliest combined translation of the Old Testament and the New from the original Hebrew and Greek, brought the Scriptures into the vernacular (spoken) Latin of the fourth century. The Vulgate remained the Bible of the Western or Latin Church until the vernacular languages of Europe became literary languages in the later Middle Ages and then in the sixteenth century the Protestant Reformation provided a powerful motive for translating the Bible into these still young languages. From the seventeenth century on, the history of Bible translation has assumed a different form around the world in each separate Christian language community.

The English Bible, King James Version (New York: Norton, 2011) presents a critical edition of the 1611 version. This version grounded the central tradition of Bible translation into English, and it deeply marked the English language. The Norton edition includes modern historical scholarship on the ancient cultures in which the Bible came, selections from the history of biblical interpretation, and examples of biblically inspired literature. The work is in two volumes: *The Old Testament*, edited by Herbert Marks, and *The New Testament*, edited by Gerald Hammond and Austin Busch. The King James Version has undergone several revisions since the late nineteenth century. The most recent American revision is the New Revised Standard Version, available as *The New Oxford Annotated Bible*, 3rd Ed., edited by Michael Coogan (Oxford, Eng., and New York: Oxford University Press, 2001), a study Bible with ample running commentary and a full complement of interpretive essays. Both of these editions contain essays on the history of English-language Bible translation down to the present.

Under the sponsorship of the Society of Biblical Literature, the *HarperCollins Bible Commentary*, Rev. Ed., edited by James L. Mays (San Francisco: HarperCollins, 2000), has a succinct commentary on every Book of the Bible. The same society also sponsored the *Harpers' Bible Dictionary*, edited by Paul J. Achtemeier (San Francisco: Harper and Row, 1985). Both the commentary and the dictionary were written by an ecumenical team of scholars. The six-volume *Anchor Bible Dictionary* (New York: Doubleday, 1992), edited by David Noel Freedman, is a similarly ecumenical effort, particularly strong on the Hebrew Bible and its ancient Near Eastern background but invaluable on the New Testament as well. Dated but still helpful, with a gloss on every proper name in the Bible, is John L. McKenzie's 1965 one-volume paperback, *The Dictionary of the Bible* (New York: Touchstone, 1995 reprint).

Raymond Brown's *An Introduction to the New Testament* (Garden City, N.Y.: Doubleday, 1997) is quite reliable and user friendly. Walter Brueggemann's *An Introduction to the Old Testament: The Canon and Christian Imagination* (Louisville, Ky.: Westminster John Knox, 2003) is equally approachable and lively. For the "Other Gospels," two collections are fundamental: the two-volume *New Testament Apocrypha*, edited by Edgar Hennecke (Philadelphia: Westminster, 1965) and *The Gnostic Scriptures,* edited by Bentley Layton (Garden City, N.Y.: Doubleday, 1987 [paperback, 1995]). Elaine Pagels's *The Gnostic Gospels* (New York: Knopf Publishing Group, 1980) has had a wide influence.

The Bible generates an unending flow of book-by-book commentaries and introductions. Beyond the introductions and dictionaries already mentioned, a judicious orientation to schools of biblical interpretation can be found in *The Cambridge Companion to Biblical Interpretation,* edited by John L. Barton (New York: Cambridge University Press, 1998).

Among historical treatments of the first Christian century, E. P. Sanders's *Jesus and Judaism* (Philadelphia: Fortress Press, 1985) places proto-Christianity in its Jewish context. Robin Lane Fox's *Pagans and Christians* (San Francisco: HarperSanFrancisco, 1988) considers early Christianity in its imperial Roman rather than its biblical or Jewish context. Rodney Stark's *The Rise of Christianity: A Sociologist Reconsiders History* (Princeton: Princeton University Press, 1996) attempts, partly from material remains such as cemeteries, to understand why Christianity spread so rapidly.

The Patristic Era (100–600 C.E.)

Paula Fredriksen's *From Jesus to Christ: Origins of New Testament Images of Christ* (New Haven: Yale University Press, 1988) roots the writing of the New Testament in the life of the earliest Christian communities. Though the letters of the Apostle Paul were written before the year 100, the picture of nascent Christianity in Wayne A. Meeks's *The First Urban Christians: The Social World of the Apostle Paul* (New Haven: Yale University Press, 1983) is illuminating for the early Patristic era as well. Robert Wilken's *The Spirit of Early Christian Thought* (New Haven: Yale University Press, 2003) is an excellent survey of patristic thought and culture. Maurice Wiles and Mark Santer compile a representative set of extracts from the early fathers of the Church in *Documents in Early Christian Thought* (New York: Cambridge University Press, 2000). *The Acts of the Christian Martyrs,* edited by Herbert Musurillo (Oxford, Eng.: Clarendon, 1972), is a compilation of all the early accounts of Christian martyrdom. Lawrence Cunning-

ham's *A Brief History of Saints* (Oxford, Eng.: Blackwell, 2005) is a historical account of the rise of the cult of the saints. The three-volume *Creeds and Confessions of the Faith in the Christian Tradition,* edited by Jaroslav Pelikan and Valerie Hotchkiss (New Haven: Yale University Press, 2003), is a comprehensive collection of all Christian creeds. J. N. D. Kelly's *Early Christian Doctrines,* 5th Ed. (New York: Continuum, 2000), is a classic account. Tomas Spidlik's *The Spirituality of the Christian East* (Kalamazoo, Mich.: Cistercian Publications, 1986) traces the development of the theology, the liturgy, and the spiritual practices of the Christian East. *Late Antiquity: A Guide to the Postclassical World,* edited by G. W. Bowersock, Peter Brown, and Oleg Grabar (Cambridge, Mass.: Harvard University Press, 1999), is a series of essays dealing with the interaction of emerging Christianity and the broad pagan culture from which it arose. William Hamless's *Desert Christians: An Introduction to the Literature of Early Monasticism* (New York: Oxford University Press, 2004) investigates the rise and early history of the monastic movement.

No Christian writer of the Patristic Era has been more widely read, down to modern times, than Saint Augustine of Hippo. His *Confessions* is a world classic, available in many translations; R. S. Pine-Coffin's edition, comprising translation and introduction (New York: Penguin, 1961), is still much admired. Peter Brown's *Augustine of Hippo: A Biography,* Rev. Ed. with a New Epilogue (Berkeley: University of California Press, 2000), updates an engrossing evocation of the man and his era.

For general histories of the period, see the first volume of the Oxford History of the Church, Henry Chadwick's *The Church in Ancient Society: From Galilee to Gregory the Great* (New York: Oxford University Press, 2001), as well as two early volumes of the Cambridge History of Christianity: *Origins to Constantine,* edited by Frances Young and Margaret Mitchell (New York: Cambridge University Press, 2005), and *Constantine to c. 600,* edited by Augustine Cassidy and Frederick Norris (New York: Cambridge University Press, 2007). Malcolm Lambert's *Christians and Pagans: The Conversion of Britain from Alban to Bede* (New Haven: Yale University Press, 2010) is a useful survey of the slow rise of Christianity from its beginnings. In *The Triumph of Christianity: How the Jesus Movement Became the World's Largest Religion* (New York: HarperOne, 2011), Rodney Stark offers a provocative sociological reading of the same period. For the slow emergence of Christian Europe, see Judith Herrin's *The Formation of Christendom* (Princeton: Princeton University Press, 1987) and Peter Brown's magisterial *The Rise of Western Christendom*, Rev. Ed. (Oxford, Eng.: Blackwell, 2003) and his later *Through the Eye of a Needle: Wealth, the Fall of Rome, and the Making of Christianity in the West, 350–550 A.D.* (Princeton: Princeton University Press, 2012). For the Greek Orthodox and Eastern Orthodox Churches, see John Binns's *An Introduction to the Christian Orthodox Churches* (New York: Cambridge University Press, 2002).

The Middle Ages and the Renaissance (600–1517)

For these periods, two volumes of the Cambridge History of Christianity are valuable: vol. 3, *Early Medieval Christianities c. 600–1100*, edited by T. F. X. Noble and J. M. H Smith (New York: Cambridge University Press, 2008), and vol. 4, *Christianity in Western Europe, c. 1100–1500*, edited by Miri Rubin and W. Simons (New York: Cambridge University Press, 2009). Eamon Duffy's *Saints and Sinners: A History of the Popes* (New Haven: Yale University Press, 2006) is an excellent and readable history of the papacy, especially good on the medieval period. The northward spread of Christianity is brilliantly recounted in Richard Fletcher's *The Barbarian Conversion: From Paganism to Christianity* (Berkeley: University of California Press, 1998).

The Rule of St. Benedict, edited by Timothy Frye, OSB (Collegeville, Minn: Liturgical Press, 1981), provides Latin and English texts of the Rule, combined with excellent essays on the history of monasticism and particular monastic practices. R. W. Southern's *Saint Anselm: A Portrait in a Landscape* (New York: Cambridge University Press, 1990) provides a full context for the emerging world of the late eleventh century. The eminent French medievalist Andre Vauchez's *The Laity in the Middle Ages* (Notre Dame: University of Notre Dame Press, 1993) provides twenty-one essays that offer

a panorama of medieval life from the lay perspective. Bernard McGinn's *The Presence of God: A History of Western Christian Mysticism*, four volumes to date (New York: Crossroad, 1992–2012), is a thorough account of the rise and development of Christian contemplative practices. Caroline W. Bynum's *Jesus as Mother: Studies in the Spirituality of the High Middle Ages* (Berkeley: University of California Press, 1982) has been pathbreaking, especially in its attention to women's spirituality in the High Middle Ages. The three-volume *Francis of Assisi: Early Documents*, edited by Regis Armstrong et al. (Hyde Park, N.Y.: New City, 2001), compiles all of the saint's writing and everything written about him in the century after his death. The French Dominican M.-D. Chenu was a pioneer in a new approach to Thomas Aquinas; his *Towards Understanding Thomas Aquinas* (Chicago: University of Chicago Press, 1964) is still useful. *The Westminster Handbook to Thomas Aquinas*, edited by Joseph Wawrykow (Louisville, Ky.: Westminster, 2005), is a reliable introduction to Aquinas and his major themes. For a broader picture of medieval Christian thought, see *The Medieval Theologians*, edited by G. R. Evans (Oxford, Eng.: Blackwell, 2000), and Yves Congar's still very useful *A History of Theology* (Garden City, N.Y.: Doubleday, 1968). The intellectual continuity between late-medieval and Reformation Europe is treated in Steven Ozment's *The Age of Reform (1250–1550): An Intellectual and Religious History of Late Medieval and Reformation Europe* (New Haven: Yale University Press, 1980).

Medieval Christianity may perhaps be most easily approached through Gothic art. Georges Duby's *The Age of the Cathedrals: Art and Society, 980–1420* (Chicago: University of Chicago Press, 1983) is about more than architecture. Henry Adams's *Mont St. Michel and Chartres*, originally published in Boston in 1904 with the support of the American Institute of Architects and available in many reprints, is similarly a study of medieval piety and the medieval imagination through two architectural masterpieces. For the first thousand years of its history, Christianity's grandest city was Constantinople, whose irreversible decline began in 1204, when it was sacked by the Franks during the Fourth Crusade. On that turning point, see Michael Angold's *The Fourth Crusade: Event and Context* (New York: Longman, 2003).

For a picture of the once extensive Christian world east of Mesopotamia at and after the rise of Islam, see Philip Jenkins's *The Lost History of Christianity: The Thousand-Year Golden Age of the Church in the Middle East, Africa and Asia—and How It Died* (New York: HarperOne, 2008). Samuel Moffett's *A History of Christianity in Asia: Beginnings to 1500* follows the spread of Christianity toward the East, while vol. 5 of the Cambridge History of Christianity, *Eastern Christianity*, edited by Michael Angold (New York: Cambridge University Press, 2006), provides an account of the story of the Orthodox Church in our period.

Reformations and the Wars of Religion (1517–1700)

Steven Ozment's *The Age of Reform* (New Haven: Yale University Press, 1980) is good for the medieval background of the Protestant Reformation. Ozment's *Protestants: Birth of a Revolution* (New York: Doubleday 1992) is a good companion to that book. For a general history of the Reformation, see Diarmaid MacCulloch's *The Reformation* (New York: Penguin, 2005). For the Catholic Reformation, see R. Po-Chia Hsia's *The World of Catholic Renewal 1540–1770*, 2nd Ed. (New York: Cambridge University Press, 2005), and N. S. Davidson's *The Catholic Reformation* (New York: Oxford, 1987). Frankly controversial but interesting on the longerterm impact of Protestantism is Brad Gregory's *The Unintended Reformation* (Cambridge, Mass.: Harvard University Press, 2012). On the remarkable seventeenth-century Jesuit missionary effort in China, see M. Brockey's *Journey to the East: The Jesuit Mission to China 1579–1724* (Cambridge, Mass.: Harvard University Press, 2007). On the spread of Catholicism to the New World, see C. R. Boxer, *The Church Militant and Iberian Expansion 1440–1770* (Baltimore: Johns Hopkins University Press, 1978).

For reference on the era of the Reformations, the following are recommended: *The Blackwell Companion to Protestantism*, edited by Alister McGrath and Darren Marks (Oxford, Eng.: Blackwell, 2004), and *The Oxford Encyclopedia of Protestantism*, edited by Hans Hillerbrand (New York: Oxford University Press, 2005). For a selection of primary sources, see *The Protestant Reformation*, Rev. Ed., edited by Hans Hillerbrand (New York: Harper Perennial, 2009). For a good selection of primary sources on the Catholic Reformation, see *The Catholic Reform*, edited by John C. Olin (New York: Fordham University Press, 1990).

Carlos Eire's *War against the Idols: The Reformation of Worship from Erasmus to Calvin* (New York: Cambridge University Press, 1986) is an excellent study of how Christian worship changed under the Reformers. Biographies of the major Reformers abound: Heiko Oberman's *Luther: Man between God and the Devil* (New Haven: Yale University Press, 1989) is thoroughly researched and highly readable. William Bouwsma's *John Calvin: A Sixteenth Century Portrait* (New York: Oxford University Press, 1989) is the work of a mature and well-regarded Reformation scholar. John O'Malley's *The First Jesuits* (Cambridge, Mass.: Harvard University Press, 1995) is a magisterial account of the religious order that spearheaded the Catholic Reformation. For an account of one of the more powerful religious women of the era, see Alison Weber, *Teresa of Avila and the Rhetoric of Femininity* (Princeton: Princeton University Press, 1990). Engaging biographies of two giants of the era whose written polemics foreshadowed later religious wars are Richard C. Marius's *Thomas More: A Biography* (New York: Knopf, 1985) and *Martin Luther: The Christian between God and Death* (Cambridge, Mass.: Belknap, Harvard University Press, 1999). On the bloodiest of the Religious Wars, see Peter H. Wilson's *The Thirty Years War: Europe's Tragedy* (Cambridge, Mass.: Harvard University Press, 2011).

Lutheranism spread beyond Luther's Germany, but Calvinism spread even more impressively beyond Calvin's Switzerland. On Calvinism as an international movement, see Graeme Murdock's *Beyond Calvin: The Intellectual, Political and Cultural World of Europe's Reformed Churches, c. 1540–1620* (New York: Palgrave Macmillan, 2004). On the later influence of Calvinism as a cultural construct, see Max Weber's endlessly discussed *The Protestant Ethic and the Spirit of Capitalism* (1904), available in many English translations.

Works on the religious literature, art, and music of the Baroque period—including studies of such towering figures as Milton, Rembrandt, and Bach—are innumerable. Especially appealing for its brevity, charm, and insight is Jaroslav Pelikan's *Bach among the Theologians* (Philadelphia: Fortress, 1986).

Encounters with Modernity (1700–1914)
Three excellent works survey this period: Gerald Cragg's *The Church and the Age of Reason* (New York: Penguin, 1960), Alec R. Vidler's *The Church in an Age of Revolution* (New York: Penguin, 1961), and Owen Chadwick's *The Popes and European Revolution* (New York: Oxford University Press, 1981). For the North American scene, see Mark Noll's *A History of Christianity in the United States* (Grand Rapids, Mich.: William B. Eerdmans, 1992). On the significance of the rise of modernity, see Owen Chadwick's *The Secularization of the European Mind in the Nineteenth Century* (New York: Cambridge University Press, 1985). On Methodism and the religion of the heart during the Enlightenment, see David Hempton's *Methodism: Empire of the Spirit* (New Haven: Yale University Press, 2005). On the Catholic Church after the Enlightenment, see Nicholas Atkin and Frank Tallett's *Priests, Prelates, and People: A History of European Catholicism from 1750 to the Present* (New York: Oxford University Press, 2003). For a comprehensive overview of Latin America, see *Christianity in Latin America: A History*, edited by Ondina Gonzalez and Justo Gonzalez (New York: Cambridge University Press, 2008). For nineteenth-century religious thinkers, see the three-volume *Religious Thought in the West*, edited by Ninian Smart et al. (New York: Cambridge University Press, 1985). On the Evangelical "Great Awakenings," see W. Reginald Ward's *The Protestant Evangelical Awakening* (New York: Cambridge University Press, 1992). On British colonialism and Protestant missionary efforts in the nineteenth and twentieth centuries, see Brian Stanley's *The Bible and the Flag: Protestant Missions and British Imperialism in the Nineteenth and Twentieth Centuries* (Ann Arbor, Mich.: University of Michigan Press, 2009). Gerald McCool's *Catholic Theology in the Nineteenth Century* (New York: Crossroad, 1977) is a useful survey about the Catholic response to the Enlightenment. For the Protestant perspective, see Karl Barth's classic *From Rousseau to Ritschl* (New York: Harper, 1959). A more recent work engaging the Enlightenment's impact on Christian theology is Philip Kennedy's *A Modern Introduction to Theology: New Questions for Old Beliefs* (London: I. B. Tauris, 2006).

The Twentieth Century and the New Millennium (1914–Present)
Vol. 9 in the massive Cambridge History of Christianity—*World Christianities, c. 1914–c. 2000*, edited by Brian Stanley and Sheridan Gilley (New York: Cambridge University Press, 2006)—is a multiauthored overview of the rapid growth and equally rapid evolution of twentieth-century Christianity. The historian Philip Jenkins has traced the demographic shift within world Christianity in *The New Faces of Christianity* (New York: Oxford University Press, 2008). In *Global Pentecostalism* (Berkeley: University of California Press, 2007), Donald Miller and Tetsunao Yamamori give a comprehensive account of the rise of charismatic Christianity in today's world. On the rise and importance of Evangelical Christianity, especially in North America, see Mark Noll's *American Evangelical Christianity: An Introduction* (Oxford, Eng.: Blackwell, 2001). *Readings in World Christian History*, edited by John Coakley and Andrea Sterk (Maryknoll, N.Y.: Orbis, 2004) provides some documentary evidence on global Christianity.

David Ford's *The Modern Theologians: An Introduction to Christian Theology since 1918* (Oxford, Eng.: Blackwell, 2005) is a sweeping survey of theological thinking in the twentieth century. Ford's *The Future of Christian Theology* (Oxford, Eng.: Blackwell, 2011) is a manifesto on the way Christian theology ought to be advanced in the new millennium. *The Blackwell Companion to Catholicism*, edited by James Buckley et al. (Oxford, Eng.: Blackwell, 2007), provides a wide sweep of Catholicism from history and culture to practices and doctrines. On the lives of modern Orthodox personalities, see Michael Plekon, *Living Icons* (Notre Dame: University of Notre Dame Press, 2002); on the current state of Orthodox theology, see Paul Valliere's *Modern Russian Theology* (Grand Rapids, Mich.: William B. Eerdmans, 2002). On the history and concepts of liberation theology, see *Mysterium Liberationis: The Fundamental Concepts of Liberation Theology,* edited by Ignacio Ellacuria and Jon Sobrino (Maryknoll, N.Y.: Orbis, 1993). Feminism has had a powerful impact on every Western religious tradition. Its impact on Protestantism is explored in *Women and Twentieth Century Protestantism*, edited by Margaret Bendroth and Virginia Brereton (Urbana-Champagne: University of Illinois Press, 2001). Hugh McLeod's *The Religious Crisis of the 1960s* (Oxford, Eng.: Oxford University Press, 2007) is a partly first-person retrospective look at a watershed decade. The impact of secularization on the contemporary world has been surveyed by Charles Taylor in the broadly historical *A Secular Age* (Cambridge, Mass.: Harvard University Press, 2007). A penetrating, postmodern philosophical engagement with the same question is Mark C. Taylor's *After God* (Chicago: University of Chicago Press, 2007).

Two recent studies are important for the contemporary mission movement of Christianity: Lamin Sanneh's *Disciples of All Nations: Pillars of World Christianity* (New York: Oxford University Press, 2008) and Dana Robert's *Christian Mission: How Christianity Became a World Religion* (Oxford, Eng.: Blackwell, 2009). In *From the Holy Mountain: A Journey among the Christians of the Middle East* (New York: Henry Holt, 1999), William Dalrymple retraces the path of a late pre-Islamic pilgrim, visits surviving Christian communities, and concludes,

elegiacally, that these Christian minorities of the Middle East are unlikely to hold out much longer. In a very different vein, in *God Is Back: How the Global Revival of Faith Is Changing the World* (London: Penguin, 2009), John Micklethwait and Adrian Woolridge suggest, arrestingly, that China's Christian population may already be the world's largest.

The Basic Sixteen Documents: Vatican Council II, edited by Austin Flannery (Northport, N.Y.: Costello, 1996), is an inexpensive and readable translation of the official documents of the Second Vatican Council. For a more comprehensive treatment, see the three-volume *Vatican II: Assessment and Perspectives*, edited by René Latourelle (New York: Paulist Press, 1989).

The bibliography on the new shape of World Christian theology is vast. Some representative samples are *Introduction to Third World Theologies*, edited by John Parratt (New York: Cambridge University Press, 2004); *Hispanic/Latino Theology*, edited by Maria Isasi Diaz and Fernando Segovia (Minneapolis: Fortress, 1996); and *Reading Other-Wise: Socially Engaged Biblical Scholars Reading with Their Communities*, edited by Gerald West (Atlanta: Society of Biblical Literature, 2007). Also of interest is M. K. Hassett's *Anglican Communion in Crisis: How Episcopal Dissidents and Their African Allies Are Reshaping Anglicanism* (Princeton: Princeton University Press, 2007).

Permissions Acknowledgments

GENERAL INTRODUCTION

Kay Ryan, "On the Nature of Understanding": From *The New Yorker,* July 25, 2011. Copyright © 2011 by Kay Ryan. Reprinted by permission of the author.

TEXT

Excerpt from THE SOUL'S JOURNEY INTO GOD, THE TREE OF LIFE, THE LIFE OF ST. FRANCIS, by Bonaventure, translated by Ewert Cousins. Copyright © 1978 Paulist Press, Inc., New York/Mahwah, N.J. Used by permission of Paulist Press. *www.paulistpress.com.*

Genesis 1–3, 12:1–3, 15:1–6, 22:1–19: Reprinted from TANAKH: THE HOLY SCRIPTURES by permission of the University of Nebraska Press. Copyright © 1985, 1999 by the Jewish Publication Society, Philadelphia.

Exodus 19–20:23: Reprinted from TANAKH: THE HOLY SCRIPTURES by permission of the University of Nebraska Press. Copyright © 1985, 1999 by the Jewish Publication Society, Philadelphia.

Deuteronomy 6:1–5: Reprinted from TANAKH: THE HOLY SCRIPTURES by permission of the University of Nebraska Press. Copyright © 1985, 1999 by the Jewish Publication Society, Philadelphia.

1 Samuel 2:1–10: Reprinted from TANAKH: THE HOLY SCRIPTURES by permission of the University of Nebraska Press. Copyright © 1985, 1999 by the Jewish Publication Society, Philadelphia.

2 Samuel 7:8–17: Scripture quotations are from the NEW REVISED STANDARD VERSION OF THE BIBLE. Copyright © 1989 by the National Council of the Churches of Christ in the USA. Used by permission. All rights reserved.

Psalm 22: Scripture taken from the HOLY BIBLE, NEW INTERNATIONAL VERSION. Copyright © 1973, 1978, 1984 by International Bible Society. Used by permission of Zondervan. All rights reserved.

Psalm 23: Extracts from the AUTHORIZED VERSION OF THE BIBLE (THE KING JAMES BIBLE), the rights in which are vested in the Crown, are reproduced by permission of the Crown's Patentee, Cambridge University Press.

Psalm 110: Scripture quotations are from THE HOLY BIBLE CONTAINING THE OLD AND NEW TESTAMENTS, REVISED STANDARD VERSION, CATHOLIC EDITION. Copyright © 1946, 1952, 1957, 1966 by the National Council of Christian Churches. Used by permission. All rights reserved.

Proverbs 8:22–31: From THE JERUSALEM BIBLE. Copyright © 1966 by Darton Longman and Todd Ltd and Doubleday, a division of Random House, Inc. Reprinted by permission of Darton Longman and Todd Ltd. and Random House LLC.

Isaiah 9:1–6: Scripture quotations are from the NEW REVISED STANDARD VERSION OF THE BIBLE. Copyright © 1989 by the National Council of the Churches of Christ in the USA. Used by permission. All rights reserved.

Isaiah 11:1–9, 56:1–8: Scripture quotations are from the HOLY BIBLE CONTAINING THE OLD AND NEW TESTAMENTS, REVISED STANDARD VERSION, CATHOLIC EDITION. Copyright © 1946, 1952, 1957, 1966 by the National Council of Christian Churches. Used by permission. All rights reserved.

Isaiah 40:1–8: Extracts from the AUTHORIZED VERSION OF THE BIBLE (THE KING JAMES BIBLE), the rights in which are vested in the Crown, are reproduced by permission of the Crown's Patentee, Cambridge University Press.

Isaiah 52:13–53: Scripture texts in this work are taken from the NEW AMERICAN BIBLE, revised edition © 2010, 1991, 1986, 1970 Confraternity of Christian Doctrine, Washington, D.C., and are used by permission of the copyright owner. All Rights Reserved. No part of the New American Bible may be reproduced in any form without permission in writing from the copyright owner.

Jeremiah 31:31–34: Reprinted from TANAKH: THE HOLY SCRIPTURES by permission of the University of Nebraska Press. Copyright © 1985, 1999 by the Jewish Publication Society, Philadelphia.

Ezekiel 37:1–14: Extracts from the AUTHORIZED VERSION OF THE BIBLE (THE KING JAMES BIBLE), the rights in which are vested in the Crown, are reproduced by permission of the Crown's Patentee, Cambridge University Press.

Daniel 7:1–14: Extracts from the AUTHORIZED VERSION OF THE BIBLE (THE KING JAMES BIBLE), the rights in which are vested in the Crown, are reproduced by permission of the Crown's Patentee, Cambridge University Press.

John 1:1–18: Extracts from the AUTHORIZED VERSION OF THE BIBLE (THE KING JAMES BIBLE), the rights in which are vested in the Crown, are reproduced by permission of the Crown's Patentee, Cambridge University Press.

The First Ecumenical Council: "The Nicene Creed" from CREEDS AND CONFESSIONS OF FAITH IN THE CHRISTIAN TRADITION, volume 1, edited by Jaroslav Pelikan. Published by Yale University Press. Copyright © 2003 Yale University. Reprinted with permission of Yale University Press.

The Second Ecumenical Council: "The Creed of Nicaea-Constantinople" from CREEDS AND CONFESSIONS OF FAITH IN THE CHRISTIAN TRADITION, volume 1, edited by Jaroslav Pelikan. Published by Yale University Press. Copyright © 2003 Yale University. Reprinted with permission of Yale University Press.

The Third Ecumenical Council: "The Formula of Union at Ephesus" from CREEDS AND CONFESSIONS OF FAITH IN THE CHRISTIAN TRADITION, volume 1, edited by Jaroslav Pelikan. Published by Yale University Press. Copyright © 2003 Yale University. Reprinted with permission of Yale University Press.

The Fourth Ecumenical Council: "On the Person and Natures of Christ" from CREEDS AND CONFESSIONS OF FAITH IN THE CHRISTIAN TRADITION, volume 1, edited by Jaroslav Pelikan. Published by Yale University Press. Copyright © 2003 Yale University. Reprinted with permission of Yale University Press.

Saint John of Damascus: From "Third Treatise" from THREE TREATISES ON THE DIVINE IMAGES by St. John of Damascus, edited by Andrew Louth. Copyright © 2003 by St. Vladimir's Seminary Press. Reprinted with permission.

Pseudo-Dionysius the Areopagite: Excerpt from "On Mystical Theology" from THE MYSTICAL THEOLOGY OF ST. DIONYSIUS, edited by Evelyn Sire. Copyright © 1999. Reprinted by permission of Holmes Publishing Group LLC.

Saint Jerome: Letter from ACW 33. LETTERS OF ST. JEROME, VOL. 1 by Charles Christopher. Copyright © 1963 by Rev. Johannes Quasten and Rev. Walter J. Burghardt, S. J. Reproduced with permission of Paulist Press in the format republish in a book via Copyright Clearance Center.

Saint Augustine: Excerpts from CONFESSIONS by Augustine, translated by F. J. Sheed, edited by Michael P. Foley. Copyright © 2006 Hackett Publishing Company, Inc. Reprinted by permission of Hackett Publishing Company, Inc. All rights reserved. Excerpt from THE CITY OF GOD AGAINST THE PAGANS, edited by R. W. Dyson. Copyright © 1998 in translation and editorial matter Cambridge University Press. Reprinted with the permission of Cambridge University Press.

Sulpicius Severus: Excerpts from "Life of Saint Martin" from NICENE AND POST-NICENE FATHERS: Second Series, Volume XI Sulpitius Severus, Vincent of Lerins, John Cassian published by Cosimo, Inc.

Saint Patrick: Excerpts from Book I of Confessions from ACW 17. THE WORKS OF ST. PATRICK, ST. SECUNDINUS by Ludwig Bieler. Copyright © 1953 by Rev. Johannes Quasten and Rev. Joseph C. Plumpe. Reproduced with permission of Paulist Press in the format republish in a book via Copyright Clearance Center. "Saint Patrick's Breastplate" from ACW 17. THE WORKS OF ST. PATRICK, ST. SECUNDINUS by Ludwig Bieler. Copyright © 1953 by Rev. Johannes Quasten and Rev. Joseph C. Plumpe. Reproduced with permission of Paulist Press in the format republish in a book via Copyright Clearance Center.

Prudentius: Excerpt from "Ode in Honor of the Passion of the Blessed Martyr Lawrence" from THE POEMS OF PRUDENTIUS, translated by Sister M. Clement Eagan. Copyright © 1962.

Saint Ephrem the Syrian: Hymn 7 from "Hymns on the Nativity" from EPHREM THE SYRIAN: HYMNS translated by Kathleen E. McVey. Copyright © 1989 by Kathleen E. McVey. Reproduced with permission of Paulist Press in the format republish in a book via Copyright Clearance Center.

Saint Romanos the Melodist: "The Standing Hymn," translated by Roger Green of the Akathistos Hymn by St. Romanos the Melodist, from THE AKATHISTOS HYMN TO THE MOST HOLY MOTHER OF GOD: WITH THE OFFICE OF SMALL COMPLINE, published 1987 by the Ecumenical Society of the Blessed Virgin Mary. Used by permission of the translator and copyright holder, Roger Green.

Anonymous: Excerpt from "The Dream of the Rood" from STONE, SKIN AND SILVER: A TRANSLATION OF THE DREAM OF THE ROOD by Richard J. Kelley and Ciarán L. Quinn. Copyright © 1999 by Richard J. Kelley and Ciarán L. Quinn. Reproduced with permission of Litho Press in the format republish in a book via Copyright Clearance Center.

Saint Athanasius of Alexandria: Excerpt from "The Life of Anthony" from THE LIFE OF ANTONY AND THE LETTER TO MARCELLINUS by St. Athanasius of Alexandria, translated by Robert C. Gregg. Copyright © 1980 The Missionary Society of St. Paul the Apostle in the State of New York. Reproduced with permission of Paulist Press in the format republish in a book via Copyright Clearance Center.

Saint Gregory of Nyssa: Excerpts from "The Life of Saint Macrina" from SAINT GREGORY OF NYSSA ASCETICAL WORKS (THE FATHERS OF THE CHURCH) by Saint Gregory of Nyssa, translated by Virginia Woods Callahan. Copyright © 1967 The Catholic University of America Press. Reprinted with permission of Catholic University of America Press in the format republish in a book via Copyright Clearance Center.

Anonymous: Excerpts from "Some Sayings of the Desert Fathers" by Thomas Merton, from THE WISDOM OF THE DESERT. Copyright © 1960 by The Abby of Gethsemani, Inc. Reprinted by permission of New Directions Publishing Corp.

Saint Benedict of Nursia: Excerpt from RULE OF ST. BENEDICT by Saint Benedict, edited by Timothy Fry. Copyright © 1981 by the Order of St. Benedict, Inc., Collegeville, Minnesota. Reproduced with permission of Liturgical Press in the format republish in a book via Copyright Clearance Center.

Saint Bede the Venerable: Excerpts from BEDE: ECCLESIASTICAL HISTORY OF THE ENGLISH PEOPLE. "The History" translated by Leo Sherley-Price and revised by R. E. Latham, translation of the minor works, new Introduction and Notes by D. H. Farmer (Penguin Classics 1955, revised edition 1968, 1990). Translation copyright © 1955, 1968 by Leo Sherley-Price. Translation of "Ecclesiastical History of the English People" copyright © 1955, 1968 by Leo Sherley-Price. Introduction copyright © 1990 by D. H. Farmer. Translation of "Bede's Letter to Egbert" and "Cuthbert's Letter on the Illness and Death of Venerable Bede" copyright © 1990 by D. H. Farmer. Reprinted by permission of Penguin Books Ltd.

Rudolf of Fulda: Excerpts from the Prologue of "The Life of Abbess Leoba" from THE ANGLO-SAXON MISSIONARIES IN GERMANY by Rudolf of Fulda, edited by C. H. Talbot. Copyright © 1954 by Sheed & Ward. Reprinted by permission of Sheed & Ward, an imprint of Bloomsbury Publishing Plc.

Anonymous: Excerpt from "Russian Primary Chronicle" reprinted by permission of the publishers from HARVARD STUDIES AND NOTES IN PHILOLOGY AND LITERATURE, VOLUME 12: THE RUSSIAN PRIMARY CHRONICLE by

Samuel H. Cross, pp. 183–189, Cambridge, Mass.: Harvard University Press. Copyright © 1930 by the President and Fellows of Harvard College.

Saint Anselm of Canterbury: Excerpt from "Meditations on Human Redemption" from THE PRAYERS AND MEDITATIONS OF SAINT ANSELM by St. Anselm of Canterbury, translated with an introduction by Sister Benedicta Ward, with a forward by R. W. Southern (Penguin Classics, 1973.) Copyright © 1973 by Benedicta Ward. Forward copyright © 1973 by R. W. Southern. Reprinted by permission of Penguin Books Ltd.

Saint Hildegard of Bingen: "Vision Twelve: The New Heaven and the New Earth" from HILDEGARD OF BINGEN: SCIVIAS by Mother Columbia Hart and Jane Bishop. Copyright © 1990 by The Abby of Regina Laudis: Benedictine Congregation Regina Laudis of the Strict Observance, Inc. Reproduced with permission of Paulist Press in the format republish in a book via Copyright Clearance Center.

Saint Bernard of Clairvaux: Excerpts from BERNARD OF CLAIRVAUX: SERMONS ON THE SONG OF SONGS, VOLUME II by Bernard of Clairvaux. Copyright © 1971 by Cistercian Publications Inc. Reproduced with permission of Cistercian Publications, Incorporated in the format republish in a book via Copyright Clearance Center.

Saint Francis of Assisi: "The Testament" from THE SAINT, VOLUME 1 OF: FRANCIS OF ASSISI: EARLY DOCUMENTS edited by Regis J. Armstrong. Copyright © 1999 by Franciscan Institute of St. Bonaventure University, Bonaventure. NY. Reprinted with permission of New City Press. Excerpt from "The Canticle of Creatures" from THE SAINT, VOLUME 1 OF: FRANCIS OF ASSISI: EARLY DOCUMENTS edited by Regis J. Armstrong. Copyright © 1999 by Franciscan Institute of St. Bonaventure University, Bonaventure. NY. Reprinted with permission of New City Press. Excerpt from Chapter 16, "How God Revealed to Sister Clare and Brother Silvester That St. Francis Should Go and Preach," from THE LITTLE FLOWERS OF ST. FRANCIS by Raphael Brown. Copyright © 1958 by Beverly Brown. Used by permission of Doubleday, an imprint of the Knopf Doubleday Publishing Group, a division of Random House LLC. All rights reserved.

Saint Thomas Aquinas: Excerpt from "Commentary on the Lord's Prayer" from ALBERT & THOMAS SELECTED WRITINGS by Saint Albertus Magnus and Thomas Aquinas, edited and translated by Simon Tugwell. Copyright © 1988 by Simon Tugwell, O.P. Reproduced with permission of Paulist Press in the format republish in a book via Copyright Clearance Center. Excerpts from SUMMA CONTRA GENTILES BOOK ONE by Sr Thomas Aquinas, Copyright © 1955 by Doubleday, a division of Random House, Inc. Used by permission of Doubleday, an imprint of the Knopf Doubleday Publishing Group, a division of Random House LLC. All rights reserved.

Anonymous: "Ave Maris Stella," translated from "Raccolta," based upon the Roman Breviary, from TREASURY OF LATIN PRAYERS, edited and translated by Michael Martin. Copyright © 2011 by Michael Martin. Reprinted with kind permission by Michael Martin.

Anonymous: "Salve Regina" from BLESSED ART THOU by Richard J. Beyer. Copyright © 1996. Reprinted by permission of Richard J. Beyer.

Wipo: "Victimae Paschali Laudes," translated from "Roman Missal," from TREASURY OF LATIN PRAYERS, edited and translated by Michael Martin. Copyright © 2011 by Michael Martin. Reprinted with kind permission by Michael Martin.

Saint Thomas Aquinas: "Pange, Lingua, Gloriosi," translated by Fr. Edward Caswell (1814–1878), from TREASURY OF LATIN PRAYERS, edited and translated by Michael Martin. Copyright © 2011 by Michael Martin. Reprinted with kind permission by Michael Martin.

Anonymous: "Dies Irae" from THE MISSAL IN LATIN AND ENGLISH. Copyright © 1962 by Baronius Press. Reprinted with permission of Baronius Press.

Dante: Excerpts from Canto I and III from THE INFERNO OF DANTE: A NEW VERSE TRANSLATION by Robert Pinsky. Translation copyright © 1994 by Robert Pinsky. Reprinted by permission of Farrar, Straus and Giroux, LLC. Canto XXXIII from THE DIVINE COMEDY by Dante Alighieri, translated by John Ciardi. Copyright © 1954, 1957, 1959, 1960, 1961, 1965, 1967, 1970 by the Ciardi Family Publishing Trust. Used by permission of W. W. Norton & Company, Inc.

Everyman: Excerpt from "The Summoning of Everyman" from EVERYMAN AND MANKIND edited by Douglas Bruster and Eric Rasmussen. Copyright © 2009 by Douglas Bruster and Eric Rasmussen. Published by Arden Shakespeare, an imprint of Bloomsbury Publishing Plc. Reprinted with permission.

Saint Catherine of Siena: Excerpts from THE DIALOGUE by St. Catherine of Siena, translated by Suzanne Noffke. Copyright © 1980 by Paulist Press, Inc. Reproduced with permission of Paulist Press, Inc. in the format republish in a book via Copyright Clearance Center.

Julian of Norwich: Excerpts from SHOWINGS by Julian of Norwich, translated by Edmond Colledge and James Walsh. Copyright © 1978 by The Missionary Society of St. Paul the Apostle in the State of New York. Reproduced with permission of Paulist Press in the format republish in a book via Copyright Clearance Center.

William Langland: Excerpts from "Passus VII" from PIERS PLOWMAN: THE C VERSION by William Langland, translated by George Economou, pp. 61–64. Copyright © 1996 by University of Pennsylvania Press. Reprinted with permission of University of Pennsylvania Press.

Margery Kempe: Excerpt from THE BOOK OF MARGERY KEMPE, translated and edited by Lynn Staley. Copyright © 2001 by W. W. Norton & Company, Inc. Used by permission of W. W. Norton & Company, Inc.

Geoffrey Chaucer: Prologue from THE CANTERBURY TALES by Geoffrey Chaucer, translated by Burton Raffel. Translation and notes copyright © 2008 by Burton Raffel. Used by permission of Modern Library, an imprint of Random House, a division of Random House LLC. All rights reserved. Excerpt from "The Wife of Bath's Prologue" from THE CANTERBURY TALES by Geoffrey Chaucer, translated by Burton Raffel. Copyright © 2008 by Burton Raffel. Reprinted by permission of Random House LLC.

Martin Luther: Excerpt from THE FREEDOM OF A CHRISTIAN by Martin Luther. Copyright © 1957 by Fortress Press. Reprinted by permission of Augsburg Fortress Press. Excerpt from "Large Catechism, The Sixth Commandment" from THE BOOK OF CONCORD: THE CONFESSIONS OF THE EVANGELICAL LUTHERAN CHURCH, translated by Theodore G. Tappert. Copyright © 1959 by Fortress Press. Reprinted by permission of Augsburg Fortress Press. Excerpt from "The Small Catechism, Preface" from MARTIN LUTHER'S BASIC THEOLOGICAL WRITING, edited by Timothy F. Lull and William Russell. Copyright © 2005 by Augsburg Fortress Press. Reprinted by permission of Augsburg Fortress Press.

W. H. Auden: "Friday's Child" from W. H. AUDEN SELECTED POEMS by W. H. Auden, edited by Edward Mendelson. Copyright © 1979 by Edward Mendelson, William Meredith, and Monroe K. Spears, executors of the Estate of W. H. Auden. Reprinted by permission of Random House, LLC, and Curtis Brown Group Ltd.

Simone Weil: Excerpts from "Reflections on the Right Use of School Studies with a View to the Love of God" from WAITING FOR GOD by Simone Weil, translated by Emma Craufurd, translation copyright 1951, renewed copyright 1979 by G. P. Putnam's Sons. Used by permission of G. P. Putnam's Sons, a division of Penguin Group (USA) LLC.

Mother Maria Skobtsova: Excerpts from "The Second Gospel Commandment" from MOTHER MARIA SKOBTSOVA: ESSENTIAL WRITINGS. Translated from the Russian by Richard Pevear and Larissa Volokhonsky. Copyright © 2003 by Orbis Books. Published in 2003 by Orbis Books, Maryknoll, New York 10545. reprinted by permission of the publisher.

Dorothy Day: Excerpts from "The Duty of Delight" from THE DUTY OF DELIGHT: THE DIARIES OF DOROTHY DAY, edited by Robert Ellsberg. Copyright © 2008 Marquette University Press, Wisconsin, USA. Used by permission of the publisher. All rights reserved. www.marquette.edu/mupress.

Paul Tillich: Excerpt from THE DYNAMICS OF FAITH by Paul Tillich. Copyright © 1957 by Paul Tillich. Renewed © 1985 by Hannah Tillich. Reprinted by permission of HarperCollins Publishers.

Pierre Teilhard de Chardin: Excerpt from "The Mass on the World" from HYMN OF THE UNIVERSE by Pierre Teilhard de Chardin. Copyright © 1961 by Editions du Seuil. English translation Copyright © 1965 by William Collins Sons & Co. Ltd. London and Harper & Row, Inc., New York. Reprinted by permission of Georges Borchardt, Inc., for Editions du Seuil.

Thomas Merton: Excerpts from "Asceticism and Sacrifice" from NO MAN IS AN ISLAND by Thomas Merton. Copyright © 1955 by The Abbey of Our Lady of Gethsemani and renewed 1983 by the Trustees of the Merton Legacy Trust. Reprinted by permission of Houghton Mifflin Harcourt Publishing Company. All rights reserved.

C. S. Lewis: Excerpts from "Charity" from THE FOUR LOVES by C. S. Lewis. Copyright © 1960 by C. S. Lewis Pte Ltd. Copyright renewed 1988 by Arthur Owens Barfield. Extract reprinted by permission of The C. S. Lewis Company and Houghton Mifflin Harcourt Publishing Company. All rights reserved.

Martin Luther King, Jr.: "I Have a Dream" by Dr. Martin Luther King, Jr. Copyright © 1963 by Dr. Martin Luther King, Jr.. Copyright © renewed 1991 Coretta Scott King. Reprinted by arrangement with The Heirs to the Estate of Martin Luther King, Jr., c/o Writers House as agent for the proprietor, New York, NY.

The Second Vatican Council: "Nostra Aetate," October 28, 1965, from THE BASIC SIXTEEN DOCUMENTS VATICAN COUNCIL II: CONSTITUTIONS, DECREES, DECLARATIONS, translated by Austin Flannery. Copyright © 1965 by Libreria Editrice Vaticana. Reprinted by permission of Libreria Editrice Vaticana.

Gustavo Gutiérrez: Excerpt from "The Task and Content of Liberation Theology" from THE CAMBRIDGE COMPANION TO LIBERATION THEOLOGY, 2nd edition, edited by Christopher Rowland. Copyright © 2007 Cambridge University Press. Reprinted with the permission of Cambridge University Press.

Desmond Tutu: Excerpts from "Aparteid's 'Final Solution'" from THE RAINBOW PEOPLE OF GOD by Desmond Tutu, edited by John Allen, Doubleday 1994.

Rigoberta Menchú: "The Bible and Self-Defense: The Examples of Judith, Moses, and David" from I, RIGOBERTA MENCHÚ: AN INDIAN WOMAN IN GUATEMALA by Rigoberta Menchú, translated by Ann Wright. Copyright © 1984 by Verso Editions. Reprinted by permission of Verso.

Czeslaw Milosz: "Campo dei Fiori," "You Who Wronged," and "Readings" from THE COLLECTED POEMS 1931–1987 by Czeslaw Milosz. Copyright © 1983 by Czeslaw Milosz Royalties, Inc. Reprinted by permission of HarperCollins Publishers.

Yeong Mee Lee: Excerpt from "A Political Reception of the Bible: Korean *Minjung* Theological Interpretation of the Bible" from *SBL Forum*, October 2005. Reprinted by permission of the Society of Biblical Literature.

Christian de Chergé: "Spiritual Testament" ("The Pentecost Letter") from THE MONKS OF TIBHIRINE: FAITH, LOVE, AND TERROR IN ALGERIA. Copyright © 2002 by John Kiser. Reprinted by permission of St. Martin's Press. All rights reserved.

Liu Zhenying (Brother Yun): Excerpt from "Back to Jerusalem" from THE HEAVENLY MAN: THE REMARKABLE TRUE STORY OF CHINESE CHRISTIAN BROTHER YUN by Brother Yun, translated by Paul Hattaway. Copyright © 2002 by Brother Yun and Paul Hattaway. Reprinted by permission of Monarch Books.

Pope John Paul II and Ecumenical Patriarch Bartholomew: "Common Declaration on Environmental Ethics" by Pope John Paul II. Copyright © 2002 Libreria Editrice Vaticana. Reprinted by permission of Libreria Editrice Vaticana.

Christian Wiman: Excerpt from "My Bright Abyss" from MY BRIGHT ABYSS: MEDITATION OF A MODERN BELIEVER by Christian Wiman. Copyright © 2013 by Christian Wiman. Reprinted by permission of Farrar, Straus and Giroux, LLC.

ILLUSTRATIONS

Christ as a young shepherd: Album / Art Resource, NY / © Artres

Christ the Ruler of All: Kharbine-Tapabor / The Art Archive at Art Resource, NY

University of Bologna lecture: Kupferstichkabinett, Staatliche Museen, Berlin, Germany / Art Resource, NY

Calvinist church interior: Kimbell Art Museum, Fort Worth, Texas / Art Resource, NY / © Artres

Kierkegaard: Album / Art Resource, NY / © Artres

Jorge Mario Bergoglio (Pope): EPA / ETTORE FERRARI / LANDOV

Saint Paul Preaching in Athens: V&A Images, London / Art Resource, NY

Ossuary: © Mark Christianson

Graffito: akg-images
The Virgin Mary as Mother of God: © Gavin Hellier / Robert Harding World Imagery / Corbis
Fresco: Cameraphoto Arte, Venice / Art Resource, NY
Funerary tablet: Scala / Art Resource, NY
Mosaic: Cameraphoto Arte, Venice / Art Resource, NY / © Artres
Illumination: © INTERFOTO / Alamy
Non Angli sed Angeli: *St. Gregory and the British Captives,* Blake, William (1757–1827) / Victoria & Albert Museum, London, UK / The Bridgeman Art Library
Aquinas: Nicolo Orsi Battaglini / Art Resource, NY / © Artres
Dante: © Manuel Cohen
The Mystic Marriage of Saint Catherine of Siena: © Image Asset Management / agefotostock
Wife of Bath: Eileen Tweedy / The Art Archive at Art Resource, NY / © Artres
The Holy Communion of the Protestants and Ride to Hell of the Catholics: Kupferstichkabinett, Staatliche Museen, Berlin, Germany / Art Resource, NY / © Artres
Luther: © The Metropolitan Museum of Art. Image source: Art Resource, NY / © Artres
Calvin: © Mary Evans Picture Library / The Image Works
Saint Teresa in Ecstasy: © Massimo Listri / CORBIS
Sor Juana: Miguel Cabrera (1695–1768) / Museo Nacional de Historia, Castillo de Chapultepec, Mexico / Jean-Pierre Courau / The Bridgeman Art Library
Profession of Faith of the Savoyard Vicar: Bibliotheque Nationale, Paris, France / Giraudon / The Bridgeman Art Library
Harnack: Project Gutenberg / Wikimedia Commons
Wesley: © National Portrait Gallery, London
Lee: Schomburg Center for Research in Black Culture / Manuscripts, Archives and Rare Books Division / New York Public Library
Dresden: Walter Hahn / AFP / Getty Images
Bonhoeffer: akg-images
King: Central Press / Getty Images
Tutu: Helmuth Lohmann / AP Photo
Milosz: Bernard Gotfryd / Getty Images
Pentecostal worship: © JO YONG-HAK / X90071 / Reuters / Corbis
Brother Yun: Photograph by Gareth Barton

Index

Acts, 136, 138
Addams, Jane, 569
Against the Heresies (Irenaeus of Lyons), 208
Agnosticism and Christianity (Huxley), 546, 547
Annals, the (Tacitus), 186, 187
Anselm of Canterbury, Saint, 294
Apologia pro Vita Sua (Newman), 526
Apology, The (Justin Martyr), 167, 168
Apology for Rational Worshippers of God (Reimarus), 476, 477
Arnold, Matthew, 551
Athanasius of Alexandria, Saint, 262
Auden, W. H., 593
Augustine of Hippo, Saint, 226
Ave Maris Stella, 329

Barth, Karl, 579
Bartholomew I, Ecumenical Patriarch, 673
Battle Hymn of the Republic, The (Howe), 519, 520
Bede the Venerable, Saint, 282
Benedict of Nursia, Saint, 270
Bernard of Clairvaux, Saint, 306
Bible
    Acts, 136, 138
    Corinthians, 140, 151
    Daniel, 107, 108
    Deuteronomy, 93
    Exodus, 89, 90
    Ezekiel, 107, 108
    Galatians, 140, 144
    Genesis, 83, 84
    Hebrews, 154, 156
    Isaiah, 101, 102
    James, 154, 158
    Jeremiah, 106
    John, 110, 111, 136, 137
    Luke, 111, 112, 124, 125
    Mark, 127, 128
    Matthew, 116, 117
    Philippians, 140, 151
    Proverbs, 96, 100
    Psalms, 96, 97
    Revelation, 159, 160
    Romans, 140, 144
    Samuel, 94, 95
Bloody Tenet of Persecution, for Cause of Conscience, in a Conference between Truth and Peace, The (Williams), 465, 466
Bonhoeffer, Dietrich, 587
Book of Common Prayer, The (Cranmer), 416, 417
Book of Her Life, The (Teresa of Ávila), 434, 435
Book of Margery Kempe, The (Kempe), 379
Brotherly Agreement at Herrnhut, The (Zinzendorf), 494, 495
Bunyan, John, 458
Burning Babe, The (Southwell), 450

Calvin, John, 412
Campo dei Fiori (Milosz), 647, 648
Canterbury Tales, The (Chaucer), 383, 384
Canticle of Brother Sun, The (Francis of Assisi), 311, 314
Catherine of Siena, Saint, 360
Chaucer, Geoffrey, 383
Chesterton, G. K., 540
Christianity and the Religions of the World (Schweitzer), 559, 560
City of God (Augustine of Hippo), 226, 230
Common Declaration on Environmental Ethics (Pope John Paul II and Ecumenical Patriarch Bartholomew I), 673, 674
Confession (Patrick), 240, 241
Confessions (Augustine of Hippo), 226, 227
Corinthians, 140, 140, 151
Cost of Discipleship, The (Bonhoeffer), 587, 589

Cranmer, Thomas, 416
Crashaw, Richard, 452
Creed of Nicaea-Constantinople, the
    (Second Ecumenical Council),
    214, 215
Cruz, Sor Juana Inés de la, 441

Daniel, 107, 108
Dante Alighieri, 342
Day, Dorothy, 607
Death, Be Not Proud (Donne), 451
de Chergé, Christian, 666
De Spectaculis (Tertullian), 210, 211
Deuteronomy, 93
Dialogue, The (Catherine of Siena), 360
Dickinson, Emily, 552
Didache, the, 171
Dies Irae, 333
Divine Comedy, The (Dante Alighieri), 342
Donne, John, 451
Dover Beach (Arnold), 551
Dream of the Rood, The, 258, 259
Duty of Delight, The (Day), 607, 608
Dynamics of Faith (Tillich), 610, 611

Ecclesiastical History of the English People
    (Bede the Venerable), 282, 283
Eckhart, Meister, 352
Edwards, Jonathan, 498
Egeria, 177
Eliot, T. S., 574
Elizabeth, a Dutch Anabaptist, 423
Elizabethan Jesuits, The (More), 426
Elliott, Charlotte, 510
Emile, or On Education (Rousseau), 478,
    479
Ephrem the Syrian, Saint, 249
Eucharistic Prayer in the Byzantine Liturgy,
    The (John Chrysostom), 180, 181
Exhortation to Martyrdom, An (Origen),
    193, 194
Exodus, 89, 90
Ezekiel, 107, 108

Fear and Trembling (Kierkegaard), 531,
    532
Firmin Lectures, The (Loisy), 488
First Ecumenical Council, the, 213
Formula of Union at Ephesus, the (Third
    Ecumenical Council), 215, 216
Four Loves, The (Lewis), 621
Fourth Ecumenical Council, the, 217
Francis of Assisi, Saint, 311
Freedom of a Christian, The (Luther), 399,
    401
Friday's Child (Auden), 593

Galatians, 140, 144
Genesis, 83, 84
German Atrocities: Aid for Refugees
    (Temple), 595, 596
Gospel of Thomas, the, 200, 201
Gregory of Nyssa, Saint, 264
Gutiérrez, Gustavo, 632

Harnack, Adolf von, 484
Heavenly Man, The (Liu Zhenying), 669,
    670
Hebrews (Letter to the Hebrews), 154, 156
[He Fumbles at Your Soul] (Dickinson), 553
Herbert, George, 452
Higginson, Thomas Wentworth, 515
Hildegard of Bingen, Saint, 300
Holdfast, The (Herbert), 452
Hopkins, Gerard Manley, 554
Howe, Julia Ward, 519
Huxley, Thomas Henry, 546
Hymns on the Nativity (Ephrem the
    Syrian), 249, 250

Ignatius of Loyola, Saint, 430
I Have a Dream (King), 624, 625
Imitation of Christ, The (Thomas à
    Kempis), 371, 372
Institutes of the Christian Religion, The
    (Calvin), 412, 414
Irenaeus of Lyons, Saint, 208
I, Rigoberta Menchú (Menchú), 643,
    644
Isaiah, 101, 102

James, 154, 158
Jeremiah, 106
Jerome, Saint, 223
John, 110, 111, 136, 137
John Chrysostom, Saint, 180
John of Damascus, Saint, 218
John Paul II, Pope, 673
Journal (Wesley), 501, 502
Journey of the Magi (Eliot), 574, 575
Julian of Norwich, 365
Just As I Am (Elliott), 510
Justin Martyr, Saint, 167

Kempe, Margery, 379
Kierkegaard, Søren, 531
King, Martin Luther, Jr., 624

Langland, William, 375
Large Catechism (Luther), 399, 406
Las Casas, Bartolomé de, 438
Lee, Jarena, 511
Lee, Yeong Mee, 658

Letter (Elizabeth, a Dutch Anabaptist), 423
Letters (Jerome), 223, 224
Letters (Pliny to Emperor Trajan and
        Trajan to Pliny), 188
Letter to the Hebrews, The, 154, 156
Lewis, C. S., 621
*Life and Religious Experience of Jarena Lee,
        The* (Lee), 511, 512
Life of Abbess Leoba (Rudolf of Fulda), 287
Life of Anthony (Athanasius of Alexandria),
        262
Life of Macrina (Gregory of Nyssa), 264, 265
Life of Saint Martin (Severus), 236, 237
Little Flowers (Francis of Assisi), 311,
        315, 316
Liu Zhenying (Brother Yun), 669
Livingstone, David, 555
Loisy, Alfred Firmin, 488
Love Divine, All Loves Excelling (Wesley),
        504
Luke, 111, 112, 124, 125
Luther, Martin, 399

Mark, 127, 128
Martyrdom of Polycarp, The, 190, 191
Mass on the World, The (Teilhard de
        Chardin), 614, 615
Matthew, 116, 117
Meditations (Anselm of Canterbury),
        294, 295
Menchú, Rigoberta, 643
Merton, Thomas, 618
Mighty Fortress Is Our God, A (Luther),
        399, 411
Milosz, Czeslaw, 647
Milton, John, 454
Mirror of Martyrs, The, see Letter
        (Elizabeth, a Dutch Anabaptist)
*Missionary Travels and Researches in South
        Africa* (Livingstone), 555, 556
More, Henry, 426
My Bright Abyss (Wiman), 677, 678

Negro Spirituals (Higginson), 515
New Impulse to an Old Gospel, A (Addams),
        569, 570
Newman, John Henry, 526
Nicene Creed, the (First Ecumenical
        Council), 213, 214
Niebuhr, Reinhold, 583
No Man Is an Island (Merton), 618
Nostra Aetate (Second Vatican Council),
        628, 629

*Ode in Honor of the Blessed Martyr
        Lawrence* (Prudentius), 246, 247

On Mystical Theology (Pseudo-Dionysius
        the Areopagite), 220, 221
*On Religion: Speeches to Its Cultured
        Despisers* (Schleiermacher), 481,
        482
On the Lord's Prayer (Thomas Aquinas),
        317, 318
On the Person and Natures of Christ
        (Fourth Ecumenical Council),
        217
Origen, 193
Orthodoxy (Chesterton), 540, 541
Our Anxiety and God (Barth), 579, 580
Owen, Wilfred, 572

Pange, Lingua, Gloriosi (Thomas Aquinas),
        332
Parable of the Old Man and the Young, The
        (Owen), 572, 573
Paradise Lost (Milton), 454, 455
Pascal, Blaise, 462
Passion of Porpotua and Felicity, The, 197
Patrick, Saint, 240
Pearl of Great Price (Smith), 505, 506
Pensées (Pascal), 462, 463
Personal Narrative (Edwards), 499
Philippians, 140, 151
Piers Plowman (Langland), 375, 376
Pilgrim's Progress, The (Bunyan), 458
Pliny the Younger, 188
*Political Reception of the Bible: Korean
        Minjung Theological
        Interpretation of the Bible* (Lee),
        658, 659
Protoevangelium of James, the, 203, 205
Proverbs, 96, 100
Prudentius, 246
Psalms, 96, 97
Pseudo-Dionysius the Areopagite, 220

Rainbow People of God, The (Tutu), 638,
        639
Readings (Milosz), 647, 650
*Reflections on the Right Use of School
        Studies with a View to the Love of
        God* (Weil), 598, 599
Reimarus, Hermann Samuel, 476
Reply to Sister Philothea (Cruz), 441, 443
Revelation, 159, 160
Romans, 140, 144
Romanos the Melodist, Saint, 251
Rousseau, Jean-Jacques, 478
Rudolf of Fulda, 287
Rule of Saint Benedict (Benedict of
        Nursia), 270, 271
Rules for Confessors (Las Casas), 438

Russell, Bertrand, 576
Russian Primary Chronicle, the, 289

Saint Patrick's Breastplate, 243
Salve Regina, 330
Samuel, 94, 95
Sayings of the Desert Fathers, 268
Schleiermacher, Friedrich, 481
Schweitzer, Albert, 559
Scivias (Hildegard of Bingen), 300
Second Ecumenical Council, the, 214
Second Gospel Commandment, The
    (Skobtsova), 602, 603
Second Vatican Council, the, 628
[*Sermon 15: On Poverty of Spirit*]
    (Eckhart), 352, 353
Sermons on the Song of Songs (Bernard of
    Clairvaux), 306
[*Seventeenth-Century Jesuit Missionary in
    China, A*] (Trigault), 446, 447
Severus, Sulpicius, 236
Showings (Julian of Norwich), 365, 366
Skobtsova, Mother Maria, 602
*Small Catechism for Ordinary Pastors
    and Preachers* (Luther), 399, 408
Smith, Joseph, 505
[*Some Keep the Sabbath Going to
    Church—*] (Dickinson), 553
Southwell, Robert, 450
Spiritual Exercises, The (Ignatius of
    Loyola), 430, 431
Spiritual Testament (de Chergé), 666,
    667
Standing Hymn, The (Romanos the
    Melodist), 251, 252
Summa Contra Gentiles (Thomas Aquinas),
    317, 322, 323
Summoning of Everyman, The, 356

Tacitus, 186
*Task and Content of Liberation Theology,
    The* (Gutiérrez), 632, 633

Teilhard de Chardin, Pierre, 614
Temple, William, 595
Teresa of Ávila, Saint, 434
Tertullian, 210
Testament, The (Francis of Assisi), 311,
    312
Third Ecumenical Council, the, 215
Thomas, The Gospel of, 200, 201
Thomas à Kempis, 371
Thomas Aquinas, Saint, 317, 332
Three Treatises on Images (John of
    Damascus), 218, 219
Tillich, Paul, 610
*To the Noblest and Best of Ladies, the
    Countess of Denbigh* (Crashaw),
    452
Trajan (Emperor), 188
Travels of Egeria, the (Egeria), 177, 178
Trigault, Nicholas, 446
Tutu, Desmond, 638

Victimae Paschali Laudes (Wipo), 331

Way of a Pilgrim, The, 520, 521
Weil, Simone, 598
Wesley, Charles, 504
Wesley, John, 501
What Is Christianity? (von Harnack), 484,
    485
Why I Am Not a Christian (Russell), 576,
    577
Why the Christian Church Is Not Pacifist
    (Niebuhr), 583
Williams, Roger, 465
Wiman, Christian, 677
Windhover, The (Hopkins), 554, 555
Wipo, 331

You Who Wronged (Milosz), 647, 650
Yun, Brother (Liu Zhenying), 669

Zinzendorf, Nicolas Von, 494